Landscape

Design, Installation, and Management

CHRISTOPHER D. HART • R. LEE IVY

Designed to help today's landscape and horticulture students gain a thorough understanding of the design, installation, and management of landscapes using modern and sustainable technology.

Guided Tour

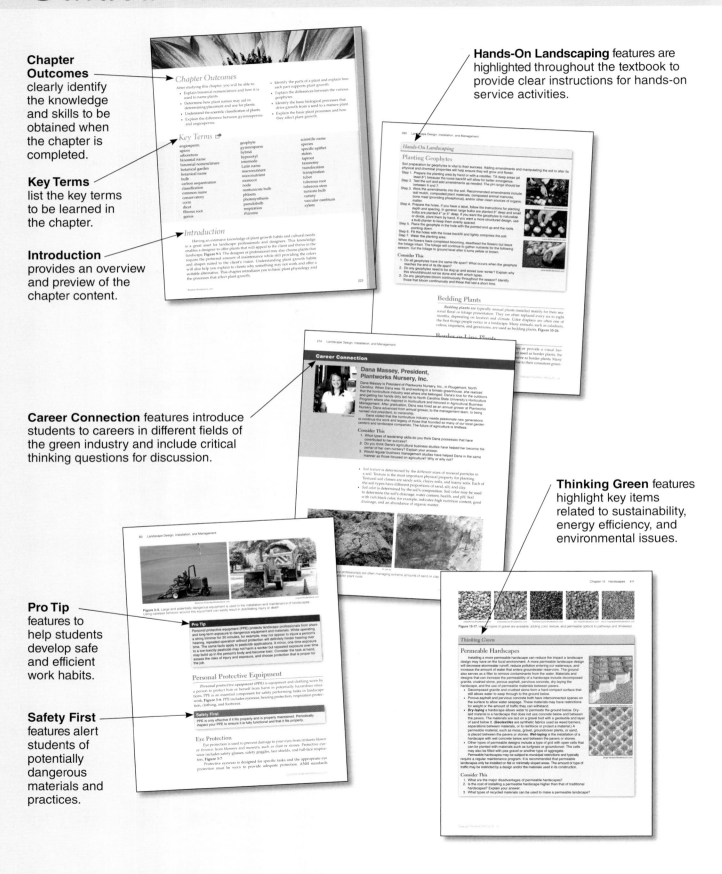

Chapter Outcomes clearly identify the knowledge and skills to be obtained when the chapter is completed.

Key Terms list the key terms to be learned in the chapter.

Introduction provides an overview and preview of the chapter content.

Hands-On Landscaping features are highlighted throughout the textbook to provide clear instructions for hands-on service activities.

Career Connection features introduce students to careers in different fields of the green industry and include critical thinking questions for discussion.

Thinking Green features highlight key items related to sustainability, energy efficiency, and environmental issues.

Pro Tip features to help students develop safe and efficient work habits.

Safety First features alert students of potentially dangerous materials and practices.

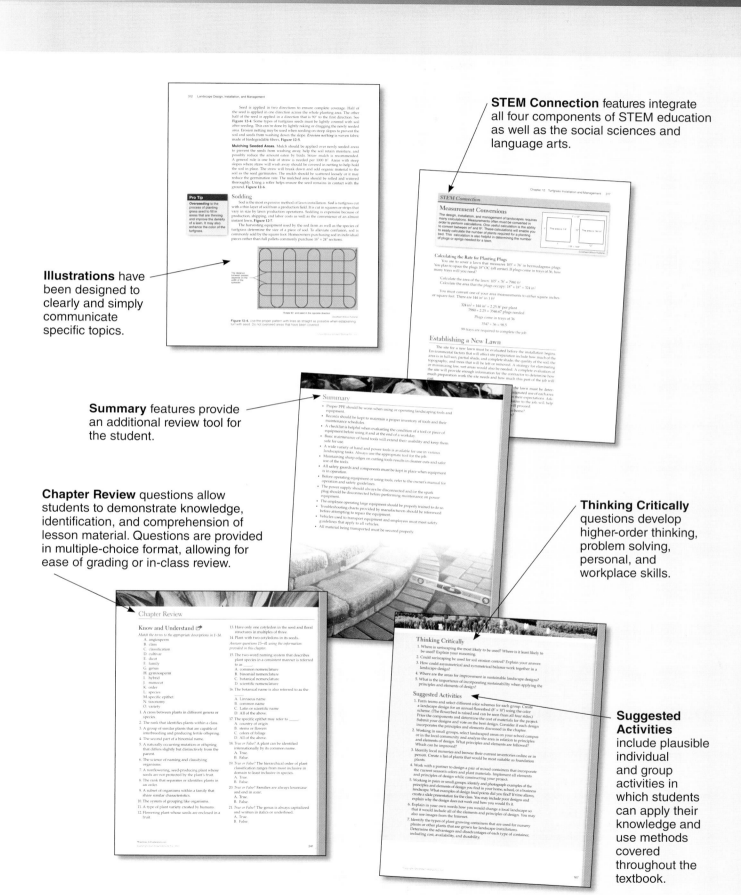

STEM Connection features integrate all four components of STEM education as well as the social sciences and language arts.

Illustrations have been designed to clearly and simply communicate specific topics.

Summary features provide an additional review tool for the student.

Chapter Review questions allow students to demonstrate knowledge, identification, and comprehension of lesson material. Questions are provided in multiple-choice format, allowing for ease of grading or in-class review.

Thinking Critically questions develop higher-order thinking, problem solving, personal, and workplace skills.

Suggested Activities include plausible individual and group activities in which students can apply their knowledge and use methods covered throughout the textbook.

TOOLS FOR STUDENT AND INSTRUCTOR SUCCESS

Student Tools

Student Text

Landscape Design, Installation, and Management introduces students to landscaping, which is a major component of the green industry. The *Landscape Design, Installation, and Management* textbook provides an exciting, full-color, and highly illustrated learning resource. The textbook is available in print and online. The online version of the printed textbook gives students access anytime from any digital device. Students can easily navigate from a linked table of contents, search specific topics, quickly jump to specific pages, zoom in to enlarge text, and print selected pages for offline reading.

Topics covered include an overview of the industry, workplace skills, safety, principles and elements of design, turfgrass selection and installation, installing hardscapes, working with clients, pest management, water features and irrigation, and much more. Students can study colorful images of the tools, plants, and pests listed in FFA's Landscape/Nursery ID lists in the text, with PowerPoint® presentations, and on the G-W Companion Website. The end of each chapter includes a bulleted summary, review and critical thinking questions, as well as activities designed for individual and team projects.

Lab Workbook

The Lab Workbook that accompanies *Landscape Design, Installation, and Management* includes two types of student activities. The first type of activity consists of questions designed to reinforce the content of the textbook. Completing these activities helps students gain a deeper understanding of the terms, concepts, theory, and procedures presented in the chapter. The second type consists of hands-on lab activities, designed to be completed in the classroom with instructor guidance and supervision. These activities provide an opportunity to apply and extend the knowledge gained from the textbook.

Online Learning Suite

The Online Learning Suite provides the foundation of instruction and learning for digital and blended classrooms. An easy-to-manage shared classroom subscription makes it a hassle-free solution for both students and instructors. All student instructional materials are found on a convenient online bookshelf and accessible at home, at school, or on the go. The Online Learning Suite includes an interactive online textbook that holds students' interest. A workbook with digital form fields for easy completion engages students for learning success. Along with e-flash cards and a variety of other learning activities, the Online Learning Suite effectively brings digital learning to the classroom.

G-W Companion Website

The G-W Learning companion website is a study reference that contains pretests, e-flash cards, matching activities, vocabulary games, review questions, and posttests. The G-W Learning companion website is conveniently accessible from any digital device.

Online Learning Suite/ Student Text Bundle

Looking for a blended solution? Goodheart-Willcox offers the Online Learning Suite bundled with the printed text in one easy-to-access package. Students have the flexibility to use the printed text, the Online Learning Suite, or a combination of both components to meet their individual learning styles. The convenient packaging makes managing and accessing content easy and efficient.

Instructor Tools

LMS Integration

Integrate Goodheart-Willcox content within your Learning Management System for a seamless user experience for both you and your students. LMS-ready content in Common Cartridge format facilitates single sign-on integration and gives you control of student enrollment and data. With a Common Cartridge integration, you can access the LMS features and tools you are accustomed to using and G-W course resources in one convenient location—your LMS.

To provide a complete learning package for you and your students, G-W Common Cartridge includes the Online Learning Suite and Online Instructor Resources. When you incorporate G-W content into your courses via Common Cartridge, you have the flexibility to customize and structure the content to meet the educational needs of your students. You may also choose to add your own content to the course.

QTI® question banks are available within the Online Instructor Resources for import into your LMS. These prebuilt assessments help you measure student knowledge and track results in your LMS gradebook. Questions and tests can be customized to meet your assessment needs.

Online Instructor Resources (OIR)

Online Instructor Resources provide all the support needed to make preparation and classroom instruction easier than ever. Available in one accessible location, the OIR includes Instructor Resources, Instructor's Presentations for PowerPoint®, and Assessment Software with Question Banks. The OIR is available as a subscription and can be accessed at school, at home, or on the go.

Instructor Resources
One resource provides instructors with time-saving preparation tools, such as answer keys, chapter outlines, editable lesson plans, and other teaching aids.

Instructor's Presentations for PowerPoint®
These fully customizable, richly illustrated slides help you teach and visually reinforce the key concepts from each chapter.

Assessment Software with Question Banks
Administer and manage assessments to meet your classroom needs. The question banks that accompany this textbook include hundreds of matching, true/false, completion, multiple choice, and short answer questions to assess student knowledge of the content in each chapter. Using the assessment software simplifies the process of creating, managing, administering, and grading tests. You can have the software generate a test for you with randomly selected questions. You may also choose specific questions from the question banks and, if you wish, add your own questions to create customized tests to meet your classroom needs.

G-W Integrated Learning Solution

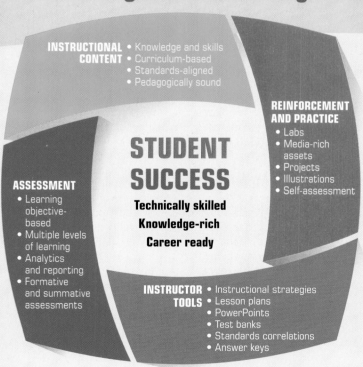

STUDENT SUCCESS

Technically skilled
Knowledge-rich
Career ready

INSTRUCTIONAL CONTENT
- Knowledge and skills
- Curriculum-based
- Standards-aligned
- Pedagogically sound

REINFORCEMENT AND PRACTICE
- Labs
- Media-rich assets
- Projects
- Illustrations
- Self-assessment

ASSESSMENT
- Learning objective-based
- Multiple levels of learning
- Analytics and reporting
- Formative and summative assessments

INSTRUCTOR TOOLS
- Instructional strategies
- Lesson plans
- PowerPoints
- Test banks
- Standards correlations
- Answer keys

The G-W Integrated Learning Solution offers easy-to-use resources that help students and instructors achieve success.

▶ **EXPERT AUTHORS**
▶ **TRUSTED REVIEWERS**
▶ **100 YEARS OF EXPERIENCE**

EMPLOYABILITY SKILLS · TECHNICAL SKILLS · ACADEMIC KNOWLEDGE · INDUSTRY RECOGNIZED STANDARDS

Landscape

Design, Installation, and Management

by

CHRISTOPHER D. HART ◆ R. LEE IVY

Publisher

The Goodheart-Willcox Company, Inc.
Tinley Park, IL
www.g-w.com

Preface

Landscape Design, Installation, and Management was created to meet the need for a comprehensive, modern, and visually exciting introduction to the study of the landscaping industry. *Landscape Design, Installation, and Management* provides learners with a breadth of knowledge of the green industry with a focus on landscaping while also creating awareness of careers and workplace skills needed to be successful. To help readers achieve these goals, the authors have incorporated supplemental activities, such as STEM connections, hands-on landscaping activities, and personalized career connections throughout the text.

The organization and content coverage of *Landscape Design, Installation, and Management* was developed with valuable insight from a panel of expert reviewers and with the certifications and skills associated with the National Association of Landscape Professionals at the forefront. The textbook content also correlates to various state standards and to exam standards for Career Skill Certification™ by Precision Exams. *Landscape Design, Installation, and Management* is presented in 22 chapters with three illustrated glossaries, which include all the items on the Nursery/Landscape CDE identification list, to help readers develop a fundamental knowledge of the landscape and green industries.

The initial chapters concentrate on occupational safety, tools and equipment, career readiness, and personal skills that are valuable in both school and work environments. Chapter 1 provides an overview of the green industry with a focus on landscaping work and businesses. Chapter 2 covers personal and professional skills needed to succeed in today's business world. Chapters 3 and 4 review safety in the workplace and while working with the tools and equipment used in the industry. An illustrated glossary of nursery and landscape tools and equipment immediately follows Chapter 4.

Chapter 5 instructs students on proper site evaluation based on important factors such as water movement and soil analysis. It also emphasizes the importance of determining landscape use, identifying rules and regulations that may affect the design, and the level of maintenance desired by the client. Chapter 5 also covers the basics of choosing plants that will thrive in new landscapes. Chapter 6 explains the principles and elements of design and how students can incorporate these elements into their designs. Chapter 7 discusses the concept of the outdoor room and how to use plants and hardscape materials to create a landscape that meets the client's needs and desires.

Plant production for the nursery and landscape industry is covered in Chapter 8. Substrates, plant propagation, field and container production, and soil types are also included in this chapter. Chapter 9 covers taxonomy, basic biology, and plant growth and development. Readers will develop an understanding of basic plant biology as well as how environmental controls can be used to manipulate plant growth. Chapter 10 provides detailed descriptions of the types and forms of plants that are used in landscape design.

Chapter 11 provides detailed descriptions and images of the common turfgrasses used to establish lawns, sports fields, and roadside erosion control. Chapter 12 covers new installations as well as turf repair and how to choose the proper turfgrass for different applications. Following chapters include lighting and water feature installation, hardscapes and basic installation procedures, and design practices used in landscape design.

Chapters 17, 18, and 19 focus on business start-ups, management, and establishing and maintaining positive client relationships. Basic accounting and business principles are included in Chapter 17 to help students understand the risks and advantages of owning their own businesses. Chapter 18 presents a methodical approach to pricing landscape projects so they are profitable and establishing and maintaining client relationships.

Chapters 20 and 21 explain proper methods for plant installation to ensure health and longevity and how to establish maintenance programs that make the best use of time and equipment to ensure a profit. The final chapter explains pest management through biological, chemical, mechanical, and cultural controls. Pest life cycles and the effect of controls at different stages is also explained in Chapter 22. Reading pesticide labels and using pesticides properly are explained in detail.

The study of these principles and embarking on a career in landscape design, installation, and management will be challenging and rewarding. We hope you enjoy the information presented and that it provides inspiration, information, and direction for your passion and pursuits.

Christopher D. Hart
R. Lee Ivy

About the Authors

Christopher D. Hart

Christopher D. Hart teaches agriculture and horticulture classes for Chatham Central High School in Bear Creek, North Carolina. Mr. Hart's courses focus on hands-on learning and producing college- and career-ready students. Mr. Hart is an alumnus of North Carolina State University where he earned a Bachelor of Science in Horticultural Science and in Agricultural Business Management. Mr. Hart also earned a Master of Science in Agricultural Education from NCSU.

Mr. Hart and his students are responsible for maintaining the school's conservatory, community garden, and six-acre arboretum. Hart and his students manage over 8000 ft² of production space in the school's container nursery, numerous greenhouses, and cold frames. Students are responsible for propagating, growing, and selling over 200 species of plants throughout the growing season.

In addition to advising the Chatham Central FFA Chapter, Mr. Hart has coached top-placing nursery landscape and floriculture teams in National FFA Career Development Events. He is the author of the lab workbook that accompanies *Horticulture Today* (Goodheart-Willcox Publisher). Mr. Hart is also a Certified Plant Professional and a Certified Pesticide Applicator.

R. Lee Ivy

R. Lee Ivy is a Senior Lecturer in the Department of Horticultural Science at North Carolina State University. He teaches courses in landscape construction, landscape maintenance, fruit and vegetable production, home horticulture, and an introductory course for students interested in horticultural science. He has been an educator for 17 years in the secondary education arena and specializes in hands-on teaching strategies and techniques. His interest in teaching stems from his respect of teachers who inspired him to make an effort, allow for challenges, and strive for high personal achievement. Childhood experiences growing peaches, vegetables, and ornamental plants sparked his interest and subsequent love of horticulture.

With a Bachelor of Science from the University of Tennessee in Ornamental Horticulture and Landscape Design and a Master of Science from North Carolina State in Horticultural Science, Ivy pursued teaching opportunities in postsecondary education. He developed hands-on teaching activities and experiences for his students in conjunction with industry and collegial partnerships. Mr. Ivy is also involved with various facets of student life, such as the Horticulture Club and Horticulture Competition Team. Travel and competition preparations allow for enhanced side-by-side partnerships with students. Most of his teaching is traditional face-to-face instruction, but he has also developed an award-winning online educational platform of project-based horticultural activities for college credit through the undergraduate certificate program and Ag-Idea, an educational partnership with universities across the United States. His efforts include recruiting the next generation of horticultural professionals through 4-H, the FFA Organization, and various career fairs. He intends to educate for sustainable landscape systems, safe food production, and a productive and rewarding livelihood.

In addition to teaching and advising, Mr. Ivy networks with green industry employers to foster job and internship opportunities for his students. A practicing landscape designer, Mr. Ivy is a Certified Pesticide Applicator and Plant Professional statewide and Landscape Industry Certified nationally.

Reviewers

The authors and publisher wish to thank the following industry and teaching professionals for their valuable input into the development of *Landscape Design, Installation, and Management*.

Tim Closs
Naaman Forest High School
Garland, Texas

David Gossman
Atwater High School
Atwater, California

Brittney Kee
Chicago High School for Agricultural Sciences
Chicago, Illinois

John Kreitzer
Upper Valley Career Center
Piqua, Ohio

Mike Liston
Tolles Career and Technical Center
Plain City, Ohio

Joe Luther
Central PA Institute of Science & Technology
Pleasant Gap, Pennsylvania

Aaron Nering
Perris High School
Perris, California

Caela Paioff
Colonial High School
Orlando, Florida

Joe Ramey
Central Nine Career Center
Greenwood, Indiana

Jodi Riedel
Wakefield High School
Raleigh, North Carolina

Melissa Trocheck
Central Montco Technical High School
Plymouth Meeting, Pennsylvania

Chris Wilder
Williston High School
Williston, Florida

Acknowledgments

The authors and publisher would like to thank the following companies, organizations, and individuals for their contribution of resource material, images, or other support in the development of *Landscape Design, Installation, and Management.*

A.M. Leonard Inc.
Brie Arthur, *Gardenuity*
Nate Bauer, A.M. Leonard Inc.
Bland Landscaping Co. Inc., Apex, NC
Brightview Landscape Services, Durham, NC
Hunter Casey, Casey Nursery Inc.
Will Crowder, Super-Sod
Daniel Currin, Greenscape Inc.
Mason Dyer, Belgard Pavers and Landscapes
Brandon Eubanks, Super-Sod
Barb Fair, North Carolina State University
BJ Fisher, Southern Showplace Landscapes Inc.
Dr. Bill Fonteno, North Carolina State University
Allison Fortner, Super-Sod
Kevin Foushee, Barefoot and Associates
Patrick Freeman, Hunter Industries
Ed Furner, Mariani Landscape, Lake Bluff, IL
Colby Griffin, North Carolina Cooperative
    Extension
Shannon Hathaway, Super-Sod
Melissa Hendrickson, North Carolina State
    University
John Hoffman, Hoffman Nursery Inc.
Brock Holtzclaw, Releaf Tree Works
Brandon Hubinek, Super-Sod
Hunter Industries
Dr. Brian Jackson, North Carolina State University
Dr. Helen Kraus, North Carolina State University
Brock Lavrack, Brightview Landscape Services
Dr. Bob Lyons
Dana Massey, Plantworks Nursery Inc.
Judson Mills, Super-Sod

Preston Montague
Josh Morrow, Super-Sod
Mike Munster, North Carolina State University
NASA
Joe Neal
Al Newsome, good-dirt.com
North Carolina Department of Agriculture
    and Consumer Services
North Carolina Plant Disease and Insect Clinic
Roger Phelps, STIHL Inc.
PlantHaven® Inc.
City of Raleigh, North Carolina
Joshua Richardson, Ruppert Landscape
Pat Scace, Missouri Botanical Garden
Tracy Sides, Landvision Designs Inc.
Hannah Singleton, North Carolina Nursery
    and Landscape Assoc.
Anne Spafford, North Carolina State University
Brandon Starnes, Super-Sod
Super-Sod, A Division of Patten Seed Company
Nathan Tart, Super-Sod
Jarred Taylor, North Carolina State University
Hillary Thompson, Super-Sod
USDA
USDA, AMS, Pesticides Records Branch
USDA Animal and Plant Health Inspection
    Services
USDA NRCS
Watts Plumbing, Heating, and Water Quality
    Solutions
Brian Whipker, North Carolina State Univesity
Yard-Nique, Morrisville, NC

Brief Contents

1 The Landscaping Industry 2
2 Workplace Skills 28
3 Occupational Safety 54
4 Tools and Equipment 84
   Illustrated Glossary: Nursery/Landscaping Equipment
   and Supplies Identification 114
5 Site Evaluation and Plant Selection 126
6 Principles and Elements of Design 148
7 The Outdoor Room Concept 168
8 Plant Production 196
9 Plant Taxonomy and Physiology 222
10 Ornamental Plants in the Landscape 244
   Illustrated Glossary: Nursery/Landscape Plant Identification 269
11 Turfgrass Selection 286
12 Turfgrass Installation and Management 308
13 Landscape Lighting and Water Features 332
14 Irrigation Design, Installation, and Maintenance 362
15 Hardscapes 398
16 Creating the Design 428
17 Starting a Business 456
18 Pricing Landscape Projects 484
19 Client Relationships 510
20 Landscape Installation 534
21 Landscape Management 564
22 Pest Management 596
   Illustrated Glossary: Pests, Disorders,
   and Beneficial Insects Identification 632

Contents

Chapter 1
The Landscaping Industry. . . 2

Impacts of the Landscaping Industry 4

The Green Industry 5

Industry Sectors 5
    Plant Production 5
    Sod Farms 8
    Research and Education 8
    Landscaping Suppliers 10
    Service Providers 10
    Landscape Design 11
    Landscaping Installation 15
    Landscape Maintenance 16
    Retailers 18

Professional Organizations 19
    AmericanHort 20
    American Horticultural Therapy Association
        (AHTA) 20
    American Society of Landscape Architects
        (ASLA) 20
    American Society of Horticultural Science
        (ASHS) 20
    International Society of Arboriculture
        (ISA) 21
    International Plant Propagators' Society . . . 21
    Irrigation Association 21
    National Association of Landscape
        Professionals 21
    Perennial Plant Association 21
    Professional Grounds Management
        Society 22
    Interlocking Concrete Pavement Institute
        (ICPI) 22
    Local Organizations 23

Professional Certifications 23

Chapter 2
Workplace Skills. 28

Setting Goals 30
    Types of Goals 30
    Vision and Mission Statements 31

Applying for a Position 32
    Résumés 32
    Letter of Application 33
    Job Application Forms 34
    The Job Interview 35

Succeeding in the Workplace 37
    Health and Hygiene 37
    Work Habits 38
    Time Management 38
    Attitude on the Job 38
    Professional Behavior 39
    Decision Making and Problem Solving 39
    Communication Skills 40
    Ethical Workplace Behavior 42
    Interpersonal Skills 43
    Conflict Management 46

Chapter 3
Occupational Safety 54

Safety and Health Agencies 56
    Occupational Safety and Health
        Administration (OSHA) 57
    US Department of Labor (DOL) 57
    National Institute of Occupational Safety
        and Health (NIOSH) 57
    US Centers for Disease Control and
        Prevention (CDC) 57
    American National Standards Institute
        (ANSI) 57

Maintaining a Safe Workplace 58

Employee Responsibilities 59

Personal Protective Equipment 60
    Eye Protection 60
    Hearing Protection 61
    Respiratory Protection 62
    Protective Clothing 63

First Aid 64
    Training and Certification 64
    First-Aid Kits 65
    Allergic Reactions 65

Workplace Safety Hazards. 66
    Plants 66
    Animals 66
    Weather Conditions 68
    Other Weather Hazards. 70

Shop Safety. 70
    Safety Data Sheets 71
    Safety Color-Coding. 71
    Chemicals and Liquid Fuels 72

Job Site and Vehicle Safety 75
    High-Visibility Clothing 76
    Work Area Barriers. 76
    Vehicle Safety 76
    High Hazard Areas 77

Tools for Sharpening Blades 100
    Grades and Grit. 101
Landscaping Power Equipment. 102
    Mowers 103
    Basic Maintenance for Power Equipment . . .105
Large Equipment. 105
    Equipment Limitations 106
    Maintaining Large Equipment 106
Troubleshooting. .107
Transportation and Hauling Equipment . .107

Illustrated Glossary
Nursery/Landscaping Equipment
    and Supplies Identification 114

Chapter 4
Tools and Equipment 84

Tool and Equipment Safety 86
    Personal Protective Equipment. 86
    Owner's Manuals 86
Record Keeping 87
    Maintenance 87
    Checklists 87
    Inventory 87
Measuring Devices .88
    Measuring Wheel 88
    Retractable Tape 88
    Winding Tape 88
    Surveyor's Tools 89
    Handheld Laser Measurer. 89
    Laser Level. 89
    Geographic Information System (GIS). 90
    Global Positioning System (GPS) 90
    Drones 90
Leveling Tools 90
Handheld Impact Tools 91
Digging and Planting Tools 92
    Shovels 92
    Other Digging Tools. 94
    Digging Tool Maintenance 95
Raking and Scraping Tools 95
Material Handling Tools 96
Pruning, Grafting, and Budding Tools 98

Chapter 5
Site Evaluation
and Plant Selection 126

Evaluating the Site. 128
    Logistics. 128
Visiting the Site 129
    Water Movement. 129
    Surveying the Site. 130
    Collecting Measurements 130
    Measuring Tools 131
    Performing a Soil Analysis 131
    Soil Compaction 132
    Freeze-Thaw Cycle 132
    Existing Structures. 132
Identifying Landscape Use 133
    Current and Future Activities. 133
    Maintenance Needs 134
Rules and Regulations 135
    Homeowner's Association. 135
Establishing a Budget 136
Choosing Plant Materials. 136
    Physical Hardiness and Life Cycle. 136
    Leaf Retention. 138
    Water Needs 138
    Environmental Adaptation 138
    Temperature for Optimum Growth 139
USDA Hardiness Zones 140
    Microclimates 141
AHS Heat Zones .141

Cardinal Directions. .141
    North-Facing Sites 141
    East-Facing Sites 143
    South-Facing Sites. 143
    West-Facing Sites. 143

Chapter 6
Principles and Elements of Design 148

Principles 150
Balance 150
Focalization 151
    Entryways 152
    Planting Beds 152
    Special Features 153
Simplicity 153
Rhythm. 154
Proportion 154
Scale. 154
Unity 155
Elements of Design .156
    Line. 156
    Form 157
    Texture 158
    Color 159
Site Considerations 161
    View Point 161
    Plant Maturity. 161
    Restrictions 161
    Cultural Requirements. 162

Chapter 7
The Outdoor Room Concept 168

Outdoor Rooms 170
    Living Area 171
    Public Area 171
    Service Area. 172
    Home and Landscape Connections 172

Property Size, Layout, and Shape 173
    Intended Use 173
    Placement of Home. 173
    Property Dimensions 173
    Property Layout 174
Outdoor Room Components 174
Walls 174
    Creating Walls Using Plant Material 176
    Creating Walls Using Building Materials. . . .178
    Fence Styles 181
Flooring. 182
    Soft Flooring 183
    Hard Flooring 185
Ceilings. 189
    Awnings. 189
    Gazebos 190
    Pergolas 191
    Trees and Shrubs 191

Chapter 8
Plant Production 196

History of Production 198
Substrates 199
    Making a Substrate. 199
Plant Propagation .202
    Sexual Propagation. 202
    Asexual Propagation 203
    Using Propagation to Manage
        the Landscape 205
Greenhouse Plant Production 205
    Plugs and Liners 206
    Acclimatization. 206
    Plant Cell Packs and Flats 207
American Standard for Nursery Stock. . . .207
Nursey Plant Production 208
    Container Production. 208
    Pot-in-Pot Production (PNP) 209
    Field Production 210
    Balled-and-Burlapped (B&B). 211
    Bare Root (BR) 211
    Transporting Nursery Stock 212
Transplants and Soil Types 213
    Soil Types. 213
    Water Movement. 215

Quarantines 215
Patented and Trademarked Plants 216

Chapter 9
Plant Taxonomy and Physiology 222

Plant Nomenclature 224
   Botanical Names. 224
   Common Names 225
Scientific Classification 226
   Phylum. 226
   Class 228
   Order 228
   Family. 228
   Genus 228
   Species 228
   Common and Binomial Names 231
Plant Parts. 231
   Roots. 231
   Stems 232
   Leaves. 235
   Flowers. 235
   Fruits. 236
   Seeds. 236
Plant Processes. 236
   Photosynthesis 236
   Respiration. 236
   Transpiration. 237
   Translocation 237
   Reproduction. 238
Plant Nutrition. 238
   Macronutrients and Micronutrients. 238
   Soil pH 239

Chapter 10
Ornamental Plants in the Landscape 244

Trees 246
   Tree Sizes 248
   Species 249
   Functions 249

Shrubs. 251
   Dwarf Shrubs 251
   Medium Shrubs 251
   Large Shrubs 251
   Evergreen Shrubs 251
   Deciduous Shrubs. 251
   Shrub Species 252
   Herbaceous Perennials. 252
Ornamental Grasses 253
Grass-Like Plants 254
Turfgrasses 255
Ground Covers. 255
Vines 256
Edibles. 258
Aquatic Plants 258
Geophytes. 259
   Color Display. 259
Bedding Plants. 260
Border or Line Plants 260
Facer Plants. 261
Foundation Plants .261
Corner Plantings 261
Topiary 262
Espalier 263
Massing. 263

Illustrated Glossary

Nursery/Landscape Plant Identification 269

Chapter 11
Turfgrass Selection 286

Turfgrass. 288
   Turf Zones 288
   Types of Lawns 289
   Other Factors to Consider 290
   Cool-Season Turfgrasses 291
   Warm-Season Turfgrasses. 296
   Blends and Mixes 300
Sustainability 301
Turfgrass Alternatives. 301
   Synthetic Turf 302
   Ornamental Grasses and Grass-Like
      Plants 302

Chapter 12
Turfgrass Installation and Management 308

Methods of Establishing Turfgrass 310
    Seeding. 310
    Sodding 312
    Sprigging and Plugging. 315
    Calculating Seed and Plant Materials 315

Establishing a New Lawn 317
    Step One: Choosing a Turfgrass 318
    Step Two: Preparing the Site 318
    Step Three: Sampling the Soil. 320
    Step Four: Amending the Soil. 321
    Step Five: Planting the Turfgrass 321
    Step Six: Maintaining the New Turfgrass . . .322

Mowing Lawns 322
    Mowing New Lawns 322

Renovating a Lawn 323
    Step One: Evaluating the Site 323
    Step Two: Taking a Soil Test 325
    Step Three: Weed Control 325
    Step Four: Preparing the Site. 326
    Step Five: Planting the Turfgrass 326
    Step Six: Maintaining New Turfgrass 327

Chapter 13
Landscape Lighting and Water Features 332

Landscape Lighting. 334
Power Systems 336
    GFCI Outlets 336
    Line-Voltage Systems 336
    Low-Voltage Systems 336
    Solar-Powered Systems 337
    Controllers. 338
    Lighting Zones 338

Lighting Fixtures and Techniques 338
    Light Fixtures 340
    Lightbulbs 340
    Lighting Techniques. 340

Types of Water Features 343
    Ponds 344
    Fountains 345
    Waterfalls 345

Equipment and Materials 346
    Electric Pumps 346
    Liners 346
    Electrical Service 347

Plant Materials 347
    Floaters 348
    Submerged Plants 348
    Erect Foliage Plants 349
    Bog and Marginal Plants 349
    Oxygenators. 349

Fish and other Aquatic Organisms 350
    Goldfish 350
    Koi. 350
    Orfes 350
    Japanese Snails 350
    Feeding Schedules 350

Constructing a Water Feature 351
    Layout and Excavation. 351
    Measuring Water Volume 351
    Calculating Pump Size. 352
    Calculating Liner Size 353
    Liner Installation 354
    Stone 354

Water Feature Maintenance 355
    Water Loss 355
    Skimmers and Filtration 356
    Predator Deterrents 356

Chapter 14
Irrigation Design, Installation, and Maintenance 362

Water Sources. 364
    Public Water Sources 365
    Private Water Sources. 366
    Retention and Detention Ponds 366

Water Movement and Pressure 367
    Maintaining Water Pressure 367

Irrigation System Components 368
    Valves 368
    Irrigation Lines 369
    Controllers. 372

Irrigation Systems 372
    Sprinkler Irrigation. 374
    Low-Volume Irrigation. 376

Irrigation Design 377
    Design Symbols. 377
    Analyzing the Area 377
    Determine Water Requirements 378
    Design Capacity 378
    Precipitation Rate 379
    Zone Placement. 379
    Sprinkler Placement 381
    Valve Placement 381
    Pipe Placement 381

Installing the System. 382
    Locating Utility Lines 382
    Point of Connection 382
    Layout and Marking. 383
    Trench Depth. 383
    Installing Pipes 383
    Installing Sprinkler Heads 385
    Installing Wires. 386
    Programming the Controller 386
    Flushing the System 387
    Finalizing the Installation 387

Maintenance and Repair 387
    Adjusting Sprinkler Heads 388
    Replacing Broken Sprinkler Heads 388
    Replacing Control Valves. 388
    Pipe Repair 388
    Wire Repair 389
    Flushing the System 389
    Winterizing the System 389

Chapter 15
Hardscapes 398

Types of Hardscapes 400
    Walkways. 400
    Driveways 401
    Patios and Decks. 401
    Stairs. 402
    Walls. 402
    Fences. 403
    Outdoor Kitchens 403
    Firepits 404

Hardscape Design .404
    Safety 404
    Pattern 405
    Water Flow. 406

Hardscape Materials 407
    Pavers 408
    Stone 408
    Wood and Composite Lumber 408
    Concrete 409
    Locally Sourced Materials. 410
    Upcycled Materials. 410
    Asphalt. 410
    Gravel 410
    Calculating Materials. 412
    Ordering Materials. 413

Tools and Equipment 413
    Grading Equipment 414
    Compactors 414
    Tools 415

Hardscape Installation 416
    Scheduling and Site Access. 416
    Marking the Area 417
    Setting the Final Grade 417
    Subsurface Preparation 417
    Topdressing. 420

Chapter 16
Creating the Design. 428

Drawing Methods .430
    Hand Drawing 430
    Computer-Aided Design (CAD) 431

Drafting Tools and Equipment 431
    Drafting Media 431
    Production Facilities. 432
    Drawing Board 432
    Pencils. 433
    Erasers 433
    Markers, Colored Pens,
        and Pastel Pencils 433

Architect's Scales and Engineer's Scales . . . 434
    Other Drawing Tools 436

Alphabet of Lines .436
    Line Widths 438

Drawing Components. 439
    Lettering. 440
    Symbols 441

Types of Drawings 444
  Viewpoints. 445
  Sketches 446
  Topographic Maps 446
  Functional Diagrams 447
  Preliminary Design 448
  Final Design. 448
  Planting Diagrams 449
Summarize Client Requirements 450

Chapter 17
Starting a Business. 456

Business Structures 458
  Sole Proprietorship. 458
  Partnership 459
  Limited Liability Company (LLC) 460
  Corporations 460
  Cooperatives 461
  Doing Business As (DBA) 461
Business Plans 462
  Business Plan Components 462
  Chain of Command 463
Mission and Vision Statements 464
  Developing a Mission Statement 464
  Vision Statement 465
Setting Goals 466
  Making Goals Specific 467
  Making Goals Measurable. 467
  Making Goals Achievable 467
  Making Goals Relevant 467
  Making Goals Timely. 467
Using Demographics. 467
  Identifying a Target Market 468
  Niche Markets. 469
Choosing a Name 469
  Business Licenses 470
  Logos 470
  Slogan. 470
  Brand Images. 470
  Choosing a Location. 470
Accounting. 471
  Bookkeeper vs. Accountant. 471
  Employer Identification Number 472

Budgets and Costs 472
  Income, Profit, and Expenses 474
  Debt 476
  Assets 476
  Liabilities 476
  Net Worth 476
  Return on Investment 477
Advertising. 477
  Online Presence 477
  Networking 478
  Community Presence. 478
  Newspaper, Television, and Radio. 479

Chapter 18
Pricing Landscape Projects. 484

Gathering Information 486
  Estimates and Bid Components 486
  Site Takeoff. 487
  Measuring Tools 487
Site Assessment 489
Project Estimates and Bids. 492
Profits and Profit Margins 492
Budgets and Costs. 493
  Direct and Indirect Costs. 494
  Operational Costs. 494
Quotes and Bids. .500
  Hourly Rates vs. Set Prices 501
  Quoting a Set Price. 502
  Bid Solicitation 503
  Competitors' Rates 504
Selling the Job 504

Chapter 19
Client Relationships. 510

Reaching Your Target Market 512
  Product. 512
  Price 513
  Promotion 513
  Place 514
  Services Marketing Mix. 515

Client Contact. 516
    Building Rapport 516
    Setting Up and Preparing for a Meeting. . 516
    Meeting the Client 516
    Gathering Information. 517
    Interpersonal Skills 518

Bid Solicitation 519
    Should You Accept the Job?. 521
    Will other Projects Be Compromised?. . . . 522
    Making a Presentation. 522

Quotes and Business Contracts 524
    Business Contracts 524

Project Management .527
    Company Hierarchy. 527
    Checking In. 528
    Following a Work Timeline. 528
    Customer Service 528

Chapter 20
Landscape Installation. . . . 534

Reading the Final Plan 536
Reviewing the Calculations 537
    Site Takeoffs. 537
    Plant Spacing. 538
    Calculating Volume 539

The Installation Process 539
    Grading 540
    Drainage. 540

Plant Delivery and Installation 541
    Staging Area 541
    Soil Amendments 541
    Order of Installation. 542
    Protecting Existing Plants 544

Planting Trees and Shrubs 545
    Moving and Placing Plants 546
    Container Plants 546
    Balled-and-Burlapped Plants 546
    Constructing a Berm 547
    Adding Mulch. 547
    Staking Trees. 548

Planting Bedding Plants. 550
    Spacing. 550
    Establishing Ground Covers 551

Planting Vines 552
    Support Structures 552

Watering 553
    Timing 553
    Methods of Application 554

Clean Up. 554

Scheduling Installation or Task
    Completion Times 555

Chapter 21
Landscape Management 564

Management vs. Maintenance. 566
Analysis and Treatment Assessment 566
    New Landscapes. 566
    Mature Landscapes 567

Management Plans .568
Fertilization 568
    Organic Fertilizers 569
    Inorganic Fertilizers. 570
    Quick-Release Fertilizers. 571
    Slow-Release Fertilizers. 571
    Controlled-Release Fertilizers. 571
    Rates of Application 571
    Fertilizer Application Methods. 573

Watering 574
    Application Methods 574
    Soil Texture 574

Mulching 576
    Depth 576
    Application 576
    Season. 576

Pruning. 577
    Areas of Growth 577
    Reasons to Prune 579
    Time for Pruning 581
    Pruning Techniques 582

Managing Annuals .584
    Soil Preparation. 584
    Watering and Fertilization 585

Winterization 585
    Mulching 586
    Pruning 586
    Compost and Fertilizing 586
    Watering. 586
    Early Fall or Late Spring Freeze 587
Sustainable Landscaping Management . . .587
Scheduling Multiple Projects 588

Chapter 22
Pest Management 596

Using IPM. 598
    Identifying the Plant and Pest. 599
    Monitoring the Pest 599
    Threshold Levels. 599
    IPM Control Methods 600
Types of Pests. 604
    Weeds. 605
    Invertebrate Pests 606
    Plant Diseases 608
    Vertebrates 610
Types of Pesticides. .611
    Herbicides 611
    Insecticides 611
    Fungicides 612
    Miticides. 612
    Molluscicides. 612
    Rodenticides 613
Chemical Structure and Toxicity. 613
Pesticide Formulations 614
    Liquid Pesticides. 614
    Pesticide Dusts 614
    Pesticide Granules 615
    Wettable Powders 615
    Aerosol Sprays. 615
    Fumigants 615

Pesticide Labels 616
    Required Information 616
    Pesticide Names 616
    EPA Registration Number 617
    Active Ingredients and Mode of Action . . 617
    Toxicity. 617
    Signal Words 618
    Lethal Dose and Lethal Concentration . . . 618
    First-Aid Instructions. 618
    Precautionary Statements 618
    Restricted Entry Interval (REI) 619
Pesticide Application. 619
    Licenses and Certifications 619
    Application Methods 620
    Mixing Pesticides 620
    Assessing the Area. 621
    Applying Pesticides 621
Storage and Disposal 623

Illustrated Glossary

Pests, Disorders, and Beneficial Insects
    Identification 632

Appendix

Pro Tips for Pruning Landscaping
    Plants 640
Average Task Times 642
Plants Commonly Used in Landscape
    Designs. 644
Plants for Wet and Dry Locations 648
Conversions and Equivalents 649
Writing and Understanding Binomial
    Nomenclature 652
Glossary 656
Index. 670

Feature Contents

Career Connection Features

Horticulture Therapist 20

Roger Phelps, Corporate Communications Manager, STIHL Inc. 22

Hannah Singleton, Manager of Professional Development 48

Daniel Currin, CEO and Owner of Greenscape, Inc. 74

Brock Holtzclaw, Arborist 106

Preston Montague, Naturalist 142

Tracy Sides, Landvision Designs Inc. 162

Edward Furner, Premier Service Director for Mariani Landscape 188

Dana Massey, President, Plantworks Nursery, Inc. 214

John Hoffman, Nurseryman 238

Brie Arthur, Garden Communicator 262

Dr. Robert Lyons, Educator, Director, Volunteer. 303

Judson Mills, Super-Sod Outlet Manager 324

Patrick Freeman, Sales Manager with Hunter Industries 357

Mason Dyer, Territory Manager, Belgard Pavers and Landscapes 420

Brock Lavrack, Senior Branch Manager for BrightView Landscape Services 447

Hunter Casey, Casey Nursery Inc. 479

Joshua Richardson, CPP, Landscape Designer, Ruppert Landscape,
    Raleigh/Durham, NC 505

Al Newsome, Entrepreneur and Art Lover. 529

BJ Fisher, President, Southern Showplace Landscapes, Inc. 552

Kevin Foushee, Turf and Ornamentals Spray Technician. 590

Colby Griffin, Extension Agent 622

STEM Connection Features

Science in Plant Production—Micropropagation 6

Reading Rulers and Tape Measures 89

Variegation 158

Nutrient Deficiency Symptoms. 234

Turfgrass Morphology 294

Measurement Conversions. 317

Calculating Seed and Plant Materials 327

Electrical Measurements 335

Pump Energy Use 347

Calculating Stone Amounts 354

Calculating Slope 419

Calculating Square Footage and Perimeter 490

Personal Pace 491
Calculating Task Times 556
Spreader Calibration. 557
Using the Soil Triangle. 575
Pesticides and Beneficials: The Wilsonville Bee Kill 611
Calibrating a Hand Sprayer. 623

Hands-On Landscaping Features

Sharpening Lawn Mower Blades 101
Living Walls. 175
Interpreting Seed Labels and Packets 202
Planting Geophytes. 260
Taking a Soil Sample. 320
Meeting the Client's Needs 523

Additional Features

Using Social Media Responsibly. 41
Case Study: Working Well with Others. 43
Developing Leadership Skills 45
Case Study: Working Safely. 59
Case Study: Staying Safe around Large Equipment. 78
Case Study: Staying Safe While Trimming Trees. 78
Gaining Knowledge and Developing Skills 143
Preserving Plants for the Future. 230
Thinking Green: Electric Mowers. 299
Thinking Green: Harvesting Rainwater 365
Thinking Green: Permeable Hardscapes. 411
Keeping Track: Installation Checklist 421
What Catches Your Eye?. 439
Keeping Track: Design Checklist 449
Developing Business Skills 464
Bids, Estimates, Proposals, and Quotes 488
The Pricing Process. 501
Thinking Green: Controlling Snails and Slugs. 607

CHAPTER

1

The Landscaping Industry

While studying this chapter, look for the activity icon ➦ to:

- **Practice** vocabulary terms with Words to Know activities.
- **Expand** learning with identification activities.
- **Reinforce** what you learn by completing Know and Understand questions.

G-WLEARNING.com

www.g-wlearning.com/agriculture

Chapter Outcomes

After studying this chapter, you will be able to:

- Explain the economic significance of the landscaping and green industries.
- Identify the sectors of the landscaping industry.
- Identify careers associated with the landscaping industry.
- Understand educational requirements for landscape industry careers.
- Explain the importance of professional organizations associated with the landscape industry.
- Describe credentials and certifications offered in the landscape industry.

Key Terms ⤤

arboriculture
arborist
aseptic culture
certified irrigation designer (CID)
cooperative extension agent
Cooperative Extension System (CES)
environmental horticulture industry
green industry
interior plantscaping
interiorscaping
irrigation system designer
irrigation technician

landscape architect
landscape contractor
landscape designer
landscape horticulture
landscape irrigation system
landscaping industry
micropropagation
nursery
plant breeding
subcontractor
tissue culture

Introduction

Have you ever considered a career in the landscaping industry? Do you enjoying being outdoors and working with your hands? Would you be interested in creating and maintaining outdoor living areas? If so, the landscaping industry offers exciting career opportunities. Whether in research, cultivation, installation, or management, work in the landscaping industry improves our outdoor spaces and our connection to nature. The impact of the landscaping industry is seen all around, including in our parks, botanical gardens, athletic fields, and golf courses, **Figure 1-1**. This chapter introduces you to the landscaping industry, career opportunities, and professional organizations.

Eric Crouse/Shutterstock.com   watchara/Shutterstock.com

Figure 1-1. There are many areas in the green industry in which a person can specialize. Golf courses, for example, require expert management and maintenance by trained individuals. City parks often receive a great amount of use and require expert installation and design as well as consistent maintenance.

Impacts of the Landscaping Industry

The *landscaping industry* consists of people and businesses that cultivate, produce, sell, install, and maintain landscape designs created by landscape architects and designers. The landscaping industry is an important part of our national economy that influences the aesthetics of our environment. Industry experts estimate that the average starting salary for a landscape professional is $46,000 and market data indicates that the average landscape contractor nets $900,000 on an annual basis with a median $291,000 in revenue. The industry in the United States has estimated revenues of $78 billion annually. It employs about one million people in over 470,000 businesses and the US Department of Labor predicts steady growth of employment opportunities. The geography of the United States is such that landscaping work is performed in parts of the country year-round.

Christopher D. Hart

Figure 1-2. Public areas often feature fun and interesting play areas for children and adults to enjoy. These areas are designed by landscape architects and installed by professionals to ensure safety and longevity.

Landscaping operations in areas with significant seasonal changes also provide services, such as snow removal, in the off-season.

We experience the aesthetic impact of the landscaping industry each day as we enjoy the beauty of landscapes in public and private areas. People living in urban areas can enjoy the outdoors in city parks across the country, **Figure 1-2**. Other positive ways in which landscaping plants affect our environment include oxygen contribution to the atmosphere, carbon dioxide absorption, and the provision of habitats and food for wildlife. Large expanses of turfgrass also serve as carbon sinks that absorb and retain carbon.

The Green Industry

The landscaping industry is part of an even larger industry known as the *green industry* or the *environmental horticulture industry*. The green industry includes plant and soil research, floriculture, viticulture (grapes), and olericulture (food plants), as well as companies that produce, rent, and sell landscape supplies and equipment. The estimated economic impact of the green industry as a whole is nearly $200 billion with over 2,000,000 full- and part-time jobs, **Figure 1-3**. The landscape segment of the green industry is referred to as landscape horticulture. *Landscape horticulture* is the cultivation and management of plants grown for aesthetic purposes, both indoor and outdoor.

Industry Sectors

The landscape industry is divided into sectors that perform the following functions:

- Produce plant materials.
- Research plant cultivation and educate the public.
- Supply plant materials and equipment.
- Provide services, such as design, installation, and maintenance.
- Purchase and sell plant materials.

Plant Production

Producers propagate and cultivate the plant materials in greenhouses and nursery fields for use in landscape installations, **Figure 1-4**. According to the USDA Census of Agriculture, these

Christopher D. Hart

Figure 1-3. Large-scale greenhouse operations grow thousands of annuals each year for homeowners and professionals to add seasonal interest and color in landscapes. These annuals are sold by nurseries, garden centers, and retail stores.

Dmytro Surkov/Shutterstock.com

V J Matthew/Shutterstock.com

Goodheart-Willcox Publisher

Figure 1-4. Commercial greenhouses and nursery fields are found across the country and often specialize in plants that are native to their area or from a similar climate.

STEM Connection

Science in Plant Production—Micropropagation

Vladimir Mulder/Shutterstock.com

Micropropagation is a form of asexual plant propagation used to reproduce plants that are identical to the parent plant rapidly. The method requires specialized equipment and sterile conditions to be successful. Technicians place small, sterilized sections of the parent plant in a petri dish, test tube, or small jar that contains a nutrient rich growing medium. The micropropagated plants are then kept in ideal growing conditions. After several steps, including multiplication and rooting, the plants are transplanted to soil and then acclimated to their environment.

Micropropagated plants are grown for many purposes, including chemical studies, pest-free plant propagation, growing large numbers of plants in a short amount of time, and to aid in the conservation of endangered plant species. The method is also useful when plant breeders are trying to increase numbers quickly so that new plants can be brought to market and when breeding species that are difficult to propagate. Micropropagation is also known as **tissue culture** or **aseptic culture**.

Consider This

1. Can you identify any plant species that have been saved with micropropagation?
2. Are there any disadvantages to micropropagation? If so, do the advantages outweigh the disadvantages?
3. Is micropropagation a controversial method of plant reproduction? Explain your answer.

Hands-On

Design a micropropagation culture "facility" with one or two classmates. The culture area and growing facility must be sterile and you must be able to control the lighting and temperature. Use the scientific method to keep detailed records and write a report with your findings.

horticultural specialty operations yield around $14 billion annually. Most producers grow a variety of plant species that are native or compatible with the local climate. However, some growers may grow species that are new and unusual and often times not native to the area, and others may grow plants specifically for interiorscapes. Many plant producers hold advanced degrees in botany or horticulture and use their knowledge and experience to raise healthy plants that will thrive in new landscapes.

Greenhouse Production

Greenhouse production includes the production of bedding, potted, foliage, and other plants used in landscape installations, **Figure 1-5**. Some greenhouse operations specialize in plant propagation from seeds or with cuttings from roots, leaves, or stems. Greenhouse operations that do not propagate plants purchase the young plants when they reach transplantable size, transplant them into larger containers, and sell the plants when they are more mature or transplant them into nursery fields. Most growers purchase transplants because it is difficult to start a large quantity of seedlings in a greenhouse that does not have the specialized structure and equipment required.

Did You Know?

Census data from the 2014 AG Census indicates that there were 23,221 floriculture producers with a combined sales volume of $13.78 billion.

A *Photology/Shutterstock.com*   **B** *T.W. van Urk/Shutterstock.com*

Figure 1-5. A—Propagation nurseries raise plants from seeds or cuttings and sell the young plants to greenhouse and nursery operations where they will be cultivated into larger, saleable plants. B—Greenhouse growers produce annuals and other herbaceous plants used to provide seasonal color.

Nursery Production

A *nursery* is a place where young plants, such as trees, shrubs, and herbaceous perennials, are cultivated for sale and planting elsewhere. Most of the plant materials in a nursery are grown to saleable size in fields, **Figure 1-6**. However, a nursery may use a greenhouse when the plant is first cultivated and a shade structure to protect the plant as it becomes acclimated to the outdoor environment. The plants are managed to various sizes based on landscaper and consumer needs. The more mature a plant is, the higher the cost. Some clients will request and pay more for mature plants in order to have an instant landscape or one that will mature more quickly. Nursery growers invest in the time it takes for plants to mature to the desired age and size. Many of the plants sold in nurseries are at least one-year old and most trees are at 7 or 8 years old. Nursery sales in the United States are more than $4 billion annually.

A *Stone/Shutterstock.com*   **B** *Andrii Zastrozhnov/Shutterstock.com*

Figure 1-6. A—Nursery producers grow trees, shrubs, and herbaceous perennials. B—The landscaping industry requires a wide variety of skills.

Sod Farms

Sod farms produce turf that is used on athletic fields, golf courses, residential lawns, and commercial landscapes. Sod farms require an extensive amount of land, regular irrigation, and high-quality soil, **Figure 1-7**. Producers must invest in specialized machinery and extensive irrigation systems. The producers must also invest in the time it takes to grow strong and well-knitted root systems before the sod can be harvested.

Sod is a labor-intensive crop with sensitive time-constraints. Harvest and delivery times must be well planned, as sod should be planted within 24 hours of harvest. The producer is responsible for handling the logistics of loading, transporting, and installing the heavy rolls of freshly harvested turf within this timeframe. Waiting longer than 24 hours will greatly affect the sod's ability to become established. Sod farms typically specialize in turfgrass species that are well suited for their area. Recent census data indicates that the 1289 sod farms in the United States average combined sales of $1.14 billion.

Research and Education

Trees resistant to disease, shrubs with extended blooming seasons, and increased plant hardiness are a few of the many advancements achieved through education and plant research. Individuals involved in this facet of the landscape industry research problems and find solutions that benefit the industry. Researchers may have science backgrounds with degrees in fields such as botany, horticulture, or forestry, and may specialize in other areas, such as plant breeding.

Botany

Botany is the scientific study of plants, including their structure, genetics, ecology, classification, and economic importance. Botanists are scientists who study and research plant growth, development, reproduction, and adaptation. Botanists may be employed in private industry, by universities, or in various government departments. Most entry-level careers require a bachelor's degree and advanced jobs require a master's or PhD.

Eric Buermeyer/Shutterstock.com   *Charles Knowles/Shutterstock.com*

Figure 1-7. Sod production is labor-intensive work that requires careful planning to ensure a high-quality product that will thrive in a newly established landscape.

Education

Educators teach horticulture and landscaping in high schools, community colleges, and universities, **Figure 1-8**. Many educational programs have greenhouses, conservatories, and arboretums in which students can experience hands-on training and hone their skills. Many educational institutions also have botanical gardens or arboretums that the students help design and maintain as part of their studies. Instructors must not only have knowledge of how to grow crops, they must have the skill to transfer that knowledge to students. Schools and trade organizations also offer industry certification at local, state, and national levels.

R. Lee Ivy

Figure 1-8. Educators teach safe equipment operation in addition to plant cultivation, installation, and management. Most programs also offer business and accounting classes as part of the curriculum.

Cooperative Extensions

The *Cooperative Extension System (CES)* is a publicly funded education program that uses knowledge gained through research and education to address human, plant, and animal needs. The program is designed to help people use research-based knowledge to improve their lives. The service is provided by the land grant universities located in each state.

A *cooperative extension agent* is the liaison between the community and the university. Extension agents conduct classes to help individuals gain licensing and certification in different fields, such as pesticide application. They also hold classes for homeowners and other individuals interested in agricultural issues, such as sustainable practices. Most extension agents are also involved in primary and secondary educational curriculum in their area. Extension agents provide people with the tools and resources needed to create successful landscapes. Entry-level positions require a bachelor's degree at minimum and higher positions require a master's degree or PhD.

Plant Breeding

Plant breeding is the manipulation of plants to improve the quality and performance of existing plants and to create new varieties. The manipulation may be performed in a greenhouse or in a biotechnology lab where scientists work on a genetic level. Plant breeding is used to modify traits, increase disease resistance, change cultural requirements, improve yields, and control growth. Plant breeding may also enable the cultivation of plants in danger of extinction due to disease or loss of environment. See **Figure 1-9**.

R. Lee Ivy

Figure 1-9. Plant breeders often work with rare and exotic species, such as the *Amorphophallus titanium*, otherwise known as the corpse flower.

Plant breeders focused on creating new ornamentals for the landscaping industry typically study the market and create or modify existing plants as demanded by consumers. Experiments and trials are commonly conducted by breeders to determine the effectiveness of the newly produced plants. Plant breeders may be self-employed or work in the public or private sectors of the industry. Entry-level jobs in plant breeding typically require a bachelor's degree with advanced jobs requiring a master's or PhD.

Landscaping Suppliers

Suppliers are the businesses that distribute materials other than plants to growers, designers, installation and maintenance professionals, and retailers. These materials include growing mediums, fertilizers, containers, tools, pesticides, and other items needed for ornamental plant cultivation, **Figure 1-10**. These companies may also supply seeds for greenhouse propagation. Landscape suppliers also distribute materials used to construct hardscapes, such as patios, decks, walkways, water features, and outdoor lighting.

Service Providers

The landscaping industry is primarily a service-based industry in which landscapers provide landscape installation, maintenance, and management services for residential and commercial properties. A landscape company may focus on a specific area or they may have divisions of the company that work on either residential or commercial design, installation, or maintenance. Working conditions vary in the service industry, as do daily routines, educational requirements, and salaries, **Figure 1-11**. The abundance of potential clients include residential property owners, municipalities, businesses, shopping malls, airports, subdivisions, housing developments, and schools.

Goodheart-Willcox Publisher

T.W. van Urk/Shutterstock.com

Figure 1-10. Suppliers provide professionals with the consumable materials needed to grow, install, and maintain commercial and residential landscapes.

Christopher D. Hart

Figure 1-11. Businesses in the landscape service industry, mow, prune, fertilize, and trim residential and commercial landscapes. Many landscape service providers also provide snow removal service.

Fotokostic/Shutterstock.com

Doug Lemke/Shutterstock.com

Figure 1-12. Public works operators work for the local government or municipality. They maintain parks, ball fields, and other properties owned by the municipality.

Public Works Segment

Cities, municipalities, and state governments may hire employees to install and maintain the landscaping in city parks, office buildings, sports fields, cemeteries, and other properties owned by the state or local government. Individuals in this segment of the industry will likely perform a wide variety of tasks as a municipal or government employee, **Figure 1-12**.

Landscape Design

Landscape design has been a profession since the 18th century in Europe. This was a period in which the wealthy had experienced gardeners create elaborate gardens throughout their properties. By the 19th century, growing cities and towns had professional designers working with architects to create parks and other green spaces where citizens could gather and enjoy the outdoors, **Figure 1-13**. Today, we have designers and more than 16,000 licensed architects designing landscapes for our homes, schools, businesses, and public spaces. These design services are valued at over $2 billion annually. The residential design market is the largest market segment.

Tupungato/Shutterstock.com

Figure 1-13. Grant Park in Chicago was established in the late 1800s on Chicago's lakefront. After a period of neglect in the 1980s, the city and park supporters helped restore the gardens, trees, and hardscapes to their original splendor.

A   *Irina Mos/Shutterstock.com*

B   *Dean Fikar/Shutterstock.com*

Figure 1-14. Many of the elaborate botanical gardens across the United States have been designed by landscape architects. They work with other horticultural professionals to choose plant materials for their physical structures as well as their beauty and interest. A—Atlanta Botanical Garden, Atlanta, Georgia. B—Japanese garden in Texas.

Landscape Architect

A *landscape architect* is a trained and licensed architect with a bachelor's or master's degree in landscape architecture. Some architects also pursue studies in horticulture and botanical science. Landscape architects design landscapes for private, commercial, and public properties, **Figure 1-14**. Depending on the architectural firm, an architect may specialize in specific types and/or size projects, such as resorts or public parks. A landscape architect must have training or experience working with challenging issues, such as steep slopes, elevation issues, and the placement of service lines and entrance and exit areas for vehicles and pedestrians.

Landscape architects may specialize in natural restoration of disturbed areas, such as wetlands or forests, or preservation planning for historic areas. Another specialization area for which demand is growing is sustainable landscaping. Most educational programs include training in the design of unconventional landscapes, such as green roofs, and sustainable landscapes with lower water and fertilization needs, **Figure 1-15**. These landscapes also include a means of managing runoff to conserve water and avoid polluting waterways.

Landscape Designer

A *landscape designer* also creates landscapes, albeit on a smaller scale than a landscape architect does. Their projects are typically limited to residential and small commercial properties, **Figure 1-16**.

Evannovostro/Shutterstock.com   *studio2013/Shutterstock.com*

Figure 1-15. Living walls insulate buildings, absorb rainfall, and help clean the air around them. Their installation also enables plant cultivation in urban areas with limited ground space.

State governments set guidelines and regulations as to which types of projects require the services of a licensed landscape architect. Landscape designers often have design training through college or certification programs but they do not have an architect's license. They may also have a horticulture or similar plant science background.

Landscape architects and designers are often responsible for much of the communication with clients, contractors, installation crews, city officials, engineers, surveyors, environmental specialists, and city planning and zoning boards. They may also have to ensure that all permits are acquired and to coordinate contractor schedules, material delivery, and the timeline for project completion.

Interiorscape Designer

Interiorscaping or *interior plantscaping* is the designing, installation, and maintenance of landscaping in indoor areas, **Figure 1-17**. Interior landscapes can transform an indoor area by adding color and texture and softening the hardscape. The plant materials also help filter and purify the air. Interiorscapes are found in a variety of settings, including shopping malls, offices, healthcare facilities, restaurants, hotels, and homes. Studies also indicate that indoor landscapes help reduce stress, create productive environments, and enhance our general well-being.

Christopher D. Hart

Figure 1-16. A landscape designer works with landscapes on a smaller scale than a landscape architect does.

Christopher D. Hart

Figure 1-17. Interiorscaping is the process of using plants to build landscape in the interior of a building or home. These landscapes may be extensive with paths and many perennials, or small areas in the center of aisles, or rest areas with seasonal plants that are consistently replaced.

Interiorscape designers follow the same design principles as traditional landscape designers. They must also work with clients to create landscapes that satisfy their client's demands. An interiorscape designer's contract typically includes the consistent care and replacement of plant materials as well as the addition of seasonal accents and plants. Many of the plants used indoors are the same species commonly used as houseplants. A designer may have a horticulture background and formal training in landscape design. A horticulture background will help a designer better understand the light, temperature, humidity, and watering needs of plant materials commonly used in interiorscapes.

Irrigation System Designer

A *landscape irrigation system* is a system designed to pump water from a source and distribute it throughout a landscape. The majority of landscape irrigation systems are installed belowground, **Figure 1-18**. An *irrigation system designer* is a person who designs and often installs or supervises installation of irrigation systems. Many designers are also responsible for system repair, maintenance, and seasonal preparation tasks. System designers must understand hydraulics, water requirements for different plant materials, and the way soil type, slope, water pressure, and the land's topography will affect the system. They must also consider water conservation, existing and proposed landscaping capacity, water flow rates, and time sequencing with existing systems when designing. A designer is often responsible for providing the client information on system use, irrigation schedules, and regular maintenance tasks, as well as emergency shutoff procedures.

The need for efficient and cost-effective irrigation systems is growing with ever increasing concerns and demands for water conservation. To ensure system efficiency, designers must keep current with technological advances and implement new water- and energy-saving technology to new and existing systems. Designers will also benefit by establishing relationships with water resource agencies that can help develop water conservation plans for specific projects.

Industry Certification. Irrigation system designers may acquire certification through various programs but certification is not necessarily required for employment. Most designers learn through on-the-job training or through manufacturer training programs. Designers seeking industry certification may become *certified irrigation designers (CIDs)* in specialized areas, such as commercial, golf course, or residential irrigation. Continuing education credits are required to maintain certifications. Irrigation designers typically have a degree in horticulture or a related field.

Figure 1-18. Irrigation designers determine water requirements of plants as well as the water supply. They must design a system that delivers water equally to all areas of the landscape.

Landscaping Installation

As with most construction projects, a variety of professionals are involved in landscape projects. The architect, designer, or other landscaping professional must coordinate any number of contractors and subcontractors to prepare or install different portions of the landscape.

Landscape Contractor

Landscape contractors are licensed professionals who coordinate and install landscape designs. Contractors often hire subcontractors to install special elements of a job that require different resources or a higher level of expertise than the contractor possesses. *Subcontractors* are contractors that specialize in specific tasks, such as building hardscapes, **Figure 1-19**. A landscape company, for example, that only installs softscape elements will subcontract another business to install the hardscape of a project. Some landscape contractors are also designers and have design-build firms. In a design-build firm, the contractor possesses the skills needed to design and install the landscape.

Landscape contractors may have backgrounds in a variety of areas, including horticulture, building construction, business, and landscape architecture. They may also have certifications in various landscaping fields. Landscape contractors are licensed by the states in which they work. However, licensing guidelines vary by state.

R. Lee Ivy

Figure 1-19. Landscape contractors may hire subcontractors to clear or grade areas or to install a hardscape. Hiring a subcontractor is often less costly for the contractor than owning large machinery that will sit unused for long periods of time or to hire additional employees to install one landscape.

Irrigation Technician

Irrigation technicians install plans developed by irrigation designers. Irrigation technicians use various styles of pipes, fittings, pumps, and controllers. Technicians also install wiring and programmable controllers and are often responsible for repairing and maintaining systems. They also establish maintenance schedules and ensure the system's efficiency, **Figure 1-20**. Irrigation technicians learn to troubleshoot and identify problems within the irrigation system and its components.

7500jacks/Shutterstock.com

Candus Camera/Shutterstock.com

Figure 1-20. Irrigation must be planned and installed properly to prevent the need to dig into a newly established landscape for repairs. Sprinklers must also be adjusted to prevent waste and ensure adequate coverage.

Figure 1-21. Most formal gardens require consistent care to retain their design.

Most technicians learn through on-the-job training or through manufacturer training and certification programs.

Landscape Maintenance

One of the most common and abundant positions available in the landscaping industry is that of the maintenance worker. Maintenance workers perform many tasks, including mowing, string trimming, edging, fertilizing, pest control, snow removal, and seasonal color installation, **Figure 1-21**. They may also replace dying or diseased plants when needed. Many individuals enter the landscaping field through maintenance positions and move up in the field through experience, training, and education.

Unlike the design and installation fields that may experience lulls, especially in downturns of the economy, the maintenance facet is usually very steady. Many landscape operations depend on maintenance contracts as their main source of income because properties always require maintenance. This is especially true with commercial sites, as businesses cannot afford to have unkempt landscapes that provide poor first impressions of their companies.

Private and Commercial Clients

Companies that focus primarily on residences must retain a certain number of clients to support their workforce. Many residential clients sign contracts that cover the entire growing season. Signed contracts ensure a steady amount of maintenance work for a company. Commercial accounts also sign contracts; however, they are often annual commitments that include snow removal during the offseason. Commercial landscape maintenance may involve the care of large properties that require multiple crews that are devoted to maintaining the job site year-round, **Figure 1-22**. Commercial landscape maintenance firms may be very large with net sales of several million dollars.

Turfgrass Maintenance

Landscape maintenance firms may specialize in turfgrass maintenance. Turfgrass maintenance workers tend to turfgrass in many locations, including residences, athletic fields, golf courses, office parks, schools, and hospitals. General landscaping firms typically tend to turfgrass while performing regular maintenance. Some turfgrass maintenance, such as that of athletic fields and golf courses, requires more attention and labor than turf on residential and commercial properties, **Figure 1-23**. This is a growing field and some universities and colleges now offer degrees in various fields of turf management. These programs also include studies focused on sustainable water use, as these large expanses of turf require a great deal of irrigation.

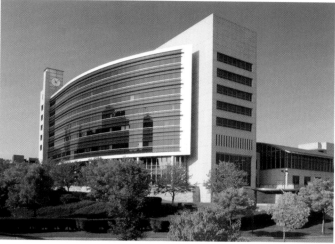

jessicakirsch/Shutterstock.com

nikitsin.smugmug.com/Shutterstock.com

Figure 1-22. Residential properties are typically smaller than commercial properties. Commercial properties are too large for smaller companies to have as clients because they cannot dedicate enough employees to maintain the landscape without compromising other client contracts.

Microgen/Shutterstock.com

Microgen/Shutterstock.com

ESB Basic/Shutterstock.com

Stefano/Shutterstock.com

Figure 1-23. Golf courses are a major division of the turfgrass industry. They require a great deal of maintenance and the use of specialized equipment. There are more than 15,000 courses in the United States using over 3000 square miles (over 2 million acres) of land.

Arborists

Arboriculture is the science of tree care and management. A professional *arborist* is a specialist trained to provide proper care, help maintain healthy trees, and give advice on removing large dying or deceased specimens, **Figure 1-24**. A trained arborist also has expertise in diagnosing and treating disease or infestations.

Most general landscape maintenance firms do not have the resources nor experience for removing large trees, whereas arborists are trained to safely climb and use the equipment needed to trim, prune, and remove large trees. Arborists also have training and expertise in caring for trees in densely populated areas where trees are often near structures and utility lines. Arborists

Goodheart-Willcox Publisher

Figure 1-24. Tree care and management is the job of an arborist. Much of their work is performed in tree canopies and requires training for safe climbing and working techniques.

often need backgrounds or degrees in arboriculture, horticulture, or forestry. Many firms require employees to obtain certification as specialists in utility or municipal work or climbing.

> **Pro Tip**
>
> There are phone apps that will search plant wholesalers and nurseries for plants by name, price, and distance.

Brokers

After the landscape plan and plant list is approved, the plant materials specified need to be located, ordered, and purchased. For example, if the design calls for a 3″ *Acer rubrum*, the contractor must install a 3″ *Acer rubrum*. In most cases, the specified plant materials are obtained from several nurseries, both local and distant. The services of a broker are often engaged to manage the logistics of locating and arranging delivery of the materials. Many brokers will pick up the needed plants and deliver them to the jobsite, **Figure 1-25**.

Retailers

Retailers, such as garden centers and mass merchandisers, sell ornamental plant materials directly to the consumer, **Figure 1-26**. Retailers typically are not involved in plant production and instead purchase plant material in bulk from production operations. Americans spend millions on annual bedding and gardening plants from retailers each year, making this a very successful division of the landscaping industry.

Successful garden centers employee a knowledgeable and helpful staff that can answer a variety of consumer questions regarding the appropriate plant choices for their landscape. Many garden centers hire seasonal help and

R. Lee Ivy

PeterVandenbelt/Shutterstock.com

Figure 1-25. Plant brokers work as an intermediary between landscapers and nurseries. They help locate plants specified on a landscape design and may deliver the plants to the site.

do not necessarily require employees to have horticulture or landscaping backgrounds. However, employees should minimally understand basic light, nutrient, and water needs for the potted and bedding plants the garden center sells. Employees should have good communication and math skills for working with customers and calculating costs and change.

Professional Organizations

Professional organizations play an important role for recent graduates and professionals working in the landscaping industry. These organi-

wavebreakmedia/Shutterstock.com

Figure 1-26. Garden centers are the final link between the producer and the end user. Garden centers are retailers who may produce and sell plants directly to consumers.

zations commonly develop certifications that set standards for all facets of the industry, **Figure 1-27**. Members receive opportunities to network, update their certifications, learn about new technologies, and learn new skills that will help them gain advancement in their careers. Some organizations also offer classes or seminars on finance and administration for small business owners. They also participate in trade shows and offer continuing education classes covering new methods, products, and technology. Many of these organizations also work with educators to ensure graduates obtain the skills employers are requesting. Membership fees in these organizations finance commodity advertisements, trade journals, educational programs, and promote the overall industry.

White78/Shutterstock.com

ingehogenbijl/Shutterstock.com

Figure 1-27. Professional landscaping and horticultural organizations help ensure that members are aware of trends and market data, as well as new technology being used in the industry. Organizations provide important information that allow growers to become more efficient and sustainable.

Career Connection

Ozgur Coskun/Shutterstock.com

Horticulture Therapist

Recent studies indicate that gardening can have a positive impact on a person's physical and mental well-being. Horticulture therapists offer classes that use plant cultivation and care to aid patient rehabilitation. A horticulture therapist also creates gardens and outdoor spaces where individuals can participate in gardening and benefit from its therapeutic effects. Horticulture therapy programs are practiced in different types of facilities, such as hospitals, nursing homes, prisons, and rehabilitation centers.

Horticulture therapists must enjoy working with people as well has have an interest in plants and gardening. A horticulture therapist typically serves as an instructor, mentor, and unofficial counselor for participating individuals. Certification programs are available through the American Horticultural Therapy Association. While there is no set educational requirement for a horticulture therapist, many positions require a degree in horticulture or a related field. Professionally trained and licensed therapists may also use gardening as part of a patient's therapy.

AmericanHort

AmericanHort is a national organization that represents professionals from all areas of the horticulture and landscaping industries, including educators, researchers, retailers, service providers, and designers. AmericanHort's mission is to unite, promote, and advance the horticulture industry through advocacy, collaboration, connectivity, education, market development, and research. Newsletters, classes, and other publications keep members in the know of current trends and demands in the industry. AmericanHort is also very active in the legislation and regulations that relate to the green industry.

American Horticultural Therapy Association (AHTA)

The *American Horticultural Therapy Association* is an organization for individuals in careers related to horticultural therapy. Their mission is to promote and advance the profession of using gardening and horticulture as therapy. The organization also supports research and development of therapeutic methods.

American Society of Landscape Architects (ASLA)

The *American Society of Landscape Architects (ASLA)* works to increase the public's awareness of and appreciation for the profession of landscape architects. The goal of the ASLA is to promote continuous learning experiences that improve and increase skills through publications, activities, and online information.

American Society of Horticultural Science (ASHS)

The *American Society of Horticultural Science* has thousands of members worldwide. ASHS represents a broad cross section of the horticultural community, including scientists, educators, students, landscape and turf managers, government, extension agents, and industry professionals. ASHS members focus on practices and problems in horticulture: breeding, propagation, production and management, harvesting, handling and storage, processing, marketing and use of horticultural plants and products.

International Society of Arboriculture (ISA)

The *International Society of Arboriculture (ISA)* is a trade organization for arborists and related individuals in the landscaping industry that work with large trees. ISA offers varying levels of certifications and professional credentials to highlight one's knowledge in the tree care industry.

International Plant Propagators' Society

The *International Plant Propagators' Society* mission of "seek and share" provides a forum for greenhouse and nursery growers to network and share practices and procedures used to produce crops for the landscaping industry. As the name suggests, IPPS has members worldwide. The IPPS hosts conferences, tours, and field days to educate its members regarding current trends and growing procedures of the industry.

Irrigation Association

The *Irrigation Association* is the leading trade organization for professionals in the landscape industry who perform tasks related to irrigation. Designers, consultants, contractors, manufacturers, and even homeowners may be members. The Irrigation Association is devoted to promoting water wise, efficient, and sustainable irrigation practices. Members are educated on methods that can help improve the efficiency of irrigation systems. The IA offers many certifications and credentials that allow its members to prove their knowledge of the industry. The irrigation association also places heavy emphasis on educating the public on sound practices of irrigation and water management.

National Association of Landscape Professionals

The *National Association of Landscape Professionals (NALP)* has over 100,000 industry professionals as members. NALP members specialize in landscape maintenance and installation, landscape and interiorscape design, irrigation, and tree care. NALP offers Landscape Industry Certifications for a wide variety of landscape professionals to display their level of experience and education. NALP also advocates with legislators and policymakers to draft legislation that is beneficial to the landscaping industry.

Perennial Plant Association

The *Perennial Plant Association (PPA)* is composed primarily of greenhouse and nursery growers of herbaceous ornamental plants. The PPA promotes the use of herbaceous perennial plants in landscape installations. The PPA has developed a Perennial Plant of the Year program to promote outstanding perennial plants and their incorporation into the landscape.

Career Connection

Roger Phelps

Roger Phelps, Corporate Communications Manager, STIHL Inc.

Roger Phelps is the corporate communications manager for STIHL Inc. STIHL produces the number one selling brand of chainsaws and a full line of outdoor power tools including blowers, trimmers, brushcutters, and construction tools. As the communications manager, Roger is responsible for managing the "story" of STIHL through event marketing, public relations, and social media. Through event marketing, Roger develops STIHL's relationships with professional associations, such as the National Association of Landscape Professionals, and with other companies and organizations. Roger's public relations team tells the STIHL story through news outlets, television, and print media. The social media team is responsible for monitoring STIHL's reputation with end users and to manage ongoing conversations with consumers and fans.

Roger encourages anyone with a passion for the green industry and communications to consider marketing as it is essential to business. As he likes to say, "You can have the greatest party in the world, but if you don't send invitations no one shows." Being able to build relationships with customers, and share a company's services, goals, and values with them is an exciting and rewarding career path. You can connect with Roger on LinkedIn.

Consider This
1. What other types of employment opportunities does STIHL Inc. offer?
2. Review STIHL's social media. Are they interesting and effective?
3. What type of educational background is required to fill a position such as Roger Phelps'?

Professional Grounds Management Society

The *Professional Grounds Management Society* is a professional organization for individuals involved in grounds management. Members manage grounds for office parks, universities, municipalities, cemeteries, and park and recreation facilities. The goal of the PGMS is to educate the industry with knowledge on safe and efficient management for the maintenance and operation of job sites.

Interlocking Concrete Pavement Institute (ICPI)

The *Interlocking Concrete Pavement Institute (ICPI)* is a North American professional trade association that represents the segmental concrete pavement industry. ICPI is considered a leader in the development and distribution of technical information about the industry and its products. Members consist of interlocking paver manufacturers, design professionals, installation contractors, and service and product suppliers. ICPI provides educational courses that result in various levels of installer certification. ICPI promotes certification to ensure installation quality and efficiency and installer competence.

Local Organizations

Members of the landscaping association should also join and become active in local horticulture-based organizations. Membership in local organizations helps professionals network with other members of the landscaping industry in their region. Local organizations may coordinate conventions and trade shows and offer continuing education. In North Carolina, for example, the Johnston County Nursery Marketing Association is a local organization that provides members access to a database of over 20 nurseries to locate plant materials.

Professional Certifications

Many trade organizations offer certifications for members of the land-scaping industry to promote their experience and competency in their areas of expertise, **Figure 1-28**. These certifications also help ensure consistency in the quality of work clients can expect and may mean the difference between winning and losing bids. Some certifications are available at both national and state levels. Many certifications require the applicant to pass a series of knowledge tests as well as practicums to demonstrate their mastery of the content. There are also fees for classes and testing for each certification and its renewal. Common national level certifications include the following:

- Certified Irrigation Technician.
- Certified Irrigation Auditor.
- Certified Irrigation Contractor.
- Certified Irrigation Designer.
- Certified Landscape Water Manager.
- Certified Agricultural Irrigation Specialist.
- Landscape Industry Certified Manager.
- Landscape Industry Certified Technician—Exterior.
- Landscape Industry Certified Technician—Interior.
- Landscape Industry Certified Technician—Lawn Care Manager.
- Landscape Industry Certified Technician—Lawn Care Technician.

R. Lee Ivy

Figure 1-28. Landscape Industry Certified Turfgrass Technicians have credentials indicating they are knowledgeable in the installation, growing, and management of turfgrass.

Certifications often evolve with changes and advancements in the industry. Trade organization websites provide the most current information regarding the types of certifications available and the steps needed to obtain or renew certifications.

Summary

- The landscaping industry is one of the fastest growing segments of the nation's agricultural economy.
- Market data suggests that the landscaping industry employs almost one million individuals in over 470,000 different businesses.
- The landscaping industry is part of an even larger industry known as the green industry or the environmental horticulture industry.
- The landscaping industry is divided into the following sectors: production, research and education, supply, service, and selling.
- Plant production for the landscaping industry is performed in greenhouses and nursery fields.
- Researchers and educators may have science backgrounds with degrees in fields such as botany, horticulture, forestry, or plant breeding.
- Suppliers are the businesses that distribute materials other than plants to growers, installation and maintenance professionals, and retailers.
- Service providers offer landscape installation, maintenance, and management services for residential and commercial properties.
- Landscape designers or licensed architects design landscapes for residential, public, and commercial sites.
- An interiorscape designer creates and often installs and maintains indoor landscaping.
- Maintenance workers perform many tasks, including mowing, string trimming, edging, fertilizing, pest control, snow removal, and seasonal color installation.
- Landscape professionals may specialize in turfgrass installation and management.
- An arborist is a specialist trained to provide proper care, help maintain healthy trees, and give advice on removing large dying or deceased specimens.
- Brokers manage the logistics of locating and arranging delivery of plant materials.
- Many occupations require formal training in horticulture or a related field.
- Professional organizations provide opportunities for members to continue their education as well as receive credentials and certifications.

Chapter Review

Know and Understand ↱

Answer the following questions using the information provided in this chapter.

1. Occupations that are a part of the landscaping industry include people and businesses that _____.
   A. cultivate grapes and produce wine
   B. create and install landscape designs
   C. specialize in agricultural irrigation
   D. All of the above.

2. The landscaping industry has revenues of _____.
   A. $25 million
   B. $78 million
   C. $25 billion
   D. $78 billion

3. Which of the following statements is true?
   A. The green industry includes businesses involved in the production and distribution of ornamental plants and landscape supplies.
   B. The green industry includes businesses that provide landscape maintenance services.
   C. The landscaping industry is a part of the green industry.
   D. All of the above.

4. Which of the following are main sectors of the landscape industry?
   A. Service providers.
   B. Research and education.
   C. Producers and suppliers.
   D. All of the above.

5. Plant production yields annually around _____.
   A. $3 million
   B. $13 million
   C. $23 million
   D. $35 billion

6. Greenhouse producers typically produce _____.
   A. trees, shrubs, and herbaceous perennials
   B. bedding, potted, foliage, and other landscape plants
   C. preformed pond liners and fish
   D. All of the above.

7. Nursery producers typically raise _____.
   A. brambles and vegetable plants
   B. turfgrasses for sod installation
   C. trees, shrubs, and herbaceous perennials
   D. worms and other soil beneficials

8. Which of the following statement about sod farming is correct?
   A. Waiting longer than 24 hours after harvest will help the sod take root quickly.
   B. Sod farms typically specialize in turfgrass species that are not common to the area.
   C. Sod farming requires an investment of time and specialized machinery.
   D. Turfgrass must be at least 7 or 8 years old before it can be harvested.

9. Botanists study and research _____.
   A. landscape design
   B. plant growth and development
   C. transport of nursery plants
   D. landscape operations

10. What roles does a cooperative extension agent serve in the landscaping industry?
    A. A liaison between the community and a university.
    B. An educator for individuals interested in agricultural issues.
    C. Conduct classes for licensing and certification in different fields.
    D. All of the above.

11. The manipulation of plants to improve the quality and performance of existing plants is referred to as _____.
    A. plant classification
    B. nursery planting
    C. plant production
    D. plant breeding

12. Businesses that distribute materials other than plants to other sectors of the landscaping industry are referred to as _____.
    A. breeders
    B. designers
    C. suppliers
    D. municipalities

13. Professionals who are formally trained, licensed, and design large-scale properties are landscape _____.
    A. contractors
    B. designers
    C. arborists
    D. architects

14. Professionals who are not licensed and typically design for residential and smaller commercial sites are landscape _____.
    A. contractors
    B. designers
    C. arborists
    D. architects

15. The designing, installation, and maintenance of landscaping in indoor areas is referred to as _____.
    A. interiorscaping
    B. indoor farming
    C. interior design
    D. mallscaping

16. Irrigation system designers must understand _____.
    A. how soil type, slope, and water pressure will affect the system
    B. how to apply sustainable practices for water conservation
    C. hydraulics and water requirements for different plant materials
    D. All of the above.

17. Why would a landscape contractor hire a subcontractor?
    A. To paint the outline for the landscape installation.
    B. To instruct the contractor's employees on plant installation.
    C. To install special elements of a job.
    D. All of the above.

18. What of the following best describes a design-build firm?
    A. The contractor subcontracts professionals to design a landscape.
    B. Subcontractors are hired to design and install each portion of a landscape.
    C. The contractor possesses skills to design and install landscapes.
    D. Subcontractors are hired to design the hardscapes of landscapes.

19. Which of the following tasks are commonly performed in the landscape maintenance industry?
    A. String trimming, pruning, edging, and fertilizing.
    B. Plant breeding and greenhouse production.
    C. Managing the logistics of plant material delivery.
    D. Irrigation system installation.

20. The science of tree care and management is referred to as _____.
    A. botany
    B. arboriculture
    C. propagation
    D. brokering

21. Why might a landscape contractor solicit the services of a broker?
    A. To manage the installation of hardscapes and irrigation systems.
    B. To manage the logistics of hiring workers to install irrigation systems.
    C. To manage the installation of rare and exotic plants.
    D. To manage the logistics of locating and arranging delivery of plant materials.

22. Retail employees should have good communication skills and a basic understanding of _____.
    A. light, nutrient, and water needs
    B. plant material brokering
    C. irrigation system repair
    D. string trimming and edging

23. How do memberships in professional landscaping organizations benefit people interested or working in the industry?
    A. Provides assistance for updating certifications and acquiring new skills.
    B. Informs and teaches members about new technologies in landscaping.
    C. Provides opportunities for networking with industry professionals.
    D. All of the above.

24. Which of the following statements best describes the advantages of professional certification?
    A. Helps ensure consistency in sod measurements.
    B. Promotes experience and competency in areas of expertise.
    C. Provides an advantage over other certified professionals.
    D. Ensures the success of small businesses.

Thinking Critically

1. How would you describe the landscaping industry to someone with no experience in the field?

2. What is the value or importance of the green industry to the US economy? How does it compare to countries with a similar economy?

3. How would you describe interiorscaping? Write a job posting, such as those found on job websites, for an experienced interiorscape designer. Include experience and education requirements for the position.

Suggested Activities

1. In a group of three or four, choose a sector of the green industry and develop a visual presentation. Discuss which areas each person will research and how many slides each person should prepare. Include factors such as employment opportunities, careers, average income, and businesses that fall under the sector. Present your slide presentation to the class. Each person should participate in the presentation.

2. Conduct a job search for employment opportunities in your area and select an open job that is of interest to you. Research the educational and certification requirements of the position.

3. Contact and interview a professional working in the landscaping industry. Prepare a list of questions before the interview. Questions should cover topics such as education, different positions held during his or her career, and reasons why he or she enjoys working in the industry. The interview may be over the phone, through email, or in person.

4. NALP annually sponsors a National Collegial Landscape Competition. Using the NALP website, select one event that you find of interest. Research the skills required to participate and achieve success in the event.

5. Research local landscaping industry certifications for your state. Are you eligible for any certifications? What requirements must be met in order to receive certification(s)?

Workplace Skills

While studying this chapter, look for the activity icon to:
- **Practice** vocabulary terms with Words to Know activities.
- **Expand** learning with identification activities.
- **Reinforce** what you learn by completing Know and Understand questions.

G-WLEARNING.com

www.g-wlearning.com/agriculture

Chapter Outcomes

After studying this chapter, you will be able to:

- Develop and analyze personal goals.
- Develop a personal mission statement.
- Explain and create professional documents for job applications.
- Identify best practices for preparing for a job interview.
- Identify habits and actions to help you succeed in the workplace.
- Develop skills to become a better team member and leader.
- Identify traits successful leaders have in common.
- Resolve conflict with negotiation skills.
- Identify behaviors and attitudes for maintaining a safe work environment.

Key Terms ↗

attitude
conflict
cover letter
ethical behavior
goal setting
leadership
letter of application
long-term goal
mission statement
negotiation
nonverbal communication

plan of action
punctual
reference
résumé
self-motivation
short-term goal
SMART goal
team
verbal communication
vision statement

Introduction

Setting challenging, achievable goals for yourself is an essential way to stay motivated and continually improve your skills, whether in school, on the job, or in other aspects of your life. When beginning your career, finding the right job is an especially important goal. You should strive to find work you can do well and enjoy, **Figure 2-1**. In addition to doing the work well, you must develop the proper habits and interpersonal skills to truly succeed at a job. This chapter prepares you to apply for a job and discusses the work habits and skills necessary to succeed in the workplace.

Toa55/Shutterstock.com   *Volkova Vera/Shutterstock.com*   *stefanolunardi/Shutterstock.com*

Figure 2-1. There are many types of careers available in the landscaping industry if you enjoy working outdoors or designing new landscapes. Working summer jobs or internships in different businesses will give you the opportunity to find what you enjoy most.

Setting Goals

Goal setting is not just saying you want or expect something to happen. *Goal setting* is the process of identifying something you want to accomplish and establishing a plan to achieve the desired result. If a person decides to save more money and sets a certain amount to save each month, he or she has set a goal and a means of reaching that goal. Goal setting is an important process to personal and professional success because it gives a person or company focus, direction, and solid targets to determine if they are succeeding.

Types of Goals

There are two main types of goals: short-term and long-term goals. *Short-term goals* list items or actions that you wish to accomplish in the near future, usually less than 12 months. *Long-term goals* state what you wish to accomplish over the span of several years or even a lifetime. Both types of goals require a plan of action. A *plan of action* is a list of individual steps that you will take to achieve a goal. Crossing each step off your list as you complete it will help you envision your success.

SMART Goals

Goals should push you into action. Using the SMART goals guidelines will help make your goals as realistic and beneficial as possible. *SMART goals* are specific, measurable, achievable, relevant, and timely.

- **Specific.** Goals must be descriptive and well defined. A specific goal provides enough detail to ensure the goal can be achieved. If you do not define exactly what you want to accomplish and why you want it, you cannot create a successful plan.
- **Measurable.** Goals must be written to provide a means of evaluating progress. If a goal is simply to increase income, it cannot be easily measured. However, if the goal states to increase monthly income by 5% for the next six months, it can be measured accurately.
- **Achievable.** Goals must be challenging and realistic. Goals that are impossible to acheive will be frustrating. However, goals that are too easy to achieve may reduce your enthusiasm and lower your performance and expectations for success.

- **Relevant.** Goals must be relevant to the path you have chosen for success in your life and career. Goals that are not consistent with your path will distract you and hamper your likeliness to succeed.
- **Timely.** All goals must have a time frame and deadlines. The time frame established for the goals should create a sense of urgency but also provide a time line that is useful for determining a plan of action.

Goals That Motivate

Motivation is essential to reaching your goals. Goals must be important and have value for you or you will not be motivated to achieve them. To help write goals that are motivational, write your goals so they relate to the highest priorities in your life, **Figure 2-2**.

Write down your goals and keep them posted where you will see them each day. You are more likely to stay focused on your goals if you make a specific plan for when, where, and how you will take or perform the action. If you want to establish a regular studying habit, for example, you could write the following sentence: "During the next two weeks I will study for one hour each day at 2:00 pm at my desk." You can also increase your chance of success by setting a reminder on your cell phone and calendar.

Vision and Mission Statements

A personal *vision statement* is a description of your personal goals for the future. A personal *mission statement* is a short summary identifying a purpose or reason of existence. Companies often use these statements to present their ideals and values to the public. As an individual, you can write personal vision and mission statements to reflect your plan for the future. It is also important for you to review the vision and mission statements of companies before you send your letter of application to ensure they reflect your personal values. Developing and using personal mission and vision statements can help you stay on the track to success, **Figure 2-3**.

Syda Productions/Shutterstock.com

Figure 2-2. If you were focused on graduating college with a degree, this would be a high priority in your life. Keeping your college degree and the opportunities it will present in mind will keep you motivated.

dizain/Shutterstock.com

Figure 2-3. Personal mission statements summarize your core ideals and values. When applying for a job, ensure your personal mission statement does not conflict with that of the potential employer.

A personal vision statement should be based in the future and serve as a road map to inspire and identify what you want to accomplish in the future. A personal mission statement can be described as your personal philosophy for not only what but who you would like to become in the future. Although there is no right or wrong way to write a mission statement, a personal mission statement should encompass all aspects of your life, not just the work aspect. Keep in mind that both statements should be revisited and adjusted as you progress toward your goal.

Applying for a Position

When you are ready to apply for employment, you will need to know the appropriate steps to take. Having a well-prepared résumé is an important first step. You will need to organize and update your portfolio. Knowing how to write an acceptable letter of application is another goal. Finally, you will want to practice your interviewing techniques. It is also extremely important that you fully read and understand the job description before you apply for a position.

Résumés

A *résumé* is a brief outline of your education, work experience, and other qualifications for work. A well-written résumé can help you get an interview. You will need to include several sections on your résumé. An example appears in **Figure 2-4**. You should tailor a copy of your résumé to the position for which you are applying. Make sure that your résumé is precise, without errors, and current. Ask a friend, instructor, or colleague to review the document to ensure there are no mistakes and that it reads well. You should also review your résumé regularly to ensure it is up-to-date with your experience, achievements, and accolades. Print your résumé on high quality, neutral-colored paper (white, gray, or cream colors). Use your printed résumé when an employer requests a résumé sent via traditional mail. You may also want to keep several copies on hand when you attend interviews.

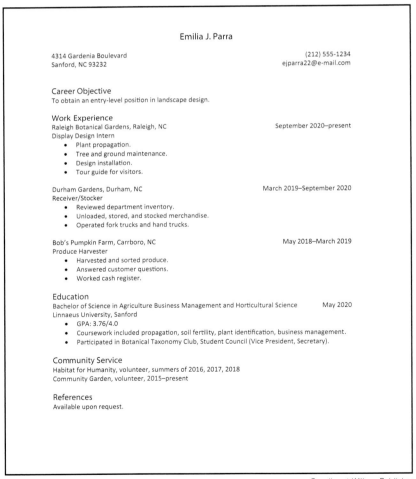

Emilia J. Parra

4314 Gardenia Boulevard
Sanford, NC 93232

(212) 555-1234
ejparra22@e-mail.com

Career Objective
To obtain an entry-level position in landscape design.

Work Experience
Raleigh Botanical Gardens, Raleigh, NC   September 2020–present
Display Design Intern
- Plant propagation.
- Tree and ground maintenance.
- Design installation.
- Tour guide for visitors.

Durham Gardens, Durham, NC   March 2019–September 2020
Receiver/Stocker
- Reviewed department inventory.
- Unloaded, stored, and stocked merchandise.
- Operated fork trucks and hand trucks.

Bob's Pumpkin Farm, Carrboro, NC   May 2018–March 2019
Produce Harvester
- Harvested and sorted produce.
- Answered customer questions.
- Worked cash register.

Education
Bachelor of Science in Agriculture Business Management and Horticultural Science   May 2020
Linnaeus University, Sanford
- GPA: 3.76/4.0
- Coursework included propagation, soil fertility, plant identification, business management.
- Participated in Botanical Taxonomy Club, Student Council (Vice President, Secretary).

Community Service
Habitat for Humanity, volunteer, summers of 2016, 2017, 2018
Community Garden, volunteer, 2015–present

References
Available upon request.

Goodheart-Willcox Publisher

Figure 2-4. A résumé is typically one page in length unless you have a great deal of experience.

Some employers request an electronic résumé that is sent via email or posted to the employer's job site. You can also post an electronic résumé to a number of online job-search sites. To create one, save your résumé as "text only" without any formatting. Review the text only résumé to make sure lines and headers break properly. Be sure to save this in a separate file from your formatted résumé. Employers may use the electronic file to search for key terms that match their descriptions of an ideal job candidate.

References

Along with the résumé, you need to develop a list of references. A *reference* is an individual who will provide important information about you to a prospective employer. A reference can be a teacher, school official, previous employer, or any other adult outside your family who knows you well.

You will need at least three references. Always get permission from each person to use his or her name as a reference before actually doing so. Your list of references, along with their titles, phone numbers, and addresses, should be kept private. Share this list only with an employer who has interviewed you and asks for your references.

You can have your references write *letters of recommendation* for you. These give an employer a more in-depth look at your skills. Choose people who know you well. Make sure you choose references who are good writers, since they will be representing you. Ask as many people as possible. Then you can choose the best letters to submit to employers.

Letter of Application

The *letter of application* or *cover letter* is often the first contact you have with a potential employer. It can make a lasting impression. It should be neat and follow a standard form for business letters. The paper should be ivory, white, or a neutral color and free of smudges and mistakes. It is best to use the same paper on which you printed your résumé. Use a standard font to give the letter a professional look. Be sure to check spelling and punctuation. Have several people read the letter and offer advice for improving it. You should mail your résumé with your letter of application.

Emilia J. Parra
4314 Gardenia Boulevard
Sanford, NC 93232
(212) 555-1234
ejparra22@e-mail.com

April 23, 2020

Mr. James Williamson
Williamson Green Designs
4392 East 134th Street
Wilton, NC 93231

Dear Mr. Williamson:

The Apprentice Landscape Designer position you advertised on the Career Finder website is exactly the type of job I am seeking. After reviewing the job description and requirements, it was clear that my experience, skills, and interests are a perfect match for this opportunity.

While obtaining my bachelor's degree in Agriculture Business Management and Horticultural Science from Linnaeus University, I gained both the theoretical knowledge and the hands-on skills required for this position. In my current position as a design intern at Raleigh Botanical Gardens, I have greatly increased my horticultural knowledge in plant identification, morphology, and environmental needs. I have also gained design skills and a better understanding of the landscape design process. I am anxious to apply the skills I have learned and to continue gaining new skills.

Please find my résumé enclosed with this letter. I would greatly appreciate an opportunity to interview for this position. Please contact me at your convenience by phone or e-mail to schedule an interview. I look forward to hearing from you.

Sincerely,

Emilia J. Parra

Emilia J. Parra

enclosure

Goodheart-Willcox Publisher

Figure 2-5. A cover letter should clearly state why you are an ideal candidate for the position. It should be easy to read and free of grammatical errors.

A sample letter of application appears in **Figure 2-5**. It is a good example to use in response to a job ad. The letter should be brief and to the point. It should include the following items:

- Title of the job you seek.
- Where you heard about the job.
- Your strengths, skills, and abilities for the job.
- Reasons you should be considered for the job.
- When you are available to begin work.
- Request for an interview.

Job Application Forms

A prospective employer may ask you to complete a job application form before having an interview. The job application form highlights the information the employer needs to know about you, your education, and your prior work experience. Employers often use these forms to screen applicants for the skills needed on the job. You might complete a form in a personnel or employment office. Sometimes you may get the form by mail or email. Many companies post an application form on their website.

The appearance of the application form can give an employer the first opinion about you. Fill out the form accurately, completely, and neatly. How well you accomplish that can determine whether you get the job. When asked about salary, write *open* or *negotiable*. This means you are willing to consider offers. Be sure to send or give the form to the correct person. The name of the correct person often appears on the form. Tips for completing the job application appear in **Figure 2-6**.

Pro Tip

Create a document that contains all the information requested in most application forms, such as the schools you have attended with their addresses and the years attended. It will save you time and effort and help ensure accuracy when filling out application forms.

✓ Follow the instructions for filling out the form. If you are asked to print, type, or use black ink, be sure to do so. Be as neat as possible.

✓ Complete every question in the form. If some questions do not apply to you, draw a dash or write "NA" (for not applicable) so the employer knows you did not overlook it.

✓ You may wish to omit your Social Security Number and write "will provide if hired."

✓ You can write "open" or "negotiable" for any question regarding salary requirements.

✓ For each former job, there may be a question asking your reason for leaving the job. Avoid writing any negative comments about yourself or a former employer.

Goodheart-Willcox Publisher; rangizzz/Shutterstock.com

Figure 2-6. Tips for completing a job application.

Online Application Forms

Many employers now request electronic applications through their company website or an independent job-search website. When filling out an online application, it is extremely important to include key terms for which the employer may search. This will help you stand out from the many other applications the employer will receive.

When preparing your application, be sure to save it in the appropriate format. If a preferred format is not given, it is best to save the application in document file format or pdf file format. This will enable the employer to find specific search terms in your document. Be sure to complete all the fields of the application. Many job-search sites have sample forms on which you can practice before attempting a real application.

The Job Interview

The interview gives you the opportunity to learn more about a company and to convince the employer that you are the best person for the position. The employer wants to know if you have the skills needed for the job. Adequate preparation is essential for making a lasting, positive impression, **Figure 2-7**. Here are some ways to prepare for the interview.

- **Research the employer and the job.** Know the mission of the employer and specifics about the job. Also, try to learn what the company looks for when hiring new employees.
- **Be prepared to answer questions.** Go over the list in **Figure 2-8** and prepare answers for each.
- **List the questions you want answered.** For example, do you want to know if there is on-the-job training or opportunities for advancement?
- **List the materials you plan to take.** This seems simple enough. However, if you wait to grab items at the last minute, you will likely forget something important.

Photgraphee.eu/Shutterstock.com

Figure 2-7. A job interview will likely be the first time the employer has visual or verbal communication with you. It is important to make a good impression.

Common Interview Questions and Responses

Question	Response
What can you tell me about yourself?	Briefly summarize your abilities as they relate to the job qualifications or your career goals. Do not provide a general life history.
Why do you want to work for this company?	Tell what you know about the company. Explain how your abilities match the company's needs.
Why do you think you would like this kind of work?	Relate the job requirements to your successful past experiences.
What are some of the projects you worked on in school?	Briefly summarize a project or coursework relevant to the job qualifications.
What other jobs have you had?	Focus on jobs with skills that relate to the job you are seeking.
Why did you leave your last job?	Be honest. However, avoid saying anything negative about your previous employer.
Have you ever been fired from a job? If so, why?	Answer honestly. If you have been fired, share what you learned from the experience. Avoid trying to blame others.
What are your major strengths and weaknesses?	Select a strength that relates to the job qualifications. Be honest when selecting a weakness, but give an example of how you have worked to improve on it.
Have you ever had a conflict with a coworker? How did you handle it?	Briefly describe the situation and how you handled it. Avoid placing all the blame on the other person. Explain what you learned from the experience.
What do you expect to be paid?	If possible, determine the salary range before the interview. Say that you are willing to discuss the salary or state a range you feel comfortable with.
What are your future plans?	Describe how the need to learn and grow is important to you. Confine your answer to the company with which you are interviewing.

Goodheart-Willcox Publisher

Figure 2-8. Interview questions help the employer establish whether you are a good fit for the position and the company. Use the questions listed here to ascertain your answers and to practice your responses.

- **Decide what to wear.** Dress appropriately, usually one step above what is worn by your future coworkers. For instance, casual clothing is acceptable for individuals who will do manual labor or wear a company uniform. If the job involves greeting the public in an office environment, a suit is more appropriate. Always appear neat and clean.
- **Practice the interview.** Have a friend or family member interview you in front of a mirror until you are happy with your responses.
- **Know where to go for the interview.** Verify the address of the interview location by checking the site beforehand, if possible. Plan to arrive ready for the interview at least 10 minutes early.

Good preparation will make you feel more confident and comfortable during the interview. Be polite, friendly, and cheerful during the process, **Figure 2-9.** Use a firm handshake. Maintain eye contact at all times. Answer all questions carefully and as completely as you can. Be honest about your abilities. Avoid chewing gum and fidgeting. Also be aware of questions you legally do not have to answer, such as those related to age, marital status, religion, or family background.

A prospective employer may ask you to take employee tests. Some employers administer tests to job candidates to measure their knowledge or skill level under stress. Since all employers support a drug-free workplace, most will likely require you to take a drug test if hired. You can ask those who have completed similar tests what to expect.

After the interview, send a letter to the potential employer within 24 hours, thanking him or her for the interview. Set yourself apart from the competition by sending a handwritten note thanking the interviewer or committee for their time and interest. Use a professional card design and write neatly. If you get a job offer, respond to it quickly. If you do not receive an offer after several interviews, evaluate your interview techniques and seek ways to improve them.

Dean Drobot/Shutterstock.com

Figure 2-9. A smile and firm handshake indicate that you are confident in yourself and your abilities.

Succeeding in the Workplace

After securing employment, adjusting to your new duties and responsibilities will occupy your first few weeks. Your supervisor and coworkers will help you learn the routine. An introduction to company policies and procedures as well as the special safety rules that all employees must know is common for new employees.

While your coworkers will be watching what you do, they will also pay attention to "how you work." How to behave in the workplace is an important lesson all employees should learn. Making an effort to do your best will help you succeed.

Health and Hygiene

As an employee, you are a representative of your company. Therefore, your employer expects you to be neat and clean on the job. Taking care of yourself gives the impression that you want people to view you as a professional, **Figure 2-10**.

Your daily grooming habits will consist of bathing or showering, using an antiperspirant, and putting on clean clothes. Regularly brushing your teeth and using mouthwash will promote healthy teeth and fresh breath. Keep your hair clean and styled in a way that will not be distracting.

Employers expect workers to dress appropriately. Many places of work have a dress code. If your workplace does not, use common sense and avoid extremes. Refrain from wearing garments that are revealing or have inappropriate pictures or sayings. Some employers have rules requiring that tattoos or piercings beyond pierced ears remain covered. Employers may

Irina Braga/Shutterstock.com

Figure 2-10. It is important to be well groomed and to dress appropriately for the interview. As a rule, you should always dress a step higher than the required dress code for employees. If you are uncertain what is appropriate, it is always better to overdress for the interview.

also have rules about wearing long hair loosely because it may be caught in machinery. Good appearance is especially important for employees who have frequent face-to-face contact with customers.

Work Habits

Employers want employees who are punctual, dependable, and responsible. They want their employees to be capable of taking initiative and working independently. Other desirable employee qualities include organization, accuracy, and efficiency, **Figure 2-11**.

A *punctual* employee is always prompt and on time. This means not only when the workday starts, but also when returning from breaks and lunches. Being dependable means that people can rely on you to fulfill your word and meet your deadlines. If you are not well, be sure to call in and let the employer know right away. If there are reasons you cannot be at work, discuss this with your employer and work out an alternate arrangement. Many people have lost jobs by not checking with their supervisor about time off.

Taking *initiative* means that you start activities on your own without being told. When you finish one task, you do not wait to hear what to do next. Individuals who take initiative need much less supervision. They have *self-motivation*, or an inner urge to perform well. Generally, this motivation will drive you to set goals and accomplish them. All these qualities together show that you are capable of working *independently*.

You are expected to be as accurate and error-free as possible in all that you do. This is why you were hired. Complete your work with precision and double-check it to assure accuracy. Your coworkers depend on the careful completion of your tasks.

Jeff Lueders/Shutterstock.com

Figure 2-11. After you are employed, it is important to understand and follow the employee code of conduct. Failure to be punctual or extensive absenteeism is unprofessional and will not be tolerated for long in the working environment.

Time Management

A good employee knows how to manage time wisely. This includes ability to prioritize assignments and complete them in a timely fashion. It also involves not wasting time. Time-wasting behaviors include visiting with coworkers, making personal phone calls, texting, sending emails, or doing other personal activities during work hours, **Figure 2-12**.

While it is important to complete all your work thoroughly, you must also be able to gauge which assignments are most important. Avoid putting excessive efforts into minor assignments when crucial matters require your attention. Even though you are still accomplishing work, this is another way of wasting time.

Attitude on the Job

Your attitude can often determine the success you have on your job. Your *attitude* is your outlook on life. It is reflected by how you react to the events and people around you. A smile and

cunaplus/Shutterstock.com

Figure 2-12. Limit personal business while working. Viewing social media or playing games during work hours may be cause for dismissal.

courteous behavior can make customers and fellow employees feel good about themselves and you, **Figure 2-13**. Clients and customers prefer to do business in friendly environments.

Enthusiasm spreads easily from one person to another. Usually, enthusiasm means a person enjoys what he or she is doing. In a sales environment, enthusiasm increases sales. On a landscape job site, enthusiasm builds a team spirit for working together.

People who do a good job feel pride in their work. They feel a sense of accomplishment and a desire to achieve more. This attitude can inspire others as well.

Professional Behavior

You will be expected to behave professionally on the job. This includes showing respect for your boss and coworkers. Limit personal conversations and phone calls to break times or lunch, **Figure 2-14**. Act courteously; remember that others are focusing on their work. Interruptions can cause them to lose concentration.

Part of behaving professionally is responding appropriately to *constructive criticism*. Every employee, no matter how knowledgeable or experienced, can improve his or her performance. If you receive criticism from a supervisor or coworker, do not be offended. Instead, use the feedback to improve yourself. The more you improve, the more successful you will be in your work.

Decision Making and Problem Solving

Employers value workers who have the ability to make sound decisions. This process applies in the workplace as well as other aspects of life. The process will help you identify the issue, identify possible solutions, make a decision, implement the decision, and evaluate the results. Having ability to solve problems on the job shows an employer that you are able to handle more responsibility. Solving problems as a group can strengthen camaraderie and help employees feel more pride in their work.

The ability to make decisions and solve problems requires *critical-thinking skills*. These are higher-level skills that enable you to think beyond the obvious. You learn to interpret information and make judgments. Supervisors appreciate employees who can analyze problems and think of workable solutions.

JP WALLET/Shutterstock.com

Figure 2-13. As an employee, you will have direct interaction with current and potential clients. A positive attitude is essential for a positive reflection of the company.

fizkes/Shutterstock.com

Figure 2-14. Falling asleep during work hours is unprofessional behavior. Getting plenty of rest at night is a healthy habit that will help you stay alert during the day.

Communication Skills

Communicating effectively with others is important for job success. Being a good communicator means that you can share information well with others. It also means you are a good listener.

Good communication is central to a smooth operation of any business. Communication is the process of exchanging ideas, thoughts, or information. Poor communication is costly to an employer, as when time is lost because an order was entered incorrectly. Poor communication may also result in lost customers.

Types of Communication

The primary forms of communication are verbal and nonverbal. *Verbal communication* involves speaking, listening, and writing. *Nonverbal communication* is the sending and receiving of messages without the use of words. It involves *body language*, which includes the expression on your face and your body posture. See **Figure 2-15**.

Lucky Business/Shutterstock.com

Figure 2-15. Do not let your body language or facial expressions show disrespect or create a negative atmosphere. The caller will also sense your negative attitude over the phone.

Listening Skills are Important. Listening is an important part of communication. If you do not understand, be sure to ask questions. Give feedback to let others know you understand them and are interested in what they have to say. Leaning forward while a person is talking signals interest and keen listening. Slouching back in a chair and yawning give the opposite signal—that you are bored and uninterested.

The message you convey in telephone communication involves your promptness, tone of voice, and attitude. Answering the phone quickly with a pleasant voice conveys a positive image for the company. Learning to obtain accurate information from the caller without interrupting that person's message is important.

Email Etiquette. Communication tools have advanced with the development of new technologies. To be an effective employee, you need to know how to communicate well with the common tools of your workplace. For example, when sending email communications, remember to think through each message as you would before sending a postal letter. Write professional emails as you would write printed business letters. Messages are often sent quickly without thought of how the recipient may interpret them. The same is true of voicemail. Keep the following in mind when using email in a professional capacity:

- Email should be descriptive but concise.
- Briefly summarize the content of the message in the subject line.
- Review and revise the material before sending.
- Check the recipients to ensure correct sends.
- Write clearly and accurately to ensure clear communication.
- Emails sent to some organizations may be public records.
- Save and keep professional email correspondence well organized.

Ongoing Development

The development of good communication skills is an ongoing process. Attending communication workshops and practicing often can keep your skills sharp, **Figure 2-16**. You should periodically give yourself a communications checkup by asking your supervisor to suggest areas that need improvement.

Using Social Media

Social media allows communication through public websites, **Figure 2-17**. This form of communication is almost immediate and can be used in both positive and negative ways. An unhappy client, for example, may post negative reviews and comments that could adversely affect the company and your job. Employers also review public websites to evaluate potential employees. If you post images of irresponsible behavior or write derogatory comments, an employer will likely remove you from their list of potential candidates. Fortunately, you may use social media to present yourself in a positive light and increase your hiring potential. Most companies have social media policies to which you must agree when you accept a job.

Master1305/Shutterstock.com

Figure 2-16. Attending a communication workshop may help you improve your communication and interpersonal skills. Many employers encourage their employees to attend workshops and often cover all costs.

Maintain a Positive Light

Using Social Media Responsibly

You can help present yourself to prospective employers in a positive light by using social media responsibly. Unprofessional or inappropriate postings, comments, and photos made on social media can ruin employment opportunities or even get you fired. Here are a few tips to help ensure your social media profile is appropriate:

- Check your privacy settings and make certain they are on private.
- Remove any postings that are set to public that may be considered inappropriate.
- Do your homework. Analyze the mission statement and vision statement of the company. Many companies will have different levels of tolerance regarding social media postings. Keep your profile professional and unbiased.
- Review your profile postings and images in their entirety. Postings made several years ago may not represent current beliefs.
- Tools from the social media site can be used to search for photos of yourself that have been added by others. Check these photos and ask that inappropriate images be removed.

Julia Tim/Shutterstock.com

Rawpixel/Shutterstock.com

Figure 2-17. When used correctly, social media can help attract new customers, maintain existing clients, and attract ideal employees.

Customer Relations Skills

Working with customers takes special communication skills. The most important aspect of customer relations is always remaining courteous. This may also require patience in some situations. When customers visit your business, you want them to have the best possible service and to leave happy. Remember that your behavior and skills at handling customers can determine if the customer will return to your business, **Figure 2-18**. The customer may spread the word about his or her experience with you to other potential customers. Make sure your customers know you appreciate their business.

Customer relations may also involve problem solving. If a customer needs help, you must provide answers as quickly and accurately as possible while remaining pleasant and polite. When a situation becomes stressful, you must be able to control your own level of stress without letting it affect your performance. At the same time, you must be able to lessen the customer's stress and attempt to eliminate its source.

Ethical Workplace Behavior

Ethical behavior on the job means conforming to accepted standards of fairness and good conduct. It is based on a person's sense of what is right to do. Individuals and society as a whole regard ethical behavior as highly important. Integrity, confidentiality, and honesty are crucial aspects of ethical workplace behavior. *Integrity* is firmly following your moral beliefs.

wavebreakmedia/Shutterstock.com

michaeljung/Shutterstock.com

Figure 2-18. Employees who are courteous and pleasant will often influence a customer to return to a store or rehire a service.

Unfortunately, employee theft is a major problem at some companies. The theft can range from carrying office supplies home to stealing money or expensive equipment. Company policies are in place to address these concerns. In cases of criminal or serious behavior, people may lose their jobs. If proven, the charge of criminal behavior stays on the employee's record. Such an employee will have a difficult time finding another job.

Interpersonal Skills

Interpersonal skills involve interacting with others. Some workplace activities that involve these skills include teaching others, leading, negotiating, and working as a member of a team. Getting along well with others can require great effort on your part, but it is essential for accomplishing your employer's goals.

Teamwork and Working Well with Others

Employers seek employees who can effectively serve as good team members. Due to the nature of most work today, teamwork is necessary. A *team* is a small group of people working together for a common purpose, **Figure 2-19**. Often, cooperation requires flexibility and willingness to try new ways to get things done. If someone is uncooperative, it takes longer to accomplish the tasks. When people do not get along, strained relationships may occur, which get in the way of finishing the tasks.

I Believe I Can Fly/Shutterstock.com

Figure 2-19. An employee who is not a team player will make a work situation unpleasant. As with a sports team, if one person does not cover his or her position, the team will not succeed.

Case Study

Working Well with Others

Raul works in the retail area of a large commercial nursery. He has recently been promoted to assistant manager. One of his new responsibilities is assigning daily assignments to the staff of retail clerks. Several of the retail clerks request they not be assigned to work with Jacob, who is the most experienced retail clerk. When Raul asks the clerks why they prefer not to work with Jacob, they are hesitant to respond. Mary speaks up and tells Raul that she is uncomfortable working with Jacob because he constantly teases her and that he is on his phone when he should be working and she ends up doing his part of the work. Jacob defends himself to Raul by saying he is only joking around and Mary lacks a sense of humor. He also denies using his phone while working.

Case Review
Discuss the following questions as a class or in groups of 2 or 3 students.
1. Is Mary being overly sensitive? Explain your answer.
2. How should Raul handle the situation?
3. How can Jacob modify his behavior to be a better coworker?
4. Does Jacob's experience make his poor behavior excusable?

A team can develop plans and complete work faster than an individual can complete the same amount of work. In contrast, a team usually takes longer to reach a decision than an individual worker does. Team members need some time before they become comfortable with one another and function as a unit. You will be more desirable as an employee if you know how to be a team player.

Team development goes through various stages. In the beginning, people are excited about being on a team. Later, disagreements may replace harmony. The good result of this is people express themselves and learn to trust the other team members. Eventually, leaders emerge and the team develops a unique pattern of interaction and goal attainment. Finally, the team becomes very productive and performs at its highest level. It takes time and a genuine desire to work together to build a strong team.

Creative ideas often develop from building on another person's idea. Honesty and openness are essential. In addition, trying to understand the ideas of others before trying to get others to understand your ideas is an effective skill to develop.

Leadership

All careers require leadership skills. *Leadership* is the ability to guide and motivate others to complete tasks or achieve goals. It involves communicating well with others, accepting responsibility, and making decisions with confidence, **Figure 2-20**. Those employees with leadership skills are most likely to be promoted to higher levels.

Leaders often seem to carry the most responsibility of a group. Other group members look to them for answers and direction. The most important role of leaders is to keep the team advancing toward its goal. Leaders do this by inspiring their groups and providing the motivation to keep everyone working together.

Good leaders encourage teamwork, because a team that is working together well is more likely to reach goals. They listen to the opinions of others

KeyStock/Shutterstock.com

Figure 2-20. Effective leaders create a positive environment that helps followers succeed.

Developing Leadership Skills

Many student organizations promote good leadership skills for work, school, and all other areas of life. To help members achieve these skills, organizations, such as the National FFA, sponsor competitions for individuals and teams. The FFA competitions, which are held at local, state, and national levels, are referred to as Career Development Events (CDEs) or Leadership Development Events (LDEs). Students develop leadership skills through training and service as officers at local, state, and national levels. Other components of FFA participation include earning degrees, participating in a chapter's program of activities (POA), performing community service, and attending leadership conferences and camps.

and make sure all team members are included in projects. Leaders also want to set a good example by doing a fair share of the work. In these ways, leaders cultivate a sense of harmony in the group.

Leadership Traits

Effective leaders have common traits or characteristics that contribute to their success. Your own demonstration of these traits can help promote a positive working environment as well as make you more eligible for promotions and advancements. Effective leaders commonly possess the following characteristics:

- **Courage.** The willingness to persist and move forward, even under difficult circumstances.
- **Confidence.** The belief in your ability to succeed and a feeling of self-assurance.
- **Integrity.** The quality of being honest, having strong principles, and treating others as you would have them treat you.
- **Enthusiasm.** Being eager to work in a manner that inspires and encourages others.
- **Optimistic attitude.** A confident and hopeful approach to situations or challenges.
- **Loyalty.** Being a reliable support for an individual, group, or cause.
- **Unselfishness.** Placing the desires and welfare of others above yourself.
- **Tactful.** Saying or doing the right thing without offending others.

Successful leaders are humble and acknowledge their mistakes or admit when they are wrong. They also make followers feel empowered and comfortable to present ideas they feel will benefit their peers. Identifying your own characteristics will help you understand where your own strengths and weaknesses lie.

Belonging to Organizations

Leading others may not be easy for some people, but everyone can improve their leadership skills with practice. Becoming involved in a school club or organization can help. Taking a role as an officer or a committee chair will give you even more practice. Many adults who are successful in the green industry participated in their local 4-H or FFA programs while in grade school and high school. These organizations have events dedicated to leadership development.

Belonging to an organization can also help you develop your teamwork skills. You will learn how to work well in a group as you plan events, create projects, and accomplish goals together, **Figure 2-21**.

Conflict Management

When you work with others, disagreements are likely to occur. Disagreements that are more serious are called conflict. *Conflict* is a hostile situation resulting from opposing views. It is important to know how to handle conflict to prevent it from becoming a destructive force in the workplace. This is called *conflict management*. A team leader has a special responsibility to prevent conflict among the team members. Several steps can be followed in managing conflict, **Figure 2-22**.

Rawpixel.com/Shutterstock.com

Figure 2-21. Joining a student or professional organization will help you improve your leadership and communication skills. You will also meet others with similar interests who might present you with employment opportunities.

Steps in Managing Conflict
1. Know when to intervene.
2. Address the conflict.
3. Identify the source and the importance of the conflict.
4. Identify possible solutions.
5. Develop an acceptable solution.
6. Implement the solution and evaluate.

Worradirek/Shutterstock.com

Figure 2-22. The ability to manage and resolve conflict in the workplace is an essential skill for people in leadership positions.

Sometimes the cause of a conflict is not so simple or easily understood. Use a positive approach and try to understand the problem from the other's point of view. Avoid jumping to conclusions and making snap judgments. Treat others with respect and in the same manner that you would like to be treated. Explore positive and negative aspects of each possible solution. If progress falls short of expectations, bring the parties back together and repeat the process. Many disagreements in the workplace can lead to productive change.

Negotiation

Often, there are times when employees and employers must negotiate on a task or work-related issue. *Negotiation* is the process of agreeing to an issue that requires all parties to give and take. The goal is a "win-win" solution in which both parties get some or all of what they are seeking, **Figure 2-23**.

Lipik Stock Media/Shutterstock.com

Figure 2-23. Negotiation is a necessary skill for working with or for other people. A client, for example, may indicate that a bid for a new landscape installation is too high for his or her budget. The landscape professional may negotiate the cost to retain and satisfy the client.

Career Connection

Hannah Singleton

Hannah Singleton, Manager of Professional Development

Hannah Singleton is the Manager of Professional Development for the North Carolina Nursery and Landscape Association. NCNLA is a nonprofit trade association dedicated to the welfare of North Carolina's green industry, with emphasis on the nursery and landscape industry.

Hannah is responsible for managing strategic professional development and educational opportunities for the industry. She develops NCNLA's annual educational plan, explores new continuing education and certification offerings, and ensures all reporting and certification thresholds are met. Singleton is also responsible for developing and delivering highly-valued events, sessions, and experiences that enhance the professional and technical skills of individuals throughout the vertically-integrated green industry. She enjoys the variety of her work, including traveling, connecting with young people, networking with nursery and landscape professionals, as well as providing new and exciting education opportunities for those professionals.

Hannah thrives in this role from her experiences as both an agriculture education teacher and nursery sales manager. Hannah holds many industry certifications herself. She advises young students and professionals interested in the green industry to find their niche. "There are a million roads to your destination; find the one that suits your passions and talents and then enjoy the ride." She says there will always be a place in the green industry for those who are passionate, hard-working, creative, and resilient.

Consider This

1. How does Hannah's experience as an agriculture education teacher contribute to her current position?
2. What appeals to you the most about Hannah's job? What appeals to you the least?

Negotiation begins with trying to understand the other party's interests. Possible solutions that meet their mutual concerns can be developed. Often, the best solution becomes clear when both parties have ample time to explain what they are trying to accomplish.

Summary

- Goal setting is the process of identifying something you want to accomplish and establishing a plan to achieve the desired result.
- Using the SMART goals guidelines will help make goals as realistic and beneficial as possible.
- Developing and using personal mission and vision statements can help you stay on the track to success.
- Mission and vision statements should be revisited and adjusted as you progress toward your goal.
- Having a well-prepared résumé is an important first step to applying for a position.
- You need to develop a list of references of people who will provide important information about you to a prospective employer.
- A letter of application is sent in with your résumé to explain who you are and why you are a good fit for the position.
- Adequate preparation for a job interview is essential for making a lasting, positive impression.
- How to behave in the workplace is an important lesson all employees should learn. Making an effort to do your best will help you succeed.
- Taking care of yourself gives the impression that you want people to view you as a professional.
- Employers want employees who are punctual, dependable, and responsible. They also want their employees to be capable of taking initiative and working independently.
- Your attitude can often determine the success you have on your job.
- Employers value workers who have the ability to make sound decisions. This process applies in the workplace as well as other aspects of life.
- Social media is a form of communication that is almost immediate and can be used in both positive and negative ways.
- Posting images of irresponsible behavior or writing derogatory comments online may cause an employer to remove you from their list of potential candidates.
- The most important aspect of customer relations is always remaining courteous.
- Ethical behavior on the job means conforming to accepted standards of fairness and good conduct.
- Some workplace activities that involve interpersonal skills include teaching others, leading, negotiating, and working as a member of a team.

- Leadership involves communicating well with others, accepting responsibility, and making decisions with confidence.
- Becoming involved in a school club or organization can help improve leadership and teamwork skills.
- It is important to know how to handle conflict to prevent it from becoming a destructive force in the workplace.

Chapter Review

Know and Understand ⤷

Answer the following questions using the information provided in this chapter.

1. The process of identifying something you want to accomplish and establishing a plan to make it happen is referred to as _____.
   A. skill setting
   B. goal setting
   C. job setting
   D. lead setting

2. What of the following best describes long-term goals?
   A. What you wish to accomplish in the near future.
   B. What you want to accomplish over the span of several years.
   C. What you list in a personal plan of action.
   D. A list of steps you choose to create a long-term plan.

3. What of the following describes SMART goals?
   A. Sporadic, miserable, atrocious, ridiculous, and timely.
   B. Simplistic, measurable, advanced, relevant, and timely.
   C. Specific, measurable, achievable, relevant, and timely.
   D. Satisfactory, misguided, accurate, restricting, and timely.

4. Why must personal goals be important and have value for you?
   A. You will not be able to achieve them.
   B. Personal goals need not have importance or value.
   C. Personal value is unimportant as long as they are SMART goals.
   D. You will not be motivated to achieve them.

5. A description of your personal goals for the future is referred to as a _____.
   A. vision statement
   B. summary statement
   C. mission statement
   D. commission statement

6. A short summary identifying a purpose or reason of existence is referred to as a _____.
   A. vision statement
   B. summary statement
   C. mission statement
   D. SMART statement

7. Which of the following sections are included on a well-prepared résumé?
   A. Career objectives and experience.
   B. Name, address, and contact information.
   C. Education history and references.
   D. All of the above.

8. The first contact with a potential employer is often a _____.
   A. mission statement
   B. cover letter
   C. résumé
   D. phone call

9. Which of the following items should be included in a letter of application?
   A. Your strengths, skills, and abilities for the job.
   B. Title of the job you seek and where you heard of the job.
   C. Reasons you should be considered for the job.
   D. All of the above.

10. For which of the following can employers legally use job application forms?
    A. To determine marital status.
    B. To screen for gender and ethnicity.
    C. To screen for skills needed on the job.
    D. To determine age and religion.

11. Which of the following can you use to prepare for a job interview?
    A. Research the company, learn specifics about the job, and know the company's mission.
    B. Dress as you would for any regular school day to indicate your professionalism.
    C. Keep a list of references on your phone and write the information on your résumé if they are requested.
    D. All of the above.

12. Which of the following habits will help you succeed in the workplace?
  A. A casual attitude toward company policies and procedures.
  B. Practicing grooming habits that keep you neat and clean.
  C. Dressing casually with garments displaying offensive sayings.
  D. Requiring constant supervision to ensure you perform your job.

13. Which qualities or habits does an employer seek in an employee?
  A. Being punctual to work and when returning from breaks.
  B. Having self-motivation and able to work independently.
  C. Prioritize assignments and complete them in a timely fashion.
  D. All of the above.

14. Which of the following statements regarding employees and work habits is true?
  A. Employees who dress in whatever manner they want to dress will advance quickly.
  B. Employees who are dependable do their part and meet their deadlines.
  C. Employees who take initiative require much more supervision.
  D. Employees who perform personal activities during work hours use time wisely.

15. Which of the following statements best describes how an employee's attitude affects his or her job performance?
  A. Doing a good job helps foster pride in your work and a desire to achieve more.
  B. Smiling and having courteous behavior will do little for a work environment.
  C. Enthusiasm on the job reduces team spirit for working together.
  D. Personal attitude has no influence on the success you have on your job.

16. While on the job, you will be expected to _____.
  A. act courteously
  B. show respect for your boss and coworkers
  C. behave professionally
  D. All of the above.

17. Having ability to solve problems on the job shows an employer that you are able to handle more _____.
  A. work hours
  B. motivation
  C. responsibility
  D. criticism

18. The process of exchanging ideas, thoughts, and information is referred to as _____.
  A. administration
  B. communication
  C. vindication
  D. altercation

19. Which of the following are the two primary forms of communication?
  A. Email and text messages.
  B. Organic and nonorganic.
  C. Verbal and nonverbal.
  D. Formal and casual.

20. Which of the following indicates that you are listening and interested in what a speaker is saying?
  A. Slouching back.
  B. Leaning forward.
  C. Yawning.
  D. All of the above.

21. Which of the following is a good practice for writing emails?
  A. Using industry slang and emojis.
  B. Using all caps to emphasize your point.
  C. Writing with common text abbreviations.
  D. Writing as though it were a business letter.

22. Which of the following will likely cause an employer to remove you from their list of potential candidates?
  A. Writing derogatory comments on social media.
  B. Posting images of irresponsible behavior.
  C. Posting inappropriate personal photos.
  D. All of the above.

23. The quality of being honest, having strong principles, and treating others as you would have them treat you is referred to as _____.
    A. enthusiasm
    B. integrity
    C. confidence
    D. courage

24. The process of agreeing to an issue that requires all parties to give and take is referred to as _____.
    A. negotiation
    B. confliction
    C. orientation
    D. socialization

Thinking Critically

1. How would you respond if a potential employer asked you if you were married during your interview?

2. Assume you are the supervisor of a landscape crew. How would you approach the issue of one of your best workers always arriving late?

3. Are workplace rules different for underage (17 or younger) employees? Explain your answer.

4. Do you think an employer should provide all PPE for his or her employees? Should an employee be responsible for the care and maintenance of their PPE? Explain your answer.

Suggested Activities

1. In a small group, develop personal mission statements. Each individual should write 2 to 4 of their most important goals. Share these goals and help each other develop mission statements using these goals as a starting point. If time allows, do the same exercise and develop individual vision statements.

2. Choose a partner and perform mock interviews for a job. Make a list of questions that an interviewer might ask, including one or two inappropriate questions on topics such as age, marital status, or religion. Alternate being the interviewer and the job candidate.

3. Make a list of your proudest accomplishments and determine what actions enabled you to achieve these accomplishments. Did your actions follow the SMART goals? Compare your results to those of your classmates.

4. Determine your short-term and long-term goals for your education. Write a plan of action for each goal.

5. Search online for employment opportunities that interest you. Using the samples in the chapter as guidelines, create a résumé and cover letter you could use to apply for the position. Exchange your résumé and cover letter with a peer and offer constructive criticism.

Occupational Safety

While studying this chapter, look for the activity icon ➦ **to:**
- **Practice** vocabulary terms with Words to Know activities.
- **Expand** learning with identification activities.
- **Reinforce** what you learn by completing Know and Understand questions.

www.g-wlearning.com/agriculture

Chapter Outcomes

After studying this chapter, you will be able to:

- Understand the importance of safety during landscape operations.
- Identify health and safety agencies that establish guidelines and enforce regulations to ensure safe work environments.
- Explain employer and employee responsibilities for maintaining a safe workplace.
- Identify personal protective techniques and equipment that should be used while conducting landscape-related activities.
- Explain and apply basic steps for administering first aid.
- Identify workplace safety hazards and explain safe practices for handling the various hazards.
- Identify and use safe practices in a shop environment.
- Understand and apply safe practices on job sites and when using motorized vehicles.

Key Terms ➘

allergic reaction
first aid
frostbite
heat cramp
heat exhaustion
heatstroke

high-visibility clothing
hypothermia
personal protective equipment (PPE)
safety data sheet (SDS)
safety hazard

Introduction

Safety is everyone's responsibility. To ensure a safe work environment, you should understand potential workplace hazards and ways to prevent accidents. While working outdoors in the landscaping industry, you may encounter poisonous plants, domestic or wild animals, and severe weather. You may also need to operate machinery and vehicles. Whether working on a job site or in the shop, you must always follow safety rules and wear proper safety equipment. This chapter will help you become familiar with occupational safety, hazards encountered in the landscaping industry, and safety rules and equipment, **Figure 3-1**.

Christina Richards/Shutterstock.com

Figure 3-1. Landscape operations can be hazardous and care must be taken to protect employees. Hazards range from working near vehicle traffic to working in a kneeling position for hours.

Safety and Health Agencies

As the Industrial Revolution gained momentum in the early 1900s, the need for work forces grew tremendously. In many cases, there was abuse and neglect of American workers, **Figure 3-2**. The government responded with acts, such as the *Fair Labor Standards Act (FLSA)* in 1938, to help establish better

Everett Historical/Shutterstock.com

Figure 3-2. Workers were abused and neglected as the Industrial Revolution grew and required greater numbers of employees. Government acts helped establish better working conditions and fair treatment for American workers.

working conditions with fair treatment and wages. Over time, the FLSA helped establish government organizations that were focused solely on worker health and welfare. These organizations include the Occupational Safety and Health Administration (OSHA), the Department of Labor (DOL), the National Institute of Occupational Safety and Health (NIOSH), the Centers for Disease Control and Prevention (CDC), and the American National Standards Institute (ANSI).

Occupational Safety and Health Administration (OSHA)

In 1970, the US Congress created the *Occupational Safety and Health Administration (OSHA)* to ensure safe and healthful working conditions for working men and women. OSHA sets and enforces workplace standards and provides training, outreach, education, and assistance. Under OSHA standards, employers are responsible for providing a safe and healthful workplace. OSHA is part of the US Department of Labor (DOL).

US Department of Labor (DOL)

The *US Department of Labor (DOL)* was established in 1913 as a direct result of organized labor's long campaign to give workers a collective voice in the government. The DOL's mission is "to foster, promote, and develop the welfare of the wage earners, job seekers, and retirees of the United States; improve working conditions; advance opportunities for profitable employment; and assure work-related benefits and rights." The DOL oversees and develops many programs, including disability, minimum water, and equal employment opportunities.

National Institute of Occupational Safety and Health (NIOSH)

The *National Institute of Occupational Safety and Health (NIOSH)* is a research agency focused on worker health and safety. NIOSH employs professionals in many fields to research health and safety issues. NIOSH is part of the US Centers for Disease Control and Prevention in the US Department of Health and Human Services.

US Centers for Disease Control and Prevention (CDC)

The *Centers for Disease Control and Prevention (CDC)* is one of the major divisions of the Department of Health and Human Services. The CDC employs professionals in many fields to research health and safety issues. Much of this research is used to develop safe protocols in handling major health issues and emergencies; however, it is also used to develop training, outreach, and education programs for the public and for worker safety.

American National Standards Institute (ANSI)

The *American National Standards Institute (ANSI)* is an organization formed by standards writers and users. ANSI manages the voluntary standards system in the United States. The standards overseen by ANSI directly impact businesses, materials, and equipment in nearly every sector, including the safety

Figure 3-3. Purchase only ANSI approved PPE to ensure you are protected. Read the tag or label before you purchase PPE.

Figure 3-4. Training and using the proper tools for each task contribute to job safety.

sector, **Figure 3-3**. ANSI is also involved in accreditation and the coordination of US standards with international standards.

Maintaining a Safe Workplace

Most people working in the landscaping industry travel each day and work in many different locations. These locations include greenhouses, nurseries, golf courses, commercial properties, private residences, and along roadways. These locations share common safety hazards but each also presents unique situations. It is an employer's responsibility to ensure each work environment is safe and that employees are aware of existing safety hazards. Employers are also responsible for providing safety training and ensuring employees understand their own responsibilities for personal safety, **Figure 3-4**.

Employers should develop safe workflow procedures and discuss procedures before, during, and after job site tasks. Supervisors should also assess and monitor work environments regularly and rectify unsafe conditions. Employers must also post safety information in a highly visible area of the workplace. Safety organizations require employers to display materials on safe work practices, such as spill prevention and cleanup procedures.

Your employer will emphasize the safety practices that employees must follow in your workplace. Employers may have restrictions on wearing long, loose hair because it can pose serious risks in landscape jobs. Long hair, loose clothing, and jewelry can be caught in moving machinery and result in serious injury. Some employers consider failure to dress safely and according to company rules a serious safety violation for which you may be dismissed.

Training

Companies may designate training days and offer incentives for those who progress through safety protocols for equipment operation and accident prevention measures. Quarterly training and daily safety meetings remind employees of dangers and encourage accountability.

Case Study

Working Safely

Sharon and Maria are working in a small engine repair shop. The majority of their customers are landscaping companies in the area. Sharon is a new employee who is certified to perform this type of repair work. Maria has been working in the shop for the past three summers and took some engine repair classes in high school. Maria notices that Sharon does not wear safety glasses when working and gives her a pair from the supply of safety equipment. When Sharon continues to work without her glasses, Maria reminds her that it is company policy to wear them. Sharon replies that she does not like wearing them because they look dumb and goes back to work.

Case Review
Discuss the following questions as a class or in groups of two or three students.
1. Why is it important for Sharon to wear her safety glasses when working on engines?
2. What should Maria do about Sharon's refusal to wear her safety glasses?
3. Is it Maria's place to ensure Sharon uses her safety glasses? Explain your answer.
4. How do you think the owner or manager will handle the situation?

Employee Responsibilities

Employees are also obligated to help maintain a safe environment for themselves and others. Employees can contribute to workplace safety by wearing the proper protective equipment, observing safety rules, reporting unsafe situations, using the correct tools, and removing malfunctioning machinery from service. They may also contribute by reviewing and understanding emergency response plans and learning basic first aid. Although it is very important to know how to respond to accidents and emergencies in the workplace, it is also very important to use safe practices to prevent accidents.

Preventing Accidents

Safety on the job is everyone's responsibility. Many workplace accidents occur because of careless behavior. Poor attitudes can also be the cause of unsafe behavior. Common causes of accidents include the following:
- Taking chances.
- Showing off.
- Forgetting safety details.
- Not wearing the proper PPE.
- Disobeying company rules.
- Daydreaming.
- Losing your temper.
- Falling asleep.

Practicing good safety habits is essential for preventing accidents and injuries on the job. A healthy worker is more alert and less likely to make accident-prone mistakes. Knowing how to use machines and tools properly is the responsibility of both the employer and employees. Wearing protective clothing and using safety equipment correctly helps keep workers safe, **Figure 3-5**.

Bankmoo Everyday/Shutterstock.com   *ungvar/Shutterstock.com*

Figure 3-5. Large and potentially dangerous equipment is used in the installation and maintenance of landscapes. Using careless behavior around this equipment can easily result in debilitating injury or death.

> **Pro Tip**
>
> Personal protective equipment (PPE) protects landscape professionals from short- and long-term exposure to dangerous equipment and materials. While operating a string trimmer for 30 minutes, for example, may not appear to injure a person's hearing, repeated operation without protection will definitely hinder hearing over time. The same facts apply to pesticide applications. A minor, one-time exposure to a low-toxicity pesticide may not harm a worker but repeated exposure over time may build up in the person's body and become toxic. Consider the task at hand, assess the risks of injury and exposure, and choose protection that is proper for the job.

Personal Protective Equipment

Personal protective equipment (PPE) is equipment and clothing worn by a person to protect him or herself from harm in potentially hazardous situations. PPE is an essential component for safely performing tasks in landscape work, **Figure 3-6**. PPE includes eyewear, hearing protection, respiration protection, clothing, and footwear.

> **Safety First**
>
> PPE is only effective if it fits properly and is properly maintained. Periodically inspect your PPE to ensure it is fully functional and that it fits properly.

Eye Protection

Eye protection is used to prevent damage to your eyes from irritants blown or thrown from blowers and mowers, such as dust or stones. Protective eyewear includes safety glasses, safety goggles, face shields, and full-face respirators, **Figure 3-7**.

Protective eyewear is designed for specific tasks and the appropriate eye protection must be worn to provide adequate protection. ANSI standards

Figure 3-6. Using safety gear and PPE helps prevent injury. Arborists are trained to safely climb and work in trees.

Tibor Duris/Shutterstock.com

A

George Dolgikh/Shutterstock.com

B

Elnur/Shutterstock.com

Figure 3-7. A—Safety goggles provide more protection from splashing fluids or liquids in mist form. B—Safety glasses have lenses with clear, yellow, orange, copper, or brown tints. Each of the colors serves a specific purpose, such as enhancing contrast and depth perception and reducing eye fatigue.

recommend the use of Z87 shatter-resistant protective eyewear when performing landscapes activities, such as cutting, sawing, pruning, and mowing. It must also be worn while working on equipment in the shop. As most landscape work is performed outdoors, it is important to purchase protective eyewear with UV (ultraviolet) protection.

Safety First

Ordinary eyeglasses and sunglasses will not provide the protection you need for some tasks. There are, however, special safety glasses and shields designed to be worn over eyeglasses.

Hearing Protection

Hearing protection must be worn when operating motorized machinery in the shop or on a job site. OSHA states that hearing protection should be used when operating equipment where the noise level is constantly 85 decibels. A normal conversation is around 60 decibels and a chainsaw is around 110. If you have to raise your voice to be heard in a noisy environment, you should be wearing hearing protection. Hearing protection reduces the noise level, thus lowering the risk of permanent or partial hearing loss. Different styles of hearing protection include earplugs and over-the-ear hearing protectors, **Figure 3-8**. Many operations develop and use hand signals and other means of nonverbal communication for use in noisy environments. These movements can be used to guide the operator as well as warn them of possible hazards.

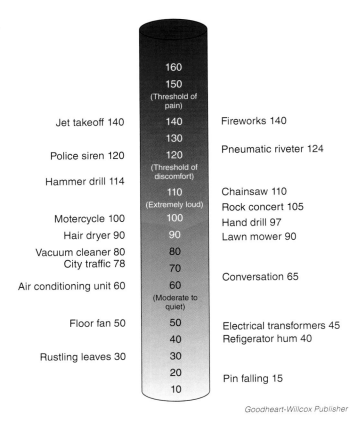

	160
	150
	(Threshold of pain)
Jet takeoff 140	140	Fireworks 140
	130
Police siren 120	120	Pneumatic riveter 124
	(Threshold of discomfort)
Hammer drill 114	
	110	Chainsaw 110
	(Extremely loud)	Rock concert 105
Motercycle 100	100	Hand drill 97
Hair dryer 90	90	Lawn mower 90
Vacuum cleaner 80	80
City traffic 78	70
		Conversation 65
Air conditioning unit 60	60
	(Moderate to quiet)
Floor fan 50	50	Electrical transformers 45
	40	Refrigerator hum 40
Rustling leaves 30	30
	20
		Pin falling 15
	10

Goodheart-Willcox Publisher

Figure 3-8. Do you find it surprising how some everyday tools are loud enough to warrant hearing protection? Most people do not realize how the things we do each day, such as blow drying our hair, can have an adverse effect on our hearing.

Respiratory Protection

Respiratory protection may also be required when working to protect your lungs from airborne particles. There are many types of protective equipment and it is important that the proper type be worn for the job. A dust mask is a very simple mask that filters dusts and other particles from the air. If chemicals are being applied, the worker may need to wear a full-face respirator. A full-face respirator protects the wearer's eyes and head and filters the incoming air so that it is safe to breath.

Respirators are available in a wide variety of styles and filtration capabilities and it is essential that the proper type be worn to ensure adequate protection, **Figure 3-9**. Keep in mind that some employers have policies restricting the amount of facial hair employees can wear because facial hair can interfere with the mask's ability to form a tight seal around your face.

Sapnocte/Shutterstock.com

Kletr/Shutterstock.com

Figure 3-9. Although every landscaping task does not require a respirator, it is advisable to wear the best respiratory protection possible. Mowing turfgrass once a week exposes a person to a great amount of dust, pollen, and other airborne particles. Mowing multiple lawns each day exposes a person to much more of the same irritants.

Protective Clothing

Protective clothing includes items such as long-sleeve shirts, pants, chaps, gloves, hats, and protective footwear. These items help protect workers from hazards, such as falling objects, sunburn, cuts and abrasions, insect stings, and chemical irritants.

Hats

Hard hats are required on landscape jobs where falling debris may cause injury. An arborist and ground crew, for example, must wear hard hats when performing tree maintenance. Hard hats may also offer some protection from chemical residue when applying pesticides or other chemicals. Soft, wide-brimmed hats can provide protection from the sun.

Gloves

Gloves can be worn to provide a better grip, provide warmth, prevent blisters, and keep wood splinters and thorns from piercing skin, **Figure 3-10**. Leather gloves are usually thicker and tougher than cloth and rubber gloves and offer protection against rough surfaces and splinters or thorns. Gloves with latex or rubber-like surfaces allow for better dexterity and grip and may provide protection from moisture or chemicals.

Footwear

Closed-toe footwear with adequate tread should always be worn when performing landscape tasks, **Figure 3-11**. A steel or composite-toe boot prevents damage from falling objects or objects flung from a machine. Proper footwear will prevent most objects from penetrating the sole and may keep your feet safe from insect and other animal bites. Sandals or flip-flops do not give adequate traction or protection.

Long-Sleeve Shirts and Pants

Although a specific task may determine which type of protective gear must be worn, many employers require all employees to wear certain clothing articles as part of their PPE. Many employers, for example, require employees to wear long-sleeve shirts and pants to protect their skin from the impact of foreign debris while mowing, string trimming, and pruning. Long pants and long-sleeve shirts also protect your skin from pesticide residue during the application of chemicals and may provide some protection from the sun. Some clothing also provides UV protection.

High-Visibility Clothing

High-visibility clothing is any type of clothing with reflective properties or made with very bright colors for ensuring that the wearer can easily be seen. High-visibility clothing is often florescent orange, yellow, or green and may have reflective strips. High-visibility clothing includes vests, hats, t-shirts, pants, and

Florin Burlan/Shutterstock.com

donate12-5/Shutterstock.com

TrotzOlga/Shutterstock.com

Figure 3-10. Gloves designed for a specific use should be used only for their intended purpose. Rubber gloves, for example, worn while moving and installing pavers, would quickly tear and leave hands exposed, and leather gloves worn while mixing chemicals would be cumbersome and allow chemicals to seep through and contact the wearer's skin.

Lyudmila Suvorova/Shutterstock.com

Lev Kropotov/Shutterstock.com

Figure 3-11. Quality footwear will protect your feet from sharp objects, spinning blades and strings, and the sting or bite from most animals and possibly minimize foot fatigue.

YolLusZam1802/Shutterstock.com

michaeljung/Shutterstock.com

Figure 3-12. High-visibility clothing protects workers' lives by making them more visible to drivers, especially in high traffic areas.

jackets, **Figure 3-12**. Many employers provide uniforms with reflective properties that satisfy all PPE requirements as well as create a professional appearance for the workers.

First Aid

First aid is help given to an injured person until full medical treatment is available. It is usually administered at the location where the injury occurs. The three main objectives of first aid are to save or preserve life, minimize injuries or prevent worsening, and to promote or hasten healing. Keep the following in mind when presented with an emergency:

- Call 911 immediately or have another person call if you are attending to an injured person.
- Do *not* endanger your own well-being. Evaluate the situation to determine if you can safely help an injured person.
- If multiple people are injured, treat the most severely injured person first.
- Get permission for care from the victim if possible and only move an injured person if their life is in danger of further injury. Moving an injured person may cause further injury.

Training and Certification

Knowing how to respond in an emergency and how to perform basic first aid are valuable skills that could save lives. Many schools and employers offer classes that provide basic first-aid training and may even work with organizations that offer certifications in first aid, CPR (cardiopulmonary resuscitation), and using an AED (automated external defibrillator). CPR is a series of compressions performed to help keep oxygenated blood flowing through the body. An AED is a portable machine that analyzes and shocks the heart to stop cardiac arrest. See **Figure 3-13**.

The primary goal of first-aid training and certification programs is to teach how to perform first aid. The initial training teaches basic first aid, such as attending to minor scrapes, cuts, and bruises, as well as how to stabilize injuries, and treat insect bites or stings, until professional help arrives. However, these programs also teach how to respond to accidents and emergencies in the workplace. Keeping calm in an emergency, for example, will help you evaluate the situation clearly and help you determine

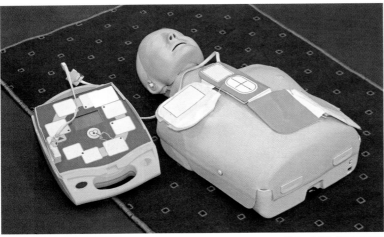

Baloncici/Shutterstock.com

Figure 3-13. Many organizations, such as a local fire department, will send a professional to a business upon request to instruct personnel on basic first aid. Many of these organizations also hold classes in a public facility.

the best course of action. Classes are available through places such as local fire departments, hospitals, community organizations, and the American Red Cross.

First-Aid Kits

Fully stocked and up-to-date first-aid kits should be kept where they are highly visible and easily accessible. Landscape industry businesses often have a workshop where tools and machinery are stored and maintained. Stationary first-aid kits can be mounted on the wall of a shop near the fire extinguisher and emergency plans, **Figure 3-14**. First-aid kits should also be kept in work vehicles and with large machinery, such as tractors, front loaders, and backhoes. It is important for all workers to be aware of locations for quick access in case of emergency. Regular reviews and restocking of kits should be scheduled.

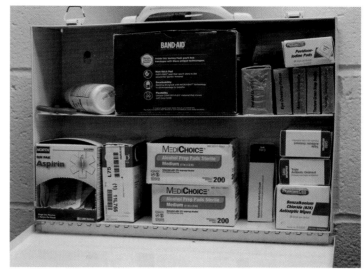

R. Lee Ivy

Figure 3-14. A wall-mounted first-aid kit should be located for ease of accessibility.

Allergic Reactions

An *allergic reaction* occurs when a person's immune system overreacts to a substance referred to as an allergen. Some allergic reactions are not severe and cause symptoms such as minor itching, watery eyes, and sneezing, while others have the potential to be life threatening. Skin conditions can also be created by exposure to allergen-holding plants. Many elements, including plants, animals, and chemicals, have the potential to cause allergic reactions. Reactions may be caused by physical contact, inhalation, or ingestion of the allergen. Allergic reactions may also be caused by bug bites or stings. In fact, many people are highly allergic to stings from common insects, such as bees and wasps.

Hives and rashes are common signs of the onset of allergic reactions. Life-threatening reactions include swelling of the victim's face, tongue, and throat. Individuals with life-threatening allergies should carry medication and alert their coworkers to their allergy and to the location of their medication. If someone is experiencing a life-threatening allergic reaction, dial 911 immediately, even if they have injected their medication.

Safety First

Although it is the employer's responsibility to ensure a safe work environment and proper training, employees must be vigilant and take the time to identify potential safety hazards each time they arrive on a job site. Workers should also know the address of the job site in case they need to inform emergency personnel of their location.

Workplace Safety Hazards

A *safety hazard* is anything that can cause injury, illness, or death. Some professions inherently present more hazards than other professions, especially those in which most work is performed outdoors where fewer factors can be controlled. For many, being outdoors is one of the benefits of working in the landscape industry. There are, however, many safety hazards related to outdoor tasks, including those presented by the plants, animals, and chemicals one might encounter or use. Workers must also protect themselves from extreme temperatures, sunlight, lightning, and severe storms.

Plants

Many types of plants can cause dermatitis or allergic reactions. Plants such as poison ivy, poison oak, and stinging nettle can cause minor itching irritation, lesions, or allergic reactions that can be life threatening. Some plants must be ingested to pose a threat, but a reaction may occur simply by touching certain plants. These types of plants are encountered when clearing overgrown areas, preparing new areas for planting, and when maintaining existing landscaping.

Some plants are more predominant in some areas of the country and some prefer specific environments. It is important to know what types of poisonous plants are in your area and how to identify them. These types of plants must be disposed of properly to prevent spreading and to limit additional hazards. See **Figure 3-15**.

Animals

Many animals, domesticated, feral, and wild, present potential safety hazards for people working in landscape environments, **Figure 3-16**. Larger animals, such as feral pigs and wild alligators, present more obvious hazards

Figure 3-15. Poison ivy, poison oak, and stinging nettle are three plants that will grow quickly once they take root. They are often found in landscapes near heavily wooded areas.

Jay Ondreicka/Shutterstock.com   *Viktor Loki/Shutterstock.com*   *frank60/Shutterstock.com*

Smileus/Shutterstock.com

Figure 3-16. In addition to black widows and diamondback rattlesnakes, there are insects that also carry disease, such as mosquitos and ticks.

as they roam freely or bask in ponds near homes and on golf courses. Other animals, such as spiders and snakes, are drawn to vegetative areas that offer protection and potential food sources. Some spiders and snakes, for example, make their habitat in woodpiles that workers may move to clear an area. The natural reaction of many of these animals is to bite or sting when they are alarmed or feel threatened. Bees, wasps, hornets, and other stinging insects have this same natural reaction.

The types of animals that workers may encounter vary by geographical location. As with poisonous plants, it is important to know what types of poisonous or dangerous animals are in your area and how to identify them. Properly identifying the type of animal that has bitten someone can mean the difference between life and death, as the antivenin and treatment used is specific to the type of venom injected. Bites from nonvenomous animals can also be very painful and run the risk of infection if not treated promptly. When possible, capture or use the camera on a phone to photograph the animal to ensure proper identification and seek immediate medical attention for the victim.

Mosquitos

According to the CDC, mosquitos may carry diseases, such as malaria, Zika virus, dengue, West Nile Virus, and Chikungunya Virus. To reduce the mosquito population, all standing water should be removed. Wearing long-sleeved shirts and long pants provides some protection, as does spraying insect repellent on exposed skin and clothing.

Ticks

The CDC also recommends quick removal of ticks before they burrow into skin. Ticks carry diseases, such as Lyme disease, Colorado tick fever, Rocky Mountain Spotted Fever, Powassan encephalitis, and Babesiousis. Ticks are found throughout the United States. Ticks are more active between April and October but especially in the summer months of June through August. Because ticks can be as small as a pinhead, they can be overlooked easily. The same methods of protection used against mosquitos will minimize risk of tick exposure.

Weather Conditions

In areas of the United States that experience more extreme seasonal changes, most landscape work is performed during the warmer months of the year. Work is performed in the warmer months because the soil is more workable and plants can be cultivated with their growth cycles. In warmer areas of the country, landscaping is performed year-round. Therefore, most landscape work is performed in hot weather and heat illnesses are common among landscape workers. Constant sun exposure, hot and humid conditions, and some personal protective equipment (PPE) all contribute to heat illnesses, such as heat cramps, heat exhaustion, and heat stroke.

Heat Cramps

Heat cramps are muscle spasms caused from the loss of fluids and electrolytes through perspiration and the lack of fluid intake. Heat cramps can be painful but do not typically result in permanent damage. Heat cramps can occur before the onset of more serious heat illnesses. Heat cramps can be prevented by keeping hydrated with water and liquids containing electrolytes to replace those lost in perspiration.

Heat Exhaustion

Heat exhaustion occurs when a person becomes dehydrated and the body's core temperature rises above a safe level. It is caused by prolonged exposure to high temperatures and high humidity when performing strenuous activity. Heat exhaustion can quickly lead to heatstroke. Signs of heat exhaustion include the following:

- Cool, pale, moist skin.
- Rapid pulse.
- Profuse sweating.
- Headache.
- Nausea.
- Dizziness or weakness.
- Heavy perspiration.

Heat exhaustion should be treated quickly. The victim should move to a cooler place and drink water and fluids designed for electrolyte replacement, such as sports drinks. Excess layers of clothing, including socks, shoes, and hats can be removed to help cool the victim. If the victim is unable to drink fluids or begins vomiting, he or she should receive immediate medical attention.

Heatstroke

Heatstroke is the most serious form of heat illness. It can occur with any previous heat-related illness, such as heat exhaustion, when the body's core temperature reaches or rises above 104°F (40°C). Heatstroke requires immediate emergency treatment because it can quickly damage body organs, including the brain, heart, and kidneys and may lead to death. Signs of heatstroke include the following, **Figure 3-17**:

- Rapid pulse.
- Lack of perspiration.
- Fatigue.

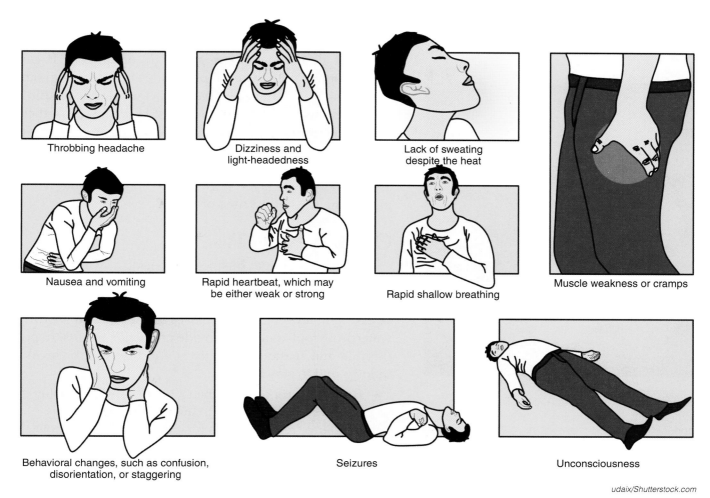

Throbbing headache

Dizziness and
light-headedness

Lack of sweating
despite the heat

Muscle weakness or cramps

Nausea and vomiting

Rapid heartbeat, which may
be either weak or strong

Rapid shallow breathing

Behavioral changes, such as confusion,
disorientation, or staggering

Seizures

Unconsciousness

udaix/Shutterstock.com

Figure 3-17. People often continue working while experiencing the first signs of heat illness. It is much wiser to pay attention to your body and rest when necessary.

- Headache.
- Nausea.
- Cramps.

Heatstroke must be treated immediately. If you suspect that someone you are working with is experiencing heatstroke, dial 911 *immediately*. The victim should be moved to a cooler place and drink water and fluids designed for electrolyte replacement if possible. Excess layers of clothing, including socks, shoes, and hats should be removed to help cool the victim. Cool compresses can be applied and the victim may be sprayed with cool water to help reduce his or her body temperature.

Sun Exposure

Extensive exposure to the sun can lead to skin problems, such as acute burns and blisters. Prolonged exposure can also cause cancerous diseases, such as melanoma. Workers can minimize skin and eye damage from the sun by taking precautions that will reduce their exposure to UV rays. Sunglasses, sunscreen, wide-brimmed

MicroOne/Shutterstock.com

Figure 3-18. Taking precautions by wearing sunglasses, hats, and sunscreen will protect oneself from the sun and its heat.

hats, and sun-protective clothing can all be used to protect against harmful UV rays, **Figure 3-18**.

Heat illness can occur gradually or quickly. It can be prevented with careful planning and by using safe work practices. Landscape workers can prevent or minimize their risk of heat illness by first being aware of their environment and preparing themselves *before* they begin working. Workers should dress for the weather and stay hydrated throughout the day. Workdays can begin earlier and breaks can be taken during peak hours to avoid working during the hottest time of the day.

Other Weather Hazards

Some landscape businesses perform work during the winter, such as snow plowing. As with overexposure to heat, overexposure to cold weather can be dangerous. Dressing in layers, wearing gloves and a hat, and wearing waterproof footwear will provide protection against hypothermia and frostbite. It is also important to take breaks indoors and to stay hydrated.

- *Hypothermia* occurs when a body loses heat faster than it can produce heat, causing a very low body temperature. Symptoms include shivering, shallow breathing, weak pulse, confusion, and loss of consciousness.
- *Frostbite* occurs when skin and its underlying tissues freeze. Mild frostbite, or *frostnip*, can be treated by warming the skin. Frostbite, however, must be given medical attention because it can damage not only the skin but muscles and bone as well. Symptoms include numbness, red, white, bluish-white or grayish-yellow skin, hard or waxy-looking skin, and blistering after warming.

Storm Weather

Storm weather also presents hazards to those working outdoors, including high winds, lightning, mixed precipitation, and freezing surfaces. Work crews should identify areas or structures at each job site that would provide them protection from the elements. Workers in wide open areas, such as a golf course, are especially susceptible to lightning. Supervisors should call workers off the course if lightning is seen in the area. Many people seek shelter under trees but this can be very dangerous as lightning often strikes the tallest object, such as a tree, and travels down the tree to the ground. The lightning may jump over to you and follow your body to the ground.

Shop Safety

Although much of the labor involved with landscape tasks is performed outdoors, there is a great deal of work performed indoors, such as tool and equipment maintenance and repair. This type of work is typically performed in a dedicated workshop that contains workbenches and stationary machines, such as a grinder, table saw, or drill press, **Figure 3-19**. For most operations, fuel, pesticides, and other potentially hazardous chemicals are also stored in the workshop. To ensure your own safety as well as that of your coworkers, it is just as important to use safe practices in the workshop as it is in the field.

Safety organizations have worked with those in all types of industry to develop universal methods of establishing a safe workplace. These methods include safety data sheets (SDS), safety color coding and labeling, and strict requirements for chemical labels and storage of chemicals and combustible/flammable liquids. Fire extinguishers should be within proximity of these substances should a fire occur.

Christopher D. Hart

Figure 3-19. Keeping shop areas neat and clean will provide a much safer and efficient work area.

Safety Data Sheets

A *safety data sheet (SDS)* is a document that provides information about a chemical, including its EPA registration number, physical and chemical properties, toxicity, and flash point, **Figure 3-20**. An SDS includes procedures for handling spills and leaks, guidelines for storage, and what types of PPE must be worn to minimize exposure. It addition, an SDS includes first-aid instructions, including what to do in the event of eye or skin contact, inhalation, and ingestion and the phone number for poison control. There is also a dedicated section for medical professionals on potential antidotes and advice for first aid.

It is mandated by OSHA that all manufacturers provide an SDS for all hazardous chemicals to ensure that anyone handling the substance has accurate information for safely handling and storing the chemical. OSHA also requires all businesses and school shops to keep the safety data sheets for all chemicals in a shop in an easily accessible location.

Safety Color-Coding

Safety color-coding has been established through OSHA and numerous other organizations, such as ANSI, to make it easier for people to identify hazardous areas in a workshop and on a job site quickly and easily. Colors, along with signal words, are used to identify specific types of hazards, **Figure 3-21**. The colors are used to identify and mark work zones and hazards and are added to the shop and/or individual pieces of equipment using tape, signs, and paint.

Kim Britten/Shutterstock.com

Figure 3-20. Reading an SDS before you work with a chemical will help you learn how to safely use the chemical. It will also help you stay prepared should an emergency arise.

ANSI-Specified Colors and Signal Words

Color	Signal	Application
Red	Danger	Used to identify a dangerous activity or condition that will result in serious injury or death if not avoided. Also used to designate fire protection equipment and flammable-materials containers.
Orange	Warning	Used to identify a dangerous activity or condition that may result in death or serious injury if not avoided.
Yellow	Caution	Used to identify a dangerous activity or condition, such as falling or tripping hazards that may result in minor or moderate injury if not avoided.
Green	Safety	Used to indicate location of safety/first-aid equipment or provide pertinent safety instructions.
Blue	Notice	Identifies activity that may lead to property damage or other issues not related to personal safety.
The following are not assigned to specific signal words or hazards. Meaning can be assigned by end user.		
Purple	Black	Combinations of Black, White, and/or Yellow
Gray	White	

Goodheart-Willcox Publisher

Figure 3-21. Implementing the ANSI-specified colors in the workshop and on machinery contribute to the creation of a safe environment. Keeping a chart posted in the workshop will help ensure personnel are aware of the colors and their applications.

Chemicals and Liquid Fuels

Landscape operations require fuel to run equipment and the use of various chemicals to fertilize plants, amend soils, and control pests. These hazardous materials must be transported to and from job sites and stored safely when not in use. OSHA has established standards to ensure the safe storage, handling, application, and disposal of such chemicals and fuels.

Fuel Storage and Transportation

Motor oil, gasoline, and diesel are all flammable liquids that must be stored and transported according to OSHA standards. Portable containers must be approved by OSHA and/or the department of transportation (DOT) and be designated solely for the purpose of storing and transporting fuels. Containers must also be clearly labeled with the type of fuel they contain. While in transport, fuel containers must be secured to prevent them from freely moving around the vehicle bed or trailer. In the shop, fuel containers must be stored in an approved hazardous storage cabinet, **Figure 3-22**.

Chemical Application and Storage

Chemicals, such as fertilizers, herbicides, and pesticides, are used in the industry to feed plants, control weeds, and manage pests. There are many regulations in place to ensure the safe handling, application, and storage of these chemicals. In addition, the application of some chemicals may *only* be performed by licensed individuals. Therefore, it is imperative for employees to understand all restrictions and safe practices pertaining to each type of chemical *before* handling or application.

R. Lee Ivy

Figure 3-22. OSHA approved fuel storage containers and cabinets are designed to keep flammable and hazardous materials safely contained and contribute to worker safety.

Although there are basic safe practices that should be followed when handling any hazardous material. Specific instructions may be included with each chemical. These instructions must be understood before an emergency occurs. Keep the following points in mind when working with chemicals:

- Do *not* handle or apply chemicals unless you have been trained to do so.
- Always read the label for safe handling and application instructions. You may also read the SDS for more detailed information.
- Do *not* eat or drink when mixing chemicals.
- Always wear the required PPE when handling and applying chemicals. This includes a long-sleeved shirt, long pants, chemical resistant gloves, protective eyewear, and shoes with socks.
- Mix chemicals in well-ventilated areas in adequate light.
- Do *not* use measuring equipment for anything other than mixing the specific chemical.
- Always add the concentrated chemical to the water when mixing. This will prevent splashing of the concentrated chemical.
- Mix only what you will be using and dispose of excess mixture in accordance with the manufacturer's instructions.

First Aid

Read the SDS and the product label *before* you handle any hazardous material. The recommended first aid is not exactly the same for different chemicals and using the wrong procedures can have adverse effects on the victim. If you are mixing chemicals in the shop, know where the eyewash station is located or ensure yourself access to fresh running water, **Figure 3-23**. If you

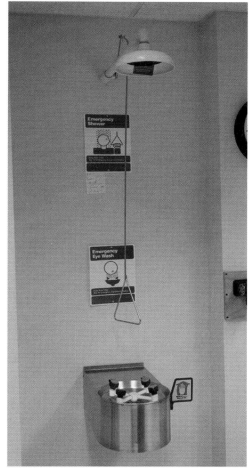

R. Lee Ivy

Figure 3-23. Many people are unaware or unfamiliar with eyewash stations and their use. All employees should be shown the location(s) and given instructions for using the station.

Career Connection

Daniel Currin

Daniel Currin, CEO and Owner of Greenscape, Inc.

Daniel Currin is CEO and owner of Greenscape, Inc., a commercial landscaping company that serves the Raleigh-Durham area. As CEO, Daniel spends his days working both in and on the business. Daniel's responsibilities range from equipping and empowering the leadership team and monitoring the company finances to casting vision and revising the structure of the organization. Daniel also spends time connecting with other industry leaders and organizations to stay on top of the ever-changing trends and climate of the green industry. "Probably the part that I enjoy the most about my job is problem-solving. As the leader of the company I need to have a pulse on the green industry and be aware of potential challenges that we may face as a company. I collaborate with other team members and industry leaders to come up with solutions that keep us surviving and thriving."

Of course, Daniel did not start day one of his postgraduate career as CEO. Greenscape was established in 1979 by Daniel's father, Michael Currin, and Daniel spent his high school summers working as a team member on a landscape crew. After his college graduation, Daniel began working full-time as a commercial management salesperson, then a commercial branch manager, and eventually stepped into the role of CEO. "I believe my time spent in several different roles over the years has allowed me to have a more holistic understanding of the company and to make the best decisions for both the company and all of our people. I would definitely encourage future green industry leaders to spend some time in various aspects of the green industry before going out on your own. It will ultimately make you a better leader."

Consider This

1. Can you see yourself as the CEO of a green industry company? What strong leadership skills do you think Daniel Currin possesses?
2. What do you think is the most challenging part of a CEO's position?
3. How do you think Daniel's high school summers on the job affect his ability to run the company?

are mixing chemicals in the field, ensure there is an easily accessible source of fresh running water, a spigot and hose for example. In most cases, it is important to flush your eyes or rinse exposed skin for an extended amount of time. You should also remove contaminated clothing to prevent further exposure.

Control, Contain, and Cleanup

Workers should not only be trained in the proper mixing and application of chemicals, they should also be trained in the process of cleaning up chemical spills. Once again, it is imperative to read the manufacturer's instructions *before* handling the chemical. It is also important to know local regulations for cleaning and disposing of contaminated materials. Knowing how best to handle a spill *before* it occurs is the safest practice. Always wear the proper PPE and keep the following three Cs in mind when handling chemical spills.

- **Control.** A chemical container that has fallen over or is damaged should be placed upright and placed in another container. A large bucket, for example, can hold the damaged container and its contents.
- **Contain.** Keep the spill from spreading. Use a spill kit or another means of keeping the spilled chemical in a contained area.

- **Cleanup.** Follow all manufacturer's instructions and local regulations for cleaning up the spilled chemicals. You must also follow instructions and regulations for disposal of contaminated cleaning materials.

Record Keeping

State and local agencies require accurate storage and record keeping of products including product identification, amount, and purchase date. Record keeping for chemical application includes product identification, amount applied, date and time of application, and reentry interval. This ensures proper longevity of chemicals and information should an application issue arise. For example, if a client's neighboring landscape is adversely affected and a complaint is made to a certifying agency, the records can be used to investigate the cause of the adverse effects, **Figure 3-24**.

Job Site and Vehicle Safety

Landscape workers are constantly traveling to and working on different job sites, often in close proximity to parking lots, walkways, and roads. It can be challenging to keep workers safe and prevent the public from endangering themselves by entering work areas. Employers can help keep employees and the public safe by training their employees how to secure an area and how to perform tasks safely.

FIELD ID/LOCATION "USDA" : _52-48 Old Creek Field_

Applicator Name and Certification Number "USDA"	Mo/Day/Year Time "USDA"	EPA Reg. Number "USDA"	Active Ingredients	Brand/ Product Name "USDA"	Restricted Entry Interval (REI)	Crop, Commodity or Site "USDA"
Bob B. Smith 200028265	5/3/02 10 am*	241-337	Pendimethalin	Prowl 3.3EC	24 hrs	cotton
	5/3/02 10 am*	100-642	Fluometuron	Cotoran 4L		

*Time is not required by the USDA pesticide recordkeeping regulations, but it is required by the WPS.

Rate	Size of Area Treated "USDA"	Total Amount Applied "USDA"	Field Notes: target pest(s); sprayer nozzles, speed, pressure, gallonage; wind & weather; crop status
1.5 pints per acre	20 acres	3.75 gallons	Sunny, wind speed 3-5 mph. Light grass infestation.
2 quarts per acre	20 acres	10 gallons	Gallonage = 10 gallons per acre. Banded at planting.

USDA, AMS, Pesticides Records Branch

Figure 3-24. The samples above are from the *USDA, AMS, Pesticides Records Branch Recordkeeping Manual* that can be downloaded from the internet. Some of the information required is from the EPA Worker Protection Standard (WPS).

High-Visibility Clothing

The first step is ensuring all employees are wearing the proper PPE, including high-visibility clothing. High-visibility clothing, such as safety vests and reflective tape on pants and shoes, increases visibility of workers to the walking and driving public, **Figure 3-25**.

Work Area Barriers

Reflective signs, cones, and portable barriers should be used to mark work areas. These signs and barriers help identify areas where the public should not enter and provide workers with a safe area to work. Road cones, for example, can be used to create a safe loading and unloading zone surrounding a landscaping truck and trailer parked in a parking lot, **Figure 3-26**.

Vehicle Safety

In the United States, there are many laws and regulations in place to keep our roadways safe. These laws apply to both drivers/operators and vehicles. It is illegal, for example, to operate a motor vehicle on the roadway without the proper driver's license. In addition, all vehicles must be insured, though there is some variation in laws from state to state regarding the minimum amount and type. Insurance is expensive and because employers are responsible for insuring their company equipment, they may not or cannot afford to employ workers with poor driving records.

Fusionstudio/Shutterstock.com

Figure 3-25. All workers should wear high-visibility clothing when they are on a worksite, even if they feel there is no hazard or danger to their well-being.

R. Lee Ivy

Figure 3-26. Taping off or placing road cones around the truck and trailer provides a secure place for loading, unloading, and refueling equipment. It will also keep the public from approaching or walking through the work area.

Commercial Vehicles

Commercial vehicles must meet the standard safety provisions required of all motor vehicles, such as rearview mirrors and functioning turn signals. However, there are many more safety provisions or regulations that commercial vehicles must meet to qualify for licensing and registration. These regulations may vary somewhat between states. It is both the employer's and operator's responsibility to ensure all vehicles and trailers are in compliance. Tractors and other slow-moving vehicles, for example, must be properly marked with a slow-moving vehicle (SMV) sign, **Figure 3-27**. Another safety feature found on many commercial vehicles is a beeper system that audibly alerts when reverse is engaged. The beeping alerts pedestrians and workers in the area that the vehicle is backing up.

Mark Herreid/Shutterstock.com

Figure 3-27. A slow-moving-vehicle sign indicates that the vehicle will maintain a slow speed on the roadway.

Hauling and Towing

Most landscape operations use detachable trailers to haul equipment and plant materials to work sites. It is imperative that the driver and/or workers know how to properly attach and load these trailers to ensure safe handling on the roadway. It is also important for the driver to adjust their driving to accommodate the additional weight and length of the trailer.

- The vehicle must have sufficient capacity to haul the weight of the trailer and its contents. The vehicle's efficiency and handling will be adversely affected if it is overloaded.
- The metal hitch establishes the physical connection that keeps the trailer and vehicle connected, **Figure 3-28**. The female connector on the trailer must fit the male connector on the vehicle to ensure a secure and safe connection.
- The wiring must be connected from the vehicle to the trailer to power the lights on the trailer.
- Proper loading of a vehicle helps with handling and stopping capabilities. It is best to center and secure the load with straps or chains over the trailer axle. If the trailer load is heaviest at the tongue or tail, it will make it difficult to steer and stop. It may also cause the trailer to fishtail (swerve side-to-side) while the vehicle is in motion, especially at higher speeds.

Sista Vongjintanaruks/Shutterstock.com

J88DESIGN/Shutterstock.com

Figure 3-28. Trailer hitches vary in size and weight holding capacity and are categorized by classes I through V. The place of purchase will guide you to the correct size and class for your needs.

High Hazard Areas

OSHA identifies falls, electrocution, being struck by something, and getting caught between something as the four highest hazard areas. Keeping work areas clean, wearing PPE, using equipment properly, and following safe practices will reduce the chance of an accident.

Case Studies

Sometimes real life examples are more effective when we learn about job hazards and how to stay safe as we work. The following two events used by the CDC and NIOSH help employers and workers develop better safety awareness and practices.

Staying Safe around Large Equipment

A crew of landscape workers was unloading a small backhoe from a trailer at a job site. The backhoe was secured to the trailer with chains, which had tightened during transport. A worker started and moved the backhoe forward a few inches to release tension on the front chains. A second worker was standing in front of the backhoe to remove the chains once they were loosened. As the driver was stepping down to help remove the chains, the backhoe lunged forward and pinned the worker between the backhoe and the rear of the dump truck to which the trailer was attached. The young worker was crushed to death.

Case Review
Discuss the following questions.
1. What precautions should the workers have taken to prevent the backhoe from moving?
2. What type of training and safety instruction would help prevent a similar accident?
3. How can employers ensure all employees understand how to stay clear of operating equipment and vehicles?
4. Would performing a job hazard analysis of all work activities help workers and employers understand work hazards? How would this type of analysis be performed?

Staying Safe While Trimming Trees

A three-man crew was cutting an 80′ oak tree using a truck-mounted aerial lift. The crew leader and the two groundsmen were taking a break. The crew leader, who was in charge of the site and was doing the tree trimming, instructed the groundsmen to remain on break, sitting on the tailgate of their truck. The truck was parked 30′ to 40′ from the oak tree. The crew leader returned to the lift and resumed trimming. He began cutting the top of the tree in sections using a chainsaw. He cut a section that was 25′ long, 7″ in diameter, and weighed almost 50 lb. He pushed the section and it fell to the ground and struck the groundsman on the head. The crew leader was unaware that the groundsman had walked into the landing zone. The victim died at the hospital.

Case Review
Discuss the following questions.
1. How could the crew have prevented the accident?
2. How could the ground be marked to indicate the landing zone?
3. What type of communication method could the workers use while loud equipment, such as the chain saw and shredder, is running?
4. Does OSHA or any other safety organization have standards that apply to this situation?
5. What information should a crew leader review with the workers to ensure that everyone understands the rules for working on site?

Summary

- Safety should be the first consideration during any landscape operation.
- Many health and safety agencies, such as OSHA, the US DOL, NIOSH, the US CDC, and ANSI, develop and enforce safe workplace standards and guidelines.
- Discussions on safe workflow procedures should be had before, during, and after job site tasks.
- Employers must post safety information, such as spill cleanup, in a highly visible area of the workplace to comply with OSHA standards.
- It is an employer's responsibility to ensure each work environment is safe and that employees are aware of existing safety hazards.
- Employees are also obligated to help maintain a safe environment for themselves and others.
- Wearing PPE is essential to protect oneself from harm in potentially hazardous situations.
- ANSI standards recommend the use of Z87 shatter-resistant protective eyewear when performing landscapes activities, such as cutting, sawing, and mowing.
- OSHA states that hearing protection should be worn when operating equipment where the noise level is constantly 85 decibels.
- Respirators vary in design and filtration capabilities. It is essential that the proper type respirator be worn to ensure adequate protection.
- Protective clothing helps protect workers from hazards, such as falling objects, sunburn, cuts and abrasions, insect stings, and chemical irritants.
- High-visibility clothing is any type of clothing with reflective properties or made with very bright colors for ensuring that the wearer can easily be seen.
- The three main objectives of first aid are to save or preserve life, minimize injuries or prevent worsening, and to promote or hasten healing.
- Allergic reactions may be caused by physical contact, inhalation, or ingestion of allergens.
- A safety hazard is anything that can cause injury, illness, or death.
- Environmental extremes can be harmful to workers conducting landscape tasks. Protection from heat and sun is essential.
- It is just as important to use safe practices in the workshop as it is in the field to ensure your own safety as well as that of your coworkers.
- A safety data sheet includes procedures for handling spills and leaks, guidelines for storage, and what types of PPE must be worn to minimize exposure.
- Motor oil, gasoline, and diesel are flammable liquids that must be stored and transported according to OSHA standards.
- While in transport, fuel containers must be secured to prevent them from freely moving around the vehicle bed or trailer.

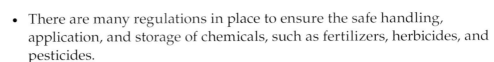

- There are many regulations in place to ensure the safe handling, application, and storage of chemicals, such as fertilizers, herbicides, and pesticides.
- State and local agencies require proper storage and record keeping of products, including product identification, amount, and purchase date.
- Record keeping for chemical application includes product identification, amount applied, date and time of application, and reentry interval.
- Employers can help keep employees and the public safe by training their employees how to secure an area and how to perform tasks safely.
- Reflective signs, cones, and portable barriers help identify areas where the public should not enter and provide workers with a safe area to work.
- It is imperative that the driver and/or workers know how to properly attach and load trailers to ensure safe handling on the roadway.

Chapter Review

Know and Understand ↪

Answer the following questions using the information provided in this chapter.

1. Which of the following agencies was created to ensure safe and healthful working conditions for working men and women?
   A. American National Standards Institute.
   B. US Department of Labor.
   C. Occupational Safety and Health Administration.
   D. Centers for Disease Control and Prevention.

2. Which of the following best describes the DOL's mission?
   A. To ensure safe and healthful working conditions for mine workers.
   B. To research and develop standards for worker health and safety.
   C. To establish better working conditions with fair treatment.
   D. To foster, promote, and develop the welfare of the wage earners, job seekers, and retirees.

3. For which of the following are employers responsible?
   A. Providing safety training.
   B. Ensuring each work environment is safe.
   C. Monitoring work environments regularly.
   D. All of the above.

4. Failure to dress safely and according to company rules may be reason for _____.
   A. promotion
   B. dismissal
   C. transfer
   D. All of the above.

5. Which of the following behaviors are common causes of workplace accidents?
   A. Poor attitudes and forgetting safety details.
   B. Showing off and taking chances.
   C. Losing your temper or falling asleep.
   D. All of the above.

6. Equipment and clothing worn to protect a person from harm in potentially hazardous situations is referred to as _____.
   A. PPE
   B. CDC
   C. DOL
   D. FLS

7. Protective eyewear worn while performing landscape activities should be _____.
   A. CDC approved
   B. Z87 shatter-resistant
   C. standard FLSA issue
   D. USDA standard Z87

8. At what noise level does OSHA recommend hearing protection?
   A. Constant 85 decibels.
   B. Between 55 and 85 decibels.
   C. When it becomes uncomfortable.
   D. Only when operating a chainsaw.

9. Which of the following is a likely reason an employer might restrict the amount of facial hair an employee can wear?
   A. It looks unprofessional.
   B. A respirator may not form a seal.
   C. He or she dislikes facial hair.
   D. It will clog a mask's air filter.

10. Which of the following articles of clothing are used as PPE?
    A. Gloves and hats.
    B. Chaps and high-visibility vests.
    C. Long-sleeved shirts and pants.
    D. All of the above.

11. To prevent objects from penetrating feet and to protect feet from falling objects, all workers should wear _____.
    A. high-top athletic shoes with closed toes
    B. leather sandals with knee-high socks
    C. footwear with adequate tread and closed toes
    D. leather shoes and thick, insulated socks

12. Which of the following is the most likely reason an employer would provide high-visibility clothing for employees?
    A. To identify crewmembers easily.
    B. To protect them from the sun and rain.
    C. To locate crewmembers easily.
    D. To ensure employees are easily seen.

13. The help given to an injured person until full medical treatment is available is _____.
    A. administered at the location where the injury occurs
    B. given to minimize injuries or prevent worsening
    C. to save or preserve a life and promote healing
    D. All of the above.

14. To help you evaluate an emergency situation clearly and determine the best course of action, you should _____.
    A. remain calm
    B. sit down and think
    C. leave the scene
    D. let someone else help

15. The best course of action to follow when someone is having an allergic reaction is to _____.
    A. give them water
    B. dial 911 immediately
    C. apply a cold compress
    D. let someone else help

16. Plants that cause dermatitis or allergic reactions are often found _____.
    A. when preparing new areas for planting
    B. while maintaining existing landscaping
    C. when clearing overgrown areas
    D. All of the above.

17. Why is it important to identify accurately the type of animal that has bitten someone?
    A. The treatment is specific to the venom injected.
    B. To capture and kill the correct animal.
    C. To pinpoint the area in which it was found.
    D. All of the above.

18. Why do outdoor workers experience heat illnesses?
    A. Insufficient fluids.
    B. Constant sun exposure.
    C. Hot and humid conditions.
    D. All of the above.

19. The most serious form of heat illness is _____.
    A. heat exhaustion
    B. heatstroke
    C. heat cramps
    D. All of the above.

20. A document that provides information about a chemical, such as its toxicity and flashpoint, is referred to as a(n) _____.
    A. PPE
    B. CDC
    C. SDS
    D. DOL

21. Flammable liquids, such as motor oil, gasoline, and diesel, must be stored and transported according to standards set by the _____.
    A. CDC
    B. DOL
    C. OSHA
    D. SDS

22. Which of the following practices should be used when working with chemicals, such as herbicides and pesticides?
    A. Do not handle unless trained to do so.
    B. Do not eat or drink when mixing chemical.
    C. Do not use measuring equipment for other purposes.
    D. All of the above.

23. To identify areas where the public should not enter and provide a safe work area for workers, work areas should be _____.
    A. marked with signs, cones, and portable barriers
    B. limited to areas with no traffic and few people
    C. blocked with any available objects or vehicles
    D. All of the above.

24. In order to drive a company vehicle, an employee must _____.
    A. ensure the vehicle is insured
    B. ensure turn signals are functioning
    C. have a valid driver's license
    D. All of the above.

Thinking Critically

1. What approach would you use if a classmate or coworker were behaving carelessly while he or she was using a chipper/shredder?

2. How would you show your understanding of your company's safety rules?

3. How would you explain to your coworker or classmate why it is important to wear PPE while using a string trimmer?

Suggested Activities

1. Work with a peer and establish a standard workflow procedure for your workplace or school shop. This should include tool safety, machinery operation, and risk reduction. Share your procedures with the class.

2. Determine the most common workplace hazards in your immediate surroundings. Compare your findings to those of your classmates and discuss how these areas can be made less hazardous.

3. Working in groups of 3 to 4, identify the best daily stretches for employees and develop a workplace challenge for overall fitness. Create incentives for those that participate and advance their health standards. Present your ideas to the class and have your classmates participate in a short round of stretches as part of your presentation.

4. In a group of 2 or 3, analyze the condition of company or school PPE and determine replacement strategies or a means of acquiring new equipment. Write a detailed report of conditions and replacement strategies. If possible, take photos of safe and unsafe areas or equipment and create a visual presentation.

5. Identify high profile areas that should display OSHA and ANSI standards.

6. Demonstrate the safe use, storage, and maintenance of every piece of equipment in the lab, shop, and classroom, include the OSHA Lockout/Tagout Program (LOTO).

7. Identify, describe, and demonstrate the effective use of safety data sheets (SDS).

8. Identify and explain the PPE that must be used when using a chainsaw, including chaps. Explain kickback and reactive forces and the means of preventing a kickback accident.

9. Locate emergency equipment, first-aid kit, SDS information, eyewash stations, shower facilities, sinks, fire extinguishers, fire blankets, telephone, master power switches, emergency exits, and emergency response plan in your lab, shop, and classroom.

Tools and Equipment

While studying this chapter, look for the activity icon ↪ to:

- **Practice** vocabulary terms with Words to Know activities.
- **Expand** learning with identification activities.
- **Reinforce** what you learn by completing Know and Understand questions.

G-WLEARNING.com

www.g-wlearning.com/agriculture

Chapter Outcomes

After studying this chapter, you will be able to:

- Identify PPE that should be worn while using hand and power tools.
- Describe basic systems of record keeping for tracking tools and maintenance.
- Describe basic guidelines for maintaining common hand tools.
- Identify common landscaping hand tools and their uses.
- Explain basic steps for sharpening tool edges.
- Identify common landscaping power tools and their uses.
- Describe basic guidelines for maintaining landscaping power tools.
- Describe basic guidelines for inspecting and maintaining large equipment.
- Perform basic troubleshooting steps on small engines.

Key Terms ➦

digging tool
geographic information system (GIS)
global positioning systems (GPS)
impact tool
inventory

leveling tool
rake
rollover protection system (ROPS)
tool maintenance schedule

Introduction

Modern tools make landscaping work easier and more efficient. For instance, using equipment, such as a skid steer, one person can grade a large lot or spread topsoil instead of a crew using wheelbarrows and shovels, **Figure 4-1**. In order to get the most out of the landscaping tools and equipment available, you must know how to select the right tool for the job and how to properly use and maintain tools and equipment. Any tool or piece of equipment can be dangerous if it is used improperly or not maintained well. This chapter describes various tools and their uses and provides maintenance and safe operation procedures for many of the tools you will encounter in the landscaping industry.

Figure 4-1. Using a wheelbarrow and shovel to spread soil over large areas is impractical unless it is not possible to move large equipment into the area.

Photowind/Shutterstock.com

Tool and Equipment Safety

The first and foremost rule is you must *not* operate any tool or equipment for which you have not been trained or authorized to operate. Taking a chainsaw up a tree, for example, can be dangerous for trained professionals, let alone for someone who does not know how or is just learning to use a chainsaw, **Figure 4-2**. Learning how to use equipment properly will help keep you and your coworkers safe and help keep the equipment in operating condition. Ask your supervisor for training on equipment operation and on checking the equipment for safety issues to ensure it is in working order.

Personal Protective Equipment

The second rule is you must *always* wear the proper personal protective equipment (PPE) to protect yourself from harm, **Figure 4-3**. Not wearing PPE while working because you think it is unnecessary or it looks unattractive is foolish and careless behavior. Failing to use PPE is also grounds for dismissal in most companies. PPE must be properly cared for to ensure it will protect the wearer as intended. Keep in mind that the type of PPE required varies by the equipment or tool being used.

Owner's Manuals

It is also highly recommended for the operator to read the owner's manual before operating any equipment. The owner's manual will include diagrams identifying components, such as the ignition, emergency brake, safety guards, instructions for use, troubleshooting guides, and maintenance instructions. Most equipment manufacturers publish owner's manuals online should you need a replacement copy.

Tobias Arhelger/Shutterstock.com

Figure 4-2. Working with a chainsaw to trim or cut down trees requires training on safe climbing and cutting with the chainsaw. It also requires head, ear, and eye PPE as well as a safety harness with ropes.

A   **B**   **C**   *Photos courtesy of A.M. Leonard Inc.*

Figure 4-3. Personal protective equipment (PPE) protects the worker against injury but also prevents long-term fatigue to extremities, the head, and body. A—Chainsaw chaps. B—Helmet with face shield. C—Chainsaw gloves.

Record Keeping

A business' record keeping is not limited to its finances. All tools and equipment must also be accounted for to ensure the purchase price, maintenance costs, and depreciation are included as part of the company's assets.

Maintenance

The appearance of tools, equipment, and employees on a job site generate the first impression of a company and the quality of its work. Great care should be taken to ensure that all tools and equipment are in good condition to keep them in safe working order and so they reflect your company in the best light possible. The most efficient means of keeping equipment in good condition is to establish *tool maintenance schedules* and record all maintenance performed. Some companies give incentives to employees who go extended periods with minimal damage to the equipment they use regularly.

Checklists

A checklist is helpful for employees to use when evaluating the condition of a tool or piece of equipment before using it and at the end of a workday. Depending on the implement, a checklist may include actions, such as checking the oil or fuel level and removing all debris. A checklist for hand tools, for example, would include the following tasks:

- Cleaning dirt or other debris from the tool.
- Checking handles for cracks or loose connections.
- Checking sharpness of metal edges or blades.
- Sanding of wooden parts as needed.
- Applying oil or sealant on wooden parts.
- Cleaning leather parts with glycerin bars or leather cleaner.
- Coating metal with a medium weight oil.
- Applying rust preventive to metal parts.

The manufacturer's recommendations for cleaning and maintaining tools may be used to establish a checklist. Keeping hand tools clean and in good condition will prolong their usefulness and it may help reduce the chance of transmitting disease or pests from one site to another. Many companies use apps on tablets or phones to keep track of tool maintenance and use.

Inventory

Keeping an accurate inventory and properly storing hand tools will ensure all tools are accounted for and that there will be enough available for a crew to perform work. An *inventory* is a complete record of the tools and equipment owned by the company. Inaccurate tool inventories may result in unnecessary expenses and lost efficiency. A tool labeling system can help keep accurate inventory. The labeling system can be as simple as paint on the handle or as complex as a bar-coded asset tag. Keeping the storage area neat and clean will also help maintain an accurate inventory and allow easy access to tools, **Figure 4-4.**

A   *Photo courtesy of A.M. Leonard Inc.*   B   *R. Lee Ivy*

Figure 4-4. A—Storage racks on a vehicle make tools accessible and ensures they will not be left behind. B—Storage areas should be labeled and kept neat to make it easy to retrieve tools and return them to a designated space.

Measuring Devices

Accurate measurements are essential to calculate the amount of materials and labor that will be needed to complete a job. There are many traditional tools used to measure landscape sites, including measuring wheels, retractable tapes, and winding tapes. Today's technology has also provided a number of electronic devices that can be used to survey and photograph job sites, including GIS, GPS, drones, cameras, computer software, and phone apps.

Measuring Wheel

A measuring wheel is used to determine linear footage by tracking the number of revolutions it makes as it is rolled across a surface, **Figure 4-5A**. Some professionals say these work best on smooth surfaces and do not work well on rough terrain. Other professionals disagree and claim if the right size wheel is used you will obtain accurate measurements. A measuring wheel reads in feet and inches or tenths of a foot, or in metric units.

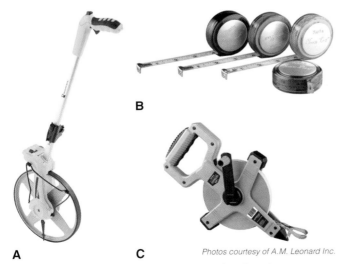

A   C   *Photos courtesy of A.M. Leonard Inc.*

Figure 4-5. Quality measurement tools allow for accuracy during the site takeoff process and when performing pricing calculations. A—Measuring wheel. B—Retractable tape. C—Winding tape.

Retractable Tape

A retractable tape is a handheld tool with a blade (typically up to 25′) that retracts into a casing, **Figure 4-5B**. These tapes can be difficult to handle alone when measuring long distances because they bend and may unhook as the user walks and lays the blade along the ground. A wider blade will not bend as easily as a narrow one and a steel blade will not stretch. Retractable tapes read in feet and inches.

Winding Tape

A winding tape is a handheld measuring tool that unwinds as the user walks along the area being measured, **Figure 4-5C**. These tapes are useful for accurate measurements of small areas. The tape may be made of fiberglass or steel. Steel is preferred because it will not stretch and skew the measurement. Measurements may be included on both sides of the tape.

Surveyor's Tools

Surveying levels (dumpy levels) and theodolites are also used to obtain accurate measurements of landscape sites. These tools can measure distances as well as vertical angles of slopes.

Handheld Laser Measurer

A handheld device projects the laser over the area being measured to a solid surface. A board can be placed at the end location if there is no flat surface. There must be a clear line of sight to the solid surface for accurate measurement. These work well on oddly-shaped property lines.

Laser Level

Laser levels are used to measure distances, elevations, and height clearances (such as ground to utility wires) as well as surface area. Long ranges and slopes are easily measured with laser devices. Most devices can download data directly to a CAD (computer-aided design) or business program to create drawings and reports. *CAD programs* are software programs for drafting designs of everything from products and landscapes to buildings and airplanes.

STEM Connection

Reading Rulers and Tape Measures

Measuring devices such as rulers and tape measures may be marked for measuring inches and fractions of an inch; meters, centimeters, and millimeters; feet, inches and tenths of an inch; or by any other system. The measuring system used to divide the spaces on a measuring device is called the *scale*. The most common linear (in a line) scale in construction uses yards, feet, inches, and fractions of an inch. There are 3 feet in a yard, 12 inches in a foot, and the inches are most often divided into halves, fourths, eighths, and sixteenths. The longest marks on the scale indicate inches. The inches on a measuring device may be divided into eighths, sixteenths, or even thirty-seconds. The second longest marks on the scale represent halves, the next longest represent fourths, and so on. The first step in reading the scale is to determine what the smallest marks on the scale represent. Count down from the whole inch to the halves, then the quarters, the eighths, sixteenths, and thirty-seconds, if they are used. Then count the number of marks from the last inch mark to the mark you are reading.

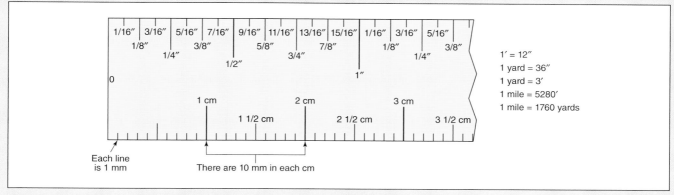

Geographic Information System (GIS)

A *geographic information system (GIS)* processes satellite images and accurately displays land, buildings, roads, and other land features. GSI can be used to view property lines and identify features in the surrounding landscape that may affect the design. A pond on the adjoining property, for example, may overflow onto the new landscape in heavy rain. Local municipalities may have GIS mapping on file. These maps provide detailed information about the site, including property lines and existing structures. Some municipalities also offer GIS services for individual properties with measuring tools and area calculators.

Global Positioning System (GPS)

Global positioning systems (GPS), especially those used by online search engines, are used to create databases of satellite images of properties around the world. The satellites also enable someone with a receiver to pinpoint an exact location. These images often include multiple views of the property. A designer or contractor can use these images to evaluate the site. The same type of GPS used on your cell phone for directions can be used to measure property. There is software and apps available that will calculate data as you walk the property while holding your phone, tablet, or other GPS receiver.

Drones

A drone is defined as an unmanned, aerial vehicle (UAV). It is essentially a remote-controlled flying robot. Drones are used in many industries to photograph or gather data on the conditions of an area. Landscape designers can use the drone to photograph a site from different viewpoints and gather measurements. It is best to contact the local municipality to ensure all regulations for drone use are followed.

Leveling Tools

A *leveling tool* is designed to indicate whether a surface is horizontal (level) or vertical (plumb) and to establish ground slopes. A leveling tool has a small, liquid-filled glass tube containing an air bubble to indicate level. The tube is sealed and fixed in a frame with a smooth lower surface. When level is achieved, the bubble rests between markings on the tube, **Figure 4-6**.

A   topimages/Shutterstock.com

B   Budimir Jevtic/Shutterstock.com

C   except_else/Shutterstock.com

Figure 4-6. A—Bubble levels are used to determine if a site is level horizontally and plumb vertically. The bubble must be between the two lines. B—Masonry level. C—Torpedo level.

In landscaping, levels are used to establish ground slopes that will direct water away from structures, prevent ponding, and keep hardscape materials horizontal or at the desired slope. A level may also be used to establish 45° angles. These devices are commonly referred to simply as levels. The different shapes, construction, and sizes make each type of level convenient for specific tasks.

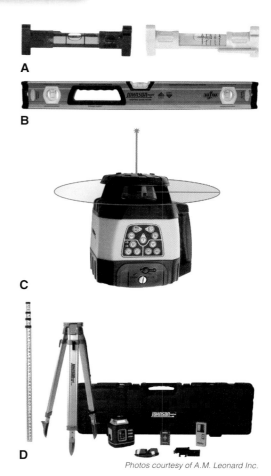

- **String Level.** A string level is used for leveling between long distance points. A string level uses a slightly curved tube filled with liquid and a bubble, **Figure 4-7A**. A string can be attached to a ground stake or fixed structure and pulled across an area. The level is attached to the string. Using a longer piece of string enables the user to check ground slopes for a larger area; however, it is more difficult to avoid a sag in the middle of the line. Any sag in the line will result in an error in the grade.
- **Torpedo Level.** A torpedo level is a small handheld level used to determine horizontal, vertical, and 45° angles, **Figure 4-7B**. A torpedo level is useful in small areas.
- **Masonry Level.** A masonry level is used for leveling and plumbing. It is longer and more accurate than a torpedo level and covers a greater distance, **Figure 4-7C**. It may also be referred to simply as a level.
- **Transit/Builders Level.** The transit level has a scope mounted on an adjustable tripod, **Figure 4-7D**. Readings are taken from a transit rod, which is placed at a distance from the level and read through the scope. (The transit rod has markings signifying feet and inches.) Transit rods are telescopic and can be extended to adjust for changes in elevation. Digital models use a rotating laser and an adjustable target on a transit rod. Digital models with remote controls allow a person to use the tool on his or her own.
- **Zip Level.** A benchmark device attached to a corded transit rod. Differences in elevation are on a digital readout.

Photos courtesy of A.M. Leonard Inc.

Figure 4-7. A string level (A), 4′ or greater masonry level (B), and/or a transit with a tripod and other components (C/D) is used to determine level. Accuracy is greater as the length of the level and its surface length are increased.

Handheld Impact Tools

Many of the tools used in other vocations are also used in landscaping. Building a wooden gazebo, for example, would require common construction tools, such as hammers and mallets. *Impact tools* are those that are used to apply force by striking an object or another tool.

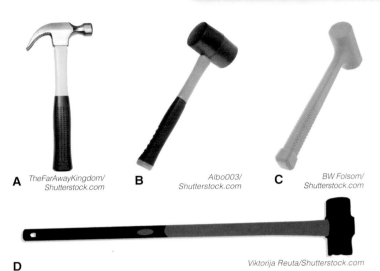

A *TheFarAwayKingdom/ Shutterstock.com*   B *Albo003/ Shutterstock.com*   C *BW Folsom/ Shutterstock.com*

D   *Viktorija Reuta/Shutterstock.com*

Figure 4-8. Impact devices are designed for specific purposes. Claw hammers (A) are useful for construction and destruction, mallets (B) and deadblow hammers (C) can be used for fine adjustments to installed materials, and sledgehammers (D) can be used during destruction and to drive rebar.

- **Hammer.** A basic hammer is a tool used for driving and pulling out nails. In addition to the basic hammer, there are many types of specialty hammers designed for specific jobs, such as a mason's hammer, which is designed to cut and set bricks, **Figure 4-8A**.
- **Mallet.** The head of a mallet may be made of rubber or a synthetic plastic, **Figure 4-8B**. It is designed to set an object in place without damaging the object's surface.
- **Dead-blow hammer.** A dead-blow hammer has a shot-filled head covered with rubber or a synthetic material and a steel handle, **Figure 4-8C**. It is designed to reduce rebound, improve the striking force of the hammer, and not damage soft surfaces.
- **Sledgehammer.** A sledgehammer has a steel head (8 lb to 20 lb) and a long handle, **Figure 4-8D**. It is swung with both hands to provide a forceful impact. A sledgehammer is used for driving rods and pipes and demolition work.
- **Tamper.** A tamper has a long handle and a flat steel head that is used for compacting and leveling soil, gravel, and other hardscape materials.

Digging and Planting Tools

Digging tools are perhaps the tools most commonly used on landscape projects. *Digging tools* are used to make holes for planting and posts and to move or spread materials, such as compost or mulch. They may also be used to help establish slope. Most digging tools serve multiple purposes.

Shovels

A *shovel* is a handheld tool with a scooped or concave blade with a curved, pointed, or flat tip. Some shovels have a D-handle at the top of the shaft for a better grip. The shaft may be made of wood or fiberglass, which is usually bright yellow or orange for visibility. Fiberglass shovels often have a section of the shaft designed for better grip.

- **Round shovel.** A round shovel has a long shaft and a rounded blade that comes to a point, **Figure 4-9A**. A round shovel is commonly used to move materials and for digging in hard, compacted soils or soil containing rocks.

Pro Tip

Spades are also used to cut through roots. This is helpful when removing shrubs and trees.

Safety First

Follow the OSHA-established guidelines for the most ergonomically correct manner in which to use a shovel. 1) Keep feet wide apart. 2) Place front foot close to shovel. 3) Put weight on front foot and use leg to push shovel. 4) Shift weight to rear foot. 5) Keep load close to body and turn feet in direction of throw.

- **Scoop shovel.** A scoop shovel has a short handle and a large, flat blade that is designed to move materials, such as mulch, stone, or even snow, **Figure 4-9B**. The blade is wide and dull and is not intended for digging.

- **Square point shovel.** A square point shovel has a square blade that is designed to move loose materials, **Figure 4-9C**. The blade is typically the same width and length of the blade on a round shovel. Square point shovels can also be used to scrape, grade, and even clean up areas in the landscape.

- **Spade.** A spade is a smaller version of a pointed shovel with a short handle and a flattened, heavier blade, **Figure 4-9D**. The extra weight allows it to cut through soils and compacted ground easier than a round shovel. The width of the blade varies by the intended use of the spade. Wider blades are useful for digging and edging large areas and narrower blades can be used for edging, prying tiles, and defining trenches.

- **Snow shovel.** Snow shovels have angled, wide plastic or metal blades designed for pushing snow, **Figure 4-9E**. A sharp edge helps the user to get under the snow for better cleaning.

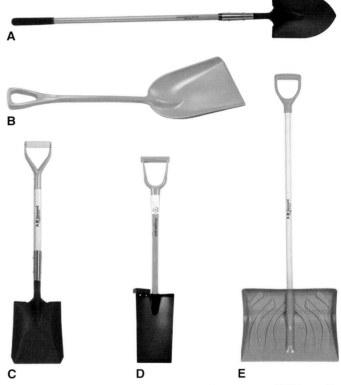

Photos courtesy of A.M. Leonard Inc.

Figure 4-9. Shovels are a key tool used for many landscaping tasks. As with the use of any tool, using the proper shovel for a specific job will ensure the most efficient use of time and effort. A—Round shovel. B—Scoop shovel. C—Square point shovel. D—Spade. E—Snow shovel.

Parts of a Shovel or Spade

The parts of a shovel or spade include the *shaft, collar, kickplate, cutting edge, socket, handle/grip,* and *blade*. The length of the shaft varies to ensure the user will have enough leverage when using the shovel. Most shafts are connected to the blade with a screw or rivet at the collar, which can be removed to replace the handle. The rounded kickplate (step) at the top of the blade enables the user to step on the shovel and drive it into the ground. Most blades are made of steel or aluminum. See **Figure 4-10**.

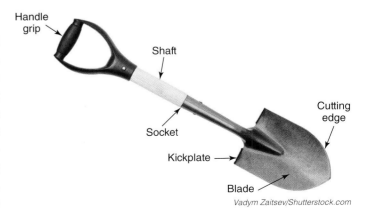

Vadym Zaitsev/Shutterstock.com

Figure 4-10. Parts of a shovel.

krolya25/Shutterstock.com

Figure 4-11. Bulb planters are useful for installing geophytes in areas where overall cultivation is not possible. This tool may be handheld and used while kneeling or with an extended handle to use while standing.

Other Digging Tools

Other types of digging tools include forks, planters, mattocks, pick axes, posthole diggers, soil knives, and trowels.

- **Bulb planter.** A bulb planter has a short handle and a cylinder-shaped blade that is used to dig holes of specific widths and depths for planting geophytes, **Figure 4-11**. The cylinder typically has depth measurements marked along the side to ensure holes are the proper depth.
- **Garden or spading fork.** A garden or spading fork has a short handle and several short, stiff tines used to turn over soil, **Figure 4-12A/B**.
- **Soil knife.** A soil knife is a small, heavy-bladed tool used for a wide variety of jobs, such as weeding, cutting roots, and digging small holes, **Figure 4-12C**.
- **Trowel.** A trowel is a small, short-handled tool with a shape similar to that of a round shovel, except the blade is typically narrower and its sides curve up more than those of a shovel, **Figure 4-12D/E**. Trowels are commonly used when installing bedding plants or preparing potted arrangements. A trowel works best in loose soil.
- **Mattock.** A mattock is a hand tool with a heavy-duty head with a medium-length shank, **Figure 4-12F**. A mattock is used for loosening hard soil, cutting through roots, digging trenches, and removing tree stumps. One end of the head is for chopping and the other is for cutting through roots.
- **Pickax.** A pickax has a short handle and a heavy-duty head with two pointed ends that are designed to break through hard ground, **Figure 4-12G**. A pickax may also be referred to as a *pick*.
- **Posthole digger.** A posthole digger has two handles connected with a hinge that allows it to be opened and closed, **Figure 4-12H**. The blades are forced into the ground in the open position to cut the hole. The handles are pulled apart to close the blades and lift the loosened soil from the hole. A posthole digger can be used to dig holes for smaller plants as well as poles and posts.

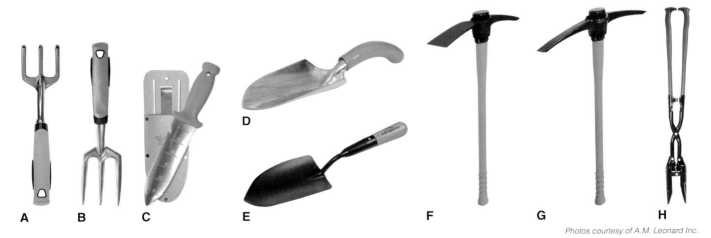

A   B   C   D   E   F   G   H

Photos courtesy of A.M. Leonard Inc.

Figure 4-12. Handheld digging tools are used for many landscaping tasks, such as planting annuals and bulbs, removing weeds, and cutting sod. Mattocks, pickaxes, and posthole diggers have specialized uses, such as disrupting compacted soils and creating deep holes. A/B—Garden fork (cultivator). C—Soil knife with sheath. D/E—Trowels. F—Mattock. G—Pickax. H—Posthole digger.

Digging Tool Maintenance

Digging tool blades may become curled or bent from use, which makes them less efficient. Curled blade edges can be straightened by placing the tool on an anvil and tapping them with a small sledgehammer to bend the metal into place. The blade edge should then be sharpened with a metal cutting file or a grinder. Sharpen the blade at the same angle and side as the original bevel of the cutting edge.

Digging tool blades should be washed with a mild detergent after each use to extend the tool's usefulness and to prevent transferring pests from one area to another. Rust can be removed from metal tools with steel wool or wire brushes. Regularly treating the blade and wooden handles with lubricating oil will prevent rust on the blade and keep the wood from drying out and cracking. Hang the tools to maintain sharp blade edges.

Safety First

Always wear eye protection, gloves, and a dust mask when sanding or grinding tools.

Pro Tip

Always allow tools to dry completely before storing or applying lubricating oil to prevent moisture from being trapped.

Raking and Scraping Tools

A *rake* is a tool designed for gathering, clearing, breaking, and leveling materials. Some have very short wood, metal, or composite handles and others have long wooden or fiberglass handles. As with most tool types, there is a variety of raking tools designed for specific uses, including garden rakes, lawn rakes, leaf rakes, thatch rakes, landscaping rakes, stone rakes, and small hand rakes.

- **Garden rakes.** A garden rake has a long handle, a short, straight head and short, curved, widely-spaced rigid tines. The head and tines are metal and do not move or bend when in use. Garden rakes are used for breaking, scraping, leveling, and grading soil. They are useful when preparing soil for seeding or laying sod. Garden rakes are commonly referred to as bow, soil, or ground rakes.
- **Leaf or lawn rake.** A leaf or lawn rake has a long handle with a plastic or metal fan-shaped head. The flexible tines are long with bent edges. These rakes are used to gather lawn clippings and leaves.
- **Thatch rakes.** Thatch rakes have long handles and a metal head with sharp, blade-like tines. Thatch rakes are designed to remove moss, thatch, and dead grass from turfgrass.
- **Landscaping rake.** Landscaping rakes have long handles and wide, flat heads. They are similar to garden rakes but typically have more tines and a wider head. They are used to spread and level substrates, such as soil or sand.
- **Stone or tarmac rakes.** Tarmac rakes have long handles and wide heads with short, strong tines. They are used to spread and level heavier materials, such as gravel. Tarmac rakes may also be called asphalt, gravel, or road rakes.
- **Small hand rakes.** These small rakes have short handles and heads similar to garden rakes. They are used for precision work between plants and in spaces too small for a standard garden rake.
- **Hoe.** A traditional hoe has a long handle and a flat, rectangular metal head that is used primarily to remove weeds in planted areas. The blade edges may be sharp on one edge or on multiple edges. A hoe may be

designed to cut on the draw or on both the push and draw of the blade. Hoes are available with many blade designs (diamond, stirrup, wing-shaped, triangular, and circles) for use in specific areas. Hoes are not designed to dig deep in the ground. Types of hoes include action, scuffle, paddle (rectangular), stirrup (circular), and Warren (triangular) hoes.

- **Edger.** An edger has a long handle with a spinning vertical blade on one end that is used to create a straight line between turfgrass and hard surfaces. See **Figure 4-13**.

Material Handling Tools

All landscaping projects require materials to be moved from one place to another. Material handling tools make it more efficient to remove and haul debris away and to place and spread materials, such as mulch.

- **Wheelbarrow.** A small cart with one or two wheels and two handles at the rear for pushing and guiding, **Figure 4-14A**. The tray or bed in which material is placed may be made of metal or heavy-duty plastic. A wheelbarrow in an invaluable tool for moving materials around a landscape site.

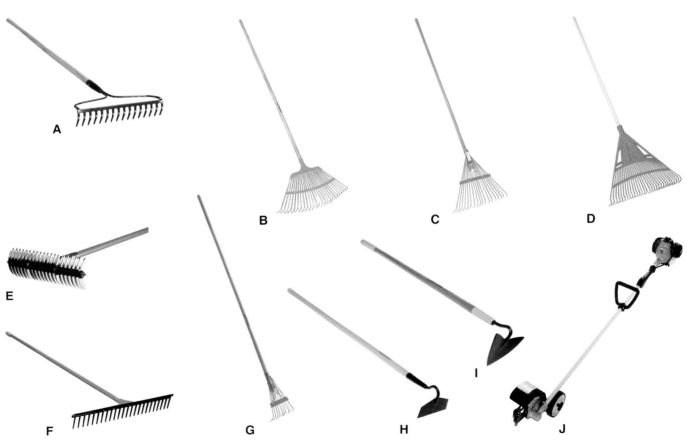

Photos courtesy of A.M. Leonard Inc.

Figure 4-13. The wide variety of scraping and raking tools presents the user with immeasurable options. Many of these tool handles are available in different materials and varying lengths. A—Garden rake (bow rake). B/C/D—Lawn rakes. E—Thatching rake. F—Landscaping or straight rake. G—Shrub rake. H/I—Hoe. J—Power edger.

- **Ball cart.** A specialized cart used to move large balled-and-burlapped plants, **Figure 4-14B**. A ball cart may also be referred to as a truck, root ball cart, or hand truck.
- **Nursery cart.** A cart used by employees and customers to move container plants, **Figure 4-14C**.
- **Mulch fork.** A garden fork with five or more tines spaced closely. A mulch fork is used to lift and move mulch materials, **Figure 4-14D/E**.
- **Debris removal tool.** A hand tool with a long, sometimes telescoping shaft that has a handle and grippers, **Figure 4-14F**. The grippers open and close the claw-type piece, which allow the user to pick up trash without bending over. This is commonly used to pick up trash before mowing.
- **Push broom.** A push broom has a long handle and a wide head with short bristles, **Figure 4-14G**. Push brooms are used for sweeping sidewalks, parking lots, driveways, patios, and other flat, hard surfaces. Push brooms are also used to sweep sand between the joints of blocks or pavers.
- **Scoop.** A scoop has a wide base and may be made of aluminum or plastic, **Figure 4-14H**. It is useful for gathering or lifting debris, sand, or light mulch.

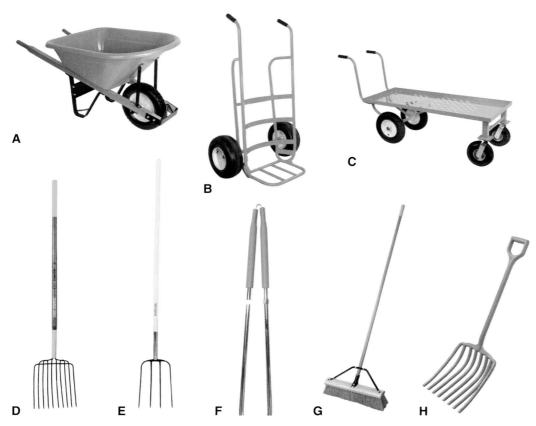

Photos courtesy of A.M. Leonard Inc.

Figure 4-14. There are many tools designed for moving landscaping materials on a job site, in nurseries, and in orchards. When used properly, the tools make work more efficient and help prevent injury to the user. A—Wheelbarrow. B—Ball cart. C—Nursery cart. D/E—Mulch forks. F—Trash picker. G—Push broom. H—Scoop.

Pruning, Grafting, and Budding Tools

Pruning shears are hand tools designed to cut through woody stems safely and without damaging the stem. This is especially important when the stem is used to grow a new plant or to prepare it for grafting. The blades on these, and all cutting tools, should be kept clean and sharp for the best results. Dull blades can be more dangerous than sharp blades as more effort is used to make the cut and your hand is more likely to slip. Dull blades will also damage the stem.

Safety First

Eye protection is always recommended when using any pruning equipment. Hard hats should be worn when working overhead.

- **Bypass pruners.** The blade alignment of bypass pruners is similar to that of scissors, but the upper blade has a convex shape and the bottom is either straight or concave, **Figure 4-15A**. These pruners are designed for cutting material up to 3/4". Bypass pruners are also referred to as *hook-and-blade pruners*.
- **Parrot-beak pruners.** Parrot-beak pruners have short handles and two concave blades designed to trap the stem between them, **Figure 4-15B**. They are used only on narrow stems.

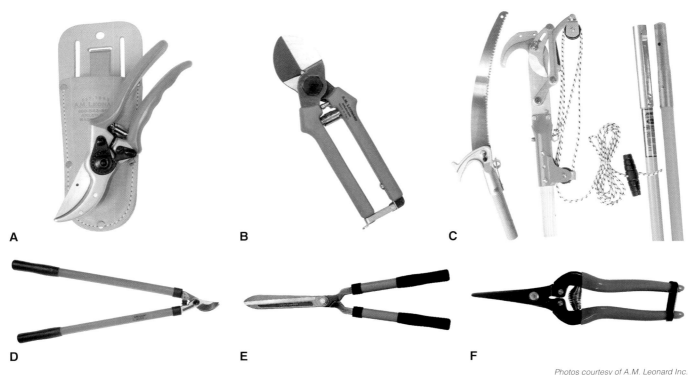

A   B   C

D   E   F

Photos courtesy of A.M. Leonard Inc.

Figure 4-15. Using the appropriate pruning tool will leave clean cuts with minimal damage to the plant. Pruning tools must be kept clean and sharp to work properly. They should also be sterilized between and after cuts when used to cut diseased materials to prevent the disease from spreading. A—Bypass pruners. B—Double-cut (parrot-beak) pruners. C—Pole pruner and saw. D—Loppers. E—Hedge shears. F—Needle-nose hand shears.

- **Pole pruner.** Pole pruners have a long shaft that enables the user to cut smaller branches that are out of reach, **Figure 4-15C**. The shaft can be made with multiple shafts or telescoping (extendable). The length of the pole varies from 8' to 16', depending on the manufacturer. A pole pruner is used on material between 2" and 4".

Pro Tip

Do *not* use anvil pruners because they will damage the stem and leave a wound. Anvil pruners have short handles and one straight, sharp blade that closes to meet an unsharpened platform blade. Anvil pruners are also referred to as *anvil-and-blade pruners*.

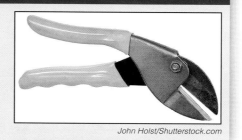

John Holst/Shutterstock.com

- **Loppers.** A hinged cutting tool with very long handles that is designed for cutting 3⁄4" to 2" material, **Figure 4-15D**. The blades are the same as those of the short-handled pruners.
- **Hedge or pruning shears.** Hedge shears are hand tools with long handles and blades made of heavier steel, **Figure 4-15E**. The blades are designed to cut a large area in one cut. Hedge shears are designed to cut herbaceous stems and will not cut woody stems cleanly. Hedge shears are useful for maintaining formal hedges, cutting back perennials, and deadheading. Smaller hedge shears are useful for trimming small amounts of plant material, **Figure 4-15F**.
- **Bow saw.** A bow saw has a curved, metal frame with a handle grip and replaceable blade, **Figure 4-16A**. A bow saw is designed to cut material between 1.5" and 6".
- **Pruning saw.** A smaller saw with a 12" to 16" blade and cutting teeth that perform on the push and pull stroke, **Figure 4-16B**. Pruning saws are designed to cut woody plants and will not gum up or bind when pruning live wood. Pruning saws can be stored in a scabbard attached to a belt for easy access.
- **Grafting tool.** A grafting tool is a specialized tool designed to cut the shoot or bud to be grafted and the rootstock to which it will be grafted. The parts can be aligned to ensure a strong and successful union.
- **Grafting knife.** A grafting knife, which has a very sharp blade, is used in various grafting methods, **Figure 4-16C**. The knife is used to make precision grafting cuts on the parts to be joined.

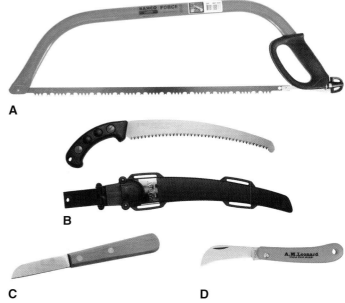

Photos courtesy of A.M. Leonard Inc.

Figure 4-16. There are many tools designed for reducing plant size and grafting materials. Keeping these tools clean and sharp will ensure the quality of cuts and the longevity of the tools. Using a sheath protects the tool and makes it easier to carry safely. A—Bow saw. B—Pruning saw. C—Grafting knife. D—Pruning knife.

- **Pruning knives** are also used when working on small precision tasks, **Figure 4-16D**.
- **Grafting band.** A grafting band is rubber material designed to hold the two plant parts being grafted in place until the parts have grown together.

Tools for Sharpening Blades

As stated earlier, dull blades can be more dangerous than sharp blades and cause damage to plant materials. The cutting blades on most tools can be sharpened using a bench grinder, sharpening stone, or file.

Safety First

The small pieces of material being removed when sharpening blades can easily strike your eyes, face, or hands. It is also possible for a blade or cutting wheel to break while the material is being sharpened. Always wear eye, face, and hand protection when sharpening tools.

- **Bench grinder.** A bench grinder is a power tool that is attached to a bench or other permanent fixture. A bench grinder has two replaceable wheels that are used to sharpen, buff, polish, or clean various materials.
- **Sharpening stone.** A sharpening stone is a natural or manufactured tool used to sharpen cutting tools. Sharpening stones come in many shapes and sizes and may be dry, whet, or oilstones. Dry stones are used dry, whetstones are wetted with water before use, and oilstones are treated with oil before use. It is important to identify the type of stone being used *before* sharpening the tool.
- **Files.** Files are metal tools with cutting ridges that are used to sharpen blades. Files are useful for on-site blade sharpening and for sharpening blades on tools that are too large for sharpening stones or bench grinders. Files may also be used to smooth and clean metal surfaces. See **Figure 4-17**.

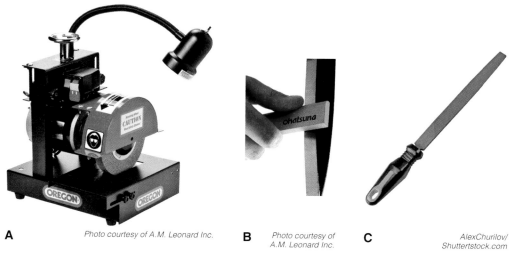

A   *Photo courtesy of A.M. Leonard Inc.*   B   *Photo courtesy of A.M. Leonard Inc.*   C   *AlexChurilov/Shuttertstock.com*

Figure 4-17. Bench grinders (A), sharpening stones (B), and files (C) are used for sharpening knives, hand tools, and blades. Each has a safe and preferred technique for operation.

Grades and Grit

Sharpening tools are available in different grades, which refers to the grit size of the abrasive particles. The grit sizes determine whether the grinding wheel, sharpening stone, or file is designed to smooth, finish, or sharpen materials.

Hands-On Maintenance

Sharpening Lawn Mower Blades

Eye protection and heavy gloves must be worn when disassembling the mower and while sharpening the blade. A face shield and respirator should be worn when using a bench grinder to sharpen a blade.

Removing the Blade

1. Disconnect the spark plug wire from the spark plug and secure the wire so it cannot accidentally reach the plug. The spark plug wire should *always* be disconnected before work begins on a lawn mower.
2. Tip the mower back toward the handle to access the blade.
3. Mark the top of the blade to ensure the blade is reinstalled in the proper position.
4. Block the blade to keep it from moving while you loosen the fastening bolt.
5. Remove the fastening bolt and any washers holding the blade, and then remove the blade.
6. Clean grass clippings and grime from the blade and housing. The blade must be clean in order to balance it accurately.

Sharpening the Blade with a Hand File

1. Secure the mower blade in a vise mounted to a workbench or other secure surface.
2. Stroke a metal file along one of the blade's cutting edges, working from a point nearest to the center of the blade to the outside edge of the blade. The file will cut during the downward stroke only. If possible, maintain the original angle of the cutting edge. If the original angle is unknown, file the cutting side to a 45° angle. File only on the angled side of the cutting edge. Continue filing until all the nicks have been removed from the cutting edge and it is clean and shiny. The blade does not need to be razor sharp.
3. After completing the cutting edge on one end of the blade, reposition the blade in the vise and sharpen the cutting edge on the other end of the blade. Take care to remove an equal amount from each end of the blade to maintain balance.
4. Use a mower blade balancer to ensure the blade is balanced. Remove additional material from the heavy end of the blade as needed to balance the blade.
5. Reinstall the blade in the proper direction and install the washers (if included) and bolt. Tighten the bolt to specifications.

Sharpening the Blade with a Bench Grinder

Wear a face mask, respirator, gloves, and long sleeves while sharpening the blade with a grinder.

1. Hold the blade with both hands and slowly move one of the cutting edges back and forth against the wheel until all nicks are removed and the cutting edge is clean and shiny. Be sure to maintain the original angle. If the angle is unknown, grind the cutting edge to a 45° angle. Grind only on the beveled portion of the cutting edge.
2. After the cutting edge on one side of the blade has been properly sharpened, perform the same procedure on the cutting edge on the opposite end of the blade. Try to remove the same amount of material from each end of the blade.
3. Once both cutting edges have been sharpened, check the blade balance. If necessary, remove additional material from the heavy end of the blade.
4. Reinstall the blade in the proper direction. Be sure to install the washers (if included) and tighten the bolt to specifications.

   Sharpening the blade regularly will maintain its efficiency because you will not have to cut areas more than once. Frayed or torn turf blade ends indicate the blade is dull.

Landscaping Power Equipment

Landscaping installation and maintenance could not be performed as it is today without portable power equipment. Mowing a professional soccer field, for example, would require a very large crew and ample time using manual push reel mowers. Using portable power tools reduces the amount of time it takes to do a job and increases the amount of power available to do a job.

Safety First

Most of the portable power equipment used in landscaping uses blades spinning at very high speeds to cut plant materials. It is essential for users to wear the proper PPE to prevent injury. Follow OSHA guidelines to determine what PPE should be worn when using portable power equipment.

- **Chainsaws.** Chainsaws are powerful tools that use a rotating toothed chain to cut through wood, **Figure 4-18A**. Chainsaws may be powered with fuel, electricity, or battery-stored energy. The cutting ability is greatly affected by the power source.
- **Cutoff or circular saw.** A cutoff saw uses a sharp spinning disc that has teeth along its edge to cut through materials, such as concrete and brick. Some cutoff saws use a continuous flow of water to cool the blade and material during cutting.
- **Rototiller.** A rototiller uses spinning blades in contact with the ground to loosen the soil and incorporate chemical or physical amendments, **Figure 4-18B**. Rototillers range in width from single row models to models as wide as 26″.
- **String trimmer.** A string trimmer has a medium-length shaft with a handle and controls at one end and a motor with a rotating plastic string at the other end. A string trimmer is used to cut turfgrass around and within mowed areas that cannot be cut with the mower, such as along fences and around poles and trees.

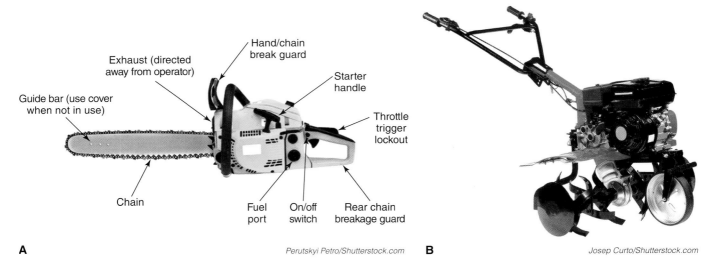

Hand/chain break guard

Exhaust (directed away from operator)

Starter handle

Guide bar (use cover when not in use)

Throttle trigger lockout

Chain

Fuel port   On/off switch   Rear chain breakage guard

A   *Perutskyi Petro/Shutterstock.com*   **B**   *Josep Curto/Shutterstock.com*

Figure 4-18. A—Chainsaws enable professionals to quickly cut trees for removal. Users must wear the proper PPE and follow safe procedures when operating a chainsaw. B—Rototillers can be used for soil compaction relief and incorporating chemical and physical soil amendments.

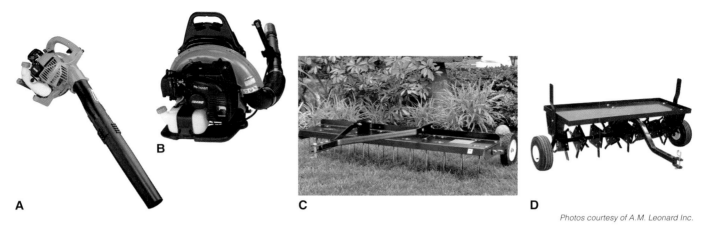

A   B   C   D

Photos courtesy of A.M. Leonard Inc.

Figure 4-19. Power tools used in landscaping are made in different sizes, with varying strength, and different types of fuel sources. String trimmers, for example, can be small, compact, use string, and have a rechargeable battery. They may also be larger, heavy-duty gas models that use chains or another type of blade to cut weeds and other plants in overgrown areas. A—Handheld blower. B—Backpack blower. C/D—Aerator attachments.

- **Leaf blower.** A leaf blower is a motorized fan that uses air to move leaves and other light debris from the landscape, **Figure 4-19A/B**.
- **Verticutter.** A verticutter uses vertically spinning blades that disrupt thatch layers in turfgrass allowing seed-to-soil contact during renovation.
- **Sod cutter.** A sod cutter is a specialized tool used to remove pieces of sod from the ground.
- **Core aerator.** A core aerator uses tines to penetrate the ground to alleviate compaction and improve water and air penetration to turfgrass root zones, **Figure 4-19C/D**. Manual aerators are also available.
- **Trencher.** A trencher is used to create narrow ditches for irrigation pipe and other utilities. Trenchers are available as walk-behind or riding machines and as attachable implements on other machinery.

Mowers

Mowing is one of the most important as well as frequent tasks performed in the landscape. Mowers are available in different sizes and styles to suit any site or situation. Mowers cut differently, have different types of blades, and different blade configurations that are designed to suit specific purposes. Common mowers include walk-behind, riding, stand-on, and zero-turn.

Walk-Behind Mowers

Walk-behind mowers are self-propelled with deck sizes ranging from around 30″ to over 60″, **Figure 4-20A**. These mowers typically use gasoline but may use propane if modified with a conversion kit. Walk-behind mowers offer a tight turning radius and are useful for mowing slopes that other mowers cannot safely mow. They are also useful in small areas where a larger mower would not fit. Using a walk-behind mower to mow steep slopes results in less trim work, which allows the job to be completed in less time. A removable sulky equipped with wheels can be attached to some walk-behind mowers to provide a seat or standing platform for the operator. Walk-behind mowers that are not self-propelled may also be referred to as *push mowers*.

A   *Juan Aunion/Shutterstock.com*

B   *Nuk2013/Shutterstock.com*

C   *Sergey Logrus/Shutterstock.com*

Figure 4-20. Mowers are chosen by use and application. Walk-behind mowers (A) give the operator opportunities for daily activity and adaptability in tight mowing locations. A stand-on (B) can reduce operator fatigue and allow for better sight lines from the operator platform. Zero-turn mowers (C) are easy to operate and quickly mow large areas. They offer comfortable seats and responsive operator controls.

Stand-On Mowers

Stand-on mowers are similar to walk-behind mowers except for the permanent standing platform and padding that allows the operator to lean comfortably against the machine, **Figure 4-20B**. Deck sizes typically range from 36″ to over 60″. Stand-on mowers can be maneuvered well in tight spots; this can be highly beneficial for landscapes in urban areas. They are typically used on lawns less than 1/2 acre.

Zero-Turn Mowers

Zero-turn mowers are ride-on mowers that provide the operator with a comfortable seated position, **Figure 4-20C**. Zero-turn mowers have a very tight turning radius and deck sizes ranging from 48″ to 72″. The larger deck sizes make the mowers more suitable for large sites (1/2 acre or more) rather than smaller lawns. Zero-turn mowers have limited maneuverability, especially on steep slopes or in damp conditions. Using a zero-turn mower may result in more trim work with string trimmers or walk-behind mowers.

Cutting Mechanisms

The manner in which mowers cut turf and the type of cutting device they use varies depending on the intended use.

- **Rotary mower.** A rotary mower uses a motorized spinning blade under a protective housing to prune turfgrass at desired heights, **Figure 4-21A**. Rotary mowers are available as walk-behind, standing, and riding mowers.
- **Reel mower.** A reel mower uses blades arranged around a drum that interface with a bed knife, **Figure 4-21B**. Reel mowers are used for manicured turfgrass settings, such as golf greens and tees. Reel mowers are also available as manual mowers.
- **Flail mower.** A flail mower uses bent T- or Y-shaped pieces of metal attached with hinges to a spinning drum to cut through heavy brush. The flexible pieces will not shatter or throw debris into the air. Some flail mowers are self-powered but many are designed as tractor attachments powered through a PTO (power take-off).

A   *Robert Pernell/Shutterstock.com*

B   *Cheng Wei/Shutterstock.com*

Figure 4-21. Rotary mowers (A) are the most common for commercial and residential landscape sites while reel mowers (B) are used for fine turf maintenance on athletic fields and golf courses.

Basic Maintenance for Power Equipment

The costs associated with purchasing power equipment is much higher than that of hand tools. Failure to maintain power equipment can result in costly damages and repairs. The best practice for power equipment maintenance is to follow the manufacturer's guidelines. This will ensure extended equipment life and keep the equipment safe for use. Basic guidelines for maintaining power equipment include the following:

- Establish a regular maintenance schedule for all equipment and tools.
- Check and change the oil and filter at recommended intervals using the proper oil and filter.
- Clean or replace the air filter according to recommendations or every 25 hours.
- Inspect blades for cracks and nicks and replace as necessary.
- Check tension on belts and chains and make adjustments as needed.
- Remove clippings and debris from equipment after each use.
- Remove fuel before long-term storage.
- Store in a protected, dry environment.

A   *Art Konovalov/Shutterstock.com*

Large Equipment

Many landscaping projects require the use of large equipment, especially new construction sites and major overhauls. Any employee who will be operating the equipment should be properly trained, whether the equipment is rented or owned by the landscaping company. Very large projects may require subcontracting a company with larger equipment.

- **Skid steer.** A skid steer is a wheeled or tracked machine with front attachments for hauling, scraping, leveling, or excavating.
- **Compact utility loader.** A compact utility loader is a walk-behind or stand-on machine used for hauling, scraping, leveling, or excavating.
- **Compact excavator.** A compact excavator is a tracked machine with a boom and bucket used for excavation and leveling. See **Figure 4-22**.

B   *R. Lee Ivy*

C   *R. Lee Ivy*

Figure 4-22. Skid steer loaders (A), compact excavators (B), and trenchers (C) are used for grading, hauling, and staging materials and digging narrow trenches for irrigation lines. Site conditions often govern their selection.

Career Connection

Brock Holtzclaw

Brock Holtzclaw, Arborist

Brock Holtzclaw is a second-generation arborist. Intrigued by his father's work as a child, Brock, delved into the world of trees and by the age of 20, he became the youngest International Society of Arboriculture (ISA) Certified Arborist in the southeast.

Brock furthered his education at North Carolina State University and obtained a degree in Horticulture with a concentration in Landscape Design. Brock has been able to combine his interests of urban tree care and spacial design into a thriving business in Charlotte, North Carolina. Three years after graduation, Brock opened the doors to Releaf Tree Works, a company that specializes in services to help with the overall health of trees, large and small. Brock leads a team of expert tree climbers, arborists, and experienced groundsmen who share a common passion for tree care. Releaf Tree Works performs tree planting, pruning, preservation, risk assessment, removal, fertilization, and emergency disaster relief.

Consider This

1. Where else besides a tree service, such as Releaf Tree Works, might an arborist be employed?
2. How much training is required to become an expert tree climber? What type of training is required?
3. What type of expenses are associated with a start-up tree service?

Equipment Limitations

While large equipment is helpful on jobs, its use can be limited by weather conditions and load capacities. For example, if a skid steer loader is hauling gravel across a clay-like soil slope, slippage may occur and the load may be lost or the operator could be injured. In addition, the site could be adversely affected. In this case, a wheelbarrow and a crew of people hauling the material may be the best choice.

Maintaining Large Equipment

All machinery must be cared for to ensure that it can be used safely. The best practice is to schedule routine inspections and maintenance according to the manufacturer's guidelines. The operator should walk around the equipment at the beginning of each workday to check for issues to determine if the machine is operable. The following are general tasks that are applicable for the use of most large equipment.

- Check the *rollover protection system (ROPS)* to ensure it is secure and in the upright position, **Figure 4-23**. The ROPS is a separate bar or a frame built into the compartment to protect operators from injuries caused by vehicle overturns. Inspect the seat belt. The ROPS should *not* be removed or left in the storage position when the machine is in operation.
- Check tires and conditions of tracks (if present) before operation. Perform maintenance for safe tire performance.

Christopher D. Hart

Figure 4-23. Rollover protection systems (ROPS) are installed to prevent injury to the driver in the event of a rollover. Seat belts should be used in conjunction with this system.

- Ensure that warning alarms are operational.
- Check the oil and fuel levels. Fill as needed with the appropriate oil and fuel.
- When checking hydraulic lines, use a piece of cardboard held over the lines to prevent injury if a line has a leak or ruptures.
- Check and replace air filters according to the owner's manual or after every 25 hours of operation (sooner if in dusty conditions).
- Inspect all pivot joints according to the schematic on the machine or in the operation manual. Apply grease as needed.

Troubleshooting

Most equipment manufacturers provide troubleshooting guides to help users determine why the equipment is not running or not running properly. Always refer to the troubleshooting chart before attempting to repair the machine. The guide may also include instructions for adjustments to remedy the situation. Troubleshooting guides always begin with the simplest solutions, such as checking the fuel and oil level and the spark plug connection.

Transportation and Hauling Equipment

Most landscaping companies own multiple vehicles for hauling and transporting equipment and employees. The standard vehicle for most companies is a truck and trailer. Safety guidelines for weight and passenger capacity apply to all vehicles as do guidelines for transporting hazardous materials, such as fertilizers, pesticides, and fuel. Operators and/or the maintenance staff should regularly inspect the vehicle to ensure everything is in working order.

- **Lights.** All lights, including headlights, taillights, turn signals, side markers, and lights on the attached trailer should be checked for connections and faulty bulbs.

- **Fluids.** All vehicle fluids, including oil, brake fluid, transmission, and power steering fluids should be checked and refilled as needed. Low levels of any fluid may indicate a leak or other issues that must be addressed.
- **Hoses and belts.** Hoses and belts are susceptible to dry rotting or tearing.
- **Brakes.** Brake fluid and pads on trucks and trailers should be checked for leaks and wear.
- **Horn.** All vehicles must have a functional horn.
- **Mirrors.** All vehicles must have a rear view mirror and a driver's side mirror. Many trucks have additional mirrors for viewing blind spots and behind the trailer.
- **Hazard lights.** Hazard lights are used to alert other drivers to a vehicle parked on the roadside, a slow-moving vehicle, or in an emergency, such as a stalled vehicle on the road.
- **Seat belts.** All seats in vehicles must have a seat belt to ensure all passengers are restrained safely.
- **Tires.** Tires should be checked regularly for proper psi and possible damage.
- **Hitch, safety chains, and breakaway cable.** These components are used to hook up a trailer, **Figure 4-24**. All should be checked for proper breakage, rust, and proper attachment.
- **Securing materials.** All materials being transported in any vehicle must be properly secured.

William Hager/Shutterstock.com   *Melissa King/Shutterstock.com*

Figure 4-24. Trucks and trailer combinations are used for hauling materials and transporting people and machinery to and from worksites. The hook-up components must be compatible (size and type) for a secure connection.

Summary

- Proper PPE should be worn when using or operating landscaping tools and equipment.

- Records should be kept to maintain a proper inventory of tools and their maintenance schedules.

- A checklist is helpful when evaluating the condition of a tool or piece of equipment before using it and at the end of a workday.

- Basic maintenance of hand tools will extend their usability and keep them safe for use.

- A wide variety of hand and power tools is available for use in various landscaping tasks. Always use the appropriate tool for the job.

- Maintaining sharp edges on cutting tools results in cleaner cuts and safer use of the tools.

- All safety guards and components must be kept in place when equipment is in operation.

- Before operating equipment or using tools, refer to the owner's manual for operation and safety guidelines.

- The power supply should always be disconnected and/or the spark plug should be disconnected before performing maintenance on power equipment.

- The employee operating large equipment should be properly trained to do so.

- Troubleshooting charts provided by manufacturers should be referenced before attempting to repair the equipment.

- Vehicles used to transport equipment and employees must meet safety guidelines that apply to all vehicles.

- All material being transported must be secured properly.

Chapter Review

Know and Understand ⤴

Answer the following questions using the information provided in this chapter.

1. *True or False?* Learning how to use equipment properly will help keep you safe and help keep the equipment in operating condition.
   A. True.
   B. False.

2. *True or False?* PPE is optional if you feel the job at hand presents no chance of injury.
   A. True.
   B. False.

3. *True or False?* The appearance of equipment on a job site can affect the public's perception of your company.
   A. True.
   B. False.

4. Which of the following tools determines linear footage by tracking the number of revolutions it makes as it is rolled across a surface?
   A. Measuring tape.
   B. Measuring roller.
   C. Measuring wheel.
   D. Measuring blade.

5. Which of the following measuring tools has a blade that extends from and returns into a casing?
   A. Winding tape.
   B. Laser tape.
   C. Roller tape.
   D. Retractable tape.

6. A measuring tool that is unwound as the user walks along a property is referred to as a _____.
   A. roller tape
   B. winding tape
   C. leveler's tape
   D. casing tape

7. Which of the following tools is used to measure distances, elevations, and height clearances as well as surface area?
   A. Laser level.
   B. Casing level.
   C. Landscaper's level.
   D. All of the above.

8. Which of the following is designed to indicate whether a surface is horizontal or plumb and to establish ground slopes?
   A. Measuring tool.
   B. Casing tool.
   C. Leveling tool.
   D. Impact tool.

9. A level used for leveling between long distance points is referred to as a _____.
   A. torpedo level
   B. string level
   C. zip level
   D. construction level

10. *True or False?* A torpedo level is longer than a masonry level and designed to cover a greater distance than the masonry level.
    A. True.
    B. False.

11. Of the following impact tools, which would be the most suitable for setting an object in place without damaging the object's surface?
    A. Sledgehammer.
    B. Mallet.
    C. Tamper.
    D. All of the above.

12. An impact tool with a steel head and a long handle that is used in demolition work is a _____.
    A. sledgehammer
    B. mallet
    C. tamper
    D. pickaxe

13. Which of the following shovels would be best or most efficient for moving materials, such as mulch?
    A. Scoop shovel.
    B. Round shovel.
    C. Pointed shovel.
    D. Spade shovel.

14. *True or False?* The extra weight of a spade allows it to cut through soils and compacted ground easier than a round shovel.
    A. True.
    B. False.

15. *True or False?* A bulb planter is a hand tool with a heavy-duty head and a medium-length shank.
    A. True.
    B. False.

16. Which of the following tools are commonly used when installing bedding plants or preparing potted arrangements?
    A. Mattock.
    B. Bulb planter.
    C. Trowel.
    D. Soil knife.

17. Which of the following rakes is used for breaking, scraping, and leveling soil?
    A. Leaf rake.
    B. Garden rake.
    C. Thatch rake.
    D. Lawn rake.

18. A rake with a long handle and a plastic or metal fan-shaped head is referred to as a _____.
    A. garden rake
    B. thatch rake
    C. turf rake
    D. leaf rake

19. A rake with a long handle and a metal head with sharp, blade-like tines is referred to as a _____.
    A. turf rake
    B. thatch rake
    C. garden rake
    D. lawn rake

20. Which of the following rakes would you use to spread and level gravel?
    A. Tarmac rake.
    B. Thatch rake.
    C. Turf rake.
    D. Tier rake.

21. Which of the following is a tool with a long handle and a flat, rectangular metal head that is used primarily to remove weeds in planted areas?
    A. Edger.
    B. Fork.
    C. Hoe.
    D. Soil knife.

22. Which of the following has an upper blade with a convex shape and a bottom blade that is either straight or concave?
    A. Anvil pruners.
    B. Bypass pruners.
    C. Parrot-beak pruners.
    D. Hedge pruners.

23. Which of the following should be used only on narrow stems?
    A. Anvil pruners.
    B. Bypass pruners.
    C. Parrot-beak pruners.
    D. Hedge pruners.

24. Which of the following pruners are designed to cut smaller branches that are out of reach?
    A. Rod pruners.
    B. Bypass pruners.
    C. Pole pruners.
    D. Shearing pruners.

25. Which of the following pruners are most likely to damage stems and leave a wound?
    A. Anvil pruners.
    B. Bypass pruners.
    C. Parrot-beak pruners.
    D. Hedge pruners.

26. A cutting tool with long handles that is designed for cutting 3/4" to 2" material is referred to as _____.
    A. grafters
    B. loppers
    C. shears
    D. pruners

27. Which of the following is designed to cut a large area in one cut?
    A. Bow shears.
    B. Grafting shears.
    C. Lopper shears.
    D. Hedge shears.

28. *True or False?* A bow saw has a curved metal frame and a replaceable blade.
    A. True.
    B. False.

29. A small saw with a 12″ to 16″ blade and cutting teeth that perform on the push-and-pull stroke is a _____.
    A. circular saw
    B. cutoff saw
    C. pruning saw
    D. reel saw

30. Which of the following are used to sharpen tool blades?
    A. Whetstone.
    B. Bench grinder.
    C. Files.
    D. All of the above.

31. A powerful tool that uses a rotating toothed chain to cut through wood.
    A. Reel saw.
    B. Cutoff saw.
    C. Chain saw.
    D. Pruning saw.

32. Which of the following uses a sharp spinning disc that has teeth along its edge to cut through materials?
    A. Reel saw.
    B. Cutoff saw.
    C. Chain saw.
    D. Pruning saw.

33. A mower that uses a spinning blade under a protective housing to prune turfgrass at desired heights is a _____.
    A. reel mower
    B. rotary mower
    C. rotor mower
    D. reclined mower

34. Which of the following mowers is used for manicured turfgrass?
    A. Reel mower.
    B. Rotary mower.
    C. Rotor mower.
    D. Reclined mower.

35. Which of the following machines uses vertically spinning blades to disrupt thatch layers in turfgrass?
    A. Vertimower.
    B. Vertitrimmer.
    C. Verticutter.
    D. Vertilator.

36. A wheeled or tracked machine with front attachments for hauling, scraping, leveling, or excavating is a _____.
    A. compact excavator
    B. compact utility loader
    C. skid steer
    D. utility excavator

37. Which of the following is a walk-behind or stand-on machine used for hauling, scraping, leveling, or excavating?
    A. Compact excavator.
    B. Compact utility loader.
    C. Skid steer.
    D. Utility excavator.

38. A tracked machine with a boom and bucket used for excavation and leveling is a _____.
    A. compact excavator
    B. compact utility loader
    C. skid steer
    D. utility excavator

39. *True or False?* The best practice is to schedule routine inspections and maintenance according to the large equipment manufacturer's guidelines.
    A. True.
    B. False.

40. Which of the following vehicle components should be inspected regularly?
    A. Lights, horn, and brakes.
    B. Hoses, belts, and fluids.
    C. Mirrors, seat belts, and tires.
    D. All of the above.

Thinking Critically

1. What criteria would you use to assess the condition of hand tools? Would the criteria for power tools be similar?

2. What are the advantages and disadvantages of using a manual reel mower?

3. What are the advantages and disadvantages of using an electric mower versus a gas mower?

4. How would you demonstrate the safe use of tools and equipment used to install and maintain landscapes?

Suggested Activities

1. Work with a partner to create a labeling and inventory system for all tools and equipment located in your school's shop. Search for apps that may be used when checking tools out of inventory. Determine if your system could be used in other school departments, such as the chemistry labs or art department.

2. Analyze the cost and maintenance of tools and equipment in your school's shop. Are there ways in which the department could manage the tools and equipment to maximize its budget?

3. Working in small groups, have each person make a list of the top 10 basic tools a landscaper should own when going into the maintenance industry. Are your answers similar? Explain why you chose the 10 tools on your list.

4. Expand on the preceding activity by comparing the advantages and disadvantages of how each tool is powered (manual, battery, gasoline).

5. Select a piece of power equipment and locate the user manual online. Develop a maintenance schedule for the chosen piece of equipment. Extend this activity by locating user manuals for each piece of equipment in the school shop and creating or updating the maintenance schedule.

Nursery/Landscaping Equipment and Supplies Identification ➦

The following equipment and supplies identification glossary contains more than 90 images of tools and materials used in the landscaping industry. This illustrated glossary has been provided to help you familiarize yourself with these implements and materials, as well as a means of studying for career development events in which their identification is a major component. The numbers in the lower, right-hand corner correlate to those on the FFA CDE ID list. This glossary is by no means all-inclusive but provides a good starting point for your studies. Use this glossary, as well as the e-flashcards on your textbook's companion website at **www.g-wlearning.com/agriculture.com** to help you study and identify these tools and materials.

Photo courtesy of A.M. Leonard Inc.

anvil-and-blade pruner **260**

Photo courtesy of A.M. Leonard Inc.

ball cart (B&B truck) **261**

JohnatAPW/Shutterstock.com

bark mulch **262**

Photo courtesy of A.M. Leonard Inc.

bow saw **263**

Photo courtesy of A.M. Leonard Inc.

broadcast (cyclone) spreader **264**

Photo courtesy of Hunter Industries, Inc.

bubbler head, irrigation **265**

bulb planter **266a**

bulb planter **266b**

bunker rake **267**

burlap **268**

compressed air sprayer
tank pressurized **269**

core aerator **270a**

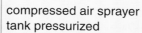

core aerator **270b**

chain saw **271**

chain saw chaps

Photo courtesy of A.M. Leonard Inc.

chain saw helmet with face shield

Photo courtesy of A.M. Leonard Inc.

chain saw gloves

Photo courtesy of A.M. Leonard Inc.

coveralls (particles/water-based liquids)

OlegSam/Shutterstock.com

cut-off machine   **272a**

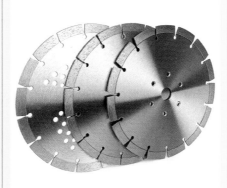

resket/Shutterstock.com

cut-off machine
diamond-edge blades   **272b**

Photo courtesy of A.M. Leonard Inc.

double-cut (parrot-beak) pruners

AJCespedes/Shutterstock.com

drip emitter   **273a**

Georgina198/Shutterstock.com

drip emitter, irrigation   **273b**

Lindasj22/Shutterstock.com

dry-lock wall block   **274**

Photo courtesy of A.M. Leonard Inc.

edger (power or hand) **275**

Photo courtesy of A.M. Leonard Inc.

edging **276**

Allison Fortner, Super-Sod

erosion netting **277a**

Photo courtesy of A.M. Leonard Inc.

erosion netting **277b**

Photo courtesy of A.M. Leonard Inc.

fertilizer injector **278**

Photo courtesy of A.M. Leonard Inc.

fertilizer tablet **279**

Photo courtesy of A.M. Leonard Inc.

garden (spading) fork **280**

Photo courtesy of A.M. Leonard Inc.

garden (bow) rake **281**

Photo courtesy of A.M. Leonard Inc.

grafting band **282**

grafting knife **283**

granular fertilizer **284**

gravity (drop) spreader **285**

ground/pelleted limestone **286**

hedge shears **287**

hoe **288a**

hoe **288b**

hook-and-blade pruners **289**

hose-end repair fitting (female) **290a**

hose-end repair fitting (male) **290b**

hose-end sprayer **291a**

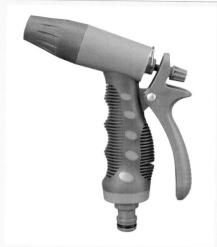

hose-end sprayer **291b**

hose-end washer **292**

hose repair coupling **293**

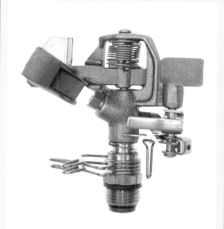

impact sprinkler **294**

landscape fabric **295**

leaf rake **296a**

leaf rake **296b**

leaf rake **296c**

Photo courtesy of A.M. Leonard Inc.

loppers **297**

Photo courtesy of A.M. Leonard Inc.

mattock **298**

Photo courtesy of A.M. Leonard Inc.

measuring wheel **299**

Photo courtesy of A.M. Leonard Inc.

mist nozzle (mist bed) **300**

Satyrenko/Shutterstock.com

mower blade balancer **301**

Christopher D. Hart

nursery container **302**

Photo courtesy of A.M. Leonard Inc.

oscillating sprinkler **303**

Photos courtesy of A.M. Leonard Inc.

peat moss **304**

Marekuliasz/Shutterstock.com

perforated water bag

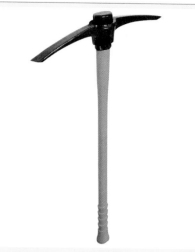

pick (pickax) **305**

planting bar **306a**

planting/earth/soil auger **306b**

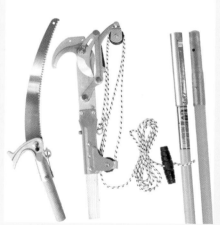

pole pruner **307**

polyethylene pipe **308**

pop-up irrigation head **309**

posthole digger **310**

power blower (hand) **311a**

power blower (back) **311b**

power hedge trimmer **312**

pot-in-pot unit **313**

pump sprayer **314**

propagation mat **315**

pruning saw **316**

push broom

reel mower **317a**

reel mower **317b**

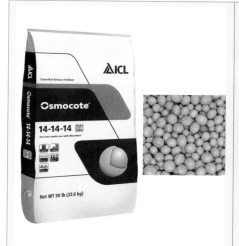

Photos courtesy of A.M. Leonard Inc.

resin-coated fertilizer   **318**

Robert Pernell/Shutterstock.com

rotary mower   **319**

Josep Curto/Shutterstock.com

rototiller   **320**

Photo courtesy of A.M. Leonard Inc.

round point shovel   **321**

Photo courtesy of A.M. Leonard Inc.

scoop (fork)

Photo courtesy of A.M. Leonard Inc.

scoop shovel   **322**

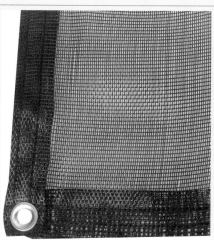

Photo courtesy of A.M. Leonard Inc.

shade fabric   **323**

Photo courtesy of A.M. Leonard Inc.

sharpening stone   **324**

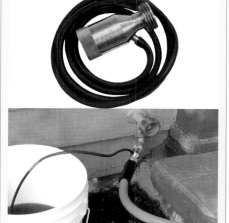

Photos courtesy of A.M. Leonard Inc.

siphon proportioner   **325**

soaker hose **326**

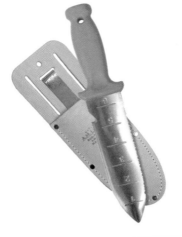

soil knife with sheath

soil sampling tube **327**

solenoid valve **328**

spade **329**

sphagnum moss **330**

square point (flat) shovel **331**

string trimmer **332**

thatch rake **333**

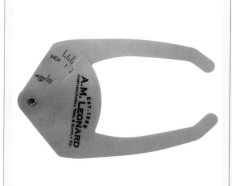

tree caliper **334**

tree wrap **335**

trowel **336a**

trowel **336b**

Christopher D. Hart

vertical mower **337**

water breaker **338**

wide-brimmed hard hat

wire tree basket **339a**

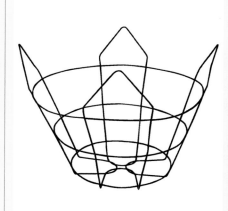

wire tree basket **339b**

CHAPTER 5

Site Evaluation and Plant Selection

While studying this chapter, look for the activity icon to:
- **Practice** vocabulary terms with Words to Know activities.
- **Expand** learning with identification activities.
- **Reinforce** what you learn by completing Know and Understand questions.

www.g-wlearning.com/agriculture

G-WLEARNING.com

Chapter Outcomes

After studying this chapter, you will be able to:

- Understand the process of evaluating a site before creating a design.
- Explain the value of visiting a site.
- Perform a soil analysis.
- Identify a client's needs and intended use of the landscape.
- Understand the impact of municipal and HOA restrictions.

- Explain why a client's budget is important to landscape design.
- Identify the plant characteristics designers use in landscape design.
- Explain how designers use plant characteristics to ensure plant survival.
- Explain how hardiness and heat zones are used when selecting plant materials.
- Determine how cardinal directions are used when selecting plant materials.

Key Terms ➦

amendment
annual
biennial
cool-season plant
deciduous
evergreen
freeze-thaw cycle (FTC)
grade
hardiness zone
heat zone map
homeowner's association (HOA)
hydrophyte
infiltration
infiltration rate

linear footage
mesophyte
microclimate
morphological
morphology
organic matter
perennial
percolation
percolation rate
pH
slope
square footage
warm-season plant
xerophyte

Introduction

Creating a new landscape design is an exciting process for both the client and the designer. When creating a design, you should understand the client's vision as well as any environmental factors that might affect the landscape, such as water drainage, erosion, and soil temperature. You will also need to choose the plants with the right growth habits and light preferences to achieve the desired landscape, **Figure 5-1**. This chapter will help you evaluate a site, discuss the client's wants and needs, and choose the best plants for a landscape.

R. Lee Ivy

Figure 5-1. Landscape designers use their knowledge of plants, creativity, and customer's preferences to develop unique and vibrant environments where people live and work.

Evaluating the Site

When creating a landscape design, you must first evaluate the site to determine what type of preparations are needed. If there are necessary alterations, such as tree and turf removal, time and resources must be allocated to that project before installation can begin, **Figure 5-2**. Preparing and surveying the site, as well as the time, materials, and equipment needed, are all part of the job cost. The landowner may not have included this type of work in their budget and you should discuss this before creating your design. Many designers create a checklist to ensure nothing is overlooked.

Logistics

Logistics must also be considered when evaluating the site. A residence with a steep driveway, for example, may pose problems for parking and ease

Paul Brennan/Shutterstock.com

serato/Shutterstock.com

Figure 5-2. Landscape sites may require many alterations due to poor conditions, such as soil compaction, poor grading, and susceptibility to erosion.

of access for employees staging materials, **Figure 5-3**. It may also make large deliveries with a semitrailer difficult. In some cases, parking and access may exist only on an adjacent property, requiring a special agreement or easement. These types of issues must be considered and remedied before the work begins. A sloped lot will also require more erosion control to be incorporated into the design. *Slope* is the rise and fall or inclination of the land surface in relation to the horizontal distance covered. A flat, horizontal piece of land is said to have a slope of zero. The slope may also be referred to as the *grade*.

Oksana Tjacheva/Shutterstock.com

Visiting the Site

Sometimes, the most valuable information can be gleaned from visiting the site. A deep well, a guy wire from a utility pole, or a low-lying swale (depression) may not be visible with aerial imaging. If the designer is unaware of the condition or object, it may adversely affect the design and its usability. It is also wise at this time to evaluate needs for protection of plant materials and existing structures. Trees that will remain on the landscape, for example, will require root protection. See **Figure 5-4**.

Water Movement

One of the most challenging site issues for many areas is the movement of water around and across the site. Visiting the site during a significant rain may reveal potential issues with runoff, erosion, and standing water. Surface water impoundment is when water remains in an area for a long period. Most terrestrial plants cannot survive in water for hours, let alone for days. Standing water may also perpetuate disease and weed populations. See **Figure 5-5**.

R. Lee Ivy

Figure 5-3. Access to planting areas may be hindered by slope or existing elements. Grading such an area is not as easy as a flat piece of ground because heavy equipment cannot work on too steep of a slope.

R. Lee Ivy

Figure 5-4. Trees require root protection from equipment and excavation damage.

R. Lee Ivy

Figure 5-5. Water coming from roofs, hardscapes, and heavy soils must be addressed when planning landscape installations.

Drainage must be addressed to minimize problems caused by water flow or stoppage. The soil texture and composition greatly affect the *infiltration* or *infiltration rate* of water movement *through* the soil profile. It also affects the speed (rate) with which the water moves *within* the soil. This movement is referred to as *percolation* or *percolation rate*. These characteristics can be evaluated by the results of a soil analysis. Steep slopes may also pose a problem for water flow and the retention of topsoil, nutrients, and soil coverings, such as mulch.

Surveying the Site

An official survey may be required depending on the site's location, local regulations, and whether the design includes fencing or other permanent structures. A licensed surveyor must be employed to perform the survey, **Figure 5-6**. The cost is minimal and the survey will ensure that all landscape features will not impose on surrounding properties.

Collecting Measurements

A designer must have accurate measurements for all areas of the property to ensure the design is created with the correct dimensions and to calculate costs of the job, **Figure 5-7**. The cost of many landscape installation and maintenance tasks, such as sod installation, mulch application, fertilization regimes, and hardscape installation, are calculated based on square footage. The amount of time, equipment, and materials needed to complete a job are also determined based on landscape measurements.

Linear Footage

Linear footage is straight line measurement. The term linear refers to a straight line, which makes a linear foot a 12″ straight line. Hard edges that are measured in linear feet include those where turf meets hard surfaces, such as brick or concrete. Soft edges that are measured in linear feet are those where the turf meets soft surfaces, such as mulch or water.

Square Footage

Square footage is a measurement of area and a two-dimensional space. Square footage is calculated by multiplying the width of an area by its length. Most properties or the portions being landscaped are not perfectly square or rectangular. However, odd shapes are also measured in square footage, albeit with additional or different calculations.

Dmitry/Shutterstock.com

Figure 5-6. Site surveys account for property lines, existing utilities, and dimensions of structures and hardscapes.

Ba_peuceta/Shutterstock.com

R. Lee Ivy

Figure 5-7. Site measurements must be accurate to ensure correct property dimensions on which materials and labor will be based.

Measuring Tools

Accurate measurements are essential to calculate the amount of materials and labor that will be needed to complete a job. Whether you use traditional tools, computer software, or handheld digital devices, using the correct tools and method for measuring will ensure accurate measurements. There are a variety of traditional tools and digital devices used to measure landscape sites, including the following:

- Measuring wheel.
- Retractable tape.
- Winding tape.
- Surveyor's tools.
- Geographic information system (GIS).
- Global positioning system (GPS).
- Handheld laser measurer.
- Laser level.

Performing a Soil Analysis

A site's productivity is greatly affected by the existing soil and its characteristics. It has been said that 80% of plant problems begin in the soil. With this in mind, it is essential to have the soil professionally analyzed. Soil analysis is the only way to know which nutrients need to be added to the soil to provide optimal growing conditions.

Soil samples are taken and tested to determine soil fertility, pH, textures, and percentages of organic matter, **Figure 5-8**. (The *pH* is a number indicating the acidity or alkalinity of a substance, such as soil or water.) Knowing which nutrients are lacking allows you to formulate soil amendments specific to the landscape's needs. Soil *amendments* are materials, such as organic matter, added to the soil to improve its physical or chemical properties. *Organic matter* is material from decayed organisms. Although it is best to take soil samples after

Marcus Holman/Shutterstock.com

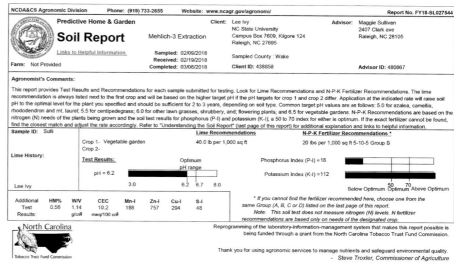

NC Department of Agriculture and Consumer Services

Figure 5-8. Soil sample results provide soil pH and nutrient levels. This information is used to determine the types of amendments needed.

grading to obtain the most accurate results, evaluating the soil before the project begins will give insight into the soil's current health. Another soil analysis may be performed after the land is graded and before planting.

> **Safety First**
>
> Always call 811 five to seven days ahead of scheduled work to have all buried telephone, gas, electrical, and water lines marked before beginning any excavation or digging.

The importance and value of soil sampling cannot be stressed enough. Soil testing will yield great benefits. An accurate soil analysis will ensure the proper application of nutrients and prevent wasted time and resources. Most importantly, it will ensure the success of the design with healthy and productive plant materials.

Goodheart-Willcox Publisher

Figure 5-9. Pedestrian traffic greatly alters soils through compaction and disruption of plant growth structures. Grass seed will not grow in such an area unless the soil is tilled and amended.

Soil Compaction

Soil compaction may also be an issue that needs to be addressed. Soil compaction inhibits plant processes, such as transpiration and respiration. Compaction can be determined through minor excavation or visual inspection of plant health (prominent weed or disease pressure). If soil compaction is not corrected, remediation efforts, such as aeration and the redirection or limitation of foot traffic, will likely be necessary in the future, **Figure 5-9**. It is common for new construction sites to have soil compaction due to the heavy machinery and foot traffic.

Freeze-Thaw Cycle

The *freeze-thaw cycle (FTC)* is a natural process in which water freezes and expands during cold weather and thaws when the temperature increases. It may occur multiple times during winter, depending on weather fluctuations. According to research by the NOAA, the freeze-thaw cycle causes changes in the soil structure, affects the cycle of water on and below the land surface, and regulates the availability of nutrients available to plants. The cycle may also affect the decomposition of organic substances and alter microbial activity. When the soil freezes, the expanding water raises the soil surface, which loosens the compacted soil. The cycle is often the cause of cracked concrete or asphalt and the shifting of pavers.

Existing Structures

A designer often must incorporate existing structures into a design, **Figure 5-10**. Aside from the main building, a lot may have a garage, shed, swimming pool, utility box, or septic field. The design may have to obscure a structure or incorporate a structure. If something is being hidden, it must also be accessible without removing or harming the plant materials. If a structure is on the adjoining property, it can be hidden with plant materials, such as a trellis with vines or a privacy hedge. If a designer is including a structure in the design, he or she must determine if a structure can be altered. A utility shed, for example, could be modified with paint and wood trim to appear as though it were a quaint cottage or potting shed.

Identifying Landscape Use

shippee/Shutterstock.com

Figure 5-10. Utility buildings and potting sheds can be integrated into the landscape. This small gardening shed uses the same wood as the fence and its rustic color to give it a sense of belonging.

The designer must understand what types of use the client has in mind for his or her new landscape before creating a design. Experienced designers may have a set list of questions for their clients to ensure they cover all aspects of the design and the customer's preferences. The designer may also have additional questions after careful evaluation of the site. Knowing what the client's needs are will help the designer determine the size of each area and the types of plant and hardscape materials that will work best in each area, **Figure 5-11**.

Current and Future Activities

The designer may ask for descriptions of current and future activities on the site and the amount of time the client expects to spend outdoors. If it is a commercial site, aesthetics and portraying professionalism may be the main goal and interaction with the site may be nonexistent, **Figure 5-12**. In a residential site, interaction with pets, kids, guests, and clients may be the main goal.

Super-Sod

Mark Herreid/Shutterstock.com

Figure 5-11. A designer considers the client's interests and needs to determine what types of plants and other materials should be used. Homeowners with pets may have specific ideas for dog-friendly areas and homeowners with children may wish for open playing areas and space for a swing set.

Figure 5-12. Commercial landscape sites typically have less foot traffic than residential sites. However, pedestrians will cut across corners if it is more convenient for them to reach their destination. A landscape designer should anticipate this behavior and create walkways that are clear and convenient to deter it.

Maintenance Needs

The level of maintenance the landscape will need also has a great deal of impact on the design. Some clients may prefer a low-maintenance landscape they can easily maintain themselves, whereas others intend to have a maintenance contract with a landscape company and are not as concerned with the amount of maintenance it will need. See **Figure 5-13**.

How often a site is used is also an important factor for determining maintenance requirements. A commercial site with a grass playing field, for example, may require regular compaction remediation to maintain healthy turfgrass on

Figure 5-13. A—A xeriscape requires much less maintenance than traditional residential landscapes. B—High use areas require additional maintenance, such as soil aeration.

the playing surface. The amount of remediation needed will vary if the number of games is limited or if daily practices and bimonthly tournaments are played. In residential areas, a play area may require frequent raking or applications of mulch if multiple children play in it on a daily basis. However, if the play area is only used during occasional visits from grandchildren, it will require less maintenance.

Rules and Regulations

Many municipalities and homeowner's associations have regulations regarding landscape installation. Many municipalities share similar guidelines for quality, planting depth, pruning, staking, watering, and species selection. Plantings must also meet additional regulations, such as ensuring safe sight lines are maintained around municipal areas. Municipalities are often more concerned with the installation of permanent structures, such as pools, sheds, driveways, walkways, and fences, than the types of plant materials being installed. They may restrict the distance from the property line a structure can be installed or the type of fencing that can be used around a pool. A municipality may also require submission of the landscape design for approval and the application for permits. The designer and the landscape professional must be aware of these restrictions before the design and installation may be undertaken.

Homeowner's Association

A *homeowner's association (HOA)* is an organization in a planned community that makes and enforces rules for the properties within its jurisdiction, **Figure 5-14**. The properties may be condominiums, townhomes, or

Imagenet/Shutterstock.com

Figure 5-14. HOAs require a standard of landscaping quality. They will provide the landscape professional with lists of acceptable plant and hardscape materials as well as maintenance requirements.

individual homes. An HOA is composed of residents from the community and is funded by all the homeowners in the community. An HOA is often responsible for hiring maintenance personnel for the common areas, including maintenance of the landscaping. An HOA is in place to regulate any proposed modifications to an individual home or its outdoor area. The organization's main goal is to maintain certain aesthetic and cleanliness standards to ensure the area retains a high quality standard and that property values are not diminished.

It is beneficial for landscape professionals to establish a proper relationship with the HOA representative and understand restrictions regarding the installation of any landscaping materials. In some cases, this person or an advisory board evaluates individual homeowner's requests and prioritizes and allocates resources to make accommodations. Establishing such a relationship will prevent misunderstandings that can lead to wasted time and materials. A landscape designer will also have to consider the HOA's restrictions or guidelines when creating his or her design.

Establishing a Budget

One of the most important discussions the designer and client must have is the client's budget. Some customers have an amount allocated while others simply want landscape issues or projects to be resolved and the budget is secondary. Once the designer knows what amount is allocated, he or she can create a design that falls within the budget range.

When the client is presented with the design, the cost of the installation should include some leeway to cover unforeseen issues that may increase the labor, materials, and time needed to complete the project. The total cost should include costs for each component or step in the process, including site preparation, surveying, materials, labor, and design. If the client cannot afford to install the complete design, the designer may present a plan that offers the installation of separate areas over a given course of time. Many designers may also present a maintenance plan and its cost when presenting the design. The project cost, estimated time of completion, and contract should be presented to the client in a timely fashion.

Choosing Plant Materials

Designers choose plants for their *morphology* or *morphological* features (physical form and structure), but they also consider other characteristics to ensure the plants thrive in the new landscape. These characteristics include physical hardiness, life cycles, leaf retention, drought resistance, and the ability to adapt to the environmental conditions.

Physical Hardiness and Life Cycle

Designers may choose plants for physical hardiness or life expectancy. Physical hardiness describes a plant's ability to grow in adverse conditions. A plant life or growth cycle is the time a plant needs to germinate, grow to maturity, and reproduce, **Figure 5-15**. The three plant life cycles are annual, biennial, and perennial.

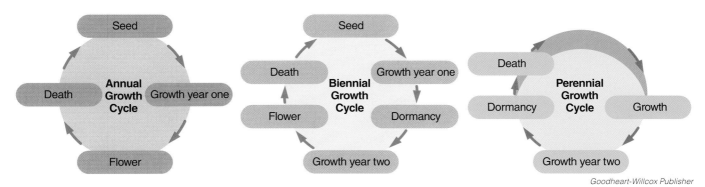

Goodheart-Willcox Publisher

Figure 5-15. Annual, biennial, and perennial life cycles. Some plants may be perennials in warmer climates and annuals in colder climates.

- *Annuals* are plants that complete their growth cycle in one growing season. All roots, stems, and leaves die at the end of the growing season.
- *Biennials* are plants that live two years to complete their growing cycle. The first year is typically a grouping of leaves near the ground. Stem growth and flowering occur in the second year.
- *Perennials* are plants that grow for many seasons. The stems, leaves, and flowers wither at the end of the season and the roots become dormant. New growth occurs at the beginning of the next season. Most industry professionals categorize perennials as plants that are 3′ to 4′ high or less, have noticeable blooms, and in some cases, are cut to the ground each year with refoliation the following spring.

Annuals, such as marigolds or petunias, have short lives and are often used to add color around perennial beds in the summer. The designer may replace the annuals with fall flowers, such as chrysanthemums. The flowers would satisfy their purpose for a few months. If the designer wanted something that would be purposeful for an extended period, he or she could use an oak tree. An oak tree would be purposeful for more than 100 years. See **Figure 5-16**.

A   *Delpixel/Shutterstock.com*   **B**   *Sean Pavone/Shutterstock.com*

Figure 5-16. A—The vibrant colors of Japanese maples make this a popular accent plant. B—It takes decades for oak trees to reach maturity. These live oaks (*Quercus virginiana*) may live up to 500 years. Here, their purpose is to frame the home's entrance and provide shade to the walkway.

A   *Derek R. Audette/Shutterstock.com*

B   *Claudio Divizia/Shutterstock.com*

Figure 5-17. A—Deciduous plants, such as this maple, have attractive bark, foliage, and fruit. B—Evergreens, such as this magnolia, provide consistent greenery and habit of growth.

Leaf Retention

A designer might use a combination of deciduous plants and evergreens to maintain interest and color after the deciduous trees and shrubs drop their leaves. ***Deciduous*** plants are trees or shrubs that lose their leaves (all at once) annually. Deciduous plants often present unique blooms, fruits, or foliage that can be integrated into a design for the growing season and architectural interest during dormancy, **Figure 5-17A**. Evergreens may be chosen for their natural shape or for their adaptability to shearing and shaping into topiaries or hedges, **Figure 5-17B**. ***Evergreens*** are plants that remain green all year. Some evergreens shed leaves or needles throughout the year, but never all at once.

Water Needs

Over time, plants adapt to the climate in which they live and may not survive extreme weather changes. Drought, for example, affects a plant's key processes, such as respiration and transpiration. Plants that do not have an adaptive means to survive an extended drought will not survive. A successful landscape professional must know which types of plants are suited to a climate and likely to thrive during extreme weather conditions, such as drought. The plant classifications, xerophyte, mesophyte, and hydrophyte, can be used to indicate a plant's water needs.

- ***Xerophytes*** are plants that live in very dry climates, **Figure 5-18A**. They have adapted to dry conditions and are installed in those areas with arid climates or very long periods of drought.
- ***Mesophytes*** are plants that thrive under typically average conditions. Most of the plants we encounter, except for desert plants, are mesophytes, **Figure 5-18B**.
- ***Hydrophytes*** are plants that are adapted to life in very wet places. Knowing that these plants thrive in extreme or intermediate conditions enables the plant selector to select specifically for small, wet areas, or wet microclimates, **Figure 5-18C**.

Environmental Adaptation

Plants native to the area will grow best, but those from other areas of the world with similar climatic and soil conditions can thrive as well. Cold-hardy plants are rarely affected by fluctuations in winter temperatures, whereas tender plants can be damaged or die due to a random drop in temperature or long duration of cold, **Figure 5-19.**

A *Pavaphon Supanantananont/ Shutterstock.com*

B *Luka Hercigonja/Shutterstock.com*

C *Istomina Olena/Shutterstock.com*

Figure 5-18. A—Xerophytes, such as cacti, tolerate coarse soils and low amounts of water. B—Mesophytes, such as goldenrod, have variable water requirements and can thrive in many types of soils with moderate amounts of water. C—Hydrophytes, such as this water hyacinth, thrive in very wet locations.

Christopher D. Hart

Figure 5-19. Many of the tender plants used in the landscape will suffer or die during cold periods. The lives of some plants can be extended by covering them before the first and subsequent frosts. Potted plants are more susceptible to the cold because their soil is aboveground and may reach colder temperatures much sooner than the ground would.

Temperature for Optimum Growth

Plants can be warm-season or cold-season plants. **Warm-season plants** typically have a longer growing season and optimum growth the warmest part of the year. Warm-season plants withstand or thrive in extended periods of high temperatures. Warm-season turfgrasses include bermudagrass, centipedegrass, and zoysiagrass, **Figure 5-20A**. Warm-season vegetables include tomatoes, melons, and squash. These vegetables have only one growing cycle.

Pro Tip

The growth of cool- and warm-season annuals is governed by the length of the growing season in a given area. The length of the growing season is estimated by determining the last spring frost date and the first fall frost date with a deviation of days before and after the frost dates. The growing season in southern areas, for example, may be April 15 to November first and June first to September 15 in northern areas.

A

R. Lee Ivy

B

RealityImages/Shutterstock.com

Figure 5-20. A—Bermudagrass is a warm-season turfgrass often used for athletic fields. B—Cool-season plants, such as cabbage and kale, thrive during spring and fall temperature cycles.

Cool-season plants thrive in the cool temperatures of early spring and fall. Some cool-season plants need cold temperatures to germinate and grow. Cool-season turfgrasses include fescue, bluegrass, and bent grass. Early blooming plants that are included in landscape designs include hellebores and pansies. Cool-season edible crops include carrots, cabbage, and kale, **Figure 5-20B**. Colorful kale is often used to add color to a landscape in the fall after the annuals are spent.

Pro Tip

Decorative kale is *not* meant to be eaten although some consider it edible. It is very bitter, tough, and chewy.

USDA Hardiness Zones

The USDA publishes a map of the United States that is divided into *hardiness zones*, **Figure 5-21**. The hardiness zones are determined by the average minimum temperature of each area. The hardiness zone for a specific plant is usually provided on the label, tag, or in the catalog description. There are also apps available to determine hardiness zones by zip codes. Over the past couple decades, hardiness zones have migrated toward a warmer classification.

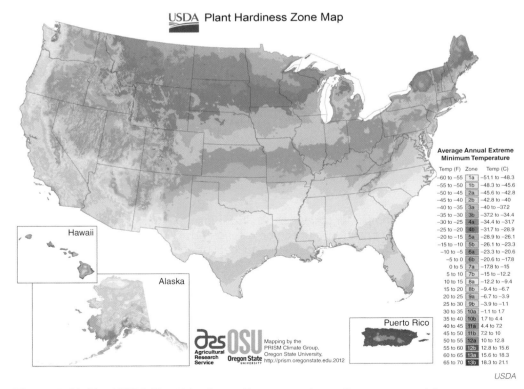

USDA

Figure 5-21. The USDA Plant Hardiness Zone map shows the average minimum temperature for each area of the country. Growers can use this information to determine what plants will grow best in a particular area.

If winter temperatures fall below the average minimum for extended periods, plants that have survived previous winters may suffer or die. The lack of colder temperatures may also affect some plants. Many fruit trees, for example, require a certain number of chill hours to regulate their growth.

Microclimates

Individual microclimates may exist within a hardiness zone, **Figure 5-22**. A *microclimate* is a small area with different environmental conditions than the surrounding area. The microclimate could slightly or greatly alter the soil and air temperatures, thus affecting plants growing in those areas. Microclimates may be created due to soil texture, nearby structures, elevation, slope, and proximity to water. New construction or changes to the topography may also create a microclimate. Existing plants may suffer or die when their environment changes.

> **Pro Tip**
>
> Many plants that are considered annuals in the North can live for years in a frost-free environment.

AHS Heat Zones

The American Horticultural Society (AHS) publishes a *heat zone map*. The heat zone map provides the average number of days that areas across the country experience temperatures over 86°F (30°C). Many garden plants have been coded with a series of numbers that coincide with the heat zones. These numbers are assigned with the assumption that the plants receive adequate water.

Cardinal Directions

To anticipate climatic conditions and the plant's response to those conditions, it is important to understand the cardinal directions specific to a site. *Cardinal directions* are the four main points of a compass.

North-Facing Sites

North-facing sites or slopes will experience cooler soil temperatures because they receive little

R. Lee Ivy

Leonardo da/Shutterstock.com

R. Lee Ivy

Figure 5-22. Microclimates are often much warmer than other areas of the landscape because they receive heat reflected from the hardscape as well as direct sunlight. The soil water may also be limited due to the amount of hardscape surrounding the plants.

or no direct sunlight. In the winter, wind exposure from cool, dry winds can adversely affect north-facing bark and can damage plants if they are not properly hydrated during the winter season, **Figure 5-23**.

R. Lee Ivy

Figure 5-23. North facing slopes are often cooler because they receive less sunlight than slopes facing south, east, or west.

Career Connection

Preston Montague

Preston Montague, Naturalist

Preston Montague is a naturalist working to improve public and environmental health through the arts, education, and landscape architecture. He is passionate about inspiring curiosity and encouraging a sense of urgency in people to affect positive change in their environment. Preston strives to help people make the connection between the health of the planet and the quality of their lives.

Naturalists often work with the US Forest Service, US National Park Service, or the US Department of Natural Resources, where they run programs to help the public understand the natural, historical, and scientific significance of our national parks. Many visit local schools to introduce students to the wonders of nature and the importance of conservation. Some of the activities a naturalist might organize include nature walks, nature photo walks, camping trips, and basic outdoor skills.

The required education is minimally a bachelor's degree in environmental education or wildlife biology. In addition to meeting the educational requirements, a naturalist must be a good communicator and have a passion for environmental issues. Teaching experience is also recommended. Many naturalists begin their careers by volunteering at local nature centers.

Consider This

1. Who are some of history's most influential naturalists? How did their work affect our national parks and forests?
2. Have you considered volunteering at a local nature center and learning more about being a naturalist?

East-Facing Sites

East-facing sites or slopes experience the first light in the morning and have lower ambient air temperature. East-facing sites can be advantageous for some blooming shrubs and partial shade-loving plants. An east-facing site may not be the best for plants needing longer duration of sunlight.

South-Facing Sites

South-facing sites or slopes experience the warmest soil temperatures due to extended sun exposure. The extended exposure causes early warming of soil temperatures in the spring. These sites will often be dry.

West-Facing Sites

West-facing sites or slopes experience the last light in the evening and have warmer ambient air temperatures. West-facing sites can be a harsh environment for some tender plants. However, the light exposure may be ideal for hardy plants and those that create shade for other plants during the warmest part of the day.

Student and Professional Organizations

Gaining Knowledge and Developing Skills

National organizations, such as the NALP and FFA, hold competitive events to help students and professionals develop good practices and skills. Many participants will earn scholarships and acquire internships through these events. Some organizations invite professionals from around the country to attend the competition and use it as a recruiting opportunity.

- The NALP (National Association of Landscape Professionals) sponsors the National Collegiate Landscape Competition (NCLC) annually. Students participate in 29 green industry related events. The NCLC is held at a different university each year and is attended by over 700 participants and over 300 industry representatives.
- The National FFA holds green industry competitions at local, state, and national levels. These competitions are referred to as Career Development Events (CDEs). The Nursery/Landscape CDE tests students' skills in aspects of maintaining landscape plants and related products, evaluating equipment and services, and landscape design.

Summary

- An essential part of the design process is meeting the client and establishing a working relationship. It is best to determine early in the project who will be the primary contact for future communication.
- Logistics of the site, such as incline, parking issues, and delivery limitations, must also be considered when evaluating the site.
- Technology, such as GPS, GIS, and drones, can be used to gain information about a property, but a site visit yields invaluable information.
- An official survey may be required depending on the site's location, local regulations, and whether the design includes fencing or other permanent structures.
- A designer must have accurate measurements for all areas of the property to ensure the design is created with the correct dimensions and to calculate accurate costs for the job.
- Soil must be professionally analyzed to determine the level of nutrients that need to be added to the soil to provide optimal growing conditions.
- A designer must establish the client's intended use for the landscape in order to create a design that will satisfy the client's needs.
- The designer and landscape company must be aware of municipal and HOA restrictions before the design and installation may be undertaken.
- The designer and client must discuss what type of budget has been allotted for the landscape.
- An understanding of plant life cycles is important before choosing plants for a specific site.
- The USDA hardiness zones are determined by the average minimum temperature of each area.
- Microclimates are small areas with different environmental conditions than the surrounding area.
- The AHS heat zone map provides the average number of days that areas across the country experience temperatures over 86°F (30°C).
- Plants can be selected based on hardiness and heat zone maps, ensuring longevity in a landscape.
- The cardinal directions of a site must be identified in order to properly place plants in the landscape.

Chapter Review

Know and Understand ⤴

Answer the following questions using the information provided in this chapter.

1. *True or False?* Preparing and surveying the site, as well as the time, materials, and equipment needed, are all part of the job cost.
   A. True.
   B. False.

2. The rise and fall or inclination of the land surface is the _____.
   A. habit
   B. alteration
   C. slope
   D. All of the above.

3. Of the following, which is the most challenging issue when evaluating a new site?
   A. Measuring the amount of daylight the site receives.
   B. Protecting existing plants, trees, or structures.
   C. Determining the existing grade of the land.
   D. The movement of water around and across the site.

4. Water movement through the soil profile is referred to as _____.
   A. infiltration
   B. percolation
   C. incorporation
   D. deterioration

5. The movement of water within the soil is referred to as _____.
   A. infiltration
   B. percolation
   C. incorporation
   D. deterioration

6. Which of the following is determined based on a site's measurements?
   A. The equipment needed.
   B. The amount of materials needed.
   C. The amount of time the job will take.
   D. All of the above.

7. Straight line measurement is referred to as _____.
   A. square footage
   B. yard footage
   C. linear footage
   D. material footage

8. Which of the following is calculated by multiplying the width of an area by its length?
   A. Square footage.
   B. Yard footage.
   C. Linear footage.
   D. Material footage.

9. The system used to view property lines and identify features in the surrounding landscape that may affect the design is a(n) _____.
   A. UAV
   B. GIS
   C. HOA
   D. LPS

10. The system used to create databases of satellite images of properties around the world is a(n) _____.
    A. UVA
    B. LPS
    C. GPS
    D. HOA

11. *True or False?* Soil samples need only be taken if runoff water has been crossing the site on a regular basis.
    A. True.
    B. False.

12. The acidity or alkalinity of a substance is indicated by the _____.
    A. UAV number
    B. drainage number
    C. analysis number
    D. pH number

13. An amendment that is commonly used to improve the soil's physical or chemical properties is _____.
    A. soil water
    B. sodium
    C. organic matter
    D. All of the above.

14. Which of the following plant processes is inhibited by soil compaction?
    A. Photosynthesis.
    B. Transpiration.
    C. Respiration.
    D. All of the above.

15. *True or False?* It is often necessary to incorporate an existing structure into a design through modification or by obscuring it with plant materials.
    A. True.
    B. False.

16. *True or False?* Current and future activities on the site are the least important factors to be considered when creating a design.
    A. True.
    B. False.

17. *True or False?* The restrictions or guidelines set by an HOA will often affect a landscape design for homes within the association.
    A. True.
    B. False.

18. The cost of a landscape installation includes which of the following?
    A. Each component and step of the process.
    B. Design, labor, surveying, and materials.
    C. Site preparation and plant materials.
    D. All of the above.

19. Plants that complete their growing cycle in two years are _____.
    A. perennials
    B. annuals
    C. biennials
    D. binomials

20. Plants that grow for many seasons are referred to as _____.
    A. perennials
    B. annuals
    C. biennials
    D. binomials

21. Plants that complete their growing cycle in one season are _____.
    A. perennials
    B. annuals
    C. biennials
    D. binomials

22. *True or False?* Evergreens are trees or shrubs that lose their leaves annually.
    A. True.
    B. False.

23. Plants that thrive under typically average conditions are _____.
    A. xerophytes
    B. mesophytes
    C. hydrophytes
    D. tetrabytes

24. Plants that are adapted to life in very wet places are_____.
    A. xerophytes
    B. mesophytes
    C. hydrophytes
    D. tetrabytes

25. Plants that have adapted to life in very dry climates are _____.
    A. xerophytes
    B. mesophytes
    C. hydrophytes
    D. tetrabytes

26. *True or False?* Cool-season plants withstand or thrive in extended periods of high temperatures.
    A. True.
    B. False.

27. *True or False?* The hardiness zones are determined by the average minimum temperature of each area.
    A. True.
    B. False.

28. Areas that have different environmental conditions than the surrounding area are known as _____.
    A. hydroclimates
    B. arid climates
    C. mixed climates
    D. microclimates

29. *True or False?* The heat zone map provides the average number of days that areas across the country experience temperatures over 86°F (30°C).
    A. True.
    B. False.

30. *True or False?* Cardinal directions specific to a site will affect soil temperature, wind exposure, and light exposure.
   A. True.
   B. False.

Thinking Critically

1. How would you explain the site evaluation process to a client?

2. You are a landscape designer installing a new landscape for a very demanding client. Soil tests indicate the land is clayey and low in nutrients and you want to add amendments. The owner does not want to pay for the additional work but you know the new plant materials will not thrive. How do you approach the situation without offending your client?

3. What approach would you use to make the soil in a chemically contaminated site usable?

Suggested Activities

1. In groups of 2 to 4, write a list of questions to ask a potential client and a list of questions a client might ask a landscape designer. Write the questions on index cards. Randomly choose 5 to 7 questions and practice asking and answering questions. Alternate positions as the client and designer.

2. Research mobile apps that can be used to assess and/or measure a site. Compare the apps and determine the advantages and disadvantages of each one. If possible, use one or more apps to assess and/or measure a site on the school campus. Measure the area using traditional methods and determine which is more accurate.

3. Determine the hardiness zone in your area. Which areas of the world share that growing condition? Choose 2 or 3 types of plants common to your area and determine if these plants could live in other areas of the world with similar growing conditions. This activity may also be performed in groups.

4. In groups of 2 to 4, identify 4 or 5 plant species in a local park or on the school campus. Determine the life cycles of each species. When do climatic conditions change their growth condition? Make a chart to track weekly changes. Include daily weather conditions and take photos each week. Determine if the plants are in their optimal growing conditions.

5. Using technology, such as the compass on your cell phone, identify the cardinal directions for a specific site on the school campus or your home. Estimate the amount of sunlight for areas around the site and how it might affect plant growth. Search online for an app that calculates light exposure over the course of the year for the same location.

6. Find a landscape with a low-lying area that is prone to holding excess water. Explain how you would evaluate the site and remedy the issue.

7. Work with a partner to create a site analysis checklist. Brainstorm all the information a landscape designer would need to develop ideas and a plan. Compare lists with your classmates and make one comprehensive list.

CHAPTER

6

Principles and Elements of Design

While studying this chapter, look for the activity icon to:
- **Practice** vocabulary terms with Words to Know activities.
- **Expand** learning with identification activities.
- **Reinforce** what you learn by completing Know and Understand questions.

G-WLEARNING.com

www.g-wlearning.com/agriculture

148

Chapter Outcomes

After studying this chapter, you will be able to:

- Describe the principles of design.
- Describe the elements of design.
- Apply the principles and elements of design to a landscape design.
- Understand the process of selecting plant material to satisfy principles of design.
- Understand how color and texture are used to create year-round appealing landscapes.
- Design sustainable landscapes.

Key Terms ↪

asymmetrical balance
balance
color scheme
distal balance
elements of design
focal point
focalization
form
formal balance
hue
informal balance
massing
principles of design

proportion
proximal balance
rhythm
scale
shade
simplicity
symmetrical balance
texture
tint
tone
unity
visual weight
xeriscaping

Introduction

Have you wondered why we find some designs more pleasing than others? The designs we find appealing typically follow the principles of design. These are basic guidelines used in all types of design work, including home decorating, clothing design, and auto engineering. In landscaping, you will apply the *principles of design* to create attractive, functional, and year-round pleasing landscapes, **Figure 6-1**. This chapter explores the principles of design and how you can use them to create appealing landscapes.

A   *Christopher D. Hart* **B**   *karamysh/Shutterstock.com*

Figure 6-1. A—A mixed perennial bed provides a habitat for insects during the summer months. B—The hardscape and softscape create an attractive image during the winter as well as the summer months.

Principles

In this chapter, we will discuss the basic principles of design and how they are used in landscape design. We will also discuss how the guidelines are implemented through the components of the landscape, such as the plants, site, structures, seasonal changes, and stages of plant growth through plant maturity. The principles of design that will be discussed in this chapter are:

- Balance.
- Focalization.
- Simplicity.
- Rhythm.
- Proportion.
- Scale.
- Unity.

Balance

Balance in landscape design is an even distribution of the visual weight of landscape materials along a central axis. *Visual weight* is the "heaviness" our eyes assign to an object. Materials that carry more visual weight in a landscape include those that are large, dark, have high contrast, and have interesting placement. Some materials, such as small stones, can carry more weight in a landscape when the viewer naturally groups them together and sees them as a whole. Landscape designers use multiple types of balance, including symmetrical, asymmetrical, and proximal or distance balance.

- *Symmetrical balance*, also referred to as *formal balance*, is a form of balance in which one side of the landscape is a mirror image of the other. It is commonly used in formal landscape designs, **Figure 6-2A**.
- *Asymmetrical balance* is achieved by placing different combinations of materials that carry the same amount of visual weight on each side of the design. Asymmetrical balance is also referred to as *informal balance*. Asymmetrical balance allows the designer to incorporate a wider variety of plant material in the design, **Figure 6-2B**.

- *Proximal* or *distal balance* is the asymmetrical balance of elements on the central axis (right and left) as well as in the field of vision (near and far). Designers consider elements that are not part of the design but will be viewed in relation to the design, such as tall buildings or distant hills or mountains, **Figure 6-2C**.

Focalization

Focalization is the use of a focal point to force the viewer's attention to a particular location. A *focal point* (area of visual dominance) is the area that constitutes that location, **Figure 6-3**. The focal point may be one object, such as a pergola or a magnificent tree specimen, or a general area, such as a patio. Flowering plants or foliage with distinctive colors are also used to create focal points. For example, the contrast of a grouping of dark-colored flowers set among light green foliage creates a strong focal point. The designer must consider plant changes that will occur throughout the growing season to ensure the landscape retains its intended focal points.

A — *randy andy/Shutterstock.com*

B — *Christopher D. Hart*   C — *Christopher D. Hart*

Figure 6-2. A—Symmetrical, or formal balance, is a mirror image of one side of the landscape. B—Asymmetrical balance, or informal balance, allows the designer to incorporate a large variety of plants into the design. Although different plants are used on each side of the walkway, both sides have the same amount of visual weight and appear balanced. C—The designer should imagine how the landscape appears up close as well as from a distance.

Figure 6-3. A wooden bench is the focal point along this walkway. Careful consideration should be made when adding manufactured materials as focal points in a design.

Entryways

In residential landscaping, the home's front door is the standard focal point of the public living area. Many designers will paint the entry door a bright color to draw the viewer's eye to the home's entrance, **Figure 6-4**. Plant materials should be selected and positioned to enhance the entryway.

Planting Beds

Planting beds must also have focal points. Where the focal point is located depends primarily on the shape of the bed. In a corner planting, for example, the focal point should be in the very corner of the design. Objects, such as statues or birdbaths, are often used to create focal points in planting beds. The purpose of a focal point may also influence its location. A sign in a commercial landscape, for example, should be placed where it is most visible to the public.

Figure 6-4. The front door is the focal point of the public living area of the landscape. Plants should be placed to draw one's eye to the entry.

The color and height of plant materials should be used to complement and guide the viewer's eye to the focal point. Shorter plants should be placed along the outside perimeter and the taller plants should be located in the center. Darker plant material is often used low in the design and near the focal point because darker colors have more visual weight. The mature height of plant materials must be considered when planning the design. Plants growing in front of the focal point should have a mature height that will not block the object or sign.

Special Features

Certain items will automatically create focal points. Water features captivate viewers by sight and sound and often are immediate focal points of an area, **Figure 6-5**. Landscape lighting used to highlight certain features of the design at night also automatically create a focal point.

Simplicity

Simplicity in landscape design is limiting the variety of material, such as types of plants or different colors, used throughout the design. Using too many types of materials will create too many focal points and make the landscape appear busy. Limiting the number of plants and materials used will create peaceful designs that are visually appealing. Repeating species of plants in the design also helps create rhythm and allows the designer to control where the eye flows, **Figure 6-6**.

BBA Photography/Shutterstock.com

Figure 6-5. Water creates a focal point within the design. Running water features also provide sound, a unique feature to add to a landscape.

Ewais/Shutterstock.com

Figure 6-6. Repeating plant species creates simplicity.

Applying the principle of simplicity also allows the landscape designer to use a smaller number of species of plants. Often times, plants in similar species will require the same cultural and maintenance requirements. Simplicity allows for easier maintenance of the landscape.

Christopher D. Hart

Figure 6-7. The logs used to create this walkway help move a visitor's eye through the landscape. The speed or pace at which the eye is drawn through the area depends on the spacing of the logs.

Christopher D. Hart

Figure 6-8. The repetition of patterns in this brick walkway draws the viewer's eye across the landscape.

Rhythm

The design principle of *rhythm* describes how the eye travels through the landscape, **Figure 6-7**. Rhythm adds a sense of motion to the design. Rhythm is implemented mainly through repetition of elements, such as plants or the type of stone used in the hardscapes. The repetition of shapes, textures, and colors through these elements creates patterns that guide the viewer through the landscape. Spacing contributes to rhythm by increasing or decreasing the pace at which the viewer's eye is drawn through the landscape. Objects that are placed close together, for example, will draw the eye to the focal point at a faster pace than the same objects spaced at greater distances.

Rhythm can be created in the repeated patterns of stone in walkways, **Figure 6-8**, consistent spacing of landscape lighting fixtures, and repeated clusters of plants in a perennial or annual border. Rhythm created by foundation plants planted in patterns is a very effective means of drawing a visitor to an entryway.

Proportion

Proportion is the size relationship between the materials used in the landscape and the landscape design as a whole. Each material used must be proportionate to the others to achieve a well-balanced, pleasing landscape. When designing the landscape for a small structure, for example, smaller plants and hardscape elements should be used. If the elements are too large for the structure, the structure will appear overwhelmed or dwarfed. Conversely, larger structures require larger materials or the structure will visually overwhelm the landscape. See **Figure 6-9** and **Figure 6-10**. Plants should be carefully selected so that they are the proper size and shape at maturity.

Scale

Scale is the size of one object in relation to the other objects in the design. Some landscape elements, such as walkways and steps, are scaled to suit the human body. The recommended width of walkways, for example, is the minimal amount of space a person needs to walk comfortably along a path. The ideal height of steps is scaled to suit the average human's stepping height to make it comfortable and safe to walk up or down the steps.

The objects used in the landscape must also be scaled to suit the space. A large water feature, for example, placed in the center of a small garden would be overwhelming. It would make the space seem crowded and it would likely make maneuvering in the garden difficult. Similarly, a small water feature placed in a large garden area would look lost or go unnoticed.

Although scale is closely related to proportion, it is different. If a design is scaled upward, for example, the sizes and amounts of all the plant materials increase, but the proportions between the materials remains the same. In other words, if a design has 3 rose bushes, 5 boxwoods, and 5 sedums, you would use 6 rose bushes, 10 boxwoods, and 10 sedum to scale upward. In this manner, you can use the same design in a larger area.

Unity

Unity is the organization of all elements in a landscape design so that they appear to belong together. Unity links all aspects of the design, **Figure 6-11**. If a design does not appear to come together as a whole, it lacks unity and the designer must determine which principles of design should be addressed.

dny3d/Shutterstock.com

Anna Frajtova/Shutterstock.com

Figure 6-9. The smaller trees are proportional to the small house. The larger trees are disproportionate and overwhelm the small structure.

Christopher D. Hart

Figure 6-10. Select larger growing plants for larger structures. Proportion is maintained in the mixed containers by using plants that grow in proportion to the containers.

ying/Shutterstock.com

Figure 6-11. Light colored materials are used to harmonize this white garden. All materials blend well; the principle of unity has been achieved.

Scorpp/Shutterstock.com

A

Christopher D. Hart

B

Figure 6-12. A—The soft plant materials soften the harsh lines created by the stone path. B—Formal landscapes typically feature straight lines and geometric shapes.

Elements of Design

The *elements of design* can be described as the "ingredients" used in a design. The selection and blending of these ingredients is guided by the principles of design. The basic elements of design used include line, form, texture, and color. Some designers also consider fragrance, size, and space as elements that may be incorporated into a landscape design.

Line

Lines used in landscape design create or define the visual paths that draw our eyes through the landscape. Lines may be straight or curved and may be static or dynamic. Static lines are those that appear to be stationary or nonmoving, whereas dynamic lines have a strong sense of movement. Straight lines are commonly considered static.

Perfectly straight lines rarely occur in nature. They should be used sparingly unless you are creating a formal landscape design, **Figure 6-12**. However, it is typically necessary to use straight lines to establish a border or separate certain areas of the landscape. The straight line created by a fence or row of screening plants can be softened with plant materials planted in front of and along the border. Walkways and planting beds should also be designed with curves to help soften harder materials, **Figure 6-13**.

A   *Christopher D. Hart*

B   *Christopher D. Hart*

Figure 6-13. Straight lines should be used sparingly in landscape designs. A—The straight hedge provides screening as well as a backdrop for the mixed perennial border. The gentle curve of the perennial border is visually appealing and helps draw the eye along the length of the bed. B—A mix of colorful annuals and perennials helps soften the lines created by the concrete structure in this downtown park.

Form

Form is the shape or silhouette of individual plants or groups of plants. Many of the plants used in formal landscapes have defined geometric shapes, such as those created by trimmed and shaped hedges. Plants with well-defined geometric shapes can easily become focal points when used in informal landscapes, **Figure 6-14**. Landscapes with geometric shapes are high maintenance. Skilled workers must regularly trim the plants to ensure they retain the desired form. The variety of plant forms available includes arching, columnar, creeping, spreading, globular, pyramidal, vase- or fan-shaped, and weeping. See **Figure 6-15**.

Barno Tanko/Shutterstock.com

Figure 6-14. Geometric shapes are visually interesting and create interest.

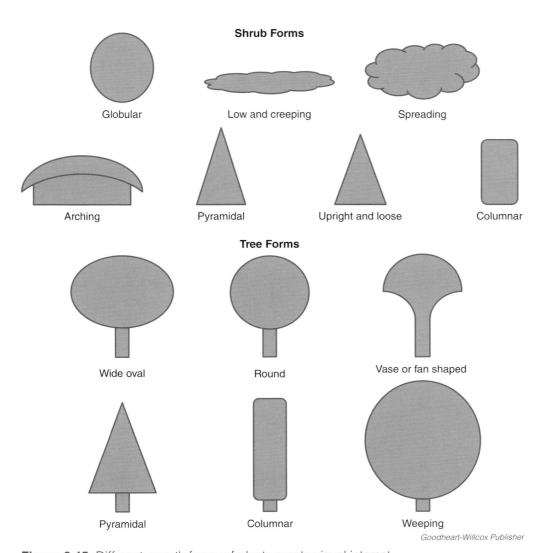

Goodheart-Willcox Publisher

Figure 6-15. Different growth forms of plants create visual interest.

Texture

Texture is both the visual and tactile surface quality of a material. In other words, textures can be seen and felt. Texture is a strong element that can add a great deal of interest to a landscape. When the viewer is near the plantings, texture comes primarily from the size, shape, and spacing of the leaves and twigs. Color, shading, and the level of leaf glossiness also influence texture. When viewed from a distance, texture comes from the plants as a whole. Light and shadows within the plantings also affect texture. See **Figure 6-16**.

Texture is described as being fine, medium, or coarse. These terms refer to how coarse or fine the surface of the material feels and looks. Plants that have large leaves are said to have a coarse texture and plants with small leaves a fine texture. Fine texture plants are suited for use in small areas. Plants with a coarse texture should be used sparingly in small areas. If plants are to be used for screening, coarse texture plants will work the best.

The designer must consider how seasonal changes will affect the textural element of the design and choose plant materials accordingly. Flowers, for example, often are short-lived and the designer must consider how the foliage will work in the design when the blooms die down. The designer must also consider the textures of hardscape materials when creating a landscape. Hardscape materials may also have coarse, medium, or fine texture. Hardscape

STEM Connection

Variegation

In addition to the wide variety of flowers available, many plants have striking foliage that can be used to add color and interest to a design. Some of the most familiar foliage patterns are those of variegated plants. The variegation occurs due to a lack of chlorophyll in the leaves. The lack of chlorophyll is not a result of the plant's environment but a result of cell mutation. The variegation may be genetic, manipulated through breeding, or occur randomly.

Consider This

1. Do variegated leaves perform photosynthesis?
2. Do variegated plants grow slower or quicker than plants without variegation? Explain your answer.
3. Why would a plant's variegation disappear?
4. Does variegation serve a purpose for a plant's growth or development? Explain your answer.
5. Are flowers ever variegated? Explain why or why not.

Johnnie Martin/Shutterstock.com   Ken Schulze/Shutterstock.com   Young Swee Ming/Shutterstock.com   alima 007/Shutterstock.com   Pavaphon Supanantananont/Shutterstock.com

PrinceOfLove/Shutterstock.com

Figure 6-16. At a distance, the mass effect of plants and other landscape elements create texture. As the viewer approaches the landscape, texture comes from the size and shape of the individual leaves and twigs as well as the hardscape materials.

materials are often the predominant texture during winter months in areas that experience drastic seasonal changes.

Color

Color is often the most striking element of design. A landscape designer must consider the color of all plant parts and not just the flower when choosing plant materials. Plants may be selected for the color they add to the landscape through their flowers, leaves, stems, and fruits, **Figure 6-17**. Annuals are commonly used for their striking display of flower or leaf color. Plants may be massed to make the most striking impact in a design. *Massing* flowers involves planting many of the same type of plant very close together.

Color Schemes

Color schemes are guidelines for combining colors in a design. Color wheels are very useful tools to have when creating color schemes in landscape design, **Figure 6-18**. The most basic colors on the wheel are the *primary colors* (red, yellow, and blue). All other colors are mixtures of these three colors. The *secondary colors* (orange, violet, and green) are those formed by mixing two of the primary colors. *Tertiary colors* are created by mixing secondary colors. Color variations, referred to as tints, tones, and shades, can be created by adding white, gray, or black to primary, secondary, or tertiary colors.

PAUL ATKINSON/Shutterstock.com   *Oksana Shevchenko/Shutterstock.com*   *Jiri Prochazka/Shutterstock.com*

Figure 6-17. Many plants add different colors to the landscape as they grow and change during the seasons.

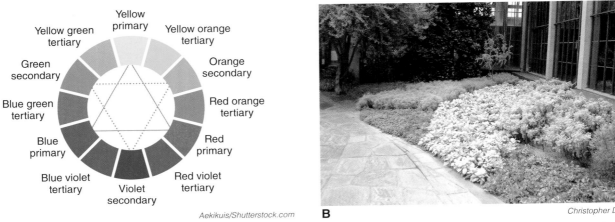

A   *Aekikuis/Shutterstock.com*   B   *Christopher D. Hart*

Figure 6-18. A—Color wheels are used to create color schemes. B—The monochromatic color scheme features plants with shades, tones, and tints of the same base color.

- A pure *hue* is a color that has not been modified.
- A *tint* is a hue that has been lightened.
- A *shade* is a hue that has been darkened.
- A *tone* is a hue to which gray has been added.

The color schemes in **Figure 6-19** indicate which colors work well together. The shapes can be rotated to indicate additional color schemes. Color wheels can be purchased at most craft stores.

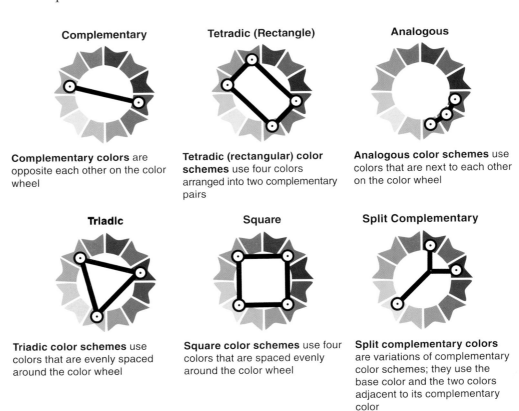

Complementary

Complementary colors are opposite each other on the color wheel

Tetradic (Rectangle)

Tetradic (rectangular) color schemes use four colors arranged into two complementary pairs

Analogous

Analogous color schemes use colors that are next to each other on the color wheel

Triadic

Triadic color schemes use colors that are evenly spaced around the color wheel

Square

Square color schemes use four colors that are spaced evenly around the color wheel

Split Complementary

Split complementary colors are variations of complementary color schemes; they use the base color and the two colors adjacent to its complementary color

Slave SPB/Shutterstock.com

Figure 6-19. Color wheels are a necessity when developing color schemes.

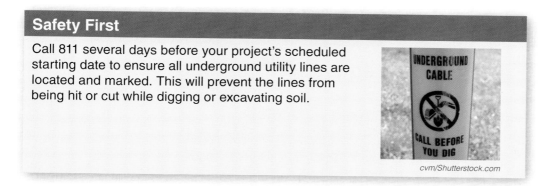

Safety First

Call 811 several days before your project's scheduled starting date to ensure all underground utility lines are located and marked. This will prevent the lines from being hit or cut while digging or excavating soil.

cvm/Shutterstock.com

Site Considerations

When first visiting a new landscape site, the designer must consider elements that might pose challenges, such as rocky terrain or a severe slope. He or she must determine if the elements can be worked into the design or if corrective measures must be taken. The designer must also consider local ordinances that require design approval because there may be restrictions that will influence the design.

Viewpoint

One should consider all directions and manners in which the landscape will be viewed before finalizing the design. Imagine how the landscape will appear to people in vehicles as they approach the site from each direction. Does the site appear balanced? Is there a sense of unity from each viewpoint? It is also important to imagine views of the landscape from inside the buildings. Consider the framing of the landscape through each window. It is also important to ensure that windows will not be blocked when plant materials reach maturity.

Plant Maturity

Mature height and width of plants should carefully be considered to achieve the desired amount of visual weight. Many landscape plants have a wide variety of growth forms, with a wide variety of visual weights. Landscape designs should always specify the exact plants that are required for the plan.

Restrictions

When designing a landscape, the designer must ensure they are aware of all legal restrictions that may affect his or her design. Many homeowner associations (HOA) dictate the type of plant and hardscape materials that can be used in a residential setting. Materials used to create the buildings within the landscape site will often determine the plant material and other hardscaping materials used to finish the landscape.

Career Connection

Tracy Sides

Tracy Sides, Landvision Designs Inc.

Tracy Sides is the owner of Landvision Designs Inc., a professional landscape design and installation firm located in Raleigh, NC. Tracy has over 20 years of experience, having worked throughout North Carolina, Virginia, and as far away as Mauritania, West Africa. He and his wife Crystal founded Landvision in 1993 with a commitment to creating exceptionally functional, enjoyable, and beautiful landscapes for their clients.

As general contractors, Landvision handles all elements of outdoor spaces, from swimming pools and outdoor kitchens to simple flowerbeds. Landvision prides itself on completing these outdoor spaces from beginning to end by employing landscape architects, landscape designers, and master artisans to implement their designs.

Tracy graduated with a Bachelor's of Science in Horticulture from North Carolina State University. He is a North Carolina Licensed General contractor, Landscape contractor, and NC Certified Plant Professional. He is a member, as well as past President, of the North Carolina Nursery & Landscape Association. He has served on several boards and committees, including the ANLA Landscape Board and the NC Landscape Contractors Licensing board.

Consider This

1. How has Tracy's years of experience helped him succeed with his own company?
2. Do you think you would enjoy working for a full-service firm, such as Landvision Designs? Why or why not?
3. Research Landvision Designs and evaluate their website, mission statement, and logo. How do these components contribute to Landvision Designs' success?

Cultural Requirements

Selection of plant material should not be made entirely on aesthetics. In order to create landscapes that are sustainable, cultural requirements must be considered before plants are selected. Selecting plants with the appropriate characteristics needed to thrive helps create a more sustainable landscape. Palm trees, for example, would not survive the winter in the northern states but do very well in more tropical climates found in states such as Florida and Georgia.

Xeriscaping

Xeriscaping is an example of choosing plants that are well suited to their environment. It is often referred to as drought-tolerant landscaping. It is important to perform a complete site evaluation when planning a xeriscape to ensure an effective water-saving design. The designer must identify the qualities and characteristics of the property, including the following:

- The amount of sun exposure each area receives.
- The amount of existing shade and its duration in each area.
- The direction of summer breezes.
- Existing slopes and other topographical features.
- Soil types and modifications to increase water absorption and retention.
- The location of drainage problems.
- The locations where rainwater and runoff can be harvested.

Plant materials should be installed in the areas most suited to their cultural requirements. Plants with low water requirements, for example, typically do well in dry spots, windy areas, exposed areas, and those areas receiving full sun (south and west side of structures). Another principle of xeriscaping is grouping plants by water requirement. Using plants native to the area will also help the xeriscape become more efficient and sustainable. See **Figure 6-20**. Xeriscaping is commonly used in the arid, southwestern part of the United States where water is scarce. Cacti and succulents thrive in this environment.

A   *Kathryn Roach/Shutterstock.com*   B   *Todd Boland/Shutterstock.com*

C   *Mary Sisco/Shutterstock.com*   D   *val lawless/Shutterstock.com*

Figure 6-20. Xeriscaping involves grouping plants with similar moisture requirements. A—Mixtures of colorful flowers, native grasses, and stones cover the sloped area and provide erosion control. B—A mixture of colors and textures provides year-round interest in those low-maintenance landscape. C—Formal planting patterns and repetition can be used to increase visual interest. D—There is a surprising amount of color that can be incorporated into a xeriscape. Cacti, such as this prickly pear cactus, often present bright, beautiful blooms.

Summary

- Principles of design are used to achieve aesthetically pleasing results in all forms of art, including landscape design.

- The principles of design are balance, focalization, simplicity, rhythm, proportion, scale, and unity.

- Balance in landscape design is an even distribution of the visual weight of landscape materials. Types of balance include symmetrical, asymmetrical, and proximal.

- Focalization is the use of a focal point to force the viewer's attention to a particular location. A focal point is the area that constitutes that location. The focal point of a residence, for example, would be the front door.

- Simplicity in landscape design is limiting the variety of material, such as types of plants or different colors, used throughout the design. Too many species of plants create landscapes that are busy and not visually appealing.

- Rhythm describes the process of how the eye travels through the landscape.

- Proportion is the size relationship between materials used in the landscape. Large buildings require large plant material; small buildings require small plant materials.

- Scale is the size of one object in relation to the other objects in the design.

- Unity is the organization of all elements in a landscape design so that they appear to belong together.

- The elements of design can be described as the "ingredients" used in a design. The selection and blending of these ingredients is guided by the principles of design.

- The basic elements of design include line, form, texture, and color. Fragrance, size, and space may also be considered elements of design.

- Lines used in landscape design create or define the visual paths that draw our eyes through the landscape. Lines may be straight or curved and may be static or dynamic.

- Straight lines should be used sparingly in informal landscape designs, as they do not naturally occur in nature. Lines should be gently curved.

- Form is the shape or silhouette of individual plants or groups of plants. Using different forms creates visual interest.

- Texture is both the visual and tactile surface quality of a material.

- When the viewer is near the plantings, texture comes primarily from the size, shape, and spacing of the leaves and twigs. When viewed from a distance, texture comes from the plants as a whole.

- Color is one of the most striking elements of design. Color may refer to flower, stem, leaf, or fruit of the plant. Various color schemes are used to generate interest in the design.

Chapter Review

Know and Understand ⤴

Answer the following questions using the information provided in this chapter.

1. A form of balance in which one side of the landscape is a mirror image of the other is _____.
   A. visual balance
   B. symmetrical balance
   C. asymmetrical balance
   D. informal balance

2. The type of balance that is achieved by placing different combinations of materials that carry the same amount of visual weight on each side of the design is _____.
   A. symmetrical balance
   B. distal balance
   C. asymmetrical balance
   D. formal balance

3. The asymmetrical balance of elements on the central axis (right and left) as well as in the field of vision (near and far) is referred to as _____.
   A. proximal balance
   B. focal balance
   C. formal balance
   D. visual balance

4. The use of a focal point to direct the viewer's attention to a particular location is referred to as _____.
   A. rationalization
   B. proximation
   C. unification
   D. focalization

5. *True or False?* In residential landscaping, the home's front door is the standard focal point of the public living area.
   A. True.
   B. False.

6. The location of the focal point in a planting bed depends primarily on the _____.
   A. color of plant materials
   B. shape of the bed
   C. shape of the plants
   D. All of the above.

7. Limiting the variety of material, such as types of plants or different colors, used throughout the design is referred to as _____.
   A. rhythm
   B. scale
   C. simplicity
   D. unity

8. Which of the following design principles describes how the eye travels through the landscape?
   A. Rhythm.
   B. Unity.
   C. Simplicity.
   D. Proportion.

9. The size relationship between the materials used in the landscape and the landscape design as a whole is referred to as _____.
   A. focalization
   B. proportion
   C. rhythm
   D. balance

10. The size of one object in relation to the other objects in the design is referred to as _____.
    A. proportion
    B. focus
    C. proximity
    D. scale

11. *True or False?* Scale and proportion are the same principle of design.
    A. True.
    B. False.

12. The organization of all elements in a landscape design so that they appear to belong together is the design principle _____.
    A. destiny
    B. simplicity
    C. unity
    D. scrutiny

13. The "ingredients" used in a design are the _____.
    A. elements of design
    B. principles of design
    C. focus of design
    D. scales of design

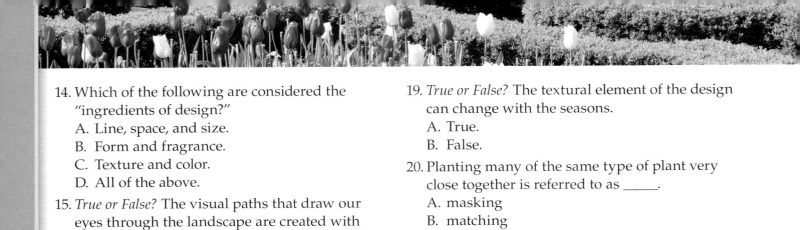

14. Which of the following are considered the "ingredients of design?"
    A. Line, space, and size.
    B. Form and fragrance.
    C. Texture and color.
    D. All of the above.

15. *True or False?* The visual paths that draw our eyes through the landscape are created with static or dynamic lines.
    A. True.
    B. False.

16. *True or False?* Perfectly straight lines are common in nature but should be used sparingly in formal designs.
    A. True.
    B. False.

17. Which of the following is the silhouette of individual plants or groups of plants?
    A. Static.
    B. Form.
    C. Line.
    D. All of the above.

18. The visual and tactile surface quality of a material is the surface _____.
    A. form
    B. shape
    C. texture
    D. line

19. *True or False?* The textural element of the design can change with the seasons.
    A. True.
    B. False.

20. Planting many of the same type of plant very close together is referred to as _____.
    A. masking
    B. matching
    C. massing
    D. All of the above.

21. Red, yellow, and blue are the _____.
    A. secondary colors
    B. tertiary colors
    C. primary colors
    D. All of the above.

22. *True or False?* The viewpoint from inside a building should be considered when designing a landscape.
    A. True.
    B. False.

23. *True or False?* The selection of plant material should be made primarily on aesthetics.
    A. True.
    B. False.

24. Drought-tolerant landscaping is referred to as _____.
    A. xeriscaping
    B. moonscaping
    C. desertscaping
    D. All of the above.

Thinking Critically

1. Where is xeriscaping the most likely to be used? Where is it least likely to be used? Explain your reasoning.

2. Could xeriscaping be used for soil erosion control? Explain your answer.

3. How could asymmetrical and symmetrical balance work together in a landscape design?

4. Where are the areas for improvement in sustainable landscape designs?

5. What is the importance of incorporating sustainability when applying the principles and elements of design?

Suggested Activities

1. Form teams and select different color schemes for each group. Create a landscape design for an annual flowerbed (8′ × 10′) using the color scheme. (The flowerbed is raised and can be seen from all four sides.) Price the components and determine the cost of materials for the project. Submit your designs and vote on the best design. Consider if each design incorporates the principles and elements discussed in the chapter.

2. Working in small groups, select landscaped areas on your school campus or in the local community and analyze the area in relation to principles and elements of design. What principles and elements are followed? Which can be improved?

3. Identify local nurseries and browse their current inventories online or in person. Create a list of plants that would be most suitable as foundation plants.

4. Work with a partner to design a pair of mixed containers that incorporate the current season's colors and plant materials. Implement all elements and principles of design while constructing your project.

5. Working in pairs or small groups, identify and photograph examples of the principles and elements of design you find in your home, school, or a business landscape. What examples of design focal points did you find? If time allows, create a slide presentation for the class. You may include poor designs and explain why the design does not work and how you would fix it.

6. Explain in your own words how you would change a local landscape so that it would include all of the elements and principles of design. You may also use images from the Internet.

7. Identify the types of plant growing containers that are used for nursery plants or other plants that are grown for landscape installations. Determine the advantages and disadvantages of each type of container, including cost, availability, and durability.

The Outdoor Room Concept

While studying this chapter, look for the activity icon to:
- **Practice** vocabulary terms with Words to Know activities.
- **Expand** learning with identification activities.
- **Reinforce** what you learn by completing Know and Understand questions.

G-WLEARNING.com

www.g-wlearning.com/agriculture

Chapter Outcomes

After studying this chapter, you will be able to:

- Identify the outdoor living areas in the landscape.
- Understand the importance of lot design in the creation of the landscape.
- Describe the different requirements and function for each area of the landscape.
- Understand the process of designing outdoor rooms.
- Identify materials used to create outdoor walls, ceilings, and floors.

Key Terms ↱

asphalt
awning
block stone
composite
concrete
flagstone
formal hedge
gazebo
gravel
ground cover
hard flooring
hedge
informal hedge
living area
mixed border

mulch
outdoor room concept
paver
pergola
privacy fence
property dimensions
public area
retaining wall
semi-privacy fence
service area
soft flooring
synthetic turf
turf
vine

Introduction

Designing a landscape is like designing an extension to someone's home. Outdoor space, just like indoor space, is used to spend time with family, entertain friends, and relax. Different areas of a landscape have different functions. As a landscape designer, you will work closely with the homeowner to determine the functions of the outdoor space in order to create an appropriate design, **Figure 7-1**. This chapter introduces the outdoor room concept and explains how you can apply this concept to create landscapes that are visually appealing as well as practical.

Figure 7-1. An outdoor room, such as this sitting area, is easily identified by its flooring, ceiling, and walls.

Outdoor Rooms

Every landscape will have different challenges and features that make the property and the project unique. The intended use, lot dimensions, property layout, and placement of the home are common factors that help determine the specific areas of the landscape. Local regulations, neighborhood policies, and homeowner associations may also determine the types of materials that can be used in a home's landscape. For example, a homeowner's association may regulate the type and color of mulch, type of fence, or type of swimming pool that may be installed, **Figure 7-2**. To avoid problems and installation delays,

Figure 7-2. Many homeowners' associations regulate landscaping designs and materials that can be used in public areas, such as mulch, which is available in a wide range of colors and materials.

designers must be familiar with all regulations that may affect their landscape design.

Just as each area of the home has a particular function, each area of the landscape should as well. These specific areas are referred to as outdoor rooms. The *outdoor room concept* states that each area of the landscape is assigned a certain function. These areas are divided into three types of spaces: the living area, the public area, and the service area.

Living Area

The *living area* is commonly referred to as the backyard of the residence and is usually more private than the rest of the property. The living area is typically a place to host cookouts, play yard games, or just relax in the sun. When designing the living area, the location of common features, such as grills, patio furniture, and fire pits, must be considered, **Figure 7-3**. The living area may also include a large, open expanse of lawn and recreational components, such as a pool, sauna, or hot tub. Entry points from the home to the living area must also be considered. Whether the main entry is from the family room, kitchen, or other common area, it is necessary to design a smooth transition that complements the home and living area.

Public Area

The *public area* is commonly referred to as the front yard. The public area should complement the home's architecture and create an inviting space. The public area typically is not designed to provide living space and, depending on the owner's preferences, may include components such as ornamental plant materials, water features, garden statues, and a decorative walkway. The public area may or may not include a large expanse of lawn.

Artazum/Shutterstock.com

Figure 7-3. The backyard is popular with families as an outdoor living area. The landscape may include soft and hard materials.

Figure 7-4. The front door is the focal point of the public area. Front doors are often painted a bright or dark color to attract the viewer's eye.

Figure 7-5. A garden shed is made into an attractive area of the landscape using proper plant selection. The informal plantings complement the shed's stone walls.

The landscape should be designed to draw the eye to the front door because it is the focal point (area of emphasis) of the public area, **Figure 7-4**. Plant material and the walkway may be used to draw the eye and guide visitors to the front door. The foundation plants, trees, and shrubs used around the home will also help soften the lines of the structure. Driveways are typically a prominent component of the public area and should be incorporated into the design. Driveways should also provide safe and efficient parking space.

The landscape design for the public area should also incorporate elements that will add interest throughout the year. This is especially important in climates that experience significant changes from season to season.

Service Area

The service area is often the smallest area of a landscape but it is of tremendous importance. The *service area* of a landscape provides the homeowner with functional space for components that are necessary but not necessarily attractive. When designing a landscape, space must be allocated for typical home components, such as air conditioning units, fuel tanks, trash can storage, and toolsheds.

Depending on the lot, the service area can be made very attractive with proper plant selection and/or structures, **Figure 7-5**. The goal of a well-planned service area is to hide items from view but still allow convenient access. Service areas should be placed in spaces that will not hinder the use of the family living area or detract from the aesthetic value of the public area. The plants and structures used for service areas must not negatively affect the component's function, such as blocking the airflow for an air conditioning unit or access to a fuel tank.

Home and Landscape Connections

When designing a landscape, designers must consider connections to the home's interior. The plant materials and structures used in the landscape should not impede or obstruct any part of the structure. For example, if the front living room of the home features a large window, the landscape components situated in front of the window should not block the view. This applies to the time of installation as well as to the landscape as it reaches maturity. Another example would be French doors that swing out into the living area. Features of the landscape design must not block the doors or endanger someone who may be sitting on patio furniture outside the doors.

Property Size, Layout, and Shape

As stated earlier, the intended use, placement of the home, property (lot) dimensions, and property layout are common factors that help determine the specific areas of a landscape. Although the layout and size of each area will vary, all designs should incorporate living, public, and service areas.

Intended Use

When designing outdoor rooms, a designer must first discuss the homeowner's intended use for the property. The intended use of the property often dictates which areas will receive the most emphasis and space. A homeowner with a large family may prefer a large, open lawn as the primary space in the living area whereas a homeowner with several small dogs may prefer a small lawn area.

Placement of Home

The placement of the home will dictate the location of each area. The designer must incorporate existing entry points from the home to the living area, public area, and service area. Other prominent features of the home and lot, such as windows and property lines, must also be considered.

Property Dimensions

The *property dimensions* (the length and width of the lot) will dictate the size of the areas. The dimensions and layout of the lot can create potential challenges for the landscape designer. For example, a corner lot is typically exposed to public view on at least two sides, **Figure 7-6**. If the homeowner requests that a large area of the yard be used as living space, extra structures or plant material may be needed to provide the homeowner with the desired level of privacy. There may also be additional restrictions on the proximity of landscape structure, such as fences, to the street or public sidewalk.

M. Niebuhr/Shutterstock.com

Figure 7-6. A great deal of the landscape of a corner lot is often exposed to public view.

Property dimensions will also dictate the size of the plants and structures needed to maintain logical proportions. Large spaces, such as a university quad, require larger plants or structures in order to create a landscape that suits the area.

Property Layout

The property layout, or shape, may also present design challenges. Builders will lay out a subdivision to maximize the number of homes that can be constructed. This typically results in oddly shaped lots. Some lots are wider in either the front or back, and others may be long and narrow. Lots that are wider in the front and narrower in the back provide ample public area and limit the living area. Lots that are long and narrow may have limited public area and a living area with little privacy. These types of lots may require additional creativity to design a landscape that meets all of a homeowner's requirements.

Outdoor Room Components

What structural components make up the interior of your home? The walls, ceilings, and floors of a home define the rooms, separating living areas from service areas and creating private and public spaces. These same components and divisions are incorporated into outdoor rooms to help define the outdoor spaces.

A wide range of materials can be used to create outdoor walls, ceilings, and floors. The design and selection of these components helps to create the overall theme and mood the homeowner desires. Each of the materials used to create the walls, ceilings, and floors have distinct advantages and disadvantages that must be considered before adding them to the design. Appearance, quality, and duration are the major qualities used to determine which materials should be used.

Walls

Outdoor walls often serve multiple functions. They may be made with a single type of material or a combination of materials. Walls may be used to:

- Frame the property.
- Provide privacy.
- Control the flow of traffic.
- Create a border, **Figure 7-7**.
- Indicate property dimensions.
- Confine pets and livestock to a specific area.
- Direct the eye to a focal point.
- Block an undesirable view.

The type of material used and the dimensions of a wall depend on many factors, including the homeowner's budget, size of the lot, proximity to neighbors, and local or residential restrictions. The type of material used will also be determined by the function the wall is to serve. For example, a homeowner

A
Spiroview Inc/Shutterstock.com

B
Jamie Hooper/Shutterstock.com

Figure 7-7. A—Walls can be used to help frame an area to minimize foot traffic. B—A neatly trimmed hedge provides a backdrop for the colorful annuals.

Hands-On Landscaping

Living Walls

A homeowner may not care to put in a fence but still want some privacy or to block something unattractive. A living wall created with plant materials is often a welcome option. Some landscaper designers prefer broadleaf evergreens with a mature height of at least 6′ because they fill in nicely and remain green throughout the year. Plants spaced too far apart will take longer to create an effective wall and may never form the desired wall if they do not grow wide enough. Spacing plants too close may cause them to appear clustered and may hamper their growth. Use the following steps to determine the number of plants needed to create an effective wall.

1. Measure the length of the area where the wall will be installed.
2. Check the spacing requirement of the plant used to create the hedge.
3. Divide the distance (length) by the spacing requirement and add one to determine the number of plants needed. Adding one to the total will ensure that there is a full plant on each end.

Example: If the length of the wall is 15′ and the Leyland cypress being installed requires spacing between 3′ and 6′, how many plants will be required?

15 ÷ 3 = 5
5 + 1= 6
Six Leyland cypress plants are needed.

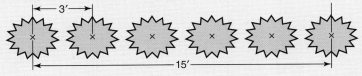

Consider This

1. Identify 2 to 3 other types of plants that would work well as a living wall. Research their spacing requirements and determine how many of each type would be needed to create a wall that is 15′ long.
2. Are there any living walls in your neighborhood? With permission from the landowner, measure the wall and note what type of plant is used and how many are in the wall. Is the wall full or is there too much open space for it to be effective as a privacy wall? Determine why the wall is/is not effective.

located in a residential setting with homes on either side of the lot may prefer a privacy fence that will not only provide privacy, but also prevent small children or pets from wandering off the property. This same type of privacy fence would be impractical for a home located in a rural setting on a large lot. A split-rail fence might be a more viable option in such a setting. Walls in a landscape may be constructed with either plant or construction materials, or a combination of the two.

Creating Walls Using Plant Material

Plant material is one of the most common and inexpensive materials used to create walls for outdoor rooms, **Figure 7-8**. However, walls created with plants often require more time and maintenance. The time needed to fill in a space and create the desired effect will depend on the plant selected.

A *hedge* is a row of shrubs used to create walls and borders. Although multiple plant species may be used, it is more typical to use the same plant throughout the hedge. In order for a plant to be used as a hedge or border, the plant must possess several characteristics, including:

- A thick, dense growth habit from the base of the plant to the tip.
- When used for privacy, the plant should be evergreen, not deciduous (seasonally shedding its leaves).
- Have a mature height that fulfills its intended purpose. For example, if the wall is going to be used for privacy, the plant must grow to a height of at least 6'.
- Physical appeal that also provides interest to the installation.

The style of a wall created with plant materials can vary to suit the landscape design. The two forms of hedges used to create walls are formal and informal.

Formal Hedges

Formal hedges are created with plants that are kept trimmed to appear uniform in size. Depending on the climate, formal hedges often require maintenance throughout the year, **Figure 7-9**. Plants that are easily sheered, such as

Smolina Marianna/Shutterstock.com

vitmore/Shutterstock.com

Figure 7-8. Walls constructed with plants often require an extended growth period to reach the desired height. These types of walls require a great deal of maintenance.

certain species of boxwoods and hollies, are typically used to create a formal hedge. Formal hedges may be used to provide privacy, create patterns, or add interest to the landscape. This type of hedge should only be used if the homeowner is willing to maintain its shape consistently. This is particularly important if a formal hedge is selected as a wall between two different properties.

Informal Hedges

Informal hedges are created with a single plant species that are allowed to grow into their natural shapes and height. An informal hedge does not require as much maintenance as a formal hedge because it is not regularly pruned to a uniform shape and height. Informal hedges have a different appearance and may not be appropriate for all landscape designs. Informal hedges may be used to provide privacy, **Figure 7-10**.

Mixed Borders

Installing a mixed border is another method of using plant material to create an outdoor wall. *Mixed borders* are created using a blend of several species of plant material, allowing the designer to incorporate plants of varying height, texture, and color into the design. Mixed borders are often used in front of privacy hedges to add interest to the landscape. When created with evergreens, the privacy hedge provides a backdrop throughout the year while the mixed border provides seasonal interest, **Figure 7-11**.

Peter Turner Photography/Shutterstock.com

Figure 7-9. Formal hedges make beautiful privacy walls when they are full and thick, making it difficult for animals or people to pass through.

Christopher D. Hart

Figure 7-10. Informal hedges may feature one type of plant material or a mixture of trees or shrubs. Informal hedges do not require as much maintenance as formal hedges.

A   *romakoma/Shutterstock.com*

B   *Del Boy/Shutterstock.com*

Figure 7-11. A—A row of column-shaped evergreens provide screening from the neighboring home. B—A mixed border featuring annuals and perennials provides color to the landscape in the early spring.

Figure 7-12. Vines require a structure, such as a trellis or arbor, on which to grow. The design of the structure determines the amount of privacy the vines provide.

Vines

A *vine* is a woody-stemmed plant that is capable of climbing up and across a structure. Vines are excellent options to create a living wall. Vines require a dedicated structure to grow efficiently and provide maximum coverage, **Figure 7-12**. Structures for vines may be as simple as a few posts anchored in the ground with wire pulled taught between the posts to an ornate trellis. Vines may be selected for their leaf color, flower color, fragrance, growth habit, or texture. Care must be taken to ensure the vines do not overcrowd their dedicated area. Vines may also be used to soften or cover a structure, such as a privacy fence.

Creating Walls Using Building Materials

Building materials, such as stone, metal, wood, composite, and vinyl, may also be used to create walls for outdoor rooms. These materials provide the client and designer with a wide variety of options to select the perfect pattern, design, and material for the landscape. Building materials vary in cost, durability, and their ease of installation.

Stone

Stone is one of the most expensive materials used to create walls. It also requires a substantial amount of labor and skill to install, **Figure 7-13**. When using stone to create a wall, the designer often incorporates it as a primary point of interest because it tends to become a focal point.

Stone may be used alone, combined with other materials, and in formal or informal landscapes. It may be used to provide privacy or define the boundaries of a space. Stone is also used in the formation of retaining walls. *Retaining walls* are used to hold back soil and allow for the change in topography of

Figure 7-13. Stone used to build hardscapes comes in a wide variety of shapes, colors, and sizes. The stone used in a hardscape should complement the home.

the site. (Retaining walls are also referred to as *dry stack walls* as they require no mortar and are placed dry.) Ornamental caps can be added to retaining walls, providing seating along the length of the retaining wall. Plant material draping over the sides of a retaining wall creates accents, **Figure 7-14**.

Metal

Wrought iron, aluminum, and chain link are the most commonly used metal fence materials. Metal fencing is used to create a border that allows the landscape to be viewed from either side. Metal fencing is often used when a client requires a secure border that does not necessarily need to create privacy.

Elena Elisseeva/Shutterstock.com

Figure 7-14. Retaining walls built with natural stones are visually appealing. Plants selected to be used around and in the retaining wall should complement the building material.

- Wrought iron fencing is one of the more expensive fence materials, **Figure 7-15A**. It is strong and durable and provides ample security. Wrought iron, which is typically painted black, may require repainting over time to inhibit rust.
- Aluminum fencing is lightweight, strong, and available in designs that mimic traditional cast iron fence designs. It is also very low-maintenance.
- Chain link fencing is an economical choice where division and visibility are both needed, **Figure 7-15B**. It is functional but not as attractive as wrought iron and aluminum fencing.

Metal fencing can be very ornate or simple in its design. It is commonly used around water features such as swimming pools where fencing is required for safety. Metal fencing can also be used in combination with stone or brick to create unique rhythm, **Figure 7-15C**.

Wood

Wood is a used to create borders and privacy fences. It is extremely versatile and available in a wide variety of styles, shapes, and sizes, **Figure 7-16**. Wood fencing can easily be customized to suit the landscape design and meet the client's needs. Wood fencing typically comes in prefabricated sections, ensuring consistency in its design and making installation easier. Wood fencing may be painted or stained to add additional interest. The wood used should be treated to ensure many years of use. Wood fencing requires periodic maintenance to maintain its aesthetic value and to ensure its durability.

Vinyl

Vinyl fencing is durable, virtually maintenance-free, and available in a wide variety of sizes, shapes, and colors. Vinyl fencing materials will not fade, warp, or splinter and do not require painting or staining. Most vinyl posts are hollow and include a section of pressure-treated lumber to add stability, **Figure 7-17**. Sections of pressure-treated wood are also used inside vinyl rails for rail-type fences and in vinyl fence panels to add stability. Vinyl fencing is more expensive to install initially, but is less expensive in the end because it requires very little maintenance.

A

kryzhob/Shutterstock.com

B

Goodheart-Willcox Publisher

C

Goodheart-Willcox Publisher

Figure 7-15. A—Wrought iron fencing is often highly detailed to create elegant fencing. B—Chain link fences securely enclose the selected area. C—A combination of wrought iron and brick create a unique fencing style.

Composite

Composite fences are relatively new to the market. *Composite* fences are made from a combination of recycled wood and plastic. They are very similar to vinyl fences but have more stability. Some styles of composite fencing also use pressure-treated wood inserts to ensure the fence's stability. Composite

romakoma/Shutterstock.com

Figure 7-16. A wooden privacy fence with a lattice top provides privacy to the homeowner. The ornamental lattice adds interest to the fence and landscape.

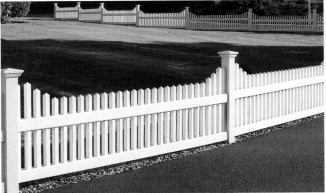

Christian Delbert/Shutterstock.com

Figure 7-17. Vinyl fences are available in different heights, colors, and styles. This durable, vinyl picket fence requires little maintenance and will provide years of service.

fencing comes in a wide variety of styles and has a long life. Decking is also commonly made out of composite materials.

Fence Styles

Once the material that works best for the design has been selected, the appropriate fencing style can be determined. The fence style used will be based on its aesthetic value and the functions it will serve. There are many fencing styles available, including privacy, semi-privacy, picket, lattice, and rail-type fences.

Privacy Fences

As the name implies, *privacy fences* are used to provide privacy to the outdoor area. Privacy fences commonly line the living area, separating it from the public areas. They are often placed along property lines. In order to provide privacy, privacy fences must be at least 6′ tall.

Privacy fences are available in a wide variety of shapes and styles, including scallop, arch, and board-on-board. The top edge of a *scallop fence* rises and falls. The lowest point in the pattern is typically in the middle of the panel, **Figure 7-18**. *Arch fences* are at their highest point in the middle of the panel. Scallop and arch designs help create visual movement. *Board-on-board fences* provide aesthetically pleasing views from both sides of the fence.

Semi-privacy fences are similar to privacy fences but are designed with more space between boards. Semi-privacy fences provide privacy but also allow light to pass through from either side. These types of fences are typically more ornate in design. Semi-privacy and privacy fences may have a combination of scallop, arch, and lattice designs at the top of the panels to create additional interest, **Figure 7-19**.

Picket Fences

Picket fences are commonly used to create borders and do not provide privacy, **Figure 7-20**. *Picket fences* are composed of three parts: the post, rail, and picket. The vertical pickets are attached to the rail and spaced less than 4″ apart. Picket fences may be scalloped or arched to provide additional interest. Picket fences range in height and can be made of wood, vinyl, composite, or metal. The spacing between the pickets allows viewing through the fence. Decorative rails and rail caps can also be used to create additional interest.

Gertan/Shutterstock.com   *Baloncici/Shutterstock.com*

AlinaMD/Shutterstock.com   *Man of the Mountain/Shutterstock.com*

Figure 7-18. Wood is an extremely versatile fence material that provides interest as well as security and privacy.

romakoma/Shutterstock.com

Figure 7-19. Semi-privacy fences feature open spaces between construction materials. The space allows for added interest while also providing privacy.

Susan Law Cain/Shutterstock.com

Figure 7-20. Picket fences included in the public area of the landscape set boundaries and add character to the home and landscape.

Lattice Fences

A *lattice fence* consists of strips of wood or vinyl that are crossed and fastened to the cross section of the panels or posts. Space is left between the strips to create a pattern of diamond- or square-shaped spaces. If the fence panels are made entirely with lattice, the fence will allow viewing from either side. Lattice is often used across the top of privacy fences to create interest.

Lattice fences create a unique pattern of lines that are visually appealing. Wood lattice is more rigid and easier to install than vinyl lattice. The design of lattice fencing makes it difficult to paint or stain.

Rail Fences

Rail fences are commonly used to establish property lines, as ornamental fences, or to contain livestock. *Rail fences* commonly feature two or three horizontal rails. Two common types of rail-type fences are the split-rail and the post-and-rail. *Split-rail fences* require special posts with cutouts into which the rails are inserted. The rails on a post-and-rail fence are attached to the posts with nails or screws. Post-and-rail fences do not require special posts and are less expensive to construct than split-rail fences.

Contemporary Fences

Just as landscaping is an art form, fence construction can be as well. Contemporary fences take advantage of being a dominant feature of the landscape and automatically become the focal point. Contemporary fences use color and unconventional materials, such as recycled pallets, shutters, roofing material, and even scrap metal, **Figure 7-21**. The design possibilities and types of materials to be used are endless and limited only by the artist's imagination.

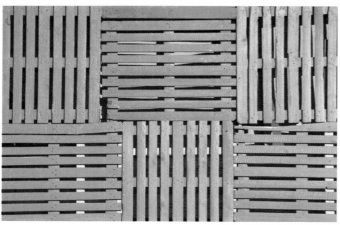

Tony Baggett/Shutterstock.com

Figure 7-21. Recycled pallets, painted orange, create a unique fencing alternative.

Flooring

Outdoor flooring is one of the most important aspects of the landscape because it is often the most abundant component and easily sets the tone for the design. The type of flooring used is determined primarily by the purpose of the outdoor space. For example, a soft material, such as turf, is typically used for large, open expanses in a living area that are intended for recreation and a hard material, such as concrete or stone, is typically used around an in-ground pool.

Outdoor flooring materials are divided into two categories: soft materials and hard materials. Soft flooring materials include many organic materials, such as turf, live ground covers, and mulch. Hard flooring is typically composed of organic or inorganic materials, such as wood, composite, concrete, stone, gravel, and asphalt. Flooring materials vary greatly in their costs, level of maintenance, and durability.

Soft Flooring

Soft flooring is used to create soft and comfortable outdoor flooring. Most soft flooring is selected for its ease of installation and low initial cost. Many soft flooring materials also capture heat from the sun and help cool the landscape. In addition, soft flooring provides a comfortable and safe surface for outdoor recreation.

Natural Turf

Turf is the most common type of flooring used in landscapes; however, it can be one of the most expensive to establish and maintain. Few components of the landscape can create as much impact as a well-groomed lawn, **Figure 7-22**.

SingjaiStock/Shutterstock.com

karamysh/Shutterstock.com

Figure 7-22. A large expanse of healthy and well-tended turfgrass greatly affects the landscape design. The viewer's eye will travel along the lawn to other plant materials.

There are many varieties of turf and each one of these varieties will thrive when planted in the proper location. A turf variety should be selected based on its characteristics, including:

- Whether it is a cool season or warm season turf.
- Wear-resistance (the amount of wear and tear the turf will tolerate).
- Drought tolerance and irrigation needs.
- Shade tolerance and light requirement.

The type of soil and level of drainage in a lot will also affect the turf's ability to thrive. Turf grasses and their establishment are discussed in detail later in the text.

Figure 7-23. Synthetic turf is used for areas that are exposed to high amounts of foot traffic.

Synthetic Turf

Synthetic turf is an alternative to natural turf for outdoor flooring. Synthetic turf is manufactured and requires little to no maintenance. Synthetic turf requires no water and is an alternative to turf in areas with limited rainfall. A variety of synthetic turfs resembling natural varieties is available. Synthetic turf has a high initial cost but costs very little to maintain and is very durable. Synthetic turf is commonly used on professional athletic fields, **Figure 7-23**.

Ground Covers

Ground covers can provide many of the same benefits of turf without the high-level maintenance, **Figure 7-24**. *Ground covers* are plants with spreading growth habits that typically reach a height of 18″ or less. Established ground covers require little maintenance when compared to other areas of the landscape. Select ground covers have excellent wear resistance and durability.

Figure 7-24. Ground covers are excellent flooring alternatives to turf. Ground covers require much less maintenance than turf and can feature unique textures and flowers.

Some ground covers can be mowed to control height. Some species have the added bonus of colorful blooms in the spring.

Mulch

Most landscape designs include areas containing mulch. *Mulch* is a decorative as well as beneficial landscape flooring material. It adds color and texture, holds moisture, prevents weeds, and adds nutrients to the soil as it decomposes. A few of the many mulching materials available include pine bark nuggets, pine straw, shredded hardwood, cocoa or pecan shells, and cypress. Inorganic mulch materials include decorative stones, such as white gravel or lava rock, brick chips, and recycled shredded rubber, **Figure 7-25**. Mulch materials are often installed as playground flooring to provide cushioning that helps prevent injury.

Christopher D. Hart

Figure 7-25. Various materials are used to create flooring in landscape designs. The asphalt parking lot and concrete walkways provide area for parking and walking. The use of pine straw mulch helps to prevent weeds in the flowerbed as well as hold moisture.

Hard Flooring

Hard flooring is used in outdoor rooms to provide a durable surface for high-traffic areas and to provide a level surface for outdoor furniture. Materials, such as wood, concrete, stone, paving blocks, brick, and asphalt, are commonly used to create walkways, driveways, and patios. Hard flooring materials and their installation have a higher initial cost than soft flooring. Flooring should be selected carefully as it often becomes a predominant component of the landscape. Depending on the material, hard flooring will reflect heat, raise the temperature of the space, and be hot to the touch.

Asphalt

Asphalt is a popular option to line pathways, driveways, and roads that receive high levels of foot traffic, **Figure 7-26**. *Asphalt* is a mixture of tar, sand, and gravel. Although asphalt is a hard paving material, it is softer than other hard paving surfaces, such as concrete or stone. Asphalt must be sealed periodically to prevent cracking and chipping.

Concrete

Concrete is an expensive, hard paving material made with water, aggregate, and powdered cement. Concrete is commonly used to construct front walks and driveways

Shuang Li/Shutterstock.com

Figure 7-26. Walkways that receive high amounts of foot traffic are commonly covered in hard paving materials, such as asphalt, to prevent compaction.

where there are large amounts of foot traffic. Concrete provides a solid, neat, and durable flooring. Concrete surfaces can be texturized to help provide traction in wet conditions and colored or stamped to add more interest.

Wood

Wood is commonly used to construct decks, walkways, and functional or decorative bridges, **Figure 7-27**. Pressure-treated wood should be used to aid in the prevention of rotting and twisting of the wood. Wood can be painted or stained to change its color. The design and installation of decks and patios are subject to local building regulations and codes. Some residential codes also dictate the type of material and design that may be used.

Gravel

Different colors and sizes of *gravel* (small pieces of loose rock) can be used as an ornamental ground cover. Rock is durable, long lasting, and provides texture, color, and interest to the landscape. Unique designs can be created using combinations of rocks of different sizes and colors. Rocks can also be placed on steep banks to help prevent erosion. Gravel can also be used in various shapes, such as in circles or waves of colors.

Pavers and Block Stone

Pavers and *block stone* are terms used to describe hard paving materials made of brick or cement. Pavers and block stone are prefabricated in various shapes and sizes. They are available in a variety of colors and textures and provide many options to create unique outdoor flooring. Standard paving patterns may be used with one or more types of pavers to create patios and walkways. Brick paving patterns include running bond, herringbone, basket weave, and stack bond, **Figure 7-28**. Pavers and block stone are usually applied on a base

Christopher D. Hart

Figure 7-27. A wooden zigzag bridge at the Sarah P. Duke Gardens in Durham, North Carolina, connects two areas of the garden.

A

R. Lee Ivy

Herringbone 45°

Herringbone 90°

Stack bond

Stack bond 45°

Basket weave

Basket weave variation

Stretcher or running bond

Stretcher or running bond 45°

B

Liubou Yasiukovich/Shutterstock.com

Figure 7-28. A—A combination of different materials creates a striking image in a walkway. B—The variety of paving patterns available give the client many options to create flooring that fulfills their vision for the landscape.

of compacted gravel and sand without the use of mortar. When installed properly, this type of flooring is long-lasting and requires little maintenance.

Outdoor Tiles

Outdoor tiles are thinner than pavers and block stone and made from a variety of materials, such as ceramic, porcelain, glass, and travertine, **Figure 7-29**. Tile is installed with a thin layer of mortar on a concrete slab. Once the tile is installed, grout is spread between the tiles and the finished surface is sealed. Outdoor tiles are hard and durable and can be made to simulate the look of other flooring materials, such as wood and stone. Tile flooring is low maintenance but long-lasting when installed properly.

Career Connection

Edward Furner

Edward Furner, Premier Service Director for Mariani Landscape

Edward Furner is the Premier Service Director for Mariani Landscape in Lake Bluff, Illinois, which is currently the largest residentially focused design/build and maintenance firm in the United States. With over 17 years of experience at Mariani, Furner successfully wears many different hats. Furner is responsible for managing quality and service expectations for Mariani's Premier residential and commercial accounts, performing quarterly site inspections, which generate comprehensive opportunity assessments, and relaying this information to production and sales teams to help keep these accounts on track to meet Mariani's quality standards.

Furner is also an employee recruiter and internal maintenance consultant for the maintenance sales team. He helps the team troubleshoot challenging client situations and offer best practices to help navigate the team toward continued success. Another role Edward enjoys is being the lead contact for the rotating summer internship program. The program brings students from around the United States to explore all aspects of Mariani to help them define a career path in the green industry, ideally with Mariani.

Edward contributes his success in part to the opportunities he enjoyed while studying at SUNY Coblekskill University and completing several internships in three different geographic regions of the United States. His participation as chair in collegiate landscape competitions, dedication as a long-time Landscape Management Committee member, and commitment to the NALP has also paid off in industry networking and within the Mariani ranks.

Furner, who is Landscape Industry Certified, was recognized in *Lawn & Landscape* magazine in 2007 as one of "The Top 35 under 35" in the landscape industry as one of 35 young professionals who are molding the industry's future. Edward continues to push the envelope in regards to improvements at Mariani Landscape and the industry as a whole.

Edward offers the following advice to those seeking a career in the green industry: "There will only be a few unique employment opportunities that present themselves in your life. Don't shy away from taking a risk, even if it takes you away from home or your comfort zone, as these opportunities are often once in a lifetime."

Consider This

1. What types of professional and personal skills does Edward Furner possess that allow him to work well in so many areas of the company?
2. Would you be willing to take a risk when a new and possibly unique employment opportunity presented itself?

Flagstone

Flagstone is used to describe stone that is cut in horizontal layers, **Figure 7-30A**. Flagstone comes in irregular shapes, which are used to create unique mosaic-type flooring. Flagstone may also be trimmed to traditional shapes and set in conventional patterns. Flagstone should be applied to a firmly compacted gravel base. The spaces between the stone will vary depending on the design, **Figure 7-30B**. These spaces can be filled in with any soft flooring material, such as gravel, ground covers, or even turf.

Wutthikrai Busayaporn/Shutterstock.com

JR-stock/Shutterstock.com

Figure 7-29. Tile is common in areas that are used for dining and entertaining. The tile can be bold with a lively and interesting pattern or subtle and elegant, displaying the natural colors and designs of the stone.

A   Elena Elisseeva/Shutterstock.com

B   packspace/Shutterstock.com

Figure 7-30. A—Flagstone may be cut into geometric shapes or used in its natural form to create a traditional path. B—The amount of spacing used between the flagstone pieces helps create different patterns.

Ceilings

Ceilings often serve aesthetic and practical purposes. The ceiling of an outdoor room typically provides protection from the elements, frames the room, and adds interest to the landscape. Ceilings may be created with manufactured or natural materials and may or may not be a permanent part of the landscape. Manufactured structures, such as awnings, gazebos, and pergolas, are commonly used in a landscape to provide homeowners with significant shelter from the elements.

Awnings

Awnings are outdoor ceilings typically made with flexible materials attached to a frame, which is attached to a structure, such as a wall, **Figure 7-31**. Awnings may be retractable to allow the homeowner coverage flexibility. Awnings are typically custom-made, allowing the homeowner to choose a color or pattern that best suits the landscape.

You Touch Pix of EuToch/Shutterstock.com

Figure 7-31. A retractable awning enables the homeowner to adjust the amount of sunlight that reaches the sitting area.

Gazebos

A *gazebo* is a permanent structure with a covered canopy and ornamental posts and railings. A gazebo can be used to provide a private space that is protected from the elements. Gazebos are usually made with wood but may also be made with other materials, such as stone, **Figure 7-32.** Vines and hanging plants may be used to add more interest and increase privacy.

Roberto Sorin/Shutterstock.com

Nalidsa/Shutterstock.com

Figure 7-32. Gazebos may be constructed of wood and feature ornamental posts and railings. The style and material used for a gazebo should match the style of the garden.

Pergolas

A *pergola* is a structure with openly spaced boards running perpendicular to each other across the top. Pergolas typically do not have sides, creating an open, airy outdoor room, **Figure 7-33**. Climbing plants are used on pergolas to create unique social areas with some protection from the elements. Trees may also be used to provide shade and interest to the space.

Trees and Shrubs

Trees and tall shrubs may also help create ceilings in outdoor rooms. Homeowners can choose from a wide variety of plant material and may choose plants for seasonal color, flowers, and the density of its leaves. Trees and shrubs should be selected carefully to avoid overpowering the room. These plant materials require maintenance to keep the desired shape and prevent them from imposing on the space. If deciduous plant material is selected, additional maintenance may be required in order to keep the outdoor room neat, **Figure 7-34**.

Christopher D. Hart

Figure 7-33. A pergola covered in wisteria is a fine addition to the landscape. Plants used on pergolas may be chosen for their floral or foliage display or for the fruit they bear, such as grapes.

Captainlookchoob/Shutterstock.com

Figure 7-34. Plant material provides unique characteristics when used as ceiling material. Decks are often built around existing trees to provide a natural shade source.

Summary

- The landscape should be an extension of the home. Windows tie the interior of the home to the outdoors.
- Before the first draft of the landscape is developed, one should have a complete understanding of how the homeowner intends to use their property.
- Just as different rooms of the home serve different functions, different parts of the landscape should as well.
- Three main areas of the landscape are the living area, public area, and service area.
- The living area should be secluded from public view.
- The living area provides areas for outdoor recreation and relaxation.
- The public area is located in the front of the property and provides the first impression of the property.
- The service area provides functional space for storage and typical home components, such as air conditioning units, fuel tanks, trash can storage, and toolsheds.
- The outdoor room is created using walls, floors, and ceilings.
- The materials selected help create the theme of the landscape.
- Outdoor walls are used to frame the property, control traffic flow, create borders, provide privacy, indicate property boundaries, block undesirable views, and contain animals.
- Outdoor flooring is one of the most important aspects of the landscape because it is often the most abundant component and easily sets the tone for the design.
- Multiple types of soft and hard flooring materials are used throughout the landscape.
- Ceilings serve aesthetic and practical purposes. The ceiling of an outdoor room typically provides protection from the elements, frames the room, and adds interest to the landscape.

Chapter Review

Know and Understand ↪

Answer the following questions using the information provided in this chapter.

1. Which of the following factors help determine the specific areas of the landscape?
   A. Lot dimensions.
   B. Property layout.
   C. Placement of home.
   D. All of the above.

2. The backyard of a residence, which is usually more private than the rest of the property, is referred to as the _____.
   A. public area
   B. service area
   C. living area
   D. common area

3. The front yard of a residence is commonly referred to as the _____.
   A. public area
   B. service area
   C. living area
   D. common area

4. The area of emphasis of the front yard is the _____.
   A. walkway
   B. garage door
   C. front door
   D. driveway

5. The area of a landscape that provides the homeowner with functional space for less attractive components is the _____.
   A. public area
   B. service area
   C. living area
   D. common area

6. *True or False?* The home's interior has no impact on the landscape design.
   A. True.
   B. False.

7. *True or False?* Appearance, quality, and duration are the major qualities used to determine which materials should be used to construct an outdoor room.
   A. True.
   B. False.

8. The type of material used and the dimensions of an outdoor wall depend on many factors, including the _____.
   A. size of the lot
   B. proximity to neighbors
   C. homeowner's budget
   D. All of the above.

9. *True or False?* Plants used to create a wall for privacy should be deciduous.
   A. True.
   B. False.

10. *True or False?* A formal hedge should only be used if the homeowner is willing to maintain its shape.
    A. True.
    B. False.

11. *True or False?* Wrought iron is the most economical choice of metal fencing.
    A. True.
    B. False.

12. A picket fence is composed of _____.
    A. pickets
    B. rails
    C. posts
    D. All of the above.

13. Fencing that consists of strips of wood or vinyl that are crossed and fastened to the cross section of panels or posts is a _____.
    A. lattice fence
    B. picket fence
    C. rail fence
    D. bar fence

14. Which of the following is one of the most important aspects of an outdoor space because it is often the most abundant component and easily sets the tone for the design?
    A. Flower colors.
    B. Outdoor flooring.
    C. Wall material.
    D. Ceiling material.

15. Which of the following is used as soft flooring in outdoor rooms?
    A. Natural turf.
    B. Synthetic turf.
    C. Ground cover.
    D. All of the above.

16. Plants with spreading growth habits that are used to create soft flooring are _____.
    A. synthetic covers
    B. ground covers
    C. turf covers
    D. All of the above.

17. Which of the following materials is used to create hard flooring for outdoor rooms?
    A. Asphalt and brick.
    B. Stone and concrete.
    C. Wood and pavers.
    D. All of the above.

18. *True or False?* Ceilings may be created with manmade or natural materials and may or may not be a permanent part of the landscape.
    A. True.
    B. False.

19. Outdoor ceilings typically made with flexible materials attached to a frame, which is attached to a structure, are referred to as _____.
    A. frames
    B. pergolas
    C. gazebos
    D. awnings

20. A permanent structure with a covered canopy and ornamental posts and railings is referred to as a(n) _____.
    A. frame
    B. pergola
    C. gazebo
    D. awning

21. A ceiling structure with openly spaced boards running perpendicular to each other across the top is referred to as a(n) _____.
    A. frame
    B. pergola
    C. gazebo
    D. awning

Match the terms to the appropriate descriptions in 22–33.
    A. composite fencing
    B. formal hedge
    C. hedge
    D. informal hedge
    E. metal fencing
    F. mixed border
    G. privacy fence
    H. retaining wall
    I. semi-privacy fence
    J. stone
    K. vine
    L. vinyl fencing
    M. wood fencing

22. A constructed wall that is used to hold back soil and allow for the change in topography of a site.

23. One of the most expensive materials used to create outdoor walls.

24. A fencing material made from a combination of recycled wood and plastic.

25. A row of shrubs that is kept trimmed to appear uniform in size.

26. A row of shrubs that is allowed to grow into their natural shapes and height.

27. Created using a blend of several species of plant material varying in height, texture, and color.

28. A fencing material that is durable, virtually maintenance-free, and available in a wide variety of sizes, shapes, and colors.

29. A row of shrubs used to create walls and borders.

30. A style of fencing that provides privacy but also allows light to pass through from either side.

31. A style of fencing used to provide privacy to the outdoor area.

32. A woody-stemmed plant that is capable of climbing up and across a structure.

33. Create a border that allows the landscape to be viewed from either side.

Thinking Critically

1. What information would you need to make a decision about installing a swimming pool as part of a landscape design?

2. How would you show your understanding of the use of ground covers?

3. What is the value of your neighborhood park or your backyard? Is the value the same for different people? Explain your answer.

Suggested Activities

1. In groups of 3 to 4, choose a residential landscape in the local neighborhood or search online for such a landscape. Each member of the group should create a bubble diagram for the chosen landscape. The diagrams must include the service area, family living area, and public area. Compare your diagrams and determine if each design includes the required components.

2. A client desires privacy from the busy side street behind their home. Work with a partner and design a mixed border for the client. Research local regulations to ensure the design does not violate the city codes.

3. Contemporary fencing uses a wide variety of materials, including recycled objects, to create interest and provide function. Choose found objects and recycled materials and design a contemporary fence. Make a scale model.

4. A homeowner wishes to have turf-type tall fescue in their backyard. The backyard measures 250' × 95'. If the grass seed is applied at the rate of 15 lb per 1000 ft^2, how many pounds of grass seed is needed?

Plant Production

While studying this chapter, look for the activity icon ⤷ **to:**

- **Practice** vocabulary terms with Words to Know activities.
- **Expand** learning with identification activities.
- **Reinforce** what you learn by completing Know and Understand questions.

www.g-wlearning.com/agriculture

Chapter Outcomes

After studying this chapter, you will be able to:

- Understand the history of plant production practices.
- Identify and determine materials required to make a substrate.
- Identify various methods of plant production.
- Describe how to measure trees and shrubs according to the *American Standard for Nursery Stock*.
- Identify the difference between plant patents and trademarks.

Key Terms ➦

acclimatize
adventitious roots
asexual propagation
balled-and-burlapped (B&B)
bare root (BR)
caliper
cultivar
cutting
division
field production
grafting
harden off
layering
liner
macropore
meiosis
microirrigation
micropore
micropropagation

mitosis
perlite
phytosanitary certificate
plant breeder
plant nursery
plug
pot-in-pot production (PNP)
progeny
propagation
propagule
sexual propagation
soilless substrate
soil pore
stalite
synthetic fertilizer
vegetative propagation
vermiculite

Introduction

You can choose from thousands of plants when creating a landscape. Understanding plant production will help you choose the right plants to create and install quality landscapes. Plant production today includes many horticultural and agricultural entities that supply seeds and seedlings to grow food and the ornamental plants you will use in landscaping. This chapter explains various methods of plant production and propagation and how you can use this information to improve landscape design and maintenance.

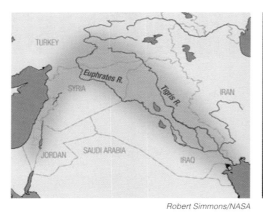

Robert Simmons/NASA

Homo Cosmicos/Shutterstock.com

Figure 8-1. The Fertile Crescent extends from the eastern part of the Mediterranean to the lower Zagros Mountains in Iraq and Iran. The Fertile Crescent lies at the meeting point of the Tigris and Euphrates rivers.

History of Production

Humans have been cultivating plants for thousands of years. Most anthropologists believe an area named the Fertile Crescent was the "birthplace" of agriculture, **Figure 8-1**. The land in this area became more suitable for growing crops as the climate changed around 10,000 BCE. Nomadic tribes began settling in this area, causing the shift to agrarian civilization. *Agrarian civilizations* are those based on agricultural production. As these civilizations grew, it was necessary to produce more food and farmers constantly sought new methods to increase their harvests.

Initially, growers collected seeds from the desired plants and stored them until planting time. Growers selected seeds from the top producing plants, hoping to grow prolific plants, but they had little control over the outcome. Some plants were reproduced through stem or leaf cuttings that were manipulated to produce roots. Eventually, the more advanced technique of grafting was used to cultivate many types of plants. *Grafting* is a technique in which a shoot or bud of one plant is inserted into or joined to the stem, branch, or root of another plant, **Figure 8-2**. One advantage of grafting is the ability to choose plant parts with desirable attributes, such as disease-resistant roots, to grow a plant that has less desirable attributes, such as low resistance to disease.

Did You Know?

Theophrastus (371 to 287 BCE), a student of Plato and Aristotle, was deemed the first scientific horticulturalist.

blackboard1965/Shutterstock.com

Bosnian/Shutterstock.com

suthiphong yina/Shutterstock.com

Figure 8-2. Grafting trees is common practice in fruit orchards. The method used to graft the plants may depend on the species being grafted.

Today, commercial horticulturists and home gardeners grow several hundred thousand species of plants using a variety of *propagation* (breeding) methods. *Plant breeders* (specialists who breed plants) can now manipulate everything from growth habit, bloom time, flower color, and foliage color to cultural requirements, **Figure 8-3**. Through the work of horticulturists and plant breeders, consumers and landscapers have more plants to choose from than ever before.

Substrates

When containerized plants were first distributed in the United States as an economic venture, they were shipped in true soil and metal cans. This type of production was challenging due to the weight of soils and shipping costs as well as the transportation of plant pathogens, such as beetles and their larva, fire ants, and soil-borne diseases, **Figure 8-4**. Growers sought an alternative substrate (growth medium) that would solve these issues. Today, virtually all container-grown plants are grown in a *soilless substrate*. A soilless substrate has several advantages over soil.

- A soilless substrate is often sterile and free of pathogens.
- Soilless substrates are lighter and more economical to ship.
- Soilless substrates are uniform and create a uniform media. The consistency of true soil changes based on the geographic location (and depth) of the harvested soil.
- The nutrient levels of soilless substrates can be controlled. The grower can create a fertilizer regime to ensure proper fertility.

Making a Substrate

Producers choose substrates based on many factors, including root stability, production goals, such as the length of time from *propagule* (plant part being used for duplication) to market, and the availability of components within a certain region. Pine bark, for example, is plentiful and easily transported across the southeastern United States because pine trees are harvested throughout the area and the bark is a by-product, **Figure 8-5**.

Base Material

The base material of a substrate is the component that makes up the majority of the substrate. Various materials are added to adjust the substrate's water-holding ability, fertility, and porosity. The materials added to the base material vary by the plant species for which the substrate is intended. Location, availability of materials, and consistency are all factors that should be considered when determining materials for a substrate. Common base materials include peat moss, hardwood bark, softwood bark, and cotton stalks. See **Figure 8-6**.

Peat Moss. Peat moss is a brown, acidic, organic material harvested from peat bogs. Peat moss can hold up to 30× its weight in water. It is used primarily to increase the moisture-holding ability of the substrate. The majority of the peat moss used in the United States is harvested from peat bogs in Canada.

Tania Zbrodko/Shutterstock.com

zawafoto/Shutterstock.com

LAURA_VN/Shutterstock.com

Figure 8-3. Plant breeders aspire to generate plants with better blooms, different colors, foliage appearance, growth habit, and disease resistance.

Pichit Sansupa/Shutterstock.com

Figure 8-4. In many areas, plant pests, such as fire ants, thwart efforts to produce quality plants.

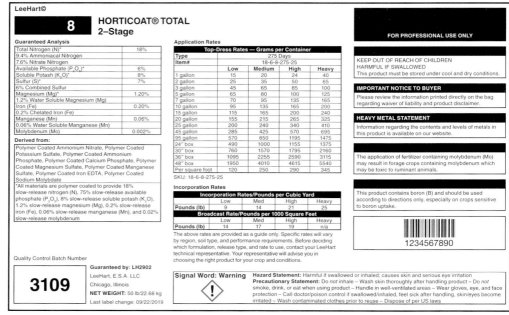

Goodheart-Willcox Publisher

Figure 8-5. Fertilizer regimes can be developed to accomplish specific plant production goals, such as expedited growth, better bloom quality, and improved fruit quality.

Photos courtesy of Dr. Brian Jackson, North Carolina State University

Figure 8-6. Potting substrates, such as peat moss, hardwood bark, softwood bark, and cotton stalks, are available regionally. A—Peat moss. B—Hardwood bark. C—Pine bark and sand. D—Softwood bark. E—Pine bark screenings. F—Cotton stalks.

Tree Bark. Hardwood and softwood bark is added to retain moisture and provide drainage. The bark provides more drainage than peat moss. The type of bark used for substrates varies by geographical region. The bark varies in size, thickness, and rate of decomposition by tree species.

Cotton Stalks. Cotton stalks and cotton gin trash are by-products in the cotton industry. The cotton waste is composted and added to substrates to improve moisture retention and improve drainage. The material may become a substitute for pine bark as many foresters now shred the bark and spread the material on the land where the trees were harvested.

Amendments

Materials added to the base material to change the water retention, nutrient content, and air-holding capacities include perlite, vermiculite, stalite, composted plant materials, aged animal waste, and synthetic fertilizers. Perlite, vermiculite, and stalite are mined in the United States and in various parts of the world. See **Figure 8-7**.

- *Perlite* is a volcanic rock that has a relatively high water content. Perlite is used to improve aeration and water retention. Perlite is mined and heated in ovens until it cracks and forms the white, round material found in planting substrates.
- *Vermiculite* is an aluminum-iron-magnesium silicate added to improve aeration. It is also heated to alter its natural form and improve its water retention capabilities.
- *Stalite* is a lightweight expanded slate added to improve its water retention, aeration, and nutrient-holding abilities. The slate used in stalite was formed from volcanic ash.
- Composted plant materials slowly release organic nutrients to plant roots. The materials used in the compost may be pathogen-free crop residue or waste from landscape installation or maintenance jobs.
- Aged animal waste products (manure) provide organic materials and nutrients. Only manure from plant-eating animals, such as cows and horses, should be used in compost. Manure should be aged about 4 to 6 weeks because fresh manure will burn plants.
- *Synthetic fertilizer* is a manufactured amendment. The nutrient content of this slow-release fertilizer is controlled by the manufacturer. This control enables the creation of formulations designed for specific plant needs. See **Figure 8-8**.

Different plant species have different requirements and there is not one substrate mixture that is appropriate for all plants. Many resources are available to assist growers with the proportions of components needed to satisfy their production goals.

A *iDEAR Replay/Shutterstock.com*

B *Dr. Bill Fonteno, North Carolina State University*

C *Dr. Bill Fonteno, North Carolina State University*

Figure 8-7. Products, such as perlite (A), vermiculite (B), and slate aggregate (C), can be added to a substrate to increase or decrease water- and nutrient-holding capacities.

A

B

C

D

A–C Dr. Helen Kraus, North Carolina State University   *D—iamporpla/Shutterstock.com*

Figure 8-8. Products, such as compost and aged animal waste, are used when producing plants. Synthetic fertilizers can be added to overcome any nutrient deficiencies in the growing substrate. A—Compost. B—Cotton compost. C—Swine lagoon waste. D—Synthetic fertilizer.

Hands-On Landscaping

Interpreting Seed Labels and Packets

Seed labels are subject to state and federal laws governing the truthful representation of contents for sale. The Association of Official Seed Certification Agencies ensures standards of seed quality and uniform methods of testing. The information given on a seed label or packet is important to the success of growing a particular plant. Variations exist among labels but labels usually include the following:

- Cultivar/release name (including species and common name) and a brief description.
- The location where the seed was grown and the name and address of the seller/grower.
- The purity of the contents desired versus other seed or inert matter.
- Noxious weed contents must be declared for conservation or turfgrasses.
- The weight of the contents.
- Lot number from the grower and processor.
- Expected germination percentage and recent test date.
- Days to germination and harvest.
- The environment needed for germination, including sun/shade and water needs.
- Planting times, depth, spacing, and growing height.
- Hardiness zones, growing regions, and flowering period.

Consider This

1. What do the days to harvest represent on a seed packet?
2. *True or False?* The hardiness zones govern the planting date of seeds.
3. How can you determine the longevity of seeds in a packet?

Goodheart-Willcox Publisher

Plant Propagation

Propagation is the process of breeding or producing more plants. Reproducing plants is a very challenging but very rewarding endeavor. Plant breeding is suspenseful and satisfying when the *progeny* (offspring) appears, **Figure 8-9**. There are two main types of propagation, *sexual* and *asexual*.

Sexual Propagation

Sexual propagation is a natural reproduction process that requires contributions from female and male plants for fertilization to occur. The biological process for sexual propagation is meiosis. *Meiosis* is a process in which a single cell from each parent divides twice to produce four daughter cells, **Figure 8-10A**. Each of these daughter cells has half the number of chromosomes (genetic information) of the parent cell. Genes from each parent cell cross over so that each chromosome contains genes from each parent.

Budimir Jevtic/Shutterstock.com

Figure 8-9. Plant breeders trial seedlings and cross-pollinated plants in progeny trials to identify desirable characteristics and select those warranting further development.

The unique combinations that result in each chromosome are responsible for genetic diversity.

The progeny may resemble the parent plants, have distinctive traits of each parent, or be greatly altered, depending on whether any of the traits are dominant or recessive. If two of the same *homozygous* (having identical pairs of genes for a pair of hereditary characteristics) plants are bred, the majority of the progeny will resemble the parents. Two homozygous red petunia plants, for example, will produce progeny with red flowers. If a homozygous red and homozygous white petunia are bred, the progeny may be plants with all red flowers. This indicates the red gene is dominant and the white gene is recessive. However, some of the offspring may have pink flowers. This indicates that neither gene is dominant nor recessive.

Sexual propagation is the simplest and least expensive method of propagation. It is also the only way some plants can propagate.

Asexual Propagation

Asexual or *vegetative propagation* is a reproduction process in which the progeny is produced from a single organism and has only the genes of that organism. The biological process for asexual propagation is mitosis, **Figure 8-10B**. *Mitosis* is a reproduction process in which a cell replicates and divides its nuclear material, and then divides itself into two daughter cells. Each of the daughter cells contains the same genetic material and the resultant plants are identical to the parent plant. Asexual propagation occurs naturally through vegetative parts of the plant, such as the roots, bulbs, or tubers.

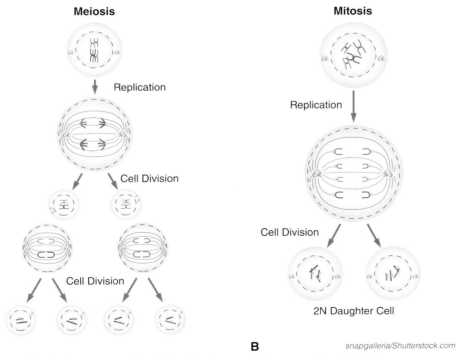

Meiosis

Replication

Cell Division

Cell Division

A

Mitosis

Replication

Cell Division

2N Daughter Cell

B

snapgalleria/Shutterstock.com

Figure 8-10. A—In the stages of meiosis (during sexual propagation), the chromosome number is halved to create sperm and egg cells. B—Mitosis is the process during asexual propagation that duplicates genetic information from one generation to the next, with little to no change in plant characteristics.

However, asexual propagation may also occur through human manipulation processes, such as cutting, layering, division, grafting, and micropropagation.

- A plant *cutting* is a plant piece that has been cut from the parent plant. The piece is placed in a suitable growing medium until it produces roots and can be transplanted. Some plants can be grown from leaf cuttings whereas others are grown from stem cuttings.

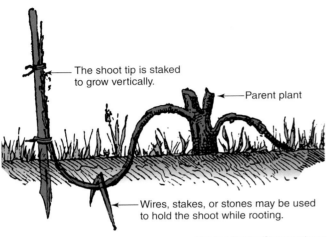

The shoot tip is staked to grow vertically.

Parent plant

Wires, stakes, or stones may be used to hold the shoot while rooting.

Morphart Creation/Shutterstock.com

Sarycheva Olesia/Shutterstock.com

Bork/Shutterstock.com

Figure 8-11. Propagation techniques, such as layering, division, and grafting, can be successfully used to duplicate unique plants. Layering and division take advantage of a naturally occurring process in many plants and grafting can be used to overcome adverse soil conditions or climate conditions.

- *Layering* is a vegetative propagation process in which stems that are still attached to the parent plant form roots. Layering occurs naturally when a branch touches the ground and adventitious roots form. *Adventitious roots* are roots that grow from any plant part other than the root. Layering techniques used in the industry include simple, compound, air, mound, and trench layering, **Figure 8-11A**.
- *Division* is a vegetative propagation process in which the crown of a plant is divided into smaller pieces that can be planted immediately to produce new plants. Each piece must have at least one bud (eye) and some roots. Division can only be used on plants that form a crown and have underground stems, such as bulbs, corms, tubers, and rhizomes, **Figure 8-11B**.
- **Grafting** is a technique in which a shoot or bud of one plant is inserted into or joined to the stem, branch, or root of another plant. Grafting is commonly used to propagate fruit trees. Types of grafts used in the industry include splice, cleft, wedge, and saddle grafting, **Figure 8-11C**.
- *Micropropagation* is a reproductive method in which plants are manipulated on a cellular level, causing them to duplicate themselves repeatedly and rapidly. Micropropagation is performed in a sterile environment. This is an expensive but very effective method of plant propagation.

Asexual propagation is often used for the commercial production of large numbers of identical plants for retail sale. The buyer is assured that the plants exhibit the same growth habits and will have a specific appearance. Asexual propagation may also be used to duplicate a unique species or cultivar for species preservation. An endangered species, for example, may be reproduced to repopulate a native area.

Asexual propagation can be time-consuming and an expensive means of plant production. It is, however, an effective means of reproducing plants with desirable traits, such as habit of growth, pathogen resistance, floral display, or production of fruit that have current and future marketability. It is also the only way some plants can reproduce.

Using Propagation to Manage the Landscape

A landscape professional with an understanding of propagation principles can choose and/or manage plants to encourage or discourage natural plant propagation. Daylilies, for example, propagate by reproducing at the crown. Leaves are produced at the crown in an arrangement referred to as a fan, **Figure 8-12**. A professional wishing to distribute daylilies to other areas of the landscape can manage the plant so maximum production occurs and desired distribution is possible. The fans can be divided and each piece can be planted in another location.

Conversely, a perennial that is a prolific seeder can be deadheaded to avoid rapid distribution of the plant within the landscape. Many species of verbena, for example, spread easily by seed distribution through birds and the wind. See **Figure 8-13**. If the flower heads are removed just before they go to seed, rapid spread can be avoided.

LianeM/Shutterstock.com

Figure 8-12. Daylilies can be propagated through division, giving the propagator multiple copies of the original plant.

Greenhouse Plant Production

Many landscape plants are propagated in greenhouses, **Figure 8-14**. Growers who specialize in propagation may cultivate plants from seed or cuttings from roots, leaves, or stems. A greenhouse producer can maximize plant production by manipulating environmental conditions, including:

- The immediate environment, including light, water, temperature, humidity, and gases, such as carbon dioxide and oxygen.

Goodheart-Willcox Publisher

Ian Grainger/Shutterstock.com

Figure 8-13. *Verbena bonariensis* is prolific in producing seeds, which need to be removed to prevent germination in other areas of the landscape. In some cases, birds, such as the goldfinch, will eat and deposit the seeds around the area.

Figure 8-14. Greenhouse environments enable producers to control the quality and amount of light plants receive. Producers also control ambient temperature, irrigation, and fertilizer regimes.

- The physiological factors, such as the substrate, nutrients, and water.
- The living factors that may benefit or adversely affect the plants, including insects, diseases, and microbial organisms.

Plugs and Liners

Greenhouse operations that specialize in plant propagation may sell their young plants to greenhouse growers who do not propagate their own plants. These growers typically purchase the plants as plugs or liners. *Plugs* are plants grown from seeds in small containers to transplantable size. *Liners* are plants with a 1″ to 3″ diameter that are grown for transplanting. Most greenhouse growers purchase transplants because it is difficult to start a large quantity of seedlings in a greenhouse that does not have the specialized equipment and structure required. It is also more efficient and economical to purchase the plugs and liners.

Acclimatization

Greenhouse plants live in a controlled environment where they are protected from the weather. They are not exposed to direct sunlight, wind, or the rain and snow and must be *acclimatized* or *hardened off* before they are placed outdoors. The acclimatization period is usually one to two weeks in a transitional environment, such as an outdoor, semishaded area protected from harsh winds. Plants that are not acclimatized are susceptible to problems, such as leaf blistering from direct sunlight and bark splintering due to freezing temperatures.

Plant Cell Packs and Flats

Plants produced in greenhouses are grown in individual containers or cell packs. The type of pot used depends on the species and its end use. Smaller plants, such as many annual bedding plants, are grown and sold in cell packs. Larger landscape plants, such as many popular perennials, are grown and sold in individual round or square pots. Growing plants in recyclable, plastic cell packs is an efficient means of maximizing the number of plants grown. It also makes shipping and selling the plants more efficient and economical.

Plants grown in cell packs are commonly sold either by flats or by the individual cell pack. A flat is a plastic tray designed to hold a number of cell packs. A standard flat measures 10″ × 20″. Insert flats (smaller trays) are used to divide the flat into smaller sections. A wide variety of insert flats is available, with varying number of plants per flat, **Figure 8-15**. The inserts also vary in size and depth. The larger the number of plants per flat, the smaller the plants.

- A 1004 tray will hold 10 cell packs with four plants per cell pack for a total of 40 plants per flat.
- A 1203 tray will hold 12 cell packs with three plants per cell pack for a total of 36 plants. A 1203 will provide more soil for plants than a 1004.

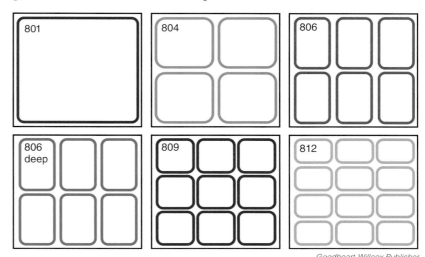

Goodheart-Willcox Publisher

Figure 8-15. There is a variety of cell configurations available. The final market may determine which to use for each type of plant species being propagated.

American Standard for Nursery Stock

AmericanHort, a national horticulture association, has published a standardized classification and grading system to ensure uniformity of product. This publication, the *American Standard for Nursery Stock*, establishes standards for the following techniques:

- Measuring plants.
- Specifying and stating the size of plants.
- Determining the proper relationship between height and caliper, or height and width.
- Determining whether a root ball or container is large enough for a particular size plant.

The standards enable buyers to choose plant materials with the assurance that plants purchased at one nursery will have the same characteristics, such as size, shape, and growth habit, as the same species purchased at another nursery. The standards also provide growers with definite parameters for measuring and labeling their products to ensure the buyer receives the product expected. Nurseries strive to maintain these standards to remain competitive. The standards can be viewed online or downloaded from the AmericanHort website.

Nursery Plant Production

Seedlings, cuttings, grafted plants, and others are grown in dedicated areas or *plant nurseries*, **Figure 8-16**. Producers can manipulate many of the same factors manipulated in greenhouses, such as growing substrates, water inputs, and nutrient availability. Pests can be controlled by encouraging beneficials (natural enemies), or by applying pest-specific chemicals. Nurseries can produce large quantities of the same species or cultivar while maintaining standardized parameters, such as height, width, growth habit, and overall shape. Production methods used in nurseries include the following:

- Container production.
- Pot-in-pot production (PNP).
- Field production.
- Bare root (BR).

Iidian Neeleman/Shutterstock.com

Ivan Popovych/Shutterstock.com

Rigucci/Shutterstock.com

Figure 8-16. Plant nurseries vary by arrangement and growing conditions. A nursery may specialize in specific types of plants, such as woody plants or herbaceous perennials.

Container Production

Most commercial plant producers grow plants in plastic containers. Growing plants in containers provides the flexibility to move the plants during their production life cycle as well as portability once the plant is marketable. Most growers use plastic containers because they are lightweight, strong, and reusable. Many nurseries offer return or buy-back programs for customers. The used containers can be sanitized and reused if they are not structurally compromised. Unusable containers can be recycled.

Containers are identified by the diameter of the top of the pot or by volume. Smaller pots are commonly referred to by their diameter. A pot with a 4″ diameter, for example, would simply be referred to as a 4″ pot. Larger containers are referred to in gallon sizes, such as 1-, 2-, 3-, and 5-gallon. The pots might also be referred to by numbers, such as #1, #3, and #5. The standards allow a specific volume range for each pot size, **Figure 8-17**.

Soilless substrates are used in containers because they weigh much less than soil and the grower can manipulate the water, nutrient, and aeration capacities. Having nutrients in the growing medium also eliminates the labor required for fertilization.

Common challenges faced in container plant production include preventing the pots from blowing over (blow-over) and reducing heat build-up

Container Volume Ranges

Container Class Specification	Container Volume Range (cubic inches/cubic cm)	Box Size Equivalent
#SP1	6.5–8 (106–131)	
#SP2	13–15 (213–246)	
#SP3	20–30 (328–492)	
#SP4	51–63 (836–1033)	
#SP5	93–136 (1524–2229)	
#1	152–251 (2492–4115)	
#2	320–474 (5246–7770)	
#3	628–742 (10,285–12,164)	
#5	785–1242 (12,860–20,360)	
#7	1337–1790 (21,913–29,343)	
#10	2080–2646 (34,090–43,376)	
#15	2768–3696 (45,376–60,589)	
#20	4520–5152 (74,096–84,457)	20″-box
#25	5775–6861 (94,669–112,472)	24″-box
#45	9356–11,434 (153,317–187,377)	36″-box
#65	13,514–16,517 (221,456–246,051)	42″-box
#95/100	20,790–25,410 (340,686–416,394)	48″-box

Goodheart-Willcox Publisher

Figure 8-17. Container charts provide growers with standard measurements for marketable plant materials.

around the root systems. Producers ingeniously combat these problems with antiblow-over devices and root ball shielding, **Figure 8-18**.

Pot-in-Pot Production (PNP)

In *pot-in-pot production (PNP)*, an insert pot housing the plant is inserted into a socket pot that may be installed over a drainage system, **Figure 8-19**. The socket pot is buried in the soil up to its rim and the growth medium in the insert pot is soilless. Pot-in-pot production provides better control over the root ball environment. The initial expense of installation due to subsurface drainage and individual irrigation spray devices is higher compared to other systems, such as containers on gravel. However, production time can be decreased and more plants can be produced quickly in the same site.

An additional advantage for the pot-in-pot production system is the protection of the root-zone. In the southeastern United States, soil temperatures at 6″ to 10″ usually remain around 55°F (12.8°C). The roots of plants installed in the sockets benefit from the consistent temperature and protection from temperature extremes and growth that is more efficient is realized. In many cases, the production cycle is 30% to 50% more efficient than

R. Lee Ivy

Figure 8-18. Growers use innovative devices, such as recycled tires, to prevent plant materials from blowing over.

Stone/Shutterstock.com

Figure 8-19. Advantages of PNP include no blow-over and the ease of harvest. Plant materials can also be grown indoors and then placed in the field without having to be repotted.

TENGLAO/Shutterstock.com

Figure 8-20. Microirrigation systems are one of the more sustainable means of watering plants in greenhouses and nurseries. More water reaches the plants than with other systems because there is less nonbeneficial evaporation.

standardized production, such as containers on gravel or black fabric. When a plant is taken from a PNP system, a landscape professional must ensure root ball protection until installation. This can be done by heeling in the root balls with organic mulch or covering the root ball with a tarp or nontransparent barrier.

Microirrigation

Microirrigation is used to water the plants efficiently. *Microirrigation* is a low-volume system of small tubes and water emitters, **Figure 8-20**. The system is metered to add water at infrequent intervals for short periods. This is advantageous for the producer because less water is needed and fertilizer can be used more efficiently. However, microirrigation systems require a higher level of maintenance than other systems because the small tubing and emitters are susceptible to clogging and damage from factors, such as animals or foot traffic.

Field Production

In a *field production* operation, plants are grown in true soil in an open field, **Figure 8-21**. The plants may come from a greenhouse or pot-in-pot operation and are typically harvested and cultivated at a size that will endure field conditions. Multiple soil types are conducive to growing plants but loose, coarse soils are preferred due to ease of digging and lower shipping weight.

Rigucci/Shutterstock.com

Goodheart-Willcox Publisher

Figure 8-21. Large shrubs and trees grown in nursery fields may not be harvested for landscape installation for 3 to 7 years after planting. Field production requires a large investment of time.

Plants grown in a field production operation are typically larger and more mature than plants grown in pots. Plants grown in field production include shrubs for screening, trees for shading, trees for streetscapes, and specimen plants. These plants can have a production cycle of 5 to 15 years. Many field plants must be harvested with large equipment due to the physical demands of digging a properly sized root ball and lifting the weight of the plant and soil, **Figure 8-22**.

Balled-and-Burlapped (B&B)

Balled-and-burlapped (B&B) is a method used to protect the root ball of plants harvested directly from the ground. Larger plants are typically harvested with a tree spade (mechanical digger), but this method of protection may also be used with plants dug by hand. The exposed root ball is placed in a non-synthetic fabric inside a wire basket, **Figure 8-23**. The basket cradles the soil and roots for handling and shipping.

Balled-and-burlapped nursery stock is commonly sold by caliper. *Caliper* is a measurement that represents the thickness of the stem, **Figure 8-24**. Caliper should be measured 6″ from the top of the root ball or soil line. If the caliper at 6″ above the ground level exceeds 4½″, the caliper should be taken again 12″ above the soil level.

Bare Root (BR)

Plant materials may also be purchased as bare roots. *Bare root (BR)* plants are free of soil and typically do not have grown stems and leaves. Nurseries commonly purchase bare root plants, **Figure 8-25**, as propagation stock. However, bare

R. Lee Ivy

Figure 8-22. Large digging machines or tree spades are used for harvesting shrubs and trees from field soils. Using a tree spade lessens damage and allows harvesting with a large root ball.

Goodheart-Willcox Publisher

Figure 8-23. When plants are removed from the ground, they may be placed in wire baskets lined with burlap. The baskets keep the root systems intact during transport and the burlap will erode after the plant is installed.

Christopher D. Hart

Figure 8-24. Tree calipers are used to measure tree trunks. They may also be used for pricing and to estimate the time a tree needs to establish roots when transplanted.

Swellphotography/Shutterstock.com

Figure 8-25. The soil is removed from some harvested plants in preparation for shipping. According to studies at Cornell University, a bare-root tree contains 200% more roots than the same tree sold balled-and-burlapped.

root plants may also be purchased by homeowners and landscape designers to obtain unique species of plants or to save costs. Bare root plants are only harvested when the plant is dormant to prevent shock. They are light and shipped easily. Bare root plants may take longer than other forms of plants to become established because they are not as developed.

Transporting Nursery Stock

Nursery stock being transported must be securely placed in the transport vehicle and protected from wind damage. Damaged plants may not thrive in the new environment and may need to be replaced, often at the nursery's expense.

Container Plants

Container plants should be secured so they do not slide or fall over when the vehicle is moving. Skilled nursery personnel often stack smaller containers by nesting rows on top and between the plants in the previous row. Stacked containers should also be secured and prevented from falling on other plants. Some trucks have rack systems designed to accommodate specific containers. If the vehicle has an open bed, the plants must be protected from the wind with a secured tarp.

Larger Plants

Semitrailers are often used to transport larger balled-and-burlapped plants or large container stock. The trailers have a raised bar at the rear of the trailer for the first row of plants to lean against. The plants will lean away from the tractor if an open, flatbed trailer is used. Each row will be laid in front of the previous row until the trailer is full. The load will be strapped and covered with a tarp to prevent movement of the plants during transport. The tarp also protects the plants from wind damage, such as leaf tattering and desiccation. Shipping in closed trailers offers more protection for plant materials, **Figure 8-26**.

R. Lee Ivy

Figure 8-26. Plants are carefully loaded for protection and proper weight distribution during shipping. Although closed trailers offer more protection than open trailers, it is more practical to ship larger trees on a flatbed trailer.

Weight Limits

When shipping orders on a semitrailer or other large truck, nursery personnel must review the planned route to determine if the truck is too heavy for bridge weight limits. If the load is too heavy and there is no alternative route, the load must be divided into smaller loads.

Transplants and Soil Types

Soil types greatly affect the formation of root systems. Plants growing in heavy, clayey soils may have tightly gathered roots whereas those growing in sandy soils may have looser, spread-out roots. The root systems absorb water differently because of their formation and the way water moves through each type of soil. Plants transplanted in a different type of soil may have difficulty adapting. To ensure transplants thrive in their new environment, the designer, installer, and maintenance professional should consider what type of soil the plants were grown in and the type of soil in the final growing environment.

Soil Types

Soil consists of four main components: air, water, minerals, and organic matter. The water and air are in the *soil pores*, spaces or gaps in the solid matter. The solid parts of the soil are the minerals and organic matter, **Figure 8-27**. The physical properties of soil include structure, texture, and color.

- *Soil structure* is the binding together of sand, silt, and clay particles. Soil structure affects water movement through the soil. Soil structure can be improved with the addition of organic matter. Soil structure is damaged when the soil is compacted.

Pro Tip

The percentage of roots can be increased by applying water in close proximity to the stem or trunk. The larger percentage of roots will help the plant adapt to its final growing environment.

Career Connection

Dana Massey

Dana Massey, President, Plantworks Nursery, Inc.

Dana Massey is President of Plantworks Nursery, Inc., in Rougemont, North Carolina. When Dana was 15 and working in a tomato greenhouse, she realized that the horticulture industry was where she belonged. Dana's love for the outdoors and getting her hands dirty led her to North Carolina State University's Horticulture Program where she majored in Horticulture and minored in Agricultural Business Management. After graduation, Dana was hired as an annual grower at Plantworks Nursery. Dana advanced from annual grower, to the management team, to being named vice president, to ownership.

Dana stated that the horticulture industry needs passionate new generations to continue the work and legacy of those that founded so many of our local garden centers and landscape companies. The future of agriculture is limitless.

Consider This

1. What types of leadership skills do you think Dana possesses that have contributed to her success?
2. Do you think Dana's agricultural business studies have helped her become the owner of her own nursery? Explain your answer.
3. Would regular business management studies have helped Dana in the same manner as those focused on agriculture? Why or why not?

- *Soil texture* is determined by the different sizes of mineral particles in a soil. Texture is the most important physical property for planting. Textural soil classes are sandy soils, clayey soils, and loamy soils. Each of the soil types have different proportions of sand, silt, and clay.
- *Soil color* is determined by the soil's composition. Soil color may be used to determine the soil's drainage, water content, health, and pH. Soil with rich black color, for example, indicates high nutrition content, good drainage, and an abundance of organic matter.

R. Lee Ivy

R. Lee Ivy

Figure 8-27. Landscape professionals are often managing extreme amounts of sand or clay. These soil types affect water and nutrient uptake for plant roots.

Water Movement

Water moves differently through different types of soils. In a clayey soil, water is tightly held in *micropores* (small spaces between soil particles). The soil will absorb moisture slowly but not retain well over time. A tree grown in sandy soil and then planted in a clayey soil will absorb moisture quickly in the *macropores*, large spaces between soil particles, **Figure 8-28**, but once the water reaches the clay layer it may not absorb as quickly and the tree may be adversely affected by the large amount of water around the roots. Conversely, a tree grown in clayey soil and then planted in a sandy soil will not absorb water from surrounding sandy soil if not directed to the immediate root ball.

With this in mind, the person procuring plants should try to match up soil types as closely as possible to make maintenance after installation more efficient. At the same time, maintenance professionals should inspect existing and/or incoming plants to anticipate differing maintenance regimes.

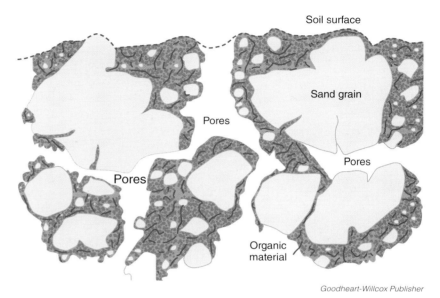

Goodheart-Willcox Publisher

Figure 8-28. The size and nature of soil particles affects the movement of water throughout the profile as well as the presence or absence of air available for exchange in and out of the roots.

Quarantines

The United States Department of Agriculture Animal and Plant Health Inspection Service (USDA APHIS) regulates the transport of live plant material. The USDA Plant Protection and Quarantine (PPQ) safeguards the agriculture and natural resources against the entry, establishment, and spread of detrimental pests and disease. Once established, nonnative species can cause a great deal of economic and environmental harm. The Japanese beetle, for example, reportedly arrived in the United States in a shipment of iris bulbs before plant inspections were standard procedure. In the larval stage, the beetle damages turfgrass. The adult beetle is an indiscriminate forager on leaves, flowers, and other plant parts, **Figure 8-29A**. The red imported fire ant from South America is another example of an invasive species whose entry into the country could have been prevented with proper inspection and quarantine.

A   *Kent Sievers/Shutterstock.com*   **B**   *Ploychan Lompong/Shutterstock.com*

Figure 8-29. Insects, such as the Japanese beetle (A) and red imported fire ants (B), displace native insects and are indiscriminate when foraging and disrupting habitats.

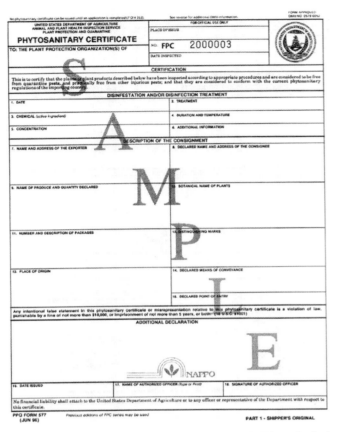

USDA Animal and Plant Health Inspection Service

Figure 8-30. Phytosanitary certificates indicate that plants are free from pests and disease.

PlantHaven®, Inc.

Figure 8-31. 'Kaleidoscope' abelia is a new cultivar of the original species of *Abelia x grandiflora*.

It was introduced to the United States through a port in Alabama. Today, the red fire ant has spread through much of the southern portion of the United States. See **Figure 8-29B**. Current quarantine maps of the United States can be found on the USDA website.

All producers must comply with local, state, and national quarantine regulations. Producers are required to treat plant material before it leaves the nursery. Plant materials can be treated with pesticide drenches of substrates or soil, or by including a granular particle in the substrate recipe. A phytosanitary certificate must also accompany plant shipments. A *phytosanitary certificate*, **Figure 8-30**, certifies that the plant is free of pathogens, insects, and weeds and meets all importing and exporting requirements.

Patented and Trademarked Plants

Many plant species and cultivated varieties (cultivars) that have been popular in the nursery trade for many years have no associated regulations. (*Cultivars* are plant varieties created by humans.) The glossy abelia, for example, is a popular low-growing shrub commonly used as a foundation or border plant. It is easily propagated through cuttings and has no patent or trademark. However, the cultivar *Abelia x grandiflora*, named 'Kaleidoscope,' cannot be propagated without a royalty payment to the patent holder. See **Figure 8-31**. This cultivar qualified for a patent because it is unique and significantly different from the original species, the glossy abelia. It also met additional requirements, such as being stable and unchanging when reproduced. Trademarked plants also require permission and royalty payments for propagation.

Plant patents last for 20 years from the date of application of the patent. During this time, it is illegal to propagate and sell the propagated plant material without a propagation license for that particular plant. It is time-consuming and expensive to apply for a plant patent. Breeders will only apply for patents for plants that are unique and are expected to be popular sellers. The breeder will receive royalties on the plants that are sold. Plants that are sold before the plant patent is approved are labeled PPAF (plant patent applied for).

Trademarking is a relatively new marketing strategy for introducing new plants into the market. A trademark is a word, symbol, phrase, and/or a design that distinguishes one brand from another. Trademarked plants often have special colored containers and unique plant tags to make the plants easily identifiable. Patented plants may also have a trademark.

Summary

- Thousands of species of plants are produced for commercial and residential applications.
- Plants propagated for sale were initially produced and shipped in true soil and metal cans but were replaced with soilless substrates and plastic containers.
- Soilless substrates are sterile and free from pathogens, lighter and more economical to ship, and allow for uniform creation of media.
- Producers choose substrates based on many factors, including root stability, production goals, and the availability of components within a certain region.
- Meiosis and mitosis are the two biological processes that give rise to sexual and asexual propagation.
- A producer may determine whether to duplicate or allow for further genetic differences through seed production based on the amount of genetic variation.
- Cutting, layering, division, grafting, and micropropagation are all ways to reproduce plants asexually.
- Landscape professionals with an understanding of plant production can better install and maintain a landscape.
- Plants grown in greenhouses and nurseries can be manipulated to expedite or slow vegetative or reproductive growth cycles.
- Plants grown in controlled environments require an acclimatization period to avoid damage once placed in the landscape.
- Standards exist to regulate the growth and sale of nursery stock to ensure consistency for markets.
- Container, pot-in-pot, field, and bare root are plant nursery production methods.
- Water management strategies must be employed in landscapes based on the type of production system.
- Care must be taken when shipping and handling nursery stock to ensure a quality product for the customer.
- Quarantines exist to prevent the unwanted spread of plant pathogens, such as insects, diseases, weeds, and microorganisms.
- Patents and trademarks are used to preserve production rights and add to the profitability of unique plant materials.

Chapter Review

Know and Understand ➦

Answer the following questions using the information provided in this chapter.

1. A technique in which a shoot or bud of one plant is inserted into or joined to the stem, branch, or root of another plant is referred to as _____.
   A. grifting
   B. grafting
   C. grating
   D. greening

2. Why are plants produced in soilless substrates?
   A. Uniform and create a uniform media.
   B. Lighter and more economical to ship.
   C. Often sterile and free of pathogens.
   D. All of the above.

3. The plant part used for duplication is the _____.
   A. propagule
   B. module
   C. pathogen
   D. All of the above.

4. Various materials are added to the base substrate material to adjust the substrate's _____.
   A. color to match the color scheme of the landscape
   B. odor so the client is not offended by the smell
   C. water-holding ability, fertility, and porosity
   D. All of the above.

5. A brown organic material harvested from bogs and used to increase water-holding ability of the substrate is referred to as _____.
   A. tree bark
   B. stalks
   C. peat moss
   D. soil

6. A volcanic rock that has a relatively high water content and is used to improve aeration and water retention of a substrate is _____.
   A. vermiculite
   B. perlite
   C. stalite
   D. synthetic fertilizer

7. An aluminum-iron-magnesium silicate added to substrates to improve aeration is referred to as _____.
   A. vermiculite
   B. perlite
   C. stalite
   D. synthetic fertilizer

8. A lightweight expanded slate added to substrates to improve water retention, aeration, and nutrient-holding abilities is referred to as _____.
   A. vermiculite
   B. perlite
   C. stalite
   D. synthetic fertilizer

9. A manufactured amendment in which the nutrient formulation can be designed for specific plant needs is referred to as _____.
   A. vermiculite
   B. perlite
   C. stalite
   D. synthetic fertilizer

10. Which of the following processes require contributions from male and female plants for fertilization to occur?
    A. Sexual propagation.
    B. Asexual propagation.
    C. Homozygous propagation.
    D. Cellular replication.

11. Which of the following is a reproduction process in which the progeny is produced from a single organism and has only the genes of that organism?
    A. Sexual propagation.
    B. Asexual propagation.
    C. Homozygous propagation.
    D. Cellular replication.

12. Which of the following is a reproduction process in which a single cell from each parent divides twice to produce four daughter cells?
    A. Meiosis.
    B. Mitosis.
    C. Microsis.
    D. Minosis.

13. Which of the following is a reproduction process in which a cell replicates and divides its nuclear material, and then divides itself into two daughter cells?
    A. Meiosis.
    B. Mitosis.
    C. Microsis.
    D. Minosis.

14. What factors can be controlled in greenhouse or nursery production operations?
    A. The immediate environment.
    B. The substrate, nutrients, and water.
    C. Insects, diseases, and microbial organisms.
    D. All of the above.

15. *True or False?* Greenhouse plants must be hardened off before they are placed outdoors.
    A. True.
    B. False.

16. *True or False?* Most annual bedding plants are grown and sold in individual 3″ round or square pots.
    A. True.
    B. False.

17. *True or False?* Larger landscape plants are grown and sold in cell packs.
    A. True.
    B. False.

18. *True or False?* The *American Standard for Nursery Stock* establishes standards for specifying and stating the size of plants and determining relationship between height and caliper.
    A. True.
    B. False.

19. Which of the following is a low-volume system that uses small tubes and water emitters to water plants?
    A. Center pivot irrigation.
    B. Sprinkler irrigation.
    C. Microirrigation.
    D. Lateral move irrigation.

20. Which of the following is the binding together of sand, silt, and clay particles?
    A. Soil color.
    B. Soil texture.
    C. Soil structure.
    D. Soil pores.

21. Which of the following is determined by the different sizes of mineral particles in a soil?
    A. Soil color.
    B. Soil texture.
    C. Soil structure.
    D. Soil pores.

22. Which of the following is determined by the soil's composition?
    A. Soil color.
    B. Soil texture.
    C. Soil structure.
    D. Soil pores.

23. *True or False?* In a clayey soil, water is tightly held in micropores.
    A. True.
    B. False.

24. *True or False?* A tree grown in sandy soil and then planted in a clayey soil will absorb moisture quickly in the macropores.
    A. True.
    B. False.

25. *True or False?* A quarantine is used to safeguard against the entry, establishment, and spread of detrimental pests and disease.
    A. True.
    B. False.

26. The document certifying that the plant is free of pathogens, insects, and weeds and meets all importing and exporting requirements is referred to as a(n) _____.
   A. USDA certificate
   B. pathogen-free certificate
   C. phytosanitary certificate
   D. progeny certificate

27. *True or False?* Plant patents last for 50 years from the date of application of the patent.
   A. True.
   B. False.

Match the terms to the appropriate descriptions in 28–38.
   A. adventitious root
   B. balled-and-burlapped (B&B)
   C. bare root (BR)
   D. composted plant materials
   E. cotton stalks
   F. cultivar
   G. cutting
   H. division
   I. field production
   J. grafting
   K. layering
   L. liner
   M. micropropagation
   N. peat moss
   O. perlite
   P. plug
   Q. pot-in-pot production (PNP)
   R. progeny
   S. propagation
   T. stalite
   U. synthetic fertilizer
   V. vermiculite

28. A plant piece that has been removed from the parent plant and placed in a suitable growing medium until it produces roots.

29. A vegetative propagation process in which stems that are still attached to the parent plant form roots.

30. A root that grows from any plant part other than the root.

31. A vegetative propagation process in which the crown of a plant is separated into smaller pieces that can be planted immediately to produce new plants.

32. A reproductive method in which plants are manipulated on a cellular level, causing them to duplicate themselves repeatedly and rapidly.

33. A plant grown from seed in a small container to transplantable size.

34. A plant with a 1″ to 3″ diameter that is grown for transplanting.

35. A nursery production system in which an insert pot housing the plant is inserted into a socket pot that may be installed over a drainage system.

36. A nursery production system in which plants are grown in true soil in an open field.

37. A nursery production method used to protect the root ball of plants harvested directly from the ground.

38. A plant variety created by humans.

Thinking Critically

1. Evaluate the contribution of micropropagation to the green industry.

2. Is micropropagation harmful to the environment? Justify your answer.

3. How would you explain asexual plant propagation?

4. Explain how you would approach an insect infestation if you were responsible for maintenance of your city's parks and landscapes.

5. What would you do if someone you knew were illegally propagating a patented plant?

Suggested Activities

1. Working in groups of 3 or 4 students, acquire samples of various growing media. Using proper techniques for sampling growing media, examine the physical and chemical properties of each type of growing media. Chart your observations and determine components and pH levels.

2. Determine the desirable properties and the advantages and disadvantages of soilless media.

3. Form groups of 3 or 4 students and identify the applicable quarantines for the pests that exist in the area where you live. Create a visual presentation for the class. Include images of the pests, where they originated, if and why they are spreading, which plants they affect and how, what methods of prevention or eradication are being used, and if they are threatening other areas/states. Each person should give one section of the presentation.

4. Identify the total number of cultivated plant species in a category, such as trees, shrubs, vines, groundcovers, perennials, ornamental grasses, fruit plants, or vegetables.

5. Choose three popular plants being sold online that are patented or trademarked. Determine the price difference between those plants and other cultivars that are not patented and trademarked. Determine the main qualities that make them different and assess whether the increase in price, if any, is necessary. If performed as a group activity, each member should choose a different plant to research. Use the information to have a group discussion.

6. Identify and contact a local plant production facility to set up a tour or invite the owner or manager to speak to your class. Prepare questions before the speaker arrives. If this is not possible, visit a local facility with a partner and speak with the manager (best to call ahead). Obtain permission to take photos. Write a short presentation.

7. Divide the class in half. One group will research the use of organic fertilizers in plant production and the other group will research the use of inorganic fertilizers. Hold a debate on the topic.

8. Research and describe the factors in planting seeds and demonstrate scarification, stratification, and planting seeds.

Plant Taxonomy and Physiology

While studying this chapter, look for the activity icon to:
- **Practice** vocabulary terms with Words to Know activities.
- **Expand** learning with identification activities.
- **Reinforce** what you learn by completing Know and Understand questions.

G-WLEARNING.com

www.g-wlearning.com/agriculture

Chapter Outcomes

After studying this chapter, you will be able to:

- Explain binomial nomenclature and how it is used to name plants.
- Determine how plant names may aid in determining placement and use for plants.
- Understand the scientific classification of plants.
- Explain the difference between gymnosperms and angiosperms.
- Identify the parts of a plant and explain how each part supports plant growth.
- Explain the differences between the various geophytes.
- Identify the basic biological processes that drive growth from a seed to a mature plant.
- Explain the basic plant processes and how they affect plant growth.

Key Terms

angiosperm
apices
arboretum
binomial name
binomial nomenclature
botanical garden
botanical name
bulb
carbon sequestration
classification
common name
conservatory
corm
dicot
fibrous root
genus

geophyte
gymnosperm
hybrid
hypocotyl
internode
Latin name
macronutrient
micronutrient
monocot
node
nontunicate bulb
phloem
photosynthesis
pseudobulb
respiration
rhizome

scientific name
species
specific epithet
stolon
taproot
taxonomy
translocation
transpiration
tuber
tuberous root
tuberous stem
tunicate bulb
variety
vascular cambium
xylem

Introduction

Having an extensive knowledge of plant growth habits and cultural needs is a great asset for landscape professionals and designers. This knowledge enables a designer to offer plants that will appeal to the client and thrive in the landscape, **Figure 9-1**. The designer or professional may also choose plants that require the preferred amount of maintenance while still providing the colors and shapes suited to the client's vision. Understanding plant growth habits will also help you explain to clients why something may not work and offer a suitable alternative. This chapter introduces you to basic plant physiology and the processes that affect plant growth.

romakoma/Shutterstock.com

Figure 9-1. A designer's knowledge of plant characteristics helps to accomplish design objectives.

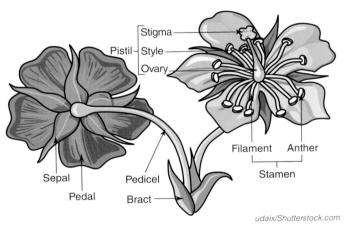

udaix/Shutterstock.com

Figure 9-2. Reproductive similarities are used for classification of plants. They may include the numbers of stamens in the flower and/or the anatomy of the fruit.

Plant Nomenclature

In 1753, Carolus Linnaeus (1707–1778) published *Species Plantarum*, a text in which he cataloged over 1300 plants. The Swedish naturalist created a classification system based solely on the flower structures of plants. He cataloged plants using the number of stamens, stamen characteristics, and the relationship of stamens to other floral parts. See **Figure 9-2**. This system forms the basis for plant classification today.

Carolus Linnaeus' ***binomial nomenclature*** (a two-word naming system) describes plant species in a consistent and methodical manner. Prior to Linnaeus' system, plant species were given different names by different botanists around the world. Most plants also had ***common names*** (a word or term in everyday language) that were specific to different regions. With Latin used as the common language, botanists around the world could communicate using universal specific names.

Botanical Names

An understanding of plant taxonomy is useful to landscape professionals when deciding which plants would work best in a particular location. Plants in the same class share many characteristics, including growth habits, structure, germination, and preferred habitat. The ***binomial*** or ***botanical name*** of plants also provides information about a plant that distinguishes it from other plants. The botanical name may also be referred to as the ***Latin*** or ***scientific name***. An understanding of plant taxonomy will also help landscape professionals communicate to customers why some plants will not work in their landscape. It will also help them identify plants with similar characteristics that will work in the landscape, **Figure 9-3**.

Botanical names follow the rules of the International Code of Botanical Nomenclature.

Specific Epithet

The first part of the name identifies the genus to which the species belongs, and the second part identifies the species within the genus. A *genus* is a subset of organisms within a family that share similar characteristics. The second part of the name is referred to as the *specific epithet*.

The specific epithet may refer to colors of foliage, stems, or flowers, country of origin, or habits of growth. The botanical name of the weeping katsura tree, for example, is *Cercidiphyllum japonicum*, **Figure 9-4A**. *Cercidiphyllum* is the genus and *japonicum* is the specific epithet noting that the country of origin is Japan. The cultivar could be 'Pendula,' which would describe its pendulous or weeping habit. The straight species, **Figure 9-4B**, would not have the pendulous growth but would likely have the same leaf shape and stem structure.

Common Names

Common names are used in many horticultural applications but they can lead to miscommunication. A bluebell, for example, may represent a specific plant in Texas but a very different plant somewhere else in the country, **Figure 9-5**. In addition, companies may assign a more "catchy" name

A
R. Lee Ivy

B
TinasDreamWorld/Shutterstock.com

Figure 9-3. A—Dwarf cultivars of a camellia can provide smaller plants and blooms that are more prolific. B—Larger growth habit and varied color of blooms are possible with camellias as with other plants.

A
R. Lee Ivy

B
CTatiana/Shutterstock.com

Figure 9-4. A—The weeping katsura tree is smaller than the upright species and has downward stretching branches. B—This katsura tree species is much taller and has upright branches.

SDeming/Shutterstock.com   Tatyana Potapenko/Shutterstock.com   Paul Maguire/Shutterstock.com

Figure 9-5. What is in a name? All three of these flowers are referred to as bluebells in their native states. Regional names cannot be used to identify a plant accurately because, as you can see, what is known as a bluebell in Virginia is very different from a bluebell in Texas or Oregon.

to the same plant for marketing purposes, adding more confusion. If the botanical name is included with the common name, the plant can be accurately identified internationally.

Scientific Classification

The system of grouping like organisms is called *classification*. The science of naming and classifying organisms is called *taxonomy*. The hierarchical order of plant classification ranges from most inclusive in domain to least inclusive in species. The three domains are Eubacteria, Archaea, and Eukaryotes. The domains are the highest and most inclusive taxonomic ranking for all living organisms. After domain, there are six kingdoms used to classify all living organisms. Plants belong to the Plantae or Plant Kingdom. See **Figure 9-6**.

- Domain.
- Kingdom.
- Phylum.
- Class.
- Order.
- Family.
- Genus.
- Species.
- Common name.
- Binomial name.

Phylum

Classifications may have several subclasses to identify a species further. Phylum, for example, is divided roughly into four major groups: nonvascular plants, seedless vascular plants, gymnosperms, and angiosperms. These subclasses may also be divided into subclasses. Angiosperms, for example, are divided into dicots and monocots.

- Nonvascular plants lack a vascular system for transporting water and nutrients, and have no roots, stems, or leaves. They also produce spores rather than seeds.
- Vascular plants have a system for transporting water and nutrients and have roots, stems, and leaves. Vascular plants include all seed-bearing plants.
- *Gymnosperms* are nonflowering, seed-producing plants. Their seeds are not protected by the plant's fruit. Many gymnosperms are used in landscapes, including firs, pines, spruces, cedars, junipers, and hemlocks, **Figure 9-7A**.
- *Angiosperms* include most flowering plants whose seeds are enclosed in a fruit. There are well over 250,000 species, including fruits, vegetables, annuals, and perennials. Angiosperms include the smallest flowering plants to the largest flowering trees, **Figure 9-7B**.
- Monocots are a subclass of angiosperms. *Monocots* have only one cotyledon (first leaves) in the seed, parallel-veined leaves, and floral structures in multiples of three. Turfgrasses and ornamental grasses are monocots.
- Dicots are also a subclass of angiosperms. *Dicots* have two cotyledons in their seeds. They have branching venation and floral structures in multiples of four and five. Roses, sunflowers, maples, tomatoes, and oaks are common dicots.

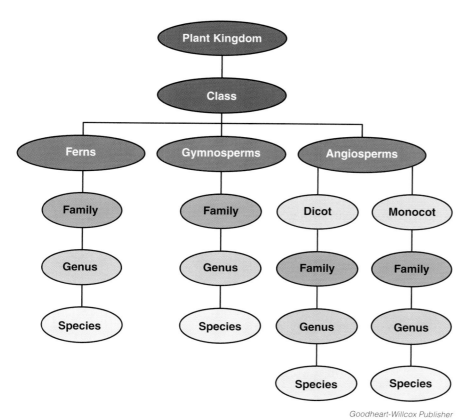

Goodheart-Willcox Publisher

Figure 9-6. Higher plants are classified by related characteristics. A large majority of landscape plants are angiosperms. Further classifications can also be useful when troubleshooting plant issues.

A   *Vizual Studio/Shutterstock.com*

B   *Zaa Chanakhan/Shutterstock.com*

Figure 9-7. A—Gymnosperms bear their seeds in an unprotected manner, such as a cone. B—Lilies are angiosperms that come in a wide array of colors, shapes, and sizes.

Class

Class is the rank that separates or identifies plants within a phylum. Classes may include subclasses describing characteristics in more detail.

Order

Order is the rank that identifies plants within a class. The identifying names end in *ales*. Orders are not used with all species because the class and family names provide sufficient identifying characteristics. Magnolias, for example, have six families and almost 60 registered taxa or groups of organisms forming a unit.

Family

A family separates or identifies plants in an order. Plants in a family have the same floral structures. The Rosaceae family, for example, includes roses, apples, and strawberries, **Figure 9-8**. The plants in this family have similar floral structures, need similar nutrient management, and have about the same growth requirements. They are also susceptible to similar diseases and insects. Families are always capitalized and end in *aceae*.

Genus

As explained earlier, a genus is a subset of organisms within a family that share similar characteristics. The genus is always capitalized and written in italics or underlined. *Quercus*, for example, is the genus for the large number of oaks. *Quercus rubra* is the red oak and *Quercus alba* is the white oak, **Figure 9-9**. One of the most recognizable shared characteristics of oak trees is the production of acorns.

Species

A plant *species* may be defined as a group of similar plants that are capable of interbreeding and producing fertile offspring. Plants with the same specific epithet belong to the same species. Specific epithets can be nouns or adjectives describing characteristics, such as appearance and growth habit. Bearded iris, for example, is *Iris germanica*, representing an herbaceous perennial that grows from rhizomes and is native to Mediterranean climates. When referring to a species, you must use the full botanical name, which is the genus followed by the specific epithet. The specific epithet is always written in lowercase and italicized or underlined and

Nella/Shutterstock.com

NinaM/Shutterstock.com

Roman Samokhin/Shutterstock.com

Figure 9-8. Roses, apples, and strawberries are in the same botanical family. Note the similarity of the flowers.

3523studio/Shutterstock.com

valzan/Shutterstock.com   *Zheltyshev/Shutterstock.com*

Figure 9-9. Oak trees are commonly recognized by the rounded lobes on their leaves and the acorns they drop each year. Their distinctive bark is also used for identification as well as their sturdy structure and shape.

never used alone. Additional examples of specific epithets include *angustifolius*, which means narrow leaves, and *multiflorus*, which translates as *many flowers*. See **Figure 9-10**.

Variety

Variety is a subclassification of a species. A *variety* is a naturally occurring mutation or offspring that differs slightly but distinctively from the parent, **Figure 9-11**. A variety must be able to reproduce and establish itself in nature. A variety is preceded by var., written in lowercase, and italicized or underlined. A common redbud, for example, is *Cercis canadensis*, which has purple flowers. A variety *alba*, has white flowers but a similar growth habit to the original (straight) species. The name would be written as such: *Cercis canadensis* var. *alba*.

Cultivar

A *cultivar* is a variety created by humans. Seedless grapes and seedless watermelons are common cultivars. Cultivars must be propagated asexually. The first letter is always capitalized and the whole name is in single quotes or preceded by the abbreviation cv. A cultivar would be written as such: *Salvia greggii* 'Furman's Red' or *Salvia greggii* cv. Furman's Red. Common cultivars include 'Conlee' azalea, 'Better Boy' tomato, and 'Natchez' crape myrtle, **Figure 9-12**. Cultivars are often used when forming the common name.

R. Lee Ivy   *Tomi Murphy/Shutterstock.com*

Figure 9-10. The straight species of *Iris germanica* (bearded iris) are not commonly sold; however, cultivars of that species are sold around the world.

MaryAnne Campbell/Shutterstock.com   *Sari ONeal/Shutterstock.com*

Figure 9-11. The white redbud is a nice variation of the more typical redbud bloom. It has a similar shape and bloom time to the species but the color variation may work well in a client's landscape scheme.

R. Lee Ivy

Figure 9-12. Many plants, such as the 'Natchez' crape myrtle, provide not only bloom and foliage interest but also architectural features and exfoliating bark.

Looking Forward

Preserving Plants for the Future

Across the country and around the world, botanical gardens, arboreta, and conservatories are used to cultivate plants of all types. These beautiful locations inspire, inform, and educate us about plants.

- **Botanical gardens** are large gardens that often have both greenhouses and outdoor areas that are open to the public. In many botanical gardens, each greenhouse is dedicated to a specific environment, such as a desert or tropical jungle. There may also be areas dedicated to butterflies or even tropical birds.

- Traditionally, an **arboretum** was a place dedicated to growing trees for study and display. Today, arboreta are more likely to be botanical gardens with living collections of trees, shrubs, and herbaceous plants, which are cultivated for scientific study, educational purposes, and for enjoyment. Some arboreta have exclusive collections of plants indigenous to a specific area or from areas around the world with similar climates.

- A **conservatory** is a greenhouse that is typically attached to a home or other structure. The plants cultivated may be primarily for display or scientific study. In the past, as ocean passages to new lands were discovered, wealthy families built conservatories in which they cultivated tropical plants collected from around the world. Many of these plants bore fruit that had been unknown or rare to people in northern climates. Some conservatories were dedicated to the study of medicinal plants.

Many arboreta and botanical gardens have children's gardens, interactive maps, hedge mazes, and locations for special events, such as weddings and parties. These events provide funding for the garden or arboretum. Many land-grant universities have partnerships with botanical gardens or arboreta, resulting in a collection that serves research, education, and extension. There are also privately funded sites that serve similar purposes.

R.A.R. de Bruijn Holding BV/Shutterstock.com

Marie-Jamieson/Shutterstock.com

Daniele Carotenuto/Shutterstock.com

Consider This

1. Is there an arboretum or botanical garden near your home or school? If so, what types of educational programs are offered?
2. Who works at an arboretum or botanical garden? What professions do the employees practice?
3. Are there any unusual or controversial studies being performed?
4. Can you volunteer or sign up for an internship?

Hybrid

A *hybrid* is a cross between plants in different genera or species. Hybrids may occur naturally or be created. Plant breeders create hybrids to combine desirable characteristics, such as habit of growth, bloom time, foliage color, and disease resistance in a single plant. Common hybrids include beans, sweet corn, and oriental lilies, **Figure 9-13**. A hybrid name is written as such: × *Fatshedera* representing a hybrid from different genera of *Fatsia + Hedera* or *Petunia × hybrid*, representing a cross of two species of petunia. The × can be placed before or in the middle of the genera, depending on how the cross was conducted, within or across genera.

Ozgur Coskun/Shutterstock.com   *Minoli/Shutterstock.com*   *Yurly Chertok/Shutterstock.com*

Figure 9-13. Hybrids, such as petunias, are commonly used for display beds, window boxes, and hanging planters. They are hardy annuals with vibrant or subdued color.

Common and Binomial Names

As explained earlier, binomial nomenclature is a two-word naming system. A binomial name consists of the genus and specific epithet. Binomial nomenclature was created to maintain consistency in plant names that could be understood internationally. Common names are names written with words or terms used in everyday language and are often specific to regions.

> **Did You Know?**
>
> Thorns and spines are modified leaves and prickles are modified stems.

Plant Parts

Plants may have six different parts: roots, stems, leaves, flowers, fruits, and seeds. The three main parts are the roots, leaves, and stem. Each of the six parts has a set of jobs to keep the plant healthy, **Figure 9-14**.

Roots

Roots gather nutrients, water, and oxygen from the soil and anchor the plant to the ground. They also provide support and store food. Roots may be fibrous, adventitious, or taproots, **Figure 9-15**. Turfgrass roots are *fibrous root* systems. They are shallow and dense and spread across the soil. Adventitious roots grow from other plant parts, such as stems or leaves. *Taproots* originate from the seed root and tend to grow downward with roots branching out from its sides. Some of the foods we eat are taproots, such as carrots and radishes. Many large tree species have taproots that serve as a strong anchor.

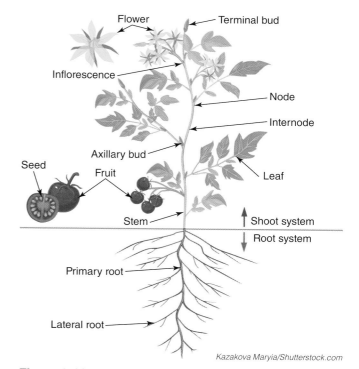

Kazakova Maryia/Shutterstock.com

Figure 9-14. All plant parts work together to capture energy, produce growth, and store nutrients for sustainable growth. Understanding the purpose of each part and process gives a horticulturalist insight into how to maintain or manipulate growth.

Fibrous Root   **Taproot**

Rattiya Thongdumhyu/Shutterstock.com

Figure 9-15. Root systems are categorized as fibrous or taproot systems. The length (depth) of a taproot depends primarily on soil characteristics, such as texture, structure, and the depth of the water table.

Stems

Stems are one of two main axes of plants. The second main axis is the root. Stems transport water and nutrients to other parts of the plant through the phloem and xylem. The *phloem* is living vascular tissue that conveys photosynthetic products throughout the plant. The *xylem*, which is also living tissue, conducts water and nutrients from the roots throughout the plant, **Figure 9-16**. The phloem and xylem are found in the layer referred to as the *vascular cambium*. Stems, which may be herbaceous or ligneous (woody), provide support for the plant and hold leaves, flowers, and branches. Herbaceous stems are frail and can be easily broken. Herbaceous stems are supported mainly by water and will wilt or bend if they lack moisture. Ligneous stems are stiff and rigid, such as tree trunks and branches. See **Figure 9-17**. Secondary growth areas occur in the vascular cambium (xylem and phloem). The primary growth areas are at the *apices*, or tips of roots and stems.

Underground Stems

Geophytes are perennial plants with an underground food and water storage organ. Geophytes spend part of their annual life cycle as a dormant, fleshy, underground structure. Geophytes are divided into seven categories: bulbs, corms, tubers, tuberous stems, tuberous roots, rhizomes, and pseudobulbs, **Figure 9-18**.

- *Bulbs* are modified stems that contain a short, fleshy basal plate at the bottom from which roots grow and which holds fleshy scales. Bulbs have the ability to store food. *Tunicate bulbs*, such as hyacinth and tulip bulbs, have a solid core of leaves covered by a thin, papery sheath. A *nontunicate bulb* has loose, fleshy scales and does not have a dry covering, such as a lily bulb. Bulbs are dug and separated when dormant.

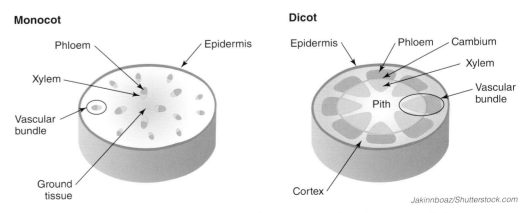

Jakinnboaz/Shutterstock.com

Figure 9-16. Stems conduct water and nutrients and provide structure and storage for plants. Xylem and phloem is arranged in vascular bundles with the cambium layer producing pith to the inside and bark to the outside.

A *rootstock/Shutterstock.com* B *Peter Turner Photography/ Shutterstock.com* C *logoboom/Shutterstock.com*

Figure 9-17. A—The herbaceous-like stems of this hosta are flexible and will die back to the ground during winter in most temperate climates. B/C—Woody stems similar to the hydrangea's store energy and provide structure for flowers and fruits and endure dormant seasons.

- *Tubers* are underground stems with nodes and internodes. (*Nodes* are the point of attachment for roots, leaves, and flowers and *internodes* are the spaces between the nodes.) Tubers serve as food storage organs. Tubers are cut into sections with two buds each. Each section will form another tuber when planted. Caladiums, anemones, and potatoes are tubers.
- *Corms* are modified enlarged stems that serve as a storage organ. Corms have nodes, internodes, and a thin, papery covering. The new corms that form on the original can be separated and planted. Crocus, gladiolus, liatris, freesia, and crocosmia are common corms.
- *Tuberous stems* are generated as the *hypocotyl* (the stem section between the upper and lower portion of the plant) swells after germination. Cyclamen and gloxinia are tuberous stems. The propagation method for tuberous stems varies by plant species.
- *Tuberous roots* are adapted for storage with shoots at one end and absorption roots on the other. Peonies, dahlias, sweet potatoes, irises, and daylilies have tuberous roots.

Tommy Atthi/Shutterstock.com   *Richard Griffin/Shutterstock.com*   *sura p singh/Shutterstock.com*   *art-TAyga/Shutterstock.com*

Figure 9-18. Geophytes are readily available for varied growing objectives, such as landscape color in early spring with tulip blooms and table displays of forced blooms.

- *Rhizomes* are modified stem structures that grow horizontally below or near the soil's surface. Rhizomes form roots on the bottom and stems on the top. Rhizomes can be cut into sections and planted. They are similar to *stolons* (modified stems immediately above the surface) but store more food. Bamboo, ginger, Solomon's seal, and certain irises are rhizomes.
- *Pseudobulbs* are swollen stems on stolons of certain orchids. They are not botanically true bulbs but do serve as storage organs. Pseudobulbs can be cut into pieces and planted.

STEM *Connection*

Nutrient Deficiency Symptoms

Symptoms of nutrient deficiency may be mistaken for issues caused by various pests, including some diseases. Chlorosis, which is the yellowing of leaf tissue due to the lack of chlorophyll, is commonly caused by nutrient deficiencies, but it may also be caused by damaged or compacted roots, high alkalinity in the soil, or a disease infestation. It is therefore vital to determine the cause of the symptom before applying a remedy. The following list provides common symptoms of nutrient deficiencies.

Macronutrients

- **Nitrogen (N).** Older leaves yellow and the rest of the plant turns light green, stunted growth and early maturity.
- **Phosphorous (P).** Older leaves turn dark green or reddish-purple, stunted growth, reduced drought tolerance, higher susceptibility to disease, leaf tips appear burnt, thin stems.
- **Potassium (K).** Older leaves wilt/curl, appear scorched, interveinal chlorosis begins at base going inward from leaf margins (yellow edges), dead leaves.
- **Calcium (Ca).** Distorted or irregularly shaped new leaves, poor fruit development, symptoms in new leaves and shoots, leaf tips appear burnt.
- **Magnesium (Mg).** Chlorosis on edges of older leaves, leaf veins remain green or have a green patch in center, poor fruit development, leaf tips become twisted.
- **Sulfur (S).** Chlorosis begins in younger leaves followed by older leaves, symptoms similar to those of nitrogen deficiency.

Micronutrients

- **Boron (B).** Deformed and discolored leaves, death of terminal buds, rotting of roots.
- **Copper (Cu).** Stunted growth and leaves turn dark green with brown tips.
- **Iron (Fe).** Chlorosis between veins of young leaves, yellow or white areas on young leaves, necrotic spots on leaf tissue, poor color of fruits.
- **Manganese (Mn).** Chlorosis between veins of young leaves, stunted growth of leaves, shoots, and fruit, dead spots, scorching on leaves.
- **Molybdenum (Mo).** Chlorosis at edges of older leaves, whole plant turns light green, yellowing or mottling on young leaves.
- **Zinc (Zn).** Terminal leaves form rosettes, chlorosis between veins of new leaves, which are stunted; short internodes, missing leaf blades.

Consider This

1. How would you determine if a plant is nutrient deficient?
2. How would you determine if the problem is caused by a lack of nutrients or by some type of pest?
3. How would you treat a nutrient deficiency?
4. What symptoms are caused by nutrient toxicity (too much of a nutrient)?
5. How would you treat a nutrient toxicity?

Leaves

Leaves are the main organs of photosynthesis and transpiration. Leaves are typically comprised of a blade (flattened portions) and a petiole (leaf stalk). Plant leaves have evolved to suit their environment. Flat leaves, for example, have more surface area to absorb more light. Thin leaves allow the sunlight to reach cells vital to photosynthesis. Thick leaves with waxy surfaces, such as those of a succulent, enable the plant to retain moisture, even during drought periods. See **Figure 9-19**.

Flowers

Flowers are the reproductive organs of a flowering plant. Flowers have sepals, petals, and stamens. These organs are attached to a flower stalk, a thickened stem called the receptacle. The petals attract pollinators and the sepals at the base of the flower help protect the developing bud. Flowering plants have female and male parts that are required for sexual reproduction. See **Figure 9-20**.

Goodheart-Willcox Publisher

Figure 9-19. Thick leaved succulents are able to endure harsh climates with little water due to their waxy cuticles and large amounts of storage cells in their leaves.

The female part is the pistil, which is located in the center of the flower. The pistil is composed of the stigma, style, and ovary. The stigma is the sticky knob at the top of the pistil. The stigma is attached to the style, which leads to the ovary containing ovules (female eggs). The male parts of the flower are the anther and filament that make up the stamen. The stamen is usually around the pistil. The anther produces pollen (male reproductive cells) and the filament supports the anther. During fertilization, the pollen land on the stigma, travel down a tube to the style and enter the ovary. Fertilization occurs when the pollen join with the ovule and the fertilized ovule becomes the fruit.

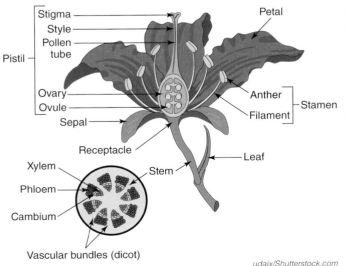

udaix/Shutterstock.com

R. Lee Ivy

Figure 9-20. Reproductive parts are easy to identify on many flowering plants, such as the lily.

A   *Bonnie Taylor Barry/Shutterstock.com*

B   *AlessandroZocc/Shutterstock.com*

Figure 9-21. A—Many flower blooms are pollinated by birds. The hummingbird's wings help spread pollen by fanning it into the air. B— Maple tree samaras twirl like helicopter blades and fall or are blown elsewhere to expand the range of the species.

Fruits

Fruits are mature ovaries that have formed because of the fertilization of the ovules. The purpose of fruit is to protect the seed inside and to aid in seed dispersal. Some fruits help seeds spread, maple seeds for example.

Seeds

Seeds are the reproductive units of both angiosperms and gymnosperms. Angiosperms are a class of flowering plants that develop seeds enclosed within an ovary. Gymnosperms do not have flowers. Their developing seeds are borne on the plants without an ovary. Seeds develop from the fertilization process. In nature, seeds are dispersed by wind, water, and animals, **Figure 9-21**.

Plant Processes

Plants use basic biological processes to drive growth from a seed to a mature plant. These processes are also responsible for producing materials plants use to reproduce. Vital plant processes include photosynthesis, respiration, transpiration, translocation, and reproduction.

Photosynthesis

Photosynthesis is a process in which plants capture energy from the sun and convert carbon dioxide (CO_2) and water (H_2O) into carbohydrate molecules that can be used as sources of energy/food.

$$6CO_2 + 6H_2O \xrightarrow{\text{light energy}} C_6H_{12}O_6 + 6O_2$$

Photosynthesis begins when a plant takes carbon dioxide from the air and water through its roots. Photosynthesis is one of the most important chemical reactions on Earth because plants take in carbon dioxide and emit oxygen. This action combats carbon buildup in the atmosphere and provides us with the oxygen we breathe. The process of *carbon sequestration* is defined as capturing CO_2 and storing it in liquid or solid forms. See **Figure 9-22**. Photosynthesis is also the beginning of the process that enables plants to produce the foods we eat.

Respiration

Respiration is a process in which the sugar produced by photosynthesis combines with oxygen to produce energy in a form that plants can use.

$$C_6H_{12}O_6 + 6O_2 \longrightarrow 6CO_2 + 6H_2O + energy$$
$$glucose + oxygen \longrightarrow carbon\ dioxide + water + energy$$

Unlike photosynthesis, which only occurs when light is available, respiration occurs constantly. Although oxygen is consumed during respiration, the plant still produces more oxygen during photosynthesis than what is consumed during respiration. The plant uses the sugars as energy for growth, seed formation, flower formation, and fruit development. Respiration is impeded in water-saturated conditions because the roots cannot draw oxygen from the soil. Variations in temperature may also affect the rate of respiration.

Transpiration

Transpiration is the process plants use to carry moisture from the roots to the small pores on the surface of the leaves. The moisture evaporates from the leaves as vapor and enters the atmosphere. Through transpiration, plants experience evaporative cooling and take in nutrients, carbon dioxide, and water. Transpiration is affected by humidity levels, temperature, wind, the plant's structure, and especially by the amount of water available. See **Figure 9-23**. Transpiration is what helps you feel cool when you sit in the shade of a tree.

Translocation

Translocation is the movement of sugar within the plant. Translocation occurs when one part of the plant moves sugar to another part of the plant that needs the carbohydrates. The source of the sugar can be an organ or any tissue that is part of the photosynthetic process, such as a leaf. Parts of the plant that receive the sugar include developing fruit, flowers, stems, developing leaves, and roots that serve as storage organs. Translocation is also the process that produces the maple syrup we enjoy on our pancakes and waffles.

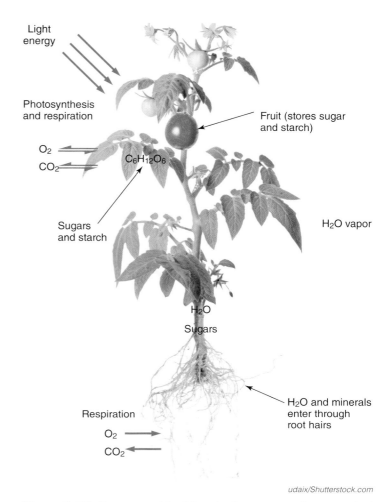

Light energy

Photosynthesis and respiration

O_2

CO_2

$C_6H_{12}O_6$

Fruit (stores sugar and starch)

H_2O vapor

Sugars and starch

H_2O

Sugars

Respiration

O_2

CO_2

H_2O and minerals enter through root hairs

udaix/Shutterstock.com

Figure 9-22. Energy and fuel for plant processes is generated through the biochemical reaction of photosynthesis. This process uses water and carbon dioxide to generate oxygen and carbohydrates when the plant is exposed to a source of energy, such as sunlight.

Goodheart-Willcox Publisher

Figure 9-23. A plant loses its turgidity when it loses too much water. Although many plants respond quickly when watered, it is very stressful for a plant to go unwatered.

Career Connection

John Hoffman

John Hoffman, Nurseryman

John Hoffman and his wife Jill own Hoffman Nursery, Inc., a wholesale nursery specializing in ornamental and native grasses. Having been in the business more than 30 years, John has developed a large network of friends and colleagues. He talks often with customers, suppliers, and employees. Having these conversations is his favorite part of the job and many business contacts have become close, lifelong friends.

Hoffman Nursery currently grows more than 140 varieties of grasses. John often speaks with plant breeders about new grasses that can be introduced into the trade. He also leads the sales team for the nursery and works with customers to help build their grass programs. It is his responsibility to move the business forward, and the future of the company is always on his mind.

John is past president of the Perennial Plant Association and has served on the board of several horticultural organizations.

Consider This

1. How is having a nursery that specializes in a specific type of plant advantageous?
2. How could the Hoffman Nursery participate in prairie restoration projects?
3. Does owning a specialty type of nursery appeal to you? Why or why not?

Reproduction

Plants reproduce sexually or asexually. Sexual reproduction occurs through *meiosis* and fertilization. Meiosis occurs through cell division in which the chromosomes are divided in half. The union of the female and male gametes is fertilization in which the plant receives half of its chromosomes from each parent. This results in a unique specimen. Asexual reproduction occurs through a process referred to as *mitosis*, during which plant cells duplicate and divide a complete set of chromosomes. This results in a specimen that is genetically identical to the parent plant. Reproduction can be affected by multiple factors but it is the lack of pollinators, such as bees, that is of primary concern in many areas of our country and around the world.

Plant Nutrition

To thrive, plants must be growing in soil environments that coincide with their growth needs. Successful plant management requires understanding how plants obtain nutrients and how to cultivate the availability of those nutrients, **Figure 9-24**. Scientists have identified 17 elements that are essential for healthy plant growth and development. These elements are divided into macronutrients and micronutrients.

Macronutrients and Micronutrients

Macronutrients are nutrients that plants need in the largest quantities. The primary macronutrients are nitrogen (N), phosphorous (P), and potassium (K). The secondary macronutrients are calcium (Ca), magnesium (Mg),

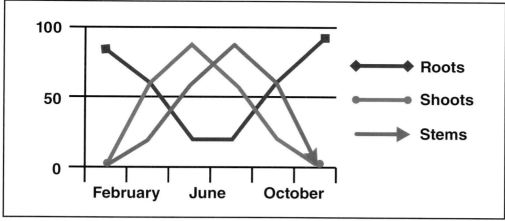

Goodheart-Willcox Publisher

Figure 9-24. Carbohydrate and sugar resources are available to different parts of the plant throughout the year.

and sulfur (S). The ***micronutrients*** are also necessary for plant health, but they are needed in very small amounts. The micronutrients are boron (B), chlorine (Cl), copper (Cu), iron (Fe), manganese (Mn), molybdenum (Mo), nickel (Ni), and zinc (Zn). Plants obtain carbon (C), hydrogen (H), and oxygen (O) primarily from water and carbon dioxide in the air, but they also acquire these essentials from the soil.

Soil pH

The pH of the soil determines the availability of nutrients. (The *pH* is a number indicating the acidity or alkalinity of a substance, such as soil or water.) If the pH is not in the acceptable range of 5.5 to 6.5 (for most plants), certain nutrients are not readily available. Azaleas, for example, need lower soil pH levels because they cannot efficiently acquire iron from the soil and soils with a lower pH provide higher amounts of iron. See **Figure 9-25**.

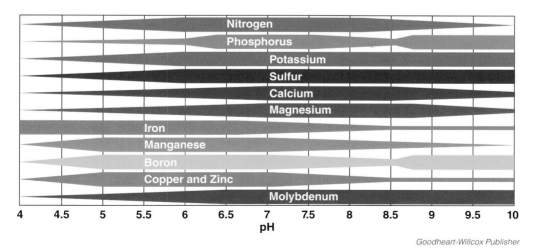

Goodheart-Willcox Publisher

Figure 9-25. The pH of the soil governs the nutrient availability to plants. At low or high pH, some nutrients are unavailable and other nutrients are available in excess. The plant may develop toxic levels of the excess nutrients. The large majority of nutrients are available in soil with a pH that is slightly below neutral.

Summary

- A binomial plant name provides information about a plant that distinguishes it from other plants.

- Common names are not a reliable way to communicate with others due to variations used in different regions.

- Genus and specific epithet make up the species name for a plant. Varieties and cultivars give further explanation of the plant's unique characteristics while hybrids can be a collection of similar plants within the classification.

- Plant taxonomy is the international science of naming and classifying organisms.

- Scientific classification is the system of grouping like organisms. The system uses a specific order of classes: domain, kingdom, phylum, class, order, family, genus, species, common name, binomial name.

- Gymnosperms are nonflowering, seed-producing plants. Their seeds are not protected by the plant's fruit.

- Angiosperms include most flowering plants whose seeds are enclosed in a fruit.

- Geophytes are perennial plants with an underground food storage organ. Bulbs, corms, tubers, tuberous stems, tuberous roots, rhizomes, and pseudobulbs are all geophytes.

- Vital plant processes include photosynthesis, respiration, transpiration, translocation, and reproduction.

- Plants use photosynthesis to capture energy from the sun and convert carbon dioxide and water into glucose sugar that can be used as sources of energy/food.

- Respiration is a process in which the sugar produced by photosynthesis combine with oxygen to produce energy in a form that plants can use.

- Transpiration is the process plants use to carry moisture from the roots to the small pores on the surface of the leaves.

- Translocation is the movement of sugar within the plant.

- Plants may reproduce sexually or asexually.

Chapter Review

Know and Understand ⤴

Match the terms to the appropriate descriptions in 1–14.

   A. angiosperm
   B. class
   C. classification
   D. cultivar
   E. dicot
   F. family
   G. genus
   H. gymnosperm
   I. hybrid
   J. monocot
   K. order
   L. species
   M. specific epithet
   N. taxonomy
   O. variety

1. A cross between plants in different genera or species.

2. The rank that identifies plants within a class.

3. A group of similar plants that are capable of interbreeding and producing fertile offspring.

4. The second part of a binomial name.

5. A naturally occurring mutation or offspring that differs slightly but distinctively from the parent.

6. The science of naming and classifying organisms.

7. A nonflowering, seed-producing plant whose seeds are not protected by the plant's fruit.

8. The rank that separates or identifies plants in an order.

9. A subset of organisms within a family that share similar characteristics.

10. The system of grouping like organisms.

11. A type of plant variety created by humans.

12. Flowering plant whose seeds are enclosed in a fruit.

13. Have only one cotyledon in the seed and floral structures in multiples of three.

14. Plant with two cotyledons in its seeds.

Answer questions 15–41 using the information provided in this chapter.

15. The two-word naming system that describes plant species in a consistent manner is referred to as _____.
   A. common nomenclature
   B. binomial nomenclature
   C. botanical nomenclature
   D. scientific nomenclature

16. The botanical name is also referred to as the _____.
   A. Linnaeus name
   B. common name
   C. Latin or scientific name
   D. All of the above.

17. The specific epithet may refer to _____.
   A. country of origin
   B. stems or flowers
   C. colors of foliage
   D. All of the above.

18. *True or False?* A plant can be identified internationally by its common name.
   A. True.
   B. False.

19. *True or False?* The hierarchical order of plant classification ranges from most inclusive in domain to least inclusive in species.
   A. True.
   B. False.

20. *True or False?* Families are always lowercase and end in *aceae*.
   A. True.
   B. False.

21. *True or False?* The genus is always capitalized and written in italics or underlined.
   A. True.
   B. False.

22. *True or False?* When referring to a species, you must use the full botanical name, which is the phylum followed by the specific epithet.
    A. True.
    B. False.

23. *True or False?* The specific epithet is always capitalized, underlined, and never used alone.
    A. True.
    B. False.

24. *True or False?* The name *Cercis canadensis* var. *alba*, is written incorrectly.
    A. True.
    B. False.

25. *True or False?* The first letter of a cultivar is always capitalized and the whole name is in single quotes or preceded by the abbreviation cv.
    A. True.
    B. False.

26. Which of the following originates from the seed root and tends to grow downward with roots branching out from its sides?
    A. Fibrous root.
    B. Adventitious root.
    C. Ligneous root.
    D. Taproot.

27. Stems are one of two main axes of plants. They serve multiple purposes, including _____.
    A. transport water
    B. provide support
    C. transport nutrients
    D. All of the above.

28. Perennial plants with an underground food and water storage organ are referred to as _____.
    A. geophytes
    B. bulbs and tubers
    C. corms and rhizomes
    D. All of the above.

29. *True or False?* A tunicate bulb has loose, fleshy scales and does not have a dry covering.
    A. True.
    B. False.

30. *True or False?* A nontunicate bulb has a solid core of leaves covered by a thin, papery sheath.
    A. True.
    B. False.

31. *True or False?* Tubers are underground stems with nodes and internodes.
    A. True.
    B. False.

32. The plant parts that are the main organs of photosynthesis and transpiration are the _____.
    A. leaves
    B. flowers
    C. stems
    D. fruits

33. *True or False?* Fruits are the reproductive organs of a flowering plant.
    A. True.
    B. False.

34. *True or False?* Flowers are mature ovaries that have formed because of the fertilization of the ovules.
    A. True.
    B. False.

35. The reproductive units of both angiosperms and gymnosperms are _____.
    A. seeds
    B. roots
    C. fruits
    D. All of the above.

36. Which of the following is a vital plant process?
    A. Respiration.
    B. Reproduction.
    C. Transpiration.
    D. All of the above.

37. *True or False?* Photosynthesis begins when a plant takes oxygen from the air and water through its roots.
    A. True.
    B. False.

38. *True or False?* One of the most important chemical reactions on Earth is photosynthesis.
    A. True.
    B. False.

39. Which of the following statements describe a plant's respiration process?
   A. Occurs constantly.
   B. Consumes carbon dioxide.
   C. Only occurs when light is available.
   D. Carries moisture from the leaves to the roots.

40. Which of the plant processes is affected by humidity levels, temperature, wind, the plant's structure, and the amount of water available?
   A. Consumption.
   B. Transpiration.
   C. Sequestration.
   D. Retention.

41. The movement of sugar within the plants is referred to as _____.
   A. transpiration.
   B. transportation.
   C. translocation.
   D. All of the above.

Thinking Critically

1. Can you identify the parts of a live plant, including the root system?

2. How would you show your understanding of binomial nomenclature?

3. Why is it necessary to use a dedicated nomenclature for identifying plants?

4. How would you determine the taxonomic ranks of an unidentified plant?

5. How would you describe the influence of light and temperature on plant growth, including phototropism?

Suggested Activities

1. Working with a partner or in a small group, research and identify geophytes adaptable to your area. Design a flowerbed with annuals, perennials, and at least three types of geophytes. The bed is 3′ × 12′ and visible from only the front and sides because it backs up to a privacy fence. Design the bed so there are flowers blooming throughout the growing season. Determine if any of the geophytes need to be dug up and stored in the winter.

2. Working with a partner, obtain three types of flowers (one of each). Determine which parts are present and which are lacking. Identify the taxonomic ranking of the flower, the root system, and the growth cycle.

3. Visit a local plant nursery, if possible, and photograph several plants and note the names on their labels. Research the plants and determine if the plants are labeled according to proper binominal nomenclature.

4. Work in a group of 3 to 4 and develop a mnemonic device to help you learn the 18 essential nutrients for plant growth.

5. Work with a partner to create a visual presentation that illustrates different nutrient deficiencies and/or toxicities and methods of treatment.

CHAPTER 10

Ornamental Plants in the Landscape

While studying this chapter, look for the activity icon to:

- **Practice** vocabulary terms with Words to Know activities.
- **Expand** learning with identification activities.
- **Reinforce** what you learn by completing Know and Understand questions.

G-WLEARNING.com

www.g-wlearning.com/agriculture

Chapter Outcomes

After studying this chapter, you will be able to:

- Identify types of plant materials commonly used in landscape designs.
- Describe the functions of trees, shrubs, and other plants in the landscape.
- List examples of ground covers, trees, shrubs, herbaceous perennials, vines, ornamental grasses, and edibles.
- Understand how to incorporate edibles into the landscape.
- Explain how plants are used to create borders and privacy screens.
- Identify constructed plant forms, such as topiaries and espalier.

Key Terms ➦

aquatic plant
bedding plant
climbing stem root
clingers
clinging stem root
dormant
dwarf shrub
edible landscaping
emergent plant
espalier
floating leaf plant
grass-like plant
heat island
herbaceous perennial
large shrub

large tree
medium shrub
ornamental grass
scrambler
shrub
small tree
specimen
submersed aquatic plant
tendril
topiary
tree
twiner
windbreak
woody plant

Introduction

Most landscape designs include a large variety of plant materials. Many of the plants are chosen for their functionality as well as their aesthetic value. These plants often serve multiple purposes, such as providing shade or privacy while adding color and interest to the landscape, **Figure 10-1**. The variety of materials available make it possible for designers to choose plants that will enhance the design, please the client, and thrive in the landscape. In this chapter, you will learn about the many types of ornamental plants and the ways they can be used in landscape designs.

Figure 10-1. Few plants provide the aesthetic beauty and functionality of trees, such as the *Jacaranda mimosifolia*/jacaranda illustrated above.

Trees

Few plants can provide the beauty of established trees. A *tree* is a woody perennial plant, typically with one main stem that grows to a mature height of at least 15′, **Figure 10-2.** A *woody plant* is defined as a plant that produces wood as its structural tissue. Trees used in landscapes may be evergreen trees and remain green throughout the year or deciduous trees, which shed their leaves annually. Although evergreens remain green throughout the year, it is important to note that they do shed leaves or needles throughout the year. How much a tree sheds may be of concern to a client that prefers a low-maintenance landscape. Evergreen magnolias, for example, litter leathery foliage throughout the year. The amount of needles that pines drop, in addition to cones, depends on the species and environmental conditions. Another factor to consider is the time a tree takes to reach maturity and its expected life span. Most nurseries offer trees of varying height or maturity. Clients may choose trees that are close to their mature height to establish a mature landscape much sooner than if younger trees were installed.

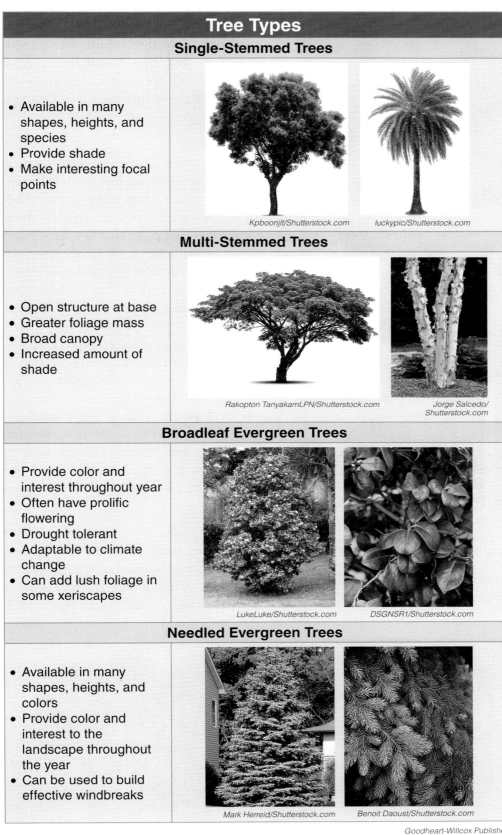

Tree Types

Single-Stemmed Trees

- Available in many shapes, heights, and species
- Provide shade
- Make interesting focal points

Kpboonjit/Shutterstock.com   *luckypic/Shutterstock.com*

Multi-Stemmed Trees

- Open structure at base
- Greater foliage mass
- Broad canopy
- Increased amount of shade

Rakopton TanyakamLPN/Shutterstock.com   *Jorge Salcedo/ Shutterstock.com*

Broadleaf Evergreen Trees

- Provide color and interest throughout year
- Often have prolific flowering
- Drought tolerant
- Adaptable to climate change
- Can add lush foliage in some xeriscapes

LukeLuke/Shutterstock.com   *DSGNSR1/Shutterstock.com*

Needled Evergreen Trees

- Available in many shapes, heights, and colors
- Provide color and interest to the landscape throughout the year
- Can be used to build effective windbreaks

Mark Herreid/Shutterstock.com   *Benoit Daoust/Shutterstock.com*

Goodheart-Willcox Publisher

Figure 10-2. Trees provide aesthetics unmatched by any other category of plant material. Large trees help frame the view and provide a backdrop for the landscape.

Christopher D. Hart

Figure 10-3. Small trees, such as this Japanese maple (*Acer palmatum*), provide interest year round. The weeping growth habit, fine textured leaves, and beautiful fall color make these trees highly desired in any landscape.

A   *Christopher D. Hart*

B   *Jill Lang/Shutterstock.com*

Figure 10-4. A—Deciduous trees provide accent in the autumn with their colorful changing leaves. B—Small trees are excellent sources of spring color. Many small trees, such as crape myrtle, have attractive flowers and ornamental bark.

Tree Sizes

Trees can be divided into two categories: small and large. *Small trees* have a mature height approximately up to 25′. *Large trees* are defined as those having a mature height over 25′.

Small Trees

Small trees are easily incorporated in landscape designs and are used more frequently than large trees, **Figure 10-3**. Small trees are often used as specimens. A *specimen* is a plant that is a focal point due to its aesthetic characteristics, including leaf color, unique growth habit, exfoliating bark, and/or floral and fruit displays.

When used as an accent, small trees complement other plants through their floral or fruiting display, **Figure 10-4A**. The flowers, fruits, and seeds can be the most exciting display for a plant during the year. Small trees used as specimens are focal points due to their aesthetic properties. These properties include interesting leaf color, unique growth habit, exfoliating bark, and/or floral and fruit displays, **Figure 10-4B**.

Large Trees

In addition to providing shade and contributing oxygen to the atmosphere, large trees may be used as windbreaks or specimens. A *windbreak* is a row or rows of trees planted to divert wind, **Figure 10-5**.

KPG_Payless/Shutterstock.com

Figure 10-5. A wide variety of plants can function as windbreaks. Windbreaks provide shelter from the wind and other elements to create a more pleasant outdoor living area.

Evergreens are often planted along the north and west sides of the property to create a windbreak because they provide protection year-round. The dense growth habit that alters the speed and direction of the wind can also be used as a sound buffer. The ability of trees to buffer sound is especially important when the outdoor living area is near a busy and noisy street. Large trees are also used as specimens in landscape designs.

Species

Some plants fall into more than one category. The plant's location and species will determine the category in which it belongs. Crape Myrtle (*Lagerstroemia indica*), for example, has many different cultivars. The cultivars range in mature heights of 36″ tall shrubs to trees that are over 30′ tall, **Figure 10-6**.

Small trees commonly used in landscape designs include Japanese maple, dogwood, crape myrtle, saucer magnolia, eastern redbud, and Japanese apricot. Large trees used in landscape designs include beech, white ash, sycamore, southern magnolia, eastern white pine, loblolly pine, and various oaks. See **Figure 10-7**.

Functions

Trees are used to create shade, add color, provide wind protection, serve as sound buffers, and provide framework for a design. Trees also sequester carbon from the atmosphere and lower temperature on heat islands. An urban *heat island* is an area in which the temperature is higher than that of the surrounding areas due to human activities. Buildings, pavement, concrete, and other structures help create heat islands, **Figure 10-8**.

Shade

Trees provide shade for outdoor living areas and permanent structures, such as

kimkwanhee/Shutterstock.com   *Jorge Salcedo/Shutterstock.com*

Figure 10-6. Cultivar selection is extremely important when selecting plant materials. Plants, such as Crape Myrtles (*Lagerstroemia indica*), are available in a wide variety of cultivars. Mature heights range from just a few feet to over 30′ tall.

A   *ZQFotography/Shutterstock.com*   **B**   *Wolfilser/Shutterstock.com*

Figure 10-7. A—Small trees, such as the Japanese apricot, provide beautiful floral displays that make strong statements. B—White ash does not provide a showy floral display, however, its growth habit and architecture make it a desirable large tree for many landscapes.

Lindy Klales/Shutterstock.com

Figure 10-8. The tree and turf between the parking spaces will be negatively affected by heat reflected from the asphalt..

Christopher D. Hart

Figure 10-9. Trees in downtown Washington, DC, provide shade along the city sidewalks.

a home or garage. The temperature in shaded areas is lower than the temperature in areas fully exposed to the sun. A designer can use shade from trees to create a more enjoyable outdoor living space, **Figure 10-9**. The direction of the cast shade depends on the size of the tree as well as the time of the year. If a large deciduous tree is desired, installation on the southwest side of a structure is recommended. Placing the tree on the southwest side of the home will provide shade cast over the house during the summer months. In the winter, a deciduous tree will shed its leaves and allow sunlight to pass through its branches and help warm the home.

Color

Color is another important function that trees provide. The leaves easily attract the eye due to the dense growth habit. The color or texture of the bark can also be used in a design. In many areas, the fall color of deciduous trees is the most noticeable aspects of trees. Maples, gums, and ginkgo trees provide striking fall color.

Framework

Few living plant materials have as much architectural impact as trees. Trees provide framework for landscape designs and help soften the sharp lines created by buildings. The variety of heights available provide the designer many options when creating his or her design.

Christopher D. Hart

Figure 10-10. Shrubs come in a wide variety of shapes, sizes, and colors. Such a wide variety allows for selection of the perfect shrub for virtually every site.

Shrubs

Shrubs are woody plants that are available in a variety of heights and have more than one stem. Depending on the species, shrubs range from 18″ to approximately 20′. Shrubs typically feature dense growth habit and are commonly used as ornamentals. They may be selected for flower color, growth habit, scent, fruit, or leaf color, **Figure 10-10.** Shrubs may be used to soften the hard surface of building's foundation or to conceal objects, such as an air conditioning unit. As a hedge, shrubs can establish boundaries or provide privacy. Shrubs that thicken and provide foliage from the ground up make effective privacy borders. Shrubs are classified as dwarf, medium, or large and may be evergreen or deciduous.

Dwarf Shrubs

Dwarf shrubs are shrubs with a mature height of less than 4′. Dwarf shrubs are commonly used in areas where short, low-maintenance plants are desired. Dwarf shrubs are ideal for use under windows and other structures.

Medium Shrubs

Medium shrubs are shrubs ranging in height from 4′ to 6′. Medium shrubs are commonly used as foundation plants. Medium shrubs used around a foundation require less pruning than large shrubs.

Large Shrubs

Large shrubs are shrubs with a mature height over 6′. Large shrubs are commonly used as corner foundation plants, hedges, and privacy screens, **Figure 10-11**. Their dense growth habit also makes them effective windbreaks and sound barriers. Large shrubs may also be pruned and formed into specimen plants that resemble trees or other shapes.

Evergreen Shrubs

Dwarf, medium, and large shrubs are all available in evergreen and deciduous forms. Evergreen shrubs effectively provide year-round interest and privacy. A designer can use different evergreen shrubs to create visual interest with varying leaf sizes, colors, and textures, **Figure 10-12.** Glossy Abeilia (*Abelia x grandiflora*) and Azalea (*Rhododendron obtusum*), for example, have ornamental leaves all year and blooms in spring, early summer, or late summer. The bloom time varies by species.

Deciduous Shrubs

Deciduous shrubs are available with a variety of leaf types, sizes, and colors. Some varieties offer a spectacular, albeit short-lived,

romakoma/Shutterstock.com

Figure 10-11. Large shrubs can be used to create a living wall that provides privacy and protection.

Christopher D. Hart

Figure 10-12. Various growth shapes and growth habits of plants can be used to create year-round visual interest.

display of flowers. The designer must consider how deciduous shrubs will impact the landscape after they lose their leaves. A combination of evergreen and deciduous shrubs are often used to create visual interest year-round.

Shrub Species

With such a wide variety of shrubs available, designers can always find one that will suit any area of the landscape. Many shrubs, such as azaleas, rhododendrons, and hydrangeas, are often selected for the beautiful and colorful blooms but they also have attractive foliage. Boxwoods make excellent shaped hedges and topiaries and provide color and interest throughout the year. Hollies are available as small evergreen shrubs to trees that grow over 80′. Hollies provide color throughout the year and berries that help sustain wildlife in the winter. Other popular shrubs include Glossy Abelia, Winter Daphne, Indian Hawthorn, Pfitzer's Juniper, and Wax Myrtle, **Figure 10-13**.

Shrub Cultivars

Cultivar selection is of utmost importance when selecting shrubs for a design because each cultivar possesses unique characteristics. *Ilex vomitoria* 'Pendula,' for example, is a large weeping evergreen shrub with a mature height of 15′. (Pendula is Latin for weeping.) It features beautiful red berries. *Ilex vomitoria* 'Nana,' dwarf yaupon holly, is a dwarf evergreen shrub with a mature height of 5′. Red fruit is rarely seen on dwarf yaupon holly. Plant breeders have also created shrubs with prolonged bloom time. Roses, hydrangeas, and azaleas that bloom multiple times throughout the year for prolonged periods can be used to provide more color and interest.

A   *Christopher D. Hart*

B   *Mccallk69/Shutterstock.com*

Figure 10-13. A—Kaleidoscope Abelia is a small shrub featuring red, green, yellow, and purple foliage. B—Azaleas offer early spring flowers unrivaled by few other shrubs.

Herbaceous Perennials

Herbaceous perennials are herbaceous plants (plant with a soft, succulent stem) that die to the ground, become dormant, and return the next growing season. When a plant is *dormant,* the buds and seeds are inhibited from growing until the environmental conditions become ideal for the plant to grow. These plants do not have aboveground woody stems. Hosta and sedum are popular herbaceous perennials. Herbaceous perennials are popular with designers and clients because they come back year after year and most require little maintenance and are easy to grow, **Figure 10-14**. They also grow larger each year and often can be divided and planted in other locations.

Some herbaceous perennials are known for their blooms and growth habits but many are chosen for their unique foliage. Most perennials are versatile and may be grown in containers, used as fillers between shrubs, or used as ground cover. Few plants can rival the ornamental impact of herbaceous perennials.

Herbaceous Perennial Species

Herbaceous perennials have been favorites of landscape designers and professional and amateur gardeners for years. Perennials, such as daylilies,

A   *Manfred Ruckszio/Shutterstock.com*   **B**   *Debu55y/Shutterstock.com*

Figure 10-14. A—Euphorbia is a drought-tolerant perennial that provides unique visual interest. B—Herbaceous perennial plants provide interesting colors and textures that can quickly become a focal point in any landscape.

daisies, and purple coneflowers, adorn residential and commercial landscapes across the country. Other popular perennials include yarrow, hollyhock, columbine, clematis, larkspur, and phlox, **Figure 10-15**.

Cultivars

Plant breeders have developed thousands of cultivars of many favorite herbaceous perennials. Over 2000 hosta cultivars have been named and each plant is unique in its height, flower color, width, and variegation pattern. *Hosta* 'Blue Mouse Ears,' for example, has a mature height of 8″ and features tiny leaves that resemble mouse ears whereas *Hosta* 'Blue Angel' has large leaves and grows to a mature height of 32″. The different cultivars enable designers to use plant species in areas where the original species may not thrive.

Ornamental Grasses

True ***ornamental grasses*** are perennial grasses belonging to the *Poaceae* family that range in size from 12″ to over 10′, **Figure 10-16**. Many people may consider ornamental grasses and grass-like plants herbaceous perennials. However, grasses are botanically different from herbaceous ornamentals and

Anna Gratys/Shutterstock.com   *Thinglas/Shutterstock.com*   *Del Boy/Shutterstock.com*

Figure 10-15. Herbaceous perennials offer unique floral and leaf color that few other plants can match.

Christopher D. Hart

Jahina_Photography/Shutterstock.com

Figure 10-16. Ornamental grasses and grass-like plants provide interesting colors, flowers, and textures. They are also great options when landscaping a site that is in full sun and receives little moisture.

are visually unique due to these differences. These grasses have a wide color range and varying leaf size and textures. They can be used as focal points easily due to their unique aesthetic qualities. The blooms and seedheads are also unique and visually appealing. Ornamental grasses also provide movement and interest during the winter season.

Ornamental grasses are very drought tolerant due to their strong fibrous root system that has very efficient water uptake. Their resistance to drought make them excellent candidates for some xeriscapes. Clump-forming species grow in neat mounds and are not invasive. However, rhizome-forming species can quickly spread if not kept under control. Designers must choose species carefully as ornamental grasses range in height from a few inches to several feet.

Job Narinnate/Shutterstock.com

MLN/Shutterstock.com

Figure 10-17. Sedges and cattails are plants that resemble grasses but are not true grass plants.

Grass-Like Plants

Grass-like plants resemble grasses but belong to different families. Carex, for example, is a type of sedge that belongs to the *Cyperaceae* family. Grass-like plants and ornamental grasses are not only aesthetically pleasing, they are very useful in problem areas of the landscape. Both types of plants, for example, can be selected to tolerate shade, wet areas, and drought. Plants can also be selected to flourish in both the cool season and the warm season. Grass-like plants include sedges, rushes, and cattails, **Figure 10-17**.

Turfgrasses

Properly installed and maintained turf makes an immediate impact on the landscape unlike any other part of the design. Turfgrass is often the base on which the site is landscaped and it often occupies a large percentage of the landscape site, **Figure 10-18.** There are many varieties of turfgrass and the designer must determine which variety will suit the landscape and meet the customer's expectations. Important characteristics to consider include wear tolerance, disease resistance, density, color, shade tolerance, drought tolerance, and maintenance requirements. The designer must also know which types grow best in warmer climates and which will thrive in cooler climates.

SingjaiStock/Shutterstock.com

Figure 10-18. A winding path of thick, healthy turfgrass creates an inviting landscape. The lawn is often the first part of the landscape that is noticed.

There are several methods of installation with varying costs, including seeding, sodding, and plugging. (These methods are explained in the following turfgrass chapters.) The client and designer must determine which method suits the project's budget. Fertilization and pest control along with maintenance procedures, such as mowing and aerating, make turfgrass very labor intensive.

Ground Covers

A ground cover is a low growing (usually less than 18″), spreading plant that can quickly cover a large area, **Figure 10-19.** Most ground covers are perennial plants that require less maintenance than most other ornamentals. These low-growing plants may be selected for their color, texture, or flowers. Ground covers are typically woody plants but may also be herbaceous. Most woody ground covers are evergreens. Ground covers are used for steep

A *ESB Essentials/Shutterstock.com*   **B** *photowind/Shutterstock.com*   **C** *EQRoy/Shutterstock.com*

Figure 10-19. A mix of ground covers is visually appealing and practical. Choose plant species that require the same environmental needs as the surrounding plants. A—Star sedum (*Sedum lineare* 'Golden Teardrop'). B—Creeping juniper (*Juniperus horizontalis* 'Golden Carpet'). C—Carpet bugleweed (*Ajuga reptans*).

or problem areas as well as to create areas requiring little or no maintenance once established.

- As an attractive alternative to turfgrass on slopes that are too steep to mow easily.
- As weed barriers by providing dense plantings that slow or eliminate weeds in areas, such as the floor of an outdoor room.
- For erosion control by slowing water flow on slopes and/or drainage areas. A woody evergreen, such as a juniper, would be a good selection.
- To landscape an area where turfgrass will not grow due to extreme site conditions.
- In place of turfgrass in areas of the landscape that are too wet or have too much shade.
- To create a landscape bed requiring little routine maintenance and where the height of plant material is important.

The ground cover selected will depend on the intended function. Ground covers, for example, are commonly used in parking lot islands. The ground covers create a bed that requires little maintenance and the short height does not block the drivers' view over the bed. The plants are also tall enough to deter people from walking through the beds. Some other types of plants can be modified to serve as ground covers. Vines, for example, can be trained to cover an area. Common ground covers include bugleweed, holly fern, and junipers, **Figure 10-20**.

Vines

A *vine* is a woody-stemmed plant with a growth habit of climbing or trailing. Vines attach to structures with tendrils, twiners, scramblers, clingers, and climbing stem roots and must have support or a structure to climb. The manner in which a vine attaches and its weight or the weight of its fruit may require a specific type of support structure.

- *Tendrils.* A tendril is a modified leaf that is used to climb by coiling around the support structure, **Figure 10-21A**. Structures should have thin poles or lattice or wire to make it easier for the tendrils to grasp. Grapes, passionflower, and sweet peas use tendrils to climb.

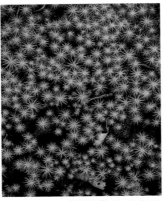

Christopher D. Hart   *J. Henning Buchholz/Shutterstock.com*   *O.C Ritz/Shutterstock.com*   *PhotoTrippingAmerica/Shutterstock.com*

Figure 10-20. Ground covers are low growing and hug the soil, making them effective for erosion prevention. The dense growth habit of ground covers also prevents weeds.

A *Zelijko Zizak Photography/ Shutterstock.com*   **B** *PeingjaiChiangmai/Shutterstock.com*

C *Jorge Salcedo/Shutterstock.com*   **D** *Terry J Taylor/Shutterstock.com*   **E** *mizy/Shutterstock.com*

Figure 10-21. Vines climb in different ways. It is extremely important to match the vine to the climbing structure to ensure the vine will climb the structure and, in some cases, not become too heavy for the structure. A—Tendril. B—Twiner (honeysuckle). C—Scrambler (roses). D—Boston ivy. E—English ivy.

- *Twiners.* Vines with a twining growth habit use their leaves or stems to wrap around a support structure. Twiners, unlike tendrils which use a modified leaf, wrap existing leaves or stems around the structure. Twining vines include clematis, wisteria, honeysuckle, and pole beans, **Figure 10-21B**. Twiners require a heavy-duty support structure.
- *Scramblers.* Scramblers are vines with very long, strong, flexible stems that must be physically attached to a climbing structure. Stems of scramblers often have thorns, **Figure 10-21C**. Climbing roses are scramblers. These vines may need a strong support structure.
- *Clingers.* These vines attach to structures with their adhesive pads and aerial roots. These vines can climb virtually on any surface. Boston ivy and Virginia creeper are common vines that have adhesive pads, **Figure 10-21D**.
- *Climbing stem roots.* Vines that climb using their stems and root structures are referred to as climbing or *clinging stem roots*. These root structures can damage paint and mortar, especially if they are pulled off the structure. These vines can climb on virtually any surface. Common vines with stem roots include English ivy and wintergreen euonymus, **Figure 10-21E**.

Although vines are a relatively small category of ornamental plants, they provide material that is unique and aesthetically pleasing. A passionflower (*Passiflora incarnate*), for example, has unique flowers that automatically make the vine a focal point, **Figure 10-22**. Vines such as honeysuckle (*Lonicera* spp.), provide a sweet fragrance that may draw the visitor to a specific location. Grape vines (*Vitis vinifera*) can be used to incorporate edibles into the landscape. Vines may become aggressive

Christopher D. Hart

kariphoto/Shutterstock.com

Figure 10-22. Passionflower is a vine with a very distinct flower and rather bland foliage. It is important to remember that plants are selected for a variety of reasons. The site along with the demands of the client will dictate selection of plant material.

and spread quickly. Before planting a vine, research available species of vines and select the best cultivar for your area.

Edibles

Edible landscaping is landscaping that incorporates edible plants in the ornamental areas of a landscape. Rather than using a dedicated area for fruit and vegetable production, both annual and perennial fruits and vegetables are planted throughout the ornamental landscaping. Edibles provide fresh food and add color, texture, and shapes to the design, **Figure 10-23**.

- Herbs, such as basil, thyme, oregano, and cilantro, have unique scents and are harvested regularly for food preparation.
- There are also edible flowers, such as marigolds, borage, sweet William, and pansies, which can be added to food dishes and used as garnish.
- Grape vines can be used as most other vines would be used with the added bonus of fresh grapes.
- Kale is often used as a border plant that provides late season color as well as food.

Many edibles have features that are similar to those of ornamental plants and can be used in the design for these features. In some instances, edibles can be used and replaced with the next seasonal crop. The types of edibles incorporated into the landscape depend on the preference of the client or homeowner.

Aquatic Plants

Aquatic plants are species that grow in water or in soils saturated with water. Aquatic plants are categorized as emergent, floating leaf, and submersed. *Emergent plants* are rooted in the soil. The leaves, stems, and flowers of emergent plants rise above the water surface. Emergent aquatic plants tolerate areas that are saturated with water and can be used in bogs and rain gardens. *Floating leaf plants* are also rooted in the ground below the water. Their leaves float on the water surface. *Submersed aquatic plants* are rooted in the soil and have most of their leaf structure below the water surface, **Figure 10-24**.

S. Quintans/Shutterstock.com

Jen Petrie/Shutterstock.com

Figure 10-23. Edible plants used can be aesthetically pleasing as well as functional.

Christopher D. Hart

Figure 10-24. Aquatic plants unique characteristics that differ greatly from other landscape plants. The pitcher plant and Venus flytrap (A/B), for example, are carnivorous plants that catch and eat small insects that wander onto their sticky surface.

Geophytes

Geophytes are plants with an underground nutrient and water storage organ. Geophytes are divided into seven categories: bulbs, corms, tubers, tuberous stems, tuberous roots, rhizomes, and pseudobulbs. Geophytes are popular with designers because most are spreading perennials that fill in areas over time. A designer can include geophytes that bloom at different times of the year to ensure color throughout the seasons. With proper planning, the landscape can have flowers blooming from spring until fall. Daffodils, crocus, and tulips bring springtime to mind because they are the earliest bloomers. These flowers may bloom when there is still snow on the ground.

Color Display

Geophytes have striking colors and are commonly used in areas needing accents or splashes of color, **Figure 10-25**. Different species that bloom at the same time are often combined in beds. Common combinations include daffodils, crocus, pansies, and tulips.

Safety First

Always call 811 to have all buried telephone, gas, electrical, and water lines marked before beginning any excavation or planting.

Anton_Ivanov/Shutterstock.com

Figure 10-25. Geophyte planting beds can create a striking display of color when they are well planned and carefully installed.

Hands-On Landscaping

Planting Geophytes

Soil preparation for geophytes is vital to their success. Adding amendments and manipulating the soil to alter its physical and chemical properties will help ensure they will grow and flower.

Step 1. Prepare the planting area by hand or with a rototiller. Till deep areas (at least 8″) because the loose backfill will allow for better emergence.

Step 2. Test the soil and add amendments as needed. The pH range should be between 6 and 7.

Step 3. Work the amendments into the soil. Recommended amendments include leaf mulch, composted plant materials, composted animal manures, bone meal (providing phosphorus), and/or other clean sources of organic matter.

Step 4. Prepare the holes. If you have a label, follow the instructions for planting depth and spacing. In general, large bulbs are planted 8″ deep and small bulbs are planted 4″ or 5″ deep. If you want the geophytes to naturalize or divide, plant them by hand. If you want a more structured design, use a bulb planter to keep them evenly spaced.

Step 5. Place the geophyte in the hole with the pointed end up and the roots pointing down.

Step 6. Fill the holes with the loose backfill and lightly compress the soil.

Step 7. Water the planting area.

When the flowers have completed blooming, deadhead the flowers but leave the foliage intact. The foliage will continue to gather nutrients for the following season. Cut the foliage to ground level after it turns yellow or brown.

aliAntye/Shutterstock.com

Liane M/Shutterstock.com

Liane M/Shutterstock.com

Consider This

1. Do all geophytes have the same life span? What occurs when the geophyte reaches the end of its life span?
2. Do any geophytes need to be dug up and stored over winter? Explain why this should/should not be done and with which types.
3. Do any geophytes bloom continuously throughout the season? Identify those that bloom continuously and those that last a short time.

Bedding Plants

Bedding plants are typically annual plants installed mainly for their seasonal floral or foliage presentation. They are often replaced every six to eight months, depending on location and climate. Color displays are often one of the first things people notice in a landscape. Many annuals, such as caladium, coleus, impatiens, and geraniums, are used as bedding plants, **Figure 10-26**.

Border or Line Plants

Plants can be used to delineate property lines or provide a visual barrier between areas. When large deciduous trees are used as border plants, the trunks provide the delineation. Hedges may also serve as border plants. Many broadleaf and narrow-leaf evergreens are chosen due to their consistent greenery and vigorous growth.

Christopher D. Hart

Figure 10-26. Bedding plants are used to provide seasonal color to the landscape. They can be used to create striking displays in window boxes by mixing species.

Goodheart-Willcox Publisher

Figure 10-27. A facer plant is used to cover the base or the stem of the plants growing behind it.

Facer Plants

Facer plants can be placed at the base of larger plants for ground coverage and contrasting colors or textures, **Figure 10-27**. Facer plants are often used at the base of large plants because their foliage is sparse due to lack of sunlight. If space allows, facer plants can be integrated into a design as a stair-step, a method of gradually increasing plant height.

Foundation Plants

Foundation plants are installed adjacent to the foundation of a structure. These plants, which are typically shrubs, can be used to create a contrast of colors and textures between the house and plant materials. These plants are often less than 4′ in height and are mostly grown for foliage display.

The same types of shrubs used as foundation plants can be used to create a low border. A low border is often less than 3′ and used to direct traffic flow or the path of the eye. In many cases, frequent shearing is needed to maintain the low border and keep the foliage growing tightly together, **Figure 10-28**.

Imagenet/Shutterstock.com

Figure 10-28. Foundation plants refer to a wide category of landscape plants that are suitable for using against the foundation of a home or other structure. Foundation plantings help to soften the stiff lines created by construction materials, such as brick and metal. Foundation plantings help the structure appear more naturalized.

Corner Plantings

A landscape designer can use plants to soften hard architectural lines and narrow the distance from the soil surface to those lines. A pyramidal plant can be installed on the structure's corners to soften outward facing vertical lines.

Career Connection

Brie Arthur

Brie Arthur, Garden Communicator

Originally from southeastern Michigan, Brie Arthur is a home gardener, author, and communicator who discovered her love of horticulture through 4-H. She studied Landscape Design and Horticulture at Purdue University and initially worked as an estate gardener at the Montrose Gardens in Hillsborough, North Carolina. She spent more than a decade as a professional plant propagator at Plant Delights Nursery and Camellia Forest Nursery before transitioning her focus on Green Industry communications through writing, public speaking, film production, and consulting. She is a published author with her debut book, *The Foodscape Revolution*.

As Vice President of Horticulture at Gardenuity, a direct to consumer on-line gardening company, Brie is able to use her plant knowledge and extensive grower network to reach consumers nationally. The goal of Gardenuity is to make growing herbs and vegetables as accessible as possible and to engage young customers by connecting growing plants to a healthy diet and clean living.

In her role as a garden industry communicator, Brie is leading the national suburban Foodscape movement; a model of community development that incorporates sustainable, local food production. She speaks internationally and is a correspondent on the PBS television show *Growing a Greener World*, sharing practical gardening advice from her one acre suburban foodscape.

In 2017, Brie was awarded the first "Emerging Professional" distinction by the American Horticultural Society. Brie serves as GWA (Garden Writers of America) National Director of Region IV representing garden communicators across the southeast United States. As a founding member of *Emergent: A Group for Growing Professionals*, she encourages an open dialogue and networking opportunities between seasoned professionals and rising green industry members. She sits on the Executive Committee for the International Plant Propagators Southern Region and is on the board of directors for the North Carolina Botanical Garden Foundation.

"*Working in the realm of garden industry communications has been an amazing transition in my career. I have control of my schedule, my pay rates, and am able to travel across the United States and beyond inspiring others to embrace the hobby of growing plants.*" —Brie Arthur

Consider This
1. Brie Arthur has held many positions in the green industry. In what ways did each experience contribute to the following position?
2. What types of personal goals would you set for yourself to follow a path similar to Brie's?
3. In what special niche of the green industry are you interested?

The same plant can be applied to an inward facing vertical line as well. Evergreens are commonly used as corner plantings because they provide foliage year-round and can be lightly pruned to maintain the pyramidal shape.

Topiary

A *topiary* is a shrub that has been pruned and sheared into an interesting shape or imaginative character. Strategic pruning is used to form the basic shape of a topiary. The early pruning is followed by repeated shearing until the plant has acquired the desired form. Topiaries need trimming or shearing on a regular basis to maintain their shape, **Figure 10-29**.

JFs Pic S. Thielemann/Shutterstock.com   *Anita SKV/Shutterstock.com*

Figure 10-29. Interesting shapes and figures are created with topiary pruning. Topiary plants require high maintenance and must be routinely sheered to maintain their desired shape.

Espalier

Espalier is a unique plant training method in which the plant is trained to grow flat against a wall or other support. Espalier can be used to create visually appealing forms and shapes against a vertical surface and to incorporate edibles into the landscape while conserving space. A fruit tree, for example, can be trained to grow against a garden wall. Espalier is often used as a focal point or at the end of a line of plants, **Figure 10-30**.

Massing

Massing is the practice of planting many of the same type of plant very close together. Massing provides sweeps of colors that create dramatic effects, especially when contrasted with monochromatic sweeps of other colors. Plants should be installed in a diagonal pattern rather than a rectangular pattern. The diagonal, staggered pattern provides more room for the plants to fully mature in width and uses more plants, **Figure 10-31**. Rectangular spacing leaves small gaps between plants. The plants must be equidistant (spaced equally apart) to ensure proper coverage is achieved.

Massed plants have lower weed pressure due to foliar shading, buffered root temperatures, and reduced water needs. Massing can be used with perennials and annuals.

Eag1eEyes/Shutterstock.com

Figure 10-30. Pyrycantha (*Pyracantha coccinea*) is commonly espalied to grow flat against a wall or other structure. Espalier plants are unique that often become a focal point of the design.

A *MaryAnne Campbell/Shutterstock.com* **B** *MyCreative/Shutterstock.com* **C** *Christopher D. Hart*

Figure 10-31. A/B—Mass plantings provide a sweep of color. C—Diagonal planting provides sufficient growing space and creates a pattern of diagonal lines that can be viewed from different directions.

Summary

- Selection of the right plant material will enhance the design, please the client, and thrive in the landscape.

- Trees are used to create shade, add color, provide wind protection, serve as sound buffers, and provide framework for a design.

- Shrubs are woody plants that are available in a variety of heights and are referred to as dwarf, medium, or large shrubs.

- Shrubs may be selected for flower color, growth habit, scent, fruit, or leaf color.

- Cultivar selection is of utmost importance when selecting shrubs for a design because each cultivar possesses unique characteristics.

- Herbaceous perennials are plants that die to the ground, become dormant, and return the next growing season.

- Some herbaceous perennials are known for their blooms and growth habits but many are chosen for their unique foliage.

- True ornamental grasses range in size from 12″ to over 10′ and are perennial grasses belonging to the *Poaceae* family.

- Grass-like plants resemble grasses but belong to different families.

- Ornamental grasses and grass-like plants are often tolerant of extreme site conditions (wet and dry).

- Turfgrass is often the base on which the site is landscaped and it often occupies a large percentage of the landscape site.

- Ground covers are low-growing, spreading plants that can quickly cover large areas. They are used for steep or problem areas as well as to create areas requiring little or no maintenance.

- Vines are plants with a growth habit of climbing or trailing by attaching to structures with tendrils, twining, and/or aerial roots. Vines require a support system.

- Edible landscaping incorporates edible plants in the ornamental areas of a design.

- Geophytes are perennial plants that are divided into seven categories: bulbs, corms, tubers, tuberous stems, tuberous roots, rhizomes, and pseudobulbs.

- Bedding plants are annual plants installed mainly for their seasonal floral or foliage presentation.

- Border or line plants can be used to delineate property lines or provide a visual barrier between areas.

- Facer plants can be placed at the base of larger plants for ground coverage and contrasting colors or textures.

Bildagentur Zoonar GmbH/Shutterstock.com

- Foundation plants, which are typically shrubs, can be used to create a contrast of colors and textures between a building's foundation and plant materials.
- Corner plants soften hard architectural lines and narrow the distance from the soil surface to those lines.
- A topiary is a shrub that has been pruned and sheared into an interesting shape or imaginative character.
- Espalier is a unique plant training method in which the plant is trained to grow flat against a wall or other support.
- Massing is the practice of planting many of the same type of plant very close together to create sweeps of colors that create dramatic effect.

Chapter Review

Know and Understand ⤷

Answer the following questions using the information provided in this chapter.

1. Which of the following are plants used in landscape designs?
   A. Herbaceous perennials.
   B. Grass-like plants.
   C. Ground covers.
   D. All of the above.

2. A plant that produces wood as its structural tissue is a(n) _____.
   A. herbaceous perennial
   B. woody plant
   C. grass-like plant
   D. All of the above.

3. *True or False?* Evergreen trees and shrubs do not shed leaves or needles throughout the year.
   A. True.
   B. False.

4. Which of the following terms best describes a plant that is a focal point due to its aesthetic characteristics?
   A. Sample.
   B. Spiritual.
   C. Specimen.
   D. Simple.

5. *True or False?* Deciduous trees are often planted along the north and west sides of a property to create a windbreak with their dense growth.
   A. True.
   B. False.

6. Trees perform which of the following functions?
   A. Create shade and add color.
   B. Provide wind protection.
   C. Sequester carbon from the air.
   D. All of the above.

7. *True or False?* A large deciduous tree is best placed on the northwest side of a home to cast shade during summer months.
   A. True.
   B. False.

8. *True or False?* Trees help soften hard lines and provide framework for landscape designs.
   A. True.
   B. False.

9. *True or False?* Cultivar selection is important when selecting shrubs for a design because each cultivar possesses unique characteristics.
   A. True.
   B. False.

10. Plants with soft, succulent stems that die to the ground and become dormant are referred to as _____.
    A. herbaceous plants
    B. dormant plants
    C. medium plants
    D. All of the above.

11. Which of the following are herbaceous perennials?
    A. Boxwood, juniper, and holly.
    B. Saucer magnolia and eastern redbud.
    C. Columbine, clematis, and larkspur.
    D. Dogwood and Japanese maple.

12. *True or False?* Ornamental grasses and grass-like plants are herbaceous perennials.
    A. True.
    B. False.

13. *True or False?* All ornamental grasses have rhizome-forming root systems and quickly spread if not kept under control.
    A. True.
    B. False.

14. Which of the following are important characteristics to consider when choosing turfgrass species?
    A. Wear, drought, and shade tolerance.
    B. Disease resistance and density.
    C. Color and maintenance needs.
    D. All of the above.

15. Of the following, which is likely to be used in place of turfgrass in areas that are wet or have too much shade?
    A. Grass-like plants.
    B. Ornamental grass.
    C. Ground cover.
    D. Boxwood shrubs.

16. Vines require a support structure to climb and attach themselves with _____.
    A. twiners
    B. tendrils
    C. aerial roots
    D. All of the above.

17. *True or False?* Vines are a relatively large category of ornamental plants.
    A. True.
    B. False.

18. Landscaping that incorporates annual and perennial fruits and vegetables throughout the ornamental plants is referred as _____.
    A. virtuous landscaping
    B. food landscaping
    C. edible landscaping
    D. This is not a landscaping method.

19. *True or False?* Emergent aquatic plants have most of their leaf structure below the water surface.
    A. True.
    B. False.

20. *True or False?* The leaves, stems, and flowers of submersed aquatic plants rise above the water surface.
    A. True.
    B. False.

21. Tuberous roots, rhizomes, bulbs, corms, tubers, tuberous stems, and pseudobulbs are _____.
    A. geophytes
    B. aquatic plants
    C. ground covers
    D. glorifides

Match the terms to the descriptions in 22–30.
    A. Bedding plants
    B. Border plants
    C. Dwarf shrubs
    D. Facer plants
    E. Foundation plants
    F. Heat island
    G. Large shrubs
    H. Large trees
    I. Medium shrubs
    J. Small trees

22. Have a mature height of less than 4′.

23. Range in height from 4′ to 6′.

24. Have a mature height over 6′.

25. Annual plants installed for seasonal floral or foliage presentation.

26. Used to delineate property or provide a visual barrier.

27. Placed at the base of larger plants for ground coverage.

28. Plant materials installed adjacent to the foundation of a structure.

29. Have a mature height approximately up to 25′.

30. An area in which the temperature is higher than that of the surrounding areas due to human activities.

31. A shrub that has been pruned and sheared into an interesting shape or imaginative character is a(n) _____.
    A. espalier
    B. massing
    C. topiary
    D. facing

32. A plant training technique in which a plant is trained to grow flat against a wall or other support is _____.
    A. espalier
    B. massing
    C. topiary
    D. facing

33. Planting many of the same type of plant very close together is referred to as _____.
    A. crowding
    B. massing
    C. forcing
    D. facing

Thinking Critically

1. How would you explain the benefits and drawbacks of planting only crabapple trees that do not bear fruit?

2. How would you explain to someone why certain tree species should not be planted near a structure?

3. How could landscaping contribute to helping reduce food shortages?

Suggested Activities

1. You and your business partner are landscaping a property that is located close to a noisy highway. The noise is unpleasant to the client and he or she would like a quiet backyard. How can this be achieved with plants? Work with a partner to find a solution.

2. Design a hedge to be used to separate property lines from an adjacent property in a residential neighborhood. The property line measures 195'. Be sure to include the number of plants that it will take to install the hedge.

3. Form groups of 4 to 5, and identify examples of screens, borders, foundation plants, or mass plantings. You may photograph examples in your neighborhood or find landscape photos online. As a group, discuss whether the effectiveness is optimized and, if not, determine the steps necessary to correct it. Create a visual presentation for the class.

4. You have a bed that you wish to plant in ajuga. It is recommended that the plants be planted 18" off center (OC). The rectangular bed measures 20' × 30'. How many plants will you need to install the bed?

5. Working in groups of 2 to 4, design an edible landscape for a small area at your school. Include a variety of edibles that will become available during different seasons of the year.

6. Review the NALP's indoor plant identification list. Obtain images of the plants listed and create a visual presentation. The images may also be used to create flashcards. Include the botanical and common names on the back of the cards.

7. Expand on the preceding activity by including pathogens, pests, and cultural damage that are common problems with indoor plants.

8. Identify and sketch the different forms of flowers and how they affect reproduction. Include the seeds and fruit of the plant and summarize their functions.

Nursery/Landscape Plant Identification ↗

The following plant identification glossary contains more than 100 plants (ranging from smaller flowering specimens, to shrubs, and trees) commonly grown and used in landscaping applications. This illustrated glossary has been provided to help you familiarize yourself with these plants, and as a means of studying for career development events in which plant identification is a major component. To help you identify the plants, each entry includes the botanical/scientific name and at least one common name. There is also a list of the names alphabetized by common names at the end of the glossary. The numbers in the lower right corners correlate to those in the CDE identification list. This glossary is by no means all-inclusive, as there are innumerable varieties and cultivars available to growers everywhere. However, it contains a good variety for you to begin your studies. Use this glossary, as well as the e-flashcards on your textbook's companion website at **www.g-wlearning.com/agriculture** to help you study and identify these common plants.

alybaba
Abelia × grandiflora/glossy abelia **101**

Bildagentur Zoonar GmbH
Abies concolor/white fir **102**

ukmooney; Frank11
Acer palmatum/Japanese maple **103**

Jonathon Billinger; Anatoly Vlasov
Acer platanoides/Norway maple **104**

Ftlombardo; Richard A. McQuirk
Acer rubrum/red maple **105**

Melinda Fawver
Acer saccharum/sugar maple **106**

Bildagentur Zoonar GmbH

Ajuga reptans/carpet bugle **107**

Charles Wayne Lytton

Antirrhinum majus/snapdragon **108**

Real Moment

Aquilegia × *hybrida*/columbine **109**

Peter Turner Photography; ArgenLant

Amelanchier arborea/
downy serviceberry **110**

photosoft

Astilbe hybrid/astilbe **111**

Supitcha McAdam

Begonia semperflorens-cultorum/
wax begonia **112**

Goodheart-Willcox Publisher

Berberis × *mentorensi*/
mentor barberry **113**

axz700; Sue Sweeney

Betula nigra/river birch **114**

Goodheart-Willcox Publisher

Brassaia actinophylla/
schefflera, octopus tree **115**

Buxus microphylla/ littleleaf boxwood **116**
photology1971

Camellia japonica/ common camellia **117**
Irina Kuzmina

Cedrus atlantica 'Glauca'/ blue atlas cedar **118**
ID1974; Grigory Stoyakin

Cercis canadensis/redbud **119**
Melinda Fawver; Real Moment

Chaenomeles speciosa/ Japanese (flowering) quince **120**
Kapustin Igor; Denis Vesely

Clematis hybrid Clematis × jackmanii/ clematis, jackman's clematis **121**
Dagmar Breu; photowind

Cornus florida/ flowering dogwood **122**
Zocchi Roberto

Cotoneaster dammeri/ bearberry cotoneaster **123**
Ian Grainger

Cotoneaster divaricatus/ spreading cotoneaster **124**
D. Kucharski K. Kucharska

F. D. Richards; Arina P. Habich

Crataegus phaenopyrum/
Washington hawthorn **125**

Goodheart-Willcox Publisher

Cynodon dactylon/
bermudagrass **126**

Skyprayer

Dieffenbachia maculata/
spotted dumb cane **127**

Steve Bower

Dracaena deremensis 'Warneckii'/
striped dracaena **128**

moritorus

Dracaena fragens 'Massangeana'/
corn plant **129**

jaroslava V

Echinaceae purpurea/purple
coneflower **130**

Bondarenko

Epipremnum species/pothos **131**

Matt Lavin: Kees Zwanenburg

Euonymus alatus/winged
euonymus **132**

Agnes Kantaruk

Euonymus fortunei/
wintercreeper **133**

Willow; Appaloosa

Fagus sylvatica/European beech **134**

Goodheart-Willcox Publisher

Festuca species/fescue **135**

Nataliia Pyzhova

Ficus benjamina/Benjamin fig **136**

Imageman

Ficus elastica 'Decora'/
decora rubber plant **137**

Devonx; Natallia Berlizeva

Forsythia × *intermedia*/
border rorsythia **138**

Peter Turner Photography

Fraxinus americana/white ash
139

topimages

*Gaillardia
aristata*/common blanketflower **140**

phriwwai

Gardenia jasminoides/
common gardenia **141**

Mark Baldwin v.apl

Ginkgo biloba/
ginkgo, maidenhair tree **142**

Gleditsia triacanthos inermis/ thornless honeylocust **143**

Sally Wallis

*Hedera helix/*English ivy **144**

KPG_Payless

Hemerocallis species/day lily **145**

reya-photographer

*Hosta × hybrida/*plaintain lily **146**

DGSHUT

Hydrangea quercifolia/ oakleaf hydrangea **147**

guentermanaus

Hydrangea macrophylla/ bigleaf hydrangea **148**

Tanya rusa; guentermanaus

Ilex cornuta cvs./Chinese holly **149**

High Mountain

Ilex crenata cvs./Japanese holly **150**

InfoFlowersPlants

*Ilex × meserveae/*meserve holly **151**

InfoFlowersPlants

274

Impatiens hybrid/impatiens
152

motorolka

Iris × germanica florentina/bearded iris
153

ANATOL

Juniperus chinensis/
Chinese juniper
154

Radovan1; VanHart

Juniperus horizontalis/
creeping juniper
155

photowind

Lagerstroemia indica/
crape myrtle
156

Janken; chinahbzyg

Leucanthemum × superbum/
shasta daisy
157

val lawless

Liquidambar styraciflua/
sweet gum
158

Lilyana Vynogradova

Liriodendron tulipifera/tuliptree
159

Peter Turner Photography; Nick Pecker

Liriope species/lilyturf
160

BONNIE WATTON

Lonicera japonica /honeysuckle
161
Calin Tatu

Magnolia grandiflora/
southern magnolia
162
Stephen Farhall

Magnolia × soulangiana/
Chinese (saucer) magnolia
163
Simon Groewe

*Mahonia aquifolia/*Oregon grape
164
Anna Bogush

Malus species/
flowering crabapple
165
Nina B; Nick Pecker

*Myrica pensylvanica/*bayberry
166
Kariphoto

Nandina domestica/
heavenly bamboo
167
Peter Turner Photography; simona pavan

Narcissus species/daffodil
168
Nanya; Isabel Eve

*Nyssa sylvatica/*sour (black) gum
169
Del Boy; Kyle Selcer

divgradcurl

Pachysandra terminalis/
Japanese spurge **170**

Nick Pecker

Paeonia hybrid/peony **171**

Vladimira

Parthenocissus tricuspidata/
Boston ivy **172**

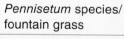

JOSHATIS

Pelargonium × hortorum/zonal
geranium **173**

Del Boy

Pennisetum species/
fountain grass **174**

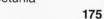

Luke Neale Photography

Petunia × hybrida/petunia **175**

Skyprayer2005

Philodendron scandens 'Oxycardium'/
heartleaf philodendron **176**

Zyankarlo; Gherzak

Picea abies/Norway spruce **177**

USDA NRCS; Bozhena Melnyk

Picea pungens/
Colorado (blue) spruce **178**

277

Pieris japonica/lily-of-the-valley
bush **179**

cynoclub BeppeNob

Pinus mugo/mugo pine **180**

photowind

Pinus strobus/eastern (weeping)
white pine **181**

Carolyn M Carpenter

Pinus sylvestris/scotch pine **182**

Ruud Morijn Photographer

Pinus thunbergiana/
Japanese black pine **183**

Manuel Ascanio; Huaykwang

Platanus × acerifolia/
London planetree **184**

simona pavan; Martin Fowler

Poa pratensis/Kentucky bluegrass **185**

Laura Glickstein

Podocarpus macrophyllus/
southern yew **186**

Nikolay Kurzenko

Potentilla fruticosa/shrubby
cinquefoil **187**

gubernat; coco312

Gabriela Beres

Prunus laurocerasus/
cherry laurel **188**

s_oleg

Prunus serrulata 'Kwanzan'/kwanzan
Japanese flowering cherry **189**

haris_M

*Pyracantha coccinea/*firethorn **190**

Photodigitaal.nl; valzan

*Quercus alba/*white oak **191**

josh Jackson; StevenRussellSmithPhotos

*Quercus palustris/*pin oak **192**

Mark Wagner jopelka

*Quercus rubra/*red oak **193**

Mark Terriberry

Rhododendron × *catawbiense/*
catawba hybrid rhododendron **194**

J Need

Rhododendron hybrid/
exbury hybrid azalea **195**

Rennes

Rosa species/
landscape shrub rose **196**

Salvia nemorosa/meadow sage

Manfred Ruckszio

197

Sedum species/sedum

Tamara Obodieieva   Starover Sibiriak

198

Solenostemon scutellarioides/coleus

Ru Bai Le

199

Sorbus aucuparia/European mountain ash

Hellen Sergeyeva; Ian 2010

200

Spiraea × bumalda/bumalda spirea

Sunny Hudson

201

Syringa vulgaris/common lilac

Ioflo69

202

Tagetes species/marigold

c12

203

Taxodium distichum/bald cypress

Photodigitaal.nl; ribeiroantonio

204

Taxus species/yew

IrynaL; InfoFlowersPlants

205

Aleksandr Nizienko; APugach

Thuja occidentalis/
American arborvitae **206**

Digoarpi

Tilia cordata/littleleaf linden **207**

guentermanaus; Melinda Fawver

Tsuga canadensis/
Canadian hemlock **208**

alabn

Tulipa species/tulip **209**

Verbena × hybrida/
garden verbena **210**

joloei

Nikolay Kurzenko

Viburnum × burkwoodii/
burkwood viburnum **211**

MaKo-studio

Viburnum trilobum/American
cranberry bush viburnum **212**

Przemyslaw Muszynski

Vinca minor/periwinkle **213**

Jordan Tan

Viola × wittrockiana/pansy **214**

ppl; unterwegs

Wisteria sinensis/
Chinese wisteria **215**

catus

Yucca filamentosa/
adam's needle **216**

Jordi Roy

Yucca gigantean; Yucca
elephantipes/giant yucca

Common Edibles for the Landscape

fedsax

Ocicmum basilicum/
small leaf Greek bush basil

Graham Corney

Coriandrum sativum/cilantro/coriander

mil87olia

Petroselinum crispun/parsley

pilialoha

Rosmarinus officinalis/rosemary

Ryan Yee

Salvia officinalis/sage

Frank Fischbach

Thymus vulgaris/thyme

Nursery/Landscape Plant Identification Latin Pronunciation

Botanical Name	Pronunciation	CDE ID#
Please note that the following list of plant names is the same list used with the preceding plant illustrations.		
Abelia × grandiflora	(ah-**BEE**-lee-ah ex gran-dih-**FLOOR**-ah)	101
Abies concolor	(**AY**-beez **KON**-kull-ur)	102
Acer palmatum	(**AY**-sir pal-**MAY**-tum)	103
Acer platanoides	(**AY**-sir plat-uh-noe-**EYE**-deez)	104
Acer rubrum	(**AY**-sir **ROO**-brum)	105
Acer saccharum	(**AY**-sir **SAK**-har-um)	106
Ajuga reptans cv.	(ah-**JEW**-guh **REP**-tanz)	107
Amelanchier arborea	(am-ul-**LANK**-ee-ur are-**BORE**-ee-uh)	110
Antirrhinum majus	(an-tih-**RYE**-num **MAY**-jus)	108
Aquilegia × hybrida cv.	(ack-wih-**LEE**-jee-uh ex **HY**-brid-ah)	109
Astilbe hybrid	(ah-**STILL**-bee)	111
Begonia semperflorens-cultorum	(bih-**GOE**-nya sem-pur-**FLORE**-enz kull-**TORE**-um)	112
Berberis × mentorensi	(**BUR**-bur-iss ex men-**TOE**-ren-see)	113
Betula nigra	(**BET**-you-luh **NYE**-gruh)	114
Brassaia actinophylla	(bruh-**SAY**-ee-uh ack-tee-no-**FILL**-uh)	115
Buxus microphylla	(**BUCKS**-us mye-kroe-**FILL**-uh)	116
Camellia japonica	(kuh-**MEEL**-yuh jah-**PON**-ih-kah)	117
Cedrus atlantica 'Glauca'	(**SEE**-druss at-**LAN**-tih-kuh)	118
Cercis canadensis	(**SUR**-siss kan-ah-**DEN**-siss)	119
Chaenomeles speciosa	(kee-**NOM**-uh-leez spee-see-**OH**-suh)	120
Clematis hybrid Clematis × jackmanii	(**KLEM**-ah-tiss ex jack-man-**EE**-eye)	121
Cornus florida	(**KORE**-nus **FLORE**-ih-duh)	122
Cotoneaster dammeri	(kuh-toe-nee-**ASS**-tur **DAM**-ur-eye)	123
Cotoneaster divaricatus	(kuh-toe-nee-**ASS**-tur dih-var-ih-**KAY**-tus)	124
Crataegus phaenopyrum	(kruh-**TEE**-gus fee-noe-**PYE**-rum)	125
Cynodon dactylon	(sye-**NOE**-dun **DACK**-til-on)	126
Dieffenbachia maculata 'Tropic Marianne'	(diff-in-**BAK**-ee-uh mak-**KEW**-lay-tah)	127
Dracaena deremensis 'Warneckii'	(druh-**SEE**-nuh dur-ah-**MEN**-siss)	128
Dracaena fragens 'Massangeana'	(druh-**SEE**-nuh **FRAY**-genz)	129
Echinaceae purpurea	(ec-kih-**NAY**-shah per-**PER**-ee-ah)	130
Epipremnum species	(ep-ih-**PREM**-num)	131
Euonymus alatus	(you-**ON**-ih-mus eh-**LAY**-tus)	132
Euonymus fortunei	(you-**ON**-ih-mus fore-**TYOO**-nee-eye)	133
Fagus sylvatica	(**FAY**-gus sil-**VAT**-ih-kuh)	134
Festuca species	(fess-**TOO**-kuh)	135
Ficus benjamina	(**FYE**-kus ben-ja-**MEE**-nuh)	136
Ficus elastica 'Decora'	(**FYE**-kus ee-**LAS**-tih-kuh)	137
Forsythia × intermedia	(for-**SITH**-ee-ah ex in-tur-**MEE**-dee-uh)	138
Fraxinus americana	(**FRACKS**-ih-nus ah-mer-ih-**KAY**-nah)	139

Nursery/Landscape Plant Identification Latin Pronunciation

Botanical Name	Pronunciation	CDE ID#
Gaillardia aristata	(gay-**LAR**-dee-uh ar-iss-**TAY**-tuh)	140
Gardenia jasminoides	(gar-**DEEN**-yuh jazz-min-oh-**EYE**-deez)	141
Ginkgo biloba	(**GINK**-oh by-**LOE**-buh)	142
Gleditsia triacanthos inermis	(gluh-**DIT**-see-uh try-uh-**KAN**-thus ih-**NUR**-miss)	143
Hedera helix	(**HED**-ur-uh **HEE**-licks)	144
Hemerocallis species	(hem-er-oh-**KAL**-iss)	145
Hosta × *hybrida*	(**HOSS**-tah ex **HY**-brid-ah)	146
Hydrangea macrophylla	(hye-**DRAIN**-jah mack-roe-**FILL**-uh)	147
Hydrangea quercifolia	(hye-**DRAIN**-jah kwer-sih-**FOE**-lee-uh)	148
Ilex cornuta cvs.	(**EYE**-leks kore-**NEW**-tuh)	149
Ilex crenata	(**EYE**-leks kruh-**NAY**-tuh)	150
Ilex × *meserveae*	(**EYE**-leks ex muh-**CERV**-ee-ee)	151
Impatiens hybrid	(im-**PAY**-shunz)	152
Iris × *germanica florentina*	(**EYE**-riss ex jur-**MAN**-ee-kuh flor-en-**TYE**-nuh)	153
Juniperus chinensis cvs.	(joo-**NIP**-ur-us chye-**NEN**-siss)	154
Juniperus horizontalis	(joo-**NIP**-ur-us hore-ih-zun-**TAY**-liss)	155
Lagerstroemia indica	(lag-ur-**STREE**-mee-uh **IN**-dih-kuh)	156
Leucanthemum × *superbum*	(loo-**KAN**-thuh-mum ex soo-**PUR**-bum)	157
Liquidambar styraciflua	(lick-wid-**AM**-bur stye-ruh-**SIFF**-loo-uh)	158
Liriodendron tulipifera	(leer-ee-oh-**DEN**-drun too-lip-**IFF**-ur-uh)	159
Liriope species	(lih-**RYE**-uh-pee)	160
Lonicera japonica	(luh-**NISS**-ur-uh juh-**PON**-ih-kuh)	161
Magnolia grandiflora	(mag-**NOLE**-yuh gran-dih-**FLORE**-uh)	162
Magnolia × *soulangiana*	(mag-**NOLE**-yuh ex soo-lawn-jee-**AY**-nuh)	163
Mahonia aquifolia	(muh-**HOE**-nee-uh ack-wih-**FOE**-lee-uh)	164
Malus species	(**MAY**-lus)	165
Myrica pensylvanica	(mur-**EYE**-kuh pen-sil-**VAIN**-ih-kuh)	166
Nandina domestica	(nan-**DYE**-nuh doe-**MESS**-tih-kuh)	167
Narcissus species	(nar-**SISS**-us)	168
Nyssa sylvatica	(**NI**-sa sil-**VAT**-ih-kuh)	169
Pachysandra terminalis	(pack-ih-**SAN**-druh tur-mih-**NAY**-liss)	170
Paeonia hybrid	(pee-**OH**-nee-uh **HY**-brid-ah)	171
Parthenocissus tricuspidata	(par-then-oh-**SISS**-us try-kuss-pih-**DAY**-tuh)	172
Pelargonium × *hortorum*	(pell-are-**GOE**-nee-um ex hore-**TOR**-um)	173
Pennisetum ruppelii	(pen-ih-**SEE**-tum roo-**PUL**-ee-eye)	174
Petunia × *hybrida*	(peh-**TOON**-yuh ex **HY**-brida)	175
Philodendron scandens 'Oxycardium'	(fill-uh-**DEN**-drun **SKAN**-denz)	176
Picea abies	(**PYE**-see-uh **AY**-beez)	177
Picea pungens	(**PYE**-see-uh **PUN**-jenz)	178

Nursery/Landscape Plant Identification Latin Pronunciation

Botanical Name	Pronunciation	CDE ID#
Pieris japonica	(**PEE**-ur-iss juh-**PON**-ih-kuh)	179
Pinus mugo	(**PYE**-nus **MYOO**-go)	180
Pinus strobus	(**PYE**-nus **STROE**-buss)	181a
Pinus strobus	(**PYE**-nus **STROE**-buss)	181b
Pinus sylvestris	(**PYE**-nus sill-**VESS**-tris)	182
Pinus thunbergiana	(**PYE**-nus thun-**BUR**-gee-an-uh)	183
Platanus × acerifolia	(plat-**AY**-nus ex ay-sur-ih-**FOE**-lee-uh)	184
Poa pratensis	(**POE**-uh pruh-**TEN**-sis)	185
Podocarpus macrophyllus	(poe-doe-**KAR**-pus mack-roe-**FILL**-us)	186
Potentilla fruticosa	(poe-ten-**TILL**-uh froo-tih-**KOE**-zuh)	187
Prunus laurocerasus	(**PROO**-nus lore-oh-**SAIR**-uh-sis)	188
Prunus serrulata 'Kwanzan'	(**PROO**-nus sur-you-**LAY**-tuh)	189
Pyracantha coccinea	(pye-ruh-**KAN**-thuh kock-**SIN**-ee-uh)	190
Quercus alba	(**KWURK**-us **AL**-buh)	191
Quercus palustris	(**KWURK**-us puh-**LUSS**-triss)	192
Quercus rubra	(**KWURK**-us **ROO**-bruh)	193
Rhododendron × catawbiense	(roe-doe-**DEN**-drun ex kuh-taw-bee-**EN**-see)	194
Rhododendron hybrid	(roe-doe-**DEN**-drun)	195
Rosa species	(**ROE**-zuh)	196
Salvia nemorosa	(**SAL**-vee-ah nem-ur-**OH**-zuh)	197
Sedum species	(**SEE**-dum)	198
Solenostemon scutellarioides	(suh-lee-oh-**STEE**-mun skoo-tul-air-ee-oh-**EYE**-deez)	199
Sorbus aucuparia	(**SORE**-bus uh-kew-**PAIR**-ee-uh)	200
Spiraea × bumalda	(spy-**REE**-uh ex bew-**MAL**-duh)	201
Syringa vulgaris	(sur-**ING**-guh vul-**GAR**-iss)	202
Tagetes species	(tuh-**JEE**-teez)	203
Taxodium distichum	(tacks-**OH**-dee-um dye-**STICK**-um)	204
Taxus species	(**TACKS**-us)	205
Thuja occidentalis	(**THOO**-yuh ock-sih-den-**TAY**-liss)	206
Tilia cordata	(**TILL**-ee-uh kore-**DAY**-tuh)	207
Tsuga canadensis	(**SOO**-guh kan-uh-**DEN**-siss)	208
Tulipa species	(**TEW**-lih-puh)	209
Verbena × hybrida	(vur-**BEE**-nuh ex **HY**-brid-ah)	210
Viburnum × burkwoodii	(vy-**BURN**-um ex **BURK**-wood-ee-eye)	211
Viburnum trilobum	(vye-**BURN**-um try-**LOW**-bum)	212
Vinca minor	(**VIN**-kah **MY**-nor)	213
Viola × wittrockiana	(**VYE**-oh-luh ex vitch-rock-ee-**AY**-nuh)	214
Wisteria sinensis	(wiss-**TEER**-ee-uh sye-**NEN**-siss)	215
Yucca filamentosa	(**YUCK**-uh fill-uh-men-**TOE**-zuh)	216

Turfgrass Selection

While studying this chapter, look for the activity icon  to:
- **Practice** vocabulary terms with Words to Know activities.
- **Expand** learning with identification activities.
- **Reinforce** what you learn by completing Know and Understand questions.

www.g-wlearning.com/agriculture

Chapter Outcomes

After studying this chapter, you will be able to:

- Identify and explain the turf zones.
- Explain how turf zones are used to choose the appropriate turfgrass.
- Describe the various types of cool-season and warm-season turfgrasses.
- Identify best practices for sustainable turfgrass management.
- Identify alternatives to traditional turfgrasses.

Key Terms 🔗

auricle
blade
blend
collar
cool-season turfgrass
leaf bud
ligule
mix
seedhead

sheath
spikelet
sustainability
sustainable turf management
thatch
turf zone
turfgrass
utility turfgrass
warm-season turfgrass

Introduction

An expanse of thick, green, well-maintained turf can be one of the most striking areas in a landscape. It is often the largest area and the foundation on which the landscape is based, **Figure 11-1**. Creating a lawn that is aesthetically pleasing, efficient, and sustainable requires a thorough knowledge of turfgrasses and their nutrient requirements. This chapter introduces you to the varieties of turfgrass and the factors you should consider before choosing the best turf for a landscape.

Shannon Hathaway, Super-Sod

Figure 11-1. A large expanse of well-maintained turfgrass is demonstrative of quality landscape installation. It is also impressionable to potential clients.

Turfgrass

Turfgrass is any species of true grass belonging to the Poaceae family that is used to make a lawn. Each of the many varieties of turfgrasses have distinctive characteristics, such as those that grow best in warmer climates and others that thrive in cooler climates. In addition to temperature preferences, other important characteristics to consider include wear tolerance, disease resistance, density, color, shade tolerance, drought tolerance, and maintenance requirements. The first step in establishing or renovating a lawn is to choose the type of grass that will be used. The turfgrass should be selected to meet the demands of the site as well as the needs of the customer.

Turf Zones

The United States is divided into three *turf zones*: cool-season, transition, and warm-season, **Figure 11-2**. The turf zone in which the turfgrass will be installed is the primary factor to consider when choosing which type to use. These turf zones or geographic areas have been established based on the following characteristics:

- Temperature.
- Available moisture.

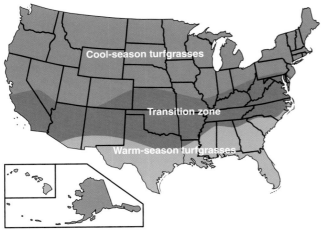

Goodheart-Willcox Publisher

Figure 11-2. The turfgrass zones can be referenced to determine which species of turfgrass will perform best in your area. It may be used with the USDA Hardiness Zone map to narrow down average temperatures for an area.

Temperature

Cool-season turfgrasses prefer an air temperature range of 60°F to 75°F (15.5°C to 24°C). Cool-season turfgrasses also have optimum growth when soil temperatures are between 50°F and 65°F (10°C and 18°C). Warm-season turfgrasses prefer an air temperature range of 80°F to 95°F (27°C to 35°C). Optimum soil temperatures for warm-season turfgrasses range from 70°F to 90°F (21°C to 32°C).

Warm- and cool-season turfgrasses will grow in the transition zone. However, some species will do better than other species because some are more tolerant of less-than-ideal temperatures. Bermudagrass, zoysiagrass, and tall fescue are turfgrass species that perform well in transition zones. The active growth periods of turfgrasses is regionally specific. A bermudagrass lawn in Florida, for example, will be green for more months of the year than a bermudagrass lawn in Virginia.

Moisture Availability

Humidity levels and temperatures vary regionally. Some species are drought-tolerant and will do well in arid climates that have little humidity. Species that are not drought-tolerant will do better in humid climates. Water availability and irrigation needs must also be considered when selecting turfgrass. When selecting a turfgrass, it is important to select cultivars that are developed for your area. It is also important to remember that irrigation may be required to establish high quality turf. See **Figure 11-3**.

Types of Lawns

Turfgrasses may also be classified according to use. Creeping bentgrass, for example, is used almost exclusively on golf greens. Turfgrasses may be classified as utility, commercial lawn, athletic field, golf course, or home lawn, **Figure 11-4**.

Allison Fortner, Super-Sod

Figure 11-3. Sod farms supply sod to landscapers and homeowners. Sod growers must follow strict cultural guidelines in order to produce high quality turf. Irrigation and well-drained soils are required to provide optimal moisture levels.

A   *Brandon Starnes, Super-Sod*

B   *Will Crowder, Super-Sod*

Figure 11-4. A—Sod is often installed in the front yard of newly constructed homes to quickly complete the landscape. B—The turf around the Panthers Stadium in Charlotte was established with Super-Sod's Elite Tall Fescue.

Utility Turfgrass

Utility turfgrass is commonly used on roadsides for erosion control. Aesthetics are not as important as practicality. Utility lawns can also tolerate being mowed only a few times each year.

Home Lawns

Home lawns are used in residential landscapes. Home lawns are commonly classified as high profile or low profile. High profile lawns require more maintenance and fertility regimes than low profile lawns. When properly grown, high profile lawns have a neater appearance than low profile lawns.

Commercial Lawns

Commercial lawns are turfgrass areas on commercial sites, such as office parks, housing developments, restaurants, malls, and shopping centers. Commercial lawns often do not have high tolerance to wear as they commonly receive little foot traffic, as they are viewed mainly from sidewalks or roads.

Christopher D. Hart

Figure 11-5. Maintaining the various turfgrasses used on golf courses requires multiple types of mowers and a knowledgeable staff.

Athletic Fields and Golf Courses

Turfgrasses planted on athletic fields and golf courses require strict maintenance and fertilizer regimens to retain their functionality and appearance. Athletic fields must be kept level and free of divots and other damage that could affect playability and player safety. Turfgrasses planted on golf courses and athletic fields must also retain their aesthetic quality. It is common for golf courses to use several types of turfgrasses cut to various heights to increase the difficulty of the sport. **Figure 11-5**.

Other Factors to Consider

Determining the proper turf zone is the primary factor used to choose a turfgrass. However, other factors should be considered. These factors apply to both warm- and cool-season turfgrasses and include the following:

- The intended use.
- The quality and pH of the soil.
- Durability in high-traffic areas.
- Duration of light exposure.
- Amount and duration of shade.
- Texture and color.
- Recommended mowing height.
- Maintenance requirements.
- Overall appearance.
- Cost of plant material and labor.

Oftentimes, the client may want turfgrass with characteristics that would not work in his or her landscape. If the above factors are considered, the landscape professional will be able to explain to the customer why a particular species will not work and offer a suitable alternative. See **Figure 11-6**.

Cool-Season Turfgrasses

Cool-season turfgrasses are those that thrive in areas with hot summers and cold, freezing winters. Their optimum growing temperature is between 60°F and 75°F (15.5°C to 24°C). Cool-season turfgrasses will stay green for most of the year, growing best in the fall and spring months. The most commonly used cool-season turfgrasses are annual ryegrass, creeping bentgrass, fine fescue, Kentucky bluegrass, perennial ryegrass, and tall fescue. Each grass possesses characteristics that can be used to determine which would be best for a particular site, **Figure 11-7**. Cool-season turfgrasses are best planted in early spring and early fall.

Christopher D. Hart

Figure 11-6. The turfgrass lining the walkway on this college campus must tolerate substantial wear from heavy traffic.

Annual Ryegrass

Annual ryegrass is a cool-season turfgrass that is medium green and has a coarse leaf texture. It is a non-spreading, bunch-type turfgrass that only lasts for one growing season. Annual ryegrass should not be used as a permanent turfgrass. Annual ryegrass is often used to overseed dormant warm-season turfgrasses to provide a green lawn during the winter months. The species is included in many grass seed mixes because of its fast germination rate. Annual

Cool-Season Turfgrasses						
	Tall Fescue (*Schedonorus phoenix*)	**Kentucky Bluegrass** (*Poa pratensis*)	**Fine Fescue** (*Festuca rubra*)	**Annual Ryegrass** (*Lolium multiflorum*)	**Perennial Ryegrass** (*Lolium perenne*)	**Creeping Bentgrass** (*Agrostis stolonifera*)
Cold Tolerance	Good	Excellent	Very good	Good	Good	Very good
Drought Tolerance	Very good	Good	Good	Fair	Good	Fair to poor
Establishment Rate	Very fast	Very fast	Medium	Fast	Medium	Medium
Growth Habit	Bunch, slight rhizomes	Spread by rhizomes	Bunch or spread by rhizomes	Bunch	Bunch	Spread by stolons and rhizomes
Height after Mowing	2.5″ to 3.5″	2.5″ to 3.5″	1.5″ to 2.5″	1.5″ to 2.5″	1.5″ to 2.5″	Less than 1/4″
Shade Tolerance	Very good	Fair to good	Very good	Fair to good	Good	Fair
Propagation (seed or vegetative)	Seed	Seed				
Texture	Coarse	Fine to medium	Fine	Coarse	Fine	Fine
Turf Zone	Cool, transitional	Cool	Cool	Cool	Cool	Cool
Wear Tolerance	Very good	Good	Poor to fair	Very good	Excellent	Good

Goodheart-Willcox Publisher

Figure 11-7. Each turfgrass species possesses unique characteristics. Carefully consider the site and needs of the client when choosing a turfgrass.

Christopher D. Hart

Figure 11-8. Annual ryegrass can be overseeded on warm-season turfgrasses to maintain a green lawn during the winter months. Annual ryegrass has only one growing season and should never be used as a standalone turfgrass.

ryegrass begins to die in the spring when temperatures exceed 80°F (27°C). Annual ryegrass is also commonly used to help prevent erosion where grass is needed quickly, **Figure 11-8**. The recommended mowing height for annual ryegrass is 1.5" to 2.5".

Creeping Bentgrass

Creeping bentgrass is a fine-textured, cool-season turfgrass that is used almost exclusively on golf course putting greens, **Figure 11-9**. It requires specialized equipment and a great deal of maintenance, including frequent mowing, fertilizing, aerating, and fungicide sprays. The species spreads through stolons and rhizomatic roots and easily migrates to other areas. It thrives in full sun when watered frequently. Creeping bentgrass tolerates foot traffic and can be repaired with plugs. The fine-textured cool-season turfgrass is mowed between 0.5" and 0.125". Creeping bentgrass is typically mowed to heights less than 1/4".

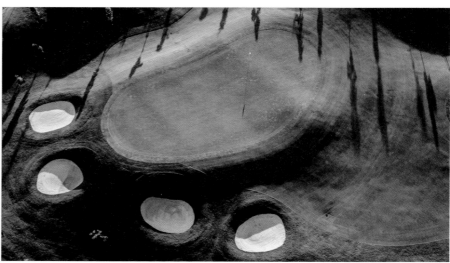

Tusumaru/Shutterstock.com
Avigator Thailand/Shutterstock.com

Figure 11-9. Penncross bentgrass is commonly used on golf course putting greens. It has strict cultural requirements.

Fine Fescue

Fine fescue is a cool-season turfgrass with an extremely fine texture, **Figure 11-10**. It has the lowest fertilizer, moisture, and light requirements of the cool-season turfgrasses. Most fine fescues are bunch-type turfgrasses. Fine fescue prefers shady areas and does not perform well in sunny locations. Fine fescue is often included in mixes of tall fescues or Kentucky bluegrass. The majority of fine fescues prefer drier soil but will need to be watered during drought periods.

The recommended mowing height for fine fescue is 1.5″ to 2.5″. Fine fescues are considered shade grasses in the United States. These turfgrasses do not tolerate high traffic due to their low wear resistance. Common names of fine fescue include red fescue, creeping fescue, and creeping red fescue.

Kentucky Bluegrass

Kentucky bluegrass is a medium- to fine-textured, cool-season turfgrass with dark green color, **Figure 11-11**. Kentucky bluegrass spreads with rhizomes to create a dense, even lawn. The rhizomatic structure also helps the turfgrass heal in worn or damaged areas. This species is best suited for the cool-season zone and may not perform as well as other species when installed close to the transition zone. As with most turfgrasses, Kentucky bluegrass prefers full sun but survives in part shade. This turfgrass will go dormant during seasons of drought and will require watering to keep it green.

Kentucky bluegrass should be mowed to a height of 2.5″ to 3.5″. Kentucky bluegrass is not as tolerant to drought or foot traffic as tall fescue is and the taller height will help the lawn during drought and with heavy traffic. Kentucky bluegrass is commonly combined with tall fescue to produce cool-season mixes that thrive in a wider variety of climates.

Perennial Ryegrass

Perennial ryegrass is a cool-season turfgrass with a fine texture, **Figure 11-12**. It is used much like annual ryegrass and is rarely used as a standalone turfgrass. The species is also used in turf mixes because of its quick germination. Perennial ryegrass is used to overseed dormant turfgrass on athletic fields and golf courses. It is preferred over annual ryegrass for overseeding because it grows denser and uniformly. Chemical and cultural control measures may be used to kill the perennial ryegrass.

Perennial ryegrass provides winter color when warm-season grasses are dormant. Failure to kill the ryegrass will result in competition between the ryegrass and bermudagrass and will create a lawn with bare spots. The playability and wear resistance of perennial ryegrass is less optimal than bermudagrass and it must be killed to allow the bermudagrass to flourish. Perennial ryegrass should be mowed at a height of 1.5″ to 2.5″.

Goodheart-Willcox Publisher

Figure 11-10. Fine fescue is an excellent choice for a cool-season turfgrass for shaded areas.

Laura Glickstein/Shutterstock.com

Figure 11-11. Kentucky bluegrass is a cool-season turfgrass with a thick growth habit and dark green color.

STEM Connection

Turfgrass Morphology

Turfgrasses have unique characteristics, structures, and growth habits and their morphology differs greatly from that of other plants. The terminology used to describe turfgrass structures is also very different from that of trees and shrubs. Developing your knowledge of the anatomy of grasses will be very helpful as you learn to identify the different turfgrass species.

- **Spikelets** are individual components of the seedhead. Spikelets make up the seedhead.
- **Seedheads** are the flowering structures of turfgrasses with characteristics unique to each turfgrass species.
- Seedheads may be classified as either a *panicle* or *spike*. An intact seedhead makes it easier to identify turfgrass species. Keep in mind that turfgrasses are typically mowed before the seedhead is visible as you look for samples of turfgrass species.
- The **sheath** is the section of the leaf blade that connects the blade to the stem. Depending on the species, the sheath may wrap around or enclose the stem.
- The **blade** is the leaf portion of the grass plant. The length and width of the blade vary greatly by species.
- The **collar** is the area on the outside of the leaf where the leaf blade and leaf sheath join. Collars may be continuous, divided, broad, or narrow.
- The **auricles** are the growth that projects from each side of the collar. They may wrap around the stem of the grass. Auricles may be long, short, or absent.
- The **ligule** is the part of a grass plant that is between the stem and leaf blade. Ligules are membranous, hairy, or absent.
- New grass blades originate in the **leaf buds**. The blades may be either rolled or folded in the bud.

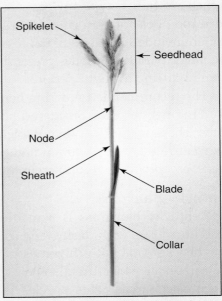

Goodheart-Willcox Publisher

Consider This

1. Collect examples of grass blades from different sources, including field and roadside grasses. Can you identify the different parts?
2. Do grasses that are considered weeds share the same morphology as desirable turfgrasses? Identify differences and similarities.
3. Do ornamental grasses share the same morphology as the turfgrasses and weed grasses? Compare the grasses and identify differences and similarities.

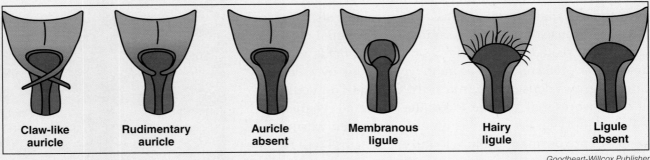

Goodheart-Willcox Publisher

Christopher D. Hart   *Jeff W. Jarrett/Shutterstock.com*

Figure 11-12. Perennial ryegrass has a thicker growth habit than annual ryegrass. Perennial ryegrass is commonly used to overseed dormant turf.

Tall Fescue

Tall fescue is a bunch-type turfgrass with a coarse texture, **Figure 11-13**. It is easily established from seed and one of the best species to plant if you desire a lawn that is green year-round. Tall fescue has a limited spreading capacity that keeps it out of beds and other mulched areas, such as at the base of trees. Due to its limited spreading ability, tall fescue may require reseeding to combat bare spots. Tall fescue requires full to part sun. The species has high resistance to summer stress caused by drought and high temperatures. This is due in part to its deep root system. In most cases, this turfgrass should not be watered daily. However, it should be watered deeply.

Christopher D. Hart

Figure 11-13. Tall fescue is a very common cool-season turfgrass. It provides an excellent lawn that is green year-round. Tall fescue is maintained at a height taller than most other turfgrass species.

Christopher D. Hart

Figure 11-14. Tall fescue is easily striped because of its taller mowing height. Striping a lawn creates unique patterns for added visual interest.

It is recommended that tall fescue have a mown height of 3″ to 3.5″. The taller height allows the grass to easily be striped, creating a nice, neat lawn, **Figure 11-14**. Due to its hardiness and durability in cool-season and transition zones, tall fescue is used in lawns, athletic fields, commercial sites, and as pasture grass. Cultivars of tall fescue should be purchased that are specific to your region in order to obtain the most appropriate seed.

Pro Tip

Lawn stripes are created by mowing adjacent paths in opposing directions. Grass blades bent toward the viewer appear dark and grass blades bent away appear lighter.

Warm-Season Turfgrasses

Warm-season turfgrasses are recommended for use only in areas where the root systems will not become damaged by winter temperatures. Their optimum growing temperature is between 80°F to 95°F (27°C to 35°C). Warm-season turfgrasses tolerate the high summer temperatures associated with the southern United States. Warm-season turfgrasses go dormant in the fall after the first frost and begin to green up slowly the following spring. Warm-season turfgrasses are best planted during the late spring and early summer. The most common warm-season turfgrasses are as follows:

- Bahiagrass.
- Bermudagrass.
- Carpetgrass.
- Centipedegrass.
- St. Augustinegrass.
- Zoysiagrass. See **Figure 11-15**.

Bahiagrass

Bahiagrass is a warm-season turfgrass with textures that range from very fine to coarse, depending on the variety. The South American tropical grass spreads with stolons and rhizomes, which creates a dense and durable turf. Bahiagrass prefers full sun but tolerates limited shade. The species requires limited fertilizers and irrigation; overwatering weakens the grass and makes it more vulnerable to disease.

The recommended mowing height for bahiagrass is 2″ to 3″ tall. Due to its dense growth, low-maintenance needs, and high drought and heat tolerance, bahiagrass works well in high-traffic or utility areas and as a means of erosion control. Bahiagrass is commonly sown in pastures and along roadsides, **Figure 11-16**. Bahiagrass performs well in soils with low fertility. This species is popular for lawns in the hot and humid Southeast and the southern states along the Gulf Coast.

Warm-Season Turfgrasses

	Bahiagrass (*Paspalum notatum*)	Bermudagrass (*Cynodon dactylon*)	Carpetgrass (*Axonopus fissifolius*)	Centipedegrass (*Eremochloa ophiuroides*)	St. Augustinegrass (*Stenotaphrum secundatum*)	Zoysiagrass (*Zoysia spp.*)
Cold Tolerance	Poor	Poor		Poor		
Drought Tolerance	Excellent	Excellent	Fair	Fair	Good	Excellent
Establishment Rate		Fast	Slow	Slow	Fast	Medium
Growth Habit	Stolons and rhizomes	Stolons and rhizomes	Stolons		Stolons	Stolons and rhizomes
Height after Mowing	2″ to 3″	0.5″ to 2″	3/4″ to 2″	1.5″ to 2″	2.5″ to 4″	1.5″ to 3″
Shade Tolerance	Fair	Poor	Good	Fair	Good (cv. dependent)	Fair
Texture	Fine to coarse	Fine	Coarse	Medium	Fine to coarse	Very fine to coarse
Wear Tolerance	Excellent	Excellent	Excellent	Poor	Fair	Excellent

Goodheart-Willcox Publisher

Figure 11-15. Warm-season turfgrasses vary greatly in growth habit and texture. Selecting the correct turfgrass for the site creates easier maintenance.

Matt Goodwin/Shutterstock.com

Goodheart-Willcox Publisher

Figure 11-16. Bahiagrass is widely used for erosion control. It can tolerate infrequent mowing that removes the majority of the leaf surface.

Christopher D. Hart

Figure 11-17. Bermudagrass can easily be identified by its blue-green tint. Brown, dead leaves at the base of the plant can be prevented by frequent mowing and proper maintenance.

Goodheart-Willcox Publisher

Figure 11-18. Carpetgrass has a coarse texture and yellow-green foliage. It is a slow growing plant and appears similar to centipedegrass.

Bermudagrass

Bermudagrass is a fine-textured, fast growing, warm-season turfgrass that spreads quickly through stolons and rhizomes, **Figure 11-17**. The root system and aggressive growth helps create a dense lawn that quickly repairs itself. It also creates a high degree of maintenance needs. Bermudagrass is extremely drought-tolerant and grows in a wide variety of soils. However, it will go dormant during periods of extended drought unless it is watered regularly. All cultivars require full sun and good drainage for optimum performance. Bermudagrass is established primarily through vegetative propagation. It can be installed as sod or with sprigs or plugs. Advancements in research and production have produced many cultivars that can be sown with seeds.

Bermudagrass is popular for use on athletic fields and golf courses due to its durability, ability to repair itself quickly, and tolerance to frequent and short mowing heights. Bermudagrass on golf courses and athletic fields may be mowed with a reel mower to a height as low as 0.5″. The recommended height for commercial and residential lawns is 1″ to 2″. It is often over-seeded with ryegrass during winter months. It is also important to note that bermudagrass can become very aggressive and difficult to contain within intended areas. Thatch may become a problem when establishing bermudagrass plantings. **Thatch** is a layer of organic matter, including dead grass clippings and live shoots, which forms between the top of the soil and the vegetation of the turfgrass. Thatch layers may become so thick that they prevent water and nutrients from reaching the roots.

Carpetgrass

Carpetgrass is a slow- and low-growing, coarse-textured grass, **Figure 11-18**. It is a creeping perennial that will quickly crowd out most other species. Carpetgrass may be established by seed or vegetative methods. The species grows well in full sun to part shade but tolerates wet and shaded areas. Carpetgrass can thrive in low-fertility locations but is not as drought-tolerant as bermudagrass and may require additional watering. The recommended mowing height is 3/4″ to 2″, but carpetgrass will tolerate the lower heights used on golf courses. Carpetgrass is similar to St. Augustinegrass and centipedegrass.

Centipedegrass

Centipedegrass is a pale green or yellowish green, warm-season turfgrass with coarse texture, **Figure 11-19**. Centipedegrass is commonly referred to as the *lazy man's grass* because of its low maintenance and fertilization requirements. Once established, it requires very little fertilizer and is relatively slow growing. The species does not tolerate heavy foot traffic,

Thinking Green

Electric Mowers

Today's electric mowers have become more reliable and affordable alternatives to gas-powered engines. The electric mowers are quieter than traditional mowers and do not release greenhouse gases into the atmosphere. Consumers can choose between push mowers and robotic models and corded or cordless mowers.

Zusha/Shutterstock.com

Consider This

1. What are the disadvantages of using an electric mower rather than a gas mower?
2. Would an electric mower be practical for mowing a baseball or soccer field? Explain your answer.
3. What types of limitations does a robotic mower have when compared to an electric push mower?

Pro3DArtt/Shutterstock.com

compaction, or high soil pH. Thatch may also be a problem with centipedegrass. This species of turfgrass may be established with seeds; however, it may take several years for a lawn to develop fully due to the slow growth rate. For faster coverage, vegetative options should be considered. Depending on the location, centipedegrass used in transition zones may be subject to winter-kill. The recommended mowing height is 1.5″ to 2″.

Craig Russell/Shutterstock.com

Goodheart-Willcox Publisher

Figure 11-19. Centipedegrass is a warm-season turfgrass that is commonly referred to as the *lazy man's grass* because of its ease of maintenance.

Christopher D. Hart

Windover Way Photography/Shutterstock.com

Figure 11-20. St. Augustinegrass has a very spongy feel due to its large stolons.

St. Augustinegrass

St. Augustinegrass has growth habits and coarse texture similar to centipedegrass, **Figure 11-20**. This species produces a very thick, dense, and spongy turf due to its large, round stolons. St. Augustinegrass must be started by vegetative means. The species is darker green and has a faster growth rate than centipedegrass. St. Augustinegrass is shade tolerant and prefers moist and somewhat fertile soils with a pH range from 5.0 to 7.5. St. Augustinegrass should be mowed between 2.5″ and 4″ tall. This species does well in coastal areas of the southeast, through the southern states, and in some areas of California.

Zoysiagrass

Zoysiagrass is one of the best selections of warm-season turfgrasses for a high profile lawn. Select cultivars of zoysiagrass may be seeded but the large majority require vegetative establishment, **Figure 11-21**. The species produces a very dense and thick carpet-like turf with its stolons and rhizomes. The thick turfgrass prevents most weeds from establishing in the lawn. Zoysiagrass is very drought tolerant and rarely requires irrigation. Depending on the species and the desired look, zoysiagrass should be mowed between 1.5″ to 3″ tall. Zoysia does not spread as quickly and profusely as bermudagrass and is easier to control.

Blends and Mixes

Many scientists recommend that a blend or mix of seeds of two to three cultivars (subspecies) of turfgrass be sown instead of a single cultivar. A *blend* is a combination of cultivars of the same species of grass. A *mix* is a combination of at least two species of turfgrass. A mix may also contain multiple subspecies. Mixes and blends can be formulated to the strengths and weaknesses of the landscape, such as growing in shady areas of the lawn. Blends and mixes are much more common with cool-season grasses than warm-season grasses. Warm-season seed is very expensive and is not commonly blended or mixed.

Christopher D. Hart

Dory F/Shutterstock.com

Figure 11-21. Zoysiagrass is similar to bermudagrass but it does not spread as easily as hybrid bermudagrass, making zoysia easier to control.

Sustainability

Sustainability is a method of using a resource so that the resource is not depleted or permanently damaged. *Sustainable turf management* uses minimal water, fertilizers, and pesticides to minimize soil contamination and prevent runoff into ground and surface waters. This is achieved through best management practices, including the following:

- Proper soil preparation.
- The use of organic soil amendments.
- Proper species selection.
- Maintaining the proper mower height.
- Mowing at proper intervals.
- Watering to proper depths.
- Applying fertilizer during the correct life cycle stage.
- Aerating at proper intervals.

All efforts should be made to provide optimal conditions to maintain the healthiest turfgrass possible, **Figure 11-22**. A healthy lawn is less susceptible to weeds, insects, and diseases and promotes biodiversity in the soil and surrounding environment. A healthy, thick lawn is also a great complement to the landscape design.

Turfgrass Alternatives

Turf is a very labor and resource intensive crop. Lawns require watering, mowing, fertilizing, weeding, aerating, and dethatching to ensure healthy, quality turf. Pesticides may also need to be applied to prevent pests. Due to

Stockforlife/Shutterstock.com   *Dejanns/Shutterstock.com*   *photowind/Shutterstock.com*   *Le Do/Shutterstock.com*

Figure 11-22. Proper management, including irrigation, mowing, dethatching, and fertilizing, creates turfgrass that is sustainable and environmentally friendly.

its high labor and input requirements, turf may not be in demand for all land-scapes. Homeowners may prefer a lawn alternative that provides many of the same benefits of turf without the high maintenance.

Synthetic Turf

Many recent advancements have been made to create a synthetic product that resembles turfgrass but does not require the maintenance of turfgrass. Synthetic turf has a higher upfront cost than traditional turfgrasses but has vir-tually no maintenance cost. Studies suggest that synthetic turf can be as much as three times less expensive than natural turf over a 20-year time period. Due to its composition, synthetic turf is not cool and the surface may become hot. Using a light-colored synthetic turf and increasing shade can help make the surface cooler during warmer months. See **Figure 11-23**.

Ornamental Grasses and Grass-Like Plants

Ornamental grasses are in the same family as turfgrass but their growth habit and cultural characteristics are much different, **Figure 11-24**. Grass-like plants are similar to plants in the *Gramaceae* family but they are not a true grass botanically. Ornamental grasses and grass-like plants come in a wide variety of heights, textures, and colors. Species can be selected that thrive in a wide variety of locations, including sun and shade as well as wet and dry soils. Grass-like plants can often tolerate mowing at the beginning of the season but do not require mowing during the growing season. Their fertilizer and main-tenance requirements are also substantially less than traditional turfgrasses.

Christopher D. Hart

Figure 11-23. The high initial cost of synthetic turfgrass may limit its use in residential lawns. However, synthetic turfgrass provides many athletic fields with low-maintenance fields that remain usable year-round.

Kathryn Roach/Shutterstock.com

Gabriela Beres/Shutterstock.com

Figure 11-24. Turfgrass alternatives offer aesthetic benefits that traditional turfgrasses cannot offer. Ornamental grasses are versatile and can be used in many areas of a landscape, including planting beds, to create borders, or as essential components of many xeriscapes.

Career Connection

Dr. Robert Lyons

Dr. Robert Lyons, Educator, Director, Volunteer

Sometimes it is best to simply follow those unexpected directions in your career rather than stick to some preconceived path. That is pretty much what happened to me as I capitalized on new opportunities as they presented themselves. My academic concentration within horticulture was floriculture and as a newly minted Ph.D. right out of graduate school, off I went to my first job at Virginia Tech with that focus in mind.

Only a few years passed before my department head (my boss!) called me and two other colleagues into his office to present us with an idea. With the impending departure of another faculty member who oversaw classic ornamental annual trials on the edge of campus, my boss posed an opportunity to convert that entire area into a teaching garden. My colleagues and I had absolutely *no* prior experience in building public teaching gardens but we became energized with the challenge of creating a new resource for our undergraduate teaching program.

In the next few years, I soon had primary responsibility for directing and managing this teaching garden. New courses in public garden management and maintenance evolved and students enrolled every semester. These students became some of the garden's greatest supporters. Former students often come up to me with stories from those courses and proudly point out plants they cultivated.

I left Virginia Tech and the gardens in 1999, when I felt I had realized as much potential as I could. My next stop was Directorship of the J.C. Raulston Arboretum at NC State University, where I resided for five years, only to leave once again to direct the Longwood Graduate Program in Public Horticulture at the University of Delaware. After 10 years, I retired from that position and now use my expertise as a volunteer at many gardens in the greater Philadelphia region. I never would have predicted all the surprises along the way in my career but I do not regret veering off in new directions when presented and I would encourage anyone to do the same!

Consider This

1. Would you be willing to move around to different jobs in different parts of the country? Why or why not?
2. What types of personal characteristics does Dr. Lyons possess that inspired him to change professional positions and take on challenges, such as the teaching garden?
3. What level of education and/or experience would you need to become the director of an arboretum, such as the prestigious J.C. Raulston Arboretum?

Summary

- An expanse of thick, green, well-maintained turf can be one of the most striking areas in a landscape.
- Blends and mixes should be sown instead of a single cultivar for best performance.
- Turfgrass selection is based primarily on the turf zone into which the landscape falls. Turf zones are determined by temperature range and available moisture.
- Cool-season turfgrasses are those that thrive in areas with hot summers and cold, freezing winters. Many species will stay green year-round.
- Each species of turfgrass has unique characteristics, including leaf texture, mowing height, growth habit, durability, and drought tolerance.
- Sustainable turf management uses minimal water, fertilizers, and pesticides to minimize soil contamination and prevent runoff into ground and surface waters.
- Synthetic turfgrass, ornamental grasses, and grass-like plants are viable alternatives for traditional turfgrass.

Chapter Review

Know and Understand ⤴

Answer the following questions using the information provided in this chapter.

1. On which of the following characteristics are the turf zones based?
   A. Color and mature height of certain grass species.
   B. Average amount of sunlight over a year.
   C. Temperature and available moisture.
   D. All of the above.

2. Cool-season turfgrasses prefer an air temperature of _____.
   A. 50°F to 65°F (10°C to 18°C)
   B. 60°F to 75°F (15.5°C to 24°C)
   C. 80°F to 95°F (27°C to 35°C)
   D. 70°F to 90°F (21°C to 32°C)

3. Cool-season turfgrasses have optimum growth when soil temperatures are between _____.
   A. 50°F and 65°F (10°C and 18°C)
   B. 60°F and 75°F (15.5°C and 24°C)
   C. 80°F and 95°F (27°C and 35°C)
   D. 70°F and 90°F (21°C and 32°C)

4. Warm-season turfgrasses prefer an air temperature range of _____.
   A. 50°F to 65°F (10°C to 18°C)
   B. 60°F to 75°F (15.5°C to 24°C)
   C. 80°F to 95°F (27°C to 35°C)
   D. 70°F to 90°F (21°C to 32°C)

5. Optimum soil temperatures for warm-season turfgrasses range from _____.
   A. 50°F to 65°F (10°C to 18°C)
   B. 60°F to 75°F (15.5°C to 24°C)
   C. 80°F to 95°F (27°C to 35°C)
   D. 70°F to 90°F (21°C to 32°C)

6. *True or False?* Only warm-season grasses will grow in the transition zone.
   A. True.
   B. False.

7. Lawns used on roadsides for erosion control are referred to as _____.
   A. commercial lawns
   B. field turfgrass
   C. utility turfgrass
   D. All of the above.

8. High profile or low profile residential turfgrass is referred to as _____.
   A. home lawns
   B. utility lawns
   C. utility turfgrass
   D. field turfgrass

9. Turfgrass installations for businesses, such as malls or office parks, are referred to as _____.
   A. commercial lawns
   B. home lawns
   C. utility turfgrass
   D. field lawns

10. Of the following, which is a factor to consider when choosing turfgrass?
    A. The quality and pH of the soil.
    B. Durability in high-traffic areas.
    C. Texture, color, and overall appearance.
    D. All of the above.

11. *True or False?* Cool-season turfgrasses thrive in areas with hot summers and freezing winters.
    A. True.
    B. False.

12. *True or False?* Cool-season turfgrasses grow best in summer months and will turn brown in the fall months.
    A. True.
    B. False.

Match the cool- and warm-season grasses to the descriptions in 13–24.
   A. annual ryegrass
   B. bahiagrass
   C. bermudagrass
   D. carpetgrass
   E. centipede grass
   F. creeping bentgrass
   G. fine fescue
   H. Kentucky bluegrass
   I. perennial ryegrass
   J. St. Augustinegrass
   K. tall fescue
   L. zoysiagrass

13. A slow- and low-growing, coarse-textured, warm-season turfgrass that will quickly crowd out other species.

14. A fine-textured, fast growing, aggressive, warm-season turfgrass that spreads quickly through stolons and rhizomes.

15. A cool-season turfgrass with an extremely fine texture and lower fertilizer, moisture, and light requirements than the other cool-season grasses.

16. A pale green or yellowish green, warm-season turfgrass with coarse texture. It is well known as the lazy man's grass.

17. A cool-season, medium green, turfgrass with a coarse leaf texture. It is a non-spreading, bunch-type turfgrass that only lasts for one growing season.

18. A bunch-type, cool-season turfgrass with a coarse texture. This grass has limited spreading ability and requires full sun.

19. A medium- to fine-textured, cool-season turfgrass with dark green color.

20. A cool-season, fine-textured turfgrass used almost exclusively on golf course putting greens.

21. This species produces a very thick, dense, and spongy turf due to its large, round stolons.

22. Perennial ryegrass is a cool-season turfgrass with a fine texture. This grass is rarely used as a standalone turfgrass.

23. This species produces a very thick, dense, and spongy turf due to its large, round stolons.

24. A warm-season turfgrass with textures that range from very fine to coarse, depending on the variety. The South American tropical grass spreads with stolons and rhizomes.

25. A combination of at least two species of turfgrass seeds is a _____.
   A. blend
   B. mix
   C. hybrid
   D. combo

26. A combination of cultivars of the same species of grass.
   A. blend
   B. mix
   C. hybrid
   D. combo

27. Which of the following apply to sustainable turf management?
   A. Applies minimal fertilizers.
   B. Prevents runoff.
   C. Uses minimal water.
   D. All of the above.

28. *True or False?* A healthy lawn is less susceptible to weeds, insects, and diseases and promotes biodiversity in the soil and surrounding environment.
   A. True.
   B. False.

29. *True or False?* Synthetic turf has a lower upfront cost than traditional turfgrasses and has virtually no maintenance cost.

Match the plant parts to the descriptions in 30–37.
   A. auricle
   B. blade
   C. collar
   D. leaf bud
   E. ligule
   F. seedhead
   G. sheath
   H. spikelet

30. The individual components of the seedhead.

31. The part of a grass plant that is between the stem and leaf blade.

32. The area on the outside of the leaf where the leaf blade and leaf sheath join.

33. The flowering structure of turfgrass.

34. The section of the leaf blade that connects the blade to the stem.

35. The point from which new grass blades originate.

36. The leaf portion of the grass plant.

37. A growth that projects from each side of the collar.

Thinking Critically

1. What facts indicate that xeriscapes are more sustainable than traditional landscapes?
2. Compare the benefits of planting seed to the benefits of installing sod for a lawn. Which do you think is better for the environment?
3. Determine if the land is harmed when sod is harvested.

Suggested Activities

1. A client comes to you for help in establishing a new lawn. The client lives in central Illinois and desires a turfgrass that is green year-round. The lawn will be a recreational area for him, his wife, and their young daughters. Which turfgrass would you recommend? Why?

2. Can you identify the parts of a blade of grass? Work with a partner to obtain and compare blades of different grasses. Include blades from grass-like plants and determine the similarities between grass-like plants and turfgrass.

3. Work with a partner and acquire photos of the turfgrasses discussed in this chapter. Gather three images for each turfgrass, one close-up of the turf, one of a blade, and one of the lawn as a whole. Create a visual presentation or a set of flash cards for studying/identifying the types of turfgrasses.

4. In groups of 4 or 5, examine the lawn areas on the school campus. Determine what type of turfgrass is present in each area. If the lawn is thriving, discuss and determine the reasons it is doing so well. If the lawn is not thriving, discuss and determine why it is failing. Discuss your findings in class and offer suggestions for improving the lawn.

5. In groups of 3 or 4, gather blades of the different grasses from around the school campus, including the sports fields. Identify the types of turf. Create a visual to share with the class. This may be on a poster board, index cards, or a slide presentation. Compare results to the other groups' identifications. How many were alike?

6. Work with a partner or small group to identify pests, pathogens, and weeds that affect turfgrass. Search for images and create a visual presentation to present to the class. Expand the activity by creating flash cards for classroom use.

7. Create a table/chart identifying horticultural characteristics of turfgrasses and ornamental grasses based on scientific principles. Include the botanical names, environmental needs, and the zones in which they grow best.

Turfgrass Installation and Management

Chapter Outcomes

After studying this chapter, you will be able to:

- Explain the methods of establishing a turfgrass.
- Calculate the amount of materials needed to properly seed, sprig, plug, and sod a new or renovated site.
- Identify the steps and procedures used to establish a new lawn or renovate an existing lawn.
- Take accurate soil samples and apply the lab's recommendations for soil amendment.

Key Terms ↪

aeration
core aeration
cyclone spreader
dethatcher
drop seeder
erosion netting
grading
overseeding
plug

plugging
rotary spreader
sod
soil amendment
space planting
sprig
sprigging
topdressing
verticutter

Introduction

Turfgrass installation and management is a large part of landscaping and the landscaping industry. Understanding the basics of turfgrass will help you create and maintain thick, healthy lawns. You may also pursue educational and career opportunities focusing on turfgrass. Many universities have dedicated programs. Career opportunities include scientific research, landscape installation and management, and turf management for golf courses or professional stadiums. This chapter explains how to establish, maintain, and repair turfgrass.

Methods of Establishing Turfgrass

Selecting a turfgrass species for a site is the first step toward producing a successful lawn. The soil must be graded, tested, and amended before installation can begin. The methods used to establish turfgrasses include seeding, sodding, sprigging, and plugging. The species and cultivar and often times the budget determine the method of installation. St. Augustinegrass, for example, is not available in seed form whereas centipedegrass is available in seed and vegetative form. The owner's budget and the time he or she is willing to wait to have a full lawn will also influence which method is used, **Figure 12-1**.

Safety First

Always call 811 to have all buried telephone, gas, electrical, and water lines marked before beginning any excavation or turfgrass installation.

Seeding

Seeding is the most common and often the most economical method of establishing turfgrass. It also takes the longest time to cover the area completely. Seed companies research and study all stages of growth and create new cultivars. Through this research and advancements in seed technology, species that were once only established through vegetative means, such as bermudagrass and zoysiagrass, are now available as viable seed.

Blue Tag

Only high quality, viable seed will ensure the desired outcome. Lower-quality seeds often contain seeds from weeds and undesired grasses. Certified seed is labeled as either blue label or gold label. Seed bags with a blue certification tag are guaranteed to contain the variety specified on the label. The blue tag also indicates that the seed is free from noxious weeds. Blue-tag seed bags with mixes and blends are certified to contain the proper percentages of each species. Certification requirements vary by grass species and from state to state. Gold label seed is certified as sod quality seed and is purer than blue label seed. See **Figure 12-2**.

Brandon Eubanks, Super-Sod

Figure 12-1. While sodding has the highest initial cost of establishing a lawn, it is the quickest method. Sod provides the homeowner or client with an instant lawn.

Seed Coating

Most grass seed has a special coating to help the seed retain moisture. This coating increases the size of the seed and the seeding rate. Always refer to the label to determine how much seed should be applied per square foot.

Rotary and Drop Spreaders

Rotary or drop spreaders are types of lawn equipment used to uniformly apply grass seed. *Rotary spreaders* have a small disc-like mechanism that turns when the device is pushed. The spreader distributes the seed in a swath that is several feet wide, **Figure 12-3A**. Rotary spreaders are also known as *cyclone spreaders*. A *drop seeder* simply drops the seed on the ground as it is pushed across the planting area. Drop seeders are typically used in areas requiring precise seed placement, such as along the perimeter of planting beds, **Figure 12-3B**.

Rotary and drop spreaders often have controls that determine the size of the opening the seed falls through. It is important to refer to the owner's manual to determine the rate that corresponds to the setting on the controller. Planting too much seed is economically unwise and it will likely create weak and spindly turfgrass.

Allison Fortner, Super-Sod

Figure 12-2. The label contains pertinent information regarding what type of seed is in the bag. The sell-by date and percentages of inert matter, weed seed, grass seed, and germination are all important information contained in a seed label.

Applying Seed

When establishing a lawn from seed, it is very important to sow at the proper rates. The spreader must be adjusted to the proper setting before the seed is applied. The label on the bag lists sowing information.

A   **B**   *Christopher D. Hart*

Figure 12-3. A—Rotary or cycle spreaders can cover a large amount of area in a single swath. B—Drop spreaders are useful for accurate placement of seeds because they only drop seed when the seeder rolls.

Seed is applied in two directions to ensure complete coverage. Half of the seed is applied in one direction across the whole planting area. The other half of the seed is applied in a direction that is 90° to the first direction. See **Figure 12-4**. Some types of turfgrass seeds must be lightly covered with soil after seeding. This can be done by lightly raking or dragging the newly seeded area. Erosion netting may be used when seeding on steep slopes to prevent the soil and seeds from washing down the slope. *Erosion netting* is woven fabric made of biodegradable fibers, **Figure 12-5**.

Mulching Seeded Areas. Mulch should be applied over newly seeded areas to prevent the seeds from washing away, help the soil retain moisture, and possibly reduce the amount eaten by birds. Straw mulch is recommended. A general rule is one bale of straw is needed per 1000 ft². Areas with steep slopes where straw will wash away should be covered in netting to help hold the soil in place. The straw will break down and add organic material to the soil as the seed germinates. The mulch should be scattered loosely or it may reduce the germination rate. The mulched area should be rolled and watered thoroughly. Using a roller helps ensure the seed remains in contact with the ground, **Figure 12-6**.

Sodding

Sod is the most expensive method of lawn installation. *Sod* is turfgrass cut with a thin layer of soil from a production field. It is cut in squares or strips that vary in size by lawn production operations. Sodding is expensive because of production, shipping, and labor costs as well as the convenience of an almost instant lawn, **Figure 12-7**.

The harvesting equipment used by the sod farm as well as the species of turfgrass determine the size of a piece of sod. To alleviate confusion, sod is commonly sold by the square foot. Homeowners purchasing sod in individual pieces rather than full pallets commonly purchase 16″ × 24″ sections.

> **Pro Tip**
>
> *Overseeding* is the process of planting grass seed to fill in areas that are thinning and improve the density of a lawn. It may also enhance the color of the turfgrass.

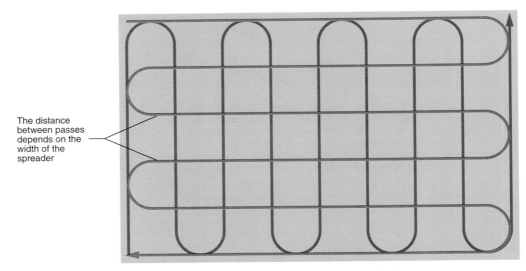

The distance between passes depends on the width of the spreader

Rotate 90° and seed in the opposite direction

Figure 12-4. Use the proper pattern with lines as straight as possible when establishing turf with seed. Do not overseed areas that have been covered.

Allison Fortner, Super-Sod

Figure 12-5. Erosion netting may be needed when establishing turfgrass on steep slopes to hold the soil in place. Pieces of sod should be laid in a staggered pattern to ensure channels for rainwater do not develop.

kao/Shutterstock.com

Figure 12-6. Turf rollers are used to push the grass seed down to ensure the mulch, seed, and soil are in contact. Rolling a newly seeded lawn will help the seed take up moisture, which will increase the percentage of germination.

Site Preparation

To ensure the sod quickly takes root and thrives, the site must be prepared properly through soil testing and the addition of sufficient amendments. It must also be watered thoroughly when the sod is initially laid. The addition of topsoil may be needed in new construction areas. Call 811 to mark the utility lines if they have not been marked or the markings are no longer in place.

Once the site is graded (leveled), it should be measured for square footage to ensure enough sod is ordered. Sod is commonly sold by the square foot, stacked on pallets, and delivered by semitrailer, **Figure 12-8**. Sod is very heavy and pallets may need to be moved nearer to the site with a forklift. Check the condition of the sod when it arrives. It should be moist but not waterlogged.

Brandon Hubinek, Super-Sod

Figure 12-7. As evident in the photos, sod creates an almost instant lawn. In addition to being labor-intensive and expensive to install, sodding is on a restricted time line for installation.

Allison Fortner, Super-Sod   *Nathan Tart, Super-Sod*   *Hillary Thompson, Super-Sod*

Figure 12-8. Sod is harvested from the sod farm, loaded on a truck, and planted just a few hours later.

The best time to lay sod is when it is delivered. If that is not possible, it must be laid within 24 hours of delivery, **Figure 12-9**. Waiting more than 24 hours will compromise its ability to take root. Sod should always be laid on moist soil. Thoroughly watering the site for a few days before the sod is delivered will create ideal conditions. The sod should be watered thoroughly for the first few days. If the sod is installed in dry areas or during a drought, it may need daily watering for a longer period.

Keep the following general rules in mind when laying sod.

- Always lay the sod so the joints overlap in a bricklike pattern. If the joints are placed in a straight line, the line becomes a channel for water.
- Sod should be laid against a straight edge first, working lengthwise across the face of the slope.
- Joints between pieces of sod should be tight. Gently pat the piece of sod to work out space between the pieces.
- The sod should be rolled with a drum roller after it is planted. Drum rollers are used to ensure the roots of the sod have good, firm contact with the soil.
- The sod must be watered thoroughly and deeply.

Brandon Starnes, Super-Sod

Figure 12-9. Once on the job site, sod should be planted immediately. Proper care and management of the sod once it arrives on the job site helps ensure the grass will properly root.

Sprigging and Plugging

Sprigging and plugging are methods of lawn installation. The plant material used may be less costly than sod but sprigging and plugging requires a great deal more labor to install properly. Sprigging and plugging should only be used on species of grasses that spread easily. A *plug* is a small section of cut sod, **Figure 12-10A**. *Plugging* is the placement of plugs at specific intervals in the lawn. Plugs are typically cut into pieces 2″ or larger. Plugs are usually planted on 6″ or 12″ centers. Sprigging and plugging may also be referred to as *space planting*. Space planting only works with turfgrasses that spread through rhizomes and stolons. The spacing of the plugs or sprigs depends on the species of turfgrass being planted. The supplier will provide spacing instructions.

A *sprig* is a cut stem with stolons that can easily root and produce new shoots, **Figure 12-10B**. *Sprigging* is planting stolons (with or without leaves) at specific intervals in the lawn. Sprigs may also be broadcasted and rolled. The spacing used to lay out the plants depends on the species of turfgrass. The closer the spacing, the more plants will be required. Closer spacing will fill in and establish the lawn sooner. Sprigs can be installed over the entire site. Tools, such as rollers, cultipackers, special planters, and straight disks can be used to ensure the sprigs and the soil have good contact.

A   **B**   *Christopher D. Hart*

Figure 12-10. A—Plugs are less expensive than sod but are limited to species of turfgrasses that are only available vegetatively. Plugs must be sown at the correct spacing to ensure complete coverage of the area. Although it is more expensive to plant the plugs closer together, closer planting will yield a full lawn faster. B—Unlike plugs, sprigs do not have soil attached to their roots. Sprigs work only on species of turfgrass that spread.

Calculating Seed and Plant Materials

The amount of seed or plant material needed depends on the method used to establish the lawn, **Figure 12-11**. All methods of lawn installation are given in a rate in relation to a specific area, which is typically square feet. The rate for sowing tall fescue, for example, might be 10 lb to 12 lb per 1000 ft^2.

- Seed is sold by the pound.
- Sod is sold by the square foot. For large jobs, it is sold by the square foot coverage area of a pallet.
- Plugs may be sold by the tray. Pieces of sod may also be purchased and cut into individual plugs.
- Sprigs and stolons are sold by the bushel per 1000 ft^2. The recommended rate for broadcasting bermudagrass sprigs, for example, is three bushels per 1000 ft^2.

Turfgrass Seeding Rates	
Turfgrass	**Amount Needed**
Annual ryegrass	4 lb to 5 lb per 1000 ft^2
Bahiagrass	5 lb to 10 lb per 1000 ft^2
Bermudagrass	1 lb to 2 lb per 1000 ft^2
Carpetgrass	2 lb per 100 ft^2
Centipedegrass	1/4 lb to 1/2 lb per 1000 ft^2
Creeping bentgrass	1 lb to 2 lb per 1000 ft^2
Fine fescue	2 lb per 1000 ft^2
Kentucky bluegrass	1 1/2 lb per 1000 ft^2
Perennial ryegrass	5 lb to 7 lb per 1000 ft^2
St. Augustinegrass	Only through vegetative means
Tall fescue	10 lb to 12 lb per 1000 ft^2
Zoysiagrass	1 lb per 1000 ft^2 (Primarily vegetative)

Goodheart-Willcox Publisher

Figure 12-11. Turfgrasses must be seeded at proper rates to ensure complete coverage. Read and follow the directions on the seed package to ensure the appropriate amount is used. It is also important to read the seed spreader to ensure the spreader is used at the correct setting.

Calculating the Rate for Planting Seed

You wish to overseed a bermudagrass lawn with annual ryegrass. The lawn measures $100' \times 250'$. How many pounds of annual ryegrass seed will you need?

You must first calculate the area to be seeded in square footage.

Area: length $\times$ width = area

$$100' \times 250' = 25,000 \text{ ft}^2$$

The seeding rate for annual ryegrass is 4 lb per 1000 ft^2.

Divide the total area by 1000 to determine the number of 1000 ft^2 sections.

$$25,000 \div 1000 = 25$$

Multiply the number of 1000 ft^2 sections by the number of pounds per 1000 ft^2 recommended for annual ryegrass.

$$25 \times 4 \text{ lb} = 100 \text{ lb}$$

100 lb of annual ryegrass seed is needed to seed the lawn.

Calculating the Rate for Planting Sod

A lawn measuring $156' \times 143'$ is to be covered in tall fescue sod. If the sod on one pallet covers 504 ft^2, how many pallets are required to complete the job?

Calculate the area: length $\times$ width = area

$$156' \times 143' = 22,308 \text{ ft}^2$$

Divide the total area to be sodded by the area covered by one pallet to determine the number of pallets needed.

$$22,308 \text{ ft}^2 \div 504 = 44.26$$

45 pallets of tall fescue sod are needed for the job.

Calculating the Rate for Planting Sprigs

You are to cover a lawn that measures $245' \times 345'$ in bermudagrass sprigs at the rate of three bushels per 1000 ft^2. How many bushels will be needed to complete the job?

Calculate the area: $245' \times 345' = 84,525 \text{ ft}^2$

Divide the total area by 1000 to determine the number of 1000 ft^2 sections.

$$84,525 \text{ ft}^2 \div 1000 = 85.5$$

Multiply the number of 1000 ft^2 sections by the number of bushels per 1000 ft^2 recommended for bermudagrass sprigs.

$$85.5 \times 3 = 256.5$$

257 bushels of sprigs are required to complete the job

STEM Connection

Measurement Conversions

The design, installation, and management of landscapes requires many calculations. Measurements often must be converted in order to perform calculations. One useful calculation is the ability to convert between in^2 and ft^2. These calculations will enable you to easily calculate the number of plants required for a planting bed. This calculation is also helpful in determining the number of plugs or sprigs needed for a lawn.

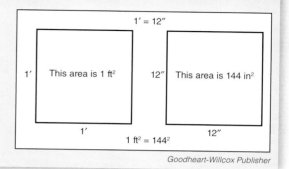

Goodheart-Willcox Publisher

Calculating the Rate for Planting Plugs

You are to cover a lawn that measures $105' \times 76'$ in bermudagrass plugs. You plan to space the plugs 18″ OC (off center). If plugs come in trays of 36, how many trays will you need?

Calculate the area of the lawn: $105' \times 76' = 7980$ ft^2
Calculate the area that the plugs occupy: $18'' \times 18'' = 324$ in^2

You must convert one of your area measurements to either square inches or square feet. There are 144 in^2 in 1 ft^2

$$324 \text{ in}^2 \div 144 \text{ in}^2 = 2.25 \text{ ft}^2 \text{ per plant}$$
$$7980 \div 2.25 = 3546.67 \text{ plugs needed}$$

Plugs come in trays of 36

$$3547 \div 36 = 98.5$$

99 trays are required to complete the job

Establishing a New Lawn

The site for a new lawn must be evaluated before the installation begins. Environmental factors that will affect site preparation include how much of the area is in full sun, partial shade, and complete shade; the quality of the soil; the topography; and trees that will be left or removed. A strategy for eliminating or minimizing low, wet areas would also be needed. A complete evaluation of the site will provide enough information for the contractor to determine how much preparation work the site needs and how much this part of the job will cost.

Once the site is evaluated, the intended use of the lawn must be determined. If there is a complete landscape design, the designated use of each area may be evident. The client should be asked to explain their expectations. Asking the following questions, as well as any others relative to the job, will help determine which turf will be used and how the job will proceed.

- Is the lawn purely an aesthetic complement to the home?
- Is the turfgrass being installed to prevent erosion?

Photos courtesy of Super-Sod

Figure 12-12. Landscaping has the ability to quickly transform a structure or an outdoor area. Sod provides an instant lawn, dramatically increasing aesthetic value.

- How much foot traffic will the lawn receive?
- What level of maintenance is desired?
- Is funding available to purchase grass in vegetative forms?
- How much time is allowed for achieving a full lawn? See **Figure 12-12**.

Step One: Choosing a Turfgrass

The first step in establishing a new lawn is to choose a species of turfgrass. The primary factors to consider are the area's climate and the turf zone.

Sean Locke Photography/Shutterstock.com

Figure 12-13. The landscape professional works closely with the client and may visit the construction site to help the client visualize where each feature and plant will be installed.

The species determines the time of the year that the lawn should be established. A discussion with the client and the professional's knowledge of turfgrass characteristics should provide the information needed to determine which species is best suited for the landscape. The characteristics that should be discussed with the client include maintenance requirements, the level of foot traffic, their preferred mowing height, and the texture and color of the turfgrasses that will work in their landscape, **Figure 12-13**. Certain species are only available as sprigs, plugs, or sod. The cost of the installation may increase depending on the species of grass selected.

Step Two: Preparing the Site

The initial site evaluation helps the landscape professional determine the work and the types of machinery needed. The site should be visited a second time to examine the area more closely and to mark trees and other objects, such as large boulders, that will not be removed. It is helpful if the client accompanies the contractor to ensure the correct trees and objects are left on the site.

The initial preparation includes debris removal, weed control, pruning and removal of trees, and grading. The order in which these actions are performed will vary by site.

- **Debris removal.** Construction materials, such as block, bricks, boards, spilled concrete, rebar, and wire, should be removed. These materials are often abundant around new construction. Large stones, fallen branches, and other organic materials will also need to be removed.
- **Weed control.** A nonselective herbicide may be applied to eliminate perennial weeds. It is best to use a nonselective herbicide that does not contain preemergent active ingredients requiring a waiting period before sowing seed. These ingredients remain in the soil and prevent germination.
- **Pruning and removal of trees.** All trees slated for removal are cleared with heavy equipment. The remaining trees should be pruned to remove dead branches, improve shape, and increase sunlight for the turfgrass where possible, **Figure 12-14**.
- **Grading.** *Grading* is smoothing the soil surface to ensure a level base and the proper slope for drainage. The slope (grade) must be at least 1% for water to drain but 2% to 3% is ideal, **Figure 12-15**. If grading must occur deeper than the thickness of the topsoil, the topsoil should be removed and piled aside. The topsoil is replaced over the graded area and smoothed to the same contour as the graded subsoil. Removing and replacing the topsoil keeps the nutrients and organic matter accessible to the turfgrass.

Special care must be taken if the slope needs to be adjusted around existing trees. It is important to tree health that the root system is not disturbed. Wood, stone, or block retaining walls can be built to maintain existing soil levels around the root system, **Figure 12-16**.

Christopher D. Hart

Figure 12-14. Branches can be removed to increase the amount of sunlight that reaches the turfgrass. Hiring an arborist to prune established trees will ensure that they are pruned properly and will not be harmed.

> **Pro Tip**
>
> Slopes greater than 15% will require additional maintenance if covered in turf. It is often recommended that slopes that are too steep to mow safely should be planted in ground covers.

A   *Christopher D. Hart*

B   *Brandon Starnes, Super-Sod*

Figure 12-15. A—A laser level can be used to determine the slope of the site when preparing a new site for lawn installation. B—Existing trees and shrubs should be properly mulched to allow ease of maintenance of the lawn as well. Properly mulched trees and plants will also help the landscaping plants conserve and hold water.

Christopher D. Hart

Figure 12-16. The original soil level around the roots of the tree should not be disturbed when the land is graded. It may be necessary to install retaining walls to maintain the original soil level.

- **Raking to final grade.** A rake, drag, harrow, or other implement raked over the topsoil will remove gravel and hard particles of soil. Raking can also be used to eliminate unwanted high and low spots. The soil may be amended before the final raking.

Step Three: Sampling the Soil

Soil samples are taken and tested to determine soil fertility, pH, textures, and percentages of organic matter. Knowing which nutrients are lacking allows you to formulate soil amendments specific to your turfgrass' needs. Samples should only be taken after grading to obtain the most accurate results. Separate samples should be taken for the lawn area and planting beds.

An accurate soil sample is composed of multiple samples from random spots through the area. Larger areas will require more samples for a better representation of the site. The lab that will be performing the tests will often provide material for taking the samples as well as instructions on how and where they should be taken.

The importance and value of soil sampling cannot be stressed enough. All turfgrasses perform at an optimal pH and nutrient level. Soil testing is the only way to know exactly the level of nutrients you need to add to your soil to provide optimal growing conditions.

Hands-On Landscaping

Taking a Soil Sample

1. Contact your local extension service or a private lab and request the materials and instructions for taking and submitting a sample.
2. Complete the paperwork with the requested information. The lab can provide the most accurate advice only if you provide detailed information about the project. In this case, you would explain that it would be a new lawn planted with seed/sod/sprigs of the chosen species.
3. Obtain a clean plastic bucket and clean soil test tube or soil probe.
4. The soil should be dry enough to crumble in your hands. If it is too wet, it will not mix uniformly.
5. Use the tube or probe to collect samples 3" to 4" deep from across the area. Place the cores (samples) in the bucket.
6. Mix the samples until a uniform mix is created. Fill the provided container or box with soil to submit to the lab.

Christopher D. Hart

Consider This
1. What types of tests can you perform at home to determine soil pH?
2. What types of tests can you perform to determine soil texture?
3. Perform a percolation test on the same soil collected for the sample. Review the sample results and determine how or if the percolation rate is affected by other components of the soil.

Step Four: Amending the Soil

The test results will reveal the soil's fertility, pH, textures, and percentages of organic matter. They will also explain which adjustments can be made to enhance the soil's fertility. *Soil amendments* are a wide variety of materials that can be added to the soil to improve performance. The most common amendments are fertilizers, lime, sulfur, organic matter, and sand. The amendments must be raked or turned into the soil to make them readily available to the turfgrass.

Step Five: Planting the Turfgrass

Once the soil is prepared, the turfgrass may be planted using one of the four methods: seeding, sodding, sprigging, or plugging. It is important to organize the crew and formulate a plan for installing the grass. If more than one person is applying seed, for example, each person can apply in one of the two directions. They must also determine a starting point to ensure the entire area is properly seeded. If sod is being laid, a starting point must be determined to ensure the proper pattern is used. If more than one person is applying seed, determine the area each person will sow. One person, for example, may begin in the front yard while another begins in the backyard. Mulch can be applied over the seed when sowing is complete. The seeded and mulched areas can then be rolled and watered.

The best time to install turfgrass depends on the region and whether the grass is a warm- or cool-season species. Cool-season turfgrasses should be planted in the spring and fall when the temperature range is between 65°F and 80°F. Warm-season grasses should be planted when the temperature range is between 75°F and 90°F, **Figure 12-17**. Grass planted when the temperatures are less than ideal may not grow and will need to be replanted. Failure to plant

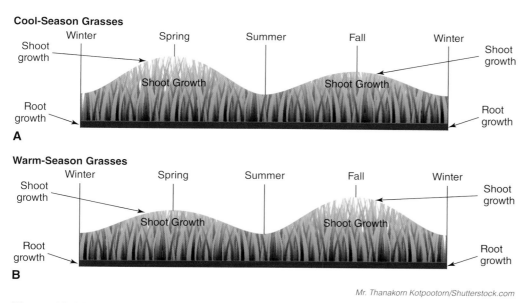

Mr. Thanakorn Kotpootorn/Shutterstock.com

Figure 12-17. A—Cool-season grasses have most of their root growth and shoot growth in the spring and fall seasons. Cool-season grasses should only be established when roots and shoots are in active growth. B—Warm-season turfgrasses have the majority of their shoot and root growth in spring and summer. Wait until the damage of frost has passed before establishing warm-season turfgrasses in the spring.

during the proper time of the year may also create a lawn that requires additional maintenance, such as watering and overseeding, to survive and thrive. In most cases, ryegrass can be used to provide a temporary green lawn until the ideal season arrives.

Step Six: Maintaining the New Turfgrass

Seedlings in newly seeded lawns should be fertilized for eight weeks to encourage root and shoot growth. The application frequency and nutrient ratio of the fertilizer will depend on the soil type and results from the soil test. Lawns started through vegetative means should be fertilized to encourage spreading of shoots and root growth. Watering regimens vary depending on the climate and the type of materials planted. Seed bags typically include instructions for recommended fertilizing and watering schedules. Suppliers of vegetative materials will provide maintenance instructions.

> **Pro Tip**
>
> *Topdressing* is both a material and method to apply a thin layer of material, such as sand or prepared soil, to the surface of a lawn. Topdressing may be used to reduce thatch buildup, smooth the surface of the lawn, to protect developing plants, and to help avoid winter desiccation. Topdressing is applied as small mounds and spread with the back side of a garden rake.

Mowing Lawns

Mowing is a major component of lawn maintenance. Maintaining sharp mower blades will ensure the best results, a lawn that is even throughout the yard. Dull blades tear, rather than cut the grass. Using dull mower blades may result in a damaged lawn with a brown cast and an uneven, ragged look. A lawn with physical damage is more susceptible to pests and disease. Cutting the lawn when it is wet may also cause physical damage. See **Figure 12-18**. The mower may become stuck and the clippings will not be discharged properly.

There are different preferred mowing heights for each turfgrass species. The different heights, however, do not affect how much grass should be cut. The rule of thumb is that no more than 1/3 of the total height of the grass should be cut and turfgrass should be mowed as soon as the grass is 50% higher than the desired height. For example, if tall fescue is to be kept 3″ tall, it should be mowed before it reaches a height of 4.5″.

Mowing New Lawns

If the lawn is newly planted, the grass should be allowed to grow and reach its suggested mowing height before the first mowing. Very sharp mower blades should be used to ensure the leaf blade is cut and minimal damage is done to the root system. New seeded lawns should not be mowed until all of the viable grass seed germinates. The root system for sodded and plugged lawns must be well developed before the first mowing. The mowing height also determines how often the lawn must be mowed. Shorter grasses, for example, may require more frequent mowing than grasses kept at a taller height.

Figure 12-18. Mowing grasses at improper heights places unnecessary stress on the turfgrass. Leaf blades cut too short struggle to photosynthesize, making it easier for weeds to take root and spread over the lawn.

Renovating a Lawn

Some landowners would prefer repairing rather than replacing their lawn. Before lawn renovation can begin, it must be determined why the current lawn is in poor condition. You must also determine whether the lawn can be repaired or if it should be replaced.

Step One: Evaluating the Site

A variety of circumstances can contribute to the poor condition of a lawn. Identifying as many issues as possible before installing new turfgrass will save money and time, **Figure 12-19**. It must first be determined whether the lawn was installed properly. If the slope is inadequate, for example, there may be an irrigation problem. You must also consider issues such as nutrient deficiencies, improper pH, soil compaction, soil porosity, available sunlight, and disease or pests. The problem might be that the wrong species of turfgrass was installed. Once you have determined what the issues are, you may begin planning the renovation.

A   **B**   *Christopher D. Hart*

Figure 12-19. A—Turfgrass is performing poorly due to heavy compaction from foot traffic. Concerns regarding the flow of pedestrian traffic should be addressed before the area is renovated. B—Turf renovation in smaller areas does not have to be extensive. The area may simply need to be aerated and reseeded to alleviate the problem.

Career Connection

Judson Mills

Judson Mills, Super-Sod Outlet Manager

Judson Mills received an Associate's Degree in Criminal Justice from Cape Fear Community College and worked for four years before he decided he needed to pursue something in which he truly had interest. Judson enrolled at NCSU and began his studies in horticultural science. During his second semester, Judson applied for an opening at Super-Sod, a division of Patten Seed Company. His employer gave him a flexible schedule so he could work full-time at Super-Sod while attending NCSU. His growing interest in the sod industry had Judson taking as many turf-related electives as he could fit into his schedule. After graduation, his employer offered him a permanent full-time position, which Judson gladly accepted.

Judson has been with Super-Sod for over 11 years, working his way from loader to outlet manager. During the course of the day Judson ensures the correct products are loaded on the delivery trucks, takes inventory of the day's fresh sod arrivals, and ensures everything from computers to forklifts are up and running. He also files reports of certified sod harvest amounts with the appropriate agencies, accounts for the previous day's harvest, and manages an amazing sales staff comprised of very knowledgeable turf experts. Judson will also take care of customer concerns over sod performance in existing lawns.

Judson says the things he loves most about his job is that every day brings new challenges and the indescribable satisfaction he receives from helping others obtain the lawn of their dreams. He also said that if he were asked what other job he would rather have, he could not answer the question. "Basically, I love what I do, and wouldn't change it for anything."

Judson also offered a few points of advice to students interested in the green industry:

- Exhibit sincere interest in everything you do on a daily basis.
- Do not procrastinate. Get your work done now because you never know what new challenge lies ahead.
- Get internships or work in different areas of the industry. One awesome experience may change the career route you have planned.
- Expand your horizons by enrolling in classes outside your major. Judson believes his horticultural degree gives him a better understanding of turfgrass production.

Consider This

1. How has Judson's attitude and work ethic helped him reach a position he truly enjoys?
2. Would you be willing to work as much as he did while attending school? Do you have the organizational skills it would require?
3. What personal goals would you set for yourself to follow a similar career path?

As you plan your renovation, you will need to determine what type of grass would best suit the location. The season and turf zone will determine when the lawn should be renovated. The same rules used with new lawns apply to renovated lawns: cool-season turfgrasses should be renovated in the late summer to early fall months and warm-season turfgrasses are best renovated in late spring to early summer. If the lawn contains very little of the desired turfgrass, all the lawn vegetation must be killed before new grass is planted, **Figure 12-20.** If all vegetation is eliminated, the steps for establishing a new lawn may be followed.

Christopher D. Hart

Figure 12-20. When the proposed area contains very little established turfgrass, it is best to spray an herbicide to kill all the vegetation before preparing the site for a new lawn.

Step Two: Taking a Soil Test

Soil sampling should be conducted to determine if the pH and nutrient levels are the issues that caused the poor lawn conditions. If these are the reasons the lawn failed, the soil must be amended. The same soil test procedures explained earlier can be used for the renovation site. However, all grass and roots must be removed from the core samples before the soil is mixed.

Step Three: Weed Control

If a lawn requires renovation, it is likely that weeds have taken over. If the weeds cover a large area, a nonselective postemergent herbicide should be used. It is important to wait several weeks before seeding to ensure the herbicide will have no ill effects on seed germination. If perennial weeds, such as bermudagrass, are persistent in the lawn, it is often recommended to kill the entire lawn and begin with a clean site. Proper application of a nonselective postemergent herbicide will remove all turfgrass and weeds. It may take several herbicide applications to control perennial weeds, **Figure 12-21**. If the site contains over 50% desirable turfgrass, a regimen of postemergent and preemergent chemicals may be used to reduce weeds. Core aeration will also help prepare the area for seeding. ***Core aeration*** is a process in which holes are made in the lawn to

R. Lee Ivy

Figure 12-21. A well-developed maintenance schedule will help prevent disorders before they become an issue in the lawn.

allow more oxygen and nutrients to penetrate the soil easily. A machine pulls plugs or cores of soil and thatch from the lawn. Core aeration is very effective on compacted soils. It may also be referred to as *aeration*.

Step Four: Preparing the Site

The degree of repair will determine how the site is prepared, **Figure 12-22**. Use a rotary mower set on its lowest setting to remove as much vegetation as possible. Once the grass is mowed, the clippings should be raked and bagged for disposal. A dethatcher or a verticutter may also be used to collect more vegetation. A *dethatcher* is any device used to remove thatch from lawns. A dethatcher may be as simple as a handheld dethatching rake or as complex as a motorized machine. A *verticutter* is described as a vertical mowing machine used to remove thatch. The area should be gone over twice. The first pass is done in one direction and the second pass is done at a 90° angle to the first. The dethatcher and verticutter will help remove any competing plant material as well as increase soil porosity and light penetration for increased germination. Do any necessary grading. Fill in any low spots to create the ideal slope of 2% to 3%.

Step Five: Planting the Turfgrass

A slit seeder may to be used to drill seed into the ground. The slit seeder is a special type of seeder that ensures the seed has good contact with the area while minimizing the area that is exposed. Rotary or drop spreaders may be used as well. Half of the seed should be applied in one direction and the other half should be applied 90° from the first direction. Reseeded areas can be covered and protected with straw mulch.

Figure 12-22. When renovating a lawn, it is important to remove as much old vegetation as possible because weeds reproduce from seed as well as roots. Extremely troubled lawns may require a complete overhaul before planting new turfgrass.

If the area to be renovated is small, plugs left from aeration of the healthy turf can be planted in the poorly performing areas. Plugs cut from strips of sod can also be used. It is important to understand that plugs can only be used on grasses that spread. They cannot be used on bunch type grasses.

Step Six: Maintaining New Turfgrass

It is very important to provide new turfgrass with the proper levels of moisture. As much as 90% of water taken up by plants is lost to the atmosphere due to transpiration. Transpiration helps keep the turfgrass cool. The top 1.5″ of soil should be kept moist when germinating seeds, **Figure 12-23**. Newly planted turfgrass may need watering two to three times a day for a few weeks. Once roots begin growing, the watering regimen should be reduced to less frequent but thorough watering to increase root development. Watering to a depth of 6″ to 9″ once per week should be sufficient. Watering early in the morning is the most efficient time to irrigate. If turfgrasses are watered later in the day, they may not dry completely before sunset and will be more susceptible to fungal diseases.

grafxart/Shutterstock.com

Figure 12-23. New turfgrass should be watered frequently to ensure the seeds germinate and the stolons and roots take hold. The frequency and amount of irrigation is gradually reduced as the turfgrass becomes established.

STEM *Connection*

Calculating Seed and Plant Materials

Calculating sod. To calculate the amount of sod needed, you must first calculate the area (length × width) in square footage. You must then divide the total area covered by one pallet to determine the number of pallets needed.

1. Calculate the rate for planting tall fescue sod for a lawn measuring 175′ × 185′. The sod on one pallet covers 510 ft².
2. Calculate the rate for planting tall fescue sod for a lawn measuring 150′ × 250′. The sod on one pallet covers 415 ft².

Calculating seed. To determine the amount of seed needed, you must first calculate the area (length × width) in square footage. You must then divide the total area by 1000 to determine the number of 1000 ft² sections. Multiply the number of 1000 ft² sections by the number of pounds per 1000 ft² recommended for the grass species.

3. Using annual ryegrass at 4 lb per 1000 ft², calculate the rate for overseeding a lawn measuring 150′ × 250′.
4. Using bahiagrass at 6 lb per 1000 ft², calculate the rate for seeding a lawn measuring 164′ × 250′.
5. Calculate the rate for seed for a lawn measuring 75′ × 120′ using fine fescue at 2 lb per 1000 ft².

Summary

- Turfgrasses can be established by seeding, sodding, sprigging, and plugging. The species of turfgrass and often times the budget determine the method of installation.

- Seeding is the least expensive method of installing turfgrass; however, it also takes the longest amount of time to create a full lawn.

- Sodding is the most expensive installation method for creating an established lawn; however, it is the quickest method.

- Sprigging is broadcasting and rolling stolons or planting stolons at specific intervals. Sprigging can only be used with turfgrass species that spread.

- Plugging is planting small sections of sod at specific intervals to ensure full coverage. Plugging can only be used with turfgrasses that spread.

- Rates for seeding, sprigging, and laying sod can be calculated to determine the exact amount of product needed.

- Establishing a new lawn requires turfgrass selection, site preparation, soil sampling, soil amending, planting the turfgrass, and a series of maintenance tasks.

- Lawn renovation requires thorough site evaluation to determine why the lawn was not successful and to determine the steps that should be taken.

- Renovating a lawn uses many of the same steps used to establish a new lawn. However, it may be more practical to completely remove the vegetation and install a new lawn.

Chapter Review

Know and Understand ↗

Answer the following questions using the information provided in this chapter.

1. *True or False?* Seeding turfgrass is the least expensive method for establishing a lawn.
   A. True.
   B. False.

2. A seed bag with a blue certification tag indicates the seed _____.
   A. is free from noxious weeds
   B. contains specified percentages of species
   C. is viable and will ensure the desired outcome
   D. All of the above.

3. The spreader that uses a small disc-like mechanism that turns when the device is pushed is referred to as a(n) _____.
   A. rotary spreader
   B. drop seeder
   C. spreader-seeder
   D. uniform spreader

4. Seed is applied in two directions to _____.
   A. create a vertical planting
   B. ensure grass grows
   C. ensure complete coverage
   D. All of the above.

5. Mulch is placed over newly seeded areas to _____.
   A. help the soil retain moisture
   B. prevent the birds from eating the seed
   C. prevent the seeds from washing away
   D. All of the above.

6. *True or False?* Sodding turfgrass is the least expensive method for establishing a lawn.
   A. True.
   B. False.

7. Which of the following actions must be taken when preparing a site for sodding?
   A. Spread seed in two directions.
   B. The ground should be soaked.
   C. Call 811 to mark the utility lines.
   D. All of the above.

8. *True or False?* The best time to lay sod is the day after it is delivered.
   A. True.
   B. False.

9. A small section of cut sod is a _____.
   A. sprig
   B. plug
   C. stolon
   D. rhizome

10. A cut stem with stolons that can easily root and produce new shoots is referred to as a _____.
    A. sprig
    B. plug
    C. clod
    D. rhizome

11. Which of the following equations is used to calculate area?
    A. Diameter × length = area
    B. Length × radius = area
    C. Length × width = area
    D. Width × diameter = area

12. Which of the following environmental factors should be evaluated before a new lawn installation begins?
    A. The amount of area that is in full sun, partial shade, and complete shade.
    B. Identifying low, wet areas that will need to be eliminated or minimized.
    C. The topography and quality of the soil.
    D. All of the above.

13. *True or False?* The species determines the time of the year that the lawn should be established.
    A. True.
    B. False.

14. The initial preparation of a site includes _____.
    A. grading, weed control, debris removal, and pruning
    B. watering, seeding, marking locations of plant materials
    C. fertilizing, grading, seeding, and marking beds
    D. All of the above.

15. *True or False?* Raking can be used to eliminate unwanted high and low spots.
    A. True.
    B. False.

16. *True or False?* Soil samples should only be taken before grading to obtain the most accurate results.
    A. True.
    B. False.

17. *True or False?* A lab can provide the most accurate advice only if you provide detailed information about the project.
    A. True.
    B. False.

18. The variety of materials (amendments) that can be added to soil to improve performance includes _____.
    A. herbicides and pea gravel
    B. lime, organic matter, and sand
    C. sulfur, sprigs, and sand
    D. All of the above.

19. *True or False?* Warm-season turfgrasses should be planted in the spring and fall when the temperature range is between 65°F and 80°F.
    A. True.
    B. False.

20. *True or False?* Cool-season grasses should be planted when the temperature range is between 75°F and 90°F.
    A. True.
    B. False.

21. To encourage root and shoot growth, seedlings in newly seeded lawns should be fertilized for _____.
    A. 24 weeks
    B. 16 weeks
    C. 8 weeks
    D. 4 weeks

22. *True or False?* Maintaining sharp mower blades will ensure the best result, a lawn that is cut evenly throughout the yard.
    A. True.
    B. False.

23. Before the first mowing of a newly planted lawn, the grass should be allowed to grow and reach _____.
    A. twice its suggested mowing height
    B. its suggested mowing height
    C. 1 1/2 times its suggested mowing height
    D. 1/4" past its suggested mowing height

24. Which of the following must be determined before lawn renovation can begin?
    A. Why the current lawn is in poor condition.
    B. If the current lawn can be repaired.
    C. Whether the current lawn should be replaced.
    D. All of the above.

25. *True or False?* Lawn renovation requires evaluation, soil testing, weed control, site preparation, and planting.
    A. True.
    B. False.

26. *True or False?* If the site contains less than 30% desirable turfgrass, a regimen of post-emergent and preemergent chemicals may be used to reduce weeds.
    A. True.
    B. False.

27. A device used to remove thatch from lawns is referred to as a _____.
    A. verticutter
    B. declipper
    C. dethatcher
    D. verticlipper

28. A special type of seeder that ensures the seed has good contact with the area while minimizing the area that is exposed is a _____.
    A. seed drill
    B. slit seeder
    C. rotary spreader
    D. drop spreader

29. *True or False?* If turfgrasses are watered early in the morning, they may not dry completely before sunset and will be more susceptible to fungal diseases.
    A. True.
    B. False.

Thinking Critically

1. Is it possible to incorporate turfgrass in a xeriscape? If so, explain how you would incorporate the turfgrass.

2. Compare the benefits of planting seed for a lawn to the benefits of installing sod for a lawn. Which do you think is better for the environment?

3. Can you identify the different parts of a blade of grass? How is the anatomy of grass different from the anatomy of an herbaceous leaf or stem?

4. Explain the purpose and benefits of overseeding a lawn.

Suggested Activities

1. Mr. Bear's lawn measures 345′ × 245′. How would you establish the lawn using bermudagrass sod? Explain your reasoning.

2. Tom Chatham wishes to cover his yard in bermudagrass sod. If his lawn measures 567′ × 234′, how many pallets of bermudagrass will he need? One pallet of bermudagrass will cover 504 ft². Tom Chatham says that is too expensive and sod is not an option. Explain what other methods are available to Tom Chatham for establishing his bermudagrass lawn.

3. Work with a lab partner to sow and grow different turfgrass seeds in 10″ × 10″ or 12″ × 12″ trays. Record your observations as the seeds sprout, grow, and eventually fill the area in which they have been planted. Take photographs throughout the experiment and use the photographs to create a visual presentation students can use to study and identify the different turfgrass species.

4. Determine how much it would cost to maintain turfgrass in your area. Measure an area on campus or your home and obtain quotes from multiple service providers. Use this information to prepare a cost estimate for maintaining a turf grass site, including materials and labor.

5. Research how turfgrass quality is measured. Obtain and prepare a turfgrass evaluation form. If time allows, present your findings to the class.

6. Working with a partner, research maintenance practices used on greens, tees, fairways, sand traps, and roughs. Prepare a visual presentation on the practices to explain how and why specific tasks are performed.

7. Research the turfgrass used on athletic fields. Describe the major characteristics of each type of turfgrass in a written or visual format.

CHAPTER 13

Landscape Lighting and Water Features

While studying this chapter, look for the activity icon to:
- **Practice** vocabulary terms with Words to Know activities.
- **Expand** learning with identification activities.
- **Reinforce** what you learn by completing Know and Understand questions.

G-WLEARNING.com

www.g-wlearning.com/agriculture

Chapter Outcomes

After studying this chapter, you will be able to:

- Identify and explain multiple functions of landscape lighting.
- Explain the differences among power systems.
- Identify the fixtures used in landscape lighting.
- Identify and compare the different lightbulbs.
- Describe different lighting techniques.
- Identify necessary components of water feature systems.
- Determine design objectives for selection and installation of components.
- Determine steps for installation of water features.
- Describe problems and explain maintenance tasks for water features.

Key Terms ↪

amperage
ampere (amp)
controller
disappearing fountain
electric current
external pump
float valve
fountain
head height
line-voltage system
Ohm's law
ohm (Ω)

perimeter
pond
pond liner
pondless waterfall
rainwater catchment
resistance
submersible pump
transformer
voltage
volt (V)
wattage
watt (W)

Introduction

Landscape designs can be enhanced with accent and ambient lighting and water features. You can use lighting in a landscape to draw attention to special features, guide visitors to an entrance, and make an area safer, **Figure 13-1**. By including a water feature with an array of aquatic plants, fish, and other organisms, you can create a landscape that is a relaxing oasis. This chapter will help you select the best lighting methods and systems for a landscape and introduce you to water feature design and installation.

Figure 13-1. The lights illuminate the façade and make the front door inviting. This illumination technique adds interest, offers safe entry, and highlights architectural features of the structure.

Landscape Lighting

Landscape lighting is used primarily to highlight features of a home, business, and landscape. However, it often serves multiple functions:

- Guiding visitors to the entryway or outdoor room.
- Creating safe areas to walk on paths, stairs, and around water features, **Figure 13-2**.
- Increasing property value.
- Adding security by deterring burglars and vandals.

Figure 13-2. The path lighting is subtle but bright enough to make the walkway safer. It is inviting and creatively placed.

Landscape lighting may be as simple as solar-powered path lights along a driveway or walkway to a home's front door. It may also be an elaborate installation with a power source, wiring, motion detectors, timers, and controllers. Many landscape operations specialize in this area due to the specific skillset required for lighting design and installation. Specialization in this area can be very profitable because the competition for these services in many areas is less than for other landscaping services.

There are different methods and types of lighting that use a variety of components. The method, materials, and system used will depend primarily on the landscape design, homeowner's associations or municipal restrictions, and the customer's budget.

STEM Connection

Electrical Measurements

Georg Ohm discovered a means of determining the relationship between voltage, amperes, and resistance. Ohm found that electrical current given current temperature and fixed resistance is proportional to voltage and is inversely proportional to resistance. The calculation of any of the three values can be made using the formula for Ohm's law:

$$\text{voltage (V)} = \text{current (I)} \times \text{resistance (R)} \quad (V = I \times R)$$

- **Ohm's law** defines the relationship between voltage, amperage, and resistance.
- **Ohms** (Ω) are the unit of measure for resistance. Ohms are represented by the omega symbol (Ω).
- **Electric current** is the flow of energy on a path. There are several forces involved in electric current and a variety of units of measurements used to describe them.
- **Amperage** is the strength of the electrical current required to power the lamp or fixture. This is important for larger systems because correct wire sizes and transformers are based on amperage. **Amperes (amps)** are used to indicate the measurement of electric current.
- **Voltage** is the potential energy between two points along an electrical conductor.
- **Resistance** is the restriction to the flowing electrical current.
- **Wattage** is a measure of the rate of energy transfer. **Watts (W)** are the standard unit of electric power, which represents the rate at which work is performed.

Most lighting fixtures are measured in watts. To calculate wattage using Ohm's law, you would multiply the amperage by volts.

- A 12-volt circuit would consume 24 watts of power if the device were drawing two amps.
- A 30-watt bulb powered by 120 volts would draw 0.25 amps (30 ÷ 120 = 0.25).
- Amps can be converted to watts for calculation of total system capacity.

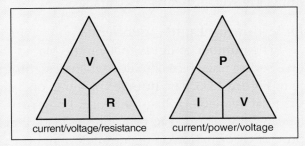

current/voltage/resistance   current/power/voltage

Power Systems

All lighting systems require a power source and wiring. The three types of power systems used for landscape lighting are line-voltage, low-voltage, and solar. *Voltage* is a measure of the amount of energy provided by or stored in an object. The voltage you use in your home for almost all electrical needs is 110V to 120V. Voltage is expressed in *volts (V)*. It is helpful to place the power source in a central location so the wires can originate around the source radially. Lighting systems are powered by 120V but the voltage is often reduced to 24V for safer installation and maintenance as well as a lower energy use.

GFCI Outlets

All outdoor outlets must be GFCI (ground fault circuit interrupter) rated. Using a GFCI will ensure service is disconnected quickly if the current is flowing along an unintended path, such as through water. A licensed electrician must be contracted to install new outdoor outlets.

jpreat/Shutterstock.com

Figure 13-3. Underground feed (UF) wire is used for in-ground applications. It can be placed in conduit for protection and/or to satisfy local electrical codes.

Line-Voltage Systems

A *line-voltage system* uses 120V, which is the same power supplied to fixtures and receptacles in the home. This voltage provides brighter and larger illumination of areas than a low-voltage or solar system. A line-voltage system is hardwired into the home's electrical system. A licensed electrician must be contracted to install the system according to local codes, such as underground feed (UF) wire or wires buried in conduit, **Figure 13-3**. Due to the permanence and installation efforts, upfront costs are higher and require additional inspections if later design changes are made. A line-voltage system uses voltage high enough to electrocute anyone who has contact with a live wire.

Low-Voltage Systems

Most residential lighting systems use low-voltage ranging from 12V to 24V. The lower voltage is achieved with a transformer that is hardwired or plugged into a 120V receptacle. A *transformer* is a device that reduces the incoming line voltage to a lower voltage with lower wattage. See **Figure 13-4**. A low-voltage system poses a much lower electrocution risk but it also limits the voltage/wattage available.

Determining Lights in a Series

The number of lights that can be placed safely on one line (in a series) must be calculated when designing the lighting system, **Figure 13-5**. The number of lights on a line is divided by the total available voltage/wattage. Long runs of lighting must be carefully planned to prevent overload. Lighting system kits provide information on the number of lights that may be placed in series and the limitations of the transformer.

Photo courtesy of Hunter Industries

Figure 13-4. An electrical transformer reduces 120 volts to 24 volts for low-voltage irrigation and lighting controllers.

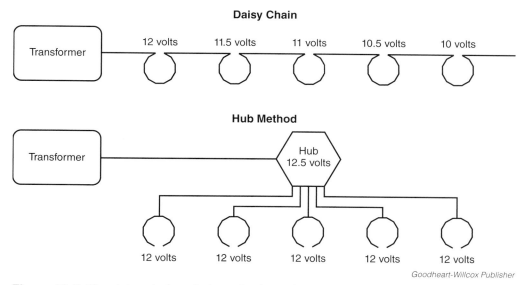

Figure 13-5. The daisy chain or hub method may be used to set landscape lighting. The method used depends on the site's power supply and light placements.

Solar-Powered Systems

Solar-powered systems use stored solar energy to illuminate the bulbs. Each light is a separate unit with its own battery, LED bulb, light sensor, controller board, and collection panel, **Figure 13-6**. Most units also have an on/off switch. The collection panel uses multiple solar cells that are wired in series to collect energy. The light will turn on when the sensor detects little or no light and turn off when it detects ample light. The collection panel must be oriented to receive as much sunlight as possible. In the United States, solar panels are usually directed to the south. Solar-powered systems will not function fully in areas that receive little sunlight, such as heavily wooded or shady areas.

A solar-powered system is a good option for locations lacking an electrical source or an established landscape in which the client does not want any soil disturbed. The initial cost for these systems can be high. However, solar-powered systems may have a better return on investment over time because there is no cost for electricity. Solar-powered fixtures have limited light output and their use is often restricted to pathways and garden beds.

Photo courtesy of Hunter Industries   Naypong/Shutterstock.com

Figure 13-6. Sun-collection panels can provide primary or supplemental power to irrigation and lighting systems.

Figure 13-7. Controllers allow on-site and remote access for irrigation and lighting applications. Settings include time of day, duration, frequency, and short- or long-term scheduling options.

Figure 13-8. Choose a controller location that is accessible. Consideration should be given to line of sight when running a trial on the irrigation or lighting system.

Controllers

The on/off schedules for line-voltage and low-voltage lighting systems are programmed with a *controller*, **Figure 13-7**. Most low-voltage system controllers include a transformer that reduces the voltage to a usable level for lighting fixtures and components. The controller can be programmed to activate the lights all at once or at different times for each zone. Newer controllers can even be manipulated with a cell phone app. Many controllers use a photocell to control the timing.

The controller should be centrally located and mounted on a permanent, fireproof fixture, such as the outside wall of a residence, commercial building, or other permanent fixtures, **Figure 13-8**. Check electrical codes to ensure the unit is properly installed.

Lighting Zones

Most lighting systems are installed in zones to distribute the power evenly on multiple lines. The controller is designed to control these zones individually or collectively. The total wattage output from the controller can be divided by the number of zones needed to determine the use load of each zone. A controller with an output of 600 W, for example, could be divided into six zones with 100 W each. The designer could install up to five 20-watt bulbs in each zone. However, the farther the bulbs are from the controller, the more likely they will suffer from wattage loss or voltage drop, **Figure 13-9**. Lengthy wires experience wattage loss because the current meets more resistance as it flows along the wire than it would meet in a shorter wire. Wattage loss occurs due to resistance of current over distance. Many designers, for example, will only place four 20-watt bulbs on a line with this capacity (100 W) to avoid the lack of wattage to an individual bulb at the end of the line.

Lighting Fixtures and Techniques

The fixtures, bulbs, and the direction of the light beam all contribute the effectiveness of a landscape lighting system. Path lighting, for example, can be bright enough to illuminate a path fully or it can be subtle and still light the pathway, **Figure 13-10**.

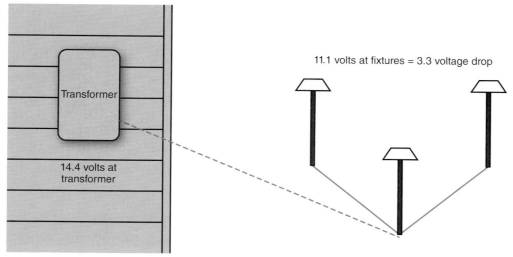

11.1 volts at fixtures = 3.3 voltage drop

Transformer

14.4 volts at
transformer

Goodheart-Willcox Publisher

Figure 13-9. The controller provides initial voltage to a lighting system. In this case, there are a total of 14.4 volts at the controller. Voltage drop occurs over distance and at each fixture. A designer can determine the number of fixtures per line using voltage drop calculations.

The amount of light used will also affect the overall effect. If too much lighting is used, it will overwhelm and wash out the landscape features. If insufficient lighting is installed, it will not make much of an impact.

Landscape designers understand how and where to install lighting for the best effect. The types of fixtures and their locations are specified on the design plans. The designer will also indicate lighting zones and the location(s) of the controller(s). It is important to note that fixtures, wires, and lighting accessories should not be visible unless they are decorative and meant to be seen.

Photo courtesy of Hunter Industries

Figure 13-10. Light fixtures can be installed to create effects that highlight landscape elements, provide safe access throughout the area, and accentuate features, such as plants, artistic elements, and structures.

Light Fixtures

Landscape lighting fixtures vary not only in design but also in the way they focus or diffuse light. Floodlights, for example, vary in light output and beam width and path lights can illuminate just the path or the path and the surrounding elements. Certain types of fixtures are decorative and functional, such as wall lanterns or sconces. Other lights, such as well lights or spotlights, are purely functional and should be hidden from view. Landscape light fixtures include spotlights, bollards, post lights, accent lights, well lights, and floodlights. See **Figure 13-11**. Using a mixture of fixtures and techniques will help create a more interesting and exciting display.

Durability

Landscape light fixtures are available in many designs and a range of costs. Inexpensive fixtures are often made of plastic and lower quality components. These types of fixtures will not endure daily sun exposure and inclement weather. Higher-quality fixtures are made with materials designed to last for years. Using inexpensive fixtures may reduce installation costs but will cost more in the end, as they will need to be replaced.

Lightbulbs

Lightbulbs (lamps) are chosen for their energy efficiency, cost, longevity, light color, brightness, and output. Bulbs may also be chosen for their compatibility with the lighting system, as some bulbs have higher energy needs. Most halogen bulbs, for example, are recommended for use with line-voltage systems only.

The latest and most efficient bulb used in landscape lighting is the LED (light-emitting diode), **Figure 13-12**. LEDs can achieve the same light output as halogen bulbs with 75% to 85% less energy (watts). The lower energy use also allows more fixtures per series. LEDs generate less heat and can use a wider voltage range than halogen bulbs. LEDs also have an estimated life that is four to six times longer than the life of halogen bulbs. Most halogen fixtures are installed with line-voltage systems. Choose LEDs with warm color temperature and high output for the best effect.

Incandescent bulbs and high-pressure sodium lamps are also used in landscape lighting. Incandescent lights are less efficient than LEDs but they are readily available and less expensive. High-pressure sodium lamps are used to light large areas and are commonly used for security rather than aesthetic purposes.

Lighting Techniques

Lighting techniques use different fixtures and placements of those fixtures to create the desired effects. To create a moonlight effect, for example, a soft light would be placed very high in a tree. The light would filter through the foliage and branches, just as natural moonlight would. Commonly used techniques include the following:

- **Cross lighting.** Illuminating a tree or garden feature from two or more sides.
- **Down lighting.** Lights are placed above a feature to create a dramatic effect. Down lighting may also be used to direct movement of visitors through narrow spaces. Down lighting and up lighting are often used together.

Fixture		Functions
Accent or spotlights		These adjustable light fixtures are used for accenting, grazing, cross lighting, and up lighting. They can be mounted focused downward to provide down lighting and moonlighting.
Bollard and post lights		Standing fixtures used to illuminate steps, walkways, driveways, decks, and pool areas.
Box shape, bullet shape, and cylinder		These fixtures focus and direct the light beams. The light surround may also cut off glare and protect the lamp and socket from debris and moisture.
Ceiling close-up, chain-hung lantern, and wall bracket		These light fixtures are mounted at entry doors, over garages, and on porches to cast either direct or diffused light outward.
Fountain and swimming pool lighting		These light fixtures are installed in sides and at ends of swimming pools and bottoms of fountains. The fixtures may be wet-niche or dry-niche. Wet-niche fixtures may be removed for lamp changes while dry-niche fixtures require access to the back of the pool shell. Many designers use colored lighting to create additional interest.
Garden light		Low-level garden lights are designed to illuminate in a broader pattern for driveways, steps, paths, flowerbeds, and perimeter plantings.
Well light or in-ground light		These fixtures are buried flush with the ground to conceal the light source. Well lighting is used to up light trees and shrubs and to graze textured walls. Well lighting placed around a tree within a retaining wall can provide safety for the area while lightly highlighting the bark and trunk.

Photo courtesy of Hunter Industries

Figure 13-11. A wide variety of fixture styles and designs can be used to create unique lighting for all areas of the landscape. Fixtures that are designed to be seen in the daylight are stylish and complement the design.

Photo courtesy of Hunter Industries

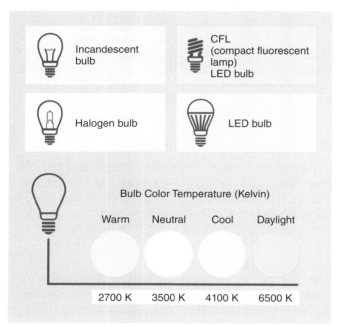

elenabsl/Shutterstock.com

Figure 13-12. Technologies, such as LED, provide more energy efficiency than traditional bulbs. Most bulb types are offered in a variety of colors and levels of brightness.

- **Flooding** or **floodlighting.** Floodlights are used to light wide building facades, architectural features, groups of tall trees, or other expansive areas. It is best to limit the use of floodlights. Floodlights are available with different beam widths to widen or lessen the expanse. Care must be taken to prevent light pollution or trespass into neighboring properties or other features.
- **Grazing.** Light is placed close to a flat surface and aimed directly up or down the surface to create dramatic light and shadow play. Grazing works especially well in landscapes with hardscapes that have uneven or irregular surface patterns.
- **Moonlighting.** Soft lights are placed high in trees (1/2 to 3/4 of the way up) to simulate moonlight filtering through the leaves and branches. Up lighting is often used with moonlighting to light the trunk or canopy.
- **Path lighting.** Decorative fixtures are installed along a pathway to illuminate the path or both the path and the surrounding area. The lighting is aesthetically pleasing and functional. Fixtures should alternate on both sides of the path.
- **Shadowing.** Shadows can be created by placing the light between the main vantage point and the item being lit. This technique works best when there is a flat surface behind the feature to catch the shadow.
- **Silhouetting.** A creative way to highlight the shape, size, and texture of a landscape feature. This technique requires a backdrop for the silhouette and a light illuminating the back of the feature.
- **Up lighting.** Lights are installed at the base shining up on a feature to accentuate height and texture. This type of lighting works well with tall trees. Placing the light at the base of the object prevents interference in the beam of light. The fixture is less likely to be damaged, as well.
- **Washing.** Shining light along a wall or hedge to create ambient lighting. The ambience can be influenced with color lighting on the wall or hedge and white light accents. See **Figure 13-13**.

eugen_z/Shutterstock.com

Figure 13-13. Lighting techniques are used to direct visitors' focus toward specific features within the landscape. The lights along the wall create a warm ambience that contrasts with the dramatic pool lighting.

General Lighting

Carefully planned lighting can minimize the number of fixtures needed and maximize the function of the installed features. Strategically placed lighting can serve multiple purposes, such as highlighting a fountain and providing ambient light to the area around the fountain, **Figure 13-14.** The fixture design and bulb output must be considered when installing lights that will serve multiple functions. Bollards, for example, are available in various heights and with designs that limit or maximize the light output. The light from a taller bollard will illuminate more area than the light from a much shorter bollard.

Types of Water Features

Water features are installed to create a relaxing ambience with the added benefit of attracting wildlife to the area. Birds, dragonflies, squirrels, and rabbits are some of the most common fauna attracted to backyard ponds. Water features can be designed to fit any landscape. They range from small bubbling fountains to elaborate ponds with cascading waterfalls and colorful fish, **Figure 13-15.** The size of a feature will depend on the space available, the client's budget, and possibly local ordinances. Most water features are placed in private garden areas, such as a backyard.

Photo courtesy of Hunter Industries

Figure 13-14. Spotlighting a centrally located fountain can reflect enough light to illuminate the surrounding seating areas and pathways.

everst/Shutterstock.com

Pirach P/Shutterstock.com

Figure 13-15. Colorful fish add movement, interest and invite visitors to spend relaxing time within a space.

Common water features include ponds, fountains, waterfalls, and pondless waterfalls. All of these features can be created as large or as small as the designer dictates.

Pro Tip

Larger ponds with higher volume are easier to maintain than small ponds. The water in a small pond will heat up quickly and provide perfect conditions for algae growth. The water may also become too warm for fish in the pond.

Ponds

Ponds created for a landscape are small bodies of standing, shallow water. Ponds can support a variety of aquatic plant materials because they are shallow enough for light to reach the bottom. Natural ponds are usually fed by underground or aboveground streams that keep the water fresh and oxygenated. Constructed ponds require pumps, water treatments, and filtration devices to do this work.

Ponds may have waterfalls, sprinklers, bubblers, misters, or hold still water, depending on the objectives of the designer or the client's desires, **Figure 13-16**. Ponds that are properly constructed and balanced with aquatic animals and plants may become self-contained ecosystems and require less upkeep. Nonchemical means of maintaining ponds include the use of porous rock that retains sediment and encourages the growth of microorganisms beneficial to the clarity and quality of the water. Landscape ponds should be 2′ to 3′ deep, especially if they contain fish. In areas where periods of freezing weather exist, ponds should be at least 3′ deep to allow overwintering areas for fish.

White78/Shutterstock.com

Figure 13-16. Aquatic features add interest and a valuable ecosystem that can be capable of supporting fish, insects, birds, and other animals.

Andries Oberholzer/Shutterstock.com

Fountains

Fountains are structures that send out a stream of water that falls into a basin of some sort and is pumped to the top to repeat the cycle, **Figure 13-17**. Water fountains are typically the simplest and least expensive means of adding a water feature to a landscape. Fountains are made from all types of material and objects. They can be formal sculptures, bubbling stones, or metal artwork made from materials such as stone, pottery, or copper. They use tubing and electric pumps to recirculate the water. Water fountains may also be constructed so the water appears to disappear when it is actually falling into a reservoir and recirculated. This type of fountain is referred to as a *disappearing fountain*.

goldenjack/Shutterstock.com

Waterfalls

Waterfalls emit water so it cascades over the top of an object, down a surface, and into a reservoir or another body of water, such as a pond, **Figure 13-18A**. Waterfalls also use tubing and electric pumps to recirculate water. The running water is never stagnant and not prone to algae or other issues more common with ponds. Waterfalls are typically louder than fountains and are therefore better at blocking outside noise.

Pondless Waterfalls

A unique way to integrate motion and sound into a landscape, garden area, or patio is with a *pondless waterfall*, **Figure 13-18B**. The hole at the base of the waterfall is dug deeper than the standard pond depth and lined with rock and gravel. As the water falls, it filters through the rock and gravel and recirculates. Water does not accumulate in the reservoir so it appears as though the water disappears into the rocks.

Zigzag Mountain Art/Shutterstock.com

Figure 13-17. Fountains range in size, shape, and function but all offer artistic interest, relaxing sound, and movement.

A   *White78/Shutterstock.com*

B   *Bubbers BB/Shutterstock.com*

Figure 13-18. A—A waterfall can mask sounds from surrounding urban areas. B—Pondless waterfalls add positive noise to an outside environment without creating an open area of water.

Equipment and Materials

Although the exteriors of water features vary greatly, most systems use the same basic equipment. The mechanical equipment should be well hidden from view. Water features use electric pumps, electrical service, tubing, and liners.

Electric Pumps

All water features require a pump and tubing to move and recirculate water. The type of pump needed depends on the size of the water feature and the demands on the pump. In a waterfall, for example, the pump must move the water from the basin to the top of the waterfall. A higher-capacity pump would be needed if the same pump were used for filtration. The two main types of pumps are submersible and external pumps.

Submersible Pumps

Submersible pumps are completely submerged in the water to hide the pump and allow it to work properly, **Figure 13-19A**. As there is no need to camouflage the pump, submersibles work well in natural settings. Submersibles are commonly used in residential applications because low volumes of water are being recirculated and the pumps are quiet. They may also be used to drain water from a pond, if necessary. Submersible pumps tend to be less energy efficient than external pumps.

A   *vseb/Shutterstock.com*

Pro Tip

If there are fish and other aquatic life in the water feature, use a submersible pump that does not use oil. If the pump seal leaks, oil may contaminate the water.

B   *smileimage9/Shutterstock.com*

Figure 13-19. A—Submersible pumps are placed in the water. B—External water pumps are used for irrigation systems and/or water garden applications.

External Pumps

External pumps are installed in dry locations, making them easier to access and service, **Figure 13-19B**. External pumps have higher pumping capacities than submersibles. They are typically not as quiet as submersibles but they are generally more reliable. Some external pumps will require little maintenance because they are completely sealed. Keeping the surrounding area clean will ensure efficient operation.

Liners

Pond liners are impermeable materials that help contain the water and prevent it from seeping into the ground. Liners may be made with concrete, preformed plastic or pliable rubber sheets designed specifically for this purpose, **Figure 13-20**. Most liners are 45 mil EPDM (Ethylene Propylene Diene Monomer). This material is highly flexible, long lasting, and safe for aquatic life. EPDM liners are available in standard sizes but may also be ordered with custom measurements.

A *photowind/Shutterstock.com* **B** *Artalis/Shutterstock.com*

Figure 13-20. A—Preformed liners are available for simple aquatic feature installations. They provide various depths for fish and plant growth. B—Flexible liners are adaptable to various depths and shapes.

Electrical Service

A 110-volt outlet is sufficient for powering pumps and feature lighting. The outlet must be GFCI rated to ensure service is disconnected quickly if the current is flowing along an unintended path, such as through water. A licensed electrician must be contracted to install a new outlet. See **Figure 13-21.**

Plant Materials

Most plants chosen for use in and around water features are plants native to the area that thrive in humid environments, **Figure 13-22.** Tropical plants are also used in ponds. However, tropical plants will not survive cold winters unless they are brought indoors. Aquatic plants are installed to add texture,

bluefish/Shutterstock.com

Figure 13-21. GFCI receptacles are used in applications in which they may be exposed to water. The GFCI is a fast-acting circuit breaker that will shut off electric power within a fraction of a second.

STEM Connection

Pump Energy Use

To determine the amount of energy a pump will use, multiply the watts (listed on the pump or box) by 24 hours and divide that by 1000, which is the kilowatt-hours per day.

(watts × 24) ÷ 1000 kW = X (watts × hours) ÷ kW = X

Multiply the number of kilowatt-hours per day by the number of days in a specific month to get the monthly use.

X × days per month = monthly energy use

Take the amount paid per kilowatt (from the electric bill), multiply that by the monthly use, and determine if the pump's energy use is acceptable.

amount paid per kW × monthly energy use = monthly cost

Consider paying more initially for energy efficient pumps to save over the life of the water feature.

weerawat nilmote/Shutterstock.com

Putt_1983/Shutterstock.com   *picturepartners/Shutterstock.com*   *vintory/Shutterstock.com*   *niteenrk/Shutterstock.com*

Figure 13-22. Aquatic plants are adapted to wet soil and shallow or standing water at various depths. They provide protection for aquatic life and interest for viewers.

Shereena M/Shutterstock.com

Figure 13-23. Water hyacinth is commonly used in water features. Its rapid growth rate and attractive bloom make it desirable for summer growing seasons. Some species are considered invasive and care must be taken to prevent spread to native wetlands.

color, and interest to water features. They also provide shade and coverage for fish and use nutrients from fish waste. They decrease algae growth and improve water quality. It is best to purchase plants from local nurseries or garden centers. The most common aquatic plants include floaters, submerged, erect foliage, bog-type, and oxygenators.

Floaters

Floaters are buoyant due to their leaf and stem structures. They reproduce rapidly and bob along the surface. If needed, floaters may be anchored with fishing line. The feathery root system provides a spawning area and hiding places for newly hatched fish. Water hyacinth, water lettuce, and duckweed are common pond floaters, **Figure 13-23**. Floaters are easily removed if they begin to cover too much of the pond surface. If floaters are annuals, they should be removed from the pond before they begin to decompose.

Submerged Plants

Submerged plants are planted in pots or planting baskets, which are placed on the bottom of the pond or on plant shelves built into the sides of the pond. The leaves and foliage float on the water surface. Many submerged plants are protected enough to survive cold winters. Common submerged plants include water lilies, lotus, water hawthorn, and ribbon grass or eelgrass.

Erect Foliage Plants

Erect foliage plants have roots below or at the water surface and display foliage and flowers a few inches or feet above the surface of the water. The main difference between these and the submerged plants is the height of foliage and flowers above the water surface. Aquatic irises, papyrus, and dwarf cattails are erect foliage plants, **Figure 13-24**.

Bog and Marginal Plants

Bog and marginal plants thrive in wet soils and add color, height, and interest to your water feature. Bog and marginal type plants can be installed in pots for partial submersion into a water feature or planted in surrounding heavy, wet soils. Bog plants vary greatly in height and colors and have a variety of leaf sizes. They are also considered perennials in many areas. Popular bog plants include reeds, rushes, horsetail, dwarf canna, and carnivorous pitcher plants, **Figure 13-25**.

Oxygenators

Oxygenators grow with some or all of their foliage below water. It is important to include oxygenators if fish and snails are in an aquatic feature. Oxygenators add oxygen to the water. It is, however, their ability to absorb waste that is the most beneficial to the water feature. These plants absorb ammonia, nitrates, nitrites, and other salts and minerals that would otherwise build up and make the water toxic. Anacharis, hornwort, and water crowfoot are common oxygenating plants, **Figure 13-26**.

Watercolorful/Shutterstock.com   *Del Boy/Shutterstock.com*

Figure 13-24. Lotus and papyrus are attractive options for water features. providing color, texture, height, and beneficial habitat.

Piyachanok Raungpaka/Shutterstock.com   *svetok30/Shutterstock.com*

Figure 13-25. Pitcher plants and horsetail are unique in their shape, texture, and structure.

IanRedding/Shutterstock.com   *Martin Fowler/Shutterstock.com*

Figure 13-26. Anacharis and water crowfoot are low-growing aquatic plants that provide green foliage and white blooms.

PANOM CH/Shutterstock.com

Figure 13-27. Aquatic snails are beneficial to aquatic features due to their algae foraging tendencies.

Fish and other Aquatic Organisms

Many installations are designed to support fish and other aquatic organisms. These add movement and interest for people of all ages. The most common addition is fish, but other organisms, such as snails, are also added for their interest and usefulness in cleaning the environment. Goldfish and koi are the most common fish added to water features. Orfes and Japanese snails are also popular additions, **Figure 13-27**.

Goldfish

Goldfish are used in many ponds because they are inexpensive and readily available. Goldfish also tend to be very hardy with few diseases. Goldfish can survive in climates where water freezes, as long as they have enough space to live below the ice. Typical stocking rates are 1″ of fish for every eight gallons of water. This rate will allow the population to be healthy and grow to an adequate size.

Koi

Koi are the most notable species in water features, **Figure 13-28**. Due to their size, koi are not usually added to smaller ponds (below 1000 gallons). Koi are very decorative with randomized markings of black, yellow, orange, whites, and tans. As they grow, they become voracious eaters and can disrupt root growth of aquatic plants if not fed regularly. Koi can be much more expensive than other fish species.

Orfes

Orfes are schooling fish that add excitement with their active feeding habits, **Figure 13-29**. Some orfes jump from the water to capture flying insects. In addition, they are compatible with goldfish and koi.

Japanese Snails

Japanese snails eat organic matter on the bottom and sides of the pond. They can be stocked at a rate of one snail per 2 ft² of pond surface. They also help maintain the pond's natural bacteria.

Feeding Schedules

Aquatic creatures need varying amounts of food throughout the seasons. It is common to minimize the amounts and frequencies of feeding during cooler temperatures to match the slowed metabolism of these creatures.

Dennis Jacobsen/Shutterstock.com

Figure 13-29. Orfes are added to aquatic environments for their foraging tendencies on mosquitoes and their docile nature with other fish.

Hung Nguyen Long/Shutterstock.com

Figure 13-28. Koi are popular additions to water features due to their unique colorations and hardiness.

Constructing a Water Feature

Once the design is complete, construction may begin. The steps used in constructing a water feature include the following:

- Layout and excavation.
- Determining volume.
- Liner installation.
- Pump installation.
- Hardscape installation.
- Plant installation.

Layout and Excavation

The layout can be painted on the ground or outlined with a rope or hose. This establishes the *perimeter*, the defining shape and the edge of the excavation area. If the pond has varied levels, the shallower area is often dug first. A small piece of equipment, such as an excavator, **Figure 13-30**, can expedite soil removal. The machine may also be used to place large stones.

Measuring Water Volume

The rough excavation is measured to ensure the dimensions and depth are accurate. For a simple geometric shape, measure the length, width, and depth and multiply those numbers to determine the cubic volume of the water. To determine total volume in gallons, multiply this number by 7.5.

Lillian Tveit/Shutterstock.com

Figure 13-30. Pond excavation is often performed with mini excavators that are able to enter small landscape areas. Their digging capabilities greatly reduce the amount of manual labor needed to prepare the area for a water feature.

Most pond designs are irregular and the volume is an estimation. Measurements must be taken from multiple directions to ensure an estimate close to the true volume. If the pond has multiple, distinct depths, each area can be measured and calculated separately. The estimated volume for each area is added to determine the total volume.

The formula for volume in gallons is average length × average width × average depth × 7.5.

$$l \times w \times d \times 7.5$$

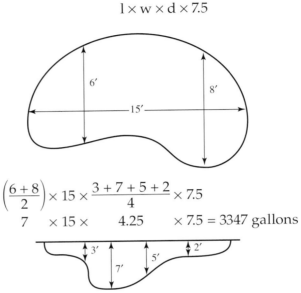

$$\left(\frac{6+8}{2}\right) \times 15 \times \frac{3+7+5+2}{4} \times 7.5$$
$$7 \quad \times 15 \times \quad 4.25 \quad \times 7.5 = 3347 \text{ gallons}$$

Calculating Pump Size

It is essential to install a pump with the proper capacity for a successful water feature. The pump must move the volume of water in the water feature at the rate desired. In some features, for example, the water is slow moving for a tranquil ambience, whereas in others it may be moving rapidly to create excitement and higher levels of sound, **Figure 13-31**.

As stated earlier, the type and capacity of the pump needed depends on the size of the water feature and the demands on the pump. The pond water should be circulated once every one or two hours. The pump must therefore be able to circulate the total water volume in this amount of time. A 500-gallon pond, for example, would require a pump that runs 500 gallons per hour (gph) to circulate the total volume in one hour. If the pond has 1000 gallons and it is determined it should circulate the water every two hours, a 500 gph pump would be sufficient.

Waterfalls

The volume of pumps used for waterfalls is calculated by first determining the head height and the desired water flow. *Head height* is the total number of feet from the top of the waterfall to the water's surface. Flow rates for waterfalls are labeled light, average, and strong. The flow rate is calculated by multiplying the desired gph by the waterfall width. If an average flow for a waterfall that is 12″ wide were desired, the width (12″) would be multiplied by 100 gph. If the head height were 5′, the waterfall would require a pump that would pump 1200 gph at 5′ head height.

Calculating Water Feature Pump Size	
Flow rate for filtration	Filtration flow rate in gallons per hour gph = 0.5 × pond volume (gallons)
Flow rate for fountains	For every inch of stream width at the top of the fountain, you need 100 gph at the height it is pumping
Flow rate for waterfalls	
Light flow	50 gph × waterfall width (in)
Average flow	100 gph × waterfall width (in)
Strong flow	200 gph × waterfall width (in)
Head height	Horizontal distance/10′ + vertical height above water level = head height
Pond volume	Pond volume (gallons) = 7.5 × average width (ft) × average length (ft) × average depth (ft)

Note: Most pump manufacturers provide information regarding their pump sizes and capabilities to help determine the capacity needed.

Goodheart-Willcox Publisher

Figure 13-31. Calculating the pump size is necessary for determining the desired flow across a waterfall or through a fountain.

Professionals recommend purchasing a pump with more capacity than needed to compensate for loss of power due to factors such as the pump's distance from the water outlet and the length of the tubing from the pump to the waterfall.

Calculating Liner Size

The liner size can be determined after the excavation is complete, **Figure 13-32**. Measure the length, width, and depth of the excavated area to determine the size needed. Ordering 15% to 20% more material than needed will ensure the liner will be usable if there are plan changes or miscalculations. The liner may be cut from a roll or custom ordered.

A *Dolgikh Pavel/Shutterstock.com* B *mvhelena/Shutterstock.com*

Figure 13-32. A—A flexible liner must be installed under water basins and waterfalls to minimize water loss. B—Preformed liners are popular for clients who request a smaller water feature.

Liner Installation

A felt barrier is laid on the bare soil before the liner is installed to protect the liner from punctures. The liner is flattened or smoothed to limit overlaps or wrinkles that may hinder regular maintenance. Once the area is covered and all flat surfaces are evident, water is added to the deepest area of the pond. This ensures that the liner will take the shape of the excavated area. The perimeter of the area is reestablished and any excess material overlapping the perimeter can be cut. The edges of the liner are folded over at least once and placed in a shallow trench around the perimeter. This will prevent the liner from being pulled into the pond as more water is added. Add soil and a few stones to the perimeter trench to hold the liner in place.

Stone

Stone is one of the most common materials used to build waterfalls, construct streambeds, and line the perimeter of water features to create a natural look, **Figure 13-33**. A designer will choose stone by size, common shape, color, and texture. Flat stones are often stacked around water feature perimeters to delineate from the surrounding landscaped areas. Stone is also placed along constructed streambeds to mimic natural streams. When placed around the perimeter, these flat stones can be used to create an overhang under which fish can hide or to create a viewing platform. The amount of stone needed for a particular water feature must be calculated using area measurements.

STEM Connection

Calculating Stone Amounts

Stone is ordered by the ton. The number of tons needed for a job can be determined by calculating the volume of stone desired.

Pond floor. Let us consider a material that will be 6″ deep in a water feature that is 20′ wide and 40′ long.

1. Calculate the square footage or area of the pond.

   area = length × width
   area = 40′ × 20′ = 800 ft²

2. Multiply the area by the depth to find volume. Convert the depth in inches to feet to prevent miscalculations.

   6″ = 0.50′
   800 ft² × 0.50′ = 400 ft³

3. Convert the volume in cubic feet to cubic yards. There are 27 ft³ in 1 yd³.

   400 ft³ ÷ 27 = 14.8 yd³

4. To convert cubic yards to tons, multiply by 1.35. This conversion is useful for most small stone materials.

   14.8 yd³ × 1.35 = 20 tons
   20 tons of material are required to cover 800 ft².

Add 5% to 10% more materials for miscalculation and on-site design changes. Adding more materials to a project is more expensive than having too much on site. Many times, the material can be used in other ways for the project.

Lisa Ewing/Shutterstock.com

Figure 13-33. Stone around water features creates a naturalistic and serene environment. Stone may be used for walls and/or as a viewing platform.

Pro Tip

Stone materials vary so much in size that most suppliers will provide calculations specific to each type of stone they sell. There are also many online materials calculators that can be used to determine how much material is needed for a job.

Water Feature Maintenance

Water features are exposed to the elements, which may add excess water and leaves and other organic debris. The open water will also evaporate and be absorbed by plants. To keep the water feature clean and functioning, debris must be removed regularly and water must be added to keep the water at the desired level.

Water Loss

Evaporation is a constant natural occurrence in which water evaporated from a body of water is replaced by flowing water or rainfall. When water evaporates from a water feature, it must be replaced manually unless there is sufficient precipitation to sustain the water level. The rate of evaporation in water features in which water flows long distances and across multiple levels is high and the need for refilling is more frequent.

A *float valve* can be used to open the water supply automatically when the water is low and close when the water returns to operational level. If the float goes below the desired level, the valve opens; if the float is at the desired level, the valve closes and remains shut. Rainwater can be used to replenish the feature in areas permitting *rainwater catchment* (rainwater storage) from roofs and other impermeable surfaces, **Figure 13-34**.

Consideration should be given to overflow in the event of heavy rainfall or snowmelt. An overflow system can easily be installed to remediate the issue.

DJTaylor/Shutterstock.com

Figure 13-34. Filtered water from a rainwater catchment may also be used to maintain the water level, as well as water the garden.

Skimmers and Filtration

A handheld or mechanical skimmer can be used to collect floating debris. A mechanical net, screen, or brush system is used with the skimmer to prevent debris and fish from entering the system, **Figure 13-35**. This can be in conjunction with a biological filtration system that allows for the growth of beneficial bacteria as well as capture of sediment.

Predator Deterrents

Predators, such as raccoons, are often attracted to landscape water features and the fish they contain. Raccoons can use the plant shelves as perches for catching fish and herons or other fish-scavenging birds may become regular visitors, **Figure 13-36**. Fish can be protected by placing nets over the water surface or by placing decoys, motion-activated sprinklers, or noisemakers near the water feature.

Austroshot/Shutterstock.com

Figure 13-35. Water skimmers, filtration components, and screens can be used to collect surface and subsurface debris.

Prairie Eyes/Shutterstock.com

Figure 13-36. Predator deterrents, such as netting and decoys, help protect fish and plants from removal and damage.

Career Connection

Patrick Freeman

Patrick Freeman, Sales Manager with Hunter Industries

Patrick Freeman currently covers the North Carolina market, representing the Hunter Residential/Commercial irrigation line as well as the FX Luminaire Low Voltage Lighting Line. His responsibilities include building relationships with distributors and contractors, providing support to Hunter's partners during product installation, training their partners on the features and benefits, as well as technical support for Hunter's product lines, and providing training on basic irrigation and lighting principles to Hunter's partners and local organizations. Patrick is also responsible for reaching sales goals and growth in his market on both product lines.

Patrick graduated from North Carolina State with a degree in Ornamental Landscape Technology with an Agribusiness Concertation. His first job in the green industry was as a spray technician at Prestonwood Country Club, where he worked his way to Assistant Superintendent. Four years later, Patrick began working with Bland Landscaping as a Residential Installation Foreman. He was quickly promoted to Irrigation Department Manager, then ultimately Vice President of Operations. Patrick was employed with Bland Landscaping for 15 years. Patrick also holds multiple licenses and certifications and works with local colleges and industry organizations.

Patrick offers the following advice to those intending to work in the green industry:

- Be professional, take pride in your work, and have a positive attitude about the process.
- Treat every task, no matter how remedial, as though it is the most important thing you will do.
- Be honest, and always do the right thing, even if it costs you. If you do this, the rest will take care of itself!
- Put yourself out there, get involved in trade organizations, and give back to the community and your school. Doing this helps you professionally, allows you to make great contacts, and serves a greater purpose for those with whom you are involved.
- You will see more doors open for you when you are involved and helping others along the way—it is a win/win proposition!
- Try different things and make sure you understand all the opportunities this wonderful industry has to offer in terms of a career!

Consider This

1. How has Patrick Freeman's positive outlook contributed to his success?
2. Did Patrick's careers follow a logical path after his college graduation?
3. What qualities do you think are needed to be a successful sales manager? Which of these qualities do you possess?

Summary

- Landscape lighting is used primarily to highlight features of a home, business, and landscape.

- Landscape lighting may be powered by line-voltage, low-voltage, or solar-powered systems.

- Lighting systems are powered by 120V but this is often reduced to 24V for safer installation and maintenance as well as for lower energy consumption.

- Controllers are used to set frequency and duration of light emission.

- Lighting systems are installed in zones to distribute the power evenly on multiple lines.

- The fixtures, bulbs, and the direction of the light beam all contribute to the effectiveness of a landscape lighting system.

- Landscape lighting fixtures vary not only in design but also in the way they focus or diffuse light.

- Lightbulbs are chosen for their energy efficiency, cost, longevity, light color, brightness, and output.

- Lighting techniques use different fixtures and placements of those fixtures to create the desired effects.

- Water features are installed to create a relaxing ambience with the added benefit of attracting wildlife to the area.

- Water features use electric pumps, electrical service, tubing, and liners.

- Tropical and native plants are used in and around water features.

- Aquatic plants are installed to add texture, color and interest, provide shade and coverage for fish, and to decrease algae growth and improve water quality.

- The most common addition to water features is fish, but other organisms, such as snails, are also added for their interest and usefulness in cleaning the environment.

- Water feature construction involves layout, excavation, volume measurement, liner installation, pump installation, hardscape installation, and plant installation.

- The type and capacity of the pump needed depends on the size of the water feature and the demands on the pump.

- Stone is used to mimic natural stacks, streambeds, and waterfalls and can be specifically arranged to accomplish design goals.

- Water features experience water loss through evaporation and plant absorption.

- To keep the water feature clean and functioning, debris must be removed regularly and water must be added to keep the water at the desired level.

- Fish can be protected from predators by placing nets over the water surface or by placing decoys, motion-activated sprinklers, or noisemakers near the water feature.

Chapter Review

Know and Understand ↗

Answer the following questions using the information provided in this chapter.

1. Which of the following are common reasons for adding landscape lighting?
   A. Draw attention to service areas.
   B. Guide visitors to the entryway or outdoor room.
   C. Make it easier for vandals to access the home.
   D. All of the above.

2. A line-voltage power system _____.
   A. will disconnect power quickly if the current is flowing along an unintended path
   B. costs less to install than a low-voltage system
   C. must be installed by a licensed electrician
   D. uses light sensors to collect energy

3. At what energy level does low-voltage lighting operate?
   A. 12V to 24V.
   B. 120V to 240V.
   C. 500V to 550V.
   D. 750V to 880V.

4. A device used to reduce the incoming line voltage to a lower voltage with lower wattage is called a _____.
   A. controller
   B. transformer
   C. circuit
   D. GFCI

5. In the United States, which direction should sun collection panels be oriented to maximize energy absorption?
   A. South.
   B. North.
   C. East.
   D. West.

6. Which of the following contribute to the effectiveness of a landscape lighting system?
   A. Pump, tubing, and head height.
   B. Filter and external pump.
   C. Bulbs, fixtures, and direction of light beam.

Match the lighting techniques to the descriptions in 7–15.

7. Lights are installed at the base shining from below a feature to accentuate height and texture.
   A. Washing.
   B. Up lighting.
   C. Moonlighting.
   D. Floodlighting.

8. Lights are used to light wide building facades, architectural features, groups of tall trees, or other expansive areas.
   A. Path lighting.
   B. Grazing.
   C. Down lighting.
   D. Floodlighting.

9. Illuminating a tree or garden feature from two or more sides.
   A. Cross lighting.
   B. Grazing.
   C. Up lighting.
   D. Shadowing.

10. Decorative fixtures installed along a walkway.
    A. Washing.
    B. Floodlighting.
    C. Path lighting.
    D. Cross lighting.

11. Lights are placed above a feature to create a dramatic effect; may be used to direct movement of visitors through narrow spaces.
    A. Moonlighting.
    B. Down lighting.
    C. Up lighting.
    D. Floodlighting.

12. Soft lights are placed high in trees, allowing the light to filter through the leaves and branches.
    A. Grazing.
    B. Washing.
    C. Floodlighting.
    D. Moonlighting.

13. Light is placed close to a flat surface and aimed directly up or down the surface to create dramatic light and shadow play.
    A. Grazing.
    B. Cross lighting.
    C. Floodlighting.
    D. Moonlighting.

14. Shining light along a wall or hedge to create ambient lighting.
    A. Up lighting.
    B. Path lighting.
    C. Grazing.
    D. Washing.

15. The light is placed between the main vantage point and the item being lit; works best when there is a flat surface behind the feature.
    A. Cross lighting.
    B. Shadowing.
    C. Floodlighting.
    D. Path lighting.

16. Which of the following statements is false?
    A. Ponds are typically the simplest and least expensive water features.
    B. Water features attract wildlife to the area.
    C. The size of a feature depends on space, budget, and possibly local ordinances.
    D. Water features create a relaxing ambience.

17. When compared to submersible pumps, external pumps are _____.
    A. easier to access and service
    B. generally more reliable
    C. typically not as quiet
    D. All of the above.

18. Which of the following statements is false?
    A. Plants are installed to add texture, color, and interest.
    B. Plants provide shade and coverage for fish.
    C. Plants use nutrients from fish waste.
    D. Plants increase algae growth and improve water quality.

19. Which of the following is *not* a type of aquatic plant?
    A. Oxygenator.
    B. Bog-type.
    C. Orfes.
    D. Floater.

20. The most common fish added to water features are _____.
    A. Japanese mollusks
    B. catfish and perch
    C. goldfish and koi
    D. None of the above.

21. The total water volume of a pond is calculated by _____.
    A. timing the water flow as it is being filled
    B. determining cubic volume and multiplying it by 7.5
    C. multiplying cubic volume by head height
    D. All of the above.

22. To circulate the total volume in one hour, a 500-gallon pond would require a pump that runs _____.
    A. 100 gallons per hour (gph)
    B. 150 gallons per hour (gph)
    C. 250 gallons per hour (gph)
    D. 500 gallons per hour (gph)

23. The water in a garden feature _____.
    A. gets warmer as the water deepens
    B. should only be replaced with rainwater
    C. evaporates and is absorbed by plants
    D. All of the above.

24. Which of the following is used to maintain a water feature?
    A. A mechanical net, screen, or brush system.
    B. A biological filtration system.
    C. A handheld or mechanical skimmer.
    D. All of the above.

Thinking Critically

1. How would you explain voltage drop and its effects on a landscape lighting system to a fellow student?

2. How would you compare and contrast the different landscape lighting systems?

3. Can you identify the different parts used in a landscape lighting system? Can you explain their functions?

Suggested Activities

1. Working in groups of 3 or 4, identify a prominent feature in a local landscape that could be accentuated by landscape lighting. Determine if power is available to that site. Sketch a layout depicting how you would install the layout. Recreate your sketch using a computer program.

2. Locate the nearest landscape lighting and aquatic gardening supplier. Make a list of materials needed for the system you designed in the previous activity. Calculate the cost of materials using the supplier's retail prices.

3. Locate a private or public garden area that would be enhanced by the addition of a water feature. Working with a partner, determine how the site would be accessed if a feature were to be installed. Design and sketch a layout of the water feature you would install. Use accurate measurements if possible.

4. Working with a partner, visit a well-designed landscape lighting system or locate images online that illustrate such a system. Determine how many fixtures exist and categorize them by uses and techniques. Explain how you would modify the lighting or why you would leave it as it is.

5. Research local electrical ordinances regulating outdoor receptacles usable in lighting or aquatic features. Identify other regulations that govern the installation of lighting systems and water features.

6. Examine an operating fountain. Locate its water and electrical source. Determine if it is operating in a manner consistent with its intended design. If not, explain how you would adjust or modify it to operate properly.

7. Locate resources, such as online calculators, to calculate the amount of stone needed for an area of your choosing. You may use a real location or a water feature of your own design. Determine the length of the streambed, height of stackable walls, and levels of a waterfall.

8. Research invasive aquatic plant and fish species in your area. Determine if local suppliers sell any of the invasive species. What harm do they cause the environment? Search government websites for measures that are used to control or eradicate these species.

CHAPTER 14

Irrigation Design, Installation, and Maintenance

 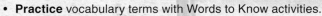

Chapter Outcomes

After studying this chapter, you will be able to:

- Identify sources of irrigation water.
- Understand the basic differences between public and private water sources.
- Identify a reclaimed water system and explain its uses.
- Explain the importance of water flow and system pressure.
- Describe the basic components of commercial and residential irrigation systems.
- Describe the different sprinkler heads, their use, and level of efficiency.
- Understand the process of designing irrigation systems.
- Understand the process of installing irrigation systems.
- Identify potential irrigation problems and solutions.

Key Terms ⟶

arc
atmospheric vacuum breaker (AVB)
backflow preventer
catch device
check valve
design capacity
detention pond
distribution uniformity
double-check valve assembly (DCV)
drip irrigation
electro-mechanical controller
emitter
friction loss
frost line
gallons per hour (gph)
gallons per minute (gpm)
galvanized piping
gear-driven rotary head
head-to-head coverage

hydraulics
impact rotary head
irrigation
irrigation zone
lateral line
mainline
micro-sprinkler head
multi-strand system
PEX (cross-linked polyethylene pipe)
point of connection
polyethylene pipe
polyvinylchloride pipe (PVC)
pop-up sprinkler head
potable water
precipitation rate (PR)
pressure vacuum breaker (PVB)
pump
quick-slip repair coupling
reclaimed water
reduced pressure assembly (RPA)

remote controller
reservoir
retention pond
riser
smart controller
soaker hose
solid-state controller
sprinkler head
sprinkler radius
stop-and-waste valve
sump pump
tamp
thread tape
trench shovel
trenching machine
trickle irrigation
turf rotor
two-wire decoder system
valve manifold
water pressure

Introduction

Many areas lack sufficient rainfall to produce and maintain high-quality turf and landscapes throughout the growing season. These areas require *irrigation*, the application of water to plants to aid plant growth, **Figure 14-1**.

Photo courtesy of Hunter Industries

Figure 14-1. An efficient irrigation system will help produce and maintain a safe and aesthetically pleasing playing surface.

When an irrigation system is properly designed and installed, it can be a very efficient and effective means of maintaining sufficient moisture. However, irrigation systems are expensive to install and maintain, and careful consideration should be taken before ground is broken. In this chapter, you will learn about the components, design, installation, and maintenance of irrigation systems.

Water Sources

The first and foremost concern for irrigation systems is the availability of water. A water source and its specific characteristics will determine the resources, tools, and materials that will be needed to design an efficient irrigation system. A public water source, for example, may not provide sufficient water pressure and may require an additional or stronger pump to be built into the system. Another example would be a public water source with more regulations than a private source, requiring a change in design or materials.

Bohbeh/Shutterstock.com

Figure 14-2. Leaking system components waste water and should be repaired as quickly as possible.

Pro Tip

Each foot of elevation change affects water pressure by 0.433 psi. Moving water uphill will require an increase of 0.433 psi for each foot of elevation change to compensate and negate the impact.

Using water for ornamental landscaping or turf can be controversial, especially in areas that regularly experience periods of drought. If the drought is severe, water restrictions may be implemented and watering ornamental landscaping and turf may be limited or prohibited. Water used in irrigation systems comes from either a public or private source, **Figure 14-2.**

Harvesting Rainwater

Metrolina Greenhouses, a large greenhouse operation in Huntersville, North Carolina, has a unique approach to collecting water to irrigate its over five million square feet of plants. Water draining from the greenhouse is collected and stored in large retention ponds. The pond water is filtered and used to irrigate the crops. Just 1″ of rain provides Metrolina with three million gallons of usable irrigation! The concrete floors in the greenhouse are also sloped so that excess water applied to the crops drains to the retention ponds as well.

Public Water Sources

Public water sources used for irrigation are typically the same sources used to provide local homes and businesses with potable water. *Potable water* is water fit for human consumption. Potable water from public systems is treated to ensure it is clean and safe to use. A public water system may draw water from sources, such as reservoirs, wells, lakes, and rivers. A *reservoir* is a constructed or natural lake that provides a water supply, **Figure 14-3**. Rainwater may also be channeled to flow into a water source.

Reclaimed Water

Some cities are implementing water reclamation systems. *Reclaimed water* is wastewater that has been treated and reused for other purposes. The treatment process removes harmful microorganisms and solid materials. The water then goes through one of several methods of sterilization. Currently, most reclaimed water is used for agricultural irrigation, watering golf course turf, and to replenish groundwater. The treated water is often cleaner than the water was originally, but many people are still uncomfortable with the prospect of using it as a potable water source. Some systems use purple piping and irrigation heads to indicate that the water in the system is reclaimed, **Figure 14-4**.

jessicakirsh/Shutterstock.com

Figure 14-3. Reservoirs provide water to residents in urban and suburban areas.

Robert Schlie/Shutterstock.com

Figure 14-4. Purple piping indicates that reclaimed water is being used for irrigation.

AuntSpray/Shutterstock.com

Figure 14-5. Submersible pumps move water to a pressure tank.

Private Water Sources

Businesses and homeowners in rural areas use private water sources because they do not have access to a public water supply. The most common private water source is a well. Modern wells use pumps and additional equipment to bring water to the surface, **Figure 14-5**. Water is pumped into the pressure tank to provide adequate water pressure to the home's plumbing. Water from some wells may require additional filtration to remove minerals and other natural nutrients before it is applied to crops.

Well Output

If a well is used to supply an irrigation system, careful consideration should be paid to the well's output and the depth of the aquifer. It may not be possible to draw water economically from wells that are extremely deep because it would be cost-prohibitive or maybe impossible to acquire an adequate amount of water flow. If a well is 450′ deep and only produces two gpm, for example, very little water would be available for an irrigation system. A well's output is the flow of water measured in gallons per minute. *Gallons per minute (gpm)* is the number of gallons of water the well/pump provides per minute. The amount of water an irrigation system applies is measured in *gallons per hour (gph)* and the output of individual sprinkler heads is commonly measured in gallons per minute (gpm).

A well providing a large volume of irrigation water may first pump the water into a pond rather than a tank. (A *pressure tank* is used in private systems where there is insufficient pressure.) A pond used to store water for an irrigation system is typically a small, often constructed, open body of water. A second pump in the pond may be required to move the water into the irrigation system. These large storage areas are helpful when wells cannot keep up with a high demand for irrigation water.

Retention and Detention Ponds

Retention and detention ponds are used to collect and filter excess irrigation and rainwater. A *retention pond* holds a permanent pool of water. Water can be pumped from the retention pond into the landscape or drain into a larger body of water, **Figure 14-6**. A *detention pond* eventually drains completely. Detention ponds are often installed to detain rainwater or snow melt and prevent flooding. When the water drains from the detention pond, the area will appear as a vegetated ditch.

Christopher D. Hart

Figure 14-6. Many commercial sites and new housing developments must have retention ponds installed to help filter runoff from walkways and parking lots.

Commercial properties and sites with large amounts of hard surfaces are often required to install retention and detention ponds to help filter and collect runoff from paved surfaces such as roads, parking lots, and walkways.

Water Movement and Pressure

Pumping water from a source and into an irrigation system is a basic process that uses hydraulics. *Hydraulics* is the science and technology of the movement of liquids. Water cannot be compressed and can therefore be forced up a well or into the irrigation lines with sufficient pressure. *Water pressure* is the force that water exerts on an area. There must be sufficient pressure applied to the water to create enough water pressure to force the water to the desired location.

Water pressure is a very important component of hydraulics. Water pressure is created through pumps and the weight of the water. Water pressure that is too low will cause spray heads to disperse water in large droplets, possibly creating improper coverage. Water pressure that is too high will cause water droplets to come out in too fine of a mist, creating drift and improper coverage, **Figure 14-7.**

Christopher D. Hart

Figure 14-7. Water pressure that is too high puts additional stress on spray heads and nozzles. It also produces a very fine mist of water that creates drift and improper coverage.

Maintaining Water Pressure

It is important to maintain a consistent water pressure in an irrigation system to ensure the system applies water in a uniform manner. The first step is to design the system with site characteristics in mind. Factors the designer should consider include the following:

- The water pressure exerted from the private or public water source.
- Gravity and friction cause water pressure loss throughout an irrigation system.
- Water moving uphill must compete against gravity.
- Increases in elevation will decrease water pressure. For each foot of uphill elevation, pressure loss is 0.433 psi.
- Water pressure increases as it flows with gravity. If irrigation pipe runs downhill, the sprinkler head at the bottom of the zone will have an increase in pressure.

Friction Loss

Water pressure is also lost through friction as it is pumped through system components. This loss of pressure is referred to as *friction loss.* The amount of water pressure lost through friction depends on the flow rate of the water and the pipe's internal texture, length, and diameter. Friction loss can be easily determined with charts from irrigation component manufacturers. This loss can be factored into the system design.

Pipe Diameter

The pipe's diameter will also affect water pressure. A smaller pipe diameter can be used to increase water pressure whereas a larger pipe can be used to lower water pressure while increasing volume. Decreasing pipe diameter while keeping the water supply constant will increase the rate of water flow. Booster pumps can also be used to increase water pressure, **Figure 14-8.**

R. Lee Ivy

Figure 14-8. Booster pumps can be used to increase pressure when water pressure is not sufficient.

Irrigation System Components

Irrigation systems require a variety of components to ensure that water moves from its source to the needed location. The types of components used will vary based on the specifications and requirements of the irrigation system. Components are used to contain, move, divert, and distribute water. Types of irrigation system components include the following:

- Pumps.
- Valves.
- Lines.
- Piping.
- Fittings (connectors).
- Controllers and timers.
- Sprinkler heads.

Pumps

A *pump* is a mechanical device used to move or distribute water from its source to where it is needed. There are many types of pumps for landscaping applications. In addition to moving water, pumps are also used to change volume and pressure. A booster pump, for example, can be added to a system to increase the system's pressure. A booster pump pulls water into an expansion tank that contains a pressurized bladder. The booster pump helps compress the air in the bladder, thus increasing water pressure.

Valves

All irrigation systems require different types of valves to control water flow at various points in the system. An emergency shut-off valve, for example, is used to cut all water supply to the system and an irrigation valve may be used to direct water only to specific sprinklers. One of the most vital valves required in all irrigation systems is the backflow preventer.

Backflow Preventers

A *backflow preventer* is an irrigation system valve that prevents water from flowing back into the water supply lines. A backflow preventer has an internal disk that opens when water is flowing out of the supply lines and closes when the water flow stops or if water begins to flow backward. Backflow preventers may also be referred to as *check valves*.

Backflow preventers commonly used in landscape irrigation systems include *atmospheric vacuum breakers (AVBs)*, *pressure vacuum breakers (PVBs)*, *reduced pressure assemblies (RPAs)*, and *double-check valve assemblies (DCVs)*, **Figure 14-9**. Local codes will determine which type of assembly is required and how that preventer is to be installed.

Control Valves

A control valve is required to connect the water supply to each individual zone. The control valve is connected to the irrigation controller through a series of wires. The irrigation controller sends an electrical signal to either open or close the control valve, thus telling the irrigation system to turn *on* or *off*. The control valve may also be referred to as a solenoid valve.

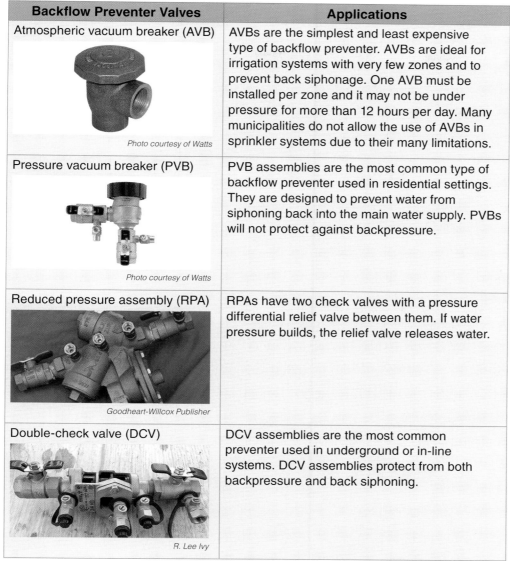

Backflow Preventer Valves	Applications
Atmospheric vacuum breaker (AVB) *Photo courtesy of Watts*	AVBs are the simplest and least expensive type of backflow preventer. AVBs are ideal for irrigation systems with very few zones and to prevent back siphonage. One AVB must be installed per zone and it may not be under pressure for more than 12 hours per day. Many municipalities do not allow the use of AVBs in sprinkler systems due to their many limitations.
Pressure vacuum breaker (PVB) *Photo courtesy of Watts*	PVB assemblies are the most common type of backflow preventer used in residential settings. They are designed to prevent water from siphoning back into the main water supply. PVBs will not protect against backpressure.
Reduced pressure assembly (RPA) *Goodheart-Willcox Publisher*	RPAs have two check valves with a pressure differential relief valve between them. If water pressure builds, the relief valve releases water.
Double-check valve (DCV) *R. Lee Ivy*	DCV assemblies are the most common preventer used in underground or in-line systems. DCV assemblies protect from both backpressure and back siphoning.

Goodheart-Willcox Publisher

Figure 14-9. Backflow preventers are available in many configurations.

Irrigation Lines

Irrigation lines are the piping used to distribute water to the sprinklers or emitters. A *mainline* is a large diameter pipe that carries water to lateral lines. A *lateral line* is a smaller diameter pipe that carries water from the mainline to the sprinkler head or emitter. A *sprinkler head* is the device attached to an irrigation line that dispenses the water. Main irrigation lines are under constant pressure. Lateral lines are under pressure only when the irrigation system is in use.

Piping Materials

Piping is made with different materials. Each type of material has unique characteristics suitable to the specific needs of an irrigation system. The most common piping materials include the following (**Figure 14-10**):

Types of Irrigation Piping

PVC pipe is one of the most common types of piping material used in irrigation systems.	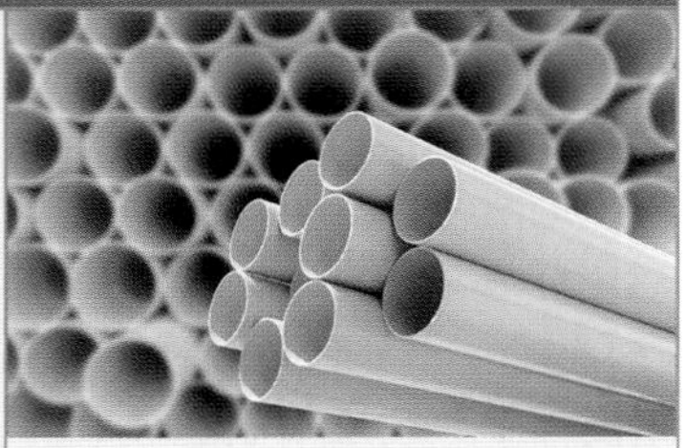 *Toa55/Shutterstock.com*
Galvanized pipe is very rigid and sturdy; however, over time the material begins to rust which eventually causes leaks.	 *MR. SURACHET PIRIYACHATKUL/ Shutterstock.com*
PEX pipe, which requires special fittings and clamping rings, is very flexible.	 *Pawel G/Shutterstock.com*
Polyethylene pipe is commonly used in drip and trickle irrigation systems.	 *Chromatic Studio/Shutterstock.com*
Copper piping is more resistant to corrosion than galvanized metal.	 *adrianmladin/Shutterstock.com*

Figure 14-10. Use of the most appropriate piping material is important to the system's efficiency and longevity.

- PVC pipe (polyvinylchloride pipe).
- Galvanized steel.
- PEX pipe (cross-linked polyethylene pipe).
- Polyethylene pipe.
- Copper pipe.

PVC Pipe. *Polyvinylchloride pipe* is more commonly referred to simply as *PVC*. PVC is one of the most common pipe materials used in irrigation systems. PVC is cost efficient, readily available, lightweight, and corrosion-resistant. PVC is available in a large variety of diameters and lengths, and can be easily cut to desired lengths. PVC fittings and pipe are easily primed and glued together. Full sections of PVC pipe are available with a bell-shaped end that allows quick connection of whole sections of pipe. PVC pipe may be buried or installed aboveground; however, extended exposure to the sun will cause the piping to break down quickly and become brittle. It is also more easily damaged or broken by equipment and machinery.

Galvanized Pipe. When *galvanized piping* (zinc-coated metal) is properly installed and maintained in an irrigation system, it has an average life span of 25 to 50 years. Galvanized pipe will eventually rust, which will lead to leaks in the system. Galvanized pipe is more rigid than PVC and is less likely to break when in contact with machines and equipment. The ends of galvanized pipe are coated with thread locker before being screwed together. *Thread locker* is a nonsticky tape that is wrapped clockwise around the male threads of a pipe to seal the space between the male and female threads. Thread locker helps create stronger, leak-proof connections. Galvanized pipe is more difficult to cut to custom lengths than other types of materials and must be threaded after it is cut and before it is connected to the system.

PEX Pipe (Cross-Linked Polyethylene Pipe). Many homes and irrigation systems are being plumbed with *PEX (cross-linked polyethylene pipe)*. PEX is made from high-density polyethylene and is very flexible. PEX pipe is white and susceptible to the sun's ultraviolet (UV) rays and must be buried or installed under a structure for protection. PEX pipe is often sold in smaller diameter and is ideal for water-saving irrigation systems, such as a drip or trickle tube. Crimping rings are used to attach pipe and fittings. A special crimping tool is required to ensure the rings are properly installed.

Polyethylene Pipe. *Polyethylene pipe* is soft and flexible, similar to PEX pipe; however, it can be used above ground. Different colors of polyethylene pipe are used for specific purposes. Brown polyethylene pipe, for example, is commonly used in drip irrigation to help the hose blend with the mulch. White polyethylene pipe reflects sunlight and is often used in installations in which the piping comes in close contact with plants.

Barbed couplings and clamps hold polyethylene pipe together. Polyethylene pipe may need to be heated with a torch to install the couplings and fittings. PEX is commonly used in water-saving irrigation systems, such as drip and trickle-tube irrigation systems. Polyethylene pipe is also commonly used to attach sprinkler heads to lateral lines.

Copper Pipe. Copper piping is used in the high water pressure areas of an irrigation system's tubing, such as around valve connections, meters, and backflow preventers. Copper piping requires copper fittings to be permanently installed by soldering or brazing. Copper pipe is more resistant to corrosion than galvanized metal.

Pipe Fittings (Connectors)

Pipe fittings or connectors are used to connect irrigation pipe. Fittings control the layout of the pipe as well as the water pressure and flow rate. Pipe fittings are available in a wide variety of shapes, sizes, and configurations to enable both simple and elaborate system designs. The basic fittings used in the landscape industry are illustrated in **Figure 14-11**.

Controllers

Irrigation controllers enable the user to apply water efficiently and effectively to the landscape, **Figure 14-12**. Newer controllers allow the user to manipulate many aspects of an irrigation system, either on site or remotely with a computer or phone app. Some of the actions an irrigation controller can manage include timing, duration, location, and the amount of water applied. Some systems may also use a rain sensor to measure rainfall and in-ground moisture sensors that will override the programmed schedule when it is raining and adequate moisture is achieved. Irrigation controllers send signals to a solenoid valve that electronically performs the action requested. These signals are sent through wires that are laid with the pipelines and attached to the solenoid valve.

Landscape irrigation systems use electro-mechanical controllers or solid-state controllers.

- *Electro-mechanical controllers* are driven by gears and motors that instruct irrigation zones to turn *on* and *off*. They are dependable but often lack many features of solid-state controllers.
- *Solid-state controllers* are more complex than electro-mechanical controllers and involve a central processing system. Solid-state controllers can manage complex irrigation schedules.
- *Smart controllers* use advanced control systems and will typically interface with a computer or smartphone. Smart controllers automatically update settings and watering schedules based on weather and other changes throughout the year. Irrigation controllers also have a seasonal setting that allows for quick adjustment and reduction of water application when it is not needed as much as in the growing season.
- *Remote controllers* work with smart controllers and can be used to open and close specific irrigation zones. Some remote controllers can operate at distances as far as two miles. Remote, battery-operated controllers are useful on valves located far from power sources.

Irrigation Systems

The two most common systems are *sprinkler* and *low-volume irrigation*. A site analysis is the first step in determining what type of system would be most appropriate. The type chosen depends on factors, such as the type of landscape being irrigated, the available water volume, and the static water pressure. Each type of system has advantages, disadvantages, and a proper place in the landscape. Installing a combination of sprinkler and low-volume irrigation often creates the most sustainable means of irrigating the site.

Pipe Fittings Used in Irrigation

	Pipefitting	Usage
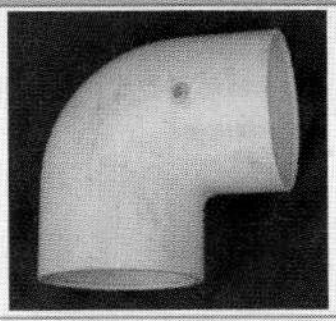	90° elbow	Making a 90° turn with pipe. A 90° turn can make irrigation systems tight and compact, but water pressure is greatly increased when such sharp turns are made.
	45° elbow	Making a 45° turn with pipe. A 45° turn is more gradual and does not have as much pressure buildup as a 90° turn.
	Pipe coupling	Joining two pieces of pipe.
	Pipe bushing	Reducing pipe size. A pipe bushing is screwed or glued into one end of a pipe. A smaller pipe is then glued into the bushing.
	Pipe reducer	Reducing pipe size. A pipe reducer is attached to the outside of the pipe.
	Pipe cap	Closing the end of a pipe. A pipe cap is not easily removed.
	Pipe plug	Closing one end of a pipe. Easily screwed on and off with a pipe wrench.
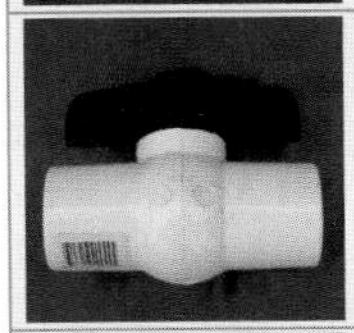	Ball valve	Cutting off the water supply to a lateral or main line. A simple way to prevent water from flowing through certain pipes.
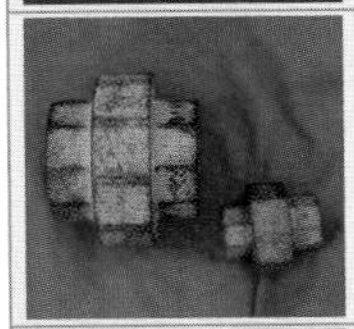	Pipe union	Removing a piece of pipe when neither side of the pipe can be turned.
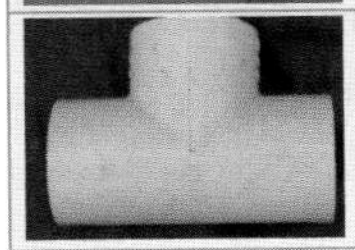	Pipe Tee	Joining three pieces of pipe.

Christopher D. Hart

Figure 14-11. Common fittings used in landscape irrigation. Fittings will vary slightly based on size and material of the fitting.

Christopher D. Hart

Figure 14-12. Irrigation controllers include time clocks for programming zones and duration of irrigation.

Christopher D. Hart

Figure 14-13. Pop-up rotary sprinkler heads are one of the most commonly used sprinkler heads. Pop-up spray heads have less moving parts than gear-driven rotary heads.

Sprinkler Irrigation

Sprinkler irrigation uses sprinkler heads to distribute water throughout the landscape. As explained earlier, a *sprinkler head* is the device attached to an irrigation line that dispenses the water. Sprinkler irrigation is the most common type of irrigation system used in the industry. The four main types of sprinkler heads are pop-up, impact rotary head, gear-driven rotary head, and large turf rotor.

Pop-Up Sprinkler Heads

Pop-up sprinkler heads are used in small areas of a landscape, such as small turf areas or beds of landscape plants. As the name suggests, a ***pop-up sprinkler head*** will pop-up when it is pressurized and in use. When pop-up sprinkler heads are not in use, they are level with the ground surface or grade, **Figure 14-13**. This allows mowing, prevents tripping, and is more aesthetically pleasing. However, they must be tall enough to clear vegetation, such as the height of the lawn, to ensure proper coverage. Pop-up sprinkler nozzles can be adjusted to fine tune the spray direction. Pop-up sprinklers provide a steady spray of water over areas ranging from 10′ to 20′. Depending on the pattern and particular sprinkler head, water output may range from 0.2 gpm to 5.5 gpm.

Gear-Driven Rotary Heads

Gear-driven rotary heads are commonly used in commercial landscape settings. The gears inside a gear-driven rotary head help propel water over a long distance in a variety of spray patterns, including:

- Full-circle (360°).
- Half-circle (180°).
- Quarter-circle (90°).
- Adjustable or variable arc nozzles, such as 40° to 360°.

The arc of a gear-driven rotary head can be adjusted to ensure proper coverage, **Figure 14-14**. *Arc* is the area of a circle irrigated by the sprinkler head. Arc is usually given in degrees or quarter sections of a circle. Gear-driven rotary heads are also concealed when not in use. Risers are used to connect the lateral line to the sprinkler head if the spray head is installed above the ground. A *riser* is a length of pipe with male pipe threads on each end. Risers are also used when pop-up sprinkler heads are used in planting beds where the irrigation system above ground will not be visible. Risers are not visually appealing and are typically placed in less conspicuous areas of the landscape.

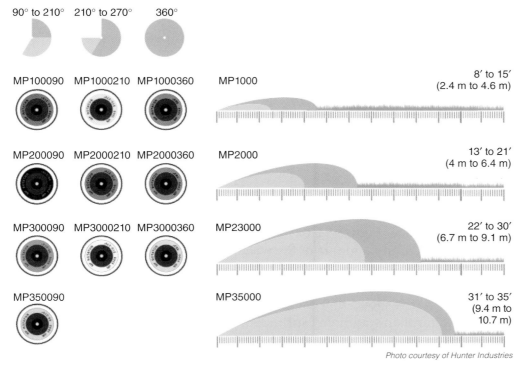

Photo courtesy of Hunter Industries

Figure 14-14. The operation and adjustment of gear-driven rotary heads varies by manufacturer. Always refer to the owner's manual to determine proper operating procedures.

The radius of some gear-driven rotary heads may be adjustable. The ***sprinkler radius*** is the distance the sprinkler head is able to throw water. Sprinkler radius is measured from the sprinkler head to the furthest point of the stream of water.

Impact Rotary Heads

An ***impact rotary head*** rotates using a spring-loaded or weighted arm that is propelled by water pressure, which causes the circular movement of the head. Impact rotary heads are installed above ground and may be portable. In a nursery setting, impact rotary heads are installed several feet above ground to maximize arc and spray patterns, **Figure 14-15**. Impact rotary heads can apply as much as 2″ of water per hour, allowing the landscaper to quickly water a large area in a short amount of time.

Turf Rotors

Large, open, grassy areas, such as athletic fields and golf courses, commonly use ***turf rotors*** to provide irrigation. Turf rotors operate in the same manner as gear-driven rotary heads but apply much larger amounts of water in a very short time. Turf rotors require a large water supply and high pressure. A single turf rotor can cover a radius of up to 200′ and dispense up to 80 gallons of water per minute. With this type of efficiency, very few rotors are needed to cover large areas and they only need to run in short time increments.

Christopher D. Hart

Figure 14-15. Impact rotary sprinklers rotate due to water pressure.

Max Lindenthaler/Shutterstock.com

88studio/Shutterstock.com

sirichai chinprayoon/Shutterstock.com

Figure 14-16. Drip irrigation is used to conserve water. It can be used in a wide variety of applications, including crop, garden, and landscape irrigation.

Low-Volume Irrigation

Low-volume irrigation systems conserve water by reducing losses from evapotranspiration and runoff. Low-volume systems are typically used to water planting beds, individual trees and shrubs, and certain crops. Many low-volume irrigation systems require pressure regulators as they operate well below water pressure supplied from typical water supply lines. Low-volume irrigation systems also require filtration to ensure the irrigation components do not become clogged.

Drip Irrigation

Drip irrigation slowly and precisely applies water to the plant root zone, **Figure 14-16**. *Emitters* are small regulators that control the quantity and rate of the water discharge. The emitters are evenly spaced along the water line or hose to water each plant. Output from drip irrigation systems ranges from 1/2 to 2 gallons per hour (gph). Research shows that drip irrigation systems use as much as 50% less water than traditional sprinkler systems. Drip irrigation may also be referred to as *trickle irrigation*.

Micro-Sprinkler Heads

Micro-sprinkler heads are much smaller than traditional sprinkler heads but also deliver water in a fan-like spray. However, the micro-sprinklers operate with a much lower water pressure. Micro-sprinkler heads are not retractable and are usually used with a riser, **Figure 14-17**. Micro-sprinkler systems conserve more water than traditional sprinkler systems but do not conserve as much water as drip systems.

Soaker Hose

A *soaker hose* is a porous hose made from recycled tires that excretes water along its entire length, **Figure 14-18**. Additional hoses may be attached to extend the hose's reach. Soaker hoses provide a quick and efficient method of supplying water where an in-ground system is not an option.

jipatafoto89/Shutterstock.com

Figure 14-17. Although micro-sprinkler irrigation conserves water, it applies more water than drip irrigation.

Michael Major/Shutterstock.com

Figure 14-18. Soaker hoses are useful for watering in areas where it may not be possible to install a permanent irrigation system.

Irrigation Design

Proper planning and design of an irrigation system will save time during the installation phase. The irrigation designer uses the landscape design as a guide because he or she must know what types of plants, hardscape, and water features are being used to determine where water is needed and what type of equipment should be used. It is also important to be aware of the landscape plans because some parts of the irrigation system are easier to install before the plants are in place. Although irrigation system designs will vary by site, all plans should include or consider the following:

- Must comply with all state and local laws and restrictions.
- Proper plant selection plays a crucial role in developing a water smart landscape.
- Must be drawn to proper scale to ensure an accurate and effective system.
- Proper scale must be used so the contractor can properly estimate the materials required to complete the project.
- Must include the location of the buildings, walkways, driveways, parking lots, and any other feature of the site.
- Should include any areas where irrigation is to be applied.
- Must identify the main water source(s).
- Designed for efficient and effective water use as well as water conservation and recycling.

Design Symbols

Special symbols are used only for irrigation design components. Some of the symbols are standard, but there are variances. Always refer to the legend on the drawing to ensure proper reference of the symbols, **Figure 14-19.** Some designers include additional information, such as the type of sprinkler and nozzle required, the size of pipe and appropriate pressure rating, location of irrigation zones, and flow rates of sprinkler heads.

Analyzing the Area

The type of land end use and the area itself will influence an irrigation system's design. An irrigation system for athletic turf, for example, will vary greatly from the design of a residential irrigation system. Before starting the design, the contractor should answer the following questions:

1. What is the water requirement of the plants included in the design?
2. What are the desires of the property owner/client?
3. Where are structures, such as walkways, streets, parking lots and driveways, located (or to be located)?
4. What are the capabilities of the site?
5. Is the main water supply line a public or private source?
6. Where are utility lines, such as electrical, gas, water, and sewer lines, located?
7. Is the water supply sufficient to support the necessary design?

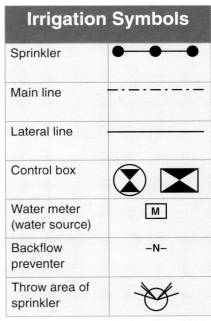

Goodheart-Willcox Publisher

Figure 14-19. The specific symbols used in irrigation system drawings will vary by designer. Refer to the legend on the plan to ensure accurate identification of the system components.

Determine Water Requirements

Determining water requirements of the landscape can be very difficult. Many factors impact water requirements, some more than others. Factors that must be considered when designing a landscape include the following:

- Day length.
- Average yearly rainfall.
- Humidity levels.
- Soil type.
- Plant species.

Soil Type

Soil types affect irrigation needs because they absorb water at different rates and have different limits as to how much water they can hold. Sandy-based soils, for example, require more frequent irrigation with less volume over a short period, whereas clay soils need less frequent irrigation with more volume over a long period.

Plant Species

The species of plants used will also have a *tremendous* impact on water requirements. The most effective and sustainable designs will have plants with similar water requirements planted in the same areas of the design. Keep in mind that most plants will require additional watering when they are first planted to ensure a healthy period of establishment. As the roots become established, they will absorb more moisture from the soil and supplemental irrigation can be reduced.

Once the irrigation system is installed and an irrigation system implemented, the only way to determine exact water requirements is by observation of the site.

Design Capacity

The *design capacity* of an irrigation system is the maximum amount of water (flow) that will be available for use at one time. The design capacity is determined by measuring water pressure and water volume. Water pressure can easily be determined by attaching a pressure gauge to the faucet nearest the water meter, **Figure 14-20**. Water pressure is measured in pounds per square inch (psi). Water volume will be determined by the size of the water meter and the size of the service line. The sizes are listed on the meter and service line. The manufacturer's chart can be used to determine design capacity simply by plugging in the sizes of the meter and service line. Manufacturer performance charts can also be used to determine precipitation rate. See **Figure 14-21**.

After the design capacity (water pressure and gpm) are determined, the number of sprinkler heads that can be in operation at the same time can be calculated. If the design capacity is 21 gpm, for example, and the sprinkler heads each use three gpm, only seven sprinkler heads may be in operation at the same time. This means you can run a maximum of seven sprinkler heads per zone.

R. Lee Ivy

Figure 14-20. Accurate water pressure readings can be taken with a pressure gauge installed near the water faucet.

Sprinkler System Design Capacity

Static Pressure psi		30	40	50	60	70	80
Water Meter	Service Line	Max gpm	Max gpm	Max gpm	Max gpm	Max gpm	Max gpm
5/8″	1/2″	2	4	5	6	7	7
	3/4″	4	6	8	8	10	12
	1″	4	7	8	10	13	15
3/4″	3/4″	4	6	8	9	10	12
	1″	5	7	10	14	17	20
	1 1/4″	5	12	17	20	22	22
1″	3/4″	4	7	8	9	12	12
	1″	5	8	14	18	20	20
	1 1/4″	5	14	24	26	30	34
Working Pressure psi		25	30	35	45	50	55

Photo courtesy of Hunter Industries

Figure 14-21. Using a sprinkler system design capacity chart will help you accurately determine the amount of water the irrigation system can displace. This information is necessary to determine the number of sprinkler heads that can be used per zone.

Precipitation Rate

Precipitation rate can be used to estimate the amount of water applied to the landscape. *Precipitation rate (PR)* is the rate at which water is applied in inches per hour. The formula for determining precipitation rate is:

$$PR = 96.25 \times \text{total gpm} / \text{Total area in square feet}$$

Factors that affect precipitation rates include sprinkler head sizes and their gpm rating, runoff, and soil infiltration rates. For example, if the site has a system capacity of 21 gpm and the area where irrigation is applied measures 3450 ft², the precipitation rate would be 0.59″ per hour.

$$96.25 \times 21 = 2021.25$$
$$2021.25 \div 3450 = 0.59″$$

A general recommendation for newly established plants is that they receive 1″ of rainfall or supplemental irrigation per week. In the above example, running the system for one hour would put out 0.59″ of water. The system would have to run almost two hours to apply the recommended 1″ of water.

Zone Placement

An *irrigation zone* is a section of an irrigation system that is controlled by a single valve. The same type of sprinkler head is used throughout a zone. The size of the area as well as design capacity will determine the number of zones required to irrigate the landscape. To ensure efficiency and adequate irrigation for the plants, each area of the landscape should be designed so that plants with similar water requirements are grouped together. These groupings can be used as a general guide to divide the landscape into multiple areas, which can then be divided into zones. The following formula may be used to determine the number of zones needed in each area:

$$\text{\# of zones (rounded up)} = \text{area gpm} \div \text{design capacity}$$

The next step is to add the output (in gpm) for each sprinkler head in the area. For example, if there are 15 sprinkler heads requiring 3 gpm each, the total area gpm is 45.

$$15 \times 3 = 45 \text{ gpm}$$

The gpm for the area is then divided by the design capacity. If the system has a design capacity of 21 gpm, it will take three zones to irrigate the area.

$$45 \div 21 = 2.14 \text{ (round up)}$$

You must round up in order to determine the specific number of zones. Refer to the simple residential irrigation plan in **Figure 14-22**. Note the two different zones required in this plan.

Once the number of zones has been determined, they can be wired to the controller to work sequentially. For example, if both the backyard and front yard of a property require three zones each, the controller should be wired so that the back three zones come on in sequential order and the zones in the front yard do the same.

Irrigation controllers are used to set the amount of time water is applied to each zone and when each zone is irrigated. Sprinklers in each irrigation zone should be closely monitored and adjusted to determine if sufficient moisture levels are being applied. Irrigation time periods will likely change throughout the growing season.

Christopher D. Hart

Figure 14-22. The sample irrigation plan indicates the number of zones required to water the area.

Sprinkler Placement

Distribution uniformity is a measure of how evenly water is applied throughout a site in each irrigation zone. Distribution uniformity is dependent on proper sprinkler placement. Distribution uniformity is also the key to creating an efficient and effective irrigation system. Head-to-head coverage should be used when placing sprinkler heads. *Head-to-head coverage* is the practice of placing sprinklers so the water from each one overlaps and reaches the next sprinkler head. If a sprinkler head's spray radius is 20', for example, sprinklers should be spaced 20' apart, **Figure 14-23**. If the spray does not reach the next irrigation head, the landscape will not be properly irrigated and there will be dry spots. Narrow and irregularly shaped areas will require additional sprinklers to ensure complete coverage.

Valve Placement

Valve placement can be determined once the number of zones and the location of sprinklers are determined. Each irrigation zone must have a control valve connecting it to the timer. The designer may choose to place all of the control valves together in a hidden spot. Valves grouped in the same location form a *valve manifold*, **Figure 14-24**. The designer may also choose to run a more direct path with the lateral lines and place the valves so that the actual valve is located inside of that irrigation zone. Placing the valve manifold where it is easily accessible makes it convenient for maintenance and repairs. The property owner may have a specific location in mind.

Pipe Placement

Although the specific distances, layout, and number of sprinklers varies between sprinkler systems, the pipes, sprinklers, lateral lines, and mainline are connected in the same basic order.

- The mainline is connected to the water supply. Main irrigation lines should be at least one size larger than the largest lateral line.

Figure 14-24. Control valves should be grouped for easier access.

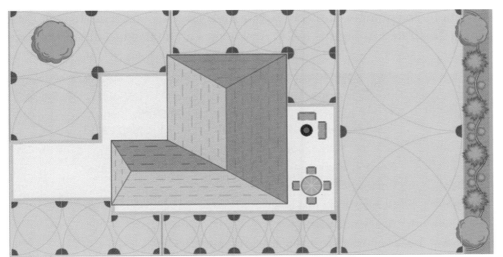

Photo courtesy of Hunter Industries

Figure 14-23. Sprinkler heads must be aligned to provide head-to-head coverage.

- A backflow preventer is installed between the mainline and the water supply to prevent backflow into the water supply.
- The zone valve manifolds are connected to the mainline.
- The sprinkler heads are connected to the lateral lines that are connected at the valve manifolds.

All system pipes should be laid with the fewest possible turns to reduce friction loss and ensure maximum water flow to the sprinklers.

Installing the System

Laws regarding who can design and install irrigation systems differ by state. Often times, irrigation contractors or landscape contractors install the irrigation system. The local government determines the requirements for obtaining a landscape irrigation certification. Local regulations should be checked before installing irrigation systems on residential properties with commercial sources of water. Commercial irrigation systems require the services of a certified irrigation contractor.

Locating Utility Lines

All telephone lines, gas lines, and water lines must be marked before digging begins. If they are not already marked for the landscape installation, call 811 to request assistance 3 to 5 days before excavation is scheduled to begin. A representative will locate and mark underground utility lines with marking paint and/or flags, **Figure 14-25**. All digging should be done within 18″ to 24″ of marked lines to reduce risk of cutting utility lines. Having these lines marked before you begin installation will save time and a great deal of frustration and fees for repair.

Point of Connection

Point of connection is the location where the irrigation system connects to the water supply. An irrigation system's point of connection is typically the pipe that connects the outside faucets. The local building codes will determine if a water meter must be installed specifically for the irrigation system of new construction. The point of connection for a high school football field's irrigation system is illustrated in **Figure 14-26**. A pipe tee can be used to direct the flow

Utility Marker Colors	
Flag Color	**Utility**
Red	Electric power lines, cables, conduit and lightning cables
Yellow	Gas, oil, steam, petroleum or gaseous materials
Orange	Communication, alarm or signal lines, cables or conduit
Blue	Potable water
Green	Sewers and drain lines
Purple	Reclaimed water
White	Proposed excavation limits or route

Goodheart-Willcox Publisher

Figure 14-25. Specific colors are used to identify the different utilities.

Christopher D. Hart

Figure 14-26. The point of connection should be easily accessible for maintenance and repairs.

of water to the irrigation control valves. Adding a shutoff valve, such as a ***stop-and-waste valve,*** will allow water going into the main water supply to be cut off and for water that is in the pipe above the ground to be drained easily for winterization.

Layout and Marking

Marking paint may be used to indicate where the irrigation lines and sprinklers are to be installed. The irrigation contractor must measure distances and follow plan specifications to ensure accurate system installation. Different colored paint can be used to indicate main lines and lateral lines and flags may be used to indicate sprinkler head placement, **Figure 14-27.**

R. Lee Ivy

Figure 14-27. Marking paint and flagging are very helpful when laying out the irrigation design before installation.

Trench Depth

Although ***trench shovels*** may be used to dig trenches for pipe installation, using a ***trenching machine*** is much more efficient. In the southeastern United States, the mainline should be buried 10″ to 12″ deep. Lateral lines should be buried 6″ to 8″ deep. The depth of irrigation lines may be regulated by local codes. The depth of the trench also depends on the frost line. The ***frost line*** is the maximum depth (in inches or millimeters) below which the soil does not freeze. Trenching machines may be leased from local rental companies. A manual sump pump may be useful to remove standing water around a broken pipe. A ***sump pump*** is a manual or electric pump that is used to move water, **Figure 14-28.**

Installing Pipes

Once the trench is dug, fittings and pipe can be placed in the trenches to allow quick installation and to ensure no components are missing. Main irrigation lines should be installed first. Once the pipe (mainline) is laid to the valve manifolds, leave enough space between the valves (6″ is recommended) to allow access for

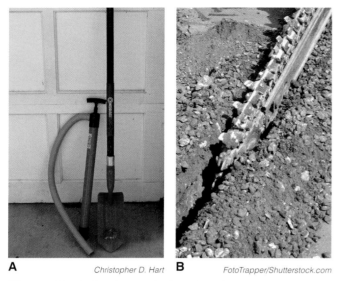

A   *Christopher D. Hart*   **B**   *FotoTrapper/Shutterstock.com*

Figure 14-28. A—A trench shovel and sump pump are useful tools for making irrigation pipe repairs. B—The small head on a trench digger makes it easier to dig around damaged pipes and connectors without causing more damage.

maintenance and repairs. It is recommended to stub and cap off one side of the valve manifold for future zone expansion. Once the valve manifolds have been installed, the lateral lines and spray heads may be installed.

PVC Pipes and Fittings

PVC pipe should be cut with a fine-tooth hacksaw and miter box, a power saw with a fine-toothed blade, or a PVC pipe cutter. Cuts must be made clean and straight and all plastic burrs must be removed before the solvent is applied. The plastic burrs may be removed from the lip of the cut pipe with a deburring tool, sharp blade, or a clean rag.

Safety First

Wear the proper respiratory protection when cutting PVC to prevent the inhalation of fine PVC particulates and work in well-ventilated areas when using solvent.

Clean the inside of the fitting and the outside of the pipe with a PVC primer to remove debris and produce a porous surface for a stronger weld. (PVC pipes are not glued but *solvent welded*.) Evenly swab a light amount of solvent to both the fitting and pipe and insert the pipe into the fitting. PVC fittings typically have a raised lip inside of the fitting. The pipe should be pushed into the fitting as far as possible for a secure fit. Once the pipe is inside the fitting it should be rotated 90° to ensure proper coverage. The solvent dries quickly so you will only have to hold it for a few seconds. See **Figure 14-29**.

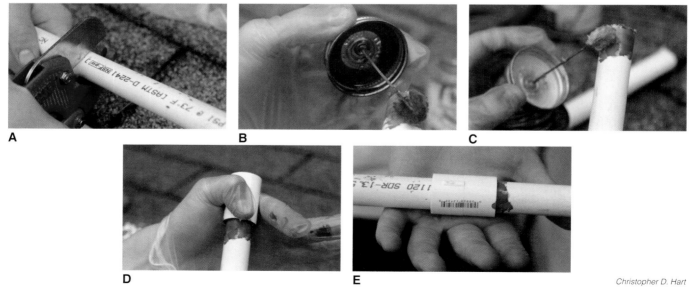

A   **B**   **C**

D   **E**   *Christopher D. Hart*

Figure 14-29. A—Use PVC cutters to cut pipe to length. B—Clean the pipe and prepare it for solvent with the primer. C—Apply solvent after the pipe is primed. D—Once the fitting is installed, rotated it 90° to ensure proper coverage of solvent on the pipe and fittings. E—A coupling used to join two pieces of PVC pipe.

Polyethylene Pipe

Barbed fittings and hose clamps are commonly used to hold flexible polyethylene pipe together, **Figure 14-30.** Depending on its size, the pipe may need to be heated before the fitting can be inserted. Most fittings have a mark or notch that indicates how deep the fitting should be inserted.

Galvanized Pipe

Galvanized pipe is screwed together with threads and thread tape. *Thread tape* is a nonsticky, stretchy white tape that provides a tight fit when joining galvanized pipe. The thread tape should be wrapped in a clockwise direction around the male end of the pipe. If the tape is wrapped in the wrong direction, it will begin to unravel when the new fittings are installed.

Installing Sprinkler Heads

Factors such as the end use, type of sprinkler head, spray radius, height, method of attachment, flow rate, and pipe diameters must be considered when installing any type of sprinkler head.

- Sprinkler heads installed on a lawn will differ from those used to water bushes or a vegetable garden.
- Lawn sprinklers are typically pop-up heads that must be installed at grade to avoid breakage from foot traffic or lawn maintenance equipment.
- Sprinkler heads must be installed at the proper height. The spray must clear foliage to ensure the arc achieves the desired reach to ensure proper coverage.
- Pipe sizing charts should be used to determine the maximum flow rates for sprinkler lines.
- The pipe should have a minimum diameter of 3/4″ connecting to the last sprinkler head.

It is also important to determine if you wish for the sprinkler head to be connected with rigid or flexible pipe to the lateral line. Connecting with flexible pipe allows the movement and exact placement of the sprinkler head. Rigid pipe offers no flexibility and it may crack if hit with a lawn mower or other equipment. Refer to **Figure 14-31.**

Methods of Attachment

Three main ways of attaching sprinkler heads to lateral lines are flexible pipe, rigid risers, and saddle fittings.

- **Flexible pipe.** Barb fittings are used to attach flexible pipe to rigid piping material. Flexible pipe allows the sprinkler head to be moved and installed exactly where it is needed.
- **Rigid risers.** Rigid risers are not flexible. If a rigid riser is used to attach a sprinkler head, there is a chance that the rigid material of the lateral line will break as well.
- **Saddle fittings.** This type of fitting is only used with polyethylene pipe. The fittings clamp onto the pipe and puncture the line. The bottom of the sprinkler head attaches to the top of the saddle fitting, **Figure 14-32.**

Christopher D. Hart

Figure 14-30. A—Polyethylene pipe may need to be heated before fittings can be inserted. B—Fittings should be inserted properly to prevent leaks. C—Hose clamps are used to secure the pipe to the fitting.

R. Lee Ivy

Figure 14-31. Flexible polyethylene pipe is used to connect the sprinkler head to the lateral line. The pipe allows for movement of the sprinkler head ensuring proper placement and flexibility.

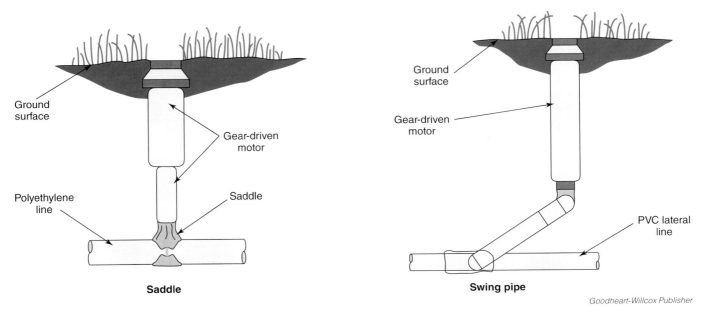

Goodheart-Willcox Publisher

Figure 14-32. Manufacturers often provide detailed images of system components.

Installing Wires

Electrical wire must be run from the sprinkler controller to each sprinkler valve. It is recommended that irrigation wire be placed 2″ to 4″ to the side or under the pipe in the pipe trench. It may also be placed in PVC conduit for protection from digging or rodent damage.

Irrigation systems are wired with one of two methods: a multi-strand system or a two-wire decoder system. The ***multi-strand system*** uses a common wire that runs from the controller to each control valve. Each control valve has a separate wire that runs directly from the control valve back to the controller. A white wire, referred to as *common* or *C*, is used to connect each zone, **Figure 14-33**. Extra wire is often included in the multi-strand system to allow for expansion of the irrigation zone. The ***two-wire decoder system*** uses two wires that run from the controller to the end of the system. A decoder is located at each valve. The decoder is assigned a specific number that the controller can send a signal to in order to open and close the valve.

All wiring for irrigation systems should be covered with an appropriate burial coating (wire insulation). All connections and wire splices should be covered with watertight connectors. All wiring, regardless of the system used, must connect back to the controller.

Programming the Controller

The location of the time clock should be determined based on available power sources. A 115V outlet is required to power the controller. Refer to the manufacturer's instructions for programming the clock.

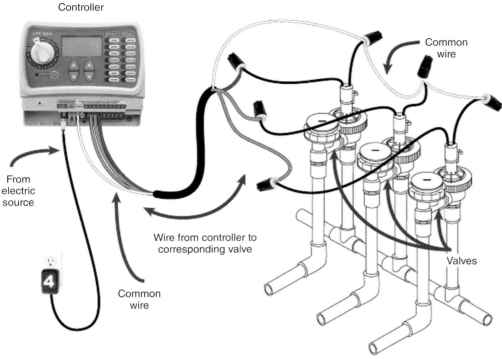

Controller

Common wire

From electric source

Wire from controller to corresponding valve

Common wire

Valves

Photo courtesy of Hunter Industries

Figure 14-33. In a multi-strand system, a common wire is connected to each control valve. One wire from each control valve also runs back to the irrigation controller.

Flushing the System

The system must be flushed before it is tested. New sprinkler head connections have temporary flushout nozzles that are left in place while the system is being assembled. Once the system is tested and soil is backfilled around the pipe, the system should be flushed. Flushing the system ensures that all debris that may have entered the pipe is flushed out. Flushing also allows you to check for leaks and proper wire connections. After the system has been flushed, the flushout nozzles can be removed and the appropriate nozzle installed.

Finalizing the Installation

Once the system has been flushed, it is time to backfill and cover the pipe. A *tamp* can be used to compact the soil to prevent settling. Once the pipe is covered, the flushout nozzles are removed and replaced with the sprinkler nozzles. The arcs can be adjusted accordingly.

Maintenance and Repair

Irrigation systems should be maintained and adjusted routinely to ensure efficiency and effectiveness and to catch problems early. Problems, such as a spike in water use, water in the valve manifold boxes, flooding around the base of a sprinkler, and water spurts or flooded areas in the ground between sprinkler heads, are indications of broken components. Broken components and poorly adjusted sprinklers waste water and will not properly cover the landscape.

Figure 14-34. Sprinkler head spray pattern and arc can be adjusted with a wide variety of tools.

Adjusting Sprinkler Heads

The most common irrigation maintenance job is the adjustment of sprinkler heads. The steps used to adjust the head will vary by manufacturer. Most require a special tool to adjust the arc. The arc should be adjusted so that water is only applied to intended areas, **Figure 14-34**.

Water that is spraying onto sidewalks, walkways, and parking lots can easily be identified through runoff. Proper coverage in irrigated areas may be more difficult to evaluate. *Catch devices* are cup-like devices that are placed at various points to collect and measure the amount of water applied during an irrigation cycle.

Replacing Broken Sprinkler Heads

Sprinkler heads are commonly broken, especially in areas of heavy foot or vehicle traffic. Replacing broken sprinkler heads is a simple task. The water supply to the zone where the head is being replaced must be shut off before repairs can be made. Different sprinkler heads should *not* be used in the same zone so it is important to use the appropriate sprinkler head replacement.

Replacing Control Valves

Irrigation systems that become unresponsive to the controller often have faulty control valves. If debris becomes lodged in the control valve's rubber diaphragm, it will diminish or block the water flow and the valve will be unresponsive. Carefully open the control valve and remove any debris before replacing the valve. Control valves come in threaded and slip options. If removing the debris does not solve the problem, replace the control valve with the appropriate size and style of control valve. Ensure all piping materials are on hand to properly reinstall the control valve.

Pro Tip

If more than one zone becomes unresponsive, there is likely an electrical problem or an issue with the controller itself.

Safety First

Call 811 to request that all telephone lines, gas lines, and water lines be marked before digging to make system repairs.

Pipe Repair

Unfortunately, underground irrigation lines can and will break. Once it is determined that a line is broken, it must be exposed for repair. If repairing the mainline, turn off the water supply and drain the system. If the broken pipe is a lateral line, ensure the irrigation zone is turned off. Use a trench shovel to carefully dig in the area of the suspected leak. Use a sump pump to remove any standing water.

Smaller diameter pipe is flexible and may be able to be repaired with new sections of pipe and couplings. Larger diameter pipe is more rigid and will often require a quick slip-repair coupling. A *quick-slip repair coupling* is a special type of coupling that is placed between two pieces of broken pipe. The special coupling expands to fit between the broken sections of pipe. It is then glued in place. It serves as a bridge to repair the section of broken pipe, **Figure 14-35.** Polyethylene and PEX pipes are flexible and can be cut and reinserted following the same steps explained earlier in the text.

Figure 14-35. A quick-slip repair coupling is used to connect larger diameter pipe that lacks flexibility.

Wire Repair

Irrigation wire that is damaged will not send the proper signals to turn on or off the system. A wire and valve locator is a handy tool that can be used to locate a break in the wire. The *wire and valve locator* generates a tone when it senses electrical current in the line. The locator is held above the ground and close to the wire while walking along its path. The locator stops emitting the tone when it no longer senses the electrical current. Once the broken wire is located and uncovered, a new wire can be run or the existing wire can be spliced together.

Flushing the System

A reduction in water pressure in irrigation systems may be caused by dirty nozzles or irrigation lines. Lines can be clogged with soil, rocks, trash, algae and other debris. Most emitters and nozzles have mesh filters to help filter debris. These filters and emitters in drip irrigation systems are especially prone to clogs. Removing emitters or nozzles and turning on the proper irrigation zone can flush irrigation lines. Emitters and nozzles should be replaced and then reinstalled in the system.

Winterizing the System

Irrigation systems in climates that experience freezing temperatures must be winterized. Water expands when it freezes and any water left in irrigation pipes may freeze and cause the pipes and/or fittings to break. The exact steps for winterizing an irrigation system depend on the layout of the system and its location. System manufacturers may also have specific instructions. Basic steps in winterizing an irrigation system are as follows:

1. Turn off the irrigation system's main water supply. Insulate or remove the backflow valve to protect it from freezing.
2. If the backflow is left in place, locate the air compressor's connection point on the backflow preventer and connect the air compressor.
3. Using the controller, open the valve farthest from the main water supply.
4. Start the air compressor and slowly increase pressure. Turn off the compressor when air is expelled from the sprinkler heads.
5. Repeat steps 3 and 4 for each valve in the system.
6. When you are finished, set the controller to rain mode. This will shut down the time clock but will still store the programmed settings in the controller.

Summary

- Many areas require irrigation because they lack sufficient rainfall to produce and maintain high quality turf and landscapes throughout the growing season.
- Public or private water sources used in irrigation systems include reservoirs, ponds, retention ponds, and detention ponds.
- Pumping water from a source and into an irrigation system is a very basic process that applies the science of hydraulics.
- The types of components used in an irrigation system will vary based on the specifications and requirements of the irrigation system.
- Mainlines are large diameter pipes that carry water from the point of connection to the irrigation system's lateral lines.
- Backflow preventers are irrigation system valves that prevent water from flowing back into the water supply lines.
- PVC, galvanized steel, PEX, polyethylene, and copper are all materials used in irrigation piping and fittings.
- Irrigation controllers send electrical signals to solenoid valves to manage timing, duration, location, and the amount of water applied.
- Sprinkler irrigation uses pop-up sprinkler heads, gear-driven rotary heads, impact rotary heads, and turf rotors to apply water to the landscape.
- Low-volume irrigation systems, such as drip irrigation, micro-sprinkler heads, and soaker hoses, conserve water by reducing losses from evapotranspiration and runoff.
- Before the irrigation system is installed, it should first be planned and designed to scale on paper. The site should be analyzed, locating existing pipes and wires at the site.
- The irrigation designer uses the landscape design as a guide because he or she must know what types of plants, hardscape, and water features are being used to determine where water is needed and what type of equipment should be used.
- The design capacity of a system determines the number of zones and sprinkler heads that a system can support. Water pressure and flow must be calculated to determine a system's design capacity.
- Marking paint and construction flags can be used to mark the location of mainlines, lateral lines, and sprinkler heads.
- Irrigation lines should be buried below the area's frost line to prevent pipelines from freezing during extremely cold weather.
- A new installation must be flushed before it is tested and backfilled. Flushing the system removes debris from the line and allows the installer to locate leaks and/or problems with the wire connections.

Chapter Review

Know and Understand ⤷

Answer the following questions using the information provided in this chapter.

1. *True or False?* The characteristics of a water source influence the resources, tools, and materials needed to design an efficient irrigation system.
   A. True.
   B. False.

2. A public water system may draw water from _____.
   A. wells
   B. rivers
   C. reservoirs
   D. All of the above.

3. Which of the following is used to indicate the water in the system is reclaimed wastewater?
   A. Red piping and heads.
   B. Purple piping and heads.
   C. Green piping and heads.
   D. Any of the above.

4. Which of the following water sources is most common in rural areas?
   A. Farm ponds.
   B. Wells.
   C. Reservoirs.
   D. Lakes.

5. *True or False?* A well's output is the flow of water measured in gallons per hour.
   A. True.
   B. False.

6. *True or False?* The amount of water an irrigation system applies is measured in gallons per minute.
   A. True.
   B. False.

7. *True or False?* The output of individual sprinkler heads is commonly measured in gallons per minute (gpm).
   A. True.
   B. False.

8. Which of the following is used in a system where there is insufficient pressure?
   A. A pressure pump.
   B. A pressure irrigator.
   C. A pressure tank.
   D. All of the above.

9. Which of the following temporarily holds excess water that eventually drains completely?
   A. A retention pond.
   B. A detention pond.
   C. An intention pond.
   D. A filtration pond.

10. Which of the following holds a permanent pool of water that may be used for irrigation?
   A. A retention pond.
   B. A detention pond.
   C. An intention pond.
   D. A filtration pond.

11. The science and technology of the movement of liquids is _____.
   A. hydroponics
   B. mnemonics
   C. hydraulics
   D. histrionics

12. *True or False?* There must be sufficient pressure applied to the water to create enough water pressure to force the water to the desired location.
   A. True.
   B. False.

13. Which of the following statements is true about water pressure?
   A. Too low results in large droplets and possibly improper coverage.
   B. Too high results in too fine a mist, creating drift and improper coverage
   C. Consistent pressure results in uniform water application.
   D. All of the above.

14. Which of the following factors must be considered when designing an irrigation system?
    A. A decrease in elevation will increase water pressure.
    B. Water pressure increases as it flows with gravity.
    C. Friction will not affect water pressure.
    D. All of the above.

15. *True or False?* The amount of water pressure lost through friction depends on the pipe's internal texture, length, and diameter and the flow rate of the water.
    A. True.
    B. False.

16. *True or False?* A smaller pipe diameter can be used to decrease water pressure whereas a larger pipe can be used to raise water pressure while increasing volume.
    A. True.
    B. False.

17. Of the following, which is a mechanical device used to move or distribute water from its source to where it is needed?
    A. Lateral line.
    B. Mainline.
    C. Pump.
    D. Valve.

18. Which of the following is used to control water flow at various points in the system or to cut all water supply?
    A. Controller.
    B. Mainline.
    C. Pump.
    D. Valve.

19. Which of the following is used to prevent water from flowing back into the water supply lines?
    A. Backflow preventer.
    B. Control valve.
    C. Backflow line.
    D. Mainline controller.

20. Which of the following is required to connect the water supply to each individual zone?
    A. Control valve.
    B. Lateral line.
    C. Mainline valve.
    D. Pump controller.

21. Which of the following is a large diameter pipe that carries water to the lines connected to the sprinkler heads or emitters?
    A. Lateral line.
    B. Mainline.
    C. Pump line.
    D. Valve line.

22. Which of the following is a smaller diameter pipe that carries water from the mainline to the sprinkler head or emitter?
    A. Lateral line.
    B. Mainline.
    C. Pump line.
    D. Valve line.

23. Which of the following is a piping material that is cost efficient, readily available, lightweight, and corrosion-resistant?
    A. PEX.
    B. Polyethylene pipe.
    C. PVC.
    D. Copper pipe.

24. Which of the following is a piping material made with zinc-coated metal?
    A. PVC.
    B. PEX.
    C. Polyethylene pipe.
    D. Galvanized pipe.

25. Which of the following is a flexible piping material made from high-density polyethylene?
    A. PVC.
    B. PEX.
    C. Copper pipe.
    D. Galvanized pipe.

26. Which of the following is a piping material that may be colored and can be used above ground?
    A. PVC.
    B. PEX.
    C. Polyethylene pipe.
    D. Galvanized pipe.

27. Which of the following is a piping material that is used in high-water pressure areas of in irrigation system's tubing, such as around valve connections and meters?
A. Copper pipe.
B. Polyethylene pipe.
C. Galvanized pipe.
D. PVC.

28. *True or False?* Fittings control the layout of the pipe as well as the water pressure and flow rate.
A. True.
B. False.

29. *True or False?* Some of the actions an irrigation controller can manage include timing, duration, location, and the amount of water applied.
A. True.
B. False.

30. Which of the following factors affect the type of system that would be appropriate for a given site?
A. The available water volume.
B. The static water pressure.
C. Type of land being irrigated.
D. All of the above.

31. Which of the following sprinkler heads are used in small areas of a landscape?
A. Pop-up.
B. Impact rotary head.
C. Gear-driven rotary head.
D. Large turf rotor.

32. Which of the following is an advantage of pop-up sprinkler heads?
A. Prevents tripping.
B. Allows mowing.
C. Aesthetically pleasing.
D. All of the above.

33. Which of the following are commonly used in commercial landscape settings?
A. Pop-up rotary head.
B. Impact rotary head.
C. Gear-driven rotary head.
D. Large gear rotor.

34. *True or False?* The area of a circle irrigated by a sprinkler head is the riser.
A. True.
B. False.

35. *True or False?* The area of a circle irrigated by a sprinkler head is the arc.
A. True.
B. False.

36. Which of the following uses a spring-loaded or weighted arm, which is propelled by water pressure?
A. Gear-driven rotary head.
B. Turf rotary head.
C. Impact rotary head.
D. All of the above.

37. Which of the following applies the large amounts of water needed on athletic fields or golf courses in a very short time?
A. Turf rotor.
B. Impact rotor.
C. Gear-driven rotor.
D. Pop-up rotor.

38. *True or False?* Drip irrigation uses emitters to apply water to the root zone and uses as much as 50% less water than traditional sprinkler systems.
A. True.
B. False.

39. *True or False?* Micro-sprinkler systems conserve more water than drip irrigation systems.
A. True.
B. False.

40. *True or False?* The irrigation designer uses the landscape design as a guide to determine where water is needed and what type of equipment should be used.
A. True.
B. False.

41. Which of the following statements apply to a landscape design?
A. Must be drawn accurately to scale.
B. Must include the location of buildings, driveways, and walkways.
C. Must identify the main water source(s).
D. All of the above.

42. *True or False?* There are no variances in the symbols different designers use to indicate system components.
    A. True.
    B. False.

43. Which of the following factors affect the water requirements of a landscape?
    A. Humidity levels, soil type, and plant species.
    B. The location of the utility lines.
    C. The height of the street curb and sidewalk width.
    D. All of the above.

44. *True or False?* Soil types affect irrigation needs because they absorb water at different rates and have different limits as to how much water they can hold.
    A. True.
    B. False.

45. The species of plants used in a design have little impact on water requirements.
    A. True.
    B. False.

46. The maximum amount of water (flow) that will be available for use at one time is an irrigation system's _____.
    A. install capacity
    B. pressure capacity
    C. design capacity
    D. base capacity

47. If the design capacity is 28 gpm and the sprinkler heads each use 5 gpm, how many heads may be in operation at the same time?
    A. 3
    B. 5
    C. 7
    D. 8

48. If the design capacity is 36 gpm and the sprinkler heads each use 8 gpm, how many heads may be in operation at the same time?
    A. 4
    B. 4.5
    C. 4.75
    D. 5

49. What would the precipitation rate in an irrigation system be if the design capacity allowed for 25 gpm and covered 4350 ft²?
    A. 0.59"
    B. 0.62"
    C. 0.47"
    D. 0.55"

50. If the precipitation rate for an irrigation system is 0.55", and it has a capacity for 30 gpm, what amount of area does it cover?
    A. 4670 ft²
    B. 5250 ft²
    C. 3790 ft²
    D. 6350 ft²

51. A measure of how evenly water is applied throughout a site in each irrigation zone is referred to as _____.
    A. head-to-head coverage
    B. uniform placement
    C. distribution uniformity
    D. sequential coverage

52. *True or False?* Valves for each zone may be placed in the same location to form a valve manifold.
    A. True.
    B. False.

53. *True or False?* All system pipes should be laid with the fewest possible turns to ensure maximum water flow to the sprinklers.
    A. True.
    B. False.

54. To reduce risk of cutting utility lines, all digging should be done within _____.
    A. 5" to 10" of marked lines
    B. 12" to 20" of marked lines
    C. 18" to 24" of marked lines
    D. 36" to 48" of marked lines

55. The point of connection is the location where the irrigation system connects to the _____.
    A. sprinkler heads
    B. risers
    C. manifold
    D. water supply

56. *True or False?* The irrigation contractor marks the location of the lines and sprinkler heads with paint before installing the system.
    A. True.
    B. False.

57. *True or False?* The frost line is the minimum depth below which the soil does not freeze.
    A. True.
    B. False.

58. A manual or electric pump that is used to move water is referred to as a _____.
    A. sump pump
    B. trench pump
    C. line pump
    D. mainline pump

59. In which order should the irrigation pipes be laid?
    A. Valve manifold, mainline, lateral lines, and spray heads.
    B. Mainline, valve manifold, lateral lines, and spray heads.

60. Which of the following tools should be used to cut PVC pipe?
    A. Fine-tooth hacksaw and miter box.
    B. PVC pipe cutter.
    C. Power saw with a fine-toothed blade.
    D. All of the above.

61. Before connecting PVC pipe to a fitting, the inside of the PVC fitting should be cleaned and _____.
    A. drained
    B. abraded
    C. primed
    D. All of the above.

62. *True or False?* Barbed fittings and hose clamps are commonly used to connect galvanized pipe.
    A. True.
    B. False.

63. *True or False?* Flexible polyethylene pipe is connected by screwing the pipes together with threads and thread tape.
    A. True.
    B. False.

64. *True or False?* The sprinkler heads installed on a lawn are the same as those used to water hedges or a vegetable garden.
    A. True.
    B. False.

65. *True or False?* Pop-up head sprinklers are installed at grade to avoid breakage from foot traffic or lawn maintenance equipment.
    A. True.
    B. False.

66. The pipe connecting to the last sprinkler head should have a minimum diameter of _____.
    A. 1/4"
    B. 1/2"
    C. 3/4"
    D. 1"

67. Which of the following methods of attachment allows the sprinkler head to be moved and installed exactly where it is needed?
    A. Rigid risers.
    B. Saddle fittings.
    C. Flexible pipe.
    D. All of the above.

68. Which of the following methods of attachment will likely break the lateral line if the attachment is broken?
    A. Rigid risers.
    B. Saddle fittings.
    C. Flexible pipe.
    D. All of the above.

69. Which of the following methods of attachment is used solely with polyethylene pipe?
    A. Rigid risers.
    B. Saddle fittings.
    C. Flexible pipe.
    D. All of the above.

70. *True or False?* Irrigation wire should be installed to the side or under the pipe in a pipe trench.
    A. True.
    B. False.

71. In a multi-strand system, the white wire connected to each zone is the _____.
   A. decoder wire
   B. odd wire
   C. common wire
   D. connection wire

72. *True or False?* A decoder is located at every other valve in a two-wire decoder system.
   A. True.
   B. False.

73. The system must be flushed before it is tested. What purpose does flushing serve?
   A. To check for leaks.
   B. To check wire connections.
   C. To remove all debris.
   D. All of the above.

74. Which of the following indicates there may be a problem with the irrigation system?
   A. Flooded area between sprinkler heads.
   B. There is a spike in water use.
   C. There is water in the manifold boxes.
   D. All of the above.

75. *True or False?* The sprinkler heads used to replace broken heads may be a different type of sprinkler head than others in the zone.
   A. True.
   B. False.

76. *True or False?* If the system becomes unresponsive to the controller, the technician should remove any debris in and around the control valve before replacing the valve.
   A. True.
   B. False.

77. *True or False?* Larger diameter pipe is flexible and may be able to be repaired with new sections of pipe and couplings.
   A. True.
   B. False.

78. *True or False?* A reduction in water pressure in irrigation systems may be caused by dirty nozzles or irrigation lines.
   A. True.
   B. False.

79. *True or False?* An irrigation system should be winterized to prevent damage from water freezing in the pipes.
   A. True.
   B. False.

80. *True or False?* The steps for winterizing an irrigation system depend on the layout of the system and its location.
   A. True.
   B. False.

Thinking Critically

1. What might happen if you placed different types of sprinkler heads in one zone?
2. How would you prioritize tasks when installing a new sprinkler system?
3. What are the advantages and disadvantages of using an underground sprinkler system?

Suggested Activities

1. Your instructor will provide you with a location on the school campus for which you will design a complete irrigation plan. Work with a partner or small group to measure the area and determine slope. Include elements for all aspects, such as the water source, the number of sprinkler heads, and the throw area of the sprinklers.
2. Expand on the preceding activity by calculating the cost of the parts, supplies, and labor for system installation. Use prices from an online supplier.
3. Calculate the maximum gpm for a system with a 3/4" water meter and a 3/4" line. The static water pressure of the system is 40 psi. Use the sprinkler system design capacity chart in **Figure 14-21** to determine the maximum gpm of the irrigation system.
3. Working with a partner, use an online GIS tool to locate your school. Using the satellite image, select an area in which irrigation will be installed (theoretically). Use the GIS system to determine the square footage of the area. Measure the square footage of additional areas on campus, such as the athletic fields, parking lot, or other areas with turf.
4. Work with your partner to design an irrigation system for one of the areas measured in the previous activity. Label main lines, lateral lines, and the throw area of the sprinklers.
5. What factors of irrigation system installation are involved in the bidding process?
6. Which local and state regulations affect the installation and use of irrigation systems in your community?
7. Compare and contrast the use of various plant irrigation methods based on plant needs, effectiveness, and economic feasibility.
8. Evaluate types of irrigation systems based on plant needs, effectiveness, feasibility, and ease of use.

CHAPTER
15

Hardscapes

Chapter Outcomes

After studying this chapter, you will be able to:

- Identify the different types of hardscapes and their functions in the landscape.
- List the elements of a hardscape that a designer must consider when creating a hardscape design.
- Identify and explain the components of a hardscape.
- List the materials used to construct hardscapes.
- Accurately calculate materials needed to construct a hardscape.
- Identify and explain the function of tools and equipment used to install a hardscape.
- Describe strategies for properly installing hardscapes.

Key Terms ➦

aggregate
brick paver
compactor
composite lumber
concrete paver
deck
dry-laying
efflorescence
face mixing
geotextile

grade
hand tamper
hardscape
patio
pattern
paving tile
permeability
pressure-treated wood
retaining wall
screed

slope
stone paver
subsurface
tamping
topdressing
vibratory tamper
walkway
wet-laying

Introduction

Landscapes often incorporate *hardscapes*, which serve as walkways, gathering areas, driveways, and focal points. Hardscapes guide the eyes through a landscape because of their unique colors, textures, patterns, and construction materials. They are often made of wood, stone, or concrete. When creating a hardscape design, you should consider the client's desires, along with the safety, functionality, installation, performance, and maintenance of the hardscape. This chapter introduces you to different types of hardscapes, hardscape materials, and installation procedures.

Figure 15-1. Hardscape areas should be designed to create inviting and relaxing areas. Plant materials, bright colors, and special lighting effects are used to enhance these areas.

Types of Hardscapes

When installing a new landscape, homeowners typically request that a type of hardscape also be included. Most hardscapes are built for functionality; however, they also serve as an important aesthetic feature. The hardscape may be a simple stone walkway to the front door, a wooden deck for family dinners, or an elaborate walkway that surrounds a pool, **Figure 15-1**. The most successful hardscapes fulfill the client's needs and complement both the softscape and the home.

Walkways

Walkways are hardscapes that provide access to and from entryways, invite visitors to walk through the garden, and provide a clear and safe means of accomplishing chores, such as taking out the trash. Walkways can also lead a landscape viewer past unique landscape features or into an area revealing a unique view or perspective, **Figure 15-2**.

Figure 15-2. Unique pathways pique a visitor's curiosity and invite them to continue walking along the path.

Standard Widths

Walkways should be wide enough for at least one person to walk comfortably. A minimum standard is 24″. It must be twice that width, or 48″, to allow two people to walk side by side or to pass each other without stepping off the path. The path must be at least 36″ wide to be suitable for a wheelchair. The width of a path should also be in proportion to the home. A large home with an expansive yard, for example, may have a path ranging from 5′ to 10′ wide.

Driveways

Driveways are often one of the largest hardscapes in residential landscapes. The standard material used for most homes is poured concrete. If it is not practical to replace a driveway, designers may have to leave the driveway as it is or perhaps line both sides with stone or bricks to make it more interesting. If the driveway is going to be newly installed or replaced, a designer may include it in the design. Driveways can be one continuous surface or divided into tire paths with groundcover between the paths. The materials used often depend on the client's choice and/or the budget, **Figure 15-3**. The design and installation of a driveway and other hardscapes may be subject to local building regulations and codes.

romakoma/Shutterstock.com

Figure 15-3. Driveways should match the home in style, material, and proportion.

Patios and Decks

Patios are recreational areas adjoining a building, such as a home, to extend the living area and are often used for outdoor dining. Patios are typically made with hard surface materials, such as stone, pavers, or concrete, and are usually at ground level, **Figure 15-4A**. These areas should be designed with sufficient space for chairs and tables and enough area for people to sit or stand and socialize. A *deck* is typically a raised platform constructed with wood or a composite made from a combination of recycled wood and plastic. Decks often have aesthetic and practical features, such as multiple levels, built-in seating and storage, firepits, and built-in lighting, **Figure 15-4B**.

A   *Ozgur Coskun/Shutterstock.com*

B   *Dariusz Jarzabek/Shutterstock.com*

Figure 15-4. A—Patios provide places to gather, dine, and socialize with family and friends. B—Decks often have multiple levels, steps, and rails, which add interest to the design and create more areas for socializing.

Patios and decks are valued for their versatility and as an extension of indoor living space. In many parts of the country, these areas are used for many months of the year for entertaining, relaxation, and as a viewing platform to observe other features of the landscape and surrounding areas.

Stairs

Outdoor stairs are needed on raised decks and in sloped areas of the landscape design. (*Slope* is the rise and fall of the land surface or a change in elevation from a fixed point. It may also be referred to as the *grade* of the land.) The stairs may be purely functional, such as one or two wooden steps leading down from a raised wooden deck, or an integral part of the design.

For safety and ease of use, outdoor stairs should be constructed at the same standard height (7″) and width (11″) used for interior stairs. The width of the step may be wider, but no less than 11″. If the surface area may become slippery when wet, each step should be textured or have some sort of traction strip to prevent falls. Stairs may be made with a variety of materials, including wood, stone, brick, poured concrete, and pavers, **Figure 15-5**.

Walls

Walls may be used for multiple purposes, including providing privacy, creating borders, confining pets, directing the eye to a focal point, or blocking an undesirable view. Walls may be created with a single type of material or a combination of materials. Hardscape walls are typically made from wood or wood composites. They may also be made from many of the same materials used for patios and other hardscapes.

Retaining Walls

A *retaining wall* is a structure that holds or retains the soil behind it to reduce soil loss through erosion as well as mitigate other soil moisture concerns, **Figure 15-6**. This type of wall is often used on sloped sites to increase the usefulness of an area by creating terraces with flat surfaces. A retaining wall may also be used to protect the roots of an existing tree before and after the landscape is installed. A low retaining wall (less than 1′) is often more aesthetic than functional. It may, however, be used to border a raised area and even provide seating if wide enough. The National Concrete Masonry Association provides instructions and diagrams on their website for building retaining walls.

aodaodaodaod/Shutterstock.com

Manfred Ruckszio/Shutterstock.com

Manfred Ruckszio/Shutterstock.com

Figure 15-5. Creative or unusual outdoor steps can be focal points that attract attention and guide visitors through the landscape. The materials used should complement both the landscape and structures, such as a home.

Figure 15-6. In many landscapes, retaining walls are necessary to keep soil and other landscape elements in place. A retaining wall can be simple and hidden with plant materials or it can be a pronounced element in the landscape.

Fences

A fence may also serve as a wall in a design. The type of fence material used will vary by its intended use and the client's desire. Fences may be made from stone, metal, wood, vinyl, or a wood composite. The materials vary mainly by appearance, capability, and cost. Fencing styles include privacy, semi-privacy, picket, lattice, and rail-type.

Outdoor Kitchens

An outdoor kitchen provides an extended cooking and dining area to the homeowner, **Figure 15-7.** This type of environment allows the host to interact more with the guests while preparing the meal. The outdoor kitchen may include a preparation area, refrigeration, cooking appliances, and a serving area. Many outdoor kitchens also include a sink with running water. An area with all these features will require professional installation of electrical wiring and plumbing for gas and water service. The appliances must be waterproof or protected from the elements to prevent damage and extend their service lives. Temporary or permanent overhead protection may also be incorporated into the design to protect the area from rain and sunshine.

Figure 15-7. Outdoor kitchens are enjoyed in many areas across the country. They may be used for everyday dining or for preparing food for larger gatherings.

Figure 15-8. Another popular feature is the open firepit. Firepits extend the utility of a living space, as many families enjoy late nights sitting around the fire. Seating may be built as part of the design, or enough space is provided to accommodate chairs.

Firepits

Firepits have become a popular addition to many landscapes. Firepits are usually integrated into the entertainment area and can range from very simple to elaborate and expensive designs. The design should complement the home and surrounding hardscape.

The area around the firepit is made of hardscape materials, such as stone or pavers, to create a safe and secure location for the fire. The center of the firepit holds the firewood or a natural gas or propane burner. All firepits must have a means for water drainage and adjustable ventilation for a successful flame. Firepit designs may be subject to local regulations and installation ordinances and may need to be submitted for review and approval, **Figure 15-8**.

Hardscape Design

Hardscape design provides an opportunity to use creativity while building function and flow through outdoor rooms and walkways. First, the designer must consider user safety when creating a hardscape design because much of the hardscape is designed for foot traffic and movement of people through the area. Other important considerations include water flow and permeability through the materials, patterns, and acceptable slope for safety and drainage.

Safety

To ensure a safe hardscape design, a designer must consider multiple aspects of the site, including the slope of the land and the amount of daylight the area receives, especially at dusk and dawn. As stated earlier, slope is the rise and fall of the land surface or a change in elevation from a fixed point. Rapid changes in slope should be avoided, as they are more likely to cause trips and falls. A designer can indicate up and down directions on steps using lighting, signage, or markings on the path. A handrail or marker post designating a change is helpful in the case of a step up or down. In the case of sight impaired persons, a series of tactile pavers may be used.

c12/Shutterstock.com   *Sumetha Suebchat/Shutterstock.com*   *Yesakova Natalia/Shutterstock.com*   *Robie Online/Shutterstock.com*

Figure 15-9. Surface textures are used to create a safe walking surface in low light and wet conditions and to add visual interest to walls and flooring.

Texture

The texture of a surface should be considered as well. A very rough texture might cause shoes to grip too much and become a tripping hazard, **Figure 15-9.** Conversely, a very smooth surface may become slick at the slightest hint of moisture.

Pattern

A *pattern* may be defined as a repeated decorative design or the recurring use of a specific element in a design. In hardscaping, patterns can be created with many types of materials and can be designed to mirror existing natural patterns or duplicate architectural patterns of existing structures. A natural pattern design in an area with rock outcroppings, for example, could be emulated in the choice and placement of material. The distinct structural lines used in a modern home could be emulated with distinct lines in the hardscape components, such as in the driveway or walking paths and with materials with straight edges. See **Figure 15-10.**

R. Lee Ivy

Figure 15-10. Pavers may be laid in traditional patterns or in unique designs. The patterns, colors, and textures create visual interest and may guide traffic flow through an area. A—Basketweave brick pattern. B—Mixed stone walkway. C—Running bond brick pattern. D—Three-pieced scallop pattern. E/F—Irregular patterns.

Figure 15-11. Hardscapes designed for water permeability enable rainwater to return to the ground and prevent it from channeling into storm drains or other offsite areas.

The materials used in hardscapes and the design itself should complement the home and softscape. Some materials lend themselves to more formal and structured patterns where others can be used to create less formal and even whimsical patterns. Many of the patterns used when laying stone, paver, or brick walkways, driveways, and patios can be identified by name.

A designer using pavers or wood will often place a soldier course (a repetition of the same material in the same pattern) around the edge of a hardscape area. This design uses the material in a *one right after the other pattern* and visually provides a border. A pattern would then be placed within the soldier course, creating more visual emphasis on the inside pattern.

Water Flow

When creating a landscape design, the designer must consider the flow of water as it contacts the surface of each hardscape material used in the design. Textured and rough surfaces often provide enough traction when wet. However, smooth surfaces may become hazardous in wet conditions. The permeability of a material will also affect water flow across the landscape.

Permeability

The *permeability* of a landscape material is measured by the amount of water it allows to pass through to the ground below. Materials that are more permeable include mulch, stone aggregates, and turf or groundcover, **Figure 15-11**. Areas covered with these materials will not deflect water unless the ground is completely saturated. Water that seeps into the ground will resupply groundwater. When using less permeable materials in a design, such as concrete, a designer must consider not only the safety factor but also where water will flow when it hits the surface. Permeable brick or concrete pavers are constructed with vertical spacer bars on the edges that create a space between the units and allow water to permeate into the soil below. Porous material, such as sand, is used between the units. This porosity also helps prevent cracking or shifting of hardscape materials during the freeze-thaw cycles of winter.

Slope

To ensure water will be directed in the desired direction, impermeable hardscapes must have at least a 1% slope. (*Slope* is the rise and fall of the land surface or a change in elevation from a fixed point.) Incorporating sufficient slope to an impermeable hardscape will ensure that water will be directed in the desired direction. The area to which the water is directed could be the lawn at the edge of a patio, flower/plant beds, a pond, or a storm drain. The slope of the lawn will direct overflow to the storm drain or other natural waterway.

In some designs, water is directed to a sub-drainage system. A sub-drainage system is a low-impact design that allows the water from the hardscape to flow into the groundwater supply. A sub-drainage system is piping below ground level that helps water drain from hard surfaces. An example would be to place a course of aggregate, such as pea gravel, over a porous sub-drainage system, **Figure 15-12**. (An *aggregate* is a collection of units, such as gravel, used together.) This course aggregate can be adhered to itself with a liquid adhesive-like substance that keeps the aggregate in place but also allows water to permeate into groundwater supplies.

When adjacent to a structure, an impermeable hardscape must have at least a 1% slope away from the structure. This will direct water away from the structure and prevent water from flowing under the structure and hardscape. If water remains under the hardscape, it will expand and possibly shift or crack the hardscape as it freezes and thaws. The proper slope is achieved by determining the vertical change across a defined horizontal distance. The units must be calculated using the same units of measurement. A simple way to ensure that slope is a 1″ drop over 8′ can be achieved by adding a level to the top of an 8′ board or string with level and measuring the distance from the ground to the board or string.

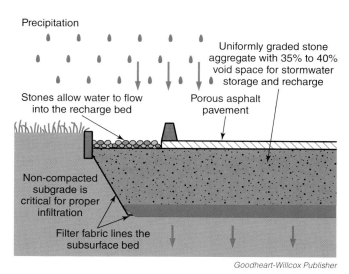

Goodheart-Willcox Publisher

Figure 15-12. Hardscape materials can provide solid walking and driving surfaces and still allow water permeability.

Hardscape Materials

A wide variety of materials, such as stone or concrete, may be used to create hardscapes. Hardscape materials must meet the client's expectations, have reasonable longevity, and accentuate the architectural features of the existing structure. Many designers choose materials based on what is available locally to simplify transport and reduce shipping costs. Unit pavers, stone, wood or wood composites, concrete, local or upcycled materials, asphalt, and gravel are some of the most common hardscape materials. See **Figure 15-13**.

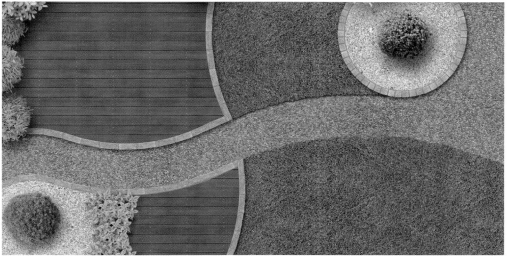

Little Perfect Stock/Shutterstock.com

Figure 15-13. A designer may use natural materials, such as wood and stone, with manufactured products, such as brick and concrete pavers, to create unique landscapes.

Pavers

Pavers are individual units of hard paving materials made of clay, stone, brick, or concrete. The type of materials used in a landscape design may depend on what is available locally. The main differences between pavers are cost, ease of handling, and durability.

- A *paving tile* is typically a glazed decorated tile that can be used as flooring or wall covering. Paving tiles come in many colors, sizes, and styles and may be made of stone, ceramic, clay, porcelain, or concrete. Paving tiles are typically much more expensive than other paving materials.
- *Stone pavers* are made of stone and are often cut into square or rectangular shapes. They may also be used in their natural, irregular shapes. Part of their beauty is their natural color variations and textures. The stones most commonly used for pavers include travertine, cobblestone, and limestone.
- Traditional *concrete pavers* are preformed and often colored units. They come in many shapes and sizes and can be used to form very simple to elaborate hardscape designs. Concrete pavers may also be stamped with a design or texture.
- *Brick pavers* may be made with concrete or clay. Unlike traditional bricks used in construction, brick pavers generally do not have holes. They are also larger and more water-resistant than traditional, rectangular bricks.

Stone

Stone is used in landscape designs for outdoor flooring, walkways, driveways, retaining walls, and even fences. Stone is also used to create natural design and as accent rocks in garden beds and other areas of the landscape. See **Figure 15-14**. Designers typically choose stone that is unique to the geographic area of the landscape.

Wood and Composite Lumber

Wood is used for hardscape fixtures, such as decking, walkways, fences, gazebos, seating, and pergolas. The type of wood used often depends on the client's

nikashmeleva/Shutterstock.com   *Sukpaiboonwat/Shutterstock.com*   *romakoma/Shutterstock.com*

Figure 15-14. Natural and shaped stones and local materials are used as accents that complement the plant materials.

preference, the structure's end use, and the types of wood available locally. The lumber from some species is more durable than others are and does not require special treatment. Less durable wood is treated with preservatives to improve their weather resistance and make them more rot and insect resistant. This type of wood is referred to as *pressure-treated wood*. Pressure-treated wood is used for hardscape structure, flooring, and railings. Due to its strength and longevity, it is also used as the structural component of hardscapes that will be completed with other wood or composites. See **Figure 15-15**. Wood hardscapes require annual maintenance, including cleaning, sanding, and resealing or staining.

Composite lumber is a hardscape material made from wood fiber and plastic. It is available in a variety of colors and textures and in the same nominal sizes as traditional lumber. Composite lumber does not splinter, is insect repellent, resists molding and rotting, and does not need to be sanded and resealed. It is environmentally friendly as it is often made with recycled materials, but it is also more expensive than most types of lumber used for decking.

> **Pro Tip**
>
> Pavers are also rated by ASTM standards. According to ASTM, pavers must be liftable with one hand, have a surface area of less than 101 in^2, have a compressive strength of 8000 psi, have less than 5% surface absorption, and comply with tolerances for area covered and thickness.

Concrete

Concrete is a traditional material used for hardscapes. Concrete pavers are commonly used but concrete may also be poured and formed on-site. Poured concrete is concrete that is transported wet and poured into prepared forms. The appearance of a poured concrete surface can be modified in various ways.

- Color can be applied to a dry concrete surface or a liquid or powder pigment can be mixed into wet concrete.
- Designs and patterns can be stamped on the concrete surface at a specific point in the drying time. These patterns may be unique in design or emulate natural stone or pavers, **Figure 15-16**.

A *Goodheart-Willcox Publisher*   **B**   *R. Lee Ivy*   **C**   *Darryl Brooks/Shutterstock.com*

Figure 15-15. A—Wood may be stained to change the color or treated with a clear coating to retain a natural look. B—Composite decking materials often mimic natural woods without the added labor of staining and treating. C—Pressure-treated wood is strong and resists rot and deters insects. It is used as a structural material for many wood or composite hardscapes but is also used to construct flooring, railings, and steps.

Figure 15-16. Concrete is commonly used for patios, walkways, and driveways. It is expensive but also versatile in that it can be stained, stamped, or texturized.

- Fibers and porous aggregate, such as gravel, stone, or sand, can be added to modify strength and permeability.
- Applying a thin layer of fine aggregate to the surface of the wet concrete (*face mixing*) to provide color and greater abrasion or texture.

Locally Sourced Materials

Many homeowners prefer a design that includes locally sourced or recycled materials. Locally sourced materials include those that are mined or harvested locally, such as a particular stone or native tree species. Using these materials is usually less expensive than importing materials and it helps support the local economy.

Upcycled Materials

Designers can incorporate pieces with historical significance, such as portions of building facades or columns from buildings that have been demolished. These types of pieces may be incorporated into hardscape elements, such as fountains, gazebos, and built-in seating, or stand alone among the plant material. Upcycling materials also keeps them from entering landfills.

Asphalt

Asphalt is a mixture of tar, sand, and gravel that creates a dark hardscape. It is softer and less expensive than many other hardscape materials and is often used for driveways and long pathways of public walking trails. Asphalt will fade to a dull gray color and become softer in extremely hot, sunny weather. Asphalt must be sealed periodically to prevent cracking and chipping. Applying sealer will also restore the original dark color.

Gravel

Gravel consists of small pieces of loose rock. The rocks come in different colors, shapes, sizes, and durability. Gravel is used for walkways, driveways, paths, and often to cover areas in which it is difficult or impractical to grow plants. As with other hardscape materials, the type chosen depends primarily on the client's wishes and its end use or how it is incorporated into a design. A solid edging will keep the gravel from traveling and properly preparing the ground below the gravel will minimize weed growth between the rocks. A commercial-grade landscaping fabric placed over the ground surface will help reduce weed growth.

Gravel is considered a low-impact material because it creates a permeable groundcover that allows water to drain. It is a common component of xeriscape designs for its permeability and ability to add color to the landscape. Common types of landscape gravel include pea gravel, churt, machine-crushed gravel, river rocks, decomposed granite, lava rocks, and crushed stone. See **Figure 15-17.**

Pro Tip

The American Society for Testing and Materials (ASTM) provides standards for paving units. The standards define dimensions, tolerances, strength, and freeze/thaw durability.

peasittichai/Shutterstock.com   *amperespy44/Shutterstock.com*   *Thamma-touch/Shutterstock.com*   *Joy Tasa/Shutterstock.com*   *trairut noppakaew/Shutterstock.com*

Figure 15-17. Various types of gravel are available, adding color, texture, and permeable options to pathways and driveways.

Thinking Green

Permeable Hardscapes

Installing a more permeable hardscape can reduce the impact a landscape design may have on the local environment. A more permeable landscape design will decrease stormwater runoff, reduce pollution entering our waterways, and increase the amount of water that enters groundwater reservoirs. The ground also serves as a filter to remove contaminants from the water. Materials and designs that can increase the permeability of a hardscape include decomposed granite, crushed stone, porous asphalt, pervious concrete, dry-laying the hardscape, and the use of permeable materials between pavers.

- Decomposed granite and crushed stone form a hard compact surface that still allows water to seep through to the ground below.
- Porous asphalt and pervious concrete both have interconnected spaces on the surface to allow water seepage. These materials may have restrictions for weight or the amount of traffic they can withstand.
- ***Dry-laying*** a hardscape allows water to permeate the ground below. Dry-laid material is a hardscape that does not use concrete below and between the pavers. The materials are laid on a gravel bed with a geotextile and layer of sand below it. (**Geotextiles** are synthetic fabrics used as weed barriers, separations between materials, or to reinforce or protect a material.) A permeable material, such as moss, gravel, groundcover plants, or sand, is placed between the pavers or stones. ***Wet-laying*** is the installation of a hardscape with wet concrete below and between the pavers or stones.
- Other types of permeable designs include a type of grid with open cells that can be planted with materials such as turfgrass or groundcover. The cells may also be filled with pea gravel or another type of aggregate.

Permeable hardscapes may be subject to municipal restrictions and typically require a regular maintenance program. It is recommended that permeable landscapes only be installed on flat or minimally sloped areas. The amount or type of traffic may be restricted by a design and/or the materials used in its construction.

Michael Dechev/Shutterstock.com

Sergii Rudiuk/Shutterstock.com

Consider This

1. What are the major disadvantages of permeable hardscapes?
2. Is the cost of installing a permeable hardscape higher than that of traditional hardscapes? Explain your answer.
3. What types of recycled materials can be used to make a permeable landscape?

Calculating Materials

Accurate site measurements are essential for calculating and ordering sufficient hardscape materials. Accurate measurements are also important when determining the cost of a project and ensuring the work is profitable for the landscape business. The amount of materials ordered should be 5% to 10% greater than the actual estimated need for the project. Ordering additional materials will ensure a sufficient amount for the job and it will also compensate for defective or broken pieces.

Square Footage

Many hardscape materials are sold by the square foot. You can determine the square footage of an area with standard calculations for geometric shapes, such as squares, circles, and triangles. See **Figure 15-18**.

Irregular Shapes

The most efficient way to determine the square footage of an irregularly shaped area is to divide the area into geometric figures, such as rectangles, circles, and triangles, determining the square footage for each shape, and adding the measurements together. See **Figure 15-19**.

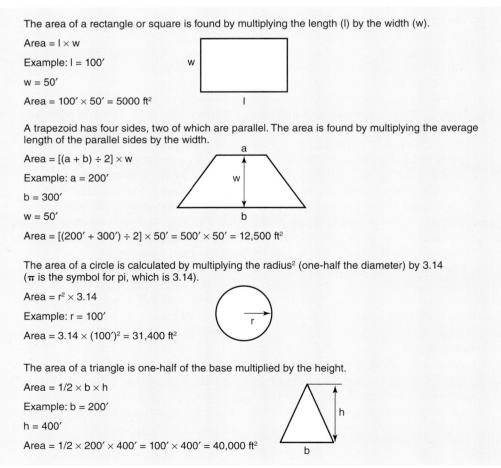

The area of a rectangle or square is found by multiplying the length (l) by the width (w).

Area = l × w

Example: l = 100′

w = 50′

Area = 100′ × 50′ = 5000 ft²

A trapezoid has four sides, two of which are parallel. The area is found by multiplying the average length of the parallel sides by the width.

Area = [(a + b) ÷ 2] × w

Example: a = 200′

b = 300′

w = 50′

Area = [(200′ + 300′) ÷ 2] × 50′ = 500′ × 50′ = 12,500 ft²

The area of a circle is calculated by multiplying the radius² (one-half the diameter) by 3.14 (π is the symbol for pi, which is 3.14).

Area = r² × 3.14

Example: r = 100′

Area = 3.14 × (100′)² = 31,400 ft²

The area of a triangle is one-half of the base multiplied by the height.

Area = 1/2 × b × h

Example: b = 200′

h = 400′

Area = 1/2 × 200′ × 400′ = 100′ × 400′ = 40,000 ft²

Figure 15-18. Two-dimensional measurements can easily be determined by using geometric shapes and applicable equations.

Any irregularly shaped area, such as a whale-shaped bed, can be reduced to one or more geometric forms. The area of each figure is calculated and added to obtain the total area.

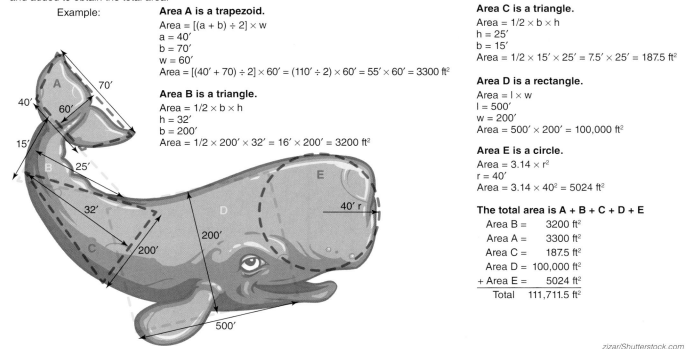

Example:

Area A is a trapezoid.
Area = [(a + b) ÷ 2] × w
a = 40′
b = 70′
w = 60′
Area = [(40′ + 70) ÷ 2] × 60′ = (110′ ÷ 2) × 60′ = 55′ × 60′ = 3300 ft²

Area B is a triangle.
Area = 1/2 × b × h
h = 32′
b = 200′
Area = 1/2 × 200′ × 32′ = 16′ × 200′ = 3200 ft²

Area C is a triangle.
Area = 1/2 × b × h
h = 25′
b = 15′
Area = 1/2 × 15′ × 25′ = 7.5′ × 25′ = 187.5 ft²

Area D is a rectangle.
Area = l × w
l = 500′
w = 200′
Area = 500′ × 200′ = 100,000 ft²

Area E is a circle.
Area = 3.14 × r²
r = 40′
Area = 3.14 × 40² = 5024 ft²

The total area is A + B + C + D + E

Area B =	3200 ft²
Area A =	3300 ft²
Area C =	187.5 ft²
Area D =	100,000 ft²
+ Area E =	5024 ft²
Total	111,711.5 ft²

Figure 15-19. Landscape areas are often irregular in shape. It is common for theme parks to install beds in the shape of animals or animated characters. A combination of squares, triangles, and circles can be used to calculate area.

Ordering Materials

Once the square footage of an area is calculated, volume must be determined before ordering materials. For example, in an area covering 1000′ it may be necessary to add 4″ of gravel as a base for a hardscape installation. The 1000 would be multiplied by 4″/12″ or divided by 3. This would equal 333.3 ft³ (cubic feet). Since there are 27 ft³ in a cubic yard, 333.3 would be divided by 27 equaling 12.3 yd³. Most often gravel is ordered by the ton and a general conversion from cubic yards to tons is needed. If the generic conversion is used, 12.3 yd³ multiplied by 0.27 equals 3.33 tons (1 yd³ = 0.27 tons).

Materials vary by weight due to their parent materials and moisture content. Always add 5% to 10% for variance when calculating with general conversion factors.

Tools and Equipment

A variety of tools and equipment is used to prepare a site for landscape installation. Hand and power tools and large equipment are used for tasks such as removing or adding substrates and leveling and grading the surface. Large equipment is also used to dig ponds and holes for large plant materials. Consideration should always be given to damage that may occur from machine operation and any space constrictions that may exist due to obstacles, such as large trees or minimal space between permanent structures. Machines with tracks tend to do less damage than wheeled loaders and may be a better option when the machine needs to travel over soft, finished areas, such as a lawn.

Safety First

Always call 811 to have all buried telephone, gas, electrical, and water lines marked before beginning any excavation work.

Grading Equipment

Most sites need to be cleared of debris, existing plant material, or thick brush, rocks, and other debris before they can be graded. The amount of clearing work and the size of the area may require the use of larger equipment, such as a bulldozer, in place of a skid-steer. Skid-steers are compact machines that can be used in both large and small areas. They are the most common machinery used for grading landscape projects, **Figure 15-20**. A skid-steer can be used to scoop and level soil and to carry large loads, such as pallets of sod or mature trees.

Safety First

Grading and other machines must be loaded and unloaded from trailers by experienced drivers wearing a safety belt. The rollover protection device must always be kept in place when the machine is being driven and loaded or unloaded from a trailer.

Compactors

In landscaping, *tamping* is the process of packing (compacting) the subsurface of a hardscape to help level the site and minimize shifting. Tampers may be power or hand-operated and the type used will depend primarily on the size of the area being tamped. *Hand tampers* have long handles with a flat metal plate attached at one end, **Figure 15-21A**. Power machines are referred to as vibratory tampers. *Vibratory tampers* are walk-behind power machines with a large metal plate that vibrates on the subsurface to compact the material, **Figure 15-21B**. Power machines significantly reduce the amount of time it takes to prepare the subsurface for hardscape installation. These tools are also referred to as *compactors*.

Roman Korotkov/Shutterstock.com

Orange Line Media/Shutterstock.com

Figure 15-20. Skid-steer loaders are available with tracks or wheels.

A　　　　　　　　　　B　　　　　　　　　　C

R. Lee Ivy

Figure 15-21. A/B—A vibratory tamper can be used to compact the subsoil and gravel base and over the installed paving materials. C—A hand tamper can be used for areas not accessible with vibratory tampers.

Tools

As with any task, using the proper tool makes the work more efficient and enjoyable. Hand and power tools that are commonly used when installing hardscapes include the following (**Figure 15-22**):

- A 4′ level for determining if a surface is level.
- A string level to determine approximate elevation changes over long distances.
- Screed boards to move sand or other materials into smooth and level surfaces.
- A paving screed tool with a long handle for leveling small areas of sand or gravel.
- Grading poles or rods are graduated rods used to determine differences in elevation. They are set for the screed board to move across. Once they are used, the remaining gaps are filled with sand or other material using a trowel or small shovel.
- A variety of shovels, including trench, flat, edging, round-pointed, pointed, square-pointed, and scoop shovels, for digging and moving materials, such as soil, gravel, and sand.
- Hard rakes to roughly level materials.
- Scoops for moving larger amounts of material from one location to another.
- Push brooms for leveling topdress material after it is applied to the final surface.
- A laser level for accurately determining elevation changes and dimensions.
- Hand chisel for scoring and creating break lines on stone, brick, or concrete.
- A mallet for driving the hand chisel into various materials.
- Paver breaker/splitter for making breaks in pavers.
- A bench or handheld cutoff saw for making cuts in pavers.
- Dust control saw for cutting pavers.
- A bundle buggy or paver cart for moving paver bundles.

JPL Designs/Shutterstock.com

Figure 15-22. Required hand tools include shovels, rakes, push brooms, dead-blow hammers, breaking or cutting tools, kneepads, and tampers.

Hardscape Installation

Many municipalities consider hardscapes impermeable surfaces even if they are constructed to meet permeable surface guidelines. This categorization typically subjects these areas to stormwater and other regulations. Once a hardscape design is completed and approved by the client, it should be submitted to the proper authority for approval. Designers who are familiar with a particular area often know local codes and incorporate this into their design. The installer or contractor may apply for permits once the design is approved.

Scheduling and Site Access

Efficient scheduling and defined access to a site helps ensure a smoother work flow. The project manager or job site coordinator must schedule employees, tool and equipment delivery, irrigation installation, and the delivery of both plant and hardscape materials. The coordinator must also anticipate site challenges, changes in weather, and changes made due to the client's preferences, and work additional time into the schedule. See **Figure 15-23**.

Existing landscape can be disrupted when new components are being installed. Defining site access, delivery pathways, and staging areas before the job begins will help minimize damage to other areas. Damage may also be limited by installing silt fences or plastic tape to indicate restricted areas and borders. Special attention should be paid to plants, such as existing trees, that will be incorporated into a design. The roots must be protected from excavation work and traffic across the canopy should be limited to prevent soil compaction and ensuing health issues.

ThomasPhoto/Shutterstock.com   Pattharawadee/Shutterstock.com

Figure 15-23. Establishing access to a site and scheduling deliveries can be a challenge for a jobsite coordinator or supervisor.

Marking the Area

After the necessary approval is given, the installer carefully measures and marks the areas where the hardscape will be installed. Straight and curved lines may be marked with chalk or spray paint or by shoveling along the border. String attached to stakes may also be used to mark straight lines. See **Figure 15-24**. This is also the time to have utility lines marked if they have not been marked or the markings are no longer intact. These markings are used as guidelines for installation. They will also give the client a better idea of where the hardscape will be installed. Once the area has been measured and marked, the installer identifies a benchmark to which all measurements are compared. The benchmark is usually the highest point of the area, **Figure 15-25**.

Setting the Final Grade

A string level, rotary transit, or digital pole level can be used to develop the final grade (slope). These devices use the established benchmark as the base dimension. The installer calculates the total depth of the materials being installed to determine how deep the ground should be excavated. The total depth of the layers is then subtracted from the benchmark to identify the point to which the ground should be excavated. To maintain a stable base, the area should not be excavated deeper than necessary and no more than 1′ around the perimeter. The backfill is set aside and used to fill in around the finished area.

Pro Tip

Polypropylene panels are gaining popularity as an alternative to compacted aggregate, especially in areas subject to damage from freezing and thawing and those with limited access. The polypropylene panel is laid on the compacted subsoil before the hardscape materials are installed. Using this material may reduce excavation and material costs.

Subsurface Preparation

One of the key elements of hardscape construction is adequate compaction of the *subsurface* (the area or layers below the final surface), **Figure 15-26**. Proper compaction will ensure that weather extremes, such as freezing, thawing, heavy rainfall, and severe drought, will not cause the surface to buckle or shift. The standard subsurface depth for walks and patios is 4″, 6″ to 8″ for driveways, and 12″ for streets.

A typical subsurface profile for a hardscape, from the lowest layer to the uppermost layer, is as follows:

- Drainage pipe (in some applications).
- Large, porous aggregate.
- Smaller aggregate, such as sand.
- The hardscape material with sand or other small aggregate filling open spaces.

Richard Thornton/Shutterstock.com

Wave_Movies/Shutterstock.com

Bildagentur Zoonar GmbH/Shutterstock.com

Figure 15-24. Work areas within a site can be identified using string, marking paint, and/or flagging.

CuteSalika/Shutterstock.com

Figure 15-25. A benchmark can be identified on a site as the starting point for elevation calculations. The benchmark should be located out of the work area.

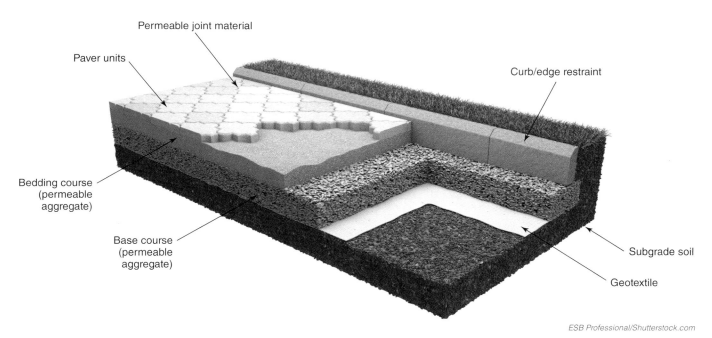

Permeable joint material

Paver units

Curb/edge restraint

Bedding course
(permeable
aggregate)

Base course
(permeable
aggregate)

Subgrade soil

Geotextile

Figure 15-26. A properly installed subsurface is necessary for quality of installation and longevity of the hardscape, free from buckling, sagging, or shifting.

As each layer is placed on top of another, smaller particles will fill in spaces between the larger particles. Compaction further forces the particles together to make a hard packed surface. The compacted aggregate is covered with a smaller aggregate, such as manufactured sand, to a specific depth (2″ to 4″). It may be necessary to install a deeper aggregate base in some areas of the country and with other hardscape materials. Check local codes and manufacturer's product recommendations. A screed board is used to *screed* (level) the material to a uniform surface, **Figure 15-27**. The top material, such as concrete pavers, is then laid and compacted with a hand or powered compactor. The designer should factor in the possibility of tree roots or excessive traffic because they may alter the performance over a long period.

Figure 15-27. Screeding creates an even surface for laying the paving materials. Poles and a straight board are commonly used.

STEM Connection

Calculating Slope

The following steps may be used to determine the slope between two points. Use feet and tenths as the units of measurement.

1. Use a survey instrument or a carpenter's level resting on a 2×4 to measure the vertical difference (v) between the two points.
2. Measure the horizontal distance (h) between the two points.
3. Calculate the slope percentage using the formula $\frac{v}{h} \times 100$ = slope percentage.

Calculating slope between two points:

Calculate slope between points A and B
v = 2′
h = 16′
2/16 = 0.125 × 100 = 12.5% slope

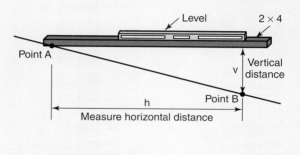

Calculate the vertical change necessary to obtain a desired slope between two points:

Calculate a 1% downslope between points A and B
h = 16
% slope = −1% elevation
A = 200.0
B = 199
16 × −0.01 = −0.16 elevation change for point B
200 − 0.16 = 199.84 elevation desired at point B

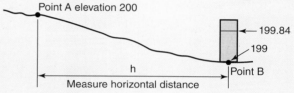

Calculate an upslope between two points:

Calculate a 4% upslope between points A and B
h = 16
% slope = 4% elevation
A = 200
B = 200
16 × 0.04 = 0.64 elevation change for point B
200 + 0.64 = 200.64 elevation desired at point B

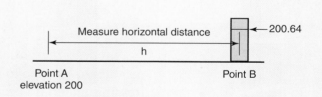

Geotextiles

Some applications require a geotextile between the subsoil and a base or aggregate layer. Geotextiles are water-permeable synthetic fabrics used as weed barriers, separations between materials, such as soil and stone, or to reinforce a material. In this case, the soil and aggregate are kept separate but water may still permeate the fabric. Overlapping seams and allowing extra material to extend up the sides of the excavated area ensures the geotextile will serve its purpose. See **Figure 15-28**.

HelloRF Zcool/Shutterstock.com   *Evannovostro/Shutterstock.com*

Figure 15-28. A water permeable fabric separates subsoil and aggregate materials to prevent the aggregate from settling into the subsoil.

Career Connection

Mason Dyer

Mason Dyer, Territory Manager, Belgard Pavers and Landscapes

Mason Dyer is the Territory Manager in the East-Central region of North Carolina. He manages residential hardscape sales and works closely with dealers and contractors in the area.

Mason began his career after graduating from East Carolina University with a bachelor's degree in geography. After graduation, Mason was employed by a landscape contractor for 20 years. While in this position, Mason's passion for hardscapes was born. His knowledge, experience, and talent helped him become a Belgard Authorized Contractor. Remodeling homes became more popular during the decline in the housing market. This increase in remodeling created more opportunities for Mason to create masterful outdoor living spaces. His award-winning installations led him and his associated company to become a leader in the industry.

In 2015, an opportunity to join the Belgard team arose and Mason took the opportunity to sell the products he was so passionate to install. He now helps contractors of all levels with industry education and various hands-on learning events. Mason is both a North Carolina Licensed Landscape Contractor and a North Carolina Irrigation Contractor and holds ICPI and NCMA certifications as well. His 24 years of experience enables him to help contractors with hardscape installations and help educate others working within the green industry. Mason feels that education is a key component in any situation. He lets contractors and others know that he is always just a phone call or email away if they have questions or need assistance.

Consider This

1. What types of personal and professional skills have helped Mason reach his goals?
2. How does his personal experience help him educate and help others?

Topdressing

Topdressing is the action of applying material over the top of a newly installed hardscape to fill in voids between the hardscape materials. The topdressing material is compacted or washed into the spaces between the hardscape materials to fill the spaces to prevent shifting and create a stronger surface, **Figure 15-29**. Common topdress materials include manufactured or polymeric sand. Manufactured sand has jagged edges that bind tightly to help lock the units in place. Polymeric sand, once wet, forms an impermeable barrier preventing weed seed germination.

Pro Tip

Efflorescence is a whitish, powdery deposit on the surface of stones that occurs when the minerals in water that has risen to the surface of the stone remain on the surface after the water evaporates. The residue can be removed with a pressure washer and scrubbing.

photowind/Shutterstock.com

R. Lee Ivy

Figure 15-29. Topdressing with sand, gravel dust, or porous rock with permeable paver systems securely locks the paving materials in place.

Keeping Track

Installation Checklist

- Determine the function and use.
- Calculate, order, and schedule material delivery.
- Coordinate delivery of tools and equipment.
- Designate pathways and staging areas.
- Lay out the area to be excavated.
- Excavate to a determined depth.
- Address subsurface issues, such as utility lines or drainage pipes.
- Install the subsurface aggregates at specified depths.
- Properly compact layers to establish a solid base.
- Install the hardscape material.
- Install edge restraint materials, such as aluminum, plastic, or wood.
- If pavers are installed, add topdress material and compact the area.
- Backfill around new installation.
- Remove tools, equipment, and excess materials.
- Police the area for miscellaneous damage and repair as needed.

Summary

- Hardscapes are walkways, gathering areas, driveways, and often focal points in a landscape design that are made of inanimate materials, such as wood, stone, and concrete.
- Walkways provide access to and from entryways, invite visitors to walk through the garden, and provide a clear and safe means of accomplishing chores, such as taking out the trash.
- Patios and decks are recreational areas adjoining a building, such as a home, to extend the living area and are often used for outdoor dining.
- Outdoor stairs should be constructed at the same standard height and width used for interior stairs for safety and ease of use.
- A retaining wall is a structure that holds or retains the soil behind it to reduce soil loss through erosion as well as mitigate other soil moisture concerns.
- A designer must consider multiple aspects of the site, including the slope of the land and the amount of daylight the area receives, especially at dusk and dawn, to ensure a safe hardscape.
- Texture may be used to help reduce slipping and falling on a hardscape surface.
- Patterns can be created with different materials and designed to mirror existing natural patterns or duplicate architectural patterns of existing structures.
- When creating a landscape design, the designer must consider the flow of water as it contacts the surface of each hardscape material used in the design.
- The permeability of a landscape material is measured by the amount of water it allows to pass through to the ground below.
- Hardscape installations require standard calculations of area, volume, and materials such as bricks and pavers.
- An impermeable hardscape must have at least a 1% slope away from an adjacent structure to direct water away from the structure and prevent water from flowing under the structure and hardscape.
- Unit pavers, stone, wood or wood composites, concrete, local or upcycled materials, asphalt, and gravel are common hardscape materials.
- Installing a more permeable hardscape can reduce the impact a landscape design may have on the local environment.
- Tamping is the process of packing (compacting) the subsurface of a hardscape to help level the site and minimize shifting.
- Tools such as leveling devices, screeds, tampers, shovels, scoops, and brooms are needed for hardscape installation.
- Efficient scheduling and defined access to a site helps ensure a smoother work flow.
- One of the key elements of hardscape construction is adequate compaction of the subsurface (the area below the final surface).

Chapter Review

Know and Understand ⤴

Answer the following questions using the information provided in this chapter.

1. Which of the following purposes does a hardscape serve?
   A. Focal points and driveways.
   B. Pedestrian access and walkways.
   C. Gathering areas.
   D. All of the above.

2. *True or False?* The most successful hardscapes fulfill the client's needs and complement both the softscape and the home.
   A. True.
   B. False.

3. How wide should a path be to be suitable for a wheelchair?
   A. At least 18″ wide.
   B. At least 24″ wide.
   C. At least 30″ wide.
   D. At least 36″ wide.

4. How wide should a path be for two people to walk side by side?
   A. At least 48″ wide.
   B. At least 36″ wide.
   C. At least 24″ wide.
   D. At least 18″ wide.

5. *True or False?* The design and installation of a driveway and other hardscapes may be subject to local building regulations and codes.
   A. True.
   B. False.

6. A recreational area adjoining a building to extend the living area and provide space for outdoor dining is referred to as a _____.
   A. deck
   B. patio
   C. retainer
   D. All of the above.

7. A raised platform constructed with a composite or wood is referred to as a _____.
   A. deck
   B. patio
   C. retainer
   D. All of the above.

8. The rise and fall of the land surface or a change in elevation from a fixed point is referred to as _____.
   A. standard height
   B. perspective
   C. grade
   D. meter length

9. At which of the following measurements should stairs be constructed?
   A. At whichever height and width matches the design.
   B. No higher or wider than 11″.
   C. The standard height and width of interior stairs.
   D. It depends on the materials being used.

10. A structure that holds the soil to reduce soil loss through erosion as well as mitigate other soil moisture concerns is referred to as a _____.
    A. retaining wall
    B. blockade wall
    C. stockade wall
    D. All of the above.

11. *True or False?* An outdoor kitchen may require professional installation of electrical wiring and plumbing for gas and water service.
    A. True.
    B. False.

12. Which of the following can make an area of the hardscape safer?
    A. Lighting on steps.
    B. Markings on paths.
    C. Handrails on stairways.
    D. All of the above.

13. *True or False?* A very rough texture is the ideal surface for walkways in a hardscape.
    A. True.
    B. False.

14. A repeated decorative design or the recurring use of a specific element in a design is referred to as _____.
    A. structure
    B. pattern
    C. design
    D. pickets

15. Which of the following is determined by the amount of water that can pass through a hardscape material?
    A. Liability.
    B. Versatility.
    C. Permeability.
    D. Opportunity.

16. *True or False?* The most permeable hardscapes are constructed with poured concrete.
    A. True.
    B. False.

17. To ensure water will be directed in the desired direction, impermeable hardscapes must have at least a _____.
    A. .05% slope
    B. 1.0% slope
    C. 3.25% slope
    D. The surface should be completely flat.

18. Which of the following materials would be most appropriately placed over a sub-drainage system?
    A. Compacted clay.
    B. Aggregate.
    C. Stamped concrete.
    D. All of the above.

19. Which of the following materials are used for hardscapes?
    A. Gravel, aggregates, and brick.
    B. Concrete and asphalt.
    C. Wood and composite lumber.
    D. All of the above.

Match the materials to the descriptions in 20–28.
    A. aggregate
    B. asphalt
    C. brick paver
    D. composite lumber
    E. concrete
    F. concrete pavers
    G. gravel
    H. paving tile
    I. pressure-treated wood
    J. stone paver

20. Small pieces of loose rock that comes in different colors, sizes, and durability.

21. A collection of units used together.

22. A glazed decorated tile that can be used as flooring or wall covering.

23. Stone cut into square or rectangular shapes or used in its original shape.

24. Preformed and often colored units that are available in many shapes and sizes.

25. A hardscape, water-resistant material made with concrete or clay.

26. A hardscape material to which preservatives are applied to improve its weather resistance and make it more resistant to rot or insects.

27. A hardscape material made from wood fiber and plastic.

28. A mixture of tar, sand, and gravel that creates a dark hardscape.

29. Which of the following is an advantage of using composite lumber instead of real wood?
    A. It does not need to be sanded or resealed.
    B. It resists molding and rotting.
    C. It does not splinter and it is an insect repellant.
    D. All of the above.

30. *True or False?* Face mixing is the application of water to the surface of wet concrete.
    A. True.
    B. False.

31. How can the appearance of poured concrete be modified?
   A. Pigment can be mixed in wet concrete.
   B. Designs may be stamped on the surface.
   C. Fibers and aggregate can be added.
   D. All of the above.

32. When pieces with historical significance, such as portions of a building façade, are incorporated into a design, it is said to be _____.
   A. upcycled
   B. renewed
   C. repeated
   D. low-impact

33. *True or False?* Gravel is considered a low-impact material because it creates a permeable groundcover that allows water to drain.
   A. True.
   B. False.

34. Churt, river rocks, decomposed granite, lava rocks, and crushed stone are all types of _____.
   A. asphalt
   B. gravel
   C. pavers
   D. sealers

35. *True or False?* Installing permeable hardscapes reduces the impact a design may have on the local environment.
   A. True.
   B. False.

36. *True or False?* Dry-laying is the application of thin layer of fine aggregate to the surface of the wet concrete.
   A. True.
   B. False.

37. *True or False?* Wet-laying is the installation of a hardscape with wet concrete below and between the pavers or stones.
   A. True.
   B. False.

38. The amount of material ordered should be 5% to 10% greater than the actual estimated need of the project to _____.
   A. cut costs by saving the extra for another job
   B. bump up the cost of the job and earn more profit
   C. compensate for defective or broken pieces
   D. All of the above.

39. *True or False?* Machines with wheels do less damage than machines with tracks.
   A. True.
   B. False.

40. Which of the following is used to compact subsurface materials?
   A. The workers' feet and body weight.
   B. A skid-steer or backhoe.
   C. A vibratory or hand tamper.
   D. All of the above.

41. *True or False?* A municipality may deem a hardscape as an impermeable surface requiring stormwater design considerations.
   A. True.
   B. False.

42. For what purpose is a rotary transit used in hardscape installations?
   A. To move materials around the landscape.
   B. It can be used to photograph the site.
   C. Determine correct depth for plant materials.
   D. The tool can be used to set the grade.

43. *True or False?* One of the key elements of hardscape construction is adequate compaction of the subsurface.
   A. True.
   B. False.

44. The standard subsurface depth for walks and patios is _____.
   A. 4″
   B. 6″ to 8″
   C. 12″
   D. 13″

45. The standard subsurface depth for driveways is _____.
    A. 4″ to 6″
    B. 6″ to 8″
    C. 8″ to 12″
    D. 12″ to 13″

46. The action of applying material over the top of a newly installed hardscape to fill in voids between the hardscape materials is referred to as _____.
    A. dry-laying
    B. wet-laying
    C. face mixing
    D. topdressing

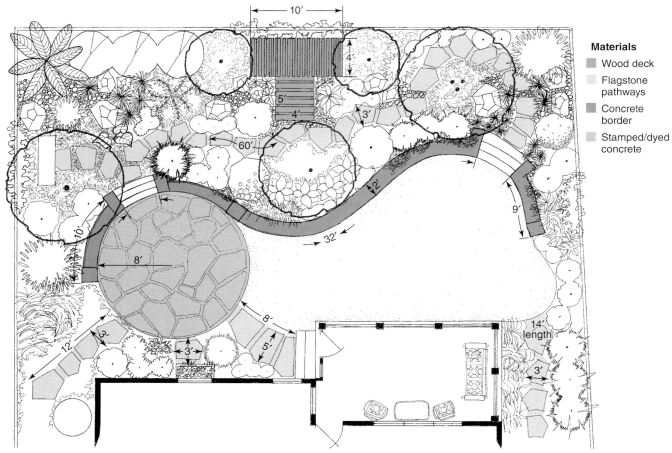

Materials
- Wood deck
- Flagstone pathways
- Concrete border
- Stamped/dyed concrete

Anne Spafford, NC State University

47. Calculate the number of 2 × 4 boards needed to construct the large area of the wood deck. The large area is 10′ × 4′ with no spacing between the boards. Each 2 × 4 is 3.5″ wide and 8′ long.

48. Calculate the number of 2 × 6 boards needed to construct the small area of the wood deck. The small area is 4′ × 5′ with a 2″ gap between boards. Each 2 × 6 is 5.5″ wide and 8′ long.

49. Calculate the square footage of the five flagstone pathways. The compacted aggregate is 4″ deep and the fine aggregate is 2″ deep.

The measurements for the pathways are 12′ × 3′, 3′ × 3′, 8′ × 5′, 14′ × 3′, and 60′ × 3′. Include 10% overage to ensure you will have enough materials.

50. Calculate the square footage of the concrete border at ground level/grade. There are three different border areas with a consistent width of 2′. The compacted aggregate is 6″ deep and the concrete is 4″ deep. The areas measure 10′ × 2′, 32′ × 2′, and 9′ × 2′. Include 10% overage in the total square footage.

51. Calculate the square footage of the circular area. The circular area has a radius of 8'. The formula for calculating the area of a circle is $\pi \times r^2$ (π is 3.14).

52. Calculate the amount of compacted aggregate and concrete (both in cubic yards) needed for the circular area. Use the square footage calculated in problem five. The area will require 6" of compacted aggregate and 4" of concrete.

53. Calculate the amount of compacted aggregate, fine aggregate, and concrete needed for all hardscape areas combined.

Site-Leveling Activities

Use different leveling devices to obtain accurate readings. Determine slope of a ramp using the different devices (string level, 4' level, rotary transit, and digital transit).

1. **String level.** Take the nylon string (already attached to the pallet) and stretch it to the end of the ramp (X). Attach the string level to determine the rise and run and then convert that to % slope.

2. **4' level.** Use the level to determine slope anywhere along the ramp. Identify the slope from your measurement [slope = vertical (height)/horizontal (distance × 100)].

3. **Rotary transit.** Collaborate with another student and level the instrument over a benchmark (Y). Shoot sites from the benchmark to bottom of the ramp (Y). Determine the rise and run and then convert that to % slope.

4. **Digital transit.** Use this device to determine the slope in similar fashion as with the rotary transit.

Suggested Activities

1. Contact your local permitting office to check the local codes for installing hardscapes. Design a simple hardscape adhering to local codes and develop a site preparation plan.

2. Working in a group of 4 to 5, photograph various locations that use hardscapes. If necessary, use images from the internet. Each member of the group should present 2 to 3 of the sites to the group and identify his or her likes and dislikes. Determine if the hardscape incorporates the elements and principles of design. Each member should explain why he or she prefers one design over another.

3. Choose an area of your yard or another potential space and create a simple patio or pathway design. Using the proposed hardscape design and space, determine the square footage of the area. If possible, choose a material from a local home improvement store and calculate the amount needed as well as its cost. Recreate your initial sketch using graphic design or drafting software.

4. Choose several types of pavers for the design created in the preceding activity. Calculate the cost of each material needed based on your measurements.

Creating the Design

While studying this chapter, look for the activity icon ➦ to:

- **Practice** vocabulary terms with Words to Know activities.
- **Expand** learning with identification activities.
- **Reinforce** what you learn by completing Know and Understand questions.

G-WLEARNING.com

www.g-wlearning.com/agriculture

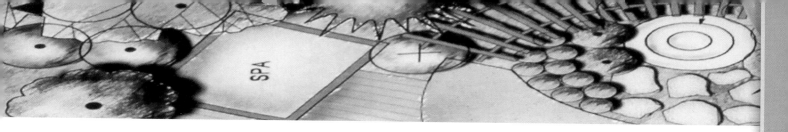

Chapter Outcomes

After studying this chapter, you will be able to:

- Understand the process of creating a landscape design.
- Identify the types of drawings used to develop and complete a landscape design.
- Determine the information necessary for developing a landscape design.
- Describe the proper deliverable format of a landscape design.
- Identify the components of a landscape design drawing.
- Use the symbols on a drawing to identify the landscape components.
- Identify the proper tools used during the design process.

Key Terms ↱

Alphabet of Lines
architect's scale
bond paper
bubble diagram
conceptual drawing
directional arrow
drafting media
engineer's scale
final design
foam board

functional diagram
graph paper
illustration board
legend
north arrow
orthographic projection drawing
perspective drawing
planting diagram
plan-view perspective
preliminary design

quadrille paper
request for proposal (RFP)
scale
sketch
sketch paper
symbol
title block
tracing paper
T-square
vellum

Introduction

A well-developed landscape design may be what convinces a potential client to choose your company to install and maintain a new landscape. Design drawings convey important information to clients, installers, and maintenance personnel, such as the plants, walkways, buildings, and water features in the landscape. Along with your ideas for the landscape, your drawings reflect your level of professionalism and attention to detail. They should be neat and well planned. This chapter helps you plan and create effective landscape design drawings.

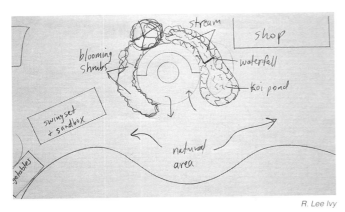

Figure 16-1. Design sketches can be drawn impromptu to convey a conceptual representation of an idea.

Drawing Methods

After discussing ideas and needs with the client, a designer may often draw a preliminary (first) sketch of their landscape design, **Figure 16-1**. The sketch can help the designer portray his or her interpretation of the client's ideas and make changes to satisfy the client's vision. The designer may also draw a rough sketch while on the site of the landscape to get a better feel for the land and identify existing structures. These rough sketches are the first steps of creating a formal design.

Hand Drawing

Traditionally, landscape plans were drawn by hand using the same drafting skills used by architects to create blueprints for buildings. Many designers still use traditional drawing techniques; however, most formal drawings are created using computer software referred to as computer-aided design or CAD. In many cases, both methods are used with the hand drawing completed first. The first hand drawing is often a full-color rendition (version) of the finished landscape, including buildings and mature plant materials, **Figure 16-2**. Additional drawings include more detailed information, such as site dimensions, names of plant materials, and construction drawings for hardscape structures.

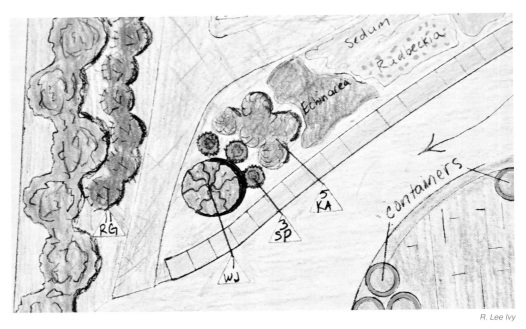

Figure 16-2. Many quality landscape designs are created by hand and often include color rendering. These plans convey the designer's ideas and concepts and reflect the wishes of the client.

Computer-Aided Design (CAD)

CAD drawings include accurate dimensions of the site with all hardscapes and plant materials in their proposed locations. The CAD drawings also include plant material names and symbols representing their place in the landscape as well as a legend key to explain the drawing's components. Additional drawings are created for parts of the design requiring more detail for the installer or builder, such as irrigation systems and structure dimensions.

The artistic rendition and the formal plans are both used when giving a presentation to the potential client. The rendition and formal design are printed on large format paper to ensure every detail is visible. Designers must be adept at hand drawing and computer-aided drawing to compete in today's market.

Drafting Tools and Equipment

Drafting designs requires a means of creating the design and media on which to draw or print the design. (*Drafting media* are the materials on which drawings are made or printed.) Designers use drawing instruments and paper specifically made for drafting. See **Figure 16-3**.

Drafting Media

The media used includes paper and film that differ in strength, translucency, erasability, stability, and permanence. Drafting media also differ in cost, with the least expensive used for beginners or preliminary sketches.

Rawpixel.com/Shutterstock.com

Figure 16-3. The final design may be transferred from paper to foam board for the client presentation. Foam boards are stiff and will not curl during your explanation of ideas for the proposed site. The plan and its graphics should be large enough for viewing by 3 to 5 people.

- *Sketch* or *tracing paper* is translucent drawing paper. It can be used over a drawing to trace the original, but it may also be used for sketching or drafting a design. Lead and ink will not spread on tracing paper but markers are likely to bleed through the paper. Some tracing paper has a preprinted outline and blank title block.
- *Graph* or *quadrille paper* has grids preprinted in a light color, usually blue. The squares that make up the grid help the designer to keep his or her scale work consistent. The paper is identified by the number of squares per inch. Graph paper is typically compatible with drawing lead or ink and with most printers.
- *Bond paper* is used primarily for printing CAD drawings because printer toner adheres well to its surface. The paper is available in various widths and roll lengths, can be translucent, and is used as an alternative to sketch paper.
- *Vellum* sheets are made of 100% cotton/rag content. A synthetic resin is used to make the paper transparent. Vellum tends to resist yellowing or becoming brittle with age.
- *Foam* or *illustration boards* are useful when making presentations. The boards are light but stiff and can be placed on an easel and remain upright. Colored pens, pencils, or markers can be used on foam board.

Figure 16-4. A request for proposal seeks parties interested in competing for a landscape installation. The RFP is the initial step of the project/client acquisition process.

Production Facilities

Landscape plan drawings are often drawn in office spaces with large-format printers and both CAD software and conventional drawing tables. These facilities typically have means of duplicating drawings or converting them to a digital format. These capabilities enable quick duplication and digital delivery to designers, code evaluators, estimators, and installers. It is also useful when multiple copies of the design are needed for an RFP (request for proposal). A *request for proposal (RFP)* for a landscape project is a process in which a potential client notifies prospective landscape companies to bid a price on the project. A municipality, for example, needing a new streetscape installed would distribute or advertise an RFP for the project. See **Figure 16-4**.

Drawing Board

A drawing board or table should be smooth without blemishes and large enough to accommodate an 18″ × 24″ sheet of paper, the most common paper size used for landscape drawings. Most drawing boards are constructed to resist warping to ensure the designer can make straight, perpendicular lines using the edge of the board to guide the *T-square*. T-squares may be constructed of wood, plastic, metal, or a combination of materials. A T-square is also used with other tools, such as triangles, to draw vertical or inclined lines. Some boards have a built-in mechanism that combines the functions of tools, such as a T-square, triangles, and protractors, into one mechanism. The vertical component of the mechanism slides along a track at the top of the drawing board. See **Figure 16-5**.

Drafting tape is used to secure paper to the drawing surface. This off-white tape is easily repositioned without tearing or marring the paper. This ensures easy adjustment to drawing positions and removal from the drafting board.

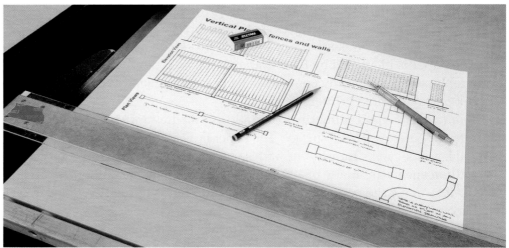

Figure 16-5. A smooth table with a straight edge is necessary to create a high quality design.

Pencils

Pencils range in hardness from 8B (very soft) to 9H (very hard). Softer leads are used to draw thicker lines and harder leads are used to draw thinner lines. Pencils may be purchased individually or in sets. Lead may also be purchased separately and inserted in a lead holder. Pencils are sharpened with a sand pad or handheld sharpener. Mechanical pencils, which do not need sharpening, are also used for drafting. Mechanical pencils lack variation in lead softness and hardness but are available in different lead sizes that can be used to achieve a variation of line thicknesses.

Erasers

Erasers vary in hardness and ability. Firm, textured rubber erasers are used to erase ink lines and soft vinyl erasers are used to erase pencil lines. Erasers should be cleaned before use by rubbing them on a piece of scrap paper. Take care when erasing as the paper may easily be torn with the friction. Use a dusting brush, not your hand, to remove shavings. Otherwise, it is more likely that the lead or ink may smear. An erasing shield can be used to protect parts of the drawing that are not to be removed, **Figure 16-6**.

Nor Gal/Shutterstock.com

Figure 16-6. An erasing shield enables the designer to erase parts of the drawing without smearing lines or removing portions of adjoining lines.

Markers, Colored Pens, and Pastel Pencils

Markers, colored pens, and pastel pencils can be used to add color, depth, and interest to a landscape design. Color brings the ideas and creativity of the designer to life and can help clients visualize the final product, **Figure 16-7**. Designers may draw over pencil lines with ink or with markers to create permanent lines once the drawing is completed.

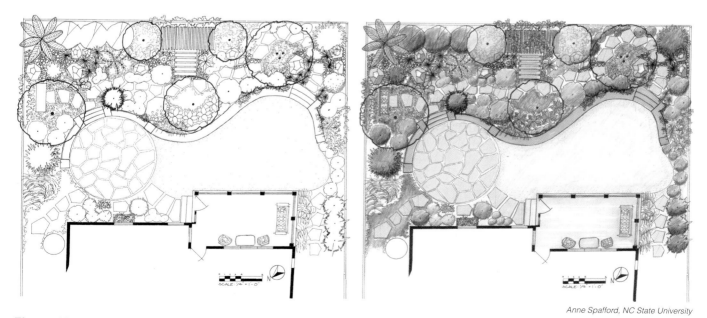

Anne Spafford, NC State University

Figure 16-7. A variety of line weights are used in black and white drawings to help the viewer distinguish different elements. Adding color to the design provides interest and detail, depth of display, leaf color, and bloom color. The addition of color also generates excitement for the client.

There are many coloring techniques used to imply texture. Broad strokes, for example, may be used to represent a *monoculture* (multiple plants or areas of the same species) of a turfgrass species or a swatch of fall color on a tree. Fine strokes, on the other hand, can be used to denote textural differences of individual plants or even leaves on a specific plant. When using markers, line thickness can be regulated by varying how much of the marker tip touches the paper and the amount of pressure applied. See **Figure 16-8**.

It is always best to purchase the best quality drawing tools that you can afford to ensure high quality results. These tools should be treated with care and properly stored to ensure extended periods of use. The pastel pencils should be sharpened with a sharp edge instead of a pencil sharpener to preserve the wax-based core. Keep in mind that dropping the pencils may crack or break the inner core.

Architect's Scales and Engineer's Scales

Architect's scales and engineer's scales are tools used to measure distances at a specific scale. A single architect's or engineer's scale typically has a triangular cross section, with each of the three sides containing four different measuring scales. See **Figure 16-9A**.

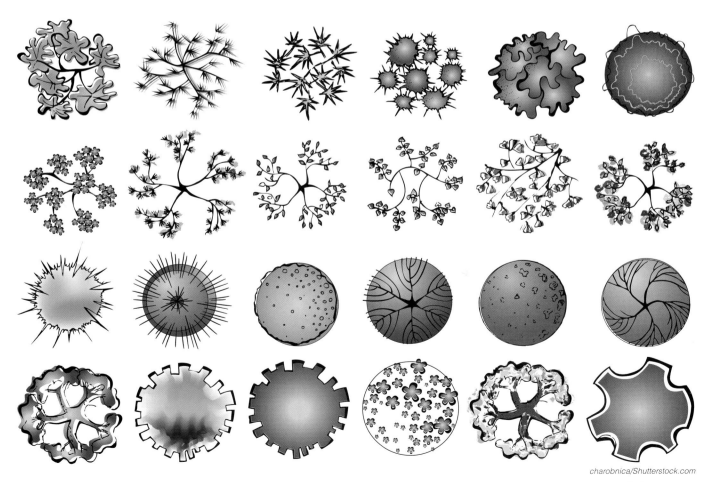

charobnica/Shutterstock.com

Figure 16-8. Designers use different line thickness to indicate or place emphasis on different plant characteristics. The perimeter and interior canopy characteristics may be emphasized.

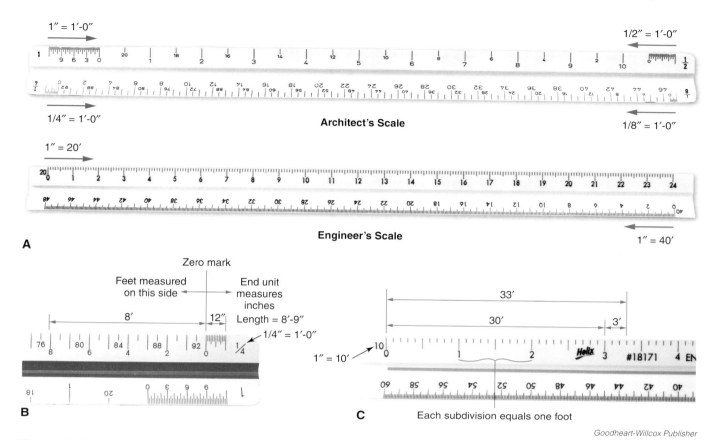

Goodheart-Willcox Publisher

Figure 16-9. It is essential that landscape designers understand how to read and use both types of scales.

Architect's scales and engineer's scales are tools used to measure distances at a specific scale. A single architect's or engineer's scale typically has a triangular cross section, with each of the three sides containing four different measuring scales. See **Figure 16-9A**.

Architect's scales measure distances relative to an actual distance of 1'-0", using scales such as 1/8" = 1'-0", 1/4" = 1'-0", and 3" = 1'-0". A scale of 1/4" = 1'-0", for example, indicates that a measurement of 1/4" on the drawing is equal to one foot on the site. Residential landscapes are typically drawn at 1/8" scale. Smaller areas are drawn at 1/4" to show details. Architect scales are also used for construction details, often at 1/2" or 1" scales.

Engineer's scales use scales in which one inch on the drawing equals a certain number of feet on the site. Common engineer's scales are 1" = 10', 1" = 20', and 1" = 30'. A scale of 1" = 10', for example, indicates that a measurement of 1" on the drawing is equal to 10' on the site. This scale is used for larger sites.

The end unit on an architect's scale is subdivided into inches or fractional parts of an inch. To measure a distance with an architect's scale, begin by selecting the appropriate scale. Align the scale so that one end of the line being measured extends into the end unit, and the other end aligns with a full unit mark. See **Figure 16-9B**.

On an engineer's scale, each major division is divided into ten units. The number at the end of each scale indicates the number of feet per inch. For example, the "10" scale represents 1" = 10'. Each inch represents 10' and each subdivision represents one foot. See **Figure 16-9C**.

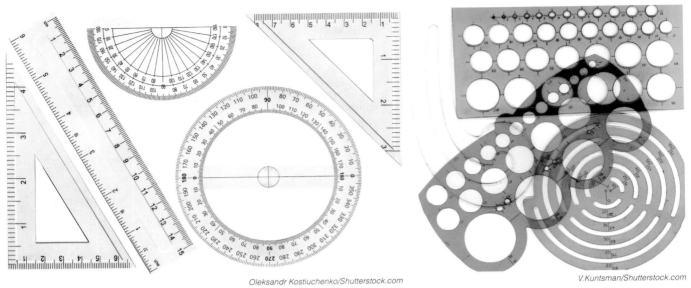

Figure 16-10. Designer's tools include 45° triangle, 30°–60° triangle, protractor, compass, French curve, flexible curves, and stencils. These tools enable the designer to draw straight and curvilinear lines.

Other Drawing Tools

Other drawing tools used in landscape design include triangles, protractors, compasses, French curves, flexible curves, templates, and stencils, **Figure 16-10**.

- *Triangles* are used to draw vertical and inclined lines. The two most common triangles are the 45° and 30° to 60° triangles. Triangles are used together or with other tools, such as a T-square, to create various angles.
- A *protractor* is used to measure and mark angles that cannot be measured with triangles and a T-square. They may be circular or semicircular.
- A *compass* is used to draw circles and arcs. Different types and sizes of compasses are used to draw circles.
- Curves that do not follow a circular arc are called irregular curves. *French curves* and *flexible curves* are used to draw curved and irregular lines. French curves are made of clear plastic and flexible curves are made of flexible plastic coated over a metal core.
- *Templates* and *stencils* are useful when a designer is drawing multiple symbols of the same size. These tools are sized to scale with the drawing and help the designer to duplicate the same size and/or species of plants. Templates and stencils have common geometric shapes or are trade specific. A landscaping template, for example, may have palm tree branch shapes and a set of graduated shrubs.

Alphabet of Lines

The **Alphabet of Lines** was developed by the American Society of Mechanical Engineers (ASME) to ensure universal meaning to the lines of drawings. Lines are drawn using different forms, such as dashes, and thicknesses (widths) to represent specific components or areas, **Figure 16-11**.

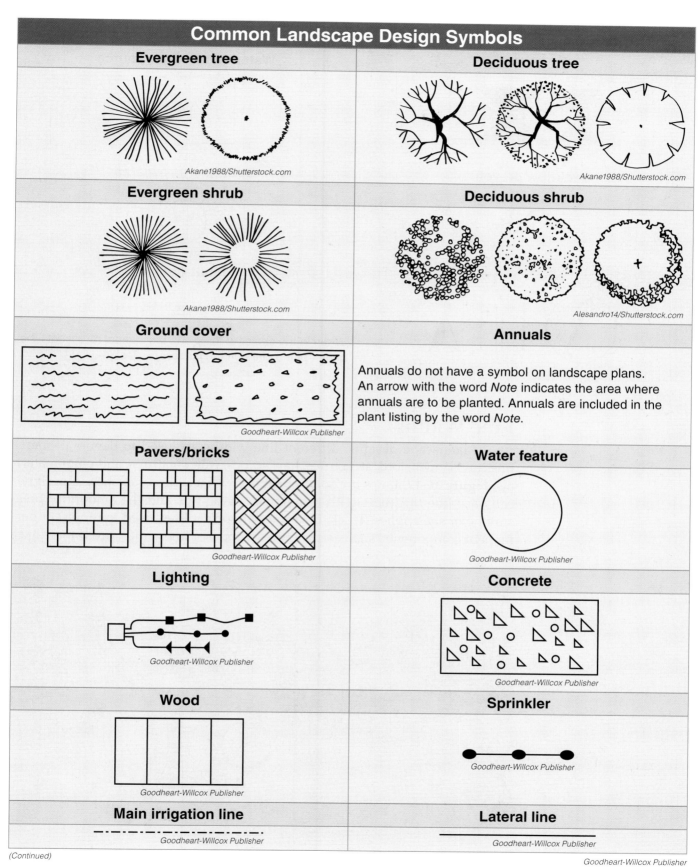

Common Landscape Design Symbols

Evergreen tree
Akane1988/Shutterstock.com

Deciduous tree
Akane1988/Shutterstock.com

Evergreen shrub
Akane1988/Shutterstock.com

Deciduous shrub
Alesandro14/Shutterstock.com

Ground cover
Goodheart-Willcox Publisher

Annuals

Annuals do not have a symbol on landscape plans. An arrow with the word *Note* indicates the area where annuals are to be planted. Annuals are included in the plant listing by the word *Note*.

Pavers/bricks
Goodheart-Willcox Publisher

Water feature
Goodheart-Willcox Publisher

Lighting
Goodheart-Willcox Publisher

Concrete
Goodheart-Willcox Publisher

Wood
Goodheart-Willcox Publisher

Sprinkler
Goodheart-Willcox Publisher

Main irrigation line
Goodheart-Willcox Publisher

Lateral line
Goodheart-Willcox Publisher

(Continued)

Goodheart-Willcox Publisher

Figure 16-11. Using standard line variations and symbols helps viewers properly interpret drawings and minimize errors.

Common Landscape Design Symbols *(Figure 16-11, continued)*

Control box	Water meter/water source
	M
Backflow preventer	**Sprinkler throw area**
-N-	
North arrow	**Plant Center**
	X or •
	When in the center of the plant, the symbol represents the center of the plant on the landscape design.

Goodheart-Willcox Publisher

Line Widths

In landscape designs, different line widths are used to denote property lines and dimensions, structures, hardscapes, water features, and plant materials, **Figure 16-12**. Lines are solid or set up with a series of dashes. A designer can vary line thickness with different drawing tips and the amount of pressure he or she applies. Thick, bold lines are object lines used to represent permanent components, such as structures, property lines, and hardscape edges.

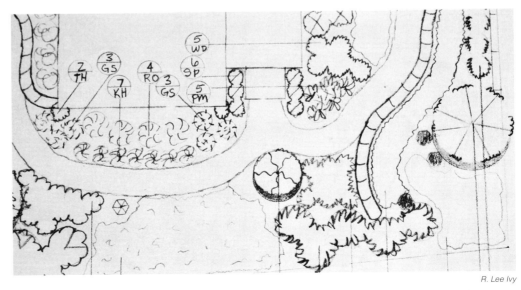

R. Lee Ivy

Figure 16-12. Different line widths are used to denote property lines and dimensions, structures, hardscapes, water features, and plant materials.

Turfgrass edges, plant material canopies, and plant materials are drawn with thinner lines.

Drawing Components

Hand drawings and CAD drawings may be created differently but they both include the same components that convey the same types of information.

- A *title block* provides site- or project-specific information, such as the client's name, property name and address, the designer's name, the date, and the scale of the drawing, **Figure 16-13**.
- The *scale* of a drawing is the size of the object in the drawing in direct proportion to the size of the actual object. A scale of 1″ = 1′, for example, indicates that 1″ on the drawing is equal to 1′ of length of the object being installed or constructed.
- A *directional arrow* indicates true north and enables the user to orient him or herself to the site. The directional arrow is also used on standard maps. A directional arrow may also be referred to as a *north arrow*.
- A *legend* is a key to the symbols used on the landscape design drawing. It explains what each symbol represents. The legend will include varied information, such as a list of plants, their names, the number of each plant needed, and their sizes at installation. It may also describe textures and types of hardscape materials.

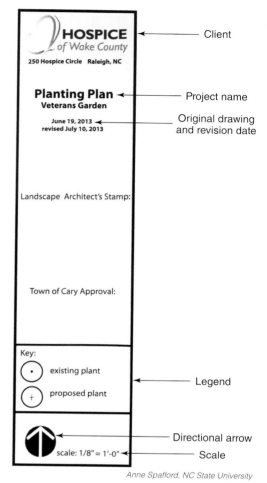

Anne Spafford, NC State University

Figure 16-13. A title block provides the site address, designer's information, a key, and the dates of the original drawing and its revisions. It may also include space for the town's stamp of approval.

Directing the Viewer's Eye

What Catches Your Eye?

When viewing a landscape design, certain elements gain the eye's attention almost immediately. Some people are drawn to the center of a drawing as they notice the textures and curves of plant canopies and curvilinear lines of landscape beds, turf areas, and hardscapes. Others first notice the heavy and thin lines of the property borders or building outlines. The designer intentionally creates lines that draw the viewer's eye through the drawing to his or her intended focal point. In the drawing on the right, for example, the viewer's eye is drawn immediately along the path. Take time to study a landscape drawing and identify the illustrator's efforts to direct your attention and highlight prominent features and components of the site.

Whitechair/Shutterstock.com

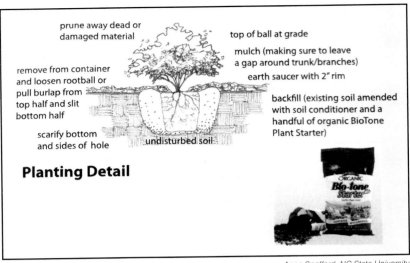

Planting Detail

prune away dead or
damaged material

top of ball at grade

mulch (making sure to leave
a gap around trunk/branches)

remove from container
and loosen rootball or
pull burlap from
top half and slit
bottom half

earth saucer with 2" rim

backfill (existing soil amended
with soil conditioner and a
handful of organic BioTone
Plant Starter)

scarify bottom
and sides of hole

undisturbed soil

Anne Spafford, NC State University

Figure 16-14. Drawing notes explain specific objectives for the landscape installation, including designer objectives and specifics about individual plants.

In some cases, planting instructions, designer notes, and site specifics are included on the drawing, **Figure 16-14**. This information can provide details to the client, such as the type of mulch being used for pathways or specifics on plant materials chosen for a shade garden. These notes may also provide the materials procurer information on specific products to purchase and deliver on a specific timeline.

Lettering

Lettering is the process of placing text on the drawing to clarify the information on the drawing. Lettering must be legible, evenly spaced, and written horizontally. All text is oriented in the same direction (horizontally) to ensure readability and eliminate the need to turn the drawing.

To keep lettering evenly spaced and horizontal, designers often draw light horizontal and vertical guidelines, **Figure 16-15**. The lines are drawn lightly so they can be easily erased. A variety of fonts can be used for lettering. Certain fonts are universally accepted as professional while others are deemed creative.

Jarred Taylor, NC State University

Figure 16-15. Designers practice writing to ensure their lettering is evenly spaced and sized. Use of this technique creates professional and consistent notation.

Symbols

Symbols are small shapes used to indicate elements of a landscape design from an aerial view (plan-view perspective). Drawing symbols in a uniform fashion will ensure that designers and other parties viewing the plan will recognize which components they represent, **Figure 16-16**. A designer can improve his or her skill and consistency by practicing drawing symbols. The same lines and patterns used to indicate texture, shadows, and other materials should be used consistently. All symbols and graphic representations of landscape components must be drawn to scale.

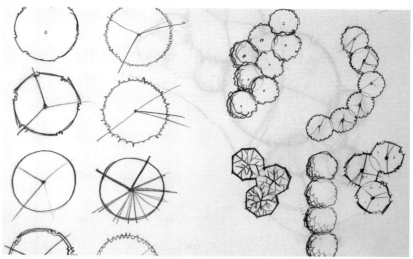

Jarred Taylor, NC State University

Figure 16-16. The symbols on a design provide unique representations of plants, showing texture, size, and shadows. These may be universal across multiple designs for uniform recognition.

Specific Plant Representations

Deciduous and evergreen plantings are distinguished with different symbols and line widths. A Japanese maple, for example, is a small deciduous tree that may be represented by thin strokes with softer edges, whereas an evergreen screening plant, such as a holly, may be drawn with thicker strokes and more jagged lines. Designer symbol use may vary but the textures and patterns will follow common stroke thicknesses. See **Figure 16-17**.

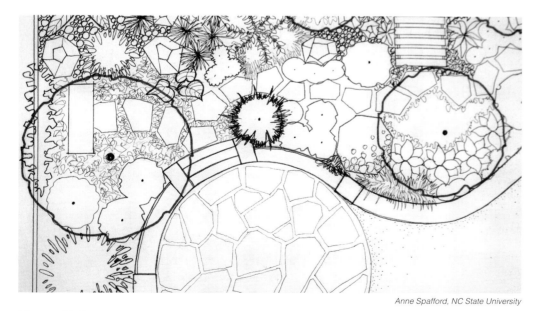

Anne Spafford, NC State University

Figure 16-17. Designers use line thicknesses or irregular strokes to create clear representations of individual plants.

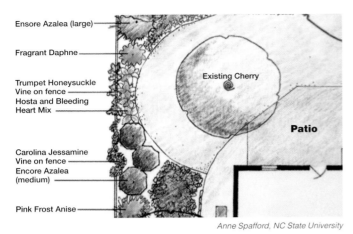

Ensore Azalea (large)

Fragrant Daphne

Trumpet Honeysuckle
Vine on fence
Hosta and Bleeding
Heart Mix

Existing Cherry

Patio

Carolina Jessamine
Vine on fence
Encore Azalea
(medium)

Pink Frost Anise

Anne Spafford, NC State University

Figure 16-18. A vine trained on a structure may be drawn linearly as compared to branches on a tree radiating from the center.

Vines

Climbing vines are represented in a linear fashion as opposed to trees and shrubs, which are drawn radiating from a center stem or trunk. In many cases, vines are trained on a fence, trellis, or other upright structure and the designer may simply apply textural graphics, **Figure 16-18**, to the structure to signify the presence of a trailing plant.

Hardscape Symbols

Hardscape symbols represent materials, such as flagstones, brick pavers, or concrete, **Figure 16-19**. The designer may indicate patterns and textures of a large hardscape area by applying the descriptive symbols to a small area. When done properly, the viewer assumes the pattern is repeated throughout the particular area.

Some materials are easily recognized due to their common shapes but other materials must be illustrated in more detail. Bricks in a rectangular pattern, for example, are easily recognized due to their common shape, but the varied shapes and 2- and 3-piece patterns of concrete pavers must be illustrated in detail, **Figure 16-20**. A flagstone pathway will include irregular lines and shapes, while indiscriminate and plain concrete walkways with expansion joints between rectangular shapes will have very little hatching. Materials that mimic other commonly used materials, such as concrete stamped with a flagstone or wood grain pattern, require different texture representation than the original material. This type of material may be identified with notes on the drawing or in a special section on the landscape plan, **Figure 16-21**.

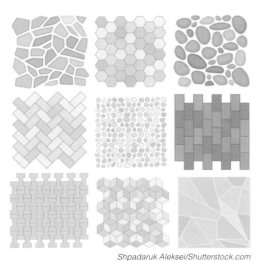

Shpadaruk Aleksei/Shutterstock.com

Figure 16-19. Hardscape materials are represented with patterns, such as basketweaves, herringbones, or common hatching.

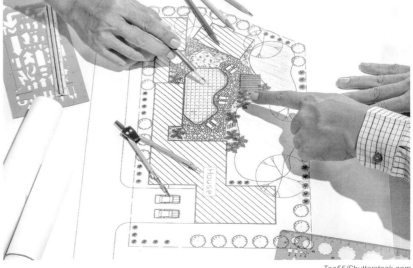

Toa55/Shutterstock.com

Figure 16-20. Many patterns drawn in groupings of three or four can be used to represent the variability of materials.

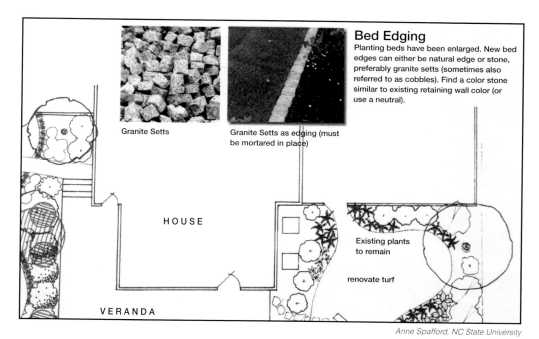

Bed Edging
Planting beds have been enlarged. New bed edges can either be natural edge or stone, preferably granite setts (sometimes also referred to as cobbles). Find a color stone similar to existing retaining wall color (or use a neutral).

Granite Setts

Granite Setts as edging (must be mortared in place)

HOUSE

Existing plants to remain

renovate turf

VERANDA

Anne Spafford, NC State University

Figure 16-21. Lines may be added along with descriptive notes when using unique patterns.

Textures

A combination of lines and dots are used to signify textures on symbols and other areas of the landscape, such as hardscape or wood materials. For example, a finely textured plant, such as common yarrow, would be represented with light lines and small dots. A large-textured plant, such as a rhododendron, would be represented by large, curved lines and larger dots or half circles.

Stippling, hatching, circling, and bubbling can also be used on symbols to provide more clarity of shape and texture on the drawing, **Figure 16-22**. These additions may represent interesting components, such as flower blooms.

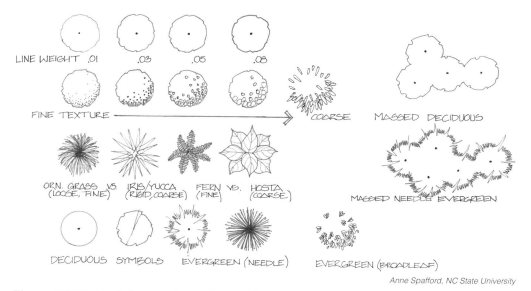

LINE WEIGHT .01   .03   .05   .08

FINE TEXTURE ⟶ COARSE   MASSED DECIDUOUS

ORN. GRASS VS
(LOOSE, FINE)   IRIS/YUCCA
(RIGID, COARSE)   FERN VS.
(FINE)   HOSTA
(COARSE)

MASSED NEEDLE EVERGREEN

DECIDUOUS SYMBOLS   EVERGREEN (NEEDLE)   EVERGREEN (BROADLEAF)

Anne Spafford, NC State University

Figure 16-22. Leaf sizes and margins can be represented by textural strokes on a design. Stippling, hatching, circling, and bubbling further represent flower sizes and leaf shapes. Broad and narrow strokes can represent textural differences.

Jarred Taylor, NC State University

Figure 16-23. Shadows provide dimensionality to a design and can help the viewer determine the design's orientation.

Shadows

Shadows are added to drawings to provide dimensionality, height-to-width ratio, and the direction of the sun, **Figure 16-23**. The shadow on a design facing north would be placed on the north side of plant materials, structures, and other landscape components that would cast a shadow.

Stencils

Stencils can be used to draw accurate and consistent standardized symbols. These tools, **Figure 16-24**, come in various sizes and contain many variations of common symbols, such as circles, and of irregular-shaped objects. Stencils can also be used to illustrate gazebos, fences, retaining walls, and other landscape components. Care must be taken when using a stencil to avoid smudging the lead or ink with the stencil as it moves across the drawing.

Types of Drawings

As explained earlier, multiple drawings are included with a landscape design. These drawings include designs for different systems, such as the irrigation or electrical system, but they also include drawings of the landscape from different views.

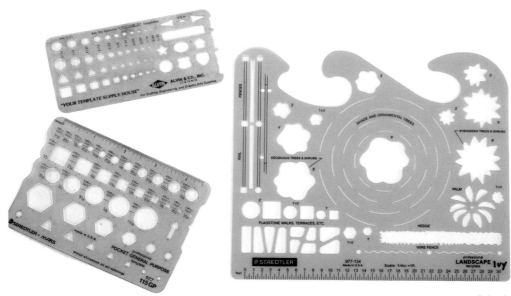

R. Lee Ivy

Figure 16-24. Various stencils are available to ensure design elements are evenly duplicated. The stencils provide uniformity and help beginning designers develop skills. With practice, the stencils may become unnecessary.

Viewpoints

- *Plan-view perspectives* provide representation of all landscape elements, their relation to each other, and the relative size of each component as seen from above, **Figure 16-25A**.
- A *perspective drawing* shows the side of a building, such as the front of a house, with its landscaping installed, **Figure 16-25B**. A perspective drawing will depict the landscape materials in proportion to the new or existing buildings.
- An *orthographic projection drawing* is a representation of the separate views of an object on a two-dimensional surface. It shows the width, depth, and height of the object and often includes dimensions. To create such a drawing, you must be able to visualize an object in three dimensions. This type of drawing is typically used in landscape design to illustrate constructed objects or structures, such as a bench or wooden deck. See **Figure 16-26**.

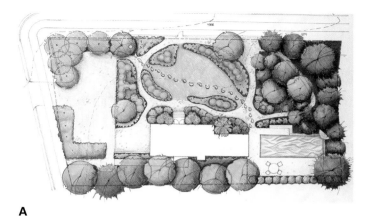

A

B   *Jarred Taylor, NC State University*

Figure 16-25. A—An overhead view or plan view gives the perspective of the overall site, its boundaries, and all components within. B—A perspective drawing provides a viewpoint as if the viewer were standing on the site. Many clients can better visualize the proposed finished product using this view.

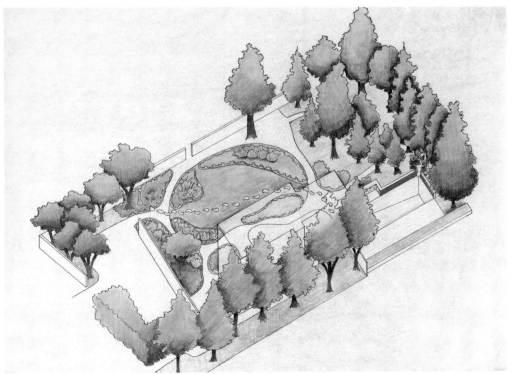

Jarred Taylor, NC State University

Figure 16-26. Orthographic drawings provide dimensionality to objects and allow better representation of each element of the design.

Sketches

Sketches are drawings of the site, proposed or existing structures, and the designer's interpretation of the client's ideas. Site analysis may also include designer notes and ideas about concealing unattractive components, such as an air conditioner, and viewpoints from various windows. Other areas, hardscapes, and neighboring issues may also be indicated on a site analysis to ensure every angle and issue is considered. See **Figure 16-27**.

Topographic Maps

Topographic maps illustrate the physical attributes of the site. The parallel lines on a topographical map are spaced at specific intervals measured in feet. Narrow spaces between lines represent rapid changes in elevation and wider distances between the lines denote gradual changes in elevation, **Figure 16-28**. Topographical maps serve several purposes, including:

- Determining how water moves across the site.
- The amount of light exposure an area is likely to receive. A south facing slope, for example, will likely be warmer during the year due to more direct sunlight.
- Identifying areas with ambient and soil temperature variations due to light exposure or cold air settling in lower areas.

Jarred Taylor, NC State University

Figure 16-27. Sketches include existing site elements as well as proposed changes, designer's notes, and client preferences. These are created after the initial meeting with the client.

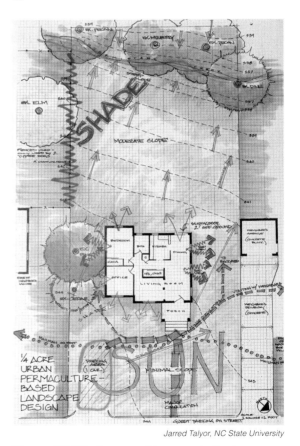

Jarred Talyor, NC State University

Figure 16-28. Topographic maps indicate elevation changes, which can be used to help predict air and water movement across a site. The contour lines, which are in 2′ or 10′ increments, represent changes in elevation across an area.

Career Connection

Brock Lavrack, Senior Branch Manager for BrightView Landscape Services

Brock Lavrack oversees BrightView Landscape Services' Raleigh and Greensboro branches as a senior branch manager. Brock's earliest management experience occurred when he ran his own small landscaping business before attending NC State. After graduation, Brock went to work at BrightView and began his career as a spray technician. (BrightView was created by a merger between Brickman Group and ValleyCrest in 2014.)

Brock's experience as a small business owner, working in the field, and on various rungs of the corporate ladder contribute to his success as a branch manager. His experiences give him knowledge and understanding of every aspect of the business that allows him to make informed decisions on everything from hiring personnel to managing financials.

Brock and Jennifer Lavrack

Brock continues to enjoy networking and maintaining relationships with those he has met over the years in the landscaping industry. He looks forward to gaining more insight and experience within the industry and continuously seeks improvements for BrightView and the industry. Brock also enjoys helping others who are seeking a career in the field.

Consider This

1. In which ways does Brock's experience as a small business owner help him manage his branches at BrightView?
2. What types of personal and professional skills do you think Brock possesses? How do these skills help him manage his employees?

Functional Diagrams

A *functional diagram* is used to roughly designate areas for specific purposes, such as dining and play areas, **Figure 16-29**. A functional diagram will also identify public, private, and utility areas. Functional diagrams are sometimes referred to as *bubble diagrams* or *conceptual drawings*.

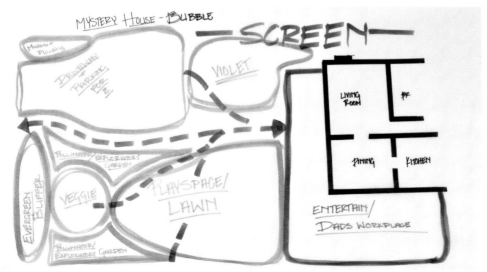

Jarred Talyor, NC State University

Figure 16-29. Functional diagrams are helpful in identifying use areas, such as flow of traffic, play areas, outdoor dining areas, and screening on property lines.

Preliminary Design

A *preliminary design* is used to identify plant selections and specific landscape elements, such as walkways, gazebos, patios, and existing utilities. This type of design can be used to discuss plant choices and the hardscape materials. Material and labor estimates may also be generated from this design, **Figure 16-30A**. A designer would begin with a surveyor's drawing or plot plan of the site that indicates property boundaries, existing structure dimensions, and details of other site characteristics.

Final Design

The final design, **Figure 16-30B**, can be presented to the client for approval. The *final design* includes all existing and proposed elements of the design. This drawing is also used by the installer as the construction or installation guide.

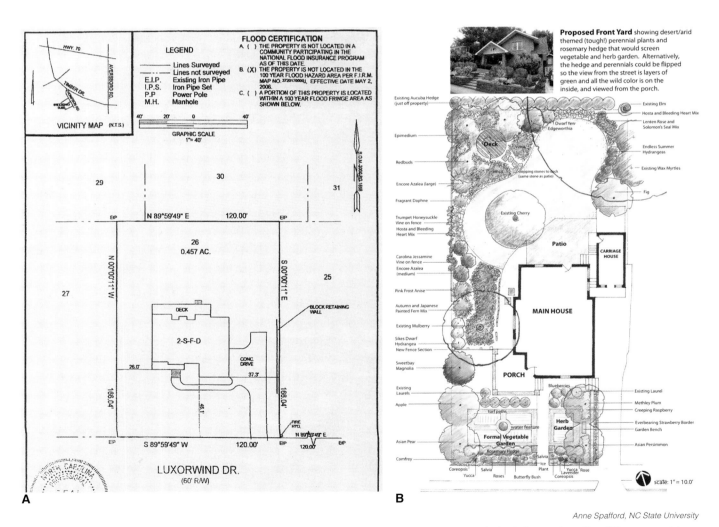

Anne Spafford, NC State University

Figure 16-30. A—A site survey or plot map/plan is used to generate the majority of site information. B—Clients would view a final design for approval before construction begins. This plan would provide all necessary information about the site and installation directives.

Keeping Track

Create a Design Checklist

- Determine client needs and site-specific information.
- Select a scale to represent the site on a workable paper size, usually 18″ × 24″.
- Place the paper on a drawing board parallel to the straight edge; use tape to secure.
- Select the appropriate drawing instruments.
- Lay out the existing components of the site.
- Determine the use areas.
- Identify focal points for specific areas.
- Develop the shape of each area.
- Select plants that fit the function of each area.
- Lay out the hardscape and utility areas.
- Label all of the elements.
- List all plants and quantities.
- Trace the final design for paper duplication or scan for digital duplication.

Planting Diagrams

A *planting diagram* shows the shape, color, location, size, and quantities of the specific plants that will be used, **Figure 16-31**. Construction details are included where specific instructions are needed.

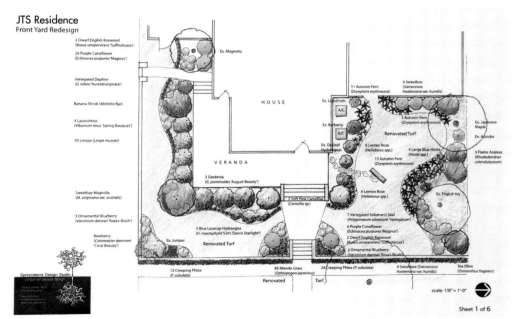

Anne Spafford, NC State University

Figure 16-31. Planting diagrams are helpful in viewing the plants chosen for a site. Colors, textures, and mature sizes can be presented to the viewer.

Summarize Client Requirements

A landscape drawing should summarize the client's expectations and give details of each of the landscape elements. These expectations and elements should be determined during the initial client meeting and displayed clearly on the landscape plan. The plan should clearly convey the overall objectives. The plan is also used to sell the project to the client while displaying professionalism and attention to detail. See **Figure 16-32**.

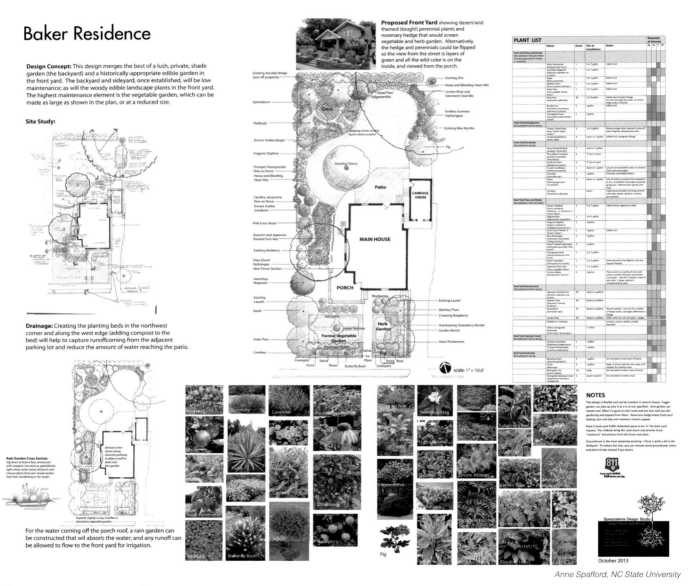

Anne Spafford, NC State University

Figure 16-32. The complete design with color images, a plant list, and an explanation of water flow and conservation may be presented to the client to help sell the project.

Summary

- A landscape design conveys information to clients, installers, and maintenance personnel.
- Landscape design drawings may be created by hand or with drafting software.
- Design drawings can be created to portray the landscape from different perspectives, including aerial views (plan view), side views (elevations), and as an object on a two-dimensional surface (orthographic projection).
- The designer must have information regarding the topography of a site, including water flow, light exposure, and areas with varying ambient and soil temperatures, before creating a design.
- The designer must have information regarding existing structures on the site as well as any proposed structures before creating a design.
- A preliminary design identifies existing landscape elements and initial concepts.
- The final design is the version that is deliverable to the client for approval. It includes all existing and proposed elements of the design.
- Landscape design drawings have many standard components, including a title block, the scale used, a directional arrow, a legend, lettering, and symbols.
- The title block contains site- or project-specific information, such as the client's name, property name and address, the designer's name, the date, and the scale of the drawing.
- A legend is a key to the symbols used on the landscape design drawing.
- Lettering is the process of placing text on the drawing to clarify the information conveyed by the drawing.
- Symbols are small shapes used on a design drawing to indicate elements of a landscape design from an aerial view (plan-view perspective).
- Symbols, textures, and shadows give the viewer valuable information about the landscape elements.
- Drafting media are the materials on which drawings are made or printed.
- Drawings can be reproduced on vellum, polyester film, or in digital format.
- Tools such as triangles, T-squares, pencils, pens, scales, compasses, and curves are used to create landscape drawings.
- Architect's and engineer's scales are used to draw objects to full, reduced, or enlarged size and to draw distances to scale.
- In landscape designs, different line widths and forms are used to denote property lines and dimensions, structures, hardscapes, water features, and plant materials.
- A landscape drawing should summarize the client's expectations, give details of each landscape component, and convey overall objectives.

Chapter Review

Know and Understand ⤴

Answer the following questions using the information provided in the chapter.

1. The computer software used to create landscape drawings is referred to as _____.
   A. RFP
   B. PDF
   C. CAD
   D. GPS

2. The materials on which drawings are made or printed is _____.
   A. drafting media
   B. prelim media
   C. board media
   D. monoculture

3. Which of the following is translucent drawing paper?
   A. Quadrille paper.
   B. Tracing paper.
   C. Bond paper.
   D. Vellum paper.

4. Drafting paper that has preprinted color grids is referred to as _____.
   A. quadrille paper
   B. tracing paper
   C. bond paper
   D. vellum paper

5. Which of the following paper is treated with a synthetic resin to make it transparent?
   A. Quadrille paper.
   B. Tracing paper.
   C. Bond paper.
   D. Vellum paper.

6. The process in which a potential client notifies prospective landscape companies to bid a price on the project is a(n) _____.
   A. RFP
   B. CAD
   C. GPS
   D. PDF

7. A drawing tool used to make straight, perpendicular lines using the edge of the drawing board is a _____.
   A. protractor
   B. triangle
   C. T-square
   D. All of the above.

8. *True or False?* Harder leads are used to draw thicker lines and softer leads are used to draw thinner lines.
   A. True.
   B. False.

9. *True or False?* A dusting brush should be used to remove eraser shavings to prevent the ink from smearing.
   A. True.
   B. False.

10. *True or False?* Designers may draw over pencil lines with ink to create permanent lines once the drawing is completed.
    A. True.
    B. False.

11. The proportional relationship between the size of the part and the size of the drawing is referred to as _____.
    A. tile
    B. schedule
    C. scale
    D. block

12. Which of the following is used to draw vertical and inclined lines?
    A. Compass.
    B. Flexible curve.
    C. Stencil.
    D. Triangle.

13. Which of the following is used to draw circles and arcs?
    A. Compass.
    B. Triangle.
    C. T-square.
    D. All of the above.

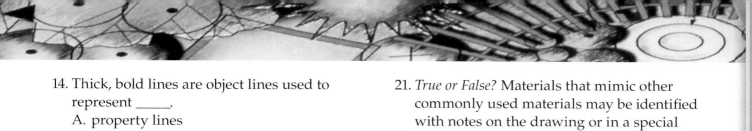

14. Thick, bold lines are object lines used to represent _____.
    A. property lines
    B. permanent components
    C. hardscape edges
    D. All of the above.

15. Which of the following provides site- or project-specific information?
    A. Legend.
    B. Template.
    C. Title block.
    D. All of the above.

16. Which of the following is a key to the symbols used on the landscape design drawing?
    A. Legend.
    B. Template.
    C. Title block.
    D. All of the above.

17. *True or False?* The process of placing text on the drawing to clarify the information on the drawing is referred to as lettering.
    A. True.
    B. False.

18. The small shapes used to indicate elements of a landscape design from an aerial view are referred to as _____.
    A. plans
    B. designs
    C. symbols
    D. All of the above.

19. *True or False?* Climbing vines are drawn radiating from the center vine.
    A. True.
    B. False.

20. *True or False?* Patterns of a large hardscape area may be indicated by applying the descriptive symbols to a small area on the drawing.
    A. True.
    B. False.

21. *True or False?* Materials that mimic other commonly used materials may be identified with notes on the drawing or in a special section on the landscape plan.
    A. True.
    B. False.

22. Textures on symbols and other areas of the landscape are signified by a combination of _____.
    A. lines and dots
    B. dashed lines
    C. hatching
    D. All of the above.

23. Which of the following is added to drawings to provide dimensionality, height-to-width ratio, and indicate the direction of the sun?
    A. Textures.
    B. Stippling.
    C. Shadows.
    D. Circles.

24. Which type of drawing provides the relative size of each component as seen from above and the representation of all landscape elements and their relation to each other?
    A. Perspective drawing.
    B. Plan-view.
    C. Orthographic projection drawing.
    D. Sketches.

25. Which of the following is a representation of the separate views of an object on a two-dimensional surface?
    A. Perspective drawing.
    B. Plan-view.
    C. Orthographic projection drawing.
    D. Sketches.

26. Which of the following shows the side of a building, such as the front of a house, with its landscaping installed?
    A. Elevation drawing.
    B. Plan-view.
    C. Orthographic projection drawing.
    D. Sketches.

27. Which of the following is used to roughly designate areas for specific purposes, such as dining and play areas?
    A. Planting diagram.
    B. Preliminary design.
    C. Functional diagram.
    D. Elevation diagram.

28. Which of the following is used to identify plant selections and specific landscape elements, such as walkways, gazebos, patios, and existing utilities?
    A. Bubble drawing.
    B. Preliminary design.
    C. Functional diagram.
    D. Planting diagram.

29. Which of the following shows the shape, color, location, size, and quantities of the specific plants that will be used?
    A. Planting diagram.
    B. Bubble diagram.
    C. Preliminary diagram.
    D. Functional diagram.

30. *True or False?* A landscape drawing should summarize the client's expectations and give details of each of the landscape elements.
    A. True.
    B. False.

Thinking Critically

1. Explain business concepts used by landscape design companies. Are they similar to those used by other landscape companies?

2. Which landscape drawing details are most important and why?

3. Describe an accessible landscape design from the point of view of someone using a wheelchair.

4. Identify a favorite deciduous and evergreen tree. Record the prominent features that would require illustration, such as the shape, foliage texture, and spacing between the branches. Draw the trees with their prominent features identified.

5. Choose a building that is important to you, such as your residence or school. View the building from a satellite image and record the most dominant lines and features. Note what would need to be transferred to a hand drawing.

Suggested Activities

1. Working in teams of 2 to 4, choose a location on the school campus to use as the site for a new design. Accurately measure and calculate the dimensions of the site and use technical drawing tools and/or software to create a landscape plan. The design plan should include scale, orientation, title box, recognized symbols, appropriate plant selection for the site, and appropriate landscape materials for the site. The design should also use the principles and elements of design.

2. Establish a baseline of information to gain from an initial client interaction. Create a questionnaire for the client to answer before the initial meeting to help the client determine what they need and want in their new landscape.

3. Identify necessary components of a landscape design kit, including design space and tools.

4. Knowing how to read a measurement scale is a needed skill. Practice using an architect's or engineer's scale and drawing simple objects to different scales.

5. Identify common landscape symbols used in landscape designs. Determine the ones you would use the most when developing a drawing.

6. Create a simple base plan and draw it at different scales. Include basic components, such as the main structure, driveway, and established walkways. Keep the amount of plant materials and planting beds to a minimum. Identify the landscape symbols in the drawing's legend.

7. Create a functional and aesthetically pleasing landscape plan. You may use the basic plan from the preceding activity and make it more elaborate. Add components, such as paths, a hardscape area, and a small water feature. Include and identify major areas of the design, such as the public, outdoor living, and service areas.

8. Explain the organization and location of activities within the landscape plan from the preceding activity. Identify the flow of traffic.

9. Identify and explain how you incorporated or applied the principles and elements of design to your landscape plan.

CHAPTER

17

Starting a Business

While studying this chapter, look for the activity icon 📲 to:

- **Practice** vocabulary terms with Words to Know activities.
- **Expand** learning with identification activities.
- **Reinforce** what you learn by completing Know and Understand questions.

G-WLEARNING.com

www.g-wlearning.com/agriculture

Chapter Outcomes

After studying this chapter, you will be able to:

- Identify and describe the five basic business structures.
- Develop a business plan to be used when acquiring credit and investors.
- Write a mission and vision statement for a business.
- Explain how to set goals and use demographics.
- Explain how to choose a name and logo and how to establish a brand image.
- Explain the purpose of basic financial reports used in business accounting.
- Determine the value of a business and define basic financial terms.
- Determine advertising strategies that generate new clientele.

Key Terms ↪

accountant
accounts payable
advertising
asset
balance sheet
Better Business Bureau (BBB)
bookkeeper
brand image
budget
business license
business plan
C corporation
capital
cash flow statement
cooperative
corporation
current asset
current liability
debt
demographics

doing business as (DBA)
employer identification number (EIN)
entrepreneur
equity
expense
fixed expense
goal
income
income statement
inventory
liability
limited liability company (LLC)
liquid asset
logo
long-term goal
long-term liability
marketing
mission statement
networking

net worth
niche market
noncurrent asset
nonliquid asset
partnership
pass-through taxation
profit
profit and loss statement (P&L)
return on investment (ROI)
S corporation
search engine optimization (SEO)
short-term goal
slogan
SMART goals
sole proprietorship
tagline
target market
tax identification number (TIN)
variable expense
vision statement

Introduction

There are many opportunities to be an entrepreneur and own your own business in the United States. An *entrepreneur* is someone who organizes and manages a business and assumes the risks involved. Starting a business is an exciting venture, but it can also be intimidating. It is best to research any new business idea before committing resources. You may also want to complete some introductory business courses to gain a broader understanding and increase your chance for success. This chapter introduces you to basic business practices and ways to promote a new business.

ESB Professional/Shutterstock.com

Figure 17-1. Seeking advice from other business owners will present you with insight gained by personal experience. Fellow business owners can be valuable resources and may be able to offer advice on business practices to suppliers, bookkeepers, and bankers.

Business Structures

The different business structures determine who owns the company and who is liable for its financial actions. Each type of business structure has advantages and disadvantages that should be taken into account when setting up a new business. It is always wise for a new entrepreneur to take time to research and understand each aspect of a business, including its structure. It is also advisable to communicate and seek advice from other business owners to determine which structure would be most beneficial, **Figure 17-1**. The five basic business structures are sole proprietorships, partnerships, limited liability companies (LLCs), corporations, and cooperatives.

Sole Proprietorship

Many individuals select a sole proprietorship structure for a new business. In a *sole proprietorship*, one individual is in a business alone, **Figure 17-2**. The owner is solely responsible for all debts incurred by the business. *Debts*

Monkey Business Images/Shutterstock.com

Figure 17-2. Owning a sole proprietorship means taking risks, trying new ideas, and providing quality services to a community.

are the money, goods, or services the company owes. The business' assets and liabilities are not separate from the owner's personal holdings. An *asset* is valuable and available property owned by a business. A *liability* is a financial obligation or debt of a company. If the business fails, the owner's personal assets may be used to settle company debts.

Sole proprietorship is the simplest business structure and perhaps the easiest for a new entrepreneur. Sole proprietors often use their own capital as an investment resource, as banks may be hesitant to provide loans to small, unproven startup businesses. *Capital* is the money needed to purchase materials and operate a business. Business capital comes in two main forms, debt and equity. A bank loan is an example of business debt. *Equity* is the difference between the business' worth minus what it owes. The owner uses pass-through taxation and the business is considered a pass-through entity. *Pass-through taxation* allows the owner to pay taxes on income from the business on his or her personal tax returns.

Partnership

A *partnership* business structure is one in which two or more people invest in and own the business. The partners have a formal agreement stating how the ownership, profits, and debts are divided between the investors, **Figure 17-3**. A company's *profit* is the money the business earns after deducting its expenses, and debts are the goods, services, or money the company owes. The agreement will also include procedures dictating how aspects of the business will be handled. It will cover things such as how a partner's passing or wish to leave the business will be handled. The partners may use pass-through taxation on the income from the business.

There are three types of partnerships: general, limited, and limited liability.

- In a *general partnership*, the partners have unlimited liability in their business. The partners are equally responsible for all debts incurred by the business. This means that personal assets of the partners are at risk if the business fails.
- *Limited partnerships (LP)* have general and limited partners. General partners manage the business and have unlimited liability. Limited partners are typically investors who are involved financially but not in the daily operation of the business. They are liable for debts only to the extent of the money they invested.
- In a *limited liability partnership (LLP)*, each of the partners has limited liability and protection from the negligence of another partner. The degree of protection that each partner receives from the LLP will vary by state.

Monkey Business Images/Shutterstock.com

Figure 17-3. The success of a business partnership depends on the ability of the partners to forge and maintain a strong, productive relationship. Identifying mutual long- and short-term goals, defining individual roles, and clearly communicating ideas of what the business should be are a few essentials of establishing a strong partnership.

Limited Liability Company (LLC)

A *limited liability company (LLC)* has the pass-through taxation of a partnership or sole proprietorship combined with the limited liability of a corporation. This allows the owners to pay a lower tax rate than corporations pay and to protect a larger amount of personal assets. Each of the owners is classified as self-employed and is required to pay self-employment taxes, such as Social Security and Medicare. Some states have term limits on LLCs and specific requirements should a partner leave or dissolution occur.

An LLC has flexibility in choosing an accounting method and how the management of the business is structured. It does not have the strict meeting and business documentation of a corporation and it allows flexibility for profit distribution among owners. An LLC may be incorporated in a different state than the one in which they operate for whatever advantages the state offers. However, there may be ongoing fees and taxes for both states.

Figure 17-4. Establishing a small business as a corporation may be the best option for some entrepreneurs. It is often easier to raise money or sell the business if it is incorporated.

Corporations

A *corporation* is a business owned by stock- or shareholders who share in profits and losses. (A business is *incorporated* legally to become a corporation.) The stockholders appoint a board to oversee the business' activities, **Figure 17-4**. The corporation is liable for the finances and actions of the business, the shareholders are not. A corporation is subject to corporate taxation in which a significant tax percentage is paid on the net income of the company. In addition, taxes are often paid twice on income from corporations. They are paid on the initial profits of the corporation and on dividends claimed by stockholders when they file their personal income tax forms.

Corporations are required to hold annual meetings of directors and shareholders and keep detailed documents and records of all corporate meetings. A corporation must also keep detailed records for all major business decisions.

S Corporations and C corporations

A business may be set up as a C corporation or an S corporation. An *S corporation* is a pass-through entity in which the business itself is not taxed and the business owner reports the business' income on his or her personal tax returns. A business may become an S corporation by filing a form with the IRS and sometimes with the state. An S corporation has more flexibility in choosing an accounting method. A *C corporation* is a separate taxpayer. The income and expenses are taxed to the corporation and not the owners. Most small business owners choose to incorporate as an S corporation to avoid the double taxation.

Cooperatives

A *cooperative* is a business structure with at least five members. Each member is an owner and has equal voting rights, regardless of his or her level of involvement. The profits are distributed among the owners. This structure is not common for landscape businesses but has been effectively operated in food production and may be adaptable to homeowners' associations or community planning groups, **Figure 17-5**.

Doing Business As (DBA)

A company may file for a *doing business as (DBA)* to operate under a name different from its legal, registered name. A DBA is required in some states for the protection of consumers conducting business with the entity. Sole proprietorships commonly use DBAs because the business' name is legally the name of the owner. The DBA allows the business owner use of the business' real name. If a sole proprietorship uses the owner's name, such as Tim Smith's Lawn Service, the business does not need a DBA. Once the DBA is registered, the owner can use the company's name to open bank accounts and enter contracts. Failing to file a DBA and doing business under a different name may incur penalties and fines. LLCs and corporations may also register for a DBA. A DBA allows the owner to operate multiple businesses without having to form a separate one for each business. This is common with franchise businesses.

Figure 17-5. Members of a cooperative share voting rights, profits, and decision-making responsibilities.

Registration for a DBA usually takes place at the county level, although some states have state level DBA registration. The fees and manner of registration will vary. Some states require the business to place a fictitious name announcement in the local classifieds. DBAs are also known as d/b/a, trading as, t/a, trade names, trade styles, fictitious business name, and operating as (OA).

Business Plans

One of the most important steps in creating a new business is to develop a business plan. A *business plan* is a document that states the mission of the business, examines its current condition, sets goals, and outlines strategies for achieving the goals. It is also very important to explain the scope of work the business will perform. It must be explained whether the company is to perform work in one area only, such as mowing and trimming, or provide multiple services, such as tree trimming and the application of agrichemicals as well as mowing and trimming. A lawn maintenance company performing tree trimming and chemical applications will need additional equipment, insurance, training, and certification. The marketing will also be different than if it was a lawn service company that mows and trims grass. *Marketing* is a process through which a business promotes and sells products or services that have value to businesses and consumers.

A business plan will explain how the business will be maintained and plans for growth. A business plan may also be used to gain investment partners and secure loans. Business plans should be reviewed periodically for evaluation and addressing changes in scope of work.

Business Plan Components

According to the US Small Business Association (SBA), a traditional business plan should include the following components:

- **Executive summary.** The summary communicates what the company is and why it will succeed. This summary also includes the service or product, mission statement, leadership structure, employee structure, and location.
- **Company description.** The description includes a detailed description of the service and product provided and a list of those served. It may also highlight the strengths of the business team and competitive advantages.
- **Market analysis.** The analysis identifies customers and competitors. It also explains why the business will offer higher quality services or those not currently offered by others in the area. An accurate market analysis requires extensive research of competitors and potential clientele.
- **Organization and management.** This section describes the legal business structure of the company, such as sole proprietorship or LLC. It also explains management hierarchy and qualifications of the people mentioned.
- **Service or product line.** This component explains the services and level of proficiency offered. It also includes research and development of any services and products and who owns the copyrights, patents, or other specific intellectual property.

- **Marketing and sales.** The marketing plan will identify potential customers and provide details of the strategy for gaining and retaining clients. This plan will change with trends and offerings of new products or services.
- **Funding requests.** This section provides a detailed plan of the amount needed and how it will be used. It should include personal and investor funding and a description of future financial plans.
- **Financial projections.** This section is the financial story of a business. For a new business, it should include projections based on market research. For an established business, financial projections can be based on the business' financial history and market research. Financial projections should cover the coming 3 to 5 years.

Chain of Command

A chain of command identifies the hierarchy of employees, beginning with the CEO and flowing down to the person or people at the lowest end of the chain. The chain of command dictates who is in charge of whom and helps clarify the responsibilities of each person or position. In a small company, the person at the top of the chain has a great deal of accountability and typically performs multiple jobs. As a company grows, the chain will expand with more management positions and positions requiring specific skill sets, such as managing personnel or record keeping. See **Figure 17-6**.

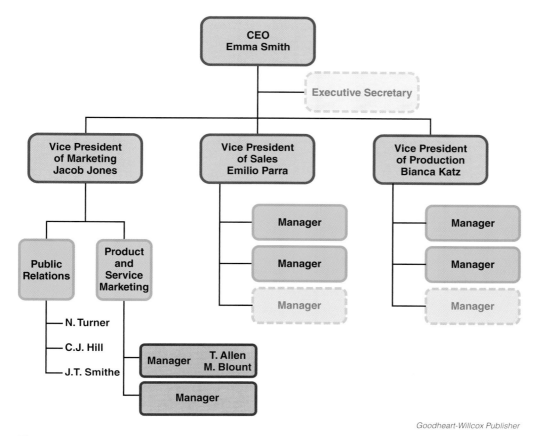

Goodheart-Willcox Publisher

Figure 17-6. The organizational structure of a business will change as a business grows. The structure must be reviewed regularly and modified to accommodate new levels of management and clearly define individual roles.

Mission and Vision Statements

A *mission statement* is a short summary of the values and purpose of a company or organization. Companies use these statements to present their ideals and values to the public. Mission statements can also be developed for individuals. A *vision statement* describes the company's goals for the future. It will commonly include specific examples of anticipated growth and achievements. It may also state beneficial effects the company anticipates for its employees, customers, and local community.

Developing a Mission Statement

There are no rules dictating the length and layout of a mission statement. However, mission statements should always be concise and define a company's goals for its customers, employees, and owners. The statement should be a true and honest reflection of the company. Mission statements should answer the following questions:

- What does the company do?
- How does it accomplish its tasks?
- What values are important to the company?
- How is the business unique?
- What makes it different from the competition?
- Why does the company do what it does? What is the company's purpose?

Reviewing the mission statements of your company's competitors and other successful businesses will give you some ideas for writing your own mission statement. It may also help you define what is unique about your business.

Student Organizations

Developing Business Skills

Some student organizations include programs that help students learn about running their own business. The National FFA organization, for example, requires students to participate in Supervised Agricultural Experience (SAE) programs. A *supervised agricultural experience (SAE)* is a student-developed project that involves hands-on learning in agriculture and natural resources. An *entrepreneurship SAE* is a hands-on learning project in which a student operates a business and is responsible for all financial risks. Students are expected to run their businesses in a professional manner using the same business principles that are covered in this chapter. Student SAEs include the following tasks:

- Using and maintaining SAE records.
- Maintaining SAE records from year to year.
- Summarizing and analyzing records.
- Devise long- and short-term goals and planning for future expansion.
- Evaluating the SAE and determining how to make it more productive and profitable.

Participating in SAEs provides students with real-life experience that they can use in the future. Many entrepreneurial SAEs provide students with income through high school and during college. Some students take their SAE business up another step and grow into a large company or sell their business for a profit.

The writing in the Bland Landscaping mission statement explains why Bland Landscaping is unique, **Figure 17-7**. It also includes information that is beneficial and enticing to potential employees as well as customers. Social media, Internet, and community involvement are used to provide specific examples of how the mission statement is implemented.

Vision Statement

Vision statements should be based in the future and serve as a road map to inspire and identify what the company wants to accomplish in the future, whereas mission statements are based in the present time and describe the company's purpose. Vision statements are living documents that should be revisited and adjusted as the company progresses.

As with mission statements, there are no set rules for writing a vision statement. The statement may be only a few sentences or short paragraphs or even presented as a list. Vision statements should be concise enough for everyone to understand the vision fully. A landscaping company's vision statement might read:

> To be recognized by our clients, our employees, and industry leaders as the best landscaping company in our target market.

Mission and vision statements are vital components of a company's success. The mission and vision statements should always be displayed prominently. Their display will serve as an inspiration to employees and stress your company's commitment to its customers. They may also attract new employees who share common ideals and goals.

We are a full-service landscaping company for commercial properties and high-end residential estates. Since 1976, we have been an innovative leader in using sound horticultural practices to keep your outdoor spaces safe and healthy.

We are committed to identifying environmental practices that help us reduce use of water, chemicals, and fossil fuels. As one of the very first Green Plus Certified companies in the nation, we strive to lead the business community as a sustainable, successful company and to be an industry leader in environmental stewardship.

Integrity is the cornerstone of our company, and we believe in operating as good corporate citizens, giving back to the community, taking care of our employees, and providing exceptional service to our customers.

BLAND LANDSCAPING CO. INC.

Bland Landscaping Co. Inc., Apex, North Carolina

Figure 17-7. Bland Landscaping has a clearly defined mission statement that is prominently displayed on their website and in their marketing materials. A mission statement gains strength when it is promoted to the public and to employees.

Setting Goals

After the vision statement is created, the company's goals must be established to help make the vision a reality. A *goal* is something that you strive to achieve. Goals for a business often include achievements such as increasing market share or efficiency, reaching more customers, or having profits double within a given period. The two main types of goals are short-term and long-term goals.

- *Short-term goals* are achievements that will be reached in the near future, usually within 12 months.
- *Long-term goals* are those that will be accomplished over the span of several years.

All goals should clearly follow the mission and vision of the company. Goals should be realistic to encourage employees to help the company achieve them. Unrealistic goals will be discouraging. Using the SMART goals guidelines will help make your company's goals as realistic and beneficial as possible. *SMART goals* are specific, measurable, achievable, relevant, and timely. See **Figure 17-8**.

Specific
- I want to start a business.
- I will solicit clients and mow lawns in my neighborhood for a profit.

Measurable
- I will be ready to sign my first client by April 25th and will aim to sign five clients by the first of May.
- I will measure my progress by the number of client contracts I have by the first of May.

Achievable
- I want to create a logo for advertising.
- I will design a company logo. I will use the logo on work shirts, equipment, and my vehicle. I will order the shirts, stickers, and magnets by the first of April.

Relevant
- Establishing my business will give me experience in time management and will help me save money for college in the fall.
- Running my own business will help me achieve financial independence.

Timely
- I will have five clients by the first of May, 10 by the first of June, and 15 by the end of July.
- I want to have enough customers by the first of May next year to need an employee to help complete the contracted jobs each week.

Goodheart-Willcox Publisher

Figure 17-8. Examples of SMART goals. Revisit your company's goals regularly to ensure you are on the track you have chosen.

Making Goals Specific

A specific goal that is clearly defined and highly detailed will ensure that a successful plan can be created. If a goal does not define exactly what and why, it will be difficult to achieve. The following questions can be used to help make a goal specific and give it focus:

- What does the company want to accomplish?
- Why is the goal important for the business?
- Who is involved?
- Where is it located?
- Which resources or limits are involved?

Making Goals Measurable

Goals should always measure outcomes, not activities, and the criteria on which they are based should be measurable. Measuring your progress will help you stay focused and meet deadlines. Measurable goals should answer the following questions:

- How much?
- How many?
- How will I know it is accomplished?

Making Goals Achievable

A goal must be realistic to be achievable. A goal that is unrealistic will be frustrating. Goals must also be challenging or you may lose enthusiasm and settle for less. The *A* in SMART may also stand for attainable.

Making Goals Relevant

A goal that is relevant focuses on something that makes sense within the broader business goal, such as growing the company and being able to contract commercial firms. The *R* in SMART may also stand for realistic.

Making Goals Timely

Setting a time frame for a goal will give it a sense of urgency. The time frame must also be realistic or there will be too much pressure to meet it. There should be specific deadlines for each intermittent goal, for example, what will be accomplished in two months, three months, and six months.

Using Demographics

Demographics are statistical data relating to population. Demographics, such as age, income, family structure, and free-time activities, can be used to identify a business' opportunities. Marketing materials can be sent directly to the people most likely to use the company's services or buy their products.

Figure 17-9. Demographics can help a business identify its target market more accurately. The demographics of your target market will affect all the choices made in developing a marketing plan.

Demographics may also be used to determine the most advantageous location for a company's headquarters. Current statistical information is available through resources such as the US Census Bureau, Bureau of Labor Statistics, Consumer Credit Data, and American Fact Finder, **Figure 17-9**. There are also online services for creating and sending surveys to potential customers.

Identifying a Target Market

A *target market* is the people most likely to buy your product or service. Knowing your target market allows you to focus marketing on those who are more likely to use your services or buy your product. Use the following steps to determine your target market:

- Determine your customer base.
- Evaluate the competition.
- Analyze your product or service.
- Choose demographics.
- Assess the decision.

Information on your target market can be found online. Review magazine articles, blogs, forums, and survey results that are focused on your target market. You may also conduct your own survey, **Figure 17-10**.

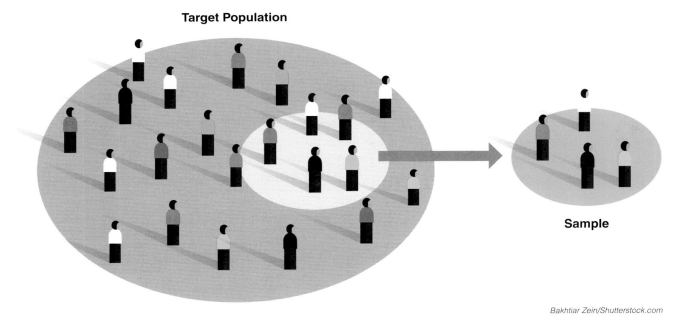

Figure 17-10. Although marketing is focused on a target market, it should not exclude those outside the targeted group.

Niche Markets

A *niche market* is a very narrow and specific segment of a larger market, **Figure 17-11**. For example, xeriscaping or sustainable landscape designs are a subset of traditional landscape designs. Many traditional landscaping companies may be able to design and install xeriscaping but would more likely refer a customer to a company that focuses on sustainable landscape designs. A niche business identifies a need that is not being addressed by competitors and offers products which satisfy that need. A niche business can corner a market because there is little or no competition.

Choosing a Name

A business name is similar to a building's foundation. If the foundation is not square, the misalignment will be amplified as the construction progresses, **Figure 17-12**. A business name does not have to explain everything the company produces; it just needs to be memorable. Keep the following points in mind when brainstorming a name.

- Review names of your competitors. Determine which names work in your opinion and which do not. Does the best name belong to the most successful business?
- Is the name trademarked? Use the search function for the US Patent and Trademark Office Database (USPTO) to see if it is already being used.
- Is the name too trendy? A name based on a trend will become dated quickly. It may also limit your business' services in consumer's eyes.
- Can it be used to create a domain name? The best domain names are short, easy to spell, memorable, and relevant to the context. Customers want to find your website quickly and easily.
- Is the name obscure or difficult to pronounce? Will it be easy to remember? The best names are easy to pronounce, sound good when spoken, and are easy to remember. Say it aloud and listen to how it sounds.

The right name can make a difference in the success or failure of a business. There are many free online tools available to help with the search. Online tools can search for the names, words, and terms people use when searching for service or product. There are also companies that specialize in branding or naming businesses.

Figure 17-11. A company that fills a niche market may be one that specializes in small water features added to mature/existing landscapes.

Figure 17-12. A business name is the first chance to identify your product, services, or personal connection to the enterprise.

Business Licenses

A *business license* is a permit issued by local, county, state, or federal authorities that allows an individual or company to conduct business. The regulations vary within each state. The type of license needed depends on the type of business and its location. Permits for a rural business, for example, will likely vary from those needed for a business in the center of town.

Logos

A *logo* is a recognizable icon, symbol, graphic design, or stylized name that identifies a company. A company may design its own logo or hire a marketing firm to do so. A new logo must be distinctive from other trademarked logos to avoid any infringement. It must also be well defined and appealing to be useful. The logo is used on vehicles, uniforms, buildings, advertising, websites, literature, products, stationery, and other company related materials.

Slogan

A *slogan* is a short, catchy phrase used with the logo that captures the company's appeal. When successful, the slogan and logo become part of the business' identity or image. The slogan should attract immediate attention and be understood immediately. The most effective slogans are short, simple, and consistent in use. McDonald's, for example, uses the slogan "Lovin' it," and Nike uses "Just do it." Take the time to write out all your company is and does in the least space possible. Write it a second time after you trim it. Trim it some more and write it a third time. Work with what remains to begin writing a slogan. Brainstorming in groups can be helpful, as can marketing firms that offer the service. Slogans may also be referred to as *taglines*.

Brand Images

Successful companies establish a brand image that people will recognize quickly. A *brand image* is the way that customers and the public perceive a company. Logos, company uniforms, color schemes, services offered, and even the type of equipment owned all contribute to the branding of the company over time.

Choosing a Location

Many successful businesses were founded in the owner's place of residence, often in the garage or workshop. As the business outgrows the available space, the owner must consider moving the business to a rented or purchased location. The new location will depend on availability, affordability, and end use. A retail space, for example, should be highly visible to attract customers driving or walking by the space. If a business' primary need for space is equipment maintenance and storage or to install a greenhouse, a location near the outskirts of town might be more appropriate, **Figure 17-13**.

Angyalosi Beata/Shutterstock.com

Hrecheniuk Oleksii/Shutterstock.com

R. Lee Ivy

Figure 17-13. When searching for a business location, a business owner must consider the amount of space needed and room for growth. If the property is out of town, it may require the extension of utility lines and the installation of a well if public water is not available.

Accounting

Every business needs a way to manage income, cash outflow, and savings. Many banks offer business accounts for ease of these operations. Compare the options for deposits, withdrawals, debit and credit card operations, and operating hours for several banks. Determine which bank has the most convenient service offerings, transaction locations, and lowest fees for the short and long term.

Bookkeeper vs. Accountant

Many people use the term bookkeeper and accountant interchangeably. There are, however, differences in education, certification, financial tasks performed, and cost.

A *bookkeeper* is a person who records the daily transactions of a business, such as processing payroll and posting debits and credits, **Figure 17-14**. A bookkeeper does not need a college degree or certification to keep a company's books. For many small businesses, a bookkeeper is sufficient once the owner has a basic grasp of accounting.

Rawpixel.com/Shutterstock.com

Figure 17-14. With a little direction, most small business owners can set up their accounting with business software. However, as a business grows, the accounting may become more complicated and require more input from an accountant.

An *accountant* is a person who interprets, analyzes, reports, and summarizes financial data. An accountant typically has a 4-year college degree in accounting and may have higher degrees of education. An accountant may become a certified public accountant (CPA) upon passing the Uniform Certified Public Accountant Examination. An accountant's fees are typically much higher than those of a bookkeeper.

It is recommended that a business owner consult with an accounting professional when the company is started to ensure he or she understands how bookkeeping and accounting function for his or her business. It can be very costly to hire an accountant to do basic bookkeeping tasks.

Employer Identification Number

In many instances, a business must acquire a tax identification number for income reporting and tax records. An *employer identification number (EIN)* is similar to a Social Security number (SSN) held by an individual. The Internal Revenue Service (IRS) uses an EIN to identify businesses with respect to their tax obligations. It may also be referred to as a *tax identification number (TIN)*. An EIN is not required for a sole proprietorship or an LLC with no employees, as the individuals operating these businesses may file taxes using their Social Security number. An EIN is also necessary to establish status with wholesalers and suppliers, and to separate personal from business assets and expenditures. An EIN may be requested through the IRS or with the assistance of a lawyer or accountant.

Budgets and Costs

A *budget* is a financial plan for the future concerning income and costs of a business. It also serves as an outline of the company's financial and operational goals, **Figure 17-15**. A well-developed budget will help a small business in many ways, including the following:

- Plan start-up needs.
- Get a business loan.
- Know your required profit.
- Plan for the things your business needs to grow and still earn a profit.
- Eliminate wasteful spending.
- Determine how much can be reinvested in the business.
- Determine when you can afford additional employees.
- Gauge whether your financial predictions are being met.

Seeking advice from your accountant or bookkeeper after you establish a budget is highly advised. A financial professional can check your numbers and help you make realistic projections regarding growth, upcoming expenses, and tax issues.

A budget should be updated regularly to be most effective. Hold monthly meetings with the management team and update the budget based on the prior month's numbers. Many business software programs include a budgeting feature that can prove to be very helpful.

Item	Price	Quantity		Revenue
Hillsborough Street Hot Dogs				
Kate Lahr		Enterprise Budget		
Income:				
Hot Dog Sales	2	28125.00		56,250.00
Soda Sales	1	14063.00		14,063.00
Total Income				70,313.00
Operating Expenses:	Price	Quantity		Cost
Hot Dogs	10	938.00		9,380.00
Buns	2	2343.00		4,687.50
Fixings	0.2	28125.00		5,625.00
Paper Products	3.75	225.00		843.75
Sodas	6	586.00		3,516.00
Utilities	4.25	225.00		956.25
Total Operating Costs	(Add this section's items)			25,008.50
Ownership Expenses				Cost
Depreciation				630.00
Repairs & Maintenance				600.00
Taxes				130.50
Insurance				348.00
Business license				1,200.00
Total Ownership Expenses	(Add this section's items)			2,908.50
Total Expenses	(Total Operating plus Total Ownership)			27,917.00
Net Income (Also called Accounting Profit)				42,396.00
Opportunity Costs	Principal	Interest rate	Time	Cost
Interest	7500	0.04	1	300.00
	Days/Year	Hours/Day	$/Hour	
Cost of your labor	225	4	10	9,000.00
Net benefit from your entrepreneurship	(Net Income minus both Opportunity Costs)			33,096.00
(Also called Economic Profit)				

Melissa Hendrickson, NC State University

Figure 17-15. A business will have multiple budgets that fit into a main budget. Each contracted project, for example, will have a specific amount of money allocated to it from the company budget. The project budget is then broken down into multiple categories, such as labor, equipment, and plant materials.

Income, Profit, and Expenses

Income is the money a business earns and *expenses* are monies paid by the company. Expenses include salaries, rent/mortgage payments, utilities, supplies, and anything else the business purchases. As stated earlier, a company's *profit* is the money the business earns over its expenses. Companies have fixed and variable expenses. A *fixed expense* is one that must be met regularly, typically on a monthly basis. *Variable expenses* are expenses that may fluctuate from month to month. There are three forms companies issue quarterly and annually, a profit and loss statement, a cash flow statement, and a balance sheet.

- A *profit and loss statement (P&L)* or *income statement* summarizes and shows the costs, expenses, and revenues over a specified time, such as a month, quarter, or fiscal year, **Figure 17-16**.
- A *cash flow statement* is used to track income and expenses. Cash flow statements are useful for predicting and budgeting income and expenses. They are also useful when making strategic decisions on how the company's resources of time, equipment, and other resources should be managed, **Figure 17-17**.

Cash Flow Budget for the Month Ending January 31, 2018

Cash Balance, Beginning of Period	0
Add: Cash Inflows	
Sales	40,000
Total Inflows	40,000
Total Available Cash	$40,000
Less: Cash Outflows	
Materials	$20,000
Wages	2,500
Salaries	3,000
Selling expenses	3,000
Office expense	500
Insurance	0
Utilities	1,000
Property taxes	1,500
Debt payments (principal on loan)	1,000
Dividends	0
Income taxes	2,000
Total Outflows	$34,500
Surplus (Deficit) Subtract outflows from inflows	$5,500
Line of Credit (use or repayment)	0
Interest Expense	$1,500
Cash Balance End of Period	$4,000

Figure 17-16. An income statement.

- A *balance sheet* is a financial statement of company assets, liabilities, and capital (equity) at a specific time. The balance sheet details the balance of income over expenses. The assets are usually divided into *liquid asset* (easily converted to cash) and *nonliquid assets* (cannot be converted quickly). The liabilities are divided into current and long-term categories.

Income Statement for the Month Ending January 31, 2018

Total Sales	$40,000
Less allowances for returns	0
Net Sales (total sales – allowances)	$40,000
Cost of Goods Sold:	
Beginning Inventory	$2,000
+ Purchases	20,000
– Ending Inventory	1,000
Cost of Goods Sold: (BI + P – EI)	$21,000
Gross Margin (NS – COGS)	$19,000
Operating Expenses:	
Wages	$2,500
Office expense	500
Insurance	0
Utilities	1,000
Property taxes	1,500
Equipment depreciation	400
Building depreciation	150
Salaries	3,000
Selling expenses	3,000
Total Operating Expenses	$12,050
Operating Income (GM – total op exp)	$6,950
Non-Operating Expenses	
Interest Expense	$1,500
Total Non-Operating Expenses	$1,500
Income before Taxes (OI – total non-op exp)	$5,450
Federal and State Income Taxes	$2,000
Net Income (Income before tax – income taxes)	$3,450

Melissa Hendrickson, NC State University

Figure 17-17. A cash flow statement.

Debt

New companies with little capital may need to borrow money and incur some debt. This may be for purchasing equipment or hiring people to complete projects in short- or long-term increments. Once a company is established, it may be necessary to purchase new equipment, lease office space, or acquire other business assets. Borrowing funds to pay for these expenses is not always the best action to take. Having to make loan payments and pay interest on the borrowed funds in addition to everyday expenses may quickly land a small business in financial trouble. New entrepreneurs should seek the advice of other successful small businesses in regards to manageable levels of debt.

Assets

An *asset* is valuable and available property owned by a business. A small landscape maintenance company, for example, may own power tools, mowers, a fuel storage tank, and a building, **Figure 17-18**. These items would be the company's assets. An asset is often used to secure loans. Together, a company's assets are called *inventory*. The two basic types of assets are current and noncurrent assets. *Current assets* have short-term usefulness for the business and *noncurrent assets* have a longer useful life for the business. In the preceding example, the equipment would be noncurrent assets and the fuel would be a current asset.

R. Lee Ivy

R. Lee Ivy

Figure 17-18. Tools and equipment are essential to any landscape business. Accurate inventory and organization allows for efficient access and maintenance.

Liabilities

Liabilities are the financial obligations or debts of a company. These debts, or *current liabilities*, are owed to creditors and suppliers. Bills that are typically due on receipt have a short time frame. These are referred to as *accounts payable*. Current liabilities include items such as wages, medical plan payments, utilities, and interest. Loans, such as the mortgage on a building, are debts paid to the lender over a specified length of time. These are referred to as *long-term liabilities*.

Net Worth

A company's *net worth* is the value of assets that exceed the liabilities. The net worth of a business should increase each fiscal year for the company's long-term health. To calculate net worth of a company, add the assets and subtract the liabilities. For example, a company with $200,000 in real estate, $100,000 in equipment, and $80,000 in annual contracts has $90,000 of liabilities from loans and outstanding payments. The net worth would be $200,000 + $100,000 + $80,000 minus $90,000, or $290,000.

Return on Investment

The *return on investment (ROI)* shows how much money a business is making compared to the money it is spending. ROI is calculated by subtracting the total amount spent from the income and dividing that amount by the income. For example, a small business earned $30,000 and spent $15,000. The ROI would be 0.50. A negative ROI indicates more money was spent than was made and a positive ROI indicates more money was earned than spent.

There is a great deal more involved with accounting than can be explained in this chapter. New business owners are encouraged to hire an accountant, at least until they are comfortable doing the record keeping themselves.

Advertising

Advertising is the act of drawing attention to a product or service. There are many ways to advertise a business, including websites, social media, newspapers, magazines, radio, and television, **Figure 17-19**. The methods that are most beneficial to a business vary by demographics and the company's target market. A *target market* is the people most likely to buy your product or service. Once a target market is identified, the best method for advertising can be identified and a budget can be allocated. Time and energy spent researching the market and means of advertising will help ensure the budget is well spent.

Dmitri Ma/Shutterstock.com

Online Presence

An online presence is a necessity for any business in operation today. Customers expect to find company information online, including the address and contact information. A professional website that is easy to navigate is a strong advertising tool. A landscaping operation can include images of completed projects along with a list of their services or products. The site can also display the company's mission, vision statements, and history. So much more can be included on a website than could ever be included in a newspaper or radio ad. Most businesses also have a visible presence on social media sites, such as Instagram, Pinterest, Facebook, Twitter, and YouTube, and many have their own blog.

IxMaster/Shutterstock.com

Figure 17-19. Advertising on local TV and radio stations are excellent methods of reaching certain target markets. Some businesses sponsor a regular program, such as one on different aspects of their industry or issues faced by small business owners.

Search Engine Optimization (SEO)

Online traffic to your website can be increased through search engine optimization. *Search engine optimization (SEO)* is a computation process that maximizes the number of visitors to a particular website by ensuring the site appears high on the list of results returned by a search engine. All major search engines have primary search results where web pages and other content are based on what the search engine considers most relevant to users, such as the location of a business. An SEO can be purchased with the work of a competent web designer.

DIY Websites

So much of what is learned by home gardeners, especially a younger demographic, comes through online viewing. The many DIY websites and videos dedicated to teaching home gardening and landscaping projects include advertising opportunities for related businesses. The ads include an active link to the advertiser's website.

Performance Reviews

Customers have ample means of spreading good and bad reviews online. A business should include real customer reviews on their website. If possible, images of the project should also be included. Performance reviews usually boost opportunity for new sales. People want to hear from previous customers and their approval of your product and the experience with your company. Testimonials and reviews give this opportunity. It is also essential to search for poor reviews online. If a client is truly unsatisfied, the problem should be addressed. False or malicious reviews should also be addressed and removed if possible.

Having a positive rating with the Better Business Bureau (BBB) is very beneficial to a small business. The *Better Business Bureau (BBB)* is a nonprofit organization focused on advancing trust in the marketplace. The BBB mediates disputes as a neutral party between the complainant and the business. A company can become a dues-paying accredited business and use the BBB trademarked logo on its marketing materials.

Networking

Networking is meeting and creating a group of acquaintances and associates to form mutually beneficial relationships with other business people and potential clients. A network is kept active through regular communication and provides mutual benefits for all involved. Many times, connections come from participation in organizations such as the Better Business Bureau or through local civic groups, **Figure 17-20**. Professional online organizations, such as LinkedIn, offer many opportunities for networking as well. Casual networking in social situations often provides opportunities to make acquaintances that also prove beneficial for the parties involved and/or their business associates.

Community Presence

Many people feel that businesses in a community have social responsibilities to that community. In other words, people in the community support local businesses and expect the businesses to support the community. Businesses can establish a strong community presence by sponsoring local sports teams and donating services to community projects.

Pavel L Photo and Video/Shutterstock.com

wavebreakmedia/Shutterstock.com

Figure 17-20. Contributing labor or materials to a community project will give volunteers, local businesses, and local government personnel a positive image of your business.

Companies can also advertise through sponsorships of local sporting arenas, such as baseball and soccer fields, to gain community and regional recognition. A business may also purchase ads shown during halftime or intermission of local basketball and hockey games.

Newspaper, Television, and Radio

If small communities are the target demographic, advertisement in the local newspaper and advertising fliers may be most effective. It may also be one of the least expensive means of advertising. Local television and radio stations may also serve as effective means of advertising. Garden and home remodeling shows inspire people to renovate their landscaping and have definitely served the landscaping industry well. These shows are often regional and the actual designers, installers, and managers are not available to the viewers due to their locale. However, the websites of these shows offer advertisement opportunities for related services and products.

In some markets, radio serves as a viable way to communicate about your products and services. Marketing segments and advertisements can be strategically played during peak times for listeners of specific demographics. Businesses may also sponsor radio shows or segments.

Career Connection

Hunter and Heather Casey

Hunter Casey, Casey Nursery Inc.

Hunter Casey is a fourth generation nurseryman and his wife, Heather, is a first generation nurserywoman. They both share a love for growing quality landscaping plants. Hunter currently serves as vice president of the family nursery, while Heather handles production inventory and helps with administration and production whenever the need arises. Hunter's daily responsibilities include potting manager, field grower, and weed management for the entire nursery. Over the years, Hunter and Heather have brought many new practices to the nursery, including liquid herbicide in containers, cover crops in field production, and new forms of production tracking.

Hunter and Heather have a passion for growing plants and love talking to young people about the nursery industry. One message they try to convey to young people interested in horticulture is that wholesale production is hard work, but at the end of the day you can take a great amount of pride in the quality of the product you have produced.

Hunter and Heather are involved in several local and state nursery and agricultural associations. Being involved in these types of organizations allows them to network with others within the agriculture and green industries. They are always looking for new and innovative ways to improve and grow their business.

Consider This

1. Which field of study would be the best preparation for managing a wholesale nursery? Explain your answer.
2. Would you enjoy owning and running a wholesale nursery? Why or why not?
3. What challenges do you think Hunter and Heather encounter with their business?

Summary

- The different business structures determine who owns the company and who is liable for its financial actions.
- The different business structures include a sole proprietorship, partnership (general, limited, limited liability), limited liability company (LLC), corporations, and cooperatives.
- A business plan is a document that states the mission of the business, examines its current condition, sets goals, and outlines strategies for achieving the goals.
- A business plan should include an executive summary, company description, market analysis, organization and management plan, service or product line, marketing and sales plan, and financial projections.
- A mission statement is a short summary of the values and purpose of a company or organization.
- A vision statement describes the company's goals for the future.
- Goals for a business often include achievements such as increasing market share or efficiency, reaching more customers, or having profits double within a given period.
- Age, income, family structure, and free-time activities are demographics used to help determine the need for landscape services.
- A business name does not have to explain everything the company produces; it just needs to be memorable.
- A new logo must be distinctive from other trademarked logos to avoid any infringement. It must also be well defined and appealing to be useful.
- A brand image is the way that customers and the public perceive a company.
- A business license is a permit issued by local, county, state, or federal authorities that allows an individual or company to conduct business.
- In many instances, a business must acquire a tax identification number for reporting income and tax records.
- A company's assets are valuable and available property owned by the business.
- Liabilities are the financial obligations or debts of a company.
- Important financial statements include income statements, cash flow statements, and balance sheets.
- The advertising methods or strategies that are most beneficial to a business vary by demographics and the company's target market.

Chapter Review

Know and Understand ⤴

Answer the following questions using the information provided in this chapter.

1. In what type of business structure is the sole owner responsible for all debts incurred by the business?
   A. Limited partnership.
   B. Corporation.
   C. Sole proprietorship.
   D. Cooperative.

2. Each of the partners in a limited liability partnership has limited liability for the company's debts and is _____.
   A. always liable for at least 50% of each partner's negligence
   B. protected from negligence of another partner
   C. not protected from negligence of the other partners
   D. None of the above.

3. Which of the following statements is true about a limited liability company (LLC)?
   A. It is subject to corporate taxation in which a significant tax percentage is paid on the net income.
   B. An LLC has the pass-through taxation of a partnership or sole proprietorship.
   C. It has a board of stockholders that oversees the business' activities.
   D. All of the above.

4. A business owned by stock- or shareholders who share in profits and losses is referred to as a _____.
   A. cooperative
   B. general partnership
   C. corporation
   D. proprietorship

5. A document that states the mission of the business, outlines strategies for achieving goals, and examines its current condition is referred to as a(n) _____.
   A. cash flow plan
   B. business plan
   C. balance plan
   D. executive plan

6. Which of the following parts of a business plan explains why the business will offer higher quality services or those not currently offered by others in the area?
   A. Company description.
   B. Executive summary.
   C. Funding requests.
   D. Market analysis.

7. Which of the following parts of a business plan describes the legal business structure and identifies the people making and guiding decisions?
   A. Organization and management.
   B. Executive summary.
   C. Service or product line.
   D. Market analysis.

8. Which part of a business plan provides a detailed plan of the amount of funding needed and its intended use?
   A. Executive summary.
   B. Funding request.
   C. Financial projections.
   D. Marketing and sales.

9. A short summary of the values and purpose of a company is referred to as a _____.
   A. balance statement
   B. vision statement
   C. mission statement
   D. goal statement

10. Goals for a business may be _____.
    A. financial achievements
    B. reached in the near future
    C. accomplished over several years
    D. All of the above.

11. Statistical data relating to population that can be used to market directly to a target market is referred to as _____.
    A. dyno-graphics
    B. demographics
    C. data graphics
    D. domain graphics

12. Which of the following questions apply to selecting a business name?
   A. Is the name trademarked by another company?
   B. Can it be used to create a domain name?
   C. Is it obscure or difficult to pronounce?
   D. All of the above.

13. Logos, company uniforms, color schemes, services offered, and even the type of equipment owned all contribute to the company's _____.
   A. accounting
   B. tax status
   C. brand image
   D. None of the above.

14. Of the following, which factors are the most influential in selecting the location of a new business?
   A. Aesthetics, soil color, and scenic view.
   B. Availability, current landscaping, and available sunlight.
   C. Affordability, building age, and landscape quality.
   D. Availability, affordability, and end use.

15. Under which circumstances does a business require a tax identification number?
   A. When the business is a sole proprietorship with no employees.
   B. When the business is an LLC with no employees.
   C. When the business has two partners using pass-through taxation.
   D. When the business is a corporation with multiple employees.

16. Which of the following statements shows the net income for a specific period?
   A. Income statement.
   B. Balance statement.
   C. ROI statement.
   D. Inventory statement.

17. Which of the following is the combination of a company's current and noncurrent assets?
   A. Inventory.
   B. Liabilities.
   C. Net worth.
   D. Taxed income.

18. Which of the following are financial obligations of a company?
   A. Long-term liabilities.
   B. Accounts payable.
   C. Current liabilities.
   D. All of the above.

19. In a successful business, which of the following increases and makes the company more valuable?
   A. Liabilities.
   B. Funding requests.
   C. Net worth.
   D. All of the above.

20. Which type of assets cannot be converted to cash quickly?
   A. Solid assets.
   B. Nonliquid assets.
   C. Liquid assets.
   D. All of the above.

21. Which of the following shows how much money a business is making compared to the money it is spending?
   A. ROI.
   B. TIN.
   C. EIN.
   D. SEO.

22. Which of the following will help a business increase its online presence?
   A. Social media.
   B. Professional website.
   C. Facebook and Pinterest.
   D. All of the above.

23. Which of the following will help increase traffic to a specific website?
   A. EIN optimization.
   B. Online optimization.
   C. Search engine optimization.
   D. Website search optimization.

24. Which of the following may be used to promote a business?
   A. Donating services to community projects.
   B. Sponsoring local sports teams or fields.
   C. Television, radio, and newspaper ads.
   D. All of the above.

Thinking Critically

1. What is the most difficult part of opening your own business? What part is the easiest? Explain your reasoning.

2. Describe the financing of a new small business from the perspective of a loan officer.

3. How would you prioritize your goals for opening your own business?

Suggested Activities

1. Work with a partner or small group and research small businesses. Define what constitutes a small business and the number of startups there are in the United States each year. Use statistics to explain the success and failure rates for new businesses. Determine if the causes of success or failure are similar among small businesses. Create a visual or oral presentation for the class.

2. Working in groups of 4 to 5, create a small theoretical company and choose a business structure. As a group, develop a company description, mission statement, and vision statement. Each person in the group should be assigned one or more positions in the company's business structure. Identify the chain of command.

3. Search online databases for demographic information in your area and identify target markets for your theoretical company. Identify the main media outlets that would be best for marketing your company.

4. Research and determine which permits and licenses are required by the local municipality for a new landscape installation and maintenance company. Download and complete an application for a license or permit as though you owned your own business. Determine if there are state regulations that must also be followed.

5. Identify three local banking institutions that offer business accounts. Compare the costs and benefits associated with the accounts. Identify any special concessions the banks have for small businesses.

6. Arrange an interview with a business owner (over the phone or in person). Discuss the pros and cons of starting and owning a business. Summarize the main points of your discussion.

7. Develop an Entrepreneurial SAE in landscape design, installation, or management. Use proper record keeping and document your day-to-day activities as they pertain to your SAE.

CHAPTER
18

Pricing Landscape Projects

While studying this chapter, look for the activity icon ➦ **to:**
- **Practice** vocabulary terms with Words to Know activities.
- **Expand** learning with identification activities.
- **Reinforce** what you learn by completing Know and Understand questions.

G-WLEARNING.com

www.g-wlearning.com/agriculture

Chapter Outcomes

After studying this chapter, you will be able to:

- Identify the components of a site assessment.
- Understand how to perform a site assessment.
- Explain the process of estimating and calculating project costs.
- Identify the components of a job estimate, quote, proposal, or bid.
- Determine accurate measurements of landscape areas.
- Define profit and calculate profit margin.
- Identify cost estimates required for accurate pricing of landscape projects.
- Describe strategies for pricing by the hour or by project basis.

Key Terms ↱

bid
bid solicitation
budget
burden
contingency
depreciation
direct cost
estimate
indirect cost
invitation to bid (ITB)
landscape estimate
markup
operational cost

operational expense
overhead
personal pace
profit
profit margin
proposal
quote
request for proposals (RFP)
request for quotations (RFQ)
site assessment
site takeoff
takeoff

Introduction

Landscape installation and maintenance professionals choose to work in the industry for many reasons, including the challenge of creating functional spaces, the enjoyment of working with their hands, and the gratification of seeing a project come to fruition. While rewarding, these activities must also be profitable. To ensure profitability, business owners must make accurate assessments of the materials and time that will be needed to complete a job, as well as an accurate estimate of their costs. This chapter explains how to assess, estimate, and bid a landscaping job that will earn a profit.

Questions for the Client

- Does the client have a particular look in mind?
- What are the client's needs/ desires in terms of maintenance?
- Is there an irrigation system installed, does one need to be installed, is this included in the budget, what is the budget for watering in the long term?
- Does the client want a landscape to provide privacy?
- Does the client want a landscape to provide edible foods?
- Does the client want a landscape to provide color?
- Does the client want a landscape to provide protection?
- Are there pets that will interact with the landscape?
- What areas of the property are to be used for specific purpose, such as including a trampoline for their children?
- Does the owner want to keep any of the plant materials, such as trees, that are on the lot?
- Do they have a good idea of what they want it to look like or are they leaving it to the professional?

Goodheart-Willcox Publisher

Figure 18-1. The estimator must know exactly what is expected of his or her company to create an accurate bid. Create a list of questions that you can use when discussing the project with a potential client.

Gathering Information

The key to an accurate bid is gathering sufficient information from the client and other contractors involved in the project. The estimator must understand the client's expectations and which parts of the project his or her company will be installing. A new landscape, for example, may require cleanup with large equipment before any work may begin. The estimator must know if another business is contracted to perform the site clearing and if he or she can omit this work from the bid, **Figure 18-1**. Ask questions if any part of the project is unclear.

Estimates and Bid Components

Many of the same elements included in estimates for new landscapes are included in estimates for maintenance jobs, although the cost and work will vary greatly. Spreading mulch, for example, is performed for new installations and established landscapes. It will take the same amount of time and work to move and spread the mulch on either type of project. However, a maintenance contract will not include costs for a designer, hardscape materials for a new patio, and freight. An estimator must calculate costs for the following components (**Figure 18-2**):

- Designer or architect.
- Labor (workers and hours).
- Machinery/equipment (including rental).
- Fuel, mileage, and travel time.
- Subcontractors.
- Hardscape materials.
- Soil testing.
- Soil amendments.
- Plant materials.
- Mulch materials.
- Freight and taxes.
- Waste disposal.
- Permits and licensing fees.
- Overhead.
- Markups.

Some of these components may not apply to a project because they were paid separately or not used for the job. A landscape designer or architect, for example, may have been contracted and paid for their services before installation begins.

Spippiri/Shutterstock.com   *au_uhoo/Shutterstock.com*   *au_uhoo/Shutterstock.com*

Figure 18-2. There are many details to consider when pricing a project. For example, it may require time to locate and ship plants to the site if any plants specified in the design are uncommon to the area. Costs for this time must also be included in the bid, especially if a plant broker is hired to locate the plants.

Site Takeoff

A *site takeoff* is a tabulation of all the landscape components and the costs associated with each component. For example, when assessing a site for maintenance costs, the estimator may count all the trees taller than 12′ and determine the cost for pruning each tree as one cost, **Figure 18-3**. The size of the lawn and the time needed to mow it would be considered another cost and the square footage of planting beds and the amount of weeding and mulch they require would be yet another cost. If it were an installation bid, the cost of the trees and the labor required for planting would be one cost. The costs for the other elements, such as shrubs and their installation, would also be included in the takeoff. The importance of calculating accurate labor, equipment, and material costs cannot be stressed enough. If these numbers are inaccurate, the job may be under- or overbid. A site takeoff may also be referred to simply as a *takeoff*.

Measuring Tools

Accurate measurements of landscape sites are essential to making a profitable bid. A bid that is high may quickly make your company a noncontender,

Marsan/Shutterstock.com

Figure 18-3. Tree pruning requires arboriculture knowledge and specialized equipment. In many states, the crew must not only be properly trained, but the workers must also be certified. If the business does not own the equipment needed, it will have to be rented, which incurs additional cost to the job.

Figure 18-4. Laser levels can be operated by one individual and have a range of a few hundred feet. Many models are self-leveling and provide rapid readings that make the work more efficient.

and anything under will reduce your profit margin. There are a variety of traditional tools and digital devices used to measure landscape sites, including the following:

- **Measuring wheel.** A traditional tool that tracks the number of revolutions it makes as it is rolled across a surface.
- **Retractable tape.** A traditional tool with a blade that retracts into a casing. These tapes can be difficult to handle alone when measuring long distances.
- **Winding tape.** A traditional handheld measuring tool that unwinds as the user walks along the area being measured.
- **Drones, cameras, and computer software.** Remote-controlled drones are flown over a property to collect data.
- **GIS (geographic information system).** A GIS processes satellite images and accurately displays land, buildings, roads, and other features found on maps.
- **GPS (global positioning system).** Global positioning systems use satellite data to calculate locations and measurements.
- **Handheld laser measurer.** A handheld device projects the laser over the area being measured to a solid surface. These work well on oddly shaped property lines.
- **Laser level.** Laser levels are used to measure distances, elevations, and height clearances (such as ground to utility wires) of a property as well as surface area, **Figure 18-4.**

The Language of Business

Bids, Estimates, Proposals, and Quotes

The terms *bid, estimate, proposal,* and *quote* mean something different to people in different industries and even within an industry. To add to the confusion, the same terms are often used interchangeably. As a small business owner, you must clearly understand what the client wants or expects in any one of the documents. Spending time and effort on creating a detailed proposal may be a poor use of your time and effort when you find the client only wants a simple estimate for a job. To avoid confusion and provide the customer with the information they want or expect, define within your own company what each term or document represents.

- A **bid** is a fixed price submitted for a specific project. A bid usually includes rates, availability, and a time frame for completion. Bids are common for projects where the scope of work is clear because the contractor can calculate costs for every aspect of the project. A bid is similar to a proposal but includes less detail.
- An **estimate** is a general estimation of what a project will cost. It is not legally binding and is subject to change once the details of the job are calculated. A quick estimate may discourage or encourage a potential client to request a more formal bid. The client may realize, for example, that the job is going to cost more than he or she expected and spare you the time of calculating a bid. Alternately, the client might be pleasantly surprised that the estimate is well within his or her budget and may request a formal quote.
- A **proposal** is a detailed explanation of all costs involved in a project, including quotes on raw materials, proposals from subcontractors, a markup of the contractor's percentage, and estimates on labor costs, taxes, and other standard costs. Depending on the language and form, a proposal may become a contract when signed by all parties involved. A proposal is more detailed than a bid and has more definite information than a quote or estimate.
- A **quote** is a fixed price offer listing the work and materials included in a project. If the job entails more work than expected, you must complete the job as agreed for the fixed price. Quotes typically include an expiration date because the price of materials and labor fluctuate. It is often wiser to give an estimate if there is potential that the job may entail more work or materials than anticipated.

Site Assessment

The bid for any landscaping project begins with a site assessment and an estimate of the job's cost based on that assessment. A *site assessment* is a complete analysis of an existing landscape for maintenance costs or for a new installation. A thorough assessment is needed to install a fully functional and sustainable landscape design, **Figure 18-5**. A site assessment for a new installation is performed to determine the possibilities and limitations of the site. A site assessment for maintenance work is performed to determine the time it will take to complete maintenance tasks, such as mowing, trimming, and pruning. The assessment for an installation job will be more extensive and detailed than an assessment for maintenance work.

All of the assessment should be done on site. This will ensure that the site condition and the steps needed for installation and/or maintenance will be accurate. The following site details to consider include the following:

- The location of the building(s) and planting areas in relation to utilities, easements, and property lines.
- Property slope and drainage. Visiting the site after a hard rain will reveal flow patterns and subsequent drainage problems.
- The influences of neighboring properties and extended views from the property.
- Existing trees, shrubs, and other plants that can be worked into a design.
- Problems with wildlife roaming through and/or eating plant materials.
- Soil types and pH. Samples should be taken from multiple areas to ensure an accurate portrayal of the site.
- Daily sun and shade conditions for all areas of the site. Assessing temperatures, wind, and humidity from these areas may also be useful.

ThomasPhoto/Shutterstock.com

Figure 18-5. The top soil on new construction sites is often scraped away before construction begins. For an accurate site assessment, the estimator must know if the builder is grading and replacing the soil or if the new soil and grading should be included in the bid.

STEM Connection

Calculating Square Footage and Perimeter

The square footage of a square or rectangular area is determined simply by multiplying the length by the width. However, many landscapes are oddly shaped. An oddly shaped area can be divided into geometric shapes for easier measurement. The measurements for each area are combined to get the total square footage of the area. After the square footage is determined, the time and cost can be calculated.

P = perimeter   A = area

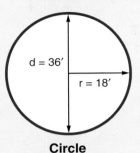

Circle

$P = 2\pi r = \pi d = 113'$
$A = \pi r^2 = 1018 \text{ ft}^2$

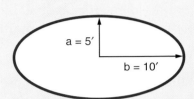

Ellipse

$P = \dfrac{2\pi\sqrt{a^2+b^2}}{2} = 49.7'$

$A = \pi ab = 157 \text{ ft}^2$

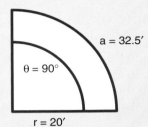

Circle Quarter

$P = 2r + a = 72.5'$

$A = \pi r^2 \times \left(\dfrac{\theta}{360}\right) = 314 \text{ ft}^2$

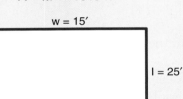

Rectangle

$P = 2l + 2w = 80'$
$A = l \times w = 375'$

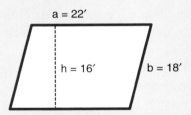

Parallelogram

$P = 2a + 2b = 80'$
$A = a \times h = 352 \text{ ft}^2$

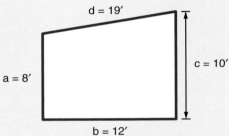

Trapezoid

$P = a + b + c + d = 39'$

$A = \dfrac{a + c}{2 \times b} = 108 \text{ ft}^2$

Square

$P = 4s = 32'$
$A = s^2 = 64 \text{ ft}^2$

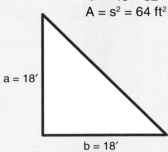

Right Triangle

$P = a + b + \sqrt{a^2+b^2} = 61.5'$

$A = \dfrac{1}{2b^2} = 324.5 \text{ ft}^2$

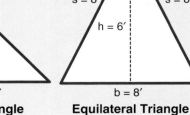

Equilateral Triangle

$P = 3 \times s = 24'$

$A = \dfrac{1}{2}\left(b \times h\right) = 24 \text{ ft}^2$

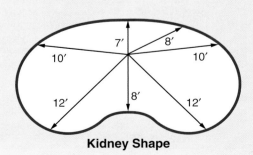

Kidney Shape

average radius $= \dfrac{8' + 12' + 10' + 7' + 8' + 10' + 12'}{7} = 9.6'$

$A = \pi r^2 = 288 \text{ ft}^2$

Alfred Sonsalla/Shutterstock.com

Yuriy Stankevich/Shutterstock.com

Figure 18-6. Trees and other plants growing along city streets and sidewalks live in microclimates. Heat radiating from the hardscapes keeps the ground warmer than it would be otherwise. Other factors that affect city microclimates include exposure to salt/deicer in winter, and the amount of sun, shade, and water they receive.

- Microclimates around the property. A *microclimate* is a small area with different environmental conditions than the surrounding area, **Figure 18-6**. Microclimates may be created due to soil texture, nearby structures, elevation, slope, and proximity to water. New construction or changes to the topography may also create a microclimate.

STEM Connection

Personal Pace

Personal pace is a manual method used to measure areas when a measuring tool is unavailable or when a rough estimate will do. The measurement is based on the average number of steps taken along a straight 100′ path. When done properly, this method can be fairly accurate.

1. Use a measuring wheel or tape to measure and mark a straight 100′ line on a level, flat surface.
2. Walk with your normal gait. Attempting to make your steps even will result in an inaccurate measurement.
3. Write the number of steps you made for each of three passes.
4. Calculate the average number of steps you made. Use the following example as a guide.
   First pass: 46 paces
   Second pass: 45 paces
   Third pass: 47 paces
   $46 + 45 + 47 = 138$
   $138 \div 3 = 46$
5. Divide 100 by the average number of paces.
   $100′ \div 46 = 2.17′$ per pace
   The average pace (pace factor) in this example is 2.17′. Once the pace is known, it is a constant that can be used at any time to calculate distance by pacing an area and multiplying that by the pace factor.

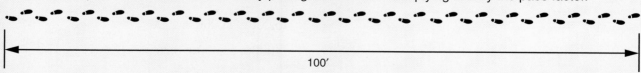

100′

Chereliss /Shutterstock.com

6. Calculate the average pace for 3 passes. Use 42, 42, and 44 for the passes.
7. Calculate the average pace for 3 passes. Use 46, 48, and 47 for the passes.

A   *karamysh/Shutterstock.com*

B   *romakoma/Shutterstock.com*

Figure 18-7. A maintenance bid for these two landscapes will be very different. A—The estimator must calculate the amount of time it will require to trim the hedges and around the planting beds in addition to mowing the lawn. B—This landscape will require less time to maintain. It has less hedges and the planting bed is much simpler. A mower with a larger deck may also be used.

Project Estimates and Bids

A *landscape estimate* is a means of roughly calculating the cost of a project based on the site assessment, design, materials, and labor. As stated earlier, a *bid* is a fixed price submitted for a specific project. A rough estimate may be solely for the client. If the client wants a rough estimate, he or she usually wants to know if the job will be within a certain cost range. If the estimator is experienced, he or she may feel comfortable giving the client a rough estimate. This type of estimate may be for simple jobs, such as replacing mulch around the trees and in plant beds. However, if the estimator is submitting a bid for a project, he or she must accurately calculate and itemize each component of the project to ensure an accurate bid and sufficient profit, **Figure 18-7**. A company's *profit* is the money the business earns over its expenses.

Profits and Profit Margins

A company's *profit* is the money the business earns after deducting its expenses. A company must make a profit to fuel growth and keep the business in operation. A *profit margin* is the ratio of profit to the cost of the project, which is the sum of all costs incurred by the job. It is typically expressed as a percentage. The following example is a calculation of the profit margin for gross profit. When calculating the profit margin on net profit, the total revenue must be revenue *after* taxes.

$$total\ revenue - project\ cost = gross\ profit\ (profit\ before\ taxes)$$

$$gross\ profit \div total\ revenue = X$$

$$X \times 100 = profit\ margin$$

Example: Green Landscaping earned $15,000 for a new installation. The project costs for the company were $11,000. How much is the profit margin on the project?

$$15,000 - 11,000 = 4000$$

$$4000 \div 15,000 = 0.26$$

$$0.26 \times 100 = 26.7\%$$

Knowing the profit margin on each service or product gives you freedom to change prices when negotiating or competing for a job. It also helps you set regular and sale prices. Profit margins are generally higher for landscape installation projects than for maintenance contracts.

Budgets and Costs

Once the scope of a project is determined, a budget must be established, **Figure 18-8**. A *budget* is the total financial resources allocated for a project. The budget for a landscaping bid or quote is a detailed list and calculation of all the costs required to complete the project. It will also indicate limits on what should be spent on each part of the project and the date of completion for each component. As the project progresses, the actual costs can be measured against the budget to see if the project is progressing according to plan and within the budget. Large commercial projects often have several budgets within the main budget, such as a direct labor budget that indicates the limits for labor costs on a job. The main budget should include the following direct and indirect costs:

- Labor costs.
- Equipment costs.
- Fuel, mileage, and travel costs.
- Subcontractor costs.
- Material costs.
- Contingency costs.
- Waste disposal costs.
- Permit and licensing costs.
- Project-specific costs.

> ## Pro Tip
> There are phone and computer apps that can identify plants and provide everything from their hardiness zones to their scientific names.

Dusit/Shutterstock.com   *Andrey_Popov/Shutterstock.com*

Figure 18-8. Careful planning and consistent reviews will keep projects within their budgets. Failure to keep accurate and consistent tracking of each task will cause frustration and loss of income.

Direct and Indirect Costs

The cost of a material or service may be direct or indirect. A *direct cost* is a price that can be attributed to a service, material, or labor used on a particular project. The fee on a piece of machinery rented for a specific job, for example, would be a direct cost. An *indirect cost* is a cost for services or activities associated with multiple projects. Indirect costs support the profit-generating activities, such as landscape design or maintenance services. Insurance premiums, rent or mortgage payments, and accounting fees, for example, are expenses that do not generate income but protect the company, pay for work facilities, and keep finances in order. Another example would be the vehicle a supervisor uses to visit project locations, haul materials, or transport crew members, **Figure 18-9**. Indirect costs are also referred to as *overhead* or *burden*. These costs (overhead) are often included as a percentage of each job.

Direct costs are typically itemized on a bid or customer billing and are paid by the customer. Small companies usually charge indirect costs as a percentage of each project. This percentage is referred to as a *markup*.

BrightView Landscape Services, Durham, North Carolina

Figure 18-9. Supervisors of landscape maintenance crews and installation teams require a vehicle to visit job-sites, meet with clients, and transport crew members.

Fixed and Variable Expenses

Overhead is referred to as a *fixed expense*, one that must be met regularly, typically on a monthly basis. Overhead costs tend to remain fixed from period to period. A business also has variable expenses. *Variable expenses* are expenses that may fluctuate from month to month. Variable expenses may increase or decrease due to multiple reasons, such as changes in sales and personnel due to a change of season, or a new promotion that requires more printing and mailing than usual.

Operational Costs

Operational costs or *expenses* include the labor, materials, and machinery used to perform a service or make a product, **Figure 18-10**. Expenses for fuel and mileage, for example, are incurred when company vehicles are used

RoadRunnerDeLuxe/Shutterstock.com   Marta Design/Shutterstock.com   Hopewell/Shutterstock.com

Figure 18-10. If overhead expenses, such as insurance, utilities, and certification fees, are not included as a percentage in each project, they will be deducted from the company's profit.

to take crews to jobs and transport materials. The business does not pay these expenses unless vehicles are performing these services. In contrast, the payments for the vehicles must be paid each month, whether the vehicle is in service or stored for the season. The vehicle payments are overhead expenses, not operational costs. Drive time, maintenance, and freight charges are also operational costs. A baseline dollar amount for breaking even on each job should be established to ensure the company would profit.

Task Completion Times

The cost for each landscaping task is determined by area (square footage) and the time (hourly rates) typically needed to complete the task. It is difficult to ensure a profit if the time taken to perform certain tasks is unknown. A moving crew, for example, may cost an average of $45 an hour. The estimator would determine the square footage of the area to be mowed and the amount of time it will take to mow the area. If it should take 1 1/2 hours according to the standard rate, the cost would be $67.50.

If a landscape company charges only by square footage, it will lose money. A small landscape company, for example, has two properties that are both 8500 ft². Property A is a wide-open area with no trees or fences and takes 30 minutes to mow. Property B has a fence and numerous trees and takes one hour to mow. If the landscaper charges $30 based on square footage only, both customers will pay $30 and the landscaper will lose money.

Although there are charts listing the average time it takes to perform a landscaping task, task times will be more accurate if the business owner times his or her own work or that of his or her employees. See **Figure 18-11**.

Equipment Time

The production rates of each piece of equipment should also be calculated. A riding lawn mower with a 52″ deck, for example, will cover more area in less time than a 20″ walk-behind mower. Knowing the production rates of each piece of equipment will also help you choose the correct equipment for the job. Proper upkeep of equipment will also keep your equipment efficient because dull blades and poorly performing equipment will likely add time to tasks. Task times should include time for loading, unloading, hauling, spreading, digging, backfilling, watering, and cleanup.

Vadim Gouida/Shutterstock.com

Losonsky/Shutterstock.com

stockcreations/Shutterstock.com

Figure 18-11. Operational costs may include labor, machinery, and materials as well as expenses associated with compensation and maintenance.

Labor Cost

Labor cost is most often the largest expense for businesses. In addition to wages, a business pays to solicit and train employees. Depending on its size, a company may also be required to pay Social Security costs, worker's compensation, and federal and state taxes on each employee. The size of the company also determines whether it must offer health-care benefits. Additional benefits may include life insurance, a pension plan, clothing allocations, and travel compensations. A percentage of all these costs must be included as part of the labor needed for a project. See **Figure 18-12**.

Labor Cost Estimate Worksheet		Your Name	
Name Jamie	**Title**	**Technician**	
a. Total Regular and Overtime Hours		2400	hours/year
b. Total Vacation Hours		100	hours/year
c. Total Sick Leave Hours		60	hours/year
d. Total Holiday Hours		60	hours/year
e. Total Hours Paid for but Not Worked		220	hours/year
(Line b + line c + line d)			
f. Total Hours on the Job		2180	hours/year
(Line a minus line e)			
Cost Items		**Cost to Employer**	
Direct Wage Costs			
1. Cash Wages or Salary		46,000	
2. Overtime Wages		0	
3. Cash Bonuses		2000	
4. Total Direct Wages		48,000	
(Sum of Lines 1, 2, and 3)			
Mandatory Wage Costs (Employer's Share)			
5. Social Security (_____%)	6.2	2976	
6. Fed. Unemployment Ins. (_____%)	6.2	2976	
7. State Unemployment Insurance (_____%)	3	1440	
8. Worker's Compensation (_____%)	2	960	
9. Medicare (_____%)	1.45	696	
10. Other _____			
11. Total Mandatory Costs		9048	
(Sum of lines 5–10)			
Value of Fringe Benefits			
12. Insurance	5	2400	
13. Retirement Contributions (_____%)		3000	
14. Uniform (Purchasing/Rental/Cleaning)		900	
15. Educational Expense		1500	
16. Transportation		3500	
17. Other _____			
18. Total Value of Fringe Benefits		11,300	
(Sum of Lines 12 through 17)			
19. Total Labor Costs		68,348	
(Line 4 + Line 11 + Line 18)			
20. Total Labor Costs/Hour on the Job		31.35	
(Line 19 divided by Line f)			

Melissa Hendrickson, NC State University

Figure 18-12. Labor costs include wages for a full-time employee, mandatory costs paid on the employee's behalf, and benefits. A billable hourly wage can then be calculated.

Equipment Costs

Equipment costs can be priced per mile or per hour. The cost for a pickup truck, for example, used to transport crew members and materials could be calculated using the mileage it accumulated on a specific job. The cost could also be calculated by the number of hours its use was dedicated to a project. Most equipment is priced on a per hour basis because most large equipment used on landscape projects must be transported to the worksite on a trailer and do not accumulate mileage in transport or on the site. This price includes the purchase or rental cost, maintenance, insurance, fees, depreciation, and replacement cost. *Depreciation* is the reduction of an asset's value over time, primarily due to wear and tear, **Figure 18-13**. Businesses use depreciation for accounting and tax purposes.

The type of tools and equipment a landscape business needs depends on the services they offer. A small lawn maintenance business, for example, would need equipment such as mowers, trimmers, pruning tools, shovels, and tools for maintaining and servicing equipment. This company would have no need for a skid steer as it would not be hauling heavy materials or moving pallets of sod.

Vehicle Cost Worksheet	
Given information	Purchase price: $45,000 Miles per year: 25,000 Length of loan: 5 years Trade-in value: $15,000
Purchase price per mile	Price per year: $6000/miles per year 25,000 = $0.24 per mile
Maintenance price per mile	Cost per oil change: $50.00 every 3000 miles Number of changes per year: 8 Cost per year: $400/miles per year 25,000 = $0.02 per mile
Tire price per mile	Cost of tires: $800 Tire life: 60,000 miles Cost per year: $333/miles per year 25,000 = $0.01 per mile
Insurance price per mile	Cost per year: $750 Miles per year: 25,000 Cost per year: $750/miles per year 25,000 = $0.03 per mile
Fuel cost per mile	Cost per gallon: $3.75 Miles per gallon: 300 miles/25 gals = 12 mpg Cost per gallon: $3.75/miles per gallon 12 = $0.31 per mile *or* Cost per tank: $93.75 cost/300 miles per tank = $0.31 per mile
Additional costs	License: $45/year Personal property tax: $150/year Inspection: $35/year Depreciation: $1000/year Total: $1230/25,000 miles per year = $0.05 per mile Total cost: $0.66 per mile Replacement cost: consider adding $0.25 per mile

Goodheart-Willcox Publisher

Figure 18-13. All equipment loses value as it ages. This decrease in value is measured as depreciation. In accounting, depreciation is used to spread the cost of the asset over its useful life. Calculations can be determined in cost/mile or cost/hour using the same format.

Vladimir1984/Shutterstock.com

R. Lee Ivy

ungvar/Shutterstock.com

Figure 18-14. It may be more efficient to purchase large equipment if it is used on the majority of a business' projects.

However, if the business agreed to perform some clearing or installation work for a customer, it could rent the large equipment needed for the job, **Figure 18-14**.

Owning vs. Renting. A business owner may rent equipment as needed per project or purchase the equipment. A business owner would likely rent equipment that is not commonly used on its projects rather than purchase it and purchase equipment that is used for most of its projects. There are advantages and disadvantages to both options.

- **Owning.** A large amount of working capital is required to purchase the equipment. If the owner does not have enough capital to purchase the equipment outright, they will need to take out a loan. The owner must cover routine maintenance costs, pay repair costs, and store the machinery when it is not in use. The owner would also need to purchase a trailer for transport and have a vehicle capable of towing the weight. While quality equipment purchases can increase the overall value of assets for many new and small businesses, careful consideration should be given to the principle that excessive debt can be burdensome and defer investment in the company and its long-term growth.
- **Renting.** Renting equipment does not require large amounts of capital to be paid. (Rental agencies typically require a refundable deposit.) Equipment is rented by the hour, per day, weekly, or monthly. It is, however, dependent on the availability of the equipment.

Fuel

Fuel is expensive and time that is spent driving to the jobsite is time that workers are not working. Logistics of the routes of the landscape crews should be considered when attaching a monetary value to the bid. If bidding on a single property that is on the other side of the city, it may not be worth the extra drive time. Fuel prices fluctuate greatly and can rise dramatically from the time a bid or quote is given to the time the job begins. There must be room in the fuel budget to cover an increase in price.

Mileage

The amount of time spent traveling to and from a project can affect the profitability as well as the ability for crews to get to other jobs. In the landscaping business, it is necessary to travel from one job to another as well as back and forth to the nursery or your business facilities. The mileage should be determined based on the average fuel and vehicle expenses. Many companies use GPS to track mileage and location of company vehicles. Travel time must be included in the budget for each job.

Subcontractors

If a subcontractor or hired labor is required, having a contract for these services is recommended. Among other things, the contract should cover each of the related cost items and state who is responsible for paying the cost. If the subcontractor's fees will be included in a quote or bid, carefully review the costs to ensure you will not have to cover anything that may be underbid.

Materials

Obtaining accurate material costs depends on accurate site measurements and the use of proper conversion rates. If a landscape operation keeps an inventory of materials, they can calculate costs based on what they paid for the materials. If a landscape operation does not keep an inventory of materials, they will have to compare prices of different suppliers and base their costs on what they will pay the supplier. Material calculations should not be used as a base multiplier for determining overall project prices, although many bids are calculated this way. Giving the client a total price without showing itemization can negatively influence the sales negotiation. Material costs should include a margin for price fluctuations. See **Figure 18-15**.

Contingencies

A *contingency* is a provision to cover unpredictable situations. If something unpredictable occurs, such as an unknown cable line being cut, the contingency will cover the additional costs of repairing the line. A small percentage of the overall job cost is typically used as a contingency fund. The percentage used often depends on the evaluation of risks an estimator notes and the potential challenges these risks may pose.

Job Cost Estimate		Name:	
Job: Binford Tool			Date: 3/20/18
Reusable Goods Costs	Cost/Unit	Units	Cost
36" self-propelled mower	$2.40/hr	130	312
20" push mower	$0.50/hr	60	30
Weedeater	$1.50/hr	80	120
Cyclone spreader	$0.40/hr	60	24
3/4 ton pickup truck	$8.75/hr	60	525
Flatbed truck	$2.80/hr	20	56
A. Total Reusables Costs			1067
Labor Costs	Cost/Hour	Hours	Cost
Bob	$10.00/hr	250	2500
Joanie	$12.50/hr	150	1875
Sammy	$14.00/hr	100	1400
B. Total Labor Costs			5775
Expendable Materials Costs	Cost/Unit	Units	Cost
Railroad ties	$4.50/tie	50	225
Hardware	$250		250
Fertilizer	$600		600
Mulch	$1.50/ft³	30	45
Plant materials	$700		700
C. Total Materials Costs			1820
D. Total Direct Costs (Lines A + B + C)			8662
E. Guarantee Costs			110.9
Overhead and Contingencies			
Overhead			1653
Contingencies			132.24
F. Total Overhead and Contingencies Costs			1785.24
Total Job Cost Estimate (Lines D + E + F)			10,558.14
Desired Profit Margin	%	10	10,55.81
Minimum Bid for Job			11,613.95
add TJCE to Proft Margin to get Min Bid			
Quote to Client			11,700

Melissa Hendrickson, NC State University

Figure 18-15. A job cost estimate is used to total all costs associated with a specific jobsite. This information is used by managers when estimating time to complete tasks, determine which materials need to be hauled to the site, and determine the cost to be passed along to the client.

Other Costs

Other costs that may be incurred include taxes, waste disposal (all materials), construction permits, and licensing. These costs must be included in the budget. There may also be costs that are site specific, such as parking fees of specialized equipment. The costs or needs for these components vary by area.

Quotes and Bids

There is no standard format for writing a bid or quote. However, a neat, highly detailed, and easy-to-read submission will definitely impress a potential client, **Figure 18-16**. Today, most companies generate quotes or bids using programs and apps that are compatible with their business software. These programs can often use stored data, such as labor hours for specific jobs, to calculate costs on a new bid or quote. Using a prepared form will help prevent omission of valid components.

Hart and Ivy Landscaping Services

1234 Marigold Avenue, Raleigh, North Carolina, 12003
321-654-9876 • Fax 321-654-9875 • handilandscape.com

Mr. and Ms. Dean
9876 Magnolia Way
Raleigh, NC, 12003
March 14, 2020

Mr. and Ms. Dean,

Thank you for allowing Hart and Ivy to develop a landscaping plan for your property. You have a beautiful home and a lot with great landscaping potential. The design Hart and Ivy proposes will maximize your property use, increase your property value, and minimize maintenance needs. We have included the following materials for your review:

- Complete layout in an aerial view of the proposed design
- Detailed drawings of the patio and walkway
- Listing of the plants included in the design and their estimated costs
- Listing of hardscape materials and estimated costs (including labor)
- Time line and cost estimates for proposed services
- Maintenance requirements
- Design and estimation fee

Labor Fees

• Design and estimation (due within 15 days of receipt of this letter)	$160.00
• Tree removal (two maples in side bed); can be completed by the first of May	$400.00
• Renovation and installation of side bed and front bed (garage); can be completed by the middle of May	$5446.03
• Renovation and installation of front and right side bed; can be completed in the fall of 2020	$4601.78
	Total: $10,607.81*

*Payments for services will be paid in half ($5303.91) at the midpoint of installation. The remainder ($5303.90) will be paid upon completion of installation.

Fully licensed, bonded, insured • Proud member of North Carolina Nursery and Landscape Association and NALP
1234 Marigold Avenue, Raleigh, North Carolina 12003   321-654-9876•Fax 321-654-9875 • handilandscape.com

Itemized Tasks

- Perform soil tests to determine proper pH and nutrient requirements. Analyze results to confirm and plan for future nutrient treatments. Amend soils based on estimated chemical needs. (Fertilization should be continued after soil tests in the coming years.)
- Remove expired plant material and wood edging. Rototill all planting areas to a depth of 6". Acquire stable compost material (1 yd³ will cover 160 ft² @ 2" deep). Acquire necessary lime and fertilizer. Work these materials into the soil with the rototiller.
- Lime should be applied in spring and fall for the next 2 years to continue to elevate the pH.
- Use 15 lb to 20 lb/1000 ft² of product (fertilizer) for each application. All plants should be fertilized in spring and fall with a complete fertilizer, such as 18-6-12 or equivalent.
- Establish the grade of the beds.
- Layout the new planting areas and develop a border (trench).
- Apply granular preemergent herbicide to the mulched areas for weed control.
- Apply high quality mulch (1 yd³ will cover 105 ft² @ 3" deep) to all areas.

Please take your time reviewing the design and its components. You may wish to make a list of questions and concerns that you can email to us or discuss at our next meeting. Hart and Ivy is fully insured and licensed to perform all of the landscaping work included in the design. Should you decide to accept our proposal, we require a nonrefundable deposit at the onset of the project. If you have any questions please do not hesitate to contact us by phone or email. Thank you once again for entrusting Hart and Ivy to create a landscape for your home.

Sincerely,

Lee Ivy and Chris Hart

R. Lee Ivy and Chris Hart

encl.

Fully licensed, bonded, insured • Proud member of North Carolina Nursery and Landscape Association and NALP
1234 Marigold Avenue, Raleigh, North Carolina 12003   321-654-9876•Fax 321-654-9875 • handilandscape.com

Goodheart-Willcox Publisher

Figure 18-16. Quotes provide a list of services and the estimated costs associated. Some quotes are also used as the contract with space for the customer and professional to sign. Clients expect to see details for installation and maintenance tasks in a neatly prepared document. The format is not as important as are the clear and concise statements.

Hourly Rates vs. Set Prices

Landscape companies installing or maintaining properties typically charge by the hour or base the contracted price on their hourly rates. If there are many unknowns on a site, such as an old septic tank that is no longer in use and deteriorated to the point of collapsing, it is advisable to bill the client at an hourly rate. The uncertainty of how the system was constructed or how long it will take to solve the issue will affect the time it takes to ensure the area above the tank will be safe for landscape installation. The hourly rate will ensure you are paid for the time spent working. If the customer is given a quote for removing or filling in the area, you will be obligated to follow through and work until the system is repaired.

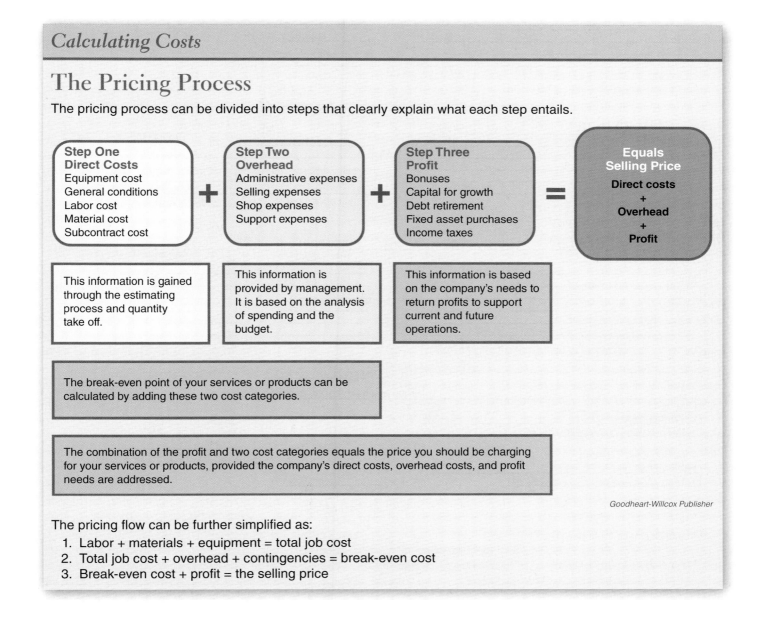

Calculating Costs

The Pricing Process

The pricing process can be divided into steps that clearly explain what each step entails.

**Step One
Direct Costs**
Equipment cost
General conditions
Labor cost
Material cost
Subcontract cost

**Step Two
Overhead**
Administrative expenses
Selling expenses
Shop expenses
Support expenses

**Step Three
Profit**
Bonuses
Capital for growth
Debt retirement
Fixed asset purchases
Income taxes

**Equals
Selling Price**
Direct costs
+
Overhead
+
Profit

This information is gained through the estimating process and quantity take off.

This information is provided by management. It is based on the analysis of spending and the budget.

This information is based on the company's needs to return profits to support current and future operations.

The break-even point of your services or products can be calculated by adding these two cost categories.

The combination of the profit and two cost categories equals the price you should be charging for your services or products, provided the company's direct costs, overhead costs, and profit needs are addressed.

Goodheart-Willcox Publisher

The pricing flow can be further simplified as:
1. Labor + materials + equipment = total job cost
2. Total job cost + overhead + contingencies = break-even cost
3. Break-even cost + profit = the selling price

Quoting a Set Price

Quoting a set price to a potential client is much like bid solicitation, albeit on a smaller scale. However, it is just as important to calculate costs accurately to ensure the job is profitable. Quotes include costs for materials, labor, licenses, permits, and other components specific to the project, **Figure 18-17**.

New Job Cost Estimate

Job Name _____

			HOURS USED		MACHINE	
MACHINERY	COST/HOUR	×	ON JOB	=	COST	
1 36″ mower	$4.57		113.20		$517.32	
2						
3 Spreader	$0.17		3.2		$0.54	
	per mile		in miles			
4 Truck	$0.55		1120.00		$616.00	
5						
6						
7						
			Total Machinery Cost		$1,133.87	

			HOURS ON	GEAR	LABOR	
LABOR	COST/HOUR	×	JOB ×	UP =	COST	
8 Supervisor	$16.56		119.6	1.4	$2,772.81	
9				1.4	$0.00	
			Total Labor Cost		$2,772.81	

					MATERIALS	
MATERIALS	QUANTITY	×	PRICE/UNIT	=	COST	
10 Fertilizer	115.20		$0.31		$35.71	
11						
12 Mulch	384.00		$4.00		$1,536.00	
13						
14						
15						
16						
17						
18						
			Total Materials Cost		$1,571.71	

		Total Machine, Labor, and Materials Cost		$5,478.39
Overhead	15 %		$821.76	
Contingencies	10 %		$547.84	
Total Overhead and Contingencies			$1,369.60	
Total Job Cost Estimate			$6,847.98	Break-Even
Profit Margin	35 %			
$6,847.98		1 +	0.35 %	
Job Cost				
		Total Job Cost Estimate	$9,244.78	
		per month	$770.40	
Actual Business Profit per Year				
$2,396.79 × 15 similar jobs		$35,951.91		
Per Month				
$199.73				

R. Lee Ivy

Figure 18-17. Using the materials calculations as a base multiplier is often done to determine total selling price. However, not all associated costs may be taken into account and the method should be avoided. Instead, actual costs should be determined and profit can be added as a calculation component of the overall project.

When discussing the cost of a project with a client, the client may wish to negotiate the price. If your profit margin is wide enough, you will have some leeway to change the price and keep the work profitable.

Bid Solicitation

A *bid solicitation* for a landscape project is a process in which a potential client notifies prospective landscape companies to bid a price for a project, **Figure 18-18**. The potential client provides the landscape companies with detailed explanations and requirements of the project. A bid solicitation may be referred to as a *request for quotations (RFQ)*, an *invitation to bid (ITB)*, or a *request for proposals (RFP)*. The bid submissions and selection process may be sealed or open to public review.

LEESVILLE ROAD LANDSCAPE
IMPROVEMENT PROJECT

ES-2016-11

ADVERTISEMENT FOR BIDS

CITY OF RALEIGH   PROJECT # ES 2016-11

Project Name: **Leesville Road Landscape Improvement Project**

Pursuant to the General Statutes of North Carolina, Section 143-128 etc. seq. sealed proposals are invited and will be received by the City of Raleigh in the office of the Engineering Servies Director until 2:00 pm, Tuesday, January 17, 2021 at which time at a meeting in Room 400, 222 W. Hargett Street, Raleigh, N. C., the sealed proposals will be publicly opened for construction consisting of furnishing and installing the following:

Approximately 1.1 miles of landscape planting along Leesville Road from Interstate 540 to New Leesville Boulevard. Project will include field layouts and adjustments, bed preparation, furnishing and installing plantings, maintaining and warranting these plantings for two years.

A hard copy and electronic copy of the plans and contract project specifications may be reviewed on line and obtained from Accent Imaging from Monday, December 12, 2016, at 8121 Brownleigh Drive, Raleigh, NC 27617, (919) 782-3332, or at www.accentimaging.com. Contract documents can be purchased from Accent Imaging for a non-refundable fee of Fifty dollars ($50.00) plus sales tax. For additional information please contact Tim Sudano at the City's Design/Construction Division by e-mail at tim.sudano@raleighnc.gov or contact the Design/Construction Division by calling (919) 996-5575.

A pre-bid conference for all contractors, sub-contractors, minority and woman owned businesses will be held at 2:00 PM on Wednesday, January 4, 2021 in Room 303, 222 W. Hargett Street, Raleigh, North Carolina 27602.

From Monday, December 12, 2020 until the date of opening the proposals, plans and specifications of the proposed work are and will continue to be on file in the office of the Engineering Services Department, 222 W. Hargett Street, Raleigh, North Carolina, during usual office hours, and are available to prospective bidders. No proposal will be considered or accepted unless at the time of its filing, the same shall be accompanied by a cash deposit, cashier's check, or certified check on a bank or trust company insured by the FDIC and authorized to do business in North Carolina in an amount equal to five percent (5%) of the proposal. In the alternative, a five percent (5%) bid bond issued by a corporate surety licensed by the State of North Carolina may be filed with the proposal. Bidders must be properly licensed under Chapter 87 of the General Statues of North Carolina and must comply with nondiscrimination provisions. The City is an equal opportunity Municipality/Owner and invites small and minority contractors to bid. The City Council reserves the right to reject any or all proposals.

This the 12th day of, December 2020.

THE CITY OF RALEIGH

Nancy McFarlane, MAYOR

Rich Kelly, P.E. Engineering Services Director

City of Raleigh, North Carolina

Figure 18-18. Bid solicitations are an opportunity to compete for projects that may be highly profitable. These can be for commercial or residential customers.

Bid solicitation is common with large commercial installations and maintenance projects. Some government projects are also contracted through bid solicitation. Business owners contemplating such a project must thoroughly read and understand the solicitation to ensure their business is able to fulfill the requirements and make a profit. Bid solicitations may be posted online or in printed media. There are many sample bid solicitations available for review online.

Competitors' Rates

Many jobs are underbid and earn little, if any, profit. The most likely reason is that the landscape professional does not have accurate measurements of the labor and task time it will take to complete a project. Some companies will simply underbid the competition or use the competition's prices as their own. Others may simply increase the competition's bid slightly and use that amount for their quote. These methods are risky as the competition's prices may not be accurate.

Selling the Job

Once the assessment is complete and the costs are calculated, the itemized list of operations is presented to the client. Some clients may choose certain tasks to be done and eliminate ones they perceive to be unnecessary. While they are the ultimate decision makers, altering or eliminating tasks will likely compromise the quality of the project. For example, in heavy clay soils where compaction and soil air is limited, remediation with tillage equipment and the addition of organic matter is very beneficial. The cost of this step can be significant, but the tilling and organic matter will increase the longevity of the plants and reduce pest problems. It is best if you can convince the client that the benefits outweigh the costs and that the landscape will be much more successful.

Include a pamphlet based on scientific principles in a sales packet or with a job estimate to give your work more credibility. The information in the pamphlet should come from reputable sites, such as a university or government site. The pamphlet *must* look professional and be without errors. The sources should be cited on the pamphlet to give the information more credibility. This information can be helpful during negotiation to convince the client to choose the quality of your work over a competitor's lower price.

Career Connection

Joshua Richardson

Joshua Richardson, CPP, Landscape Designer, Ruppert Landscape, Raleigh/Durham, NC

Joshua Richardson is a professional landscape designer for Ruppert Landscape. Ruppert Landscape is a large commercial landscape company with construction and management branches along the eastern region of the United States. Joshua has worked on interesting projects such as a native prairie garden, a children's garden, and on many commercial landscape renovations and custom landscape water features.

Joshua recognized his passion for plants and landscape design after taking his first horticulture class in high school during his first year. Joshua has been working in the commercial landscape industry since he graduated from North Carolina State with a bachelor's degree in landscape design. He works with customers to enhance and renovate the landscapes of large commercial properties. Joshua stresses the importance of listening to a client's needs in order to provide a design that meets the client's budget. As a landscape designer, Joshua works in the office rendering landscape designs and outdoors, performing site assessments or guiding a crew to make the design a reality.

Joshua encourages anyone interested in the landscape design field to pursue college education in the field to learn design aspects and techniques. He states that it is vital for a landscape designer to have great knowledge of a large library of plants to design successful landscapes. Joshua emphasizes the importance to be on the forefront of new techniques, products, and technology in the design field. These aspects of the industry are always evolving and continued learning is important to be successful as a landscape designer.

Consider This

1. What aspect of Joshua's job do you find the most interesting?
2. What part of a designer's work would be the most challenging for you?
3. How important do you think it is for a designer to stay informed about new techniques and technology? How does this knowledge affect a designer's ability to create new landscape designs?

Summary

- A site assessment is a complete analysis of an existing landscape for maintenance costs or for a new installation.
- All of the assessment should be done on-site to ensure that the site condition and the steps needed for installation and/or maintenance will be accurate.
- A landscape estimate is a means of roughly calculating the cost of a project based on the site assessment, design, materials, and labor.
- Site measurements can be taken with digital equipment, using GPS or GIS technologies, with manual tools, and by pacing.
- A company's profit is the money the business earns over its expenses. A company must make a profit to fuel growth and keep the business in operation.
- A profit margin is the ratio of profit to the cost of the project, which is the sum of all costs incurred by the job.
- A budget must be established once the scope of a project is determined.
- Material calculations should not be used as a base multiplier for determining overall project prices.
- Overhead includes all costs associated with operating a business not directly tied to one specific project.
- A contingency percentage is added to total job cost to offset any complications or issues experienced during a project.
- Landscape companies installing or maintaining properties typically charge by the hour or base the contracted price on their hourly rates.
- Clients should be apprised of all tasks to be performed during a project and only allowed to eliminate those that will not affect overall project quality.

Chapter Review

Know and Understand ➥

Answer the following questions using the information provided in this chapter.

1. A complete analysis of an existing landscape for maintenance costs or for a new installation is a site _____.
   A. measurement
   B. assessment
   C. evaluation
   D. investigation

2. *True or False?* An assessment for maintenance work is performed to determine the possibilities and limitations of the site.
   A. True.
   B. False.

3. Which of the following best describes a landscape estimate?
   A. A detailed list of materials and labor.
   B. Profit margin subtracted from total price.
   C. A rough calculation of a project's cost.
   D. The rough total of all indirect costs.

4. Which of the following components are included in a landscape estimate?
   A. Cost of labor, machinery, waste disposal, and permits.
   B. Cost of plant and mulch materials, and soil amendments.
   C. Cost of overhead, subcontractor, and hardscape materials.
   D. All of the above.

5. Which of the following is a tabulation of all the landscape components and the costs associated with each component?
   A. Site takeoff.
   B. Site assessment.
   C. Site measurement.
   D. Site design.

6. *True or False?* A low bid may reduce your profit margin on a job.
   A. True.
   B. False.

7. What is the square footage of a rectangular lot that measures 65′ × 95′?
   A. 9175 ft²
   B. 6175 ft²
   C. 3175 ft²
   D. 7175 ft²

8. When calculating the profit margin on net profit, the total revenue must be revenue _____.
   A. plus project cost
   B. minus project cost
   C. after taxes
   D. before taxes

9. Which of the following is an indirect cost included in the project cost?
   A. Labor.
   B. Plant material.
   C. Overhead.
   D. Mileage.

10. Which of the following is a direct cost included in a project cost?
    A. Mortgage.
    B. Labor.
    C. Utilities.
    D. Vehicle payment.

11. Which of the following is considered burden?
    A. Insurance premiums.
    B. Accounting fees.
    C. Mortgage payments.
    D. All of the above.

12. An expense that must be met regularly, typically on a monthly basis is a(n) _____.
    A. fixed expense
    B. variable expense
    C. operational expense
    D. All of the above.

13. Of the following, which most accurately describes the calculation of labor costs?
    A. Calculated by the efficiency of individual workers.
    B. Calculated by the condition of the equipment.
    C. Calculated by the task time required to complete the job.
    D. Calculated by fuel, mileage, and freight charges.

14. Which of the following is the reduction of an asset's value over time?
    A. Reduction.
    B. Depreciation.
    C. Deduction.
    D. Itemization.

15. What are the advantages to renting equipment?
    A. Limited capital needed.
    B. Costs for maintenance and repair.
    C. Storage space needs and costs.
    D. All of the above.

16. Which of the following statements is true?
    A. Businesses use GPS to track fuel prices.
    B. Subcontractor's fees are included in a quote.
    C. The mileage rate is set by the IRS.
    D. All of the above.

17. Why would a contingency be included on a bid or quote?
    A. To cover unpredictable situations.
    B. To cover the additional costs.
    C. To maintain the profit margin.
    D. All of the above.

18. Why would a business owner charge by the hour instead of giving a set price for a job?
    A. It is easier to account for each cost of a project.
    B. To simplify the accounting needed for the job.
    C. To ensure payment for the time spent working.
    D. All of the above.

Thinking Critically

1. You have a small landscape maintenance company with a consistent client base. You have determined that you need to raise prices for your services to keep making a profit. How would you approach your clients to let them know you were raising prices? What would you say to a client who was canceling your services because of the price increase?

2. How would you convince a client to retain your services even though your price is higher than that of two lawn service companies that are lowballing local jobs?

Suggested Activities

1. In a group of 3 or 4, research and compare site assessment guidelines found online. Use your research to create a new, usable assessment checklist. Share your checklist with the class and determine what you did not include.

2. Work with a partner and measure the lot where you live or a small area on the school campus. Prepare a detailed estimate and proposal for a simple, new landscape installation or a regularly scheduled landscape maintenance job for an existing landscape. Write the estimate as a preliminary document.

3. Create a landscape site analysis for a new landscape installation by surveying the site, locating the utilities, and making recommendations for grade changes. With permission, this can be performed on a site currently under renovation.

4. Working with a partner, find an image of a professional landscape installation. Decide on reasonable measurements of the lot (create your own) and create a bid for a landscape maintenance project that includes all costs, expenses, and markups. Write the bid in a professional format.

5. Calculate the square footage of the following oddly shaped gardening bed. Calculate each geometric shape individually and add the measurements to obtain the total square footage.

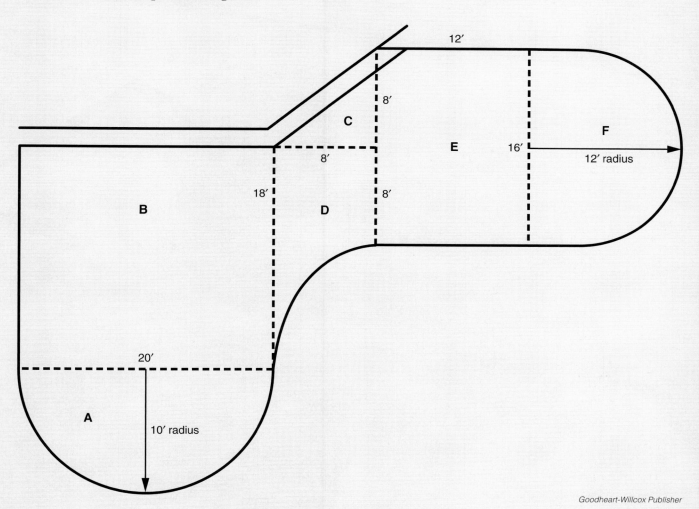

Goodheart-Willcox Publisher

CHAPTER

19

Client Relationships

While studying this chapter, look for the activity icon  to:
- **Practice** vocabulary terms with Words to Know activities.
- **Expand** learning with identification activities.
- **Reinforce** what you learn by completing Know and Understand questions.

G-WLEARNING.com

www.g-wlearning.com/agriculture

Chapter Outcomes

After studying this chapter, you will be able to:

- Explain and apply the four Ps of marketing.
- Identify methods used to reach potential clients in a target market.
- Prepare for meeting a potential client, including scheduling and dressing properly.
- Identify ways in which to make a positive impression to potential clients.
- Listen carefully to a client's needs and build a rapport with the client.
- Understand basic guidelines for presenting a landscape bid or quote.
- Decide which clients and opportunities are advantageous to your company.
- List components of a landscape quote and a bid.
- Explain the elements of a business contract.
- Identify tactics used to introduce clients to members of the landscape company.
- Explain the importance of establishing and following a work timeline.

Key Terms ➦

breach of contract
business contract
consideration
customer service
four Ps of marketing
institutional promotion
intention
marketing mix
offer
place
price

product
promise to perform
promotion
promotional mix
site manager
terms and conditions
time requirement
unique selling proposition (USP)
value
value proposition
work timeline

Introduction

To grow your business, you will need to attract new clients. First, determine the target market. The most practical way to spend an advertising budget is to focus on the people most likely to use the business. Second, promote the business using media, such as television, newspapers, or the internet, that people in the target market use often, **Figure 19-1**. The goal is for people in the target market to see the promotional material on a daily basis. Finally, sign new clients and provide them with services that exceed their expectations. This chapter introduces you to ways to grow your business, including effective marketing methods, best practices for meeting and greeting clients, and agreeing to business contracts.

Monkey Business Images/Shutterstock.com

Goodluz/Shutterstock.com

Figure 19-1. Does your target market read the newspaper on a daily basis? Do they watch TV or do they get most of their news online? Spending a marketing budget on a medium not used by your target market is not money well spent.

Reaching Your Target Market

As discussed in Chapter 17, *Starting a Business*, a target market is the people most likely to buy your product or service. Once the target market is determined, the most effective marketing and advertising methods can also be determined. *Marketing* consists of various activities through which a business promotes and sells it goods or services in order to make or generate a profit. Large and small companies use the four Ps of marketing to successfully promote their goods and services. The *four Ps of marketing* are product, price, promotion, and place. The four Ps help businesses understand and satisfy customer demand. The *marketing mix* is the strategy for using the four Ps. It consists of the decisions made about product, price, place, and promotion for a product or a business, **Figure 19-2**.

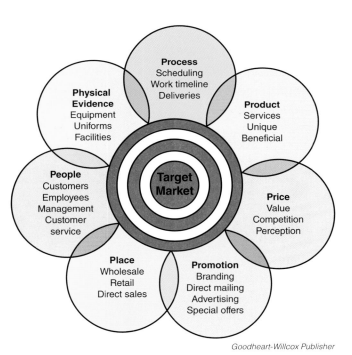

Goodheart-Willcox Publisher

Figure 19-2. Marketing professionals have added physical evidence, people, and production to the original four Ps. Marketing agencies often present the client with a list of questions pertaining to the marketing mix. The list helps the client define their goods or service in detail, which helps the marketing agency produce a more successful campaign.

Product

The *product* is the good or service being offered that fulfills consumers' needs and demands. Research should be conducted to identify consumer needs, get feedback, and confirm the product or service meets consumer needs. It is also necessary to determine what makes the product unique and the benefits it offers the consumer. This is called a unique selling proposition (USP). The *unique selling proposition (USP)* is a statement that highlights the benefits and special features of a product or business. It expresses how the product or business is different from and better than the competition. The research methods can include customer reviews online or through mailings and feedback from the sales team on customer views. A lawn maintenance service, for example, may use sustainable practices, such as composting all yard waste, **Figure 19-3**.

Price

The *price* is the amount the consumer pays for the product or service. The price of a good or service must meet the following requirements:

- It must cover the cost of producing and selling the product.
- It must generate sufficient profit for the business.
- It must be what customers are willing to pay.

The price is linked to the value consumers perceive it has rather than the actual value. *Value* is the relative worth of something to an individual person, which changes from person to person. The *value proposition* is an explanation of the value of a product compared to other similar products. If a product is priced higher than or lower than its perceived value, consumers may not purchase it. A product can be assessed by comparing it to competitor prices and features. Customers may be willing to pay more if they believe in the value of the product.

Promotion

Promotion is the communication aspect of marketing. The goal of a product promotion is to promote specific goods or services offered by a business. Product and service promotions are designed to increase sales. It includes strategies, such as advertising, sales promotions, social media marketing, search engine marketing, public relations, company newsletters, and email marketing. The combination of these strategies is considered the *promotional mix*.

LianeM/Shutterstock.com   *Alison Hancock/Shutterstock.com*

Figure 19-3. Leaves and chipped brush can be composted to provide valuable organic matter to planting beds. Composted leaves and brush provide a low-cost sustainable mulch that can be used to prevent weeds and hold moisture.

Additional methods of promotion include word of mouth, referrals, business cards, promotional fliers, and employee uniforms and vehicles with the company name and logo displayed. Word of mouth and referrals often come from clients that are pleased with their service and recommend services to their neighbors, friends, and other businesses. A specific color from the logo used consistently on promotional materials will also help consumers recognize your brand image. See **Figure 19-4**. An *institutional promotion* focuses on promoting the company rather than its products in order to increase awareness of the business and create a favorable view of the brand.

Place

The *place* of goods and services is how they will get to the customer. Place includes the activities involved in getting goods and services to customers. To make effective placements, it must be understood where consumers will buy your service or product. If you sell wholesale nursery plants (goods), for example, you may choose to offer them to wholesale customers online, by cold calling, or directly to a business through salespeople. (Wholesale nurseries do not sell to the general public.) You may also have to limit your promotions locally to minimize shipment or transportation costs. A wholesale nursery may also attract new customers by participating in trade shows with a company booth showcasing the plant materials it grows.

A service business, such as a landscape maintenance business, may use the same approach toward homeowners and commercial businesses. They might also use mass mailing and local radio and television channels. A landscaping business earns profits by providing consumers with specialized services that meet their needs and wants. Service businesses do not sell goods, but instead perform activities and share specialized knowledge with their customers.

Goodheart-Willcox Publisher

Figure 19-4. Logos placed on company equipment helps to promote the company. Care should be taken at all times when using company equipment; the operator's actions are a reflection of the company.

Promotion is necessary to make consumers aware of your product or service and build preference for your brand.

Successful application of the four Ps has been proven to be effective in product or service success. Keep in mind that the four Ps are interdependent and must be planned with each other in mind. The four Ps must be balanced in a marketing plan to place your business in the most favorable light and reach your target market. See **Figure 19-5**.

Services Marketing Mix

Some marketing professionals have updated the marketing mix by adding three Ps to the method. The three Ps are people, physical evidence, and process.

People

The demeanor and attitudes of your employees is crucial for your company's success. Employees should be instructed on how they are expected to behave when working with or being around customers. Crew members on an installation job, for example, should not be speaking or behaving offensively. Your people are as much a part of the business as its goods and services. Customers do *not* differentiate the people who work for a business and the business itself.

Physical Evidence

Clients will judge your company, not only by the quality of its service, but the testimonials from previous customers, before and after comparisons, and the physical presence of your equipment and employees. Marketing professionals have said that customers think of companies or brands by a single attribute, either negative or positive. Positive reviews will boost your credibility and likely earn more business. Battered and dirty trucks and trailers appear neglected and will give a poor impression, whereas well-maintained equipment shows the company values the equipment and the impression it makes on others. Employees with clean uniforms and neat appearance will also be a positive influence, one in which it appears you and your employees care about the impression they give their clients.

Processes

Process refers to the systems that affect the service, such as employee punctuality. If employees are late to work they will be behind schedule and may not perform a service that was scheduled and confirmed with a client. Other processes that may affect your company include organized scheduling of employees and jobs, timely delivery of materials and equipment, and cleaning a site when the work is completed.

stoatphoto/Shutterstock.com

Figure 19-5. A marketing strategy is used to determine how the company will identify and reach potential customers. A marketing strategy for a garden center, for example, would be designed to attract local homeowners and gardeners, whereas a marketing strategy for a wholesale nursery would be designed to reach wholesale customers, such as landscapers and garden centers.

Client Contact

Once the marketing plan is in place and active, clients will contact the business. It is essential that online links work without incident and telephone calls and emails are followed up in a timely manner. Failing to follow up promptly will give potential customers a poor impression of your business. It is also important to respond in a professional and pleasant manner.

Building Rapport

Rapport developed between the company spokesperson and the prospective client may also influence the client's decision. A client may be willing to pay a higher cost if they feel their relationship with the landscaping company will be positive. Businesses soliciting landscaping services may also look for a landscape company with similar beliefs. For example, the homeowner's association of an apartment or condo complex in which there is a great deal of focus on sustainable practices may hire a landscaping company specifically because it uses sustainable practices.

Setting Up and Preparing for a Meeting

During the first contact, listen to the client's needs to determine if the project is something your business offers. If so, ask for the address and schedule a date to meet the client on-site. If the project is something your company does not offer, you may refer them to another business that can meet their needs. This is an effective means of networking with other businesses that may also refer business to your company. Ensure the client has your cell phone number or set up call forwarding so you will not miss a call.

To make a good impression when you meet the prospective client, dress professionally and be prepared. Bring all necessary materials, including tools for measuring, blank contracts, and electronic devices used for taking photos and inputting data. Your company vehicle should be clean as should your shoes in case you are invited into the home or office.

fizkes/Shutterstock.com

Figure 19-6. The individual that meets with the prospective client for the first time must present a positive and professional image. The prospective client will base impressions of the landscaping company on this first interaction.

Meeting the Client

An essential part of the process is meeting the client and establishing a working relationship. There is only one chance to make a first impression and whoever meets the client first must ensure the company is well represented. The client should be greeted professionally and confidently with a firm handshake and good eye contact, **Figure 19-6**.

Personal Attire

Proper attire should always be worn when meeting a client. If you are attending a more formal meeting, it may be best to wear business attire, such as a suit and tie. For a less formal meeting, in a residential setting for example, casual office wear is usually acceptable. Wearing a shirt with a company logo and standard issue pants is positive reinforcement of your company's professionalism. It is always best to err on the side of caution and overdress for your meeting. If you work on-site or visit sites regularly, you may want to keep clean clothes and shoes on hand in case you have an impromptu meeting.

Primary Contact

Initial meetings establish communication and offer opportunities to relate the goals of the company and better understand the desires of the client. Many residential jobs have more than one person involved in the decision-making. If this is the case, it is best to determine who will be the primary contact for future communication. This will prevent misunderstandings and problems that may ensue due to miscommunication.

Commercial Contracts

Commercial projects typically have a ***site manager*** representing the company. The site manager will likely be the main contact handling all issues between businesses and the landscaping company, **Figure 19-7**. A multiuse mall, for example, may have multiple business owners contributing ideas for the landscaping. A point person is necessary to convey collective ideas and needs to the landscape professional, such as preferences for colors and the presence or absence of plant fragrances.

Gathering Information

Some project costs can be determined on-site once the lot measurements are known. The estimator may be able to calculate costs for a simple maintenance job, for example, once measurements are taken and tasks are tabulated. The information gathered during this meeting will depend on the type of work being done. A new design and installation project, for example, will require much more work upfront with the client than a maintenance project will require.

sirtravelalot/Shutterstock.com

Figure 19-7. A site manager is often the main contact between the client and the landscape company. The site manager is ultimately responsible for ensuring the landscape is being installed or maintained up to the standards of the client.

Figure 19-8. A new landscape involves planning, grading, installation of plants, and installation of hardscape materials. Much interaction is required between the client and the site manager to ensure that the landscape meets the need of the client.

It will also require extensive site preparation tasks, design work, and new plant materials, all of which must be discussed with the client, **Figure 19-8**.

In smaller companies, people often wear multiple hats and perform several jobs. The first person meeting the client may be the owner who may also be the estimator and salesperson.

Interpersonal Skills

Interpersonal skills are those used when interacting with others, including clients and coworkers. Learning how to speak and listen to customers in a way that makes them comfortable and makes a good impression is essential for a successful business.

Listening Skills

An important part of communication is being a good listener. Carefully listen to the prospective client to understand what they hope to gain from using your company's services. Keep notes and pay special attention to ensure the project needs are noted and if there are any areas or problems you can address that other companies may overlook. Providing creative solutions to these issues may give your company an edge over other companies toward signing the client. Address each of the prospective client's needs and indicate how your company can meet and exceed these needs.

Verbal and Nonverbal Skills

Verbal skills are those used when speaking, listening, and writing. Nonverbal skills are those used to send and receive messages, such as the expression on your face and your body posture. In addition to using good listening skills, you must use a clear voice that is easily heard and understood when you are speaking. To ensure you are heard and understood, respectfully face the person to whom you are speaking. Keep the following points in mind when communicating professionally:

- If you do not understand, be sure to ask questions.
- Lean forward while a person is talking to signal interest and keen listening.
- Answer the phone quickly with a pleasant voice to convey a positive attitude.
- Think through each email message as you would before sending a postal letter.
- Use social media to present yourself and your business in a positive light.
- Always remain courteous when speaking on the phone or in person.

Bid Solicitation

As discussed in Chapter 18, *Pricing Landscape Projects*, a bid solicitation for a landscape project is a process in which a potential client notifies prospective companies to bid a price for a project. The prospective client provides the landscape companies with detailed explanations and requirements of the project. These types of projects are typically large commercial or government landscape maintenance or installation jobs, **Figure 19-9.** Bids submitted for government jobs are public information that may be viewed by other companies, but bids for private companies are typically closed bids in which only the bidder and the prospective client have access to the information. Having access to other submitted bids enables companies to compare costs and determine if they are under or overbidding a job.

Svineyard/Shutterstock.com

Vadim Ratnikov/Shutterstock.com

Antwon McMullen/Shutterstock.com

Figure 19-9. Commercial and municipal contracts may entail many sites, seasonal tasks, and storm cleanup. Smaller companies may not have the employees nor equipment to fulfill the contracted work without jeopardizing other commitments.

It may also help a company confirm whether they can do the job and/or earn a profit. Consider the following points when submitting a bid:

- Calculate *all* costs to gain a clear idea of profit margins *before* submitting the bid, **Figure 19-10**.
- Potential jobs that are logistically demanding or requiring additional capital resources may be bid on the higher range to reduce the risk associated with obtaining the new client.
- Bidding on the higher range increases the profit margin and provides more room for potential error.
- Jobs may be bid on the lower range if the company believes that they can make a profit in other areas of the landscape.
- The company may bid the maintenance of the property low with the hope of obtaining a more lucrative installation job at the same site.
- The company may also bid on the lower range if the property owner has other potential job sites.

Some landscaping companies are simply too small to serve large commercial accounts and some small properties are not large enough to benefit commercial landscaping companies. Smaller companies typically have a maximum property size that they can service based on the number of employees, the amount and type of equipment owned, and the overall mission of the company.

Lucas Bischoff Photograph/Shutterstock.com

Figure 19-10. The steep inclined streets in San Francisco offer city landscape professionals with creative as well as architectural challenges. Unique features of a site will increase the labor required to install and maintain the area. Large areas of shrubs, annual beds, and mulched areas add additional expense to the property maintenance and should be factored when calculating the bid.

Should You Accept the Job?

Clients that are looking for landscaping services will typically receive bids from several companies. It is important to note that not every potential client will be a good match for the landscaping company. Some clients will be focused on finding the least expensive quote and may not be as concerned with quality. Others will value quality and understand that quality labor, preparation, and installation is more costly. When bidding with other landscaping companies, it is important to remember the mission and vision of your company.

As a business owner, you have to ask yourself a few important questions after the initial client meeting. You must first determine if you want to be involved in the project. Could this be a beneficial client for your company's goals and structure? What will it do for your company? Would the job help you develop a relationship with an established building contractor or influential homeowner in a neighborhood or new development, **Figure 19-11**? Might the landscape site help gain prestige for your company? Could the job help your company gain entrance into a potential market? Commercial clients may own multiple sites, such as a bank with multiple branches or a landlord with multiple residences or complexes. Working with such a person or business may entail all of the properties he or she owns.

Johnny Habell/Shutterstock.com

Figure 19-11. A company might gain a larger contract, such as for a new development, by performing another smaller or less profitable job.

Referring another Company

If you choose *not* to do the job, it is important to professionally and formally tell the client. This decision must be made before any agreements are made to keep your company's reputation intact. It is always in your best interests to know your limits and prevent getting in over your head. Making promises or implying that you will definitely do the job when you most likely will not take it will create negative publicity for your company. You can still build good rapport with the customer by explaining honestly why you cannot take the job and referring the client to another reputable company.

Pro Tip

Commercial properties may have specific guidelines for landscape maintenance to ensure the site is maintained to the standards of the corporation. This is common for franchises or chain businesses.

R. Lee Ivy

Figure 19-12. Some jobs require equipment that a business might not own and the company will have to lease or purchase the equipment to complete the project. The additional costs must be calculated and included in the total cost of the project.

After you consider how the job will benefit your company, you must determine if it will generate a profit. If a relationship with this client may present opportunities for future profitable work, then a compromised profit margin may be acceptable.

Will other Projects Be Compromised?

The next consideration is whether your company will be able to perform tasks or complete the project without compromising other commitments. Would you have to purchase or rent more equipment or hire more employees? Can you afford to do so? Would your acquisition of plant materials or equipment tie up working capital set aside for other purposes? If the answer is yes to any of these questions, discussions within the company should be given due time and consideration, **Figure 19-12**.

Making a Presentation

In certain situations, a company must give a visual presentation to the management group responsible for choosing a landscaping company for a site, **Figure 19-13**. The presentation may have guidelines and be limited to a specific amount of time. If making a presentation, follow these basic guidelines for a successful presentation:

- Carefully read all guidelines before preparing the presentation.
- Stay within the given time limit and be respectful of others' time.
- Use visual aids with little text. Do *not* read the text word for word.
- Use bullet points with short, concise points.

Monkey Business Images/Shutterstock.com

Figure 19-13. Prior to selecting a maintenance or installation company, clients will often want a visual representation of what the company is proposing. A strong visual presentation that clearly conveys your message will increase your chance of being awarded the job or contract.

- Use color combinations that are appealing and easily read and seen by the audience.
- Proofread, proofread, and proofread some more. Grammatical and spelling errors reflect poorly on you and your company and may determine whether the bid is won or lost.
- The introduction should gain the audience's attention as well as summarize what will be discussed in the presentation.
- The body of the presentation should include the benefits of your company and explain why your company should be selected.
- The conclusion should summarize the main points that were discussed in the presentation.

Hands-On Design

Meeting the Client's Needs

Joe and Sam Jones are seeking your expertise. They have recently remodeled a home in an established neighborhood and have selected your company to develop the landscape plan. There are no trees or other plant materials on the site. The Jones family has the following desires for their landscape:

- A fenced-in backyard to provide privacy from their adjacent neighbors.
- A small area featuring a raised bed for seasonal vegetables (10′ × 10′).
- A small patio that is large enough for a grill and patio set.
- A storage area for yard tools and patio cushions.
- An area for the garbage and recycle containers.
- A finished parkway that requires little maintenance.
- An irrigation system with remote control.
- Low-maintenance plants because the clients do not have time to devote to maintenance.
- Seasonal flowers that bloom throughout the growing season.

Develop a landscape plan that fully meets the demands of the clients. Ensure all components are drawn to scale.

Consider This

1. Were you able to incorporate all of the required elements?
2. What was the most difficult component to incorporate?
3. Did you have other components that you thought would complement the design?

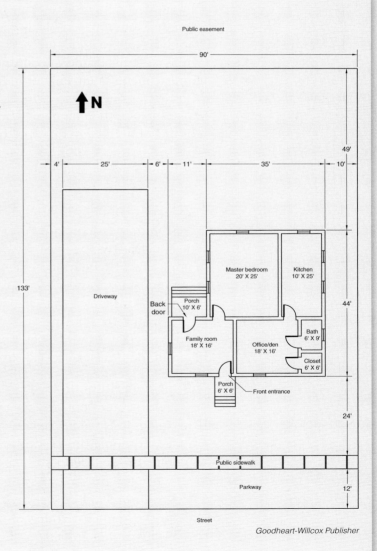

Goodheart-Willcox Publisher

Quotes and Business Contracts

Once again, the type of work being performed will determine how the contract is structured and what information it will include. Tasks included in the contract for a new design and installation project may include designer or architect fees, labor, machinery/equipment costs, subcontractors, hardscape materials, soil testing and amendments, plant materials, and mulch materials. A maintenance contract will typically list services to be performed, materials included, time schedules, and material disposal.

If a job includes the creation of a new design, the design will have to be approved before costs can be calculated for the project. The design costs may be included if the company installing the landscape is also contracted to create the design. However, if a prospective client has a professionally created design, he or she may be pricing installation costs between multiple companies and the quote will be prepared accordingly.

A quote detailing the services to be provided or the components of the project is prepared and presented to the prospective client. A business contract is drawn based on the details in the quote and any additional costs that apply. It will include the cost of labor, machinery/equipment (including rental), mileage, travel time, subcontractor costs, hardscape materials, soil testing, soil amendments, plant materials, mulch materials, freight and taxes, waste disposal, permit and licensing fees, and costs that are specific to the job. It will also include the payment schedule and a timeline identifying when each step of the job will begin and be completed. If the client accepts the terms outlined in the contract, both the customer and the authorized business representative will sign the contract.

Business Contracts

A *business contract* is an agreement between two or more competent parties, such as two people or two businesses. Categories generally have to do with employment, sale or lease, tenancy, service, and general business contracts. A small business owner may have contracts for borrowing money, renting equipment, to purchase or sell goods and services, or to have a partnering agreement with other businesses. He or she may also have employment contracts if employees are hired. There are also contracts for subcontractors, consultants, and marketing services, **Figure 19-14**.

Contract Elements

A business contract is legally enforceable if is agreed upon by both parties and includes specific elements, including an offer, a promise to perform, terms and conditions, time requirements, consideration (usually money), intention, and form. Well-defined elements will help prevent misunderstandings that could occur if any were omitted from the contract.

- An *offer* can be a service or product presented for sale. Items in a store, for example, are offered for acceptance or purchase to the public.
- The *promise to perform* specifies what each party will be providing as well as a promise to uphold the terms of the contract. This may also be referred to as an agreement or acceptance.

Hart and Ivy Landscaping Services
1234 Marigold Avenue,
Raleigh, North Carolina, 12003

321-654-9876   Fax 321-654-9875   handilandscape.com

TO: _____

_____

_____

LANDSCAPING
MANAGEMENT AGREEMENT

Order number:	Date of order:
Phone:	Order taken by:
Approximate start date:	☐ Seasonal contract ☐ One-time job
Job Number:	☐ Repeat customer ☐ Other _____
Job Location:	
Approximate completion date:	

LAWN MAINTENANCE

	CHARGE
☐ Weekly _____	
☐ Bi-weekly _____	
☐ Off-site disposal of turf clippings _____	
☐ Monthly cultivation of bed area _____	
_____	
_____	
Begin _____ End _____	

FERTILIZATION/WEED CONTROL PROGRAM

	CHARGE
☐ Crab grass control _____	
☐ Turf fertilization _____	
☐ Spring _____	
☐ Early summer _____	
☐ Late summer _____	
☐ Fall winterization _____	
☐ Organic Fertilization _____	
☐ Early summer _____	
☐ Late summer _____	
☐ Fall winterization _____	
☐ Broadleaf weed control _____	
☐ Late spring _____	
☐ Late summer _____	

BED CARE

	CHARGE
_____ Applications of weed control to beds _____	
_____ Fertilization _____	
☐ Mulching _____	
Type of mulch _____	
_____	
Amount of mulch _____	
_____	

SPRING CLEAN UP

	CHARGE
☐ Aeration _____	
☐ Dethatching _____	
☐ Mowing/trimming maintained areas _____	
☐ Clean up turf areas _____	
☐ Clean up bed areas _____	
☐ Cut back perennials _____	
☐ Pruning (trim/shape) _____	
☐ Off-site disposal of debris _____	

FALL CLEAN UP

	CHARGE
☐ Bi-weekly mowing of maintained areas _____	
☐ Clean up turf areas _____	
☐ Clean up bed areas _____	
☐ Pruning (trim and shape) _____	
☐ Aeration _____	
☐ Winterization _____	
_____	
☐ Transplanting _____	
_____	
☐ Off-site disposal of debris _____	
Begin _____ End _____	

GRUB CONTROL

	CHARGE
☐ Early summer _____	

GUTTER CLEANING

	CHARGE
☐ Spring _____	
☐ Fall _____	
☐ Other _____	

Additional services which may be needed shall be provided at $_____ per hour, per person, plus material.

Billing will begin on the first day of the first month of contract period and will be submitted on the first of each month until the end of the contract period.

Upon signing, this proposal becomes a legally binding contract. A two-week written notice is required should either party wish to cancel this contract.

Hart and Ivy Landscaping is not responsible for damage to sprinkler heads, hoses, children's toys, cable lines, gas lines, and invisible dog fences, etc., that occur as a result of normal operations.

OTHER PROJECTS

DESCRIPTION	MATERIAL	LABOR	CHARGE

Hart and Ivy Landscaping hereby proposes to furnish material and labor in accordance with the above specifications.

_____
Authorized Signature

_____
Date

Acceptance of proposal: the above specifications are satisfactory and are hereby accepted. Hart and Ivy Landscaping is authorized to do the work as specified. Payment to be made as outlined above.

_____
Authorized Signature

_____
Date

Total materials	
Total labor	
Subtotal	
Tax	
Total	

Figure 19-14. Contracts used for landscape maintenance should be detailed and specific. The contract should clearly lay out which maintenance tasks will be performed and their frequency.

- The *terms and conditions* explain in detail how the service and product will be rendered. It also specifies the rights and obligations of each party, including the amount and date payment is due and how long the agreement will remain in effect. Possible remedies for breach of contract by either party may also be included in this section. Special terms are included in this section, such as whether the contract can be canceled for any reason, such as a breach of contract. A *breach of contract* occurs if one party does not meet the terms of the contract.
- The *time requirement* outlines the delivery of products or services, including the dates and times.
- The *consideration* explains what each party will gain from the business arrangement. In a landscape maintenance contract, for example, the consideration received by the hiring party is landscape maintenance and the landscape company receives payment for its services. The consideration, or payment, may also be a trade of services or products. The payment terms may be included in this section.
- *Intention* indicates that both parties intend for the contract to be legally binding.
- *Form* refers to the physical format of the contract. Contracts for many types of transactions, such as selling or purchasing real estate, must be in writing and signed to be legally binding.

Indypendenz/Shutterstock.com

Figure 19-15. Verbal contracts are easy and quick to complete but they offer no protection for the client nor the company. Contracts at the very minimum should explain the details of the project, price to be charged, and should be signed by both parties.

Verbal vs Written Contracts

A contract may be verbal or written. Verbal or spoken contracts rely on the good faith of the parties involved and can be difficult to enforce, **Figure 19-15**. It is advisable to have all contracts written and signed by all parties. For agreements made without a signed contract, all documentation generated for the agreement, such as emails, quotes, or discussion notes, should be saved to help identify the terms of agreement.

Leases as Contracts

Small businesses often rent office or shop space and large equipment when needed. Real property leases involve renting buildings, land, or other physical space. The lease includes the cost, definition of the space, how the space can be used, what you are allowed to change, and whether the landlord pays for alterations and improvements. Equipment leases can be for everything from office machinery, such as a copier, to skid loaders and dozers. These leases typically include cost, time allowance, liability, statements regarding damage, and conditions of deposit.

The Small Business Association (SBA) advises that business owners seek legal and professional advice before signing a contract. The SBA also recommends that owners read every word, including the small print, and cross out blank spaces so they cannot be altered after the contract is signed. The SBA website is an excellent resource for information on contracts as well as many other issues faced by small businesses.

Project Management

Once the bid is awarded, the salesperson should introduce the site manager or client to the person in charge of the site as they will be directing and performing the daily or week-to-week work. Once again, if there is more than one person involved in the decision making, it is best to determine who will be the primary contact for future communication and to exchange contact information. Ensuring the client is comfortable with their company contact is essential to keeping the client content. The client must also know whom to contact if they have concerns or there is a problem with their site.

Company Hierarchy

The hierarchy of landscape companies varies. In smaller companies, the owner may also be the salesperson and crew foreperson. In larger companies, there is often an account manager and a crew foreperson. The account manager is responsible for communicating with the client and ensuring all contracted work is being performed to their satisfaction. The account manager is not on the job every day but may visit the work site regularly. The crew leader is on the work site daily to manage the working crew. The crew leader (foreman/woman) ensures the contracted work is completed to specifications. The crew leader answers directly to the account manager, **Figure 19-16**.

ALPA PROD/Shutterstock.com

Figure 19-16. A crew leader is responsible for communication between the landscape workers and the account manager. They are a go-between for management and the workers. Crew leaders must be well-organized to organize the logistics of performing the job.

Alison Hancock/Shutterstock.com

Sigur/Shutterstock.com

Figure 19-17. Leaf removal is a very important task that occurs during the fall months. Leaf removal allows the landscape to appear neat and well kept. Collected leaves make excellent compost and leaf mulch for future plantings.

Checking In

Company management should periodically check in with client during the job and after the job is complete to ensure they are pleased with the services. Showing concern and taking care of issues promptly can speak volumes for a company and will help the company retain clients. Clients who are content with landscape work are also more likely to recommend the company to other businesses or friends and family.

Following a Work Timeline

The timeline established in the contract serves as a work timeline for the crew. The ***work timeline*** lists all tasks that must be completed during the installation or maintenance of a landscape. In an installation contract, dates are included to indicate when specific tasks are to be completed, such as the installation of the hardscape or irrigation lines. Dates specified on maintenance contracts usually refer to periods of time in which each task is to be performed. For example, mowing will done during the spring, summer, and fall months on a weekly or biweekly schedule, pruning will be conducted annually during the appropriate season, and leaves will be removed in the fall, **Figure 19-17**.

Work timelines are important because they allow planning and labor scheduling and give clients a reasonable expectation of when a job will be performed or completed. It is easier for a manager to schedule work tasks on all sites if there is a timeline established. Pruning, for example, requires special equipment and training and must be performed at certain times of the year. The manager can schedule a pruning crew to complete the pruning on all job sites within a period of time. This enables the use of the crew and equipment to be limited to the least amount of time possible, which reduces costs.

Customer Service

Customer service is taking care of the customer's needs efficiently and delivering helpful service before, during, and after the customer's needs are met. Good customer service adds value to the product or service and helps establish a relationship and hopefully a loyal client. The saying that the "customer is always right" carries a lot of weight and should be the prominent guiding principle in business. If a customer has complaints, efforts should be made to remediate the issue as quickly as possible. Satisfying a complaint may require a clear explanation of the cause, such as inadequate watering, and options for remediation. Even if the cause of the issue is due to the customer's neglect, it may be necessary to compromise and offer the customer a means of repairing the issue. The compromise may require a reduction in cost for material replacement or labor. Poor customer service reflects badly on any company and disgruntled clients can spread their dissatisfaction just as quickly as posting a good review, **Figure 19-18**.

ponsulak/Shutterstock.com

Figure 19-18. Customer service is extremely important, perhaps now more than ever. Clients have numerous methods to praise or criticize your company that within minutes can be viewed by thousands of potential customers. Workers should be trained and aware that their actions may be recorded and broadcasted.

Career Connection

Al Newsome, good-dirt.com

Al Newsome, Entrepreneur and Art Lover

As a child, Al Newsome spent much of his time with his two grandfathers in North Carolina. One was a farmer and the other an avid gardener. From early on, it was clear gardening was in his DNA. Al began his green industry career doing yardwork for neighbors when he was thirteen. When he was 15, he acquired a contract with a home builder to maintain the lawns of their newly-built, unsold homes. He went to North Carolina State University and majored in horticulture, all the while thinking that one day he would have his own nursery. Al soon discovered he liked the creative aspect of gardening and started his own design-build landscape firm while still a senior in college. The company grew over the next 16 years, especially with the addition of a retail store. The store, named The City Gardener, sold garden accessories and furniture and featured the garden art of many artists.

Al sold his company and currently works with Ball Horticultural Company, introducing new plant varieties to the trade and developing marketing programs and strategies for growers and retailers. Al and his wife Suzy Newsome have formed Good Dirt, a company featuring sustainable garden products. The main mission of Good Dirt is to help gardeners of all levels be successful at gardening.

Consider This

1. How difficult do you think it is to run your own business while you are still in college? Explain your answer.
2. What type of personal skills and habits would you need to be successful in your studies and your business simultaneously?
3. It is common for people working in the green industry to move into different areas. Which areas interest you? How would you plan your career path?

Summary

- Referrals are one of the best ways to generate new clientele and projects.

- Once the target market is determined, the most effective marketing and advertising methods can also be determined.

- The four Ps of marketing, product, price, promotion, and place, are a tool used to help understand what the product or service can offer consumers and how to plan a successful promotion campaign.

- Flyers, commercials, social media, websites, and branding materials are all means of increasing the presence of branding within the community.

- Failing to follow up phone calls and emails promptly will give potential customers a poor impression of your business.

- To make a good impression when you meet the prospective client, dress professionally and be prepared. Potential clients should be greeted with a firm handshake and direct eye contact.

- There is only one chance to make a first impression and whoever meets the client first must ensure the company is well represented.

- An important part of communication is being a good listener.

- Rapport developed between the company spokesperson and the prospective client may influence the client's decision.

- A bid solicitation for a landscape project is a process in which a potential client notifies prospective companies to bid a price for a project.

- It is important to note that not every potential client will be a good match for the landscaping company.

- Taking on a job might compromise other commitments.

- The type of work being performed will determine how a business contract is structured and what information it will include.

- A quote detailing the services to be provided or the components of the project is prepared and presented to the prospective client.

- A business contract is drawn based on the details in the quote.

- Once the bid is awarded, the salesperson should introduce the site manager or client to the person in charge of the site as they will be directing and performing the daily or week-to-week work.

- Company management should periodically check in with client during the job and after the job is complete to ensure they are pleased with the services.

- Work timelines are important because they allow planning and labor scheduling and give clients a reasonable expectation of when a job will be performed or completed.

- The saying that the "customer is always right" carries a lot of weight and should be the prominent guiding principle in business.

Chapter Review

Know and Understand ⤷

Answer the following questions using the information provided in this chapter.

1. A tool used to help understand what a business has to offer and to plan a successful advertising campaign is referred to as _____.
   A. a 4-point media blasting
   B. 4 ways to reach your market
   C. the top 4 advertising methods
   D. the 4 Ps of marketing

2. The communication aspect of marketing is _____.
   A. promotion
   B. prominence
   C. presentation
   D. principle

3. The manner in which marketing materials are presented to the customer is referred to as _____.
   A. presentation
   B. preference
   C. placement
   D. publication

4. *True or False?* The demeanor and attitudes of a company's employees has little effect on a company's reputation.
   A. True.
   B. False.

5. *True or False?* Battered and dirty equipment may negatively influence a client's perception of a company.
   A. True.
   B. False.

6. Why would it be advantageous to refer someone to another business that could better serve their needs?
   A. It is good to share business with others.
   B. It is an effective means of networking.
   C. It makes them aware of other local companies.
   D. It is not advantageous to do so.

7. When preparing to meet a prospective client, it is important to _____.
   A. bring all necessary materials
   B. wear clean, professional clothes
   C. err on the side of caution and overdress
   D. All of the above.

8. You can make a good impression when meeting a prospective client by _____.
   A. arriving promptly
   B. establishing good eye contact
   C. greeting with a firm handshake
   D. All of the above.

9. On many commercial projects, the person who represents the company is referred to as the _____.
   A. crew foreperson
   B. site manager
   C. sales representative
   D. site specialist

10. Bids submitted for government jobs are _____.
    A. public information
    B. closed to the public
    C. subject to submission fees
    D. reviewed by private companies

11. Potential jobs that are logistically demanding or requiring additional capital resources may be bid on the _____.
    A. lower range to increase profit
    B. lower range to reduce risk
    C. higher range to reduce risk
    D. higher range to reduce profit

12. On which of the following reasons might a company decide a job would not be beneficial to accept?
    A. It would compromise other commitments.
    B. It would not help gain entrance into a potential market.
    C. It would require too much capital for materials.
    D. All of the above.

13. When giving a visual presentation for a bid, it is best to _____.
    A. use long lines of text with bullets
    B. stay within the given time limit
    C. read the slide text word for word
    D. All of the above.

14. *True or False?* A business contract is drawn based on the details in the quote and any additional costs that apply.
    A. True.
    B. False.

15. The business contract element that specifies what each part will be providing and an agreement to uphold the terms of the contract is the _____.
    A. terms and conditions
    B. time requirement
    C. promise to perform
    D. intention and form

16. The business contract element that explains what each party will gain from the business arrangement is referred to as _____.
    A. consideration
    B. intention
    C. formation
    D. contraction

17. *True or False?* When there is more than one person involved in decision making, it is essential to determine who will be the primary contact for future communication to prevent issues due to miscommunication.
    A. True.
    B. False.

18. *True or False?* The foreperson is responsible for communicating with the client and ensuring all work is performed to their satisfaction.
    A. True.
    B. False.

19. *True or False?* The account manager is at the job site daily to manage the working crew.
    A. True
    B. False

20. *True or False?* Clients who are content with your company's landscape work are more likely to recommend your company to other people.
    A. True.
    B. False.

21. A detailed work timeline for a maintenance contract specifies tasks are to be performed _____.
    A. over periods of time
    B. on specific dates
    C. before the hottest part of the day
    D. at specific hours of the day

22. *True or False?* A landscape company should not compromise a solution to a customer's complaint if the issue is due to the customer's neglect.
    A. True.
    B. False.

Thinking Critically

1. You have a small lawn service business and had to raise prices due to higher expenses. A long-term client refuses to pay the cost increase on his lawn service. How would you handle this issue?

2. How would regular maintenance needs change if a client were holding garden parties once a month?

3. How would you react to a prospective client with a lucrative project who was extremely rude when you met her on the potential site?

Suggested Activities

1. In groups of 3 to 4, identify companies known for their customer service. List the practices that help them stand out from other companies in their industry. Make a short list of personal experiences with poor customer service. Use your results in a class discussion comparing good customer service practices with poor practices.

2. Working in pairs, measure a property and write a quote for an annual landscape maintenance contract. Base your costs on prices local landscape companies charge for similar work. Would the prices be different if a sole proprietorship company operating from his or her garage was performing the work?

3. Choose a landscaped site on school grounds and develop a work timeline for a landscape company installing the same design. Be sure to include all areas of landscape installation or maintenance.

4. Work with partners to practice meeting clients for the first time. Create a fictional installation and/or maintenance project. Write a list of questions the client might ask and one that a landscape professional would ask the client about the job. Include a scenario in which the client is being rude or difficult. Act out the meeting. Practice good habits for creating a good first impression.

5. Working with a small group or partner, practice responding to the needs of a customer or client. Choose a type of landscaping business and use different scenarios, such as care advice, equipment, treatments, clinical diagnoses, or dealing with an unsatisfied customer. Take turns being the customer and employee.

CHAPTER

20

Landscape Installation

While studying this chapter, look for the activity icon  **to:**

- **Practice** vocabulary terms with Words to Know activities.
- **Expand** learning with identification activities.
- **Reinforce** what you learn by completing Know and Understand questions.

G-WLEARNING.com

www.g-wlearning.com/agriculture

Chapter Outcomes

After studying this chapter, you will be able to:

- Identify the components of a final landscape plan.
- Explain how on-center spacing is used when installing plants.
- Calculate the number of plants needed for a given area.
- Calculate the volume of landscape materials, such as mulch, needed to cover a given area.
- Define and explain the importance of slope.
- Explain the order in which plant materials are installed.
- Properly install and stake trees and shrubs.
- Identify and apply the steps used to install plants other than trees and shrubs.
- Identify plants in need of water and irrigate them correctly.
- Calculate the time a given landscape task will take to complete.

Key Terms 🔗

berm
field capacity
girdling
guying
landscape fabric
on-center (OC) spacing

planting depth
rootbound
staking
sunscald
tree wrap

Introduction

Installing a design is one of the most exciting and labor intensive parts of a landscaping project. The installer works from the final plans to make the landscape design a reality. The final plans include everything from how the site should be graded to how the plants should be watered. The installer schedules crew members, equipment delivery, hardscape installation, and plant delivery and installation to complete the project on time. This chapter provides instruction for calculating materials, fertilizing, planting, and caring for a new installation.

Reading the Final Plan

The final plan or design is the drawing used as a guide for the landscape installation. Aside from the design drawing, the final plan includes a title block, legend, planting diagram, notes, and a directional or north arrow. See **Figure 20-1**.

- The *title block* provides project-specific information, such as the client's name, property name and address, the designer's name, the date, and the scale of the drawing. The *scale* is the size of the object in the drawing in direct proportion to the actual object. A 1:8 scale, for example, indicates 1" on the drawing represents 8' in the landscape.
- The *legend* explains what each symbol represents and includes a list of plants, their names, the number of each plant needed, and their sizes at installation. It may also describe textures and types of hardscape materials.
- A *planting diagram* shows the shape, color, location, size, and quantities of the specific plants that will be used and provides detailed planting instructions for select trees and shrubs used in the design. It also includes information, such as spacing requirements, planting depth, mulching depth, berm construction, and staking methods.
- Other information on final drawings includes hardscape materials and paving patterns, designer notes, and additional site specifics. These notes can be used by the materials procurer when purchasing materials and arranging deliveries.
- The *directional* or *north arrow* is included to ensure proper orientation of the plan and its installation.

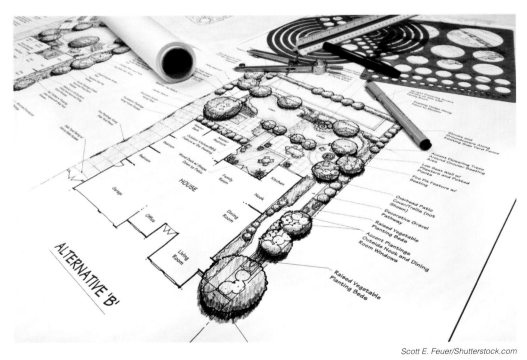

Scott E. Feuer/Shutterstock.com

Figure 20-1. The landscape design contains all the information needed to properly install and even bid the landscape installation. Plant and hardscape materials are clearly labeled to ensure the design is completed as intended.

Reviewing the Calculations

The installer must review the plan thoroughly and note any discrepancies before any work is performed. He or she may want to recalculate materials, such as the amount of topsoil and mulch that will be needed, and review the planting area sizes and the quantities of plants indicated for each area. The installer should also walk the site and look for problem areas that may have been overlooked or underestimated, **Figure 20-2**. A thorough review of the plan and site will help ensure all issues can be addressed before the project installation begins.

Figure 20-2. The installer should walk through the site prior to installation to ensure that problem areas are addressed and sufficient materials are ordered. Failing to preview the site prior to installation may lead to delays.

Site Takeoffs

A *site takeoff* is a tabulation of all the landscape components and the costs associated with each component. The costs include the labor, materials, equipment, and any other costs incurred by the project, **Figure 20-3**. The installer may review the site takeoff and the itemized bid to ensure every component of the job has been calculated accurately. This is advisable when somebody else has performed the initial measuring and material calculations or if the installer has not visited the site. It is also advisable to ensure that the number of plants on the plan matches the number specified in the legend and to compare these numbers to the plants delivered for installation. The plan is also used to determine the number of work hours needed to install the landscape and to schedule work crews accordingly.

Figure 20-3. The measurements and information gathered with a takeoff are useful when pricing and bidding landscape work. Sites with large open areas have fewer individual plants to install and most of the job would be installing the turfgrass. Sites with curves and large amounts of plant material are more labor intensive and require more time for installation.

Plant Spacing

The number of plants needed for an area is calculated by the amount of space each plant needs, **Figure 20-4**. The ideal range of space that should be left between plants depends on each plant species. *Hemerocallis* 'Buttered Popcorn', for example, should be spaced 18" to 24" from the next plant. The distance between plants is measured from the center of each plant. This is referred to as *on-center (OC) spacing*. OC is typically used only with groundcovers and smaller herbaceous plants. Using the minimum distance between plants will allow the plants to fill in the area more quickly. Placing the plants too far apart may lead to empty space between them, even when the plants reach maturity. Weeds will quickly take root in the open space between plants.

Christopher D. Hart

Figure 20-4. Placing plants, such as begonias, at equidistant spacing will ensure complete and uniform coverage. Proper spacing is also beneficial because it ensures that plants will not crowd each other.

Calculating Plant Materials

The area of the bed and the spacing specified on the final drawing is used to calculate the number of plants that will be needed to fill an area. Plants that are to be spaced 18" OC, for example, will each require an area that measures 18" × 18", **Figure 20-5**. Use the following steps to calculate how many plants will fill the area.

Problem: The bed measures 15' × 5' and the plants are to be placed 18" OC.

1. Calculate the area (square footage) of the bed.

$$15' \times 5' = 75 \text{ ft}^2$$

2. Determine how much area each plant requires.

$$18" \times 18" = 324 \text{ in}^2$$

3. Convert the in² to ft² by dividing the in² by 144 (144 in² = 1 ft²).

$$324 \text{ in}^2 \div 144 = 2.25 \text{ ft}^2 \text{ per plant}$$

4. Divide the area to be landscaped by the space needed per plant.

$$75 \div 2.25 = 33.33$$
$$34 \text{ plants required}$$

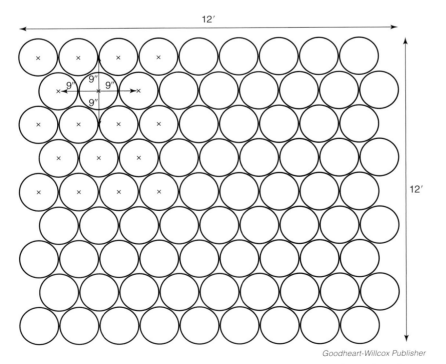

Goodheart-Willcox Publisher

Figure 20-5. Sixty-four plants spaced 18" OC will fill a 12' × 12' bed.

Calculating Volume

Landscape materials, such as mulch, sand, gravel, and concrete, are purchased in volume by the cubic yard. Volume is calculated with the formula *length × width × height* (l × w × h = v) or *area × height* (a × h = v). The height is the depth of materials. Use the following steps to calculate the volume of gravel needed for the patio base.

Problem: How many cubic yards of gravel are needed to install 6″ deep on a 10′ × 10′ patio.

1. Calculate the area of the patio.

$$10' \times 10' = 100 \text{ ft}^2$$

2. Convert 6″ to feet. (12″ = 1′)

$$6 \div 12 = 0.5'$$

3. Calculate the volume of the area.

$$100 \text{ ft}^2 \times 0.5' = 50 \text{ ft}^3$$

4. Divide ft³ by 27 to calculate cubic yards. (There are 27 cubic feet in one cubic yard.)

$$50 \text{ ft}^3 \div 27 = 1.85 \text{ yd}^3$$

$$1.85 \text{ yd}^3 \text{ of gravel is needed}$$

Each cube is 1ft³

1 yd³

3′

3′

3′

Safety First

Always call 811 to have buried telephone, gas, electrical, and water lines marked before beginning any excavation work.

The Installation Process

After the major site preparation is completed, the site is graded. The *grade* or *slope* is the rise and fall of the land surface in relation to the horizontal distance covered, **Figure 20-6**. A slope of 15%, for example, indicates that a site will rise or fall 15′ vertically over a 100′ span. Slope controls the direction and speed of runoff in the landscape. Water should drain away from structures, such as buildings, and should flow to a safe area in the landscape. The slope used around structures varies by site, but a slope of at least 1% is needed to move water. The slope must be steep enough to move water but flat enough to maintain the functionality of the landscape.

Artazum/Shutterstock.com

Figure 20-6. Slope is extremely important to water drainage and must be taken into account when installing hardscape and plant materials. Water must drain away from structures. The slope must also be managed so that maximum use of the site is achieved.

Grading

The steps taken to create slope will vary based on whether it is new construction or a renovation. In new construction, the site is graded to accommodate the new structure and hardscapes as well as the landscape. This requires the use of large machinery, such as loaders or bulldozers, to move materials and smooth the surface, **Figure 20-7**. The site may also require the delivery and addition of new topsoil.

A renovation project may entail some grading, depending on the extent of the project and if there are any problems, such as drainage issues. Hand tools such as shovels and rakes are often enough to correct small issues with grading. Surveying levels can be used to ensure adequate slope is created. Refer to Chapter 15, *Hardscapes*, for more detailed instruction on establishing slope.

Cathy Kovarik/Shutterstock.com

Figure 20-7. Heavy equipment may be required if large adjustments need to be made in slope.

Drainage

Oftentimes, small drainage issues will not be realized until after the landscape is installed. The drainage capabilities of the site will be tested after heavy rainfall or prolonged irrigation. Standing water, wet spots in the lawn, or flooded structures are clear indications of a drainage problem, **Figure 20-8**. It may be necessary to install drainage to channel the water effectively. Oftentimes, a discreet, shallow ditch cut into the lawn will solve the issue.

A   *Goodheart-Willcox Publisher*

B   *Annette Shaff/Shutterstock.com*

C   *Kamol Jindamanee/Shutterstock.com*

Figure 20-8. A—A low area in this concrete walkway has collected runoff from a quick afternoon thunderstorm. B—If the wet area persists, drainage may need to be installed to alleviate the issue. Low areas in lawns hold moisture and can present difficulty when mowing. C—A drain may be installed along the problem area in the lawn to prevent standing water.

Plant Delivery and Installation

Plant installation is often the most time-consuming part of a project. Locating plant species specified in the design is time consuming as well. Plant materials will likely be ordered from multiple suppliers to obtain the correct species in the sizes specified. It can be challenging to plan the pickup or delivery of plants when they are supplied by multiple sources. If the landscaping company has adequate storage space, they may have large orders for multiple sites delivered and stored in a staging area before taking them to the individual sites. A plant broker may also be hired to locate and arrange deliveries to the jobsite.

Staging Area

A staging area where plants can be sorted and kept safely should be available when the plants arrive, **Figure 20-9**. The list of plants on the design or planting diagram can be used to ensure everything needed has been delivered. The plants should also be inspected for damage and overall condition before the delivery is accepted. Plants must be watered and protected with mulch if they will not be installed on the day of delivery. A plant should be fully turgid (full of water) before planting to reduce stress and enable the plant to adapt to its new environment more easily.

Soil Amendments

The success of newly installed plant materials is dependent on the physical and chemical composition of the soil. Soil amendments are added to the planting areas while they are being prepared for installation. In plant beds, for example, amendments are worked into the top 8″ to 12″ of soil, **Figure 20-10**. Adding the proper amendment can improve soil qualities, such as increasing the availability of air in clay soils and water-holding capacity of sandy soils. Amendments such as aged pine bark, organic compost, and leaf mold are commonly used. These materials should be incorporated at a rate of 20% to 30% by volume and cultivated into the root zone.

thatcha698/Shutterstock.com

Figure 20-9. Prior to installation, plants are often grouped together. Grouping plants together allows one to take inventory and to ensure that the correct plant materials arrive on the jobsite.

Chatree.l/Shutterstock.com

Figure 20-10. Organic matter may be added to the planting bed before installing new plants. Organic matter provides nutrients as well as increases the moisture-holding ability of the soil.

- **Compost.** Organic materials, such as animal manures and kitchen and yard waste, can be used to improve soil qualities. The pH and nutrient content must be stable before the compost is used in garden beds because compost that is too rich to support plants may burn up the leaves and root system.
- **Leaf mold.** This organic material can be acquired at many municipal yard waste facilities. Leaf mold must be tested for pH and heavy metals.
- **Tree bark.** Mulches are different from amendments in that they are placed on top and only amend over a long period, whereas amendments alter the soil in short order.

Materials to Avoid

Materials to avoid include peat moss, sand, uncomposted hardwood bark and fresh wood chips, and sawdust.

- **Peat moss.** It is expensive and often must be shipped long distances.
- **Sand.** When mixed with clay and water, it becomes as hard as brick.
- **Uncomposted hardwood bark** and **fresh wood chips.** These draw nutrients from plant roots as the microorganisms use the nutrients as an energy source for breaking down the material.
- **Sawdust.** It also draws nutrients from the plant because it requires decomposition by microorganisms.
- **Wood ashes.** These are often high in pH and micronutrients.

When planting individual trees or large shrubs, soil amendments are incorporated directly into the planting hole. The planting diagram will specify how the amendments are to be incorporated.

Fertilizers high in nitrogen should be avoided at planting because most nursery plants are grown with slow-release fertilizers that remain in the soil included when the plant is harvested. The slow-release fertilizers last for several months and will continue to provide nutrients that help the roots become established. Using an unsuitable amendment when planting will lead to more maintenance tasks because stressed plants are more susceptible to pests and disease.

Order of Installation

The crew leader will have a plan prepared for the order of plant installation to ensure everything is planted per design specifications. Some plants are installed before others because their installation would otherwise damage materials in the surrounding area. A very large tree, for example, would be delivered and installed with a tree spade, skid steer loader, or tractor. Preparing the hole for such a tree and the large machinery used will disturb the surrounding soil and any plant materials that have been installed.

After the large material has been installed, the remaining plants should be set on the ground in their locations. Setting the plants in place before installation will ensure proper spacing. It will also be easy to take inventory and determine if everything has been delivered. It is also a good practice to plant materials after the hardscape is completed to prevent damage to the plants, **Figure 20-11**.

Jo Ann Snover/Shutterstock.com

Figure 20-11. Plant material should be installed after the hardscape to prevent damage to the plants and to ensure the plants are in the correct locations. If plants are installed first, they may be planted in the path of the hardscape.

Shrubs and smaller trees are typically installed first for the same reasons as large trees. Many of the perennials and bedding plants are placed at the foot or in front of shrubs and trees and would be in the way if they were planted first. If the planting area were backed by a border, such as a fence or hedge, workers would begin at the border and work their way forward. If the planting area is exposed on all sides, workers may begin in the center and work outward or from one side to the other, **Figure 20-12**. If multiple crews are scheduled, the first crew may install the trees or shrubs that form the border or backdrop and the second crew would follow them and install the smaller trees and shrubs. A third crew may be responsible for installing the herbaceous perennials and annuals. Turf is typically installed after all other plant materials are installed to minimize traffic on sod or seeded areas.

Alexander Zamaraev/Shutterstock.com

Figure 20-12. When installing a circular flower bed, it is often best to begin planting in the center of the bed and work toward the outside of the circle. If there is a different plant in the center of the circle, it should be planted first.

R. Lee Ivy

Figure 20-13. In addition to protecting the trunk and branches of a tree, care should be taken to protect the root system by minimizing the amount of foot traffic and heavy equipment going over the area surrounding the tree.

Protecting Existing Plants

Plants that will remain on-site, such as mature trees, must be protected from excavation and installation activities, **Figure 20-13**. The roots of a tree may extend a distance up to three times the canopy, which makes them susceptible to damage and growth disruption during landscape installation. Foot traffic and the movement of heavy equipment across a landscape site can compact the soil above the roots, causing adverse effects on the roots to obtain water, nutrients, and air. Digging may also disturb or damage root systems. Strategically locating delivery pathways and staging areas for materials can help prevent or alleviate growth problems for existing plants, **Figure 20-14**.

Pro Tip
The first year of installation is the most important for each plant. The second year is as important for the large trees.

Christopher D. Hart

Figure 20-14. Plywood placed on the ground helps spread the weight evenly across the surface area of the planting bed and lawn area. The roots of trees in the surrounding area, such as this large oak, are protected and soil compaction is minimized.

Planting Trees and Shrubs

The single most important factor when planting trees and shrubs is how deep they are planted, which is referred to as the *planting depth*. If they are planted too deep, the roots may drown and suffocate. If the hole is too shallow, the plant may fall over easily or dry out quickly due to insufficient moisture availability. The references used to determine planting depth are the top of the root ball for balled-and-burlapped plants and the top of the soil line for container plants, **Figure 20-15**.

The proper dimensions for a planting hole is 1.5 to 2 times wider than the width and the same depth as the root ball. A wide planting hole helps to amend the soil adjacent to the root ball and provides room for adjusting and ensuring the plant is straight. Balled-and-burlapped and container trees and shrubs should be planted in a hole with a flat bottom. The hole for bare root trees planted directly in the landscape should have a mounded bottom to prevent crowding of the roots. It is important that the base of the plant be located on solid soil and not loose backfill to prevent the soil from settling. Loose backfill may be used to fill the space around the roots.

Planting time is also a good time to prune and remove dead or damaged tissue. Thin-barked trees that are planted in the fall may require tree wrap to prevent sunscald. *Sunscald* is an injury that occurs in the winter on young, thin-barked trees when they are exposed to bright sun and cold temperatures. The damage may appear as though the bark has split open, sunk in, or died. *Tree wrap* is a light-colored material made specifically for wrapping around young tree trunks to reflect the sun and keep the bark at a more consistent temperature, **Figure 20-16**. Tree wrap also protects the new trees from wildlife rubs and damage from string trimmers and lawn mowers. Apply the wrap from the soil line to the second or third branch. Overlapping the edges will allow the wrap to shed water. Plastic guards or other materials may also be used.

A   B   *ckeyes888/Shutterstock.com*

Figure 20-15. A—The soil surface of container plants is not constricted with any type of material and the roots are covered with ample soil. The surface should be even with the ground surface when planted. B—As there is typically a minimal amount of soil below the burlap wrapping, the top of the root ball is used to determine where the tree should be level with the ground surface.

A   *Goodheart-Willcox Publisher*   B   *Photo courtesy of A.M. Leonard Inc.*

Figure 20-16. A—Sunscald is caused when the sun shines on the stem of a plant while the roots are frozen and unable to supply the plant with sufficient moisture. B—Breathable fabric designed for wrapping young trees provides sun protection.

Matthew Corley/Shutterstock.com

Figure 20-17. Container plants should *never* be carried by the stem. They should only be carried by supporting the bottom or holding on to the sides of the container. These plants should also be left in the container until the ground is ready for installation.

Christopher D. Hart

Figure 20-18. Roots on this asparagus fern need to be broken apart before the plant is installed. This can usually be done gently by hand.

Moving and Placing Plants

Trees and shrubs should not be carried by the stem alone because it can cause damage to the plant. Smaller plants can be carried by supporting the base by hand, with a wheelbarrow, or hand truck dolly. Plants are removed by tilting the container and slowly easing the soil out into the installer's hand. It is easier to remove the plant if the soil is damp. Larger plants are often moved and placed in the hole with mechanical equipment. See **Figure 20-17**.

> **Pro Tip**
>
> Containers must be washed thoroughly with a disinfectant before being reused to ensure there are no pathogens or contaminants that could be introduced to a new plant.

Container Plants

Containers should be removed from the base of the plant and saved for reuse or recycling. If the plant is rootbound, the roots may need to be cut and straightened before being covered with soil. The roots of a plant that is *rootbound* have outgrown the pot and are circling the inside perimeter of the container, **Figure 20-18**. A variety of tools or methods can be used to cut the root ball or break it apart. The root ball of smaller herbaceous perennial plants or annual plants can usually be divided by hand. Larger plants, such as trees and shrubs, may require the use of a shovel or a large knife to split the root ball. Take care to prevent damaging the plant. PPE, such as eye and hand protection, should be worn when cutting a root ball.

Balled-and-Burlapped Plants

The nylon strings at the top of the root ball should be cut and removed when planting balled-and-burlapped trees and shrubs. The burlap is unpinned and folded as far back as possible within the planting hole. The wire basket may also be folded back. Trying to remove the burlap and the wire basket completely will likely cause damage to the root system, whereas leaving it in place will do no harm. Some nurseries use treated burlap that will not decompose as quickly as untreated burlap. Ask the supplier if the burlap on their trees is treated. You may cut off as much of the treated burlap as possible to prevent plant issues in the future. The basket and burlap will eventually break down in the soil. Leaving the wire basket in place also helps create a solid root ball, which may reduce the need for staking. See **Figure 20-19**.

Backfill

After the tree is positioned straight at the proper height, backfill is added to fill in the space around the root ball, **Figure 20-20**. Soil amendments, such as bark, fertilizer, or other organic materials, may be added to the planting hole to improve soil structure. The backfill should lightly be tapped to eliminate unnecessary air pockets in the soil.

Constructing a Berm

Once the tree is planted, a berm is installed. A *berm* is an earthen mound 4″ to 6″ tall installed around the drip zone of the tree. The berm is constructed with the soil removed from the planting hole. After the berm is created, the plant should be mulched with 3″ to 4″ of desired materials. The berm provides an area around the plant in which water can collect to ensure that it receives sufficient moisture as well as provide nutrients directly to the tree. It also makes it easier for mowing around the plant.

Adding Mulch

After mulching, the plant should be watered to help settle the soil, **Figure 20-21**. It is important to water newly installed plant materials deeply to reduce stress and help them become established. Apply water until it reaches field capacity. *Field capacity* is achieved when the capillary pores of the soil profile are full of water. Newly planted trees and shrubs need an average of 1.5″ of water per week to become established. If rainfall is insufficient, irrigation must be provided.

Zigzag Mountain Art/Shutterstock.com

Figure 20-19. Digging the hole 1.5 to 2 times the width of the root ball allows for enough adjustment to move the tree until it is straight and plumb. It also allows for soil amendments to be added.

photowind/Shutterstock.com

Figure 20-20. Backfill is used to fill in the area around the root ball and to create berms around large trees and shrubs. Placing backfill on a tarp conserves the soil for reuse and simplifies cleaning of the surrounding area.

Thom Friend/Shutterstock.com

Ozgur Coskun/Shutterstock.com

Figure 20-21. On average, one person can apply 1.5 cubic yards of mulch per hour, depending on the distance that must be traveled to apply and spread the mulch.

Geography may also affect the type of mulch used. Pine straw, for example, is commonly used in the southeastern United States because pine trees are plentiful in that area and the pine straw is economical and readily available. Depending on the species and size of the bale, one bale will cover 40 ft² and 3″ deep or 50 ft² and 2″ deep. The bark from the pine trees is a by-product of the lumber industry that is used as mulch.

- **Hardwood bark.** In other parts of the country, hardwood bark, such as oak, maple, and hickory, is readily available. These materials should be aged for 3 to 6 months before application. This will ensure the proper carbon to nitrogen ratio and lessen the amount of weed seeds that transfer to landscape settings.
- **Inorganic products.** Inorganic products, such as gravel and rock, are commonly used for specific designs and can be purchased and transported to all areas of the country. These materials require a barrier on the soil so they do not settle over time.

If other materials are chosen, they should be tested for stable nutrients and may be varied in their texture. One product that many people appreciate are colorized ground pellets. Common colors are black, brown, and red. As with the choice of any other material, a designer would choose so that the viewer focuses on the plant material and not on large amounts of mulch. In the example of red mulch, it has its usefulness but often detracts from the aesthetic value of the plant materials.

Pro Tip

Not only is mulch visually appealing, it is also practical. Proper application of mulch helps prevent weeds, holds moisture in the soil, and minimizes soil erosion.

Staking Trees

Staking trees is the use of stakes or posts and wire, rubber, rope, tree tie webbing, or nylon cords to provide the trees support, anchorage, and protection from winds, **Figure 20-22**. Trees are typically top heavy and the root system of a

Ingrid Maasik/Shutterstock.com

LuckyViewfinder/Shutterstock.com

Chanawee Champakerdthapya/ Shutterstock.com

Andrii Zhezhera/Shutterstock.com

Figure 20-22. Landscape professionals and gardeners may use manufactured devices or a variety of other materials to support young and vulnerable trees.

newly planted tree is not developed enough to anchor and support the top part of the tree. Staking helps keep the plant stable while the root system is developing. Staking a tree is expensive and often visually unappealing, and studies indicate that trees are physiologically better not being staked. It is recommended that the support system should only be used when absolutely necessary. When trees are not staked, they develop larger root systems and are less likely to have girdled or damaged trunks. *Girdling* is a condition that occurs when the growth of the trunk is restricted, **Figure 20-23**. Failing to remove staking in a timely manner will likely hinder the growth of the trunk. However, certain trees in certain situations require the support. The method of staking that should be used for each tree is specified with the planting instructions.

Samuel Acosta/Shutterstock.com

Figure 20-23. Girdling occurs when staking material is left too long on a tree. The bark of the tree begins to grow around the support structure.

Using Stakes

Short stakes or taller poles or posts may be used to stake a tree. The short stakes are driven into the ground (preferably within the edge of the berm) angled away from the tree and the nylon rope or cording is attached to the stakes and the tree trunk. (Notches on the stakes hold the rope/wire in place.) The height at which the cording is attached to the tree can be determined by running your hand along the trunk to the point where it feels unsteady. The cording should be attached to the tree as low as possible while still providing support for the tree. See **Figure 20-24A**.

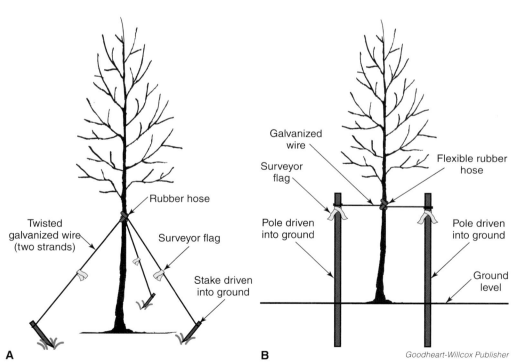

Goodheart-Willcox Publisher

Figure 20-24. Whether stakes or posts are used depends on location and aesthetic preference. Short stakes and wires (A) are less visible than posts (B) but may present more of a tripping hazard, especially to children running through the yard. Poles or posts installed parallel to the tree are also easier to anchor into the soil than short spikes driven at angles.

Christopher D. Hart

Figure 20-25. Guying is used on larger trees, such as this sabal palm in Florida. Guy wires attach to hooks or eyelets that are anchored deep in the ground.

Using three stakes offers more protection than using only two stakes. One of the stakes should be installed on the side of the prevailing winds. The other two stakes should be evenly spaced from the initial stake to provide even support around the tree. The top of the stakes should be high enough that they are easily seen and are not a tripping hazard.

Using Posts or Poles

Poles or posts are also driven into the ground within the edge of the berm so that they are parallel to the tree, **Figure 20-24B**. Wire is then attached to both the tree and the posts. Wire is commonly used, as it is easy to tighten. The wire around the tree is covered with a durable, rubber hose to prevent the wire from rubbing or digging into the tree. As with the stakes, one post should be placed on the side of prevailing winds and the other two or three should be evenly spaced from the first post.

Guying

Guying is a form of staking used to steady large trees. Guying uses anchoring devices that are driven deep into the ground with only a few inches left above the soil surface, **Figure 20-25**. The location and spacing of the devices follow the same placement as stakes or posts.

Removing Stakes

Staking should be removed once the tree is established. A rule used by installers is that staking is required for one year per inch of caliper. The stakes for a 1″ caliper tree, for example, can be removed in 12 months.

Planting Bedding Plants

The methods used for planting bedding plants are much simpler than those used for planting trees and shrubs. As the name suggests, bedding plants are planted in a prepared bed of amended, loose, high quality soil. Planting in a prepared bed is much easier than planting trees and shrubs, as the soil is loose and the holes needed are much shallower, **Figure 20-26**. Some planting beds are covered with landscape fabric before planting. *Landscape fabric* is a tight woven textile laid on top of the soil and covered with mulch to prevent the growth of weeds.

Spacing

Bedding plants are planted in rows with a uniform distance between plants. The rows are staggered to ensure full coverage and create interesting lines of plants when viewed from different directions. The created lines are visually appealing and create striking planting beds. The manner or order in which bedding plants are installed is personal preference.

Ivan Smuk/Shutterstock.com

Figure 20-26. Beds must be prepared before planting to ensure the best results. Compost or other materials can be worked into the soil easily and the improved soil structure allows for ease of planting.

Planting

When installing bedding plants, it is important to ensure that the plant to be installed is not rootbound. Because bedding plants are typically much smaller than trees and shrubs, the root ball can easily be broken by using your hand or a soil knife. The plant should be installed so that the root ball of the plant is level with that of the soil.

Establishing Ground Covers

Ground covers are available in woody and herbaceous form. Herbaceous ground covers, such as liriope, mondo grass, and pachysandra, may be planted and installed in the same manner as bedding plants. Woody ground covers, such as junipers, are commonly sold in larger containers and are installed in the same manner as shrubs. See **Figure 20-27**.

Spacing

The two most important factors for installing ground covers are plant spacing and depth. Ground covers must be spaced so the area fills in evenly. Spacing plants closer together will ensure the area fills in quickly; however, it will be more costly because more plants will be required. The plant should be installed with its soil level at the soil level in which it is installed. Diligence in pulling or treating weeds is important to prevent weeds from taking root in the space between the young plants.

A   *Summer_Kang/Shutterstock.com*

B   *divgradcurl/Shutterstock.com*   **C**   *photowind/Shutterstock.com*

Figure 20-27. Ground covers are excellent choices to add beauty and prevent erosion. Once established, they require much less maintenance than a lawn. A—Liriope. B— Pachysandra. C—Juniper.

Career Connection

BJ Fisher

BJ Fisher, President, Southern Showplace Landscapes, Inc.

BJ Fisher is the operations manager and president of Southern Showplace Landscapes Inc., located in Concord, NC. Southern Showplace has both residential (70%) and commercial clients (30%). Southern Showplace installs Suntrust and Bank of America commercial landscapes from Memphis, TN to Orlando, FL.

BJ loves the landscape industry because every project, homeowner, and customer is different and presents unique challenges. As president, BJ ensures that the landscape on each project is installed in a proper horticultural manner and that the customer is satisfied with the project from start to finish.

BJ advises young landscape professionals to find a landscape career that they love. There are plenty of opportunities that are currently wide open in the green industry. He also says that his education at the community college and university levels was vital and helped fast-track him to where he is today. BJ received an associate degree in landscape gardening from the local community college and a bachelor degree at North Carolina State University in horticultural science.

Consider This

1. Which area would you find more interesting, residential or commercial landscaping design? Explain your answer.
2. How does BJ's involvement throughout the design and installation process contribute to his success?
3. Visit the Southern Showplace Landscapes website and review its social media presence. How effective is the company's online presence? Explain your answer.

Planting Vines

Vines are woody-stemmed plants with climbing or trailing growth habits. Vines typically have a much greater spread than ground covers. Vines use tendrils, twiners, scramblers, adhesive pads, and climbing stem roots to climb. Vines can provide vertical interest and soften vertical edges. Vines may be used to create a living, colored wall or a ceiling for an outdoor room. Large trees may also provide support that vines need. As with many other plants, a vine's seasonal floral display can be the most exciting display during the year, **Figure 20-28**.

Support Structures

Selecting the appropriate growing structure for vines is very important because they can spread quickly into undesirable areas, have difficulty grasping the structure, or become too heavy for the structure. Woody vines, for example, often have a fast growth habit and will become very heavy over time, requiring a strong structure. There are also vines that may spread across the ground and others that do not climb on their own and must be attached to a structure. Trellises, arbors, gazebos, poles, walls, fences, and lattice are common structures used to provide support to vines. They must also have an appropriate support structure to reach their maximum performance.

Christopher D. Hart   *visionteller/Shutterstock.com*   *JeniFoto/Shutterstock.com*

Figure 20-28. Vines require a support structure to provide optimal conditions for the plant's success. Vines may be trained to create interesting shapes, such as an arch above a garden gate. When in full bloom, vines can provide a vibrant and colorful display.

> **Pro Tip**
>
> Zip or bread ties can be used to attach vines to the growing structure to help guide the vine in the desired direction.

Watering

Watering newly installed plants is extremely important to their establishment, **Figure 20-29**. The new landscape plants need an average of 1.5″ of water per week. If this does not occur naturally through precipitation, it must be supplied through irrigation. As water needs differ between plant species and water-holding capacity varies with soil types, each plant should be used as a guide to determine when water is needed. Most plants should be watered just before they begin to wilt.

Timing

The amount of time allowed between watering should also be monitored. Allowing the soil to dry somewhat between watering will encourage root growth, as the roots will seek moisture. If the soil is not allowed to dry, the roots will not develop and may rot. It is better to water longer and less frequently than it is to water for less time more frequently. Watering for longer periods will allow the water to leach completely through the root zone of the soil profile.

elina/Shutterstock.com

Figure 20-29. Thoroughly watering plants after installation helps settle the soil and provide the roots with moisture.

Methods of Application

If the new landscape has an irrigation system, the controller can be adjusted to ensure the new plants are watered sufficiently. Any new plants installed out of the irrigated areas must be watered with a hose, aboveground sprinkler, or other means. Water bags are used on trees and large shrubs, especially when the plants are located in an area that is difficult to irrigate. The bags are filled with water and slowly release water to the plant. Water trucks equipped with a tank, pump, and hose are useful in public parks with limited water sources and in urban areas for watering planters, hanging baskets, curbside trees, and flower beds, **Figure 20-30**.

The contract established between the client and the landscape company should explain who is responsible for watering the plant material once it is installed. As an incentive, many landscape companies will provide the clients with a warranty on plant material if they are selected to maintain the site.

Clean Up

Cleaning up each workday and at the completion of the job reflects positively on you and your company. At the end of each workday, materials not yet installed should be left as neat as possible and out of the way. Leaf blowers and push brooms are very helpful tools during the cleanup process. Creating and using a checklist at the end of a project is useful to ensure the site is clean and presentable.

- All trees, weeds, and soil cleared from the initial site must be disposed of properly.
- Empty plastic containers should be sorted, stacked, and removed for recycling or reuse.
- Plant labels or tags attached to installed plant material must be removed.
- Soil and other debris should be swept and/or washed from all surfaces, including sidewalks and parking lots.

> **Pro Tip**
>
> Check local landfill guidelines prior to hauling off debris. Many landfills will take yard debris but will not take soil or fill dirt. The yard debris is shredded and later sold as mulch.

A   *Misterfullframe/Shutterstock.com*

B   *Mikhail Olykainen/Shutterstock.com*

Figure 20-30. A—Water trucks are used to provide water to areas that do not have automatic irrigation. Newly installed trees and shrubs, as well as annuals and bedding plants, often require more water than mature plants. B— Perforated water bags are placed at the base of trees. The bags are filled with water, which slowly drips into the soil, ensuring newly installed trees and shrubs receive sufficient moisture.

Scheduling Installation or Task Completion Times

As discussed in Chapter 18, *Pricing Landscape Projects*, the cost for each landscaping task is determined by area (square footage) and the time (hourly rates) typically needed to complete the task. It is difficult to ensure a profit if the time taken to perform each task is unknown. The person performing the takeoff would determine the square footage of the area to be covered and determine how much time and how many workers it will take to complete the task.

Landscape associations have calculated the time it takes to perform basic installation tasks in an attempt to establish standard production rates, **Figure 20-31**. It is important to note that these production rates are estimates of the time required to perform a given task. Experienced landscape contractors will be able to generate more accurate information based on location, time of year, the plant material being installed, the quantity being installed, and each crew's abilities. Having an estimation of the amount of time it takes to complete a job also enables the contractor to schedule and plan other projects.

Pro Tip

Task completion times will be more accurate if the business owner uses the average time it takes his or her employees to complete the tasks.

Container Shrubs	Plants Installed per Hour
1 gallon	17
3 gallon	10
5 gallon	6
15 gallon	1.5

Container Trees	Hours to Install Each Tree
15 gallon	0.75
30 gallon	2
45 gallon	2.25
65 gallon	3

Balled-and-Burlapped Trees	Hours to Install Each Tree
6′ to 8′ tall	1.5
1″ caliper	1.25
2″ caliper	1.75
3″ caliper	4.5

Goodheart-Willcox Publisher

Figure 20-31. Labor rate charts are useful when bidding and scheduling landscape jobs. The charts provide an estimate of the amount of time it takes to perform common landscape tasks.

STEM Connection

Calculating Task Times

Establishing task times is an important component of calculating the cost of a landscape project. Having accurate times enables efficient scheduling of crews, equipment, and material deliveries. It also enables the company to maintain its profit margin on each project. Review the following calculation of task times using the information in **Figure 20-31**.

- 34 1-gallon shrubs
- 20 3-gallon shrubs
- 4 15-gallon trees
- 4 yd³ of mulch

Calculate the time per task and the total time needed to complete the job.
- If 17 1-gallon shrubs are installed per hour, 34 1-gallon shrubs would require 2 hours.
- If 10 3-gallon shrubs are installed per hour, 20 3-gallon shrubs would require 2 hours.
- If 1 15-gallon tree requires 0.75 hours, 4 15-gallon trees would require 3 hours.
- If spreading 1.5 yd³ of mulch requires 1 hour, 4 yd³ of mulch would require 2.67 hours.
- **Total:** The job could be completed by one crew member in 9.67 hours.

The preceding times were calculated for one crew member performing the installation. If multiple crew members are performing the work, it will take much less time.
- One crew member requires 9.67 hours.
- Two crew members require 4.84 hours.
- Three crew members require 3.22 hours.
- Four crew members require 2.42 hours.

The crew leader can assign tasks for multiple projects using the time estimations as needed. If three crew members were assigned to install the plants in the example, the project could be completed in one day, leaving the crew members available for other jobs during the week. Using the worker production standards found in **Figure 20-31**, calculate the time per task and the total time needed to install the following plants.

Plant	Quantity	Size	Time Per Plant	Total Time Per Species
Acer palmatum 'Virdius'	2	2″ caliper		
Ilex 'Steeds'	5	5 gallon		
Loropetalum chinensis 'Ruby'	7	3 gallon		
Magnolia 'Brackens Brown Beauty'	1	1″ caliper		
Cryptomeria 'Globosa Nana'	2	3 gallon		
Total time needed to install all plants				

kdevvy/Shutterstock.com   *Bridgette Rodriguez/Shutterstock.com*   *bengy/Shutterstock.com*

The ***Acer palmatum***/Japanese maple comes in a variety of colors and sizes. The tree is often used as a focal point of the landscape because of its flowing shape, interesting textures, and bright display.

Material/Fertilizer Spreader Calibration

Spreader calibration is performed to ensure the correct amount of fertilizer, seed, or pesticide is applied uniformly over the target area without causing plant injury. Calibration requires equipment adjustment and delivery rate (output) calculation. To prevent unsatisfactory results, spreaders should be calibrated every time they are used to ensure they are in working order.

Information Required
- The spreading width of the spreader. The swath width of a common spreader is 10′.
- The time it takes you to walk 100′.
- The amount of material you would need to get a uniform application over the area using 2 to 4 passes.
- **Fertilizer:** 5.5 lb of 18-6-12 fertilizer is required to achieve 1 lb N/1000 ft^2.
- **Calculate:** The calculation for this fertilizer is 1 lb/0.18 = 5.5 lb/1000 ft^2.
- Assume it takes you 22 seconds to walk 100′ (10′ × 100′ = 1000 ft^2).

Procedure
1. Place a plastic bag over the mouth of the spreader to catch the fertilizer.
2. Set the spreader at a setting and turn the crank for 22 seconds to collect the fertilizer.
3. Weigh the bag and adjust the spreader setting until you are getting the desired weight.
4. Determine the number of passes. If the desired total is 5.5 lb and you plan for 2 passes, the target application rate per 1000 ft^2 is 2.75 lbs.
9. If the desired rate is 50 lb per 1000 ft^2, calibrate to 25 lb per 1000 ft^2 for uniform coverage.

Fertilizer Application
Once the spreader is calibrated, break into groups and apply the product to a specific area. Record the amount of fertilizer, herbicide, seed, or lime applied to specific areas.

Square Footage: _____

Rate:_____

Product: _____

Equipment: Handheld Rotary Spreader

Spreader Setting: _____

Total Poundage: _____

Summary

- Information provided with the final design includes the types and quantities of plant materials that are required for the site.
- A thorough review of the plan and site will help ensure all issues can be addressed before the project installation begins.
- A site takeoff includes the cost of materials, labor, time, equipment, and any other costs incurred by the project.
- Landscape plants are planted on-center. On-center spacing is calculated by measuring the distance from the center of one plant to the center of the next plant.
- The number of plants needed to install the landscape can be found in the legend.
- Calculations may be used to determine the exact numbers of bedding plants, herbaceous perennials, and ground covers needed.
- Installation may be begin after the site is graded.
- An area for staging plants should be established before the plants are delivered.
- Soil amendments are added while the planting areas are being prepared for the installation.
- The larger plants, such as trees and shrubs, are installed first to avoid damage to the smaller bedding plants.
- If the planting area were backed by a border, such as a fence or hedge, workers would begin planting at the border and work their way forward.
- If the planting area is exposed on all sides, workers may begin in the center and work outward or from one side to the other.
- Plants that will remain on-site, such as mature trees, must be protected from excavation and installation activities.
- The planting depth for trees and shrubs depends on the species. However, correct depth for plants may be determined by the soil level of the plant to the ground level (surface).
- Staking and guying should be done only when necessary.
- Watering is extremely important to the establishment of a newly installed landscape. Plants should be watered thoroughly and deeply.
- Once the job in finished, the site should be cleaned and all debris removed.
- The total time needed to complete a job may be calculated using standard production rates based on the type of plant and the number of people doing the work.

Chapter Review

Know and Understand ⤤

Answer the following questions using the information provided in this chapter.

1. Which of the following is included on the final plan?
   A. Directional arrow and notes.
   B. Plant list and planting diagram.
   C. Legend and title block.
   D. All of the above.

2. A 1:8 scale indicates 1″ on the drawing represents how many feet in the landscape?
   A. 1′ to 8′
   B. 8′
   C. 16′
   D. 18′

3. What is the actual length of a line that measures 10″ on a drawing with a 1:8 scale?
   A. 8′
   B. 16′
   C. 40′
   D. 80′

4. The shape, color, location, size, and quantities of the specific plants that will be installed is shown on the planting _____.
   A. notes
   B. scale
   C. diagram
   D. address

5. *True or False?* The directional arrow is included to ensure all plant supports face north.
   A. True.
   B. False.

6. *True or False?* There is no need to revisit a site or review a plan once it is finalized.
   A. True.
   B. False.

7. If twelve 14″ plants must be spaced 18″ OC, what distance should there be from the center of one plant to the center of the next plant?
   A. 12″
   B. 14″
   C. 18″
   D. 32″

8. If a planting bed measures 15′ × 5′ and the plants must be placed 14″ OC, how many 10″ plants will fill the area?
   A. 45
   B. 55
   C. 90
   D. 105

9. If a planting bed measures 18′ × 5′ and the plants must be placed 12″ OC, how many 12″ plants will fill the area?
   A. 45
   B. 55
   C. 90
   D. 105

10. Mulch is to be applied to a 15′ × 20′ flower bed. If mulch is applied 3″ deep, how many cubic yards of mulch is required to complete the job?
    A. 2.78 yd^3
    B. 3.78 yd^3
    C. 4.78 yd^3
    D. 5.78 yd^3

11. How many cubic yards of mulch is required to mulch a flower bed that measures 12′ 6″ × 4′ 2″? Assume the mulch is to be applied 3″ deep. (Do not forget to convert the inches to feet.)
    A. 1 yd^3
    B. 0.48 yd^3
    C. 13 yd^3
    D. 3 yd^3

12. *True or False?* A slope of 18% will rise or fall 18″ vertically over a 100′ span.
    A. True.
    B. False.

13. Which of the following professions sources and arranges delivery of plant material?
    A. Plant breeder.
    B. Plant designer.
    C. Plant broker.
    D. Plant stager.

14. What is the primary purpose of a staging area?
    A. An area for removing plants from pots.
    B. An area to keep damaged plants.
    C. A sorting and storage area for plants.
    D. All of the above.

15. *True or False?* Soil amendments, such as fertilizer, are inserted in each planting hole before a bedding plant is installed in the hole.
    A. True.
    B. False.

16. *True or False?* Some plants are installed before others because their installation would otherwise damage materials in the surrounding area.
    A. True.
    B. False.

17. *True or False?* If the planting area were backed by a border, such as a fence or hedge, workers would plant from the front of the bed and work their way toward the border.
    A. True.
    B. False.

18. For which of the following reasons do mature trees remaining on a site require protection during excavation and installation activities?
    A. Roots cannot obtain water, air, and nutrients easily from compacted soil.
    B. Damaged tree roots will prevent the new plants from growing.
    C. Damaged tree roots will alter the fertility of the surrounding soil.
    D. All of the above.

19. The single most important factor when planting trees and shrubs is the _____.
    A. proper fertilizer
    B. spacing between plants
    C. planting depth
    D. backfill

20. How much wider should the planting hole be than the root ball?
    A. 3″ to 4″ wider.
    B. 1 1/2 times wider.
    C. 1 1/2 to 2 times wider.
    D. 1″ to 2″ wider.

21. An injury that occurs in the winter on thin-barked trees when they are exposed to bright sun and cold temperatures is referred to as _____.
    A. sunburn
    B. sunscald
    C. winter burn
    D. All of the above.

22. *True or False?* Newly installed plants become rootbound when the roots cannot penetrate the surrounding soil.
    A. True.
    B. False.

23. *True or False?* The wire basket and burlap should be removed after the tree is placed in the hole to prevent root damage.
    A. True.
    B. False.

24. An earthen mound 4″ to 6″ tall installed around the drip zone of a tree is referred to as a _____.
    A. berm
    B. hill
    C. perimeter zone
    D. mulch line

25. What is the purpose of adding mulch to landscape beds?
    A. To hold moisture.
    B. To deter weeds.
    C. To increase aesthetic value.
    D. All of the above.

26. Water should be applied to newly installed landscape plantings until the soil reaches _____.
    A. field capacity
    B. complete saturation
    C. full coverage
    D. All of the above.

27. Staking trees provides trees with _____.
    A. anchorage
    B. wind protection
    C. support
    D. All of the above.

28. *True or False?* When trees are not staked, their root systems are underdeveloped or fail to become established.
    A. True.
    B. False.

29. Which of the following statements regarding staking is true?
    A. Cording should be attached as low as possible.
    B. One stake should be on the side of prevailing winds.
    C. Three stakes offer more protection than two stakes.
    D. All of the above.

30. *True or False?* Poles used for staking are perpendicular to the tree trunk.
    A. True.
    B. False.

31. Guying is a form of _____.
    A. pruning large trees
    B. fertilizing large trees
    C. supporting large trees
    D. slowing tree growth

32. Approximately how many years will it take for a tree with a caliper of 2″ to become established?
    A. 12 months
    B. 16 months
    C. 24 months
    D. 48 months

33. *True or False?* Spacing of annuals and ground covers does not matter as the plants naturally spread and will cover in the area.
    A. True.
    B. False.

34. Which of the following is used by vines to climb a structure?
    A. tendrils or twiners
    B. adhesive pads
    C. scramblers
    D. All of the above.

35. *True or False?* Having an estimation of the amount of time it takes to complete a job is useful for scheduling crews and determining labor costs.
    A. True.
    B. False.

Thinking Critically

1. What criteria would you use to assess the installation of a new landscape?

2. What details are the most important when choosing plants for a landscape?

3. Why are accurate measurements of space and materials important when pricing a landscape project?

4. What suggestions would you present if plants specified in a design were not available?

5. Are there trends in landscaping designs? What differences are there between today's styles and those of 20 years ago? What drives these changes? Analyze different landscape design styles and identify the different aesthetic and environmental factors of each style.

Suggested Activities

1. In groups of 4 to 5, make a list of 50 common landscape plants. Divide the list between group members. Each group member is to research the plants on their list and create 5″ × 7″ flash cards. Images of the plants should be on one side and the name (Latin and common) and environmental needs on the other side. Images should be of a mature plant, leaves, fruits, and seeds. The environmental needs should include planting zone, mature height, spacing distance, light and shade needs/tolerance, and other pertinent facts. Use the flash cards to study and learn about each plant's environmental needs. This activity may also be used to produce a visual presentation designed for review.

2. Working with a partner or in a small group, prepare an area and install a tree or shrub. Photograph each step of the work. Create a visual presentation of a systematic guide for installing a tree or shrub. Each member of the group should help with the installation and perform a portion of the presentation.

3. Calculate the number of plants needed to cover the flower bed. Petunias placed 6″ OC will be used to cover a 15′ × 20′ flower bed. How many plants will be needed?

4. You are to install petunias in a flower bed that measures 10′ × 5′. It is recommended to space petunias 12″ to 18″ OC. Your supplier is only able to supply one flat of petunias. How should the plants be spaced so that the area can be planted using only one flat?

5. Mulch is to be applied 3″ deep to a flower bed measuring 25′ 3″ × 12′ 4″. How much should you charge to complete the job? Assume your company has a labor rate of $40 per person per hour and one person can apply 1.5 yd³ per hour. You purchase the mulch for $30/yard.

6. Bagged mulch is on sale at $10 for 5 bags at your local hardware store. The bags contain 2.8 ft³ of mulch. Your local landscape supplier's cost for bulk mulch is $30/yard. Which is the better deal?

7. The current landscape plan calls for ten 3-gallon containers and the local nursery has the plant only in 5-gallon containers. One person can install ten 3-gallon containers in one hour. One person can install six 5-gallon containers per hour. How much time will it take to install the ten 5-gallon containers?

8. You have the following landscape to install. Assuming that you have a workday of 7 hours, can a crew of four install the landscape in one day? Refer to **Figure 20-32**.

Quantity	Plant/Container Size	Time Needed Per Plant/Material	Total Time Needed
12	2" caliper		
5	5-gallon		
30	3-gallon		
10	1" caliper		
15	Yards of mulch		
		Total time for job	

9. Obtain soil samples from various places on the school campus and/or from home. Working with a partner, determine the pH for each sample. Research and determine what should be added to each soil to adjust its pH.

10. Review your home lawn or that of a neighbor or relative (with permission) and determine what type of fertilizer would work well on the turfgrass. Consider the characteristics of the type of turfgrass and what type of care it would need for optimum performance. Develop a maintenance program that includes a fertilization schedule. If possible, apply the fertilizer and track the lawn's performance.

Landscape Management

Chapter Outcomes

After studying this chapter, you will be able to:

- Explain the difference between managing and maintaining a landscape.
- Identify which components of a landscape should be analyzed when reviewing a potential job site.
- List the tasks that are performed when maintaining a landscape.
- Explain the difference between organic and inorganic fertilizers.
- Understand and explain the differences among fertilizers.
- Identify the proper timing of maintenance techniques, including fertilizer application, watering, mulching, and pruning.
- Determine when to apply mulch and the amount needed.
- Explain reasons for pruning, identify where pruning cuts should be made, and determine the time pruning should be performed for specific plants.
- Explain winterization tasks for various plants.
- Assess sustainability of current and future practices.
- Determine the most efficient ways to conduct maintenance practice.

Key Terms ↗

adventitious bud
branch collar
bud
complete fertilizer
controlled-release
  fertilizer (CRF)
deadheading
epicormic root
epicormic shoot
fertilizer
fertilizer injector
flower bud
frost heave
gradual restorative pruning

growth bud
hard pruning
heading
heading back
heterophyllus
incomplete fertilizer
inorganic fertilizer
landscape management
leaf axil
organic fertilizer
outward facing bud
pruning
quick-release fertilizer (QRF)
recurrent growth

rejuvenation pruning
restorative pruning
shearing
single-nutrient fertilizer
slow-release fertilizer (SRF)
sucker
terminal bud
thinning
transplant
water-insoluble fertilizer
water-soluble fertilizer
water sprout
wood bud

Introduction

The goal of any landscape manager is to keep a landscape clean, healthy, safe, and attractive throughout the year. Landscapes must be able to withstand many environmental changes, including weather, rainfall, and pests. Landscape managers develop plans to deal with these issues and ensure the landscape continues to thrive. This chapter introduces you to the planning and tasks involved in landscape management.

Management vs. Maintenance

To *maintain* something means to prevent its deterioration or to keep it the same. Some landscape companies specialize in maintenance that keep

landscapes in the same neat and clean condition. On a weekly or biweekly schedule, they mow lawns, trim hedges, edge walkways, and may aerate and fertilize lawns, **Figure 21-1**. They also winterize and open irrigation systems, clean up debris in the spring, rake leaves in the fall, and lay mulch as needed. For many clients this is sufficient. Other clients, however, want a service that not only performs these basic services but also want a company that *manages* their landscape.

Landscape management is the application of management principles to foster growth and adjust maintenance plans to coincide with natural changes due to weather, pests, and other unforeseen events. A landscape management service understands that the plants in a landscape are constantly changing and they identify issues early and create a plan of action to resolve those issues.

welcomia/Shutterstock.com

Figure 21-1. Landscape management tasks include lawn care, pruning, nutrient management, irrigation management, debris removal, and aesthetic improvements, such as the application of mulch.

Analysis and Treatment Assessment

The first step in managing a landscape is to analyze the site and condition of the plant materials, including the lawn. A newly planted landscape and a mature landscape will have different needs.

New Landscapes

The plant materials in a newly planted landscape should be in good condition and the soil should be providing adequate nutrition, **Figure 21-2**. The main goal of treatment at this point is to ensure all plants develop healthy root systems in their new environment. Treatment entails adequate watering, proper mowing, and the addition of nutrients as needed.

Jamie Hooper/Shutterstock.com

Figure 21-2. A newly installed landscape will not require additional nutrition if the site has been prepared properly. The soil and amendments should provide adequate nutrition for a given amount of time.

Mature Landscapes

The plant materials in a mature landscape may also be in good condition, especially if the owner is knowledgeable and has used best practices in maintaining the landscape, **Figure 21-3**. The landscaper may take soil samples and carefully examine plants for signs of disease or pests. The soil samples will help determine what soil types are found throughout the site if any nutrients are lacking. Treatment would include standard maintenance tasks and a plan for pruning, aeration, dethatching, fertilization, and any site-specific tasks, such as cleaning and winterizing a water feature.

If the plant materials in a mature landscape are in poor condition, the assessment will be more extensive. The landscaper will note damaged or diseased plants and the condition of the turfgrass,

karamysh/Shutterstock.com

Figure 21-3. A mature landscape that is maintained properly provides visual appeal, heating and cooling benefits for adjacent buildings, water quality improvements on the landscape site, and habitat for beneficial insects, birds, and other small animals.

as well as overgrowth and unsafe areas. It must be determined *why* the landscape is in its current state before any work is performed. The conditions could be from neglect, over fertilizing, poor mowing practices, poor drainage, rampant infestation, or disease. Soil tests will reveal if the condition of the soil is partly to blame. Treatment may require the removal and replacement of plant materials and fertilization. If conditions are poor enough, a complete or partial renovation may be warranted, **Figure 21-4**.

sokolovski/Shutterstock.com

Figure 21-4. A landscape in poor condition detracts from the visual appeal and value of a property and may also be in violation of local ordinances. It is often more efficient to clear the existing materials and update the site with a new installation.

Management Plans

The differences found on each site warrant tailored management plans for each landscape, **Figure 21-5**. Maintenance schedules and tasks will change as a site matures or returns to its original glory. Many of the same materials and tasks are used to maintain each landscape, albeit in different amounts and at different times of the year. The following tasks are performed on most landscaped sites.

- Fertilization.
- Irrigation.
- Mulching.
- Pest control.
- Aeration.
- Pruning.
- Shearing.
- Mowing.
- Edging.
- Winterization.

Fertilization

A *fertilizer* is a substance that is spread on the ground or mixed in the soil to help plants grow by providing nutrients that plants obtain naturally from the soil.

Sanlyn/Shutterstock.com

Figure 21-5. Topography and water movement across a site require the most adjustment for growing healthy plants. Property that is higher than street level, for example, may require careful planning and construction of retaining walls to maintain a usable and maintainable landscape.

Fertilizer is added to soil because these ingredients must be replenished as they are absorbed by plants, including turfgrass, to keep the plants healthy. Keep in mind that if nutrients are lacking in fall and spring, growth is limited the following season, **Figure 21-6**. Fertilizers may be organic or inorganic and quick-release, slow-release, or controlled-release.

Organic Fertilizers

An *organic fertilizer* is composed of organic materials, such as plants, vegetable peelings, and/or manure. Home gardeners often use compost from kitchen waste and yard waste as fertilizer. The nutrients provided by organic fertilizers are released as the materials decompose. Organic materials improve the texture of soil and improve its aeration and drainage or water retention capabilities.

The content of an organic fertilizer determines which nutrients it provides. Feather meal from a poultry house, for example, is high in nitrogen (as high as 12% to 14%), and cottonseed meal (a byproduct of cotton ginning) provides 3% to 10% of nitrogen, phosphorous, and potassium. These fertilizer materials also provide micronutrients and microorganisms that are of benefit to the soil ecosystem and plant growth, **Figure 21-7**.

szymonbielinski/Shutterstock.com

Figure 21-6. Nutrient deficiencies cause stunted growth, including small leaves, shortened stems, and underdeveloped root systems. Healthy nutrient levels provide adequate growth and can help plants resist attacks from pathogens and other pests.

Pro Tip

Never apply fresh manure as it may have a scorching effect on plants.

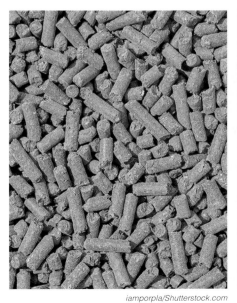

iamporpla/Shutterstock.com

Danie Nel Photography/Shutterstock.com

Krit Leoniz/Shutterstock.com

Figure 21-7. Organic fertilizers, such as pelletized animal manures, vermicompost, and composted kitchen scraps, improve soil ecology and provide valuable nutrients for plant growth.

Other commonly used organic fertilizers include composted manure from herbivores (plant-eating animals), bone meal, blood meal, shellfish, seabird guano, bat guano, and fish emulsion or fish meal. Each material provides certain nutrients, **Figure 21-8**. These fertilizers are available commercially. Landscape companies with ample facilities may compost yard waste materials for later use. The choice to use organic fertilizers may be based on a client's request or the landscape company's mission to use sustainable practices.

Inorganic Fertilizers

Inorganic fertilizers are manufactured from materials other than plants or animals. Most of the nutrients in inorganic fertilizers are from raw mineral sources, such as potassium from salt mining operations, which are processed in a form that is readily available to plants. The numbers on the bag indicate the percentage of nutrients needed in the largest amounts by plants. The nutrients listed on the side of the bag indicate the ratio of the three primary ingredients: nitrogen, phosphorus, and potassium. A fertilizer may be complete, incomplete, or a single-nutrient.

- A *complete fertilizer* is one in which nitrogen (N), phosphorous (P), and potassium (K) are all present (N, P_2O_5, K_2O). A complete fertilizer is most often used for plant maintenance and growth needs. Fertilizers with three numbers, such as 15-15-15 and 20-5-10, are complete fertilizers.
- An *incomplete fertilizer* is one that lacks one of the three primary macronutrients (N, P, and K). It is often used to provide specific growth results, such as flowering or production of fruit. Fertilizers with two numbers and a zero, such as 14-0-14 and 18-46-0, are incomplete fertilizers.
- A *single-nutrient fertilizer* is one that has only one of the three primary macronutrients. These fertilizers can be used to correct deficiencies in soils and/or promote growth. Fertilizers with two zeros and one number, such as 3-40-0 and 0-46-0, are single-ingredient fertilizers.

Organic Fertilizers	
Composted manure from herbivores (plant-eating animals)	Low in nutrients but very valuable as a soil improvement element. *Only composted manure should be used. Fresh manure will scorch plants.*
Bone meal	Provides calcium and phosphate. Used to stimulate flowering and root system growth. Used on bulbs, flowers, and fruit trees.
Blood meal	High in nitrogen. Promotes green, leafy growth. Overapplication can burn plant roots.
Shellfish	High in calcium, contains some phosphorous, and trace minerals. Aids in stimulation of flowering and root system growth.
Seabird guano	High content of nitrogen, phosphorous, potassium, and some trace elements. Used to stimulate flowering and root system growth.
Bat guano	High content of soluble phosphorous, nitrogen, potassium, and some trace elements.
Fish emulsion or fish meal	High calcium content and some phosphorous and other trace minerals. Aids in stimulation of flowering and root system growth. May scorch plant roots.

Goodheart-Willcox Publisher

Figure 21-8. Many types of organic fertilizers are available locally through nursery suppliers.

The common ratios used for landscape plants are as follows. The higher amount of nitrogen reflects the higher need of that nutrient for plant growth.

- 3-1-2 (18-6-12) (common ration for trees and shrubs)
- 4-1-2 (20-5-10) (common ration for turf grasses)
- 1-1-1 (10-10-10) (general fertilizers for soils that are not deficient in any one ingredient)

Quick-Release Fertilizers

The least expensive fertilizers are quick-release fertilizers. *Quick-release fertilizers (QRF)* are not coated and the nutrients are released when the fertilizer is exposed to moisture in the air and/or when the product contacts plant materials or soil. A quick integration into the soil allows rapid absorption by plants and visible growth results. The challenges with these products include off-target applications, runoff, and overapplication that results in plant tissue burn. These nutrients may also be washed away before the plant has absorbed them. Quick-release fertilizers are also referred to as *water-soluble fertilizers*.

Slow-Release Fertilizers

A *slow-release fertilizer (SRF)* has a thin resin-based coating, which wears slowly and meters the release of nutrients over time, depending on the activity of organisms in the soil. The rate, pattern, and duration of release are not controlled. The use of SRFs decreases nutrient losses and can decrease the amount of fertilizer used over time. Slow-release fertilizers are also referred to as *water-insoluble fertilizers*.

Controlled-Release Fertilizers

The release of nutrients by a *controlled-release fertilizer (CRF)* is over a specific time, at a specific rate. CRFs are not dependent on soil microbes and water. The release rate of CRFs is influenced primarily by temperature and somewhat by water acting on the coating. As the temperatures rise in the spring, for example, fertilizer is released as the plant needs nutrients for root growth, bud break, and flower and shoot development. The coatings have different thicknesses and pore sizes through which water and nutrients pass. Controlled-release fertilizers are the most expensive of the three fertilizers discussed.

Rates of Application

Rates of application are based on growth objectives. The first being establishment, followed by growth (top and root), and maintenance. In the case of establishment (root growth) for plants, the timeline governs the application and rates.

- **Perennials.** The roots achieve biomass equilibrium with the shoots within weeks.
- **Shrubs and small trees.** The roots need 1 to 2 years to achieve biomass equilibrium with the shoots.
- **Trees.** The roots of larger trees need 2 to 3 years to achieve biomass equilibrium with the shoots.

First Objective: Establishment

For the 1st year, a rate of 1 lb of nitrogen per 1000 ft^2 per year (1 lb N/M/yr) is adequate to ensure growth for landscape trees, shrubs, vines, groundcovers, and perennials. Applying more nitrogen than the recommended amount in the first year promotes shoot growth and discourages root growth. When a plant is *transplanted* (displaced from its original growing conditions), the balance of root to shoot ratio is disrupted. It is therefore necessary to reduce top growth and encourage root growth to obtain the correct ratio. See **Figure 21-9**.

Second Objective: Growth

During the 2nd or 3rd year, a rate of 2 lb to 4 lb N/M/yr encourages growth for the top and root system. At this point, a plant may fully occupy its space in the design. Additional nitrogen may not be needed if a plant is surrounded by managed turf. The turfgrass requires high rates of nitrogen and the nearby plants may have sufficient access to the nitrogen.

Third Objective: Maintenance

A return to the rate of 1 lb N/M/yr ensures adequate maintenance while not encouraging excessive amounts of growth, which would require additional maintenance, such as pruning and leaf cleanup. The root zone pH and nutrient levels surrounding mature trees should be monitored through soil testing because trees greater than 30 years of age do not respond to extra amounts of nutrients.

Figure 21-9. Successful plant growth is dependent on a healthy root system. To maintain itself, a plant allocates nutrients to the most needed location. If there is excess nitrogen available, the shoots and stems gain those nutrients and the roots remain underdeveloped.

Fertilizer Application Methods

Soil types, plant species, and available labor must be considered when determining which fertilizer application method should be used. Surface applications are the most economical and effective methods with nutrients that are mobile, such as nitrogen and potassium. Application is relatively easy as long as the soil is not compacted and it has minimal slope. Additional methods include the following (**Figure 21-10**):

- *Fertilizer* is placed in holes bored in the ground with an auger in a grid pattern around a plant or group of plants. This method works well with compacted soils and reduces the potential for surface runoff.
- *Liquid fertilizer* applications enable rapid nutrient uptake but have an increased potential for surface runoff. Liquid fertilizers may be applied with water using a fertilizer injector. A **fertilizer injector** is a tool that dilutes and mixes the fertilizer with water being applied to the plants. A compressed air sprayer or pump sprayer may also be used to apply liquid fertilizer.
- *Spikes* and *nutrient briquettes* are used in conjunction with an auger or during planting. The spikes and briquettes are convenient to apply but they are expensive in comparison to other fertilizers.
- In some cases, where a high value plant is under attack from pathogens (insects or diseases), *injections* at the base of the trunk are used to bypass the application and absorption process and achieve immediate absorption. This process is specialized and should be conducted by a trained individual to ensure the correct dosage is used and to avoid plant damage.
- Nutrients, such as phosphorus, calcium, and magnesium, should be incorporated *prior* to planting because they are mostly immobile in soils. Incorporating the nutrients also helps minimize potential surface runoff.

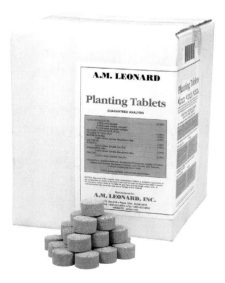 

Photos courtesy of A.M. Leonard Inc.

Figure 21-10. Fertilizer briquettes and spikes are convenient application methods but are typically more expensive than other formulations, such as liquid or granules.

Torychemistry/Shutterstock.com

Figure 21-11. Plants in landscape areas that receive excess water for extended periods of time will experience root rot and overall plant decline.

Kamil Jany/Shutterstock.com

Figure 21-12. Irrigation systems that are designed and installed properly are efficient for watering lawns and other plant materials.

Pro Tip

The best time to water landscaping plants is early in the morning. Watering early in the morning minimizes evaporation and enables increased absorption into the soil.

Watering

The consistent availability of water is essential for root establishment when new plants are first installed. The water should be applied directly to the plant with a water hose. This purges the excess air from the soil pores and replaces the air with water for the immediate uptake by the roots. Stress caused by lack of water can jeopardize the plant's health, cause underdeveloped roots, and may possibly cause the plant's death. An excess of water may cause roots to rot, **Figure 21-11**. Root rot is more likely to occur in heavy soils and during rainy periods. Soil that is waterlogged for more than two weeks causes problems for newly installed plants.

Application Methods

Water can be applied to root systems through broadcast applications over a large area or can be directed to the area immediately around the root system. The property owner may choose to install an irrigation system, especially on large properties with expansive lawns, **Figure 21-12**. If there is an irrigation system in place, it should be programmed to add more water during high growth periods and little, if any, during dormancy. In colder climates, the irrigation system is turned off and winterized.

Woody plants (trees, shrubs, vines, and groundcovers) grow roots most efficiently during spring and fall. Research shows that woody plants need 1″ to 2″ of water per week for adequate development and the avoidance of rot. The higher volumes of water are needed during spring, summer, and fall. Once plants are established, supplemental water may only be needed during excessively hot and dry seasons. The irrigation scheduling for herbaceous plants is similar to the schedule for woody plants because they follow similar growth patterns. Well-established plants will have lower water needs than new plantings.

Soil Texture

The soil texture and composition greatly affect the infiltration rate of water movement *through* the soil profile. It also affects the rate (speed) water moves *within* the soil. This movement is referred to as the percolation rate. The texture of the soil also affects the size and number of soil pores that are available and the water-holding capability of the soil. The frequency of water application is determined, in part, by the infiltration and percolation rates of the soil.

Textural soil classes are sandy soils, clayey soils, and loamy soils. Each of the soil types have different proportions of sand, silt, and clay, **Figure 21-13**.

- The typical infiltration rate for sandy soils is > 0.8″/hour. Therefore, water application to coarse-textured soils, such as sand, occurs more often at lesser volumes.
- The typical infiltration rate of clayey soils is 0.01″/hour. Therefore, water application occurs less often at higher volumes.

The amount of time it takes for a soil volume to drain and reaerate must also be considered. Sandy soils drain within one day and reaerate within two days, whereas clayey soils drain in three days and reaerate in three days. Given this information, the watering schedule is tailored to match the soil type and the plants' needs.

Figure 21-13. Soil composition and color is determined primarily by the soil's parent material, which is the soil's underlying geological material.

STEM Connection

Using the Soil Triangle

Rather than being one type of soil, most soils are a combination of the soil separates sand, silt, and clay. The standard textural classes on the triangle are based on the relative quantities of the soil separates, with each side of the triangle representing one of the separates by percentage. The grid lines, which align with the percentages, are used to help determine the soil class.

- The percentage of sand is read by following the grid lines from bottom right to top left.
- The percentage of clay is read by following the horizontal grid lines from left to right.
- The percentage of silt is read by following the grid lines from top right to bottom left.
- The point at which all three lines intersect indicates the soil's textural class.

You can follow any two of the component percentages on the triangle to determine the percentage of the third and find the name (class) for the soil type. For example, let us assume we have a soil with 40% sand and 20% clay.

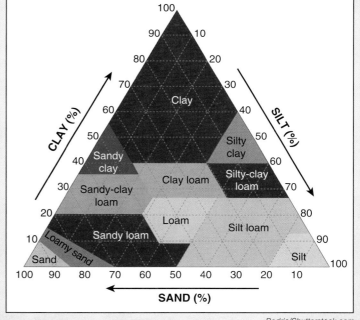

1. What is the percentage of silt? What is the soil's textural class?
2. What would the percentage of silt be if the soil were 35% sand and 35% clay? What is the soil's textural class?

Consider This

1. What types of simple tests can be used to separate soil particles? How are the soil separates measured?
2. Why is clay the largest textural class?
3. What is the maximum amount of clay in loam?
4. How would potting soil react to a hydrology test? Explain your answer.
5. What does the soil color indicate about a soil's texture?

Mulching

Mulch applied to beds and around trees is aesthetically pleasing, reduces weeds, and helps preserve soil moisture, **Figure 21-14A**. The type of mulch used depends on the designer and/or homeowner, as it is available in many shapes, sizes, textures, and color.

Depth

Mulch applied to a newly planted landscape should be 3″ deep. Annual application to replace mulch that has decomposed should be 1″ to 2″ to ensure adequate coverage. Anything less than 1″ is not beneficial and anything over 3″ hinders root growth. One cubic yard of bark mulch will cover 100 ft², 3″ deep.

Application

Due to weight and size differences, some mulches can be applied more quickly than others can. Mulch can be delivered in bulk to the site and then transported manually with a wheelbarrow or some other means to the planting areas. Some materials can be blown into place with a machine, **Figure 21-14B**.

Season

Mulch is applied after leaves have fallen, during the dormant season, and before spring green up. It is easier to apply mulch after deciduous plants drop their leaves. Some sites require a second application of mulch in late summer to freshen the look of the landscape and provide better contrast with the plant foliage and blooms. Mulch applied in early spring replaces mulch that has settled and decomposed during the winter season

A   *Ozgur Coskun/Shutterstock.com*   B   *ND700/Shutterstock.com*

Figure 21-14. Bagged mulch can be easily transported to landscape areas. Large amounts of mulch are effectively and economically applied using mulch blower trucks and long hoses.

Pruning

Pruning is the selective removal of stems, branches, or other parts of a plant to achieve a specific goal, **Figure 21-15**. Careless pruning can cause damage to plants and/or ruin the plant's appearance, which also negatively affects the landscape as a whole. However, a poor landscape can be greatly improved when plants are pruned by a professional. Pruning for most plants should be performed during certain periods in a plant's growth cycle, such as when it is dormant or after flowering. It is therefore important to understand plant growth cycles and the affect pruning has on buds and shoots as well as how to perform cuts.

Areas of Growth

In addition to knowing when to prune, you must know *where* to prune. Cutting in the wrong place may hinder flowering, cause the plant stress, or leave the plant more susceptible to insects and disease. The stem structures of trees, shrubs, and plants vary but each plant requires a bud and a node to produce flowers and leaves. It is essential to identify buds correctly to prune plants successfully.

- A *bud* is a stem's primary growing point. It may be a wood or growth bud, a flower bud, or a leaf bud.
- A *wood bud* or *growth bud* is one from which wood branches grow. It is pointed and grows flush with the branch and may appear scaly.
- *Flower buds* are larger than growth buds and have a soft, downy surface. Flowers bloom from flower buds, which may then produce fruit.
- The primary growth areas are at the *apices*, or tips of stems and roots. These are terminal buds. A *terminal bud* is defined as the growth bud at the tip of a branch or stem. When the terminal bud is removed, the remaining buds on the branch are stimulated to grow.
- *Lateral buds* develop on the sides of a stem. Lateral buds may be wood, leaf, or flower buds. They grow in a *leaf axil*, which is the upper angle between the leaf and stem.

igorstevanovic/Shutterstock.com   *Christian Delbert/Shutterstock.com*

Figure 21-15. It is imperative to understand growth habits and cycles before pruning shrubs and trees. It is also important to use tools that are designed for the type and size of stem or branch you are cutting.

(Left to right) djgis/Shutterstock.com; Saifuldb/Shutterstock.com; Kazakov Maksim/Shutterstock.com; Flower Studio/Shutterstock.com

Figure 21-16. The ability to identify trees, shrubs, and other plants by their buds is a useful skill for landscape professionals, especially when they are pruning. Buds vary in size, location, shape, and even color.

- The point of attachment for all leaves, roots, and flowers is the *node*. Much growth occurs at the nodes. The space or length of stem between nodes is referred to as the *internode*. Adventitious buds may form on internodes. *Adventitious buds* are those that develop from places other than nodes or leaf axils.
- An *outward facing bud* is any growth bud facing away from the center of the tree. See **Figure 21-16**.

Where a pruning cut is made is important because pruning cuts are made to direct growth. A cut below a node results in dieback of the stem to the next node, which results in an unsightly appearance. A pruning cut made above the node will direct growth outward.

Vegetative buds that originate in leaf axils and at the tips mentioned before can be seen while unseen buds below the bark of many plants give rise to *epicormic shoots* or *roots*. These are also called *latent buds* whose growth is activated by a mechanical alteration to the bark or greater influence of light. For example, when a cutting is taken from a stem and a root develops given the correct growth environment, or as limbs are removed and bark is exposed to light giving rise to new buds that form into shoots. See **Figure 21-17**.

Pro Tip

Always prune back to buds that are aiming in the direction you want the new limbs to grow. This is typically upward and outward.

Charoenkrung.Studio99/Shutterstock.com

Kutlayev Dmitry/Shutterstock.com

Figure 21-17. Epicormic shoots may be a symptom of stress in a tree. Trees that have been overly pruned or have been damaged during a storm may grow epicormic shoots to compensate for the loss of leaf surface, which greatly affects the tree's ability to perform photosynthesis. A tree will grow these shoots primarily when it needs to increase amounts of photosynthesis.

Reasons to Prune

Whether it is used to control the size or influence flowering, pruning is considered a stimulant for growth. When part of a plant is removed, the plant's energy is focused on healing the cut and the remaining parts of the plant, which stimulates growth. However, a plant's response to pruning depends on the plant's growth habit, its age and size, timing (season), and the severity of the pruning. Pruning, depending on the degree and timing of the cut, can strengthen a stem, induce flowering, or cause branching. The most common reasons for pruning plants include the following:

- **To direct growth.** Direct growth to a specific area or away from another object.
- **To influence flowering and fruiting.** Pruning may be used to increase the number of flowers and fruits on a plant or reduce the number to produce fewer flowers and fruit with a greater display or fruit size, **Figure 21-18**.
- **To maintain health and appearance.** Removing damaged, dead, or diseased material to ensure plant health and to increase or decrease the density of the foliage.
- **To rejuvenate.** Pruning may be used to promote the growth of younger stems that yield brighter bark and/or more flower and fruiting capabilities.
- **To control size.** Altering the shape and form of a plant. This is the most common and misused technique that is highly discouraged.

Figure 21-18. Fruit trees are pruned differently from landscape plants because of their need for high air movement and sunlight within the canopy. Pruning fruit trees is also necessary for disease reduction and adequate ripening of the fruit.

A   *Yukikazu/Shutterstock.com*

B   *Jeanie333/Shutterstock.com*

Figure 21-19. A—The art of Japanese bonsai uses standard pruning principles to produce small trees that mimic the shape and scale of full-size trees, such as the ginkgo illustrated above. B—Espalier is the process of training trees against a flat surface, such as a wall, fence, or trellis. The process is often used in small gardens to conserve space.

- **To produce specialty forms.** Training into shapes or against structures to display unique characteristics of the plant or accentuate architectural characteristics of a structure, **Figure 21-19**.
- **To promote safety.** Removing dead, diseased, or weak branches to prevent breaking and falling, removing branches hanging over a structure, and/or connection to live power lines. It is also important to remove these branches to prevent breakage that would cause damage to the tree.
- **To stimulate terminal growth.** The apical dominance of buds on the terminal causes all lateral growth to yield to terminal growth when lateral buds/branches are removed. Cutting back the lateral buds stimulates terminal growth. This is common with young plants if they require training to promote growth in height or shape.
- **To stimulate lateral growth.** The removal of the terminal buds/branches stimulates lateral growth.
- **To remove unwanted or undesirable growth.** Undesirable growth includes branches that are hanging too low or crossing other branches, suckers, and water sprouts. *Suckers* are unwanted shoots that grow near the base of the trunk and *water sprouts* are thin branches that typically grow straight up from lateral branches, **Figure 21-20**.

An understanding of the end goals is imperative to good pruning. Plans for pruning should include objectives, the size range and location of branches to be removed, the percentage of the live crown to be removed, and the techniques and tools to be used.

Pro Tip

The phrase, "follow the 3 Ds when pruning," refers to pruning dead, damaged, and diseased materials.

R. Lee Ivy

Figure 21-20. Root suckers and water sprouts occur from dormant buds below the bark of the plant. These buds grow due to mechanical damage of the bark or increased sunlight. This growth is commonly removed to allow the canopy to return to its natural form.

Time for Pruning

The best time for pruning varies with plant species. Pruning cuts are made during specific periods in the growth cycle to achieve the desired results. Conifers, for example, have one flush of growth in the spring and hollies have *recurrent growth* (multiple flushes of growth) during the growing season. A landscape professional with knowledge of growth patterns can schedule pruning and avoid exposing bare stems or removing flowers. A traditional evergreen azalea, for example, sets its flower buds in the summer before the following spring's flowering season. If pruning occurs after the flower buds are formed, the floral display is compromised. See **Figure 21-21**.

Some plants only produce flowers on the current seasons' growth, not on the established growth. Pruning these plants before or during flowering will not compromise the floral display. Many hydrangeas, for example, produce flowers on the current season's growth and will bloom multiple times during the season after pruning. Perennials are pruned after they have gone dormant, when ground covers or vines have grown out of desired spaces, or dead or damaged materials are discovered, **Figure 21-22**.

Woody plants are pruned mostly during the dormant season to avoid insect and disease attacks. However, corrective pruning may be done throughout the year using sharp pruning tools and proper cutting angles to allow the wound to close.

V J Matthew/Shutterstock.com

Figure 21-21. Flowering shrubs, such as azaleas, should be pruned after flowering and before the next year's flower buds are formed to avoid compromising the floral display.

Paolo Trovo/Shutterstock.com   *abinkung/Shutterstock.com*

Figure 21-22. Ground covers are useful for covering areas that are difficult to mow or grow other ornamental plants. Most ground covers will spread quickly over the desired area but will easily overcome the intended boundaries if not pruned.

Did You Know?

A *heterophyllus* plant develops different leaf forms on the same plant. *Osmanthus heterophyllus*, for example, has spiny and entire leaf margins.

Growth Season

In most areas of the United States, optimum time of root growth is during late winter and early spring followed by mid to late fall. Some areas experience soil freezing and root growth is slowed while most areas experience high soil temperatures in the summer, which also slows growth.

Pruning Techniques

Pruning should be performed with the natural growth habit of the plant so that the plant's appearance reflects its fundamental form and character. In other words, a properly pruned tree will look as natural. Common pruning techniques include heading, thinning, rejuvenation pruning, deadheading, and shearing.

Goodheart-Willcox Publisher

Figure 21-23. Heading back can be used to thin the canopy of the plant as well as reduce overall size.

Goodheart-Willcox Publisher

Figure 21-24. Thinning cuts remove water sprouts, crossing branches, and improve the shape and spacing of branches.

Heading or Heading Back

Heading or *heading back* removes the terminal portion of shoots or limbs to a live bud or branch. This reduces overall size and stimulates lateral (horizontal) branching near the cut. See **Figure 21-23**. When pruning large limbs, an angled cut made at the branch collar enables proper sealing of the wound. The *branch collar* is a swollen area at the base of a branch that is at a 30° to 45° angle from the trunk.

Thinning

Thinning removes an entire shoot or limb to its point of origin from the main branch. The removal of older branches stimulates flowering and fruiting growth and provides increased light penetration and better air movement through the tree, which reduces disease and insect activity. Thinning trees reduces the density at the edge of the crown, not the interior. See **Figure 21-24**.

Rejuvenation Pruning

Rejuvenation pruning removes the majority of the plant material to stimulate juvenile growth and thickening of the plant over time. The severe cutback, which leaves 6″ to 12″ of the plant above ground, should be made after the growing season or just before new growth in the spring. This method is used on small shrubs, perennials, ornamental grasses, frost-damaged plants, ground covers, and vines. This type of pruning works best with shrubs that have several stems rising directly from the ground. Rejuvenation pruning may also be referred to as *restorative* or *hard pruning*. *Gradual restorative pruning* is the removal of branches over several years. See **Figure 21-25**.

Deadheading

Deadheading is the removal of dead blooms on perennials and small shrubs during blooming. Deadheading some plants encourages new flowers to bloom. The stems can be cut back on many plants after blooming. Deadheading is also effective on many annuals, such as petunias. See **Figure 21-26**.

Shearing

Shearing is a pruning method that removes large amounts of plant material at one time with no regard to the natural structure. This technique is used to create and maintain formal landscapes and to create neat and effective screens with hedges. Evergreen and deciduous shrubs that respond best to shearing are those with short internodes, short leaves, dense branching, and a slow growth rate. Shrubs that respond well to shearing include boxwood, privet, yew, and buckthorn.

Some spring or summer blooming perennials are sheared by half to encourage regrowth and additional flowering. These same perennials are often sheared to the ground at the end of the season to prepare for the next season's new growth. A few perennials that respond well to shearing include asters, daisies, Russian sage, and tall phlox.

Christina Richards/Shutterstock.com

Figure 21-25. Rejuvenation pruning encourages new growth, which results in brighter and more productive stems with more flowers (on flowering shrubs).

Handheld or power pruning shears with long blades can be used for smaller branches on shrubs and for most perennials. Loppers may be used to shear wider branches. To reduce cleanup time after shearing, rake back mulch and place a tarp along the base of the plants to catch clippings. See **Figure 21-27**.

Jason Kolenda/Shutterstock.com

Figure 21-26. Deadheading is the removal of dried and discolored flowers. Deadheading may increase repeated blooms on some flowering plants.

Ivan Smuk/Shutterstock.com

Figure 21-27. Shearing shrubs produces a neat and formal look. Shrubs are often sheared with the top being slightly narrower than the bottom. This ensures sufficient sunlight for the entire plant, which will help keep it full from top to bottom.

Spring_Summer/Shutterstock.com

Tadeas Skuhra/Shutterstock.com

Figure 21-28. Annuals are grown in nurseries with highly nutritious substrates to ensure healthy plants with vibrant colors. Petunias are very popular as a summer accent plant due to the wide variety of colors available and their hardiness.

Severe Pruning

In some instances, severe pruning is necessary. Severe pruning typically involves cutting the plant to a height of 6″ to 12″ above the ground. This type of pruning is usually due to severe damage or dieback due to insect or other pathogen attacks. This may be a precursor to removing the plant if it becomes a regular occurrence.

Managing Annuals

With their decorative foliage and floral displays, annuals are a great addition to any landscape. Annuals are used in hanging pots and planters, to fill entire beds, create interesting designs, to accent perennials, and to replace spring flowers as they die, **Figure 21-28**. In many parts of the country, summer annuals are replaced with annual fall plants for continuous color. Annuals can be chosen for their color, texture, height, width, or growth habits and environmental needs. Hardiness zones and maintenance requirements must also be considered.

Many professionals use plants from the same grower or breeder because of their past performance. Organizations, such as All-America Selections (AAS), independently test and judge flowers and edible varieties in North America and rank them by garden superiority. Various universities and botanical gardens also field test plants for hardiness, pest resistance, foliage or floral display, and overall performance. The results and winners' lists are published, highlighting the plant's desirable attributes.

Soil Preparation

Soil preparation is essential before planting annuals to ensure continuous blooms and full, shapely growth. If an entire bed is to be planted with annuals, the ground can be tilled and soil amendments can be worked into the soil, **Figure 21-29**.

Koliadzynska Iryna/Shutterstock.com

Ivan Smuk/Shutterstock.com

Figure 21-29. Working fertile amendments in annual flower beds before planting will yield rapid foliage and floral growth. Rapid growth is encouraged because annual flowers have limited time to yield aesthetic appeal.

Preemergent herbicides may also be worked into the soil. When annuals are installed in beds or areas with perennials, care must be taken to avoid damage or disturbance to the established plants. Amendments can be worked into the backfill or added directly to the holes. When planting, take care to release plants properly from cell packs to avoid damage to the roots.

Keep in mind that planting depth, spacing, and light and nutritional needs vary by plant species. This information is used to ensure plants installed in each area of the landscape have similar needs.

Watering and Fertilization

To keep plants healthy and ensure continuous, vibrant color, annuals must receive adequate water and fertilization. Liquid or slow-release fertilizers can be added weekly or as needed. If provided, follow the grower's recommendations. Maintenance of annual beds includes hand weeding as needed and removal of spent flowers for some species.

Winterization

Many landscape plants will survive winter with little care, however, preparing the landscape for winter will help plants stay healthy and become productive in the next growing season. Tender and new plants are especially vulnerable and must be protected if they are to survive the winter, **Figure 21-30**. An understanding of each plant's needs for winter protection is essential to successful winterization. Bearded iris, for example, is said to be prone to rot and should not be mulched for the winter. Some plants have cold hardiness traits and use an acclimation process triggered by shorter day length and cooling temperatures in the fall to prepare for the winter. These plants may not require much in the way of winterization.

ubonwanu/Shutterstock.com   *photowind/Shutterstock.com*

Figure 21-30. In many climates, plant protection is necessary for marginally hardy plants or during unique climatic fluctuations. These young evergreens are protected from harsh winter winds with burlap and this rhododendron is surrounded with spun bond, a nonwoven material designed for this purpose.

Mulching

One of the first steps for winterizing most plants is laying down mulch. The mulch insulates the soil and will prevent frost heave, especially for shallow-rooted perennials. *Frost heave* occurs when the freezing and thawing of the soil pushes plants out of the soil and exposes the roots and crowns to freezing air and drying winds. Mulch will also help the soil retain moisture.

Chemical amendments and mulching recommendations for perennials are the same as for trees and shrubs. However, additional mulch or covering of some type provides tender perennials and plants, such as roses, with additional protection from the cold.

Pruning

Pruning or cutting down perennials will help eliminate hiding places for pests and diseases. Perennials should not be pruned until they have gone dormant. However, some perennials, such as ornamental grasses or plants with interesting seedheads, provide interest in the landscape during winter and are often left until spring, **Figure 21-31**. As explained earlier, woody plants are pruned mostly during the dormant season to avoid insect and disease attacks.

Compost and Fertilizing

Plants should not be fertilized within 3 to 4 weeks of winter, as this will encourage growth. However, compost may be added to provide nutrition for soil and improve the soil's texture. The compost will break down slowly and release nutrients over time.

Watering

Water can be added until the ground freezes, allowing for survival through the winter season. In many areas, winter precipitation is enough to sustain plant systems. Plant damage may occur if plants experience drought during the cold season. Therefore, a manager must determine when to add water or when the plant's water content is adequate to endure cold periods. Soil probes inserted around the roots will determine moisture content.

Figure 21-31. Fruit, flowers, and seedheads provide interest and movement during winter months. They can also be food sources for wildlife during the cold season.

Early Fall or Late Spring Freeze

Many plants are damaged when exposed suddenly to freezing temperatures, **Figure 21-32**. The lack of acclimation time leaves the plants more vulnerable to the cold. Plants are also vulnerable to cold damage when they come out of dormancy due to warmer temperatures from extended sun exposure and are exposed suddenly to a late spring freeze. It is important to understand this process to anticipate client's questions and/or schedule maintenance, such as pruning of damaged material.

Timofey Zadvornov/Shutterstock.com

Safety First

Pet feces and animal waste, such as bones or meat, should never be added to a compost pile. These materials may contain pathogens that cause illness and death in humans. The person handling the compost or ingesting food that has come in contact with the compost can be infected. Other materials that should not be added to compost include diseased plant materials, invasive weeds, and plants such as poison ivy or poison oak.

Sustainable Landscaping Management

Sustainable landscaping is the use of planned methods to offset negative environmental impacts, such as reducing waste, decreasing runoff, and conserving water and energy. These strategic methods include using gray water for irrigation, composting lawn waste, and aerating turf to prevent compaction, **Figure 21-33**.

Peter Turner Photography/Shutterstock.com

Figure 21-32. Frost and cold damage can occur with dramatic temperature changes. Many plants will recover but their visual display may be delayed or reduced.

Jean Faucett/Shutterstock.com

Photo courtesy of Hunter Industries

Figure 21-33. Sustainable practices, such as the reuse of gray water for irrigation and composting of commonly discarded products, such as Christmas trees, are favorably recognized by homeowners and commercial clients.

Sustainable landscaping management begins with a carefully planned design that considers how the lot, growing conditions, and water flow will affect the landscape materials and determine its needs. A landscape professional may also evaluate an existing site and determine ways in which the landscape could be altered to make it more sustainable. The new design and proposed changes must be discussed with the client before any modifications are made to the design or the landscape.

Management tasks that will help improve sustainability include the following:

- **Water.** Ensure there are no leaks in irrigation systems, adjust sprinklers to prevent overspray onto hardscape services, and use rainwater whenever possible.
- **Pest management.** Develop and use integrated pest management (IPM) to reduce the need for pesticides. IPM includes the introduction of beneficials (desirable insects) to control pests and disease. Eliminate invasive plants.
- **Soil.** Aerate compacted soil to prevent erosion and runoff, add organic materials to soil, and encourage the homeowner to compost kitchen waste for use in the landscape.
- **Compost.** Compost yard waste, use mulching mowers, and use local materials (plants and hardscapes) as much as possible, **Figure 21-34**.
- **Recycle.** Use recycled construction materials and permeable hardscape materials.

Another sustainable practice is leaving leaf litter under woody ornamentals as a mulch and weed barrier. Collections of leaves from specimen or shade trees from other areas can also be chopped and returned as mulch. However, if there are diseases or insects in the area that overwinter in leaf litter, the practice of repurposing the leaves on-site should be avoided and fresh mulch should be applied.

Kunanui/Shutterstock.com

Figure 21-34. Composting can be practiced by large- and small-scale producers. The resulting product can be returned to the benefit of the landscape.

Scheduling Multiple Projects

To ensure profitability and customer satisfaction, projects must be carefully planned. The timing of material and equipment delivery, the presence of sufficient personnel, task times, travel time, vehicles needed, and equipment delivery are all important parts of a job that must be accounted for in the project schedule.

Task Completion Times

Knowing the amount of time it takes to complete each task, such as planting a large tree or applying mulch, is a major component of a project schedule, **Figure 21-35**. It will be difficult to schedule the number of workers needed at each job site if task times are unknown. For example, it is sometimes more efficient for one person to perform a task rather than a team of two or three workers. The other workers could be at a different job site completing tasks that require more than one person. However, it may be more practical for the entire crew to complete the first job quickly and then move to the second job if they are riding together in a company vehicle and the job sites are not near each other. This would save fuel and time and enable the crew to move on to a third job if needed.

Safety First

Safety should be the first concern when assigning tasks and crews. It may be unsafe for a single crew member to perform certain tasks, such as trimming taller trees or using a chain saw, at a job site alone.

Logistics

Planning a route from the base to each job is also an important component of the project schedule. As explained in the preceding paragraph, it may be more efficient for the crew to complete a job together before moving to the next job. The most efficient route should be planned so the crews avoid peak traffic times and do not backtrack. The mileage and fuel between jobs is also tracked to ensure their cost is covered.

Most companies use a GPS to track vehicles and calculate travel times. An investment in this technology can minimize inefficiencies and allow employees to be as productive as possible. The task times for each job may also be entered in the computer program or written on time sheets. A job board, **Figure 21-36**, may be placed in the main office to map out the best routes in conjunction with the weekly schedule of clientele and tasks to be completed at each site.

welcomia/Shutterstock.com

Figure 21-35. More accurate pricing is ensured when each task has a time associated with the process.

Phovoir/Shutterstock.com

Figure 21-36. Companies use planning boards or scheduling software to coordinate crew routing and task completion across multiple sites.

A crew may also use their time more efficiently by assigning and planning the order of the tasks to be performed or even parking the vehicle strategically. Parking the vehicle in the center of a business parking lot, for example, enables the crew to work the property in a clockwise direction and maintain a minimal distance from the vehicle. If the job is linear (in a line), employees and equipment can be dropped off at one end and the vehicle can be parked at the other end. The crew would work its way back to the truck.

Pro Tip

Daily safety briefings held before the crews begin working should also include review of the day's jobs to confirm everyone knows where and when they will be working throughout the day.

Career Connection

Kevin Foushee

Kevin Foushee, Turf and Ornamentals Spray Technician

Kevin Foushee is a trained spray technician specializing in the treatment of turf and ornamentals. Kevin's interest in the green industry began when he became involved with his FFA chapter in high school. The friendships he developed with advisors and peers as they competed in Career Development Events have become cherished, lifelong connections. Winning a national championship in the Nursery/Landscape competition inspired Kevin to pursue a career in the landscaping industry and become a professional spray technician.

In his work, Kevin's goal is to enrich lawns and landscapes with precisely timed applications of pesticide, herbicides, insecticides, and fungicides. Kevin hopes that his work encourages others to keep and enjoy properly maintained lawns and to use sustainable practices. Kevin is a graduate of the North Carolina State Horticultural Science Department.

Consider This

1. How has Kevin's involvement in FFA contributed to his success?
2. Do you find this area of the green industry interesting? Why or why not?
3. Have you participated in FFA or NLPA competitions? Has your participation inspired you to pursue a career in the green industry? Explain your answer.

Summary

- Landscape companies specializing in maintenance keep a landscape in the same neat and clean condition and mow lawns, trim hedges, and edge walkways on a weekly or biweekly schedule.
- A landscape management service performs maintenance tasks but also adapts its service to changes due to weather, pests, and other unforeseen events. They also identify issues early and create a plan of action to resolve those issues.
- The first step in managing a landscape is to analyze the site and condition of the plant materials, including the lawn.
- The differences found on each site warrant tailored management plans for each landscape.
- Tasks that are performed when maintaining a landscape include fertilization, irrigation, mulching, pest control, aeration, pruning, shearing, mowing, edging, and winterization.
- Organic fertilizers are composed of organic materials, such as plants, vegetable peelings, and/or manure whereas inorganic fertilizers are manufactured from materials other than plants or animals.
- Fertilizers have differing amounts of each ingredient and differing means of releasing ingredients.
- Professionals must understand proper timing of maintenance techniques, including fertilizer application, watering, mulching, and pruning.
- Mulch applied to beds and around trees is aesthetically pleasing, reduces weeds, and helps preserve soil moisture.
- Mulch applied to a newly planted landscape should be 3" deep. Annual application to replace mulch that has decomposed should be 1" to 2" to ensure adequate coverage.
- Pruning is the selective removal of stems, branches, or other parts of a plant to achieve a specific goal.
- Professionals must understand reasons for pruning, identify where pruning cuts should be made, and determine the time pruning should be performed for specific plants to ensure successful pruning results.
- Common pruning techniques include heading, thinning, rejuvenation, deadheading, shearing, basal pruning, and severe pruning.
- With their decorative foliage and floral displays, annuals are a great addition to any landscape.
- Many landscape plants will survive winter with little care; however, preparing the landscape for winter will help plants stay healthy and become productive in the next growing season.
- Winterization tasks include mulching, pruning, adding compost, and watering.
- Assess sustainability of current and future practices.
- Determine the most efficient ways to conduct maintenance practice.
- Sustainable landscaping management begins with a carefully planned design that considers how the lot, growing conditions, and water flow will affect the landscape materials and determine its needs.
- A landscape professional may evaluate an existing site and determine ways in which the landscape could be altered to make it more sustainable.
- Carefully planned scheduling of multiple projects and crew members will reduce wasted time and help keep all projects on schedule.

Chapter Review

Know and Understand ↱

Answer the following questions using the information provided in this chapter.

1. *True or False?* Maintenance and management are the same thing.
   A. True.
   B. False.

2. A landscape service that adapts to changes due to weather, pests, and other unforeseen events is a _____.
   A. marathon service
   B. management service
   C. maintenance service
   D. marketing service

3. *True or False?* A newly planted landscape and a mature landscape will have the same maintenance needs.
   A. True.
   B. False.

4. Which of the following is performed when analyzing a mature landscape?
   A. Examine plants for disease or pests.
   B. Determine if trees need pruning or removal.
   C. Take several soil samples.
   D. All of the above.

5. Which of the following tasks are performed on most landscaped sites?
   A. Mulching and mowing.
   B. Fertilization and aeration.
   C. Edging and mowing.
   D. All of the above.

6. *True or False?* When a plant is transplanted, the balance of root to shoot ratio is increased.
   A. True.
   B. False.

7. *True or False?* Plants surrounded by turf need additional nitrogen because the turf takes all of the nitrogen from the soil below and near the turf.
   A. True.
   B. False.

Match each term to the descriptions in 8–15.
   A. complete fertilizer
   B. controlled-release fertilizer
   C. incomplete fertilizer
   D. inorganic fertilizer
   E. organic fertilizer
   F. quick-release fertilizer
   G. single nutrient fertilizer
   H. slow-release fertilizer

8. A fertilizer composed of materials, such as plants, vegetable peelings, and/or manure.

9. A fertilizer manufactured from materials other than plants or animals.

10. A fertilizer in which nitrogen (N), phosphorous (P), and potassium (K) are present.

11. A fertilizer that lacks one of the three primary macronutrients.

12. A fertilizer that contains only one primary macronutrient.

13. A fertilizer that releases nutrients when it is exposed to moisture in the air and/or when it contacts plant materials or soil.

14. A fertilizer that releases nutrients over time, depending on the activity of organisms in the soil.

15. A fertilizer that releases nutrients over a specific time, at a specific rate.

16. *True or False?* When new plants are first installed, sporadic application of water is adequate for root establishment.
    A. True.
    B. False.

17. *True or False?* Once plants are established, supplemental water may only be needed during excessively hot and dry seasons.
    A. True.
    B. False.

18. The rate of water movement *through* the soil profile is referred to as the _____.
    A. infiltration rate
    B. movement rate
    C. flow rate
    D. All of the above.

19. The rate (speed) water moves *within* the soil is referred to as the _____.
    A. infiltration rate
    B. penetration rate
    C. percolation rate
    D. movement rate

20. Mulch applied to a newly installed landscape should be _____.
    A. 1″ deep
    B. 2″ deep
    C. 3″ deep
    D. 4″ deep

21. The selective removal of stems, branches, or other parts of a plant to achieve a specific goal is referred to as _____.
    A. pruning
    B. prying
    C. prevention
    D. All of the above.

22. A stem's primary growing point is a(n) _____.
    A. root
    B. internode
    C. inset
    D. bud

23. The bud at the tip of a branch or stem is the _____.
    A. terminal bud
    B. axil bud
    C. outward bud
    D. flower bud

24. *True or False?* The lateral buds grow more vigorously when the terminal buds are removed.
    A. True.
    B. False.

25. On which of the following does a plant's response to pruning depend?
    A. The number of flower buds on each branch.
    B. The plant's growth habit and age.
    C. The number of branches in the crown.
    D. All of the above.

26. Unwanted shoots that grow near the base of the trunk are referred to as _____.
    A. downward shoots
    B. water sprouts
    C. apices
    D. suckers

27. Thin branches that typically grow straight up from lateral branches are referred to as _____.
    A. downward shoots
    B. water sprouts
    C. apices
    D. suckers

28. *True or False?* The best time to make pruning cuts varies by plant species.
    A. True.
    B. False.

29. *True or False?* Plants that flower only on the current season's growth should be pruned before flowering to ensure abundant blooms.
    A. True.
    B. False.

30. Which of the following types of pruning removes the terminal portion of shoots or limbs to a live bud or branch to reduce size and stimulate lateral growth?
    A. Thinning.
    B. Restorative.
    C. Rejuvenation.
    D. Heading back.

31. Which of the following types of pruning removes an entire shoot or limb to its point of origin from the main branch?
    A. Thinning.
    B. Restorative.
    C. Rejuvenation.
    D. Heading back.

32. Which of the following types of pruning removes the majority of the plant material to stimulate juvenile growth and thickening of the plant over time?
    A. Thinning.
    B. Restorative.
    C. Rejuvenation.
    D. Heading back.

33. The removal of spent blooms on perennials and small shrubs during blooming is referred to as _____.
    A. back heading
    B. deadheading
    C. thin heading
    D. All of the above.

34. This technique is used to create and maintain formal landscapes and to create neat and effective screens with hedges.
   A. Scoring.
   B. Shearing.
   C. Searing.
   D. Spreading.

35. Pruning that involves cutting the plant to a height of 6″ to 12″ above the ground is referred to as _____.
   A. shear pruning
   B. sear pruning
   C. severe pruning
   D. starve pruning

36. What causes plants to begin the acclimatization process?
   A. Shorter day length and cooling temperatures.
   B. Shorter day length and warmer temperatures.
   C. Longer day length and warmer temperatures.
   D. Longer day length and cooling temperatures.

37. Which of the following occurs when the freezing and thawing of the soil pushes plants out of the soil?
   A. Soil heave.
   B. Frost heave.
   C. Winter heave.
   D. Plant heave.

38. *True or False?* Perennials should be pruned just before they become dormant.
   A. True.
   B. False.

39. *True or False?* Plants become more vulnerable to the cold if there is a lack of acclimation time.
   A. True.
   B. False.

40. Which of the following should *not* be placed in a compost pile?
   A. Seabird guano.
   B. Cow manure.
   C. Dog or cat feces.
   D. Fish emulsion.

41. The use of planned methods to offset negative environmental impacts, such as reducing waste, decreasing runoff, and conserving water and energy, is referred to as _____.
   A. conservative landscaping
   B. sustainable landscaping
   C. reduction landscaping
   D. strategic landscaping

42. *True or False?* Sustainable landscaping may begin with the design of a new landscape as well as the modification of an existing landscape.
   A. True.
   B. False.

43. *True or False?* Checking for leaks in irrigation systems and adjusting sprinklers to prevent overspray onto hardscape surfaces help improve sustainability.
   A. True.
   B. False.

44. Which of the following can be managed in such a way as to make a landscape more sustainable?
   A. Water.
   B. Soil.
   C. Compost.
   D. All of the above.

45. *True or False?* Knowing how much time it takes to complete each task, such as planting a large tree or applying mulch, is a major component of a project schedule.
   A. True.
   B. False.

Thinking Critically

1. Are there steps that can be taken to reduce the need to prune? Explain your answer.

2. Which do you think is better, letting plants grow and die down naturally or pruning the plants? Justify your answer.

3. How would you explain the difference between the types of buds?

4. How do plants react to top or crown pruning? Should the crown of a newly planted tree be removed? What are the long- and short-term effects of crown pruning a transplant?

Suggested Activities

1. Working with a partner, collect soil samples from three locations on the school campus. (Mark the samples with the locations.) Conduct a percolation test on each soil sample and determine the percolation rate. Were the percolation rates different? Which soils would be appropriate for growing plants?

2. Expand on the preceding activity by performing hydrology tests with the same soils. Determine if and how the percentages of each soil separate affect the percolation rate.

3. Research online for local sources of organic amendments and determine availability, pricing, and delivery options. Compare the costs to those of inorganic fertilizers. Which is more expensive?

4. Working in a group of 3 to 5 students, obtain images of recently pruned plants. You may use online images if you are unable to take your own photos. Create a visual presentation showing different plants that have been pruned using the same technique. You may also include examples of poor pruning. Share your presentation with the class.

5. Work in a small group to identify plants that will live in your climate zone. Each person should be assigned a different type of plant, such as flowering perennials for sun, small ornamental trees, flowering shrubs, and perennials for shade. (You may want to limit the number of plants per person.) Search online or visit local nurseries to gather information and images of each plant. Create a digital library or a visual presentation to share with the class.

6. Pollarding, coppicing, and topping are "pruning" methods not discussed in the chapter. Work with a partner to create a visual presentation that explains each of these methods. Include multiple images of each and explain the advantages and disadvantages of using these methods. You may also want to include historical uses of these methods.

7. Some states, such as Florida, have created a list of landscape principles that are considered friendly to the local environment. Work with a partner to create a guide for sustainable and environmentally friendly landscaping. Use Florida's guide as a model for your list.

While studying this chapter, look for the activity icon to:
- **Practice** vocabulary terms with Words to Know activities.
- **Expand** learning with identification activities.
- **Reinforce** what you learn by completing Know and Understand questions.

G-WLEARNING.com

www.g-wlearning.com/agriculture

Chapter Outcomes

After studying this chapter, you will be able to:

- Identify necessary steps to implement and use an IPM plan.
- List and explain the differences among pest control methods.
- List the types of common pests that cause damage to plant materials.
- Explain the life cycles of weeds and identify characteristics that ensure their survival.
- Explain the life cycles of insects and why this knowledge is important to their control.

- Identify common causes of plant diseases and their methods of control.
- Identify and explain the basic differences among types of pesticides.
- Identify the different pesticide formulations and explain their application.
- Read and understand the components of a pesticide label.
- Understand the processes used to apply pesticides safely and effectively.
- Apply procedures used to store and apply pesticides safely.

Key Terms ⤴

action threshold
acute toxicity
bacteria
beneficials
biological control
broadcast
chemical control
chronic toxicity
complete metamorphosis
contact insecticide
cultural control
drench
EPA registration number
exclusion control
foliar spray
fungicide
fungus
general-use pesticide
herbicide
host
incomplete metamorphosis

insect
insecticide
integrated pest management (IPM)
invertebrate
LC_{50}
LD_{50}
lethal dose
mechanical control
metamorphosis
miticide
mode of action
molluscicide
nonselective herbicide
nymph
pathogen
pest
pest eradication
pest prevention
pest suppression
pesticide

pesticide formulation
pesticide label
physical control
phytotoxicity
plant disease
postemergent herbicide
preemergent herbicide
restricted entry interval (REI)
restricted-use pesticide
rodenticide
sanitation control
scouting
selective herbicide
signal word
surfactant
systemic insecticide
threshold level
toxicity
vertebrate
virus
weed

Introduction

To develop and maintain high-quality landscapes, you will need to be able to properly identify and control pests. Pest management should be considered in all stages of landscape design, installation, and maintenance. You will often need to consider your client's wishes when managing pests. Some may expect pristine high-quality turf that requires frequent application of chemicals, while others may request that only organic pest management tactics be used. This chapter discusses how to prevent, identify, and control common pests.

Using IPM

Integrated pest management (IPM) is a combination of pest management techniques designed to minimize the use of hazardous materials to control pests. In the green industry, a *pest* is any organism that can cause damage or harm to plants and their growth, **Figure 22-1**. The pests that affect plants in landscapes, nurseries, and greenhouses include insects, vertebrate animals, weeds, parasites, and diseases.

Pest management strategies are based on a combination of factors, such as the size of the area, degree of the problem, life cycle stage of the pests, type of plants affected, and the time of year. Once it is determined that a problem exists, the following basic steps can be used to implement an IPM program:

1. Correctly identify the pest and plant.
2. Monitor the pest to be managed.
3. Determine if pest population has reached threshold level.
4. Consider the management choices.
5. Implement the tactic or tactics that control the pest with the least harm to the environment.
6. Record and evaluate the results.

Pro Tip

A well-planned IPM program will not only keep plants healthy, it will also reduce the amount of chemicals needed and the cost of effective pest control.

Lertwit Sasipreyajun/Shutterstock.com

JKI14/Shutterstock.com

Figure 22-1. Powdery mildew is a common problem for roses. It is easily diagnosed by the powderlike substance on the leaves and the unhealthy blooms.

Identifying the Plant and Pest

The first step of pest control is to properly identify the pest and plant. The plant will often offer clues to the problem because some plants are more prone to certain pests, such as whiteflies on poinsettias. Proper identification of the plant can narrow a large list of pests. If the pest is not identified correctly, the control measures used to treat it 'will be ineffective and may even cause damage. It is also very important that the person evaluating a situation can distinguish between a healthy plant and a plant that is unwell. Many plants have unique colors, shapes, and patterns that may appear as pest damage or plant disorders to the untrained eye, **Figure 22-2**.

Monitoring the Pest

Growers and workers that visit jobsites regularly should always be alert to potential problems because identifying the issue early makes it much easier to control. The regular checking of landscapes, greenhouses, nursery fields, or other areas for pests while they are manageable is referred to as *scouting*, **Figure 22-3**. The method used to scout varies by pest and the type of area being monitored. Pest damage may easily be seen by simply walking through the landscape. Weeds in the lawn and damage from vertebrates are visible and easily spotted. Diseases and insect damage often require a closer inspection of individual plants. Insect traps and sticky cards are commonly used by greenhouse and nursery producers to collect small samples of insects. The insect population is then evaluated to determine control measures.

Landscapes are usually evaluated through visual observations; whereas sweep nets and weed counts are commonly used in fields and insect traps are most common in greenhouses.

Threshold Levels

A *threshold level* is the point at which the pest reaches an unacceptable level and corrective action must be taken. Some pests have a very low or high threshold level; whereas others have no threshold. Some pests, for example, have potential to cause extensive damage in the future if they are allowed

Goodheart-Willcox Publisher

Figure 22-2. Cultivars have unique colors and variegation patterns. It is extremely important to know what a healthy plant looks like to ensure a proper diagnosis is made. If a plant does not appear healthy, the plant and environment will provide clues as to the disease or pest.

sezer66/Shutterstock.com

GSPhotography/Shutterstock.com

Figure 22-3. Scouting for pests is an extremely important step in the pest control process. Greenhouses require consistent monitoring to prevent pests from reaching threshold levels. Workers should be trained to observe their surroundings and identify potential pests when performing routine maintenance tasks, such as watering or trimming.

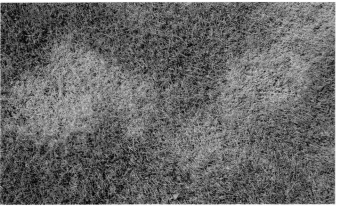

SingjaiStock/Shutterstock.com

Figure 22-4. Threshold levels indicate the level of pest damage that is acceptable. For example, a small amount of turf damage may be tolerated by a homeowner but would be unacceptable on a professional golf course. A well-developed pest management plan will indicate threshold levels for specific pests and plants.

victoras/Shutterstock.com

ND700/Shutterstock.com

Figure 22-5. Hand weeding is labor intensive and provides immediate results. Herbicide application requires less labor but may take an extended period of time before the results are visible. Postemergent herbicides will quickly kill the weed but the weed will still be visible as it dies. The client will often follow the professional's advice as to which control measure is most appropriate.

grow, mate, and breed, **Figure 22-4**. The population may increase greatly the following season as the larvae hatch and repeat the cycle. The threshold level is determined by the potential damage a pest may cause, be it high or low, and sometimes by the owner's tolerance. A few sprigs of clover, for example, on a residential lawn may not bother the homeowner but the same clover on a professional sports field or putting green would not be tolerated. Threshold levels may also be referred to as *action thresholds*.

IPM Control Methods

At this point, the groundskeeper, landscaper, or greenskeeper must determine which IPM control methods and methods of application would be the most appropriate, **Figure 22-5**. When possible, the least intrusive methods should be tried before moving on to the more toxic or potentially harmful methods. Types of IPM controls include:

- Cultural.
- Sanitation.
- Exclusion.
- Physical and mechanical.
- Biological.
- Chemical.

Prevention, Suppression, and Eradication

Each method of control is designed to prevent, suppress, or eradicate the pest. *Pest prevention*

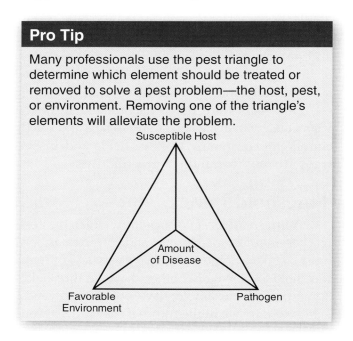

Pro Tip

Many professionals use the pest triangle to determine which element should be treated or removed to solve a pest problem—the host, pest, or environment. Removing one of the triangle's elements will alleviate the problem.

Susceptible Host

Amount
of Disease

Favorable
Environment

Pathogen

Robert Blouin/Shutterstock.com

Figure 22-6. Select species of crepe myrtle are prone to various diseases, such as powdery mildew. Diseases can be prevented in part by planting disease-resistant cultivars.

involves any action that is taken to prevent the pest damage from occurring. Planting resistant cultivars, for example, is a prevention method, **Figure 22-6**. Using preemergent herbicides is also a pest prevention technique. The use of prevention techniques will often reduce future needs for pesticides and herbicides. Using a preemergent herbicide, for example, to control crabgrass in the lawn will alleviate the need for additional applications of herbicide to control crabgrass once the lawn emerges.

Pest suppression involves treating existing pest problems to keep insect damage below a threshold. Plant producers often take a suppression approach knowing that there will be some insects on their plants; however, they closely monitor and scout to ensure damage levels do not exceed their thresholds. *Pest eradication* is the complete elimination of the pest. Repeatedly setting mole traps in a lawn, for example, is an eradication method, **Figure 22-7**.

Cultural Controls

Implementing an effective IPM regime begins long before signs of pests are found. *Cultural controls* begin with using best practices to install and manage a landscape. Proper soil preparation, for example, will ensure plants are receiving sufficient nutrition and the roots can easily grow. Other cultural controls include the following:

- Performing a site assessment and establishing a plan to prepare the site.
- Installing plants that are resistant to diseases and best adapted culturally to the environment.
- Installing plants at the correct depth and using supports when necessary.

A   Floki/Shutterstock.com

B   9Gawin/Shutterstock.com

Figure 22-7. A—Whiteflies are not uncommon in greenhouses and are almost impossible to completely eradicate. Growers keep them below threshold levels using suppression measures. B—Termites can cause extreme damage to wooden structures and many homeowners have preventive measures in place. If termites are found on a site, they *must* be eradicated and preventive measures should be set in place.

Kratka Photography/Shutterstock.com

Figure 22-8. An infected or dying tree is removed for safety reasons and to prevent the disease from spreading.

littlenySTOCK/Shutterstock.com

Figure 22-9. Sanitation can be as simple as picking up trash and debris. Not only is trash unsightly, it offers additional habitats for pests.

- Using the correct spacing to ensure the plants are in optimal conditions with sufficient air and light. Plants that are crowded are more prone to pests.
- Establishing and following a maintenance time line.
- Removing dead, diseased, and damaged portions of the plant, **Figure 22-8**.
- Pruning as needed at the proper time and locations to control growth.
- Removing or moving plants that are doing poorly in their current location.
- Watering and fertilizing on schedule to ensure proper nutrients and sufficient water are being provided.
- Dethatching and aerating turfgrass on schedule.
- Mowing turfgrass at proper heights and applying appropriate amounts of water and fertilizer.
- Cleaning, sharpening, and storing tools and equipment properly.

Sanitation Controls

Effective *sanitation controls* require the landscape or production area to be kept as clean as possible. Keeping the growing and equipment areas neat and clean will minimize the attraction of pests. Cleaning all tools and equipment between locations will reduce the chance of transmitting pests from one area to another. Mowing with sharp mower blades, removing debris, and pruning damaged or diseased tissue are also sanitation controls, **Figure 22-9**.

Pro Tip

Sanitizing your work shoes between locations or before entering a nursery or greenhouse will minimize the odds of transmitting pests between areas.

Exclusion Controls

Exclusion control is the use of screens, traps, and other barriers to prevent pests from causing damage. Greenhouse vents are commonly covered with insect screens to prevent insects from entering the growing area. Fences and other barriers are used to help protect areas from vertebrate pests, such as geese or deer, **Figure 22-10**.

Physical and Mechanical Controls

Physical and *mechanical controls* directly remove or kill pests and may also prevent pests from reaching the host plant with barriers or traps. (A *host* is a live organism on which the pest is living.) Physical and mechanical control methods include hand picking, spraying with water, and cutting to remove damaged tissue. Hand pulling, using hoes, and applying flame torches (in limited areas)

Artazum/Shutterstock.com

Figure 22-10. A home garden can be protected from deer and other animals with a secure fence. This type of measure would be impractical and less effective around a large nursery.

Simon Kadula/Shutterstock.com

Gabor Tinz/Shutterstock.com

can be used to remove weeds, **Figure 22-11**. Installing barriers, such as metal or plastic edging, can prevent the unwanted spread of many plants and laying landscape fabric before planting will help minimize weeds.

Biological Controls

Biological control uses living microorganisms or natural predators to control pests. These natural predators are referred to as *beneficials*. Two commonly used beneficials are the lady beetle or ladybug that feeds on destructive aphids and mites, and the praying mantis, which feeds on several common insect pests. Parasitic wasps are also popular beneficials as they feed on caterpillars, moths, and beetles in the egg, larva, and pupa stage. See **Figure 22-12**.

Beneficials can be purchased from greenhouse and pest management supply companies. Beneficials are often introduced on a weekly basis over several weeks to control the insect. The exact regimen depends on the quantity and type of pest and whether it is an indoor or outdoor environment.

Figure 22-11. A well-developed pest management plan uses different methods to control pests. The pest number and threshold levels will determine the appropriate course of action.

thechatat/Shutterstock.com   Visual Intermezzo/Shutterstock.com

Figure 22-12. Beneficial insects can be very helpful in landscapes and production settings. Beneficial insects feed on plant-damaging insects, such as aphids and whiteflies, and do not cause damage to plants.

Chemical Controls

Depending on the pest, *chemical control* is often the last technique used when following an IPM regimen. Chemical controls are an important part of pest management and may sometimes be the only option to treat an area. Pesticides are divided into categories that are each specific to a particular problem or pest. A *pesticide* is a chemical used to control insects, weeds, fungi, rodents, and other pests, **Figure 22-13**. It is recommended to begin treatment with the least toxic control and progress to more toxic chemicals if necessary.

Types of Pests

As stated earlier, a *pest* is any organism that damages plants or impedes their development. The damages caused by live pests are referred to as a *biotic* disorders. Some pests attract others, which may make the issue more difficult to treat. Keep in mind that plant damage may be caused by other agents, such as lawn trimmers or excessive fertilization. Other nonliving agents that cause plant damage include lawn mowers, lightning, herbicides, road salt or deicer, and drought, **Figure 22-14**. The damages caused by these nonliving agents is referred to as *abiotic* disorders. The illustrated glossary at the end of the chapter includes images of common landscape pests. The pests that affect plants include weeds, birds, rodents, mammals, insects, snails, nematodes, and plant pathogens (organisms that cause disease in plants).

Dziurek/Shutterstock.com

Figure 22-13. Chemicals should be applied *only* after the plant and pest are properly identified. The pesticide label includes the names of the pests and plants for which the pesticide is approved. It is illegal to use the pesticide in a manner that does not follow the label's restrictions.

Todd Lipsky/Shutterstock.com

Figure 22-14. High winds will often cause damage to established shade trees. Depending on the location of the damage, often little can be done besides complete removal.

Weeds

A *weed* may be defined as any unwanted plant, **Figure 22-15**. If not controlled, weeds can thrive in all areas of the landscape, including gardens, planting beds, sidewalk cracks, parking lot islands, and the small spaces between concrete slabs or pavers on driveways. Weeds are undesirable because they compete with desirable plants for nutrition and water and will often take over areas and crowd out landscaping plants, such as turfgrass. They are also typically unattractive and often serve as allergens that affect the skin or sinuses of many people. The labor and material costs involved in their removal also increases the costs of plant production and landscape maintenance.

Weed Characteristics

Weeds are aggressive plants that can thrive in most environmental cultures due to characteristics that ensure their survival. Common weed characteristics include the following:

- The ability to thrive in a wide array of cultures.
- A very rapid growth and reproduction rate.
- The ability to withstand drought.
- Staggered germination times.
- Long-term survival of buried seeds.
- Seed dormancy and dispersal mechanisms.
- Ability to propagate sexually and asexually.

Weed Classifications

Weeds are classified in the same manner as other plants. A weed may be a cool-season or warm-season plant and it may have an annual, biennial, or perennial life cycle. *Cool-season weeds* grow best when the average daily temperature is below 70°F and *warm-season weeds* grow best when the average daily temperature is above 70°F. The growth habit (life cycle and season) of the weed will help determine the method of control that will be most effective. Weeds may also be classified by their leaf types, such as broadleaf, grass, or sedge, **Figure 22-16**. As with any pest, it is important to identify the weed before applying any type of control to ensure the control will be effective.

Christopher D. Hart

Figure 22-15. Weeds have a detrimental effect on landscape and production plant growth. Weeds compete for air, sunlight, water, nutrients, and space. Preventing and removing weeds will help maximize plant growth.

Uriy/Shutterstock.com

sianc/Shutterstock.com

arousa/Shutterstock.com

Figure 22-16. As with any pest, weeds must be accurately identified for effective control. A combination of selective preemergent and postemergent herbicides can be used to kill weeds without causing damage to the lawn or planting bed.

Invertebrate Pests

Invertebrates are animals lacking a backbone, such as lady bugs and aphids. *Insects* are small invertebrates with an exoskeleton, three distinct body regions, and three pairs of legs, **Figure 22-17**. Most insects also have wings.

- The *exoskeleton* is a hardened external skeleton.
- The three body regions are the head, thorax, and abdomen.
- The *antenna*, *eyes*, and *mouthparts* are attached to the head.
- The *thorax* is the middle body segment to which the legs and wings are attached.
- The *abdomen* contains the digestive system and other organs.

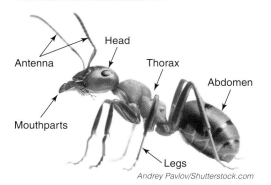

Andrey Pavlov/Shutterstock.com

Figure 22-17. True insects have three distinct body regions: head, thorax, and abdomen.

Growth and Development

Understanding an insect's growth and development is essential to successful control because different controls are more effective during each stage of an insect's life cycle. For example, the larval stage of a Japanese beetle is a grub. Most grubs are easily controlled with a granular insecticide that would be ineffective as a control for the adult beetles.

The changes an insect undergoes through its life cycle are referred to as *metamorphosis*, **Figure 22-18**. Metamorphosis may be complete or incomplete. In *complete metamorphosis*, an insect goes through four stages: egg, larva, pupa, and adult. In *incomplete metamorphosis*, an insect goes through three stages: egg, nymph, and adult. (A *nymph* is a juvenile insect.)

The caterpillar attaches itself to a plant stem

The chrysalis (pupa) forms

The egg hatches into a small caterpillar

The caterpillar completes the cycle as a butterfly

An adult female lays eggs that are fertilized by the male

Kim Howell/Shutterstock.com

Figure 22-18. Insects damage plants differently during different growth stages. Beneficial insects, such as butterflies, also undergo complete metamorphosis.

Thinking Green

Controlling Snails and Slugs

Snails and slugs are members of a large group of animals known as *mollusks*. The most obvious difference between the animals is a large shell. Snails have shells and slugs do not. These small pests feed on plant foliage, leaving holes on larger leaves and completely consuming leaves of seedlings. Many homeowners combat these pests effectively using organic controls instead of using chemical molluscicides.

- Sprinkling diatomaceous earth around the affected plants. Diatomaceous earth is made from fossilized remains of diatoms, which have a broken glass-like texture that slugs and snails avoid. Diatomaceous earth must be applied regularly as it is ineffective once wet.
- Spreading crushed egg shells around the plants. The abrasive texture deters snails. The egg shells also provide nutrients, such as calcium, to plants as they decompose.
- Creating mulch with seaweed and mixing it in the soil around the plants. The snails and slugs are deterred by the iodine smell. Seaweed also adds nutrients to the soil. These pests are also deterred by the smell of mint, rosemary, and thyme. These edible plants can be planted near the problem areas and provide fresh herbs as well.
- Picking them off by hand in the cover of night when the pests are more active. Use a flashlight to help search under leaves and around plants for successful picking.

Consider This

1. How effective are organic controls compared to chemical controls?
2. Do snails and slugs have a useful purpose in the landscape?
3. How many other types of effective organic controls can you find? Research the topic and create a small poster explaining the methods and their effectiveness.

Ivan Marjanovic/Shutterstock.com   *Starover Sibiriak/Shutterstock.com*

Mona Makela/Shutterstock.com

Ngukiaw/Shutterstock.com

Pest Damage

Insects affect plants in different ways during each stage of plant growth and during each life cycle stage of the insect. Insects may kill or deform plants by laying eggs in plant tissues, feeding on roots, leaves, and stems, tunneling or boring into stems, sucking sap, or transmitting disease. The most visible type of damage is caused by the feeding behavior of pests. Depending on their mouthparts, pests bite, crush, bore, chew, pierce, suck or rasp, siphon, or sponge on plant leaves, stems, flowers, fruit, and roots.

- *Chewing insects* cause damage by biting, chewing, crushing, or grinding plant parts. Chewing insects include beetles, cutworms, caterpillars, snails, slugs, and grasshoppers.
- *Piercing and sucking insects* cause damage by puncturing the plant and sucking sap from the leaves and stem. Common piercing and sucking insects include aphids, mealy bugs, mites, scale, and whiteflies. Damage from piercing and sucking insects includes yellow spotted leaves, stunted growth, and visually unappealing leaves.
- *Rasping and sucking insects* rasp or break the leaf surface and suck sap. Thrips are common rasping and sucking insects. Thrips' damage is a speckled white pattern on plant leaves. See **Figure 22-19**.
- *Siphoning insects* dip a coiled tube into a liquid food, such as nectar, and draw (or siphon) the liquid. Siphoning insects, such as butterflies, do little or no damage to plants.
- *Sponging insects* have two sponge-like structures that collect liquid food and move it into a food canal. Sponging insects, such as houseflies, may easily transmit diseases from other sources.

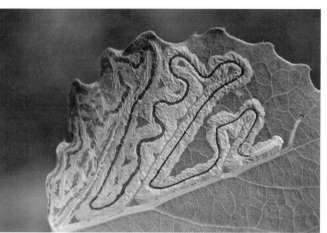

Belozorova Elena/Shutterstock.com

Figure 22-19. Insects cause damage in several ways. Leaf miners, for example, damage plants by boring tunnels between the layers of the leaf.

Plant Diseases

Plant diseases are disorders caused by infectious pathogens. A *pathogen* is an organism or agent, such as a virus, fungus, or bacteria, that causes a disease. Once plants become infected, there is little that can be done to rid the plant of the malady. Infected plants should be removed and discarded carefully to prevent the disease from spreading. Spraying uninfected plants with the appropriate pesticide will help prevent the disease from spreading.

Viruses

Viruses are considered nonliving organisms for several reasons, including their lack of cells and the inability to reproduce on their own. The name of the virus typically indicates the plant and symptoms in which the virus was first discovered. Although a virus is often named for a specific plant, it does not mean that only that specific plant is susceptible to that virus. Tobacco mosaic virus (TMV), for example, attacks members of the Solanaceae family, including tomatoes, peppers, poinsettias, and tobacco, **Figure 22-20**. Plants infected with a virus function improperly and exhibit symptoms such as leaf curling, streaking, mottling, or ring-shaped spots. Viruses enter greenhouses and landscapes in many ways, including infected propagation material, on workers' clothes or shoes, and insects.

Fungi

A *fungus* is a specialized organism that attaches itself to a host and decomposes the host as it absorbs nutrients from it, which eventually results in plant rot and death of the plant, **Figure 22-21**. Most plant diseases are caused by fungi. Most fungi prefer dark, moist locations and are likely to grow in areas that are overwatered and/or stay damp due to poor airflow. Common fungal diseases include damping off, rust, and powdery mildew.

Bacteria

Bacteria are single-celled, nonaggressive microorganisms that cannot penetrate plant foliage or stems. Bacteria infect plants through wounds and openings caused by pruning, cuts, and cracks. They may also enter through natural openings or be injected by insects. The most obvious symptoms occur on the infected plant's foliage, which may defoliate prematurely. There is no cure for bacterial diseases, so the diseased plants may be pruned to remove the infected areas or removed from the landscape. The blades of the cutting tool must be sterilized with a bleach/water mixture (1:9) or another disinfectant between cuts to prevent spreading. Overgrowth, leafspots, wilts, and galls are common symptoms of bacterial diseases, **Figure 22-22**.

Plant Pathology/Shutterstock.com

Figure 22-20. Tobacco mosaic virus (TMV) affects a wide range of plants, most of which are in the Solanaceae family. TMV can be identified by the yellow mosaic pattern it causes on the leaves.

Lukas Zajicek/Shutterstock.com

Figure 22-22. Galls are abnormal growths that appear on many parts of trees. Galls are caused by a wide variety of pests, including insects and mites. Galls result after a pest infects the plant and causes it to produce the extra growth.

Grandpa/Shutterstock.com

Tunatura/Shutterstock.com

Manfred Ruckszio/Shutterstock.com

Figure 22-21. Certain species of roses are particularly susceptible to fungal diseases, such as powdery mildew and black spot. Fungal diseases can be prevented through the use of fungicides or by planting resistant cultivars.

A — Davydele/Shutterstock.com
B — Christian Delbert/Shutterstock.com
C — Randy Bjorklund/Shutterstock.com
D — Taras-studio/Shutterstock.com

Figure 22-23. Vertebrates, such as voles and moles, are very destructive pests. A/B—Voles are plant eaters and feed on plant roots. Damage is clearly evident as the damaged plants die. C/D—Moles feed on earthworms, grubs, and other insects in the soil. Moles are tunneling creatures that make underground pathways that make the lawn feel spongy and leave holes with mounds of soil across the lawn.

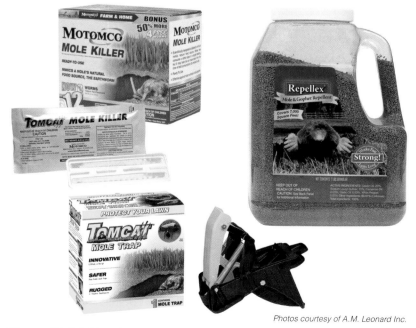

Photos courtesy of A.M. Leonard Inc.

Figure 22-24. Vertebrates are commonly controlled with baits and traps. Check local regulations regarding the control of vertebrates before purchasing and applying controls.

Vertebrates

Vertebrates are living organisms with a backbone, such as birds, deer, and rodents. Vertebrate pests most often cause physical damage to plants. Voles, for example, burrow underground and cause damage to plant roots and lawns, **Figure 22-23**. The root system may be reduced to the point that it is unable to take up water and nutrients and the plant may soon die.

As with other pests, the type of vertebrate causing damage should be identified before control measures are taken. The primary defense against vertebrate pests is erecting barriers, such as netting or fencing, and installing traps to capture the pests, **Figure 22-24**.

Types of Pesticides

Pesticides are designed to target specific types of pests and are identified as such. Pesticide categories include herbicides, insecticides, fungicides, molluscicides, and rodenticides.

Herbicides

Herbicides control and eliminate weeds. All herbicides are either selective or nonselective and either preemergent or postemergent. *Selective herbicides* will only target certain weeds and will not harm the surrounding plants or turfgrass. *Nonselective herbicides* will kill any plant the chemical contacts. *Preemergent herbicides* target weeds before they germinate. They are typically applied at the beginning of the weed's growing season. Many preemergent herbicides include fertilizer that adds nutrients to plants while preventing weeds. *Postemergent herbicides* target weeds after they have germinated.

Insecticides

Insecticides are toxic chemicals used to control harmful insects. Insecticides kill pests in different ways. A *contact insecticide*, for example, poisons and kills pests when the insecticide comes in contact with the pest's body.

STEM Connection

Pesticides and Beneficials: The Wilsonville Bee Kill

In 2013, a large bee kill occurred in Wilsonville, Oregon, an area in which many horticultural crops are cultivated. A maintenance crew sprayed a product containing dinotefuran on 55 blooming linden trees in a shopping center parking lot to control aphids. As bees are the primary pollinators for linden trees, many were collecting pollen from the new blooms. The dinotefuran killed more than 50,000 bumblebees. Such a loss can represent hundreds of wild bee colonies.

Dinotefuran is classified as a neonicotinoid, which is a systemic chemical absorbed into the plant tissues. These long-lasting chemicals can make the plants themselves toxic to insects. There was a temporary ban of the chemical's use in the United States, but it is currently labeled for use in landscape settings. The chemical is banned in Europe.

PavlovaSvetlana/Shutterstock.com

Consider This

1. What other pesticides are harmful to beneficial insects, such as the bumblebee?
2. Are there any controls in place to prevent another large bee kill?
3. Are the pesticides, such as neonicotinoids, found in honey or other foods?
4. Which flowers, fruits, and other food crops depend on bees for pollination?
5. What examples of environmental damage can you find to justify the ban of a specific chemical used in weed or pest control?

Contact insecticides are effective for pests that are easily seen or when quick removal is desired. Contact pesticides will also kill insects when they eat plant surfaces that are coated with the insecticide. These pesticides are most effective for insects with chewing mouthparts. Poisons that are ingested are referred to as *stomach poisons*.

Insecticides are also designed to work systemically through the plant. *Systemic insecticides* enter the plant's stems, leaves, and roots and are ingested when insects feed on the plant. Systemic insecticides are effective for insects with piercing/sucking mouthparts. Systemic pesticides are not immediately effective because the active ingredient must first be taken in by the plant. Systemic insecticides may be applied as a drench or foliar spray.

Fungicides

Fungicides are crop-specific insecticides designed to prevent fungi from spreading. Fungicides are used preventively rather than to control an actively growing fungus. Fungicides are typically applied as a drench or foliar spray.

Miticides

Miticides eliminate the tiny spider-like organisms referred to as mites, **Figure 22-25**. Miticides kill the insect by contact or through ingestion. Miticides are commonly applied as a foliar spray.

Molluscicides

Molluscicides control mollusks, such as snails and slugs, which feed on leaves, **Figure 22-26**. Molluscicides are typically granular and spread around the plants. The mollusks feed on the poison granules.

ALEX2016/Shutterstock.com

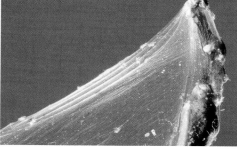

Aptyp_koK/Shutterstock.com

Yuangeng Zhang/Shutterstock.com

Figure 22-25. There are many types of mites that cause plant damage. Insecticides may not effectively control mites because they are anatomically different than insects. Use miticides labeled for the specific mite and plants for effective control.

Kletr/Shutterstock.com *Starover Sibriak/Shutterstock.com* *Artush/Shutterstock.com*

Figure 22-26. Snails and slugs are nocturnal mollusks that feed on leaves. In addition to the holes in plant leaves, snails and slugs often leave a silvery trail.

Rodenticides

Rodenticides are designed to eliminate rodents ranging from moles and mice to gophers and woodchucks. Rodenticides are used in granular or block-shaped pieces that are most commonly used as bait in a trap. Rodenticides often include a desiccant that removes all the liquid from the rodent's body, leaving a dry carcass that will not rot.

Chemical Structure and Toxicity

Pesticides are grouped according to their chemical structure, which determines their toxicity to pests and the time they remain in the environment, **Figure 22-27**. Different chemicals within each group can be used to control different types of pests.

- *Organophosphates* are one of the most toxic forms of synthetic pesticides. They typically only last for a few months in the environment.
- *Organochlorines* are an older group of pesticides that endure for an extended time in the environment. Organochlorines may cause acute toxicity in humans and wildlife due to their prolonged life and potential buildup in their bodies over time.
- *Carbamates* are one of the safest forms of synthetic organic pesticides. Carbamates break down quickly in the environment.
- *Prytethroids* are a relatively new class of pesticides that are low in toxicity to mammals and birds. Prytethroids bind tightly to soil and organic matter, which reduces damage due to leaching.
- *Botanicals* are pesticides derived from plants or plant parts, **Figure 22-28**
- *Insecticidal soaps* use potassium-based fatty acids to control soft-bodied insects. The soaps damage the insect's cell membranes on contact with the pest.

Thananya Apiromyanon/Shutterstock.com

Figure 22-27. The formulation of chlorinated hydrocarbons causes them to last longer than other pesticide formulations and take more time to break down in the environment.

Santhosh Varghese/Shutterstock.com *Jitlada Panwiset/Shutterstock.com*

Figure 22-28. Neem oil is a botanical pesticide derived from the seeds of the neem tree (*Azadirachta indica*). The oil is used to control a wide variety of insects.

Pesticide Formulations

A *pesticide formulation* is the format of the mixture of ingredients used to create the pesticide. Most pesticides are available in one or more of the following formulations:

- Liquid.
- Dust.
- Granules.
- Wettable Powder.
- Fumigant.
- Aerosol.

Liquid Pesticides

Liquid pesticides are concentrated formulations that must be diluted with water before application. Liquid pesticides are mixed with detergents, surfactants, and other chemicals. *Surfactants* are surface-active ingredients that are added to a pesticide to help the pesticide adhere to the targeted area. They are not abrasive to nozzles but can degrade rubber hoses and gaskets. They are more dangerous to handle then other formulations because they are absorbed quickly through the skin. They also are more likely to cause plant injury, **Figure 22-29**.

Pesticide Dusts

Dusts are ready-to-apply dry formulations made with very fine particles. The active ingredient is typically mixed with a talc-like powder but some formulations are made purely of the active chemical. Dusts typically have a signal word of caution because they are easily carried by wind and may easily contact the applicator's skin, eyes, nose, and mouth, **Figure 22-30**.

A *Photomontage/Shutterstock.com*

B *Fotokostic/Shutterstock.com*

C *Gavin Baker Photography/Shutterstock.com*

Figure 22-29. Liquid pesticides are applied in a variety of ways. New technology is used to program drones to spray plants (A), thus limiting the exposure for employees. Tractors (B) can also be programmed to spray specific amounts in areas that need more or less treatment. Aerial application (C) is used to treat fields efficiently. Planes are especially useful when the ground is too wet for tractors.

Photo courtesy of A.M. Leonard Inc.

Figure 22-30. Pesticide dusts are applied dry with a duster. Dusts typically have very low toxicity levels because they drift easily, which makes it difficult to contain application to a specific area.

Pesticide Granules

Granules are dry pellets commonly applied to the soil with spreading equipment. Granular pellets are individual pieces with enough weight to mitigate drift. Most seeding and fertilizer spreading equipment can be used to apply granules. Water-soluble granules are mixed with water and applied as a liquid, **Figure 22-31**.

Wettable Powders

Wettable powders (WP) are mixed with water and applied as liquids. The powder particles are suspended in the liquid and do not dissolve. Phytotoxicity is generally low and the pesticides are somewhat safer to handle than liquid concentrates. *Phytotoxicity* is a poisonous effect by a substance, such as a pesticide, on plant growth. However, wettable powders are abrasive and cause extensive wear on pumps and nozzles.

Aerosol Sprays

Aerosol sprays are pesticides in gas form under pressure. Aerosols are convenient for small areas but too expensive and impractical to use on larger areas. The chemical is premixed and ready to apply. Aerosol sprays do not require special spray equipment as the nozzle is built into the can. Due to the small treatment area and higher cost, aerosol sprays are typically marketed as homeowner products. Wasps and hornets are pests commonly treated with aerosol cans of pesticide that have an extended reach. The gas should only be used on still days or in protected areas because it is easily carried by a breeze.

LaMiaFotografia/Shutterstock.com

Fotokostic/Shutterstock.com

Figure 22-31. Granules are applied with the same type of spreader used to seed a lawn. The granules are heavier than dust formulations and do not drift.

Fumigants

Fumigants are also pesticides under low pressure in gas form but they are typically much more concentrated than aerosol formulations, **Figure 22-32**. Fumigants are used to treat large, enclosed areas, such as a greenhouse, but may also be used to treat soil. The sprayer creates very fine droplets that drift throughout the area to be treated. The entire contents of the can are pressurized and released or applied after the pesticide handler leaves the area. No one is allowed to enter the area until after the REI is reached.

Jaral Lertjamekorn/Shutterstock.com

Figure 22-32. Aerosol sprays are premixed and ready to use. These premixed sprays are more commonly used by homeowners to kill pests, such as wasps and ants.

Pesticide Labels

The *Federal Insecticide, Fungicide, and Rodenticide Act (FIFRA)* is a US federal law that regulates pesticides to protect applicators, consumers, and the environment. FIFRA mandates the language and standards used on chemical pesticide labels. A ***pesticide label*** is a lengthy document attached to the container that includes the information needed to apply the chemical safely and accurately. The Environmental Protection Agency (EPA) is responsible for interpreting labeling standards and ensuring that they are followed.

The pesticide label is considered a legal and binding agreement between the applicator and the manufacturer. When applying pesticides, it is important to understand that it is a violation of federal law to use the product in a manner that is inconsistent with the labeling.

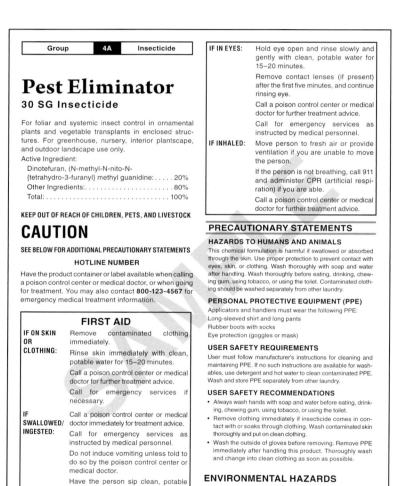

Goodheart-Willcox Publisher

Figure 22-33. The pesticide label contains all information needed to properly apply the chemical. It is imperative for the person mixing and applying a pesticide to carefully read and follow the label for safe and effective application.

Required Information

The EPA requires specific information to be included on the pesticide label attached to the chemical container. The manufacturer may also include information designed to market and promote the chemical. Information found on pesticide labels includes the following (**Figure 22-33**):

- Pesticide name.
- EPA registration number.
- Active ingredients.
- Signal words, **Figure 22-34**.
- Precautionary statements.
- Environmental hazards section.
- First-aid instructions.
- Storage and disposal instructions.

Pesticide Names

Pesticides may be referred to by a brand name, chemical name, or common name. The *brand name* is a name that is created by the chemical company to market the product. The *chemical name* is the scientific name that states the structure of the chemical's active ingredient. The *common name* is a shorter version of the chemical name. All chemicals with the same chemical or common name will have the same active ingredient. For example, RoundUp® is the brand name for the active ingredient glyphosate. Glyphosate is used as the common name and N-phosphonomethyl glycine is the chemical name.

Signal Word	Toxicity	Toxicity Category	LD$_{50}$	LC$_{50}$	Approximate Amount to Cause Fatal Harm
Danger	High	I	0 to 50 mg/kg	0 to 2000 ppm	A taste to a teaspoon
Warning	Moderate	II	50 to 500 mg/kg	2000 to 20,000 ppm	A teaspoon to a tablespoon
Caution	Low	III and IV	500 to 5000 mg/kg	Over 20,000 ppm	Over one ounce

Goodheart-Willcox Publisher

Figure 22-34. The signal word is used to indicate the toxicity of a chemical.

Generic Pesticides

Once a chemical manufacturer's patent expires, other manufacturers can legally manufacture the same product under a different name. These products are often referred to as generic because they do not use the original brand name. Although the product may be made by a different manufacturer and have a different brand name, the common name and chemical name remain the same. Generic pesticides are often less expensive than the original brand name pesticide.

EPA Registration Number

The *EPA registration number* is assigned to a pesticide after it has been reviewed and verified by the EPA. The number certifies the product has been reviewed and has minimal risk when the label's directions are followed. The EPA number does not indicate that the EPA supports the product or guarantees its effectiveness.

Active Ingredients and Mode of Action

The active ingredients are those that "perform the control." Multiple inactive ingredients may also be included in the formulation to preserve and help distribute the active ingredients. The *mode of action* indicates how the pesticide effectively controls or eliminates the pest. The mode of action is identified by a number and classification. For example, chemicals with a mode of action of 4a are classified as neonicotinoids. Neonicotinoids are a class of insecticides that damage pests by affecting a protein responsible for nerve action. It is important to use different modes of action when treating pests to ensure the pest does not develop resistance.

Safety First

Although some chemicals are more toxic than others, all chemicals should be treated in the same safe manner when they are being mixed and applied.

Toxicity

The *toxicity* of a pesticide is its ability to poison organisms. *Acute toxicity* is a measure of the pesticide's toxicity after a single exposure and *chronic toxicity* is its toxicity after repeated exposures over time. After each exposure, a small amount of the pesticide is stored in the organism's body and may build to a harmful or fatal level.

mark_vyz/Shutterstock.com

Photo courtesy of A.M. Leonard Inc.

Figure 22-35. Employers are responsible for providing the appropriate PPE for employees. They must also provide emergency hand and eyewashing stations in the event of pesticide exposure. All employees should be trained to respond to pesticide exposure.

TFoxFoto/Shutterstock.com

ND700/Shutterstock.com

Figure 22-36. The REI states how long individuals must remain out of a treated area. All areas that are sprayed must be clearly labeled to prevent persons from unknowingly entering the area.

Signal Words

The terms caution, warning, and danger are *signal words* used to indicate the potential threat level a chemical poses to human health. The term *caution* indicates the chemical poses minimal harm to human beings. The term *warning* indicates the chemical is dangerous and can have a negative impact on human beings. Chemicals identified with the word *danger* are the most toxic and can only be purchased by licensed applicators, **Figure 22-35**.

Lethal Dose and Lethal Concentration

A *lethal dose* is the amount of a toxin that will cause death to a human being. The letters LD and the number 50, written as LD_{50}, are used to indicate the lethal dose that kills 50% of the test population. LD_{50} values are expressed in mg of chemical per kg of body weight. The less of a chemical it takes to cause fatal harm, the more toxic the chemical. The lower the LD/LC values, the more toxic the chemical. LC_{50} stands for the lethal concentration of the chemical in the air. The LC_{50} is expressed in ppm. Toxicity levels may also be represented by toxicity categories I, II, III, or IV. Toxicity category I is the most toxic and toxicity category IV is virtually nontoxic.

First-Aid Instructions

The first-aid section on the label explains what actions should be taken if someone is poisoned by the pesticide. The first-aid protocol on a label is specific to the chemical contained and it is wise for the applicator to read the protocol before using the pesticide to be better prepared for an emergency. If someone has been poisoned, call 911 and a poison control center (the number may be on the label) and keep the label with you so you can answer questions from the operator(s).

Administer first aid as described on the label until medical help arrives. The label should be sent to the hospital with the victim to ensure the toxin is properly identified and treated. For most chemical contact, fresh water can be used to rinse exposed skin and eyes. Do not induce vomiting unless it is indicated as treatment on the label. See **Figure 22-36**.

Precautionary Statements

Precautionary statements state which type of personal protective equipment (PPE) must be worn when mixing and applying the chemical. The toxicity level and method of application will determine which type of PPE should be worn. Employers are required by law to supply workers applying pesticides with the proper PPE.

Restricted Entry Interval (REI)

The restricted entry interval (REI) will also be included on the pesticide label. The *restricted entry interval (REI)* is the amount of time that must pass before a person can enter an area after it has been treated with the pesticide. For example, if a greenhouse grower sprays a chemical with an REI of 12 hours, workers must wait 12 hours after the pesticide application was completed before entering the work area without wearing proper PPE. A sign indicating the restrictions must be posted on any area under an REI, **Figure 22-37**.

Arcady/Shutterstock.com; Goodheart-Willcox Publisher

Figure 22-37. A pesticide applicator license indicates that the applicator has been trained to ensure he or she can safely apply chemicals. Each state has specific requirements for obtaining an applicator's license.

Safety First

Signs stating that an area has been treated with a pesticide must be in a language understood by most people in the area. A sign written in English and Spanish, for example, is appropriate for many areas of the United States.

Pesticide Application

The laws and regulations concerning the use and application of pesticides are in place to protect people, wildlife, bodies of water, and the air around us. These regulations are not optional and must be followed by those working with, selling, purchasing, and applying pesticides. The national standards established by the EPA and USDA permit states to create and provide pesticide applicator certification and training programs.

Licenses and Certifications

Pesticides are listed as either restricted-use or general-use. *Restricted-use pesticides* have potential to cause extensive damage if used improperly and therefore require special licensing to purchase and apply. Restricted-use pesticides may be applied *only* by trained and certified applicators. Certified applicators must undergo training and pass state exams to earn their certification. Certified applicators must also renew their certification periodically through education and/or testing. *General-use pesticides* are those available to the public. The instructions for use on the label of general-use pesticides are the extent of legal restrictions for their application. Individual states may also require licensing to purchase general-use pesticides, **Figure 22-38**.

NinaMalyna/Shutterstock.com   *ZoranOrcik/Shutterstock.com*   *Goodheart-Willcox Publisher*

Figure 22-38. Foliar application, broadcasting, and drenching are three common methods of pesticide application. It is imperative for the applicator to read the label to ensure the pesticide is mixed correctly and the proper application method is used. Select insecticides can be applied as a foliar spray or a drench, depending on the pest and the concentration.

Christopher D. Hart

Figure 22-39. The most dangerous time when working with chemicals is when the applicator is mixing the formulation because the chemical is in its most concentrated form. Some pesticides have different PPE requirements for mixers and applicators—*always* read the label to ensure the proper PPE is being worn.

Photo courtesy of A.M. Leonard Inc.

Figure 22-40. Spill kits should be readily available when mixing chemicals in the shop or on-site. All employees should know the location of the kit and how to use it.

Application Methods

The form of the pesticide and the area being treated often determine how the pesticide is applied. A *foliar spray* is used to apply the pesticide to the leaves of the plants. When a pesticide is applied to the soil and absorbed by the plant, it is referred to as a *drench*. Pesticides that are *broadcast* are spread uniformly over the area to be treated. Granule pesticides are typically broadcast. See **Figure 22-39**.

Mixing Pesticides

Many pesticides are not designed for immediate application. Most liquid pesticides, for example, are shipped in concentrated form and require the addition of water before application. The person mixing a pesticide *must* wear the proper PPE to ensure their safety, **Figure 22-40**. It is also imperative for the mixer to read the directions on the label *before* beginning to prepare the pesticide to ensure they understand the mixing procedure and are aware of the hazards and first-aid protocol. Although there are differences in pesticide ingredients and mixing procedures, all personnel should use the following practices and safety measures when mixing pesticides.

- Wear the appropriate PPE. This may include long pants, long-sleeved shirt, rubber gloves, respirator, goggles, and protective shoes.
- Do not eat or drink when mixing pesticides.
- Mixing is considered dangerous because the pesticide is in its most concentrated form.

- Keep dedicated mixing equipment for pesticides. Mixing equipment, such as spoons, measuring cups, and containers, should clearly be labeled to prevent them from being used for any other purpose.
- Dedicate a sprayer to herbicides and another to pesticides. Sprayer damage may occur if the sprayer is not cleaned thoroughly between use of herbicides and other pesticide types.
- Mix in a well-ventilated area or outdoors if possible.
- Pour the chemical into the water. This minimizes the possibility of the concentrate splashing the mixer in the face.
- Mix the chemical only at the recommended rate. Increasing the rate will *not* proportionally increase the effectiveness of the chemical.
- Mix only enough chemical for the job at hand.
- If a spill occurs, follow the manufacturer's instructions and clean the area immediately. Control the spill, contain the spill to a specific area, and dispose of the chemical according to the manufacturer's instructions, **Figure 22-41**.

Photo courtesy of A.M. Leonard Inc.

Figure 22-41. Pesticides must be stored in their original container inside a locked cabinet dedicated to pesticides. All chemicals should be stored safely and securely and always out of the reach of children.

Assessing the Area

The surrounding environment and weather should be assessed before the pesticide is applied to ensure the chemicals reach their intended target and do not endanger any organisms or nearby bodies of water.

Weather

Chances of rain, wind, and extreme temperature are very important environmental factors to consider when applying pesticides. Wind can cause the pesticide to drift to surrounding areas and rain may wash the chemical prematurely from the host plant. Certain ambient temperatures can cause the chemical composition of select pesticides to change. Thoroughly read the label to understand how, when, and where the pesticide should or should not be applied.

Applying Pesticides

The first step of pesticide application is reading the manufacturer's instructions for application. Failure to apply the pesticide correctly will result in reduced effectiveness of the chemical and may cause environmental damage. The second step is ensuring the applicator is wearing the appropriate PPE to prevent skin contact or ingestion of the chemicals. All personnel should use the following practices and safety measures when applying pesticides.

- Always read the label to determine application rates and methods and appropriate PPE.
- Always read the label carefully to ensure the plant and disorder will be effectively controlled.

Career Connection

Colby Griffin

Colby Griffin, Extension Agent

Colby Griffin is the Horticulture Extension Agent for the North Carolina Cooperative Extension in Franklin County. He developed his love of horticulture as a child while helping in the family vegetable garden and as he began developing the landscape around his parents' home. When Colby began his undergraduate work at NC State, his goal was to become an extension agent. Colby worked at a garden center, landscape company, and local historic site on the ground crew before finally reaching his dream career.

Colby assists homeowners with everyday gardening questions and develops programs that give them tools for tackling problems in their home landscapes. He also assists local farmers with pest or disease problems. The major vegetable crops that Colby works with are leafy greens, strawberries, peppers, and pickling cucumbers. Franklin County also has a large population of landscape professionals for which Colby is active in providing the needed continuing education credit opportunities and classes. He hopes that by being readily available to growers, he will become a vital link for them between what is going on in the field and the research being conducted at NC State University.

Colby wants young people interested in horticulture to know that Cooperative Extension can provide one of the best avenues for expanding their horticulture knowledge. "Being an extension agent allows me to use a variety of horticulture skills on a daily basis. I enjoy being able to talk to farmers and the public about what is happening in their fields and home landscapes." Colby says that Cooperative Extension continually provides professional educational opportunities and events that help deepen his knowledge of horticulture and agricultural sciences.

Consider This

1. Does Colby's job interest you? What aspect of the position would you enjoy the most? Explain your answer.
2. Which types of FFA or NALP programs and events would help prepare you for a job as an extension agent?
3. Consider contacting your local extension agent and inviting him or her to speak to your class about his or her work. Prepare questions ahead of time.

- Ensure the area to be sprayed is clear of people and/or domesticated animals.
- Only apply the chemical if the weather permits.
- If applying as a foliar spray, spray until the pesticide begins to drip from the leaves. Finer water droplets help increase foliar coverage but droplets that are too fine may drift to other areas.
- Pay careful attention to sources of water. Many pesticides have restrictions as to the legal distance between the area of application and bodies and sources of water.
- Triple rinse the sprayer with clean water when application is completed. Pressurize the sprayer and spray water to ensure the wand and spray tube are clean.
- Remove and clean PPE as needed.
- Store the equipment and pesticides in the proper locations.
- Thoroughly wash your hands and face or shower.

Storage and Disposal

Proper storage and disposal is essential to minimize the potential for contamination or harm to individuals and the environment. As always, follow the manufacturer's instructions for storage and disposal as well as any state or federal regulations. Keep the following points in mind:

- Pesticides should *always* be stored in their original container.
- Pesticides should be stored in a secure location that is inaccessible to children and untrained individuals.
- Empty pesticide containers should be triple rinsed and punctured before disposing. Triple rinsing the pesticide ensures all residual pesticide is removed. Puncturing the empty container ensures unknowing individuals will not use the pesticide container for another purpose.
- Contact the local municipality or disposal companies that may collect or have drives to collect hazardous chemicals.

STEM Connection

Calibrating a Hand Sprayer

Sprayer calibration is performed to ensure the correct amount of pesticide is applied uniformly over the target area without leaving excessive pesticide residue or causing plant injury. Calibration requires equipment adjustment and delivery rate (output) calculation. To prevent unsatisfactory results, hand sprayers should be calibrated every time they are used to ensure they are in working order. Use plain, clean water to determine the device's calibration.

Calibrating a Hand Sprayer for Lawn Application

1. Inspect the sprayer for damage. Check hose connections for leaks and replace worn O-rings as needed in the nozzle, trigger, and pump. Replace the nozzle if it is worn or damaged, as the spray pattern will be distorted.
2. Measure a 10′ × 25′ test area similar to the area you will be spraying.
3. Fill the sprayer with water to a specific level. Many sprayers have measurement markings along the side.
4. Using the same nozzle, pressure, and walking speed that you will use when applying the pesticide, spray the premeasured area. Move the wand evenly over the area.
5. Determine the amount of water (volume) needed to refill the tank to the same level in Step 2.
6. Multiply the volume from Step 5 by 4 to determine the volume of spray mixture you will need to spray 1000 ft². Most pesticide manufacturers indicate application rates per 1000 ft².
7. Determine how much pesticide is needed for each gallon of water and for each tankful. Refer to the pesticide label to determine the ratio of water to pesticide.
8. Calculate the number of full tanks and the total amount of pesticide needed to cover the intended area.

Safety First

Check the label to determine the minimum volume to apply per 1000 ft². If the volume in Step 6 is less than what is specified on the label, the mix would be too concentrated. Repeat Steps 3 to 6 but decrease your walking speed in Step 4 to increase the sprayer's output.

Summary

- IPM is a series of pest management techniques that are used to minimize the use of hazardous materials to control pests.

- A pest is any organism that can cause damage or harm to plants and their growth. A host is a live organism on which a pest is living.

- A pest must be identified correctly before treatment. If the pest is not identified correctly, the control measures used to treat it will be ineffective and may even cause damage.

- Scouting is the regular checking of landscapes, greenhouses, nursery fields, or other areas for pests while they are manageable. The person evaluating a situation must be able to distinguish between healthy plants and plants that are unwell.

- A threshold level is the point at which the pest reaches an unacceptable level and corrective action must be taken.

- The different pest control methods are cultural, sanitation, exclusion, physical and mechanical, biological, and chemical.

- Cultural controls include site assessments, use of disease-resistant plants, proper planting, following a maintenance time line, performing 3 Ds, pruning, watering, fertilizing, dethatching, aerating, mowing, and keeping tools clean and sharp.

- Effective sanitation controls require the landscape or production area to be kept as clean as possible.

- Exclusion control is the use of screens, traps, and other barriers to prevent pests from causing damage.

- Physical and mechanical controls directly remove or kill pests and may also prevent pests from reaching the host plant with barriers or traps.

- Biological control uses living microorganisms or natural predators (beneficials) to control pests.

- Chemical control is the application of pesticides to control or eliminate pests.

- Plant damage may be caused by other agents, such as lawn trimmers, excessive fertilization, lawn mowers, road salt or deicer, and drought.

- The pests that affect plants include weeds, birds, rodents, mammals, insects, snails, nematodes, and plant pathogens (organisms that cause disease in plants).

- Weeds are undesirable plants because they compete with desirable plants for nutrition and water and will often take over areas and crowd out landscaping plants, such as turfgrass.

- Weeds thrive in most cultures, grow rapidly, reproduce rapidly, have strong drought resistance, staggered germination times, long-term survival of seed, use dormancy, have good dispersal mechanisms, and can propagate sexually and asexually.

- Understanding an insect's growth and development is essential to successful control because different controls are more effective during each stage of an insect's life cycle.
- In complete metamorphosis, an insect goes through four stages: egg, larva, pupa, and adult. In incomplete metamorphosis, an insect goes through three stages: egg, nymph, and adult.
- Plant diseases are disorders caused by infectious pathogens, such as a virus, fungus, or bacteria.
- Pesticide categories include herbicides, insecticides, fungicides, molluscicides, and rodenticides. They are used for weeds, insects, fungi, mollusks, and rodents, respectively.
- Pesticide controls are designed to prevent, suppress, or eradicate pests.
- Herbicides may be selective, nonselective, preemergent, or postemergent.
- Insecticides may be contact or systemic formulations.
- Fungicides are used preventively rather than to control an actively growing fungus.
- Miticides kill the insect by contact or through ingestion.
- Molluscicides are typically granular and spread around the plants. The mollusks feed on the poison granules.
- Rodenticides are used in granular or block-shaped pieces that are most commonly used as bait in a trap.
- Most pesticides are available in one or more of the following formulations: liquid, dust, granules, wettable powder, fumigant, and aerosol.
- A pesticide label is a lengthy, legal document attached to the container that includes the information needed to apply the chemical safely and accurately.
- A pesticide label must include the name, EPA registration number, active ingredients, signal word, precautionary statements, environmental hazards, first-aid instructions, and storage and disposal instructions.
- The terms caution, warning, and danger are signal words used to indicate the potential threat level a chemical poses to human health.
- LD_{50} and LC_{50} are values used to indicate a measure of a pesticide's toxicity. The lower the LC_{50} or LD_{50} number, the more toxic the chemical.
- The reentry interval (REI) is the amount of time that must pass before a person can enter an area after it has been treated with the pesticide.
- The person applying a pesticide must be trained and/or certified to apply restricted-use pesticides in all states and may also need a license to apply general-use pesticides.
- Restricted-use chemicals may only be purchased and used by licensed applicators.
- Pesticides must be applied in accordance with the manufacturer's instructions and with any applicable state or federal regulations.

- The first step of pesticide application is reading the manufacturer's instructions. Failure to apply the pesticide correctly will result in reduced effectiveness of the chemical and may cause environmental damage.
- Proper storage and disposal of pesticides is essential to minimize the potential for contamination or harm to individuals and the environment. The manufacturer's instructions for storage and disposal as well as any state or federal regulations must be followed.
- Pesticides should *always* be stored in their original container.
- Pesticides should be stored in a secure location that is inaccessible to children and untrained individuals.

Chapter Review

Know and Understand ↱

Answer the following questions using the information provided in this chapter.

1. *True or False?* IPM is a combination of pest management techniques designed to encourage the use of pesticides to control plant pests.
   A. True.
   B. False.

2. Which of the following is a step used to create an IPM program?
   A. Determine if pest population has reached threshold level.
   B. Record and evaluate the results.
   C. Identify the pest and understand its biology.
   D. All of the above.

3. If the pest is not identified correctly, the control measures used to treat it _____.
   A. may cause damage
   B. will be just as effective
   C. are punishable by law
   D. All of the above.

4. *True or False?* Landscapes are usually scouted for pest problems through visual observations.
   A. True.
   B. False.

5. Which of the following is the point at which a pest reaches an unacceptable level and corrective action must be taken?
   A. Hatching level.
   B. Foothold level.
   C. Threshold level.
   D. Control level.

6. Which of the following are pest control methods used in IPM?
   A. Biological, chemical, and cultural.
   B. Actionable, clinical, and elemental.
   C. Manageable, structural, and divisional.
   D. All of the above.

7. Which of the following strategies involves any action that is taken to stop the pest damage from occurring?
   A. Pest suppression.
   B. Pest eradication.
   C. Pest prevention.
   D. Pest supplication.

8. Which of the following strategies is used for the complete elimination of a pest?
   A. Pest suppression.
   B. Pest eradication.
   C. Pest prevention.
   D. Pest supplication.

9. *True or False?* Pest eradication involves treating existing pest problems to keep insect damage below a threshold.
   A. True.
   B. False.

10. Which of the following actions is used in cultural control?
    A. Installing disease-resistant plants.
    B. Following a maintenance time line.
    C. Using best practices to install a landscape.
    D. All of the above.

11. Which type of pest control requires the landscape or production area to be kept as clean as possible?
    A. Optimization.
    B. Annihilation.
    C. Sanitation.
    D. Transmutation.

12. Which of the following tactics are used with the exclusion control method?
    A. Removing dead, diseased, and damaged plant portions.
    B. Dethatching and aerating turfgrass on schedule.
    C. Installing screens, traps, fences, and other barriers.
    D. All of the above.

13. Hand picking and spraying water are both examples of _____.
    A. exclusion controls
    B. physical controls
    C. biological controls
    D. All of the above.

14. Using living microorganisms or natural predators to control pests is which type of control?
    A. Sanitation control.
    B. Annihilation control.
    C. Biological control.
    D. All of the above.

15. *True or False?* Chemical controls are an important part of pest management and may sometimes be the only option to treat an area.
    A. True.
    B. False.

16. *True or False?* Plant damage may be caused by nonliving agents.
    A. True.
    B. False.

17. Which of the following inorganic agents cause plant damage?
    A. Lawn mowers and string trimmers.
    B. Excess salt or fertilization.
    C. Extended drought.
    D. All of the above.

18. Of the following, which are common pests that cause damage to plant materials?
    A. Nematodes and plant pathogens.
    B. Weeds, birds, and rodents.
    C. Insects and snails.
    D. All of the above.

19. Weeds have many natural characteristics that ensure their survival, such as the ability to survive in many environments and _____.
    A. a very rapid growth and reproduction rate
    B. the element of beauty they add to the landscape
    C. attractive and very strong scents
    D. All of the above.

20. *True or False?* Weeds have the same life cycles as desirable annual and perennial plants.
    A. True.
    B. False.

21. *True or False?* Different controls are more effective during each stage of an insect's life cycle.
    A. True.
    B. False.

22. *True or False?* In incomplete metamorphosis, an insect goes through four stages: egg, larva, pupa, and adult.
    A. True.
    B. False.

23. Insects may kill or deform plants through which of the following actions?
    A. tunneling or boring into stems
    B. feeding on roots and stems
    C. laying eggs in plant tissues
    D. All of the above.

24. *True or False?* Sponging insects may easily transmit diseases from other sources.
    A. True.
    B. False.

25. Which of the following is considered a pathogen that infects plants?
    A. Virus.
    B. Bacteria.
    C. Fungus.
    D. All of the above.

26. *True or False?* A virus is a specialized organism that attaches itself to a host and decomposes the host as it absorbs nutrients from it.
    A. True.
    B. False.

27. *True or False?* Fungi are treated with preemergent herbicides.
    A. True.
    B. False.

28. *True or False?* Bacteria are treated with selective herbicides.
    A. True.
    B. False.

29. Which of the following best describes selective herbicides?
   A. Will kill any plant the chemical contacts.
   B. Will only target certain weeds.
   C. Target weeds before they germinate.
   D. Target weeds after they have germinated.

30. *True or False?* Preemergent herbicides target weeds before they germinate.
   A. True.
   B. False.

31. *True or False?* Postemergent herbicides target weeds before they germinate.
   A. True.
   B. False.

32. *True or False?* A contact insecticide is effective for insects with chewing mouthparts.
   A. True.
   B. False.

33. *True or False?* Systemic insecticides are most effective for insects with chewing mouthparts.
   A. True.
   B. False.

34. Which of the following is used preventively rather than to control an actively growing plant disease?
   A. Miticide.
   B. Molluscicide.
   C. Fungicide.
   D. All of the above.

35. Which of the following is used to control snails and slugs?
   A. Rodenticide.
   B. Molluscicide.
   C. Fungicide.
   D. All of the above.

36. Which of the following pesticide formulations must be diluted with water before spraying?
   A. Aerosol.
   B. Granules.
   C. Liquid.
   D. All of the above.

37. Which of the following best describes pesticide dusts?
   A. They are concentrated formulations.
   B. May be made purely of the active chemical.
   C. Its particles are suspended in liquid before application.
   D. All of the above.

38. *True or False?* Aerosols are convenient and most practical for use on larger areas.
   A. True.
   B. False.

39. *True or False?* Fumigants are used to treat large, enclosed areas, such as greenhouses.
   A. True.
   B. False.

40. *True or False?* A pesticide label is considered a legal and binding agreement between the applicator and the manufacturer.
   A. True.
   B. False.

41. Which of the following are required on all pesticide labels?
   A. Active ingredients and first-aid instructions.
   B. Signal words and precautionary statements.
   C. Pesticide name and EPA registration number.
   D. All of the above.

42. Which of the following signal words indicates the chemical poses minimal harm to human beings?
   A. Danger.
   B. Caution.
   C. Warning.
   D. Toxic.

43. Which of the following signal words indicates the chemical is dangerous and can have a negative impact on human beings?
   A. Danger.
   B. Caution.
   C. Warning.
   D. Toxic.

44. Which of the following signal words indicates it is the most toxic and can only be purchased by licensed applicators?
   A. Danger.
   B. Caution.
   C. Warning.
   D. Toxic.

45. Which of the following chemicals is the most toxic?
   A. LD_{50} 2 mg/kg
   B. LD_{50} 20 mg/kg
   C. LD_{50} 200 mg/kg
   D. LD_{50} 2000 mg/kg

46. *True or False?* The pesticide label should be sent to the hospital with the victim to ensure the toxin is properly identified and treated.
   A. True.
   B. False.

47. The amount of time that must pass before a person can enter an area after it has been treated with the pesticide is the _____.
   A. PPM
   B. FPI
   C. LDC
   D. REI

48. *True or False?* The applicator is required to post a sign indicating the area has been treated with a pesticide.
   A. True.
   B. False.

49. Which of the following have potential to cause extensive damage if used improperly and therefore require special licensing to purchase and apply?
   A. Restricted-use pesticides.
   B. General-use pesticides.
   C. Certified-use pesticides.
   D. Special-use pesticides.

50. *True or False?* Pesticides should *always* be stored in their original container.
   A. True.
   B. False.

51. *True or False?* Puncturing the empty container ensures unknowing individuals will not use the pesticide container for another purpose.
   A. True.
   B. False.

Thinking Critically

1. What examples of environmental damage can you find to justify the ban of a specific chemical used in weed or pest control?

2. How does the effectiveness of biological controls compare to that of chemical controls? Can the effectiveness of biological controls be heightened? Explain your answer.

3. How would you explain the life cycle of insects and the effect of various insecticides at different life cycle stages?

4. What would you do if you knew of someone who was disposing of old pesticides by dumping them on the ground near a local pond or stream?

5. Explain the risks and benefits associated with the materials and methods used in plant management.

Suggested Activities

1. Working in a small group, photograph or download images of pesticide labels. Determine if each label includes all of the required information (pesticide name, EPA number, active ingredients, signal words, precautionary statements, environmental hazards, first-aid protocol, and storage and disposal instructions). What additional types of information is on each label? Are the labels easy to read and understand? Are there ways to improve the readability?

2. Work with a partner of in a small group to evaluate the controls used in your school's horticultural program. Develop a plan that could be used at your school to implement IPM strategies. Compare your IPM plan to those of your classmates and determine which strategies would be most appropriate?

3. Work with a partner to locate pests in your school greenhouses or on plants on school campus. What are the pests? What damage do they cause? Photograph the pests and plant damages as well as healthy plants of the same species. Create a visual presentation and explain your findings. Include the types of controls you would use to control or eliminate the pests.

4. Work with a small group to create a short video or visual presentation on how to safely mix and apply pesticides. You may use plain and colored water to represent the two fluids. You may also demonstrate how failing to follow protocol can endanger the person mixing and those around him or her.

5. What happens when the beneficials have eliminated most of the pests and no longer have an adequate food supply? Work with a partner and research the topic. Write a short report or create a visual presentation on how scientists are helping to solve this problem. Begin your research with *banker plants*.

6. Pesticides and fertilizers are common water and soil contaminants. Work with a partner or small group to identify best management practices to reduce pollution. Create a short visual presentation to explain your findings.

7. Research nonpoint and point source pollution. Under which category do pesticides and fertilizers fall? Explain how pollution affects or enters a watershed.

8. Research the common pests, pathogens, and invasive and poisonous plants in your state. Determine if actions are being taken to eliminate or control the pests. Prepare a short video or visual presentation on the origin of the pests, their impact on the environment, and the measures needed to eliminate and control them.

Pests, Disorders, and Beneficial Insects Identification ↗

The following pests, disorders, and beneficial insects identification glossary contains a small sampling of:

- Common pests and the damage they cause to plants and trees.
- Common plant diseases that affect plants worldwide.
- Common weeds that affect ornamental and agricultural plants.
- Beneficial insects used to control pests.

This illustrated glossary has been provided to help you familiarize yourself with these pests, damage, diseases, weeds, and beneficial insects as well as a means of studying for career development events in which their identification is a major component. The numbers in the right-hand corners correlate to those on the CDE ID lists. This glossary is by no means all-inclusive, but provides a good starting point for your studies. Use this glossary, as well as the e-flashcards on your textbook's companion website at **www.g-wlearning.com/agriculture** to help you study and identify these pests and disorders.

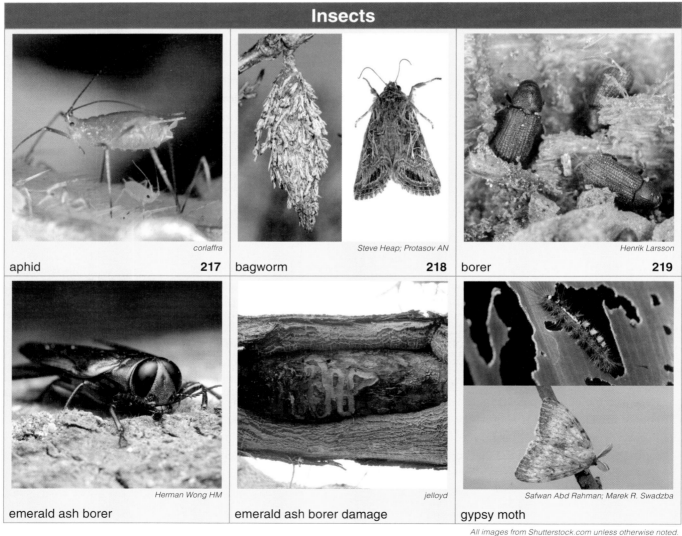

Insects

corlaffra	*Steve Heap; Protasov AN*	*Henrik Larsson*
aphid **217**	bagworm **218**	borer **219**
Herman Wong HM	*jelloyd*	*Safwan Abd Rahman; Marek R. Swadzba*
emerald ash borer	emerald ash borer damage	gypsy moth

All images from Shutterstock.com unless otherwise noted.

Japanese beetle

Kent Sievers

leafhopper **220**

YapAhock

leaf miner (damage) **221**

topimages

scale **222**

Decha Thapanya

spider mite **223a**

D. Kucharski; K. Kucharska

spider mite damage **223b**

D. Kucharski; K. Kucharska

slug **224a**

Lisa S.

snail **224b**

Pascal Lagesse

snail/slug damage **224c**

Savo Ilic

whitefly   *fotosav*   **225**

white grub   *D. Kucharski; K. Kucharska*   **226**

Diseases

anthracnose   *mykhailo pavlenko*   **227a**

anthracnose   *tippawan cholviriyanant*   **227b**

apple scab   *Vilor*   **228**

black spot   *Manfred Ruckszio*   **229**

botrytis   *Floki*   **230**

canker   *Lertwit Sasipreyajun; Kapong_pumpui*   **231**

cedar-apple rust   **232**

samray; jelloyd

crown gall (on rose)   **233a**

North Carolina Plant Disease and Insect Clinic

crown gall   **233b**

Goodheart-Willcox Publisher

tobacco mosaic virus

Plant Pathology

damping off

HelloDecenmber

fireblight   **234**

Grandpa

powdery mildew   **235**

Grandpa

oak galls

jelloyd; Hecos

oak galls

Ariene Studio; colin robert varnell

oak galls

root rot/sloughing **236a**

root rot/sloughing **236b**

sunscald

sunscald

Weeds

Poa annua/annual bluegrass **237**

Plantago major/broadleaf plantain **238**

Plantago lanceolata/buckhorn plantain **239**

beckysphotos; F.Nedi

Stella media/chickweed **240**

Christian Delbert; marekuliasz

Digitaria sanguinalis/crabgrass **241**

Nadezhda Kulikova; Marykit

Taraxacum species/dandelion **242**

guentermanaus; pullia

Lamium amplexiaule/henbit
(dead nettle) **243**

arousa

Cyperus rotundus/nutsedge **244**

Anna Gratys; Ole Schoener

Chenopodium album/lambs quarters

Sinelev; Kimberly Boyles

Oxalis corniuculata/oxalis **245**

Volodymyr Nikitenko; wasanjai

Portulaca oleracea/purslane **246**

Ruth Swan; Elvan

Trifolium species/clovers **247**

Elena Elisseeva; K Steve Cope

Toxicodendron radicans/poison ivy

Jerry-Rainey; Sundry Photography

Toxicodendron diversilobum/poison oak

S.O.E.; Fotokostic

Urtica dioica/stinging nettle

Physiological Problems

North Carolina Plant Disease and Insect Clinic

frost/freeze injury (bark splitting)   **248a**

North Carolina Plant Disease and Insect Clinic

frost/freeze injury   **248b**

Barb Fair, NC State University

iron deficiency   **249**

North Carolina Plant Disease and Insect Clinic

leaf scorch/drought burn/winter burn
(on holly)   **250**

Barb Fair, NC State University

nitrogen deficiency   **251**

Scott Latham; Barb Fair, NC State University

pot-bound roots   **252**

Barb Fair, NC State University

string trimmer/mower injury **253**

Goodheart-Willcox Publisher

herbicide injury **254**

Beneficials

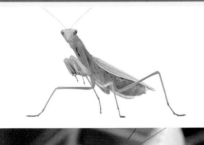

Eric Isselee; Dr. Morley Read

praying mantis **255**

Yellowj; Jolanda Aalbers

lady beetle **256**

Melinda Fawver; Sean McVey

paper wasp (drone and queen) **257**

Henri Koskinen; corlaffra

lacewing **258**

Garmasheva Natalia; Rocket Photos – HQ Stock

spiders **259**

Appendix

Pro Tips for Pruning Landscaping Plants	
Pruning Established Trees	
Respond to client's needs	As a professional, use your knowledge to decide whether pruning is necessary or healthy for the tree
Remove	Dead, damaged, and diseased materials (3 Ds) Water sprouts Root suckers (may also be sprayed) Crossing branches
Major pruning	Winter to budbreak, trees can wall off wound quicker during this time
Minimal pruning	Between budbreak and leaf expansion Between later summer and leaf fall (remove less than 30% of wood)
Light or corrective pruning	Anytime
Proper pruning cuts	Heading, back to bud or branch Thinning, remove entire branch
Pruning Young or Newly Planted Shade and Screening Trees	
First five years of care are critical to health and success of trees	
First year after planting	Establish a central leader
	Pruning at planting is not advisable because it slows root growth
Corrective pruning	Remove dead, damaged, and diseased materials (3 Ds)
	Remove crossing branches
	Topping is never advisable because it causes weakening
Next 2 to 5 years	Select scaffold branches (foundation branches)
	Wide angle of attachment from trunk to branch (45° to 60°)
	Vertical spacing: 12″ to 18″
	Radial spacing: 5″ to 7″ per 360°
	Remove branches that are too low, have a sharp angle of attachment, are within 4″ to 6″ of scaffold branches, and outgrown leaders
Pruning Shrubs and Perennials	
Rhododendrons, azaleas, other native flowering shrubs	Natives withstand pruning, whereas hybrids are not easily pruned
Flowering shrubs and perennials	Deadheading after flowering can cause rebloom for some species
Ornamental grasses	Cut back before new growth appears
	New growth may also be flat topped

(Continued)

Pro Tips for Pruning Landscaping Plants *(continued)*

Pruning Woody Plants

Deciduous	Prior to budbreak (winter through dormancy)
	Prior to full leaf expansion (after budbreak in late spring) to retard shoot growth
	May have irregular forms and growth from the base or main framework
	Pruned unwanted branches at the base of the plant and 20% to 25% of older branches every 2 to 3 years to maintain dense canopy, dependent on client's preferences
Broadleaf evergreens	Can be pruned during the growing season selectively or indiscriminately
	Rapid growth rate and shape can be manipulated to suit client preferences
Narrowleaf evergreens	Slow growing, growth from terminal buds or close to terminal with dense outer shell of foliage
	No latent buds, therefore renovation pruning is not practiced

Pruning for Flowers

	If there are flowers on current season's growth, prune when dormant
	If flowers are on previous season's growth, prune after flowering to prevent damage to following year's flower buds

Pruning for Berries

	Prune selectively before flowering in spring or after fruiting to prevent damage to the following year's flower buds

Pruning for Stem Color

	Prune every 2 to 3 years during the dormant season to encourage new stems vibrant in color (1- and 2-year-old wood has best color)
	Prune after flowering in mid-June for best color in winter; for current season color, prune when dormant

Shearing Plants

Commonly used to reduce plant size and/or create screening	For formal hedges, use plants with small leaves, short internodes, dense branches, and latent buds
	Changes plant's natural form and produces dense upright growth and shades out bottom of plant unless bevel is cut in angling out from the top to the base
Renovation pruning	May be required every 3 to 5 years to generate new growth from within the canopy and to keep density of hedge

Specialty Pruning

Espalier	Trees are trained on a trellis or wall as focal point or interest piece from initial planting
Pollarding	Heading back to same place on 1- to 2-year-old wood following basic time periods for the species
Topiary	Plants are trained on frames and consistently trimmed from planting into various shapes; plants that are not trained on frames are manipulated and sheared into the desired form
Bonsai	Plants are maintained as miniature versions through pruning and branch manipulation using wires; maintenance does not always adhere to seasonal patterns if the plants are in a manipulated environment, such as a greenhouse

Goodheart-Willcox Publisher

Average Task Times

Turfgrass Operations

	Equipment Needed	Average Completion Time (minutes)	Per Unit	Tasks Included
aeration	walk-behind aerator	10	1000 ft²	unloading/loading
chemical amendments (lime, fertilizer)	walk-behind/chest-mounted spreader	3	1000 ft²	unloading/loading, mixing
edging (hard)	gas-powered edger	3	100′	unloading/loading
edging (soft)	gas-powered edger	5	100′	unloading/loading
mowing	52″ zero turn	4	1000 ft²	unloading/loading
scouting	note-taking equipment	1	1000 ft²	note-taking
spot spraying	backpack sprayer	10	1000 ft²	unloading/loading

Tree and Shrub Operations

	Equipment Needed	Average Completion Time (minutes)	Per unit	Tasks Included
chemical amendments (lime, fertilizer)	walk-behind/chest-mounted spreader	5	1000 ft²	unloading/loading, mixing
mulching bark	mulch fork, wheelbarrow	30	1000 ft²	hauling, spreading
mulching straw	knife for cutting bale string	10	1000 ft²	spreading
1.5 yd³ of mulch	mulch fork, wheelbarrow	60		hauling, spreading
pruning	hand pruners, loppers	20	Tree	hand pruning, debris cleanup
pruning	hand pruners, power shears	5	1000 ft²	pruning, debris cleanup
scouting	note-taking equipment	1	1000 ft²	note-taking
spot spraying	backpack sprayer	10	1000 ft²	unloading/loading

Annual Color Beds Operations

	Equipment Needed	Average Completion Time (minutes)	Per Unit	Tasks Included
maintenance	hand pulling of weeds, deadheading	10	1000 ft²	pull weeds, deadhead, fertilize
planting	trowels	400	1000 ft²	lay out and install plants
soil preparation	rototiller or hand fork	200	1000 ft²	add chemical amendments and organic matter, rototill

Installation Operations

	Equipment Needed	Average Completion Rate (area)	Per Unit	Tasks Included
brick pavers on sand	solid base, screeded sand, 2-person crew	20 ft²	hour	brick staging and placement
seeding	walk-behind spreader	9000 ft²	hour	spreading of seed, moisture retention application (straw)
irrigation trenching	mechanical trencher	60′	hour	adequate depth of trenching

(Continued)

Average Task Times *(continued)*

pipe installation	by hand	80′	hour	installation and backfill
irrigation head application	by hand	80′	hour	head placement, backfill, and hand tamping

Plant Installation

	Equipment Needed	Average Completion Time (minutes)	Per Unit	Tasks Included
addition of soil amendments	fertilizer spreader, wheelbarrow, hand tools	200*	1000 ft²	unloading/loading
installation of ground covers/ vines	wheelbarrow, hand tools	1 to 10*	per ground cover or vine	digging, backfilling, watering
installation of perennials/ ornamental grasses	wheelbarrow, hand tools	1 to 10*	per ornamental grass	digging, backfilling, watering
installation of shrubs	wheelbarrow, hand tools	5 to 20*	shrub	digging, backfilling, watering
installation of trees	wheelbarrow, hand tools	30 to 60*	tree	digging, backfilling, watering
site grading	utility loader	60*	1000 ft²	unloading/loading
soil excavation	utility loader	90*	1000 ft²	unloading/loading

*All operations can be altered by changing the size of the installation crew; generally, a two-person crew is more efficient than one person, while a four-person crew may be less efficient than a three-person crew. The size of the plant material also affects efficiency.

Individual Plant Installation

Plants	Plants Installed per Hour
1-gallon container shrub	17
3-gallon container shrub	10
5-gallon container shrub	6
15-gallon container shrub	1.5
Container Trees	**Hours to Install Each Tree**
15-gallon container tree	0.75
30-gallon container tree	2
45-gallon container tree	2.25
65-gallon container tree	3
Balled-and-Burlapped Trees	**Hours to Install Each Tree**
6′ to 8′ B&B tree	1.5
1″ caliper B&B tree	1.25
2″ caliper B&B tree	1.75
3″ caliper B&B tree	4.5

Goodheart-Willcox Publisher

Plants Commonly Used in Landscape Designs

Trees

Small Trees (mature heights of approximately 20′)

Please note the exact classification will vary by cultivar as the height and width of plants changes dramatically based on the cultivar.

Acer buergeranum, trident maple	*Ilex* 'Nellie R. Stevens,' Nellie Stevens holly
Acer palmatum, Japanese maple	*Lagerstroemia indica*, crape myrtle
Cedrus atlantica 'Glauca Pendula,' blue atlas cedar	*Magnolia* × *soulangiana*, saucer magnolia
Cercis canadensis, eastern redbud	*Prunus mume*, Japanese apricot
Cornus species, dogwood	

Large Trees (mature heights of at least 40′)

Acer platanoides, Norway maple	*Pinus strobus*, eastern white pine
Acer rubrum, red maple	*Pinus taeda*, loblolly pine
Cryptomeria japonica, cryptomeria	*Platanus occidentalis*, sycamore
× *Cupressocyparis leylandii*, leyland cypress	*Quercus alba*, white oak
Fagus grandifolia, American beech	*Quercus falcata*, southern red oak
Fraxinus americana, white ash	*Quercus palustris*, pin oak
Ginkgo biloba, ginkgo	*Quercus phellos*, willow oak
Liquidambar styraciflua, sweetgum	*Quercus virginiana*, southern live oak
Magnolia grandiflora, southern magnolia	*Taxodium distichum*, bald cypress
Metasequoia glyptostroboides, dawn redwood	*Tsuga canadensis*, Canadian hemlock
Nyssa sylvatica, black gum	*Ulmus americana*, American elm

Shrubs

Dwarf Shrubs

Abelia × *grandiflora* 'Little Richard,' glossy abelia	*Ilex crenata* 'Helleri,' helleri holly
Berberis thunbergii 'Crimson Pygmy,' barberry	*Ilex vomitoria* 'Nana,' dwarf yaupon holly
Buxus sempervirens 'Suffruticoa,' dwarf boxwood	*Ligustrum japonicum* 'Rotundifolium,' curlyleaf ligustrum
Daphne odora, winter Daphne	*Nandina domestica* 'Gulf Stream,' nandina
Gardenia jasminoides 'Radicans,' dwarf gardenia	*Raphiolepis indica*, Indian hawthorn
Hydrangea macrophylla, florist's hydrangea	*Rhododendron obtusum*, azalea
Ilex cornuta 'Carissa,' carissa holly	*Spirea japonica* 'Goldmound,' spirea

Medium Shrubs

Abelia × *grandiflora* 'Edward Goucher,' glossy abelia	*Ilex crenta* 'Compacta,' compacta holly
Aucuba japonica, Japanese aucuba	*Ilex crenata* 'Rotundifolia,' round-leaf holly
Buxus microphylla var. japonica, Japanese boxwood	*Juniperus chinensis* 'Pfitzeriana,' pfitzer's juniper
Callicarpa americana, American beautyberry	*Pieris japonica*, Japanese pieris
Euonymus alatus 'Compacta,' burning bush	*Prunus laurocerasus* 'Zabeliana,' zabel laurel
Gardenia jasminoides, gardenia	*Spirea thunbergii*, spirea
Ilex cornuta 'Dwarf Burford,' dwarf burford holly	

(Continued)

Plants Commonly Used in Landscape Designs *(continued)*

Large Shrubs

Camellia japonica, Japanese camellia	*Ilex × attenuata* 'Fosteri,' fosteri holly
Camellia sasanqua, sasanqua camellia	*Ilex × attenuate* 'Savannah,' Savannah holly
Elaeagnus pungens, elaeagnus	*Ligustrum japonicum*, Japanese privet
Euonymus japonica, Japanese euonymus	*Loropetalum chinensis*, Chinese fringe flower
Hibiscus syriacus, rose of Sharon	*Myrica cerifera*, wax myrtle
Hydrangea paniculata, hydrangea	*Photinia glabra*, red photinia
Ilex cornuta, Chinese holly	*Pyracantha coccinea*, scarlet firethorn
Ilex opaca 'Greenleaf,' American holly	*Rhododendron catawbiense*, catawba rododendron
Ilex vomitoria, yaupon holly	

Herbaceous Perennials

Achillea species, yarrow	*Echinacea purpurea*, purple coneflower
Ajuga species, bugleweed	*Gaillardia aristata*, blanket flower
Alcea species, hollyhock	*Hemerocallis* species, daylily
Aquileagia hybrida, columbine	*Heurchera* species, coral bells
Buddleia davidii, butterfly bush	*Hosta* species, hosta
Clematis species, clematis	*Iberis sempervirens*, candytuft
Coreopsis species, tickseed	*Leucanthemum superbum*, shasta daisy
Delphinium species, larkspur	*Phlox paniculata*, garden phlox
Dianthus species, sweet William	*Phlox subulata*, creeping phlox
Digitalis species, foxglove	*Rudbeckia hirta*, black-eyed Susan

Turfgrasses, Grass-Like Plants, and Other Grasses

Cool-Season Turfgrasses

Agrostis stolonifera, creeping bentgrass	*Lolium* species, ryegrass
Schedonorus phoenix, tall fescue	*Poa pratensis*, Kentucky bluegrass
Festica rubra, fine fescue	

Warm-Season Turfgrasses

Cynodon dactylon, bermudagrass	*Stenotaphrum secundatum*, St. Augustinegrass
Eremochloa ophiuroides, centipedegrass	*Zoysia tenuifolia*, zoysiagrass
Paspalum notatum, bahiagrass	

Turfgrass Alternative Options for Sun

Bouteloua gracilis, blue grama	*Deschampsia flexuosa*, crinkled hair grass
Carex cherokeensis, Cherokee sedge	*Eragrostis spectabilis*, purple love grass
Carex divulsa, grassland sedge	*Juncus tenuis*, path rush
Carex rosea, rosy sedge	*Sesleria autumnalis*, autumn moor grass
Carex texensis, Texas sedge	*Sporobolus heterolepis*, prairie dropseed
Deschampsia cespitosa, tufted hair grass	*Sporobolus heterolepis*, 'Tara,' dwarf prairie dropseed

(Continued)

Plants Commonly Used in Landscape Designs *(continued)*

Turfgrass Alternative Options for Shade

Carex appalachia, Appalachian sedge	*Carex pensylvanica*, Pennsylvania sedge
Carex eburnean, bristle-leaf sedge	

Ground Covers

Ajuga reptans, ajuga, bugleweed	*Juniperus horizontalis*, creeping juniper
Cotoneaster dammeri, bearberry cotoneaster	*Pachysandra terminalis*, Japanese spurge
Cyrtomium falcatum, holly fern	*Phlox subulata*, moss pink
Euonymus fortunei, wintercreeper	*Sarcocca hookeriana* var. *humilis*, Himalayan sweet box
Iberis sempervirens, evergreen candytuft	*Sedum* species, stonecrop
Juniperus conferta, shore juniper	*Vinca major*, periwinkle

Grasses and Grass-Like Plants

Acorus gramineus, sweet flag	*Miscanthus* species, maiden grass
Calamagrostis × *acutiflora*, feather reed grass	*Muhlenbergia capillaris*, muhly grass
Carex species, sedge	*Panicum virgatum*, switch grass
Festuca glauca, blue fescue	*Pennisetum* species, fountain grass
Juncus species, rush	*Schizachyrium scoparium*, little bluestem

Vines

Clematis, clematis	*Passiflora incarnata*, purple passion flower
Ficus pumula, weeping fig	*Trachelpspermum jasminoides*, confederate jasmine
Gelsemium sempervirens, Carolina jessamine	*Vitis vinifera*, grape
Hedera helix, English ivy	*Wisteria* species, wisteria
Lonicera species, honeysuckle	

Geophytes

Spring Flowering	Late Summer and Early Fall
Anemone species, windflower	*Allium giganteum*, giant allium
Arum cornutum, voodoo lily	*Begonia tuberhybrida*, tuberous begonia
Caladium species, angel wings	*Convallaria* species, lily of the valley
Cannas × *generalis*, canna lily	*Frittilaria* species, crown imperial
Colocasia species, elephant ear	*Gladiolus* species, sword lily
Crocosmia species, montbretia	*Hyacinthus* species, common hyacinth
Crocus species, crocus	*Iris* species, garden iris
Dahlia species, dahlia	*Lycoris* species, spider lily
Eucomis species, pineapple lily	*Narcissus* species, narcissus
Eremurus species, foxtail lily	*Oxalis* species, wood sorrel
Hippeastrum papillio, amaryllis	*Scilla siberica*, Siberian squill
Lillium asiatic, Asiatic lily	*Trilium* species, trillium
Tulipa species, garden tulip	*Zephyranthes* species, rain lily
Zantedeschia species, calla lily	

(Continued)

Plants Commonly Used in Landscape Designs *(continued)*

Common Edibles for the Landscape

Actinidia kolomikta, hardy kiwi	*Cucurbita* species, squash	*Punica granatum*, pomegranate
Allium cepa, onion	*Cynara cardunculus* var. *scolymus*, artichoke	*Rubus* species, caneberries, such as blackberry, raspberry, dewberry
Allium sativum, garlic	*Vaccinium* species, blueberry	*Salvia officinalis*, sage
Allium schoenoprasum, chives	*Diospyros kaki*, Asian or Japanese persimmon	*Solanum lycopersicum*, tomato
Brassica oleracea var. *sabellica*, kale	*Ficus carica*, fig	*Solanum melongena*, eggplant
Capsicum species, garden pepper	*Lactuca sativa*, lettuce	*Spinacia oleracea*, spinach
Citrullus lanatus, watermelon	*Malus domestica*, apple	*Thymus vulgaris*, thyme
Cocumis sativus, cucumber	*Mentha* species, mint	*Triticum* species, wheat
Coriandrum sativum, cilantro	*Origanum vulgare*, oregano	*Zea mays*, corn
Cucumis melo var. *cantalupensis*, cantaloupe	*Paseolus vulgaris*, common beans	
Edible flowers, such as borage blossoms, calendula, hibiscus, lavender, nasturtiums, pansy, roses, sage flowers, violets, and zucchini blossoms are also grown as edible landscaping plants.		

Goodheart-Willcox Publisher

Plants for Wet and Dry Locations

Trees

Wet Locations	Dry Locations
Acer rubrum, red maple	*Acer campestre*, hedge maple
Amelanchier arborea, service berry	*Ceris canadensis*, eastern redbud
Betula nigra, river birch	*Fagus sylvatica*, European beech
Diospyros virginiana, persimmon	*Fraxinus*, ash
Gleditsia tricanthos, honey locust	*Ginkgo biloba*, ginkgo
Ilex opaca, American holly	*Juniperus virginiana*, eastern red cedar
Nyssa sylvatica, black gum	*Koelreuteria paniculata*, golden-rain tree
Quercus nigra, water oak	*Platanus × acerifolia*, London plane tree
Salix species, willow	*Quercus rubra*, red oak
Taxodium distichum, bald cypress	*Zelkova serrate*, Japanese zelkova

Shrubs

Wet Locations	Dry Locations
Aesculus parviflora, bottlebrush buckeye	*Berberis thunbergii*, Japanese barberry
Fatsia japonica, Japanese fatsia	*Chaenomeles speciosa*, flowering quince
Fothergilla species, fothergilla	*Cotinus coggygria*, smokebush
Ilex vomitoria, yaupon holly	*Juniper* species, junipers
Myrica cerifera, wax myrtle	*Ligustrum* species, privet
Sabal minor, palmetto	*Potentilla fruticoa*, cinquefoil
Thuja occidentalis, American arborvitae	*Rosa rugosa*, rugosa rose
Viburnum opulus, cranberry viburnum	*Yucca filamentosa*, yucca

Ground Covers

Wet Locations	Dry Locations
Ajuga species, ajuga	*Ajuga* species, ajuga
Bignonia capreolata, cross vine	*Chasmanthium latifolium*, northern sea oats
Campsis radicans, trumpet creeper	*Cotoneaster adpressus*, creeping cotoneaster
Gelsemium sempervirens, Carolina jessamine	*Hemerocallis* species, daylily
Lonicera sempervirens, trumpet honeysuckle	*Hypericum calycinum*, St. John's wort
Wisteria frutescens, American wisteria	*Sedum* species, sedum
	Vinca minor, periwinkle

Herbaceous Perennials

Wet Locations	Dry Locations
Canna species, canna	*Agastache rupestris*, hyssop
Crinum species, crinum	*Buddleia* species, butterfly bush
Eupatium purpureaum, Joe pye weed	*Coreopsis* species, tickseed
Hibiscus coccineus, swamp hibiscus	*Echinacea purpurea*, coneflower
Iris sibirica, Siberian iris	*Gaillardia aristata*, blanket flower
Lobelia cardinalis, cardinal flower	*Nepeta* species, catmint
Monarda species, bee balm	*Salvia nemorosa*, salvia
Tiarella cordifolia, foam flower	*Veronica* species, speedwell

(Continued)

Plants for Wet and Dry Locations *(continued)*

Ornamental Grasses and Grass-Like Plants

Wet Locations	Dry Locations
Acorus gramineus, sweet flag	*Festuca glauca*, Elijah blue fescue
Arundo domax, giant reed	*Miscanthus* species, maiden hair grass
Carex species, sedges	*Muhlenbergia*, muhley grass
Equisetum hyemale, horsetail rush	*Panicum virgaum*, panic grass
Schizachyrium scoparium, little bluestem	*Pennisetum*, fountain grass

Goodheart-Willcox Publisher

Conversions and Equivalents

Length

US Customary to SI Metric

Multiply	By	To Determine
inches (in/″)	25.4*	millimeters (mm)
inches (in/″)	2.54*	centimeters (cm)
feet (ft/′)	0.3048*	meters (m)
feet (ft/′)	30.48*	centimeters (cm)
yards (yd)	0.9 or 0.9144*	meters (m)
miles (mi)	0.07646	kilometers (km)

SI Metric to US Customary

Multiply	By	To Determine
millimeters (mm)	0.04 or 0.0393701	inches (in/″)
centimeters (cm)	0.4 or 0.3937008	inches (in/″)
meters (m)	3.3 or 3.280840	feet (ft/′)
meters (m)	1.1 or 1.093613	yards (yd)
cubic meters (m³)	35.31	cubic feet (ft³)
cubic meters (m³)	1.308	cubic yards (yd³)
kilometers (km)	0.6 or 0.621371	miles (mi)

Weight

US Customary to SI Metric

Multiply	By	To Determine
ounces (oz)	28.0 or 28.349523125*	grams (g)
ounces (oz)	0.028 or 0.028349523125*	kilograms (kg)
pounds (lb)	0.45 or 0.45359237*	kilograms (kg)
short ton or ton	0.9 or 0.90718474*	tonnes or metric tons (MT/t/T)

SI Metric to US Customary

Multiply	By	To Determine
grams (g)	0.35 or 0.03527396	ounces (oz)
kilograms (kg)	2.2 or 2.204623	pounds (lb)
tonnes or metric tons (MT/t/T)	1.1 or 1.1023113	short ton or ton

(Continued)

Conversions and Equivalents *(continued)*

Volume

US Customary to SI Metric

Multiply	By	To Determine
teaspoons (tsp or t)	5.0	milliliters (ml)
tablespoons (tbsp or T)	15.0	milliliters (ml)
fluid ounces (fl oz)	30.0 or 29.57353	milliliters (ml)
cups (c)	0.24	liters (l)
pints (pt)	0.47 or 0.473176473*	liters (l)
quarts (qt)	0.95 or 0.946352946*	liters (l)
gallons (gal)	3.8 or 3.785411784*	liters (l)
cubic inches (in³)	0.02 or 0.016387064*	liters (l)
cubic feet (ft³)	0.03 or 0.028316846592*	cubic meters (m³)
cubic yards (yd³)	0.76 or 0.764554857984*	cubic meters (m³)

SI Metric to US Customary

milliliters (ml)	0.2	teaspoons (tsp)
milliliters (ml)	0.67 or 0.06667	tablespoons (tbsp or T)
milliliters (ml)	0.03 or 0.03381402	fluid ounces (fl oz)
liters (l)	61.024 or 61.02374	cubic inches (in³)
liters (l)	2.1 or 2.113376	pints (pt)
liters (l)	1.06 or 1.056688	quarts (qt)
liters (l)	0.26 or 0.26417205	gallons (gal)
liters (l)	0.035 or 0.03531467	cubic feet (ft³)
cubic meters (m³)	61023.7 or 61023.74	cubic inches (in³)
cubic meters (m³)	35.0 or 35.31467	cubic feet (ft³)
cubic meters (m³)	1.3 or 1.3079506	cubic yards (yd³)
cubic meters (m³)	264.0 or 264.17205	gallons (gal)

Area

US Customary to SI Metric

Multiply	By	To Determine
square inches (in²)	6.5 or 6.4516*	square centimeters (cm²)
square feet (ft²)	0.09 or 0.09290304*	square meters (m²)
square yards (yd²)	0.8 or 0.83612736*	square meters (m²)
square miles (mi²)	2.6	square kilometers (km²)
acres (ac)	0.4 or 0.40468564224*	hectares (ha)

SI Metric to US Customary

square centimeters (cm²)	0.16 or 0.1550003	square inches (in²)
square centimeters (cm²)	0.001 or 0.00107639	square feet (ft²)
square meters (m²)	10.8 or 10.76391	square feet (ft²)
square meters (m²)	1.2 or 1.195990	square yards (yd²)
square kilometers (km²)	0.4	square miles (mi²)
hectares (ha)	2.5 or 2.471054	acres (ac)

Temperature

US Customary to SI Metric

Fahrenheit (°F)	5/9 (after subtracting 32)*	Celsius (°C)
Celsius (°C)	9/5 (then add 32)*	Fahrenheit (°F)

(Continued)

Conversions and Equivalents *(continued)*

Liquid Measure

Gallons	Quarts	Pints	Ounces	Cups	Tablespoons	Teaspoons	Milliliters
1	4	8	128	16	256	768	3480
	1	2	32	4	64	192	960
		1	16	2	32	96	480
			1	1/8	2	6	30
				1 (8 oz)	16	48	240
					1	3	15
						1	5

Equivalents

0.1 gallon = 13 ounces	0.4 gallon = 51 ounces	0.75 gallon = 96 ounces / 3 quarts
0.2 gallon = 26 ounces	0.5 gallon = 64 ounces / 2 quarts	0.8 gallon = 102 ounces
0.25 gallon = 32 ounces / 1 quart	0.6 gallon = 77 ounces	0.9 gallon = 115 ounces
0.3 gallon = 38 ounces	0.7 gallon = 90 ounces	1.0 gallon = 128 ounces / 4 quarts
1 gallon of water = 8 1/3 lb	1 ft^3 of water = 62 1/2 lb	
12″ = 1′	1760 yd = 1 mile	1 mile^2 = 640 acres
3′ = 1 yd	144 in^2 = 1 ft^2	1 acre = 43,560 ft^2
5280′ = 1 mile	1 yd^2 = 9 ft^2	

*Exact

Goodheart-Willcox Publisher

Writing and Understanding Binomial Nomenclature

Parts of a Botanical Name

Binomial nomenclature is a two-word naming system that uses Latin to name plant species in a consistent and methodical manner. Without this system, plant species were given different names around the world. Most plants also had common names that were specific to different regions of the world. Before this system, plant species were given different names around the world.

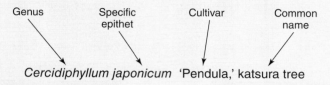

Genus   Specific epithet   Cultivar   Common name

Cercidiphyllum japonicum 'Pendula,' katsura tree

sur-sid-ih-FILL-um juh-PON-ih-kum

- The first part of a botanical name is the name of the *genus*, which is a subset of plants that share characteristics.
- The second part of the name is the *specific epithet*, which may refer to many features of the plant, for example, colors of foliage, stems, or flowers, country of origin, or habits of growth, who found it, or nothing at all.
- Together, the genus and specific epithet constitute the *species* name. The word species is both singular and plural; thus, it is used to indicate one or multiple species. Species is abbreviated as *sp.* (singular) or *spp.* (plural).

Cornus species, dogwood
Colocasia sp., elephant ear

- When the word species or its abbreviation is included in a name, it is lowercase and *never* italicized.
- The last part of the botanical name is the *common name*, which varies by geographical location.

Capitalization and Italicization

The capitalization and italicization of botanical names follows the rules of the International Code of Botanical Nomenclature. These rules also help make the names consistent internationally.

Genus in italics   Specific epithet in italics   Common name   Genus underlined   Specific epithet underlined

Centaurea cineraria, dusty miller *or* <u>Centaurea cineraria</u>, dusty miller

sen-tore-EE-uh sin-ur-AIR-ee-uh

- The genus name is always written with an initial capital letter and written in italics or underlined.
- The names of genera (plural of genus) are treated as nouns.
- The name of a genus can be abbreviated to its first letter when several species of a genus are listed in sequence.
- A genus may contain a single species to more than one hundred species or even a thousand or more (though this is rare).
- The specific epithet always begins with a lowercase letter and is written in italics or underlined.
- The specific epithet is usually considered an adjective that modifies the genus. It also agrees in gender with the genus.
- The common name is written in lowercase unless it is a proper noun. It is neither italicized nor underlined.

(Continued)

Writing and Understanding Binomial Nomenclature *(continued)*

Cultivars

A *cultivar* is a variety created or selected by humans. The term is derived from the term: *cultivated variety*. Cultivars are clearly distinguished by one or more characteristics, which they retain when reproduced.

Genus   Specific epithet   Cultivar name in single quotes   Cultivar name capitalized and preceded by cv.

Salvia greggii 'Furman's Red' or *Salvia greggii* cv. Furman's Red

SAL-vee-uh GREGG-ee-eye

- A cultivar is always capitalized and written in single quotes or preceded by the abbreviation *cv.* It is neither italicized nor underlined.
- A cultivar name cannot be in Latin and may not be the same as the botanical or common name of a genus.
- The name in quotes is the *cultivar*, which is a variety of the plant created by humans.
- A cultivar name may be trademarked and/or patented.

Hybrids

A *hybrid** is a cross between plants of different genera or species. Hybrids may occur naturally or be created. The × may be placed before or in the middle of the genera, depending on how the cross was conducted, within or across genera.

× *Fatshedera*
fats-HED-ur-uh
Phlox × *procumbens*
FLOCKS pro-KUM-benz

- The × before the genus indicates that the plant is a hybrid of two genera. For example, × *Fatshedera* is a hybrid between the different genera *Fatsia* and *Hedera*.
- *Phlox* × *procumbens* is a hybrid resulting from a cross between the species *P. stolonifera* (creeping phlox) and *P. subulata* (moss phlox).
- The multiplication symbol (×) is used to indicate the cross, not the letter x. If multiplication symbol (×) is not available, an x may be used.
- The × is neither italicized nor underlined.

* There can be only one correct name corresponding to a particular hybrid formula; this is the earliest legitimate name at the appropriate rank, and other names corresponding to the same hybrid formula are synonyms of it.

Variety

A *variety* is a naturally occurring mutation or offspring that differs slightly but distinctively from the parent.

Genus   Specific epithet   Variety name preceded by var.

Cercis canadensis var. *alba*. is a variety of *Cercis Canadensis*

Cercis canadensis var. alba.   Species and variety names underlined

SUR-siss kan-uh-DEN-siss var. AL-buh

- A variety name is written in lower case and italicized or underlined.

(Continued)

Writing and Understanding Binomial Nomenclature *(continued)*

Pronunciation

In the United States, botanical names are usually pronounced with English letter sounds as opposed to those used in classical Latin. The pronunciation will vary by dialect. The following rules will help you correctly pronounce botanical names.

- There is no silent *e* at the end of words in botanical names.

- A final vowel is always voiced.

> *Quercus buckleyi*, Texas red oak
> KWURK-us BUCK-lee-**eye**
> *Rhododendron catawbiense*, Catawba rhododendron
> roe-doe-DEN-drun kuh-taw-bee-EN-**see**

- The *ae* and *oe* are treated as the letter *e*.
- The *ae* and *oe* may be pronounced as a long *e*. For example:

> *Acer crataegifolium*, hawthorn maple
> AY-sur kruh-**tee**-jih-FOE-lee-um
> *Actaea racemosa*, bugbane
> ack-**TEE**-uh ray-sem-OH-zuh

- The *ae* and *oe* may be pronounced as a short *e*. For example:

> *Aesculus parviflora*, bottlebrush buckeye
> **ESS**-kew-luss par-vih-FLORE-uh

- The *ae* and *oe* are now often written as *e*.

- When the letter *c* precedes ae or oe, it is pronounced as though it is followed by the letter *e*, such as in the word *ceiling*.

> *Caesalpinia cacalaco*, cascalote
> **seez**-al-PYE-nee-uh kah-kuh-LAY-koe

- When the letter *g* precedes ae or oe, it is pronounced as though it is followed by the letter *e*, such as in the word *geology*.

> *Galanthus nivalis* subsp. *reginae-olgae*
> guh-LAN-thus nih-VAY-liss ruh-JYE-nee-OL-**jee**

- The letters *ch* are pronounced as a *k*.

> *Geranium wallichianum*
> jur-AY-nee-um wuh-li**ck**-ee-AY-num

- The letters *th* are pronounced as they are in the word *thinking*.

> *Gleditsia triacanthos*, honey locust
> gluh-DIT-see-uh try-uh-KAN-**th**us

- Some initial consonants are silent when followed by a consonant.

> *Pseudotsuga menziesii*, Douglas fir
> **s**oo-doe-TSOO-guh MEN-zeez-ee-eye

(Continued)

Writing and Understanding Binomial Nomenclature *(continued)*

- Words with two syllables are stressed on the first syllable.

Pteris, brake fern
TEER-iss

- The vowel of the first syllable is short when followed by two or more consonants.

Hosta fortunei
HOSS-**tuh** FOR-tune-ee-eye

- The vowel of the first syllable is long when followed by a single consonant.

Sedum rupestre, blue spruce sedum
SEE-dum roo-PESS-tree

- Words with more than two syllables are stressed on the second to last syllable, if the vowel of that syllable is followed by two or more consonants, which makes the vowel short, or if the vowel is long.

Narcissus tazetta
nar-SI**SS**-us tuh-ZETT-uh
Nymphaea
nim-**FEE**-uh

- Words with more than two syllables are stressed on the third to last syllable, if the preceding rule does not apply.

Nepeta or *Clematis*
NEP-ih-tuh or **CLEM**-ma-tis

- Some double consonants may be treated as single consonants.

Chionochloa rubra, red tussock grass
kye-on-oh-KLOE-uh ROO-**br**uh

- The *sh* or *ess* sound may be given to the letters *c* and *t* if they are followed by the letter *i*.

Veronica gentianoides
vur-ON-ih-kuh jen-**shee**-ay-noe-EYE-deez
Betula occidentalis, water birch
BET-you-luh ock-**sih**-den-TAY-liss

- The letter *x* is pronounced as two separate consonants due to its *ks* sound.

Taxus baccata, English yew
TAC**KS**-us buh-KAY-tuh

Glossary

A

acclimatization. The gradual introduction of greenhouse plants to the outdoor environment. Also referred to as *hardening off.* (8)

accountant. A person who interprets, analyzes, reports, and summarizes financial data. (17)

accounts payable. Bills that are due on receipt or in a short time frame. (17)

action threshold. The point at which the pest reaches an unacceptable level and corrective action must be taken. Also referred to as *threshold level.* (22)

acute toxicity. The measure of a pesticide's toxicity after a single exposure. (22)

adventitious buds. Buds that develop from places other than *nodes* or *leaf axils.* (21)

adventitious roots. Roots that grow from any plant part other than the root, such as from the stem or leaves. (8)

advertising. The act of drawing attention to a product or service. (17)

aeration. A process in which holes are made in the lawn to allow more oxygen and nutrients to penetrate the soil easily. A machine pulls plugs or cores of soil and thatch from the lawn. Core aeration is very effective on compacted soils. May also be referred to as *core aeration.* (12)

aggregate. A collection of units, such as gravel, used together. (15)

allergic reaction. A situation in which a person's immune system overreacts to a substance referred to as an allergen. (3)

alphabet of lines. A standardized collection of the different types of lines used in design drawings. (16)

amendment. The materials added to soil to improve its physical or chemical properties. (5)

amperage. The strength of the electrical current required to power a lamp or other fixture. (13)

amperes (amps). Term used to indicate the measurement of electric current (amperage). (13)

angiosperms. Plant classification which includes most flowering plants whose seeds are enclosed in a fruit. (9)

annual. A plant that completes its growth cycle in one growing season. All roots, stems, and leaves die at the end of the growing season. (5)

apices. The tips of roots and stems. (9)

arboretum. A place dedicated to growing trees for study and display; a botanical garden with living collections of trees, shrubs, and herbaceous plants, which are cultivated for scientific study, educational purposes, and for enjoyment. (9)

arboriculture. The science of tree care and management. (1)

arborist. A specialist trained to provide proper tree care, help maintain healthy trees, and give advice on removing large dying or deceased specimens. (1)

arc. The area of a circle irrigated by a sprinkler head. (14)

architect's scale. A drawing tool used to draw objects to full, reduced, or enlarged size and to draw distances to scale. (16)

aseptic culture. A form of asexual plant propagation in which a small section of the parent plant is placed in a nutrient-rich growing medium to rapidly reproduce plants that are identical to the parent plant. Also referred to as *micropropagation* or *tissue culture.* (1)

asexual propagation. A reproduction process in which the progeny is produced from a single organism and has only the genes of that organism. Also referred to as *vegetative propagation.* (8)

asphalt. A hard paving material made from a mixture of tar, sand, and gravel. (7)

asset. Valuable and available property owned by a business. (17)

asymmetrical balance. A form of balance achieved by placing different combinations of materials that carry the same amount of visual weight on each side of the design. Also referred to as *informal balance.* (6)

atmospheric vacuum breaker (AVB). The simplest and least expensive type of *backflow preventer.* (14)

attitude. A person's outlook on life; a reflection of how a person reacts to the events and people around him or her. (2)

auricle. The growth that projects from each side of the collar on a blade of grass. (11)

awnings. Outdoor ceiling material typically made with flexible materials attached to a frame, which is attached to a structure, such as a wall. (7)

B

backflow preventer. An irrigation system valve that prevents water from flowing back into the water supply lines. Also referred to as a *check valve.* (14)

bacteria. Single-celled, nonaggressive microorganisms that cannot penetrate plant foliage or stems. Bacteria infect plants through wounds and openings caused by pruning, cuts, and cracks. (22)

balance. An even distribution of the visual weight of landscape materials along a central axis. (6)

balance sheet. A financial statement of company assets, liabilities, and capital (equity) at a specific time. (17)

balled and burlapped (B&B). A method used to protect the root ball of plants harvested directly from the ground. The exposed root ball is placed in a natural fabric inside a wire basket for secure handling and shipping. (8)

bare root (BR). A nursery method of harvesting and selling plants; the plants are free of soil and typically do not have grown stems and leaves. (8)

bedding plants. Plants installed mainly for their seasonal floral or foliage presentation. (10)

beneficials. The natural predators that are introduced or released in an area to control pests. (22)

Note: The number in parentheses following each definition indicates the chapter in which the term can be found.

berm. An earthen mound 4″ to 6″ tall installed around the drip zone of the tree. A berm is also a larger ridge or embankment installed for various reasons, such as to provide privacy or dampen noise. (20)

Better Business Bureau (BBB). A nonprofit organization focused on advancing trust in the marketplace. (17)

bid. A fixed price submitted in an itemized format for a specific project. (18)

bid solicitation. A process in which a potential client notifies prospective landscape companies to bid a price for a project. Also referred to as a *request for quotations (RFQ)*, an *invitation to bid ((ITB)*, or a *request for proposals (RFP)*. (18)

biennial. A plant that lives two years to complete its growing cycle. The first year is typically a grouping of leaves near the ground; stem growth and flowering occur in the second year. (5)

binomial name. A two-word name that includes a genus and specific epithet for a plant species. Also referred to as the *botanical, Latin*, or *scientific name*. (9)

binomial nomenclature. A two-word naming system that describes plant species in a consistent and methodical manner. (9)

biological control. A pest control method in which living microorganisms or natural predators are used to control pests. (22)

blade. The leaf portion of a grass plant. (11)

blend. A combination of cultivars of the same species of grass. (11)

block stone. Hard paving materials made of brick or cement; available in a variety of shapes and sizes. (7)

bond paper. A drafting media that is used primarily for printing CAD drawings because printer toner adheres well to its surface. (16)

bookkeeper. A person who records the daily transactions of a business, such as processing payroll and posting debits and credits. (17)

botanical garden. A large garden that often has both greenhouses and outdoor areas that are open to the public. (9)

botanical name. A two-word name that includes a genus and specific epithet for a plant species. Also referred to as the *binomial, Latin*, or *scientific name*. (9)

branch collar. A swollen area at the base of a branch that is at a 30° to 45° angle from the trunk. (21)

brand image. The way that customers and the public perceive a company. (17)

breach of contract. A situation in which one party does not meet the terms of a contract. (19)

brick paver. A paving unit made with concrete or clay formed in a rectangular shape. (15)

broadcast. A method use to apply a pesticide in which the pesticide is spread uniformly over the area to be treated. (22)

bubble diagram. A preliminary design drawing used to note designated areas for specific purposes, such as dining and playing. Also referred to as *functional diagrams* or *conceptual drawings*. (16)

bud. A stem's primary growing point. It may be a *wood* or *growth bud*, a *flower bud*, or a *leaf bud*. (21)

budget. A financial plan for the future concerning income and costs of a business. (17); the total financial resources allocated for a project. (18)

bulb. A modified stem with a short, fleshy basal plate at the bottom from which roots grow and which holds fleshy scales. (9)

burden. All costs associated with operating a business that are not directly tied to one specific project. Also referred to as *overhead* or *indirect costs*. (18)

business contract. An agreement between two or more competent parties, such as two people or two businesses. Categories generally have to do with employment, sale or lease, tenancy, service, and general business issues. (19)

business license. A permit issued by local, county, state, or federal authorities that allows an individual or company to conduct business. (17)

business plan. A document that states the mission of the business, examines its current condition, sets goals, and outlines strategies for achieving the goals. (17)

C

caliper. A measurement that represents the thickness of a plant stem. (8)

capital. The money needed to purchase materials and operate a business. (17)

carbon sequestration. A process in which CO_2 is captured and stored in liquid or solid forms. (9)

cash flow statement. A financial report that tracks income and expenses. (17)

catch device. A cup-like device that is placed at various points to collect and measure the amount of irrigation water being applied during an irrigation cycle. (14)

C corporation. A business structure in which the corporation is a separate taxpayer and the income and expenses are taxed to the corporation and not the owners. (17)

certified irrigation designer (CID). A person certified in the design and/or installation of landscape irrigation systems. (1)

check valve. An irrigation system valve that prevents water from flowing back into the water supply lines. Also referred to as a *backflow preventer*. (14)

chemical control. A pest control method in which a pesticide is used to control insects, weeds, fungi, rodents, and other pests. (22)

chronic toxicity. The toxicity of a pesticide after repeated exposures over time. (22)

classification. The scientific system of grouping like organisms. (9)

climbing stem root. Vines that climb using their stems and root structures. Also referred to as *clinging stem roots*. (10)

clinger. A vine that attaches to structures with its adhesive pads and aerial roots. (10)

clinging stem root. A vine that climbs using its stems and root structures. Also referred to as *climbing stem roots*. (10)

collar. The area on the outside of the leaf where the leaf blade and leaf sheath join. (11)

color scheme. The guidelines for combining colors in a design. (6)

common name. A word or term for a plant used in everyday language. The variations often cause confusion or misidentification of a plant. (9)

compactor. A power or hand tamping tool with a metal plate that is used on the subsurface of a hardscape to compact the material. Also referred to as a *hand tamper* or *vibratory tamper*. (15)

complete fertilizer. A plant fertilizer in which nitrogen (N), phosphorous (P), and potassium (K) are present. (21)

complete metamorphosis. A form of metamorphosis in which an insect goes through four stages: egg, larva, pupa, and adult. (22)

composite. Hardscape material made from a combination of recycled wood and plastic. (7)

composite lumber. A hardscape material made from wood fiber and plastic. (15)

conceptual drawing. A design drawing used to note designated areas for specific purposes, such as dining and playing. Also referred to as *bubble diagrams* or *functional diagrams*. (16)

concrete. An expensive hard paving material made with water, aggregate, and powdered cement. (7)

concrete paver. A preformed paving unit made of concrete. (15)

conflict. A hostile situation resulting from opposing views. (2)

conservatory. A greenhouse that is typically attached to a home or other structure. The plants cultivated may be primarily for display or scientific study. (9)

consideration. The portion of a contract that explains what each party will gain from the business arrangement. (19)

contact insecticide. A chemical pesticide that poisons and kills pests when the insecticide comes in contact with the pest's body. (22)

contingency. A contract provision that is used to cover unpredictable situations. (18)

controlled-release fertilizer (CRF). A fertilizer that releases nutrients over a specific time, at a specific rate. (21)

controller. Device that manipulates the on/off schedules for line-voltage and low-voltage lighting systems. (13)

cool-season plant. A plant that thrives in the cool temperatures of early spring and fall. (5)

cool-season turfgrass. A grass that thrives in areas with hot summers and cold, freezing winters. Their optimum growing temperature is between 60°F and 75°F (15.5°C to 24°C). (11)

cooperative. A business structure with at least five members. Each member is an owner and has equal voting rights, regardless of his or her level of involvement. (17)

cooperative extension agent. The liaison between the community and a university who conducts classes on various agricultural, horticultural, and landscaping topics for professionals and members of the public. (1)

Cooperative Extension System (CES). A publicly funded education program that uses knowledge gained through research and education to address human, plant, and animal needs. (1)

core aeration. A process in which holes are made in the lawn to allow more oxygen and nutrients to penetrate the soil easily. A machine pulls plugs or cores of soil and thatch from the lawn. Core aeration is very effective on compacted soils. May also be referred to as *aeration*. (12)

corm. A modified enlarged stem that serves as a storage organ. (9)

corporation. A business owned by stockholders or shareholders who share in profits and losses but are not personally liable for the business' financial transactions. (17)

cover letter. A brief and to-the-point letter that accompanies an applicant's résumé. It is often the first contact you have with a potential employer. Also referred to as a *letter of application*. (2)

cross-linked polyethylene pipe (PEX). A white, high-density polyethylene pipe that is very flexible. It is susceptible to the sun's ultraviolet (UV) rays and must be buried or installed under a structure for protection. (14)

cultivar. A plant mutation or offspring created by human manipulation. (9)

cultural control. A pest control method in which cultural methods are used to help prevent pest problems, such as using best practices to install and manage a landscape and installing disease-resistant plants. (22)

current asset. Valuable and available property that has short-term usefulness for a business. (17)

current liability. A financial obligation or debt of a company to creditors or suppliers that is typically due on receipt. (17)

customer service. Taking care of the customer's needs efficiently and delivering helpful service before, during, and after the customer's needs are met. (19)

cutting. A plant piece that has been cut from the parent plant and is used to propagate a new plant. (8)

cyclone spreader. A piece of lawn equipment used to broadcast seed in a swath that is several feet wide. Also referred to as a *rotary spreader*. (12)

D

deadheading. The removal of dead blooms on perennials and small shrubs during blooming. (21)

debt. The money, goods, or services a company owes. (17)

deciduous. Trees or shrubs that lose their leaves annually. (5)

deck. A hardscape that adjoins a home and is used for recreational purposes. Decks are typically raised platforms constructed with wood or a composite. (15)

demographics. Statistical data relating to population, such as age, income, and family structure. (17)

depreciation. The reduction of an asset's value over time, primarily due to wear and tear. (18)

design capacity. The maximum amount of water that can be used at any given time in the irrigation system. (14)

detention pond. A constructed pond that temporarily holds excess water that eventually drains completely. (14)

dethatcher. Any device used to remove thatch from lawns. (12)

dicot. A plant that has two cotyledons, branching venation, and floral structures in multiples of four and five. (9)

digging tool. A tool used to make holes for planting and posts and to move or spread materials, such as compost or mulch. (4)

direct cost. A price that can be attributed to a service, material, or labor used on a particular project. (18)

directional arrow. An arrow on a landscape design drawing that indicates true north and enables the user to orient himself or herself to the site. (16)

disappearing fountain. A water feature in which the water seems to disappear but is actually falling into a reservoir and recirculated. (13)

distal balance. The asymmetrical balance of elements on the central axis (right and left) as well as in the field of vision (near and far). Also referred to as *proximal balance*. (6)

distribution uniformity. A measure of how evenly water is applied throughout a site in each irrigation zone. (14)

division. A vegetative propagation process in which the crown of a plant is divided into smaller pieces that can be planted immediately to produce new plants. (8)

doing business as (DBA). A form of registration that allows a business to operate under a name different from its legal, registered name. (17)

dormant. A period in which the buds and seeds of a plant are inhibited from growing until the environmental conditions become ideal for the plant to grow. (10)

double-check valve assembly (DCV). A common backflow preventer used in underground or in-line systems. (14)

drafting media. The materials on which landscape design drawings are made or printed. (16)

drench. A method used to apply a pesticide in which the pesticide is applied to the soil and absorbed by the plant. (22)

drip irrigation. A low-volume irrigation system that slowly and precisely applies water directly to the plant root zone. Also referred to as *trickle irrigation*. (14)

drop seeder. A piece of lawn equipment that simply drops the seed on the ground as it is pushed across the planting area. It is used for more precise placement of seed. (12)

dry-laying. The construction of a permeable hardscape that does not use cement below and between the pavers. (15)

dwarf shrub. An evergreen or deciduous woody plant with a mature height less than 4'. (10)

E

edible landscaping. Landscaping that incorporates edible plants in the ornamental areas of a landscape. (10)

efflorescence. A whitish, powdery deposit on the surface of stones that occurs when the minerals in water that has risen to the surface remain on the surface when the water evaporates. (15)

electric current. The flow of energy on a path. (13)

electro-mechanical controller. Irrigation system controller that is driven by gears and motors that instruct irrigation zones to turn on and off. (14)

elements of design. The "ingredients" used in a design; the selection and blending of these ingredients (line, form, texture, and color) is guided by the principles of design. (6)

emergent plant. An aquatic plant whose roots are in the soil and the leaves, stems, and flowers rise above the water surface. (10)

emitter. A small regulator that controls the quantity and rate of water discharge in a drip irrigation system. (14)

employer identification number (EIN). A number assigned by the IRS to identify a business with respect to their tax obligations. Also referred to as a *tax identification number (TIN)*. (17)

engineer's scale. A drawing tool used to draw objects to full, reduced, or enlarged size and to draw distances to scale. (16)

entrepreneur. A person who organizes and manages a business and assumes the risks involved. (17)

environmental horticulture industry. The industry that includes plant and soil research, floriculture, viticulture, and olericulture, and companies that produce, rent, and sell landscape supplies and equipment. Also referred to as the *green industry*. (1)

EPA registration number. An identification number assigned to a pesticide after it has been reviewed and verified by the EPA; certifies the product has been reviewed and has minimal risk when the label's directions are followed. (22)

epicormic root. A new plant growing from the root of another plant. (21)

epicormic shoot. A shoot growing from a previously dormant bud on the trunk or limb of a tree. (21)

equity. The difference between the business' worth minus what it owes. (17)

erosion netting. A woven fabric made of biodegradable fibers which is designed to prevent soil and newly-planted seeds from washing down the slope. (12)

espalier. A unique training method in which a plant is trained to grow flat against a wall or other support. (10)

estimate. A general estimation of what a project will cost. (18)

ethical behavior. Conforming to accepted standards of fairness and good conduct. (2)

evergreen. A plant that remains green year-round; some shed needles or leaves throughout the year but never all at once. (5)

exclusion control. A pest control method in which screens, traps, and other barriers are used to prevent pests from causing damage. (22)

expense. Monies paid by the company for salaries, rent/mortgage, utilities, supplies, and other business purchases. (17)

external pump. A water feature pump that is installed in a dry location. They have higher pumping capacities and are easier to access and service than submersible pumps. (13)

F

face mixing. Applying a thin layer of fine aggregate to the surface of the wet concrete to provide color and greater abrasion or texture. (15)

fertilizer. A substance that is spread on the ground or mixed in the soil to help plants grow by providing nutrients. (21)

fertilizer injector. A tool that dilutes and mixes the fertilizer with water being applied to the plants. Some injectors are adjustable, while others apply at a fixed rate, such as 1:16. (21)

fibrous roots. Root systems that are shallow and dense and spread across the soil, such as those of turfgrass. (9)

field capacity. A condition that occurs when the capillary pores of the soil profile are full of water. (20)

field production. A nursery cultivation operation in which plants are grown in true soil in an open field. (8)

final design. The finished landscape drawing that is also used as the construction document for use by the installer. (16)

first aid. The help given to an injured person until full medical treatment is available. (3)

fixed expense. A business expense that must be met regularly, typically on a monthly basis. (17)

flagstone. Natural hardscape material that is used as an accent or to create outdoor flooring. (7)

float valve. A valve installed in a water feature that opens and closes the water supply with a float on the water surface. If the float goes below the desired level, the valve opens; if the float is at the desired level, the valve closes and remains shut. (13)

floating leaf plant. An aquatic plant whose roots are in the soil and leaves float on the water surface. (10)

flower bud. A bud from which flowers bloom, which then produce fruit. (21)

foam board. A drafting media that is light but stiff and can be placed on an easel and remain upright. Also referred to as *illustration board*. (16)

focal point. An area of visual dominance in a landscape design to which the viewer's attention is drawn. (6)

focalization. The use of a focal point to force the viewer's attention to a particular location. (6)

foliar spray. A method used to apply a pesticide to the leaves of a plant. (22)

form. The shape or silhouette of individual plants or groups of plants. (6)

formal balance. A form of balance in which one side of the landscape is a mirror image of the other. Also referred to as *symmetrical balance*. (6)

formal hedge. A row of shrubs created with plants that are kept trimmed to appear uniform in size; used to create an outdoor wall. (7)

fountain. Structure that sends out a stream of water that falls into a basin of some sort and is pumped to the top to repeat the cycle. (13)

four Ps of marketing. A tool used to help understand what the product or service can offer consumers and how to plan a successful promotion campaign. The four Ps are product, price, promotion, and place. May also be referred to as the *marketing mix*. (19)

freeze-thaw cycle. A natural process in which water freezes and expands during cold weather and thaws when the temperature increases. (5)

friction loss. The loss of water pressure as the water is pumped through system components. (14)

frostbite. A medical condition that occurs when skin and its underlying tissues freeze. (3)

frost heave. A condition that occurs when the freezing and thawing of the soil pushes plants out of the soil and exposes the roots and crowns to freezing air and drying winds. (21)

frost line. The maximum depth (in inches or millimeters) below which the soil does not freeze. (14)

functional diagram. A preliminary design drawing used to note designated areas for specific purposes, such as dining and playing. Also referred to as *bubble diagrams* or *conceptual drawings*. (16)

fungicide. A chemical pesticide that is crop-specific and designed to prevent fungi from spreading. (22)

fungus. A specialized organism that attaches itself to a host and decomposes the host as it absorbs nutrients from it. (22)

G

gallons per hour (gph). The amount of water an irrigation system applies in one hour. (14)

gallons per minute (gpm). The number of gallons of water the well/pump provides per minute. (14)

galvanized piping. Zinc-coated metal piping used in irrigation systems. (14)

gazebo. A permanent structure with a covered canopy and ornamental posts and railings. (7)

gear-driven rotary head. A sprinkler head that is gear-driven and capable of propelling water over a long distance in a variety of spray patterns. (14)

general-use pesticide. A pesticide that is available to the public. (22)

genus. A subset of organisms within a family that share similar characteristics. (9)

geographic information system (GIS). A system that processes satellite images and accurately displays land, buildings, roads, and other land features. (4)

geophyte. A perennial plant with an underground food storage organ. (9)

geotextile. A synthetic fabric used as a weed barrier, separation between various materials, or to reinforce or protect a material. (15)

girdling. A condition that occurs when the growth of the trunk is restricted. (20)

global positioning system (GPS). A system to create databases of satellite images of properties around the world. The satellites also enable someone with a receiver to pinpoint an exact location. (4)

goal. Something that you strive to achieve. (17)

goal setting. The process of identifying something you want to accomplish and establishing a plan to achieve the desired result. (2)

grade. The rise and fall or inclination of the land surface. A flat, horizontal piece of land is said to have a slope of zero. It may also be defined as the change in elevation from a fixed point. Also referred to as *slope*. (5); the rise and fall of the land surface or a change in elevation from a fixed point. Also referred to as *slope*. (15)

grading. Smoothing the soil surface to ensure a level base and the proper slope for drainage. (12)

gradual restorative pruning. A pruning technique in which the majority of the plant material is removed over a period of 3 years to stimulate juvenile growth and thickening of the plant over time. (21)

grafting. A propagation technique in which a shoot or bud of one plant is inserted into or joined to the stem, branch, or root of another plant. (8)

graph paper. A drafting medium with preprinted grids that help the designer keep his or her scale work consistent. Also referred to as *quadrille paper*. (16)

grass-like plant. Any of various plants with leaves that resemble grass leaves but belong to different families of plants. (10)

gravel. Small pieces of loose rock used for ground cover, walkways, driveways, and as an ornamental means of ground cover. (7)

green industry. The industry that includes plant and soil research, floriculture, viticulture, and olericulture, and companies that produce, rent, and sell landscape supplies and equipment. Also referred to as the *environmental horticulture industry*. (1)

ground cover. Plants with spreading growth habits that typically reach a height of 18″ or less; may be used to create soft, outdoor flooring. (7)

growth bud. A bud from which wood branches grow. Also referred to as a *wood bud*. (21)

guying. A form of *staking* used to steady large trees. (20)

gymnosperms. Nonflowering, seed-producing plants. Their seeds are not protected by the plant's fruit. (9)

H

hand tamper. A compacting tool with a long handle with a flat metal plate attached at one end. Also referred to as a *compactor*. (15)

hardening off. The gradual introduction of greenhouse plants to the outdoor environment. Also referred to as *acclimatization*. (8)

hard flooring. Outdoor flooring made from materials such as wood, concrete, stone, paving blocks, brick, and asphalt. (7)

hardiness zone. A zone of the country that is determined by the average minimum temperature of each area. (5)

hard pruning. A pruning technique in which the majority of the plant material is removed to stimulate juvenile growth and thickening of the plant over time. Also referred to as *rejuvenation pruning* or *restorative pruning*. (21)

hardscape. A walkway, gathering area, driveway, and other structure made of inanimate materials, such as wood, stone, and concrete. (15)

head height. The total number of feet from the top of the waterfall to the water's surface. (13)

heading. A pruning technique in which terminal portions of shoots or limbs are removed down to a live bud or branch to reduce size and stimulate lateral growth. Also referred to as *heading back*. (21)

heading back. A pruning technique in which terminal portions of shoots or limbs are removed down to a live bud or branch to reduce size and stimulate lateral growth. Also referred to as *heading*. (21)

head-to-head coverage. The practice of placing sprinklers so the water from each one overlaps and reaches the next sprinkler head. (14)

heat cramp. A muscle spasm caused from the loss of fluids and electrolytes through perspiration and the lack of fluid intake. (3)

heat exhaustion. A condition that occurs when a person becomes dehydrated and the body's core temperature rises above a safe level. (3)

heat island. An area in which the temperature is higher than that of the surrounding areas due to human activities and hardscape structures. (10)

heatstroke. The most serious form of heat illness. (3)

heat zone map. A map of the United States that provides the average number of days that areas across the country experience temperatures over 86°F (30°C). (5)

hedge. A row of shrubs used to create walls and borders in the landscape. (7)

herbaceous perennial. An herbaceous plant (plant with a soft, succulent stem) that dies to the ground and returns the next growing season. (10)

herbicide. A chemical pesticide designed to control and eliminate weeds. (22)

heterophyllus. A plant that develops different leaf forms on the same plant. (21)

high-visibility clothing. Any type of clothing with reflective properties or made with very bright colors for the purpose of ensuring that the wearer can easily be seen. (3)

homeowner's association (HOA). An organization in a planned community that makes and enforces rules for the properties within its jurisdiction. (5)

host. A live organism on which a pest is living. (22)

hue. A pure color that has not been modified. (6)

hybrid. A cross between plants in different genera or species. (9)

hydraulics. The science and technology of the movement of liquids. (14)

hydrophyte. A plant that is adapted to life in very wet places. (5)

hypocotyl. The stem section between the upper and lower portion of the plant. On tuberous stems, this portion swells after germination. (9)

hypothermia. A medical condition that occurs when a body loses heat faster than it can produce heat, causing a very low body temperature. (3)

I

illustration board. A drafting medium that is light but stiff and can be placed on an easel and remain upright. Also referred to as *foam board*. (16)

impact rotary head. A sprinkler head that rotates using a spring-loaded or weighted arm that is propelled by water pressure. (14)

impact tool. A tool used to apply force by striking an object or another tool. (4)

income. The money a business earns. (17)

income statement. A financial statement that shows net income for a specific period, such as a month, quarter, or fiscal year. Also referred to as *profit and loss statement*. (17)

incomplete fertilizer. A plant fertilizer that lacks one of the three primary macronutrients [nitrogen (N), phosphorous (P), and potassium (K)]. (21)

incomplete metamorphosis. A form of metamorphosis in which an insect goes through three stages: egg, nymph, and adult. (22)

indirect cost. A cost for services or activities associated with multiple projects. Also used to describe *overhead*. (18)

infiltration. The manner in which water moves through the soil profile. (5)

infiltration rate. The rate in which water moves through the soil profile. (5)

informal balance. A form of balance achieved by placing different combinations of materials that carry the same amount of visual weight on each side of the design. Also referred to as *asymmetrical balance*. (6)

informal hedge. A row of shrubs created with a single species of plants that are allowed to grow into their natural shapes and create an outdoor wall. (7)

inorganic fertilizer. A soil amendment manufactured from materials other than plants or animals that is designed to provide nutrients to plants. (21)

insect. A small invertebrate with an exoskeleton, three distinct body regions, and three pairs of legs (may also have wings). (22)

insecticide. A chemical pesticide used to control harmful insects. (22)

institutional promotion. Focuses on promoting the company rather than its products in order to increase awareness of the business and create a favorable view of the brand. (19)

integrated pest management (IPM). A combination of pest management techniques designed to minimize the use of hazardous materials to control pests. (22)

intention. The portion of a contract that indicates that both parties intend for the contract to be legally binding. (19)

interior plantscaping. The designing, installation, and maintenance of landscaping in indoor areas. (1)

interiorscaping. The designing, installation, and maintenance of indoor landscaping. (1)

internode. The spaces between the *nodes* on a stem. (9)

inventory. The combined assets of a company. (17)

inventory (tool). A complete record of the tools and equipment owned by the company. (4)

invertebrate. An animal lacking a backbone, such as ladybugs and aphids. (22)

invitation to bid (ITB). A process in which a potential client notifies prospective landscape companies to bid a price for a project. Also referred to as a *bid solicitation*, a *request for quotations (RFQ)*, or a *request for proposals (RFP)*. (18)

irrigation. The application of water to plants to aid plant growth. (14)

irrigation system designer. A person who designs and often installs or supervises installation of irrigation systems. (1)

irrigation technician. Trained personnel who install, maintain, and repair landscape irrigation systems. (1)

irrigation zone. A section of an irrigation system that is controlled by a single valve. (14)

L

landscape architect. A trained and licensed architect with a bachelor's or master's degree in landscape architecture. (1)

landscape contractor. A licensed professional who coordinates and installs landscape designs. (1)

landscape designer. A professional who creates landscapes on a smaller scale than a landscape architect does. Their projects are typically limited to residential and small commercial properties. (1)

landscape estimate. A means of roughly calculating the cost of a project based on the site assessment, design, materials, and labor. (18)

landscape fabric. A tightly woven textile laid on top of the soil in planting beds and covered with mulch to prevent the growth of weeds. (20)

landscape horticulture. The cultivation and management of plants grown for aesthetic purposes, both indoor and outdoor. (1)

landscape irrigation system. A system designed to pump water from a source and distribute it throughout a landscape. (1)

landscape management. The application of management principles to foster growth and adjust maintenance plans to coincide with natural changes due to weather, pests, and other unforeseen events. (21)

landscaping industry. The industry that consists of people and businesses that cultivate, produce, sell, install, and maintain landscape designs created by landscape architects and designers. (1)

large shrub. An evergreen or deciduous plant with a mature height over 6′. (10)

large tree. A tree with a mature height over 25′. (10)

lateral line. A smaller diameter pipe that carries water from the mainline to the sprinkler head or emitter. (14)

Latin name. A two-word name that includes a genus and specific epithet for a plant species. Also referred to as the *binomial, botanical,* or *scientific name.* (9)

layering. A vegetative propagation process in which stems that are still attached to the parent plant form roots. (8)

LC$_{50}$. The lethal concentration of a chemical in the air. (22)

LD$_{50}$. The lethal dose of a pesticide that kills 50% of the test population. (22)

leadership. The ability to guide and motivate others to complete tasks or achieve goals. (2)

leaf axil. The upper angle between the leaf and stem. (21)

leaf bud. The location on a stem of grass in which a new grass blade originates. (11)

legend. A key to the symbols used on the landscape design drawing. (16)

lethal dose. The amount of a toxin that will cause death to a human being. (22)

letter of application. A brief and to-the-point letter that accompanies an applicant's résumé. It is often the first contact you have with a potential employer. Also referred to as a *cover letter.* (2)

leveling tool. A tool designed to indicate whether a surface is horizontal (level) or vertical (plumb) and to establish ground slopes. (4)

liability. A financial obligation or debt of a company. (17)

ligule. The part of a grass plant that is between the stem and leaf blade. (11)

limited liability company (LLC). A business structure that has the pass-through taxation of a partnership or sole proprietorship combined with the limited liability of a corporation. (17)

linear footage. Straight line measurement. (5)

liner. A greenhouse plant with a 1″ to 3″ diameter that is grown for transplanting. (8)

line-voltage system. Landscape lighting system in which the power comes directly from the building's electrical service. The system is hard-wired into the electrical service. (13)

liquid asset. Valuable and available property of a business that is easily converted to cash. (17)

living area. The backyard of the residence, which is usually more private than the rest of the property. (7)

logo. A recognizable icon, symbol, graphic design, or stylized name that identifies a company. (17)

long-term goal. Item or action that you wish to accomplish over the span of several years or even a lifetime. (2); a business achievement that will be reached over the span of several years. (17)

long-term liability. A business' debts that are paid to the lender over a specified length of time. (17)

M

macronutrients. The nutrients plants need in the largest quantities: nitrogen (N), phosphorous (P), and potassium (K); calcium (Ca), magnesium (Mg), and sulfur (S). (9)

macropore. A large space between soil particles that may hold air or water. (8)

mainline. A large diameter pipe that carries water to lateral lines. (14)

marketing. An advertising process through which a business promotes and sells products or services that have value to businesses and consumers. (17)

marketing mix. A tool or management process used to help understand what the product or service can offer consumers and how to plan a successful promotion campaign. May also be referred to as the *4 Ps of marketing* (*product, price, promotion,* and *place*). (19)

markup. Charge added to a bill to help cover a business' overhead costs. (18)

massing. Planting many of the same type of plant very close together. (6)

mechanical control. A pest control method in which pests are directly removed or killed and prevented from reaching the host plant with barriers or traps. Also referred to as *physical control.* (22)

medium shrub. An evergreen or deciduous woody plant ranging in height from 4′ to 6′. (10)

meiosis. The biological process for sexual propagation in which a single cell from each parent divides twice to produce four daughter cells. Each of these daughter cells has half the number of chromosomes (genetic information) of the parent cell. (8)

mesophyte. A plant that thrives under typically average conditions. (5)

metamorphosis. The changes an insect undergoes through its life cycle. (22)

microclimate. A small area with different environmental conditions than the surrounding area. (5)

microirrigation. A low-volume irrigation system that uses small tubes and water emitters to slowly release water to the plants. (8)

micronutrient. The nutrients plants need in very small amounts: boron (B), chlorine (Cl), copper (Cu), iron (Fe), manganese (Mn), molybdenum (Mo), nickel (Ni), and zinc (Zn). (9)

micropore. A small space between soil particles that may hold air or water. (8)

micropropagation. A form of asexual plant propagation in which a small section of the parent plant is placed in a nutrient-rich growing medium to rapidly reproduce plants that are identical to the parent plant. Also referred to as *tissue culture* or *aseptic culture.* (1); an asexual reproductive method in which plants are manipulated on a cellular level, causing them to duplicate themselves repeatedly and rapidly. (8)

micro-sprinkler head. A much smaller sprinkler head that delivers water in a fanlike spray at a low water pressure. (14)

mission statement. A short summary identifying a person's purpose or reason of existence; a personal philosophy for not only what, but who, a person would like to become in the future. (2); a short summary of the values and purpose of a company or organization. (17)

miticide. A chemical pesticide that eliminates tiny spider-like organisms referred to as mites. (22)

mitosis. The biological process for asexual propagation in which a cell replicates and divides its nuclear material, and then divides itself into two daughter cells. Each of the daughter cells contains the same genetic material and the resultant plants are identical to the parent plant. (8)

mix. A combination of at least two species of turfgrass. (11)

mixed border. A planted area used to create an outdoor wall using a blend of several species of plant material. (7)

mode of action. The manner in which the pesticide effectively controls or eliminates the pest. (22)

molluscicide. A chemical pesticide used to control mollusks, such as snails and slugs. (22)

monocot. A plant that has only one cotyledon, parallel-veined leaves, and floral structures in multiples of three. (9)

morphological. See *morphology.* (5)

morphology. The physical form and structure of plants. (5)

mulch. A loose landscaping material that adds color and texture, holds moisture, prevents weeds, and adds nutrients to the soil as it decomposes. (7)

multi-strand system. A method of wiring an irrigation system that uses common wire running from the controller to each control valve. Each control valve has a separate wire that runs directly from the control valve back to the controller. (14)

N

negotiation. The process of agreeing to an issue that requires all parties to give and take. (2)

net worth. The value of a business' assets that exceed the liabilities. (17)

networking. Meeting and creating a group of acquaintances and associates to form mutually beneficial relationships with other business people and potential clients. (17)

niche market. A very narrow and specific segment of a larger market. (17)

node. The point of attachment on a stem for roots, leaves, and flowers. (9)

noncurrent asset. Valuable and available property that has a long-term usefulness for a business. (17)

nonliquid asset. Valuable and available property of a business that cannot be converted to cash quickly. (17)

nonselective herbicide. A chemical pesticide that will kill any plant the chemical contacts. (22)

nontunicate bulb. A bulb with loose, fleshy scales and no dry covering. (9)

nonverbal communication. Communication by the sending and receiving of messages without the use of words. (2)

north arrow. An arrow on a landscape design drawing that indicates true north and enables the user to orient himself or herself to the site. Also referred to as a *directional arrow.* (16)

nursery. A place where young plants and trees are cultivated for sale and planting elsewhere. (1)

nymph. A juvenile insect. (22)

O

offer. A service or product presented for sale. (19)

ohms (Ω). The unit of measure for resistance. (13)

Ohm's law. Defines the relationship between voltage, amperage, and resistance with the mathematical formula: voltage (V) = current (I) × resistance (R) (V = I × R). (13)

oncenter (OC) spacing. The installation of plants with the same spacing using the center of each plant as the point of measurement. (20)

operational cost. The cost of labor, materials, and machinery used to perform a service or make a product. These costs do not accrue when the labor, materials, and machinery are not performing a service or making a product. Also referred to as *operational expense.* (18)

operational expense. The cost of labor, materials, and machinery used to perform a service or make a product. These costs do not accrue when the labor, materials, and machinery are not performing a service or making a product. Also referred to as *operational cost.* (18)

organic fertilizer. A soil amendment composed of organic materials, such as plants, vegetable peelings, and manure, that is worked into the soil to improve soil texture and provide nutrients to plants. (21)

organic matter. Material from decayed organisms that is added to soil to improve its physical and chemical properties. (5)

ornamental grasses. Perennial grasses belonging to the *Poaceae* family; range in size from 12″ to over 10′. (10)

orthographic projection drawing. A representation of the separate views of an object on a two-dimensional surface. It shows the width, depth, and height of the object and often includes dimensions. (16)

outdoor room concept. The outdoor room concept states that the landscape is a direct extension of the home. Each area of the landscape should serve a certain function. (7)

outward facing bud. A growth bud facing away from the center of the tree. (21)

overhead. All costs associated with operating a business that are not directly tied to one specific project. Also referred to as *burden* or *indirect costs.* (18)

overseeding. The process of planting grass seed to fill in areas that are thinning and to improve the density of a lawn. It may also be used to enhance the color of the turfgrass or provide winter color. (12)

P

partnership. A business structure in which two or more people invest in and own the business. (17)

pass-through taxation. This type of taxation allows a business owner to pay taxes on income from the business on his or her personal tax returns. (17)

pathogen. An organism or agent, such as a virus, fungus, or bacteria, that causes a disease. (22)

patio. A recreational area that adjoins a building, such as a home, to extend the living area and is often used for outdoor dining. Patios are typically made with hard surface materials, such as stone, pavers, or concrete, and are usually at ground level. (15)

pattern. A repeated decorative design or the recurring use of a specific element in a design. (15)

pavers. Hard paving materials made of brick or cement; available in a variety of shapes and sizes. (7)

paving tile. A glazed, decorated tile that can be used as flooring or wall covering. (15)

percolation. The speed or manner in which water moves *within* the soil. (5)

percolation rate. The speed or manner in which water moves *within* the soil. (5)

perennial. A plant that grows for many seasons. The stems, leaves, and flowers die at the end of the season and the roots become dormant. New growth occurs at the beginning of the next season. (5)

pergola. An open structure with openly spaced boards running perpendicular to each other across the top. (7)

perimeter. The defining shape and the edge of the excavation area. (13)

perlite. A volcanic rock that has a relatively high water content. It is used to improve a substrate's aeration and water retention. (8)

permeability. A measurement of the amount of water that passes through a hardscape material to the ground below. (15)

personal pace. A manual method used to measure areas when a measuring tool is unavailable or when a rough estimate will do. The measurement is based on the average number of steps taken along a straight 100′ path. (18)

personal protective equipment (PPE). Equipment and clothing worn by a person to protect himself or herself from harm in potentially hazardous situations. (3)

perspective drawing. A design drawing that shows the side of a building, such as the front of a house, with its landscaping installed. (16)

pest. Any organism that can cause damage or harm to plants and their growth. (22)

pest eradication. The complete elimination of the pest. (22)

pesticide. A chemical used to control insects, weeds, fungi, rodents, and other pests. (22)

pesticide formulation. The format of the mixture of ingredients used to create a pesticide. (22)

pesticide label. A lengthy document attached to chemical containers that includes the information needed to apply the chemical safely and accurately; considered a legal and binding agreement between the applicator and the manufacturer. (22)

pest prevention. Any action that is taken to prevent pest damage from occurring. (22)

pest suppression. Treating existing pest problems to keep insect damage below a threshold. (22)

PEX (cross-linked polyethylene pipe). A white, high-density polyethylene pipe that is very flexible. It is susceptible to the sun's ultraviolet (UV) rays and must be buried or installed under a structure for protection. (14)

pH. The number indicating the acidity or alkalinity of a substance, such as soil or water. (5)

phloem. A living vascular tissue that conveys photosynthetic products throughout a plant. (9)

photosynthesis. A process in which plants capture energy from the sun and convert carbon dioxide (CO_2) and water (H_2O) into glucose sugar that can be used as sources of energy/food. (9)

physical control. A pest control method in which pests are directly removed or killed and prevented from reaching the host plant with barriers or traps. Also referred to as *mechanical control*. (22)

phytosanitary certificate. An official document that shows a plant has been inspected and appears to be free of pathogens, insects, and weeds and meets all importing and exporting requirements. (8)

phytotoxicity. A poisonous effect by a substance, such as a pesticide, on plant growth. (22)

place. The manner in which promotional or advertising materials are presented to the customer. (19)

plan of action. A list of individual steps taken to achieve a goal. (2)

plant breeder. A person who specializes in breeding plants; breeders can manipulate everything from growth habit, bloom time, flower color, and foliage color to cultural requirements. (8)

plant breeding. The manipulation of plants to improve the quality and performance of existing plants and to create new varieties. (1)

plant disease. A disorder caused by an infectious pathogen. (22)

plant nursery. A place where young plants and trees are cultivated for sale and for planting elsewhere. (8)

planting depth. The total depth at which a plant is planted. (20)

planting diagram. A landscape design drawing that shows the shape, color, location, size, and quantities of the specific plants that will be used in the landscape. (16)

plan-view perspective. A design drawing that provides representation of all landscape elements, their relation to each other, and the relative size of each component as seen from above (aerial view). (16)

plug. A greenhouse plant started from seed and grown in a small container to transplantable size. (8); a small section of cut sod used to fill in bare areas or to install a new lawn. (12)

plugging. The placement of plugs at specific intervals in the lawn. Also referred to as *space planting*. (12)

point of connection. The location where the irrigation system connects to the water supply. (14)

polyethylene pipe. A black, soft piping material that can absorb the sun's UV rays. It is commonly used in water-saving irrigation systems, such as drip and trickle-tube irrigation systems. (14)

polyvinylchloride pipe (PVC). One of the most common pipe materials used in irrigation systems. PVC is cost efficient, readily available, lightweight, and corrosion-resistant. (14)

pond. A small body of standing, shallow water created for a landscape water feature. (13)

pondless waterfall. A water feature that simulates a natural waterfall in which the water seems to disappear but is actually falling into a reservoir and recirculated. (13)

pond liner. An impermeable material that helps contain the water and prevent it from seeping into the ground. (13)

pop-up sprinkler head. A sprinkler head that pops up when in use. (14)

postemergent herbicide. A chemical pesticide that targets weeds after they have germinated. (22)

potable water. Water fit for human consumption. (14)

pot-in-pot production (PNP). A nursery cultivation method in which a plant is grown in an insert pot and that pot is placed in a socket pot that has been sunk into the ground. The system makes watering and moving the plant easier than growing the plant in the ground. (8)

precipitation rate (PR). The rate at which water is applied (with an irrigation system) in inches per hour. (14)

preemergent herbicide. A chemical pesticide that targets weeds before they germinate. (22)

preliminary design. A landscape design drawing used to identify plant selections and specific landscape elements, such as walkways, gazebos, or patios. (16)

pressure-treated wood. Wood that is treated with preservatives to improve its weather resistance and make it more rot and insect resistant. (15)

pressure vacuum breaker (PVB). A common backflow preventer used in residential settings. (14)

price. The amount the consumer pays for the product or service. (19)

principles of design. The basic guidelines used to create attractive, functional, and year-round pleasing landscapes. (6)

privacy fence. A fence designed to block the fenced area from public view. (7)

product. The good or service being offered that fulfills consumers' needs and demands. (19)

profit. The money a business earns after deducting its expenses. (17)(18)

profit and loss statement (P&L). A financial statement that summarizes and shows the costs, expenses, and revenues over a specified time, such as a month, quarter, or fiscal year. Also referred to as an *income statement*. (17)

profit margin. The ratio of profit to the cost of the project, which is the sum of all costs incurred by the job. (18)

progeny. The offspring of plants. (8)

promise to perform. The portion of a contract that specifies what each party will be providing as well as a promise to uphold the terms of the contract. (19)

promotion. The communication aspect of marketing. (19)

promotional mix. The combination of promotional strategies, such as advertising, sales promotions, social media marketing, search engine marketing, public relations, company newsletters, and email marketing. (19)

propagation. The process of breeding or producing more plants. See also *asexual*, *sexual*, and *vegetative propagation*. (8)

propagule. A plant part being used for duplication. (8)

property dimensions. The length and width of the lot. (7)

proportion. The size relationship between the materials used in the landscape and the landscape design as a whole. (6)

proposal. A detailed explanation of all costs involved in a project, including quotes on raw materials, proposals from subcontractors, a markup of the contractor's percentage, and estimates on labor costs, taxes, and other standard costs. (18)

proximal balance. The asymmetrical balance of elements on the central axis (right and left) as well as in the field of vision (near and far). Also referred to as *distal balance*. (6)

pruning. The selective removal of stems, branches, or other parts of a plant to achieve a specific goal. (21)

pseudobulb. A swollen stem on the stolon of certain orchids. (9)

public area. The front yard of a residence. (7)

pump. A mechanical device used to move or distribute water from its source to where it is needed. (14)

punctual. Always being prompt and on time. (2)

Q

quadrille paper. A drafting medium with preprinted grids that helps the designer keep his or her scale work consistent. Also referred to as *graph paper*. (16)

quick-release fertilizer (QRF). A fertilizer that releases nutrients when it is exposed to moisture in the air and/or when it contacts plant materials or soil. Also referred to as a *water-soluble fertilizer*. (21)

quick-slip repair coupling. A special coupling used to attach two pieces of pipe. (14)

quote. A fixed price offer listing the work and materials included in a project. (18)

R

rainwater catchment. Rainwater storage from roofs and other impermeable surfaces. (13)

rake. A tool that uses tines designed for gathering, clearing, breaking, and leveling materials. (4)

reclaimed water. Wastewater that has been treated and reused for other purposes. (14)

recurrent growth. Multiple flushes or periods of growth. (21)

reduced pressure assembly (RPA). A backflow preventer with a pressure differential relief valve between two check valves. (14)

reference. An individual who will provide important information about you to a prospective employer. (2)

rejuvenation pruning. A pruning technique in which the majority of the plant material is removed to stimulate juvenile growth and thickening of the plant over time. Also referred to as *restorative pruning* or *hard pruning*. (21)

remote controller. An irrigation system controller that operates from long distances. (14)

request for proposals (RFP). A process in which a potential client notifies prospective landscape companies to bid a price for a project. Also referred to as *request for quotations (RFQ)*, an *invitation to bid (ITB)*, or a *bid solicitation*. (18)

request for quotations (RFQ). A process in which a potential client notifies prospective landscape companies to bid a price for a project. Also referred to as a *bid solicitation*, an *invitation to bid (ITB)*, or a *request for proposals (RFP)*. (18)

reservoir. A constructed or natural lake that provides a water supply. (14)

resistance. The restriction to the flowing electrical current. (13)

respiration. A process in which the sugar produced by photosynthesis combines with oxygen to produce energy in a form plants can use. (9)

restorative pruning. A pruning technique in which the majority of the plant material is removed to stimulate juvenile growth and thickening of the plant over time. Also referred to as *rejuvenation pruning* or *hard pruning*. (21)

restricted entry interval (REI). The amount of time that must pass before a person can enter an area after it has been treated with the pesticide. (22)

restricted-use pesticide. A pesticide that has potential to cause extensive damage if used improperly and therefore requires special licensing to purchase and apply. (22)

résumé. A brief outline of your education, work experience, and other qualifications for work. (2)

retaining wall. A wall built with hardscape materials; used to hold back soil and allow for the change in topography of the site. (7); a structure that holds or retains the soil behind it to reduce soil loss through erosion as well as mitigate other soil moisture concerns. (15)

retention pond. A constructed pond that holds a permanent pool of water. (14)

return on investment (ROI). The return on investment states how much money a business is making compared to the money it is spending. (17)

RFP (request for proposal). A process in which a potential client notifies prospective landscape companies to bid a price on a project. (16)

rhizome. A modified stem structure that grows horizontally below or near the soil's surface; also serves as a food storage organ. (9)

rhythm. A principle of design which adds a sense of motion to a landscape design; also how the eye travels through the landscape. (6)

riser. A length of pipe with male pipe threads on each end. It is used to connect the lateral line to the sprinkler head when the spray head is installed aboveground. (14)

rodenticide. A chemical pesticide (typically in the form of bait) designed to eliminate rodents ranging from moles and mice to gophers and woodchucks. (22)

rootbound. A condition in which the roots have outgrown the pot and are circling the inside perimeter of the container. (20)

ROPS (rollover protection system). A separate bar or a frame built into the compartment to protect operators from injuries caused by vehicle overturns. (4)

rotary spreader. A piece of lawn equipment used to broadcast seed in a swath that is several feet wide. Also referred to as a *cyclone spreader*. (12)

S

S corporation. A pass-through entity in which the business itself is not taxed and the business owner reports the business' income on his or her personal tax returns. (17)

safety data sheet (SDS). A document that provides information about a chemical, including its EPA registration number, physical and chemical properties, toxicity, and flash point. (3)

safety hazard. An object or situation that can cause injury, illness, or death. (3)

sanitation control. A pest control method in which the landscape or production area is kept as clean as possible. (22)

scale. The size of one object in relation to the other objects in the design. (6); the size of the object in a landscape design drawing in direct proportion to the size of the actual object. (16)

scientific name. A two-word name that includes a genus and specific epithet for a plant species. Also referred to as the *binomial*, *Latin*, or *botanical name*. (9)

scouting. The regular checking of landscapes, greenhouses, nursery fields, or other areas for pests while they are manageable. (22)

scrambler. A vine with very long, strong, flexible stems that must be physically attached to a climbing structure. (10)

screed. To use a straight-edged board to level material to a uniform surface. Also refers to the board itself. (15)

search engine optimization (SEO). A computation process that maximizes the number of visitors to a particular website by ensuring the site appears high on the list of results returned by a search engine. (17)

seedhead. The flowering structure of turfgrass. (11)

selective herbicide. A chemical pesticide that will only target certain weeds and will not harm the surrounding plants or turfgrass. (22)

self-motivation. An inner urge to perform well. (2)

semiprivacy fence. A fence that allows a small amount of viewing from the public area; wider spaced boards allow light to pass through from either side. (7)

service area. An area that provides the homeowner with functional space for components that are necessary but not necessarily attractive. (7)

sexual propagation. A natural reproduction process that requires contributions from female and male plants for fertilization to occur. (8)

shade. A *hue* that has been darkened. (6)

shearing. A pruning method that removes large amounts of plant material at one time with no regard to the natural structure; used to create and maintain formal landscapes and to create effective screens with hedges. (21)

sheath. The section of the leaf blade that connects the blade to the stem. (11)

short-term goal. Items or actions that an individual or business wishes to accomplish in the near future, usually less than 12 months. (2)(17)

shrub. A woody plant that may be evergreen or deciduous. These plants are common ornamentals that range from 18" to approximately 20'. (10)

signal word. Terms used to indicate the potential threat level a chemical poses to human health. (22)

simplicity. A principle of design which states that the variety of material, such as types of plants or different colors, should be limited throughout the design. (6)

single nutrient fertilizer. A plant fertilizer that contains only one primary macronutrient. (21)

site assessment. A complete analysis of an existing landscape for maintenance costs or for a new installation. (18)

site manager. The main contact handling all issues between a business and a landscaping company that is installing or maintaining a commercial property. (19)

site takeoff. A tabulation of all the landscape components and the costs associated with each component. Also referred to as a *takeoff*. (18)

sketch. A rough drawing of the site, proposed or existing structures, and the designer's interpretation of the client's ideas. (16)

sketch paper. A drafting medium that is translucent and can be used over a drawing to trace an original or used for sketching a design. (16)

slogan. A short, catchy phrase used with the logo that captures the company's appeal. Also referred to as a *tagline*. (17)

slope. The rise and fall or inclination of the land surface. A flat, horizontal piece of land is said to have a slope of zero. It may also be defined as the change in elevation from a fixed point. Also referred to as *grade*. (5); the rise and fall of the land surface or a change in elevation from a fixed point. Also referred to as *grade*. (15)

slow-release fertilizer (SRF). A plant fertilizer that releases nutrients over time, depending on the activity of organisms in the soil. Also referred to as *water-insoluble fertilizer*. (21)

small tree. A tree with a mature height approximately up to 25′. (10)

smart controller. An advanced irrigation system controller that interfaces with a computer or smart-phone. (14)

SMART goal. An acronym used to describe goals that are specific, measurable, achievable, relevant, and timely. (2)(17)

soaker hose. A low-volume irrigation system that uses a porous hose that excretes water along its entire length. (14)

sod. Turfgrass cut with a thin layer of soil from a turfgrass production field. It is laid on prepared soil to create an almost instant lawn. (12)

soft flooring. Outdoor flooring made with organic materials, such as turf, live ground covers, and mulch. (7)

soil amendment. A wide variety of materials that can be added to the soil to improve performance. Common amendments are fertilizers, lime or sulfur, organic matter, and sand. (12)

soilless substrate. A plant growth medium that contains no soil. The growth medium is manufactured with a combination of materials to create an ideal substrate; it can be manipulated to meet the needs of specific plants. (8)

soil pores. The spaces or gaps in the solid matter of soil. (8)

sole proprietorship. A business structure in which one individual is in business alone and is wholly liable for all debts incurred by the business. (17)

solid-state controller. A complex irrigation system controller that uses a central processing system. (14)

space planting. The placement of plugs or stolons at specific intervals in the lawn. Also see *plugging* and *sprigging*. (12)

species. A group of similar plants capable of interbreeding and producing fertile offspring. (9)

specific epithet. The second half of a scientific name for a plant species. It is usually descriptive of a plant feature or in honor of someone's name or a place. (9)

specimen. A plant that is a focal point due to its aesthetic characteristics, including leaf color, unique growth habit, exfoliating bark, and/or floral and fruit displays. (10)

spikelet. The individual component of turfgrass seedheads. (11)

sprig. A cut stem with stolons that can easily root and produce new shoots. (12)

sprigging. Planting stolons (with or without leaves) at specific intervals in the lawn. Sprigs may also be broadcasted and rolled. Also referred to as *space planting*. (12)

sprinkler head. The device attached to an irrigation line that disperses the water. (14)

sprinkler radius. The distance the sprinkler head is able to throw water. (14)

square footage. A measurement of area used to represent a two-dimensional space. (5)

staking. The use of stakes or posts and wire, rubber, rope, or nylon cords to provide the trees support, anchorage, and protection from winds. (20)

stalite. A lightweight, expanded slate added to improve a substrate's water retention, aeration, and nutrient-holding abilities. (8)

stolon. Modified stems located immediately above the ground surface. (9)

stone paver. A paving unit made of natural stone that is cut into square or rectangular shapes or used in its natural, irregular shape. (15)

stop-and-waste valve. A shutoff valve that allows water going into the main water supply to be cut off and for water that is in the pipe above the ground to easily be drained for winterization. (14)

subcontractor. A contractor who specializes in specific tasks, such as building hardscapes. (1)

submersed aquatic plant. An aquatic plant with roots in the soil and most of the leaf structure below the water surface. (10)

submersible pump. A water feature pump that is completely submerged in the water to hide the pump and allow it to work properly. (13)

subsurface. The area made up of layers below the final material of a hardscape. (15)

sucker. An unwanted shoot that grows near the base of the trunk. (21)

sump pump. A manual or electric pump used to remove water from a hole. (14)

sunscald. An injury that occurs in the winter on thin-barked trees when they are exposed to bright sun and cold temperatures. The damage may appear as sunken or dead bark. (20)

surfactant. A surface-active ingredient that is added to a pesticide to help the pesticide adhere to the targeted area. (22)

sustainability. A method of using a resource so that the resource is not depleted or permanently damaged. (11)

sustainable turf management. A management system that uses minimal water, fertilizers, and pesticides to minimize soil contamination and prevent runoff into ground and surface waters. (11)

symbol. A small shape used to indicate elements of a landscape design from an aerial view (plan-view perspective). (16)

symmetrical balance. A form of balance in which one side of the landscape is a mirror image of the other. Also referred to as *formal balance*. (6)

synthetic fertilizer. A manufactured substrate amendment that allows the creation of nutrient formulations for specific plant needs. (8)

synthetic turf. Manufactured alternative to natural turf. (7)

systemic insecticide. A chemical pesticide that enters the plant's stems, leaves, and roots and is ingested when insects feed on the plant. (22)

T

tagline. A short, catchy phrase used with the logo that captures the company's appeal. Also referred to as a *slogan*. (17)

takeoff. A tabulation of all the landscape components and the costs associated with each component. Also referred to as a *site takeoff*. (18)

tamp. A tool used to pack soil with repeated light strokes. (14)

tamping. The process of packing (compacting) the subsurface of a hardscape to help level the site and minimize shifting. (15)

taproots. Roots that originate from the seed root and grow downward with roots branching out from its sides. (9)

target market. The people most likely to purchase your product or service. (17)

tax identification number (TIN). A number assigned by the IRS to identify a business with respect to their tax obligations. Also referred to as an *employer identification number (EIN)*. (17)

taxonomy. The science of naming and classifying organisms. (9)

team. A small group of people working together for a common purpose. (2)

tendril. A modified leaf that is used by vines to climb by coiling around the support structure. (10)

terminal bud. The growth bud at the tip of a branch or stem. (21)

terms and conditions. The details of a contract that explain how the service and product will be rendered. (19)

texture. The visual and tactile surface quality of a material. (6)

thatch. A layer of organic matter, including dead grass clippings and live shoots, which forms between the top of the soil and the vegetation of the turfgrass. Thatch layers may become so thick that they prevent water and nutrients from reaching the roots. (11)

thinning. A pruning technique in which an entire shoot or limb is removed to its point of origin from the main branch. (21)

thread tape. A nonsticky, stretchy white tape that provides a tight fit when joining galvanized pipe. (14)

threshold level. The point at which the pest reaches an unacceptable level and corrective action must be taken. Also referred to as *action threshold*. (22)

time requirement. The portion of a contract that outlines the delivery of products or services, including the dates and times. (19)

tint. A *hue* that has been lightened. (6)

tissue culture. A form of asexual plant propagation in which a small section of the parent plant is placed in a nutrient-rich growing medium to rapidly reproduce plants that are identical to the parent plant. Also referred to as *micropropagation* or *aseptic culture*. (1)

title block. A component of a landscape design drawing that provides site- or project-specific information, such as the client's name, property name and address, the designer's name, the date, and the scale of the drawing. (16)

tone. A *hue* to which gray has been added. (6)

tool maintenance schedule. A means of keeping records of maintenance performed and when it should be performed in the future. (4)

topdressing. A material and method to apply a thin layer of material, such as sand or prepared soil, to the surface of a lawn to improve lawn health and protect plants from desiccation. (12); the action of applying material over the top of a newly installed hardscape to fill in voids between the hardscape materials. (15)

topiary. A shrub that has been pruned and sheared into an interesting shape or imaginative character. (10)

toxicity. The ability of a pesticide to poison organisms. (22)

tracing paper. A drafting medium that is translucent and can be used over a drawing to trace an original or used for sketching a design. (16)

transformer. A device that reduces the incoming line voltage to a lower voltage with lower wattage. (13)

translocation. The movement of sugar within the plant. (9)

transpiration. The process plants use to carry moisture from the roots to the small pores on the surface of the leaves. (9)

transplant. To displace a plant from its original growing conditions and install it in another location. (21)

tree. A woody perennial plant, typically with one main stem that grows to a mature height of approximately 15′. (10)

tree wrap. A light-colored material made specifically for wrapping around young tree trunks to reflect the sun and keep the bark at a more consistent temperature. (20)

trench shovel. A hand tool used to dig trenches for pipe installation. (14)

trenching machine. A machine designed to efficiently and accurately dig trenches for irrigation system lines. (14)

trickle irrigation. A low-volume irrigation system that slowly and precisely applies water directly to the plant root zone. Also referred to as *drip irrigation*. (14)

T-square. A drawing tool used to make straight, perpendicular lines using the edge of the board to guide it. (16)

tuber. An underground stem with nodes and internodes; functions as a food storage organ. (9)

tuberous root. A root that has adapted to store food; it has shoots on one end and absorption roots on the other. (9)

tuberous stem. An aboveground storage structure; it is attached to the main stem of the plant and develops branches and leaves on the other end. (9)

tunicate bulb. A bulb with a solid core of leaves covered by a thin, papery sheath. (9)

turf. Grass that is grown specifically to create a lawn. (7)

turfgrass. Any species of true grass belonging to the *Poaceae* family that is used to make a lawn. (11)

turf rotor. A type of irrigation head that is used to apply water to large areas, such as athletic fields and golf courses. (14)

turf zone. One of the three geographical zones used to help determine which type of turfgrass should be used in a specific area. (11)

twiner. A vine that wraps its leaves or stems around a support structure. (20)

two-wire decoder system. A method of wiring an irrigation system that uses two wires running from the controller to the end of the system. A decoder is located at each valve. The decoder is assigned a specific number that the controller can send a signal to in order to open and close the valve. (14)

U

unique selling proposition (USP). A statement that highlights the benefits and special features of a product or business. (19)

unity. The organization of all elements in a landscape design so that they appear to belong together. (6)

utility turfgrass. Turfgrass that is commonly used on roadsides to prevent erosion. (11)

V

value. The relative worth of something to an individual person, which changes from person to person. (19)

value proposition. An explanation of the value of a product compared to other similar products. (19)

valve manifold. Created when a number of valves are grouped in the same location. (14)

variable expense. A business expense that may fluctuate from month to month. (17)

variety. A naturally occurring mutation or offspring that differs slightly but distinctively from the parent. (9)

vascular cambium. A layer of a plant stem that contains the *xylem* and *phloem*. (9)

vegetative propagation. A reproduction process in which the progeny is produced from a single organism and has only the genes of that organism. Also referred to as *asexual propagation.* (8)

vellum. A drafting medium made of 100% cotton/rag content. The paper is treated with a synthetic resin to make it transparent. (16)

verbal communication. Communication that involves speaking, listening, and writing. (2)

vermiculite. An aluminum-iron-magnesium silicate added to improve aeration in a substrate. (8)

vertebrate. A living organism with a backbone, such as birds, deer, and rodents. (22)

verticutter. A vertical mowing machine used to remove thatch. (12)

vibratory tamper. A walk-behind power machine with a large metal plate that vibrates on the subsurface of a hardscape to compact the material. Also referred to as a *compactor.* (15)

vine. A woody-stemmed plant with a growth habit of climbing or trailing by attaching to structures with tendrils, twining, and/ or aerial roots (or holdfasts). These plants must have support; can be used to create an outdoor living wall. (7)

virus. A nonliving organism that infects plants; it cannot reproduce on its own and must have a host. (22)

vision statement. A description of a person's goals for the future. (2); a statement that describes a company's goals for the future. (17)

visual weight. The "heaviness" our eyes assign to an object. (6)

volt (V). A unit to measure the force of an electric current. (13)

voltage. A measure of the amount of energy provided by or stored in an object; the potential energy between two points along an electrical conductor. (13)

W

walkway. A hardscape that provides access to and from entryways, invites visitors to walk through the garden, and provides a clear and safe means of accomplishing chores, such as taking out the trash. (15)

warm-season plant. A plant with a longer growing season and optimum growth during the warmest part of the year. (5)

warm-season turfgrass. A grass recommended for use only in areas where the root systems will not become damaged by winter temperatures. Their optimum growing temperature is between 80°F to 95°F (27°C to 35°C). (11)

water-insoluble fertilizer. A plant fertilizer that releases nutrients over time, depending on the activity of organisms in the soil. Also referred to as a *slow-release fertilizer.* (21)

water pressure. The force that water exerts on an area. (14)

water-soluble fertilizer. A plant fertilizer that releases nutrients when it is exposed to moisture in the air and/or when it contacts plant materials or soil. Also referred to as a *quick-release fertilizer (QRF).* (21)

water sprout. A thin branch that typically grows straight up from lateral branches. (21)

watt (W). The standard unit of electric power, which represents the rate at which work is performed. (13)

wattage. A measure of the rate of energy transfer. (13)

weed. Any unwanted plant. (22)

wet-laying. The installation of a hardscape with wet cement below and between the pavers or stones. (15)

windbreak. A row or rows of trees/shrubs planted to divert wind. (10)

wood bud. A bud from which wood branches grow. Also referred to as a *growth bud.* (21)

woody plant. A plant that produces wood as its structural tissue. (10)

work time line. The time line in a contract that lists all tasks that the landscape company must complete during the installation or maintenance of a landscape. The work time line includes specific dates or time periods in which each step will be performed. (19)

X

xeriscaping. Drought-tolerant landscaping in which the plants chosen will require little irrigation once established. (6)

xerophyte. A plant that is adapted to life in very wet places. (5)

xylem. Living tissue in a plant stem that conducts water and nutrients from the roots throughout the plant. (9)

Index

A

Abelia × grandiflora/glossy abelia, 269f
Abies concolor/white fir, 269f
abiotic disorders, pests, 604
accidents, prevention, 59–60
acclimatize, 206
accountant, 472
accounting, 471–477
    assets, 476
    bookkeeper vs accountant, 471–472
    budgets and costs, 472–473
    debt, 476
    employer identification number (EIN), 472
    income, profit, and expenses, 474–475
    liabilities, 476
    net worth, 476
    return on investment, 477
accounts payable, 476
Acer palmatum/Japanese maple, 269f
Acer platanoides/Norway maple, 269f
Acer rubrum/red maple, 269f
Acer saccharum/sugar maple, 269f
action threshold, 600
acute toxicity, 617
adventitious bud, 578
adventitious roots, 204
advertising, 477–479
    community presence, 478–479
    networking, 478
    newspaper, television, and radio, 479
    online presence, 477–478
aeration, 326
aggregate, 407
AHS heat zones, 141
Ajuga reptans/carpet bugle, 270f
allergic reaction, 65
Alphabet of Lines, 436–444
    drawing components, 439–440
    lettering, 440
    line widths, 438
    symbols, 441–444
amendment, 131
Amelanchier arborea/downy serviceberry, 270f
American Horticultural Society (AHS), 141
American Horticultural Therapy Association (AHTA), 20
American National Standards Institute (ANSI), 57
American Society of Horticultural Science (ASHS), 20–21
American Society of Landscape Architects (ASLA), 20
American Standard for Nursery Stock, 207
AmericanHort, 20, 207
amperage, 335

ampere (amp), 335
analysis and treatment assessment, 566–567
    mature landscapes, 567
    new landscapes, 566
angiosperm, 227
annual bluegrass (*Poa annua*), 636f
annuals, 137
    managing, 584–585
    soil preparation, 584–585
    watering and fertilization, 585
Antirrhinum majus/snapdragon, 270f
anvil-and-blade pruners, 99
aphid, 632f
apices, 232
Appendix
    average task times, 642–643
    conversions and equivalents, 649–651
    individual plant installation, 643
    plants commonly used in landscape designs, 644–647
    plants for wet and dry locations, 648–649
    pro tips for pruning landscaping plants, 640–641
    writing and understanding binomial nomenclature, 652–655
aquatic plants, 258–259
Aquilegia × hybrida/columbine, 270f
arboretum, 230
arboriculture, 17
arborist, 17
arc (sprinkler), 374
architect's scale, 435
architect's scales and engineer's scales, 434–436
    other drawing tools, 436
aseptic culture, 6
asexual propagation, 203
asphalt, 185
asset, 476
Astilbe hybrid/astilbe, 270f
asymmetrical balance, 150
atmospheric vacuum breaker (AVB), 368
attitude, 38
auricle, 294
awning, 189
Azadirachta indica (neem tree), 613

B

backflow preventer, 368
bacteria, 609
bagworm, 632f
balance, 150
balance sheet, 475
ball cart, 97
balled-and-burlapped (B&B), 211

    planting, 546
bare root (BR), 211
    planting, 545
bedding plants, 260, 550–551
    cell packs and flats, 207
    ground covers, 551
    root ball, 551
    spacing, 550–551
Begonia semperflorens-cultorum/wax begonia, 270f
beneficials, 603, 639f
Berberis × mentorensi/mentor barberry, 270f
berm, 547
Better Business Bureau (BBB), 478
Betula nigra/river birch, 270f
bid, 488
    accepting job, 521–522
    making presentation, 522–523
    referring another company, 521–522
    solicitation, 503, 519–523
biennial, 137
binomial name, 224
    pronunciation, 283–285
binomial nomenclature, 224
biological control, 603
biotic disorders, pests, 604
blade, 294
blend, 300
block stone, 186
bond paper, 431
bookkeeper, 471
border or line plants, 260
borer (insect), 632f
botanical garden, 230
botanical name, 224
botany, 8
bow saw, 99
branch collar, 582
brand image, 470
breach of contract, 526
brick paver, 408
Brassaia actinophylla/schefflera, octopus tree, 270f
broadcast, 620
broadleaf plantain (*Plantago major*), 636f
bubble diagram, 447
buckhorn plantain (*Plantago lanceolata*), 636f
bud, 577
budgets, 136, 404, 472, 493–500
    contingencies, 499
    definition, 472, 493
    direct and indirect costs, 404
    equipment costs, 497–498
    equipment time, 495
    establishing, 136
    fixed and variable expenses, 494
    fuel, 498
    labor costs, 496

Note: Page numbers followed by *f* indicate figures/images.

materials, 499
mileage, 498
operational costs, 494–500
subcontractors, 499
task completion times, 495
waste disposal, 500
building materials
composite, 180–181
metal, 179
stone, 178–179
vinyl, 179–180
walls, 178–181
wood, 179
bulb, 232
bulb planter, 115
bunker rate, 115
burden, 494
burlap, 115
business contract, 524
business license, 470
business name, 469–471
brand image, 470
business license, 470
location, 470–471
logos, 470
slogan, 470
business plans, 462–463
chain of command, 463
components, 462–463
business structures, 456–483
accounting, 471–477
advertising, 477–479
business plans, 462–463
choosing a name, 469–471
mission and vision statements,
464–465
setting goals, 466–467
sole proprietorship, 458–459
using demographics, 467–469
Buxus microphylla/littleleaf boxwood, 271*f*
bypass pruners, 98

C

CAD programs, 89
calculations, 537–539
calculating plant materials, 315, 327,
538
materials, 412
planting plugs, 317
planting sod, 316
planting sprigs, 316
plant spacing, 538
pond liner size, 353
precipitation rate, 379
seeding rate, 316
site takeoff, 537
slope, 419
square footage and perimeter, 490
stone, 354
task times, 556
volume, 539
water volume (pond), 351
caliper, 211
Camellia japonica/common camellia, 271*f*
capital, 459

carbon sequestration, 236
cardinal directions, 141–143
east-facing sites, 143
north-facing sites, 141–142
south-facing sites, 143
west-facing sites, 143
cash flow statement, 474
catch device, 388
C corporation, 460
Cedrus atlantica 'Glauca'/blue atlas cedar,
271*f*
ceilings, 189–191
awnings, 189–190
gazebos, 190
pergolas, 191
trees and shrubs, 191
Centers for Disease Control and Prevention
(CDC), 57
Cercis canadensis/redbud, 271*f*
certifications, 23
certified irrigation designer (CID), 14
Chaenomeles speciosa/Japanese (flowering)
quince, 271*f*
chain saw, 115
chaps, gloves, helmet, 115–116
check valve, 368
chemical control, 604
chemicals and liquid fuels, 72–75
chemical application and storage, 73
clean up, 74–75
first aid, 73–74
fuel storage and transportation, 72–73
record keeping, 75
chickweed (*Stellaria media*), 637*f*
chronic toxicity, 617
clean up, 554–557
scheduling installation/task completion, 555
Clematis hybrid Clematis × jackmanii/clematis,
jackman's clematis, 271*f*
clients
relationships, 510–533
bid solicitation, 519–523
contact, 516–519
project management, 527–529
quotes and business contracts, 524–526
target market, 512–515
climbing stem root, 257
clingers, 257
clinging stem root, 257
clovers (*Trifolium* species), 637*f*
collar, 294
color, 159–161
scheme, 159–160
wheels, 160
common name, 224
communication skills, 40–42
customer relations, 42
email etiquette, 40
listening skills, 40
ongoing development, 40–41
using social media, 41
compactor, 414
complete fertilizer, 570
complete metamorphosis, 606
composite, 180
composite lumber, 409

compost and fertilizing, 586
compressed air sprayer tank, 115
computer-aided design (CAD), 89, 431
conceptual drawing, 447
concrete, 185
concrete paver, 408
create hardscapes, 409–410
conflict, 46
management, 46–48
negotiation, 47
conservatory, 230
constructive criticism, 39
contact insecticide, 611
contingency, 499
control valves, replacing, 388
controlled-release fertilizer (CRF), 571
controller
irrigation, 372
lighting, 338
cool-season plant, 140
cool-season turfgrass, 291–296
annual ryegrass, 291–292
creeping bentgrass, 292
fine fescue, 293
Kentucky bluegrass, 293
perennial ryegrass, 293
tall fescue, 295–296
cooperative, 461
cooperative extension agent, 9
Cooperative Extension System (CES), 9
copper piping, 371
core aeration, 325
core aerator, 115
Coriandrum sativum/cilantro/coriander, 282*f*
corm, 233
corner plantings, 261–262
Cornus florida/flowering dogwood, 271*f*
corporation, 460
Cotoneaster dammeri/bearberry cotoneaster,
271*f*
Cotoneaster divaricatus/spreading
cotoneaster, 271*f*
cover letter, 33
coveralls (particles/water-based liquids),
116
crabgrass (*Digitaria sanguinalis*), 637*f*
Crataegus phaenopyrum/Washington
hawthorn, 272*f*
critical-thinking skills, 39
cultivar, 216, 229
cultural control, 601
current asset, 476
current liability, 476
customer service, 528
cut-off machine, 116
cutting, 204
cyclone spreader, 311
Cynodon dactylon/bermudagrass, 272*f*, 298

D

dandelion (*Taraxacum* species), 637*f*
deadheading, 583
debris removal tool, 97
debt, 458
deciduous, 138
shrubs, 250

deck, 401
demographics, 467–469
    niche market, 469
    target market, 468
depreciation, 497
design
    Alphabet of Lines, 436–444
    architect's scales and engineer's scales, 434–436
    balance, 150–151
    creating, 428–455
    design capacity, 378–379
    drafting tools and equipment, 431–434
    drawing methods, 430–431
    elements of design, 156–161
    focalization, 151–153
    principles and elements, 148–167
    proportion, 154
    rhythm, 154
    scale, 154–155
    simplicity, 153–154
    site considerations, 161–163
    summarize client requirements, 450
    types of drawings, 444–449
    unity, 155
detention pond, 366
dethatcher, 326
dicot, 227
Dieffenbachia maculata/spotted dumb cane, 272*f*
digging/planting tools, 92–95
    bulb planters, 94
    maintenance, 95
    shovels, 92–93
direct cost, 494
directional arrow, 439, 536
disappearing fountain, 345
diseases of common plants, 634–636
    anthracnose, 634
    apple scab, 634
    black spot, 634
    botrytis, 634
    canker, 634
    cedar-apple rust, 635
    crown gall, 635
    damping off, 635
    fireblight, 635
    oak gall, 635–636
    powdery mildew, 635
    root rot/sloughing, 636
    sunscald, 636
    tobacco mosaic virus, 635
distal balance, 151
distribution uniformity, 381
division, 204
doing business as (DBA), 461
dormant, 252
double-check valve assembly, 368
double-cut (parrot-beak) pruners, 116
Dracaena deremensis 'Warneckii'/striped dracaena, 272*f*
Dracaena fragens 'Massangeana'/corn plant, 272*f*
drafting tools and equipment, 431–434
drawing methods, 430–431
    computer-aided design (CAD), 431
    hand drawing, 430

drawings
    final design, 448–449
    functional diagrams, 447
    planting diagrams, 449
    preliminary design, 448
    sketches, 446
    topographic maps, 446
    types, 444–449
    viewpoints, 445
drench, 620
drip emitter, 116
drip irrigation, 376
drones, 90
drop seeder, 311
drop spreader, 118
dry stack wall. *See also* retaining wall.
dry-laying, 411
dry-lock wall block, 116
dwarf shrub, 251

E

Echinaceae purpurea/purple coneflower, 272*f*
edger (power or hand), 96, 117
edible landscaping, 258, 282*f*
efflorescence, 420
electric current, 335
electrical wire, 386
electro-mechanical controller, 372
elements of design, 156–161
    color, 159–161
    definition, 156
    form, 157
    line, 156
    texture, 158–159
email etiquette, 40
emerald ash borer, 632*f*
emergent plant, 258
emitter, 376
employee responsibilities, 59–60
employer identification number (EIN), 472
employment
    attitude on the job, 38–39
    decision making and problem solving, 39
    health and hygiene, 37–38
    professional behavior, 39
    succeeding, 37–48
    time management, 38
    work habits, 38
engineer's scale, 435
entrepreneur, 457
environmental adaptation, 138–139
environmental horticulture industry, 5
EPA registration number, 617
epicormic root, 578
epicormic shoot, 578
Epipremnum species/pothos, 272*f*
equipment and tools, 114–125*f*
equity, 459
erosion netting, 117, 312
espalier, 263
estimates, and bid components, 488
ethical behavior, 42
Euonymus alatus/winged euonymus, 272*f*

Euonymus fortunei/wintercreeper, 272*f*
evergreen, 138
exclusion control, 602
expense, 474
external pump, 346

F

face mixing, 410
facer plants, 261
Fagus sylvatica/European beech, 273*f*
Fair Labor Standards Act (FLSA), 56
Federal Insecticide, Fungicide, and Rodenticide Act (FIFRA), 616
fence styles, 181–182
    contemporary, 182
    lattice, 182
    picket, 181
    privacy, 181
    rail, 182
fences, hardscapes, 402
Fertile Crescent, birthplace of agriculture, 198
fertilization, 568–573
    application methods, 573
    controlled-release fertilizers, 571
    injector, 117, 573
    inorganic fertilizers, 570–571
    label, 200*f*
    organic fertilizers, 569–570
    quick-release fertilizers, 571
    rates of application, 571–572
    slow-release fertilizers, 571
    tablet, 117
fertilizer. *See* fertilization.
Festuca species/fescue, 273*f*, 293, 295
fibrous root, 231
Ficus benjamina/Benjamin fig, 273*f*
Ficus elastica 'Decora'/decora rubber plant, 273*f*
field capacity, 547
field production, 210
final design, 448
firepits, 403
first aid, 64–65, 73–74
    allergic reaction, 65
    kits, 65
    training and certification, 64–65
fish/aquatic organisms, 350–351
    feeding schedules, 350–351
    goldfish, 350
    Japanese snails, 350
    koi, 350
    orfes, 350
fixed expense, 474, 494
flagstone, 188
float valve, 355
floating leaf plant, 258
flooding or floodlighting, 342
flooring, 182–189
    hard flooring, 185–189
    mulch, 185
    soft flooring, 183–185
flower bud, 577
flowers, plant parts, 235
foam board, 431

focal point, 151
focalization, 151–153
foliar spray, 620
form, 157
formal balance, 150
formal hedge, 176
Forsythia × intermedia/border forsythia, 273*f*
foundation plants, 261
fountain, 345
four Ps of marketing, 512
Fraxinus americana/white ash, 273*f*
freeze-thaw cycle (FTC), 132
friction loss, 367
frostbite, 70
frost heave, 586
frost line, 383
fruits, plant parts, 236
functional diagram, 447
fungicide, 612
fungus, 609

G

Gaillardia aristata/common blanketflower, 273*f*
gallons per hour (gph), 366
gallons per minute (gpm), 366
galvanized piping, 371
garden (bow) rake, 117
garden (spading) fork, 117
garden rakes, 95
Gardenia jasminoides/common gardenia, 273*f*
gazebo, 190
gear-driven rotary head, 374–375
general-use pesticide, 619
genus, 225
geographic information system (GIS), 90
geophytes, 232–234, 259–260
geotextile, 411, 419
Ginkgo biloba/ginkgo, maidenhair tree, 273*f*
girdling, 549
Gleditsia triacanthos inermis/thornless honeylocust, 274*f*
global positioning system (GPS), 90
goals, 30–32, 466–467
    goal setting, 30, 466
    SMART goals, 30
    vision and mission statements, 31–32
    workplace skills, 30–32
grade, 129, 402
grading, 319, 540
grading equipment, 414
gradual restorative pruning, 582
grafting, 198, 204
    band, 100, 117
    knife, 99, 118
    tool, 99
granular fertilizer, 118
graph paper, 431
grass-like plants, 254, 302
gravel, 186
gravity (drop) spreader, 118
grazing, 342
green industry, 5
greenhouse plant production, 205–207
    acclimatization, 206

plant cell packs and flats, 207
    plugs and liners, 206
greenhouse production, 6–7
ground cover, 184, 255–256
    establishing, 551
    permeable hardscape, 411
ground/pelleted limestone, 118
growth bud, 577
guying, 550
gymnosperm, 227
gypsy moth, 632*f*

H

hand tamper, 414
hard flooring, 185–189
    asphalt, 185
    concrete, 185–186
    flagstone, 188–189
    gravel, 186
    outdoor tiles, 187
    pavers and block stone, 186–187
    wood, 186
hard pruning, 582
harden off, 206
hardiness zone, 140
hardscapes, 398–427
    asphalt, 410
    calculating materials, 412–413
    concrete, 409–410
    design, 404–407
    driveways, 401
    fences, 403
    firepits, 403
    gravel, 410
    installation, 416–421
    locally sourced materials, 410–413
    marking the area, 417
    ordering materials, 413
    outdoor kitchens, 403
    patios and decks, 401–402
    pattern, 405–406
    pavers, 408
    setting the final grade, 417
    stairs, 402
    stone, 408
    subsurface preparation, 417–420
    tools and equipment, 413–416
    topdressing, 420
    walkways, 400–401
    walls, 402
    water flow, 406–407
    wood and composite lumber, 408–409
head height, 352
heading, 582
heading back, 582
head-to-head coverage, 381
health and hygiene, employment, 37–38
heat cramp, 68
heat exhaustion, 68
heat island, 249
heat zone map, 141
heatstroke, 68
Hedera helix/English ivy, 274*f*
hedge, 176
hedge or pruning shears, 99, 118

Hemerocallis species/daylily, 274*f*
henbit (*Lamium amplexicaule*), 637*f*
herbaceous perennial, 252
herbicide, 611
heterophyllus, 581
high-visibility clothing, 63, 76
hoe, 95, 118
homeowner's association (HOA), 135–136
homozygous, 203
hook-and-blade pruners, 118. *See also* bypass pruners.
horticulture therapist, 20
hose repair coupling, 119
hose-end repair fitting (female), 118
hose-end repair fitting (male), 119
hose-end sprayer, 119
hose-end washer, 119
host, 602
Hosta × hybrida/plaintain lily, 274*f*
hue, 160
hybrid, 239
Hydrangea macrophylla/bigleaf hydrangea, 274*f*
Hydrangea quercifolia/oakleaf hydrangea, 274*f*
hydraulics, 367
hydrophyte, 138
hypocotyl, 233
hypothermia, 70

I

Ilex cornuta cvs./Chinese holly, 274*f*
Ilex crenata cvs./Japanese holly, 274*f*
Ilex × meserveae/meserve holly, 274*f*
illustration board, 431
impact rotary head, 375
impact sprinkler, 119
impact tool, 91
    handheld, 91–92
Impatiens hybrid/impatiens, 275*f*
income, 474
income statement, 474
incomplete fertilizer, 570
incomplete metamorphosis, 606
indirect cost, 494
industry certification, 14
industry sectors, 5–19
    greenhouse production, 6–7
    landscape design, 11–14
    landscape maintenance, 16–18
    landscaping installation, 15–16
    plant production, 5
    retailers, 18–19
    service providers, 10–11
    sod farms, 8–10
    suppliers, 10
infiltration, 130
infiltration rate, 130
informal balance, 150
informal hedge, 177
inorganic fertilizer, 570–571
insecticide, 611
insects, 606
    illustrated, 632–634
institutional promotion, 514

integrated pest management (IPM), 598–604
    control methods, 600–604
    identifying plant and pest, 599
    monitoring pest, 599
    threshold levels, 599–600
intention, 526
interior plantscaping, 13
interiorscaping, 13
Interlocking Concrete Pavement Institute
    (ICPI), 22
International Plant Propagators' Society, 21
International Society of Arboriculture (ISA),
    21
internode, 233
interpersonal skills, 43–46, 518–519
    leadership and traits, 44–45
    listening skills, 518
    teamwork, 43–44
    verbal/nonverbal skills, 519
inventory, 87, 476
invertebrate, 606
invitation to bid (ITB), 503
Iris × germanica florentina/bearded iris, 275*f*
Irrigation Association, 21
irrigation systems, 362–397
    analyzing area, 377
    components, 368–372
    controllers, 372, 386–387
    design, 377–382
    design capacity, 378–379
    design symbols, 377
    designer, 14
    flushing system, 387
    installing, 382–387
    irrigation lines, 369–372
    layout and marking, 383
    low-volume irrigation, 376
    maintenance and repair, 387–389
    pipe installation, 383–385
    pipe placement, 381–382
    plant species, 378
    point of connection, 382–383
    precipitation rate, 379
    pumps, 368
    soil type, 378
    sprinkler head installation, 385
    sprinkler irrigation, 374–375
    sprinkler placement, 381
    system components, 368–372
    technician, 15
    trench depth, 383
    utility lines, 382
    valve placement, 381
    valves, 368–369
    water movement and pressure, 367
    water requirements, 378
    water sources, 364–367
    wires, 386
    zone, 379
    zone placement, 379–380

J

Japanese beetle, 633*f*
job
    application forms, 34–35

interview, 35–37
job site and vehicle safety, 75–77
    high hazard areas, 77
    high-visibility clothing, 76
    vehicle safety, 76–77
    work area barriers, 76
Juniperus chinensis/Chinese juniper, 275*f*
Juniperus horizontalis/creeping juniper, 275*f*

K

L

lacewing (insect), 639*f*
lady beetle, 639*f*
Lagerstroemia indica/crape myrtle, 275*f*
lambs quarters (*Chenopodium album*), 637*f*
landscape architect, 12
landscape contractor, 15
landscape designer, 12
landscape estimate, 492
landscape fabric, 119, 550
landscape horticulture, 5
landscape installation, 15–16, 534–563
    bedding plants, 550–551
    calculations, 537–539
    clean up, 554–557
    drainage, 540
    final plan, 536
    grading, 540
    installation process, 539–540
    plant delivery and installation,
        541–544
    planting trees and shrubs, 545–550
    tools and equipment, 413–416
    vines, 552–553
    watering, 553–554
landscape irrigation system, 14, 362–397
landscape lighting/water features, 332–361
    constructing water feature, 351–355
    equipment and materials, 346–347
    fish and aquatic organisms, 350–351
    landscape lighting, 334–335
    lighting fixtures/techniques, 338–343
    plant materials, 347–350
    power systems, 336–343
    water feature maintenance, 355–357
landscape maintenance, 16–18
    arborists, 17–18
    brokers, 18
    private and commercial clients, 16
    turfgrass maintenance, 16
landscape management, 564–595
    analysis and treatment assessment,
        566–567
    fertilization, 568–573
    management plans, 568
    management vs maintenance, 566
    managing annuals, 584–585
    mulching, 576
    pruning, 577–584
    scheduling multiple projects, 588–590
    sustainable, 587–588
    watering, 574–575
    winterization, 585–587

landscape projects, 484–509
    budgets and costs, 493–500
    gathering information, 486–488
    profits and profit margins, 492–493
    project estimates and bids, 492
    quotes and bids, 500–504
    selling the job, 504
    site assessment, 489–491
landscape use, 133–135
landscaping industry, 3–27
landscaping rake, 95
large shrub, 251
large tree, 248
lateral line, 369
Latin name, 224
    pronunciation, 283–285
lawn. *See also* turfgrass.
    amend soil, 321
    athletic fields and golf courses, 290
    choosing turfgrass, 318
    commercial lawns, 290
    establishing, 317–322
    evaluate site, 323–325
    home lawns, 290
    maintain, 322, 327
    mowing, 322–323
    planting turfgrass, 321–322, 326–327
    site preparation, 318–320, 326
    soil sample, 320
    soil test, 325
    types, 289–290
    weed control, 325–326
layering, 204
LC_{50}, 618
LD_{50}, 618
leadership, 44
leaf axil, 577
leaf bud, 294
leafhopper (insect), 633*f*
leaf miner (insect), 633*f*
leaf rake, 119–120
leaf retention, 138
leaves, plant parts, 235
LED technology, 342
legend, 439, 536
lethal dose, 618
letter of application, 33
Leucanthemum × superbum/shasta daisy, 275*f*
leveling tools, 90–91
liability, 459, 476
licenses and certifications, pesticide appli-
    cation, 619
lighting fixtures/techniques, 338–343
ligule, 294
limited liability company (LLC), 460
linear footage, 130
liner, 206
line-voltage system, 336
Linnaeus, Carolus, 224
Liquidambar styraciflua/sweet gum, 275*f*
liquid asset, 475
Liriodendron tulipifera/tulip tree, 275*f*
Liriope species/lilyturf, 275*f*
living area, 171
logo, 470
long-term goal, 30, 466
long-term liability, 476

Lonicera japonica/honeysuckle, 276*f*
loppers, 99, 120
low-volume irrigation, 376

M

macronutrient, 238
macropore, 215
Magnolia grandiflora/southern magnolia, 276*f*
Magnolia × soulangiana/Chinese (saucer) magnolia, 276*f*
Mahonia aquifolia/Oregon grape, 276*f*
mainline, 369
maintenance and repair
    adjusting sprinkler heads, 388
    flushing system, 389
    irrigation systems, 387–389
    pipe repair, 388–389
    replacing broken sprinkler heads, 388
    replacing control valves, 388
    winterizing system, 389
    wire repair, 389
Malus species/flowering crabapple, 276*f*
marketing, 462
marketing mix, 512
markup, 494
massing, 159, 263
material handling tools, 96–97
mattock, 94, 120*f*
measurements, 130–131
    conversions, 317
    linear footage, 130
    measuring tools, 131
    site evaluation, 130
    square footage, 130
    square footage and perimeter, 490
    volume, 539
measuring devices/tools, 88–90, 487–488
    drones, 90
    geographic information system (GIS), 90
    global positioning system (GPS), 90
    handheld laser measurer, 89
    laser level, 89
    measuring wheel, 88, 120*f*
    reading rulers and tape measurers, 89
    retractable tape, 88
    surveyor's tools, 89
    winding tape, 88–89
measuring wheel, 88, 120*f*
mechanical control, 602
medium shrub, 251
meiosis, 202, 238
mesophyte, 138
metamorphosis, 606
microclimate, 141, 491
microirrigation, 210
micronutrient, 239
micropore, 215
micropropagation, 6, 204
micro-sprinkler head, 376
mission statement, 31, 464–465
mist nozzle (mist bed), 120
miticide, 612
mitosis, 203

mix, 300
mixed border, 177
mode of action, 617
molluscicide, 612
mollusks, 607
monocot, 227
monoculture, 432
morphological, 136
morphology, 136
mower blade balancer, 120
mowers, 103–105
    cutting mechanisms, 104–105
    stand-on, 104
    walk-behind, 103
    zero-turn, 104
mulch, 185
mulch fork, 97
mulching, 312, 576
    depth, application, and season, 576
    mulching seeded areas, 312
multi-strand system, 386
Myrica pensylvanica/bayberry, 276*f*

N

Nandina domestica/heavenly bamboo, 276*f*
Narcissus species/daffodil, 276*f*
National Association of Landscape Professionals (NALP), 21
National Institute of Occupational Safety and Health (NIOSH), 57
negotiation, 47
net worth, 476
networking, 478
niche market, 469
node, 233
noncurrent asset, 476
nonliquid asset, 475
nonselective herbicide, 611
nontunicate bulb, 232
nonverbal communication, 40
north arrow, 439
nursery, 7
nursery cart, 97
nursery container, 120
nursery plant production, 208–213
    balled-and-burlapped (B&B), 211
    bare root (BR), 211–212
    container production, 208–209
    field production, 210–211
    pot-in-pot production (PNP), 209–210
    transporting nursery stock, 212–213
    weight limits, 213
nursery production, 7
nursery/landscape plant identification, 269–285*f*
nutrient deficiency symptoms, 234
nutsedge (*Cyperus rotundus*), 637*f*
nymph, 606
Nyssa sylvatica/sour (black) gum, 276*f*

O

occupational safety, 54–83
    first aid, 64–65
    jobsite and vehicle safety, 75–78

    maintaining safe workplace, 58–60
    personal protective equipment, 60–64
    safety and health agencies, 56–58
    shop safety, 70–75
    weather hazards, 70
    workplace safety hazards, 66–70
Occupational Safety and Health Administration (OSHA), 57, 71, 93
Ocimum basilicum/small leaf Greek bush basil, 282*f*
offer, 524
Ohm (Ω), 335
Ohm, Georg, 335
Ohm's law, 335
on-center (OC) spacing, 538
online presence
    advertising, 477–478
    DIT websites, 478
    performance reviews, 478
    search engine optimization (SEO), 477
operational cost, 494
operational expense, 494
optimum growth, temperature for, 139–140
organic fertilizer, 569–570
organic matter, 131
ornamental grasses, 253–254
ornamental plants, 244–285
    aquatic plants, 258–259
    bedding plants, 260
    border or line plants, 260
    corner plantings, 261–262
    edibles, 258, 282*f*
    espalier, 263
    facer plants, 261
    foundation plants, 261
    geophytes, 232–234, 259–260
    grass-like plants, 254, 302
    ground covers, 255–256
    massing, 263
    ornamental grasses, 253–254
    shrubs, 251–253
    topiary, 262–263
    trees, 246–250
    turfgrasses, 255
    vines, 256–258
orthographic projection drawing, 445
oscillating sprinkler, 120
OSHA, 57, 71, 93
outdoor room concept, 168–195
    ceilings, 189–191
    components, 174
    flooring, 182–189
    outdoor rooms, 170–172
    property size, layout, and shape, 173–174
    walls, 174–182
outdoor rooms, 170–172
    home and landscape connections, 172
    living area, 171
    public area, 171–172
    service area, 172
outward facing bud, 578
overhead, 494
overseeding, 312
oxalis (*Oxalis corniculata*), 637*f*

P

Pachysandra terminalis/Japanese spurge, 277f
Paeonia hybrid/peony, 277f
paper wasp (insect), 639f
parrot-beak pruners, 98
Parthenocissus tricuspidata/Boston ivy, 277f
partnership, 459
    general, 459
    limited liability (LLP), 459
    limited (LP), 459
pass-through taxation, 459
patents and trademarked plants, 216
path lighting, 342
pathogen, 608
patio, 401
pattern, 405
pavers, 186, 408–409
    ASTM standards, 409
paving tile, 408
peat moss, 120, 199
Pelargonium × hortorum/zonal geranium, 277f
Pennisetum species/fountain grass, 277f
percolation, 130
percolation rate, 130
Perennial Plant Association (PPA), 21
perennial, 137, 571
perforated water bag, 121
pergola, 191
perimeter, 351
perlite, 201
permeability, 406
personal pace, 491
personal protective equipment (PPE), 60–64
    eye protection, 60–61
    hearing protection, 61–62
    protective clothing, 63–64
    respiratory protection, 62
perspective drawing, 445
pest, 598
pest eradication, 601
pest management, 588, 596–631
    chemical structure and toxicity, 613
    pesticide formulations, 614–615
    pesticide labels, 616–622, 616f
    pesticides, 611–613
    storage and disposal, 623
    types of pests, 604–610
    using IPM, 598–604
pesticide labels, 616–619
    active ingredients and mode of action, 618
    EPA registration number, 618
    first-aid instructions, 618
    lethal dose and lethal concentration, 618
    names, 616–617
    precautionary statements, 618
    required information, 616
    restricted entry interval (REI), 619
    signal words, 618
    toxicity, 617
pesticides
    aerosol sprays, 615
    application, 619–622
    applying, 621–622

dusts, 614
formulations, 614–615
fumigants, 615
fungicides, 612
granules, 615
herbicides, 611
insecticides, 611
labels, 616–619
liquid, 614
miticides, 612
mixing, 620–621
molluscicides, 612
powders, 615
rodenticides, 613
storage and disposal, 623
pests
    damage, 608
    illustrations, 632–638f
    invertebrates, 606–608
    plant diseases, 608–610
    types of, 604–610
    vertebrates, 610
    weeds, 605
pest triangle, 600
Petroselinum crispum/parsley, 282f
Petunia × hybrida/petunia, 277f
PEX (cross-linked polyethylene pipe), 371
pH, 131
    soil, plant nutrition, 239
Philodendron scandens 'Oxycardium'/
    heartleaf philodendron, 277f
phloem, 232
photosynthesis, 236
physical control, 602
physiological problems
    frost/freeze injury, 638
    herbicide injury, 639
    iron deficiency, 638
    leaf scorch/drought burn/winter
        burn, 638
    nitrogen deficiency, 638
    pot-bound roots, 638
    string trimmer/mower injury, 639
phytosanitary certificate, 216
phytotoxicity, 615
Picea abies/Norway spruce, 277f
Picea pungens/Colorado (blue) spruce, 277f
pick (pickax), 121
Pieris japonica/lily-of-the-valley bush, 278f
Pinus mugo/mugo pine, 278f
Pinus strobus/eastern (weeping) white pine,
    278f
Pinus sylvestris/scotch pine, 278f
Pinus thunbergiana/Japanese black pine, 278f
pipe
    diameter, water movement and pres-
        sure, 367
    galvanized, 385
    installing, 383–385
    irrigation fittings, 372f
    placement, 381–382
    polyethylene pipe, 385
    PVC pipes and fittings, 384
    safety, 384
    repair, 388–389
place, 514–515
plan of action, 30

plant breeder, 199
plant breeding, 9
plant delivery and installation, 541–544
    materials to avoid, 542
    order of installation, 542–543
    protecting existing plants, 544
    soil amendments, 541–542
    staging area, 541
plant diseases, 608–610, 634–635f
    bacteria, 609–610
    fungi, 609
    viruses, 608–609
plant materials, 347–350
    bog and marginal plants, 349
    choosing, 140
    environmental adaptation, 138–139
    erect foliage plants, 349
    floaters, 348
    leaf retention, 138
    oxygenators, 349–350
    physical hardiness and life cycle,
        136–137
    submerged plants, 348
    temperature for optimum growth,
        139–140
    water needs, 138
plant nomenclature, 224–226
    botanical names, 224–225
    common names, 225–226
    specific epithet, 225
plant nursery, 208
plant nutrition, 238–239
    macronutrients and micronutrients,
        238–239
    soil pH, 239
plant parts, 231–236
    flowers, 235
    fruits, 236
    leaves, 235
    roots, 231
    seeds, 236
    stems, 232
    underground stems, 232–234
plant processes, 236–238
    photosynthesis, 236
    reproduction, 238
    respiration, 236–237
    translocation, 237
    transpiration, 237
plant production, 196–221
    American Standard for Nursery Stock,
        207
    greenhouse plant production, 205–207
    history, 198–199
    nursery plant production, 208–213
    patented and trademarked plants, 216
    propagation, 202–205
    quarantines, 215–216
    substrates, 199–202
    transplants and soil types, 213–215
plant species, irrigation design, 378
plant taxonomy and physiology, 222–243
    plant nomenclature, 224–226
    plant nutrition, 238–239
    plant parts, 231–236
    plant processes, 236–238
    scientific classification, 226–231

planting bar, 121
planting depth, 545
planting diagram, 449, 536
planting/earth/soil auger, 121
plan-view perspective, 445
Platanus × acerifolia/London planetree, 278f
plug, 206, 315
plugging, 315
Poa pratensis/Kentucky bluegrass, 278f, 293
Podocarpus macrophyllus, southern yew, 278f
point of connection, 382
poison ivy (*Toxicodendron radicans*), 638f
poison oak (*Toxicodendron diversilobum*), 638f
pole pruner, 121
polyethylene pipe, 121, 371
polyvinylchloride pipe (PVC), 371
pond, 344
pond liner, 346
pondless waterfall, 345
pot-in-pot unit, 122
pop-up irrigation head, 121
pop-up sprinkler head, 374
postemergent herbicide, 611
posthole digger, 94, 121
potable water, 365
Potentilla fruticosa/shrubby cinquefoil, 278f
pot-in-pot production (PNP), 209
power blower (back), 122
power blower (hand), 121
power equipment
    basic maintenance, 105
    chain saws, 102, 115f
    cutoff or circular saw, 102
    landscaping, 102–105
    leaf blower, 103
    mowers, 103–105
    PPE, 86
    rototiller, 102
    string trimmer, 102
    verticutter, 103
power hedge trimmer, 122
power systems, 336–343
    controllers, 338
    GFCI outlets, 336
    lighting zones, 338
    lights in series, 336
    line-voltage systems, 336
    low-voltage systems, 336–337
    solar-powered, 337
praying mantis, 639f
precipitation rate (PR), 379
preemergent herbicide, 611
preliminary design, 448
pressure vacuum breaker (PVB), 368
pressure-treated wood, 409
price, 513
principles of design, 149
privacy fence, 181
product, 512–513
Professional Grounds Management Society, 22
professional organizations, 19–23
    American Horticultural Therapy Association (AHTA), 20
    American Society of Horticultural Science (ASHS), 20
    American Society of Landscape

Architects (ASLA), 20
AmericanHort, 20
    Interlocking Concrete Pavement Institute (ICPI), 22
    International Plant Propagators' Society, 21
    International Society of Arboriculture (ISA), 21
    Irrigation Association, 21
    National Association of Landscape Professionals (NALP), 21
    Perennial Plant Association, 21
    Professional Grounds Management Society, 22
profit, 459, 492
profit and loss statement (P&L), 474
profit margin, 492
progeny, 202
project management, 527–529
    checking in, 528
    company hierarchy, 527
    customer service, 528–529
    work time line, 529
projects
    logistics, 589–590
    scheduling, 588–590
    task completion times, 589
promise to perform, 524
promotion, 513–514
promotional mix, 513
propagation, 199, 202–205
    asexual propagation, 203–205
    manage landscape, 205
    mat, 122
    sexual propagation, 202–203
propagule, 199
property dimensions, 173–174
property size, layout, and shape, 173–174
    intended use, 173
    layout, 174
    placement of home, 173
    property dimensions, 173–174
proportion, 154
proposal, 488
protective clothing, 63–64
    footwear, 63
    gloves, 63
    hats, 63
    high-visibility clothing, 63–64
    long-sleeve shirts and pants, 63
proximal, 151
pruning, 577–584
    areas of growth, 577–580
    growth season, 582
    knives, 100
    professional tips, 640–641
    saw, 99, 122
    shears, 98–99
    severe, 584
    techniques, 582–584
    time, 581–582
Prunus laurocerasus/cherry laurel, 279f
Prunus serrulata 'Kwanzan'/kwanzan Japanese flowering cherry, 279f
pseudobulb, 234
public area, 171–172
pump, 368

pump sprayer, 122
punctual, 38
purslane (*Portulaca oleracea*), 637f
push broom, 122
Pyracantha coccinea/firethorn, 279f

Q

quadrille paper, 431
quarantines, 215–216
Quercus alba/white oak, 279f
Quercus palustris/pin oak, 279f
Quercus rubra/red oak, 279f
quick-release fertilizer (QRF), 571
quick-slip repair coupling, 388
quote, 488
quotes and bids, 500–504
    bid solicitation, 503–504
    competitors' rates, 504
    hourly rates vs set prices, 501
    quoting set price, 502–503
quotes and business contracts, 524–526
    business contracts, 524–526
    contract elements, 524, 526
    leases as contracts, 526
    verbal vs written, 526

R

rainwater catchment, 355
rake, 95
raking and scraping tools, 95–96
reclaimed water, 365
record keeping
    checklists, 87
    inventory, 87–88
    maintenance, 87
    tools and equipment, 87–88
recurrent growth, 581
reduced pressure assembly (RPA), 368
reel mower, 122
reference, 33
rejuvenation pruning, 582
remote controller, 372
request for proposal (RFP), 432, 503
request for quotations (RFQ), 503
reservoir, 365
resin-coated fertilizer, 123
resistance, 335
respiration, 236–237
restorative pruning, 582
restricted entry interval (REI), 619
restricted-use pesticide, 619
résumé, 32–34
    letter of application, 33–34
    references, 33
retaining wall, 178, 402
retention pond, 366
return on investment (ROI), 477
rhizome, 234
Rhododendron × catawbiense/Catawba hybrid rhododendron, 279f
Rhododendron hybrid/exbury hybrid azalea, 279f
rhythm, 154
riser, 374

rodenticide, 613
rollover protection system (ROPS), 106
rootbound, 546
Rosa species/landscape shrub rose, 279f
Rosmarinus officinalis/rosemary, 282f
rotary mowers, 104, 123
rotary spreader, 311
rototiller, 102, 123
round point shovel, 123

S

Salvia nemorosa/meadow sage, 280f
Salvia officinalis/sage, 282f
scale, 633f
S corporation, 460
safety data sheet (SDS), 71
safety, hardscape design, 404
safety hazard, 66
sanitation control, 602
scale (drawing), 154, 439
scale (insect), 633f
scheduling/site access, 416
scientific classification, 226–231
    class, 228
    common/binomial names, 231
    cultivar, 229
    family, 228
    genus, 228
    hybrid, 230
    order, 228
    phylum, 226
    species, 228–229
    variety, 229
scientific name, 224
    pronunciation, 283–285
scoop, 97
    fork, 123
    shovel, 123
scouting, 599
scrambler, 257
screed, 418
SDS, 71
search engine optimization (SEO), 477
Sedum species/sedum, 280f
seedhead, 294
seeding, 310–312
    applying seed, 311–312
    blue tag, 310
    mulching seeded areas, 312
    rotary and drop spreaders, 311
    seed coating, 311
    turfgrass, 310–312
seeding rates
    planting plugs, 317
    planting sprigs, 316–317
    seed, 316
    sod, 316
seed label, interpreting, 202
seeds, 236
selective herbicide, 611
self-motivation, 38
semi-privacy fence, 181
service area, 172
services marketing mix, 515
    people, physical evidence, processes

(3Ps), 515
sexual propagation, 202
shade, 160
shade fabric, 123
shadowing, 342
sharpening blades, 100–101
sharpening stone, 123
shearing, 583
sheath, 294
shop safety, 70–75
    chemicals and liquid fuels, 72–75
    safety color-coding, 71–72
    safety data sheet, 71
short-term goal, 30, 466
shovels, 92–93
shrubs, 251–253
    cultivars, 252–253
    dwarf, 251
    evergreen, 251–252
    herbaceous perennial species, 252–253
    large, 251
    medium, 251
    species, 252
signal word, 618
silhouetting, 342
simplicity, 153–154
single-nutrient fertilizer, 570
siphon proportioner, 123
site assessment, 489–491
site considerations, 161–163
    plant maturity, 161
    restrictions, 161
    viewpoint, 161
site evaluation and plant selection, 126–147
    AHS heat zones, 141
    budget, 136
    cardinal directions, 141–143
    evaluating site, 128–129
    identifying landscape use, 133–135
    logistics, 128–129
    measurements, 130
    plant materials, 136–140
    rules and regulations, 135–136
    surveying, 130
    USDA hardiness zones, 140–141
    visiting site, 129–133
    water movement, 129–130
site manager, 517
site takeoff, 487, 537
sketch, 431, 446
slogan, 470
slope, 129, 402, 406
    calculating, 419
slow-release fertilizer (SRF), 571
slug, 633f
    controlling, 607
    molluscicides, 612
small tree, 248
smart controller, 372
SMART goals, 30, 466
snail, 633f
    controlling, 607
    molluscicides, 612
soaker hose, 124, 376
social media, 41
sod, 312–314
    cutter, 103

farms, 8–10
    research and education, 8–10
    site preparation, 313–314
soft flooring, 183–185
    ground covers, 184–185
    natural turf, 183–184
    synthetic turf, 184
soil
    amendment, 321
    analysis, 131–132
    compaction, 132
    knife with sheath, 124f
    pH, 239
    pore, 213
    sampling tube, 124
    triangle, using, 575
    taking samples, 320
    type, irrigation design, 378
soilless substrate, 199
sole proprietorship, 458–459
solenoid valve, 124
Solenostemon scutellarioides/coleus, 280f
solid-state controller, 372
Sorbus aucuparia/European mountain ash, 180f
space planting, 315
spade, 124f
species, 228
specific epithet, 225
specimen, 248
sphagnum moss, 124f
spider mite, 633f
spiders, 639f
spikelet, 294
Spiraea × bumalda/bumalda spirea, 280f
sprig, 315
sprigging, 315
sprinkler head, 369
    adjusting, 388
    installing, 385
    methods of attachment, 385
    replacing, 388
sprinkler irrigation, 374–375
    gear-driven rotary heads, 374–375
    pop-up sprinkler heads, 374
    sprinkler placement, 381
    sprinkler radius, 375
    turf rotors, 375
square footage, 130
    calculating, 490
    hardscape materials, 412
square point (flat) shovel, 124f
staking, 548
stalite, 201
stand-on mowers, 104
stinging nettle (*Urtica dioica*), 638f
stolon, 234
stone paver, 408
stop-and-waste valve, 383
string trimmer, 124f
subcontractor, 15
submersed aquatic plant, 258
submersible pump, 346
substrates, 199–202
    amendments, 201
    base material, 199–200
    cotton stalks, 200–201

making, 199–201
    tree bark, 200
subsurface, 417
sucker, 580
sump pump, 383
sunscald, 545
surfactant, 614
sustainability, 301
sustainable turf management, 301
symbols (design), 441–444
    hardscape symbols, 442
    plant representation, 441
    shadows, 444
    textures, 443
    vines, 442
symmetrical balance, 150
synthetic fertilizer, 201
synthetic turf, 184
Syringa vulgaris/common lilac, 280*f*
systemic insecticide, 612

T

Tagetes species/marigold, 280*f*
tagline, 470
takeoff, 487
tamp, 387
tamping, 414
taproot, 231
target market, 468, 477, 512–515
    place, 514–515
    product, 512–513
    promotion, 513–514
    services marketing mix, 515
tarmac rakes, 95
task completion times, 409, 589, 642–643
    calculating, 556
tax identification number (TIN), 472
Taxodium distichum/bald cypress, 280*f*
taxonomy, 226
Taxus species/yew, 280*f*
team, 43
tendril, 256
terminal bud, 577
terms and conditions, 526
texture, 158
thatch, 298
thatch rake, 95, 124*f*
thinning, 582
thread tape, 385
threshold level, 599
Thuja occidentalis/American arborvitae, 281*f*
Thymus vulgaris/thyme, 282*f*
Tilia cordata/littleleaf linden, 281*f*
time management, 38
time requirement, 526
tint, 160
tissue culture, 6
title block, 439, 536
tone, 160
tool maintenance schedule, 87
tools/equipment, 84–125
    compactors, 414
    digging and planting tools, 92–95
    equipment limitations, 106
    grading equipment, 414

hand and power tools, 415
handheld impact tools, 91–92
hardscapes, 413–416
landscaping power equipment, 102–105
large equipment, 105–107
leveling tools, 90–91
maintenance, 106–107
material handling tools, 96–97
measuring devices, 88–90
personal protective equipment, 86
pruning, grafting, and budding tools, 98–100
raking and scraping tools, 95–96
record keeping, 87–88
safety, 86, 416
tools for sharpening blades, 100–101
transportation and hauling equipment, 107–108
troubleshooting, 107
topdressing, 322, 420
topiary, 262–263
toxicity, 617
tracing paper, 431
transformer, 336–337
translocation, 237
transpiration, 237
transplant, 572
transplants and soil types, 213–215
    water movement, 215
trees, 246–250
    caliper, 125
    color, 251
    framework, 251
    functions, 249–251
    shade, 250
    sizes, 248–249
    species, 249
    types, 247
    wrap, 125, 545
trees/shrubs
    backfill, 547
    balled-and-burlapped plants, 546–547
    berm, 547
    container plants, 546
    guying, 550
    moving and placing plants, 546
    mulch, 547–548
    planting, 545–550
    removing stakes, 550
    staking trees, 548–550
trench shovel, 383
trencher, 103
trenching machine, 383
trickle irrigation, 376
trowel, 125
truck and trailer combinations, 108
T-square, 432
Tsuga canadensis/Canadian hemlock, 281*f*
tuber, 233
tuberous root, 233
tuberous stem, 233
Tulipa species/tulip, 281*f*
tunicate bulb, 232
turf, 183
turfgrass, 288–300
    alternatives, 301–303
    blends and mixes, 300

calculating seed and plant materials, 315–317
cool-season, 291–296
definition, 255, 288
establishing new lawn, 317–322
installation and management, 308–331
methods of establishing, 310–317
mowing lawns, 322–323
ornamental grasses and grass-like plants, 302–303
renovating, 323–327
seeding, 310–312
seeding rates, 315–317
selection, 286–307
sodding, 312–314
sprigging and plugging, 315
sustainability, 301
synthetic turf, 302
turf zones, 288–289
types of lawns, 289–290
warm-season turfgrasses, 296–300
turf rotor, 375
twiner, 257
two-wire decoder system, 386

U

unique selling proposition (USP), 512
unity, 155
up lighting, 342
USDA Animal and Plant Health Inspection Service (USDA APHIS), 215–216
USDA Census of Agriculture, 5
USDA hardiness zones, 140–141
    microclimates, 141
USDA Plant Protection and Quarantine (PPQ), 215
US Department of Labor (DOL), 57
utility lines, locating, 382
utility turfgrass, 290

V

value, 513
value proposition, 513
valve manifold, 381
valves
    backflow preventers, 368
    control valves, 368
    irrigation system components, 368–369
variable expense, 474, 494
variegation, 158
variety, 229
vascular cambium, 232
vegetative propagation, 203
vehicle safety, 76–77
    commercial vehicles, 77
    hauling and towing, 77
vellum, 431
verbal communication, 40
Verbena × hybrida/garden verbena, 281*f*
vermiculite, 201
vertebrate, 610
vertical mower, 125
verticutter, 103, 326
vibratory tamper, 414

Viburnum × burkwoodii/burkwood vibur-num, 281*f*
Viburnum trilobum/American cranberry bush viburnum, 281*f*
viewpoint, 161
vine, 178, 256–258, 552–553
    support structures, 552–553
Vinca minor/periwinkle, 281*f*
Viola × wittrockiana/pansy, 281*f*
virus, 608
vision statement, 31, 464–465
visual weight, 150
volt (V), 336
voltage, 335–336

W

walk-behind mowers, 103
walkway, 400–401
walls, 174–182
    building materials, 178–181
    fence styles, 181–182
    living walls, 175
    plant material, 176–178
warm-season plant, 139
warm-season turfgrasses, 296–300
    Bahiagrass, 296–297
    bermudagrass, 298
    carpetgrass, 298
    centipedegrass, 298–299
    St. Augustinegrass, 300
    zoysiagrass, 300
washing, 342
water breaker, 125
water features, 343–345
    calculating pump size, 352–353
    constructing, 351–357
    electric pumps, 346
    electrical service, 347
    fountains, 345
    landscape lighting, 343–345
    layout and excavation, 351

liner installation, 354
liner size, 353
liners, 346
maintenance, 355–357
measure water volume, 351–352
ponds, 344
predator deterrents, 356
pump size, 353*f*
skimmers and filtration, 356
stone, 354–355
water loss, 355
waterfalls, 345, 352
water flow, hardscapes, 406–407
water pressure, 367
    friction loss, 367
    maintaining pressure, 367
    pipe diameter, 367
water sources, 364–367
    private, 366
    public, 365
    reclaimed water, 365
    retention and detention ponds, 366–367
    well output, 366
water sprout, 580
watering, 553–554, 574–575
    application methods, 574
    methods of application, 554
    soil texture, 574–575
    timing, 553
water-insoluble fertilizer, 571
water-soluble fertilizer, 571
watt (W), 335
wattage, 335
weather conditions, 68–70
weeds
    characteristics, 605
    classifications, 605
    control, 325
    herbicides, 611
    illustrations, 636–637*f*
wet-laying (hardscape), 411
wheelbarrow, 96

whitefly, 634*f*
white grub, 634*f*
wide-brimmed hard hat, 125
Wilsonville bee kill, 611
windbreak, 248
winterization (landscape), 585–587
winterizing, irrigation systems, 389
wire and valve locator, 389
wire repair, 389
wire tree basket, 125
Wisteria sinensis/Chinese wisteria, 282*f*
wood bud, 577
woody plant, 246
work habits, 38
work time line, 528
workplace
    employee responsibilities, 59–60
    maintaining safe workflow, 58–60
    safety hazards, 66–70
    training days, 58
    workplace behavior, 42–43
workplace skills, 28–53
    goals, 30–32
    succeeding in workplace, 37–48

X

xeriscaping, 162–163
xerophyte, 138
xylem, 232

Y

Yucca filamentosa/adam's needle, 282*f*
Yucca gigantean; *Yucca elephantipes*/giant yucca, 282*f*

Z

zero-turn mowers, 104

Comprehensive Training Manual For Healing And Freedom

How To Minister To Spiritual, Mental, Emotional, Physical, Relational, Sexual and Addictive problems

STEVE PIDD

Revised 2020 English Only Version

ABOUT US

Steve and his wife Em have spent the majority of their Christian life serving as Senior Pastors in a local Church environment.

They have been involved internationally in schools training and ministering in the areas of healing and freedom for over 20 years.

They have developed and conducted their 'School of Healing and Freedom' (SOHAF) in various locations in Australia and across the World during that time.

In more recent years their ministry abroad has mainly involved teaching and mentoring Pastors and leaders, as well as churches, to be equipped in the area of healing and freedom ministries.

Steve is the founder and International Director of Agape Orphanage Network Australia Inc. For information on how to help children in need please go to the website: www.aon.org.au

For information regarding 'School of Healing and Freedom' (SOHAF) go to the website: www.418centre.org The ministry name is based on Luke 4:18.

CONTENTS

FORWARD   6

UNIT ONE   The Gospel of the Unders and Overs   8

UNIT TWO   The Church and the Holy Spirit   46

UNIT THREE   The Healing Streams of God   70

UNIT FOUR   Part 1: Truth Encounters: A Biblical Perspective   109

UNIT FIVE   Principles for understanding demons or evil spirits   186

UNIT SIX   Discernment   221

UNIT SEVEN   Dealing with Fear   239

UNIT EIGHT   Ungodly Control and Insecurity   252

UNIT NINE   Low self-image, Inferiority and Pride   264

UNIT TEN   Rebellion, anger and bitterness   270

UNIT ELEVEN   Sex 'Gods idea!'   286

Appendix One   Sample Sessions   344

Appendix Two   Popular Redemption Scriptures   348

Appendix Three   Other Resources from 418Centre   350

Forward

Having attended a great many conferences over the years my observation is that the modern church is largely concerned with matters such as leadership, growing the numbers in your congregations, or church planting.

There is no doubt at all that these are wonderful and necessary topics to facilitate the building of the Kingdom of God.

There is, however, very little focus on healing ministries and as a consequence the doctors are the first port of call for physical problems. For many churches, even large city congregations, if there are mental or emotional issues the people are sent to psychiatrists or Christian counselors trained in secular techniques.

In contrast if we look at the Jesus model, His focus was on healing the sick, freeing those with demonic bondages and healing the broken hearted.

Apparently, His disciples freely received this ministry from Christ themselves <u>before</u> they were commissioned to take the good news to the World.

> *Matthew 10:8 Heal the sick, raise the dead, cleanse those who have leprosy, drive out demons. <u>Freely you have received</u>, freely give. NIV (Emphasis mine)*

Perhaps we could look at it in this way. Imagine if you were putting together a football team and selecting your players. "Alright, I choose that man over there with one leg, the blind guy, that deaf fellow, the man with one eye, those chaps with the back braces on, and those cripples."

Then you launched them out onto the field, yelling with great enthusiasm and encouragement; "Go get them guys!" It doesn't make much sense to me, but many of us have been around churches where the focus is on trying to motivate broken people to live a victorious life of faith. We have all seen the fallout and problems from people with unresolved issues active in a church environment.

Remember the 'Vasa'

There is an old Swedish warship housed in a museum in Stockholm called by the name of 'Vasa.' She was commissioned to be built by the King of Sweden Gustavus Adolphus for use in the war with Poland-Lithuania and was constructed 1626-27. Upon completion she was considered to be one of the most powerful warships in the world at the time.

A tremendous amount of resource was put into her, and she presented with rich and ornate decorations. She was loaded with large and powerful guns. Unfortunately, all of the expense and efforts went into her appearance and equipment for war. Not enough time was spent on the design and what was done below the waterline out of sight.

The result was that she appeared to be a splendid, dangerous and formidable enemy, when in fact she was unstable in her foundation and not well ballasted. Sadly only 1400 meters into her maiden voyage she encountered a gust of wind which caused the ship to capsize and sink. The guns had just been fired as a grand salute to onlookers as the vessel left Stockholm.

Forward Cont.

The lesson for us appears to be that if we spend all of our time on presentation and how things look, and neglect dealing with the sub surface problems of the church we may not ever even get into battle.

If we train people in leadership, and develop or release gifts but don't deal with the unresolved issues in their lives, are we building on sand?

We have found that if we focus on the people being set free, the gifts and leadership come with motivation that God is pleased to bless.

At times I have ministered to leadership teams of larger churches and have been amazed at what is often going on in the background.

I thoroughly believe that healing the brokenhearted and setting the captives free was the main ministry of Jesus for a very good reason.

If we want to be the stable church that God is pleased to anoint, we may need to consider spending a little more time on working below the water line and sorting out the areas that are not always visible.

UNIT ONE

The Gospel of the Unders and Overs

Basis and Biblical Reference

In this opening unit we want to lay out a reference point or a basis for TRUTH that we can refer back to. We tend to receive sermons and messages in our church or study environments on a range of subjects, without having an overview, or general understanding of the foundations of our Christian faith.

This then is a 'whirlwind tour' of the Gospel, a framework or skeleton from which we can check if the statements in our various units and studies are accurate and sound doctrinally. It is vitally important that whatever we teach is compatible and complies with the overall counsel and instruction of the scriptures.

Study 1: The Spiritual Realm and the Unseen World

I once heard someone say that you can only see about 5% of what is actually present in our World. When you think about it, we could compile quite a long list of things that we accept as existing and impacting life, and yet we cannot actually see them. Can I suggest a few to get you thinking: Germs, bacteria, oxygen, nitrogen and all the other elements of the air. Gravity is a 'force' and there is electricity, colors, wind, radiation, smells, sounds, static electricity, heat and cold, magnetism, UV rays and I could go on for some time. These are naturally occurring invisible items and forces that we readily believe in and accept.

What about a few man-made things that we cannot see? We have radio waves that are there and can skip around the globe. There are multiple TV channels in the air and if you have the right receptor you can pluck it right out of the power of the air. If you have a smart phone you can receive the messages that are there but invisible, receive your emails, watch the football, view the news, have a text message or social media come through. We can even talk to someone on the other side of the World face to face. We could go on to talk about satellites, remote controls for your TV, garage door and so on, and on.

Whether we are talking about naturally occurring invisible items, or man-made inventions, the point is that we readily accept the unseen World in this context. We believe in all of these things even though we cannot see them. We have FAITH in their ability to <u>produce results</u> and <u>outcomes</u> even though many of them are not visible or discernable to the natural senses. We accept them, and work with them, even though we often don't know how or why they work.

UNSEEN SPIRITUAL BEINGS

So, to this point we have not even mentioned the unseen spiritual beings that are behind virtually everything that happens on Earth.

Jesus used the example of the wind to explain to Nicodemus in Johns gospel chapter 3 that we easily accept its ability to make things happen, and see its effects even though we don't actually see it. Nicodemus was trying to understand how Jesus was able to perform supernatural signs. Jesus was saying that there were unseen spiritual forces behind the things that He was doing….in this case, the miracles coming through the person of the Holy Spirit.

> *John 3: 8 "The wind blows where it wishes, and you hear the sound of it, but cannot tell where it comes from and where it goes. So is everyone who is born of the Spirit." NKJV*

So, we acknowledge the existence of spiritual beings and their interplay with mankind, whether from the Kingdom of God, or the Kingdom of Darkness. In fact, largely everything that happens on the Earth, good or bad, happens through human cooperation with either one or the other of those Kingdoms. We could say that this influence may happen directly or indirectly, and work through humanity, whether by deception and ignorance, or willful submission.

> *Ephesians 6:12 "For we do not wrestle against flesh and blood, but against principalities, against powers, against the rulers of the darkness of this age, against spiritual hosts of wickedness in the heavenly places". NKJV*

Every one of these unseen beings does their work through human participation and cooperation. Someone has well said that every evil thing done in the Earth has human fingerprints on it……manipulated and inspired by an unseen being. Of course, we could extend that statement to include every good act as well.

SPIRITUAL INSPIRATION
Example 1
In the Gospel of Luke, we see Jesus pointing out to His disciples James and John, that they were unaware of which <u>type or manner</u> of spirit that they were under the influence of. They were deceived about their own motives, and consequently, thinking that this was their OWN ideas they easily cooperated with another spirit.

Many people in the Church environment, and not just the world, readily participate with other spirits such as rejection, resentment, unforgiveness, self-justification, immorality and the like, thinking that this behavior and these responses are simply their <u>own idea</u>.

> *Luke 9:55 But He turned and rebuked them, and said, "You do not know what manner of spirit you are of. NKJV*

Example 2
In the NIV we find a well worded passage referring to Job being aware that his friends were not speaking by their own knowledge, but that they were in fact receiving their inspiration from another source.

> *Job 26:4 Who has helped you utter these words? And whose spirit spoke from your mouth? NIV*

> **Note:** This concept that is translated in the NIV is conveyed in the original Hebrew language.

Example 3

In Matthew Chapter 16 we see Peter receiving a wonderful revelation from the inspiration of the Spirit of God regarding the person of Jesus.

> *Matthew 16: 15-17* ¹⁵ *"He said to them, "But who do you say that I am?"* ¹⁶ *Simon Peter answered and said, "You are the Christ, the Son of the living God." ¹⁷ Jesus answered and said to him, "Blessed are you, Simon Bar-Jonah, for flesh and blood has not revealed this to you, but My Father who is in heaven.*

Very soon after this we see him making another comment that is inspired by a spirit that is not the Spirit of God. Jesus, discerning this other source, rebukes the spirit that is manifesting through Peter. I am sure that it would have come as a shock to Peter, that his well-meaning, but worldly thinking could have come from another spirit. We also need to be careful that we are not 'double agents' at times working unwittingly for another kingdom!

> *Matthew 16:23 But He turned and said to Peter, "Get behind Me, Satan! You are an offense to Me, for you are not mindful of the things of God, but the things of men." NKJV*

LESSON 1

Many times, we just assume that our thinking is simply OUR own thinking, when in fact it could be inspired by a spiritual entity.

LESSON 2

We can be used by either spiritual Kingdom and virtually everyone is at times working for the other side without realizing it. We need TRUTH from the Spirit of truth and to have developed discernment from the Word of God.

LESSON 3

Jesus didn't say "come out" as the problem was not a demon inside Peter in this instance; it was a spirit working through him from the outside, and because of his beliefs he came UNDER and submitted to Satan working through him.

In the following verse we see Cain being pressured by a being who was promoting sin. It was taking advantage of his emotional state, and influencing him to choose an evil course of action. It is noteworthy that Cain believed that acting out in this way would satisfy his emotional state, and resolve his problem. In other words, Cain believed that 'sin' was what he needed to fix his life circumstance and make him content. This is the basic deception behind sinful attitudes and activities.

We have found over the years that meeting 'perceived' emotional needs **is the greatest predictor** of behavior. The root behind most sin and submission to evil spiritual powers begins here. For example, we commonly find that many people in adultery suffer from rejection, and it is the perceived sense of acceptance that they seem to receive in the ungodly relationship that leads them into the situation. It 'seems' as though it will make them happy, but it never really does. It is the devil's solution to their rejection, not God's. King David seemed to be completely oblivious to his sin with Bathsheba. Later he realized that he needed to look deeper, understanding that his sin was proceeding from an unclean heart. We will look at this in more detail later.

> *Genesis 4:6-7* *⁶ Then the LORD said to Cain, "Why are you angry? Why is your face downcast? ⁷ If you do what is right, will you not be accepted? But if you do not do what is right, <u>sin is crouching at your door</u>; it desires to have you, but <u>you must master it</u>." NIV*

The Lord was pointing out that if Cain submitted to the spiritual pressure to do wrong that he would come UNDER its power. We see this principle of giving authority and power over ourselves, through submission, to spiritual beings that are encouraging ungodly behavior and actions that are sinful and offensive to God. <u>*Note: sin in both the Old and New Testaments means an 'offence'.</u>

> *Romans 6: 16 Don't you know that when you offer yourselves to someone to obey him as slaves, you are slaves to the one whom you obey--whether you are slaves to sin, which leads to death, or to obedience, which leads to righteousness? NIV*

> *2 Peter 2: 19b....for a man is a slave to whatever has mastered him. NIV*

PRINCIPLE: Anything that we SUBMIT to we come UNDER and give it authority OVER ourselves in that area. *(Note: the prefix sub means under. For example, a submarine = under the water.)*

> *Romans 6: 13-14 ¹³ Do not offer the parts of your body to sin, as instruments of wickedness, but rather offer yourselves to God, as those who have been brought from death to life; and offer the parts of your body to him as instruments of righteousness. ¹⁴ For sin shall not be your master, because you are not under law, but under grace. NIV*

> *James 4: 7-8 ⁷ Therefore <u>submit</u> to God. Resist the devil and he will flee from you. ⁸ Draw near to God and He will draw near to you. Cleanse your hands, you sinners; and purify your hearts, you double-minded. NKJV*

The preceding passage refers to putting yourself under the authority of God, and refusing to submit to the Devil. We do this by seeking after God, and His order, rather than running away from, ignoring or hiding from Him because of our sin, as Adam and Eve did. Cleansing our hands is referring to our deeds, and purifying our hearts is dealing with our desires for sin and other things.

Jesus and spiritual influences

Jesus himself lived under the constant inspiration of the seven spirits which constitute the sevenfold ministry of the Holy Spirit. We will touch on this in more detail in later units.

Isaiah 11:1-2 ¹There shall come forth a Rod from the stem of Jesse, And a Branch shall grow out of his roots. ² The Spirit of the LORD shall rest upon Him, The Spirit of wisdom and understanding, The Spirit of counsel and might, The Spirit of knowledge and of the fear of the LORD. NKJV

Verse 3 goes on to point out that Jesus was not going to rely on the sense realm. Because He fully understood and discerned what was manipulating both people and circumstances, He was going to make His judgments and decisions on that basis.

³ His delight is in the fear of the LORD, And He shall not judge by the sight of His eyes, Nor decide by the hearing of His ears; NKJV

Let us now briefly look at the revealed nature and activities of some spiritual entities.

Study 2: Spiritual Beings and human cooperation

So, we not only recognize the reality of the spiritual realm or heaven lies, but in practical terms acknowledge that the Earth was created by and from that realm by God. It is therefore superior in every way to the natural World. Consequently, when we as re-born spiritual beings learn to walk in the spirit, we are no longer confined to the basic principles of this World but have access to the <u>super</u>natural or <u>above</u> natural power of God.

ANGELS

Angels are mentioned more than 300 times throughout the scriptures which is a notably significant amount. The Bible reveals that their purpose in regards to us is to serve those who are receiving salvation.

Psalm 91:11 For He shall give His angels charge over you, To keep you in all your ways. NKJV

Hebrews 1:14 Are they not all ministering spirits sent forth to minister for those who will inherit salvation? NKJV

An excellent biblical example of this is the story of Elisha and his servant in 2 Kings Chapter 6. At that time Elisha the prophet was warning the King of Israel of every plan of the King of Syria. When the King of Syria found out that it was Elisha that was foiling his plans, and that Elisha was in the city of Dothan he sent horses, chariots and a great army there and surrounded the city.

When Elisha's servant rose up early in the morning he went out and saw the great army surrounding them and was afraid. His master instructed him not to be fearful and asked the Lord to let his servant see in the spirit, as apparently, he could. His servant then saw that there were many more angelic beings present in the unseen realm who were there for them, than those in the visible realm that were against them.

Most people rarely see in the spirit, but if we could we would realize that indeed if God is for us who can be against us! I have heard quite a number of personal testimonies from credible people who have seen angels in this modern era. Some of them are small children who would not even know what an angel was.

APPARENT FUNCTIONS OF ANGELS

Angels in scripture appear to fit into specific roles and activities.

We see the angel Gabriel appear a number of times in the book of Daniel and also in the book of Luke. He is bringing messages or instruction to Daniel, Zacharias and later Mary. It appears that his role is that of a messenger.

> *Revelation 12:7-9* ⁷ *And war broke out in heaven: <u>Michael and his angels fought</u> with the dragon; and the dragon and **his angels** fought,* ⁸ *but they did not prevail, nor was a place found for them in heaven any longer.* ⁹ *So the great dragon was cast out, that serpent of old, <u>called the Devil and Satan</u>, who **deceives the whole world**; he was <u>cast to the earth</u>, and his angels were cast out with him. NKJV (Emphasis mine)*

From the preceding verses and other passages in scripture we can deduce that Michael and his angels are some kind of warrior angels. Some theologians believe that he may be responsible for around one third of the angels. In verse 9 we also note that the Devil or Satan also has angels, which are now cast down to the Earth. Satan, (meaning opposer or adversary) was formerly named Lucifer which means 'shining one' or 'bringer of light.' Some theologians propose that his role in the Heaven lies may have been in the area of worship; certainly, he was privileged and was some kind of guardian.

> *Ezekiel 28:14-17* ¹⁴ *I ordained and anointed you as the mighty angelic guardian. You had access to the holy mountain of God and walked among the stones of fire.* ¹⁵ *"You were blameless in all you did from the day you were created until the day evil was found in you.* ¹⁶ *Your great wealth filled you with violence, and you sinned. So I banished you from the mountain of God. I expelled you, O mighty guardian, from your place among the stones of fire.* ¹⁷ *Your heart was filled with pride because of all your beauty. You corrupted your <u>wisdom</u> for the sake of your splendor. So I threw you to the earth and exposed you to the curious gaze of kings. NLT*

In the end his sin problem was PRIDE, which led to REBELLION. So, we could say that the root of his sin and wickedness was the distorted desire for SELF realization of his person, and living for SELF in that context. This led to SELF promotion, which caused him to seek to not be submitted to God.

> *ISAIAH 14:12-14* ¹² *"How you are fallen from heaven, O Lucifer, son of the morning! How you are cut down to the ground, You who weakened the nations!* ¹³ *For you have said in your heart: '<u>I will</u> ascend into heaven, <u>I will</u> exalt my throne above the stars of God; <u>I will</u> also sit on the mount of the congregation On the farthest sides of the north;* ¹⁴ *<u>I will</u> ascend above the heights of the clouds; <u>I will</u> be like the **Most High**.' NKJV (emphasis mine)*

Lucifer, now Satan, wanted to be like God, receiving worship for himself, and be **<u>above or over</u>** everything and everyone. In his rebellion he wanted his OWN THRONE, ruling and being his own god. He no longer wanted to be <u>under</u> authority.

LESSON
We could say then that 'SELF in pride' is the original basis for sin and rebellion against the knowledge of God.

WHAT WAS THE SIN OF SATAN AND HIS ANGELS?

1. He wanted to be praised instead of worshipping God. It was all about his own glory, and his sense of SELF being exalted.
2. Consequently he (they) no longer wanted to submit to Gods will. This was rebellion, and God was not going to tolerate it in His Heavenly kingdom.

 LESSON
This is something that we should really pay attention to. Even Satan's wisdom became corrupted for the sake of his SELF realization and SELF promotion.
Ezekiel 28:17b You corrupted your <u>wisdom</u> for the sake of your splendor; NKJV

The scriptures warn us about the dangers of following a similar pathway.

> *Proverbs 26:12 Do you see a man wise in his own eyes? There is more hope for a fool than for him. NKJV*

In the case of Satan, the outcome of his rebellion was inevitable.
Note: Rebellion is setting yourself against authority, or refusing to work within instituted boundaries, which is lawlessness.

> *Revelation 12:9 So the great dragon was cast out, that serpent of old, <u>called the Devil and Satan</u>, who **deceives the whole world**; he was <u>cast to the earth</u>, and his angels were cast out with him. NKJV (emphasis mine)*

So, our observation here is that Satan and one third of the angels were cast down to the earth. Also noteworthy is that he now deceives the WHOLE world. (Christians are meant to progressively be the exception. Remember that Jesus brought us grace to release us from the power of sin, and TRUTH to make us free from the captivity of deception.)

> *John 1: 17 For the law was given through Moses, but <u>grace</u> and <u>truth</u> came through Jesus Christ. NKJV (emphasis mine)*

CONSIDERATION
If you were God and you had now lost one third of your angels what would you do?
Is it conceivable that God might create a place to test those who will be entering into His kingdom in the future? Clearly He would not want more proud rebellious SELF willed beings running around who did not want to submit to Him......
.....is there a biblical New Testament basis for this kind of thinking?

> *Galatians 5: 16-21 ¹⁶ I say then: Walk in the Spirit, and you shall not fulfill the lust of the flesh. ¹⁷ For the flesh lusts against the Spirit, and the Spirit against the flesh; and these are contrary to one another, so that you do not do the things that you wish. ¹⁸ But if you are led by the Spirit, you are not under the law.*

By implication, if you are **<u>led</u>** by the Spirit you are not SELF willed or SELF seeking, you are Spirit seeking, and looking to His will and commands.

> *¹⁹ Now the works of the flesh are evident, which are: adultery, fornication, uncleanness, lewdness, ²⁰ idolatry, sorcery, hatred, contentions, jealousies, outbursts of wrath, selfish ambitions, dissensions, heresies, ²¹ envy, murders, drunkenness, revelries, and the like; of which I tell you beforehand, just as I also told you in time past, that <u>those who practice such things **will not inherit** the kingdom of God.</u> NKJV (emphasis mine)*

We could summarize all of the works of the flesh, (or sin nature as some translations render it) as meeting the perceived needs of the fallen 'SELF' life. All of the things listed are either living for <u>self</u>-gratification for the body or some <u>self</u>-realization or <u>self</u>-promotion for the emotional life and <u>self</u>-worth. So apparently if you are living continually entirely for yourself, with no consideration of cooperating with the Holy Spirit, or fulfilling Gods commands, you may have a serious problem.

Contrast this with the fruit of the Spirit, or walking in, with, or after the Holy Spirit. You will notice that most of these 'fruits' or evidences of the Holy Spirits workings, are not about your<u>self</u>, but rather about your attitudes and behavior towards others.

> *Galatians 5: 22-25 ²² But the fruit of the Spirit is love, joy, peace, longsuffering, kindness, goodness, faithfulness, ²³ gentleness, self-control. Against such there is no law. ²⁴ And those who are Christ's have crucified the flesh with its passions and desires. ²⁵ If we live in the Spirit, let us also walk in the Spirit. NKJV*

We have found over the years that as people receive self-image, identity, and emotional healing, that they become increasingly less concerned with self, and more interested in helping others.

So, the issue is do you feel conviction about your fleshly behavior, and whether or not you are interested in God's answers for dealing with it. It is how you regard your behavior that God is interested in here. (Psalm 66:18) Do we justify it and have not the least intention of changing, or do we want to deal with it in the ways that God has provided?

If we are trying to find God's help in changing, we are under grace. If our genuine desire is to change, and do things that please God, it shows a preference for Him and His will over self and self-will. Hebrews chapter 10 verse 14 says that by the sacrifice of Jesus those who are being sanctified have been 'perfected forever.' So, we can deduct from this statement that if we are seeking to walk with the Holy Spirit in the process of sanctification we have already, past tense, been made perfect before God. IF we are engaged in the process of being sanctified through the work of the Holy Spirit facilitating the Word of God in our lives we are under grace.

Sanctification is positioned in the 'continuing present tense' which means that it is an ongoing work. But if we do not want to be sanctified, and are happy with our current attitudes and behavior, are we perfected? Indeed, God gives grace, we do not take it. It is conditional on His Lordship and our submission as we come <u>under</u> Him.

> *Hebrews 10:14 For by one offering He has <u>perfected forever</u> those who <u>are being sanctified</u>. NKJV (emphasis mine)*

The Bible calls this change of thinking to 'repent.' The Greek word for repent is Metanoeo which means to 'change your thinking' and 'reconsider your ways.' John the Baptist was looking for 'fruit' or evidence that suggested that your thinking and ways were different.

Matthew 3:8 Therefore bear fruits worthy of repentance. NKJV

Hence, 'the Kingdom of heaven is at hand;' reconsider what you are doing, how you are living and thinking and which spirit you are serving. The result of this decision will be turning away from that nature and way of living which was <u>under</u> the power of Satan.

This attitude of wanting to turn then places us <u>under</u> the grace of God and free from sin. Some believers feel that they can take the grace of God and return to a self-seeking lifestyle where your life revolves around yourself. A true sign of a change of thinking is if your life revolves around God and seeking Him out. His response is walking with you through life and you dwelling in His presence.

2 Chronicles 15:2b The LORD is with you while you are with Him. If you seek Him, He will be found by you; but if you forsake Him, He will forsake you. NKJV

Just as with Jesus He is looking for 'followers.' His purpose is not to follow us and serve us with what we want for ourselves.

Someone has said that you will know if you have died to yourself if you no longer argue with God.

It has been pointed out that Gods love language is obedience. If we are wanting to submit to Him, and conform to His perfect ways it proves that we love Him.

John 14: 15 If you love me, you will obey what I command. NIV

We will cover the act of 'repentance' in more detail further on in the unit.

LESSON
If God is truly Lord of our lives we will be dealing with self-seeking, self-willed behavior, and be looking to Him for what He wants for our lives on a daily basis.

SONS OF GOD
In the Old Testament there are a number of references to the 'Sons of God.' I will list some here for your further study.

Genesis chapter 6 verses 2 and also 4.
Job chapter 1 verse 6 and also chapter 2 verse 1.

There are some other references but the point that I am trying to make here is that these 'sons' of God appear to be angels.

In the New Testament we find references to the Son of God (Jesus) and to 'sons of God' being <u>us</u>! These are those of us who have chosen to follow God, walk after the Spirit, and deal with the old self preferring nature which was living for sin. *(Let me note again: sin in both Hebrew and Greek means <u>offence</u>).*

> *Romans 8:13-14* ¹³ *For if you live according to the flesh you will die; but if by the Spirit you put to death the deeds of the body, you will live.*
> ¹⁴ *For as many as are led by the Spirit of God, these are sons of God.*

If we are looking for God and what He wants we are <u>under</u> the leading of the Spirit of God. We do this because we have a living faith in Him, and this faith produces deeds confirming our sonship.

> *Galatians 3:22 But the Scripture has confined all <u>under sin</u>, that the promise by faith in Jesus Christ might be given to those who believe. NKJV (emphasis mine)*

And also;

> *Galatians 3:26 For you are all <u>sons of God</u> through faith in Christ Jesus. NKJV (emphasis mine)*

So, the New Testament 'sons of God' are people who have actions that prove that they believe in God, and have changed how they live as a result of that belief. This does not mean that they have overcome all sin....it means that they want to. This attitude puts them under grace.

> *James 2: 17-18* ¹⁷ *In the same way, faith by itself, if it is not accompanied by action, is dead.* ¹⁸ *But someone will say, "You have faith; I have deeds." Show me your faith without deeds, and I will show you my faith by what I do. NIV*

Could we then propose that if the Old Testament Sons of God are angelic spirit beings, some of which have fallen from grace through disobedience.... that it is conceivable that the New Testament 'sons of God' are being tested in obedience for eternity?

Is God replacing His fallen angels? We cannot say for sure and scripture is not definite, but there is enough evidence, that I personally certainly want to disengage from anything to do with behavior stemming from the fallen nature. Setting ourselves in obedience and faith in the word of the Most High God seems a very wise course to take. Jesus did state that we will at least be 'like' or 'equal' to the angels. Either way it is a great privilege to be called sons, and we should definitely endeavor to live accordingly.

> *Luke 20: 35-36* ³⁵ *"But those who are counted worthy to attain that age, and the resurrection from the dead, neither marry nor are given in marriage;* ³⁶ *"nor can they die anymore, for they are <u>equal to the angels and are sons of God</u>, being sons of the resurrection. NKJV (emphasis mine)*

God must have been grieved at the rebellion of His angels. These spiritual beings apparently were entrusted with authority, responsibility, free will and choice just as we have been.

LESSON
God is not looking to break our free will and choice, He is desiring for us to bow it down, because we choose to be His children.

Study 3: The fall of Satan and the arrival of man

Having established the existence and implications of the unseen realm let us now piece together a theological overview of what has happened. We need to know the truth for our own knowledge, and also to be able to give a good account to help others clearly understand.

We have already noted that Satan and his angels have been cast down specifically to the earth having been defeated in the war in heaven.

> *Revelation 12:7-9* *⁷Then there was war in heaven. Michael and the angels under his command fought the dragon and his angels. ⁸And the dragon lost the battle and was forced out of heaven. ⁹ This great dragon--the ancient serpent called the Devil, or Satan, the one deceiving the whole world--was* <u>thrown down to the earth with all his angels</u>. *NLT (emphasis mine)*

So, the situation was that Satan and his angels were now on earth. It appears that Satan has not lost his cleverness or indeed his powers, but he evidently is now limited in his ability to use them. Jesus spoke of His own eyewitness account of seeing his fall. He also gave us authority OVER all of the power of the enemy. We exercise this by <u>faith in God that it truly is so</u> because the Word of God states it to be.

> *Luke 10:18-20* *¹⁸ And He said to them, "I saw Satan fall like lightning from heaven. ¹⁹ "Behold, I give you the* <u>authority</u> *to trample on serpents and scorpions, and* <u>over</u> *all the* <u>power</u> *of the enemy, and nothing shall by any means hurt you. ²⁰ "Nevertheless do not rejoice in this, that the spirits are subject to you, but rather rejoice because your names are written in heaven." NKJV (emphasis mine)*

Clearly, Jesus gave us authority over the literal power of the enemy. When we are operating in the nature of God, submitted in obedience, then the Holy Spirit's power is far greater than the power of Satan. The Holy Spirit then facilitates the word of God being ministered through us and brings it to pass.

There is a caution in verse 20 in the preceding passage to not begin to think that we are something because of what is happening through us, lest we become swollen up in pride as was our adversary. The things that happen around us come to pass because God said they would if we believe His Word, and because the Holy Spirit then makes them a reality, not because we are greater than anyone else. In this we must become as 'little children,' unassuming, and with a simple faith that if God our Father said it, then it is so.

WHAT HAVE SATAN AND HIS ANGELS LOST?

They formerly had responsibilities and authority to fulfill these responsibilities. So even though they apparently still have their gifts and abilities they now no longer have anywhere to exercise them.

> *2 Peter 2:4 For if God did not spare the angels who sinned, but cast them down to hell and delivered them into chains of darkness, to be reserved for judgment; NKJV*

> *Jude 1:6 And the angels who did not keep their positions of authority but abandoned their own home--these he has kept in darkness, bound with everlasting chains for judgment on the great Day. NIV (emphasis mine)*

I used to work for a company developing their business for them in 3 different states in our nation. I was responsible for growing their enterprise and was given a credit card in order to finance and carry out my activities. On the top of the card was the name of the company. Further down under this was my name. They authorized me to use the card to carry out my work for them, but it had a credit limit. As I was faithful with my work for them and produced results, I was given access to greater funds. It was my skills, gifts and abilities, but it was their resource and commissioning to work on their behalf. This was in a designated area, and for a specific goal nominated by them. So, as I was faithful UNDER authority, my area of authority, influence, and empowerment to complete my task was increased.

> *Luke 19:17 "And he said to him, 'Well done, good servant; because you were faithful in a very little, have authority over ten cities.' NKJV*

So, these angels abandoned their responsibilities and the authority that they had over their particular areas. It would be like me not staying submitted to my employer, they would have soon no longer authorized my credit card. It would not mean that I had lost my capabilities, just that I no longer had anywhere to exercise them. It appears that God does not take back the gifts and abilities that He has given His created beings.

> *Romans 11:29 For the gifts and the calling of God are irrevocable. NKJV*

LESSON

Authority is linked to responsibility. It is given so that we can fulfill our God given purposes, not so that we can have prestige or power. Authority is not for us to be above others, or Lord our position over any other person. For example, fathers and mothers have authority over their children, and are responsible for their being raised in the counsel of the Lord.

MAN ENTERS THE SITUATION

We now have a circumstance in which Satan and his angels are cast out of heaven where they formerly had authority to exercise their gifts and abilities. They still have these gifts, but now no longer have anywhere that they are permitted to use them, finding themselves cast down to the earth.

Enter, man, who has delegated <u>authority over</u> the earth. He has been given a mandate and responsibility to rule over the earth and subdue it or bring it <u>under</u> authority.

<u>**Note:**</u> Many people want to have authority over people, property or projects but not so many want to take responsibility for that which they have authority over. PRINCIPLE; Authority is not to make you someone, or to control others, (self-realization and promotion) it is to give you the ability to look after that which you are responsible for. Hence the servant of the Lord in leadership is to be a servant of all...not Lording their position over those that they are responsible for. This means exercising authority with the good of the other persons or people in mind, not personal power, glory or control. In that sense people that you lead are not a part of your ministry, they ARE your ministry. You are responsible to look after them.

> *1 Peter 5:2-4 ² Be shepherds of God's flock that is under your care,
> serving as overseers--not because you must, but because you are
> willing, as God wants you to be; not greedy for money, but eager to
> serve; ³ not lording it over those entrusted to you, but being examples
> to the flock. ⁴ And when the Chief Shepherd appears, you will receive the
> crown of glory that will never fade away. NIV*

As an example of delegated authority, we know that many nations were under the rule of
the British Empire. Governor Generals were placed in charge of, or given dominion over, to
rule on behalf of the British leadership. These people had delegated authority to rule over
and subdue the nations that they were responsible for.

Adam found himself in this situation. As he was obedient to God for all that he had been
placed in charge of, he was given the power and authority to exercise and fulfill that
responsibility.

> *Genesis 1: 26-28 ²⁶ Then God said, "Let Us make man in Our image,
> according to Our likeness; let them have <u>dominion over</u> the fish of the sea,
> <u>over</u> the birds of the air, and over the cattle, over all the earth and <u>over</u>
> every creeping thing that creeps on the earth." ²⁷ So God created man in
> His own image; in the image of God He created him; male and female He
> created them. ²⁸ Then God blessed them, and God said to them, "Be fruitful
> and multiply; fill the earth and subdue it; have <u>dominion over</u> the fish of the
> sea, over the birds of the air, and <u>over every living thing</u> that moves on the
> earth." NKJV (emphasis mine)*

We must note here that they were given the responsibility to work together to rule over the
earth. It appears from the account in Genesis chapter 2 that the instructions about the
tree of knowledge of good and evil were given to Adam before God made Eve. So, it was the
responsibility of the man to uphold the Word of God that he had been given in regards to
the tree on behalf of his family.

> *Genesis 2: 15-17 ¹⁵ Then the LORD God took the man and put him in the
> Garden of Eden to tend and keep it. ¹⁶ And the LORD God commanded the
> man, saying, "Of every tree of the garden you may freely eat;
> ¹⁷ "but of the tree of the knowledge of good and evil you shall not eat, for in
> the day that you eat of it you shall surely die." NKJV*

So now we have man and woman on the Earth with dominionship or jurisdiction <u>over</u> all
that God had made them responsible for. As they remained <u>submitted</u> to him in obedience
and stayed <u>under</u> His instructions, they had power to fulfill their work.

Now we also have Satan who is cast down to the Earth. He still has his abilities but there is
nowhere that he is authorized to use them.

Note: Just because Satan has gifts and abilities it does not mean that he is right
with God. If we have gifts and abilities given to us by God, that does not necessarily
automatically make us right with God. If we use them for our own purposes, in a wrong
spirit or attitude such as pride, or for self-gain of some kind, such as personal glory, fame
or money, we may not fare well at the judgment. We cannot assume that we or others
are right with God because we have gifts. God is looking for the fruit of the spirit as the
right motivation. Fruit without gifts will limit our impact for the gospel, but gifts without
fruit will not produce what God is looking for either.

Note cont.

I have seen ministers who appear to believe that they are right with God because He has given them gifts, power, even healing through them and bringing people to salvation. Seemingly some areas around their lives do not add up to a sanctified life. I know of a Pastor who was seeing people regularly saved, filled with the Spirit and healed through his ministry. At the same time, he was sexually abusing young girls in his church. He was justifying himself, in at least one case, seeing himself as being like King David, and the girl as being like his Bathsheba. We cannot know the background of this man, how he arrived in such a place or if he eventually repented and was forgiven. This is for God to judge and not me, but it is a caution for all of us to minister in the 'fear of the Lord' as Jesus did. We would be foolish to assume that because God is using us that He for some reason is overlooking deliberate sin.

Matthew 7: 22-23 *[22] "Many will say to Me in that day, 'Lord, Lord, have we not prophesied in Your name, cast out demons in Your name, and done many wonders in Your name?' [23] "And then I will declare to them, 'I never knew you; depart from Me, you who practice lawlessness!' NKJV*

 LESSON
A gift is not a guarantee of salvation, it is a responsibility with an expectation of a fruitful outcome, as is well illustrated for us in the story of the talents. This can be studied in detail in Matthew Chapter 25:14-30

THE NATURE OF MAN
Man is created in the image of God a 'triune, tripartite or three part' being.

We would be surprised if it were any other way as God is Father, Son and Holy Spirit. They work together. As someone put it; the Father thinks it, the Son speaks it and the Holy Spirit makes it happen. We see Jesus confirming this in the Gospels only saying what He heard the Father say, and only doing what He saw the Father do. He also did nothing of His own ability, but the Holy Spirit brought it to pass through Him as Jesus pleased the Father by doing His will.

In the New Testament we know these three parts in man as Spirit, Soul and body.

THE HUMAN SPIRIT
Created order is **Spirit** (ruling over the whole person in submission <u>under</u> God), **soul** (covered and subjected by the spirit,) and then finally **the body** playing out the decisions of the spirit and soul. Many in our times are ruled by bodily lusts or soulish priorities and desires.

1 Thessalonians 5:23 Now may the God of peace Himself sanctify you completely; and may your whole spirit, soul, and body be preserved blameless at the coming of our Lord Jesus Christ. NKJV

The Human spirit mirrors the functions of the Holy Spirit, (in His image). Firstly, the Human spirit gives life just as the Holy Spirit gives life.

James 2:26 For as the body without the spirit is dead, so faith without works is dead also. NKJV

The Holy Spirit communicates truth as the 'Spirit of truth.' Our spirit registers inside us what the truth is.

> *1 Corinthians 2:11 For what man knows the things of a man except the spirit of the man which is in him? NKJV*

The Holy Spirit brings conviction; in the human spirit we call this our conscience.

The Human Spirit communicates comfort and strength empowering us. The same function is true of the Holy Spirit. We could say that if we have the Holy Spirit then all of our faculties are enhanced.

> *Proverbs 18:14 The spirit of a man will sustain him in sickness, But who can bear a broken spirit? NKJV*

The Holy Spirit is creator. The human spirit is creative, inspired.

The Holy Spirit empowers and facilitates, as does the life and power given to the body and soul by the human spirit.

It is the human spirit that makes the connection with God as spirit to Spirit. And it is the human spirit that God joins Himself to, or as it is in the Greek, (kollao) He glues or sticks Himself to our spirit.

> *1 Corinthians 6:17 But he who is joined to the Lord is one spirit with Him. NKJV*

> *John 4:24 "God is Spirit, and those who worship Him must worship in spirit and truth." NKJV*

THE HUMAN SOUL

The soul is considered to be the 'will' the 'mind' and the 'emotions.' We see this played out in life as; "I want," "I think" and "I feel".

The centre or middle of the will, mind and emotions, is what the Bible calls the 'heart,' which has a deep influence on all of the activities of the soul. We will discuss this in full in a later Unit.

THE HUMAN BODY

The body has its own desires for pleasures and the Worldly things on offer. In its fallen state it contributes to the 'flesh' or 'sinful nature.'

The body and soul are programmed by their environment and can be subdued and brought back into Gods order, ruled by the human spirit under the influence of the Holy Spirit. This happens through sanctification by the Holy Spirit, renewing of the mind through the word of God, and often the healing of brokenness in the 'heart' or centre of the soul.

FUNCTIONS

Perhaps we can illustrate here some biblical parallels for the spirit, soul and body concept.

New Testament:	Spirit	Soul	Body

Old Testament: Innermost place   Inner parts   Outer man
                             (God Conscious)   (Self-Conscious)   (World Conscious)

O/T Temple Typology: Holy of Holies   Holy Place   Outer courts

Remember Jesus referred to both His body and our bodies as 'temples.' The physical picture of the temple building in the Bible always gives us functional pictures of the parts of our humanity. Perhaps we could add one more analogy to a practical understanding of how they work together.

Computer: Internet   Programs   Hardware
                          (Access to outside   (Programs/training) (The machine)
                           information)

LESSON

We are as a human being, a unit made up of different parts and functions. We can dissect these to study and find out the areas which may need ministry, so that we can restore God's order and bring healing and freedom.

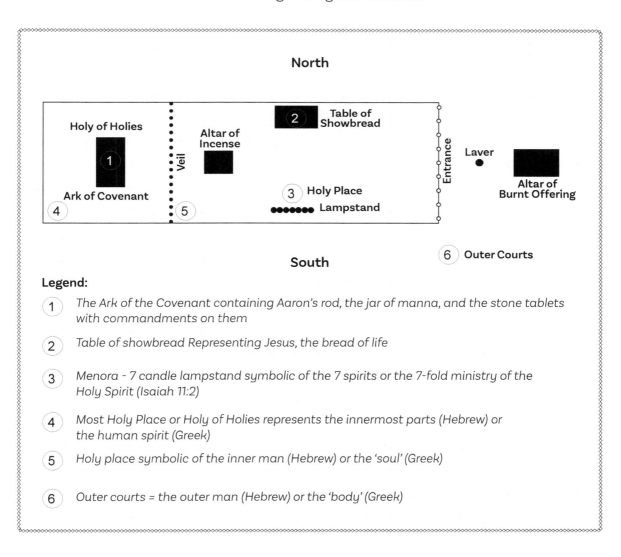

Legend:

1. *The Ark of the Covenant containing Aaron's rod, the jar of manna, and the stone tablets with commandments on them*

2. *Table of showbread Representing Jesus, the bread of life*

3. *Menora - 7 candle lampstand symbolic of the 7 spirits or the 7-fold ministry of the Holy Spirit (Isaiah 11:2)*

4. *Most Holy Place or Holy of Holies represents the innermost parts (Hebrew) or the human spirit (Greek)*

5. *Holy place symbolic of the inner man (Hebrew) or the 'soul' (Greek)*

6. *Outer courts = the outer man (Hebrew) or the 'body' (Greek)*

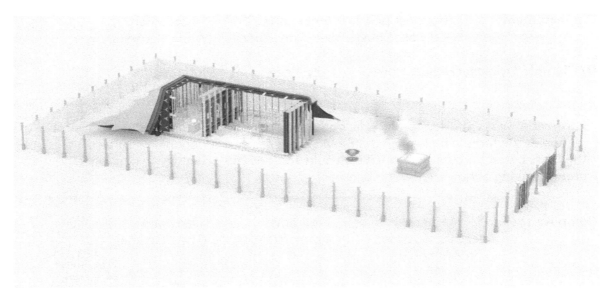

Pictured Above: Sanctuary tabernacle 3d rendering of the wilderness tent described in Exodus.

Study 4: The fall of man

We have established that man is created in Gods image and placed on the Earth to rule on Gods behalf. Satan has been thrown down to the Earth along with his angels. Now came the meeting of the fallen spiritual being with Adam and Eve.

Genesis 3:1 Now the serpent was the shrewdest of all the creatures the LORD God had made. "Really?" he asked the woman. "<u>Did God really say you must not eat any of the fruit in the garden?</u>" NLT (emphasis mine)

What just happened?
1.   The devil just created some areas of doubt.
-            Firstly, about the integrity of God's Word.
-            Secondly about whether or not God was withholding something good from them. He was implying that God was not good, loving or protective.

2.   Satan created a perception of God, which opened them to wrong belief. Wrong belief about someone's character leads to doubt and unbelief about their positive motives and intentions.

3.   Satan directly called God a liar when in Genesis 3:4 he told the woman that if she ate from the tree that they wouldn't die. In believing Satan to be truthful they accepted that God was not. In so doing they made Satan the source of truth to be followed, evidently believing that he was the good provider and placed themselves under his deceptive instructions. This is the basic situation that unregenerate man lives under today, whether he is ignorant of it or not. Consequently, mankind still ascribes power to Satan in the Earth through submission and obedience.

*Genesis 3:3-4 ³ "It's only the fruit from the tree at the center of the garden that we are not allowed to eat. God says we must not eat it or even touch it, or we will die." ⁴ "**You won't die!**" the serpent hissed". NLT (emphasis mine)*

> (It is not surprising that the final covenant that we find ourselves under is one whereby everything comes to us by faith alone.)

> *Romans 1: 17 For in the gospel a righteousness from God is revealed, a righteousness that is by faith from first to last, just as it is written: "The righteous will live by faith." NIV*

That is, faith in what God has said, His Word. Faith in His character, nature, ability and good loving intentions for us. It is worth noting that when believing in, and accepting Gods perfect love was no longer the covering, deception came, and fear came as well! We could define fear as the expectation of negative things happening, and faith as expecting good outcomes.

> In considering Satan's counsel they were coming <u>under</u> another word......when this doubt and perception was created, it led to a misinterpretation, or misunderstanding of the situation............followed by a conclusion.... and this produced a decision.... which led to an action. The action was disobedience, transgression or rebellion.... the first SIN.... which resulted in a consequence!

As we recall 'sin' means 'an offense.' So, the first sin was doubting Gods character, love, goodness and protective intentions for us. (Note: none of us likes being misunderstood, and we are very imperfect...how much more offensive would it be for a perfect God?)

DEFINITION AND STATEMENT

Sin then, comes through being deceived into misinterpreting the TRUTH of a situation....and what is actually good or best for us!

We can say then that sin is most often OUR BAD SOLUTIONS to our 'PERCEIVED' or ACTUAL needs and circumstances.

The devil continues to work exactly this way today.... distorting the TRUTH and offering us his solutions to our situations.... deceiving us by causing us to misinterpret what is happening. He manipulates the whole World this way causing war, misery in relationships, and also in hurting and damaging individual lives.

For Adam and Eve this was causing them to submit to Satan, coming <u>under</u> him through doubt and unbelief. They were not 'seeing' what was going on. It is not surprising that the mission of the Apostle Paul involved helping those who were perishing to see the truth.

> *ACTS 26:18 'to open their eyes, in order to turn them from darkness to light, and from the power of Satan to God, that they may receive forgiveness of sins and an inheritance among those who are sanctified by faith in Me.'*
> *NKJV*

PARADISE LOST

God had given Adam and Eve access to everything in the garden except for one tree...... the tree of the knowledge of good and evil. By all accounts they had everything they could possibly need in every way. The garden was beautiful to look at and evidently, they even were able to have time with God Himself.

> *Genesis 3:8-9 ⁸ And they heard the sound of the LORD God walking in the garden in the cool of the day, and Adam and his wife hid themselves from the presence of the LORD God among the trees of the garden. ⁹ Then the LORD God called to Adam and said to him, "Where are you?" NKJV*

A number of years ago a man in our church was asking questions about sex and even wanting to know about my sex life. It was clear that he wanted to push the boundaries and was fishing for how far he could go without getting himself into trouble. When I returned home, I told my wife about the discussion. Her comment was: "It's almost as if people think that what God has given isn't enough!"

This is clearly the case that Satan always puts before us. He suggests or implies that what God has given us is not enough. In this case Adam and Eve had all they needed. Satan suggested that it was not enough, and that God was keeping good things from them. He proposed that they needed to break out of the boundaries, limitations and rules to get what they needed to make them happy.

This is the basis of rebellion and lawlessness and if we cooperate and submit to it, then that nature of Satan is imprinted on us.

Today media promotes every kind of evil. Drugs, perverted sex, violence and revenge, living for food, travel, oversized homes, money and living for pleasure, social ascendancy.... or success in the eyes of the World are among many things portrayed as being 'what you need' to make you happy.

Satan still deceives the World into thinking that what God has given is not enough....and that you need to be your own god and provision, to throw off the limits and get what you want for yourself. He subtly suggests that there will be no consequence for this self-seeking behavior.

> *Genesis 3:2-4 ² "Of course we may eat it," the woman told him.*
> *³ "It's only the fruit from the tree at the center of the garden that we are not allowed to eat. God says we must not eat it or even touch it, or we will die." ⁴ "You won't die!" the serpent hissed. NLT*

I see many Christians today addicted to T.V. or other media who never read their Bibles. (Some reports suggest that only about 2% of Christians ever read their Bible from cover to cover – that is less than 2 in every 100) Without the knowledge of Gods Word for the most part they leave themselves open to being Worldly or Carnal Christians. They have been conformed to the thinking and standards of the World. John in his gospel to the believers and in his three other New Testament books mentions the 'World' around 100 times, most often as a negative influence. The devil has found a way through media to give people enormous doses of 'World' in very short spaces of time. People know 'good and evil' and many things that they would be better off not knowing through the injection of media into their lives. All kinds of fears and distortions are propagated through the screens that are placed before us.

Again, we can't help but wonder if the devil is whispering as people view, "surely you won't die!" But many are the spiritually walking dead.

In translations such as the New King James version the word 'Christian' is used only twice. Many things in the World are called 'Christian' but do not look much like the Kingdom of God in practice.

In the New International version, the term 'believers' is used around 20 times, 10 times as often as 'Christians.'

But if we go to the term 'disciple' or 'disciples' we find it mentioned about 270 times. So, in God's economy do you think He is looking for 'Christians', 'believers', or 'disciples'? True disciples have <u>discipl</u>ined themselves to seek first the Kingdom of God and His righteousness, and to not be conformed to the World. To die to living for self, resist the devil, walk after the Spirit, and put off the deeds of the flesh.

[Further study; Matthew 6:33, Romans 12:2, Matthew 23:25, Romans 8:1-5 + 13-14, James 4:7-8.]

"YOU WILL BE LIKE GOD"

Having challenged Gods integrity, truthfulness and trustworthiness, the temptation moved on to what was on offer to 'supposedly' bring more satisfaction with life. Firstly, Satan appealed to them by offering a promotion in status. Most likely he deceived the other fallen angels into following him by offering them a 'higher' position than they currently had. The problem again not being happy with what you have.

> *Genesis 3:5 "God knows that your eyes will be opened when you eat it. You will become just like God, knowing everything, both good and evil." NLT*

This was at the root of Satan's own fall, the desire to be 'like God.' He now was deceiving mankind by proposing the possibility of self-promotion. We see today mankind under this deception working feverishly to solve all of their own problems without God. Man puts his faith today in what man can do; it is the gospel of man. It began in the garden with accepting this belief and desire that man could be like God. As we see mankind even today looking to science and technology to resolve his own issues faithlessly without the Lord. We see him blinded by the counterfeit miracles that are being worked with natural materials. That is not to say that we do not appreciate the efforts of the people who are trying to make the world a better place, and their achievements. Indeed, the created order part is that man is still trying to subdue the earth and rule over it, which is admirable. The 'fallen' part is that man now no longer believes that he needs God to do this. He will do it on his own as his 'own god.'

> *2 Thessalonians 2:9-10 ⁹ The coming of the lawless one will be in accordance with the work of Satan displayed in all kinds of counterfeit miracles, signs and wonders, ¹⁰ and in every sort of evil that deceives those who are perishing. They perish because they refused to love the truth and so be saved. NIV*

Perhaps the name of this 'lawless one' is <u>technology</u>, a part of which is media. Certainly, the spirit behind technology seems to be manipulating and programming the World, conforming people to an agenda. The subtlety of this is that much of it seems to serve mankind in giving him what he 'needs' to be satisfied with life. For example, we see the proliferation of things such as pornography, with reportedly more than 33% of the internet being devoted to this devastating bondage.

Is media the new tree of knowledge of good and evil? With care, discernment and discipline it can be a good servant, but without restraint it appears to be a very bad master.

LESSON

The power that Satan has over mankind comes through deception followed by submission.... whether or not people even believe that the devil exists is irrelevant.

THE FALL

There are two words that we should pause to consider the meaning of here because they both hold significance for our walking in righteousness. Firstly, the word for temptation which in the Greek, in the tense of tempt, is 'peirazo.' This literally means to 'test' or 'examine', to scrutinize, to entice.

The second word is sin. Which as we have already related, in both Hebrew and Greek, sin means 'an offence' or 'to offend.' So, we are tested and examined in regards to how we see God and His gifts to us, His love and faithfulness. Sin then is when we choose something other than what He has given, doubting His nature. He then, evidently, is offended by us rejecting Him and the things that He offers us as a result of His goodness.

> *Genesis 3:6 The woman was convinced. The fruit looked so fresh and delicious, and it would make her so wise! So she ate some of the fruit. She also gave some to her husband, who was with her. Then he ate it, too. NLT (emphasis mine)*

LESSON

Basically, behind all sin choices is that which Satan was proposing about the forbidden tree in the garden. 'Good things are being kept from you...this is what you need, this will make you happy.' Perhaps we can add to this; 'don't trust God to have your best interests in His heart, get what you want/need for yourself.'

Today he works exactly the same way, programming us by the ways of the world through contact with others, media or some other medium.

SUMMARY

We can observe three elements and areas to the temptation.

1. Be like God; be your own empowerer and the setter of what is appropriate for you in terms of how you live, and what is permitted for you. In other words, be your 'own' spiritual covering. This is seemingly to do with the fall of the **spirit of man**.

We see the beginning of the decline of the U.S. as a Christian nation when the Bible was taken out of the schools in the early 1960's. We could liken this to taking the steering wheel off in your car....it is unlikely that you will stay on the road for very long. Without the counsel of God through His word everyone began to do what was right in their own eyes. By the end of the 1960's and early 1970's people were adopting attitudes such as 'look after number 1' (self) and 'if it feels good do it' (self on the throne) and 'if its right for you its right' (be your own god).

What followed was all manner of negative behaviors increasing exponentially. Alcoholism, drugs, violence, broken homes, immorality, mental problems etc. etc. all went off the charts as man decided to throw off the limits, just as he did in the Garden of Eden. This decline is well illustrated and reflected in much of the media, materials and attitudes coming out of that nation today. There are still many holding up a standard there, but the general population, as in most Western nations, has largely removed the Bible and the Word of God as being the tree of life.

2. So, that is apparently the corruption of the 'human spirit,' and then the woman saw that it was good for 'making you wise!' She evidently saw a benefit for her soul in the area of wisdom.

3. And finally she saw that it was desirable as food. Clearly, they had plentiful supplies of food, but now considered that they could please the bodily element of their flesh through eating this food.

In 1 John Chapter 2 we see a New Testament parallel warning for believers in our times.

> *1 John 2:16-17* [16] *For all that is in the world; the lust of the flesh, the lust of the eyes, and the pride of life; is not of the Father but is of the world.*
> [17] *And the world is passing away, and the lust of it; but he who does the will of God abides forever. NKJV*

Lust of the flesh = desires and things for our body

Lust of the eyes = things that will supposedly make us emotionally satisfied (*E.G. new house or car, perhaps someone else's wife or husband or sexually stimulating images.*)

Pride of Life = could be to meet a perceived emotional 'need' such as low self-image. But it certainly is a s*piritual attitude* and covering that is aligned with Satan and not the Kingdom of God.

But all of these things are of the World and will not provide for us what they deceptively promise.

> **Note:** Lust here denotes wanting that which is forbidden. To enjoy good food and pleasure is not sin. To enjoy things that look good are not sin.... such as beautiful scenery or your own wife. These are given by God for us; we can be thankful for them and they are enough. It is wanting things that are forbidden that constitute lusts.

> *1 Timothy 6:17b But their trust should be in the living God, who richly gives us all we need for our enjoyment. NLT*

 LESSON
The world system under the influence of the devil offers many things that supposedly will make you happy....this is generally the exact opposite of the truth.

FEAR AND 'PROJECTION'

So, as we round out our thinking about the fall of man, we see that they now were aware of things that God had been protecting them from. They had taken themselves out from UNDER the covering of LOVE, Protection and Provision. Their guilt now produced anxiety and they were aware that they had become their own protection and provision in a hostile environment. This need for protecting yourself, and looking out for what might happen that could bring harm, is called fear.

We know that the remedy for this is being touched by God with His truth in all areas, spirit, soul and body. We will discuss how to appropriate receiving from Gods freedom from fear in later units. (Note: Guilt comes when we have done something that we shouldn't have, or not done something that we should have.)

> *1 John 4: 18-19* [18] *There is no fear in love; but perfect love casts out fear, because fear involves torment. But he who fears has not been made perfect in love.* [19] *We love Him because He first loved us. NKJV*

Projection is where we will no longer take responsibility for our sin, or even our part in a negative ungodly relationship. It is where we want to blame others for our behavior rather than take responsibility for our part in it, and accept that we need to seek God and His help for change.

> *Genesis 3:8-12* [8] *Toward evening they heard the LORD God walking about in the garden, so they hid themselves among the trees.* [9] *The LORD God called to Adam, "Where are you?"* [10] *He replied, "I heard you, so I hid. I was afraid because I was naked."* [11] *"Who told you that you were naked?" the LORD God asked. "Have you eaten the fruit I commanded you not to eat?"* [12] *"Yes," Adam admitted, "but <u>it was the woman</u> you gave me who brought me the fruit, and I ate it." NLT (emphasis mine)*

Adam blamed his wife for their sin. He would not accept responsibility either for his participation in the sin or for not standing up for the instruction and Word of God he had received.

Remember apparently God had given the instructions to Adam before He created Eve to work with him. The responsibility was then on Adam, the first man.

In our modern western society, we still see today that very often man doesn't want to take responsibility for his family, or even have a family to be responsible for. Spiritually he is easily swayed away from God and very often it is the women who lead the family back to church.

As a consequence, many modern women, justifiably, do not feel confident that they will be properly looked after and protected by the man. They often take over the leadership of the household, because the men, like Adam, are weak in their convictions and not responsible in their actions.

This is an ungodly order in the household that causes a lot of problems in the family and society. Most women are simply not equipped for the pressures of operating a household as leader on her own, and as a result many suffer considerably.

LESSON

At the root of anxiety and insecurity issues for mankind is separation from an all-powerful God who is more than able to meet all of our needs.

SUMMARY OF THE SITUATION

1. So now we have God in heaven, the sovereign owner of the universe. Man, on Earth who had until now nothing between him and his creator. Up to this point mankind had authority and power over the World while they continued to remain UNDER God's authority through obedience to His instructions.

2. Satan had been cast down to the Earth still having abilities but with no authorization or place to use them.

3. In doubting God man has accepted Satan's authority and integrity OVER that of God, and by doing so in obedience to him has come UNDER the power of Satan.

4. There is now another spiritual entity in between mankind and God. God will always be over all, so Satan, a created being remains UNDER God. Man, however is now UNDER Satan and is cut off from God spiritually. It is now that the 1st of the devils lies begins to come in to play. God is the source of power and life. The devil had stated that they would not die if they disobeyed. Being spiritually separated from God it was now inevitable that they must begin to die.

Perhaps we could liken it to a solar panel which derives its power and energy from the sun. If heavy cloud comes in between, or it is night and darkness is the covering, then it is just a matter of time that the power it has stored will run out. As the sin of man increased and sin proliferated, it is not surprising that man's days became shorter and shorter as he is separated increasingly from the ways of God, whose power is the source of life.

Interestingly we see that following Gods ways and commands even today will add time to our power and life on the Earth.

> Proverbs 3:1-2 [1] My son, do not forget my law, But let your heart keep my commands; [2] For length of days and long life And peace they will add to you. NKJV

Principle: All deception is rooted in moving you away from, and taking your eyes off what God has said. This includes adding to it or twisting it to suit your purposes.

Study 5: The 'ruler' of the World

Satan now had 'dominion' over all of the areas of the Earth that Adam had been given authority over. Consequently, he rules over every person who has not been redeemed by Christ Jesus. None of us were 'born again' from the womb. We are all saved by grace through faith. Each of us must make the decision to come out from 'under' the influence of the devil.

The New Testament makes no arguments that this is the case. Let me catalogue a few scriptures that highlight Satan's ongoing position in the Earth for all who have not come back 'under' the authority of God through the sacrifice of Jesus.

> *Matthew 4:8-10* *⁸ Again, the devil took Him up on an exceedingly high mountain, and showed Him all the kingdoms of the world and their glory. ⁹ And he said to Him, "All these things I will give You if You will fall down and worship me." ¹⁰ Then Jesus said to him, "Away with you, Satan! For it is written, 'You shall worship the LORD your God, and Him only you shall serve.'" NKJV*

Jesus did not dispute that Satan could give him the Kingdoms of the World, or that he had them in His power. Jesus refused to submit and come UNDER the authority of the devil, citing in contrast to Adam and Eve obedience to Gods Word as His reference for living. Note the temptation was the desires of the eyes and perhaps the pride of life. He began in verse 3 with trying to get Jesus to turn stones into bread, the weakness of the flesh.

It is worth noting here that the devil even tried to tempt Jesus by using the Word of God.

> *Matthew 4:5-7* *⁵ Then the devil took Him up into the holy city, set Him on the pinnacle of the temple, ⁶ and said to Him, "If You are the Son of God, throw Yourself down.* **For it is written:** *'He shall give His angels charge over you,' and, 'In their hands they shall bear you up, Lest you dash your foot against a stone.'" ⁷ Jesus said to him, "It is written again, 'You shall not tempt the LORD your God.'" NKJV (emphasis mine)*

What was actually wrong here? The Word of God is always true and Jesus could have thrown Himself down and expected angelic intervention. The problem was that it was initiated by the wrong spirit. It was proposed as manipulation, so if Jesus had submitted to another will He would have come 'under' its authority.

Example: Suppose a man says: 'It is written', a woman should submit to her husband. The Word is true, but if her free will is compromised or the spirit behind it is control or self-seeking, then it is not of God and initiated by another ungodly power working through the man. A woman submits to her husband in Gods order because the man is sacrificially loving and caring about her, not because he is manipulating her to care about him, or give him what he wants for himself. In any event Biblically she chooses to do it because the bible says that is how she should live.

> *John 14:30 "I will no longer talk much with you, for the ruler of this world is coming, and he has nothing in Me. NKJV*

In the preceding passage Jesus called the devil the ruler of the world. There is no dispute from Jesus that it was so.

Interestingly He pointed out that the devil had nothing in Him that would allow him any power or authority. He had no sin or areas of deception that would lead to submission that would put him under the devil. Perhaps more importantly he had no areas of wrong believing that he could use to manipulate or tempt Jesus. Jesus knew perfectly that the

Father loved Him, and also, He had a correct picture of the person of God Himself. His self-image and emotions were not compromised by areas of wrong belief either. So, His relationship with Father God was complete.

Someone said that the roots of many of our problems are separation from God, ourselves or others in some area. It is of prime importance then that our thinking about those relationships is accurate and based on Gods truth.

AFTER THE CROSS

Following are some other names for Satan that indicate that his position has not changed in regard to unredeemed humanity. These references are after the completed work of the cross and indicate that the devil's position has not changed. It's the status of the believer that is different in Christ.

> *2 Corinthians 4:3-4* ³ *But even if our gospel is veiled, it is veiled to those who are perishing,* ⁴ *whose minds the **god of this age** has blinded, who do not believe, lest the light of the gospel of the glory of Christ, who is the image of God, should shine on them. NKJV (emphasis mine)*
> *Ephesians 2:1-3* ¹ *And you He made alive, who were dead in trespasses and sins,* ² *in which you once walked according to the course of this world, according to the **prince of the power of the air**, the spirit who now works in the sons of disobedience,* ³ *among whom also we all once conducted ourselves in the lusts of our flesh, fulfilling the desires of the flesh and of the mind, and were by nature children of wrath, just as the others. NKJV (emphasis mine)*
>
> *1 John 5:19 We know that we are children of God, and that the whole world is **under** the control of the evil one. NIV (emphasis mine)*

THE RESCUE PLAN OF GOD

The purpose of God in all of His covenants is for man to be in authority <u>over</u>; if we will submit to authority <u>under</u> the Lordship of Gods ways…. the head represents authority, deciding what will happen…. the tail gets dragged around wherever the head decides. We see many in our time just being dragged around by the ways of the World and other influences that they are in bondage to.

> *Deuteronomy 28:13 "And the LORD will make you the head and not the tail; you shall be <u>above only</u>, and <u>not be beneath</u>, if you heed the commandments of the LORD your God, which I command you today, and are careful to observe them. NKJV (emphasis mine)*
>
> *Matthew 8:8-10* ⁸ *The centurion replied, "Lord, I do not deserve to have you come under my roof. But just <u>say the word,</u> and my servant will be healed.* ⁹ *For I myself am a man <u>under</u> authority, with soldiers under me. I tell this one, 'Go,' and he goes; and that one, 'Come,' and he comes. I say to my servant, 'Do this,' and he does it."* ¹⁰ *When Jesus heard this, he was astonished and said to those following him, "I tell you the truth, I have not found anyone in Israel with such <u>great faith</u>. NIV (emphasis mine)*

> **Note:** In Matthews Gospel chapter 8 we see the great example of these principles with the story of the centurion man's sick servant. The centurion appeared to understand that Jesus operated <u>under</u> the authority of the supreme being God. As a result of whom he was <u>under</u> the authority of, He was in authority <u>over</u> lessor entities. Therefore, the centurion man deduced that Jesus' word alone would be sufficient to decide the outcome of his servant's malady. Jesus considered this man's understanding of His position of authority, and consequent belief in His abilities to resolve the situation, to be 'great faith.'

LESSON
Understanding who God is, His faithfulness and ability to fulfill His word, and His true attitude towards us is the basis of 'genuine faith.'

Study 6: The 'GOOD' News of the Gospel

Up until this point we have seen only bad news with mankind coming under the power of a cruel new master. Amazingly, Adam, the 1st man submits to Satan in Paradise whilst surrounded with beauty, where he had everything. All that he could ever need and more. Jesus as the 2nd Adam refuses to submit whilst in the desert where He had absolutely nothing. Not even a piece of bread to eat.

Remember, He established His dealings with the devil based on 'it is written.' In other words, His foundation for refusing the devils offers was coming from that which God had said. This placed Him under the authority of the word of God and His instructions. This is what the 1st Adam failed to do. The Word of God then is our foundation as we are followers of Christ Jesus, 'the Word made flesh.'

He was the 'Word made flesh' in the sense that His life was an enactment of living the life described in the Word. He only behaved and reacted as the Word said He should. He lived the life that was revealed in scripture that He should live. His mission and purpose were the fulfilling of what the Word said He would do.

For us to be conformed to Christ's likeness as the Word made flesh, then we also need to be conformed to the Word of God as well. In other words, we should become the Word living out through our person (clothed in flesh) as well, being both 'hearers and doers.' Not stepping outside of the boundaries and counsel of the Word of God.

> *James 1: 22 Do not merely listen to the word, and so deceive yourselves. Do what it says. NIV*

> *Romans 8: 29 For those God foreknew he also predestined to be conformed to the likeness of his Son, that he might be the firstborn among many brothers. NIV*

Consequently, Jesus refused to submit to another spiritual being, or be coerced towards another agenda that was outside of the revealed will of God through His Word. In Genesis chapter 3 right back where the fall occurred, we see God announcing that Jesus would come and destroy the total authority that the devil had over mankind. The 'head,' of course, we understand as being the symbol of authority that we have already described. The Genesis passage points to injury for Jesus in His process of taking complete authority over those who would believe in Him from Satan.

> *Genesis 3:15 "And I will put enmity between you and the woman, and between your offspring and hers; he will crush your head, and you will strike his heel." NIV*
>
> *1 John 3:8 He who does what is sinful is of the devil, because the devil has been sinning from the beginning. The reason the Son of God appeared was to destroy the devil's work. NIV*

Remember anything under your feet is something under your authority. So, the passage is saying that Satan is always and was always under the authority of God. Jesus never submitted to Satan's agendas and never sinned, so the devil had no authority over Him, and even the cross was a striking at Jesus' foot as He walked over him crushing his power.

1 John 3:8 explains that destroying the work of the devil in our lives was the purpose of Jesus the Christ coming to earth. We note here that John the Baptist preached repentance, Jesus preached repentance, and the Apostles preached repentance. We will clarify what this means in a moment, but suffice to say that if we are not going to change how we regard our participating with Satan, and move to cooperation with God, then Jesus cannot complete this work and fulfill His promise.

 LESSON
Submitting to Satan's agenda for our lives through sin, puts us under his authority, and allows him to bring about outcomes that are contrary to God's best purposes and intentions for us. For example, if you are a Christian and drink a bottle of Whisky a day for 20 years you shouldn't be surprised if you have a damaged liver. Did God want that for you? No! Did the devil? Yes! The counsel of scripture clearly warns against drunkenness.

THE SIGNIFICANCE OF THE BAPTISM OF JESUS

As an act of obedience Jesus presented himself to His cousin John for baptism. John's baptism was a baptism of repentance and so this confused John as Jesus was without sin.

> *Matthew 3:13-17 ¹³Then Jesus came from Galilee to John at the Jordan to be baptized by him. ¹⁴ And John tried to prevent Him, saying, "I need to be baptized by You, and are You coming to me?" ¹⁵ But Jesus answered and said to him, "Permit it to be so now, for thus it is fitting for us to fulfill all righteousness." Then he allowed Him. ¹⁶ When He had been baptized, Jesus came up immediately from the water; and behold, the heavens were opened to Him, and He saw the Spirit of God descending like a dove and alighting upon Him. ¹⁷ And suddenly a voice came from heaven, saying, "This is My beloved Son, in whom I am well pleased." NKJV*

There are two points that we will highlight here that are very important to our story.

1. Jesus was without sin and consequently had nothing to repent of. We know however that He was going to go to the Cross to pay the penalty of death that was to be

the outcome for us because of our sin. He was going to fulfill the law in full. So, as we consider this, we must examine the question; 'can sin be forgiven without repentance?'

> *Luke 24:46-47* [46] *He told them, "This is what is written: The Christ will suffer and rise from the dead on the third day,* [47] *and* <u>*repentance and forgiveness of sins*</u> *will be preached in his name to all nations. NIV (emphasis mine)*

If Jesus were to go to the Cross to deal with our sin, without first identifying with our sin in repentance on our behalf, the work of the cross would have been void.

CONSIDERATIONS ON 'REPENTANCE' AND 'GRACE'

In this modern era, we have what is known as the 'grace message,' and we also have the 'repentance message.' So, which one is valid? We could say that the 'repentance message' without grace will likely produce legalism. Equally, the 'grace message' without repentance can result in lawlessness. Jesus put these into context for us in Luke chapter 24 when He proclaimed what our message would be. Let us repeat this passage here now emphasizing it as in another context.

> *Luke 24:46-47* [46] *He told them, "This is what is written: The Christ will suffer and rise from the dead on the third day,* [47] *and* <u>*repentance and forgiveness of sins*</u> *will be preached in his name to all nations, beginning at Jerusalem. NIV (emphasis mine)*

Note: The NKJV use the word remission rather than forgiveness which is equally valid from the original language.

Remember, repentance means 'change your thinking' and 'reconsider your ways' which will result in turning from your current attitudes and actions. The consequence of this promised by Jesus is forgiveness.

Really when the Apostle Paul was speaking of God's grace, he was not proclaiming a new message or revelation, he was reinforcing that God's graciousness, <u>IS</u> His forgiveness, and the resultant remission of our sins. He understood that it comes to us through our repentant attitudes. It begins with Gods generous offer of forgiveness through Christs sacrifice, the outcome of which is a change of thinking towards God and His Kingdom.

> *Romans 2:4-5* [4] *Or do you show contempt for the riches of his kindness, tolerance and patience, not realizing that God's kindness leads you toward repentance?* [5] *But because of your stubbornness and your unrepentant heart, you are storing up wrath against yourself for the day of God's wrath, when his righteous judgment will be revealed. NIV*

The NLT brings out Gods gracious patience with us in encouraging us to change our thinking in how we regard him, and subsequently our attitudes and behavior.

> *Romans 2:4 Don't you realize how kind, tolerant, and patient God is with you? Or don't you care? Can't you see how kind he has been in giving you time to turn from your sin? NLT*

There is a significant story just before Jesus announced in Luke chapter 24, that the message that we are to bring, is to encourage people to reconsider what they value and are living for. And also explain the offer of forgiveness and the blotting out of our sins through Christ Jesus. The story is of the men crucified with Jesus in Luke Chapter 23.

> *Luke 23:39-43* *³⁹ One of the criminals who hung there hurled insults at him: "Aren't you the Christ? Save yourself and us!" ⁴⁰ But the other criminal rebuked him. "Don't you fear God," he said, "since you are under the same sentence? ⁴¹ We are punished justly, for we are getting what our deeds deserve. But this man has done nothing wrong." ⁴² Then he said, "Jesus, remember me when you come into your kingdom." ⁴³ Jesus answered him, "I tell you the truth, today you will be with me in paradise." NIV*

Was one criminal less of a sinner than the other? No. One criminal had sufficient fear of God and knowledge of Jesus to take responsibility for his behavior, confessing that he was a sinner who needed saving. In so doing he was 'changing his thinking' about what was acceptable. Repentance established; Jesus proceeded to proclaim forgiveness.

LESSON

It is not whether or not we are sinless that brings forgiveness, because none of us are. It is how we regard sin in our hearts that matters. We will examine in a moment how the Apostle Paul in Romans chapter 7 was struggling with areas of sin. The point is that he WAS struggling, which means that his attitude was repentant. His thinking was that he didn't want to sin, and this in turn qualified him for forgiveness through the grace of God.

THE CHANGING OF THE PRIESTHOOD

2. Another important aspect of Jesus' baptism was the changing of priesthood under the New Covenant. We see in Leviticus 8:6 Aaron and his sons, the original priests, being baptized or washed by Moses to confirm their ordination.

Zacharias the father of John the Baptist was in the priestly line and served in the temple. So, it is symbolic that John being born of the line of priests should now be baptizing Jesus immediately before He began His ministry.

Later we know that Caiaphas the serving high priest who examined Jesus before the crucifixion tore his own robe in apparent frustration. Under the law this rending of his garment disqualified him from being high priest (Leviticus 21:10).
In contrast Jesus also wore the one-piece garment of a priest. Lots were cast for His robe, and it was never torn leaving Him as legitimate to be our high priest.

> *Hebrews 11:12-19* *¹² For when there is <u>a change of the priesthood</u>, there must also be <u>a change of the law</u>. ¹³ He of whom these things are said belonged to a different tribe, and no one from that tribe has ever served at the altar. ¹⁴ For it is clear that our Lord descended from Judah, and in regard to that tribe Moses said nothing about priests. ¹⁵ And what we have said is even more clear if another priest like Melchizedek appears, ¹⁶ one who has become a priest not on the basis of a regulation as to his ancestry but on the basis of the power of an indestructible life. ¹⁷ For it is declared: "You are a priest forever, in the order of Melchizedek." ¹⁸ The former regulation is set aside because it was weak and useless ¹⁹ (for the law made nothing perfect), and a better hope is introduced, by which we draw near to God. NIV (emphasis mine)*

THE HOLY SPIRIT COMES UPON HIM TO BEGIN HIS MINISTRY

The Holy Spirit came upon Him at His baptism and we hear the Father expressing His pleasure at the obedience of His Son. I think this is something that every human being needs to hear. We need to know that we are giving God pleasure in our existence. Notably I have read that in His culture that you were not considered a full adult until thirty years of age, so this was the appropriate time for Him to begin His ministry.

> *Luke 3:22-23* *²² And the Holy Spirit descended in bodily form like a dove upon Him, and a voice came from heaven which said, "You are My beloved Son; in You I am well pleased." ²³ Now Jesus Himself began His ministry at about thirty years of age, being (as was supposed) the son of Joseph, the son of Heli. NKJV*

Prior to His baptism we see Him doing no miracles. A part of His ministry to us was to model how we should walk in the Spirit in terms of behavior. (Exhibiting the fruit of the Spirit). He also showed us how to move in the power of the Spirit through the gifts of the Spirit.
We note that Jesus was 'led' into the desert FULL of the Holy Spirit. But it is important to observe that after He overcame His fleshly needs and the temptation of the devil in terms of His self-realization, remaining faithful to the Word of God, that He returned in the POWER of the Holy Spirit.

> *Luke 4:1-2* *¹ Jesus, **full of the Holy Spirit**, returned from the Jordan and was led by the Spirit in the desert, ² where for forty days he was tempted by the devil. He ate nothing during those days, and at the end of them he was hungry. NIV (emphasis mine)*

> *Luke 4: 14 Jesus returned to Galilee in the **power of the Spirit**, and news about him spread through the whole countryside. NIV (emphasis mine)*

In Luke 4:18 we see the reason for the Holy Spirit being upon Him and we will discuss this in more detail in Unit 2.

Throughout all of this testing Jesus was on Earth just like we are in terms of His location. He still enjoyed unbroken relationship with the Father as He was never separated from God as we have been by sin, submission and cooperation with the devil. He remained in authority over Satan at all times, and we see Him exercising this position over demons when He began His ministry.

When we are saved through faith in Christ Jesus, we find ourselves in the same position as Jesus. In terms of location we are found in this hostile environment called Earth. But in terms of Spiritual authority we are seated in the heaven-lies with Him and OVER all of the power of our enemy. We exercise this position by faith that the Word of God says it is so. Even if we are having a bad day, and don't feel very much in authority over our situation, the spiritual reality is that we are!

A father or mother may not live as though they have authority over their children, and consequently not exercise it, but the fact remains that this is their position if they will take it up and appropriate it.

> *Ephesians 2:6, 8-9* *⁶ And God raised us up with Christ and seated us with him in the heavenly realms in Christ Jesus, ⁸ For it is by grace you have been saved, through faith--and this not from yourselves, it is the gift of God-- ⁹ not by works, so that no one can boast. NIV*

SIN AND RIGHTEOUSNESS

Sin, or transgressing Gods Word positioned Adam under Satan and Separated from God. Righteousness and living only within the boundaries of God's Word positioned Jesus, the second Adam, the second sinless man born, under God and over Satan and all of his works.

> *1 Corinthians 15:45-49* ^{*45*} *And so it is written, "The first man Adam became a living being." The last Adam became a life-giving spirit.*
> ^{*46*} *However, the spiritual is not first, but the natural, and afterward the spiritual.* ^{*47*} *The first man was of the earth, made of dust; the second Man is the Lord from heaven.* ^{*48*} *As was the man of dust, so also are those who are made of dust; and as is the heavenly Man, so also are those who are heavenly.* ^{*49*} *And as we have borne the image of the man of dust, we shall also bear the image of the heavenly Man. NKJV*

Study 7: The New Covenant

So, we see Jesus bringing in the New Covenant for mankind. This Covenant was to be by Faith alone with Jesus bringing about a complete redemption. He fully paid for every provision for us on the cross. We have salvation, healing and deliverance from our enemies all included, and we have nothing that we can do to earn it. Jesus did it all, a finished work, and we access all of His provisions appropriating them all, and receiving them by Faith.

> *Romans 1:17 This Good News tells us how <u>God makes us right in his sight</u>. This is accomplished from <u>start to finish by faith</u>. As the Scriptures say, "It is through faith that a righteous person has life." NLT (emphasis mine)*

Some people point to the finished work of the cross and claim that they have everything by claiming the scriptures. They have what we might call a 'Word only God.' In the New Covenant everything is accessed by faith. It is a reversal of the situation in the Garden in the sense that man fell, and lost his position through doubt and unbelief. He is now restored and redeemed, receiving all of Gods provisions in Jesus through faith based on truth alone. Indeed, it appears that God has largely limited Himself to responding to the activity of faith. It is not so surprising then that Jesus, as we have mentioned, was so impressed with the Centurion man in Matthew chapter 8. He seemed to have fully grasped this concept of being <u>under</u> to be <u>over</u>.

> *Matthew 8:8-10* ^{*8*} *The centurion answered and said, "Lord, I am not worthy that You should come under my roof. But only speak a word, and my servant will be healed.* ^{*9*} *"For I also am a man <u>**under**</u> authority, having soldiers <u>under</u> me. And I say to this one, 'Go,' and he goes; and to another, 'Come,' and he comes; and to my servant, 'Do this,' and he does it." 10 When Jesus heard it, He marveled, and said to those who followed, "Assuredly, I say to you, I have not found such <u>great faith</u>, not even in Israel! NKJV (emphasis mine)*

If you read Isaiah chapter 61:1+2 there are the promises of God regarding preaching the good news to the poor, setting the captives free, healing the broken hearted and so on. It was the 'Word only,' and didn't help anyone that we know of until Jesus arrived around 600 years later as 'the Word made flesh.' He then announced in Luke 4:18 that He was now going to fulfill that prophecy. It required that there was someone with faith and alignment with the Word and will of God, to now go and act it out in the power of the Holy Spirit.

Remember with creation that God had something in mind. Then Jesus spoke it into being and the Holy Spirit made it a reality. Just the Word as a concept without someone to action it, and the Holy Spirit being involved to fulfill it, is what I mean by a 'Word only' God.

We can quote the scripture, but it requires faith and activity for it to become a 'living Word,' before it normally benefits anyone. For example, some people will claim a 'written word scripture' for years, for something like healing with no results. Yet that same word reveals that God has provided gifts of healing, and people with faith to act out the word on your behalf. Someone with the ability to work with the Holy Spirits gifts to see you helped. A person who has works, knowledge and experience in your area of need that God can touch your life through. (That is not to say that you cannot be that person yourself, releasing the Holy Spirit to confirm the Word of God through your own faith if you have it.)

> *James 2:20 But do you want to know, O foolish man, that faith without works is dead? NKJV*

> *1 Corinthians 12:4-11 ⁴ There are diversities of gifts, but the same Spirit. ⁵ There are <u>differences of ministries</u>, but the same Lord. ⁶ And there are <u>diversities of activities</u>, but it is the same God who works all in all. ⁷ But the manifestation of the Spirit is given to each one <u>for the profit of all</u>: ⁸ for to one is given the word of wisdom through the Spirit, to another the word of knowledge through the same Spirit, ⁹ to another faith by the same Spirit, to another gifts of healings by the same Spirit, ¹⁰ to another the working of miracles, to another prophecy, to another discerning of spirits, to another different kinds of tongues, to another the interpretation of tongues. ¹¹ But one and the same Spirit works all these things, distributing to each one individually as He wills. NKJV (emphasis mine)*

APPROPRIATING GODS PROVISIONS BY FAITH

We know that God so loved the World that He sent His only son to pay for its sin, so that all could be saved. Is everyone saved? No! The opportunity of salvation is paid for everyone, but received only by those who believe that Gods Word is true in this regard. The Word says that it is there as a promise and an indication of the will of God, paid for by Jesus, but it requires faith to actively claim it for it to become a reality.

> *John 3:16 "For God so loved the world that He gave His only begotten Son, that whoever believes in Him should not perish but have everlasting life. NKJV*

And so it is with every promise of God. You do not normally come into salvation and automatically receive freedom from all bondages, broken heartedness, or the need for physical healing. When do you get them? When you know about them and accept them by faith. This often means receiving through a ministry that God has placed in His body to provide for your needs. As someone has said; 'God's goodness is for those who will accept it.'

If you are in a Church that teaches that healing is not for today, or perhaps the baptism in the Spirit and speaking in other tongues is no longer available, you will most likely never receive them. You appropriate them by faith, which is trusting God for them, and believing that they are yours. If you don't believe that they are for today then for you according to your faith they are not. When do we get the promises of God? When we hear the good news about them and lay hold of God in Faith to receive them.

Personally, I believe that the deliverance of Israel from Egypt is a picture for us all. In bringing them out of Egypt God did everything for them, they had to do nothing. It was a supernatural translation from captivity to freedom. In the same way God redeems us completely from sin and Satan's captivity through the work of the cross. There is nothing for us to do but receive.

But next they came to the Promised Land. For them to possess the promises that are there, they have to have an active faith with corresponding actions. God had already said that He would give them the land. They all agreed that it was a good land, but they did not all believe that God was with them, and trustworthy to be able to deliver on His promises.

In much the same way after our initial salvation many of the promises of God need to be contended for by active faith. Otherwise we all agree that Gods promises are good, but being passive, deceived or intimidated by the enemy prevents us pressing in with God for the provisions that Jesus paid for. Even in this Old Testament example, the principle remains that without active faith we miss the fullness of Gods provision.

> *Hebrews 3:19 So we see that they were not able to enter, because of their unbelief. NIV*

THE CROSS AND THE END OF JESUS' EARTHLY MINISTRY

As we jump to the end of Jesus' time on Earth, we find Him in the garden of Gethsemane with His disciples. We see a battle going on within Him. His Spirit relating directly to God wants to fulfill the will and mission of God that He has been tasked with. Having come into human form as we are, He is a living soul, and He has a body. The emotional pressure from the knowledge of what He was about to face, both on His soul and body, was overwhelming.

We see the disciples falling asleep under the duress of the situation that they found themselves in. As He sees them unable to stay awake, I believe that He was noting the effect on them, but also acknowledged His own internal battle between His spirit and soul. Yet again He chose not to <u>sub</u>mit to preferring self, and remained <u>over</u> the circumstances choosing the will of the Father.

> *Matthew 26:38-42 ³⁸ Then he said to them, "My <u>soul</u> is overwhelmed with sorrow to the point of death. Stay here and keep watch with me." ³⁹ Going a little farther, he fell with his face to the ground and prayed, "My Father, if it is possible, may this cup be taken from me. Yet not as I will, but as you will." ⁴⁰ Then he returned to his disciples and found them sleeping. "Could you men not keep watch with me for one hour?" he asked Peter. ⁴¹ "Watch and pray so that you will not fall into temptation. The <u>spirit is willing, but the body is weak</u>." ⁴² He went away a second time and prayed, "My Father, if it is not possible for this cup to be taken away unless I drink it, may your will be done." NIV (emphasis mine)*

In all of this He remained in the 'power of the Spirit' rather than seeking His personal comfort in the 'weakness of the flesh.'

THE CRUCIFIXION

Mark chapter 15 reveals Jesus being nailed to the cross at the 3rd hour. (9.00am) At the same time the Passover lamb that was symbolic of Jesus as the lamb of God was moved from the temple court and tied to the altar.

Jesus had been questioned and examined by the priests and found without sin. The symbolic lamb had also been examined and found to be without spot or blemish as well.

At the 6th hour (12.00pm) darkness fell over the Earth until the 9th hour (3.00pm). Every family had to participate in the Passover in the temple. As a result, it may well have been that very few were at the crucifixion, beyond the Romans who were attending.

At the 9th hour (3.00pm) the temple lambs throat was cut, at the same time Jesus...the Lamb of God, announces "it is finished."

He dies physically.
This means of execution was peculiar to the times and yet it was prophesied that He would die in this manner.

THE CURTAIN
We know that when He died that the curtain in the temple was torn from top to bottom. This curtain was between the Holy Place and the Holy of Holies. You will remember from earlier in our studies that the Holy place, as a symbol is representative of the human soul, and the Holy of Holies represents the human spirit, and the place where the presence of God resides most strongly.

The picture that we have now, is that through the sacrifice of Jesus, the way is now open for us to again come into the presence of God, through faith in the work of Jesus.

> Hebrews 10:19-22 [19] Therefore, brothers, since we have confidence to enter the Most Holy Place by the blood of Jesus, [20] by a new and living way opened for us through the curtain, that is, his body, [21] and since we have a great priest over the house of God, [22] let us draw near to God with a sincere heart in full assurance of faith, having our hearts sprinkled to cleanse us from a guilty conscience and having our bodies washed with pure water. NIV (emphasis mine)

We know that death could not hold Him down and that inevitably having paid for our sin He must rise again. As a result, we now have an empty cross and a seated Christ who intercedes for us, the High priest of our confession.

WHERE DO WE NOW FIND OURSELVES?
Why has God done all of this for us when we acknowledge that all of us have sinned and lived for ourselves. I believe that God would be denying Himself, His own nature and faithfulness if He did not make a way for us. The fact is that through Adam and Eves sin and submission that Satan came to us, and we became captives sold into slavery. (Clearly sin began with Satan and his angels before mankind was created).

So, we could say that nobody on Earth from that point on asked to be in the situation that they are in, or have the weaknesses and faults that they have. ALL fall short of the glory of God, there is no one righteous, not even one (Romans 3:10).

We could say that every human on Earth no matter how bound, deeply deceived into sin, hurt, broken or damaged they are, asked for these issues.

We say when we see someone with something out of Gods order; "something happened." We cannot judge, we do not know how they arrived at this place, or in the condition that they are in. So, God <u>cannot</u> **not** offer them grace, mercy and another chance….it would not be fair. The fact is that His very throne is established on the foundation of justice.

> *Psalm 89:14 Righteousness and justice are the foundation of Your throne; Mercy and truth go before Your face. NKJV*

God in His wisdom knows that our cooperation and submission to sin is based on being deceived and misinterpreting, or having come to the wrong conclusions about our situations.

For example, life may have taught us that we are a bad person. This then becomes 'our truth' but it is not God's truth. Nonetheless if we believe that we are bad we will most likely live accordingly.

Study 8: The Grace of God

The grace of God then is to deal with why we sin rather than sin itself, which was dealt with by Jesus on the cross. Jesus Himself acknowledged that it was deception that caused sinful activities and asked the Father for our forgiveness. We all put Him on the cross, because we all have sinned, and it was necessary to pay the price for it all. Remember this was the plan and will of the Father to open the way for us to be able to be back in relationship with Him.

> *Luke 23:34 Then Jesus said, "Father, forgive them, for they do not know what they do." NKJV*

In this passage, basically He was alluding to the fact that they/we don't know why they/we were doing what they/we were/are doing. So, by implication He knew that He was about to pay for their/our sin. Consequentially, we could say that grace is implying: 'Father I will pay for their sin, but I will also send the Holy Spirit, who will work with them bringing truth to help them deal with why they are deceived into sin.'

> *John 16: 13 "However, when He, the Spirit of truth, has come, He will guide you into all truth". NKJV*

We see two mechanisms at work through the work of the cross.

1. Redemption: The first is what we might call that which <u>God will do **for** you</u>. This work of redemption is forgiveness of sin, and perfecting of us before God the Father, so that He can receive us, and we can relate with Him. Redemption comes to us through the finished work and ministry of Jesus, and includes all kinds of healing and freedom through faith and the ministry of the Holy Spirit. This is a completed work which cannot be added to by our own efforts or works.

2. Sanctification: The second is the process of sanctification which is an ongoing work of the Holy Spirit as we walk with Him. The cross opened the way for the outpouring of the Spirit of truth and the commencement of His ministry. This second part we would describe as that which <u>God will do **in** you</u>. It is an ongoing work which is not yet completed in us. It includes receiving sufficient truth to access the provisions of redemption.

> *Hebrews 10:14 For by one offering He has perfected forever those who are being sanctified. NKJV*

As we have previously stated, and now reinforce, perfecting us forever is a past tense statement. Those who are being sanctified is continuing present tense. In other words, it is ongoing. So, Jesus dealing with our sin and making us right with the Father is a finished work. Possessing the land of our souls, subjecting our bodies, and walking in the authority of our inheritance is an ongoing process.

As we have said, we lost our position through deception, and it is restored in a practical way through being sanctified by the truth.

> *John 17:17 "Sanctify them by Your truth. Your word is truth. NKJV*

Truth is a very strong theme of the New Testament appearing around 110 times. We need to base our lives around seeking Gods truth to grow into healthy children.

> *John 8:31-32 ³¹ Then Jesus said to those Jews who believed Him, "If you abide in My word, you are My disciples indeed. ³² "And you shall know the truth, and the truth shall make you free." NKJV*

Interestingly the Bible connects evil with having a lack of truth.

> *1 Corinthians 13:6 Love does not delight in evil but rejoices with the truth. NIV*

In any case we see a just God remembering that we are dust, (created humans) and making a way for us to return to Him.

To put His justice and mercy into perspective, let me relate the following excellent story which I read in one of my devotionals.

FIORELLO LA GUARDIA; THE JUST JUDGE

Fiorello was Mayor of New York City for three terms from 1934 through until 1945.
One bitterly cold night he decided to preside as judge over a night court. An old woman was brought in for stealing a loaf of bread.

She explained that she had taken it to feed her family who were starving. As judge, Fiorello responded that he had to punish her stating that the law makes no exceptions, there must be a consequence, and payment for the offence was required.

"I must fine you $10 dollars" was his verdict. This was a considerable amount of money in the times. The rent for a house for a month in those days was around $22 and an average weekly wage was around $30.

He then reached into his own pocket and took out a ten-dollar bill.

'Here's the $10 to pay your fine, which I now remit.' He threw the $10 bill into his own hat and declared, "I'm now going to fine everybody in this courtroom fifty cents for living in a town where a person has to steal a loaf of bread in order to eat. Mr. Bailiff, collect the fines and give them to this defendant."

After the hat was passed around, the incredulous old woman left the courtroom with a new light in her eyes and $47.50 in her pocket to buy groceries! This is between $1,500 and $2,000 based on today's average wage in the U.S.

The law demanded that she be punished, suffer consequences, and pay for her actions. Justice held the environment and circumstances accountable, and required that she be extended grace.

This is a great picture of the Gospel for us. We did not ask to be born into the environment of a sinful world or our particular circumstances. Some perhaps grew up with issues such as a bad home life or generational influences affecting their lives.

A just God then says, the fine must be paid, but I will pay it.

Not only did you do nothing other than be born into this world to earn this free gift of forgiveness', but I am also going to bless you with every spiritual blessing in the spiritual realms. Just like the old lady in the story we come before the judge with nothing but guilt and empty handedness. However, just as she did, we leave pardoned and blessed beyond our wildest imaginations. We have a fair judge, and a Gospel or Good news that seems too good to be true. But it is!

> *Ephesians 1:3-8* *³ Praise be to the God and Father of our Lord Jesus Christ, who has blessed us in the heavenly realms with every spiritual blessing in Christ. ⁴ For he chose us in him before the creation of the world to be holy and blameless in his sight. In love ⁵ he predestined us to be adopted as his sons through Jesus Christ, in accordance with his pleasure and will--⁶ to the praise of his glorious grace, which he has freely given us in the One he loves. ⁷ In him we have redemption through his blood, the forgiveness of sins, in accordance with the riches of God's grace ⁸ that he lavished on us with all wisdom and understanding. NIV*

SUMMARY

Before we move on to Unit two, let us summarize the outworking of the New Covenant as it relates to us and our lives in an ongoing manner:

1. Redemption: 'That which God does **for** us'
                          A completed work, finished and paid in full
2. Sanctification: 'That which God does **in** us'
                          An ongoing work of the Holy Spirit
3. Mission: 'That which God does **through** us'
                          This comes as we understand our redemption,
                          and as we cooperate with the Holy Spirit in the
                          work of sanctification, it opens the way to works
                          of faith...

> *James 2:17-18* *¹⁷ In the same way, faith by itself, if it is not accompanied by action, is dead. ¹⁸ But someone will say, "You have faith; I have deeds." Show me your faith without deeds, and I will show you my faith by what I do. NIV*

Gods intentions for the mission of the Church are taken up next in Unit 2. Some further reference will be made to sanctification in terms of our attitudes to cooperating with and submitting to the Holy Spirit. The main body of accelerated sanctification will be detailed in Unit 4, Truth Encounters, which will explain a process that the Holy Spirit uses to bring this about.

UNIT TWO

The Church and the Holy Spirit

Introduction

Let us begin recapping in broad terms three themes that we find in the New Testament in regards to our walk with God:

1. REDEMPTION – 'What God will do <u>for</u> you'
2. SANCTIFICATION – 'What God will do <u>in</u> you'
3. MISSION – 'What God will do <u>through</u> you'

Study 1: God's intentions for mankind

1. REDEMPTION

We have covered this largely in Unit one. We saw how Jesus Christ paid the price for us for our sin and its consequences. As a result, we now belong to Him and are able to access by faith all of His benefits. Jesus' work is finished, and we receive through faith by the ministry of the Holy Spirit.

Psalm 103:2-4 ² Bless the LORD, O my soul, And forget not all His benefits: ³ Who forgives all your iniquities, Who heals all your diseases, ⁴ Who redeems your life from destruction, Who crowns you with loving kindness and tender mercies. NKJV

2. SANCTIFICATION

Some people believe that when you are born again and receive the Holy Spirit that God has finished the work in you. As a result, much of the Church remains passive, deceived, captive and broken.

The truth is that receiving the Holy Spirit is the <u>beginning</u> of His ministry to you and through you. We will discuss what this might look like in detail in later units. For the moment, let us say that His work of sanctification is accomplished through freeing us from areas of deception, and this by bringing Gods truth to mind and heart.

John 17:17-18 ¹⁷ "Sanctify them by Your truth. Your word is truth. ¹⁸ "As You sent Me into the world, I also have sent them into the world. NKJV

In the preceding verse we see that the process of sanctification is the activity of receiving truth at every level of our beings.

John 16:13 "However, when He, the Spirit of truth, has come, He will guide you into all truth" NKJV

It is the work and function of the Holy Spirit, or Spirit of truth, to bring this truth to us, wherever in our person that it is required.

> John 8:32 *"And you shall know the truth, and the truth shall make you free."* NKJV

Let me note here that much of the focus of the Church has been ministering to the mind and seeking to bring change to lives by applying truth here. This is very necessary as 'a part' of sanctification. However, many have a great deal of truth in the mind but it has not set them free, this is because they also need truth in the heart. This is a neglected area of ministry which is to be a major part of that which the Spirit of Christ will do in us.

As previously stated, we are devoting a later unit titled 'Truth Encounters' to explaining this ministry.

Many have come into the Kingdom as born-again believers, possibly been filled with the Spirit, and even learnt to work in gifts of the Spirit. They may even have taken up a leadership role without having received ministry in this area. King David understood that he needed truth in a deeper place than his conscious mind.

> Psalm 51: 6 *Surely you desire truth in the inner parts; you teach me wisdom in the inmost place. NIV*

Bible scholars indicate that 'inner parts' could also be translated 'heart' in this passage as the New Living version has it. The point is that King David was acknowledging that his sin with Bathsheba proceeded from deception in a deeper part of his being.

Many confuse the 'heart' with the mind and therefore come to the conclusion that the 'renewing of the mind' will resolve any issues that a believer may face. 'Renewing of the mind' is I believe conforming the conscious thinking to the ways of God, as opposed to being conformed to the thinking of the world.

This is certainly a very important part of our transformation, but does not resolve every issue.

3. MISSION
This Unit relates to the mission of the New Testament church.

The church being the 'ekklesia' as it is in the Greek language, which means the community of believers or saints. Together as the body of Christ we are to be doing His work on Earth. So, in essence we are to continue the ministries that He was doing, as His ambassadors or representatives. There are a great many activities termed as 'discipling' in the Christian World. I believe fundamental discipling is learning to do the things that He was doing. The needs of the World are the same today as they were in His time when He came to us as the 'Son of man,' healing the sick, setting the captives free, and healing the broken hearted. Certainly, these items were central in His own earthly ministry, and were the activities that He commissioned the early 'disciples' to continue.

> John 20:21-22 [21] *Again Jesus said, "Peace be with you! As the Father has sent me, I am sending you."* [22] *And with that he breathed on them and said, "Receive the Holy Spirit. NIV*

THE SPIRIT OF THE LORD AND THE ANOINTING

In the modern church world, there are all kinds of teachings around about the 'anointing.' Fundamentally the anointing of the Holy Spirit is His presence to facilitate particular Kingdom tasks as He wills. (We see this in the Old Testament where people were chosen to be anointed as prophets, Kings, priests or some other function.) Our concentration then is on the mission that the Lord has given us. We can be sure that the Holy Spirit will make our faith driven activity a reality, as we operate in the revealed will of God.

> *Mark 16:20 Then the disciples went out and preached everywhere, and the Lord worked with them and confirmed his word by the signs that accompanied it. NIV*

What we must observe here is that the work of God is always about helping people. Gifts or the 'anointing' are not about us personally, to make us feel good or be impressive to our fellow man. If the motives of our hearts are right then we will want to be as is our Father in Heaven, and we will just want to, in love, help our fellow man. The most powerful way to do that will not be in our own abilities, which is often religious activity, but as co laborers with God who has the power to bring real change.

Study 2: Living According to the Spirit

> *John 16:7 "Nevertheless I tell you the truth. It is to your advantage that I go away; for if I do not go away, the Helper will not come to you; but if I depart, I will send Him to you. NKJV*

Jesus considered that we would be in a better place if He returned to heaven and sent the Holy Spirit to us. In His flesh body, manifested as the son of man, He was limited by problems such as distance, and exposure, in terms of how many people He could help. He taught the disciples how to live according to the Spirit in regards to behavior and attitudes. He also trained them in how to work with and be led by the Holy Spirit and to allow Him through them to set people free. He did no recorded works that I am aware of prior to His own baptism and subsequently being filled with the Holy Spirit.

We can confirm then that He did no works as a man, but only began to fulfill His calling as the 'word made flesh' when He allowed the Holy Spirit to work in and through Him.

Clearly, His ultimate intention was for many disciples to be trained to minister to the needs of a hurting and captive humanity just as He did.

This working through many 'sons' and 'daughters,' meant that He would be able to reach the entire world with Gods goodness and offer of salvation.

It is worthy of note that there are activities of the Holy Spirit that came with the beginning of His dispensation and ministry through believers. I am speaking of functions in line with that which scripture had already revealed that He would be manifesting, such as leading us into 'all truth.' Speaking in tongues and the gifts of the Spirit were not recorded as present through believers until the beginning of the Holy Spirit era.

Although Jesus demonstrated all of the gifts of the Holy Spirit, it appears that they only became available for all believers when the Spirit was poured out. For example, speaking in other tongues did not occur until the Holy Spirit was poured out in Acts chapter 2. We should not be surprised then if Holy Spirit ministries such as 'Truth Encounters' which we will cover in Unit 4, are specific to this time. It is not an extra Biblical event, or non-scriptural in that He is called the 'Spirit of truth.' It is a thoroughly biblical concept that it is a major part of His ministry to bring truth to whatever area of our being that is in deception.

Perhaps we could even go so far as to take the liberty to comment that the outpouring of the Spirit of truth, means that being filled with the Spirit is largely to be filled and permeated with Gods truth. That is that all parts of our members are in the light and aligned with the Word of God.

> John 16:13 *"However, when He, the Spirit of truth, has come, He will guide you into all truth" NKJV*

LIVING AS THE ANOINTED CHURCH

The criteria for us to be the church that God is pleased to anoint, is for us to be led by the Spirit as Jesus was.

> *Luke 3:22 And the Holy Spirit descended in bodily form like a dove upon Him, and a voice came from heaven which said, "You are My beloved Son; in You I am well pleased." NKJV*

Having received the Holy Spirit, the next thing that happened was that He was led by the Spirit into the wilderness, being 'filled with the Holy Spirit.'

> *Luke 4:1 Then Jesus, being <u>filled</u> with the Holy Spirit, returned from the Jordan and was led by the Spirit into the wilderness, NKJV (emphasis mine)*

In the wilderness He dealt with that which we might describe as the 'self-life.' This is in terms of putting what you could have, or want for yourself, aside in favor of being where the Spirit wanted Him to be. This meant denying physical wants and items that He was fully entitled to, such as the most basic thing for the body, food, all for the sake of the will of God.

Later as we know the devil came and tempted Him offering Him the same things that he had tempted Adam and Eve with in the beautiful Garden of Eden.

The devil tempted Him to turn the stones into bread. Eve saw that the food was good to eat. The devil let Him see the kingdoms of the world and their glory. Eve was impressed by what she saw.

> *Genesis 3:6 So when the woman saw that the tree was <u>good for food</u>, that it was <u>pleasant to the eyes</u>, and a tree desirable to <u>make one wise</u>, she took of its fruit and ate. NKJV (emphasis mine)*

As we know each time Jesus was tempted, He used the written word of God as His reference point for which spirit He was going to align with. So, the devil's final temptation was using the written word of God in order to get Jesus to bow down and submit to him. The written word is always true, but if it is initiated by the wrong spirit, and out of context to manipulate, then it can bring you under the authority of the work of Satan.

Eve was tempted to be special, being made wise by eating the fruit, and would become like God. In this final effort from the devil Jesus was tempted to prove that He was 'someone special.' Had He not already known that He was, being already full of truth and complete in the Fathers love, He may have been susceptible. This action would have been an act of self-promotion, which was Satan's own downfall. So, to follow the Spirit of God, Jesus dealt with, and refused, all of the aspects of the fallen self-life which were instigated by the devil.

> *1 John 2:16 For all that is in the world; the lust of the flesh, the lust of the eyes, and the pride of life; is not of the Father but is of the world. NKJV*

Having dealt with what the World offered, the elements of the 'fallen self-life,' and also the devil who works through the first two, Jesus returned in the 'power of the Spirit.'

> *Luke 4:14 Then Jesus returned in the <u>power of the Spirit</u> to Galilee, and news of Him went out through all the surrounding region. NKJV (emphasis mine).*

This all happened immediately before Jesus announced the beginning of His ministry and the confirmation of the Prophetic word of Isaiah 61, that a person who came in the flesh, would make the Word true by the working of the Holy Spirit through Him.

> *Luke 4:18-19 [18] "The Spirit of the LORD is upon Me, Because He has anointed Me To preach the gospel to the poor; He has sent Me to heal the brokenhearted, To proclaim liberty to the captives And recovery of sight to the blind, To set at liberty those who are oppressed; [19] To proclaim the acceptable year of the LORD." NKJV*

The preceding verse is only one of two places in the New Testament where the anointing of the Holy Spirit on Jesus was mentioned. Christ means the 'anointed one' or in Hebrew, the 'Messiah,' and so the fact that He was anointed was evident in His name. On both occasions where it does directly mention His anointing, the purpose of the anointing of the Holy Spirit, is to minister to humanity which are afflicted by the works of the devil.

> *Acts 10:38 "how God anointed Jesus of Nazareth with the Holy Spirit and with power, who went about doing good and healing all who were oppressed by the devil, for God was with Him. NKJV*

What does all of this mean to us?
So, why is the anointing of the Holy Spirit on the Church today? Is it there to make us feel good, and He does! Or is it to empower us to do the works of Jesus today by the manifestation of the Holy Spirit working through us also?

> *John 20:21-22 [21] So Jesus said to them again, "Peace to you! As the Father has sent Me, I also send you." [22] And when He had said this, He breathed on them, and said to them, "Receive the Holy Spirit". NKJV*

We all have an anointing from the Holy One to continue this work of proving Gods love, acceptance and grace to His hurting creation, and to set the captives free. When we read the scriptures or hear the word preached, we know if we are hearing the truth or not. Our renewed human spirit acknowledges the truth even though our minds need renewing and our broken hearts need healing.

> *John 1:20 But you have an anointing from the Holy One, and all of you know the truth. NIV*

HOW DO WE WALK IN THE 'ANOINTING' ON US?

We know that the Holy Spirit uses people by working through them, and giving gifts as He decides is appropriate and commensurate to their sanctification, development and character. But how do we qualify to be used by Him in this way so that we can serve God's purposes in the World?

Jesus showed us the way. He began, having received the Holy Spirit, to now be led by the Spirit. If we are going to be led by our own desires, priorities and self-promotion, then we will probably not be too attentive to what the Holy Spirit may have for us.

When Jesus said to take up our own cross, deny our 'selves' and follow Him, He was saying that we need to lay aside our own 'fallen self' tendencies that want to have what the world offers. Jesus' own cross meant doing something that He would prefer not to do, for the sake of the Fathers will, and laying aside things that He could have had, even life. Our 'cross' may be laying aside a career or some other thing that we could have for our 'selves'. These represent the lives we lose, in favor of fulfilling the will of God.

When we lose this inferior natural life, we gain a super abundant life in the spirit.

> *Romans 8:14 For as many as are led by the Spirit of God, these are sons of God. NKJV (emphasis mine)*

In a very basic form, we note that the works of the 'flesh,' 'sin nature,' or 'fallen nature' as listed in the book of Galatians chapter 5 and verse 19-21 all stem from some form of 'self-realization.' If we go on to the fruit of the Spirit, we see that they are attributes such as goodness, kindness, patience, love, which are characteristics directed outwardly and purposed towards dealing well with others rather than self-seeking.

So, they are 'fruit' or evidence that you are being led by the Spirit and cooperating with Him.

> *Galatians 5:18 But if you are led by the Spirit, you are not under the law. NKJV (Emphasis mine)*

In order for the works of the flesh or sin nature to be dealt with, many times in addition to being led by the Holy Spirit, we need ministry from Him by some means to set us free. But we may need to let go of our own ideas and our 'right to our self,' before we are prepared to entertain receiving help from others who 'walk in the spirit.' This leads us to another Biblical example regarding how we relate to working with the Holy Spirit as junior partners.

Strong's concordance instructs us that the word translated 'walk' is in the Greek language 'peripateo' from which I imagine we derive words such as 'patio' where we walk. Permit me to expand its meaning from the original language, and underline a few key meanings that relate to our attitude towards our relationship to the Holy Spirit.

4043. Peripateo, to tread all around, i.e. walk at large (espec. as proof of ability); fig. to live, deport oneself, **follow (as a companion or votary)**:--go, **be occupied with**, walk (about).

So, in a very real sense our lives are to be spent walking around with and following our companion, being occupied with His priorities for us.

If our personal focus is on Him and His plans for an abundant life for us, then we will not be preoccupied with our inferior 'fallen self' interests.

To put the following passage in context our 'lusts' are our strong desires to meet our own perceived needs or wants. It does not mean that all strong desires or the enjoyment of life is evil, but rather that selfish desires that are forbidden such as immorality are lusts.

> *Galatians 5:16 I say then: Walk in the Spirit, and you shall not fulfill the lust of the flesh. NKJV*
> *Galatians 5:16-17* ¹⁶ *So I say, live by the Spirit, and you will not gratify the desires of the sinful nature.* ¹⁷ *For the sinful nature desires what is contrary to the Spirit, and the Spirit what is contrary to the sinful nature. NIV*

Finally let us look at what we may expect to see working in and through us as the Spirit has increasing sway through our willful cooperation. But first let us examine one more passage to put in context how a true disciple, usable by God, will regard the Holy Spirit.

> *Romans 8:1 There is therefore now no condemnation to those who are in Christ Jesus, who do not walk <u>according</u> to the flesh, but <u>according</u> to the Spirit. NKJV (emphasis mine)*

Aside from the obvious implication that those who walk according to the 'flesh,' fallen, or sin nature may well still potentially be subject to condemnation, I want to focus on this word 'according.' What I am saying is not those who struggle with 'self' issues so much, because they often require healing and release from captivity. But more on those who do not give the Holy Spirit His rightful place.

The dictionary definitions for 'accord' and 'according to' mean; in agreement and harmony with, consistent with; in a manner corresponding and conforming to; on the authority of the pattern of; and carries the sense of giving place to, and according position to.

Although that is a lengthy description of the word, I think it is worth thinking over, in the sense of fully understanding how we qualify to be exempt from condemnation. And how we're promoted as being those who are in Christ Jesus, and living according to the Spirit.

God gives grace, we do not presume to take it. I was once talking with a Christian man who was living a carnal, self-centered lifestyle, with no indication of wanting to serve God. He was explaining to me how he was under grace and could live how he wanted.

I attempted to convey to him that God gives us grace so that we can learn to do His will, and not so that we can continue to live for our own will and wants. If we are in genuine relationship with Him, under His Lordship, then His wants will become our wants as we choose to bow down under His will.

Then we know that all things that we need will be added to us and everything we could need for our enjoyment will be given.

(Matthew 6:33, 1 Timothy 6:17) Indeed, those things that are in His will, and that He wants for us, are far better than anything that we could try to provide for ourselves.

> *1 Corinthians 6:19-20* ¹⁹ *Or do you not know that your body <u>is the temple of the Holy Spirit who is in you</u>, whom you have from God, and <u>you are not your own?</u>* ²⁰ *For you were bought at a price; therefore glorify God in your body and in your spirit, which are God's. NKJV (emphasis mine)*

Study 3: Old Testament prophecy of the Holy Spirit through Jesus

To really comprehend the work of the Holy Spirit through the Church we firstly need to understand His work through Christ. Remember, Jesus as a man showed us how to work with the Holy Spirit. This was in terms of how to act and deal with our fellow man in regards to attitudes and behavior (fruit of the Spirit)....and also how to minister to people in the Spirit by faith in releasing gifts. (Gifts of the Spirit)

There are particular characteristics of the ministry of the Holy Spirit which should become increasingly evident is us as we follow the Spirit in sanctification. These were apparent in the ministry and person of Jesus, our model to follow.

> *Isaiah 11:1-2* ¹*A shoot will come up from the stump of Jesse; from his roots a Branch will bear fruit.* ² *The Spirit of the LORD will rest on him-- the Spirit of wisdom and of understanding, the Spirit of counsel and of power, the Spirit of knowledge and of the fear of the LORD. NIV*

From the passage we note 'Jesse' as being the father of King David, in whose line Jesus was born as the Son of man. The passage is teaching us that what is known as the sevenfold ministry of the Holy Spirit or the seven Spirits will rest on Jesus and work through Him.

There are various references to the seven Spirits in the book of Revelation 1:4, 3:1, 4:5 and 5:6.

They together represent the activities or manifestations of the Holy Spirit that we would expect to see through a believer. In a sense, perhaps we could call them, the 'tools or equipment' of the Spirit to work out the will of God in helping people, and establishing the Kingdom in them.

I am sure that many people would have had moments when they were supporting someone with counsel, and heard themselves say something very wise. It is easy in those situations to feel that you are quite clever, when in fact it is the inspiration of the Holy Spirit that has come out of your mouth.

Perhaps 20 years ago now a number of men were gathered having prayer and breakfast together. The conversation worked around to someone asking the question; "do you think Adam was filled with the Spirit?" When the meeting finished, I drove home and my wife was having her early morning devotions in our carport. As I got out of the car, she met me with the question; "do you think Adam was filled with the Spirit?"

Of all the possible biblical questions that could have come my way, she asked me this on that same morning. In fact, I have never been asked that before or since that I can recall. It seemed to me that the Holy Spirit was saying that He had much more to do with guiding our thinking than we were aware of!

The 'tools or equipment' of the Holy Spirit?

In this portion of the study we will mention the fruit of the Spirit, the ministry of the spirit, and the gifts of the Spirit.

THE FRUIT OF THE SPIRIT

We have already described that the fruit of the Spirit is largely directed towards considering and preferring others. The works of the flesh or 'fallen self' nature is all about self-gratification and self-promotion and self-realization. This relates to meeting the perceived 'self' needs, coming from a distorted identity, which is the result of the fall of man that we were born under. King David understood this well.

> Psalm 51:5-6 ⁵ Behold, I was brought forth in iniquity, And in sin my mother conceived me. ⁶ Behold, You desire truth in the inward parts, And in the hidden part You will make me to know wisdom. NKJV

Often the fruit of the Spirit appears as a result of the Holy Spirit ministering to these perceived 'self-conflicts.' As the wounded self is sanctified by truth, we become less needs oriented, and effortlessly begin to love and consider the needs of others. The fruit of the Spirit then, is usually evidence of His ministry to us, as opposed to being the result of self-effort.

While the deceptive beliefs remain, then the corresponding behavior will also be present.

Sometimes it is dealing with deliberate self-centeredness, stemming from the programming of the world system. This is resolved through the renewing of the mind. At other times it is resolving heart beliefs that produce the behavior. Either way, we could say that the fruit of the Spirit is the evidence of the influence and work of the Holy Spirit in our being.

You do not therefore try harder to be joyful, peaceful, or loving for example. Rather it is evidence that He has further influence and consequent cooperation from your being as you receive His truth.

> Galatians 5:22-24 ²² But the fruit of the Spirit is love, joy, peace, longsuffering, kindness, goodness, faithfulness, ²³ gentleness, self-control. Against such there is no law. ²⁴ And those who are Christ's have crucified the flesh with its passions and desires. NKJV

In saying this I believe that your human spirit is regenerated, born again and complete in Christ. It is a matter of participating with Him as He works through the healing of your heart that results in a soul and body that are in order. King David certainly understood that this was the root cause of his selfish and fallen sinful behavior. He knew that his own spirit had to be committed to the process, and that without the Holy Spirit's work that this would never be achieved.

> Psalm 51:10-11 ¹⁰ Create in me a clean heart, O God, And renew a steadfast spirit within me. ¹¹ Do not cast me away from Your presence, And do not take Your Holy Spirit from me. NKJV

There are those who believe that we will achieve the fruit of the spirit simply by our own self effort or the capabilities of our minds. My daughter once gave me a key ring that was engraved with the instruction to be 'joyful always,' and then after a semi colon, to 'pray continually.' I am not sure when the semi colon was added, but to me it was like saying; 'Be clean,' break, 'shower daily,' as if they were two separate, unconnected activities. The joy comes as a result of our communication with God, not because we simply decide to be happy. Therefore, removing any obstacles to that relationship becomes paramount in our Christian journey.

1 Thessalonians 5:16-17 [16] *Be joyful always;* [17] *pray continually. NIV*

THE MINISTRY OF THE SPIRIT

The fruit of the Spirit then is evidence of the nature of the Holy Spirit changing our attitudes and behavior.

There are also attributes of the Holy Spirit that equip us, or give us the tools to minister to others; hopefully we are able minister in the right spirit and motivation. Having received healing and freedom ourselves, it is a normal consequence, to now become aware of the needs of others, and to want to give out that which we have 'freely received' ourselves. Let me repeat that most times, if we are still wounded or in bondage, we will be, often unconsciously, preoccupied with our real or perceived 'self needs.'

> *Matthew 10:8 "Heal the sick, cleanse the lepers, raise the dead, cast out demons. Freely you have received, freely give. NKJV (emphasis mine)*

I am not suggesting that these attributes that I am about to list only appear when all of the fruit is fully established in us, more that they grow along with the fruit.

So, what are these characteristics that empower us to fulfill the call, and work out the anointing that is on us for our time?

Isaiah prophesied that the Spirit of the Lord would be on Jesus to minister to the broken hearted, free the captives and so on in Isaiah 61 and Jesus quoted from this passage in Luke 4:18, announcing that He was now going to fulfill that which the prophet had seen happening around 600 years earlier.

> *Isaiah 11:2 The Spirit of the LORD will rest on him-- the Spirit of wisdom and of understanding, the Spirit of counsel and of power, the Spirit of knowledge and of the fear of the LORD. NIV*

As we have stated already, the preceding list reveals what is known as the 'seven spirits' or sevenfold spirits of the Holy Spirit. There are other references to them, particularly in the book of Revelation where they are mentioned four times. This was a time when the Apostle John was writing to the believers in such a way, as only they would understand, as they already had the scriptures.

> *Revelation 4:5 And from the throne proceeded lightnings, thunderings, and voices. Seven lamps of fire were burning before the throne, which are the seven Spirits of God. NKJV (emphasis mine)*

> *Revelation 5:6b stood a Lamb as though it had been slain, having seven horns and seven eyes, which are the seven Spirits of God sent out into all the earth. NKJV (emphasis mine)*

God gave us physical examples or 'types' in the Old Testament that we understand to be representative of spiritual realities. We see what is known as the, 'Menora,' standing in the Holy place in the temple as representative of the Holy Spirit. In type, the Holy of Holies was where the presence of God dwelt. Here we find the Ark of the Covenant containing the two stone tablets of the Ten Commandments, Aaron's rod, and a pot of manna. This area of the temple is considered to be representative of the human spirit.

You may recall that he who is joined to the Lord is one spirit with Him. (1 Corinthians 6:19) We are consequently now considered to be the temple of the Holy Spirit.

Under this new relational Covenant, the Commandments were going to be written on our renewed, sensitive to God, hearts.

> *2 Corinthians 3:3 Clearly you are an epistle of Christ, ministered by us, written not with ink but by the Spirit of the living God, not on tablets of stone but on tablets of flesh, that is, of the heart. NKJV*

Before you came to the curtain which separated the Holy of Holies was a room called the Holy place which we understand to be, in type, the soul.

Note: A 'type' is something that contains characteristics that make it identifiable. It is patterned or constructed in a particular way, with a consistent structure or theme. The Bible gives us natural, visible types, to illustrate spiritual or invisible realities. Romans 1:20 Example: Jesus said 'destroy this temple' speaking of His person, Spirit, Soul, and body, and that He would raise it up again. They thought that He was referring to the literal temple.... but Jesus knew that this was a 'type' of the human person.

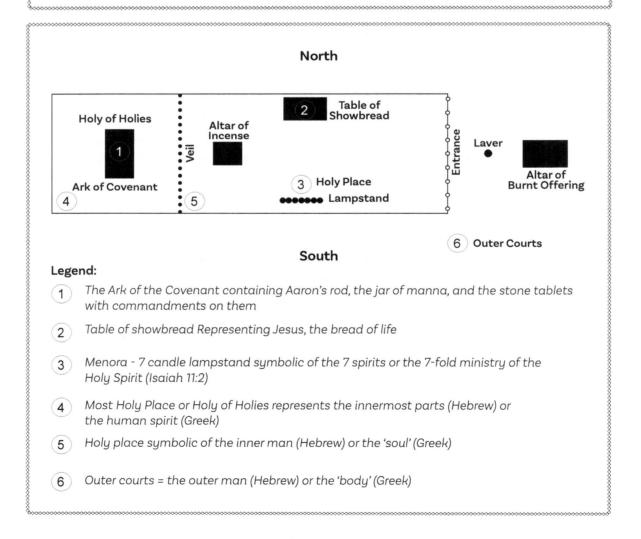

North

Holy of Holies

1

Ark of Covenant

4

Veil

5

Altar of Incense

2 Table of Showbread

3 Holy Place
●●●●●●● Lampstand

Entrance

Laver
●

Altar of Burnt Offering

6 Outer Courts

South

Legend:

1 *The Ark of the Covenant containing Aaron's rod, the jar of manna, and the stone tablets with commandments on them*

2 *Table of showbread Representing Jesus, the bread of life*

3 *Menora - 7 candle lampstand symbolic of the 7 spirits or the 7-fold ministry of the Holy Spirit (Isaiah 11:2)*

4 *Most Holy Place or Holy of Holies represents the innermost parts (Hebrew) or the human spirit (Greek)*

5 *Holy place symbolic of the inner man (Hebrew) or the 'soul' (Greek)*

6 *Outer courts = the outer man (Hebrew) or the 'body' (Greek)*

After that the outer courts which interface with the world are representative of the body. In the Holy place, (soul), amongst some other articles were the Menora, and the table of showbread, representing the bread of the presence. You may recall Jesus described Himself as the bread of life in John chapter 6, that we must eat from, indicating that in a sense we consume His presence as our daily provision.

The Menora was a candle stand with seven arms made of pure gold. These arms bore the candles which were representative of the seven spirits of the Holy Spirit; perhaps it was placed in this area because of His working out from the Spirit and presence of God, through the human faculties, mind and soul.

It is common to find these spiritual manifestations in isolation or grouped together in places throughout the scriptures.

>*Deuteronomy 24:9 Now Joshua the son of Nun was full of the spirit of wisdom. NKJV*

In the following passage from Proverbs we see six of the seven spirits or attributes grouped together.

>*Proverbs 8:12-14* [12] *"I, <u>wisdom</u>, dwell together with prudence; I possess <u>knowledge</u> and discretion.* [13] *To <u>fear the LORD</u> is to hate evil; I hate pride and arrogance, evil behavior and perverse speech.* [14] *<u>Counsel</u> and sound judgment are mine; I have <u>understanding</u> and <u>power</u>. NIV (emphasis mine)*

This list of spiritual attributes or equipment should become increasingly evident in our lives. The Holy Spirit then works through us in our work for others as revealed in Isaiah 11:2 in the following ways:

1. The Spirit of the LORD – we understand this to be the Revelatory Spirit, as seen in prophecy. It knows the mind of God for a particular situation. Let me propose that in the NT this manifestation of the Holy Spirit is revealed as 'the mind of Christ.'

> So, we could propose that this Spirit is the knowing of what the Lord is thinking about a particular situation. Walking after the Spirit of Christ becomes asking Him; "what do you want me to do or say here Lord?"

2. The Spirit of wisdom   3. The Spirit of understanding
4. The Spirit of counsel   5. The Spirit of power (or might)
6. The Spirit of knowledge (to some degree perhaps this refers to the knowledge of God, and the ways, statutes and precepts of God)
7. The Spirit of the fear of the Lord

I think that sometimes the modern church is guilty of seeking the power of God, and neglects the other works of the Spirit. In any case these are the manifestations of the

Holy Spirit, and we should expect to see these operating as evidence of His activities and presence. As we scan the list, it should become evident that most of the operations of the Spirit will then be most apparent through words.

It is notable that at times the works of Jesus were attributed to wisdom and knowledge rather than power.

> *Mark 6:2 And when the Sabbath had come, He began to teach in the synagogue. And many hearing Him were astonished, saying, "Where did this Man get these things? And what wisdom is this which is given to Him, that such mighty works are performed by His hands! NKJV (Emphasis mine)*

FOR FURTHER REFERENCES TO GROUPINGS OF THESE CHARACTERISTICS

> *Psalm 111:10 The fear of the LORD is the beginning of wisdom; all who follow his precepts have good understanding. To him belongs eternal praise. NIV (emphasis mine)*

> *Proverbs 1:1-7 ¹ The proverbs of Solomon son of David, king of Israel: ² for attaining wisdom and discipline; for understanding words of insight; ³ for acquiring a disciplined and prudent life, doing what is right and just and fair; ⁴ for giving prudence to the simple, knowledge and discretion to the young-- ⁵ let the wise listen and add to their learning, and let the discerning get guidance--⁶ for understanding proverbs and parables, the sayings and riddles of the wise. ⁷ The fear of the LORD is the beginning of knowledge, but fools despise wisdom and discipline. NIV (emphasis mine)*

> *Proverbs 9:10 "The fear of the LORD is the beginning of wisdom, and knowledge of the Holy One is understanding. NIV (emphasis mine)*

We will move on to study the practical manifestation or appearing of these seven spirits in the New Testament.

Study 4: Jesus and the Gifts of the Spirit
We are always looking to Jesus as our model for all that we do. If He did it, we want to do it. If it doesn't look like something that He would have done, or how He acted, then we should not be drawn into it. Being in nature God, of course He worked perfectly with the Holy Spirit to complete the works of the Father for those in need around Him.

Consequently, as the Spirit of the Lord was on Jesus, He demonstrated the entire sevenfold ministry of the Spirit in His own earthly ministry.

He prophesied frequently. We see Him understanding what people were thinking at times. (Matthew 9:4 + Luke 17) He gave counsel and taught about the Kingdom with an authoritative knowledge of God. He had knowledge of, for example, the history of the Samaritan woman at the well. He displayed power regularly with miracles. In the garden of Gethsemane, He exhibited the fear of the Lord, in preferring the Fathers will over self. And notably, as mentioned previously, we see people attributing the signs that He was performing to wisdom and not merely power.

Mark 6:2b "Where did this Man get these things? And what wisdom is this which is given to Him, that such mighty works are performed by His hands! NKJV

THE GIFTS OF THE SPIRIT

We have just detailed the seven Spirits that represent and manifest the work of the Holy Spirit through us. Now we look to the New Testament gifts of the Spirit, moving beyond the gospels and into the epistles. We see clearly the work of the Holy Spirit manifesting the 7 Spirits through the church as He wills. We would we be surprised if the gifts did not match up producing the same prophesied attributes and activities here, as described throughout the scriptures, and collated in Isaiah 11:2!

So, the gifts are the practical outworking of the seven Spirits. Let us list them here and make a comparison;

OT	NT
Spirit of the Lord	Prophecy
Spirit of wisdom	Word of wisdom
Spirit of Knowledge	Word of Knowledge
Spirit of power	Working of miracles (Greek 'power')
Spirit of counsel	Different types of healings
Spirit of understanding	Discerning of Spirits

(Note if you discern something you understand that which you are looking at.)

1 Corinthians 12:4-7 ⁴ There are diversities of gifts, but the same Spirit. ⁵ There are differences of ministries, but the same Lord. ⁶ And there are diversities of activities, but it is the same God who works all in all. ⁷ But the manifestation of the Spirit is given to each one <u>for the profit of all</u>. NKJV (emphasis mine)

We can observe here that all of the different activities of the Spirit are for our benefit. As we examine the next verses, we can all possibly identify with having given someone counsel, or heard wisdom, knowledge or understanding come out of our mouths that was much more than our personal cleverness or intellect. Perhaps we did not previously recognize or acknowledge it as being a gift, or inspiration from the Spirit of Christ.

1 Corinthians 12:8-10 ⁸ for to one is given the <u>word of wisdom</u> through the Spirit, to another the <u>word of knowledge</u> through the same Spirit, ⁹ to another faith by the same Spirit, to another <u>gifts of healings</u> by the same Spirit, ¹⁰ to another the <u>working of miracles</u>, to another <u>prophecy</u>, to another <u>discerning of spirits</u>, to another different kinds of tongues, to another the interpretation of tongues. NKJV (emphasis mine)

As we consider the following verse can I suggest that the number of gifts that work through you emerge over time, and that you are released into them increasingly as your character is conformed to Christ Jesus, as the Word of God. You may also find that you are drawn to some particular gifts or enabling, that specifically help you facilitate and dispense your calling. Your calling and election is the choice of God, and not something you decide. You don't choose your calling, in a sense, it chooses you.

1 Corinthians 12:11 But one and the same Spirit works all these things, distributing to each one individually as He wills. NKJV

The working and evidence of the presence of the Holy Spirit through His church remains the same. Prophecy, wisdom, knowledge, healings and miracles through the power or might of God.

With the absence of the fear of the Lord in this passage, without doing a deep study we can confirm that they all have an expression. Fear of the Lord, and a subsequent healthy sober minded self-perspective, as we are in awe of Him, opens us up to being candidates for the gifts of the Spirit. Further it keeps us in cooperation with the leading of the Spirit, as we avoid the consequences of walking after the sin nature.

If Jesus required the Spirit of Fear of the Lord as a part of His equipping to achieve His purposes on Earth, then how much more should we cherish it as He did?

> *Isaiah 11:2-3* *² The Spirit of the LORD shall rest upon Him, The Spirit of wisdom and understanding, The Spirit of counsel and might, The Spirit of knowledge and of the fear of the LORD. ³ His delight is in the fear of the LORD, And He shall not judge by the sight of His eyes, Nor decide by the hearing of His ears. NKJV (Emphasis mine)*

It is noteworthy in verse 3 of the preceding passage that Jesus was going to live by knowledge coming from the Holy Spirit, through the Seven Spirits manifestation on Him, rather than through His senses.

I think by now that we have established what the working and anointing of the Holy Spirit looked like on Jesus, and should therefore look on us, His church. Let us now examine what the New Testament teaches us about the PURPOSE of the presence and anointing of the Holy Spirit upon us.

In terms of our personal growth and sanctification the Holy Spirit is working in us to conform us to the likeness of Christ. (Romans 8:29, Ephesians 4:13) In regards to our calling He is working through ascension ministries to equip us for the work of the ministry, each fulfilling our particular role in the body of Christ.

> *Ephesians 4:11-13* *¹¹ And He Himself gave some to be apostles, some prophets, some evangelists, and some pastors and teachers, ¹² for the equipping of the saints for the work of ministry, for the edifying of the body of Christ, ¹³ till we all come to the unity of the faith and of the knowledge of the Son of God, to a perfect man, to the measure of the stature of the fullness of Christ. NKJV*

THE PURPOSE OF THE SPIRIT OF THE LORD UPON US

We have noted already that the Holy Spirit and His anointing is on the church for exactly the same reason as it was on Jesus. Namely to fulfill the MISSION of reaching, saving, healing and freeing captive people that God loves.

> *John 3:16-17* *¹⁶ For God so loved the world that he gave his one and only Son, that whoever believes in him shall not perish but have eternal life. ¹⁷ For God did not send his Son into the world to condemn the world, but to save the world through him. NIV*

Scholars place the prophecy from Isaiah 61 regarding the ministry of Jesus at almost 700 years before His birth. As we look at the passage, we can make two observations.

1. There is no evidence that this promise of God helped anybody until Jesus came in the flesh and was baptized with the Holy Spirit coming upon Him.

In other words, it required someone for the Holy Spirit to work in and through before the Isaiah 61 'Word' could be fulfilled.

> *1 John 5:6-7* ⁶ *This is He who came by water and blood; Jesus Christ; not only by water, but by water and blood. And it is the Spirit who bears witness, because the Spirit is truth.* ⁷ *For there are three that bear witness in heaven: the Father, the Word, and the Holy Spirit; and these three are one. NKJV*

The situation is the same today, we have the Word and we have the Holy Spirit, but God is looking for His Sons, Daughters, and saints, living the Word, to be available to work through......which leads us to our second point.

2. When Jesus quotes Isaiah 61 in Luke 4:18 He only reads as far as verse 2. This covers His ministry. But the Isaiah 61 passage goes on to describe what 'they,' those who have 'freely received' will be doing!

> *Isaiah 61:1-2* ¹ *"The Spirit of the Lord GOD is upon Me, Because the LORD has anointed Me To preach good tidings to the poor; He has sent Me to <u>heal the brokenhearted</u>, To proclaim <u>liberty to the captives</u>, And the opening of the prison to <u>those who are bound</u>;* ² *to proclaim the acceptable year of the LORD, NKJV (emphasis mine)*

Jesus quotes to here in Luke 4:18-19, referring to His own Earthly ministry.

> *Luke 4:18-19* ¹⁸ *"The Spirit of the LORD is upon Me, Because He has anointed Me To preach the gospel to the poor; He has sent Me to heal the brokenhearted, To proclaim liberty to the captives And recovery of sight to the blind, To set at liberty those who are oppressed;* ¹⁹ *To proclaim the acceptable year of the LORD." NKJV*

The passage continues in Isaiah 61 including our work:

> *And the day of vengeance of our God; To comfort all who mourn,* ³ *To console those who mourn in Zion, To give **them** beauty for ashes, The oil of joy for mourning, The garment of praise for the spirit of heaviness; **<u>That they</u>** may be called trees of righteousness, The planting of the LORD, that He may be glorified."* ⁴ *And **<u>they</u>** shall rebuild the old ruins, **<u>They</u>** shall raise up the former desolations, And **they** shall repair the ruined cities, The desolations of many generations. NKJV (emphasis mine)*

> **Note:** We have already mentioned 'types' in scripture which refer to illustrations that give us a picture. We have already proposed that the 'temple' refers to the human person. Wherever we find cities or walls in scripture, again they refer to the human personality. So, when the Bible is talking about repairing 'ruined cities,'(For example Isaiah 58:12), it is pointing to bringing about wholeness from the brokenness of humanity.

Proverbs 25:28 Like a city whose walls are broken down is a man who lacks self-control. NIV

The New Testament word for 'save' includes the concept of being made whole. This follows the general theme of Gods restoration of fallen humanity, which, as we have pointed out was the main activity of Jesus on Earth. It was also that which He commanded us to do,

and sent the Holy Spirit to facilitate it happening. Following is the full meaning of the Greek word 'sozo,' which is normally translated, 'save.'

4982. sozo, sode'-zo; from a prim. sos (contr. for obsol. saos, "safe"); to <u>save, i.e. deliver or protect</u> (lit. or fig.):--<u>heal</u>, preserve, <u>save</u> (self), do well, <u>be (make) whole</u>.
Strongs Concordance (emphasis mine)

The concept is very consistent throughout scripture in terms of why God is with you and why He anoints you. If you want more anointing care about helping God help people more! By way of example let's have a brief look at another Isaiah passage, which is consistent with the work described in Isaiah chapter 61.

Isaiah 57:15 For thus says the High and Lofty One Who inhabits eternity, whose name is Holy: "I dwell in the high and holy place, With him who has a contrite and humble spirit, To revive the spirit of the humble, And to revive the heart of the contrite ones. NKJV

Study 5: Physical and emotional healing

We see the heart of God in commissioning Jesus to do 'good' by healing those under the power of the devil.

Acts 10:38 how God anointed Jesus of Nazareth with the Holy Spirit and power, and how he went around doing good and healing all who were under the power of the devil, because God was with him. NIV

Jesus taught about the Kingdom of God, and then demonstrated its benefits by healing the sick. He then 'discipled' and trained His followers into doing the same. We consider this to be a 'hear,' 'see' and 'do' process. Hear about the Kingdom, see me do it, and then go and do it yourself.

Having attended a great many conferences over the years, my observations are that the modern church is largely concerned with matters such as leadership, growing the numbers in congregations, or church planting. There is no doubt at all that these are wonderful and necessary topics to facilitate the building of the Kingdom of God.

There is, however, very little focus on healing ministries and as a consequence, doctors are usually the first port of call for physical problems. For many churches, even large city congregations, if there are mental or emotional issues, the people are sent to psychiatrists or Christian counselors trained in secular techniques.

In contrast if we look at Jesus as the model, His focus was on healing the sick, freeing those with demonic bondages and healing the broken hearted. His disciples freely received this ministry from Christ themselves before they were commissioned to take the World.

> *Matthew 10:8 "Heal the sick, raise the dead, cleanse those who have leprosy, drive out demons. <u>Freely you have received, freely give</u>." NIV (emphasis mine)*

Perhaps we could look at it this way. Imagine if you were putting together a football team and selecting your players. "Alright, I choose that man over there with one leg, the blind guy, that deaf fellow, the man with one eye, those chaps with the back braces on, and those cripples." Then you launched them out onto the field, yelling with great enthusiasm and encouragement; "Go get them guys!"

It doesn't make much sense to me but many of us have been around churches where the focus is on trying to motivate broken people to live a victorious life of faith. We have all seen the fallout and problems from people with unresolved issues active in a church environment.

THE HOLY SPIRIT IN US

As we have stated Jesus did not begin His ministry on Earth until He was filled with the Holy Spirit. For Him this occurred concurrently with His water baptism which is something which happens occasionally.

> *Luke 4:1 Then Jesus, <u>being filled</u> with the Holy Spirit, returned from the Jordan and was <u>led by the Spirit</u> into the wilderness, NKJV (emphasis mine)*

This 'filling' with the Holy Spirit happened immediately before His correction of the fall in His confrontation with the devil in the wilderness. This was followed by His announcing of the fulfilling of His ministry in Luke 4:18. Notably Jesus' appeared to immediately go out and look for His church in the form of Peter and the others, to begin the training and discipling process immediately. This is a very good indicator that His purpose and intention was always to train His church how to work with the Holy Spirit to fulfill the Fathers will.

He taught His disciples that the coming of the Holy Spirit, also known as the Spirit of Christ would work from within them.

> *John 14:16-17 ¹⁶ And I will ask the Father, and he will give you another Counselor to be with you forever-- ¹⁷ the Spirit of truth. The world cannot accept him, because it neither sees him nor knows him. But you know him, for he lives with you and <u>will be in you</u>. NIV (emphasis mine)*

The obvious outworking of this promise was first evidenced in Acts chapter 2 and continues to this day for all believers who understand this promise and desire to be filled as Jesus was, to do the works that Jesus did, and does by His Spirit today.

> **Note:** In the New testament the Holy Spirit is typically referred to as: Holy Spirit 93 times / Spirit of God 12 times/ Spirit of Truth 4 times/ Spirit of Christ 2 times.

> *1 Corinthians 6:17 But he who unites himself with the Lord is one with him in spirit. NIV*

He is the power that works from within us, and His Spirit is entwined with our spirit. Literally from the Greek language glued to our human spirit. It is His power from within us that facilitates the works of God in our times. The only limitation for Him is our faith, our thinking, and our understanding of God, our identities and our position in Him. Anything is possible through the work of the Holy Spirit in us.

> *Ephesians 3: 20 Now to him who is able to do immeasurably more than all we ask or imagine, <u>according to his power that is at work within us</u> NIV (emphasis mine)*

To keep perspective, we realize that we are simple, flawed human beings, perfected by Christ and presented to the Father without spot or blemish. Qualified to receive the Holy Spirit, and to do the works of God through the sacrifice of Jesus alone, so we cannot boast.

> *Ephesians 2:8-10 ⁸ God saved you by his special favor when you believed. And you can't take credit for this; it is a gift from God. ⁹ Salvation is not a reward for the good things we have done, so none of us can boast about it. ¹⁰ For we are God's masterpiece. He has created us anew in Christ Jesus, <u>so that we can do the good things he planned for us long ago</u>. NLT (emphasis mine)*

> *Colossians 1:21-22 ²¹ This includes you who were once so far away from God. You were his enemies, separated from him by your evil thoughts and actions, ²² yet now he has brought you back as his friends. He has done this through his death on the cross in his own human body. As a result, he has brought you into the very presence of God, and you are holy and blameless as <u>you stand before him without a single fault</u>. NLT (emphasis mine)*

The treasure that we have is the Holy Spirit who joins with our spirit, and it is His power that works through us. We will describe this more in Unit 3 under 'Gifts.'

> *2 Corinthians 4:7 But we have this treasure in earthen vessels, that the excellence of the power may be of God and not of us. NKJV*

At times it is good to remind ourselves that the works come from the great one who is in us, who is greater than the one in the World. We are His temple, His dwelling place.

> *1 John 4:4 But you belong to God, my dear children. You have already won your fight with these false prophets, because the Spirit who lives in you is greater than the spirit who lives in the world. NLT (emphasis mine)*

In this regard we can join with Jesus in acknowledging that God prepared our bodies for His inhabitance, to do His will in the Earth.

> *Hebrews 10:5-7 ⁵ Therefore, when He came into the world, He said: "Sacrifice and offering You did not desire, But a body You have prepared for Me. ⁶ In burnt offerings and sacrifices for sin You had no pleasure. ⁷ Then I said, 'Behold, I have come; In the volume of the book it is written of Me; To do Your will, O God.'" NKJV*

Study 6: Receiving the Holy Spirit

Jesus often created pictures or used analogies to explain spiritual principles in a way that was easy to understand. At one time He used the example of not putting New Wine in Old wineskins. My wife and I used to own a vineyard and well understand that new wine ferments and expands, and it needs to be contained in a way that allows for this growth. The 'type' of the New Wine is that of the Holy Spirit poured out. I believe that Jesus was saying that if He were to put the Holy Spirit in your hard, unregenerate human spirit that is not sensitive to God or the Holy Spirit that you could not contain His presence.

> Matthew 9:17 *"Nor do they put new wine into old wineskins, or else the wineskins break, the wine is spilled, and the wineskins are ruined. But they put new wine into new wineskins, and both are preserved." NKJV*

He is indicating that your human spirit must be made new, born again first to be able to cope with the expansion that the Holy Spirit will bring. So, scripture indicates that He works on three fronts in His regeneration of mankind. He firstly puts a new human spirit in us. Then He puts a teachable, sensitive heart in us.... remembering that this is the centre of our soul. And then He puts His Spirit in us to facilitate and empower all of His works.

> Ezekiel 36:26-27 *²⁶ I will give you a new heart and put <u>a new spirit</u> **in you**; I will remove from you your heart of stone and give you <u>a heart of flesh</u>. ²⁷ And I will put <u>MY SPIRIT</u> **in you** and move you to follow my decrees and be careful to keep my laws. NIV (emphasis mine) *[Note: my Spirit is in capitols letters creating a distinction from a new human spirit in verse 26]*

Once a person has resolved from scripture that it is Gods intention to renew their human spirit, and to indwell them by joining His Spirit to theirs, it is a relatively simple process to see them receive the infilling of the Holy Spirit. The only time that there may be a problem is if the person still holds doubts that this is for today. Or perhaps that God considers that they are not worthy to receive. Some believe that it is only for special people which is faulty doctrine and has no Biblical basis.

HOW TO PRACTICALLY HELP A PERSON RECEIVE THE HOLY SPIRIT

Some people simply pray for people to receive the Spirit. Others lay on hands. Personally, I often don't even pray for people to receive. I normally explain to them that this is Gods idea and desire, and that Jesus already made them right with the Father so that the Holy Spirit can come into them.

My personal testimony is that I was alone with God, pruning vines in my vineyard, when I received the gift of the Spirit. Nobody prayed for me or laid hands on me. In the book of Acts Chapter 10 we see the Apostle Peter in the middle of preaching his message to the centurion Cornelius and the other believers gathered. It appears that God so much wanted to baptize them with the gift of the Holy Spirit that He did not wait for Peter to finish his discourse.

> Acts 10:44-45 *⁴⁴ While Peter was still speaking these words, the Holy Spirit came on all who heard the message. ⁴⁵ The circumcised believers who had come with Peter were astonished that the gift of the Holy Spirit had been poured out even on the Gentiles. NIV (emphasis mine)*

> The point is that we don't need a formula, we often only need to activate the gift.

ACTIVATING TONGUES

Many years ago, I was praying with a Chinese lady who wanted to be baptized in the Spirit and speak in tongues. I had convinced her that God wanted her to have the gift, and had shown her from the Bible where it explained that this was for today. The problem was that I had never led anybody into the Holy Spirit Baptism before. The thought came into my mind to pray in the Spirit short sentences, and have her imitate what I was saying, and that she would trip over her tongue and receive her own prayer language. When I followed this prompting that is what happened, and I have been leading people to speak in tongues the same way ever since. At times this will be large groups from the front of a meeting, other times individually in prayer lines where often as many as 20, 30 or more people will be filled one at a time.

Some people get their own tongue very quickly, others are very good at remembering and imitating what you have said. Eventually however, if you persevere some words that I have not said in my prayer language begin to creep in. Let me reiterate, many other people do this in other ways. This is simply how I do it, and offer it if you do not know what to do, as a means to help get people going. The main thing is that they receive.

THE MINISTRY OF THE HOLY SPIRIT THROUGH US

In terms of ministry, a person comes to you with a problem; it is God who has the answers and power to resolve it. Our part is to be equipped to be the little piece of fuse wire that makes the connection between their need and Gods power and promised provisions. In this sense we make His Word 'flesh,' or in other terms give it an expression in the natural realm. We do this through being a 'door' aligned with the Word of God that the Holy Spirit can confirm and make manifest His abilities through.

It's truly a privilege that God allows us to co labor as His children in the family business in this way. As stated, in terms of personal growth on our journey we are becoming conformed to the likeness of Christ through our cooperation, decisions, attitudes, and behavior as we receive His Truth. This creates an increasing door for the Holy Spirit to continue the ministry of Christ through us.

We measure our progress against the word of God in terms of our actions and deeds. If we are to be conformed to Christ, we will also be conformed to the Word of God as He was.

> *Romans 8:29 For those God foreknew he also predestined to be conformed to the likeness of his Son, that he might be the firstborn among many brothers. NIV*

We too, will become people full of grace and truth. Someone has said that there is no junior Holy Spirit. In other words, we all receive the same Spirit. The question is, are we letting Him work through us, is the door open….and in some measure, how much of us has He got use of in terms of cooperation, submission, knowledge and understanding of His ways and will?

> *John 1:14 The Word became flesh and made his dwelling among us. We have seen his glory, the glory of the One and Only, who came from the Father, <u>full of grace and truth</u>. NIV (emphasis mine)*

Another 'type' that we find in the scriptures is that of 'doors' and 'gates.' Jesus informed us in Matthew chapter 16 verse 18 that the 'gates' of hades will not prevail. He was referring to people who are hosting demonic forces through cooperation and participation, giving the nature of Satan access to the natural realm through the 'gate' of their personality.

In the Old Testament we see reference to us being a spiritual entry point for God into our realm. It has been well said that both God and Satan are looking for access to the Earth to manifest their nature and have an expression.

Psalm 24:7-9 [7] *Lift up your heads, O you <u>gates</u>! And be lifted up, you everlasting <u>doors</u>! And the King of glory shall come in.* [8] *Who is this King of glory? The LORD strong and mighty, The LORD mighty in battle.* [9] *Lift up your heads, O you <u>gates</u>! Lift up, you everlasting <u>doors</u>! And the King of glory shall come in. NKJV (emphasis mine)*

We are therefore referred to as 'gates' and 'doors' that are entry points for God to come into our environment and bring change. As we behold Him and obey His will in faith He has His expression.

POTENTIAL IN THE HOLY SPIRIT

If Billionaire Bill Gates approached me and invited me to be a partner in his business, and stated that whoever works for him now works for me. And that whatever finances and resources he had I could now use to grow his business. I would now consider that I had significant potential.

How much more potential than that we have when God comes to us, gives us the Holy Spirit, and then invites us to share in the work of the Kingdom. Bill Gates plus anyone has a lot of possibilities, but this is nothing compared to the Holy Spirit plus anybody at all, no matter how insignificant or foolish we may be in the eyes of the world!

> *Mark 16:20 Then the disciples went out and preached everywhere, and the Lord worked with them and confirmed his word by the signs that accompanied it. NIV*

Study 7: The God Dimension

Having realized that God will do His work coming in through us, we then need to open our minds so that He can have as much access as possible to do His will in the Earth. In order for us to reach our potential in God through the Holy Spirit, we have to begin to think in another dimension. The Earth is a created program that has rules and limitations. But God is outside of those and is not limited or confined to the basic principles of this Earth. The Universe was created by Him from the spiritual or heavenly dimension, and this realm is far greater and does not have the limitations that the natural world does. Supernatural, simply means, above natural.

God is not limited to the program, guidelines and limitations of this world. He is of a superior dimension, and is wanting to move us out of the program and introduce us into understanding our limitless potential in His supernatural dimension.

> *Colossians 2:8-10* [8] *See to it that no one takes you captive through hollow and deceptive philosophy, which depends on human tradition and <u>the basic principles of this world</u> rather than on Christ.* [9] *For in Christ all the fullness of the Deity lives in bodily form,* [10] *and you have been given fullness in Christ, who is the head over every power and authority. NIV (emphasis mine)*

God operates multi-dimensionally, and is wanting us to realize that as His children we are as well. All things are possible to those who believe. God is the God the God of the impossible. Yes, He is with us in the small day to day details of life as well, knowing every hair on our heads.....

> *Matthew 19:26 But Jesus looked at them and said to them, "With men this is impossible, but <u>with God all things are possible</u>." NKJV (emphasis mine)*

....but as we look through the scriptures God is revealed over and over doing things that are impossible, and even seem almost ridiculous to our natural minds. God has no limitations. Let me just suggest a few sample events from the Old Testament to illustrate the principle that God does things that are above what is possible in the natural world, and that are beyond the confines of the program and basic principles that the World operates under.

An old man, (Moses) has a staff that becomes a serpent. God uses it to perform various miracles to deliver His people including parting the Sea so that they can walk across on dry ground. (Exodus 14)

We see God open the mouth of a donkey, so that he can rebuke Balaam, who is wanting to work against the will of God for personal gain. (Numbers 22)

We see a prophet called Elijah bringing about a miracle where a woman's jar never runs out of oil and her bin never runs out of flour. (1 Kings 17) Another prophet of God named Elisha throws a stick into the water and causes an axe head to float. (2 Kings 6)

We see men thrown into a fiery superheated furnace and suffer no harm. (Daniel 3)

These are all impossible events in the natural realm that God worked through people who were drawn into His dimension, and there are many more.

JESUS MOVES THE THINKING OF THE DISCIPLES

The point is that God is above the limitations of the world. In the New Testament we see Jesus trying to get the disciples to understand this, in order for them to be able to launch His church with supernatural signs. In Matthew chapter 14 we see Jesus doing a miracle by feeding 5,000 men and also women and children with 5 loaves of bread and 2 fish. There were 12 baskets of leftovers. Again, for natural man this is ridiculously impossible. Notably Jesus then 'made' the disciples get into the boat and cross the lake without Him.

> *Matthew 14:22 Immediately Jesus <u>**made**</u> the disciples get into the boat and go on ahead of him to the other side, while he dismissed the crowd. NIV emphasis mine)*

Why did He do this? He was trying to get them to think beyond what was possible. At 3am He came to them walking on the water...defying and totally disregarding the natural laws of buoyancy. Evidently Jesus was trying to alter their thinking about the limitless abilities of God, to move them into His dimension. I believe that this is why He allowed Lazarus to die, so that He could raise their faith and lift their expectations. (John 11:14-15)

> *Mark 9:23 Jesus said to him, "If you can believe, <u>**all**</u> things are possible to him who believes". NKJV (emphasis mine)*

In the story of Jesus walking on the water we see Peter seeking a word from Jesus to confirm that he could also operate in this supernatural dimension. We know that while he had his eyes on Jesus, and faith in the words that he had from Jesus, that he did walk on the water. Then he became aware of the natural circumstances that were around him and he began to sink. We could say that while we are focused on the word of God to us, and His dimension, we will walk over our natural circumstances. But when we are focused on the basic principles of this world we will be in doubt and conflicted, and come *under* our situation.

Jesus cited the reason for Peter beginning to sink as being a lack of faith. Asking Peter, why did he doubt. Doubt meaning, be in two minds, wavering about what he believed, reasoning out his circumstances and possibilities…. instead of trusting the words of Jesus alone.

> *Matthew 14:28-31* ²⁸ *"Lord, if it's you," Peter replied, "tell me to come to you on the water."* ²⁹ *"Come," he said. Then Peter got down out of the boat, walked on the water and came toward Jesus.* ³⁰ *But when he saw the wind, he was afraid and, beginning to sink, cried out, "Lord, save me!"* ³¹ *Immediately Jesus reached out his hand and caught him. "You of little faith," he said, "why did you* **doubt***?" NIV (emphasis mine)*

In Marks gospel chapter 11 we see Jesus cursing a fig tree. Reportedly He was not being unfair to the tree…. even though it was out of season there should have been an edible blossom called naphtha. So, in a sense He cursed the tree because there was no sign of it being fruitful at all. His words being charged with power from another dimension the tree died from the roots up.

The disciples were amazed that the words of Jesus carried such supernatural power. Again, Jesus used it to move their thinking towards understanding that they could also speak through faith and release power from Gods dimension.

> *Mark 11:22-24* ²² *"Have faith in God," Jesus answered.* ²³ *"I tell you the truth, if anyone* **says** *to this mountain, 'Go, throw yourself into the sea,' and does not doubt in his heart but believes that* **what he says will happen***, it will be done for him.* ²⁴ *Therefore I tell you, whatever you ask for in prayer, believe that you have received it, and it will be yours. NIV (emphasis mine)*

In Matthews gospel chapter 17 we see the story of Jesus and Peter needing money to pay the temple tax. Jesus instructed Peter to go and throw out his fishing line, and that in the mouth of the first fish that he caught he would find a four-drachma coin. Exactly the amount needed to pay the tax for the two of them. In terms of what is possible in the natural world this would seem ridiculous. Peter had probably caught hundreds of thousands of fish in his lifetime. Now he was being told that the first fish that he caught would have exactly the right amount of money in its mouth for what they needed.

In all of this I am encouraged, that even in those times where they did not have all of the distractions and programming of media, they still had to see miraculous signs to move them into God's limitless dimension. After feeding the 5,000 we see a little later Jesus feeding 4,000. He comments that the disciples are still struggling with understanding this dimension.

> *Matthew 16:8-10* ⁸ *Aware of their discussion, Jesus asked, "You of little faith, why are you talking among yourselves about having no bread?* ⁹ ***Do you still not understand?*** *Don't you remember the five loaves for the five thousand, and how many basketfuls you gathered?* ¹⁰ *Or the seven loaves for the four thousand, and how many basketfuls you gathered? NIV (emphasis mine)*

We know that finally, after 3 years of intensive discipling, they were released and empowered by the Holy Spirit to demonstrate and take the gospel of the Kingdom of God the ends of the Earth.

In the next Unit we will look at the Healing streams that God has provided to meet the needs of a hurting humanity. They all require people of faith to work through, who have in some measure reframed what is possible in the power of the Spirit, as they touch the Kingdom of God, and His limitless abilities.

UNIT THREE

The Healing Streams of God

LESSONS ON DEALING WITH PEOPLE'S ISSUES

Before we even consider the outworking of Gods healing streams through us, it is worth pausing and considering the necessity of having our inner world in good order, so that we can be 'stable' vessels for the ministry of the Holy Spirit to work through.

THE RIVER OF GODS PROVISION

As we move on to the healing streams, let us briefly detail seven problems that afflict mankind. We have covered the seven spirits that are the manifestation of the Holy Spirit given to work through believers to resolve these issues.

7 areas or problems that require Gods ministry through the Holy Spirit:
1. Spiritual freedom - clearly our own human spirit needs to be reborn and set free from sin - often people struggle with demonic spirit bondages
2. Emotional wholeness – many diseases stem from imbalanced feelings
3. Mental problems – a high percentage of mental issues are inner belief based
4. Relational issues – these come as we interact from our perceptions of self
5. Physical healing – our bodies are the end of the line in terms of hormonal balances in relation to our inner thought life (if these thoughts and beliefs are not at ease we have; dis-ease)
6. Sexual disorder – our sexuality often needs to be healed and reoriented
7. Addictive bondages – these often begin as our bad solutions to our pain or are 'self'-pleasing issues from perceived need.

We have covered seven basic problems that beset humanity, and the seven Spirits of the Holy Spirit that equip us to meet these needs, which according to the Apostle Paul are common to man. 1 Corinthians 10:13

Now I would like to propose seven healing streams that flow together to become the river of God that bring gladness to the inhabitants of the city of God.

> Psalm 46:4 "There is a river whose streams make glad the city of God, the holy place where the Most High dwells." NIV

These streams, or ways that God heals, often work together just as do the gifts of the Spirit. Combined constituting Gods healing river towards wholeness.

These provisions of God were promised by the Father, paid for and demonstrated by Jesus Christ the Son, and facilitated to us today by the Holy Spirit. God has committed to meeting every need that we may have.

> Philippians 4:19 And my God will meet all your needs according to his glorious riches in Christ Jesus. NIV

SEVEN SPIRITS FOR THE SEVEN BASIC ISSUES OF MAN

To recap from Unit 2, the 'equipment' of the Holy Spirit to deal with these 7 main problems is the 7 Spirits that are outlined in Isaiah Chapter 11. We have already covered these in some detail in Unit 2, so we will not go over them again here. It is good to keep them in mind however when we cover the Healing stream of gifts. They are in fact implicated in all of the healing streams in one way or another.

> *Isaiah 11:2 The Spirit of the LORD will rest on him-- the Spirit of wisdom and of understanding, the Spirit of counsel and of power, the Spirit of knowledge and of the fear of the LORD. NIV*

Now we have the 7 basic problem areas that mankind suffers with. We have 7 Spirits that God uses to deal with these areas. And now we are going to look at 7 Healing Streams that the Holy Spirit works through to meet every need.

SIGNIFICANT WORDS AS WE CONSIDER THE HEALING STREAMS

Healing is largely a matter of putting things back into Gods order. In other words, becoming whole, in the sense of being restored by Him, and becoming in His likeness. As we have described physical wellness comes as a result of the affect of the Holy Spirits ministry to our spirit and soul.

> *3 John 1:2 Dear friend, I pray that you may enjoy good health and that all may go well with you, even as your soul is getting along well. NIV*

This concept of freedom and healing coming through wholeness is held in the words translated from the Greek language as 'saved' and 'salvation.'

Saved = 4982. **sozo**, sode'-zo; from a prim. sos (contr. for obsol. saos, "safe"); to save, i.e. **deliver or protect** (lit. or fig.):--**heal**, preserve, save (self), do well, **be (make) whole.** (Emphasis mine: reference, Strong's concordance)

Being saved then includes being *delivered* from captivity, being *healed* of areas where the devil has had ground, and being made *whole*.... all of which are usually the same thing. As we come into mental, emotional, relational and spiritual wholeness our bodies reflect the same. This wholeness in Christ is a result of deliverance from the power that Satan has had over us through our deception, and consequent cooperation.

Salvation = 4991. **soteria**, so-tay-ree'-ah; fem. of a der. of G4990 as (prop. abstr.) noun; rescue or safety (phys. or mor.):--**deliver, health**, salvation, save, saving. (Emphasis mine: reference, Strong's concordance)

REVIVAL

In light of this we understand 'revival' from a Biblical perspective as something that happens in the human heart and spirit. A 'revival' is when this affect of the influence of the Holy Spirit on the human heart happens to, and changes enough people to impact a city, a region or even a nation. The Bible says that God is with the humble, to work through them in ministering to bring revival to a hurting humanity.

> *Isaiah 57:15 For this is what the high and lofty One says-- he who lives forever, whose name is holy: "I live in a high and holy place, but also with him who is contrite and lowly in spirit, (also translated as humble in spirit) to revive the spirit of the lowly and to revive the heart of the contrite. NIV (emphasis mine)*

Where do we find this in the New Testament? An early 'revival' or offer of 'revival' found in Acts chapter 3 where the Apostles Peter and John had just demonstrated the supernatural power of Gods dimension by raising up and healing the cripple man who was begging at the gate called Beautiful. This exposure to Gods abilities convicted those who witnessed the event of the reality of God. Paul, seizing the opportunity afforded by the astonishment of the people at the works of God, recommended that they change their thinking in regards to the Kingdom of God. He proposed that if they changed their thinking that God would bring revival to them.

> Acts 3:19 **Repent**, then, and turn to God, so that your sins may be wiped out, that **times** of **refreshing** may come from the Lord. NIV (emphasis mine)

Allow me highlight three words from this verse in the Greek language.
1. Repent = 3340. **metanoeo**, met-an-o-eh'-o; from G3326 and G3539; **to think differently** or afterwards, i.e. **reconsider** (mor. feel compunction):--repent. (Emphasis mine: reference, Strong's concordance)
2. Times = 2540. **kairos**, kahee-ros'; of uncert. affin.; **an occasion, i.e. set or proper time**:--X always, opportunity, (convenient, due) season, (due, short, while) time, a while. Comp. G5550. (Emphasis mine: reference, Strong's concordance)
3. 'Refreshing' = 403. **anapsuxis**, an-aps'-ook-sis; from G404; prop. **a recovery of breath**, i.e. (fig.) **revival**: --revival. (Emphasis mine: reference, Strong's concordance)

I am not sure why anapsuxis is normally translated as refreshing because the full meaning appears to be lost. But if we piece these words from the passage, we come up with something like this as a paraphrase.

If you will think differently about God and consequently reconsider your ways, then God has a proper time for you now, where you will have your sins wiped out, (redemption) and you will have the breath of life revive you and make you whole through the presence of God in your life. (sanctification)

With these concepts in mind, we begin to explore the healing streams of God, armed with an understanding of what purpose and outcome that God is seeking through them.

The 7 Streams
STREAM 1 'FAITH PRINCIPLES'

Whatever kind of healing that we are talking about, or whatever stream that God chooses bring freedom through, for us to receive God's provisions there will be faith involved. In its most fundamental form faith and believing in God is; to be persuaded or convinced that you can trust in God. If He has said something then we expect that it will be so.

Believe: Greek *Pisteuo*; to have faith (in, upon, or with respect to, a person or thing), commit (to trust), put in trust with.
Faith: Greek *Pistis*; persuasion, i.e. conviction.

God has limited Himself to working through faith in the Earth. This makes the condition of the church in terms of believing pretty important in terms of bringing restoration to fallen humanity.

> John 6:28-29 ²⁸ Then they said to Him, "What shall we do, that we may work the works of God?" ²⁹ Jesus answered and said to them, "This is the work of God, that you believe in Him whom He sent." NKJV

Why has He set these limits? I believe it is because the first sin, and the basic reason that mankind fell was their lack of belief and trust in the nature of God. It was apparently offensive to God, that Adam and Eve did not have faith that He was a good and loving God, who had their best interests in His heart. This may give us a clue to the meaning of Romans 14:23, which states that; '*whatever is not from faith is sin.*' In other words, anything that we do that does not trust in the benevolent nature of God is offensive to Him.

The scriptures use many words describing His person. Here are just a few: Merciful, gracious, just, righteous, abounding in love, compassionate, faithful, patient……and so on. So, anything that we do that does not have this picture of God as its foundation is built on a wrong premise. It is not the truth, and is an area that we are deceived in. This is what happened to Adam and Eve. They were deceived into doubting God's integrity, the protective nature of His commands, and whether or not He was not loving, and actually withholding something good from them. Something that the serpent suggested that would be beneficial for them, make them happy and meet their needs.

So, we see the father of faith, Abraham, as somebody who trusted God's person unequivocally. It was this absolute trust in the nature of God that made God deem him as righteousness…. not his efforts to be righteous in his own strength through self-effort or personal piety.

> *Romans 4:20-22* [20] *He did not waver at the promise of God through unbelief, but was strengthened in faith, giving glory to God,* [21] *and being fully convinced that what He had promised He was also able to perform.* [22] *And therefore "it was accounted to him for righteousness." NKJV*

We can then summarize the situation that we find ourselves in this way.

God wants to give us everything, consequently He sent Jesus to pay for our offenses and sins we commit because of our inherited doubt and ignorance of His goodness. We access these through faith in Christ Jesus which releases the Holy Spirit to make Gods provisions for us a reality. So, in order for us to receive we must have a right picture of His kindness, and be able to receive and accept His promises.

This appears to be a reversal of what happened in the Garden of Eden where mankind fell out of Gods blessings through doubt and unbelief. Now we receive everything by faith, trusting in the integrity of His word to us. In this we could say that the New Testament or Covenant is a Covenant of Faith.

> *Romans 1:17 For in the gospel a righteousness from God is revealed, <u>a righteousness that is by faith from first to last</u>, just as it is written: "The righteous will live by faith." NIV (emphasis mine)*

> *Romans 1:17 This Good News tells us how God makes us right in his sight. <u>This is accomplished from start to finish by faith</u>. As the Scriptures say, "It is through faith that a righteous person has life." NLT (emphasis mine)*

We could say then that we receive all of the promises of God through faith in His nature, which was demonstrated by Jesus who healed 'all' who came to Him.

It's clear from scripture that without faith it is impossible to please God. In other words, if we think of Him in the right way, believing in His person as revealed in the Bible, He is very pleased. But if we regard Him in the wrong way then it is impossible to please Him.

> *Hebrews 11:6 So, you see, it is impossible to please God without faith. Anyone who wants to come to him must believe that there is a God and that he rewards those who sincerely seek him. NLT*

As we lay this foundation for the Stream of healing by faith, we see that in Jesus' home town they could not believe and this meant that they could not receive. Familiarity with Him stemmed the flow of faith which was required to release the power of God in their situations. Perhaps they were thinking along the lines of; "didn't He help his father Joseph make our table and chairs?"

We see this in a church environment when people are familiar with sitting in church, doing the service a particular way, and never seeing healing. Then if one of their own ministers try to pray for the sick, they know him as the man from the church barbeque, or fellowship night. Faith and expectation are not released. Often healing evangelists are stylized, which creates an; 'I haven't seen this before, I don't know what to expect,' type setting which opens the way to believing for something to happen. Often, they come in with a fresh message, and fresh personal faith based on testimonies of what has happened as they travel.

> *Mark 6:3-6 ³"Is this not the carpenter, the Son of Mary, and brother of James, Joses, Judas, and Simon? And are not His sisters here with us?" And they were offended at Him. ⁴ But Jesus said to them, "A prophet is not without honor except in his own country, among his own relatives, and in his own house." ⁵ Now He could do no mighty work there, except that He laid His hands on a few sick people and healed them. ⁶ And He marveled because of their unbelief. Then He went about the villages in a circuit, teaching. NKJV*

Over the years we have learnt that miracle healing can be difficult in your own home church as people become familiar with you. A few years ago, we amalgamated our long-term church and took on another congregation who had lost their Pastor. We ministered there four years before finally transitioning it to a new leader in order to concentrate on our other ministry demands.

For the first few months that we were there I was able to work in words of knowledge and people were healed, but as they became more familiar with us you could see the expectation gradually *drying up*. It was time to bring in other people that they did not know, who weren't 'from their hometown,' as a contact point for their faith.

LESSON
If we can convince people that God is trustworthy and willing and able to meet their needs then anything can happen. The late healing Evangelist William Branham, who ministered through the 1950's and 60's reported, as I recall, that God told him that if he can 'get the people to believe then anything is possible.'

This means that it falls to the church to accurately represent God in all of His wonderful attributes, to inspire faith, and to position people to receive His abilities and power.

> *Mark 10:27 Jesus looked at them and said, "With man this is impossible, but not with God; all things are possible with God." NIV*

We as the ministers need to have faith and be convinced of Gods trustworthiness, and be able to position others to receive through our knowledge of God and testimony of His works.

> John 14:12 I tell you the truth, anyone who has faith in me will do what I have been doing. He will do even greater things than these, because I am going to the Father. NIV

GIVING FAITH

Once someone has experienced God healing people, it is very difficult to convince those people that He won't. This applies to emotional healing, deliverance, or physical healing. Some people have stronger faith in some areas than others because they mainly work in one stream and as a result have experienced God's provisions mostly in that setting. A few years ago, we went directly from one nation to another where the faith dynamics were considerably different. Fortunately, we had been in the country that had been far more open to physical healing first. When we came to the second nation, we had to persevere for a little bit longer to get the breakthroughs. I recall going along the prayer line and some people were being healed, beginning with some changes from the initial prayer, improving more or being totaled healed on the second occasion, and then coming right through as we continued to pray.

There was one woman towards the end of the line with some kind of lung problem. As I prayed for her, she reported over and over again no change. The fact that I had just experienced God healing so many people in the previous country meant that I simply could not let go of trying to get her free. Eventually we ran out of time and she was still reporting no change. A few minutes after we began to hear testimonies from the front, she joined the line and testified that something had happened with her. She said that it was as if fresh wind had come into her lungs. She was a middle-aged woman, and had had the problem since she was a small child.

The point is that if we had not had fresh experience of that which God wants to do, I would not have pressed through. It is amazing how many people are healed when we persist in prayer rather than giving up when nothing or not much happens immediately.

LESSON
Our personal faith is infectious and other people are impacted and moved by it if we are convinced ourselves. One sign of these personal convictions in regards to Gods goodness, power, and intention to heal, is our perseverance with the person needing ministry for the Lord.

PERSISTENT FAITH

Possibly my favorite healing story is from the American Apostle Che Ahn [1]. We get so hung up on instant miracles that people often give up on their healing before they reach the church door to head home. As his story goes a man came up to him in a prayer line and in an accident his finger had been cut off at the second knuckle. His teenage daughter had been helping him trim the hedges when she unintentionally cut off his finger with the hedge clippers. He demonstrated his faith saying; *Pastor, I believe God wants to grow my finger back, and I want you to stand with me in faith.* Che Ahn agreed with him, as he put it, hoping for the best.

---

[1] Reference book. Say Goodbye to Powerless Christianity. Destiny Image publishers. Author: Che Ahn

A couple of months later the man was back in the prayer line. As he approached the apostle he was smiling and as the story goes held up his hand to show his brand-new finger complete with a new nail! Che humbly reported that at the time he may not have believed that the finger would grow back. It was the man's faith to receive that brought about the results. We modern Christians have to some extent been programmed by microwaves and fast food chains. We expect to go through the drive through requesting; *One physical healing, two deliverances, and complete emotional restoration to go thanks.*

In reality, healing and deliverance is a journey that has miraculous moments here and there. Sometimes patience and perseverance are developed as we contend for the faith.

Another man that I know of had terminal liver cancer. He went to one healing meeting after another all over the country and finally received His healing. Having received the object of his faith he then proceeded to have his own healing ministry. Clearly it was the certainty of God's promise in his heart that made him persevere. Some people spend years, *standing on the word*, and never receive because they are trying to make something happen by their own will and effort. If we come as *little* children, we are not trying to do anything, we are just presenting ourselves because Abba daddy said to. If we have received then we will know immediately or discover it in due course as the evidence of the healing appears.

 LESSON
Persistence in believing will always produce a result. Faith will have its outcome.

RECEIVING FAITH

Jesus often asked questions such as; *do you believe that I can do this*? He also made comments such as; *your faith has healed you, according to your faith* and so on. He was looking for faith to receive in the person whom He was to minister to. Of course, He had perfect faith Himself, but without them being able to receive it would be like trying to tip water into a jar with the lid still on.

We learnt a lesson about people's faith to receive on one of our first times overseas preaching a healing gospel. We were in a developing nation in the Pacific and God was miraculously healing various physical problems. I recall preaching and praying for the sick in one church and then being raced off an hour away to do the same in another congregation. A couple of days later we were back at the original church and my wife and I were approached by the Pastors wife. She came up to us and enquired; *did you see that lady who you prayed for the other day who was carried in*? We responded that we did and she went on to explain what had happened. *Did you know that she had terminal cancer and notice that she walked out of the meeting by herself after prayer? The following day she was walking around the hospital by herself and the day after she was released to go home.* My wife incredulously proclaimed wide eyed; *really.* I gently elbowed her and whispered in her ear that this is what we have been telling these people that God wants to do for them. *Don't look too surprised or they may not expect it to keep happening.* As comical as this was, we learnt the lesson that their receiving faith was why God was touching them. Indeed, they had more faith in what God would do through us than we did at the time ourselves.

 LESSON
Accurately teaching the word of God, or sharing stories of what God has done can often raise faith to receive in people, and produce results beyond what we would ourselves have expected.

FAITH AND BEING 'FULLY CONVINCED' AT 'HEART' LEVEL

Being fully convinced, I believe is something in the heart rather than mental assent or wishful thinking. We can believe in theory, for anything in our minds, but belief in our hearts comes largely from experience of God doing what He said that He would do. At times we have had no experience of God confirming His word because of our environment, or we have heart beliefs that prevent us from believing that God would want to prove His word in or through us.

We will cover this in more detail in following Units. Let us say though that this could be because we believe in our hearts that we are not worthy, not really loved, not cared about, or good enough depending on what was programmed into us as children.

So, healing of beliefs in our hearts can open up new realms of faith as can attending meetings where God is proving His word through a person of faith. In any case Jesus said that we can have whatever we believe in our hearts, having dealt with doubt, as opposed to what we believe in our minds.

> *Mark 11:22-24* ²² *So Jesus answered and said to them, "Have faith in God."*
> ²³ *"For assuredly, I say to you, whoever says to this mountain, 'Be removed and be cast into the sea,' and **does not doubt in his heart**, but believes that those things he says will be done, he will have whatever he says.*
> ²⁴ *"Therefore I say to you, whatever things you ask when you pray, believe that you receive them, and you will have them." NKJV (emphasis mine)*

LESSON
Many times, we need truth for our own inner heart beliefs or the inner beliefs of the hearts of others, in regards to for example, worthiness to minister or receive, before we have faith that God can move through.

DEALING WITH DOUBT AND UNBELIEF

So how do we deal with our doubt and unbelief? In two Corinthians chapter ten and verse five we see that we are to demolish and destroy arguments that set themselves up against the knowledge of God. The Greek word here that is translated; as *arguments* is *logismus*, and it means; computation, i.e. (fig.) reasoning, imagination, thought. It is reasonably obvious that we get words such as logic from this root word. So, the passage is really saying to pull down and destroy all logical reasoning out, and trying to compute and understand the word of God.

There is no working out the word of God. Think about it. Jesus walks on water, talks to storms, drachmas appear in fish's mouths, He feeds five thousand with next to nothing, axe heads float, water becomes wine, seas part for the Israelites to cross, donkeys talk to their riders … shall I go on.

> *2 Corinthians 10:5 "We demolish **arguments** and every pretension that sets itself up against the knowledge of God, and we take captive every thought to make it obedient to Christ" NIV (emphasis mine)*

The point is that you cannot reason out something that you will never be able to understand. The things that God does are not natural. So, then the word of God and His promises are technically not logical or possible. They cannot therefore be worked out. They can only be received.

We need to take control of our thought life and refuse to try to work it out, otherwise your reasoning is going to go into; *Maybe God doesn't heal today, or He only heals in Africa where they don't have many doctors, or He will only heal good people, but He won't heal me because I am not good enough!* Etc.

I have heard that if you buy a loaf of white bread today that by the time the grain has been broken down and processed by man that there is no nutritional value left in it for us. When we begin to process the word of God, and manize it, instead of taking it whole and untouched, we render it of no value to us either.

Smith Wigglesworth who very clinically dealt with his own unbelief, proclaimed his well-known default position. *God said it, I believe it, that settles it.* In other words, there is no more to think about, and nothing to work out; I trust His integrity, promises and ability without question. He also made the statement that; *carnal (worldly) reasoning will always land you in the bog of unbelief.*

I taught on these principles in Africa recently, and on the Sunday morning the young man leading worship that day gave in his own language a testimony, and received a round of applause. Although I did not know what had happened, I was told after the service that having heard these principles, he became inspired and decided to try it out and see if it was true. He stepped out boldly praying for a lady with a disease and she was healed.

Whether you want to receive your own healing or help in the ministry to others you need to take captive, and deal with your doubt and unbelief. Once you have decided to refuse to even think about the possibility of God not being true to His word, it can be helpful to meditate over and over on His nature. When you are receiving or praying for others you can be expecting something to happen based on your meditations regarding how God is towards us.

LESSON
The issue is very often not whether or not we have faith, because we have all been given a measure which will grow if we feed it. The problem most times is that we concurrently have wrong beliefs which produce doubt and unbelief. These need to be resolved in order for faith alone to be our default position.

HAVING 'GIVING FAITH' WITHOUT POSITIONING THOSE IN NEED FOR 'RECEIVING FAITH'

I did one of our two-week healing schools for a church some time ago, and in the course of the school God faithfully demonstrated every kind of healing that I taught on. At the end of the two weeks my personal faith was at an all-time high. I was brimming with faith and felt that anything would happen that I prayed for.

I went directly into another church the following weekend. They brought up a lady who was suffering from breast cancer. I prayed for her with great faith and expectation and the power and anointing of God was on her quite strongly. A few months later I heard that she had died. What had happened? I realized that I had not taught her the word, prepared her, or done anything to evoke her faith to receive.

Additionally, the environment that she was in was one of an expectation of a negative outcome because her husband and children had seen his first wife die a few years earlier. I learnt that my faith to give is not as important as is the ability of the person to receive.

Our work then is to raise the faith of the people through teaching and testimony to position them to receive.

Reading the great healing Apostle Smith Wigglesworth, I noted that there were occasions where he would go to minister in a home and would not immediately pray for the sick person. He commented once that *there was not an atom of faith in the house*. He would proceed to minister the Word of God in order to deal with the environment, and then he would pray sometimes the next day and get his result.

In the case of the Apostle Paul in the book of Acts, we observe him seeing faith in a man who was responding to his teaching. Evidently others in the room had problems as well but were not moved by faith and convinced at heart level that God wanted to touch them. So, it is good for us to be aware of the effects of our sharing, testifying, teaching or preaching in terms of raising faith for people to understand and receive.

> *Acts 14:9-10 9 This man heard Paul speaking. Paul, observing him intently and seeing that he had faith to be healed, 10 said with a loud voice, "Stand up straight on your feet!" And he leaped and walked (NKJV).*

LESSON
It is vitally important to build an environment of faith based on truth, so that the people are positioned to receive. This may take time if you are in a religious environment, or where there has been no teaching or experience of Gods healing and freeing abilities.

TIMES WHEN YOU MAY NOT 'FEEL' FAITH
Let me briefly contrast this with times when I have taught all week and been very tired by the time it comes to the prayer line. I am too worn out to feel much personal faith and at times have prayed very feeble prayers indeed, and yet the subject has still been healed.

One such instance was in Asia some time back. At the end of a week of teaching and ministering we were heading back to our hotel. On the way some of the Pastors took us to the home of an old lady who needed prayer. When I prayed for her, she became quite irate and pointed to her eyes. She was apparently blind. I laid my hand over her eyes and prayed a tired prayer commanding them to open. Almost immediately she was counting the fingers of an excited young Pastor across the table. She certainly did not get healed by my energetic faith, and looking at her I don't think that she personally had either faith or unbelief. The Pastors however had seen people being healed on the school through the week and they had great expectations.

LESSON
Faith does not need to be felt emotionally, although often you do feel it as your emotions are the outworking of your beliefs. It is your inner conviction. In fact, you may be more aware of faith, because you are deliberately choosing it, when you begin in different kinds of healing ministries. Later, you just 'know' that this is what God does, and not have any special feelings. This is still faith.

BELIEVING FOR YOURSELF
Many times, it is more difficult to believe for yourself than it is for others. This is probably because you have experiential knowledge of your symptoms being present each day. Most

times rather than try hard, we need to keep it simple, and seek out the healing gifts that God has placed in the body to meet these needs. In Australia a great many people are trying to resolve their problem themselves by some means. God has placed healing gifts in the body for a reason and they can help us to receive.

Even Smith Wigglesworth suffered from appendicitis and almost died [2]. It was a praying woman of faith and a young man who came and addressed the problem that brought about his healing. He was apparently unable to believe and come to faith for his own cure. In fact, as the story goes when they visited Wigglesworth's home the young man jumped up on the bed and commanded the spirit causing the appendicitis to go, and before Smith could tell him that he couldn't possibly have a demon, it left. So clearly, he had no faith for cure by those means at that time either.

We need to be convinced of God's goodness and power, and trust His character and willingness to set us free. This believing response is the basis of both our salvation and Him empowering us to overcome in the World.

> John 5:4 *"For whatever is born of God overcomes the world. And this is the victory that has overcome the world; our faith." NKJV*

LESSON
At times you may need the ministry of others to help you receive for yourself.

HOW SHOULD HEALING LOOK?

Many people don't receive their healing because they believe that it should look some particular way, or that they should feel this or that. I would estimate that with most of the people that we see healed physically through our ministry nothing obvious happens. This can be true also of deliverance or baptism in the Holy Spirit. One minute they are sick or have demonic power working in them and the next minute they don't. One minute they can't speak in other tongues, and the next moment they can.

Jesus actually admonished the man in John chapter 4, and I imagine all of those present, for needing to see something happen before they believed and would receive. The man had come to Jesus requesting healing for his son.

> John 4:46-53 *46 So Jesus came again to Cana of Galilee where He had made the water wine. And there was a certain nobleman whose son was sick at Capernaum. 47 When he heard that Jesus had come out of Judea into Galilee, he went to Him and implored Him to come down and heal his son, for he was at the point of death. 48 Then Jesus said to him, "Unless you people see signs and wonders, you will by no means believe." 49 The nobleman said to Him, "Sir, come down before my child dies!" 50 Jesus said to him, "Go your way; your son lives." So the man believed the word that Jesus spoke to him, and he went his way. 51 And as he was now going down, his servants met him and told him, saying, "Your son lives!" 52 Then he inquired of them the hour when he got better. And they said to him, "Yesterday at the seventh hour the fever left him." 53 So the father knew that it was at the same hour in which Jesus said to him, "Your son lives." And he himself believed, and his whole household. NKJV (emphasis mine)*

---

[2] Smith Wigglesworth on Healing. Publisher: Whitaker House

Nobody reported seeing anything happen; the boy was simply healed because his father believed the word that Jesus spoke. Some people have preconceived ideas in regards to perhaps something that they have seen in a meeting or on U tube, and believe that all healings should look this way or it *didn't work*. When you consider that our thinking is the limiting factor, and when our minds get in the way, then our expectations block the work of God through faith. Remember the devil is forever defeated, the only power he has over you is the areas of deception that you hold. This could include receiving and accepting the thought that you cannot be healed or freed.

At times I have been in churches where there may be a cripple or the like who has been in the church for many years. As a result, the people are used to them being in that condition. So, you are dealing with mass expectation of how he should look and be. We could say that the mind in regards to what God can, or wants to do, is the limiting factor. Perhaps people have seen him prayed for many times before.

There is the well-known story of the lady who touched the hem of Jesus garment in Matthew Chapter 9 and received her healing. If you can picture the event with the crowd all around them, and the disciples urging Jesus to hurry or they will miss the last bus. The woman touches His hem and is healed. Who knew that something had happened? Most likely nobody other than Jesus who felt the power go out of him, and the lady who felt that she was healed. The others didn't see anything happen, and there is no evidence that she fell to the ground or shook for ten minutes, or any other event that some might expect should be present for healing. She simply touched His hem and was healed.

I have often seen people looking bored because they don't see much happening in healing meetings and assume that nothing is going on. Very often, but not always, the minister can feel the flow of the power going through Him, and the person receiving can feel themselves being touched. God does not need to be showy and comes as He pleases.

I think that we need to be bottom line Christians, and be all about caring about people and not putting on a show. The testimonies are how we know that God has been working.

I heard a story of two healing ministers in modern times. Reportedly one of them prayed in a very dignified gentle manner and people would be healed without anything obvious happening. When the other man would pray for people they would shake violently and fall to the ground.

On one occasion as the more dignified man went through a particular town, he went past a healing meeting being conducted by the other man. He commented to his driver that the way that this man prayed and that what happened when he did was unseemly. As they drove on, he began to get a headache. Inquiring of the Lord he was instructed to go back and get prayer from the other man. When he did, apparently he shook violently, fell to the ground, and got up healed. Regardless of the validity of the story it does raise the point that if we take a; *that's not how you do it* approach we may well miss our healing.

God will come through various ministers as He pleases. Whether this is to do with the personality of the minister that the Holy Spirit is working through or not, I could not say. We do however have to have our eyes fixed on Christ the healer and not the man that He is working through. In any case it is important to not get hung up on seeing something happen or particular methods. Simply pray with faith and leave the details to God.

Remember it is largely the person's ability to receive that matters, and your job is to position them with truth about God to release their faith. It is not somebody with a big name or ministry that has healed you. Seven times in the gospels according to Jesus it is; *Your faith has healed you.*

I have a friend who is a well-known minister from Uganda. At one time he was running a gospel crusade in Kenya, and at the end of the service he began to pray for the sick. He remembered a sick man who had been brought in on a stretcher and laid under the platform, so he went and prayed for him. After he had prayed, he began to walk away and the crowd erupted. It turned out that the man was not in fact sick, but actually dead. After prayer he had sat up on his stretcher to everyone's amazement. The point is we just pray for God to touch the subject, refuse to doubt His goodness, and you never know what might happen. Certainly, the dead man didn't have any unbelief to complicate the issue, which leads me to the next portion of this stream.

LESSON
God heals many different ways. He does not always work the same way and has a variety of expressions depending on the person that He is working through, or the environment.

FAITH VERSES UNBELIEF
Faith puts us *under* God's provision and outcome. This is evidenced by Abraham who was fully convinced that God could do that which He said He would do. As we have said, once we have our convictions about God's promises and intentions for us, we need to leave the details to Him in terms of how it will look and when it will take place. Doubt, unbelief and skepticism put us, or keep us under Satan's outcome, which will not be positive, changing or redemptive in nature.

One day I was praying for a lady who was booked in for an operation, and the power of God was on her heavily. We needed three or four people to hold her up through the ministry time. She had been the last person in the prayer line, and so after we had finished, I headed for the church cafe to get into the coffee queue. From where I was standing, I was not visible to the lady, and she had entered the kitchen to talk to some friends. From this position I could hear her explaining to another lady how pleased she was that God had provided somebody to look after her after her operation. I was thinking back to 5 minutes earlier when she could not stand up, as she was overwhelmed with the healing power of God.

I later reflected on the situation and how her expectation was set on the outcome of the operation and not the power of God. She doubted that His power would heal her and did not believe that anything would change. In a sense she had switched off whatever God wanted to do immediately after the prayer.

I have seen many times when asked how people are feeling immediately after prayer, they may make statements such as; *at the moment I have no pain.* This can mean that they are struggling to get their minds around what has just happened. There is every chance that if challenged that they will accept and receive the return of their symptoms before they even get home. This is according to the faith and expectations that they hold, based on their knowledge of God and His word. I have seen a number of people who have had some symptoms beginning to come back who have stood on the word and refused to accept the sickness or injury again.

One time I prayed for three people who responded to a word of knowledge for the same back problem. When I prayed for them one of them fell to the ground, shook and stood up proclaiming that they were healed. The other two reported nothing. The following week I enquired of each of them as to their condition. The one who had manifested and reported healing had the back problem back again. The other two both independently said the same thing as each other, and that was that the day after prayer the problem was worse, but the following day that they were both healed, and reported remaining healed. So, what happened? I think that the two people just accepted it for whatever it was going to be, not having doubt or unbelief, and the other who was sensitive to the Holy Spirit was probably also sensitive to unholy spirit, and when some symptoms came, they received their problem back. We need to be fully convinced that if the son sets you free, then you are free indeed.

We have already quoted that Jesus said that we can have whatever we believe in our hearts if we do not doubt. The basis of the word translated as doubt holds the meaning of intellectual deciding, judging, wavering, hesitating or contending. In other words, the matter isn't settled, you are not fully convinced.

> Matthew 21:21-22 ²¹ *So Jesus answered and said to them, "Assuredly, I say to you, if you have faith and do **not doubt**, you will not only do what was done to the fig tree, but also if you say to this mountain, 'Be removed and be cast into the sea,' it will be done.* ²² *"And whatever things you ask in prayer, believing, you will receive." NKJV (emphasis mine)*

Each of us has been given a measure of faith. So, having faith, however undeveloped, is not the problem as we only need a mustard seed of faith. The issue then is usually not how much faith we have, it is how much unbelief. Both can exist in us at the same time. I have ministered in churches that were not denominationally predisposed to healing and the working of the Holy Spirit. As Jesus did, I have sometimes spent a week ministering one on one behind closed doors healing the sick and hurting. As the testimonies have circulated through the church there has been expectation building, and we have been able to see people healed in a prayer line by the following Sunday.

So, the issue really is not about having a great amount of faith, it is more about dealing with unbelief or wrong beliefs. At times you hear of prayer chains where they try to get 500 people praying for a sick person. May I gently suggest that this is unbelief and fear that God will not hear, and that He needs many to persuade and pressure Him? My Bible says that healing was His idea and not ours; we don't have to talk Him into it! He already promised, paid for it, and commanded that we minister it. If we simply receive without doubting it is ours.

I was ministering to a young lady who had been abused one day. She wanted to share something very personal with me, and so requested that everyone would go behind the window in the door whilst she revealed what was troubling her. As they went out, she said desperately, "pray for me that I will be healed!"

I said to the departing group of ladies, "don't pray for her, you don't have to talk God into this…it's His idea!" God healed her. He is committed enough to our healing that He already paid for it Himself.

 LESSON
The expectations of what God will do for them is a strong indicator of their believing in regards to faith. At times you can see faith in expressions such as a dawning realization in relation to what God wants to do, or a look of expectation. Other times you see nothing. What you do not want to see or hear is doubt or unbelief.

CHOOSING FAITH

Whether you want to receive your own healing or help in the ministry to others you need to take captive, and deal with your doubt and unbelief. Once you have decided to refuse to even think about the possibility of God not being true to His word, it can be helpful to meditate over and over on His nature. When you are receiving or praying for others you can be expecting something to happen based on your meditations regarding how God is towards us. There is an appendix of redemption scriptures in the back of the book to consider as a basis for your healing and freedom.

> Psalm 103:2-4, 8, 13 [2] *"Praise the LORD, O my soul, and forget not all his benefits,* [3] *who forgives all your sins and heals all your diseases,* [4] *who redeems your life from the pit and crowns you with love and compassion,* [8] *The LORD is compassionate and gracious, slow to anger, abounding in love.* [13] *As a father has compassion on his children, so the LORD has compassion on those who fear him"* (NIV).

Let me make a final observation relating to doubt and unbelief. Some people think that if you don't pray a particular way, or for the right thing, or long enough, then healing won't happen. Laying on hands and a prayer such as; *be healed in the name of Jesus* really is all that you need. Let me reiterate, you do not have to talk God into it; this is His idea, and as we have said, He even commanded us to go out and heal the sick. You may need to work through the doubts of the people that you are ministering to though, before you see or sense enough expectation to pray for them. You need to be convinced yourself first before you will sway them. Your faith needs to be greater than their doubt and unbelief. The late Smith Wigglesworth was so convinced of Gods ability and desire to heal that he moved many in his audiences to his point of view. I know of modern healing ministries who operate the same way.

I once prayed for a lady who wanted prayer to confirm a positive outcome to a cancer operation that she'd had. I heard a couple of days later that, at the same time, God had healed her back and she no longer needed her brace. I didn't even know that she had a bad back, and so I certainly didn't pray the right prayer, if there is such a thing, but God knew. We don't need to get everything right; we just have to believe that in His love and compassion that He will do whatever is needed.

I recall one well known American evangelist being asked by a lady; *I know that you can heal headaches, but I have cancer!* His reply was something along the lines of; *Lady, I can't heal anything, but God can and it doesn't make much difference to Him what you've got!*

Famous people both from the past, and those in the present age, who have *faith healing ministries* are so convinced of God's willingness and ability to heal that they convince many other people in their meetings that this is so. Some expound powerfully the promises from the word; others share testimonies or demonstrate healing in their meetings, or a combination of all. The key is that they are so persuaded from their own experiences of God, that others are moved from their normal believing to the faith of the minister, and as a result they become open to God's power and ability as well.

 LESSON
It is God who does the healing. We cannot understand how He does it, we can only know that He does. We don't, therefore have to know everything about what we are praying for in the stream of faith healing.

SUMMARY

The most important work then in any kind of healing ministry is to position the subject under Gods provision, submitted to Him and trusting in His ability and promises. Remember, whatever we submit to has power <u>over</u> us. This applies to whether we are submitted to Satan's challenge to Gods nature which produces doubt and unbelief, and puts us <u>under</u> his outcomes, or we are submitted to God in faith to receive His provisions.

> *2 Peter 2:19b ....for a man is a slave to whatever has mastered him. NIV*

There is an excellent example of this in the book of Daniel chapter 3 where Daniels friends refused to submit to fear and intimidation. They refused to bow down and worship other gods, instead making a faith proclamation about the abilities of God to deliver them.

This placed them 'under' the power of God and released supernatural provision and miraculous protection.

> *Daniel 3:17-18* ¹⁷ *If we are thrown into the blazing furnace, the God we serve is able to save us from it, and he will rescue us from your hand, O king.* ¹⁸ *But even if he does not, we want you to know, O king, that we will not serve your gods or worship the image of gold you have set up." NIV*

STREAM 2 'UNDER THE ANOINTING'

The second healing stream that I am proposing is the anointing, which is the presence of God, and can be the tangible power of God. It can come as the result of faith that has risen through gifts, testimonies, teaching or an act of faith for example. Equally faith can come as a result of the anointing or presence of God in a meeting.

> *Luke 5:17 "Now it happened on a certain day, as He was teaching, that there were Pharisees and teachers of the law sitting by, who had come out of every town of Galilee, Judea, and Jerusalem. And the power of the Lord was present to heal them." NKJV (emphasis mine)*

We have already pointed out that the *Spirit of power* is one of the seven Spirits or a part of the sevenfold ministry of the Holy Spirit. When people are talking about *the anointing*, they are often referring to the power of God, and so we will largely focus on this expression of the Holy Spirit in this unit. Clearly, *the anointing* or presence of God is also tangible at other times, such as, worship services, prayer meetings or ministry sessions to the hurting and broken, as well as for many people who feel His presence with them.

LESSON
The gifts work together. For example the presence or anointing of the Holy Spirit can produce faith, which in turn can create an environment for gifts, which produce healing.

THE ANOINTING, IN THE SENSE OF POWER FOR HEALING

There are two words translated in the New Testament as power. The first word is *exousia* which means *authority* type power, such as you would exercise over others submitted to you in specific areas. An example of this would be in the book of Acts where the Apostle Paul is stating that his mission is to turn people from the deception that they are under. This deception is causing them to submit to Satan and give him power (authority) over them through their submission. The word power in the following text is *exousia* which means *authority* type power.

*Acts 26:18 'to open their eyes, in order to turn them from darkness to light, and from **the power** of Satan to God, NKJV (emphasis mine)*

Reference, Strong's concordance: 1849. exousia, from G1832 (in the sense of ability); privilege, i.e. (subj.) force, capacity, competency, freedom, or (obj.) mastery (concr. magistrate, superhuman, potentate, token of control), <u>delegated influence:--authority, jurisdiction, liberty, power, right, strength</u>.

The Greek word for literal power in the New Testament is *dunamis* which means literal or miraculous power, force or might. We get words such as dynamo or dynamite from this root. This is the power to heal that was described in the previous passage, and also in stories such as the power that healed the lady who touched the hem of Jesus' garment in Matthew chapter 9 verse 20. Another example of *dunamis* power would be the literal power of God working in and through us that we observe from the following passage in Ephesians.

*Ephesians 3:20 Now to Him who is able to do exceedingly abundantly above all that we ask or think, according to the **power** that works in us. NKJV (emphasis mine)*

Reference, Strong's Concordance: 1411. Dunamis, = from G1410; force (lit. or fig.); spec. miraculous power, ability, abundance, meaning, might (-ily, -y, -y deed), (worker of) miracle (-s), power, strength, violence, mighty (wonderful) work.

In the following passage we see on this occasion exousia translated as authority rather than power. Also, we note that this time the word for *the power* of the enemy is dunamis, meaning that the enemy has some literal power, but Jesus is giving us dominion, jurisdiction or authority over it. We sometimes see this when we exercise, for example, authority over a demon in somebody, and the demon uses its power to have a physical manifestation as it exits. Jesus had occasions such as in Mark chapter 1 verse 26 when a spirit convulsed the man as it exited.

Luke 10:19 "Behold, I give you the authority to trample on serpents and scorpions, and over all the power of the enemy, and nothing shall by any means hurt you. NKJV

LESSON
So, the distinction is that exousia power as authority is like a badge that we wear, an authorization from the kingdom of God. However, *dunamis* power as literal power is a manifestation of *the anointing* of the Holy Spirit, in or through us.

ATTRACTING THE ANOINTING OR PRESENCE OF THE HOLY SPIRIT

We have at times ministered in places where the people are so hungry for the touch of God that they receive easily. There can at times be a powerful presence of God come in as the prayer line begins and the Holy Spirit moves on people. I remember one occasion where people were being touched, healed and delivered, and the presence of God was so strong that we became very bold. With His power so eminent you nearly felt like asking if they had any dead people. It is almost as if His nearness gives you confidence that anything is possible.

How strong the presence of His anointing might be in a meeting is not something that we can control, although we can observe. It does however appear that where there is hunger for

His presence, expectation, humility and genuine worship you can certainly expect a strong manifestation.

At times people are spontaneously delivered or healed when the anointing of the Holy Spirit comes upon them. In different countries across the World I have seen people go into spontaneous deliverance when I pray for them. Notably, the power of God passing through you or from within you on these occasions feels the same even though the results vary. For example, it feels the same to me whether God is healing someone, delivering them, perhaps taking them down under the power or giving them a touch of His presence.

Remember we are just the door or channel that God comes in through, we are His entrance into an environment, what happens next is as the Spirit wills. At such times it is not a mental exercise, or even whether you are praying or not. I recall one-time many years ago in Africa, going along and simply ministering the Spirit through my hands......I was not saying or praying anything because of the language dynamics in the room. It was clear that people were being touched but not much more was happening. I look back amused, reflecting on how God may see these things. At the time I made the comment in my mind to God that; "Lord, I am doing the tipping but not much is happening!" The next person I ministered to fell out on the floor and convulsed in deliverance, and then the next, and so on right until the end of the line.

At times people are healed or set free by the Holy Spirit while teaching is in process.

LESSON

The Holy Spirit comes as He pleases. When He comes in as the power of God through us, we mostly cannot predict what He might do or how He might touch a person. We are gates and doors to His Kingdom provisions.

SEEKING THE 'ANOINTING'

It can be distressing as at times we hear of people doing strange things to get the anointing. The Holy Spirit seems to be particularly attracted to obedient people and humble people. We know that Jesus had the Spirit without measure so He is always our model in all things. We can look to Him for the secret to the anointing.

> *John 5:19 Then Jesus answered and said to them, "Most assuredly, I say to you, the Son can do nothing of Himself, but what He sees the Father do; for whatever He does, the Son also does in like manner. NKJV*

Clearly the 'anointing' or presence of God is strongest when we are looking to God for His will and purposes, and reliant on His abilities and not what we can do through our own efforts.

> *John 8:29 "And He who sent Me is with Me. The Father has not left Me alone, for **I always do those things that please Him**" NKJV (Emphasis mine)*

Most of the great healing ministries of the past understood that the way to having God come increasingly through you, was a process of getting yourself out of the way. Self can block the flow and make you a dam rather than a river. You need to be not about yourself, but rather others, and living for His glory and not your own. Then even if you imagine yourself as a funnel, and the funnel has a few cracks in it, most of what is tipped in will still go through. So it is with us. Although we are imperfect, if we hold our *funnel* up to God for

Him to pour His Spirit through to minister to the people, there will be enough tipped in by Him to achieve the result.

In terms of enlarging your funnel, it will cost you something of losing your life to gain a more abundant life in the Spirit. The natural life is not necessarily sinful, it is simply inferior. You can have a life on Earth and have things that are not essentially bad, but if you want God to use you, then this natural life may need to go on the altar in preference for being used by Him. Smith Wigglesworth explained this process of walking increasingly as a clear channel for God in this way; *All of me none of God - less of me more of God - none of me all of God.*

'SPECIAL' ANOINTED PEOPLE

Many years ago, I was at a church where they were talking about the amazing *anointing* on their leader, and how they all wanted prayer from him for the *anointing* as if it was something that could be randomly handed out and given from this man. My first thoughts were about when Samuel selected King David. He was ready to anoint his impressive older brothers, but God showed him, not this one, not this one, until David came in and it was clear that he was the one. What I take from this is that God is very selective about who He anoints, and for what purpose. Even the great Prophet Samuel could not make this call or select who was to receive the anointing. I think that we can cheapen the anointing with this type of thinking.

> *1 Samuel 16:6-13* *[6] So it was, when they came, that he looked at Eliab and said, "Surely the Lord's anointed is before Him." [7] But the LORD said to Samuel, "Do not look at his appearance or at the height of his stature, because I have refused him. For the Lord does not see as man sees; for man looks at the outward appearance, but the LORD looks at the heart." [8] So Jesse called Abinadab, and made him pass before Samuel. And he said, "Neither has the LORD chosen this one." [9] Then Jesse made Shammah pass by. And he said, "Neither has the LORD chosen this one." [10] Thus Jesse made seven of his sons pass before Samuel. And Samuel said to Jesse, "The LORD has not chosen these." [11] And Samuel said to Jesse, "Are all the young men here?" Then he said, "There remains yet the youngest, and there he is, keeping the sheep." And Samuel said to Jesse, "Send and bring him. For we will not sit down till he comes here." [12] So he sent and brought him in. Now he was ruddy, with bright eyes, and good-looking. And the LORD said, "Arise, anoint him; for this is the one!" [13] Then Samuel took the horn of oil and anointed him in the midst of his brothers; and the Spirit of the LORD came upon David from that day forward. So Samuel arose and went to Ramah (NKJV).*

God has called you for what He has called you, and you need to grow in your own anointing as you make room for God to rule on the throne of your heart. If you look inside and He is not sitting on the throne there, and you are, then that is a very good place to start on coming into the *anointing.* These people were suggesting that this man had a special *anointing* that was causing healing to happen around his life. In the night I wrestled with this concept inquiring of the Lord as to how you get a special anointing such as this. The answer came in the form of a scripture from John's gospel:

> *John 14:1 "I tell you the truth, **anyone** who has faith in me will do what I have been doing. He will do even greater things than these, because I am going to the Father" NIV (emphasis mine).*

This resolved the issue of 'special *anointing*' for me. It is a matter of simple faith in God, and this might well release anointing, but it is for *anyone* who chooses to believe and trust God! When we step out and present ourselves for God to use, we create a channel, or door that the anointing can come through. Very often in a meeting the anointing, power of the Spirit, (Spirit of Power) becomes manifested when we begin to minister to people, not before.

LESSON
People that we may term as 'anointed' are usually those that have yielded themselves to the Holy Spirit. They have removed self-preference, wanting to do what pleases God. This makes them a wide channel for God to come through. This is not something that was imparted to them in a prayer line.

LAYING ON HANDS TO RELEASE THE ANOINTING

Finally, laying on of hands is a channel for the power of God to flow through. Some people feel it and others don't. That is not the point. Why does the laying on of hands work? Because Jesus said to do it! I have been in meetings where the people were spiritually not very alive. So, there was virtually no tangible presence of God in the room beyond that which came through my hands when I prayed for people. They still received deliverance. It reminded me of Jesus in His own home town, He could not do mighty miracles because of the unbelief of the general population, but He could still see individuals healed through His hands.

> *Mark 6:5-6 ⁵ Now He could do no mighty work there, except that He laid His hands on a few sick people and healed them. ⁶ And He marveled because of their unbelief" NKJV*

We can see that because of the dynamic of unbelief that what the Holy Spirit could do through Jesus was limited. This applies to setting a dynamic of faith in our churches, and eventually our culture. This can take time, and if we are leaders, we must make sure that our people have continuous exposure to the gifts and people called that He has provided in His body.

We can see why Jesus taught about the Kingdom, and what God wanted for them before He ministered. He raised faith first through people having a right understanding.

The streams often overlap as they run into the same river. For example, the anointing or presence of God brings faith, but equally faith ushers in the presence of God.

LESSON
The power of God will flow through the laying on of hands. Some people will receive this, and in others you will sense resistance because of their beliefs.

STREAM 3 'GIFTS'

Gifts raise faith in the supernatural ability and intervention of God into our situation. Often people covet gifts so that they will appear to be someone, or better than other people. God is looking for people who will seek gifts because of a genuine motivation to see people receive His help and provision. In this case they are expressing gifts because of love for Him and for people. This places you 'in the Spirit' in the sense of being aligned with the nature, purpose and ministry of the Holy Spirit. It makes you a genuine candidate for Him to use you, choose you and gift you.

We do not necessarily come into the gifts because we do a seminar on how to operate in them, although we need to do that as well. Many people who have never done training, but have walked with God, not necessarily seeking gifts have simply discovered that something works through them.

A BASIS FOR THE GIFTS OF THE SPIRIT

As a foundation for our study let me graft in the gifts of the spirit as listed in 1 Corinthians chapter 12.

> *1 Corinthians 12:1-11* [1] *Now concerning spiritual gifts, brethren, I do not want you to be ignorant:* [2] *You know that you were Gentiles, carried away to these dumb idols, however you were led.* [3] *Therefore I make known to you that no one speaking by the Spirit of God calls Jesus accursed, and no one can say that Jesus is Lord except by the Holy Spirit.* [4] ***There are diversities of gifts, but the same Spirit.*** [5] *There are differences of ministries, but the same Lord.* [6] *And there are diversities of activities, but it is the same God who works all in all.* [7] *But the manifestation of* ***the Spirit is given to each one for the profit of all***: [8] *for to one is given the word of wisdom through the Spirit, to another the word of knowledge through the same Spirit,* [9] *to another faith by the same Spirit, to another gifts of healings by the same Spirit,* [10] *to another the working of miracles, to another prophecy, to another discerning of spirits, to another different kinds of tongues, to another the interpretation of tongues.* [11] ***But one and the same Spirit works all these things, distributing to each one individually as He wills.*** *NKJV (emphasis mine)*

USING THE GIFTS

As we have said *spiritual gifts raise faith*. For someone to call out your details through a word of knowledge as you sit in a service shows that God knows you, and knows what your needs are. In the 1950s and 60s, William Branham from the U.S. was a famous healing evangelist. He used the word of knowledge to great affect calling out people with specific details such as where they were from, and street numbers, and this opened people up to the supernatural realm sparking off faith. He used to say that it was like lifting himself up to look over a fence, the higher he raised himself the more he could see.

Very few of us will ever be gifted to this level but we can all work in the gifts if our motivation is right. If you want to look good or be someone it may not be for you. However, if your motivation is that a person may go home without some ailment or other if you step out, and you just want to help, then you can be reasonably sure that what comes into your mind as you reach out will be from God.

Some time ago I was reading an article about fitness training and they mentioned the term; *hard gainers*. What this refers to is that some people are naturally athletic and only have to look at weights or do exercise and they put on muscle or get into shape. This seems to be true of spiritual gifts as well. Some are very gifted or *pre-wired* by God for spiritual gifts and it is easy for them, while others of us are *hard gainers*. The thing to know is that we can still get there and help people; it just might take some of us a little longer to learn how to position ourselves to hear from God. I think some of us who have to learn the process and work for it a little more, may at times be those who may be going to help others to get going as well.

King David learnt to trust that God was with him in the place of obscurity by killing lion and bear whilst tending his father's sheep. This was necessary before he was thrust into the limelight with Goliath. So it is that we often learn to trust that we are hearing God's voice whilst we are ministering to others in environments such as helping people through *Truth Encounters*. (Truth Encounters is a form of mental/emotional healing which will be covered in detail in Unit 4) .

I recall one morning calling out in the service that there was a lady who had been having headaches since she was a child. A lady of around 50 years old responded. I prayed a simple prayer commanding the spirit of infirmity to go and nothing visible or obvious happened. A few weeks later she realized that she had not had a migraine. At the time of writing nearly 5 years on she still has never had the complaint again. Normally we would minister to the roots of the migraines with *Truth Encounters*. But the lesson is that we know that God does not call out a complaint so that everyone knows that they have the issue, but rather because He is intending to heal them.

STEPPING OUT

I used to consider words of knowledge akin to loosening all of the wheel nuts off on your car, and speeding around a curvy road that ran along the edge of a cliff. In other words, you have a strong sense of an element of risk. After a while, you find that if your heart and motivation are right that God will always come through.

Two or three years ago in Kenya I called out a man with a liver problem and described him. This was the first word of knowledge that I had done in the meeting with several hundred Pastors attending. No response. I think God just smiles. The next few words that I had the people responded and were healed. Phew!

The following morning there was a lot of noise at the back of the church and the Pastor that I had described with the liver problem came in, and proceeded to testify that he had been healed when I called the word of knowledge, while he was still in Hospital! The lesson, God is faithful. If you will step out, He will step in!

People commonly come to you after the service and have not come out for fear or some other reason. A few years ago, again my first word of knowledge in a large church in Uganda, was a man with a head injury sitting in a particular area. No response. Between services he emerged, confirmed that this was where he was sitting and that he had the head injury. It's good to remember that the important thing is to help them and not your reputation.

Some people like to make spiritual gifts a part of their identity and worth, and feel that if they operate in them that they are somehow superior to others. The truth is that anyone can be used if they make themselves available. We often work in some activation on our schools so that people learn how simple it is. I recall one such meeting where we had several hundred Pastors attending the School of Healing and Freedom that we run. I invited anyone who wanted to be guided into bringing a *word of knowledge* to come forward. Nobody moved. Who wants to be the Pastor who didn't have a *word*, I get it! After a minute or two, four of five guys from the band came out. With a little guidance each of them called someone out. All of the complaints were there, and when they prayed for the people, all of them were healed which is what usually happens. The point is that God will use anyone who is willing to help and is prepared to trust Him. Many of the people that we train most likely go on to be much better at getting words than I am, and that is the point of discipling. Probably the reason that I expect that others will be able to get words is that I am so ordinary myself. As a result, I think that in all areas of ministry we train people in, that if I can do it, then anyone can.

If you don't reach out for a word you will never get one. If you have opportunity, ask God for a word that will help someone receive from Him, and you may be surprised at what comes into your mind. But I recommend that if you aren't going to bring it don't ask for it.

In my early days with this I was sharing in a healing elective at a conference. I had asked God for a couple of words and had something come to mind. As I went along, I called out the first one and she responded and I prayed for her. I thought; *Phew, made it.* And being relieved, I thought, *I will just leave it there.* The problem was that on the way home I was convicted that the other lady that I had had the *word* for may have gone home sick, and may have not had another opportunity for healing in her environment. I decided to not hold back if I had a word again in the future.

A couple of years ago one of our team was preaching in a large church in Africa, and in the course of the service I received a word regarding a man with trouble and pain in both his kidneys. The problem was that it was a very busy service and our team member had an altar call, so I had no opportunity to call him out for prayer. Through the week I was teaching afternoons and evenings at the church. On the Wednesday night service most of the church attended so I decided to see if he was there. I called out the complaint and where the man had been sitting in the Sunday service, and he responded and was healed.

The lesson is that God is faithful and His word will not return to Him void, but will accomplish all that He has purposed for it. In my experience I see the highest percentages of people are physically healed through a word of knowledge, and the greater the detail the greater the faith response.

THE INNATE ABILITY TO CONNECT TO THE DIMENSION OF GOD

We could perhaps use the analogy of the modern 'smart phone' to help us understand how the Holy Spirit works within in us, as a pathway to access another realm. Firstly, a smart phone is a machine with various features and capabilities already put in it by the designer. So, it can operate as a unit on its own without connection to outside resources. It has for example, storage and the ability to hold programs such as games, Bibles and so on. It has functions such as a calculator, clock, calendar and so forth that operate independently from its own programs and resources already loaded into the machine.

Secondly, it has a receptor that can connect it to the power of the air and receive messages and so on from outside of the unit. In much the same way we have programs, or things that we have learnt that can operate in our soul without outside sources. We can reason, calculate and remember items held in storage. We also have a spirit that has the capacity to pick up from outside sources. This human spirit is very limited in its fallen state because the program that it operates from is corrupted. So now signals received or perceived are distorted and unclear.

When the Holy Spirit comes into us and joins to our human spirit we are now connected to and have direct access to God's dimension.

So, in a sense the Holy Spirit is like a receptor in us, that is, a door to the spiritual Kingdom of God. As with a smart phone we can go 'online' with God and receive information and power that are coming from Him as the source. We could perhaps liken it to going 'online' and playing worship music from an outside source on our smartphone. The music is coming 'through' the smartphone, but is being accessed from an invisible realm.

In much the same way, with spiritual gifts, we deliberately connect with, and go 'online' with God to receive a message or instruction that comes through us, but did not originate with us.

If we are living a life of desiring intimacy with God, we will find that we are 'online' much of the time sharing our thoughts. From that place it is relatively easy to go the next step and seek to receive something specific. It is a spiritual connection with God who is Spirit that needs to be nurtured for the gifts to flourish.

> *John 4:23-24* [23] *Yet a time is coming and has now come when the true worshipers will worship the Father in spirit and truth, for they are the kind of worshipers the Father seeks.* [24] <u>*God is spirit*</u>*, and his worshipers must worship in spirit and in truth." NIV (emphasis mine)*

HOW CAN I RECEIVE A WORD OF KNOWLEDGE OR PROPHECY?

You begin by making yourself available to God and looking to Him to put something into your mind to help or encourage someone. We were doing a healing school in a camp environment at one time, and as we were drawing towards the end of the week it occurred to me that we had not reached out for a word of knowledge yet. So, I enquired of the Lord if there was a person that He wanted to touch. A throat problem came into my mind followed by the picture of the face of a person who had been attending the school. When I stood up a little later, I asked the lady if she had a throat problem and she confirmed that she did. The Pastor asked if we should pray for her. I commented that we were about to have communion which includes the healing provision of Jesus' broken body. After communion the lady reported that she was healed. The point is, would I have had something put in my mind if I had not reached out? No. So we begin by giving our mental faculties to God for His use.

The old saying is that; *God talks how you listen.*

Most gifts raise faith. Once one person is healed their testimony will raise further faith in others. There is a gift of faith where at times the faith that God has developed in you is not sufficient for the situation, and now, as you reach out you have a supernatural faith that is His. This faith refuses to accept an unresolved situation. I am sure that Jesus already knew that if the man in Matthew chapter 12 and verse 13 stretched out his hand that he would surely be healed. So, gifts are a stream or channel that God uses for healing various maladies.

LESSON

We can be looking for some big lightening bolt supernatural experience or word from God. The truth is that most times we have communication from Him in a simple way through our senses. We can test if it is God or not by asking ourselves a question. Did I deliberately come up with that through my thought and effort, or did it just come into my mind or I sensed it when I turned my attention to Him?

How to work with the Gifts of the Spirit
WORDS OF WISDOM

A '*Word of Wisdom*' is probably more common than people realize. Have you ever been sharing with someone and you hear wise words and understanding come out of your mouth? You may have attributed it to your own mind and knowledge, and yet, you know that you did not think it through to come to those conclusions. This could happen when sharing with someone, explaining scripture and application, or counselling someone in order to help them in their situation. Although you may not have acknowledged that it is the inspiration of the Holy Spirit, it most likely is Him working through your faculties as *the Spirit of Counsel.* (Isaiah 11:2)

Consequently, I think that *Word of Wisdom* is one of the more common, and unintentional manifestations and gifts of the Spirit. Unlike other gifts it is probably more often than not, not deliberately reached out for. It is very often just there when we need it. We are after all one with Him in Spirit, and so what we think are simply our thoughts are often mixed with His thoughts. (1 Cor. 6:17)

In all of the gifts we can have *the mind of Christ* and *know* things. (1 Cor.2:16)

We can of course reach out for a *word of wisdom*. After preaching a service at a church that we were visiting a young woman came over to our table. She stated that she was a nurse and about to go to work. She explained that the woman that she was caring for was bitter against God because she had lost her husband. The young lady asked, *have you got any wisdom for me, what can I tell her?*

In this case I was reaching out to the Lord even though it was organic, and I was not praying or going into some altered state or something. I was simply turning the attention of my mind to Him. I told her; *tell her that the Lord doesn't always get what He wants either. He does not want to see people suffer or be unhappy.*

I believe that this was a *word of wisdom*, and it was unmeditated on by me, I just suddenly understood it and relayed it.

On reflection afterwards, thinking it through, I would say that this is the truth. God does not want to see hungry children, wars, abuse or any other manifestations of the fallen world that we see. God has allowed people free will and choice, and therefore the people to blame are anyone in the world who is disobedient to His will. If every time I came to your house, I hit you over the head with a piece of wood, who would have the lump? You would! Who sinned? I did. Does God want me to do that? Never. The point is God does not force us….but He is always there to help us and meet our needs if we follow Him. The result of giving us this free will and choice is that God mostly lets us have what we want, rather than insisting on what He wants. Noteworthy though is that He is looking for a love response. If we love Him, we will obey Him.

WHO CAN WORK IN GIFTS, HOW DO YOU QUALIFY?
Jesus said that if we ask for bread God will not give us a stone. (MT 7:9)

So, it begins with desire to further the work of God. Good ground for us is a church environment where the gifts are taught and the work of the Holy Spirit is valued. Someone said that gifts are like kids receiving lollies or sweets, they have to be received. Depending on your calling, you are often drawn towards a particular gift which you can see will be valuable helping you achieve your task. For example, and apostolic person or an evangelist might be drawn to word of knowledge to facilitate healing ministries and so on.

Other people simply discover that they have a gift. My wife, even as a young believer, without effort began getting pictures for people. These were largely unbidden, often coming at prayer meetings, and she instinctively knew what God meant for the person by

the picture. So, we could say that some people are already 'wired' or intended by God to operate in a particular gift.

Still others come into gifts as their relationship with the Holy Spirit matures, or as they are exposed to ministries working in them. Others begin when they are set free from things such as fear or low self-image that hold them back.

As time goes by a believer may find other gifts becoming available to them.

HOW TO RECEIVE A PROPHETIC WORD OR A WORD OF KNOWLEDGE
When we talk about the gifts of the Spirit a mistake that is made is that people often look for some big thing. As we have already described we are one with God in spirit and so often the thoughts that sound in our mind like our own thoughts are actually His. Naturally this is most likely going to be the case when we give Him our attention and seek Him for something to help or encourage someone.

Remember God is pleased by faith, which is trusting in His goodness and provisions. As a consequence, we can be sure that He is pleased when we step out and learn by experience…. even if we don't get everything right to begin with…His pleasure is on us like any good Father because we are having a go.

With this mindset we can approach the gifts relaxed, not pressured, not straining or trying hard….and practice listening to inspired thoughts that will seem very much like our own. One difference is that we are looking for something to help others, and so you can be pretty sure that whatever is imprinted on your mind is God. (That is assuming that you are listening, and attentive to what comes into your mind, and not deliberately trying to make something up!)

 LESSON
We do not receive from God by trying hard. It is the practice of giving Him our attention, and being aware of what we are receiving.

SO HOW WILL THE HOLY SPIRIT SPEAK TO US?
The old saying is that *'God talks how we listen'*. Some people think in words, others in pictures. So, the Holy Spirit may put things into our minds in the following ways: Thoughts, pictures, impressions, sudden understanding, scriptures and so on.

A friend of mine who is a well-known international prophet says that sometimes it begins like the faintest impression, but as you look at it more detail will begin to appear. It is like a photo developed in a dark room. As you isolate it and close out other things that could detract from seeing it clearly form begins to appear.

Beginners might get a picture, or some words or know something and bring that. For someone who by reason of use has developed their senses they might receive one thing, and then another, and another….and as they loop these things together, they may bring quite a long word. But at the beginning may only receive one thing. The point is that we need to be faithful to bring the thoughts and phrases that God gives us, or share the pictures and impressions. We have to step out.

 LESSON
When we are faithful with little, we can be given much. So, it is good to develop a gift, this could include study from others about how the gift works.
So, we go through a little process that looks something like this; (eventually it happens automatically when we are in a situation that demands gifts)

1. Reach out for inspiration from God…. open your mind and give Him your attention. (this can be likened to 'going online' with the internet, connecting up)

2. Something comes into your mind that is not the result of conscious thought. (In other words, you did not think *what can I come up with*, there was just something there, in the mailbox, so to speak. You have mail!)

3. The message or word is examined. If it is prophecy, you will be looking at, *what is God wanting to communicate to this person?*

4. Now you step out and bring the message/ or word. How you do this will depend on your personality, but you should be natural and not try to assume some form or 'wear someone else's armor,' just be yourself, otherwise you are not basing what you are doing on truth. If you are not trying to be falsely spiritual, the Holy Spirit will quickly take and confirm the word to the heart of the hearer.

5. The word is then received by the person and confirmed by their response whether or not it is correct and for them. Some people will have an emotional response as the Holy Spirit touches something deeply inside them.

6. Now, if received, it falls to the person to respond to the word in an appropriate way. One of my good friends, Faylene Sparkes, has an amazing, well developed prophetic gift, and she puts it this way. If God is giving you a word to do with the plans that He has for you then you can take it as: *an invitation to become, God prophecies to your potential, it is not a done deal.* You still have to walk with God into your destiny and at times sow into where God wants to take you, which requires faith.

Prophecy will not be condemning, it will not be demanding that you try harder or telling you that you are not doing enough, it will be encouraging, strengthening and comforting.

> *1 Corinthians 14:3 But everyone who prophesies speaks to men for their strengthening, encouragement and comfort. NIV*

All can prophecy, but not all are prophets. Some people are called to equip the saints in this area, and have been drawn to developing this gift and making it their main ministry.

Perhaps the clearest way to illustrate the difference between prophecy and the word of knowledge would be in explaining activations, where we help people begin to work in these gifts. Fundamentally *prophecy* is receiving a communication for a person or people from God. A *word of knowledge* is going to also be inspired information, but will normally relate to a condition that the person has. This could be a physical problem, or an emotional, relational, financial, or other kind of circumstance that God is wanting to resolve. It is received in the same way as prophecy, with the differentiation that you are not looking for what God is wanting to communicate to the subject, but rather what their problem is so that He can meet the need.

 LESSON
Some people will be more drawn to one gift that another. This often relates to the particular 'tools' that they may need to outwork their calling.

ACTIVATIONS
We often have to *'activate'* people by getting them to give God the use of their faculties and minds, turning their attention to receiving from Him. We do this with simple exercises, taking very small steps and giving God the opportunity to put something in our minds.

STEPS TO ACTIVATING PROPHECY
1. Have your group break into pairs, preferably people that they do not know, or know well. Have them face each other, with each of them facing a wall.

2. Now you have them meet the Holy Spirit half way, so to speak, by giving him some kind of landing pad…by giving them something fairly simple to reach out for. So, this means that they are not just standing around waiting for something to come into their mind. For example, we ask the Holy Spirit to put a person from the Bible on their minds. Then we ask them to ask God why He put this particular character in their minds, and what is He saying about the person being prophesied over because He gave them this person.

3. We have them take it in turns sharing what they received with each other.

4. We then repeat the process asking the Holy Spirit to bring to mind items such as a scripture, could be an activation, words of a song another, something from nature, (E.G. Jesus called Peter a 'rock' and prophesied that because of this solidness He was going to build His church on him) and so on. You can make up your own. By the time your group has done three or four activations in a row other thoughts that haven't been propagated will begin to come to mind. Eventually with practice and repetition they will be able to reach out, and God will just put something in their minds without prompting. Some will be more gifted and pick this up more quickly than others. Often once the thoughts begin to come there is a spontaneous flow of thought. *We first saw activations of this type modelled through the ministry of Faylene Sparkes*

STEPS TO ACTIVATING WORD OF KNOWLEDGE

1. I will quite often ask if there are people in the meeting who have never given a *word of knowledge*. I will usually ask 3 to 5 people to come out the front and to line up facing the congregation.

2. I will then ask the Holy Spirit to imprint a physical complaint on their minds. It could be something like a particular back problem, or a knee injury or perhaps some kind of sickness.

3. Once they have called out the complaint that has come into their minds, *(and remember it will seem like their own thoughts, and could be words or a picture, or even feel something sympathetic in their own body)* We are then looking for detail to raise faith.

4. So, now I ask them if they have a slight leaning to one side of the building, left, or right? Once they have chosen a side, I again ask them that if they had to pick would they think the person was at the back of the meeting, middle or front.

5. Next we have the complaint and where we feel that the person might be sitting. Next we check to see if there is a sense of what gender they might be. If they don't have a leading about where they are sitting or about gender, we do not push it but most people do have a sense.

6. Now we announce something such as; there is a lady sitting down the back on this side of the building who has a kidney problem. Over the years I have been amazed at how often following this process to activate people who have never given a *word of knowledge*, that the person and complaint is exactly there. God is faithful! Sometimes in large churches I have seen the members of the church get very excited as the subject of *the word* puts their hand up…. proving that gifts of the Spirit can work easily through any of them. Nearly always everyone who participates receives a word from the Holy Spirit.

7. We have the people who have been identified come out to be prayed for by the person who received *the word*. The exciting thing is almost every time the person getting prayed for receives healing for their affliction.

IN THE SERVICE OR OUT OF THE SERVICE

We have just described how people might receive during a service; they could even wait on the Lord for something whilst sitting in church. Another way that you can receive from the Lord is to open your mind to *a word* before the meeting even begins. If you are a minister you can be asking the Lord for something even as you lay in bed in the morning. At times this affords time to let it develop in your mind and you may receive a great deal of detail which can release significant faith.

Words of knowledge can raise faith in a meeting and open the way for a lot of healing even beyond using the gift.

Note: God is not the author of disorder. You need to be submitted to the authority of the leaders in whatever environment that you find yourself in. It is important that you have permission to operate spiritual gifts in places where you are not in charge.

LESSON

Praying in the spirit as a part of your daily routine develops a sensitivity to the presence of the Holy Spirit which makes it easier to access the gifts. They are His gifts, not yours, so you need to make sure that you give Him plenty of use of your faculties to help you receive. *The first time that I saw an activation of this type was through the ministry of Ron Strode.*

DISCERNING OF SPIRITS

Different people seem to have different ideas about exactly what discerning of spirits is as a gift. To *discern* is to recognize or find out, and carries the sense of being able to distinguish one thing from another. In this context, discerning of spirits is understanding what you are looking at. *(Spirit of Understanding. Isaiah 11:2)*

This could apply to demonic influence on a person's life, or whether or not their own human spirit is co operating with worldly or satanic precepts. We see Jesus exercising this gift, naturally seeing which spiritual influence the disciples James and John were under. Notably He did not tell a demon to come out, knowing that this was spirit working over them from outside their being.

> *Luke 9:55 But He turned and rebuked them, and said, "You do not know what manner of spirit you are of". NKJV*

It could also relate to people discerning the presence and affect of the Holy Spirit, in an individual or even in a meeting.

OTHER GIFT SUMMARIES

Here we will briefly comment on the remaining gifts in the 1 Corinthians 12 passage.
<u>Gift of faith:</u> We have already mentioned a supernatural faith that is beyond our normal faith that can be present at times.

<u>Gifts of Healings:</u> Some people consider that this applies to the fact that each individual healing is a gift, which could well be the case. There are in addition to physical healings, healing of the broken hearted, healing of relationships and so on. So, I think that healings plural may apply to these different works of the Spirit in bringing healing to different areas of the human person.

<u>Working of Miracles:</u> Some translations say the *working of miracles*; others use terms such as *miraculous powers.* In the Greek language it certainly refers to the operation of literal *dunamis* power (Spirit of Power. Isaiah 11:2). This is power that most commonly comes through the hands of a believer, and is not the result of cognitive effort. It is simply there.

<u>Different kinds of tongues:</u> This is generally accepted as a tongue that is different from your normal prayer language, and is a form of prophecy which is usually interpreted by another believer who is given the meaning of the message brought in tongues.

STREAM 4 'REPENTANCE'

Many people do not want to *change their thinking or reconsider their ways*, which as we have stated is what *repent* essentially means. They are happy being in control of their own lives and doing what they want. And yet an unrepentant heart is often a large blockage to receiving healing of any kind.

> *Galatians 6:7-8* [7] *"Do not be deceived, God is not mocked; for whatever a man sows, that he will also reap.* [8] *For he who sows to his flesh will of the flesh reap corruption, but he who sows to the Spirit will of the Spirit reap everlasting life." NKJV*

You can imagine somebody who reads in the Bible that drunkards will not inherit the kingdom of God, but they persist in drinking a bottle of whisky a night. Why would they be surprised if they end up with liver disease? Is that what God wants for them? No.

I have never seen God not be prepared to free someone from an emotional, physical or spiritual problem regardless of the condition of their lives. So, we are not confusing repentance with only being able to be healed if you do everything right, never sin, and are perfect. The fact that you come to God wanting His help to change is repentance. However, many do not come, being content in their own solutions and so do not receive their freedom …. or perhaps want healing so that they can get into more mischief.

> *James 4:1-3* [1] *What causes fights and quarrels among you? Don't they come from your desires that battle within you?* [2] *You want something but don't get it. You kill and covet, but you cannot have what you want. You quarrel and fight. You do not have, because you do not ask God.* [3] *When you ask, you do not receive, because you ask with wrong motives, that you may spend what you get on your pleasures. NIV*

GOD KNOWS THE END FROM THE BEGINNING

Let us qualify the need for repentance through the eyes of grace and mercy. A man responded to a word of knowledge a number of years ago and was set free from a spirit of infirmity and healed. We discovered three years later that He was in an adulterous relationship at the time of the prayer, and yet God healed him and he remains healed to this day!

Would you have healed him? Perhaps not? When the relationship was exposed three years after the healing the man responded by coming to get help. He had been in denial, and had not let himself accept what he was doing just as King David had done with Bathsheba. He received emotional healing of the rejection that led him into the relationship, and deliverance from associated spiritual strongholds. His Christianity continues to bloom and increase today. Underneath he hated himself for what he was doing all of the time. God looks on the heart and knows the end from the beginning; just like Zacchaeus he knows who will repent.

Let me reiterate, repentance is the desire to follow God's ways not necessarily the ability within yourself to achieve it, or having already attained it. Very often we need God's help to accomplish repentance, and the changing of our thinking and reconsidering our ways is an ongoing journey. It begins with accepting the fact that we are out of order with God's ways. We confess and agree with how He sees our issue and take responsibility for our part in it.

REPENTANCE AND ALIGNMENT

Many people ask God to step in and change their situation or circumstances. At times they bemoan, God why don't you do something? God could quite rightly be forgiven by responding, *I did, I sent forth my Word and if you did it, and obeyed it, as a hearer and doer your situation would be healed and rectified!*

On many occasions I have seen people going through horrendous emotional turmoil with their marriage partner. People outside the relationships struggle to understand why God does not step in and resolve the situation. After all, they are Christians. The people themselves pray to God to fix the relationship, or shut off from God considering Him to be unfair or uncaring because nothing is changing. What is going on?

The truth is that usually one or more of the people in the relationship are unrepentant about their attitudes. This could be either because they know the Bible but don't want to follow its instructions, feeling that somehow it does not apply to them. Or possibly they simply have never read it, or are ignorant of what it says having not been taught.

The most common reason for relational disharmony is simple lack of forgiveness. In other words, one or both of the partners simply cannot forgive the other person for not measuring up to what they think that they should be. They have set up a standard of what they want, or feel that the other person should do or be for them, and are continually offended that the person falls short. Someone has said that we *should not let what someone is not get in the way of appreciating who they are.* The Bible puts it this way.

> *Proverbs 19:11 A man's wisdom gives him patience; it is to his glory to overlook an offense. NIV*

It is to our glory to overlook an offense because we are exhibiting the nature of the glorious one, our God. He is gracious, abounding in love and forgiveness. As His children so we should also be!

When I was a young Christian, I used to boast about the Word of God that everything in the Bible works…. if you do it. It's true! *(I wrote inside the cover of my first Bible what B-I-B-L-E meant to me: Blueprint Inside Bearing Life Everlasting)*

This lack of forgiveness often leads to another sin in the form of control. If you don't accept people as they are, or how you think that they should be, (according to you, not God) then you will often impose your will on theirs and try to make them conform to the image that you have for them. This is a perversion of created order and the will area, and could be termed as low-grade witchcraft. For people who exhibit this kind of behavior there is often a lot of turmoil in their relationships, their emotions and their bodies. Repentance must come first so that God can begin to minister to these problems.

Sadly, churches are largely unequipped to help repentant people to receive God's freedom through the ministry of the Holy Spirit. In any case the scripture can't be reshaped to suit yourself, and the statements on unforgiveness and its implications for a lack of blessing and resolution in your circumstances remains.

> *Matthew 6:14-15* ¹⁴ *For if you forgive men when they sin against you, your heavenly Father will also forgive you.* ¹⁵ *But if you do not forgive men their sins, your Father will not forgive your sins. NIV (Emphasis mine) [Remember a sin against you is something that is offensive to you]*

Unfortunately, unforgiving Christians often can't understand why their lives are full of torment and they feel tortured in their situations, soul and body. Matthew Chapter 18 sheds some light on this. It is never Gods desire that we undergo discipline and suffering. However, extending grace and forgiveness truly are not optional.

> *Matthew 18:34-35* ³⁴ *"And his master was angry, and delivered him to the torturers until he should pay all that was due to him.* ³⁵ *"So My heavenly Father also will do to you if each of you, from his heart, does not forgive his brother his trespasses." NKJV*

LESSON
We need to be aligned with the ways of the Kingdom for the provisions of God to flow freely to us. Perhaps we could liken it to disconnecting the drain pipe from the roof of your house, and then wondering why our water tank is not full. We have to have the pipe both connected, and properly lined up to receive the supply when it comes.

GOD LOOKS AT THE HEART AND ENCOURAGES US TO REPENT

I was at a healing meeting that an acquaintance was running at one time and a lady came out and received healing through his ministry. He asked if her husband was in the meeting and she reported that she didn't have a husband, she had a partner and he was present. Between meetings a Pastor friend was speaking of the lady and asked me if I would have drawn alongside her and let her know that she was living in sin? I responded that I would not; I would have a coffee with her and talk about how amazing God is and how awesome her healing was. Eventually, somewhere down the track, at the right time, no doubt her relationship would come up. Our mission is to connect people to God, not to make them perfect. He already did that through redemption, so we need to have grace and patience as they grow in their desire to respond to God's goodness and kindness with repentance.

> *Romans 2:4 "Or do you despise the riches of His goodness, forbearance, and longsuffering, not knowing that the goodness of God leads you to repentance?" NKJV*

This lady did not have a problem with God, or the Evangelist who the healing came through. But she might well have had issues with a church that dealt with her in a way other than the revealed character of God. Later her *partner* came up for prayer and received healing as well.

We could suggest then that repentance is an attitude of the heart that God is looking for, as opposed to having no weaknesses or shortcomings. He is looking for us to choose Him as a response towards His goodness and the freedom that He brings to us. So, if we posture His warnings in that way as a matter of love, we see it all in a different light.

> *John 5:14 Afterward Jesus found him in the temple, and said to him, "See, you have been made well. Sin no more, lest a worse thing come upon you" (NKJV).*

His merciful dealings with our failings demand that we rethink how we are going to live. When the woman who had been found in adultery was brought to Jesus, He knew that ALL sinned and fell short of the glory of God without exception. The church is a group of ALLS who have received His grace. When the accusers put themselves under His authority for a decision, He challenged any without sin to cast the first stone, knowing full well that under the law if they claimed to be without sin, they would have to be stoned themselves. Jesus forgave and extended grace to the woman instructing her to rethink and change how she lived. As someone put it there are no special sins.

> *John 8:10-11 ¹⁰ When Jesus had raised Himself up and saw no one but the woman, He said to her, "Woman, where are those accusers of yours? Has no one condemned you?" ¹¹ She said, "No one, Lord." And Jesus said to her, "Neither do I condemn you; go and sin no more". NKJV*

REPENTANCE AND EXPECTATION

Evangelists running healing meetings early last century would look for expectation of healing in the eyes of those coming for prayer and considered this to be visible faith. They were fairly certain in those days that those who had no intention of attending church or ever serving God need not to expect to get healed.

> *1 John 3:21-22 ²¹ "Beloved, if our heart does not condemn us, we have confidence toward God. ²² And whatever we ask we receive from Him, because we keep His commandments and do those things that are pleasing in His sight". NKJV*

Our hearts could condemn us because we have no intention of changing our ways or following God, or because we have a condemning belief about ourselves that needs healing first. In our times I have even seen God heal even skeptics, as He knows where they will go from there. They may well prove to be the best at testifying to His power and willingness to heal. It is often unchurched people with no expectations of what should happen who are touched by God in healing meetings, as opposed to those who have had the experience of sitting in a Church with wrong beliefs, and consequently have never seen anyone healed.

STREAM 5 'SANCTIFICATION'/ [RIGHTEOUSNESS?]

As we are conformed to the likeness of Christ, as we have mentioned, we will also be conforming to the Word of God. This holds health benefits for us, for example, we no longer respond by holding bitterness, resentment or unforgiveness. Instead of releasing negative hormones, as we grow in love, grace, joy, acceptance and positive emotions we release healthy chemicals into our bodies.

I once read an article that stated that our bodies should be slightly alkaline and disease cannot prosper within us. Along with a long list of foods that it claimed were acidic was a list of negative emotions that also produced acidity. Dealing with these toxic responses through finding our way to line up with the Word of God therefore is a doorway to health.

> *Proverbs 3:6-8* ⁶ *"In all your ways acknowledge Him, And He shall direct your paths.* ⁷ *Do not be wise in your own eyes; Fear the LORD and depart from evil.* ⁸ *It will be health to your flesh, And strength to your bones" NKJV*

The following passage encourages us to meditate deeply, deliberately and continually on the word of God. It carries a promise that as we are hearers and doers that these alignments with God's order will bring health into your physical being.

> *Proverbs 4:21-23* ²¹ *"Don't lose sight of my words. Let them penetrate deep within your heart,* ²² *for they bring life and radiant health to anyone who discovers their meaning.* ²³ *Above all else, guard your heart, for it affects everything you do" NLT*

An area of the medical world known as Bio psychiatry proposes that if we could have everybody thinking properly then no one would get sick. As we have described already, this is because there would be chemical and electrical balance in the body and all of the 12 major systems would work together in perfect harmony.

In a sense when Christ is given the headship of His body then it works together in harmony, because it outworks in the natural world all of His perfect thoughts and ways. When our head has perfect Biblical thoughts and deeds we can expect to be in perfect health as well. For the world this is simply an unrealistic ideal. For the body of Christ, as we conform to the word, and our thinking is sanctified by the Holy Spirit, and we have our hearts healed, we can expect the final outworking to be improved health and longevity.

> *Psalm 92:13-14* ¹³ *"Those who are planted in the house of the LORD Shall flourish in the courts of our God.* ¹⁴ *They shall still bear fruit in old age; They shall be fresh and flourishing" NKJV*

LESSON
As our thinking is made Holy through sanctification, then the end of the line is our outer person or body which conforms to our thought life. Perfect thoughts, beliefs and consequent actions result in physical health.

SIN AND SICKNESS
Another element of sanctification, through receiving God's truth and conforming to His word, is knowing the truth about redemption and God's promise of healing. Sin and sickness are linked and so when we examine the scriptures, we see them both being dealt with at the same time.

> *Psalm 103:2-3* ² *"Praise the LORD, I tell myself, and never forget the good things he does for me.* ³ *He forgives all my sins and heals all my diseases." NLT*

In the case of the paralytic man we see Jesus saying directly that forgiving sin and healing of the body are exactly the same thing. He could have said that the man's sins were forgiven and let them carry the man out on his stretcher. The evidence that his sins were forgiven was his healing by Jesus.

> *Matthew 9:5-6* ⁵ *"Is it easier to say, 'Your sins are forgiven' or 'Get up and walk'?* ⁶ *I will prove that I, the Son of Man, have the authority on earth to forgive sins." Then Jesus turned to the paralyzed man and said, "Stand up, take your mat, and go on home, because you are healed!" NLT*

Notably a ministry of the Church is to proclaim the forgiveness of God to the World.

> *John 20:21-23* ²¹ *So Jesus said to them again, "Peace to you! As the Father has sent Me, I also send you." ²² And when He had said this, He breathed on them, and said to them, "Receive the Holy Spirit. ²³ "If you forgive the sins of any, they are forgiven them; if you retain the sins of any, they are retained."* NKJV

Even with communion we see that Jesus paid for our sins with His blood as the Lamb of God and also provided for our healing with His broken body (1 Corinthians chapter 11). The book of James chapter 5 and verses 15 and 16 require that as a preface to the prayer of faith making us well that we confess our sins. There have been significant healing revivals that have occurred in previous eras as well as our own times that have been based around the confession of sin in this way.

This is accepting that we are out of order and that sin is implicated in our problem.

Confess simply means *say the same as*. So, we are taking responsibility for our actions and behavior and saying the same about it as does the word of God. This agreement with God deals with the Lordship issue and nullifies our rebellion making us candidates for healing.

The final scripture that I am going to use to illustrate the connection between forgiveness of sins and healing, points us back to the stream of repentance. In the middle of the verse it relates to changing our thinking in regards to what we are living for. This is an important component of being positioned to receive the healing promised through redemption.

Peter is quoting from Isaiah 53:5 which says by His wounds *you are* healed pointing ahead in time to the cross, whereas the New Testament passage says that *you have been* healed pointing back to the finished work of Jesus.

> *1 Peter 2:24 "He himself bore our sins in his body on the tree, so **that we might die to sins** and live for righteousness; by his wounds **you have been** healed." NIV (emphasis mine)*

It is noteworthy that the message that we are instructed to preach is repentance and forgiveness of sins. In other words, change our thinking in regards to how we live and what or whom we are living for in terms of our choices and actions. The forgiveness of God is the grace that He extends to us as we repent and change our thinking about the things of God. (Luke 24:47). Sadly, this message no longer appears in some of the newer translations.

> *Luke 24:47 and repentance and forgiveness of sins will be preached in his name to all nations. NIV*

NOTE: the word translated 'forgiveness' is 859. Aphesis (Reference, Strong's Concordance) which contains the additional meanings: G863; freedom; (fig.) pardon: --deliverance, forgiveness, liberty, remission. These as a response to our change of thinking, reconsidering our ways in a positive light.

LESSON

So, when we propose a grace message that does not include a change of thinking (repentance), in terms of how we regard our behavior in the light of Biblical standards, then our concept is inaccurate.

STREAM 6 'SPIRITUAL RELEASE'

We will cover this subject with all of Unit 5 being devoted to it. We can state here however that many problems, including the spiritual, mental, emotional, relational, sexual, addictive and often physical issues have a demonic component.

Often what we believe opens the door, and leads us towards giving a place to the devil.

> *Ephesians 4:27 nor give **place** to the devil. NKJV (emphasis mine)*

Place in the Greek language = topos > means a location, or position. We could say by extension, somewhere to stand or to operate from. There will be more detail in Unit 5.

Offering *a place* can be our solution to our deceptive perception of reality, and this causes us to choose the sin that the World offers. We have the dynamic of pressures from the World that propose, as in the garden, that following the sins on offer are what we need, and will make us happy.

> *1 John 2:15-16 ¹⁵ Stop loving this evil world and all that it offers you, for when you love the world, you show that you do not have the love of the Father in you. ¹⁶ For the world offers only the lust for physical pleasure, the lust for everything we see, and pride in our possessions. These are not from the Father. They are from this evil world. NLT*

This encouragement to take up sinful practices comes through sources such as worldly media, but also often through relationships and people who are bound themselves, although they may not be aware of their captivity, and willfully participate.

> *1 Corinthians 15:33 Do not be misled: "Bad company corrupts good character." NIV*

Giving *place* to the devil, as a course of action, can also be a predictable response to belief based hurt or distortions of our identity's. If you don't believe the devil exists or seeks your cooperation you will see no problem with your behavior. The door at times is a generationally inherited weakness or propensity to particular sin, and we will discuss this in a later module.

In the event that a spirit has come through a breach, via a weak mental or emotional moment, a demon may be present to hold onto this weakness. Our thinking and beliefs release hormones and neurotransmitters in order to chemically elaborate the feelings or responses to our thoughts that we call emotions. When these hormones and belief-based emotions are imbalanced then our physical self will be prone to disease. Considering that demons amplify, intensify, and replay beliefs producing emotions, we see that they can greatly accelerate, worsen and promote an environment producing the likelihood of disease and other issues.

Often, we see physical healing come when a *spirit of infirmity* (weakness) is addressed. The *ground* or *terrain* that it has many times are the deceptive *beliefs* that are held, which eventually produce disease. Of course, disease can be present because of emotional imbalances without demonic interference, but it may not be as serious, or it may emerge more slowly as we age. Obviously spiritually influenced cultural environments such as high sugar and high fat diets, alcoholism, drugs and so on contribute to the ability for the diseases to prosper and proliferate as the body's defenses are broken down.

The problem that we are often confronted with is that we may be aware of the spiritual element of an issue in a person, and as a result, we very much want to see them free. However, it is very difficult to get a demon out of a person who does not believe they have one, or deliver those who are not prepared to deal with the ground that gives it *place* through healing or repentance. So, no matter how much you want to cast out spirits, you need to remember that you have authority over evil spirits and not the person's free will. Clearly if they have placed themselves in your prayer line, they have put themselves under provisions that might come through you to help them. Even the Gadarene demoniac with his legion of demons came to Jesus for help.

> Mark 5:6 *"When he saw Jesus from afar, he ran and worshiped Him." NKJV*

Some Biblical exceptions to requiring the desire of a person to be free seems to be if a person is in a meeting or interfering with the business that God has you on. In those arenas you are under the authority of Christ, and consequently over the power of the enemy to achieve the outcome that God has purposed for the ministry time.

Some time ago we were ministering in Micronesia and a woman who was suffering from terminal cancer was set free in a prayer line from a spirit, along with a great release of grief. Many people carry a great sadness relating to matters such as the loss of identity or lack of affirmation that they have suffered. This can be associated with bitterness towards others who have damaged self-worth, as well as resentment towards self, for not being what is seemingly needed to be valued. In this case, we later heard that, the result of her deliverance was healing of her body. So, the spiritual power which had a *place* working within was implicated in her disease. Unit 5 is devoted to this subject entirely, but suffice to say here that being freed from evil spirits is a major healing stream. Some people suggest that one third of Jesus ministry was setting people free from demons.

> Luke 6:18-19 ¹⁸ *as well as those who were tormented with unclean spirits. And they were healed.* ¹⁹ *And the whole multitude sought to touch Him, for power went out from Him and healed them all. NKJV*

STREAM 7 'TRUTH ENCOUNTERS'

Unit 4 is entirely devoted to explaining this important stream which has implications for bringing healing and freedom to all of the 7 major problem areas that afflict mankind. A *Truth Encounter* is when the Holy Spirit sets a person free from a wrong belief that is held in their *hearts*.

> John 8:32 *"And you shall know the truth, and the truth shall make you free."* *NKJV*

The Bible states that the things that are able to affect our *hearts* are involved and related to every part of our lives.

> Proverbs 4:23 **Above all else**, *guard your heart, for it affects* **everything** *you do. NLT (emphasis mine)*

The Apostle Paul states that the problems that we have are not unique to ourselves, but rather that we all struggle with the same things because we have all been programmed in our hearts to believe similar things.

> *1 Corinthians 10: 13 No temptation has overtaken you except such <u>as is common to man</u>; but God is faithful, who will not allow you to be tempted beyond what you are able, but with the temptation <u>will also make the way of escape</u>, that you may be able to bear it. NKJV (emphasis mine)*

We all struggle with problems that are common to humanity, because we share common *beliefs*, often relating to our identity, which open us to temptation. The way of escape is many times the ministry of the Holy Spirit in bringing *truth* to these *wrong beliefs*.

THE NEED TO BE SET FREE ON THE INSIDE

I recall hearing a story from a minister whose group had been ministering to the hurting and lost. One day a prostitute came for prayer. She had lost an eye to a disease and now was suffering with the disease in her remaining eye. As the story went, not only did God heal the diseased eye as a response to prayer, but He also did a creative miracle and replaced the other eye. She was back in prostitution within a week! There was a profound miracle in her body, but no response or healing in her soul or spiritual condition.

I remember a man who one night had an amazing miracle healing in his leg. He then went home and proceeded to abuse his wife and children. Nothing had happened in resolving the issues in his soul. In God's order I believe there is a high priority on mental, emotional and resultant relational healing.

> *Matthew 5:29-30 [29] "If your right eye causes you to sin, pluck it out and cast it from you; for it is more profitable for you that one of your members perish, than for your whole body to be cast into hell". [30] "And if your right hand causes you to sin, cut it off and cast it from you; for it is more profitable for you that one of your members perish, than for your whole body to be cast into hell." NKJV*

In Unit 4 we will describe some of the many cases of physical healing that we have seen as a result of dealing with *beliefs of the heart*. These have occurred in the process of having a soul that prospers.

Many people cannot receive healing by faith because they believe in their hearts that they are not worthy or important, or perhaps that God does not care about them. More often than people realize, these beliefs need to be resolved before they can accept healing for their bodies through the provisions of the cross. Anything is possible if you have faith, so it is reasonable that in a meeting where believing for a miracle is running high, that if your body can be healed, then deliverance or some level of emotional release is of course possible.

Typically, in a really good meeting where many are receiving various kinds of healing by faith, there can be as many as 5 or 10% of people receive physical healing. Can I suggest then that the figures for emotional healing, if it is occurring, would not be expected to be greater than this percentage? In contrast, almost all of people who come for release through *Truth Encounters* and commit to the process predictably receive their freedom. So, God heals any way that you are able to receive.

If people cannot receive physical, emotional healing or deliverance in a faith meeting, that does not mean that God has given up on freeing them. We should not be saying; *Oh well, you didn't have enough faith, try again another time!* It may well be that God has a different pathway to healing, and He certainly never gives up on being committed to fulfilling the provisions of His Word to us.

Another point is that if only 5 or 10% of people are able to receive healing in a faith meeting, what is happening with the other 90 – 95% of people. Normally they have wrong believing or doctrine in the mind which needs to be resolved through good teaching. They may also hold wrong believing in the heart which needs to be dealt with through healing by the Holy Spirit.

Remember that there are thoughts that you hear in your mind, and also thoughts that you may not necessarily hear or be aware of, that are automatized and are proceeding from your heart. We have already quoted Hebrews chapter ten and verse fourteen which states that those who are being sanctified are already perfected through Christ. God declares us as perfect and this means that to Him, we are both sinless and healed through Jesus who dealt with both of those needs for us on the cross. We receive this provision by believing it sufficiently that we come to Him in faith for His promise. Many don't receive because they do not seek Him or His gifts in this regard because of unbelief or wrong believing. So, we could say that most people have enough faith, a tiny mustard seed, to be changed, but hold incorrect beliefs at some level that nullifies the positive confession.

Some people say that we need to get our hearts right with God. More often than not I think we need to bring our hearts to God and He makes them right. King David certainly understood that it was God who would create a clean heart in him and not his own self effort. (Psalm 51:10)

> *Psalm 51:10 Create in me a clean heart, O God, And renew a steadfast spirit within me. NKJV*

It is clear from scripture that God is the only one who knows what is in our *hearts*. In Unit 4 we will work through how we can cooperate with Him in giving Him access to our inner parts as King David did.

> *Psalm 139:23-24* [23] *Search me, O God, and know my heart; test me and know my anxious thoughts.* [24] *See if there is any offensive way in me, and lead me in the way everlasting. NIV*

Understanding ministry to our hearts which are broken is probably the most important Unit on the school in terms of total transformation.

> *Hebrews 4: 12 For the word of God is living and powerful, and sharper than any two-edged sword, piercing even to the division of soul and spirit, and of joints and marrow, and is a discerner of the* **thoughts and intents of the heart**. *NKJV (emphasis mine)*

As we proceed to Unit 4 we will illustrate that the heart has beliefs that produce thoughts. Dealing with these are critical to our wholeness in every area.

UNIT FOUR

PART 1: Truth Encounters: A Biblical Perspective

HOW WE BEGAN MINISTERING 'TRUTH ENCOUNTERS'

In the early 1990s we had an elderly man in our Church who used to tell me how he had been wonderfully set free of the problems he carried. The vehicle of his freedom was a process he termed the 'healing of the memories.' He was in his 80s at the time and reported that these miraculous changes had occurred in the early 1960s. He would periodically reminisce about the amazing changes that God had brought into his life through that ministry. He was a delightful old man of God who went on to live until he was 94 years old.

In those days I did not fully understand the concept, and to be honest, at the time for me it was all about setting people free from demonic influences and teaching them to come into line with Biblical principles in order to stay free. That is still good advice, but we have come to understand that there is usually much more to the picture of being completely free than this.

Around that time, I read a book by an Australian man by the name of Thomas Foster. His publication was titled 'Miracles of Inner Healing.' This was first available in 1975 and had a subheading on the front cover stating, 'How Jesus Heals Your Memory.' Although I found the topic interesting, I was fairly convinced that what we were doing was all that was needed.

A few years later I met one of his daughters and her husband. They remain good friends to this day. They have been in ministry themselves for many years and report that they first heard Thomas Foster speak on the subject in the early 1970s. There was a later edition of the publication which I believe is still reprinted from time to time today. Later I went on to find two books on the priority of inner healing, written by David Seamands entitled; 'Healing for Damaged Emotions.' (First printing 1981), and the second entitled 'Healing of Memories' (First printing 1985).

OUR FIRST EXPERIENCES OF GOD HEALING IN THIS WAY

In 1998, we had a lady booked in for a ministry session with a fear problem. At that time, 'healing of the memories' as it was called, did not fit into my World. It was still not a part of what we understood as to how to help people get the freedom that God has promised for us. We had however come to realize from the scriptures that beginnings were important. When the man in Mark chapter nine brought his mute son to Jesus for freedom, Jesus asked him this question,

> Mark 9:21 "How long has this been happening to him?" And he said, "From childhood" NKJV.

Another example noting beginning points would be the woman who was bent over with the Spirit of Infirmity in Luke chapter 13.

Luke 13:11 "And behold, there was a woman who had a spirit of infirmity eighteen years, and was bent over and could in no way raise herself up" NKJV.

Something happened eighteen years ago that was an entry point for the spirit, and apparently nineteen years ago she did not have the problem.

It became clear to us that Jesus was looking for the origin of the problem; the *beginning point.* This indicated that there was some event or experience which was the starting place for what was going on now. In other words, the beginning point for ministry is an individual being asked to re-member *and describe* what had happened at a particular time in their lives? We knew enough from the scriptures to know that whatever problem a person came to us with, *something had happened somewhere* to produce the issue. This 'cause and effect' could be an event of some kind or possibly a generational influence behind the presenting situation.

In the case of this lady with the fear issue, we began asking questions regarding what she feared and where it had come from. It didn't take long and we accessed a memory that held the fear feeling and the belief producing the anxiety. As was my custom I prayed for her, asking God to set her free and addressing the spiritual dynamics that I believed to be behind the fear. She was sitting with her eyes closed remembering the event and focusing on the feeling of fear. Instead of simply feeling freer, we could see that she was having some changing facial expressions. After a few moments she opened her eyes and reported being peaceful in the memory and the fear being gone.

My wife and I had been watching her and looking at each other and wondering what was going on. We proceeded to ask her what had happened. She explained to us that once we had identified what she was afraid of, and prayed for her, God had given her a picture. What the picture meant to her had resolved the belief that she held about the situation in her memory. She remains a friend today. At the time of writing, it was around 20 years ago that she was set free. She has remained free of the belief that produced the fear. As an aside, pictures are 'one way' that God communicates with people. Indeed, some people 'think in pictures.'

As I thought through what happened in this time of ministry, I came to understand that she could not deal with her feelings with her conscious mind. The beliefs producing the emotions were learnt in a past event. It was a conscious event at the time that it happened, but what she decided at the time of the event went from being head knowledge and thoughts in her mind, to being beliefs that she held in her heart. I will explain this conclusion in detail in another chapter.

In any case, this ministry experience had me searching out my few books on 'Healing of the Memories' to take another look. It was also the beginning of seeing a great many people predictably and regularly being set free through this type of ministry. Since then, in Australia and across the World, we have taught and ministered this model of ministry, as being a part of what God offers, along with other streams that bring healing and freedom.

OTHERS IN MINISTRY WHO WERE HAVING SIMILAR EXPERIENCES

Around 5 years later we began to hear of others who were having the same kind of freeing moments when trying to help people afflicted with emotional and mental issues. I began collecting their writings and video materials to glean whatever I could in order to be as effective as possible helping others.

I found that there were people doing this ministry from all kinds of Christian backgrounds. There were some using a lot of psychology terminology who did not believe in the gifts of the Spirit or that healing is for today, ranging through to people who pursue extra biblical manifestations as a component of their faith. The common denominator is that they were all good genuine people, regardless of their theological backgrounds and beliefs, who desired to serve God in helping the broken hearted and setting the captives free. All of them were reporting some positive results, with God working through them to change people's lives.

Most of the models that I looked at had done some great work in putting together teaching and training manuals to help the body of Christ to be fully equipped in this area of ministry. I encouraged people in our church at the time to look at a variety of manuals and teachings for a balanced approach.

Some ministries experienced something in a simple prayer event as we did, and then developed what had happened into extensive training courses. These studies can greatly help those who learn from books. We have trained people, and seen others who would never complete a training manual, who have proven to be brilliant at setting people free once they receive some mentoring and understand some simple principles.
We progressively developed our own teaching materials, drawing directly from what I found the scriptures to say on the subject. So, although our ministry practices may be very similar to what others are doing, our basis and doctrine on the subject might be considerably different. This book is our offering and contribution to add to what others are bringing to light on this important and much needed ministry.

'TRUTH ENCOUNTERS'

Truth Encounters, and other Biblically endorsed areas of ministry, need to be underpinned by a Statement of Faith (see appendices). We respectfully make some distinctions in our statement of faith that may perhaps be different in terms of the beliefs of other ministries doing this work. This is not pertaining to who is right, it is how we understand and experience the truths revealed in the Bible. We first heard the expression 'Truth Encounter' quite a number of years ago used by Pastor Mike Connell from New Zealand. During his address, he made a comment that sometimes we have 'Power Encounters' and at other times we have 'Truth Encounters.' It was such a good way of describing what we were experiencing in this area of ministry that we adopted the term, 'Truth Encounters.' Pastor Mike may have had something entirely different in mind when he used this term.

Study 1: Truth Encounters and 'The Fall of man'

Why does the truth make us free? We begin by considering how man came into bondage. Every activity, good or bad, that occurs in the Earth is a result of what people believe. It is the result or consequence of their choices and what they decide that they want to do. This begins at the individual level and outworks itself on the World stage with the instigation of events such as war. For everything to work in harmony, beginning with the internal workings of our bodies and extending to our relationships with God, others and even ourselves, we require TRUTH AT EVERY LEVEL OF OUR BEINGS.

Satan continues to work very hard to prevent this from happening, opposing God's perfect ways for mankind. The Bible gives us a very instructive picture of the working of Satan to bring about the fall of man, stating that,

> *Genesis 3:1 "Now the serpent was the shrewdest of all the creatures the LORD God had made." "Really?" he asked the woman. "Did God really say you must not eat any of the fruit in the garden?" NLT*

What just happened? The devil just brought Adam and Eve under his counsel by deception. The deception came about by creating a perception about God's love, integrity, goodness and provision for them. 'Really,' implied that God was not caring and was in fact keeping something good from them. Clearly this was *not the truth.*

> *1 Corinthians 13:6 "Love does not delight in evil but rejoices with the truth." NIV*

We can say that what we *believe* and perceive to be 'true' is the basis of all wrongful behavior and activity within the Earth today. The preceding verse implies that without truth, or if we deny the truth, we may be led into evil. Activities may seem right to us and good at the time and we often justify our acceptance of wrong doing. For Adam and Eve, this *false perception* created by Satan produced doubt and, as a result, they did not interpret the situation correctly. This *misinterpretation* led to *a conclusion*, from which they made *a decision* which produced *an action*. The action was disobedience; and rebellion against the Word of God. Throwing off Biblical laws and limits is known as sin.

We could summarize this simply by saying that sin comes through *misinterpreting* the *truth* of a situation and, consequently, what is actually best for us. For Adam and Eve, they saw that the tree *was* good. But in truth it was not good for them. They were much happier before, enjoying all of the many things God had given them in innocence and without guilt.

The devil continues to work in exactly the same way with humans to this day. He deceives us about who God really is and His attitude toward us, and then programs us with wrong beliefs about our own identities. Through this he manipulates humanity to serve and submit to him. His deception is behind every problem and area of suffering that is known to man.

Truth then, becomes the basis of freedom from captivity; it is the basis of faith which releases all of God's provision. It is the tool that sets us free and places us back *over* the influence of the deceiver that man has submitted to and come *under.*

Saul, later known as Paul, received direct instruction from the Lord that his ministry was going to be opening the eyes of those to whom he was to minister. They were under the power of Satan through deception, and they needed to correctly see and interpret their situation as the *beginning point* in turning back to God. The book of Acts records that the ministry would be:

> *Acts 26:18 "... to open their eyes, in order to turn them from darkness to light, and from the power of Satan to God, that they may receive forgiveness of sins and an inheritance among those who are sanctified by faith in Me.' NKJV*

When we are converted, I believe we receive truth in our human spirit and something changes in us and in our relationship to God. This is termed by some as the 'New Creation.' (2 Cor 5:17, Gal 6:15) It is still our choice to follow, put on and develop this new spiritual seed, this new or born-again spirit that we have been given.

> *Ezekiel 36:26-27* ²⁶ *I will **give you a new heart** and **put a new spirit in you;** I will remove from you your heart of stone and give you a heart of flesh.*
> ²⁷ *And I will put **my Spirit** in you and move you to follow my decrees and be careful to keep my laws. NIV (Emphasis mine) [Also Ezekiel 11:19+20]*

The preceding passage holds 3 components:
1. A new heart in us soft towards God
2. A new human spirit
3. His Spirit (in capitols)

Jesus eluded to this when He stated that He would not put new wine in old wine skins. Our old human spirit (Wineskin) cannot grow with, and expand to accommodate the growth of the Holy Spirit. (The New Wine) First we need Him to put a new human spirit in us and then we can contain the Holy Spirit. (Mat 9:17) We can of course ignore the new life which is sensitive to God and not give place and prominence to the seed of the new creation which is meant to grow being renewed in the knowledge of God. It is still a choice, but now we have an option.

> *Colossians 3:9-10* ⁹ *Do not lie to each other, since you have taken off your **old self** with its practices* ¹⁰ *and have put on **the new self**, which is **being renewed in knowledge** in the image of its Creator. NIV (emphasis mine)*

Some people think and teach that we should just simply walk around proclaiming that we are a new creation and that all of our problems will just fall away. However, the following passage relates that we need to deliberately deal with the issues that give the old deceived self and its desires power. And then go through the process of renewing our minds to the ways of God, including choosing to live a holy life.

> *Ephesians 4:22-24* ²² *You were taught, with regard to your former way of life, to put off your **old self**, which is being corrupted by its deceitful desires;* ²³ **to be made new** *in the attitude of your minds;* ²⁴ *and to **put on the new self**, created to be like God in true righteousness and holiness.*
> *NIV (emphasis mine)*

In any case we now *know* we are children of God, sensitive to the Spirit of God. And yet sometimes we don't feel like it. Our minds are not yet renewed and we struggle with the programming in our hearts. Jesus said in John's gospel that the truth would make us free. Specifically,

> *John 8:32 "And you shall know the truth, and the truth shall make you free."*
> *NKJV*

In practice I have found that we need truth in every area of our being, not just our minds. I will explain this in detail as we continue. In addition, Jesus promised that we are going to be freed with truth through the ministry of the Holy Spirit. He was going to want to inhabit every part of our person with truth, *all truth*. We could say then that one aspect of being 'filled with the Spirit' is to be filled with truth. Specifically,

> *John 16:13 "When the Spirit of truth comes, he will guide you into all truth."*
> *NLT*

Study 2: Why grace?

When we are led *"into all truth"* (NLT, John 16:13), we come to new understandings of the grace of God. From Adam and Eve on, we are all born under the deceptive power of Satan. I think that we can accurately state that nobody asked for this to be the case. We need to remember that God is *a just God.* As a consequence, we see Jesus going to the cross and asking the Father to:

Luke 23:34 "… forgive them, for they do not know what they are doing"

That is, forgive us for the things that we do that have put Him in the place of needing to pay the price for our sin. He was seemingly speaking of the people who were physically putting Him on the cross at the time, but it rings true of all sinners who made His crucifixion necessary for their redemption.

So, if I can paraphrase His request in light of the lack of truth that we have just discussed, and note this as being the root of our behavior and sin. He appears to be saying; 'Father, forgive them, for they have no knowledge of what is behind what they are doing.' In other words, they/we do not understand the beliefs that have led them to interpret the situation in the way they have, or what has caused them to take the actions that they have. He knows full well why we do what we do! So, we see Him asking for grace for us in our sin.

> *John 1:17 "For the law was given through Moses, but grace and truth came through Jesus Christ." NKJV*

I propose then, that the implications of the grace of Jesus going to the cross for us is a rationale something like;

'I will fulfill your will Father and take care of their behavior and resultant sin, but I will also send the Spirit of truth to guide them into understanding as to why they do what they are doing.'

He was making us perfect and presentable to the Father while sanctifying us through a continuing journey of receiving truth in the inner parts. We see this confirmed in Hebrews (10:14), which states that we were perfected, past tense, through the sacrifice of Jesus.

> *"For by one offering He has perfected forever those who are being sanctified." (NKJV)*
> Amen.

We are however on an ongoing journey of being made Holy through sanctification, which is postured as continuing in a present tense.

Many people confuse redemption with sanctification. Redemption is the finished work of Jesus in making us perfect before the Father. Many people somehow think that everything was finished at the cross, including healing and sanctification. The evidence is that churches are full of sick people with all sorts of emotional and behavioral problems. To support their doctrine, we would have to assume that these believers are not actually in the Kingdom and are therefore unsaved.

It would also mean that the gifts that the Holy Spirit works through believers are also not necessary to facilitate promises such as healing that Jesus won for us. The truth is that, as we have been alluding to, redemption came through Jesus Christ and, through the cross, all of God's blessings are paid for and now available to us. His mission was finished but the era and work of the Holy Spirit was just about to begin. Sanctification then is the *ongoing* work of the Holy Spirit to us and in us.

As we have said some people seem to believe that if we just think of ourselves as being a 'new creation' then we will be completely whole. And yet, there are many Christians who struggle with sin, sickness, wrong reactions, damaged emotions, addictions, imperfect relationships, areas of deception, fear and anxiety etc.

We are indeed a new creation, in the sense that we are spiritually connected with, and in a new place with God. We now have a heart that is sensitive to God and is desiring relationship with Him. The old life that had no interest in God has passed away. Through the sacrifice of Jesus on the cross we are now back in direct relationship with God, our potential is now unlimited.

Healing, freedom, and sanctification are now available, along with the gifts of the Spirit, to facilitate the work of God. An example of this would be; God so loved the world and Jesus died for the sins of all. Are all people in the World saved? No, although He loves the World and desires that none perish, not all love God, so not all are saved because not all access the provisions of the cross through faith. In the same way, not all believe that healing, deliverance, or the healing of a broken heart are for today or for them personally. Consequently, they do not receive the fullness of their redemption.

Mankind fell from grace as the result of doubting the integrity of God's word to us; by implication, His good intentions, love, and plans for us all. God has now limited Himself to faith to access all of His provisions. This seems reasonable to me, as nobody likes being misunderstood or thought of incorrectly, and we are human. How much more having a wrong idea of a perfect and wonderful God. The evidence reveals that we will only receive what we believe that God has provided for us, which means that we reverse the fall in that we trust in His character and provisions. This is what Adam and Eve did not do. In the event that we believe that the Word of God says what it means and means what it says, we can perhaps summarize and reiterate our New Testament relationship and interaction with Him in the following way;

Redemption	=	that which God does **for** you
Sanctification	=	that which God does **in** you
Mission	=	that which God does **through** you.

After we understand what God has done for us, we can then work with Him in allowing and pursuing that which He wants to do in us! The final outworking of this will see us positioned to serve God in whatever works He has predetermined to do through us.

GRACE THAT PRODUCES A HEART RESPONSE

Strong's concordance states that an aspect of the Greek word *Charis*, which is translated *grace*, is an effect of His grace as 'the divine influence on the heart.' What a beautiful picture of the work of the Spirit of truth in encouraging us to seek out God's truth for our growth as a response to all that He has done for us. Grace is given, not taken; it is not something that we should receive without thanksgiving. It should elicit in us a heart of praise and a life laid down and dedicated to God. Sadly, many miss this and, having been forgiven, return to a self-centered life as 'Lord' of their own lives.

A WONDERFUL ILLUSTRATION OF REDEMPTION AND GRACE

Let me repeat the illustration from Unit 1 as a picture of grace and redemption.

I recently read a story about one of New York city's most popular mayors by the name of Fiorello LaGuardia. His 3-term service was during the 1930s and 40s. He reportedly was not happy about people who exploited the poor. One bitterly cold night the mayor decided to preside over night court. An old woman was brought in charged with stealing a loaf of bread. She explained that her family was starving. LaGuardia's response was, "I've got to punish you. The law makes no exception. I must fine you ten dollars." (I worked out that in today's money, in Australia, that would be close to $300). Having said that he reached into his own pocket and paid the fine for her trespass, placing the $10 into his own hat. He then declared, "I'm going to fine everybody in this courtroom fifty cents for living in a town where a person has to steal bread in order to eat!" * As the story goes, the incredulous old woman left the courtroom with a new light in her eyes and $47.50 in her pocket to buy groceries. This could be as much as $1,500 today; a lot of groceries indeed.

It is a great picture of the Gospel. The law demanded that she be punished, but grace insisted on blessing. Indeed, the price for her trespass must be paid. But the person presiding over the law paid the price himself. The law held her accountable, but justice and righteousness held her environment and circumstances accountable.

> *Psalm 89:14 As it is written, "**Righteousness and justice** are the foundation of Your throne; **Mercy and truth** go before Your face." NKJV (emphasis mine)*

What did she do to earn the great blessing and forgiveness that she left with? Nothing at all, she surely sinned. We come to God with our sin, and we walk away with so many blessings; it's amazing. Fiorello LaGuardia was looking past the sin as to why she sinned.

All have sinned but God was looking at *why* we sin. As we have just seen in Psalm 89, the very foundation of God's throne is justice. (Also, see Deuteronomy 32:4) He would be denying His very nature to not extend grace and help in freeing and sanctifying a fallen and suffering humanity. Jesus paid the penalty demanded by the law, and then sent the Holy Spirit to ensure the provisions of God are received and to resolve the reasons for the offense to begin with. The mission of the Church therefore, is to serve the Father as Jesus did. We do this by ministering God's grace, co laboring with the Holy Spirit in bringing truth, freedom and healing to the captives.

Gods Little Devotional Bible   HB HONOR Books

Study 3: Understanding the Biblical meaning of the 'Heart'

Before we can fully appreciate the ramifications of receiving truth in the processes of sanctification, healing and freedom, we first need to study where truth needs to be applied.

THE MINISTRY OF JESUS

> *John 16 says that "however, when He, the Spirit of truth, has come, He will guide you into all truth." NKJV (John 16:13)*

The application of this passage relates to the Holy Spirit guiding us into 'ALL' truth. *All* means every area that requires truth. We tend to read this as meaning doctrinal truth, revelation, and understandings for our minds. This is certainly *a part* of how we will know the truth that will set us free. For example, hearing the good news of Christ Jesus can bring us redemption. Renewing the minds of believers is a high priority for the modern church in an information-based world. There is no doubting that this is very important for learning and following the ways of God. The disengaging of the World is, no doubt, the responsibility of the believer in disciplining their mind to the things of God. We certainly need to be *hearers* and *doers* in terms of knowing how we should live and act. We have a mandate as follows:

> Romans 12:2 *"And do not be conformed to this world but be transformed by the renewing of your mind." NKJV*

THE HEART

There is another area of our being that is however largely neglected by the modern church. This part of our person also requires truth, and is often directly related to us receiving wholeness and freedom. Once He had received the Holy Spirit, Jesus announced amongst other things that He was going to 'Heal the broken hearted,' and 'set the captives free.' He was quoting Isaiah 61 where the Old Testament prophet had listed what the activities of Jesus would be when the Holy Spirit came upon Him. Notably these words had not previously been fulfilled; it required that there was a person aligned with the Word and will of the Father whom the Holy Spirit could work through. With the coming of Jesus as Christ the result was that the Isaiah 61 Word became flesh and had a manifestation and expression in the Earth. We read in Luke 4,

> Luke 4:18-19 *" 18 The Spirit of the LORD is upon Me, Because He has anointed Me To preach the gospel to the poor; He has sent Me **to heal the brokenhearted,** To proclaim liberty to the captives And recovery of sight to the blind, To set at liberty those who are oppressed; 19 To proclaim the acceptable year of the LORD." NKJV (emphasis mine)*

Jesus modeled to us how to walk in the Spirit in terms of behavior and attitudes, as well as how to minister in the Spirit, expressing the gifts of the Spirit. He did no works of His own ability and began His own ministry when He received the Holy Spirit and began to be led by the Spirit.

What He introduced to us was meant to be the beginning of the Luke 4:18-19 ministries for mankind and not the end. The plan was that Spirit led believers would continue the works and example modeled by Jesus. This is very much the reason the Spirit of the LORD is upon us today. We read,

> John 20:21-22 *" 21 So Jesus said to them again, 'Peace to you! As the Father has sent Me, I also send you. And when He had said this, He breathed on them, and said to them, 'Receive the Holy Spirit." NKJV*

The Gospels do not directly tell us how He healed the Broken Hearted. We do understand that the words that He spoke to people were powerful to heal, in that He was and is God Himself. Today, we still see people receive their healing when they receive a word from the Spirit of Christ. Some people struggle with this concept, but it is as simple as; 'my sheep hear my voice.' In fact, believers will seek to listen diligently knowing that His words are Spirit and life. John states,

> John 6:63 *"It is the Spirit who gives life; the flesh profits nothing. The words that I speak to you are spirit, and they are life." NKJV*

Further, Jesus promised that when we know the truth it will make us free. Specifically,

> *John 8:32 "And you shall know the truth, and the truth shall make you free."*
> *NKJV*

WHAT IS THE BIBLICAL FUNCTION OF THE 'HEART'?

> *Mark 12:30 "And you shall love the LORD your God with all your **heart**, with*
> *all your **soul**, with all your **mind**, and with all your **strength**. This is the first*
> *commandment" NKJV (emphasis mine)*

Here are four clear and distinct areas that the Bible reveals as individual in function. Your *strength* is considered to be your forcefulness, ability, might or power. Your *soul* is generally accepted to be your mind, will and emotions in terms of the sum of whom you are as a person; I think, I will and I feel.

In this passage your *mind* is also singled out and the word that it is translated from, means, your capacity and faculty to be able to reason, understand, and imagine. It has the ability of conscious thought leading to conclusions. For example, it has the function of being able to compute and think through a mathematical problem and to produce an answer. It is very much a conscious activity and would include deliberately memorizing and voluntarily storing information. We could summarize the mind as your thinker or your computer which has the ability to store or access information.

We come now to what the Bible refers to as our *heart*. For the sake of the study, I will quote the function and operation of the *heart*, as translated from the Greek directly from the very reputable Strong's Concordance.

> *2588. kardia; **the heart**, i.e. (fig.) **the thoughts or feelings** (mind); also (by*
> *anal.) the middle: --(+ broken-) heart (-ed) (emphasis mine).*

It appears from the original language that the scripture is referring to a deeper area of the personality that holds thoughts which produce feelings and behavior. I am proposing that these thoughts and feelings are coming from beliefs that were once conscious thoughts or beliefs involuntarily learnt by experiences and events. They were significant conclusions or interpretations arrived at in the past that are stored or *taken* to heart. These thoughts, beliefs or feelings have usually come as a result of the programming of life, as deliberate training or experiential beliefs stemming from events.

We may no longer know them as beliefs or thoughts but rather as feelings, behavior or responses to particular situations. This is further confirmed in the Bible with the statement that the word of God is able to access this deeper place. Hebrews 4, verse 12 states,

> *Hebrews 4:12 For the word of God is living and active. Sharper than any*
> *double-edged sword, it penetrates even to dividing soul and spirit, joints*
> *and marrow; it judges **the thoughts** and attitudes **of the heart**. NIV*
> *(emphasis mine)*

So evidently our hearts have thoughts and attitudes that need to be discerned or judged. Jesus actually named one means of doing this as listening to what people are saying. We can measure this against the word of God to see if the thought, intent, motivation or attitude is correct. For example, someone may be heard saying; "that's just how it is with me, I'm never going to be good enough." And yet, the word of God says that we are

His creation and through Jesus we are just fine as we are! However, we discern that the preceding thought and statement is sourced from the heart. Scripture says,

*Matthew 12:34 "You brood of vipers, how can you who are evil say anything good? For out of the **overflow of the heart** the mouth speaks." NIV (emphasis mine)*

It is a principle that often the words that come out of us locates us in terms of what our inner beliefs are. The New Living Translation presents it in this way:

Matthew 12:34b For whatever is in your heart determines what you say. NLT

Our heart, or *middle* as Strong's concordance describes, has a lot to do with how we live, act and react. Might I suggest that the heart is the middle or centre of the soul, that is, the centre of the mind, emotions and will. And that most of our decisions or acts of our will proceed from the influence of these inner thoughts/beliefs and emotions. Consequently, it is vital to have truth in our hearts in order to experience wholeness and abundance in our lives. 1 Corinthians 4:5 says:

*1 Corinthians 4:5 "Therefore, judge nothing before the appointed time; wait till the Lord comes. He will bring to light what is hidden in darkness and will expose the **motives** of men's **hearts**. At that time each will receive his praise from God." NIV (emphasis mine)*

Let me suggest some of the outworking's and implications proceeding from the beliefs held in the heart. In fact, we have found that every kind of problem known to man can be found *beginning* here. As a sweeping statement, this includes things that we suffer as a result of the condition of other people's hearts. This is clearly confirmed in scripture:

Proverbs 4:23 "Above all else, guard your heart, for it affects everything you do." NLT

Above all else, protecting what goes into your heart is a compelling and vitally important instruction; this includes whatever we allow in through our conscious decisions. We can consistently and deliberately expose ourselves to the things of God through voluntary activities such as storing up the word of God, or we can be conformed to the World by various forms of media and exposure to negative influences. As I have suggested the evidence from scripture is that the 'heart' is the middle, central point or junction of the soul. That is the mind, will and emotions, and consequently it has a direct affect and influence on the function of them all.

Study 4: The role of memory
VOLUNTARY AND INVOLUNTARY MEMORY

Voluntary memory
Permit me to introduce some terms that we can use to help us understand the different ways that we can have things *stored up* in our hearts. One way is that we have information that we have decided to consciously learn and then retain through repetition. This could include the 10 times table or the scriptures. We could also have memory that affects us from Worldly things that we have decided to expose ourselves to. These things which we have

taken into our hearts will have an influence on how we live by way of future decisions, motivations, activities, what we think about, and behavior. This kind of memory or *heart belief* is to do with how we shape what we understand and perceive about the world around us. It pertains to things such as our morality, skills, and functionality.

Automatized thinking

As an adult, most likely if you exit your shower or bath and begin to dry yourself with a towel, it will not be a deliberate conscious exercise. You are possibly thinking about how your day will go or something else. At one time when you were learning how to dry yourself, it was a deliberate conscious effort involving your mind. Now if you involve your conscious thought with something like, "do I dry this arm or this arm next?", you might find that your minds involvement creates confusion with your processes that are now automatic.

I quite like music, and as an adult I will sometimes memorize a song in order to be able to just play it. I find that if I just let it come out of my heart it happens automatically, but if I begin to consciously think about which note is coming up next, I almost always mess it up.

Many of the feelings, responses, decisions and activities that we go through are done automatically in this way. For example, the mental activity of deciding what is suitable for us to watch on TV. It was once something that we worked out with our conscious mind, but now our responses and actions come automatically from the conclusions and interpretations about life that we *already* hold in our hearts. Jesus very emphatically stated that many of our actions come from the prior encoding of this deeper place. Matthew says,

> Matthew 15:18-19 "¹⁸ But the things that come out of the mouth **come from the heart**, and these make a man 'unclean.' **For out of the heart** come evil thoughts, murder, adultery, sexual immorality, theft, false testimony, slander." NIV (emphasis mine)

We could quite easily add a large number of good and bad deeds that come from the heart to that list. Jesus was just giving us a sample of negative activities that come from what has been stored in the heart. It is worth considering as the modern church that Jesus really took the Pharisees to task for focusing on outward appearances and neglecting dealing with *the issues of the heart* in the people they were responsible for. They were giving them religious rules on how they should look and what they should do, instead of helping them find freedom by a relationship with God, and accessing His provisions through the Holy Spirit. That is not to say that we don't want to present well as a church, but we need to major on ministering to the broken hearted as Jesus did.

> Luke 11:39 Then the Lord said to him, "Now you Pharisees make the outside of the cup and dish clean, but your **inward part** is full of greed and wickedness. NKJV (emphasis mine)

A little later he admonished them for giving them outward religion and rules without setting the people free from the problems that have caused their negative behavior to begin with. Religion is seen as follows; 'This is what you do to be right with, or please God!' or 'This is how you do it, how you should look, what you should say!' These are human created standards and efforts for practicing Christianity.

> Luke 11:46 "Yes," said Jesus, "how terrible it will be for you experts in religious law! For you crush people beneath impossible religious demands, and you never lift a finger to help ease the burden." NLT

For those of us who are leaders we should take counsel from the book of Ezekiel on how God regards us if we do not prioritize the healing of His people over building our own little Kingdoms on Earth. We have a God given responsibility to try to meet the needs of the people in our care. Understandably sometimes we do not know how to do this, and as a result God provides training such as this.

> *Ezekiel 34:2,4* [2] *"Son of man, prophesy against the shepherds of Israel, prophesy and say to them, 'Thus says the Lord GOD to the shepherds:"Woe to the shepherds of Israel who feed themselves! Should not the shepherds feed the flocks?*
>
> *And;*
>
> [4] *"The weak you have not strengthened, **nor have you healed those who were sick, nor bound up the broken,** nor brought back what was driven away, nor sought what was lost; NKJV (emphasis mine)*

Involuntary memory

Involuntary memory is *beliefs* that you have taken into your *heart* that were not intentionally or purposefully learnt. These beliefs have also become 'automatized' and so we no longer know them as conscious *thoughts or beliefs*; we may now know them as only feelings, emotions or responses and behavior.

Remember our definition of 'the heart' as being *thoughts and feelings* from our *middle or central part*. These may come to us involuntarily through experiential learning in, for example, feelings of rejection received in a historical event, or perhaps fear, anger or inferiority learnt through life.

We have already stated that the conscious mind interprets events and comes to *conclusions* which then become *beliefs* that are stored in our *hearts*. These *beliefs* that are in our *hearts* are recorded there usually through repetition or significant events. In terms of critical matters such as our identity and how we think others view us, the Bible tells us that we are most influenced as children. Science confirms what the Bible has always said, that a child's brain is plastic and formative in terms of self-awareness and identity up until around 10 years old. In Hebrew, **a child** is regarded to be between infancy and adolescence. Adolescence is considered to begin at around 10 years old, so biblically a child is less than 10 years old.

> *Proverbs 22:6 "Train a child in the way he should go, and when he is old he will not turn from it." NIV*

20 years and thousands of hours of ministry have confirmed that most people's identity beliefs, proceed from situations, that have been found in the *heart* and are sourced in memories before the age of 10 years old. An *identity belief* is one that has to do with who you 'are' and how you perceive that others see you. It is *your* reality or *truth* about your-'self.' Very often a spirit other than the Holy Spirit has helped you interpret life and come to the conclusion that you now hold about yourself. Even in a Christian household those who were meant to help *guard our hearts* may have unintentionally been the source of our programming.

How many people have grown up in households where as a child you were informed that; *'little children should be seen and not heard!'* At that moment you have had fed into your heart that you are some kind of lesser humanity that should not have a voice.

SITUATIONAL BELIEFS

A *situational belief* is one that has come from an event or theme in life that has programmed you to believe something which could affect how you perceive your identity, but also how you feel about life in general. Many children today are in a situation where a parent has left them and gone out of the home. Their experience has perhaps taught them that, *'people cannot be trusted to care about you, you are not safe or important.'*

A sample of identity beliefs includes: *'I am not loved/lovable, I am worthless, not good enough, not important, I am a nothing, I don't matter,' etc. etc.*

A sample of situational beliefs includes: *'There is no one there to protect me; no one cares about me, nobody wants me, I am not as good as others, I won't be able to do it,' etc.*

REPETITION

Reportedly the brain has little cells called 'Microglial' cells which account for 10-15% of all of the cells found in the brain. A part of their function is to clear up cellular debris. They are like little vacuum cleaners that go through your brain and suck up and dispose of useless information that is not reinforced within 24 to 48 hours. General information is considered important enough to be kept *through repetition.* We see this with the ten times table, or perhaps repeatedly being dealt with in a particular way while growing up. This will program and reinforce what you believe to the point of it becoming a permanent belief.

A Biblical example can be found with God telling Joshua five times to be strong and courageous. He seems to be saying; 'you need to meditate on this, take it *to heart,* and make it your default position, because when you see those angry guys with spears coming over the hill you will need to have your default position and response settled way down deep inside of you. Then you don't need to think about it because you have it as an *automatic* response.'

CRITICAL MOMENTS OR EVENTS

Information deeply encoded in *significant* emotional or traumatic *events,* including moments of weakness, or episodes containing fear or extreme stress, are taken to *heart and remain.* Most seventy-year old's will not remember what they had for breakfast on their first day of school. There is no reason for your brain to store in memory that information as it has no real bearing on your life. They may however remember beliefs recorded through interpreting events related to the anxieties of the day, and the acceptance of others in a new environment.

We have found that anything that you can remember from your childhood was a significant moment in either a positive way or negative way. It may have been a time where you were coming to some conclusion about yourself or your situation. Once you have decided that you are, for example, inferior, you are going to interpret future situations in the same way. It is a *heart belief* that you now carry and you are, in a sense, what you think you are *in your heart.* You will make your decisions based on those beliefs. For example, if you have learnt through experience that you are not very smart with remembering words you will probably avoid spelling contests like the plague. They will only potentially confirm what you already believe about yourself and expose that perceived weakness to everyone else.

Significant emotional or traumatic events are burned deeply into your memory through an electro-chemical process called protein synthesis. This could be events such as being embarrassed in a school room, a fearful event of perhaps nearly drowning, and range through to the trauma of seeing porn on a smart phone where the deeply recorded images can reportedly last a lifetime.

Study 5: Grasshoppers and faith

Proverbs 23:7 "For as he thinks in his heart, so is he. "Eat and drink!" he says to you, But his heart is not with you." NKJV

Notice that this passage does not state *as the man thinks in his mind*. The passage suggests that the man has invited you for a meal and that is the good intention that he has towards you. But he has a conflict between his conscious choice and what is going on for him at heart level. Perhaps he heard a great message about hospitality at church and is trying to live it out, however he grew up in a poor household where they often didn't have enough to eat. That which he now wills to do is in conflict with the anxiety coming from his previous experiences and the beliefs held inside him about there being enough. The reality may well be that he has plenty but he is going to default to his previous programming every time.

As he thinks in his heart, so is he. A profound old saying puts it this way: **'It's not what you think you are, but WHAT YOU THINK, you ARE!'** In other words, you will live your life according to what you think about yourself. Let us reinforce this thought by repeating the scripture from Proverbs,

> *Proverbs 4:23 "Above all else, guard your heart, for it affects everything you do." NLT*

A great example of this in the scriptures is that of the Israelites. While God was doing everything, they were doing fine. It is the picture of redemption where God performs the complete activity for them in delivering them from the slavery and the subservience that they were under in Egypt. In the same way God does everything through Jesus and delivers us from the slavery of the law and sin.

God was then looking for them to participate with Him in occupying a land that He had set apart for them. He even tells them that He had gone before them and had given them the land. By faith they can walk into their inheritance. It would be wonderful, and they all agree that it is a good land. So, what is the problem, what holds them back from entering into this promised life walking in the provision of God? Numbers 13:33 records the problem as a reconnaissance report stating,

> *"We even saw giants there, the descendants of Anak. We felt like grasshoppers next to them, and that's what we looked like to them!" NLT*

The Israelites had grown up as slaves. They had grown up with low self-image and inferiority as they were being treated as some kind of lesser beings. This lack of confidence now emanated out of them and was discerned by their potential opponents.

Often people criticize the modern church for its lack of faith and power. Remember that many have grown up in a broken, rejective family and society. Like the Israelites, they would like to move into the Promised Land but they have been taught that they are not good enough, or not worthy to carry God's power and provision. They need first to be set free at *a heart* level.

The Promised Land for believers is the 'abundant life to the full' that Jesus announced He came to bring. Sadly, just as with the Israelites, many never come into it because of their **unbelief**, that is, **wrong belief** about themselves and how God sees them. They give mental assent to the scriptures but can never exercise *heart faith* and trust in God to live the life that He wants for them. It is noteworthy that Jesus said that we can have whatever we believe in *our hearts* as opposed to what we believe with our minds.

> *Mark 11:23 says "For assuredly, I say to you, whoever says to this mountain, 'Be removed and be cast into the sea,' and **does not doubt in his heart**, but believes that those things he says will be done, he will have whatever he says." NKJV (emphasis mine)*

Doubt comes from a wrong belief about God. It began with Adam and Eve who doubted God's integrity and genuinely perfect intentions for them. It started with 'did God really say?' When we hold wrong beliefs about God at *a heart* level, we may hear a great inspirational message about what we should be doing, and then decide as a mental activity to try, having been convinced in our minds, only to be disappointed because we do not really believe God for the outcome.

Genuine faith is not about what you can get God to do for you by believing Him for something. True faith is about having a correct picture of who He is and His plan for you. Often, we need to hear His voice, as Jesus did, before He began His ministry confirming that you are His child and that He is pleased with you. He may not be pleased with everything you do but He is most likely pleased with who you are. He understands why you do what you do even though you do not. If your heart condemns you, God is greater than your heart. (1 John 3:20)

People often quote that faith comes through hearing, and hearing the Word of God, and encourage you to read your bible more to grow in faith. In the Greek language there is the word 'Logos' which is the written word of God, and the word 'Rhema' which refers to the spoken word of God. The Romans passage that we are discussing uses the word 'Rhema.'

> *Romans 10:17 says, "So then faith comes by hearing, and hearing by the word (Rhema) of God." NKJV (emphasis mine)*

So, faith or trust in God comes to us when God speaks to us in some way. This could include reading the Word at times if the Holy Spirit is highlighting a passage. But in regards to bringing *truth to your heart*, it is when God speaks to what you *believe* that your picture of God and yourself consistently changes. This releases true trust and faith in Him.

Study 6: 'Strongholds' and spiritual warfare

Many years ago, we were ministering through Micronesia and our host took us for a tour around the Island of Guam. He showed us the concrete bunkers that the Japanese had built before the coming battle in order to hold the ground or territory that they occupied. The Bible says in Ephesians chapter 4 and verse 7 to not give the devil a place. The Greek word translated as 'place' is the word, topos. It means a place, a location, a position, a spot or a home.

In much the same way as the Japanese made strongholds **before** the battle began, the devil establishes **a place** in our *belief systems* through deception and misinterpretation.   Later, as the Apostle Paul found out, when the Spirit of truth comes on the scene there is an internal battle and conflict for the ground or place of the heart that has already been occupied.

Many people believe that when they are feeling bad or anxious that they are under some kind of spiritual or demonic attack. Most times what is actually happening is that *beliefs* that the person already holds are being stressed or triggered through the environment or situation that they find themselves in. Perhaps they are confused by Paul's later statement in Ephesians regarding wrestling spiritual powers which states:

> *Ephesians 6:11-12 " ¹¹ Put on the full armor of God so that you can take your stand against the devil's schemes. For our struggle is not against flesh and blood, but against the rulers, against the authorities, against the powers of this dark world and against the spiritual forces of evil in the heavenly realms." NIV*

In fact, he is more likely to be making reference to the fact that, although you are dealing with humans, flesh and blood, it is the negative spiritual dynamics projecting from them onto you that is your problem. In other words, it is not the people themselves that are attacking you. It is the spirits manipulating the people through *their* areas of deception which give place and cooperation with the powers that you are actually dealing with.

Jesus floated the concept of human participation with spiritual inspiration at various times in the gospels. It is wrong believing that opens us to being potential unwitting hosts to unholy spirit. This is exemplified in the following passage:

> *Luke 9:54-55 " ⁵⁴ And when His disciples James and John saw this, they said, "Lord, do You want us to command fire to come down from heaven and consume them, just as Elijah did?" But He turned and rebuked them, and said, "You do not know **what manner of spirit you are of**." NKJV (emphasis mine)*

In other words, James and John were not aware of what type of spirit they were cooperating with. Peter was inspired by the Spirit of God but was soon found to be working for the other side. This is true of all of us. People can do something wonderful in the love of God, and later be heard gossiping, criticizing or judging another believer. The truth is that, if we don't get our hearts cleaned out, we can at times be found to be double agents and on occasion working unintentionally for the other side! In contrast,

> *Matthew 16:15-17 " ¹⁵ He said to them, "But who do you say that I am?" Simon Peter answered and said, "You are the Christ, the Son of the living God." Jesus answered and said to him, "Blessed are you, Simon Bar-Jonah, **for flesh and blood has not revealed this to you, but My Father who is in heaven.**" NKJV (emphasis mine)*

Peter had a wonderful *Rhema* word from the Father. A few short verses later, his inspiration was coming from another source which he was open to, through his previous programming in life. I am fairly sure that Jesus, much to Peter's dismay, was addressing the spirit behind the idea. This would have been quite confronting for Peter to be exposed for his co-operation and deception.

> *Matthew 16:22-23 ²² Then Peter took Him aside and began to rebuke Him, saying, "Far be it from You, Lord; this shall not happen to You!" But He turned and said to Peter, "**Get behind Me, Satan!** You are an offense to Me, for you are not mindful of the things of God, but the things of men." NKJV (emphasis mine)*

Jesus could clearly see the spirit that He was contending with coming through the man Peter, even though Peter was unaware. It is clear that very often the things that men have in mind are inspired by Satan. Nothing spiritual happens on Earth without human participation, this includes the works of God. There will be prayers and deeds motivated by faith behind Gods activities as well. When people are rejective, competing or putting you down for example, and you are feeling anxious or depressed it is most likely tapping into a belief that you already hold and not a spiritual attack. Of course you acknowledge that it is the spirit behind the persons negative projections that you are actually dealing with.

Study 7: Beliefs produce feelings or what we term emotions

We have seen that the Israelites were unable to take up their destiny because of beliefs of inferiority which produced feelings of fear and inadequacy. If they had instead been programmed by life that they were equal or if they had received healing from their previous beliefs, they would have felt confident and full of faith! Sadly, the covenant that they were under did not include the ministry of the Spirit of truth, so they did not have the opportunity for freedom from their inner thoughts that we find ourselves with.

THOUGHTS AND FEELINGS

A feeling or emotion is the result of a belief that has been accessed. In fact, it is your chemical bodies' version of what you believe. So, a thought or belief and feelings or emotions are one and the same. Some time ago I was reading a book where Charles Finney made the statement that '*feelings follow thoughts.*' This is a profound statement in its application to what we are discussing about the heart. You do not simply have a feeling because you have a feeling. It is emanating from something that you already *believe*:

- If you *believe* that nobody loves you, then you will feel sad.
- If you *believe* that no one cares about you, you may feel angry.
- If you *think* that there is no protection for you, your emotion will probably be anxiety.
- If you *believe* that you will never ever be able to be what people expect you to be, then you will feel overwhelmed and hopeless, which is the basis of endogenous depression. Endogenous meaning, having an internal origin.

> *Proverbs 12:25 says, "Anxiety **in the heart** of man causes depression, But a good word makes it glad." NKJV (emphasis mine)*

A feeling or emotion is a chemical elaboration of *a belief* through the release of hormones or neurotransmitters. It is a *thought or belief* that your body makes into a *feeling or emotion* through these chemicals. For example, a fear belief will release particular hormones such as adrenaline and the stress hormone, cortisol, so that your body can make your thoughts something that you can feel. These hormones have other functions in your bodies so when you have long term negative emotions, they become imbalanced, and this is the basis for disease.

STORY: TWO LITTLE BOYS

In order to help people understand this principle I often use the following story when I am preparing them for ministry. There were two little 5-year-old boys walking down a street in their town. One of them noticed a motorbike across the road and went over to look at it. As the other boy continued down the road a dog came out of the gateway of a nearby house and bit him on the leg. In that moment of trauma, it was deeply encoded in him that dogs can hurt and frighten you. His mind has made a very good memory of the event, and he is now on guard against the possibility of it happening again. In order to counteract this ever-present fear, he reads numerous books about how dogs are man's best friend and that most of them will never hurt you. He is trying to counteract his involuntary heart belief with voluntary information from his mind.

This is often what we do in church and wonder why people never change or have limited growth. We give them lots of information to learn for their problems and tell them how they should think, perhaps sometimes not unlike the Pharisees. The Jesus model was to heal their broken hearts and set the captives free. I will explain what I mean by this statement a little further on, but back to our story for the moment.

As he grows up and becomes a teenager he is often invited to his friends' houses and really wants to go, but underneath there is a nagging hesitation and anxiety. He is not consciously thinking it but underneath the thought that there may be a dog at their house is producing the anxiety. So, his inner beliefs are beginning to affect his life choices.

Many years later the 5-year-old boys are again together walking and are now 40 years old. As they go along a small dog comes out of a laneway near them wagging his tail. The man who was bitten has an immediate physical fear response, even though with his mind he is trying frantically to apply the knowledge that he has about dogs and is telling himself how it looks so friendly. His *heart belief* that dogs sometimes bite you is greater than his *logical conscious knowledge* that the dog looks really friendly. The outworking is the release of fear hormones and a very uncomfortable feeling in his physical body.

His friend on the other hand has an entirely different response. He feels happy, warm and 'fuzzy.' What is the difference; it's the same dog? Growing up as a small boy, his family had a friendly dog that played with him, climbed all over him and licked his face. The emotions that he was feeling were coming from *different beliefs* about the same situation stored in his heart. So, the same situation was producing opposing responses based on what they already *believed*.

CAPTIVITY

Many people are tormented and held captive to *beliefs* that they hold about themselves, their worth, or their situations. For example, a number of years ago we had a black dog we called 'Misty.' As a pup she used to go out of the yard and get lost if we weren't home. As a result, if we went out, we would tie a rope to her collar and connect it to a fence post to keep her from running away. Of course, she tried to get loose for a while but eventually gave up. When she was older, I would tie the rope to her collar but not bother to tie up the other end. She no longer tried to get away; she had attempted to before and learnt that it was impossible. She was captive in her thinking to her previous situation.

This was now *belief-based behavior* or responses. This was not necessarily an emotion for her anymore although originally it may have been frustration. Now it was *belief-based behavior* that she was captive to.

Many people are held captive to what they perceive to be true. These inner thoughts indeed may come from an episode or training that at one time was true. A lot of actions, activities and responses come from previous programming, and although consciously with our minds we want to do something, we find that we cannot do what we want to do, there is something opposing us.

The Apostle Paul came to understand this clearly in his own walk. Many people like him wish to follow the things of God as they come into a New Creation potential, being on a new footing with a reborn spirit. They now have the Holy Spirit to guide them, and the word of God to instruct them. Just like Paul however, they often find themselves with one foot on the accelerator and one foot on the brake.

A PROGRAM BEHIND THE PROGRAM

In our early days of teaching this ministry I was operating one of the first versions of Microsoft PowerPoint from my Laptop computer to facilitate the presentation. My computer was not running properly and was taking a very long time to perform normally simple tasks. The man who had sold me the computer was actually in the congregation and so I invited him up to the platform to resolve the issue. He took one look at the computer and pointed to a little green light that was flashing. "There," he said, "there is a program running behind the program, and that is why it is not functioning properly!" With that he, with a blur of hands across the keyboard, far too fast to ever remember what he did, turned off the 'scanning' program that was operating in the background. It was going on underneath, with no obvious evidence on the screen other than its poor operation and the little green light flickering. This was a light bulb moment for me. I suddenly understood Romans 7 and the Apostle Paul's dilemma in a new way. Not only *his* discomfort, but also many other Christians who want to live according to the word of God.

There is something going on in the background that is affecting the operation of the will. This other 'program' needs to be switched off by the Holy Spirit before you can be all that you can be and do all that you choose to do without hindrance.

If you can imagine the screen as the conscious mind which will only display what you actively choose to think about. If you think about fruit or perhaps a hot dog, you will now have something on the screen of your conscious mind. But while you think about what you have decided to think about, behind this may be feelings of anxiety or depression coming from a deeper place, your *heart*, that are not conscious. These are other programs behind what you are deciding to do with your mind need to be addressed. You want to think and react in all of the ways that you see in scripture with your conscious mind but something else is in play.

I sometimes think that we read in the Bible, for example, about the fruit of the Spirit as ways that we should decide to act. This is certainly true in the sense of our conscious decisions, but in practice these fruits are more often the results of the work that the Holy Spirit has done in our *hearts*. We could use the example of choosing to be joyful, but for many, this will be impossible without being made free from *beliefs* for example producing guilt, shame, inadequacy or anxiety etc.

Study 8: The example of the Apostle Paul's dilemma

In Romans chapter 7:15-25, we see a battle going on in the 'members' or different areas of the Apostle Paul's being. This is the case for many people in the church today.   Let us summarize the problem in this way. Their spirit is reborn of the Holy Spirit, a new creation, (John 3:5-8) so they are now connected to the Father and the Kingdom of God, but there are areas where wrong believing still has 'a place.' They are hungry for the truth and want to live out the Word of God as a response to the leading of the Holy Spirit. So spiritually they are willing, and in their conscious minds they want to walk after God. However, pulling against them is their old programming at *heart level*. They have what they know and confess to be true from the word of God, but it is not setting them free. They appear to be double minded. Their confession, and their responses, behavior and actions do not match.

These people are on a journey of renewing their minds with truth, but another part of them is defaulting to their old ways of acting. Their bodies and *hearts* want to continue to conform to the responses, attitudes, motivations, habits and associations that have been programmed into them through life in the World.

In Romans 7, Paul is not suffering from some personality disorder. His Spirit is alive to, and wanting the things of God, but there already exist *contrary beliefs* held in his heart producing automatic feelings and behavior. His body is still in the habit of playing out the feelings coming from these beliefs, and most likely whatever he does to cope with these emotions. These are probably his automatic solutions for gratification, self-realization and identity. In order to understand this clearly, in the following verse let's make his spirit led man to be in bold letters, and his 'flesh' person (which I propose is his unsanctified heart and body, sometimes called the sin nature, or Adamic, Carnal or fallen nature) to be underlined.

> Romans 7:15 "*I don't understand <u>myself</u> at all, for I really want to do what is right, but <u>I</u> don't do it. Instead, <u>I</u> do the very thing I hate.*" NLT (emphasis mine)

It is like that person in church who hears a message on forgiveness. A part of them wants to forgive and be in line with the Kingdom, and they even know that they should. But another part of them wants to justify itself and hold on to the resentment. Internal peace is gone as flesh clashes with spirit.

Mostly, the truth in this case is that whatever the person who is not being forgiven is doing or has done is not the main problem. The issue is usually that something that is offending is touching a belief that the person holds, and this causes some kind of emotional reaction. For example, you may not be forgiving a spouse for seeming to not care about your needs. The probability is that somewhere in your history you were treated as though you do not matter or are not important. So, the real issue behind the resentful response that you are trying not to have, is the pain of believing that you do not matter for some reason. The unforgiveness is the *fruit* of the hurt that is held and not the actual *root* of the behavior.

The problem then is the belief that is held in the unsanctified or unhealed part of *the heart*. The Spirit of truth has to bring truth, healing and sanctification to this belief before that area of the heart can come into harmony under the covering of the Spirit. Otherwise it will continue to contest what kind of behavior is most appropriate as a response to life situations. This appears to be the kind of dilemma that Paul was found in.

> Romans 7:22-23 " ²² *For I delight in the law of God according to the* **inward** *man. But I see another law in <u>my</u> members, warring against the law of my mind, and bringing <u>me</u> into captivity to the law of sin which is in <u>my</u> <u>members</u>.*" NKJV (emphasis mine)

Let us try to give another picture of what this could look like in practice. A person is waiting for the Sunday church service to begin. The Pastor or minister comes in and walks right past them without the least sign of recognition. The person feels quite upset but tries to tell themselves that it is ok, and not to worry about it. It's all good, after all they have lots of friends. It happens again the next week and they have a little anger and begin to notice little faults with the minister and shares them with others. **They** know that _they_ should not be doing this, but what **they** know _they_ should not do, _they_ do. What is happening here?

The person knows that they should forgive the minister. If they looked at and identified that upset feeling they would find that they are being made to feel unimportant. An area that does not yet have truth, that has previously been programmed, teaching them that they are unimportant is being accessed. Out of them are coming retaliatory responses that they know are wrong but that they cannot seem to stop. The _truth_ is that they have misinterpreted the situation, believing and holding a perception that the minister did not value them. In actual fact the minister considers them a valuable part of the church family, but immediately before the service he is trying to make sure that all the music is in order, the preaching is ready to go, and the equipment is all working and so on.

Is this resolved by the person trying harder to solve their concern? They are already trying as hard as they can to go with their convictions from scripture about how they should be, and they are feeling condemned because they cannot seem to resolve it with their good intentions, knowledge of scripture, and their own efforts to work it out with their minds.

> Romans 7:24-25 "Oh, what a miserable person **I** am! Who will free _me_ from this life that is dominated by sin? Thank God! The answer is in Jesus Christ our Lord." NLT (emphasis mine)

THE ANSWER IS JESUS CHRIST OUR LORD. SO HOW CAN WE BE FREE?

King David made a profound statement in regards to God's intentions and method for healing, sanctifying and freeing us. When he talks about God's desire for truth in the inner parts, you will see how this lines up with healing broken hearts, setting the captives free and working through the process of sanctification. _Inner parts_ in the Old Testament scripture that we are about to quote can, according to Hebrew scholars, also be translated as _the heart_. The _inmost place_ refers to the human spirit. Personally, I believe that our re-born human spirit already receives and witnesses to the truth of God's word by the work of the Holy Spirit. However, our _hearts_ or _inner parts_ need the truth that God wants us to know in order for us to be set free.

> Psalm 51:5-6 says, "Surely I was sinful at birth, sinful from the time my mother conceived me. Surely you desire **truth in the inner parts**; you teach me wisdom in the inmost place." NIV (emphasis mine)

Noteworthy, King David acknowledges the passing of the sin nature through the generations to him right at the point of conception. The King also acknowledged that it was his heart that needed cleaning. Psalm 51 was written following David's sin with Bathsheba. Somehow, he had for some time managed to deny his sin and contrived some way to justify his behavior. Many people seem to be content to live on the surface of their being not seeking out the root reason for their activities. As Jeremiah 17:9-10 states,

> "The heart is deceitful above all things, And desperately wicked; Who can know it? I, the LORD, search the heart, I test the mind. Even to give every man according to his ways, According to the fruit of his doings." NKJV

It becomes very apparent that each of us need to let the LORD search our hearts, as most often we are not aware of why we do what we do, or where it is coming from. We can join with King David in inviting the Holy Spirit to help us find out what we believe at a heart level and set us free. It is like putting the anti-virus program on your computer to remove the corrupted files so that the machine runs how it was intended. Scripture says,

> Psalm 51:10 "Create in me a clean heart, O God, And renew a steadfast spirit within me." NKJV

Adam and Eve ran *from* God. Through Jesus we can now run boldly to God for freedom through His truth in our hearts. Psalm 139:23-24 expresses this desire as follows;

> "Search me, O God, and know my heart; test me and know my thoughts. Point out anything in me that offends you, and lead me along the path of everlasting life. NLT

Study 9: Sanctification, healing and freedom come through truth

We have already quoted the verse that *the truth will make us free*. This freedom begins by acknowledging that our captivity comes through what we believe that is not truth. Such as not understanding sound doctrine in regards to our minds but also importantly what we hold to be true at heart level. It is clear that sanctification comes through truth from God.

> John 17:17 says, "Sanctify them by Your truth. Your word is truth." NKJV

That is a fairly unchallengeable and straightforward statement. Our minds are renewed by truth and our hearts are healed and released from captivity to wrong beliefs in the same way. If then, sanctification comes through truth, it is fair to deduce that being guided into truth by the Spirit of truth is the way of sanctification at every level.

> John 16:13 "When the Spirit of truth comes, he will guide you into all truth." NLT

This is why we have come to refer to this ministry as 'Truth Encounters.' It is when we have an encounter with the Holy Spirit and He reveals truth to us. He speaks to us as sheep who hear His voice and we are changed. The Holy Spirit has been sent to us through Jesus, who has extended us grace for our sins, but also is influencing our hearts to seek and walk in the truth. As previously stated, Strong's concordance presents *Charis*, the word from which grace is translated in the following manner.

485. charis,; from G5463; graciousness; lit., fig. or spiritual; espec. (the divine influence upon the heart) acceptable, benefit, favor, gift, grace

It appears from the Bible that the very reason for the coming of Jesus was to bring us the grace of God, and then restore us to wholeness through the truth. The ministry of the Holy Spirit then in this era is vital in every way.

> John 1:17 For the law was given through Moses, but **grace and truth** came through Jesus Christ." NKJV (emphasis mine)

Study 10: What is a Broken Heart and who are the broken hearted?

Let us first examine God's priority regarding those suffering in this area. We have already identified from the Greek language in the New Testament that the *heart* is *beliefs* or *thoughts* that are manifested or matched by corresponding *feelings or emotions*. In the Old Testament the word that is translated as *heart* from the Hebrew language *Leb* also relates to your centre, your intellect, will and is widely used for feelings.

The central place of motivation for your inner thoughts, which produce feelings and influence your decisions and responses, is your *heart* and the *beliefs* held there. This is well supported by the context of the Psalms of David that we have recently quoted. So, when this area is out of order, not whole, or not as God intended, it means problems for us.

BROKEN?

In the Gospel of Luke chapter 4 we see the statement that the Spirit of the Lord is upon Jesus to Heal the Broken Hearted. I think that we have thoroughly dealt with what *the heart* means, but what does it mean for a heart to be '*broken?*' Luke 4:18 speaks to this brokenness as follows:

> "*The Spirit of the LORD is upon Me, Because He has anointed Me To preach the gospel to the poor; He has sent Me to heal the* **brokenhearted***, To proclaim liberty to the captives.*" NKJV (emphasis mine)

If our hearts are our *central beliefs that produce emotions*, then how does that relate to being broken? I think that we can deduce that if our thinking and feelings are not whole or as they were intended to be, then they are broken and need healing/fixing. We have already established that this is done by receiving truth from the Spirit of truth. The Greek word 'suntribo' translated 'broken' literally means *broken, crushed, shattered, or bruised.*

If you have a clock and it has a slightly bent hand on it you would call it broken. If it is smashed to pieces you would also consider it to be broken. Whether you are a little bit broken or you are completely shattered, you are still broken because you are not in the working order that the designer intended. You are not whole. The application here is relating to the state of your heart. So, if your *beliefs and feelings* are in any way not as they were intended to be, then you are broken.

None of us have perfect truth about ourselves, or about how God really feels about us, therefore we are ALL broken hearted. The only question is how broken, and where are we in the process of sanctification and healing? Now we can see clearly why God desires truth in our hearts. It relates directly to our journey into wholeness and freedom from captivity in every area of our lives.

Many people have had their self-image *broken* down through negative statements and constant criticism. Others are *crushed* under the burden of expectations to perform and please others. Some have had their lives *shattered* through such traumas as physical or sexual abuse. Still more have had their sense of well-being *bruised* through anxiety about being loved and valued. All of the *beliefs* resulting from this treatment and programming, constitute the brokenness of the human person in *the heart.*

The Greek word 'sozo', normally translated as 'saved' on examination carries a much fuller meaning. As well as saved, it includes; *to be healed, to be delivered and to be made whole.* God did not save us for eternity only, He had in mind for us to be transformed and bring Him glory through our lives on Earth. We have seen that as people are made whole and healed of their brokenness, others see the changes. In turn this proves the integrity of God and the promises in His Word.

IMPLICATIONS OF A 'BROKEN HEART' AND CAPTIVITY FOR WRONG BELIEFS

Let me outline again seven of the basic problems that assail mankind. I will not address them in detail here but you will see that each of them is directly impacted by what we *believe.*

1. Spiritual bondage

This relates firstly to remaining unsaved and a slave to the ruler of this world. Our blindness and lack of knowledge regarding our situation keeps us submitted to this spiritual being. Secondly, we often see areas of demonic strongholds as a part of the mechanism of serving or being held in sin. It is often an undiagnosed element, and comes as result of giving *ground* and permitting the *strongman goods.* So, giving place to, and co-operating with unholy spiritual entities, is also based on our bad solutions to our problems which stems from *our wrong beliefs.*

2. Mental soundness

Beliefs producing fear and anxiety are tormenting and can lead to all kinds of *masking* behavior. The vast majority of mental problems that are observed begin with *beliefs* at a *heart* level with chemical imbalances being the outworking. It is also true that some people are born mentally handicapped in some way and others have mental impairment through events such as damage from an accident or drug abuse. In the case of *belief based* mental issues, there will usually be coinciding emotional and physical implications. One scientific study that I read of recently cited that because of the diseases normally present with mental illness, that the corresponding effect on your physical health could take up to 20 years off your life. Along with this because of these sicknesses your quality of life would also be radically impaired.

3. Emotional peace

If our minds and thoughts are not at peace then our feelings and emotions will also be out of order. You do not simply have an emotion; remember it is a *thought* coming from *a belief* first.

4. Relational wellbeing

If you have mental inner thought issues along with emotional damage, your responses will also be out of order in relationships. Typically, your wrong *belief-based* hurts will react with the faulty inner thoughts of others, making it very difficult to have harmonious interactions.

5. Sexuality

We have even found that in order to come together fully in sexual union there are usually *beliefs* that need to be dealt with first. This can be basic inner thoughts that affect other areas of life such as; "You don't really care about me; what I want is not important!" Leading to conclusions such as; "you are just using me; you don't really value me; you are selfish and only care about what you want!" Other kinds of brokenness stemming from feelings proceeding from sexual abuse also commonly need to be rectified.

These can be *identity beliefs* such as; "I am dirty, it's my fault or I did something that this has happened so I must be a bad person. With sex I'm trapped, powerless," and so on.

When trying to initiate the sexual act, all of these *beliefs* will produce unwanted feelings and anxiety. For some who have been abused they will run from sexual activity because of fear and how it makes them feel, making normal marital activities almost impossible without healing. Others will conclude that because they are already ruined, defiled, dirty or bad, then why bother trying to be good; they then become promiscuous. Sadly, this is often the case with sex workers such as prostitutes who have lost their self-value.

Another way that sexuality can be out of order is through belief-based gender confusion. Sexual sin such as adultery or fornication usually proceed from emotional issues such as looking for acceptance, so again all of these things as Jesus stated are *heart issues*.

6. Addictive problems and besetting sins
Addictions are usually related to masking behavior or coping mechanisms for *heart based*, unresolved emotional issues. They are in effect our solution to our pain or anxiety which lay us open to setting up chemical cycles, associations and bondage to habits to cover our feelings.

7. Physical health
Our bodies are the end of the line in terms of our *thought life*. How you think about yourself and life will have a direct effect on your health in either a positive or negative way. Your body will flag or play out your *inner thought life* as your physical feelings are the chemical elaboration of the thoughts. It begins as a thought, becomes a feeling, which in terms of your body is a chemical release. We could say then that if your inner and outer thoughts are positive then it will be reflected in your body, hence the mind/body connection.

Study 11: Physical healing through healing the broken heart
When we have a thought or belief it goes to the part of the brain called the hypothalamus. This part of the brain oversees, amongst other systems, the central nervous system and the endocrine or glandular system. These glands release hormones into our bodies that are involved in many body functions. In terms of your chemical/physical body, hormones make your world go around.

Perhaps this is most easily demonstrated in some basic life activities. If you begin to think about your favorite food, your hypothalamus will begin to perform the relevant functions to get your body ready to eat. You may now find your stomach grumbling as the hormones involved begin to wind up your gastric system. If you think about a sexual encounter your body will release the appropriate hormones to prepare you for the physical act. Men are far more likely to have a rapid response to these thoughts because, according to the scientists, they have on average 20 to 25 times as much of the sex hormone testosterone. So, guys, it is advisable to avoid potential discomfort, by not thinking about sex before you have cleared the appointment with your wife.

So, we can see the fundamental outworking of our thoughts in our bodies through these simple illustrations. A cheerful or happy heart that is content with life and at peace with self and God will release hormones that promote health and well-being. The word of God says,

> Proverbs 17:22 "A cheerful heart is good medicine, but a crushed spirit dries up the bones." NIV

A heavy heart, loaded down with *negative beliefs* will produce hormone imbalances which lead to disease. We say that if your mind is not at peace or at *ease*, you are open to *dis- ease* in your physical body.

A BULL IN A FIELD

As an example of how this can play out in our bodies, let us look at two hormones in the hormonal cascade that affect each other and need to be in balance with each other. One is called cortisol, which is a stress hormone. It has anti-inflammatory properties and helps mediate actions such as blood sugar balances and so on. There are a number of other hormones that we need to function and be healthy that are in turn made from cortisol. There is another hormone on the other side of the cascade known as DHEA (Dehydroepiandrosterone) also from which many other hormones that we need are made. Amongst other things DHEA is implicated in mood and a sense of wellbeing.

Imagine finding yourself in a field with a snorting bull staring you down. Might I suggest that in that moment you do not need to be in a good mood and feel that all is right with the World! You actually need to have a stress response and go into flight fairly quickly. This is typically what happens with such a threat. Hormones that you need to get you out of the situation such as cortisol rise rapidly and hormones that give you a sense of well-being or are not important in the moment diminish. After the situation is resolved these levels go back to normal.

But what if your stress is coming from a fear related to people such as fear of rejection, failure, or performance anxiety to do with the expectations of others? It is very hard to avoid all humans. There are billions of them and invariably you will need to deal with some of them at some point in time. Anxiety issues related to whether you perform to expectations, or receive acceptance or not, are ever present, daily stressors. Hormonally, this means that your chemicals stay out of balance long term, and usually become more exaggerated over time. This is a common phenomenon in a society founded on achievement, conformity to expectations and success in return for value, significance and worth.

So now you have too much of one hormone and not enough of the other as an outworking of your way of life and culture. Normally, over time, the imbalance of these hormone values become more and more exaggerated. Simplistically this is a typical example of the pathways to disease. Each negative emotion will have some kind of unhelpful effect on your physiology and health.

SCIENTIFIC STATISTICS

Modern science confirms what the Bible has always stated, that if our soul is functioning well then the outcome will be health. The most recent statistics that I have heard is that around 90% of diseases proceed from emotionally rooted chemical imbalances. I would suggest that possibly the other 10% are to do with our bad solutions to our emotional problems such as drugs, alcohol, excessive food or even at times prescription medication which can carry a considerable number of side effects. I am not sure that we can lay all of our diseases at the feet of cultural issues, such as a high sugar diet as some do. However, these and other substances that we ingest certainly create an environment for disease to prosper and proliferate.

> 3 John 1:2 says, "Dear friend, I pray that you may enjoy good health and that all may go well with you, even as your soul is getting along well." *NIV*

The preceding passage confirms that if our souls, that is our mind, will and emotions, are in good order then our bodies will also be healthy. As we have seen, the state of our souls and physical well-being are directly linked to the condition and beliefs of *our heart*. In practice we have seen this to be the case over and over again. If our thought life is conformed to the word of God, both at the voluntary conscious level and also in the heart, we can expect the result to be health. Proverbs 4:20-23 puts it this way,

> *"Pay attention, my child, to what I say. Listen carefully. Don't lose sight of my words. Let them penetrate **deep within your heart** for they bring life and **radiant health** to anyone who discovers their meaning. Above all else, guard **your heart**, for it affects everything you do." NLT (emphasis mine)*

I have read somewhere that there is an area of modern medicine known as bio psychiatry. The premise of this model is that if they could get people to think correctly then nobody would be sick. The concept is correct, however without the power and ministry of the Holy Spirit I suggest that it is impossible for them to attain.

The New King James version translates this passage as the 'issues of life' that come from the heart. Health is certainly an issue that many have to deal with.

> *Proverbs 4:20-23 " ²⁰ My son, give attention to my words; Incline your ear to my sayings. ²¹ Do not let them depart from your eyes; Keep them in the midst of your **heart**; ²² For they are life to those who find them, And **health to all their flesh**. ²³ Keep your **heart** with all diligence, For out of it **spring the issues of life**. NKJV (emphasis mine)*

THE EXAMPLE OF A THYROID GLAND HEALED
A young lady in her mid-20s came for ministry with a presenting problem of her thyroid counts being, as she put it, *off the charts*. Her doctor was going to start her on hormone treatment immediately. I suggested that we work on the anxiety beliefs that she held that were producing the problem. We spent about an hour investigating and ministering to her anxieties. The next week she returned to her doctor reporting that she was well. His response to the blood test that followed was; *that can't be right, it is all in balance*. And so, he ordered another test which also proved to be perfect. An unexpected bonus from the ministry time was that she reported delightedly, that *the best part was that she didn't have a panic attack*, as she normally would when they did the blood test. Even her anxieties about the blood test were *belief* based.

A BROKEN HEART HEALED, LEADING TO RELEASE FROM A PHYSICAL MALADY
A number of years ago we were ministering in a large church in a rural city in Australia. A lady in her 50s was on the list to come for help and she was suffering from a variety of emotional problems. She was very eager to be set free and so her session went unusually quickly. Most of her problems were as a result of a considerable amount of sexual abuse in her early life. After around 45 minutes she reported that she was completely at peace and so we concluded our time together.

About 2 to 3 weeks later I received a message from her reporting all of the many benefits from the session. Unexpectedly she also reported that she no longer had to be hospitalized weekly for treatment to her liver and kidneys. I was not even aware that she had a problem as she had not mentioned it. Consequently, I had not prayed for her healing, it was simply a byproduct of her *broken heart* being healed by the Spirit of Christ.

At times we deliberately target beliefs that produce disease, and other times it happens unbidden as a result of the healing and release from captive thoughts and feelings taking place. We have seen various problems, such as for example arthritis or asthma, being healed without direct prayer. Somewhere in the process of an emotional release, the body comes back into order and they simply disappear. That is certainly not to say that God does not heal the body in a number of other ways, it is a way that we see God healing the sick.

THE POWER OF LIFE AND DEATH

> *Proverbs 18:21 "The tongue has the power of life and death, and those who love it will eat its fruit." NIV*

This proverb suddenly becomes very powerful in its potential power to break a *heart*. For example, in its simplest form, when a child is told that they are stupid, useless or in some way inadequate, it becomes a part of the programming of the identity or self-beliefs within their hearts. The echoes of these beliefs are literally a breeding ground for negative emotions eventually leading to disease and finally premature death. Not only might they impact on the length of life, they will almost certainly have an effect on the quality of life. Fortunately, Jesus promised us that He came to set the captives free in order for us to have abundant life to the full.

If we have been crushed by negative words, it will be difficult to have a *cheerful heart* that releases healthy hormones. A *heavy heart* that has been crushed this way will load our human spirit down in its ability to empower our bodies to function properly.

> *Proverbs 18:14 says "A man's spirit sustains him in sickness, but a crushed spirit who can bear?" NIV*

The heavy weight of a *broken heart* will sap away the life-giving function of the human spirit. We have already seen that a crushed or broken spirit dries up the bones. Other authors have already documented that the blood cells making up the immune system are manufactured in the bone marrow. If this is dried out it becomes pretty obvious that this can lead to some pretty serious diseases that have their etiology or causation in immune cell production or disruption.

AUTOIMMUNE DISEASE

Statistics vary, but a general figure of 1 out of every 7 to 10 people in the U.S. suffer from what is termed autoimmune disease. I imagine that the numbers would be similar across the developed World. There are more than 80 of these diseases listed. Some Christian commentators consider the root of the autoimmune component of diseases to be self-rejection, and we have found this to be the case.

Remember your body is the end of the line for your thought life. If, at a *heart level* you do not accept yourself then, your body will play out those thoughts. In essence you yourself become the enemy of your own acceptability because of some kind of perception that you hold about your worthiness. Your body then *follows your thoughts* by attacking itself. Some state that your immune system will then attack the weakest link in the chain. If you have stress, fear or anxieties this may be your thyroid or your adrenal glands for example. If you are overweight and your pancreas is overworked you may be a candidate for diabetes. At times we see people who are enormous and massively overweight or morbidly obese but they are not diabetic. They certainly have created an environment for the disease but emotionally they do not seem to hold inner beliefs that make them predisposed.

EVERYTHING STARTS WITH A THOUGHT

I have come to the conclusion that everything begins with a thought that is shaped by what we *believe*. Further, the *beliefs of the heart* are most powerful in terms of their implications because we do not usually know what they are or how to rectify them without the Holy Spirit. The outworking's of these range from your own personal inner health and relationships, right through to world leaders with low self-image making decisions based on their emotional needs and beginning world wars. The *thoughts of the heart* are the principle issue with implications for everything. How we are programmed becomes critical. 1 Corinthians 2:10-11 states,

> *"But God has revealed them to us through His Spirit. For the Spirit searches all things, yes, the deep things of God. For what man knows the things of a man except the spirit of the man which is in him? Even so no one knows the things of God except the Spirit of God." NKJV*

Study 12: Gods own perspective for those suffering in this area

Before we begin with how to practically work with the Spirit of truth in applying this ministry, let us examine God's position and provision towards this ministry. Do we need to talk God into helping us, or is it His idea?

DO YOU WANT MORE OF THE PRESENCE OF GOD, OR ANOINTING ON YOU?

Let us begin with a couple of Old Testament passages firstly encouraging our involvement and commitment to the ministry, and then a prophetic account of what those who respond to these passages will be doing.

> *Isaiah 57:15 states, "For this is what the high and lofty One says-- he who lives forever, whose name is holy: "I live in a high and holy place, but also with him who is contrite and lowly in spirit, to revive* **the spirit of the lowly** *and to* **revive the heart** *of the contrite." NIV (emphasis mine)*

We have to 'tease out' the exact meaning from the Hebrew that this passage comes from. He is saying that, He is with the contrite (Heb. Dakka - meaning, crushed or destroyed) and the lowly in spirit (Heb. Shaphal – meaning depressed). He is with them to revive them (Revive Heb. Chayah – meaning, to make alive, quicken, recover, repair, restore (to life), revive, save, to make or be whole).

This is much the same meaning as the NT Greek word 'sozo'. His promise is also to revive their *hearts*, which coming from the Hebrew word *Leb*, as we have pointed out means *the feelings, intellect and will*. Or perhaps we could position it this way; the feelings proceeding from our beliefs which affect our choices.

In the New Testament we have words such as 'Anapsuksis' which is normally translated as 'refreshing' but in the Greek it is actually, 'recovery of breath' or '*revival*.' So, whatever you think about what '*revival*' is, from a Biblical perspective, it is bringing life back to an individual's spirit and heart. A *revival* is when enough people are revived to change a community, city or even a nation.

> *Acts 3:19 says, "Repent, then, and turn to God, so that your sins may be wiped out, that times of* **refreshing** *(Anapsuksis, - recovery of breath, revival) may come from the Lord." NIV (emphasis mine)*

The basis of this is **repent**. This literally means to 'think differently,' or 'reconsider how you think.' Once we have changed our minds about how we regard God and His kingdom, it falls to Him to *revive* us and bring us to *wholeness*. As we know, in Luke chapter 4 and verses 18 -19, Jesus unraveled the scroll of Isaiah and quoted from chapter 61 regarding what He was now about to do. However, in Isaiah 61 the chapter goes beyond what Jesus reads and details what those that had received healing of *their* broken hearts and freedom from captivity were going to do. Isaiah 61:1-3 notes that,

> *"The Spirit of the Lord GOD is upon Me, Because the LORD has anointed Me To preach good tidings to the poor; He has sent Me to heal the brokenhearted, To proclaim liberty to the captives, And the opening of the prison to those who are bound; To proclaim the acceptable year of the LORD, And the day of vengeance of our God; To comfort all who mourn; To console those who mourn in Zion, to give them beauty for ashes, The oil of joy for mourning, The garment of praise for the spirit of heaviness."*

Up until this point He is talking about what He, in the first instance, will do for us. Next, He shifts to what the results of this ministry to us will be, and the passage moves on to what we who have received from Him will be doing:

> *Isaiah 61:3-4 "* *3 That* **they** *may be called trees of righteousness, the planting of the LORD, that He may be glorified. And* **they** *shall rebuild the old ruins,* **they** *shall raise up the former desolations, and* **they** *shall repair the ruined cities, The desolations of many generations." NKJV (emphasis mine)*

I believe that in *type*, the ruined cities refer to the broken human personality. Jesus referred to His own body as being a temple. The Bible also states that we are the temple of the Holy Spirit. So, the picture of the temple, or a city is not an uncommon portrayal of the human personality in the scriptures. This position is strengthened from other passages which refer to setting yourself on helping people receive the promises, such as Isaiah 58. Another example is that found in Proverbs 25:28.

> *"Like a city whose walls are broken down is a man who lacks self-control."* *NIV*

This passage refers to the ability of a man to resist and defend his person from participating with outside spiritual pressure. For example, normal emotional control being compromised through drugs or alcohol abuse.

As we round out our thoughts on the subject of Truth Encounters from a Biblical perspective, we can be encouraged to note in the following passage some powerful promises for our own healings as we set and position ourselves to free others. My wife and I can confirm that God is faithful to His word. We have progressively received healing and freedom ourselves as we have dedicated our lives to ministering to others.

> *Isaiah 58:6-12 "* *6 Is not this the kind of fasting I have chosen: to loose the chains of injustice and untie the cords of the yoke, to set the oppressed free and break every yoke? 7 Is it not to share your food with the hungry and to provide the poor wanderer with shelter-- when you see the naked, to clothe him, and not to turn away from your own flesh and blood?*
> *8* **Then your light will break forth like the dawn, and your healing will quickly appear;** *then your righteousness will go before you,* **and the glory**

of the LORD will be your rear guard. ⁹ *Then you will call, and the LORD will answer; you will cry for help, and he will say: Here am I. "If you do away with the yoke of oppression, with the pointing finger and malicious talk,* ¹⁰ *and if you spend yourselves in behalf of the hungry and satisfy the needs of the oppressed, then your light will rise in the darkness, and your night will become like the noonday.* ¹¹ *The LORD will guide you always; he will satisfy your needs in a sun-scorched land and will strengthen your frame. You will be like a well-watered garden, like a spring whose waters never fail.* ¹² *Your people will rebuild the ancient ruins and will raise up the age-old foundations;* ***you will be called Repairer of Broken Walls,*** *Restorer of Streets with Dwellings. NIV (emphasis mine)*

It is clear in the New Testament that Jesus discipled His followers into doing what He did. The Father's Will shall always involve ministering to, or supporting, those who are helping people to receive salvation, healing and freedom. If the Father is all about meeting the needs of the people He created, then it is inevitable that His children will be dedicated to the same activities.

PART 2: Ministering Truth Encounters

INTRODUCTION

We are going to begin to look at the practical aspects of knowing what to do to connect a person with the Holy Spirit for a 'Truth encounter.' I would like to make a couple of comments here before we begin. Firstly, although we are spending a lot of time talking about the ministry, we could sum up the whole process in a couple of lines.

> *We are looking to identify that which we* _believe in our hearts_ *that is causing some kind of issue and asking God to set us free by bringing His truth to our inner parts.*

Second, some people get hung up on questions such as "where is this in the Bible?" and "why do we need to do this?" The Bible makes it clear that we need to have a clean heart created in us, that we need God's truth in our hearts, and that His sheep WILL hear His voice. So, we are asking Him to answer specific questions once we identify the *belief-based thoughts* that are producing our problems.

"WHY DO WE NEED TO DO THIS TYPE OF MINISTRY?"

In our modern society we are flooded by all kinds of media. For many people, a few spare minutes means an opportunity to check their emails or Facebook, or perhaps relax in front of the Television. Added to this is the complicated, activity-based lifestyles that we lead. I propose that by the time evening came, one hundred years ago, saints such as Oswald Chambers most likely had their Bible and a candle to fill in their nights. So, to sit with God and relate with Him regarding the source of their issues would have been a comparatively uncomplicated endeavor. Most of us can point to times where the Holy Spirit has communicated something to us that has brought some kind of change. In fact, we are in a time of the outpouring of the Spirit of Truth as never before in history.

So, this ministry is aimed at purposefully, deliberately and diligently at bringing specific areas, issues and hurts to the feet of the Father for His truth. Most Christians want to be free to be all that they can be in service to God. They want to bring Him glory by modeling and giving evidence to His provision and love by seeing it manifested in their lives. Let us look at how we can receive truth for ourselves and then help others.

Study 13: Accessing the Heart via the mind and emotions

SCREENS, ICONS, PROGRAMS

For the sake of an illustration, let us imagine your conscious mind as a screen; perhaps as a television (TV) screen. In today's world there can often be up to 100 channels or more on our TV. On a normal TV set you can only view one channel or program at a time. We described in Study 7 how in much the same way, if I begin to talk about a hot dog or your favorite meal you may now have a picture on the screen of your mind. To access that picture of food you had to put whatever else you were thinking about to the side and change channels briefly. Your conscious mind is much like a computer in this respect, having been designed to be a sequential processor, or in other words to focus on one task at a time.

In a ministry session then, we are tuning into the fear, rejection or whatever other channel in order to view and connect with it. Thinking now of a hot dog, if we focus on it long enough, we will begin to have something happen in our stomachs as a reaction to the thought. In the same way as we begin to concentrate on, and embrace our fear or other issues, bringing them onto the screen of our conscious minds, we will have a chemical bodily response that we call emotion or feelings.

We can now begin to look for *the belief* and inner thoughts producing the emotion. Whether we present with a negative emotion and identify *the belief* producing it, or have a negative belief and let ourselves feel it, is immaterial. The important thing is that we connect them both on the conscious screen of our minds. Usually people will come presenting with negative emotions such as anxiety, fear, anger, rejection, bitterness and so on. Some people will look for help because of how they are reacting in relationships or to life.

As you listen to their story or problem you will most likely hear the beliefs behind the emotions come out in words. I usually have a piece of paper or a notebook with me, and record statements that I believe may be connected *to beliefs*. Jesus said that we will hear the overflow of the heart from the mouth: Matthew 12:34b states,

> *"... for out of the overflow of the **heart** the **mouth** speaks." NIV (emphasis mine)*

For example, in the course of telling their story, somebody might say something such as; 'school was a difficult time for me, but that's not surprising, I can never keep up with the other kids!' When the time comes for ministry, we could say to them something along the lines of, 'I heard you say before that you can never keep up with the other kids; is that true?' Now, as they concentrate on that statement and connect with the feeling that goes with it, we can ask a further question to find out *the belief of the heart*. 'What does that make you, if you can't keep up with the other kids?' Their possible answer may be something such as; 'I must be dumb!'

The next thing that we want to do is find the place where they first learned this; the critical moment when they 'took it to heart.' There is always a historically matching memory. They may report something along the lines of, 'when I was in grade 3, I could not do my times table and the teacher embarrassed me in front of the class.' So, I would probably say something along the lines of, 'so in that moment you believed that you **are** dumb because you could not do the times table?' Response 'Yes.'

Then I would say something such as, 'Lord, Fred believes that he is dumb and can't keep up with other people because he could not do his times table. His truth is that *he is dumb*; what is your truth for him?' As 'Fred' now has *the belief*, the matching negative feeling, and the historical event pulled up onto the screen of his mind it is time to ask God to reveal *His* truth to set him free. Whatever, God does in that moment will set 'Fred' free simply because He is God. The key for *us* is helping Fred is finding what is *believed in his heart*.

We tend to remember whatever is stored in the moment of emotional weakness and vulnerability. Surrounding details are not necessarily a part of interpreting the event so much as what is happening in the moment. God could remind him that he had been off sick and was not present when the instruction to learn those times tables was given.

Remember, this whole event including *beliefs* were beneath the surface in the heart all along. They needed to be deliberately accessed and brought into the conscious mind to be processed. It is apparently normally necessary to know what you believe before you can present it to the Lord to address it with His truth.

DEALING WITH MULTIPLE BELIEFS

Rounding out our illustration of a television screen, let us consider the multiple channels again. When we first began this ministry, people would come to us for help, and in a session, we might work through 2 or 3 *beliefs* and feelings that were a problem. They would usually report how free they felt, and we would be thinking that we had just worked with the Lord to fix up their whole lives! In some cases, people were happy with their new freedom, but many times we would be contacted with a report that they were struggling again. Upon investigation we would find out that everything resolved in the previous session was still settled, but there were other new issues. We have found this to be the case in ministering to others as well as receiving healing for ourselves. Most of us have a significant number of *channels* that need to be *reprogrammed*.

By way of example, someone may come presenting a problem of fear. They may have a fear of rejection, failure, flying, abandonment, or lack of protection or provision and so on. Each of these fears is *a different belief* and stem from various historical events. You can only have one of these *channels or programs* running in your conscious mind at a time. It is necessary to go through them one at a time and switch them off individually, so to speak. You only need one fear program still running to feel, for example, anxiety. Typically, as you go through ministering to each belief the intensity becomes less and less until they are completely free.

That is not to suggest that every fear needs to be dealt with before your anxiety is completely gone. It is usually fear related to people that is ever present, such as fear of rejection. It is difficult to not deal with people as there are billions of them on the Earth. A fear of flying, for example, may produce no anxiety at all because you simply choose not to fly. However, if you have to fly for some reason, your *belief-based* anxiety will quickly be present and need to be resolved.

THE 'GOLF' PRINCIPLE

I once saw a picture of the famous golfer Tiger Woods standing beside a pile of golf balls that would fill a shopping trolley. He was basically practicing producing the same swing over and over. The courses may change, the competition varies, the conditions will be different, but he is doing the same thing over and over.   In much the same way we have a handful of questions that we use over and over to help people identify that which they believe. Sometimes we will be visiting fear channels, other times switching of all of the rejection or bitterness channels. On occasions we will be finding the beliefs behind sin.

Some people will be very emotionally connected and receive the ministry easily. Others will have defenses and objections or be people who want to resolve their own problems with their minds and have not been able to. Whatever comes to us, as co laborers with the Holy Spirit, we patiently and graciously give our time, repetitively, asking the same handful of questions!

After a while, once you become familiar with the process you will find yourself ministering a *truth encounter* driving with someone in a car, across a table at lunch, in a prayer line or more purposefully in a prayer room at some location. The point is that once you learn the simple process you will be applying it over and over to different cases. It is very rewarding to see God setting people free, and Him allowing us the privilege of being involved.

'ICONS' AND 'SHORTCUTS'

Before we move on, I want to push out the parameters of the screen in the conscious mind analogy. Up to this point, we have discussed it as a television screen in order to illustrate that some people may have many *channels and programs* that need to be worked through, and others just a few. It doesn't actually reflect on you as a person how many *negative beliefs* that you have collected. It is a bit like being clothed by life. Someone's clothing may be expensive and plentiful; another's may be dirty and tattered. In the end we are all the same, just people clothed by different circumstances and conditions.

We know that God looks at who you are and not the outer appearance, this includes weighing justly your circumstances and how you arrived where you are. We cannot then judge anyone's behavior in any way. Something happened to produce the responses, everyone has a story, and if nothing negative happened to you then you can consider yourself blessed. You need to know though, that if you were the product of the same situations, then you would probably hold the same beliefs and produce the same attitudes and behavior. These responses to beliefs I call, *universal reactions*. They are predictable reactions to beliefs that are held. I will illustrate these in a later study.

COMPUTER SCREENS

Most people today have seen a computer screen. We can use this as an analogy to further examine how our conscious mind operates. On most screens are little pictures called *icons* which have some kind of symbol depicting the program that they represent. The program is in the unit stored in a deeper place. On my computers you have to click a button twice with the pointer on the icon to open the program.

The point is that these icons connect you to programs that are there underneath whether you open them or not. In the case of operating the computer most of these are opened as a deliberate act. This can be the case with our minds. For example, we can purposefully open the *time to cook the dinner* program which holds all the information that we have stored and held as data about preparing food. It will come up onto our screen and we will access what we know to complete the task. In my case all there is when I open the *prepare dinner program* is, '*buy Pizza.*'

ASSOCIATIONS

With regard to our minds, these programs are often accessed by situations or circumstances automatically. We call these *associations*. Perhaps the simplest way to explain this would be something like the ringing of your telephone. Your brain *associates* the sound with somebody wanting to talk to you. It then opens the *program* containing information on how to answer the phone in your memory, and most likely selects the most suitable response, depending on whether you expect it to be a friend or a grumpy employer.

Emotionally, we operate along much the same lines. Perhaps we are starting a new job in a crowded office. Without deliberately wanting to, we access an anxiety belief. Stored in the memory in the file along with the belief is *how do I react in this situation*? The belief could be something like, *people won't like me unless I do what they want and make them happy*, and this has been learnt from a historical event. The response to the situation, also stored in the memory, could be something such as, to entertain them and be funny. This may have been how they gained acceptance and fitted in as a child in similar situations. So, the behavior coming from the *I need to perform to be accepted belief* is a mask.

People often present with these types of situations on their *shopping lists* for healing. They would most likely come into a session reporting anxiety in these environments. We have them *click on the I am uncomfortable in group situations* icon on the screen of their conscious minds. By that I mean, concentrate on this type of situation and how it makes them feel. Then, we identify a matching historical event with the same emotions in it and clarify what is believed that produces the feelings. Once we have these elements, we can invite the Spirit of truth to minister freedom to them.

SHORTCUTS

Before we move on from the screen analogy, I would like to point out that these icons are readily accessible shortcuts to the programs within the computer that bypass the normal pathways. This is a helpful picture for us in terms of resolving habitual sin cycles. Let us create a common scenario.

A married woman struggles with rejection having never had true love and acceptance in childhood. As a consequence, deep inside she believes that she is *not loveable* or *good enough to be noticed*. The spouse, because of their own issues, is always at work, playing golf or at the pub with his friends. He feels that he has shown love by getting her a nice house and a car. Along the way she meets a nice man at work who comments on her hair. Later he invites her for a coffee.

Up until this point the whole process is going through the normal pathways of feeling that this is wrong, knowing that you shouldn't be doing it, but at the same time, mistaking the good feeling of being cared about as love. Usually your emotional needs will be the greatest predictor of your behavior, and eventually she moves past the self-conflict into an illicit relationship. After the first time, the person no longer works through the normal pathways regarding whether or not the sin should be entered into. Now this is the apparent solution to their rejection and they *shortcut* the process and go straight to the sinful activity. Without being set free from the underlying rejection beliefs, she can easily fall into further affairs. Typically, with both men and women, when their rejection is resolved they struggle to see how they could have gotten into the situation to begin with.

Another example could be a man addicted to pornography. At one time he felt convicted and guilty. But eventually when the opportunity or situation presents for him to access the sin, it is now a shortcut and he goes directly to the sin without inner opposition. His heart is hardened and he no longer goes through any thinking process that would hold resistance or objection, he goes directly to the sin.

2 Peter 2:19b says, "for a man is a slave to whatever has mastered him." NIV

Many sins have an emotional *need* component as the original trigger which needs to be resolved. Christians are not any different to anyone else in terms of their humanity and emotional needs. They are not the same as other people, however, in that they have the opportunity to be set free.

In summary then, as a tool to help our understanding, we know that when people look to us to connect them to God for healing, we need to get them to go through the exercise of connecting, consciously and deliberately, with information that they hold in their hearts. Some are hesitant to do that and you may need to spend some time working through getting them to look at the problem, and bring it up onto the *screen* of their conscious mind. Quiet rooms and a one on one session are ideal for this where possible. If they are prepared to, I have them focus on their thoughts or feelings, and go to what I term *periscope depth*. This is where they begin to concentrate on, and explore, what is underneath in the heart.

> **Note:** We can only minister to whatever a person is wanting help with. It is entirely up to them. God will not make them get ministry and neither should we. Our job is to offer healing if they desire it. We can encourage people to work through everything that they can find. Some people will, for example, be pleased to get rid of a fear or the like, but are happy to keep their pride and rebellion. It's almost as if they go, 'thanks for that God, but I am taking over again and am satisfied with my own solutions!' This is between God and the person; it is not our place to judge, only to be equipped to help when possible. We can only work with whatever issue that they present with.

Study 14: Sources of & Influences on Heart beliefs

THE GENERATIONAL PRINCIPLE

> *Exodus 20: 5-6, states, "For I, the LORD your God, am a jealous God, visiting the iniquity of the fathers on the children to the third and fourth generations of those who hate Me, but showing mercy to thousands, to those who love Me and keep My commandments." NKJV*

Doing the mathematics, Almighty God offers mercy to one thousand generations for those who show their love by keeping His commandments. That is 250 to 333 times more that He wants us to be blessed; than He wants us to be disciplined! If there are no consequences then there is no fear of God. However, this passage makes it abundantly clear that He wants to encourage us and reward us for showing our love for Him. God's love language is obedience.

> *John 14:15 "If you love Me, keep My commandments." NKJV*
> *John 14:15 "If you love me, you will obey what I command." NIV*

The *visiting* in Exodus 20:5 is like a *drawing to*. On face value, it almost seems as if the father's sin in a particular area, becomes an area where the children will be tested to see if they love God and prefer His commandments and ways. Will they seek Him to be free from their sins and weaknesses?

Have you ever wondered why, in a neighborhood, some of the residents are alcoholics, while others will never have a drink in their lives but are drawn like a magnet to horror movies, drugs, violence or pornography? This is the outworking of the *visiting* on the family line. Under the curse of the law this was the consequence of iniquity. It continues today for those who remain under the judgment of the law, not having believed that Jesus fulfilled the law and took the penalty of the curse in their place. Sin is defined by the law, it did not begin with the law; it began with Satan and entered the human generation line through Adam and Eve.

POSITIONS ON GENERATIONAL PRINCIPLES

Let me give you three distorted positions that Christians often hold pertaining to generational principles:

1. It was 'all done at the cross.'

This doctrine proposes that Jesus ended the penalty of the curse and so there are now no effects on Christians. This is a *positionally* true statement. Jesus did pay for our freedom from the curse of the law; hence all of His part was *done at the cross*. But we need to know that all of these promises are under the New Covenant which is mediated and accessed by faith. In the event that this were automatic and operative without the faith component there would be no sick Christians, no mental, emotional, relational issues or sin addictions to be dealt with. It is reasonably obvious that this is not the case. All of these maladies one way or another relate to the curse of sin through our generations all the way back to Adam.

The truth remains though, that Jesus did pay for the curse that passes through the generation lines, and largely we appropriate that provision of freedom through the ministries of the Holy Spirit. Water baptism is an ideal time to pray against dynamics coming through the family, as you are choosing to put the old life behind. We have seen evidence such as repeated accidents as a result of a family curse stop when we have prayed specifically against them at water baptism. But again, you will only be able to access by faith those things that you are aware of. As a consequence, many other areas are discerned later in further ministry settings.

> *Galatians 3:13 "Christ redeemed us from the curse of the law by becoming a curse for us, for it is written: 'Cursed is everyone who is hung on a tree.'"*
> *NIV*

Still others believe that traits passing from generation to generation simply do not exist. In a practical sense, observing even our physical characteristics and mannerisms and those of our parents and ancestors quickly dispels this thought. Even practices such as architecture or diet have a generational influence.

2. All of your healing and freedom will come through dealing with generational issues.

This group has you renouncing everything that you can possibly think of. Personally, I have not seen freedom come to many people using this model. If your generational influences have become your personal sin then you need to confess, repent and be ministered to and set free. It can become an excessive practice that is meaningless. I have seen people with issues that could be easily ministered to, endlessly and fervently going through books renouncing all kinds of sins of their ancestors.

The truth is that Jesus DID take the penalty of that curse for you. Now by faith and through the ministry of the Holy Spirit you can be set free. Self-effort in renouncing will not yield much without Him. A minister led by the Spirit may help you with the prayer of faith in these times. In the Old Testament we see that Balaam could not curse the people of God as they were protected. The method that was used to expose them and bring a curse on them was by getting them to participate in the sins of the societies around them.

3. The children eat sour grapes.

In arguing that generational influences are not relevant to Christians, people often quote the book of the major prophet Ezekiel in order to imply that generational principles are no longer in effect.

> *Ezekiel 18:1-3* ¹ *The word of the LORD came to me again, saying;* ² *"What do you mean when you use this proverb concerning the land of Israel, saying: 'The fathers have eaten sour grapes, And the children's teeth are set on edge'?* ³ *"As I live," says the Lord GOD, "you shall no longer use this proverb in Israel." NKJV*

If these people were to look further to the same account in the book of Jeremiah, they would see a fuller explanation of this. Remember, they are both prophetic books speaking of a time to come.

> *Jeremiah 31: 29-34* "²⁹ *In those days they shall say no more:* **'The fathers have eaten sour grapes, And the children's teeth are set on edge.'** ³⁰ *"But every one shall die for his own iniquity; every man who eats the sour grapes, his teeth shall be set on edge.* ³¹ *"Behold, the days are coming, says the LORD, when I will* **make a new covenant** *with the house of Israel and with the house of Judah;* ³² *"not according to the covenant that I made with their fathers in the day that I took them by the hand to lead them out of the land of Egypt, My covenant which they broke, though I was a husband to them, says the LORD.* ³³ **"But this is the covenant that I will make with the house of Israel after those days, says the LORD: I will put My law in their minds, and write it on their hearts; and I will be their God, and they shall be My people.** ³⁴ *"No more shall every man teach his neighbor, and every man his brother, saying, 'Know the LORD,' for they all shall know Me, from the least of them to the greatest of them, says the LORD.* **For I will forgive their iniquity, and their sin I will remember no more."** *NKJV (emphasis mine)*

Clearly, the expanded Jeremiah passage refers to the new covenant of provision through faith which was established for us by Jesus. You will find this in the book of Hebrews Chapter 10 in the New Covenant directly quoting Jeremiah. (See previous and following highlighted passages). So, we can deduce that the prophetic biblical statement that was made by Jeremiah and Ezekiel regarding 'sour grapes' referred to the covenant that we are now under. It was not something for their times.

> *Hebrews 10:16-17* "¹⁶ **This is the covenant that I will make with them after those days, says the LORD: I will put My laws into their hearts, and in their minds I will write them,"** ¹⁷ *then He adds,* **"Their sins and their lawless deeds I will remember no more."** *NKJV (emphasis mine. The same as Jeremiah 31:33-34)*

HOW THEN SHOULD WE REGARD GENERATIONAL PRINCIPLES?

As we have already established, Jesus paid the price for our freedom from generational influences. We consider co-laboring with the ministry of the Holy Spirit as a part of facilitating that freedom in a person's life. Because Jesus has already paid for their release then we can now simply consider generational influences as another potential source for their problem.

Let me give a very simple example of this. Imagine a parent has suffered from rejection from their own family. Remember the nature of God is always accepting. God did not reject man, man rejected God. Rejection then, not being one of the ways of God, can be considered as iniquitous or fundamentally, a sin-based activity. In this simple illustration then we see that the parents sinned against the child in not accepting them. Almost certainly they also suffered areas of rejection from their generations. Our sample parent then, having not received acceptance for their person will most likely continue the cycle, Christian or not, until it is broken.

Are we then getting them to renounce rejection when they come for help? No, we don't even necessarily need to know that it is generational. We are simply ministering to the beliefs that are now held as a result of the rejection. Now, as they have acceptance themselves on the inside, the cycle is broken and they will be carriers of love and grace. Their children may also need some ministry if they have already been affected by the rejection.

When we are dealing with emotional and *heart-based* healing, regardless of the source the ministry is the same, although we may observe that the source is generational. The ministry is actually appropriating the freedom from the curse that was promised under the New Covenant.

DELIVERANCE FROM GENERATIONALLY TRANSMITTED WEAKNESSES

Although not directly related to our 'Truth Encounters' subject, I will mention here that at times, deliverance of an evil spirit can go along with the ministry. A number of years ago I was ministering to an elderly lady who had suffered with guilt from an event early in her life. She eventually confessed that she had performed a sexual act with a dog. As well as ministry to the beliefs that she held relating to the event, she was delivered from a generational spirit drawing her to the bestiality act. She had never confessed this episode to another person prior to seeing me.

A few years later her middle-aged daughter also came for emotional healing. Towards the end of the session she confessed something that she had never told anyone before. When she was a young girl, she had also had sex with a dog. She also needed deliverance from the unclean spirit compelling her to this act.

Once you have seen a few of these cases there are no further doubts regarding generational influences. They were both lovely people, and both exemplary Christians, but there was an area of weakness that had come to them that they had not chosen.

Over the years we have seen many people set free from influences which cause them great guilt and condemnation. They are so relieved to realize that they are not inherently evil people, but something happened in their generations further upstream that they did not ask for. Their specific area of *visiting* was not something that they had read about in the will!

HEREDITARY DISEASE

If you attend doctors for some kind of chronic illness or disease, they will usually ask you if it is in the family. Physiologically they may test and observe some kind of genetic predisposition for the onset of the disease. We have already previously discussed studies that propose that as many as 90% of diseases stem from emotional imbalances.

I would like to suggest, and have noted over many years, that what actually passes through families are particular emotional problems that create an environment for that specific malady. For example, hereditary self-rejection will give opportunity for autoimmune problems to proliferate in a family line. So, dealing with rejection which has led to self-rejection will remove the predisposition for further generations to suffer. I have observed other troubles such as bitterness and resentment in families that suffer from illnesses such as cancer and arthritis. For the glorious Church that will shine in these dark times, disease prevention may well be just as important as cure.

EPIGENETICS AND SECULAR SCIENCE

Incidentally, modern secular science confirms the biblical generational principle. Most of that which the modern world is discovering relating to people can be found in your Bible which was written thousands of years ago by the creator of everything! It is already well documented that disease can be hereditary or generational. Epigenetics is an area of science that is stating that habits, behavior and addictions, for example, are also transmitted through the family.

The following statement is quoted from an article on Epigenetics that I was sent. The passage is from a Neuropsychologist, where Dr. Timothy Jennings explains:
*The choices we make – the foods that we eat, the things that we watch – can affect how DNA is expressed. When we have kids, we pass on the sequence to them. So, if we become addicted to stuff, we can pass along to our children gene instructions that make them more vulnerable to addictions. So, take pornography addiction, for instance, since it's the fastest growing epidemic in today's church. According to a recent study, 68% of Christian men are addicted to porn. Most likely, they are unaware of the hereditary ramifications of viewing porn. It doesn't happen generally with one exposure to pornography. It's the repetitive volitional exposure to pornography that will cause this type of gene expression change to happen". *Dr. Jennings has a U-Tube series explaining Neuroplasticity and Epigenetics*

In practice, we have usually found that the parents of men addicted to porn have also had the problem. Christians are not exempt from these principles and temptations in the World, but we do have the option of freedom. This is just one example. We acknowledge that whether we are dealing with *beliefs* that need truth, or sin problems that need deliverance or other ministry, generational sources are something that we need to be aware of.

CONCEPTION

Our next source is at conception. We have just discussed how dispositions towards beliefs, physical predispositions, behavior and even habits can pass to us, generationally and spiritually. This would pass to us at conception. It is well documented that the point of life beginning is as the sperm meets the egg and that there is at that moment a little *fireworks* display. For many Christians we would accept this to be the time where the human spirit and soul were placed within that first single fertilized cell. The scientists tell us that this flash of light is the moment when life begins.

We thank our mothers and fathers for joining with God in creation in providing our chemical bodies. But indeed, our spirits and souls are created by our Father in Heaven, who purposed us for Himself to spend eternity with Him. However, we are looking at the challenges we face that hinder our fruitfulness on the journey as we prepare for that time.

TRANSFERENCE AT CONCEPTION

In the following passage, King David ties his weakness and subsequent iniquity with Bathsheba to sinfulness that he received right at conception. Notably, in Psalm 51, verse six, he cites the solution and best defense against self-deception and sin as being truth in the inner parts, or heart as some translations render it.

Psalm 51:5-7 ⁵ *Surely I was sinful at birth, sinful from the time my mother conceived me.* ⁶ *Surely you desire **truth in the inner parts**; you teach me wisdom in the inmost place.* ⁷ *Cleanse me with hyssop, and I will be clean; wash me, and I will be whiter than snow. NIV (emphasis mine)*

Many years ago, we were traveling interstate between cities. I was asked by a person that I knew if we would be prepared to minister to a relative of theirs as we passed through their city. On the way to the home of the subject I did a little research on the internet regarding their disease. They were suffering from an unusual heart disease, and according to the medical information that I read on the internet it began at *conception*. This amazed me that medical etiology of the disease stated that it began at the time of a couple of cells receiving life. There is no heart, so how physically can heart disease begin here if you are basing your study on physiology and scientific evidence and not spiritual concepts?

It turned out that, as is the case with many forms of heart disease, fear was at the root. In this case, fear of death was the problem, which could indeed, be passed at conception. The Lord gave the person a picture which they reported as resolving the fear that was received at conception.

As a source, I will not spend much time on conception as it is relatively unusual for a belief to be birthed right in that moment. However, it is good to be aware of the possibility. None of these sources of beginnings are places that you deliberately look for or suggest. It will usually come from the person that you are working with.

Let me offer this story to illustrate what I am saying. Please note again that it is a fairly rare occurrence, which has presented on a few occasions in more than 20 years of facilitating this kind of ministry. I would hate to spark off a group of people targeting ministry to *conception* as Christians tend to do.

Important note: People seem to love; 'this is how you do it' models. This is the exact opposite of how this ministry works. We are not directive at all as to where the ministry should go. But as we explore what people are '*feeling and believing*,' as the beginning point, with the direction of the Holy Spirit we *discover* the source.

A young lady was presenting with a feeling of defilement and a sense of being unclean. As we asked her questions and explored her history, we could find no event that would cause her to feel that way. An impression came into her mind of her father forcing himself on her mother in rape. The source of the defilement and uncleanness having been revealed she was subsequently set completely free. As I have stated, this is a very rare and unusual case, and I would certainly discourage anyone from suggesting this as a source to anybody that you are helping. If it is something that you need to know, the Holy Spirit will reveal it most likely to the person.

PRENATAL, 'BEFORE BIRTH'
I have digressed a little here and there but we are looking to find the beliefs that we hold in our hearts that are not God's truth or perspective. In the case of taking in beliefs *prenatal* or while we are still in our mother's womb, we need to realize that these *beliefs* were initially feelings. Later, when we have words, we can describe the feelings with words. The words are

a verbal explanatory version of the feelings or emotions and are one in the same. There is a great deal of science and evidence that indeed a child is impacted by that which both the mother and father are thinking and doing whilst the child is still in the womb [3].

We see instances in the Bible, such as John the Baptist, leaping in the womb when Mary was visiting, carrying the unborn Jesus.

> *Luke 1:41 says, "And it happened, when Elizabeth heard the greeting of Mary, that the babe leaped in her womb; and Elizabeth was filled with the Holy Spirit." NKJV*

This is an area that you may commonly find yourself ministering in. Again, it is vital that you do not suggest this as the source. When you have exhausted all other possibilities of where beliefs may have begun, and there are no memories then this is a possible source.

> **Note:** Many people who do not immediately have memories may have suppressed them over time because they are too painful or fearful. There are other reasons for not immediately being able to access memory which we will discuss in a later chapter.

A feeling of not being wanted in a prenatal setting may later be described in words as the belief that no one wants you or perhaps that you are unacceptable. Put simply, rejection is non-acceptance. I have noted, over the years, some predictable beliefs emerging when a child is not accepted when they are known by the parents to be present: 'I don't belong, I am an intruder, I shouldn't be here, I am not wanted, I am not loved...'

There of course can be other reasons coming from memories and events that can cause you to hold those same beliefs. I reiterate that it is vital to not try to take people to a source that you believe may be the root. Just begin with the presenting problem and work backwards into their inner reality.

For example, we have all seen people who come into church, are warmly accepted, loved and valued. Eventually they find a reason to move on, and so they go to many churches, finally, sadly often leaving church altogether. Many times, the reason is, that no matter how much love that they receive, if they hold a belief in their hearts that they *do not belong, are not an accepted part of the group, not really loved, wanted or valued*, they will eventually leave.

All of these beliefs promote anxiety for them in the form of fear of rejection. Once having been rejected, we fear it happening again. This is the most common kind of fear and anxiety, fear of man.

OTHER KINDS OF BELIEFS FROM PRENATAL INFLUENCES

It is very much the case that we can receive any kind of belief that the mother is feeling. If a father has left the mother because he found out that she was pregnant, she will most likely feel she is *not important* or valued. The child may grow up believing that men will not be there for them and that they do not value you or treat you as important or valuable. This is likely to be a possible root to behavior such as extreme *self-importance* and is behind issues such as narcissistic attitudes. So, the solution to feeling that you are *not important* becomes

---

3 *For further study: The Secret Life of the Unborn Child by Thomas Verny M.D. with John Kelly*

being the only one who *is important*. There can, of course, be other events in childhood where these same beliefs have taken hold. A mother, who already has small children and is struggling to manage in some way, may produce a child who has imbibed the mothers' anxious feelings and goes through life stressed from a belief that they will not be able to cope.

AN EXAMPLE OF HOW SPECIFIC SITUATIONS PRODUCE MATCHING BELIEFS

I teach on prenatal beginnings in our School of Healing and Freedom, and a number of years ago there was a young lady in her mid-twenties attending the sessions. When I began explaining this area, she reported to me later that in her mind she thought to herself, *As if Steve!* The next morning, she was booked in for a ministry session and she was set free from some fears and different problems coming from her memories. Eventually we came to a belief that we discovered began when her mother found out that she was pregnant with her. The situation that she wanted help with was that she had always felt excessively responsible for her mother's life and happiness. Now in her mid-twenties their relationship was such that the daughter's role was that of mother, and the mother looked to the daughter to resolve her problems. The mother even rang up during the ministry session for advice.

As the young lady focused on the feeling of being responsible, and I asked some questions to refine the emotion and belief, the situation unfolded. She remembered her mother, who was 17 years old at the time of discovering the pregnancy, once saying to the unborn child something along the lines of, *you've ruined my life.* For mum, it was the end of being able to do whatever she wanted and she wasn't prepared. The child now believed that she was responsible for the mothers' happiness and it played out in life and their relationship. When God brought perspective, she was greatly relieved to be free of the burden, and promptly booked her mother in for a ministry session for her issues as well!

The point is that we can be very vulnerable to the thoughts and feelings of our parents in the prenatal setting. I could write for some time stories such as people with fear of water that were at Sea in storms in a prenatal event and numerous other situations that are the basis of a person's troubles.

People are going to receive freedom in different ways in their healing moments as God touches them and sets them free. I recall one lady suffering from prenatal rejection reporting something like a warm blue star touching her heart as she felt the pain emanating from her lack of acceptance.

KEEPING IT SIMPLE

Whether prenatal or from another source, you can make an educated guess as to what a person may have been thinking in a given situation or circumstance. As an example, it is common to find a child that has, for instance, been abandoned by the Father either before birth or in early childhood now holding a fear of abandonment. Beliefs such as, *there is no one there for me, there is no one there to protect or provide for me, men don't think I am important*, or other predictable beliefs are common. Once abandoned, insecurity will be a large part of their life, and having been abandoned then the fear of it happening again will be a prominent anxiety. People with these kinds of wounds will typically be controlling and possessive around relationships, often needing constant reassurance that those around them will be there for them. So, it begins in the mind with a fear of abandonment belief such as, I could be left alone, and ends in the body with physical problems such as Asthma.

Adopted children may have beliefs such as *where is everybody (familiar) gone? There is no one there for me.'* (That is the people that should be there). This can create a considerable amount of fear, anxiety, and even depression.

HELPING LOCATE A PERSON CLOSE TO THEIR BELIEFS

So, as ministers, in our efforts to help we can look at a situation or circumstances, make an educated guess and propose what might be believed, and offer it as a suggestion. This could come out in a statement from you, for instance in a situation where it is known that parents decided not to keep you, as, *So, do you feel like you are not wanted?* People actually know what they feel if they are honest. They will either say *yes, I do, no, not really, or that's close, but it is more like this or this!* You have simply landed them near their belief. Before you invite the Lord to bring truth there, you might ask a further question such as; *do you feel that there is any reason that you were not wanted?* They may reply that they just feel like they were not wanted, and that is the belief that they hold, or they may respond with something along the lines of *I feel as though I was not wanted because I was in the way*, or some other kind of qualifying belief.

> **Note:** If a child is rejected pre-birth, or even after birth and they are feeling not wanted, then even though the parents might change their mind and accept the child later, or perhaps decide to stay together, the child will still have already received the rejection in that initial moment of emotional breach.
>
> Whatever the source, the thoughts and beliefs that have been encoded in the heart will match that which you would reasonably expect to be taken in given the content of the event.

NOTE REGARDING SUGGESTING POSSIBLE BELIEFS

Some ministries doing this kind of work would never suggest a possible belief. Their guidelines could be something such as that the person must discover the belief themselves. I could never see any practical reason for this. People come to you to help them identify whatever it is that they believe is causing their problem. Basing your suggestions on what you would expect could be reasonably taken in as a belief can make a session dramatically shorter, which leaves you more time to minister into other areas. I have never seen anyone agree with a suggested belief to please me. They either say, *yes exactly, almost, but it's more like this, or, no, that is not it.*

The more ministry experience that you have, the more discernment and skill you have at helping identify beliefs. Of course, it is not a technique or *method* that has to be followed. The same results are achieved simply by asking questions. Suggesting belief options is simply a tool that may be appropriate in some situations. It may prove to be helpful with, for example, some subjects who don't quite understand what it is that you are looking for.

GENDER CONFUSION WITH PRENATAL INFLUENCES AS ONE POTENTIAL SOURCE

Many times, I have found people who feel that they should have been the opposite gender. This often stems from people wanting the child to be born a particular sex. A few years ago, when I was teaching Pastors on this in Africa, one of the hosts took the platform after I had finished the session. He bravely proclaimed that when his daughter was in his wife's womb, and given that they had wanted a boy, he prayed and prophesied over the child that it would be a male. Now, he confessed, as a grown-up girl, when he leaves the house she puts on his clothes. It really is best to leave the selection to the creator.

At times I have ministered to some farmer's daughters who illustrate this affect. Their hair is cut like men's hair, they wear men's overalls, and they can often outwork the men on the farm. It is not uncommon for them to also exhibit lesbian tendencies. The farmers have wanted boys to help with the farm work and so these girls have felt from before birth which position in the family that they should fulfill. Remember, as a principle, *as a person thinks in their heart so are they!* (Proverbs 23:7). These girls think in their *hearts* that they should be boys. That is how they are in terms of their gender orientation and behavior. This then becomes the basis of their identity. In the same way I have ministered to men who believed that they should be girls and have various predictable distortions of their personality.

Note: There are other reasons for gender disorientation and preference.

A FINAL NOTE IN RELATION TO PRENATAL MINISTRY IF IT PRESENTS AS THE SOURCE

Spiritually, God intended for us to be accepted, valued, received and loved right from our very beginnings. A rejective spirit is from another kingdom which is not the kingdom of God. In the event that our commencement to life and relationships was under rejection there is often a spirit there which also needs to be dealt with. Once the person is connected to the feelings and beliefs, postured to receive from God in whatever way He chooses to touch them, simply tell the spirit of rejection, fear or whatever else to go. Most times this is not a dramatic deliverance. For example, the person may suddenly have some emotion as the spirit leaves, cough as it comes out on the breath or exhibit involuntary deepened breathing. Quite often you will not see much happen but the person will simply report feeling lighter.

AM I 'QUALIFIED' TO MINISTER HEALING OR FREEDOM?

You do not need to have some big ministry to do this, as it is firstly, the work of the Holy Spirit, the finger of God. It is in the name of Jesus Christ, not your name that you are commanding it to go. Remember redemption! Regardless of how you see yourself at the moment, the Father sees you as perfect, (Hebrews 10:14), seated in the heavenlies with Christ (Ephesians 2:6). Positionally, over all of the works of the enemy, in Christ, with authority over all of the power of the enemy (Luke 10:19). This is regardless of whether or not you are a brand-new Christian or having a good or bad day!

He made us and anointed us with the Holy Spirit so that we could do these good things! We just need the heart of God in wanting to see people helped by receiving His provisions. It is not about personal perfection or being good enough in our own eyes. This ability to have the Holy Spirit work through you, as you are, is the grace of God. He surely smiles and is pleased when we have enough faith to trust Him at His word.

> *Ephesians 2: 8-10 " ⁸ God saved you by his special favor when you believed. And you can't take credit for this; it is a gift from God. ⁹ Salvation is not a reward for the good things we have done, so none of us can boast about it.*

*¹⁰ For we are God's masterpiece. He has created us anew in Christ Jesus, **so that we can do the good things he planned for us long ago**." NLT (emphasis mine)*

Peter had to realize his own human weaknesses, and all of God's supply and provision, before he was suitable to humbly serve God. Peter denied Jesus proving his humanity. In spite of this failure, Jesus' next instructions to him were to go and feed His sheep. Now aware that he was to work in the grace of God's provisions, the power of the Holy Spirit and the name of Jesus, he was ready to serve. He now was able to make the following statements which we should all humbly identify with:

> *Acts 3:12 So when Peter saw it, he responded to the people: "Men of Israel, why do you marvel at this? Or why look so intently at us, as though by **our own power or godliness** we had made this man walk"?*

And

> *Acts 3:16 "And His name, **through faith in His name**, has made this man strong, whom you see and know. Yes, **the faith which comes through Him** has given him this perfect soundness in the presence of you all." NKJV (emphasis mine)*

Later we see this principle of total reliance on God and His righteousness was acknowledged by the Apostle Paul. Along with Peter, a key to his success was the knowledge of his own imperfect human nature. As with us, he was still undergoing the process of sanctification.

> *Acts 14:3 "Therefore they stayed there a long time, speaking boldly in the Lord, who was bearing witness to the word of His grace, granting signs and wonders to be done by their hands."*

> *Acts 14:15b, "We also are men with **the same nature as you**." NKJV (emphasis mine)*

They acknowledged willingly, that they had the same nature as these men. In the Greek language, the word translated *nature* means *similarly affected, like passions*. They were pointing out that they were aware of their human weaknesses and propensities, and without the Grace of God and the works of the Holy Spirit, these things would not be happening.

The point that I am making is that you don't step back from taking authority over an evil spirit because you are not perfect in your own eyes. That is the best place to be! His grace is sufficient for you. You are, through Jesus, perfect in God's eyes and that is all that matters. In the unlikely event that you are actually perfect in all of your ways, then you no longer need Jesus to make grace available to you. However, if that is the case, you most likely are in deception and have some serious pride issues which, incidentally, seem to be on the top of the list of things that God does not like!

A key to all kinds of ministry is to base your worthiness and consequent authority to minister, in the name of Jesus, on the completed work of redemption, as opposed to where you are up to in the ongoing work of sanctification. It is also wise to base your own worthiness in qualifying for any kind of healing or freedom, on the redemptive work of Jesus rather than where you have come to in your own version of being good enough. God very pointedly marks out that our own efforts at righteousness, as opposed to His provision through Jesus falls along way short.

*Isaiah 64:6, "**All** of us have become like one who is unclean, and all our righteous acts are like filthy rags; we all shrivel up like a leaf, and like the wind our sins sweep us away. NIV (emphasis mine)*

*Romans 3:10 As it is written: "There is **no one righteous**, not even one. NIV (emphasis mine)*

God Himself not only heals our diseases; He deals with the reason for the disease to begin with. I have never seen God not heal or free a person physically, emotionally or spiritually if they receive from Him with a simple faith. This includes people with some fairly unsanctified behavior and attitudes at times.

*Psalm 103:2-4 ² Praise the LORD, O my soul, and forget not all his benefits, ³ who forgives **all** your sins and heals **all** your diseases, ⁴ who **redeems your life** from the pit and crowns you with love and compassion. NIV (emphasis mine)*

ADDRESSING THE EVIL SPIRIT

Most times, if you have the person connected to their feelings and beliefs, and you address a spirit as we have said, you may see a sudden release of emotion, or they may simply report that they feel lighter or free. They may report that, at the moment that you told the spirit to go, God communicated with them in some way. It really doesn't matter whether you address the spirit in a whisper or a yell. It is not volume or some kind of show that releases the person, it is the place of authority that God has given that matters. Equally important is the permission of the person and their desire for you to address the spirit. It is largely a matter of exposing the spirit and its hold that makes the ministry effective.

I know, in different nations across the world, a number of little, very old ladies, who are very adept at casting out demons without changing the tone of their voices. So physical size, personality, emotional intensity or strength really are not relevant; it is really about understanding the authority that you have in the name of Jesus.

The example of the Canaanite woman, in Matthew chapter 15, is an excellent illustration of spiritual authority. The woman came with a presenting problem of a demon troubling her daughter. Jesus is not recorded as saying or praying anything regarding the demon or going to the lady's house. He simply said that as a response to the woman's faith that her child would be set free. There is no mention of a manifestation. Notably the story describes the result of the child being set free as healing. Other times we see demons come out just in the presence of Jesus or later the Apostles in the book of Acts.

*Matthew 15:22 A Gentile woman who lived there came to him, pleading, "Have mercy on me, O Lord, Son of David! For **my daughter has a demon in her**, and it is severely tormenting her."*

*Matthew 15:28, "Woman," Jesus said to her, "your faith is great. Your request is granted." And her daughter **was instantly healed**. NLT (emphasis mine)*

DEMONIC AMPLIFICATION

Demonic dynamics will be discussed in more detail in a later Unit. I want to point out that, the *belief* that matches the emotional breach is often the entry point for a demon stronghold. Dealing with *the beliefs* that give ground to the spirit is far more important than the spirit itself.

If you put your favorite songs through an amplifier, it is the same music, but now it has power. Evil spirits or demons, as we also know them, work in much the same way. You can have an emotional problem without having a spirit attached, which is going to be the case in most *Truth Encounters* sessions. You can hold the same belief, but the pain or response is now magnified by a demonic entity. This is why I believe people will often report some measure of emotional release or freedom in a prayer line, at a healing meeting or church service. The presence of the Holy Spirit has caused the evil spirit to move off.

Prior to our working in *Truth Encounters* we would cast out demons. Some people would report a measure of improvement, and others would be back in the same condition a week later. The problem was that we drove the rats away but didn't clean up the rubbish, being the negative beliefs causing the brokenness, pain or anxiety.

I am often in churches where the ministers proclaim that God is going to move and heal everyone's hurts and issues in the service. I have not yet seen this happen, although God can do absolutely anything so it is possible. The only predictable way that I have ever seen God completely freeing people from *heart-based beliefs* is through some kind of *Truth Encounter.*

HEALED OF ANOREXIA NERVOSA

A number of years ago I was attending a healing meeting and I saw a man there with his wife and daughter whom I had seen in other healing meetings in another state. He also recognized me so we were chatting together. As we went along, he reported that he was there because his daughter had anorexia nervosa and had been hospitalized in a critical condition, as I recall more than once. I could see the desperation in his eyes and encouraged him to have faith and expect a breakthrough. I realized that he had brought her to a number of healing meetings with no result in the past.

My experience told me that people may get some partial help through deliverance in a prayer line, but that usually they are freed by dealing with the beliefs. Feeling that I should offer some help, I hesitantly said something along the lines of: *This is an excellent ministry, so there is every chance for her healing this weekend! But, if you don't get the breakthroughs that you are looking for, we see God bringing healing to these kinds of complaints in other ways.* And I gave him my card.

A month or two later I received an email reporting that she had been in hospital again and could we help. When we were near their town we dropped in and did a session with their daughter at their local church. We then headed off to minister somewhere else and heard nothing further. A year or so later we were in a meeting in their state and after the service the glowing mother came up to me and reported that from the time of her session, the daughter had simply improved and put on weight returning to health.

God can do anything, but personally I have not seen complete emotional healing in a normal prayer line. We do at times minister a *Truth Encounter* in prayer lines but only on rare occasions, or if it has just been taught and people are aware of the source of their issues.

---

4 *The depth of the pain can also have a bearing on the strength of a spirit and its power and influence in the host person.*

> **Important Note:** I never think about evil spirits when I am ministering in a Truth Encounter. I am focused purely on finding the beliefs. If there is one present, and you understand demonic dynamics, you will become aware that it is involved. Don't go looking for spirits. Most times with *Truth Encounters*, if there is a spirit implicated it will leave when the beliefs are resolved and you may not even be aware that there was one actively working [4]. This is because the spirit is usually involved in the sinful responses or reactions to the hurtful belief. Once the hurt is resolved the person no longer needs or wants to respond in this way, which is a gift of repentance. (2 Timothy 2:25 NKJV) So, you can see that the spirit has a hold because of their willful cooperation. In a very practical way, the truth has made them free.

Examples of this could be issues such as; bitterness, unforgiveness, rebellion, pride, self-pity, anger, control, fear and so on. Most of the time these issues are present without any obvious demonic stronghold or amplification. Both you and the person being ministered to may never even become aware of the demonic presence that was possibly involved at some level.

For more information on spiritual issues see Unit 5 on dealing with demonic influences.

Study 15: Memory

Most of the time we are helping people, and indeed the majority of their problems, are going to be found in *beliefs* learnt or interpreted as *conclusions about their identity* or the situation found in their memories. We will therefore examine how these *beliefs* may be deposited in the *heart*.

Some people question whether or not accessing memory in a ministry setting is a valid activity. If I asked most people what John 3:16 says, they would quickly respond; 'God so loved the World....' How do they know this? They remember it. How to find your way home, sit on a chair, speak, or do anything at all, is based on learning and remembering. Memory is therefore related to every single action that we perform, including breathing.

Some people put up questions such as why do we have to look back? They quote the Apostle Paul, who urges us to forget the things which are behind. In the following passage and its preceding verses, you will see that he is not talking about ignoring life-shaping memories. He is in fact talking about forgetting his achievements as a Pharisee which he now counts as *rubbish*.

> *Philippians 3:13-14 "[13] Brethren, I do not count myself to have apprehended; but one thing I do, forgetting those things which are behind and reaching forward to those things which are ahead. [14] I press toward the goal for the prize of the upward call of God in Christ Jesus." NKJV*

Others comment that you shouldn't spend your whole life looking into the past. I agree that we should be moving on and working for the Gospel. But we also set aside specific times where we deliberately deal with issues from our past. I recently heard a comparison between a rowing boat and a canoe or Kayak race. In a rowing boat you are moving forward but looking back all the time. Whereas, in a canoe or Kayak you are looking at where you are going and moving forward. On occasions, however, even in a Kayak it is good to look back and see if anything from behind needs to be considered and dealt with. Checking what is going on behind out of sight that might affect the outcome of your race?

In terms of negative beliefs and emotions, it is a critical part of the healing process. The initial memory where a belief is taken in, is the place with the most detail for accurately examining and *identifying the conclusion* and *consequent belief* from the circumstances taken to heart.

It is good to note that memory does not simply relate to the past, it also has implications for the future. For example, if someone has had an event where they were perhaps publicly embarrassed, they will now be on the lookout for potential places or situations where this could happen again. This will then be a source of low-grade anxiety and will often be present in gatherings. The long-term effects of this will have an outworking in the physical body as being the end of the line for the sub-surface thought.

The scientists tell us that a small almond shaped section of nervous tissue in the brain named the *Amygdala* is responsible for memory and emotions. It is considered by some to be the fear centre. When something significant such as embarrassment occurs, the Amygdala is activated, and its response could be something such as; *That wasn't good; I better make a good memory of that so that I can make sure that it doesn't happen again!* From the initial event, memory projects the new belief about possible repeat situations out into the future to try to prevent a repeat occurrence.

All fears or responses to particular stressors have their beginnings in memory of some kind. The possible exception to this may be a fear that has passed through the generation line.

CRITICAL EVENTS

The first time that we do anything is a significant moment in terms of encoding information about how we perceive that activity. Our early impressions of how we perform in areas such as the school environment for example, are a common place of memory where people arrive in a session. How our parents and teachers regarded and assessed our efforts will affect the way in which we view our person and ability to perform and meet requirements. We could perhaps be compared to a sibling who is academically interested and gifted and come away with some kind of inferiority belief or low self-image. Typically, these would be unconscious inner thoughts such as; *I am not as good as others. I'm dumb, a loser, useless, not like other people, a failure* etc. etc.

This certainly has impact when we are deciding about our *identity* as a child, and while our brain is plastic and impressionable. Later in life we will use those beliefs to interpret other critical first-time events such as sexuality. Usually if the initial experience is not positive, they will see those activities through the filter of their existing *self-image beliefs*, having already learnt that they are *inferior* or *cannot perform as others can*. They will use these preexisting beliefs to reach a conclusion about whether or not the activity is positive and reinforcing or yet another place for anxiety.

> **Note:** In much the same way as parents and teachers should remove pressure and help a child see their academic endeavors in a positive light, the church should help their newly-weds with realistic expectations to help them to qualify their performance in the learning process of areas such as sexuality and relationships. This would hold true for other significant first-time events such as speaking or sharing in a Church service.

TRAUMAS AND EPISODES

A number of years ago we were conducting our healing school and a Chinese lady came into the session with her husband. All the way through the teaching she would cough every few seconds, not being deliberately disruptive, just unable to prevent it. The next day she made an appointment to be on the ministry list to receive some help. As we interviewed her it came to light that she had been in an accident crushing her chest, and this was the beginning point for her coughing. She was a very brave lady and connected with the fear belief proceeding from the trauma, which was as I recall; *I am going to die.*

As she remembered the event and connected with *the belief and feeling,* we invited the Lord to bring His truth. In this instance, because she was connected with the event, a spirit of fear of death was exposed and manifested, and then came out. At the same time God communicated to her regarding *the trauma belief.* She was free and sat quietly throughout the day, finally testifying to her healing in the evening service. She was healed and freed from some other problems, and as a result, was so pleased that she translated all of the considerable amount of school notes into Chinese for use in her own nation.

Notes:
1. It is unlikely that if we had gone after the spirit of fear that we would have had the same success in seeing her set free from it. Identifying and feeling the belief which the spirit rode in on at the point of weakness exposed it, and brought it into the open with nowhere to hide. Dealing with the belief closed the emotional breach that gave it place.

2. We are not hunting for demons, even in traumatic situations, we are looking for the beliefs encoded as that is where the problem really lies. If there is some evidence of demonic replay, stronghold or amplification then simply tell it to go. I usually do this while I have the person focus on the beliefs producing the feelings. This way the spirit is exposed. The same can be applied to dealing with areas such as lust problems. Being exposed to pornography for example can be a type of trauma which is deeply encoded in the memories. If there is a lustful spirit there then having the person think the thoughts from the trauma can in some cases cause the demon to be brought to the surface because you have connected with that which it holds!

3. Let me reiterate here, don't go looking for demons, but be aware that they may be present particularly in regards to trauma. Most *Truth Encounters* you will not even give demons a thought. (More on Spiritual dynamics in Unit 5).

EPISODES

By *episodes,* I am referring to individual events where beliefs were the conclusions arrived at in that critical moment. For example, sexual or physical abuse which are usually extremely traumatic in nature. Your parents, forgetting to pick you up for school, might be a one-time episode where you conclude that you're *not important, and really don't matter.* But it may not be traumatic, because even though you are feeling hurt because of the omission, you are having a great time with the other kids in the playground.

SEXUAL ABUSE

To be abused sexually is a traumatic episode which can affect many areas of the personality. From the damage and brokenness involved, there emanates rejection, fear, confusion, degradation and low self-image. This is a significant area, when you consider that indications in the western world are that, as many as minimally fifty percent of women have had some form of inappropriate sexual behavior acted out on them. This could range from being touched by a friend of the family or relative right through to penetrative sex with a small child. Having ministered to a great many of these victims, I can offer hope that God will faithfully set you free. I also offer a list of possible beliefs that are commonly present with people who have been offended against in this way.

Inferiority
I am dirty, unclean, not like other people, ruined, a nothing, or, I'm bad.

Confusion
I am overwhelmed, and don't know or understand what is happening.

Guilt
Somehow this is my fault. I have done this. At times children will get attention, value and importance, at a neighbor's house when they have been receiving none at home. This may include sexual behavior. The guilt is too much to bear because they know that at some level that they wanted to be there. On occasions I have ministered to people who have felt guilty because they have felt physical pleasure in the act. Nerve endings are nerve endings; they do not discriminate between whether an event is appropriate or not, they simply report sensations. So, if they felt pleasure then it was not their fault either, but this is something that they need perspective from the Lord on. More often abused people would report pain.

Fear
This can be in the form of being overwhelmed physically and emotionally and not understanding what is happening. Beliefs such as; *I cannot cope, it is too much to bear, I am trapped, overpowered, there is nobody here to protect me,* may also be present. Further, fear from threats from the perpetrator over being harmed if they tell anyone, or being afraid to tell parents because it is a relative or even that they expect punishment from their harsh family may also be present.

If the abuse continues, with subsequent events, usually these later times are interpreted through whatever beliefs are already held from the initial episode. This could be the person believing that it is happening again because; *they* are bad, dirty, naughty or some other belief that they already hold as being true about themselves.

Some of the sad outcomes from sexual abuse are that once a person has concluded at heart level that they are bad or dirty, then why even try to be good; after all they are ruined and spoilt anyway. The result of this kind of inner dialogue can be a promiscuous lifestyle. Perhaps they have learnt that sexual acts give you favor, *love* or acceptance from men.

They exact opposite of promiscuity is the issue that you most commonly deal with, and that is sexual dysfunction. The act of sex by association connects you with all of the fears, feelings of sex as being dirty, guilt and defilement. Enjoyment and participation of sex is no longer an option for you. This can be a great barrier to having a wholesome, complete and intimate relationship with your spouse. Sadly, in this age a high percentage of males have also been abused.

I ministered to a man some time ago who reported that before he and his wife were married, they had had a very active sex life. (I am not making comments on the appropriateness of this behavior here). After they were married, she shut down and the sex life that they had enjoyed ended. Once I had ascertained that she had been abused as a child, I explained to him that most probably before they were married, she felt as though she was in control and could walk away at any time. After they were married, she would have unconsciously been feeling as though she didn't have a choice any more, wasn't in control, and now she had to have sex. Possibly she also felt that she was trapped and couldn't get away. These were all unconscious thoughts that she had learnt in the abusive episode. Unintentionally her inner beliefs were now being triggered and her emotional priorities dictated her behavior. Whatever the inner thinking, God has a greater truth to set you free.

REPETITIVE THEMES

God Himself encouraged repetition as a means of making our beliefs permanent memory, or our *default position*. For example, we recall Joshua being told five times to be strong and courageous. In other words, meditate on your responses until they are an automatic neural pathway. God is saying here that you need to set up a *shortcut* to how to react when you are under attack. Then, you no longer need to think it through, it is already decided who you are and how you are and for that matter how God views you. Repetitive themes from childhood, when our brains are *plastic*, malleable, and particularly impressionable, become long term beliefs that we hold.

> *Deuteronomy 6: 6-9 " ⁶ And these words which I command you today shall be in **your heart**." ⁷ "**You shall teach them diligently to your children**, and shall talk of them when you sit in your house, when you walk by the way, when you lie down, and when you rise up." ⁸ "You shall bind them as a sign on your hand, and they shall be as frontlets between your eyes."*
> *⁹ "You shall write them on the doorposts of your house and on your gates. NKJV (emphasis mine)*

God is instructing Israel to have repetitive exposure to His commands so that they become *heart* beliefs and permanent pathways. Someone once said to me; *isn't filling up with scripture like brainwashing*!? I am not sure about you but by the time I began walking seriously with the Lord my brains needed washing! In any case I would also like to highlight from the passage, the command to *diligently* teach them to the children. God the creator of our beings knew how important it is for our children to receive His word in that critical time of plasticity when we are deciding about life. Prevention, and being able to walk with God minimizing areas of serving the enemy, leaves us less open to being hurt, and in a much better place to be fruitful. However, even if we are incorrectly programmed God is always holding out His hand offering healing and help.

REPETITION IN MODERN LIFE

For many people the very important pre-adolescent time is a period where they are being told or shown that nothing that they are doing is good enough. We have educational systems which cater for people whose minds think along particular lines. Most likely, very similar to the academics and educators who prepared the system. History is littered with billionaires, inventors, entrepreneurs and successful people who did not function well at, or even complete, school.

For many people, school for example, is a place where they can be repeatedly confronted with learning that they are second rate or inferior. Families that have high demands on performance or perfection and don't offer love, encouragement and acceptance are environments of repetitive reinforcement of this inadequacy.

I remember my son when he was first learning to ride a bike. He wobbled around the front yard taking out the new tree that my wife had planted. He then disappeared down the sideway from where an enormous crash emanated. When I went around to find out if he was alright, he had ridden into the BBQ knocking it into the tin shed. He made some kind of statement such as; *I can't do it, I suck!* My response to him was something along the lines of; *you're doing great, it took me more goes than that to get as far as you did! Really?* he said looking encouraged. What just happened? I guarded his heart by helping him interpret the situation in a positive light.

> **Note:** Before you feel that you have failed on your own parenting journey, I was not always so impressive with my parenting skills; we all have to learn.
>
> The point is that if we are always encouraging, always finding the positives, then we are keeping their heart self-beliefs in God's order. As the Apostle Paul put it:
>
> > *2 Corinthians 10:8, "... for even if I boast somewhat freely about the authority the Lord gave us for **building you up rather than pulling you down**, I will not be ashamed of it ..."* NIV (emphasis mine)

Many people have only ever experienced criticism and disapproval, being programmed over and over again with their shortcomings and failings. Those who are around my age or older grew up in the *little children should be seen and not heard* generation. The implication of this statement is that you are some kind of second-class citizen as a child, not significant, valuable or important. And that is exactly what a great many people believe inside, that they simply don't matter, or that they are a nuisance, in the way, unacceptable or feel as though they are a nothing. Those who were meant to be guarding their hearts were unwittingly programming them through repetitive reinforcement that in some way they are not good enough.

In defense of all parents I would like to add that most fathers and mothers love their children. They would not deliberately hurt their families and would certainly have done things differently if they had understood the ramifications. In some measure the church is responsible for having failed to teach its members how to protect their children in this vital area. In any case, most are likely parenting out of that which they have received themselves, and the modeling that has passed through the generation lines.

Today, most children receive their training from media, much of which is run by people from the *children should be seen and not heard* generation and is slanted towards *my rights* generation which is a knee jerk reaction to being made to feel second rate. It is not too surprising to see this response from children of that era, leading to giving children full rights and decision-making authority long before they have the knowledge and wisdom to cope with running their own lives.

Possibly, an inner decision to not put that inferiority onto their children came as a result. Consequently, many modern children grow up under the belief that they are special. They *are* special to God, but in life they are no more special than anyone else, and when they grow up it is often a shock for them to find this out. We, as the Church have to take responsibility for equipping our people in how to Biblically train our children and bring them up in the counsel of the Lord.

UPGRADE INFORMATION

We don't want to confuse the healing of our *heart beliefs* with the renewing of our minds. There are many things that we learn through life that are not deeply recorded. We are talking here about areas such as *identity beliefs*. This is for God to free us from. But if we simply have wrong beliefs about how to do life then receiving improved information will renew our minds.

Let me say here that most of the changes in how we live and see things come to us through reading our Bibles or hearing the word taught. If this were not so, then why would we even bother to preach and teach. All that we are talking about here relates to areas and issues that we cannot overcome through better information. If we read in the Bible that we should build each other up and not judge each other, we might think; *well that is a better way of living than that which I am doing now!* And having made the decision we become a *hearer and doer* of the Word.

There is a great old story of a lady who was cooking a roast. Her friend was watching her and asked her; *why do you cut the roast in half before you put it in the oven?* The lady replied; *I actually don't know, my mother always did it that way so I will have to ask her!* When the question was presented to the mother her response was; *Oh, I only have a small oven, so I have to cut it in half, but you have a big oven and that is not necessary for you!*

The lady just received better information on how to do life. To keep this ministry in balance and perspective, there is still a preeminent place for Biblical advice (Counseling) and Bible teaching. In fact, on many occasions as we go along with the healing ministry there is a concurrent thread of teaching running through the sessions. I have unfortunately known of people who become proficient in the *Truth Encounters* ministry who have, as a result, felt that they are qualified to give advice on, for example, relationships. Some of them do not have sound Biblical knowledge and consequently their own relationships are not in order. This is something that Pastors who allow groups to minister under the covering of their church may need to take note of. Beware that a person who is equipped and now helping and seeing people set free is not going beyond the guidelines that you allow for the ministry.

Study 16: Types of Beliefs

Other ministries use different names for identifying types of beliefs. Over 20 years of working in this area we have found that they commonly fall into one of the following categories. It helps to know what type of belief you are dealing with because you then understand the kind of circumstances in a memory that you are looking for.

IDENTITY BELIEFS – ABOUT SELF

Identity beliefs relate to that which you perceive about who you are and how you are. Rather than a lengthy discourse let me suggest some common beliefs reflecting how one's identity is seen:

"I'm not loveable, I'm unacceptable, not enough, less than others, stupid, a nothing, dumb, ugly, a failure, a loser, useless, weak, I don't matter, am not important" and so on. Notice that they are all beliefs relating to your identity, they are about 'self.'

These types of *heart* beliefs are at the root of many anxieties. Unconsciously you are worried about people discovering your shortcomings or reinforcing them. When I am preparing people for ministry, I often explain identity beliefs to people using a story which I have constructed but is based on stories that I have heard over and over again.

Sample story

Imagine someone who has come to you is reporting how much anxiety they are going through. How I would deal with it may run something like this;

Fred: I have a terrible problem with anxiety.

Me: Can you give me an example of how it affects you?

Fred: I was at work the other day and heard the main door behind me open; I had an anxiety attack and reached for my pills.

Me: If you stop and think about the situation for a moment, what was it that you were worried about when you heard the door open?"

Fred: Thoughtful pause; Mmmmmm...I was nervous that it may have been the boss.

Me: And if it was, what are you worried about happening?

Fred: He may have come over and looked at my work!

Me: And if he did, what do you think could happen?

Fred: He might tell me that it was no good.

Me: I am sure that that is not a good feeling. I want you to close your eyes and feel what it is like for him to tell you that your work is not good enough, and let your mind connect you with other historical places where you have felt just like that.

Fred: Pause; I have just remembered that when I was in kindergarten, I was doing a painting with some other kids and the teacher was coming along looking at everyone's work. The first person was Mary and the teacher said that Mary's painting was so creative, and then Johnnie's was so neat and all in the lines. When she saw mine, she said, it was the biggest unrecognizable mess that she had ever seen in her life!

Me: As you look at that criticism and rejection, I want you to look for the conclusion and belief about yourself that you came to.

Fred: With some emotion; I'm useless, not as good as others.

Me: Let's ask the Lord what He considers to be true about you being useless and inferior. Just concentrate on those beliefs and feelings and listen.

Fred: Pause; He said, why would He have called and chosen me if I was useless. He said that all of His children are created equal, they have different gifts but none are better than another. I have just remembered that I was the best reader in the group!

Me: So how do you feel about people discovering that you are useless and not as good as them now?

Fred: Honestly, I feel that I am fine just as I am. And I am just the same as everyone else, the same only different, different in a good way, unique!

Identity beliefs also have a bearing on our relationships and how we respond, react to, and deal with others. They also reflect on how we relate to ourselves, and ultimately God. Truly, *as a man thinks in his heart, so is he*, in terms of how he reacts to others, and also how he sees himself.

Proverbs 23:7 "For as he thinks in his heart, so is he." NKJV

Let us propose that a person thinks that they are not good enough because they do not do things well enough. By now we know that this is a belief that was learnt in an event earlier in life. As a result, if that person feels, whether it is true or just a perception, that you are criticizing something that they are doing then you can expect some kind of angry response. They are angry at you for making them feel that which they already unconsciously believe, but they are also angry at themselves for not being able to do things well enough. Whenever negative emotions are present, they may be directed outwardly as a reaction, but they also exist inwardly connected to an area of hurt as well. So, this person might struggle to forgive you for how you are making them feel, but they probably haven't any forgiveness for themselves either for being the person who you can find fault with, because of their perceived imperfections and shortcomings.

This will also reflect in your relationship to God. You will be a double minded man. In your human spirit, which is now one with the Holy Spirit, you know that you are loved and accepted. But in your *heart*, you *believe* that you are not good enough because you cannot do things well enough. Therefore, how could God consider you as good enough, when you don't believe that you are yourself at heart level!

> *James 1:6-8 " ⁶ But let him ask in faith, with no doubting, for he who doubts is like a wave of the sea driven and tossed by the wind. ⁷ For let not that man suppose that he will receive anything from the Lord; ⁸ he is a double-minded man, unstable in all his ways." NKJV*

Sometimes we believe in God's goodness mentally, but the lack of faith in our hearts is because of our doubts about our worthiness to receive. Jesus pointed out that we can have whatever we believe in our hearts, not our heads. So, for faith to flow we have to believe that God is greater than our hearts. We need to receive His truth about our value and worth.

> *Mark 11:22-23 ²² So Jesus answered and said to them, "Have faith in God." ²³ "For assuredly, I say to you, whoever says to this mountain, 'Be removed and be cast into the sea,' and **does not doubt in his heart**, but believes that those things he says will be done, he will have whatever he says." NKJV (emphasis mine)*

We had not been involved in this ministry all that long, when one day I noticed my wife getting a bit agitated as I was wiping down the kitchen bench. I commented to her that I could see that me doing this was making her angry. After a short time, we identified that to her it seemed as if I was implying that she was not doing a good enough job, that she was an untidy person. After a short period of ministry into the memory where she had first learned this, and truth from the Lord, her whole attitude changed. Now instead of being upset, she felt it could be a good idea while I was helping to sweep the floor and put out the rubbish as well!

SITUATIONAL BELIEFS

As the name suggests, these are beliefs which have come out of a situation and may or may not relate to your identity. Phobic beliefs fall under this category. An example of this type of belief might be something such as having panic attacks in small spaces where you feel captive, such as an elevator. As you focus on the feeling you might, for example, identify that the anxiety about small spaces might be that you will not be able to breath. As your mind does a data match with other places holding those feelings you remember as a small boy playing football at school. You managed to get hold of the ball and five or six boys jumped on you and held you down. In that moment you were crushed, trapped and struggled to breathe. As you focus on the situation, we ask you what will happen if you can't get away and breathe. The response is; "I can't breathe, I am going to die!"

There is nothing here relating to identity, it is all to do with the situation. As we have the person embrace the *fear feeling* and *the belief* that they are trapped, can't get away, and are going to die because they cannot breathe, we ask God for His truth. Which could simply be words, or a realization that they did not die, or some other communication that sets them free?

Story
Some time ago I was waiting with our lady bank manager in her office for some other staff to come in to work out a financial proposition that we were putting together for a church development. While we were waiting, we were casually chatting and she made the comment; *I see that you travel overseas quite a lot.* I affirmed her statement, and she went on to say that she would love to be able to travel but she has a fear of flying. I said to her that our ministry experience is that often when people are afraid to fly that it usually began with a traumatic memory along the lines of perhaps a child being in a swimming pool and getting out over their heads. They can no longer touch the sides and they cannot swim. They feel like they are out of control and are going to die. When they go on an airplane their mind automatically makes the connection. *You are not in control, can't touch the bottom, there is nothing solid beneath you and therefore you could die!*

She looked at me in amazement and said; *I just remembered when I was a small girl, I lived in the country and was in the local swimming pool. I went out too far into the deep end and thought that I was going to die!*

The point is, it is a belief from a situation, nothing to do with identity. These are just simple terms we use to differentiate between types of beliefs. Incidentally, there can be many other situations that can produce a fear of flying. I recently encountered a lady with three different reasons from three individual memories that caused her to be afraid of flying.

A few years ago, my wife ministered to a lady who had a fear of flying. Her husband was very frustrated because they were getting older and he was eager to go adventuring. She received ministry for this fear and some other issues and then they went home. We did not see them again for a number of years, but eventually we ran across them again. I remembered her fear of flying and enquired about how she was going with it. She responded excitedly that they had now been around the world several times.

OBJECTION BELIEFS
These are beliefs where for some reason there is an objection held that stops the person from proceeding to the memory or receiving from the Lord. An example of this could be something as simple as somebody believing that they are doing the wrong thing if they allow the possibility that their parents were anything less than perfect. Before they will go to places where, perhaps their identity was damaged, you will need to find out and deal with why they think that being real about their parents is doing the wrong thing. You are not seeking to dishonor the parents, rather find the source of your own problems.

At other times people will come into a session and you can observe that they are very tense. Sometimes I will simply suggest something along the lines of; *do you believe that you won't be able to do this ministry?* or *Are you afraid that I will be disappointed if you cannot do this?* They often look a bit surprised but respond with a ready; *Yes! How did you know?*

We need to deal with the fear of failure memory first. This may be a place where they may have disappointed someone by not being able to do what was expected, or perhaps a place where everyone else could achieve and they could not, or something similar.

I recall one man being hesitant to let himself connect with his memory. I asked him what he believed that made him object to seeing the content of his historical event. He reported that he was afraid. I requested that he focus on the fear and identify and clarify exactly what it was that produced the anxiety. He told me that he was afraid that he would be out of control, which was clearly to do with what was going on in the memory. I asked him to focus on the belief and invited the Lord to bring His perspective. The man sat quietly for a moment and then opened his eyes and looked up at the same time making the statement; I **am** out of control!

This communication from the Lord meant something to the man in his inner parts. It was good truth as we all have very limited control over the World we live in, even the actions of those close to us. We never really know if an aircraft is about to come through our roof or the stock market may have just crashed and we have missed the news! The truth is that we are all largely not in control, but God is, and He is able to protect us. This resolved the resistance issue and the man proceeded into his memory for freedom.

Perhaps a final story in order to illustrate another way that *objection beliefs* may present and impact the ministry time. First, I note that you do not need to look for these; you will simply observe that they are present. And secondly, you will not run across them in every session, they will be involved occasionally.

OBJECTIONS TO LETTING GOD SPEAK TO YOU

Periodically you will encounter people who hold beliefs that prevent them from receiving from God. These could be simple thoughts such as; *I'm not worth His time, of course He will free others, but He doesn't care about me, and everyone else can do it, (hear from God) but I won't be able to, I will get it wrong and He will be angry with me!*

These beliefs have been learnt in specific memories that are best dealt with first. You may recognize that there is some kind of blockage to them hearing from God, and this is probably the main cause. Still other people hold beliefs that God does not interact with people today, or at times we run across those who have been trained in another ministry model and refuse to listen for God's voice because; *this is not the way we do it!*

Story

A number of years ago, we were ministering to an attractive young lady who was needlessly jealous of other women. She was successfully ministered to and received freedom in other areas but her jealousy problem remained. It caused major problems in her relationship with her fiancée who could not even watch the news on television because there might be a pretty weather girl. If there was a magazine around with a girl on the cover it was quickly put away. If they were at church, he was watched constantly in case he looked at another girl. If she even thought that he may have noticed another girl, real or imagined she flew into a rage. As a perceived solution to her jealousy she had become very controlling in her relationship.

We identified the source as being a time where, as a small girl of around 3 or 4 years old, the family would receive visits from a friend who was a handsome young man. He would fool around playfully with the little girl and gave her attention which made her feel special and loved. She concluded that this special affection and attention was only for her. One day the young man brought his girlfriend along with him. The family had known that he had a girlfriend but the little girl did not. For her, this was an intensely traumatic moment. She was devastated that someone else clearly had a greater measure of the attention and affection of the young man. She was overcome with jealousy. We could summarize jealousy as; *you have what I would like to have.* She also felt incredibly inferior. Here was a mature adult girl with modern clothes and a fully-grown shapely figure. She concluded along the lines that, she was; *Not enough, and could not be what she needed to be. The other girls were better.*

Later, as an attractive adult woman herself, this thinking was unreasonable. She continued to fear losing her male partner and to be jealous of other girls who could take him away because, unconsciously in her heart, she was afraid that he would see another girl who was more, and prefer her. This for her was a logical inner conclusion which matched her historical event. Having identified and confirmed these beliefs with her we invited God to communicate the truth to her to set her free.

In other things that we had dealt with her she had no problem in hearing from God and receiving her healing, but this was different. So up to this point we can see that she didn't have an issue with going to the original memory or accepting her beliefs. Now, however, she held an *objection* to having God speak to her and receive freedom from her jealousy and resultant ungodly control.

We eventually worked out that she believed that if she let go of the control through healing, then her fiancée would go ahead and prefer another girl. So, for her, the jealousy was tied in with what she perceived to be true, and control over the situation that she was insecure about, was her solution to the problem. She simply did not want to be free because she felt that staying in control was going to protect her from losing her man. Sometime later when she realized that she would lose her man anyway because of her jealousy and control, she committed her will to the process. She then received truth about her beliefs and was delivered of the spirit holding the jealousy and controlling behavior.

I want to point out that the spirit was not the problem, her will was the issue. The spirit had come in on the sins of jealousy and control, beginning with the emotional breach that was created with the shock of discovering the adult girlfriend. She was deceived unwittingly into believing that controlling her male boyfriends was the solution to the perceived situation. This opened her to cooperating and participating with a sinful attitude inspired by an unholy spirit.

As long as she believed that the control served a purpose for her, the spirit had ground to magnify, amplify and hold her bound. As the spirit worked through her it also held the fiancée in bondage, not being free to relate with females in a normal way or even watch television. Simply trying to cast out the spirit without identifying the belief that gave it place is normally a fruitless exercise. In a sense she held the spirit to herself believing that it was serving a purpose for her. Of course, she was unaware of the spiritual element of what was happening. Once she permitted herself to be freed of the beliefs behind the jealousy there was no need for the *protection* afforded by the controlling attitudes.

The same is true with deliverance from all sin-based issues. Until you are willfully convinced that you need to fall out of agreement with the sin, then you will most probably stay in bondage. It is vitally important therefore, to understand that genuine repentance is the basis of deliverance. Repentance in the Greek language means; *change your thinking, reconsider your ways.* Often, we are unwilling or unable to do that until we discover what it actually is that we are thinking in *the heart* that puts us in a place of harboring or hosting ungodly actions that give place to the devil. Hence, this is one application of the verse; *you shall know the truth and the truth shall make you free.*

*2 Timothy 2:25-26 " ²⁵ In meekness instructing those **that oppose themselves;** if God perhaps will **give them repentance** to the acknowledging of the truth, ²⁶ And that they may recover themselves out of the snare of the devil, who are taken captive by him at his will." KJV (emphasis mine)*

> **Note:** The word of God teaches us what sin is so that we will know what manner or type of spirit we are cooperating with.
>
> *Luke 9:55 But He turned and rebuked them, and said, "You do not know what manner of spirit you are of." NKJV*

> **Note:**
> Not all controlling behavior or jealousy has a spirit resident inside the person. It is still cooperating with an unholy spiritual influence even if it is weaker and from outside the host person. This will be explained in Unit 5

However, if as in this case there is a blockage, or there is an unusually strong resistance to ministry, you may find that a spirit on the inside is the cause. It is more attached to the responses or solutions to the hurt rather than the pain itself. Chasing the spirit will not bring the freedom; dealing with the hurt that produces the need for the ungodly reactions and activities, which sometimes opens the door to an evil spirit, is the most important focus. Once the truth is received, freeing the person from the troubling belief, then the spirit may manifest, or simply leave once the reason for its presence, is removed.

GOING TO THE DEEP PLACE WHERE THE BELIEF RESIDES

This ministry can be carried out anywhere and at any time. For the best possible results, I find that a quiet room, in preferably a one on one situation affords the person receiving ministry the best possible opportunity to concentrate without distraction. I do remember situations such as ministering to a man who was suicidal on the side of a very busy street. There were noisy cars and motorbikes' roaring past, but the man seemed to be unaffected, and to my amazement, was able to focus on the source of his pain and receive his freedom.

Normally we try to have a quiet room. Having heard their story and made a few notes about areas that may need ministry I encourage them to go to what I call, *periscope depth.* In other words, close their eyes, shut out the outer world and concentrate on the inner deeper place of the heart.

BELIEFS, FEELINGS AND MEMORIES

At times, as you hear the story and the presenting problems, you will note statements that reflect *inner beliefs.* At other times, some emotion will come up, but it does not seem to be at that time connected to the belief. I liken this to those multi story concrete car parks that are in many cities today. Each level has a number which is usually painted on the various doors to the stairs and exits on that level. It is almost as if, from this door over here, you hear a *belief statement* that does not hold feelings. But from another door over there proceeds some *emotion.* They do not seem to be connected here on level 5, but as you ask questions and embrace the thoughts and feelings eventually you end up in the basement, at the initial memory where the *first-time belief* was taken to heart. So, the *basement* holds the circumstances in the memory which produced the conclusion, which became a permanent belief that produces and matches the emotions.

SECONDARY MEMORIES HOLDING THE SAME BELIEFS

Often people will not go directly to the first memory where the belief was interpreted and encoded. For example, someone who believes that they are not as good as other people may have memories later in life or even recently that seemed to confirm this thinking. This could be a marriage break up or failure to perform in secondary school. You could be stopping off here to connect more intensely with the emotions or to refine the belief. Ultimately, as we have previously stated, their *identity beliefs* will have begun before the age of 10 years old.

For many years, we fostered both long term and short-term children, so we can confirm from experience that what both the Bible and science say about this being the critical formative age is true. Into your family come children who are *pre-packaged* with their inner thinking about themselves and life. The same can be said about everyone who walks through the door of your church. *Something happened* that they most likely didn't ask for; they are clothed by life. Our mission is to be equipped to help them, offering God's answers and provision.

Very commonly, the beginning point for a ministry session, is the report of the subject having been triggered in a relationship or particular situation. In the event that the emotion from the belief is strong in the current relationship, but not so strong in the initial memory, you can have the person switch backwards and forwards from the strong feelings from the present time to the event held in memory state. This will help to identify and accept the accuracy of the thoughts and feelings from the source.

INTERPRETING OTHER PEOPLE'S LIVES THROUGH OUR OWN BELIEFS

We have already highlighted that our lives, behavior and responses are shaped by what we believe in our heart. It also affects how we perceive the situations of other people, and indeed how we see life.

> Proverbs 4:23, "Above all else, guard your heart, for it **affects everything** you do." NLT (emphasis mine)

A person who grew up in poverty will be able to empathize with poorer people in the World. A Pastor who grew up being treated as though he was not important or significant, will not let anyone out of the door on Sunday, until they have been greeted and made to feel that they are valuable.

What we believe about ourselves and life is projected onto others even if they do not hold the same beliefs. We expect that they would feel the same as us. Someone who grew up with injustice will consider it vital to stand up for those who are oppressed.

On a number of occasions, I have had mothers come to me in a very distraught condition because their daughters are going through a marriage break up. When I suggest that these situations are probably stirring up beliefs within them, I usually receive a response along the lines of; *shouldn't a mother be feeling this for their child?* Yes, they should, but I encourage them to take the opportunity to investigate and see if any of the feelings that are present are connected to their own experiences. Usually once we have worked through all of the emotions that the situation has provoked in them, they are only left with a mental sympathy for their child's circumstances. In other words, *all* the feelings that they were experiencing were tied to interpreting what their daughters should be going through by their own inner beliefs. The daughters probably have their own historically based reactions to the situation.

COMMON BELIEFS, DIFFERENT PERSONALITIES

After a period of time doing this ministry, you begin to find repetitively that there are some very common beliefs that you deal with over and over again. What does change is the differing personalities of the people that you are working with. Some people are very emotional while others have little emotion and are largely cognitive, mind-based people.

I have seen at times that some *brands* of inner healing seem to think that if you cry you are being touched by the Holy Spirit and being healed. In much the same manner people can think that a person crying in the church service is being healed by the Holy Spirit. That is possible, but I think that most times the presence of the Spirit may be softening emotions. We tend to bless the emotion and pray something such as; *more Lord, bless them more, heal them Lord.* If we asked them a few questions we may find that, for example, it was that song about the Father that moved them, because their father left when they were a child, or something similar.

The key to the healing is identifying the belief, not the degree of the emotion. Someone who experiences feelings intensely may struggle with emotions daily. A more stoic person may simply get on with life but have issues, such as anxiety, or belief-based behavior such as the need to succeed, being regarded, or being right. The emotional person may have a dramatic time in the ministry session and express a great sense of relief and freedom.

The more cognitive person may only feel enough to identify and resolve the belief. They may not report much more than that the belief no longer feels true. Just because they lack the euphoria does not mean that they are not free. They are more likely to experience what has happened in terms of how they see life, their sense of peace and wellbeing, and notice that old responses and reactions have disappeared when certain stressors are present.

WAYS IN WHICH WE REMEMBER

1. Emotionally:

Fear, anxiety, rejection, grief, unworthiness etc. We access memory by connecting with the initial places that hold these feelings.

2. Pictures:

Memory events from very early life may just be a vague impression rather than a clear picture. Some people have incredibly vivid memories with amazing recall of detail. This can relate to the level of trauma and corresponding strength of the picture. Some people can have memory pictures that are not connected to emotions. They may have pushed the emotions down because they are too frightening or painful to look at.

One lady I was working with told me the story of having to get her own birthday cake as a child because her birthday had been forgotten. She was laughing about it as though it were a funny story. The emotions did not match the situation. She should have been feeling hurt and sad. It is necessary to accept the true feelings in the memory to identify that which you have believed.

3. The body:

(Somatic) headache, stress, breathing, tension, stress, muscles, nausea, aches and pains, etc. Have you ever had that sick, dread feeling in the pit of your stomach? This is a probable body memory connecting you to a belief learnt in a previous situation. In a ministry setting you would have the person focus on this feeling and look for other places where they may have felt the same.

4. Senses:

Smells, sounds, taste, and touch etc. A commonly used example of this is music from your past which may make you feel happy or sad. The song is associated with a time in your life which may have been positive or negative. It may relate to bringing you to a visual event that contains something significant. Some people do not like to be touched or hugged. It connects them to times where touch may have meant something negative. You can have them focus on the thought of being touched and this will often bring a memory to them which contained these feelings.

5. Words:

Some phrases or unkind nicknames may be joined to unpleasant memories that are to do with the shaping of heart beliefs.

Sample questions

As you begin to work in this ministry, or even examine your own thoughts, you will find that there are only a certain number of questions available to use and I suggest some here. You can of course be creative and come up with your own.
"What will happen if … ?" (e.g. …'you have to fly overseas').

Note: We call fear the **what if spirit**! so **what will happen if**? is a good basic question for fear, anxiety, stress or insecurity.

"How does it feel to think that…?"   (e.g. …'there is nobody to protect you').
"How does this make you feel … ?"   (e.g. …'to think that you don't matter').
"Why do you think … ?"   (e.g. …'no one cares about you').
"What does this mean about you … ?"   (e.g. …'that everyone else is able to succeed').
"What does it make you … ?"   (e.g. …'if you are the person who is ignored').
"What do you believe is true about you … ?   (e.g. … if someone has perhaps, learnt that they are stupid in an event).

Typical belief samples

Fear:	"This or that could happen!"
Anger:	"They don't care about me!" "This is not how things should be!"
Rejection:	"Nobody wants me, I don't belong, am not a part of this."
Stress:	"I can't cope!" "It's hopeless." (Depression)
Sadness:	"I am not loved."
Rebellion:	"It's not fair!"

Performance anxiety / inferiority: "I cannot do what others can do, or what is expected."
Insecurity: "People aren't doing what they should be doing."
Bitterness / resentment: "I will not forgive them for what they have done" or at times, "what they have not done that they should have!"

All of these kinds of perceived beliefs affect relationships and often produce sin responses and reactions.

THE DEMEANOR OF THE MINISTER

If you are going to be effective in this ministry you will need to become a good listener. Slow to speak and quick to listen is great wisdom. You hear what a person is saying to gather information and note cues that may point to beliefs. In addition, you are looking to God for prompts, inspiration and information. I have already discussed the car park analogy. Occasionally, once you gain some experience, it may be obvious to you what a person believes. However, if you suggest it, they may well deny it. It will not be until you arrive in the *basement* that the belief is alive and significant to them.

If you are not yet mature as a Christian, or indeed free from your own issues, you may have a need or tendency to be vocal about all that you know and think. This may not inspire the vital trust that is needed for a person to share their most intimate details. The need for confidentiality is absolutely critical. I have shared a number of testimonies and stories in this publication. If I think that a story might be helpful in the teaching and training environment, I will ask permission to share it. Without a person's consent I do not talk about details of anyone's ministry time. It is something personal between them and God. People coming for help will usually sense whether or not it is safe to open up the areas that their lives are built on with you.

POSITIONING

The most important area of any healing or freedom ministry is to have the person aligned to receive from the Lord. Jesus taught about the Kingdom of God before He ministered. It is vitally important that people understand what the issue is, and what God offers in terms of resolving your problem. Therefore, explaining or teaching about the ministry is key. This can come in the form of your own explanations, a work up book, video or audio teaching.

In an environment, such as attendees of our healing school, people who want ministry already know what to expect and how it works. In other settings, where possible, to be thorough and most effective, we will do a work up session first where we explain and teach about the ministry. We have found that God will not usually override a person's free will and choice. Consequently, He will only do for people that which they want and choose. This can be frustrating for some new ministers. They can see the answer to the problems and try to push people to deal with their issues. Jesus only ministered to those who came to Him. Given that He was preaching repentance, and many did not want to reconsider their ways or change their thinking about their lifestyles, possibly many did not come. Our job is to teach what God has made available as best we can, and then be equipped to serve Him in helping those who come.

BEING READY

Most people who have been through teaching on the subject or a workup session now see their problem and come to receive their freedom. Once in a while, I have someone who does the workup and, even though they now see the source of the issues, they feel that it is not something that they want to do. A small percentage never return, but many times they will return, weeks months or even years later, desperate, reporting that they are now ready to do whatever is necessary to be set free. I have come to realize that although we finish work for the day, the Holy Spirit goes home with them, and never ceases to work with and encourage them.

COMMON REASONS WHY PEOPLE MAY NOT COME FOR MINISTRY

1. Ignorance

They simply do not know about this opportunity for freedom or they have received a distorted picture of it from some source.

2. Fit

It does not fit into their theological or ministry method framework.

3. Pride

Pride is the most common reason. Many people are full of their own opinions and views. Having some knowledge, they become *puffed up*. They want to fix the problem themselves without help from others, working it out in their own minds. Remember the Pharisees who considered themselves above the common sinners. Jesus at one time rebuked them for searching the scriptures because they thought that the written word alone would provide eternal life.

Pride says, *I will fix me!* in a sense, following on from the temptation in the garden to be *as or like God!* Pride wants to set up a monument to self to bow down to and be, in a way, your own god. Jesus pointed out that the scriptures actually do not fix you without Him, the word made flesh. He is the person whom the Holy Spirit can work through and meet your needs. The principle is the same for receiving the promise of eternal life, and also receiving other provisions that come through Jesus.

> John 5:39-40 "*39 You diligently study the Scriptures because you think that by them you possess eternal life. These are the Scriptures that testify about me, 40 yet you refuse to come to me to have life." NIV*

The beginnings or ground that gives place to pride is found in inferiority and low self-image. Pride, or making yourself above others, in your own thinking is the devil's solution for the perceived weakness that you hold about yourself at heart level.

Proud people are probably the ones who stay away from receiving help more than any others. Their behavior, or how they appear, is often the exact opposite of a person's inner belief. For example, a person who walks around appearing self-important and superior almost certainly believes in their hearts that they are not important and are inferior. Now, the only viewpoint that holds any importance for them is their own. They will have the attitude that you better listen to them and often hold the floor in conversations. King Solomon was not kind in his appraisal of these hurting people in many of his writings.

> Proverbs 26:12 "*Do you see a man wise in his own eyes? There is more hope for a fool than for him." NIV*

For a proud person to admit to any kind of weakness or imperfection strikes at the core of their sense of inferiority. And after all, what could anybody possibly know that they do not! The result is that many with pride issues avoid ministry. There can at times be an evil spirit involved in the resistance to help. Even if there is not a demon on the inside, pride certainly proceeds from spiritual influences even from the outside.

A while ago we had a new lady coming to our church who asked me if she could come for some help with her problems. She asked me if I could make sure that I don't tell the other leaders that she was coming. I replied with something like, *Sure, no problem. But I don't think that they would pay much attention, as many of the congregation comes for sessions and most of the leaders receive ministry themselves!* This seemed to put her at ease. The point is, isn't this what normal church life should look like anyway?

4. Control

We have already discussed that many people want to be in absolute control of their lives. For some of these persons, to be able to trust another with the deep things of their lives is very difficult.

5. Fear
There are those who are simply too afraid of what might happen, what you might think about them, or what they may have to face to consider opening up for help.

6. Denial
Some people simply will not accept they have problems, or they may have a part in faulty relationships. These people expect that their own emotional well-being would be fine if everyone around them did what they think they should be doing. This is called *projection*, where you deny your issues and blame shift your situation, feelings and responses onto everyone else. It is not surprising that we see the first instance of not taking responsibility for our own behavior right back at mankind's beginnings in Genesis.

> *Genesis 3:11-12* [11] *And he said, "Who told you that you were naked? Have you eaten from the tree that I commanded you not to eat from?"* [12] *The man said, "The woman you put here with me--she gave me some fruit from the tree, and I ate it." NIV*

WHY DO WE NEED HELP?
Some people ask why they need to sit down with someone to do this ministry. Let me offer a couple of reasons.

1. If you don't commit to some kind of appointment then you will probably never get around to it. I used to say to people that it is a bit like going to the dentist, we put it off as long as we can. (Around 15 years ago I read of someone else making almost the exact same comparison).

2. To begin with, you most probably don't have the skills to find your beliefs, and you may find it hard to connect to deep painful events without experienced support. Eventually it may be possible to minister to yourself as it is a very simple process.

3. Discernment. If you've ever played the game of golf you will know that everyone will tell you how to improve and what you are doing wrong. Even bad golfers will give you advice, sometimes bad advice. The point is that they *can* see that you are doing something wrong. You cannot see your own swing, because you are in it, they can. However, they may not know what they are looking at.

   Discernment in its simplest form, is being able to understand what you are seeing or looking at. It's a good idea to get your advice from a Golf pro whose own game is working well, rather than a *hacker* who is struggling with his handicap. Clearly the same is true in ministry; don't take advice from just any well-meaning Christian, it is worth checking the life and experience of the person that you are seeking help from.

SHOPPING LISTS
By the time a person has listened to teaching on *Truth Encounters* or has done a work up session, they should have a basic understanding of the ministry process. Many by now may have noteworthy memories coming to them. Anything that is a memory is significant or it would not be remembered to begin with. Few people can remember what they had for breakfast on a particular day 2 years ago; let alone many years ago because it really is not important.

We now ask the person to begin to put on their *shopping list* the areas that they may suffer with and are looking for freedom in. This can be known problems, such as never feeling that they are worth anything, or perhaps a fear of storms, or it can be a set of reactions that they have to specific situations.

A reaction example:

This may be something along the lines of; *I get very, very angry when my husband leaves his clothes on the floor.* This could come from some kind of belief such as, *nobody cares about me, and what I want.* A self-belief may be holding hurt behind that thinking, along the lines of; *I'm a nothing, I just don't matter.* The *I'm a nothing* is going to be the identity belief that holds the emotional pain. The anger is not the problem but is a predictable response to being made to feel like this.

Their *shopping list* may contain a list of issues that they are aware of, and also a number of *trigger* circumstances. We encourage them to simply write down any situations that produce negative emotions. Anything that makes them feel angry, sad, fearful, indignant, rejected, inferior, unimportant and so on. A *shopping list* could look something like;

> *I just never feel worthy of being noticed.* (Looking for historical match).
> *My husband always seems uninterested in what I want ….! etc. etc.*

Some new ministers get nervous that they won't know what to do. As long as you remember that you are looking for *the beliefs that produce the feelings*, you are on the right track. We are not trying to give you methods, but rather principles. I am quite sure that my wife ministers very differently to me, but we are both looking for the same thing.

The people already have the problems so you don't have to find any. In addition, God has the answer for them already. Your job is only to help them find that which they *believe in their hearts*, then open it up to God to provide His truth. You can only minister to whatever they come in with for help. You may discern other issues, but if they do not want assistance in those areas, then you acknowledge their choices.

We can summarize the areas of responsibility along these lines;

Our part:
- To teach or instruct them in understanding the ministry.
- To help them identify and clarify the beliefs in their *hearts*.

The person's part:
- To be willing to seek out and note their issues.
- To be prepared to embrace and accept their beliefs, emotions and memories.

The Holy Spirit's part:
- To guide and inspire the minister and person in the session.
- To reveal God's truth and bring freedom.

WAYS THAT GOD MAY COMMUNICATE WITH PEOPLE

An old saying says that *God talks how you listen.* He made your brain and soul exactly how He intended it to be. Some people think in words, others in pictures or impressions; let me offer some of the common ways that God might communicate truth to you.

1. In words:

I tend to think in words, so mostly when God uses my mind to communicate truth to me it comes in words. Interestingly I have noticed that as I have become more and more free that I also receive pictures and impressions at times either for myself or others. Some people get stuck here because they are waiting for flashes of light and a booming voice, or an audible word from outside your body. I explain it this way. My computer is set up with the fonts, letter styles, writing size and so on that I like. If I were to give it to you and ask you to write me a note, when you returned it to me, I might exclaim; *that is just my writing!* That's true; you just used my faculties or equipment to communicate your message to me.

In the ministry room, having identified the heart belief, I simply encourage people to let their minds go. When they hear something, occasionally people might explain that it just seemed like their own thoughts, but they heard this or that. We test and see whether or not it is God by looking at the old belief. Perhaps a person may have always thought that they were dumb. It felt true to them. Now they look for the belief and cannot find it, or it is no longer true; it has always been true to them, but it is gone.

2. *Pictures or impressions:*
Many people think in pictures. I remember a man who was suffering from a rejection belief of some kind. When this man spent time with his own children, he would put his face up against their face as a sign of love and affection, indicating acceptance and connection. The man was focusing on his belief and feeling that he was rejected, and God gave him a picture, an impression of the Heavenly Father putting His face against the mans. Needless to say, he was deeply touched and moved. However God communicates to us, it is like a *prophetic now word* applied to our historical event.

In fact, I was ministering to a young man one day and as he embraced the heart belief that he held, the Holy Spirit took some words from a prophetic word that he had received a number of years earlier, and applied it to his belief, bringing healing. Why did it not bring healing before? The young man did not know what he believed in his heart up until this time when we exposed it. Then the Holy Spirit applied the words to the belief.

3. *Scriptures:*
Very often the Holy Spirit will use a scripture that people know well in their minds and apply it to issues in their hearts. By way of example, I was ministering to a lady recently and she was in a memory where she was struggling to keep up with the other children in being able to do her school work. As a result, she had come to a conclusion and belief that she still suffered with daily along the lines of; *I am dumb because I cannot do the schoolwork like the other kids.* As she concentrated on the school memory and felt the belief, the Lord put into her mind the book of Ecclesiastes: *Everything is meaningless!*

For her, this meant that the activity that she was basing her identity on really did not matter. This brought her freedom. If the reference that she was measuring herself against was meaningless, then the conclusion that she arrived at had no basis and could not be true either. This was not a conscious act on her part to think differently, it was the result of the truth which the Holy Spirit communicated to her. Education is good, but it is a 'man' activity, and may not relate very much to what a person will be doing in life.

4. *Realizations:*
Several years ago, I ministered to a young man who came with the presenting problem of feeling as though he was responsible for everything that went wrong in his family life, his workplace, and even to some extent the world. As he connected with the feeling, we arrived at the place where he learnt a belief something like; *It's my fault if bad things happen.* As a small boy he was traveling in the back seat of the family car. They had an accident with another car as they entered an intersection. It was an emotionally traumatic event for the little boy. His father whipped around and said sharply, *have you got your seatbelt on?*

Now, it may seem ridiculous, but in that emotionally charged moment the boy thought; This bad thing is my fault because I haven't gotten my seat belt on! These thoughts are burned deeply into our brains in moments of crisis through an electro-chemical process known as protein synthesis.

As we explored the memory, he discovered that afterward it turned out that he did in fact have his belt on. He now realized that the truth was that it was not his fault at all. He had believed that it was because, after the moment of shock, it was too late to reinterpret the belief for him as a child after the emotional intensity subsided because the belief was in his heart. But now many years later the Holy Spirit reminded him of the complete picture and set him free.

Personally, I believe that one of the reasons that this ministry is so effective is that God dwells in eternity and not time (Isaiah 57:15). He is everywhere all of the time. He is already there ten years from now, and He is there in your memory, whether you knew of Him or not, as a child. So, we can identify your belief up here in time, and counsel you about it with minimal change. But when He speaks into, and helps you reinterpret your event with His truth, He is actually there!

Another example of a realization could be a child coming into a room where mother and father are having a heated argument. In that moment the child believes that it is somehow their fault. Looking back and exploring the memory through the eyes of God they now realize, as they see more of the picture that was not as emotionally intense, that the parents were already fighting before they entered the room. So, how could it be their fault? God will at times bring freedom through realization. I have also seen at times people being set free at the moment where they realize why they believe what they believe, and where it came from, and for them that is the healing.

5. Sensations, feelings, knowing:

God is indeed very creative in how He communicates with us. Normally we do not know what He is going to do, or how He will do it. Sometimes He will give us insight into what He is about to say or do. I think in part this is on the job training for words of knowledge and learning to hear his voice for ourselves.

I recall one lady who had suffered severe physical abuse, and as she was accessing memories and beliefs, there was a light coming into the picture. When the light came in, she felt peaceful and calm, safe. I was frantically going through my theology to make sure that this was something Biblical. Remembering, Jesus, light of the world reassured me that this was something that God might do. The bottom line was that her fears were resolved.

Other people report simply feeling love. Still more, report that they just know that the beliefs they held are not true. I remember asking one lady after a session what she now thought of God. She thought about it for a moment, and then replied; *He's clever, He's very clever!* Amen. Our God is indeed very clever.

6. Through our senses

One lady that we ministered to had come with the presenting problem of struggling to believe God for provision. She was actually a woman of great faith in most areas of her life. However, as a child she was never sure that they were going to have food to eat, and the belief that she took to heart as a result of that anxiety was at the root of the problem. Immediately after we asked God to communicate His truth to her, she asked a question; *who has got the bread? I can smell bread!* After assuring her that no one had bread I asked her what the smell of bread meant to her. She reported that it meant that; *there will always be enough.* For her this resolved the issue, and as a result of her new expectations of God providing, over the next few months her family situation changed dramatically.

Through our senses seems to be a much less common way that God uses, but it happens from time to time.

WIRING

Sometimes God will multitask and use the ministry room as a training ground for you or the recipient. Remember before David went up against Goliath, he found that God was with him in the private place, killing both lion and bear. He honed his skills as a shepherd boy before he was put into public ministry.

God is always about helping people, and He uses our time doing so to learn about Him and His goodness as we see His love, grace and ability to help His children. As we are faithful in little, it is a training ground for other things. Many times, as people hear from God in their healing moment, it becomes obvious for some of them, that God has put in them faculties such as receiving pictures easily. As they learn to understand what God is saying through the pictures and they reach out to Him for what He is communicating to them, they realize that they could reach out for something for others as well. So, ministry times can be a birthing place for prophetic ministries as they not only discover their gifting, but also get free enough and in the truth enough to use them. (That is in part, not having the words from God convoluted through their own soulish heart beliefs.)

WARNING

Many ministries have gone off the rails and brought the ministry into disrepute by suggesting how God should communicate with them. For example, I have heard of people suggesting to picture Jesus in the memory. This is a recipe for disaster, licensing potential deception. I have had people report seeing Jesus in their memories perhaps two or three times in 20 years of ministering *Truth Encounters*. Even these were many years ago, and I cannot be sure that they had not been exposed to other ministries who practiced this and, as a consequence, thought that this was what was expected.

My wife has also been ministering this way for perhaps 10 or 12 years and has rarely seen it either. Our work is to simply help the person identify what it is that they believe, and then pass the ministry time over to the Holy Spirit to communicate truth as He sees fit. We are the assistants in the ministry, not the directors.

Study 17: Problem areas that you may periodically encounter

CONSCIOUS OBJECTIONS

We have already discussed that some people will simply not want ministry for some reason; they might propose that they are a new creation so there is nothing left to do, and point to the finished work of the cross. If you cannot help them negotiate these conscious objections then you simply acknowledge their free will and choice. They may simply not agree with this form of ministry and either decide to resolve their problems themselves, or feel that another approach is better for them.

We can only teach about the ministry as best we can and testify to what we have seen and heard in terms of the results that we have experienced. Some ministers feel that now that they see the problems for what they are, and know the answer, that they need to push people to go to God for healing. God Himself does not force anyone to do anything; it is not in His nature. We see this in how Jesus dealt with the disciples recognizing their free will and choice.

John 6:66-67 [66] *says that, "At this point many of his disciples turned away and deserted him.* [67] *Then Jesus turned to the Twelve and asked, "Are you going to leave, too?" NLT*

He could have proclaimed, *hey you guys, you can't go, I have invested a lot of time in you!* Instead, He enquired as to what they willed to do and which course of action that they had decided on.

SUPPRESSION

If you suppress something then you restrain, subdue, repress, or hold it back; like a sneeze, a cough or a yawn, at an inappropriate moment. When we are talking about suppressing memories, we are saying that you have chosen to not permit yourself to look at it for some reason. Perhaps it holds guilt, shame, rejection or some other unsavory emotion in it. So, we restrain it from coming onto the screen of our minds, pushing it back, as a willful act denying it, and eventually over time, we have repressed it to where we can no longer readily access it. The neural pathway that connected us to the event has gone from a strong four lane highway with street lights, to a broken-down potholed dirt track. It is now barely accessible, and we do not want to go to it in any case.

Usually if people have chosen to remember memories no more as an act of their will, then to see those pictures they now have to choose to see them again. They are still there, in storage, it is just that the connection to them has become weak. I have found that often when people now decide to explore those memories for healing that they come back a piece at a time. Just as they faded out as the connection became weak, now as they try to find them the pathway begins to strengthen.

I recall many young ladies who have pushed down abusive memories. When they have chosen to access the memories, they have come back as little snippets and pieces of pictures. As they have been able to accept each piece then another will emerge. Of course, it does not need to be an abusive situation, it could be something along the lines of denying that your father or mother did not love you. As a result, you push the place where you learnt this out of reach.

Possibly it is the memories you have suppressed, or at times it is the emotion that should be in the memory that has been pushed away. I have heard somewhere that; *you have to feel it to heal it.* This applies in this ministry because many times you have to examine the feeling to see what belief is producing it. Therefore, having at least some emotion matching the belief is important.

DISSOCIATION

I have a wrist watch that has written on the back of it, Waterproof to 30 meters. I have often wondered what happens at 31 meters when the pressure becomes too great. Theoretically at least the outside circumstances become too great for it to deal with and it is overwhelmed, crushed, and broken.

> *Proverbs 18:14 "A man's spirit sustains him in sickness, but a crushed spirit who can bear?" NIV*

Not being able to cope with, or bear a situation, can cause the mind to overload and disconnect from the event. Modern homes often have a circuit breaker on the electrical system in case the wiring is overloaded and damage might occur. If this looks like happening, it simply breaks the connection that allows the power to flow into the situation.

Mentally we seem to have the same kind of protection in our wiring. If something is happening to us that we cannot bear, then the mind disconnects or dissociates from what is going on.

Over the years, I have found this to be a common phenomenon with traumas such as sexual abuse. If a twenty-year-old person was being sexually imposed on, in perhaps a rape or coercive sexual encounter, they nowadays, would normally have at least a basic understanding of the sexual act. If the same abuse is played out on, for example, a four-year-old, they have no understanding whatsoever of that which is going on. It is overwhelming and they cannot cope, so they disconnect from the event.

Often, they will project their minds onto some other activity to escape from the situation. After the event, the emotions and memories from the event remain compartmentalized and shut off because of the extreme feelings such as fear and powerlessness that they contain. There is usually some kind of belief *objecting* to connecting to the contents of the memory. This could be thoughts such as; *if I go there, I will not be able to cope, I will be out of control, I will die,* and so on. These need to be identified and resolved.

Story
A number of years ago, we were doing a school in another state, and there was in attendance, a young married man. From time to time his wife would appear for short periods of time but seemed unwilling to be very involved with the group. We were having a break and the Pastor asked if I would see the young lady and explain about the ministry. I agreed, and not knowing what her issue was, I went through how the *Truth Encounters* ministry worked. She thanked me and left. A little later the Pastor came back and informed me that she wanted ministry but did not have any memories relating to her problem.

Once we began the session, I found that her presenting symptom was that she was unable to have a sexual relationship with her husband because of the feelings that it produced in her. The emotions that she described were consistent with someone who had been abused. As she tried to connect the feelings with a historical event which matched that which she was experiencing, she reported that she had no memories whatsoever. I explained to her that there was some kind of belief that she had that prevented her from seeing what had happened to her, and that it had been an act of her will not to see the memories for that reason. I went on to encourage her that it will also be an act of her will to see why she objected to seeing her memory pictures.

After concentrating for a moment, she announced that it had been a member of family, a close relative who had done it. The perpetrator was considered to be an exemplary Christian and she believed that she could not possibly accept the event because of the closeness of the relative. She further believed that, because of their relationship to the father and mother, she could not tell her parents what had happened. This overload caused her to completely disconnect with the memory altogether. Once this was resolved, she was able to accept that which had happened to her and process the beliefs from the abuse and be healed.

A couple of years ago I was in that town again and she came over and greeted me. She had two small children in her arms and another holding her hand, so I am guessing that the original issue was resolved.

Before our children grew up and I would be driving them to school, they would often comment to each other, *Dad's dissociated!* They would see the glazed look and disconnection from the trip to school, as I was thinking in my mind through some ministry case or wrestling with understanding a scripture. The difference is that there was no reason for me to not reconnect with reality. For people who have suffered trauma and disconnected there is a reason.

The ministry in this situation is exactly the same. You just have to have their will aligned, and work through the objection belief before the healing can come. Usually, as with other beliefs, once the beliefs have been taken to heart in an abuse, these beliefs will now be associated with any later abuses and used to qualify these events as well. Other beliefs can of course be added from later times of offence if the circumstances or situation is different.

These memory bubbles, containing a younger version of you, hold reasons made by your will at the time as to why you do not want to see the event. It is valuable to remember that the current version of you is the *executive member of the board* if you like, and holds ultimate sway in exerting and committing your will.

PERSONAS, MASKS AND DENIAL

The Pharisees and teachers of the law adopted a religious image which presented themselves as Holy men who were right with God. Many people who feel that they are not good enough as they are, will adopt some kind of mask or persona that they feel will make them acceptable.

We moved areas a lot when I was going through school, and I had to make new friends and fit into a new town environment many times. One of the ways that I found that made me accepted was to be the *funny guy*. For me this became my mask and you really could not get any deeper than jokes with me.

For some preachers, they don't feel that they are good enough just being themselves, and when they take to the platform you wonder who this new person is that you have not seen before. They are a mixture of their favorite speakers, which they know are accepted! For some people it is difficult at first for them to let you get behind their created image of themselves. You need patience and love to have them trust you sufficiently to take the mask off and own their inadequacies. These images often are not based on truth in regards to who they really are.

Denial and self-justification is also another possible hindrance to helping people receive ministry. If they feel that they have, for example, *every right to be angry*! Often, they will not be prepared to look at what it is in their lives that has been tapped into producing the response. Many people deny that they have any issues at all. It is everyone else that is at fault! As the saying goes; *everyone is messed up except for you and me, and now we mention it, I am not that sure about you!*

IS THIS COUNSELING?

We do not consider this type of ministry to be counseling. We are not giving instructions regarding efforts that people should undertake to resolve their problems. We simply teach them about what God will do for them if they want to receive from Him. Then, if they choose to connect with the beginnings of their presenting issues, we assist them in defining that which they believe in their hearts. Rather than this being something that they can do, these sessions are all about letting God do what He promised to do in setting them free.

In the event that we do offer them some teaching in a session, we are simply forwarding the advice or counsel that the Bible gives us all. We are not telling them that they have to do this. We are simply helping them see how their lives could function better from a Biblical standpoint. As with all the instruction of scripture, it is entirely our choice as to whether or not we do it. Our work in the ministry room is to help them to receive from God in order for them to be able to live in God's order.

IS THIS PSYCHOLOGY?

Physiology is the biological study of the living organisms of the body. Doctors understand the parts of the body and for the most part understand from these studies how the organs of the body function. They are not wrong about their observations and have some success in treating various maladies, and we are thankful to God for their efforts. We acknowledge of course that only the work of the Holy Spirit can bring miraculous, complete, and many times instant healing.

The New Testament is written in the Koine Greek language, and the word for soul is from the Bible; 'psuche.' In Latin the word for soul is; 'psyche,' which they identify as the identity or personality. Words such as psychology or psychiatry therefore refer to doctors who study and help people with the problems which relate to their souls.

The beginning of these studies historically points back to around 140 years ago. The Bible is the ultimate book explaining the activities of the soul pre-dating man's observations by a considerable amount of time. So, is what we are presenting: a study of the soul? Yes. Personally, I have never read a psychology book and simply began trying to help people by referencing the bible to find out how to do it. I had a break over Christmas in 2017 and the thought came into my mind to examine what they say that the unconscious or subconscious represents, and so I read a couple of internet articles on the subject.

The prefixes: un = not, and sub = under or below

The articles considered this as thought that is not conscious thought, or thought that is going on *under* the consciousness. From the various articles that I read; nobody seems to be able to clearly define which is which. In conclusion, what they noted that they are observing is the activities and issues presenting that are largely the same as that which the Bible says about the *heart*. Many of the things that they have learnt about the soul are not wrong; they are just limited without the Holy Spirit in terms of how they can resolve them. Just as with their observations of the body, they are limited with their treatments, so too are these soul doctors limited in that which they can offer. We appreciate their efforts and acknowledge that they bring some measure of help. The discovery and development of psychology was heralded as a great move forward for mankind's ability to heal himself, but if they had read a Bible, they would have found that the information in its fulness was there all along.

Very often people have come to us for help after many years of $200 a session visits to a psychologist. Dr. Jesus proceeds to consistently resolve their issues at no cost having already paid the price Himself. I am in no way trying to diminish the efforts or knowledge of these professionals; I am simply saying that God can do what they/we cannot.

FLOW CHART

The ministry process:

A person comes to you with a problem. This could be a mental, emotional, relational, addictive, spiritual, sexual or physical issue.

↓

They may have been *set off* or *triggered* by a life situation producing for example: anxiety, anger, sadness, bitterness, resentment, guilt, inferiority, rejection and so on.

↓

Your role is to help them focus on these feelings and reactions and to identify the beliefs which they believe at *heart* level, and which they may no longer immediately consciously access.

↓

The key components that you are trying to connect here are: The emotions, the beliefs producing the emotions, and the matching memory pictures. (No pictures prenatal, perhaps a feeling or a sense of something)

↓

You have them focus on the presenting feelings and using questions help them to discover the beliefs producing the emotion, OR

↓

If they have a belief, such as, *I just never think that I am good enough*, have them connect with the feeling that should be associated with such a thought. (The emotion often comes up as the story is related or the memory is accessed and described.)

↓

Request that they let memories come to them or willfully look for the memory picture, if they don't already have it, which contains the thoughts and feelings. (With some pictures that are remembered, it is not always immediately obvious as to why the beliefs have been interpreted here.)

↓

Having refined and identified the belief that was learnt, invite God to bring Truth. (You can be creative in how you request this to avoid being repetitive, but using phrases such as, *Lord, would you like to show Fred how you see this situation? Lord, would you touch Fred by revealing your Truth to replace what he perceives as the truth here? Lord, what would you like Fred to know about the belief that he holds?* and so on.)

Note:

How you address God in this setting is up to you. Some people just say; 'God can you please …' others might invite Jesus to minister to the person. This is also Biblical as it is the Spirit of Christ who is communicating with them. Someone else might ask the Holy Spirit, or the Spirit of truth to free them with the truth. I often just say 'Lord,' but at times, mix it up a bit. I have never seen God hold back His blessing because we did not get the method exactly correct. If you really felt the need to be pernickety and be doctrinally accurate in regards to this, you could offer a prayer such as, *Father, in the name of Jesus, would you please bring your truth to 'Fred' through the Holy Spirit.* (And then seek ministry for your own fear of getting it wrong; cheeky grin!)

I offer this guideline as an example of how a ministry could flow, to help with what you are looking for, where you are looking, and how you look. In practice it all happens quite naturally and organically as you listen to a person's story and ask questions when appropriate. The Holy Spirit really will inspire your thoughts. When you first begin, feeling like you don't know what to do is a common, expected part of stepping into something new. You are beginning with far more information than I had. In the early days I would commence a session with someone, and if we seemed stuck or I did not know how to proceed I would announce that I felt it was a good place to finish for the day. Then I would go and pray and try to work out what I should do next.

WHERE TO FROM HERE?

In many of units after unit 5 of this publication, I examine being able to discern or understand the types of beliefs that are producing specific feelings, attitudes or responses. Some of these issues are matters such as rejection, rebellion problems, low self-image, fear and so on. At the end of each of these, I will attach scenarios of typical cases relating to those particular issues. In Unit 5 we will study the ways in which spiritual influences interact with, and are implicated, in the beliefs. When are influences spiritual? Always. We are primarily spirit beings in a spiritually manipulated world. So, we are going to try and clarify how this affects us.

UNIT FIVE

Principles for understanding demons or evil spirits

Study 1: Spiritual dynamics and setting the captives free

There have been very few weeks over the last nearly 30 years where we have not been dealing with demons in some setting or another. We have come to some understandings as to how they generally operate over that time. As we begin to discuss the connection between evil spirits and ministering to people, I want to make a couple of points very clear up front.

Firstly, we do not go into a ministry session looking for demons, generational problems or entry points from any other source. If we come from a *methods*, or *this is what you do, follow this process* type training, we will often gravitate to being directive and preempting what the problem might be. I have seen ministries that work through a particular list of *demons*, or we *break this or that* as their standard ministry model, and, many times, they see very few or limited results.

We begin with *what is your problem*? Along the way we may become aware of demonic power being involved. Even when these spirits are discerned, our primary interest is the *ground, terrain, activity*, or <u>belief</u> that gives them place and not the spirit itself. The devil and His demons are completely and utterly totally defeated and there is no other way to regard him.

> *Luke 10:19-20 "* [19] *I have given you authority to trample on snakes and scorpions and to overcome* **all** *the power of the enemy; nothing will harm you.* [20] *However, do not rejoice that the spirits submit to you, but rejoice that your names are written in heaven." NIV (emphasis mine)*

If you accept the preceding and following verses, then our complete authority over Satan is obvious. The only thing that remains to be done to ensure your freedom is to identify the topos or ground that the devil has been given to stand on and resolve it.

> *Colossians 2:15 "And having disarmed the powers and authorities, he made a public spectacle of them, triumphing over them by the cross." NKJV*

We can accurately say then, that for a believer, the devil is not the problem, rather it is the area of our *thinking or inner believing* that gives him ground and deceives us into moving our will to participate with him. So, we really are not *demon focused*, instead we are targeting the presenting problem that a person carries, being aware that at times it might be empowered and amplified by an evil spirit.

Our mission, in co laboring to set the captives free, is to resolve wrong believing and areas of deception working under the ministry of the Spirit of Truth.

Luke 11:20 "But if I cast out demons with the finger of God, surely the kingdom of God has come upon you." NKJV

Examining beliefs at a heart level is the quickest way that I have seen to expose the ground held by many evil spirits. The beliefs themselves may be the ground for the demons, or the resultant sin choices and behavior may give them place.

THE SPIRITUAL OR UNSEEN REALM
As we begin to look at this area, we should not have a problem with seeing the world as being manipulated from an unseen realm. I can only imagine the thousands of mobile phone calls, SMS messages, radio waves, emails, television station transmissions, Facebook pictures and so on that are all around me in the invisible realm at any given time. Add to that the unseen power of gravity, prismatic color, temperature, magnetic fields, static electricity, etc. etc. etc., there is indeed a great deal that we cannot see that affects our world. I cannot see how a television remote changes the channels or another *bipper* puts up my garage door, but they do! All of these examples, and we have not even mentioned unseen spiritual beings interplaying and manipulating the world system through mankind.

WHAT ARE DEMONS OR EVIL SPIRITS?
Although many people have various theories about what demons are and where they come from, the Bible does not specifically state any of this. It does however reveal their nature and activities, and also how we are to deal with them. By observation however, we can say that they are bodiless spirits. The terms *demon, evil spirit,* or *unclean spirit,* according to the famous Bible teacher Derek Prince, are interchangeable. To be demonized is considered to have or be under the influence of an evil, unclean spirit or a demon. Some early translations used phrases such as, *possessed with devils,* or *possessed with the devil.*

> ### Note:
> *Devils'* is considered to be a mistranslation for demons as the person of the devil is *diablos* speaking of Satan himself and used only in the singular. Demon is translated from *diamon* or *diamonion.*

Some took this to be that the devil possessed the entire person, whereas in reality, *demons* often possess or have control of areas of the human personality or body. In truth, a believer is redeemed and possessed only by Christ. The control of these areas is certainly by degrees ranging from one part of the person having strongholds, through to many areas. Mostly demons are not always manifested or seen all of the time.

A long time ago I worked with a man who, in a given situation, would exhibit demonic facial and behavioral changes. He was in fact a good man, who had an unresolved problem area that appeared only on rare occasions when particular circumstances presented. At the other end of the scale, I have worked with an extreme case where all that was constantly visible was demons and where the person virtually was completely run by the evil spirits. This is extremely unusual and I have never seen another case even close to this level of demonization. Usually the demons hold areas of a person in the soul or body.

I liken the personality to your neighborhood. Most of the houses are fine, but there are one or two residences that are noisy and have wild parties. Sadly, we cannot normally arrange evictions for these neighbors as we can with demons. So, we can say that these spirits without bodies can hold areas that have become available to them for inhabitation. The demons do not have a choice in this as it is whatever is yielded to them through some kind of agreement, weakness or cooperation from the host.

'IN' A SPIRIT

The late Derek Prince pointed out that a passage such as Mark chapter 5, verse 2 could also be rendered as a man in an unclean spirit rather than *with*.

> *Mark 5:2 "And when He had come out of the boat, immediately there met Him out of the tombs a man with an unclean spirit." NKJV*

A lady came to a home group that we were running in the mid-1990s complaining of having had an unusual outburst of anger. Armed with the information from Derek Prince's observation about being *in a spirit*, I proceeded to ask her if she had been near anybody who was an angry person. I had known her for a number of years and she had always presented as very calm and amiable. She responded that she had been with a man who was a very angry person indeed, and that she had had the outburst in his company. People who carry demonic spiritual dynamics will often have an almost magnetic spiritual atmosphere that you need to avoid being pulled into. It is trying to illicit a reaction in you to have some measure of control over your behavior. For example, rejection rejects, pride will make you feel inferior, rebellion will treat you unjustly and disrespectfully to try to create the same responses in you that gave the spirits place in the host. That certainly does not mean that you will automatically receive that spirit, but it does mean that it now has had an expression through you as well as the host.

The spirit realm is a 2-way street. One day I was sitting in a group with some other Pastors and I was getting clear visions and strong words of knowledge for members of the group. Whilst I do have words of knowledge and so on, normally visions for me would be more like impressions. After a while I realized that I was seated beside a well-known and regarded prophet. I concluded that my proximity to him had me *sitting in his gift* and that was the reason for the abnormal pictures etc.

In summary we can say that we need to be aware of the spiritual dynamics of people that we are dealing with and that discernment is our best defense against receiving or responding to someone else's junk. We can see it many times as being something beyond the normal levels of a person's problems, to the amplified or unnatural tangible invisible influence of an unseen entity. If you are aware, you can often see the presence of a spirit on a person as a facial expression of for example, grief, low self-image or lust. You can also see them in body language such as pride and arrogance, perhaps rebellious or aggressive attitudes.

Although demons do not have a body, they seek a house or host to inhabit. They exhibit all the normal faculties of a soul. They showed *knowledge and comprehension* of knowing Jesus and also Paul. They displayed thought and decision or will when they decided to return to their house. In James chapter two it says even the demons tremble which indicates that they have emotion. Legion in Mark chapter 5 knew who he was as a soul, and in this case had sufficient power over the vocal cords of the man to speak, communicate and express himself.

At times you will be aware that speech coming from a person is demonically influenced even though there is not complete control as in the case of the demoniac in Mark 5. In these cases, it will be more of a mixture with the person's own personality and there will not likely be a complete voice change. This could be something in the order of; *I hate you!* or *I'm such a loser!* where the intensity of the emotion or statement may be an indicator of a resident spirit. Even at the minimum end of the scale, as we have already pointed out, Jesus identified the source and inspiration behind Peter's comments in Matthew 16:23 as having originated with Satan, although operating from outside of his person.

ACTIVITIES OF DEMONS

The late Derek Prince compiled the following list of the activities of demons from both scripture and personal involvement with deliverance ministry. In my experience it is completely accurate.

1.	Demons Entice or tempt.	(James 1:14)
2.	They deceive.	(I Timothy 4:1-2)
3.	Spirits enslave.	(Romans 8:15) [This would include besetting sins]
4.	They torment.	(2 Timothy 1:7; 1 John 4:18)
5.	Demons drive or compel.	(Luke 8:29)
6.	Evil spirits defile.	(Titus 1:15)

LESSON
Demons work to deceive, oppose, destroy and rob us of peace and produce disharmony and division at every opportunity.

Study 2: Unholy spirits, are they inside or outside?

SPIRITUAL INFLUENCE FROM OUTSIDE

Spiritual pressures that come from outside of us largely come through the programming of the world. This could be in the form of cultural dynamics, for example, the western world is highly sexualized in our times. As a consequence, we are bombarded with ungodly sexual themes and images which proceed from demonic influences. These are *coverings* or spiritual powers that have found cooperative people or groups to work with and follow them. This submission gives them power. It is highly unlikely that the devil or his cohorts are watching you or following you personally. His attacks on you will usually come through people who are unwittingly following him. They are thinking that how they are behaving or dealing with you is simply something that *they* independently want to do; after all the devil doesn't exist.

So, we have extremes, with some people thinking that the devil is able to attack you as a spiritual being without the use of a host person or some kind of medium such as media. Then at the other end of the scale, the devil just doesn't exist at all. In the case of Jesus' dealings with Satan through Peter, Jesus pointed out that the access came through Peter's *man* thinking which was programmed into him by the world system.

> *Matthew 16:23 But He turned and said to Peter, "Get behind Me, Satan! You are an offense to Me, for you are not mindful of the things of God, but the things of men." NKJV*

By implication, the things of men are the things of Satan, the influencer and controller of the fallen world. Notice that Jesus did not say *come out*. Peter did not have a demon inside him, rather he was submitting to the spiritual environment and training coming through his society. We see in the story of Job that he attributed some of the thinking and comments coming from his friends to their lack of discernment in regards to what spirit they were being inspired by. This may have been a shock to them as quite probably they thought that all of their ideas we coming from their own wisdom.

Many of the thoughts that we have, very possibly proceed from some kind of spiritual influence that we are open and attentive to because of our training. This is certainly true when we renew our minds to the ways of God and through His word conform to His Spirit.

> Job 26:4 "Where have you gotten all these wise sayings? Whose spirit speaks through you?" NLT

Again, we see that the way of thinking that gave place to the devil, and a consequent door through their minds and then mouths, was a non-biblical mindset from worldly wisdom. We also note, to attack Job with negative thoughts, which incidentally may well have affected him, required hosts for the spirits to get at him though. The fact that he was able to discern the source was protective for him in not receiving what they were trying to put on him.

We have, in a previous study, cited Jesus pointing out to His disciples that they were unaware of the type of spirit that they were being influenced by.

> Luke 9:55 But He turned and rebuked them, and said, "You do not know what manner of spirit you are of." NKJV

Yet again we see that He did not cast a spirit out of them because it was not resident inside them. It was worldly thinking inspired by the proud Satan controlled environment that they were still operating in.

CAN SATAN ATTACK YOU AT WILL?

Many Christians seem to have the idea that Satan can attack you out of a *clear blue sky* so to speak, anytime that he wants. This thinking suggests that he can attack you at will without some kind of agent to work through or exposure to some kind of medium or prior programming to tempt you. Their concept proposes that the devil might suddenly decide to attack you with fear, or to hold you back in your walk, just because he chooses to. In my experience I have never seen anyone attacked by fear who was not presented with a potentially anxiety inspiring situation, or more commonly holding a previously existing fear belief from a historical source.

To believe this would be to believe that someone who has never suffered with bitterness or lust for instance could suddenly be attacked with resentment for no reason or struggle with immoral thoughts. To take this further, this kind of thinking proposes that you could, without contact with another human being, or any kind of advertising, exposure or encouragement suddenly be overcome by a power drawing you into alcoholism, drugs, violence, and the occult or horror movies. This is absurd really, but there are a lot of people who spend time on *spiritual warfare* against a non-existent threat.

Believing that the devil can do this is giving him much more power than he actually has. He is roaming around, but he tempts through media or temptations to cooperate with him through some kind of peer pressure or reaction to offences from other people. Jesus preached repent, in other words change your thinking about what you allow yourself to join with and be exposed to, saying that the Kingdom of heaven is at hand to cooperate with.

> Isaiah 14:16 Everyone there will stare at you and ask, 'Can this be the one who shook the earth and the kingdoms of the world? NLT

Satan is not omnipresent as is God. He is limited in his ability to personally monitor individuals. In the case of God who *is* omnipresent, I knew of him because a person taught me about Him as a small child. In my teenage years and early twenties, I had largely walked away from Him and scarcely gave Him a thought. Even He did not put *God thoughts* into my mind. He eventually used a person to refire my faith. So, normally in the first instance, even God does not approach a person who has no knowledge of Him without the use of a person.

> *Romans 10:14 How then shall they call on Him in whom they have not believed? And how shall they believe in Him of whom they have not heard? And how shall they hear without a preacher? NKJV*

In conclusion, we could say that as we resolve our fallen nature tendencies by dying to that which the world offers, and deal with deceptive beliefs held at a heart level, the devil has no place from which to bother us. I know many mature and free Christians who are only aware of the devil in the setting of getting others free of his influences. The only power that he actually has, is in what he has already trained you to believe, such as to live in fear, or, that you are not acceptable and so on. These *beliefs* give him access to how you respond to life and deal with others, which now gives him opportunity to provoke or tempt others through your ungodly activities and attitudes towards them. The other way he can affect you is in what you choose as a result of your beliefs. This may outwork as it did in the garden in thinking that something sinful and forbidden is what you need to make your life better. Indeed, the Apostle Paul knew that the people's eyes were closed to the deception and activities of Satan, and that this was the source of his power over them.

> *Acts 26:18 '... to open their eyes, in order to turn them from darkness to light, and from the power of Satan to God, that they may receive forgiveness of sins and an inheritance among those who are sanctified by faith in Me.' NKJV*

In all of this, participation and submission to him are an unwitting form of worship in that you prefer his guidelines for living over God's. In this sense, the devil inhabits the praises of *his* people!

> *Ephesians 2:1-3* [1]*"As for you, you were dead in your transgressions and sins,* [2] *in which you used to live when you followed the ways of this world and of the ruler of the kingdom of the air, the spirit who is now at work in those who are disobedient.* [3] *All of us also lived among them at one time, gratifying the cravings of our **sinful nature** and **following its desires and thoughts**. Like the rest, we were by nature objects of wrath." NIV (emphasis mine)*

Most of what we believe was programmed into us growing up. And this, through people who were giving us thinking and believing that did not line up with God's ways. Therefore, it becomes reasonably obvious where most of our problems begin from, and where the solutions for freedom lie.

COLLECTIVE HUMAN SPIRIT

Sometimes what we think is an evil spirit is actually the collective power of a cooperative human spirit which is open to working in the devil's ways. For example, drunken parties, drugs or orgies, or the agreement of the corporate human spirit of our society on matters such as; *fornication is not sinful or pornography is normal and acceptable*. This is human spirit streaming in behind the devils wishes because it suits the self-indulgent fallen nature.

It is a power dynamic which creates a spiritual environment in much the same way as football matches or rock concerts have a spiritual/emotional atmosphere as the human spirit opens up and gets involved. That is not suggesting that football or a music concert is demonic, only that it has an atmosphere that has a corporate spirit emanating from a dynamic of collective human spirit in unison that can be felt and caught up in.

RANDOM ATTACKS FROM SATAN

So, am I saying that God or unholy spirits cannot put thoughts in your mind from outside your person? No. What I am proposing is that it appears that neither God nor His opposer randomly put thoughts in your mind without *eliciting or evoking your attention* by some means. If you watch a horror movie and then have bad dreams in your sleep it is because you gave Satan your attention and handed him your mind. He is going to try to get to you through the world system, people, and through your existing beliefs.

In much the same way we choose to communicate with God in prayer and seek Him for His counsel. So then when we open ourselves to His input, we ask, seek, knock, then we receive something, otherwise we probably won't hear much. Once we have committed our lives to Him, He has every right to give us His thoughts if we are looking to Him and giving Him our attention. For example, if I am seeking Him for a sermon, I will get more inspirational ideas than if I am engaged in a building project at home and my faculties are focused there. I often have a notebook or at least a pen available in a church service because as we are all giving Him our attention, and He is near inhabiting our praises, I often easily get thoughts and inspiration. But these are times of deliberate focus on Him. The door is wide open as we are choosing to communicate with Him.

Of course, if His Spirit resides *inside* of us and we are one in spirit with Him then he has full access to our faculties all of the time. In much the same way, if we have a spirit inside of us holding onto an area of our thinking then that demon will be a constant influencer towards those kinds of thoughts.

The devil has no power whatsoever, or ability to attack us or put thoughts in our minds without us beholding him, thinking about him or being attentive. Many Christians are deceived into thinking that he has power to attack us and that if we say this or that, he will test us. Or if you press in to God or are active in the gospel he will go after you. This is deception leading to fear.

My wife and I have ministered the gospel and taught on healing and deliverance in many developing countries. We have never feared anything happening and have never had any oppression or attacks on us, ever. That is not arrogance; it is simply what the Bible says. If God is for us, who can be against us? If you think that the devil can attack you then you are putting your faith in him as being greater than God, and that he is not defeated at all, which is faith in reverse, that we know as fear.

If that is the case, you may be right, because you are giving him power that he does not have through your deception. We never even give the possibility that the devil can touch us a thought. In fact, I don't think about him at all, beyond recognizing his activities through others that need help so that his works can be destroyed. God is *the* power and we are in Him. His ability to protect us is unchallengeable. When the Lord says that it is time to go home it is time. God Himself oversees all of our circumstances; He allows them for our shaping and refining.

> Luke 10:19 *"Behold, I give you the authority to trample on serpents and scorpions, and **over all** the power of the enemy, and **nothing** shall by any means hurt you." NKJV (emphasis mine)*

Jesus suffered not because the devil was able to overpower Him, but because He was yielded to the Father's will in suffering for our sake. The same could be said of Paul and the others. They chose to put themselves in harm's way for the cause of the gospel. It was their will and not that of the devil that caused their tribulations. They willfully exposed themselves to human beings through whom the devil could operate, in the hope of saving them.

> *Matthew 26:53-54 " ⁵³ Or do you think that I cannot now pray to My Father, and He will provide Me with more than twelve legions of angels? ⁵⁴ "How then could the Scriptures be fulfilled, that it must happen thus?" NKJV*

Satan means the adversary, enemy or opposer which can be applied personally to the devil, but also encompasses all of the spiritual opposition to God working with him. So, attacks that come from the devil will usually come through people who are submitted to him in some area. This could be in the form of someone rejecting or being violent towards you and range through to a fellow teenager showing a schoolmate pornography on a smartphone. Either way his attack has not come from nowhere but rather evil spirit has found a manifestation in the natural realm through a *door or gate*. Jesus said that the *gates of hell* will not prevail. In other words, those who let the devil use them for his work, whether unwittingly or not, won't have the victory over believers who constitute the church.

> *Matthew 16:18 "And I also say to you that you are Peter, and on this rock I will build My church, and the gates of Hades shall not prevail against it." NKJV*

Someone once said that both God and Satan are looking for a manifestation in the Earth. Like Peter, at times we can be double agents, where one moment we are exhibiting the Spirit of God in love, gentleness, kindness and so on. Later we find ourselves working for the other side and giving him an expression through criticism, fault-finding, or rejecting someone. We truly do need to make our focus worshipping God. Our behavior and attitudes being doors and gates for His Spirit only, giving Him a manifestation in the Earth.

> *Psalm 24:7 "Lift up your heads, O you gates! And be lifted up, you everlasting doors! And the King of glory shall come in." NKJV*

We need to come to the truth about whose spirit we are allowing to work through us, and often that requires receiving truth in the inner parts or heart before we are able to know what manner of spirit that we are of.

> *John 4:24 "God is Spirit, and those who worship Him must worship in spirit and **truth**." NKJV*

 LESSON
God and the devil are both looking for your cooperation and submission. They both seek to elicit or evoke your attention through some means. They are not of course equal, Satan being a created being who has limited time in the Earth.

SPIRITUAL INFLUENCE FROM INSIDE

When a spirit finds a way inside a person it has much greater influence over them, and becomes entwined in the personality or body. This is true of the Holy Spirit indwelling a believer as well. Obviously, there is no comparison between the power of the Holy Spirit and a demon, but in many ways, the Holy Spirit also limits His power in us, and through us, to willful cooperation. Whether speaking of the Holy Spirit or an unholy spirit we could say that when they are inside, they have greater access and influence on our thoughts and faculties. The Holy Spirit normally comes inside when the person is ready and open to His presence. He does not force His way in. On the other hand, a demon will take any opening possible to find a way into a host person.

Jesus gave us the example of the wineskins. I believe that when a person is born again, he now has a new sensitivity to God and the Kingdom of heaven. This would be likened to a new wineskin. He now has a new soft regenerated human spirit which can expand and grow in the things of God. The Bible uses the picture of the New Wine as the Holy Spirit being poured out. We need a new spirit or a new wineskin to hold the new wine, which is the Holy Spirit who will continue to mature, ferment and expand in us when He comes inside.

> *Matthew 9:17 "Nor do they put new wine into old wineskins, or else the wineskins break, the wine is spilled, and the wineskins are ruined. But they put new wine into new wineskins, and both are preserved." NKJV*

The book of Ezekiel bears this out confirming in the following passage that God will soften our hard hearts, (soul) and put in us a new spirit, (human spirit) which can be joined to His Spirit so that we can worship in spirit and in truth, joined spirit to Spirit. The following passage illustrates this, with our new spirit, (small 's') and God putting in His Spirit. (Capitol 'S')

> *Ezekiel 36:26-27* *[26] I will give you a new heart and put **a new spirit** in you; I will remove from you your heart of stone and give you a heart of flesh. [27] And I will put **my Spirit** in you and move you to follow my decrees and be careful to keep my laws. NIV (emphasis mine)*

The Bible teaches us that we are one spirit, joined to the Lord. The Greek word translated here is *kollao* which literally means glued or stuck together. This powerful joining makes it impossible to be closer with Him in spirit.

> *1 Corinthians 6:17 "But he who is joined to the Lord is one spirit with Him." NKJV*

It is worth pointing out that the Strong's concordance cites an element of the word *Charis* from which *grace* is translated, as *the divine influence upon the heart*. This sheds a different light on the grace of God. A large part of this grace is His influencing us away from ungodly behavior and serving Satan. Because of the presence of the Holy Spirit, we can have *the mind of Christ* if we choose to listen.

Let me propose that whether you are a Christian or not, if you have a demon inside you, then you can have the mind of that evil spirit as well. It is not that the evil spirit is more powerful than the Holy Spirit; it is that you choose to follow it for some reason. When the Apostle Paul encourages the believers to work out their *salvation*, he did not exclusively mean their passage into heaven. He knew that this was provided for through redemption. Salvation is translated from the Greek word *soteria*. Strong's Concordance presents it this way: *4991. Soteria, noun; rescue or safety (phys. or mor.):--deliver, health, salvation, save, saving.*

Paul was implying that you need to work on your deliverance from the devil. This, we are proposing, is by receiving light and truth which will result in your healing in every area of your being.

> *Philippians 2:12 "Therefore, my beloved, as you have always obeyed, not as in my presence only, but now much more in my absence, work out your own **salvation** with fear and trembling." NKJV (emphasis mine)*

Again, we see the Greek word sozo translated as saved, carrying in it the sense of more than simply being saved for eternity: *4982. sozo, to save, i.e. **deliver** or protect (lit. or fig.):--**heal**, preserve, save (self), do well, **be (make) whole** (Emphasis mine).* It also points to deliverance from the opposer, as well as healing, and importantly being made whole, which is the result of sanctification through truth.

> *Ephesians 2:8 "For by grace you have been **saved** through faith, and that not of yourselves; it is the gift of God, 9 not of works, lest anyone should boast." NKJV (emphasis mine)*

We can conclude that a major part of our freedom and protection from evil spirits, whether they are inside or out, is by responding to the divine influence of the Spirit of Christ and receiving healing, deliverance and wholeness from His ministry.

> *1 Thessalonians 5:23 "Now may the God of peace Himself sanctify you completely; and may your whole spirit, soul, and body be preserved blameless at the coming of our Lord Jesus Christ." NKJV*

If demons are influencing us from outside of the body the Bible instructs us to resist them.

> *James 4:7 "Therefore submit to God. Resist the devil and he will flee from you." NKJV*

If they are operating inside the body, we are to cast them out in the name of Jesus Christ.

> *Matthew 8:16 "When evening had come, they brought to Him many who were demon-possessed. And He cast out the spirits with a word, and healed all who were sick." NKJV*

Sometimes I hear people say that a Christian can't have a demon. I think the question is more like can a demon have a Christian, or at least an area of one? As an obvious example, most statistics that I have heard, cite that well over 50% of Christian men regularly look at pornography. I rest my case.

A DEMON UNDER EVERY BUSH

Some people who are excessively demon focused may be looking for a *demon under every bush!* Whilst that may be true to some extent, it is not a healthy way to approach this area of ministry. There is probably a spider under every bush as well but we don't really pay much attention unless it relates to something that we are doing.

The other end of the scale is to ignore the possibilities of demons altogether and come up with some unbiblical theology that excludes them. A common one is that a Christian cannot have a demon. This is often based on the premise that God cannot exist with evil and so He cannot infill a believer and have the demon remain. However, He does indwell believers and most often sin and sickness remains and dwells with Him. He is not condoning or participating with it, but nor is He removing Himself from it. At the beginning of the book of Job we see God seemingly casually chatting with Satan. Apparently, He has no problem being in the presence of an evil spiritual entity.

Let me propose that not only can a believer have a demon, but in fact deliverance from them is our bread or a provision for us that is not available to others.

> *Mark 7:27 But Jesus said to her, "Let the children be filled first, for it is not good to take the children's bread and throw it to the little dogs." NKJV*

In this passage the woman was looking for deliverance for her daughter from a demon. Jesus was pointing out that it was something that was for the children of God. She showed herself to be just such a person, coming ahead of time under the new covenant of faith as a means to receive God's provision. It is worth observing that the daughters' problem was a demon, but that the result of it leaving was healing. Sometimes the work of an evil spirit produces sickness of some kind.

> *Matthew 15:28 Then Jesus answered and said to her, "O woman, great is your faith! Let it be to you as you desire." And her daughter was healed from that very hour. NKJV*

Being set free from demons then, is a part of God's children's provision. Consequently, Jesus instructed the disciples as a part of their job description to deal with them. So, to not be prepared to use His name and authority in this way could be seen as disobedience to His command.

> *Matthew 10:1 "He called his twelve disciples to him and gave them authority to drive out evil spirits and to heal every disease and sickness." NIV*

I was once dealing with a man who had come into our church from a denomination that taught that a Christian could not have a demon. He began sharing this point of view with a young believer who was influenced by him at the time and was also a part of the church. The problem was that the young man who he was imposing his doctrine on had had a powerful deliverance the evening before and had witnessed his wife being set free as well from an Occult spirit. This would be expert on demons quickly changed his position from a *Christian can't have a demon, to, that's not how I do it*!

To say that a Christian cannot have a demon is a bit like saying that they cannot have sin or sickness. The overwhelming evidence is that they both can and do, although the intention of God, as modeled by Jesus, is that they should not have either. Respectfully might I suggest that we could perhaps spend a little less time on matters such as how the Sunday service looks and a little more time on delivering the promises of God to His people? That is not to say that the service isn't important, but if that is all we have to offer those who attend how biblical are we?

 LESSON

God is desiring to fill us with His Spirit as Jesus was to empower us to walk in His ways and have abundant life. Satan seeks to come inside us also and occupy areas of our being with demonic power for greater influence, stealing our peace and destroying our lives if possible.

> *Luke 4:1 Then Jesus, **being filled with the Holy Spirit**, returned from the Jordan and was led by the Spirit into the wilderness. NKJV (emphasis mine)*

John 10:10 The thief comes only to steal and kill and destroy; I have come that they may have life, and have it to the full. NIV

Study 3: The Strong man's goods

A number of years ago I was pulling down an old house on our property in order to build a new one on the site. In the meantime, we had a large shed and I set up my office and a lounge room in there. There was also a lot of furniture stacked in there. While I was working outside some of the children came out screaming that there was a snake in the building. Now I could have taken the attitude that I would just deal with it if it showed up. However, I felt that it was my duty and responsibility to find where it had come in and seal that off and then expose it and deal with it so that it could not cause harm.

As I have said, if we become aware that a *demon* is in the house, we have a duty to those that we are responsible for, to find out where it came from and evict it as soon as possible. When we were in Kenya at one time, we were awakened to the sound of mosquitoes who had gotten in through the net. I would not rest until I had found the holes where they came in and patched them up. I then made sure that I tracked those insects down and eliminated them before I tried to sleep. I know that in the night with their buzzing, it will rob our peace and ruin our functionality and mood for the following day. Consequently, it is prudent for me to deal with them as soon as possible. First, as with the snake, I have to expose where it is hiding and block up the place where it has come in!

LESSON
It is vitally important to deal with any relevant entry point when dealing with evil spirits.

EXPOSING THE ENEMY THROUGH TEACHING

It has been proposed that fully one third of Jesus' recorded ministry to people in the gospels was dealing with demons in some way. We know that before He ministered, He often taught the people. A number of years ago we were ministering in a large church in the Pacific and immediately prior to lunch I had taught on rejection. There was a young lady who brought the meal to us at the Pastors house, and as she put the food in front of us, I noticed that she had tears in her eyes. I commented to her; *The rejection teaching touched you didn't it?* She responded that it did. I asked her if she wanted me to pray for her and she indicated that she did. Across the table I took authority over the spirit of rejection and commanded it to go in the name of Jesus. She had a manifestation and I asked her if it had gone. She informed me that it had and so we proceeded to eat our lunch. The point is that this was easily done because she saw her problem. If the setting had been right, *Truth Encounters* would have been a good option for further healing. If she had not understood the source of her issue and the spiritual element of her problem, most probably nothing would have happened.

In the mid-1990s an intellectual lady came for some ministry advice. As she described her problem it became evident to me that she was also carrying a spirit of rejection. I explained this to her and how it worked but she was struggling with the concept, and so thanked me and left. Several months later she returned and confirmed that she now believed that what I had explained was true. Now that she had seen the spiritual element of her problem, it was only a matter of moments and she was free. She later reported that she was now able to get on with people whom she formerly struggled with and generally felt better.

I want to make the point that if I had tried to cast out the spirit without her having a realization that it was present; I would have been wasting my time. God will not necessarily set her free because I want her to be free. He will set her free when, by her own will, she wants Him to free her, which will normally require her understanding her need. If this were not the case then God would automatically set everyone free of everything without the consent of their free will and choice. Even the demoniac in Mark chapter 5 came to Jesus and fell down before Him. Jesus often said things such as; *do you want to be made well?* (John 5:6).

Another factor that I would like to mention regarding this lady's ministry was that at that time we did not minister *Truth Encounters* and although she reported improvement and that the *power* had gone out of her rejection, she was still not completely whole in that area. A few years later she returned for further ministry in which the *truth made her completely free.*

 LESSON
People need to understand their problem, so that they can commit their will to the process.

WHAT ARE THE STRONG MAN'S GOODS?

A strong man's *goods or possessions* are those things which he holds that strengthen his position. The Greek word translated as *goods or possessions is huparchonta*, which also means *that which one has*, or *his property.*

> Luke 11:20-21 [20] *But if I drive out demons by the finger of God, then the kingdom of God has come to you.* [21] *"When a strong man, **fully armed**, guards his own house, his **possessions** are safe." NIV (emphasis mine)*

Let me suggest that he is fully armed with areas of deception that protect those areas that he considers his property, possessions or goods. These possessions that give him *a place* are the beliefs that we hold that cause us to serve him and participate with him. For example:

- A spirit of bitterness will hold hurts and beliefs resulting from being hurt or abused.
- A spirit of rebellion will hold beliefs relating to injustice.
- A spirit of pride will hold beliefs relating to inferiority.
- A spirit of self-pity will hold beliefs to do with nobody caring about the host and so on.
- The one who is stronger is the Spirit of truth, because truth overpowers the power of deception just as light dispels darkness.
- So is the spirit the problem or, is the property or possessions that he holds that give him a place, the issue?

> Ephesians 4:27 *" ... nor give **place** to the devil." NKJV (emphasis mine)*
> Ephesians 4:27 *" ... and do not give the devil a **foothold**." NIV (emphasis mine)*

Giving the devil a foothold or a place to stand, through what we believe and the resultant way that we act, is the true nature of the problem. Again, we look to the original Greek language and see that *foothold* and *place* come from the word *topos* which means a location, a home, or even an opportunity. So often through what we *believe* we consciously or unconsciously yield a portion of our personality, soul or body for the demon to stand on. Being *fully armed* relates to his ability to protect his position. For example, if his possessions which give him place are *beliefs* relating to inferiority then his ability to defend those beliefs are the pride response that comes from those beliefs. Now he is safe because the host will not go to anyone for help because their pride will not allow them to be *under* another person. Remember this is because the solution to inferiority that the devil suggests is to make you *over* or *above* everyone else in pride. This means that you believe that you know more or better and have more wisdom than anyone else. If we continue to use the same examples the *fully armed* component of injustice beliefs is the rebellion reaction. Now the person is captive because they cannot submit to another.

In the case of a control spirit, the person's insecurity is the issue. To trust another would mean that they are no longer in control, and this is the defense of the strongman and so on. This is why ministering to the *root heart belief*, rather than trying to cast out the demon by attacking his defenses is a far more effective and permanent way of dealing with the spirit. He is now weak and easy to cast out because he has lost his *possessions* which gave him a *place* and so this is also a gentler approach for the person.

Many times, the spirit is attached to sinful behavior, attitudes, reactions and responses that are retaliatory by nature. The name of the demon is the name of ungodly sinful activities such as unforgiveness, resentment, bitterness, ungodly control, rebellion, pride, hatred, self-rejection, fear of rejection and so on. I need to point out that all of these can and do exist without the presence of a demon inside the host. Either way *the beliefs* need to be dealt with to remove the areas that the devil can work through from outside, or that are strongholds of evil spirits on the inside.

Two of the main ways that the demons have *a place* then, is firstly by holding people captive to pain and hurt coming from heart beliefs. Secondly, they are from responses that you believe will resolve the issues proceeding from these beliefs. This could, along with the emotional reactions that we have described, include things such as lustful or immoral activities, violence, addictive behavior, theft, lying, criticism, and so on.

How right was Louis Pasteur when he made an observation relating to the destructive power of the unseen enemy that we now know as germs! *The germ is nothing, the terrain is everything!* In a spiritual sense we could replicate this principle by saying that the demon is nothing, the environment or *beliefs* that give him *place* are everything. The only hold he has on us to use us, manipulate us, and keep us in bondage is some area of deception or wrong believing in the mind, heart, or both. The germ is nothing and consequently our focus is not on him, he simply *flags* the real problem. Once we know the type of *root belief* and likely circumstance that it was learnt in, we can deal with the terrain.

LESSON
The best way to take away *the armor* of the 'strongman' is to remove his possessions that give him place. The armor is usually the ungodly responses that come from *the beliefs* that he possesses.

THE 'DUNG' GOD
Jesus described Satan as *Beelzebub* which means the *dung god*, or the *lord of the flies*. This gives us a great perspective on how God regards demons. They are nothing, they are just like flies. The only power that they have is whatever you are deceived into giving them, which is why when you know the truth it will set you free. I think that most of us who started out with a *cast out the demons'* focus, and neglected healing the broken hearts, would agree

with me that many times we would shoo away the flies on Monday only to find that we had to do it again a week later. Some people would stay free, or have a measure of deliverance but many, even though they may have had powerful deliverances and manifestations, would return bound again.

Whereas when we take the *Truth Encounters* model, we see them completely free in the area ministered to, and are often not even aware if there was a demon there or not, because we took his goods in which he trusted in. It is much gentler for the person than attacking a fully armed spirit if we remove that which he trusts in. In short, clean up the dung and there is no further reason for the flies to be there. They need food and the dung heap as their place. The fly is nothing; the dung is *everything*!

SWEPT AND EMPTY

When Jesus used the picture of that which the spirit considers to be *his house*, or *place that he inhabits* He states that if this abode, which is based on the possessions of the demon is left empty, then it is likely that the evil spirit will return. Why is this?

Let me propose that the property of the demon that gave him place was the *deceptive beliefs* that the host or person held. So, if the house is left empty and not filled with God's truth through the ministry of the Spirit of truth, then there is nothing stopping him from returning. If knowing the Truth will set you free, and if this is done by the Spirit of Christ, then you will remain free indeed.

> Matthew 12:43-44 43 *"When an unclean spirit goes out of a man, he goes through dry places, seeking rest, and finds none.* 44 *"Then he says, 'I will return to my house from which I came.' And when he comes, he finds it empty, swept, and put in order." NKJV*

 ## LESSON
If we have not cleaned up the dung*, then the flies will stay around, or return if we have shooed them away. *The dung is the wrong beliefs that are evident as we are measured against the word of God. For example, if we believe that we are not loved or loveable, when the Bible clearly says that we are.*

REPENTANCE AND DELIVERANCE

Once a spirit has established a strong hold on your hurts or sinful reactions, he is going to *replay them* as inner thinking or addictive and often repetitive behavior. He is also going to *amplify* your responses and the intensity of emotion that you hold. People with demonic powered beliefs may often not be able to control their feelings and have an inordinate response in how they react to stressors.

When we talk about repentance, people normally consider it to mean to turn from your sin. This turning is actually a byproduct of repentance. The word translated as *repent* from the original Greek language is *Metanoeo* and it means to *think differently* or *reconsider*, or *to change one's mind*. When we think differently about what we are doing, reconsider our ways and then change our minds, the byproduct will be turning from sin. In the first instance we need to know that our thinking and resultant deeds are wrong to begin with, and we do this through learning the ways of God from His word. In the epistle 1 John and chapter 3 we see that Jesus came to destroy the works of the devil.

> *1 John 3:8 "He who sins is of the devil, for the devil has sinned from the beginning. For this purpose the Son of God was manifested, that He might destroy the works of the devil." NKJV*

Having established that Jesus came to destroy the works of the devil that were operating in and through mankind, we now observe that He came preaching; *repent for the Kingdom of heaven is at hand.* Why?

He did this because in order to destroy the devil's works in us, he needs us to stop cooperating with our enemy by our own will and volition. He needs for us to think differently, reconsider our ways and change our minds to living the ways of the Kingdom of God. We do this by renewing our minds and then deciding that we want to be hearers and doers of the word. But as we have described in an earlier chapter the Apostle Paul had set himself in this stance as he outlined in Romans chapter 7, but was unable to do that which he had decided to do with his conscious mind. He needed a change of thinking at heart level as well before he could fully live out his repentance, and this is a gift of God through healing ministries such as *Truth Encounters* and deliverance.

> *2 Timothy 2:24-26* [24] *"And the servant of the Lord must not strive; but be gentle unto all men, apt to teach, patient,* [25] *In meekness instructing those that* **oppose themselves***; if God peradventure will give them* **repentance to the acknowledging of the truth***;* [26] *And that they may recover themselves out of the snare of the devil, who are* **taken captive by him** *at his will." KJV (emphasis mine)*

As in the case of Paul, these people oppose themselves because how they want to act with their minds is not in agreement with how they do actually act, which is based on the deceptive *beliefs* that they hold in their hearts. The final result is that they remain in bondage to the devil acting out his will and manifesting his nature. They are often doing this even though they are believers, in part because they believe that their actions are *just what they want to do,* and are not aware of the devil's involvement. In 2 Timothy chapter 2 and verse 25 that we have just read it refers to the change of thinking or repentance coming as a result of *acknowledging the truth.*

Our mission is to gently instruct them and teach them the truth about the roots of their issues and how they can receive freedom from captivity. Mostly evil spirits have a place in us through something that we believe either consciously or unconsciously. This could include not believing that a part of the problem is a demon.

SPIRITUAL 'ARMOR'
Whilst we are mainly focused on the issue, or the 'dung', it is good to be aware of the possibilities of spiritual interference, which is why I am writing this whole section.

Story
At one time a lady traveled a long way to receive *Truth Encounters* ministry. Before we began the ministry session, and following a prompt, I prayed for her and she received the baptism in the Holy Spirit as evidenced by her speaking in other tongues. As we proceeded to go through her memories, we identified the beliefs in her heart, as we normally would, and God communicated things to her that were consistent with what would normally happen.

This is the only time that I have ever seen this, but at the end of the session she reported that all of her problems were the same and that her new Holy Spirit tongue seemed ridiculous to her. Again, I felt prompted to ask if I could pray for her against a spirit before she left and she responded that this would be alright with her. I took authority over *a spirit of doubt and unbelief* and commanded it to leave and come off her mind and emotions. Nothing obvious happened.

A couple of days later she was booked to come in for another session before she made the long journey home. I was not particularly looking forward to this time together because all that we usually saw God free people through, did not seem to have had much effect on her. When she arrived, she alighted from her vehicle beaming and reported that she was all healed and loved her new prayer language. The spirit of doubt and unbelief had been blocking her from receiving any of the things that had happened in her prayer session. Once the spirit was gone, she had a download and was completely set free. Following is an excerpt from the testimony that she emailed to me a week later;

"Steve and Em, wow you would not believe the changes in me!! But then of course you do believe!! Praise the Lord…here we go…just overflowing with the Holy Spirit like the incredible hulk, just wants to burst out, the heaviness, anxiety, confusion, sadness, back pain, sleeplessness…all gone, zapped, now light, joyous, calm, strengthened."

And so it went on, including no longer needing her medication for a physical problem. The point is that, if we were not aware of the possibility of a spirit or spirits being involved, it is unlikely that she would have received her healing.

Story
On another occasion I was ministering to a young lady who had suffered considerable sexual abuse. God was faithfully setting her free from the beliefs that she held from the painful memories. As the Lord resolved one particular memory, she reported joy and peace in regards to her new freedom. She asked me a question not relating to emotion from the event. In this instance she had been sodomized and her question was in regards to whether or not I thought this could have been implicated in a problem with moving her bowels. I shot up a quick thank you prayer as I had missed it, and could have left her with this problem for life.

I related to her that there may well be a spirit of infirmity that attached to her as a result of the ungodly act towards her. At this point some of you may be thinking why should she get a spirit when she did not do anything wrong? This is a reasonable question so let me briefly digress.

If you went to your neighbors' house and they hit you over the head with a piece of wood, who sinned? They did. Who has the lump on the forehead? You do. Sin creates an opening just as when parents deeply or repetitively reject their children, and the child receives a corresponding spirit. It would be rare for a person to ask for or want a demon; something has happened to them, usually that they did not ask for.

In the case of this young lady, she was a victim of an ungodly sexual bond and along with the emotional trauma this created an entry point for the spirit. I will explain this more fully under the heading *integrity*. I simply addressed the spirit of infirmity that had come in through the lustful activity and told it to go. She looked a little bit uncomfortable for a moment and then told me that it had gone. A few days later I received a phone call from her and she reported that her system was now working perfectly. Again, if we were not aware of the possibilities of a spirit operating, she could have gone on through life with the problem.

In Unit 3, speaking of gifts I mentioned a lady who came to me after a meeting where I had spoken and ministered in their church. She asked for some wisdom for a lady that she was looking after who was bitter and angry against God because her husband had died. I suggested that she tell the lady that; *God does not always get what He wants.* He does not want wars, children abused or people saying nasty things to each other. He has in some sense limited Himself in evidently giving all of His creation free will and choice. He is not pleased, and eventually will judge using the Word of God to measure. Even for believers He in some measure has limited His activities to faith which is based on how we see His character.

LESSON
Whilst concentrating on bringing truth to see people set free, it is good to be knowledgeable and attentive to other things that may be going on.

Study 4: Names of demons and touching the spirit realm

Some people feel that they need to know the names of all the demons and get them right before they will leave. You can simply say something such as; *you spirit that is attached to this or that, leave in the name of Jesus.* There are books around with pages of lists of the names of demons. At one time I remember reading a book with one of these lists and thinking how will I remember the names of all these evil spirits? A scripture that I had read came to remembrance in my mind about the *lying spirits* in 1 Kings 22:22. In this passage the prophets were looking to say what the Kings wanted to hear in order to receive their acceptance and favor. The usual reason that people tell lies is a fear of rejection and it is the most common reason that I have found that causes people to lie.

I have dealt with a number of people where this has become a demonic problem and they simply cannot tell the truth even when they want to. The basis of freedom in these people in the first instance came with resolving the rejection beliefs, but I digress.

In the case of the prophets wanting to please the Kings and say what they wanted to hear, this opened them to having a spirit attached to them.

> *1 Kings 22:21-23* ²¹ *"Then a spirit came forward and stood before the LORD, and said, 'I will persuade him.'* ²² *"The LORD said to him, 'In what way?' So he said, 'I will go out and be a lying spirit in the mouth of all his prophets.' And the LORD said, 'You shall persuade him, and also prevail. Go out and do so.'* ²³ *"Therefore look! The LORD has put a lying spirit in the mouth of all these prophets of yours, and the LORD has declared disaster against you."* NKJV

What I learnt from studying and meditating on the passage is that the spirit was not a *lying spirit*, it was just a generic nondescript spirit. It was only able to attach itself to that which was yielded to sin, in this case lying. It could not go and be a spirit of lust or bitterness because that was not the area of the personality or body that was being made available to sin. So, the name of a spirit is simply the area of the person that they hold. If it's bitterness, its bitterness, lust, lust, lying, lying and so on. It exists there because it has access to the person in some way, often through their unwitting yielded ness in following sinful behavior, attitudes and responses.

Many in the church seem to have this idea that the devil already has spirits with special names, functions and job descriptions in stock, that he can send at will to attack people. You can almost imagine how some might think this would look in the spirit world; *We are running low on spirits of bitterness in New York, could you send 5,000 more please? And we need another 10,000 spirits of lust to drive the porn industry in London!* In all probability a spirit that may have previously functioned as bitterness because of the participation of its last host, could well have a role of insanity or mental illness in the next person that they are able to inhabit.

When they run through generation lines, they seem to be able to promote the same *beliefs* and ground to operate on that was in previous generations. As a result, you may see for example issues such as ungodly control, lust, unforgiveness or rejection run through families, with corresponding physical maladies, until someone receives freedom from Christ Jesus.

TOUCHING THE SPIRIT REALM

When I was a young man, we used to go camping in canvas tents. This material was excellent at keeping out the rain and weather. The only problem that it had was that to some extent the material seemed to soak up the water to the point of saturation as a part of its ability to have the rain runoff. So, if you touched the material anywhere when it was raining that was now a place where it leaked. The spirit realm is very much like this. We are always surrounded by spiritual elements and wherever we touch it, that is where we have given it access to leak into our environment.

Let me suggest some areas where we may create openings, and if there is demonization that goes with it then the following list of examples could all be the names of demons. We could address them as; *you spirit that has been involved in holding Fred into 'rebellious' behavior.* (This assumes that we have dealt with the injustice beliefs already or concurrently.) These are some sample areas of the human person that spirits may influence or affect:

- Emotional breaches;   fear, bitterness, rejection, inferiority Etc.
- Mental problems;   doubt, unbelief, fantasy, withdrawal, insanity. Etc.
- Moral issues;   pornography, fornication, adultery, lying, theft. Etc.
- Relational disharmony;   mockery, criticism, judgment, religion, rejection Etc.
- Spiritual alliances;   the occult, false religion, witchcraft. Etc.
- Physical bondage;   addictions, lusts, altered states, violence, infirmity.

These are all potential areas of exposure to the spirit realm if we touch it or there is an opening through which it can enter. You will note that virtually all of these are tied to thoughts coming from *beliefs*, which precipitate and present in decisions. This should re center us on the need for truth at every level of our being so that we can make good protective choices.

 LESSON
To know what kind of demon or evil spirit we are dealing with we simply look at its function and the area of stronghold in the person.

Study 5: Breaches

INTEGRITY

Most probably when you hear the word *integrity* you think of a business man or similar who conducts their dealings in an upright and trustworthy manner. The word integrity actually means; *the state of being entire, or whole.* As an example, if you could imagine your skin as a God given barrier to protect you from the elements as well as various bacteria and diseases. While my skin holds its unbroken integrity and remains whole you could pour, for example, hepatic B virus over my arm and I would not be harmed. But if you created a small cut or opening in the wholeness of my skin then I would become infected and get sick.

We have already mentioned that the word for being *saved* is *sozo* and that a part of the meaning of that word includes to *deliver* or *protect* and coming to *wholeness*. The more whole we are in regards to truth about God, ourselves, how to deal with others, and the spiritual world that we have, the more delivered we are. This is our best protection against possible infection from the spiritual realm and this is why children are the most vulnerable, because they have the least amount of truth and understanding. They need our spiritual protection and instruction to bring them up in the counsel of the Lord.

The most whole person who ever walked the Earth was Jesus. He stated that because the devil had no *wrong beliefs in Him* in regarding Himself, (*identity*) how Father God saw Him, or why people were used as instruments of the devil to try to get to Him. Because of the level of truth that He had inside He was without sin; the result was that the devil couldn't touch Him. Wholeness is our best protection.

> John 14:30 *"I will no longer talk much with you, for the ruler of this world is coming, and **he has nothing in Me**." NKJV (emphasis mine)*

When we have a break or breach in our spiritual or emotional integrity, it is a potential entry point for a spirit. This could be a time of fear or trauma. It could be a time of abuse where our understanding of the situation is overwhelmed and we are out of control. It could also be at a time where we are on drugs or drunk, and our normal resistance and mental integrity is weakened, and now we do something sinful that we would not normally do.

In a ministry setting we are aware of possible breaches in our wholeness of some kind that may have given place to a spirit. We are looking to repair the breach in the walls of the human personality so that the people again have normal resistance to spiritual inroads.

> Isaiah 58:10-12 *¹⁰ If you extend your soul to the hungry And satisfy the afflicted soul, Then your light shall dawn in the darkness, And your darkness shall be as the noonday. ¹¹ The LORD will guide you continually, And satisfy your soul in drought, And strengthen your bones; You shall be like a watered garden, And like a spring of water, whose waters do not fail. ¹² Those from among you Shall build the old waste places; You shall raise up the foundations of many generations; **And you shall be called the Repairer of the Breach**, The Restorer of Streets to Dwell In. NKJV (emphasis mine)*

Walls were intended to keep the bad things out and protect the good things inside. Physically, a healthy body will include a good immune system that can deal with all of the attacks that may come. In much the same way a healthy soul carries its own protection. Some spiritual and emotional building materials that are used to strengthen the walls of the human personality and keep the temple in good condition are such items as; love, acceptance, grace, truth, value, significance, encouragement, worth, freedom, respect, honor, forgiveness, kindness, protection and so on.

We children of God have been given the privilege of working with the Holy Spirit to help repair people's lives, and for Him to receive the glory for that which He does in them. This is well illustrated in the following beautiful typology from Isaiah.

> *Isaiah 61:3-4* *³ To console those who mourn in Zion, To give them beauty for ashes, The oil of joy for mourning, The garment of praise for the spirit of heaviness; That **they** may be called trees of righteousness, The planting of the LORD, **that He may be glorified.**" ⁴ And **they** shall rebuild the old ruins, **They** shall raise up the former desolations, And **they** shall repair the ruined cities, The desolations of many generations.*
> *NKJV (emphasis mine)*

INTEGRITY TO INTEGRATION

Many people are unaware of, or unable to discern the spiritual dynamics that may be at work inside of them. Often times they leave getting help until it is too late and they have a trail of hurt children and broken relationships or a physical problem.

A long time ago I developed a low-grade tooth ache in a slowly rotting tooth. As with most people I didn't particularly like the dentist's chair and so I put up with it for several years. Eventually it did get worse and I did go to get it taken out. I recall the very irate dentist sweating profusely as he wrestled for a very long time with his pliers on this rotten tooth. He became increasingly frustrated as pieces broke off as he struggled to remove the offending article. As he wiggled the last piece loose, interspersed with grunts I recall him saying between pushing it back and forth; *Don't EVER, EVER leave it this long again*!

Very often we minister to people who have a trail of relational or other damage behind them. You can't help but think that if they had done something much sooner their lives and the lives of those around them would have been much more abundant. Sadly, the modern church is often either not equipped to offer help to them, or prioritizes other activities. Jesus spent His time healing people and setting them free, and everything else proceeded from that.

LESSON
Our best defense against spiritual inroads is wholeness. If we don't get our issues dealt with others around us will suffer as a consequence.

WORKING IN THE DARKNESS

In Australia we have termites or white ants as we know them. We used to live in an area where they were highly active. They are not unlike the demonic realm in the sense that they work in the dark and hate being exposed to the light because they will die. We once owned an old house that had an infestation. Very often the first sign that they were there was a hole in your skirting or architrave where, when you pushed on it, your finger would go right through. By that stage the damage was done and your framing was usually extensively damaged. The only way to avoid this was through regular examinations from an expert who was equipped to detect them and knew the signs to look for.

I do not say lightly that today there is evidence everywhere that the body of Christ is quite badly infested. We need to train up an army of helpers to get her into an irresistible condition to attract a hurting world. God can of course resolve all issues if He is given the opportunity to do so.

Once a spirit has breached the integrity of a person through some means and come inside, it will entwine itself with your personality in that area. From experience I would say that a demon is limited to work in you in the area or place that has given it ground. By this I mean that a spirit that causes you to be violent has no ability to lead you into false religion or lustful behavior. Its function and area of influence is limited to that which has given it access and place. If the member of your personality that is given to the devil is, for example, your sexuality through choosing to view pornography, then it follows that lust will be the stronghold outcome rather than say bitterness.

> *Romans 6:12-13* ¹² *Therefore do not let sin reign in your mortal body, that you should obey it in its lusts.* ¹³ *And do not present your members as instruments of unrighteousness to sin, but present yourselves to God as being alive from the dead, and your members as instruments of righteousness to God. NKJV*

Although many times a spirit will come to us as a result of the sins of others which have created breaches in us, in the preceding verse we see that at times the demon has come as a result of opening a door through our willful cooperation. This happens even though we may be unaware of the spiritual implications at the time. If we continue using the common problem of pornography as an example, a person may or may not receive a spirit of lust from a one-time viewing. However, if people have continued and repeated exposure, submitting to the spirit power behind the offense, you can be reasonably sure that they are giving a strong place in their sexuality where a spiritual stronghold will be established and make a *home*.

People who have become bound by this have reported the *replay of images* and an *amplification* of their sexual urges and chemical responses as a result of the thoughts. So, is this a spirit of lust that has brought its nature in, or is it just a generic spirit which now holds a specific area of your being, namely your sexuality? Again, the scriptures point to the likelihood that it is not the nature of a spirit that has a hold on you; it is rather an area of your own person that has been yielded to the spirit and distorted.

> *James 1:14-15* ¹⁴ *But each one is tempted when he is drawn away* **by his own desires and enticed**. ¹⁵ *Then, when desire has conceived, it gives birth to sin; and sin, when it is full-grown, brings forth death. NKJV (emphasis mine)*

I am not suggesting for a moment that every time you sin that you are going to receive an evil spirit. I am proposing that all sin is not from God, so anytime that we sin we are serving Satan and, at times, if this is repetitive or an emotional breach, this could open us up to demonization. *(An emotional breach could include an adrenaline rush from high danger activities, horror movies or excitement from something that we view that is beyond levels that God intended).* For the most part the *ground* for demons entering is prepared and made available in the earlier years of life from conception to adolescence.

 **LESSON**
We can open a door to a spirit by engaging in activities that are beyond Gods created order.

ENTWINED

Let's continue examining sexuality as an easily understood area of our person that can be open to demonic activity through some form of immorality. Once engaged in lustful behavior the spirit inside has entwined itself with your sexuality and you have, to some measure, become one with it in your thoughts in regards to sexual matters. As a result, the sexual ideas, desires or tendencies you have are now all influenced by the demon inside of you.

We could say that it has come in through some kind of breach in the integrity of your person and has now moved to being integrated with your sexuality. If you are unaware of this influence then you now think that it is only *your thoughts and ideas* that move you towards ungodly sexual activities. So, you do not hesitate to go ahead with this behavior because you simply think that it is what you alone want. You think it is just your thoughts that you are having.

The same could be said for retaliatory or revengeful thoughts that you may be having if you hold unforgiveness. You simply think that it is what you want, and what will please you, and so you don't hesitate to act out further in sin. This could apply to any area of distorted behavior or attitudes that we are in bondage to, and that are *replayed* or *amplified* as an expression. We need to discern it by identifying that which is out of order with Gods plans for our attitudes and actions. This is done by measuring these thoughts and deeds by the Word of God and the counsel of the Spirit of God.

> John 6:63 *"It is the Spirit who gives life; the flesh profits nothing. The words that I speak to you are spirit, and they are life. NKJV*

It is often difficult to receive deliverance and separation from an integrated spirit until the person understands, to some degree, the concept that a part of their thoughts are not actually them. After all, why would you want a part of yourself cast out?

Let us propose a case of say somebody addicted to smoking or excessive food intake as possibly a form of comfort for inner pain from *identity beliefs*. Now they feel prompted to have a cigarette or go to the refrigerator. If they think that it is simply their own thinking then they won't hesitate to go ahead and act out. But if they realize that it could be a demon within them compelling them to continue in the behavior that will result in them being robbed of health or bring on premature death, they may be ready for separation. The devil is a liar, a thief and a murderer; he will always be working against you reaching your potential for abundant life.

In regards to the examples that I have used, I would say that, *in my opinion*, only a percentage of smokers have a spirit attached to their addiction. Most of the smokers that I know of, wish that they could give up. This is strong indicator that their will and thinking is not completely compromised or influenced excessively. I have at times heard people say of cigarettes; *I just love them!* Most people would say that they enjoy some of their smokes but a lot of them are just out of habit. On more than one occasion when I have heard the, *I just love them* statement, I have commented to the host that actually maybe they do not love them, and that it is probably a spirit that they are entwined with that loves them, and that this in part is what is speaking out of them.

I have on a couple of occasions offered to cast them out. Each of the times when I have said this, the spirit has risen in their throats. In every instance the men have said *not now* being shocked at the revelation that their habit was perhaps spirit driven. Evidently, they needed time to decide whether or not they actually wanted to stop and work out what was what, and decide whether the spirit was a friend or an enemy! Later I know that one of them did give up, others I have not seen again.

In the case of food addictions as a means of comfort, clearly not every time will it be an evil spirit. If it is extreme and out of control then it is a possibility that this is a part of the problem, most likely along with rejection and other emotional issues. Once we have integrated with a spirit, we can use terms such as participating with, following, or cooperating with the ungodly internal entity. We have to begin by changing our thinking about it in repentance and then fall out of agreement with our working with it as a basis for being set free.

 LESSON
Separation begins with seeing and understanding the true source and nature of the problem, and choosing willfully to be disconnected from it.

PHYSICAL OR MENTAL PROBLEMS

Once a demon has integrated and amplified, for example emotional issues, you can expect some kind of outworking in the physical body and or mental health areas. For instance, there are various reasons that people hear voices, but very often it is echoes from things learnt in painful memories that are demonically replayed. Remember, dealing with the connected *inner beliefs* is the basis of the freedom and not merely shooing away the flies.

A lady was set free from a spirit of rejection. The rejection had been the foundation for bitterness and resentment in her life which in turn affected her physiology. By the age of thirty years old if she was sitting down for more than a couple of minutes when she stood up, she would hobble around until she could get her arthritic ankles moving. Her father was the same and his mother before him. Perhaps a month after her deliverance someone noticed that she no longer *hobbled* when she stood up and it was realized that she was healed. The point is that nobody prayed for her to be healed from the arthritis. It was a cause and effect healing and a byproduct of being set free from rejection. Almost 30 years later she is still healed and has never *hobbled* again, whilst others in her family who never received ministry have chronic arthritic and associated resentment issues.

As we have dealt with emotionally rooted issues, whether demonic or not, we have seen many physical ailments such as asthma, hormonal problems, inflammatory issues, allergies and so on simply disappear. All without any direct prayer. We can include various *mental illnesses* with all kinds of interesting names that detail the fruit associated with the malady. The point here is that we need to be aware of the possibility of a spiritual component relating to a person's problems and be aware that evil spirits don't respond to counseling, you can't get them saved or disciple them, and you can't inner heal them! The ground needs to be dealt with and they need to be evicted. I recall ministering to a 70-year-old lady who was set free from an unclean spirit. She was sad as she made the comment after receiving her freedom that it had ruined her and her husband having fullness in their married life.

LESSON
Demons often magnify emotional and consequent hormonal balances that lead to, or hasten disease or weakness in the body.

INFIRMITY

Luke 13:11 "And behold, there was a woman who had a spirit of infirmity eighteen years, and was bent over and could in no way raise herself up." NKJV

Apparently, prior to eighteen years earlier, the woman did not have a spirit of infirmity and she was healthy and well. Something happened! Strong's concordance informs us that the Greek word asthenia from which we have the word infirmity contains the following meanings: *Feebleness (of body or mind); malady; frailty: disease, infirmity, sickness, weakness.*

We can conclude that whenever we are praying for a disease, sickness or malady that has taken hold as the result of a weakness in the body, there is a strong possibility that a *spirit of infirmity* is holding the body into that condition. It has most likely taken hold when the physical integrity or wholeness of the person was weakened and breached through trauma, or longer-term hormonal imbalances caused by emotional 'dis' ease from faulty *heart beliefs*, or some other kind of breakdown of the body's normal defenses such as immune problems.

People are healed after a simple prayer commanding the spirit to go. Many times, the emotional components of the disease need to be ministered to, and also beliefs emanating from trauma dealt with to take away the ground that the spirit holds. If we don't do this then, although the spirit is gone and healing may result, we have left the door open, so to speak, and they may end up with the same or another sickness. If people prayed against the spirit of infirmity more, and the recipients of the prayer understood what this meant, we would see many more people being healed.

Not surprisingly this can extend to physical injuries where a weakness has occurred through events such as accidents. We could say; *you spirit that has come in through weakness leave* and expect the same results.

I recall that Smith Wigglesworth used to command spirits to come out of the damaged knees of miners and this would result in healing. May I suggest that this is probably because their knees were weakened over time through their work, and the weakness was created by their form of employment? I have prayed with individuals commanding a *spirit of infirmity* to leave without seeing anything obvious happen, and later heard that the person involved discovered that they no longer had their illness.

In summary, we could say that arthritis is a kind of infirmity or weakness created by beliefs producing emotional and consequent hormonal balances. The same could be said of cancer, migraines and many other illnesses. We could say that cancer is one kind of infirmity or weakness, migraines another, arthritis another and so on.

INSANITY

The majority of this publication is directed towards how to become increasingly sound of mind and whole of body. To be insane simply means to be unsound in mind.

*Hosea 9:7 "The days of punishment have come; The days of recompense have come. Israel knows! The prophet is a fool, The spiritual man is **insane**, Because of the greatness of your iniquity and great enmity." NKJV (emphasis mine)*

We see various mental illnesses which have a spirit of insanity involved. People such as drug addicts' risk being open to this problem through opening the door by voluntarily going into altered states that make their mind not sane, not sound or whole, and seeking unreality as a means of pleasure, escape from life or pain.

Let me tentatively propose that the modern church, in seeking the *power of God* for the wrong reasons, may unwittingly at times open themselves up to insanity. Where leaders have low self-image issues, they may seek to be the *most spiritual* church and have *more blessing and power from God* than other churches. This competitive spirit may open them to readily embracing any manifestations as being from God, and consequently create an opening for other spirits. These extra biblical manifestations are not outlined in the Word of God as something that will be a function of the Holy Spirit, as are for example gifts.

I fear that this may be another expression of a religious spirit. We call the *religious spirit* the *try hard spirit*. When the pendulum swings too far one way this will be legalism where you try hard to be better than everyone else by getting everything right and keeping the letter of the law. At the other end of the scale when the pendulum swings back past centre the people involved will be trying hard to be the more spiritual and in their own eyes superior to others. Trying hard to be good enough for God or others is usually a sign of an inner belief that you are not enough and this inferiority opens us to pride. I thoroughly believe in the power of God and enjoy seeing people, touched, healed and delivered.

A number of years ago some churches that I know of embraced some such manifestations where people would be gripped by strange movements and actions. Some friends that I knew reported that they did this every week, but that they also saw some of the people who were manifesting at these meetings drunk and smoking at the hotel the following evening. Apparently being touched by the *power of God* was not affecting any change in these individuals. My personal experiences of seeing the power of God is mostly in the Holy Spirit bringing healing or deliverance as it was demonstrated with Jesus. I understand that making these comments will make me unpopular with some people but let me explain a little more fully why I offer these observations.

Around 27 years ago we took in a 9-year-old insane boy who was virtually totally demonized. Particularly in the first few years as we worked through the different dimensions of his problems we witnessed all kinds of crazy laughing and strange manifestations. To say the least, we became very familiar with full blown insanity. One night I attended one of these meetings and witnessed virtually the same behavior through these well-meaning Christian people. At one point as many of them were on the floor under the influence of this spirit suddenly the crowd parted and I had a few second snapshot of a well-known man doing exactly the same crazy laughing as our foster son had been doing. It is indelibly imprinted on my mind to this day. I am not referring to the laughter movement that went through many churches on which I have no comment.

My intention is not to hurt anyone or diminish them as good people, children of God or excellent ministers of the gospel. I am simply trying to alert areas of the body of Christ that may not be aware of this, and that not every spirit is the Holy Spirit. I cannot see any way that making people behave in this way would bring glory to God. If I was an unbeliever and walked into such a meeting, I would probably conclude that if I became a Christian that there would be a reasonable chance that I might end up with epilepsy or similar.

LESSON
We have to careful about what we yield or submit to.

POSSIBLE ENTRY POINTS

We have already covered some of these major topics in detail.

- Trauma or loss of mental or emotional integrity
- Sin responses, or reactions coming from emotional pain or abuse such as, unforgiveness, bitterness, hatred, or rebellion etc.
- Sin *solutions* stemming from efforts to resolve emotional pain; Lusts, excessive use of substances such as food, alcohol, drugs, or escape into media and unreality, immoral relationships, addictions etc.
- Involvement in the Occult, witchcraft, or false religions as being the worship of other gods.

GENERATIONALLY INHERITED SPIRITS

In a sense all sin is generational, because for mankind it began with Adam and Eve, and has traveled through the generations up to this point in history. Often the drawing to the family weaknesses opens us to also committing the same sins and giving place to the devil through our own submission and compliance.

We were working with a Chinese lady one day and she was having emotional healing and deliverance from various spirits. In the course of the Holy Spirit setting her free her body began to contort into various unnatural shapes. Once she was free from these generational demons my wife asked her if this was some kind of dragon spirit because of the particular way her body had conformed as they exited, and she confirmed that it was so.

I was watching a current affairs program on television a number of years ago and they stated that chemical and genetic habits passed through the sperm and ovaries from mum and dad to the child. The report went on to say that they have not worked out how yet, only that it must be so because of the evidence in behavior. It would certainly be a difficult thing to understand if you remove the spiritual element. In other cases, there have been twins separated at birth that have grown up distantly and exclusively of each other who have both independently exhibited the traits of their parents.

'SOUL TIES'

Another area that we have not touched on and has become popular in church jargon, is an opening for demonic entry that has been dubbed a *soul tie.* Although difficult to find under that terminology in most modern translations, the principle refers to some kind of connection of the soul whereby some ungodly element passes from one person to another.

So, if we replaced the term *soul tie* with the word *relationship* then you discover that the whole Bible from cover to cover is talking about the interaction of the souls of humanity, and the consequent impact that it has upon us.

A godly *soul tie* or *relationship* then would be something such as parents ministering love and acceptance to their children, or believers building each other up and encouraging one another. But clearly there are many negative things that can be imparted to us from the souls of others in relationships.

> *1 Corinthians 15:33 "Do not be misled: Bad company corrupts good character." NIV*

So perhaps at the least end of the *soul tie* scale we could suggest something such as a boy in year 4 at school looking to a lad in year 6 who he thinks is *very cool*. The older boy swears and uses bad language so as a result of the younger boys' agreement and coming in line with wanting to be like the very cool year 6 lad, he also begins to swear. So, something ungodly, sin, has just passed through their relationship. In this case, when the younger boy gets a little older, he decides that actually it is not cool to swear and decides to stop. This change of thinking or repentance as we know it, then breaks the tie.

At times, if the connection is stronger then, the relational joining can be an opportunity for a spirit to pass. This could be through an illicit sexual relationship, where a spirit relating to the one flesh joining sits over the connection, holding them together. People report suffering from depression or having suicidal thoughts or lust problems that they have never known before, but that their partners in the ungodly act suffer from.

> *1 Corinthians 6:16 And don't you know that if a man joins himself to a prostitute, he becomes one body with her? For the Scriptures say, "The two are united into one." NLT*

We were once ministering to a man who confessed an illicit adulterous relationship from, as I recall, around 12 years earlier. As he was sharing what had happened his mobile phone suddenly went off and it was this lady, whom he had never had contact with in all of that time. Evidently his thinking and talking about her had enlivened an existing connection in the spirit. Jesus often healed or delivered people without needing to be present because distance is not relevant in the spiritual realm.

Another man once came to me reporting that he still had dreams about a girlfriend that he had been with before he was married many decades earlier. He was a good Christian man with a lovely wife whom he loved, and together they had a large family. It troubled him and he wanted to be free. As we discussed what had happened, he revealed that this girlfriend was immediately before his conversion. When he came to the Lord, he asked her if she would ever be interested in God, and the response was no. With his new-found faith he thought it through and decided that she was not for him and broke the relationship. So, the mind and will part of his soul had disconnected but his emotions had not because he had loved the girl. The Lord set him free with the realization of what had happened, and though dealing with the emotional component.

If someone is struggling with some kind of *relational* or *soul tie* to another then their part in their freedom is to voluntarily disconnect from any memories of the other person. For example, I have ministered to a number of men who have had previous sexual partners who, now married, feel as though when they are having marital relations with their wives that there are 3 of them in the bed. These men are usually still allowing themselves to think about this past partner from time to time which keeps the tie alive. Our advice with any kind of soul tie is for them to remember them no more. This means pleasures, adventures together or whatever memories might bind them, and get rid of any articles that might promote these thoughts and remind them of the past.

The critical element of breaking the tie is not the spirituality of the minister or the power of God, it is the will of the person to disconnect. If they are genuinely prepared to do that, then if you feel that there is a spiritual power involved then you can address the spirit that binds them together, or anything that is known of that has come to them through the other person. Again, *breaking soul ties or generational links* is not the first place that I would go as a method, but rather is something that you deal with as it comes up in the course of resolving areas where they require the Lord's healing and freedom.

LESSON
A common way that a spirit may find an entry point is through relationships and joining with others in sin, or a connection through an ungodly event with another person being acted out on us.

OBJECTS AS 'LINKS'

A number of years ago in the course of ministry it was revealed by a lady of around 45 years old that we were working with, that she talked to her teddy bear. As she explained about her relationship to the toy it became apparent that her connection with it was more than a natural emotional fondness. The discussion about the bear had come up as we were finding it difficult to break her free from a spirit connection of witchcraft to her adoptive mother, who gave her the teddy and practiced the craft. The next time she came in she brought the toy with her and really struggled with the thought of relinquishing it. Eventually she gave it to me and when she did the spirit came out of her. Now instead of being possessive of the bear she became indignant and went into our lounge room and threw it in the fire. I am not in the habit of removing people's childhood toys from them, but in this case, it was a tie to the witchcraft coming through the mother.

TRANSFERENCE

Some people fear that a demon can simply pass to you for no reason, and this is very much not the case. As we have already described there has to be an opening in the wholeness of the person. This could be through someone willfully opening the door, through to something such as an ungodly tie or cooperation and alliance in sin with another person. It could also come as transference through the generation line or through an opening such as submitting to significant fear. This fear could come through the violent or abusive behavior of another acted out on you, or fear generated through some kind of occult ritual or witchcraft type behavior.

The idea that you could be near another human and without some kind of breach in the integrity of your person, that a spirit could just pass to you is not the case. I have previously mentioned taking in a demoniac boy who was initially completely run by evil spirits. Our children and other foster children, sat with him, slept in the car, or at times the same room as him. They sat at the same table with him to eat, and particularly in the early days there were usually fully manifested spirits operating. Nobody ever received anything from him although he had a great many quite powerful spirits still within him.

> Proverbs 26:2 *"Like a flitting sparrow, like a flying swallow, So a curse without cause shall not alight."* NKJV

LESSON
A spirit cannot simply come into you without some kind of door, opening or exposure to something that creates an entry point.

MANIFESTATIONS

Some people get hung up on the type of things that they expect to see when a person is delivered of an evil spirit. They may feel that there should be loud shrieks or the person slithering across the floor. There is a wide variety of manifestations that may happen ranging from those types of lively encounters to seeing nothing at all, with the person simply reporting that something left, they feel free, lighter, peaceful or joyous. This is in part to do with the type of spirit that you are dealing with, and sometimes how much you have undermined its position before you have told it to go. If it is emotionally based, it will be much easier on the host if you do the healing work first. Sometimes upon commanding them to leave you may see an unexpected eruption of emotion which can be quite deep if the pain has been traumatic. A spirit may rise in their throat and come out with coughing or some other kind of appearance such as involuntary deepened breathing.

The more dramatic manifestations are often connected with involvement in activities such as witchcraft or the Occult.

We leave all of those things to the Holy Spirit as the finger of God. Our job is just to be obedient as God's mouthpiece and command them to go. Don't be surprised by what happens or doesn't happen, the main thing is that the person is free.

One night I was praying for a man in the kitchen at church and when I addressed the spirit that was troubling him, I did not see anything happen. I said to him, not to worry about not seeing anything, it must go and that I sensed that it had. He replied; *Oh no it went alright; it came in from my shoulders and went out through the top of my head!* This was an unusual manifestation, but don't be surprised by anything when you are dealing with the spiritual realm.

GETTING STARTED

Not long after I began studying books about demons we took in a little girl as a foster child. To begin with, if I approached her, we would see her face twist up and contort. This was unusual because I normally had a great rapport with little children. We concluded that most likely she had previously suffered some kind of abuse from a man. Eventually I won her over and she would not let me put her down. Some months went by and eventually her mother was moving to another district and so she needed to be placed in care in that area.

From what we had read, and now understood, it was apparent that her ongoing issues were demonic in nature. This put me in the very uncomfortable place of either stepping out with my little bit of faith, or leaving her with issues that may hamper her for the rest of her life. When we put her to bed one night, I took authority over the spirits that we perceived were there and commanded them to go in Jesus name. She responded with a massive prolonged yawn and then turned over and went to sleep.

At that time, we lived next door to my wife's sister, who at times my wife would go to visit. Normally when she did this our little foster girl would have facial contortions and manifest. The day after prayer my wife proceeded to go next door and the little girl had no response whatsoever and sat happily playing with her toys. It was a miracle. My wife had been praying that her next foster parents would be Christians as well, which turned out to be the case. They later reported that she was a perfect little girl not exhibiting any of the behavior that we had seen before the prayer event. So, although we have talked a lot about understanding the work and activities of demons here, at the end of the day you fix your attention and concentration on the Holy Spirit, and in the name of Jesus and tell them to leave.

LESSON
You will probably never experience a demon leaving a person that you are helping if you don't command it to go in Jesus name. There will not necessarily be a big manifestation with most 'garden variety' demons if you have done the healing work or there is genuine repentance if it is a sin issue. On rare occasions, if the subject is extremely violent for example, you may need help from someone more experienced.

THE NAME OF JESUS
It's good to remind ourselves that spirits don't respond to our name, and that God really doesn't need us to set people free. A number of years ago we had a particularly powerful time delivering a lady from demonic power which included a physical healing. I remember afterwards walking around the back of the church hall praying and feeling a bit like I was God's man for the hour. I did not like the feeling of pride and prayed to the Lord to get rid of it because I could not make it go away.

Later that evening we were conducting a training session and discussion time on deliverance. We put on an old Derek Prince VHS on the subject which was probably 10 years old at the time. We had seen it many times over the years but on this occasion when we got to the end part of the tape, where he commanded various spirits to come out, the lady sitting beside me manifested a demon, and it came out and she was free. It was quite humorous because the pride that I had felt in the afternoon was gone as well. It was as though the Holy Spirit was saying; *I don't really need you I can use anything!*

Study 6: Final thoughts on healing and freedom ministries

OUR PART IN THE SESSION
We have already stated that the key to helping people come into the provisions of God is all about positioning them to receive. In the case of deliverance, if nothing is happening with the person, or if there is but they are not getting free then most probably it isn't to do with your spirituality, and certainly not with the authority of Christ.

Remember, we are ministering based on our faith in the name of Jesus, the will of the Father, and not because of our own Holiness or godliness.

> *Acts 3:12 When Peter saw this, he said to them: "Men of Israel, why does this surprise you? Why do you stare at us **as if by our own power or godliness (Note: also godliness can be translated holiness)** we had made this man walk? NIV (emphasis mine)*

and

> *Acts 3:16 **By faith in the name of Jesus,** this man whom you see and know was made strong. It is Jesus' name and the faith that comes through him that has given this complete healing to him, as you can all see. NIV (emphasis mine)*

Let me suggest some areas that you might need to work through which could be blocking their ministry outcome:

1. Revelation

If they have not understood the nature of their problem and been able to accept the spiritual component, they may struggle to get free. Jesus taught them first.

Hosea 4:6, "My people are destroyed for lack of knowledge" NKJV

2. Confession

To confess means to say the same as. It is when we say the same as God does about our problem, rather than to deny it or try to justify it. Then we are in a good place to receive freedom. If, for example, we have a demonic element to bitterness, but in our minds feel that we have every right to hold our unforgiveness and bitterness then we may struggle to receive our freedom. We are not falling out of agreement with the spirit and into agreement with the word of God or taking responsibility in our part of the activity.

3. Repentance

If we are not prepared to *change our thinking* or *reconsider our ways* then we may block our freedom. In the case of inner thinking, we may need the beliefs dealt with, before we can cooperate for the deliverance. For example, if we have had a fear producing episode, that has given us fear beliefs, then unwittingly we may want the spirit to remain because we have the perception that it helps to protect us in some way.

4. Forgiveness

A common reason that people don't receive freedom is because they refuse to forgive others. Again, there may need to be healing of the hurts before the spirit loses its place, and consequently the will of the person becomes to no longer participate.

Matthew 6:14-15 [14] *"For if you forgive men their trespasses, your heavenly Father will also forgive you.* [15] *"But if you do not forgive men their trespasses, neither will your Father forgive your trespasses. NKJV*

5. The 'strongman's goods'

We have explained this already in detail and this is why most often deliverance is along with Truth Encounters where necessary, rather than the other way around. As we have said, many of these problems can exist without having demonic power on the inside that needs to be evicted.

6. A mouthpiece

Once we have covered these positioning issues, all that remains is commanding the spirits to leave in the name of Jesus. You are simply God's mouthpiece; it is the Holy Spirit's work to manifest the promise of deliverance. I have seen many spirits come out of people, and I am well aware that it is the goodness of God, faith in Jesus name, and the work of the Spirit that has accomplished this, and not because I am anyone special.

SPONTANEOUS DELIVERANCE

I have experienced in different settings across the world, times when praying for people in a meeting that they manifest a spirit and it convulses them as it comes out, as they did in Jesus' time on the Earth.

Mark 9:26 Then the spirit cried out, convulsed him greatly, and came out of him. And he became as one dead, so that many said, "He is dead." NKJV

I very often have no idea what the spirit is. It is the presence of the Holy Spirit on the person that causes the reaction as He comes in through us. Usually it is to do with the individual that I am praying for. If the Holy Spirit is operating in power, I have experienced times such as once when I was praying for a lady standing in the front row, four or five ladies standing in the rows behind went into deliverance. In these instances, it is simply what the Holy Spirit is doing, and for me it feels the same as when someone is healed or touched in some way as a result of the anointing. Making ourselves available simply makes us a door or gate that the Spirit can work through and do whatever He wants.

At times people receive some kind of deliverance along with baptism in water or in the Spirit. This does not necessarily mean that they are free of everything. Equally many times people have been set free of a spirit in a prayer line and we have seen nothing obvious, or they have felt nothing, but the resulting evidence is that they are free in that area.

I recall as a young believer having found out that my great grandfather had been high up in freemasonry. I prayed a simple prayer to disconnect with anything to do with it and suddenly something left me. It was as if someone put a vacuum cleaner over me and something rushed out of the top of me. I was left thinking, *that didn't just happen* but knowing that it did. What, if anything, it was actively doing in me at the time I could not say, but clearly it had found a home down the family line!

FALLEN NATURE OR DEMONS?

So, is your sin problem or bad habit demon powered or just your fallen nature and lack of self-discipline? When I was a young believer wrestling with this question, I had a little vision. It was a sieve and in it were three little stones. What I understood from the picture was that our fallen nature goes through the sieve of the Word of God which, if attended to and cooperated with, should filter our ungodly activities. At times though, there are a few issues that need to be ministered to and removed manually.

If you press in, pray, build yourself up in the Holy Spirit and discipline yourself to study the word and avoid unhealthy exposure to the world, and;

- You take ground and improve over time, even though you might be taking two steps forward and one step back, then your problem is most likely external pressure, unresolved beliefs, or fallen nature tendencies that have not been dealt with.

- Your problem gets worse than before, then in that instance it is probably an evil spirit within you that you are dealing with. We are mainly talking habits and sin here as opposed to hurts. A spirit, if it is still armed with some unresolved possessions such as deliberate sin or emotional pain then it will immediately seek rise up, exert pressure, and bluff you that it is too strong for you, in order to get you or the minister to give up.

This could come in a form such as struggling with negative or lustful thoughts, confusion, discouragement, self-rejection, or a manifestation in the prayer setting. It is a *stronghold*.

There is personal responsibility that the person receiving ministry must be prepared to take.

1. Man is responsible for his choices and responses. Once you realize that you are participating with another will that is operating inside of you, then you must conclude that there is no substitute for repentance.

2. It has been well said that deliverance will not give a person self-discipline, as it must be learned, practiced and exercised. It brings order to a person's life. The devil does most of his work through disorder. [5]

---

5 *Pastor Carroll Thompson 1977*

Proverbs 25:28 "Like a city whose walls are broken down is a man who lacks self-control." NIV

The best defense then, is restoring God's order to the life of the person. Remember that the demon can be cast out but the *place* or *topos* cannot be cast out. It must be brought under the authority of Christ or be healed. Unless the ground is dealt with, the deliverance may not be maintained which is why the main focus is on *Truth Encounters*. Notably the word disciple is used around 300 times in the New Testament, and Christian only 2 or 3 times. From God's perspective which should we be? There are all kinds of things called *Christian* in our world, but *disciples* are a little harder to find.

The strength of the enemy will depend on the amount of submission and cooperation that he has received. So, the human will and desire is a very important factor in coming to freedom. Several years ago, I ministered to a man who suffered from sexual, alcohol, and other addictions. A strong motivator for seeking Gods freedom was the fact that he was about to lose his family. In the course of his *Truth Encounters* ministry time he had a glimpse of his own possibilities in Christ, which further encouraged him to seek a full healing. He was freed from his issues and later, along with his wife, they entered into this ministry and began setting others free as well. We need to overcome passivity and desire our freedom so that we can possess the land.

FIGHTING WITH A DEMON

In the event that, as a minister, you find yourself fighting with a demon for some reason, let me suggest a couple of possibilities as to why;

1. The person has unforgiveness, unhealed belief areas, deception, lack of repentance, a failure to confess something relevant, or doubt and unbelief.

2. You may actually be wrestling with your own doubt and unbelief that the battle is over. Or, that you are worthy to have been given complete authority over all of the works of the enemy.

If you are fighting, it may be because you have been taught that the enemy is not defeated and has not been totally disarmed, or that Jesus has triumphed (Colossians 2:15). In that case you believe that you have to fight which is not true. The only power that the demon actually has, is willful or deceptive cooperation from the host.

Jesus never argued with demons because He knew that He was in the Father and that the Father was in Him. Now we are seated in Christ (Ephesians 2:6). Jesus never told us to fight with demons He instructed us to expel them and set the captives free.

> *John 14:10-14* [10] *"Do you not believe that I am in the Father, and the Father in Me? The words that I speak to you I do not speak on My own authority; but the Father who dwells in Me does the works.* [11] *"Believe Me that I am in the Father and the Father in Me, or else believe Me for the sake of the works themselves.* [12] *"Most assuredly, I say to you, he who believes in Me, the works that I do he will do also; and greater works than these he will do, because I go to My Father.* [13] *"And whatever you ask in My name, that I will do, that the Father may be glorified in the Son.* [14] *"If you ask anything in My name, I will do it. NKJV (emphasis mine)*

SATAN'S POSITION HAS CHANGED?

Some people have suggested that Satan's position changed at the cross. Did his position change? He is still called the god of this age, the ruler of the World, and the prince of the power of the air in the Epistles, after the cross. I would suggest that he is still causing wars, disharmony, sickness and deception just as he always did.

Did Gods position change at the cross? No. He was always in authority over Satan and all of creation so His position didn't change either. Whose position did change then? The believers' position changed. We went from being under the devil to being over all of his power. We do not however have authority over human will. So, if for some reason they are submitting to the devil through deception or choice, they may be allowing the demon to remain.

FINALLY

Let me say that, although I have discussed the topic of demons or evil spirits at length, in ministry they are not our focus and I rarely think about them. The purpose of this section is simple awareness of their workings so that they can be discerned if present. Let me encourage you again to not make the ministry about looking for them. In practice you are working on the person's *wholeness* and you may simply, with the permission and cooperation of the person, cast one out here and there as you go along where applicable.

DO I THROW AWAY MY BIBLE?

Will *Truth Encounters and deliverance* solve all my problems and make the World perfect? No. The world is a hostile environment. Jesus said that the Kingdom of God *will be within* you. So, your inner world needs to be built on the foundation of Jesus, the Word made flesh. This foundation of the living word, God's truth, on the inside, is that which is needed for you to be at peace in the World just as Jesus was. Let me reiterate;

> John 14:30 "I will no longer talk much with you, for the ruler of this world is coming, and he has nothing in Me." NKJV

From a quick study of the Greek language, as revealed in Strong's concordance, Jesus is saying in the preceding verse that there is no area of hold, no ability to affect Him, no wrong beliefs possessed by the evil one to manipulate Him. Further, there is no condition in Him such as not knowing who He is, what His purpose is, or how Father God sees Him, that gives the devil any influence over Him in this earthly environment. He stood *complete* and *whole*, and untouchable in truth. This is what we need to seek for ourselves as a part of the process of being conformed to the likeness of Christ.

LESSON

Jesus has made us perfect to the Father through redemption. This foundation in Christ qualifies us to minister. (Hebrews 10:14) [We may not be perfect to each other or even ourselves...our basis and qualification is that Jesus made us right with God so that we can do the works prepared for us.] So, as we step in with our mustard seed of faith looking to God and not our own abilities, we are often surprised at what happens.

> Ephesians 2:8-10 ⁸ God saved you by his special favor when you believed. And you can't take credit for this; it is a gift from God. ⁹ Salvation is not a reward for the good things we have done, so none of us can boast about it. ¹⁰ For we are God's masterpiece. He has created us anew in Christ Jesus, **so that we can do the good things he planned for us** long ago. NLT (emphasis mine)

UNIT SIX

Discernment

In this Unit we will be exploring some of the most common types of beliefs that we deal with. Jesus said that you can tell the type of tree that you are dealing with by the fruit that it produces. We are going to look at different kinds of *fruit* that would be associated with particular root systems. It is one thing to be a *fruit spotter* and observe that people have issues, and quite another to be a tree doctor who not only sees the fruit, but understands how to minister to the tree or root system producing it. In these next units we provide an overview of these problems.

Study 1: Rejection - Broken heartedness

As we begin to look at the subject of rejection in brief, let us first define it and put it into perspective. Rejection is *non-acceptance*. The definition of rejection includes the following:

- to refuse to acknowledge or accept
- to forsake
- to refuse to have or use
- to cast or throw away as useless, worthless, or unsatisfactory
- to refuse to love
- to discard as unwanted or not filling requirements.

Many people hold *heart beliefs* that they are not wanted, don't belong, or perhaps that they are not loved or loveable. Still others feel as though they are worthless, not cared about, will never be good enough, or don't measure up to what is wanted. They feel that they fall short of the expectations of others. These beliefs all drop into the category of rejection, or not being accepted.

In the Garden of Eden mankind submitted to Satan and rejected God as Lord. They rebelled against His commands in regards to the tree of the knowledge of good and evil. Whatever kinds of spirit that you participate with and submit to, you give authority to them over you in the area of your submission. Rejection was now a covering power that all future mankind was born under as a consequence of the fall.

I have previously pointed out that God never rejected humanity, rather we rejected Him. This was joining with Satan who had rejected God's Lordship in favor of *self-realization*. God is always redemptive and immediately He promised to repair the situation for His creation as we see in the following passage.

> *Genesis 3:15, "And I will put enmity between you and the woman, and between your offspring and hers; he will crush your head, and you will strike his heel." NIV*

In this verse, God was informing Satan, the instigator of the rejection of God by man, that he was going to have his head crushed by a male offspring of woman. This is, of course, is speaking of Jesus, who was going to suffer being struck on the heel. We need to point out here that the head represents authority, and correspondingly the feet step on, over or above their environment.

Jesus never lost authority. He only suffered in His heel as He crushed the head or authority of Satan as He walked through His mission. A part of this process was taking our rejection by being rejected Himself. He then dealt with the rebellious sin that put us under this power, in order for us to return to relationship with the Father.

> Isaiah 53:3-4 ³ "He was despised and **rejected** by men, a man of sorrows, and familiar with suffering. Like one from whom men hide their faces he was despised, and we esteemed him not. ⁴ Surely, he took up our infirmities and carried our sorrows, yet we considered him stricken by God, smitten by him, and afflicted." NIV (emphasis mine)

I have never yet met a human being who did not have some evidence of the fruits of rejection in their lives. We were all born under this element of the fall. In my opinion, rejection is the *tap root* to most of our problems, and I consequently hold it up as being an area of prime importance. Not being received and accepted by another produces separation in relationships and cuts us off from love and nurture. This is true in terms of how we relate to God, but also how we receive others and even ourselves. If we don't believe that we are acceptable then we will struggle to receive love.

Without the assurance of love, we are going to have anxiety problems as is well evidenced in modern society. Articles vary slightly but figures generally indicate around one in ten Australians being on medication for anxiety and as many as one in five reporting that they suffer from it. These are the statistics for those who admit to having the problem. Statistics in the U.S.A. appear to be very similar.

> 1 John 4:18 "There is no fear in love. But perfect love drives out fear, because fear has to do with punishment. The one who fears is not made perfect in love." NIV

When we have our *heart beliefs* resolved, and also understand fully at a conscious level as well, that through redemption Christ dealt with our punishment and separation from the Father completely, we can then receive His love.

 LESSON
Man rejects God. The Lord is by very nature accepting and embracing, wanting that none should perish, but rather that all would change their thinking about Him and His Kingdom. (2 Peter 3:9) We could say then that God loves the whole World, enough to send His son to pay for our sin, (John 3:16) but not everyone loves and accepts Him. As with Adam and Eve people are deceived about His true nature and character.

THE POTENTIAL DAMAGE OF NO ACCEPTANCE

Around twenty years ago I heard a story from an English Bible teacher named Ruth Hawkey [6]. The account that she related helped me to fully understand the potential damage to humans who do not receive nurture in the form of love and acceptance.

---

6 Ruth Hawkey is the author of several publications relating to healing and freedom

The setting was an overloaded institution in Eastern Europe who had in their care 97 children between 3 months and 3 years old. Now remember that mankind's most basic need is to have love and acceptance communicated to them; connection. Because of the lack of staff, there was no time available for physical or emotional nurture. Reportedly, at 3 months there were signs of abnormality with the children losing their appetites, exhibiting poor sleep patterns and their eyes were becoming vacant and looking into space. At 5 months some were exhibiting serious deterioration. They were whimpering and their faces would become twisted and distorted if anyone approached them and tried to pick them up. As the story goes 27 died the first year with no physical reason; they were considered to have shriveled up on the inside. 7 more died the second year and the survivors suffered with severe psychological disorders. There have been many such studies by people such as Rene A. Spitz that confirm the types of damage that these settings can produce.

We can testify to having seen many of these issues and manifestations present with very rejected children that we have fostered over the years. The point is that the result of not receiving love and acceptance from the parents, and subsequent lack of bonding and nurture can have pronounced effects on one's total person. These examples are of an extreme nature but they stand to illustrate that rejection has a profound impact on the human person; the only remaining question is to what degree it has touched us.

POSSIBLE BEGINNING POINTS FOR REJECTION BELIEFS
1. Prenatal:
That is, beginning before birth whilst still in the womb. Gods intention was for us to be accepted and wanted and that was to be our spiritual covering. But if we are not accepted, even in the womb then the spirit over us is rejection and we are imprinted with that on our souls, along with corresponding beliefs. For example, many children conceived in the depression years exhibited significant rejection problems. Birth control was not being used in those days, as a consequence there were often large families. Parents would often conclude that they didn't want another child has they were having enough trouble feeding the ones that they already had, and as a result not be readily excepting of the new family member.

Generational rejection
The late Noel Gibson, who was expert on rejection, and wrote a number of excellent books on the subject, stated that hereditary or generational rejection will always show up in the baby. In other words, if the rejection is in the family line you can expect it to manifest in the child.

2. Adoption/ Fostering
We have previously discussed the resultant *beliefs* proceeding from the separation choices, decisions and situations leading to adoption and fostering. In the case of adoption many times the decisions are made before the birth of the child. Even though the child may find themselves in a loving and accepting family the rejection issues and beliefs will automatically be there.

In the case of fostering, there is usually a significant reason why they need to be fostered out to begin with. Children are very often egocentric and lay the reason for be moved out of the family at something that they have done, or not done. Remember these conclusions are not because of conscious deliberate mental effort, but rather a conclusion or interpretation from the experience of the situation. In any case most times they will carry rejection, having concluded that they are unacceptable in the family unit for some reason. This often times may be merely *a perception*, coming from the appearance that the parents don't want them. The truth may well be that the parents are so embroiled in their own situation that they cannot cope with the child.

3. Parenting issues

Modeling
Many parents simply cannot communicate love and acceptance. This can stem from them never having had it modeled to them in terms of to how to show the worth, value, love and acceptance that a child needs. It continues then as a generational cultural omission that leaves a breeding ground for children to come to their own conclusions regarding whether or not they are acceptable.

Empty 'love tanks'
Some parents have not received love and grace themselves so they are emotionally bankrupt and have nothing to give. They are themselves rejected and many of the efforts around their lives are in trying to meet the needs of their own wounded selves. Sadly, rejected people are most often rejective; *rejection rejects.*

Absentee
At times parents are absentees in their dealings with their families, and often at critical times where children are coming to conclusions about themselves. This can result from circumstances such as hospitalization, traveling for work, or even working long hours to provide for the family. They may also be physically present but emotionally unavailable. Perhaps they are addicted to drugs, alcohol, television, digital games and media in order to escape their own pain and consequent relational problems.

Physical bonding

It has been said that physical bonding and nurture is especially important from the mother who has been gifted to be relational and present, meeting the everyday needs of life. The fathers tend to be more task oriented looking to longer term provisions and developments for the family. He is more likely to be focused, for example, on building an outboard motor so that his family doesn't have to row the boat home. His tendency is to be a provider and problem solver. In the family dynamic, identity comes largely from his encouragement and approval.

Money

We live in a world that holds financial wealth at a premium. Often in the western world we will see parents substituting material giving for time, attention and genuine interest in a child. Somehow, we have come to a place where we believe that if we have given them the latest media games to occupy them, this is love. Children know if you are just trying to get them out of the way. This is interpreted in their *hearts* with *beliefs* of unimportance, and lack of worthiness to be given time and relationship.

Other priorities

I once heard a story of a child attending a Pastors kids camp. She arrived wearing gaudy, out there, strikingly decorated clothing. She featured a big brightly colored Mohawk down the middle of her head. I suggest that somewhere deep inside that person was a cry proceeding from their heart, possibly something along the lines of; *Would somebody please notice me, anyone, please!*

Being a Pastor I can empathize that it is all too easy to fall into being busy ministering to everyone else, preparing a message or studying the Bible. The truth is that children don't need a huge amount of time; you're not that much fun anyway because, after all, you are an adult. But they need a minute or two here and there to know that they are more important than whatever you are doing. I am sure that as the little children come to us, we, like Jesus, need to make time for them. I am convinced that God is more than pleased if you put your Bible down for a time so that they can understand how important they are.

Pastors are just an example; it could be any other activity, but the responsibility for modeling the heart of God should begin with us as parents. Parents have been given the responsibility to represent God in all aspects of His character. We have found that the *God picture* that most people hold is a projection off the parenting that they have received. If you never have time for them, they will expect that God is also too occupied creating universes to listen to their needs. If you are always too busy, then the expectation will be that God doesn't have time for them, or that they are a nuisance. So, if father was harsh and critical then that is how they tend to see God. If they believe that the father, (or at times mother) didn't love them, then God doesn't love them either.

If you are often absentee, they won't even bother praying to God, because He is off somewhere sleeping on a cloud. If you don't take time correcting them and teaching them to respect authority and consequences for action, then they are likely to grow up without the fear of God and find themselves making choices that can eventually destroy or negatively impact their lives. So, many times in ministry we find that the image that people have of God is a projection or extension of how the parents, the father in particular dealt with them.

Conditional acceptance

A number of people hold rejection beliefs learnt through only receiving acceptance if they perform and meet the standards set for them. These expectations could relate to behavior, academic or other achievements. Fundamentally what is being projected onto them spiritually and emotionally is; *If you don't measure up by doing this or that then you are not good enough, and therefore not acceptable!"*

Some parents have such high standards for their children that they create a breeding ground for performance anxiety and depression. If a child is only ever criticized and told that they are not enough, then the consequent belief will be that no matter how hard they try, they will never be able to be what they need to be for acceptance. This is an overwhelming belief that produces hopelessness and eventually depression. Inside the person, inevitably, the heavy load of never being able to meet expectations is too much and they become depressed. The devil offers them a way out and often times suicide is attempted. It is wonderful when people access a *depression belief* and God speaks something into their memory and you hear them report something like *I'm ok! meaning, I am ok as I am … I can just be, I don't have to strive to be enough; I am enough because I am me!*

Christian parents can be as guilty as anyone of metering out conditional acceptance based on performance. A fear that our children may not be good enough for God, leads us to impose all kinds of religious standards on them. In turn they grow up seeing God as a person who is watching to make sure that you get everything right. One mistake and He will punish you. God actually doesn't expect us to be perfect. He knows that we are created beings in a hostile fallen environment, complete with our old nature which has a tendency towards sin, a world full of temptations and a spiritual enemy who is constantly trying to deceive and gain sway over us. Sometimes we need to forgive ourselves for being merely created beings formed from dust, God has! And then we can extend this grace and understanding that we have received from Him by not demanding others and our children to meet our standards.

Psalm 103:10-14 ¹⁰ *"He has not punished us for all our sins, nor does he deal with us as we deserve.* ¹¹ *For his unfailing love toward those who fear him is as great as the height of the heavens above the earth.* ¹² *He has removed our rebellious acts as far away from us as the east is from the west.* ¹³ *The LORD is like a father to his children, tender and compassionate to those who fear him.* ¹⁴ *For* **he understands how weak we are; he knows we are only dust**. *NLT (emphasis mine)*

Some parents use their child's success as a part of their own value, to help shore up their own rejection and how they are perceived by society.

Inappropriate discipline

Excessive correction without love leaves a child to conclude that they don't matter; they are nothing, they simply live to fulfill all your wants and needs. If you have a genuine motivation towards the child, they understand this and will receive the discipline. If they feel that this is all about conforming their lives to you being pleased, and that you do not care about them or that which they want or need, that is, them, themselves, then this will read on their hearts as injustice, which will produce rebellion. The same is true of not taking time to discipline your child. They sense that you cannot be bothered and that therefore their lives are an inconvenience to you. You do not accept the responsibility for the outcome of their lives, and therefore they do not matter to you.

When our daughter was beginning to stand and wobble around the furniture at perhaps 10 months old, she would touch a pot plant or something and look around to see if this was ok or not. I would say, no. Then she would touch it again and look to see what would happen. I would get up and calmly go over and give her a gentle little smack on the hand. This only occurred a few times and at that early age she learnt that no didn't mean; *maybe, or If you try long enough you will get your way, or If you want to you can, because after all you have rights!* She learnt that no meant no. From then on there was no further need to test this because she already knew what would happen. No domestic violence, and I never ever saw our children throw a tantrum, ever. Correction was done in love and as early as possible.

At the same time, we had a friend with a daughter the same age. This father's response to his daughters testing of boundaries was; *give them what they want and they will leave us alone!* Even small children understand this as that they are not worth the time.

There is an old jazz song that goes something like; *it ain't what you do, it's the way how you do it, that's what gets results!* This is profoundly true. If you discipline your child in anger with a statement such as; *You are really annoying <u>me</u>; now you are going to really cop it!* Who is it all about? You! It's about what you want, and how they need to be to be good enough for your love and acceptance.

The problem is that often parents don't take the time to disciple their children and eventually their behavior becomes so unruly that the parents explode in anger and frustration. But if your child needs discipline and you calmly take them aside and give them a hug and say something like; *You know I love you so much, you are not a naughty child, you have done a naughty thing. We don't want you to grow up to have a sad life and get into trouble. So, I have to punish you.* Then having metered out appropriate justice where the punishment fits the crime you give them another big hug saying; *I don't like having to do that to you, but I love you so much that I needed to, and hope that we never need to do it again.* Who has this been about? Them! It has been about what they need and their good, and they will receive it and even appreciate it. But when it is all about you, you can expect problems. It is the spirit that it is delivered in.

Feel free to disagree with me; this is my opinion and my experience. As a Pastor I have had young parents with babies ask about how to bring up their children. Using these kinds of principles, I have seen their children growing up happily, knowing the boundaries, well behaved, secure, and tantrum free. I recall one young couple who were continually receiving praise for their exemplary children.

I have already mentioned that we were in a foster care program for a number of years. Some of the children who came to us had been branded ADD. Using these kinds of principles, these children would calm right down when they came into our home. After a time, I began to interpret ADD in many cases as Appropriate Discipline Disorder. Many of these problems did not exist when the Bible was the basis of raising your children. We are in Africa doing ministry most years for, on most occasions, more than a month at a time. I have never yet seen a tantrum or a badly-behaved child. As the Africans are influenced increasingly by western values and humanistic approaches to parenting, it seems to be just a matter of time and they will have the same issues as we do. *It ain't what you do; it's the way how you do it, that's what gets results!*

> Proverbs 22:6 *"Train up a child in the way he should go, and when he is old he will not depart from it."*

> Proverbs 22:15 *"Foolishness is bound up in the heart of a child; The rod of correction will drive it far from him." NKJV*

The Bible treats dealing with children, correcting them in love as a matter of prime importance. Clearly physical discipline is something only to be done where necessary, but if a child learns it early enough you can expect a good self-controlled life for them into the future. In much the same way as we do not consciously access heart beliefs that largely dictate our choices and behavior, if we have grown up under discipline, we may no longer consciously know why we have a strong need to do what is right. It is in our programming.

When my children became adults, they have enjoyed playfully pushing the limits with me with teasing and so on. I still see in them a restraint as to how far they should go. They may not consciously remember exactly what will happen, but there remains a sense of consequence. Someone has said that respect comes before love. If they do not respect us who are meant to be representing all aspects of God to them, then in all probability, they will not have the necessary fear and awe of God that will protect them. If we do not love our children enough to correct them then they may well grow up lawless. This will inevitably leave them unable or not wanting to submit to the ultimate authority figure, God the Father.

Sadly, we see over and over in these times children from Christian families grow up and walk away from God because they only want their own way. The parents cannot understand what has happened. They have unwittingly brought them up in the ways of the World and not the ways of God. Often times they are afraid to discipline their children because of their own fear of rejection which tells them that they will be rejected if they bring correction.

> Proverbs 23:13 *"Do not withhold correction from a child, for if you beat him with a rod, he will not die. 14 You shall beat him with a rod, and deliver his soul from hell." NKJV*

2 Timothy 3:1-4 [1] *"But know this, that in the last days perilous times will come:* [2] *For men will be lovers of themselves, lovers of money, boasters, proud, blasphemers,* **disobedient to parents**, *unthankful, unholy,* [3] *unloving, unforgiving, slanderers, without self-control, brutal, despisers of good,* [4] *traitors, headstrong, haughty, lovers of pleasure rather than lovers of God."*
NKJV (emphasis mine)

4. Rejection through Abuse

Verbal, emotional, mental, sexual and physical abuses are all strong sources of rejection. The *language of the spirit* or the attitude behind all of these is something along the lines of; *You don't matter, you are just rubbish that has to fit into what I want, you are nothing.* At heart level, matching beliefs are now held about your self-worth and acceptability. These acts destroy how you perceive yourself, your identity, value and importance.

Study 2: Results of rejection or non-acceptance

1. A love 'vacuum'

A person who has not experienced acceptance will often be, what is sometimes termed as, needy. In other words, they always need some kind of help, support or encouragement from others. Sometimes these people will suck the life out of those around them desperately trying to get you to meet the inner need they have. Very hurt people can have an emotional whirlpool that draws everyone and everything into it as a solution to their emptiness. This can include a propensity towards lusts, possessions, acknowledgement from achievements, possessiveness and jealousy around relationships. Problems such as hoarding can fit in here, where a person may feel that belongings connect them to a World where they feel unwanted.

These people will often crave acceptance from *parental figures* such as ministers, or will worship a sports hero or movie star. This person becomes the centre of their lives as a kind of replacement of the absent key figures of a father or mother. Many times, homosexual tendencies fit in here, with psychological studies reporting a high incidence of this behavior being a response to not having received love and acceptance from a primary care giver in the critical early stages of life [7] .

The need for acceptance and love can also be found as a strong motivator behind sex outside of marriage, adultery and even issues such as the epidemic of pornography. These illicit movies offer men the emotional stimulus of these supposedly accepting women being pleased with the efforts of the men portrayed in the pictures. Having dealt with many men with this addiction, I have come to the conclusion that porn for men is primarily about the acceptance and success in relationships that is craved. Clearly there is an additional highly exciting sexual stimulation component as a complication.

When men fear failure or rejection in relationships pornography is an easy option, where there are no risks or needs to deal with working through harmonizing relationships. In a twisted kind of way often their emotional needs are met through seeing men received the way that they would like to be, and affirmed as they would like to be. Men with healthy emotional, relational and sexual relationships at home normally weather these worldly temptations effortlessly. [8] The truth is that nothing and no person can completely fill this *belief-based* love and acceptance vacuum. Only God can bring wholeness to these broken hearts with His truth and love.

---

7 *That is one of a number of reasons for these practices.*
8 *There are other issues in play with addiction to pornography that often need to be dealt with.*

2. Narcissistic behavior

Narcissism is defined as an abnormal love and admiration for oneself. It is reasonably obvious that this is the person's solution to not being loved, regarded or treated as being important. From repeated dealings with *narcissistic behavior* I have concluded that the underlying beliefs are normally something such as; I *am not important and therefore not loved."*

Their countermeasure to this heart belief is that in their own eyes not only are they important, they are in fact the only person who is important, and they are indeed the most important of all people. This is in essence love of self, and is based on self-promotion in their own eyes. This being the case, it is natural that what <u>they</u> think, want, and do is of the utmost importance. They have a tendency towards grandiosity and an inflated picture of their abilities and superiority as a human being. This by implication places everyone else as lemmings and lesser humanity. Because self is now firmly on the throne, they are prone to the whole self-syndrome. Self-consumed, self-centered, self-indulgent, self-justified, self-gratifying, self-important, self-protective, self-righteous, self-deceived and selfish, etc. etc.

In a Christian setting, unfortunately, these people believe for instance that they are going to be mightily used as prophets to the nations, or carry mighty anointing, are apostles and so on. Sadly, many are never used, because they cannot begin with small things or to serve under authority because it is beneath them. God Himself opposes the conformity to Satan's likeness in pride that has occurred in them through their broken heartedness.

It is very difficult for these people to admit weakness; (the deception is that the shortcomings that they are unaware that they carry are in fact only self-perceptions – and are not true anyway) they have built walls around the monument to self to protect the image of acceptability and importance from being attacked. Very often these people present as harsh or intense.

Perhaps the *my rights* attitude that we find in society today comes under this extreme focus on self. Possibly believing and fearing that nobody really considers that you are important, have worth, or deserve protection and provision, you then insist and demand that you are looked after.

3. Hermits and extroverts

Some people respond to rejection by hiding from people in order to avoid rejection. Even in company they present as withdrawn. In a sense they have accepted that they are unacceptable and not good enough, and are therefore afraid to come out of their protective shell. Others will gravitate to wearing a mask and becoming, for example, the life of the party in order to be acceptable. When they go home, they are very often emotionally exhausted from the effort to rise up and be what they perceive is necessary to be wanted and accepted by people.

Others exhibit what is known as *harmonizing behavior*. This usually occurs when they have learnt in childhood that they need to be whatever other people want them to be in order to receive acceptance. This means that they never really have their own identity, and suppressing who they are to please others often leads to mental issues and maladies later in life. Some Christian commentators have suggested that problems such as Alzheimer's disease stems from these kinds of confusion about identity beliefs. I have witnessed that these components are certainly present on several occasions.

4. Loneliness

Another result of rejection is poor bonding and the inability to make close relationships. Beliefs such as, *I am not wanted, don't belong, not worthy or worth acceptance, am not cared about* and so on, presents a strong inner case for not receiving the affection of another, yourself, and even God. We all really do need to hear; *This is my child, in whom I am well pleased.* While we cannot accept ourselves, we will struggle to accept others as well. This makes healing and freedom in this area a vital part of returning to God's perfect order.

Matthew 19:19 "You shall love your neighbor as yourself." NKJV

5. Emotional immaturity

Some of us older folk who are *digital immigrants* find ourselves in a world where if you cannot get your smart phone to work you ask a 4-year-old to set it up for you. This might be an exaggeration, but often times by early teenage years, our children are very worldly wise on many fronts that we were never exposed to. Emotionally however, they have not developed. They have knowledge but it is not balanced with emotional maturity. Much of this can be laid at the feet of insufficient parenting and nurture. Modern society and living standards now, many times, requires both husband and wife in the workplace to sustain lifestyles.

Coupled with this is the phenomenon of children being overwhelmed with decisions that they are given and not yet equipped to make. In other words, they are made responsible for their lives before they have the knowledge and understanding to cope. I recall seeing a fast food advertisement where a very small child was having one choice after another fired at them. *Is it this kind of food time or this kind? Is it playing time or home time?* and so it went. At this age it is possibly better to say; *sit up here and eat your dinner. Go and play for ten minutes and then we are going home!*

Parenting is a bit like having a length of rope. To begin with your child is completely under control and once they learn some self-control you slowly feed out more rope to them, letting them have more and more control, now a mix of self-control and your control. Finally, as they reach adulthood you throw them the last little bit of rope and they have full control, having gradually learnt self-control and taking responsibility for choices over time. Now your job as parent is finished in that area and you can take up your role as a support and friend. But if you give them all of the rope at the beginning they are out of control, not having matured in self-control and knowledge. More commonly trauma and abuses arrest the normal development of emotions as the wounded child distances themselves from harmful identity beliefs in order to cope with life.

Some people may come for ministry who still feel and behave like a child in some ways. Along with the beliefs about our identity and acceptability that is stored in your mind, is the, *how do I respond when I am hurt like this* information. This is why people at 40 years old or more can have an argument with their spouse and they both walk away and as they cool off, they are thinking; *that was childish, we behaved like 8-year old's!* In all probability, that was where you first took in the belief about yourself that you reacted to, and also the response which was now automatic.

6. Fear of rejection

Once a person has had the pain and negative experience of rejection, they will now be on watch to protect themselves from further rejection. Other fears such as fear of failure or fear of embarrassment, and so on, fall under this category. You must ask yourself, what will happen if you fail? In the past, most likely, you have learnt that this means you will not receive acceptance. Why did you feel embarrassed? Because you felt that something that you did or said was unacceptable!

'FRUIT' OR POSSIBLE SIGNS OF A FEAR OF REJECTION

Independence

If I am afraid that you might reject me, then an unconscious decision might be something such as, *I won't need you or your acceptance, and then I don't need to worry about you rejecting me! I will meet my own needs and be my own provision.*

Self-Pity

Feeling sorry for yourself could run closely with this kind of inner thinking. *Poor me, nobody cares about me. I feel sorry for me!* Inside we are singing that *somebody done somebody wrong song.* This nobody cares about me belief may at times also have an outward manifestation; *You must hear my story, how I have been wronged and then you should feel sorry for me too!* It can lead to controlling behavior and attitudes; *I must make people care about me, because nobody does!* This unconscious inner thinking stems from insecurity about being accepted and loved. The problem is, that if you *make* people care about you, do things for you and love you, is that you know inside that YOU made them do it, rendering it meaningless.

You can imagine if God pinned us to a wall poking us relentlessly in the chest with a giant finger saying; *Love me, you must love me!* In the end, for fear of being crushed, we would capitulate and acknowledge our love for Him. This would mean nothing to Him because He made us do it. And yet He extends free will and choice to mankind, which sadly we abuse. It is His, love, mercy and kindness that leads us to repentance, not His control. Where self-pity is, there is often times also resentment, bitterness, unforgiveness, and retaliation towards others and often self. Until healing comes to the broken heart it will be difficult to forgive. Once you have identified and resolved the belief/s producing the hurt, the person usually moves from; *It's all your fault for making me feel this way, to it's not your fault, you have your own issues to deal with.*

King David had it right when his spirit man was encouraging his soul that God had the answer to his pain and negativity.

> *Psalm 42:5-6,11* *⁵ "Why am I discouraged? Why so sad? I will put my hope in God! I will praise him again - my Savior and ⁶my God! Now I am deeply discouraged, but I will remember your kindness; ¹¹ Why am I discouraged? Why so sad? I will put my hope in God! I will praise him again-- my Savior and my God!" NLT*

The late Noel Gibson wrote a number of excellent books on rejection in the 1990s. His wife Phyl gave us permission to reference his material after his death. He suggests some of the following, as symptoms that suggest the need for healing from rejection: In the brackets is my expansion.

A. Refusing comfort.   (This could include throwing tantrums or sulking.)

B. Rejection of others.   (If you reject someone first, if they reject you back then you can justify it to yourself – you feel that if you blow their candle out, then yours will burn more brightly!)

C. Signs of emotional hardness. (Harshness, criticism, judgment, the tongue)

D. Skepticism, doubt, unbelief. (This stems from not being able to trust. Fearing people's motives towards you)

E. Aggressive attitudes.   (Feeling that aggression/anger, disapproval, in a verbal or physical form is the logical way to ward off further rejection)

F. Thoughts of revenge.   (Retaliation of some kind coming from resentment to perceived hurt)

G. Argumentativeness.   (Point scoring and the need to win an argument and be right all of the time as a countermeasure to the low self-image coming from rejection - simply cannot agree or accept another's point of view).

I recall working with a man many years ago, and no matter what you said or suggested his response was always; *I know!*" One day he was driving a truck on a highway and I was the passenger. The traffic lights turned red and there was a police car pulling up at the lights coming the other way. I began to draw his attention to the lights, and that there was a vehicle stopping immediately in front of us. Before I could get more than a few words out he responded; *I know!* Referring to the fact that he had seen the police car, he had not however seen the vehicle in front and I will leave it to your imagination as to what happened next. Needless to say, it was an unpleasant experience stemming from the inability to believe that someone else may know something that you do not.

H. Stubbornness'/defiance.   (People who feel that they have been wronged or aren't being accepted and dealt with fairly very often simply will not cooperate – feeling that their treatment is not fair, or unjust)

When I was a little boy, I felt that I had been wronged with an event with my older brother. As a result, when I was punished for the crime without having, in my opinion, been properly heard I refused to cry or be penitent. As an extension to this we see rebellion, fighting and resistance to authority.

I. Burying emotions   (Noel made this statement in one of his books which I took careful note of; *Some bury their emotions but tend the grave continually!*)

I took this to mean that while they do not permit themselves to feel the pain, there is a lot of time spent in making sure that the *body of rejection* is not forgotten. This could be in the form of self-pity, or resentment as to how they had been hurt and rejected.

J. Inner vows.   (I thought I would add inner decisions to this list).

There is another reason why rejection *beliefs and feelings* can be buried or suppressed. For example, many times I find people who have closed down their emotions, using their capacity for self-control in an ungodly way on themselves. Often times this comes from a place in the childhood history such as being told that; *big boys or just boys don't cry.* Therefore, your acceptance becomes based on your not expressing emotion. Your conclusion and inner decision, or vow, is then something along the lines of; *If I am not accepted when I display emotion,* then I will not have emotion! Somebody has helped you misinterpret life and now you are bound by *a belief in your heart* that after a while you will not consciously be aware of. You require God's truth and perspective in this regard to be made free.

> **Note:**
> You never simply don't have emotions, even if you suppress them, they will often come out in your body as disease or your mind as mental illness. Jesus exhibited a full range of emotions in weeping, joy more than His companions, anger at times and so on because that is God's order. We deny our feelings at our own peril.

7. Self-rejection

This occurs when you accept rejection as being a correct assessment of your acceptability, worth and value. In a sense you continue to replay the rejection beliefs that you hold as now being your truth. In a ministry setting you will hear *self-rejection statements* overflowing from *the heart* out of the mouth. These will give you strong insights into the beliefs that people hold. It is extremely common for those who have rejection to also have fear of rejection and self-rejection issues. As they share their story or problem you may hear and note such statements as: *I'm just not good enough, I'm stupid, useless, a loser, hopeless, ugly, such an idiot, never do it right, am not as good as others*, and so on.

I was in the U.K. studying many years ago and befriended a very cultured Englishman named Charles. Towards the end of our studies he asked me a question. He enquired of me, *Are you always so sardonic?* I responded, *I don't know Charles, what on Earth does sardonic mean?* As I now understand it, it means laughingly mocking or being derisive, and in this context, he meant towards myself. In other words, I was making jokes at my own expense, kidding around about my shortcomings. It was however, reflective of some inner issues that I later had to deal with. At that time, I did however decide that if God had accepted me then He was more likely right than I was and so I needed to stop rejecting myself. That dealt with my mind in regards to the behavior, later my heart was healed as well. This criticism of self, as an inward expression, will normally be accompanied outwardly by criticism of others because of the low self-image that it proceeds from.

False humility can probably come under this banner as well. With an attitude and presentation based around; *well I am just no one and nothing, I am not worth noticing, don't worry about me!* This is not humility; this is low self-image. You can, in fact, be quite confident, but still be aware that in comparison to God you are just a created being. So, humility is actually a healthy perspective of your humanity. You have your God given strengths and weaknesses just like everyone else, you are neither greater, nor lesser, you are simply you!

SELF-ACCUSATION, SELF-CONDEMNATION AND SELF-BITTERNESS

When self-rejection is extreme, it can at times extend to self-hatred because of your perceived unacceptability and inadequacy. Some Christian commentators consider this to be at the root of autoimmune disease. In the heart the belief is that you are not enough, a failure, not what you should be. This, through your shortcomings, makes you the enemy of your own acceptability. Your immune system then plays out its role of destroying the enemies of your wellbeing, which in this case has been inwardly decided to be you! Spiritually and emotionally you are now against yourself because of that which you believe about yourself in your heart.

The experts tell us that the immune system will then attack the weakest link in the chain, often being the organ that is most under load. This could be our stress system such as our thyroid or adrenal glands or other bodily organs. Commonly our pancreases are under such a load because of overeating which makes them the weakest link and we could develop diabetes. The bad diet then, is only creating an environment for the disease to be established and prosper.

Why are many people very obese and have no diabetes and others only slightly overweight and contract the disease? This could be a strong indicator of how prolific the self-rejection issue is today, projecting out of not being accepted in the home or the breakdown of the family unit.

Where self-rejection exists fruits such as guilt and self-condemnation will often be present. Guilt relates to believing that you have done something that you should not have done, or perhaps more likely in this situation, guilt believes that you have not done something that you should have. Hence the guilt is connected to the self-rejection via the mechanism of believing that you should do or be more and have failed.

Story
A number of years ago a man came to me presenting with diabetes. I asked him if he carried a fear of rejection, self-rejection and guilt. After he had thought about it for a while, he reported that he did. We did some brief *Truth Encounter* sessions over the next few weeks dealing with memories containing guilt that produced anxiety and self-rejection beliefs. At the conclusion of the ministry times I also prayed for his healing. After each session he reported that his blood sugar levels came down 2 points. I would not suggest that we make this a guideline for ministering to diabetics as it was an isolated case. However, we did target these emotions deliberately because there are ministries which consider diabetes to be rooted in the specific emotional dynamics of anxiety connected to rejection, fear of rejection, self-rejection, self-hatred, guilt, and depression [9].

We can readily see how this ties together. Depression often comes from hopelessness about ever being able to perform well enough or be enough to be accepted. As a result, you are constantly anxious and fearful about being rejected for not being or doing enough. You then reject yourself for being a failure and feel guilty about not pleasing others or achieving their standards.

So, to minister to these *belief based* negative emotions, the question is not so much do you have fear of rejection or self-rejection and guilt, as it is to why do you feel guilty and what do you believe that has led you to reject yourself?

Another lady came for ministry at one time with another autoimmune disease called Multiple Sclerosis. She was quite slim and had been a fitness instructor. As we went through the preliminary work up session explaining *Truth Encounters*, I commented to her that if she had been overweight, she may have had diabetes instead. She related to me that her sister was overweight and she did, in fact, have diabetes. They both grew up in the same family environment and most probably held the same or similar rejection beliefs.

OUTWARD SIGNS OF SELF-REJECTION
We have just discussed some potential inner workings of self-rejection; there are also some very obvious outward manifestations that may be encountered. Self-punishment for not being acceptable or not accepting yourself could present in behavior such as *cutting*, or children banging their heads against the wall or hitting themselves. This self-punishment is a sure sign that they are angry and frustrated with themselves. Adults might try to self-destruct with alcohol or drug abuse. Others try to comfort themselves with food and can at times set up a self-destructive cycle. Now overweight, they consider themselves to be even less acceptable by the standards set up by modern media. Still others may go the other way

---

9 *In His Own Image by Dr. Art Mathias. In my opinion, the specific fear that you are dealing with is fear of rejection, which is very often present with rejection and self-rejection.*

with excessive gym work or excessive exercise or dieting to try to make themselves better and good enough. Some may have other performance and success-based goals such as career or wealth. These can also be to do with receiving love, acceptance, significance, value and worth from a performance-based world system which is for the most part rejective.

CANNOT, 'WILL NOT' RECEIVE ENCOURAGEMENT

We have already mentioned self-pity. Many people cannot receive affirmation, the inner rejection belief regarding their unworthiness is like a force field that cannot accept any encouragement as being true. For some self-pity is a kind of distorted *good feeling* which is a kind of demonic counterfeit for love. Often people suffering from self-rejection will present as negative, pessimistic, and are unable to receive because of unbelief. The underlying belief is something such as; *if I reject me, surely you must too!*

NEGATIVE SELF-IMAGE AND COMPARISON

Commonly, self-rejection proceeds from *memories and events* where a person has been compared to a sibling, or another student, and as a consequence has felt that they are inferior. If this is the case then usually you will find that they still have a problem with comparison in order to rate their acceptability today.

The truth is that God does not mass produce humanity as we do cell phones, where you can have a black one or a silver one and otherwise, they are all exactly the same. Each one of us is an individual, we are one of a kind masterpieces that God created for Himself to spend eternity with.

> 2 Corinthians 10:12b *"But they, measuring themselves by themselves, and comparing themselves among themselves, are not wise." NKJV*

Once we have received healing from beliefs stemming from comparison, it is wise to take the counsel of scripture and not compare ourselves with others. If we do, we will either decide that we are better and be swollen up in pride, or decide that we are lesser, and enter into inferiority and self-rejection. Just accept that you are an awesome individual creation that cannot be compared to any others. There are no other versions of you in existence, found in history or planned for the future. Thank and praise God as King David did for making you, you. That is not pride; it is acceptance of yourself and who God created you to be. You are the work of His hands; you did not after all create yourself!

> Psalm 139:14-17 [14] *"I will praise You, for I am fearfully and wonderfully made; Marvelous are Your works, And that my soul knows very well.* [15] *My frame was not hidden from You, When I was made in secret, And skillfully wrought in the lowest parts of the earth.* [16] *Your eyes saw my substance, being yet unformed. And in Your book they all were written, The days fashioned for me, When as yet there were none of them.* [17] *How precious also are Your thoughts to me, O God! How great is the sum of them!" NKJV*

DISTORTED SELF-IMAGE

Self-rejection produces a distorted self-image. It can be like a belief based demonic hedge stopping people from receiving love, acceptance and belonging. It can cause people to reframe things that are said to them according to the *inner heart beliefs* that are held. Genuinely motivated suggestions for doing tasks another way or improving functionality from a friend, spouse or employer are heard, reframed by beliefs, and perceived as an attack on competency and worth.

My wife and I have ministered to many pretty girls who believed that they are quite ugly and unacceptable. This often begins as a child when they perhaps had a skin rash or similar, and possibly someone was unkind at school. Maybe they had a little bit of childhood chubbiness. The point is that the belief that they took to heart has distorted their image of themselves and consequently they now reject themselves. I mentioned this phenomenon whilst teaching on a school recently along with some other problems that apply here. A pretty young girl burst into tears and had to go out and receive ministry. I later found out that an incorrect self-belief about her looks was the cause of the outburst.

SELF-REJECTION SYMPTOMS

A) **Low self-image:** – rejection crushes the personality
   "If they think that I am hopeless, useless etc.......then I must be!"

B) Proceeding from the depths of **low self-evaluation** comes **inadequacy and insecurity**
   "I am not enough; I don't feel safe to come out and be me!"

C) **Sadness, grief, sorrow:** These are outward signs of a wounded or crushed spirit...
   .... the evidence of deep hurt. Many people have a 'tragic look' on their faces as a result.

> *Proverbs 17: 22 A cheerful heart is good medicine, but a crushed spirit dries up the bones. NIV*
>
> *Proverbs 18: 14 The spirit of a man will sustain him in sickness, But who can bear a broken spirit? NKJV*

D) **Self-accusation, Self-condemnation:** This is where they are unable to forgive themselves and take all of the blame for the rejection. They constantly put themselves down, and cannot receive praise or encouragement. Many will punish themselves for the way that they *perceive* that they are. Underneath there is inner dialogue going on that is producing the attitudes to themselves and emotional turmoil. *"I will never get any better, I will never be good enough!"*

E) **Worry, anxiety or depression:** *"I don't know what to do to resolve this. I can't cope. What will happen if I don't fix it?"*

F) **Frustration and anger:** often this is directed at not being able to achieve standards, goals or expectations, real or perceived, that relate to qualify you to receive acceptance, love, significance, value or worth. *Negativity, pessimism or hopelessness* may also be present, proceeding from a belief that things cannot changed and expectations will not be met. Inner self talk could be along the lines of; *"I'm too useless, it's hopeless, I just can't do it!"*

G) **Inability or refusal to communicate:** This could be in the form of 'sulking' or 'packing a sad, 'or 'being in a huff' etc. The underlying idea behind the behavior is probably retaliation for how the subject is being made to feel, but it can also be a plan to cut off the source of the rejection.

SAMPLE MINISTRY TO REJECTION BELIEFS SCENARIO
A person approaches you for help.

Step 1:   Explain the process to the person, and what you are looking for, namely *heart beliefs*. This process could include having them read, view or listen to material explaining the ministry.

Step 2:   The person comes for the actual ministry session.

Note: They already have the problem that they are struggling with so you don't need to come up with anything. It is not your job to fix their whole life, just try to help them with whatever is presenting at the time.

Listen to their story and the issue that they are bringing to you. Make notes of the things that they say that may be clues to what they *believe*. Writing things down is good as it means that you don't miss things that may need to be visited, and you don't need to interrupt their story.

Step 3:   Ministry Example

Fred: I felt very uneasy when I went to try out for the church choir!
Me: Why do you think that you were uncomfortable in that setting?
Fred: I think that I felt that I did not belong there, I was not a part of it.

This could indicate a possible belief such as; *I am not wanted*, or *I am not accepted*.

Step 4:   We have them concentrate on the feeling produced by the thought that they do not belong, and are not a part of it; rejected by the group. We are looking for the earliest possibly historical place where they learnt beliefs that caused them to feel this way.

Fred: I have just remembered my first day of school. There was a group of kids playing and talking together and they ignored me!
Me: As you concentrate on the memory and feel that rejected feeling, why do you think that they ignored you?
Fred: Pauses and explores the memory. I think it is because I am not like them, I am new and so they don't want me. This must be true because they are all accepting each other, but I am on the outside!
Me: Let's ask the Lord what His truth, the real truth is. Lord what do you want Fred to understand about that time where he felt that he was not wanted because he is not like them, because he is new?
Fred: The Lord is reminding me, that these kids went to Kindergarten together and already knew each other. I couldn't get in to Kinder because they were full up.
Me: So, are you not wanted because you are different?
Fred: No, I am the same; I have just not built relationships yet. Later I did make some good friends there.
Me: How do you feel about the church choir now?
Fred: I feel excited about it now; I will be making some new friends it will just take a little time.
Me: Perhaps close in prayer thanking the Lord for His healing, or I may enquire as to whether or not there are other things which require ministry.

Clearly this example is not going to be as deeply painful as rejection often is. Some people may have very painful traumatic rejection situations from some kind of abuse or absence of love in the home. Other people may have a *profile of rejection* composed of multiple less painful beliefs.

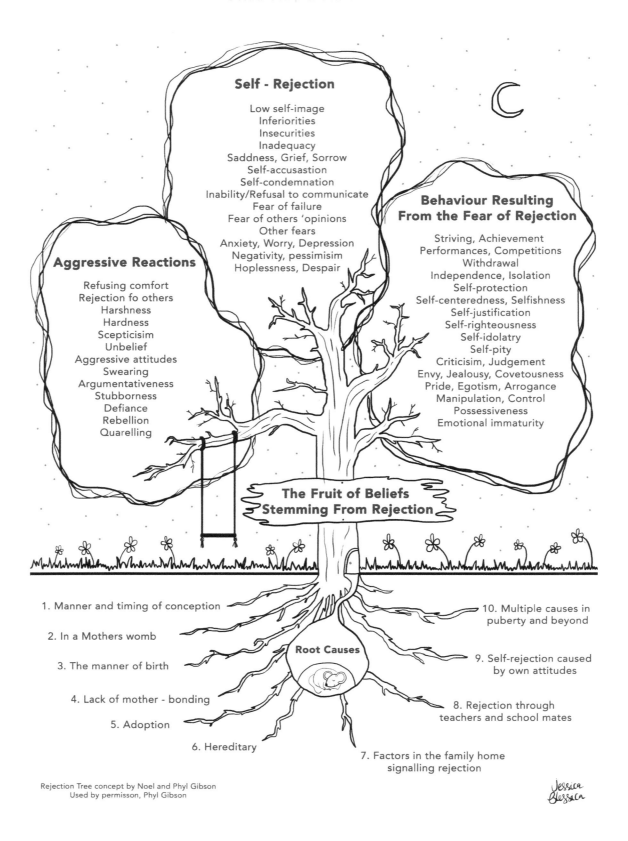

Self - Rejection

Low self-image
Inferiorities
Insecurities
Inadequacy
Saddness, Grief, Sorrow
Self-accusastion
Self-condemnation
Inability/Refusal to communicate
Fear of failure
Fear of others 'opinions
Other fears
Anxiety, Worry, Depression
Negativity, pessimisim
Hoplessness, Despair

**Behaviour Resulting
From the Fear of Rejection**

Striving, Achievement
Performances, Competitions
Withdrawal
Independence, Isolation
Self-protection
Self-centeredness, Selfishness
Self-justification
Self-righteousness
Self-idolatry
Self-pity
Criticisim, Judgement
Envy, Jealousy, Covetousness
Pride, Egotism, Arrogance
Manipulation, Control
Possessiveness
Emotional immaturity

Aggressive Reactions

Refusing comfort
Rejection fo others
Harshness
Hardness
Scepticisim
Unbelief
Aggressive attitudes
Swearing
Argumentativeness
Stubborness
Defiance
Rebellion
Quarelling

**The Fruit of Beliefs
Stemming From Rejection**

1. Manner and timing of conception

2. In a Mothers womb

3. The manner of birth

4. Lack of mother - bonding

5. Adoption

6. Hereditary

Root Causes

10. Multiple causes in
puberty and beyond

9. Self-rejection caused
by own attitudes

8. Rejection through
teachers and school mates

7. Factors in the family home
signalling rejection

Rejection Tree concept by Noel and Phyl Gibson
Used by permisson, Phyl Gibson

Jessica
Blessen

UNIT SEVEN

Dealing with Fear

WE NOW CONSIDER TWO TYPES OF FEAR

Study 1: Circumstantial fear

What I term *circumstantial fear* is anxiety that is relating to a current event, such as a storm, a particular financial situation, or some other present tense happening. These do not relate to anything that you already believe from fearful times in the past.

For example, we were recently booked to run a number of healing schools in Kenya at the same time as they were running elections. These are often volatile and violent times in Kenya and many people including some Kenyan ministers warned us not to come. My wife and I both prayed about it and together had peace about the trip and so decided to go and fulfill our commitments anyway. When we arrived many of the Pastors commented that we must be very brave. The truth is they had been through anxious times with elections before, but we had no precedent or beliefs about potential harm to influence our decision. So, we were not actually brave, we simply had an absence of fear which is not the same thing. Courageous people push through their fears despite difficult circumstances.

I recall reading once that Napoleon's bravest general at one time could not mount his horse because his knees were shaking so violently. Reportedly he looked down at his legs and said something along the lines of; *If you knew where I was taking you next, you would shake much more than that!* He was not prepared to submit to fear and let it dictate his activities. I am sure that once he was in battle the fear would have been displaced.

LESSON

We always have a choice. For Christians if God is for us who can be against us? (Romans 8:31) For believers the only real choice is faith.

A PRACTICAL THEOLOGY OF DEALING WITH 'CIRCUMSTANTIAL FEAR'

The Bible gives us a theology of how to deal with fear in our present circumstances where there is no historical precedent. It shows us how to practically deal with fears that are new situations, by displacing them in choosing trust and having faith in Him. This of course assumes that we are free from *fear beliefs* stemming from the past. I am told that there are 366 *fear nots* in the Bible. That is one for each day of the year and even leap year is covered. In the event that you are captive to a fear that came to you before you knew how to respond, or had God in your life, then you most probably need to be set free by a *Truth Encounter* with the Holy Spirit.

Before we examine how to be set free at *heart level* from *historical fear beliefs* let us first examine what our mindsets or *default position* should be in regards to submitting to *circumstantial* fear. There are some excellent pictures of this that Jesus gave us in the gospels. In Matthew 14, we see the story of an event that produced fear in the disciples that had no historical precedence. The setting is that Jesus had just fed the five thousand people multiplying five loaves and two fish. I believe that one aspect of what He was doing was to move the Apostles from the basic principles of the World in terms of what was possible, to understanding that all things are possible with God. God is never confined or limited to the program that this World runs on.

I take heart that the Apostles were a little slow picking this up. After the feeding, rather than travel across the lake with them as He usually would, He *made* them go ahead.

> *Matthew 14:22 "Immediately Jesus* **made** *the disciples get into the boat and go on ahead of him to the other side, while he dismissed the crowd." NIV (emphasis mine)*

I believe that He did this purposefully in order to challenge their believing and God picture with yet another supernatural act. As you read the following verses keep in mind that they had never seen anyone walk on water before and so had no previous beliefs from any such experience. This was an entirely new situation and *circumstance* that they were dealing with.

> *Matthew 14:25-31 [25] During the fourth watch of the night Jesus went out to them, walking on the lake. [26] When the disciples saw him walking on the lake, they were terrified. "It's a ghost," they said, and* **cried out in fear***. [27] But Jesus immediately said to them: "Take courage! It is I. Don't be afraid." [28] "Lord, if it's you," Peter replied, "tell me to come to you on the water." [29] "Come," he said. Then Peter got down out of the boat, walked on the water and came toward Jesus. [30] But when he saw the wind, he was afraid and, beginning to sink, cried out, "Lord, save me!" [31] Immediately Jesus reached out his hand and caught him. "You of little faith," he said,* **"why did you doubt?"** *NIV (emphasis mine)*

Their response was automatically fear, where Jesus was trying to move their default position to being faith. Notably Peter did have enough trust and faith in Jesus to step out on His word. The principle here is that while he looked to Jesus he was doing fine, but when he heeded his circumstances, he was not fine. We could say that faith makes you float and puts you above or over your circumstances, but fear makes you sink and puts you under the power of your circumstances. Faith can make us walk over our situations because it is centered in a supernatural or *above* natural being.

 LESSON
Fear will make you subject to natural outcomes, as a result of being submitted to your surroundings and senses.

JESUS TALKS TO THE STORM

In Mark Chapter 4 we see Jesus assessing where the disciples were up in terms of their moving from *circumstantial fear* to a faith response in God. We call fear the *what if spirit*. As an opposite to faith, real fear believes that another spiritual being can have the final say in outcomes, producing something negative. I have been at sea in storms and you can imagine some of the thoughts behind the fear in the boat. *What if* Peter's repair on the hull doesn't hold? *What if* we cannot bail the water out quickly enough? *What if* Luke's knots don't hold on the mast, he is after all a physician? *What if* Jesus doesn't wake up and tell us what to do. There may have been a whole myriad of beliefs and thoughts that together gripped them with fear.

> Mark 4:39-40 ³⁹ *Then He arose and rebuked the wind, and said to the sea, "Peace, be still!" And the wind ceased and there was a great calm.*
> ⁴⁰ *But He said to them,* **"Why are you so fearful?** *How is it that you have no faith?"* NKJV (emphasis mine)

Jesus attributed their fear to their lack of faith. We will either submit to or come *under* one or the other. In regards to new situations, it is always a choice which we will make. Many times, how we decide to respond is based on our previous experiences of God coming through for us.

Jesus always seemed committed to releasing His disciples into the supernatural potential of the faith dimension. He took them through many situations that were possibly places of choosing to believe. One such time, was after feeding the 5,000. He now fed the 4,000 in the hope that the dawning of understanding would come to them. We can all thank God that He is so patient with us in our journey out of fear into faith. He is in fact the author and finisher of our faith (Hebrews 12:2). Whatever page we are on in the book of the pilgrimage into faith that we are on, we can be sure that he will complete the good work that he began in us. (Philippians 1:6) In any case the disciples were not yet thinking about the supernatural potential of faith. We can take heart, later of course when they understood, they turned the world upside down.

> Matthew 16:8-9 ⁸ *But Jesus, being aware of it, said to them,* **"O you of little faith,** *why do you reason among yourselves because you have brought no bread?* ⁹ **"Do you not yet understand,** *or remember the five loaves of the five thousand and how many baskets you took up?* NKJV (emphasis mine)

Jesus pointed to remembering previous things that God had done, as the means by which to reprogram your expectations to a place of faith. We could perhaps summarize our part in releasing God into our situations, and that which He wants to do through us, something such as this;

Unbelief	expects	nothing to happen.
Fear	expects	something bad to happen.
Faith	expects	something positive to happen.

Defining fear under another name

You may know fear in one of its many forms, for example, anxiety, stress, distress, worry, tension, restlessness, dread, apprehension or insecurity. Additionally, we might add in hopelessness, helplessness, doubt or unbelief. They are forms of fear because they do not include the presence, power or willingness of God to resolve whatever we are confronted with.

To summarize fear, we could define it as; *An expectation of a negative outcome.*

I was doing some study quite a few years ago on what different people had to say about fear. Some books cited the existence of over 5,000 known fears. I wondered how I might manage to remember all of these fears. A thought came into my mind; *fear is whatever you are afraid of!* Hardly a blinding revelation, but nonetheless it resolved the issue once and for all for me. When we are ministering to others or even examining our own selves, it is not necessary to work through a list, simply identify what it is that the person is afraid of.

Good fear

We use the term *a universal emotion*, as being a predictable feeling or response that can be distorted by the devil as a consequence of the fall. God gave us fear as a protective instinct. As a result, we don't normally play on highways or near cliffs. We don't as a rule, kiss snakes on the lips, this is simply not smart.

I am not sure of the origins, but I recall the story of a Pastor who was visiting town and decided to drop in on a member of his congregation. When he arrived, even though the door was not locked nobody responded to his knocking. He amused himself by leaving a note on the door which he considered was very clever.

> *Revelation 3:20 "Behold, I stand at the door and knock." NKJV*

On Sunday, after the service, one of the deacons approached the minister with an envelope that had been addressed to him and which was found in the offerings.

> *Genesis 3:10 "I heard you in the garden, and I was afraid because I was naked; so I hid." NIV*

We can say that there is *good, wise* God-given fear that protects us. This includes the fear of God which helps to protect us from negative outcomes. The distorted version of fear deceives us that we need to protect ourselves, when it is in fact not necessary or beneficial. It is the fear of things that we are not meant to fear, or times when we can exercise faith to displace fear, that I am talking about.

Fear began in the garden, where man no longer believed that God had their best interests at heart, and was keeping things from him. In essence they doubted that He was good and really loved them. This was unbelief, or probably more aptly, wrong belief which is the basis of all of our anxieties. As a result, as we understand and receive God's love and acceptance both in our minds and hearts, we find ourselves being freed from our many fears. I have sometimes asked for a show of hands in congregations where we are ministering, of people who have no fear at all. As yet I have not seen a hand raised anywhere.

> *1 John 4:18-19 18 "There is no fear in love; but perfect love casts out fear, because fear involves torment. But he who fears has not been made perfect in love. 19 We love Him because He first loved us." NKJV*

Equally we could say that the antithesis or natural enemy of fear, faith, also proceeds from believing that there is no longer any need to expect negative outcomes for us. This knowledge of His love for us, both mind and heart, receives that God has shown His love first by redeeming us and paying the penalty for our transgressions.

 LESSON
God gave us fear for our protection, as with everything else that God created, the devil seeks to distort it and destroy us through it.

Fear as faith in reverse

I recall a fine sounding worldview that goes something such as: *Hope for the best, expect the worst, and take what comes.* Thinking such as this proposes that we really have no input into our destinies and outcomes. It denies or discounts interaction and results proceeding from the abilities of God, or submitting to satanic spiritual powers.

Let us contrast Job with Daniel's friends, Shadrach, Meshach and Abednego. In the case of Job, everything was going well. He was highly regarded, wealthy, healthy, and had, by all appearances, a good family. Then everything around him began to fall apart. To what did he attribute and note as a precursor to these happenings?

> *Job 3:25 "What I feared has come upon me; what I dreaded has happened to me." NIV*

In contrast, we see Shadrach, Meshach and Abednego, and everything was not going well. However, they still refused to bow down to anyone or anything other than God. They refused to fear, and chose to put themselves under God's ability in faith regardless of the outcome. This took them out from under the potential outcome that Satan would have had for them, and put them under the supernatural power and provision of God.

> *Daniel 3:17-18 ¹⁷ "If we are thrown into the blazing furnace, the God we serve is able to save us from it, and he will rescue us from your hand, O king. ¹⁸ But even if he does not, we want you to know, O king, that we will not serve your gods or worship the image of gold you have set up." NIV*

The outcome of their faith decision, and choosing to refuse fear in their circumstance, was finding the Lord in their trial with them, and the final result being them having favor and witness with their oppressors. Notably, they were not spared from the trial but were triumphant in the midst of it as a result of their choice.

> *Daniel 3:25 He said, "Look! I see four men walking around in the fire, unbound and unharmed, and the fourth looks like a son of the gods." NIV*

I was in Nigeria a number of years ago and there was a lady who was directing witchcraft type stares at me in order to create an opening through fear in me. I remember thinking, not arrogantly, but confidently; *lady, do you think I am going to submit to fear from you when God is for me!* Later in a church service, she was delivered by the local minister of the spirit associated with her practices.

I will spare you the whole story of how I ended up in a first-class seat on the way to England at one time, but I did. Seated beside me was a doctor who was calmly reading a book. As I looked out from my high window on this 747 my attention was drawn to how the engine was wobbling around on the wing. For a moment I felt anxious, until it occurred to me what was happening. I inwardly made the statement; *I like flying, go and find someone else to bother!* Within seconds the doctor that I was sitting with suddenly became very agitated and left his seat and went out and I assume vomited. My guess is that there was someone in the aircraft quite close to us with fear issues that were of a demonic nature, and this spiritual dynamic was reaching out trying to impact us. As we go through life we are challenged with situations where we need to make faith choices and refuse to submit to the pressures of the enemy.

 LESSON
Whatever we submit to has power over us to bring about an outcome, even if we submit through deception rather than willful choice. Truth then is our best defense.

> **Note:** These are rare isolated incidences to illustrate how to respond to our presenting circumstances out of our understanding of Biblical perspective. 99.9% of my fears have been *historically rooted* which I will explain in a moment.

Programming

It takes only the briefest examination to see that the devil is busily programming the world with fear via media. Horror movies, violence, end of the world films, plane crashes, disasters, and so on litter our screens. Shows where people are cut up to be examined, medical series, and so on abound. Those who have time to view television or other media are inundated with fearful images and themes. Personally, I fly too often to be interested in spoiling my journeys by watching air crash investigations or the like. We are filled with the possibilities of *negative outcomes* daily, ranging from global warming to a world financial crisis. This may have more impact than you realize.

I recall reading conclusions from researcher Brandon S. Centerwall who was looking at the effects of television on programming. He discovered that homicide rates in the U.S., where gun laws are comparatively loose, from the time that they had television in 1945 through to 1974, increased 93%. As a reference, they also looked at Canada who had very strict gun laws and had television over the same period of time, and saw almost the same rise of 92%. South Africa did not have television until the early 1970s, and so over the same period homicides went down 7%. After 1975 with the introduction of television, their rates went up 130%. We can reasonably conclude that it was the programming in behavior of the human soul through media that produced the changes and not the access to guns.

Some time ago, before I became full time in ministry, I worked part time to help support us. I met with a client at one time and upon enquiry as to how his previous day had been, he responded with; *Terrible thanks, I was admitted to hospital with panic attacks!* I felt prompted to ask him if he viewed horror movies. When he responded *no.* I thought I had missed it. Then he followed on with the comment; *I used to, I used to watch a lot.* Indeed, we need to be very careful about what we fill up on, and are exposed to, as the seed will bring its harvest.

 LESSON
The law of sowing and reaping applies with fear. We need to be very careful what we expose ourselves to, and fill up on.

Setting the 'default position' of faith

It seems reasonably obvious that God did not give us or intend for us to be subject to a spirit of fear. We must realize that Satan is the instigator of bringing us into the bondage of fear. This invisible enemy will be seeking to bring to pass the object of our fear as we accept and submit to his plan for negative outcomes for us. Moving from fear to faith, as far as how we think in our minds is often a progressive journey as we hear from the counsel of God instructions such as; *Do NOT worry about your life, what you will eat, tomorrow,* and so on. *Do NOT be anxious. Cast ALL your anxiety on Him.* (Matthew 6:25-34; Philippians 4:6; 1 Peter 5:7, NIV). If God says do not then I do not see another way to live other than His perfect order.

> *Joshua 1:9 "Have I not commanded you? Be strong and of good courage; do not be afraid, nor be dismayed, for the LORD your God is with you wherever you go." NKJV*

Joshua was going to be confronted with many potential opportunities to worry and fear negative outcomes. In all five times through the book of Joshua he was instructed to be strong and make the choice to be courageous. Repetition makes a deep impact on our memory. When it is reinforced with decisions to obey and make this our *default response*, it becomes a part of our thinking and being.

In Australia we have a lot of bushfires. A study on resident's responses to these fires showed that those who meditated and rehearsed their fire escape plans, acted out accordingly when the stressful challenges came. Those who had no plan of how to respond tended to be overwhelmed and panicked, at times resulting in their deaths. It has been well said that fear and faith are equal in that they both expect an outcome. It becomes vital as to whether we are under Satan's deception and responding to *perceived fear*, as he gives us his perspective on potentially negative events, or faith, allowing God to produce His outcomes.

Remember fear exists because we have a *negative expectation* in regards to God's attitude towards us, or our worthiness to receive from Him which relates to our next area, *historical fear*. Every time that we expect or entertain a negative outcome, we are submitting to a spiritual power that is challenging God's word and nature, just as it happened in the Garden of Eden.

Perhaps the first ever fear was, fear of missing out, based on the tree of the knowledge of good and evil. Today the fear of missing out is called the *new* phenomenon abbreviated as FOMO. It is related to people addicted to media who cannot go for very long without checking their media for fear of missing out on the latest post etc.

LESSON
Magnifying the Lord, and His power, love and abilities towards us is for our good, not His vanity. It doesn't matter how big we make Him in our lives, He is always many times greater than what we could imagine. Magnifying Him in our meditations grows our faith, and makes the choice to trust Him more obvious and eventually automatic.

Renewing our 'minds' in regards to fear

If we do not live progressively in the counsel of scripture in regards to dealing with fear, there is a strong chance of you ending up with what we term a *fear profile*, where your practiced fear thinking becomes a permanent part of you; your default position. We need to discipline ourselves, filling our minds with the instructions of scripture in terms of how to deal with *circumstantial fear*.

The bottom line is that God is *the power* and he is right behind His word to perform it. The devil, on the other hand, is a created being who is limited to creating scenarios and perceptions to deceive you into submitting to fear. In scripture, there is usually an antidote to fear along with the acknowledgement of the pressure of fear to impact us. There are examples of declarations that we can make to reinforce our decisions, and to make faith our default position and automatic response. I will list a few examples for your consideration;

> *Proverbs 29:25 "The fear of man brings a snare, But whoever trusts in the LORD shall be safe." NKJV*

> *Isaiah 26:3 "You will keep him in perfect peace, Whose mind is stayed on You, Because he trusts in You." NKJV*

Psalm 56:3 "Whenever I am afraid, I will trust in You. 4 In God (I will praise His word), In God I have put my trust; I will not fear. What can flesh do to me?" NKJV

Psalm 118:6 "The LORD is on my side; I will not fear. What can man do to me?" NKJV

Romans 8:31-32 ³¹ What, then, shall we say in response to this? If God is for us, who can be against us? ³² He who did not spare his own Son, but gave him up for us all--how will he not also, along with him, graciously give us all things? NIV

Effects of fear

Spiritually   Robs us of our faith, therefore removing our power and potential.
Mentally   Confusion, mind racing, trying to solve the problem.
Emotionally   Takes our peace, torments, feels bad.
Physically   Many negative effects on the body and health.
Fruitfulness   Makes us unfruitful, binds us and stops us walking into our *promised land* of abundant life and limits that which God can use us for.

The problem with us accepting fear as a reasonable response, is that in order to do so we have to downsize God and His love and power to match our beliefs. We have to believe that He is not in control, cannot protect or provide for us, or does not really love or care about us. In that instance, we have to re-define fear in our lives as doubt and unbelief.

We often think of fear as being adrenaline releasing heart pumping anxiety of some kind, but many times it is low grade in the form of daily stress, worry or anxiousness. This every present kind of fear is usually emanating from *heart beliefs* that we hold from sources located in our history.

Study 2: Historical fear

We have just spent a considerable amount of time on examining the instructions of scripture in regards to how we should deal with present tense or potential future fear *circumstances* that we may encounter. However, the vast majority of fear projects from beliefs we hold which we have already learnt in *historical* negative events, or fearful environments in the past. Even if we are presented with a potentially anxious situation in the present which does not have precedence, if we still hold unresolved *fear beliefs* from the past, we will automatically have expectations of a negative outcome by interpreting the possibilities of the event based on our previously existing beliefs. As a result, virtually all people who come for ministry presenting with fear and anxiety issues need to be set free from the beliefs that they have learnt from past experiences.

We have two types of fear, being circumstantial or historical in nature. We also have two kinds of fear beliefs. As we have detailed in the *Truth Encounters* section, we can hold beliefs that come from *situations* that relate to the events where we learn them, and also beliefs that relate to our *identity*. These beliefs are also marked and distinct in the area of fear.

Fear from Situational beliefs

Phobic type fear, or phobias, where people have specific fears tend to fit into this category. (*Phobos* is the Greek word from which fear is translated in the New Testament). For example, a person may present with a fear of tight spaces or elevators. As you have them focus on their fear, you are looking for a memory that holds matching feelings or circumstances as with those that they are currently experiencing. Their fear of tight spaces is not going to be to do with their identity, who they are, or whether they are good enough. We might ask them a question such as; *What is it that you are afraid of happening in the enclosed space?*

They could perhaps respond with something such as; *I will be trapped and I won't be able to get away.* I would then enquire as to what will happen if they can't get away. You may get for example a response such as; *I won't be able to breathe, and if I can't breathe, I will die.*

These beliefs can, many times, be established before going to the memory, or later in the memory examining the matching feelings. I would ask them to really embrace the feeling and ask them if there is *a historical place* where they felt exactly like this. That is, they are trapped, can't get away, can't breathe, and as a consequence in the memory, they believe that they will die. This is the *actual belief producing the fear*, in this case, that *they are going to die.*

This could have come from a situation such as the story we related in an earlier chapter where a boy gets hold of the football in a game, and then has several heavy guys on top of him pressing the football into his chest. It is a matching set of circumstances to potentially being in an elevator or on an aircraft for instance. You could be trapped, not in control of the situation, and in the end as a consequence you could die. Mostly anxiety attacks or panic attacks come from these underlying beliefs. We see people set free from these attacks as the subsurface beliefs are identified and dealt with.

In the case of our footballer, once we have identified the belief producing the emotion and the source of the thoughts with the matching circumstances, we ask the Lord for His truth. We tend to deeply encode the belief in the intense moment. The Lord may say something such as; *I didn't let you die; it was just a moment and you were free; I will always watch over you*, or some other kind of freeing truth. God is very creative in how He sets the captives free.

At times there may be a spirit attached to the fear. If that is the case you will become aware of the probability by the intensity of the fear. Don't make casting out demons a part of *your method* in dealing with these fears. If there is a spirit there, it may simply leave when the truth sets them free. Do be aware of the possibility. I never go into ministry thinking about demons, looking for them, or expecting that deliverance from them will be a part of the ministry. To me it would be like going shopping and expecting every time that you were out that you would have to deal with somebody who was going to be rude to you. I just go out to get what I am wanting, and at times a person becomes involved that I have to deal with who, for instance, is trying to take my parking space and prevent me from getting where I want to go.

In the case of ministry, the problem is still the problem, and that is the belief producing the negative emotion. We continue to go after the belief and if there is an evil spirit involved powering up the fear response, we simply tell it to go in the name of Jesus. Think of it as shooing away a fly while you are trying to cook a barbeque. A spirit is only as big as you make it in your thinking. Either you believe that the Bible is true and you have complete authority over them in Jesus name or not. If you believe that Jesus' is the name above all names you will have no problems. I will explain more on this is section four.

We can summarize dealing with these kinds of fears by saying that we are simply looking for a *situation* where the belief/s were taken in. If you recall, we talked about the *Amygdala* area of the brain which is reportedly considered to be the fear centre. When a negative incidence occurs, it responds with something such as, *you better make a good memory of that so that we can watch for it and prevent it from happening again!'*

Some people say that fear is;

False **E**vidence **A**ppearing **R**eal

This is true to a large degree in that fear is usually a projection towards something that *might happen* based on previous experience, rather than something that definitely will happen. The World may well end, but we actually don't have much to do with when that could happen. Certainly, fear will not prevent it from happening or change the time of that possible occurrence by one second.

Note: There are times when there is a generational fear that has come through practices such as freemasonry or witchcraft curses. This comes through the sins of the ancestors who have been submitted and involved in ungodly practices further up the family line. For example, with freemasonry there could be something such as a fear of being buried alive. Usually telling the spirit behind that to go will greatly lesson the fear, although there may be beliefs involved as well.

Why would you investigate if freemasonry or other possible sources are present? Because there are no memories or known prenatal events that connect with the fear.

Fear from Identity beliefs

As you understand by now, what we term *identity beliefs* relates to who you are, how you are, and what you consider to be true about your *'self.'* I will not go into a lot of detail here because we have already detailed these in the preceding studies; these are the sources of negative *self-beliefs* which we may now fear being reinforced. These project from incidences producing rejection, inferiority, injustice, insecurity, abuse and so on. I will suggest a few common beliefs that people may hold as a result of being exposed to these negative influences; *I'm weak, stupid, inferior, can't do it, not as good as others, not wanted, don't belong, am not worth caring about, am a nothing, not important* etc.

Once life has programmed these negative inner thoughts into you, you now fear that they will be proven to be true. You may fear that people will discover these *supposed* weaknesses in your person. Additionally, you may fear that people will not want you, or will think poorly of you because of these *perceived* shortcomings. For example, if you believe that you are a failure and cannot meet people's expectations, you will fear disappointing people and not being able to do those things that they require. The freedom from the fear regarding these beliefs about yourself comes once you no longer hold them as being true about you.

Situation or phobic beliefs will trigger if you are suddenly confronted with a stressor that you cannot avoid. Many people control their environments so that this will not happen. If you are afraid to drive in the city you will possibly catch the train and as a result have no anxiety when you go to town. However, *identity-based fears* are hard to avoid because they are often ever present in your dealings with other human beings. In my opinion and experience, these *identity-based anxieties* are usually the fear, stress or anxiety beliefs that are mostly implicated in disease.

Two categories of fear

At the time that I was pondering on the long lists of fears that were offered to us, I came to the conclusion that generally all fears seemingly fall broadly under 2 categories.

Fear of harm

This would obviously relate to being hurt or abused physically or in some other harmful way and would include anxieties projecting from accidents and traumas. It could also take in situations such as fear of no protection or no provision or even lack of finances. These would all mean that some kind of harm to your state of being would be the result. Fear of being out of control may stem from places where you were out of control and some kind of hurt was the result.

Fear of rejection

The other broad category I would consider many fears to come from is fear of rejection. Under this we will find such subtitles as *Fear of man, fear of failure,* and *fear of embarrassment* etc.

Why would you fear man?
>He may not accept you for who you are.

What will happen if you fail?
>People will reject your efforts and consequently you!

Why would you be embarrassed to begin with?
>This is because some kind of weakness or supposed inferiority has been exposed with the expectation that people will reject you because of it.

In our minds:
>We *know* that we should not even care about the 'praises of men.'
>We *know* that being accepted and loved by God is not conditioned to our performance, abilities or success in man's eyes.
>We *know* that God will be pleased by our faith, in not submitting to fear but rather trusting Him in everything, and trusting Him and stepping out in service.

However, *knowing this* in our minds and wanting to hold these attitudes and produce corresponding actions does not remove *the heart beliefs* that oppose our freedom. We really do need God to set us free to be all that we can be for His glory. I don't find people who want fear or who don't want to be free to serve the Lord. Most hate it, and long to be free. It is not however, a matter of merely changing your thinking or reading books and becoming experts on fear. I have not seen anyone set free that way. It is the truth at *heart level* that makes you free.

>Romans 7:15 *"For what I am doing, I do not understand. For what I will to do, that I do not practice; but what I hate, that I do."* NKJV

Physical manifestations of fear

Earlier in these writings, I described some physical outworking of fear problems in the body such as allergic reactions, skin problems, asthma and so on. I will not go into further detail here, only to say that these problems are evidence of the spiritual issue of fear working out in the body via the beliefs and emotions, and then finally producing a physical manifestation in the physiological balance of the afflicted person.

I was working in *Truth Encounters* with a young lady one night and as we moved into her anxiety-based beliefs she broke out all over with little lumps. Initially I thought it must have been because earlier in the day she had been at the river with friends, and there are a lot of mosquitoes there and she must have been repeatedly bitten. As we talked about the lumps it became apparent that it was hives resulting from touching into the places of anxiety that she had in her memories. The Bible describes us as doors and gates. Both God and Satan are looking for an expression from the spiritual realm into the natural realm through what we believe. Our thoughts, decisions, actions and reactions make an opening to the spirit world. This young lady's case was a demonstration of a spiritual/emotional malady having expression in the physical realm.

> Psalm 24:7 *"Lift up your heads, O you gates! And be lifted up, you everlasting doors! And the King of glory shall come in." NKJV*

Wholeness in our souls, and consequently our bodies, is an expression of the Spirit of God having worked in us.

> 3 John 1:2 *"Beloved, I pray that you may prosper in all things and be in health, just as your soul prospers." NKJV*

Sample ministry: Situational or phobic fear

Me: "What can we help you with today?"

Fred: "Well I have a fear of flying."

Me: "So what are you afraid might happen when you get on an aircraft?"

Fred: Ponders "I feel as though I will be out of control"

Me: "I want you to focus on that thought and the feeling that goes with it and see if you remember a time in your life where you felt just like that."

Fred: "I remember being pushed down a steep hill in a little cart we had made. The big kids put me in and sent the cart racing down the hill towards the trees."

Me: "What did you believe might happen while you were afraid?"

Fred: "I guess I felt that I was going to get hurt and nobody could stop it happening. I was terrified!"

Me: "Let's hold that belief up to the Lord that 'nobody can stop what's going to happen, and I will get hurt.'" (Prayer asking the Lord to bring His truth)

Fred: "I just remembered that actually one of the big kids ran after me and eventually did stop the cart before it hit the trees."

Me: "So what does that mean to you?"

Fred: "Well it means that God will always find a way to protect me. He is always in control."

Me: "So think about flying now, are you still afraid of being out of control?"

Fred: Pauses "No. I am still a bit fearful though it is nowhere near as much!"

Me: "Alright focus on the residual fear and see if you can work out what you are afraid of."

Fred: "I have been on a plane before and it felt like there was nothing solid underneath me….it was a scary feeling."

Me: "Okay, I want you to concentrate on the anxious belief that there is nothing solid underneath you." "Lord, would you help Fred to connect with a place where he felt just like that before?"

Fred: "As soon as you said that I remembered being on a cliff edge when we were kids and it caved in underneath me. I slid down the face of it and into the river."

Me: "So you felt as if there was nothing solid under you? And what was the consequence or fear expectation about that situation?"

Fred: "I thought that I was going to die!"

Me: "Alright, I just want for you to embrace that anxiety and belief in that memory that because there is nothing solid under you, you will die."

Fred: Pauses "Do you know, that is just not true. What came to mind was the scripture that talks about the circle of the Earth. It's just hung out there in space with nothing under it just because God put it there and supports it, nothing under it, but still suspended."

Me: "So if you think about there being nothing solid under you on a plane how do you feel about it now?"

Fred: "You know it's really okay….!"

Me: "How do you feel about flying now Fred?"

Fred: "Do you know, it's weird but I think that I am a bit excited!"

Perhaps we might say a prayer thanking the Lord or certainly make a comment about how amazing our God is in setting us free and acknowledging Him as being the one who has done the freeing. Either way, God is glorified as He fulfills His promise and the session closes.

Sample ministry: Identity belief-based fear

Me: "What seems to be the problem?"

Fred: "I have been asked to do communion in church next Sunday, but I am petrified and haven't been able to sleep!"

Me: "I want you to imagine yourself up there in front of all those people. As you feel that anxiety I would like you to examine it and try to work out exactly what it is that you are afraid might happen."

Fred: Pause "I am afraid that I might not be able to do it properly."

Me: "I would like you to feel that anxiety about not doing it properly, and as you do let your mind connect you with a place that held those feelings. It will be somewhere where you actually couldn't do what was expected."

Fred: Ponders "I remember in school when I was about 7 years old. The teacher wanted me to write some cursive text on the blackboard, and I wrote it back the front. The teacher made a big fuss over it making fun of me in front of the whole class and I recall being incredibly embarrassed."

Me: "As a result of not being able to do it, and the intense embarrassing moment in front of the class, what conclusion about yourself did you come to?"

Fred: Pause, thoughtful "I'm dumb. I must be dumb because I could not do it right."

Me: "As you feel that embarrassment and the belief that you are 'dumb' because you could not do it, let us ask the Lord what the real truth is."

Prayer: "Lord Fred things that he is dumb because he could not do the cursive writing on the board. What do you want him to know about that situation?"

Fred: "Well, I didn't hear any thoughts. But I just sort of understood that none of us had actually been taught cursive yet. And the teacher liked to mock us and make fun of us. She sort of deliberately put me in that position to make sport of me."

Me: "So are you dumb because you could not do it?"

Fred: "No, the truth is that none of us could yet. I am feeling that I was alright, there is nothing wrong with me, but I think that the teacher had some issues. I forgive her."

Me: "Picture yourself doing communion on Sunday, how do you feel about messing it up now?"

Fred: "I actually feel fine about it; I will work out how to do it as best I can and really everything doesn't have to be perfect. After all, we are all family."

> **Note:** A situation such as public speaking typically may evoke a response from more than one historically learnt fear producing belief. As each one is ministered to the intensity of the anxiety normally goes down. If you just process the beliefs one by one eventually you will achieve peace. It is of course normal to be a little nervous if it is a new situation.

UNIT EIGHT

Ungodly Control and Insecurity

Study 1: Godly control versus ungodly control

Clearly God wants His Kingdom run in an orderly way, not out of control but in an organized fashion, under instituted authority. This godly control of course is meted out in the right spirit and needs to be appropriate. We could say that we are to be responsible and have authority over certain areas, beginning with our own behavior. For example, Adam was to be responsible for the garden and indeed the subduing of the Earth. He was given the list of instructions before Eve was created, so it fell to him to cover and be responsible for how she responded to the temptation. Instead of eating of the fruit he should have made some kind of statement such as; *God told us not to eat of that tree and so I am not touching it. Can I recommend that you don't eat it either and that you don't talk to snakes anymore?*

In 1 Kings chapter 21 we see King Ahab being too weak to appropriately execute his authority. The result was that his wife Jezebel presumed authority and control, and manipulated the outcome of the situation. To swing the pendulum all the way back past centre the other way, many nations have men dominated societies. Christians in these societies often use the Bible to strengthen their case of their wives being treated as second class citizens who must submit to them. This is actually a manifestation of a controlling spirit. The man's responsibility, in terms of how he sets a Biblical Holy Spirit led environment in the relationship, is the only part that he needs to worry about as an act of his free will. He cannot reasonably expect his wife to respond to him by doing her part, if he, as the covering, and the stronger member does not provide for her that which she needs.

> *Ephesians 5:25-29* ²⁵ *"Husbands, love your wives, just as Christ also loved the church and gave Himself for her,* ²⁶ *that He might sanctify and cleanse her with the washing of water by the word,* ²⁷ *that He might present her to Himself a glorious church, not having spot or wrinkle or any such thing, but that she should be holy and without blemish.* ²⁸ *So husbands ought to love their own wives as their own bodies; he who loves his wife loves himself.* ²⁹ *For no one ever hated his own flesh, but nourishes and cherishes it, just as the Lord does the church." NKJV*

It is not the man's role to force or manipulate the woman to submit to him. His part is only, by 'his own' free will and choice, to fulfill God's intentions for him in the relationship. The woman in turn has her instructions in the Bible on how she should respond to his godly attitudes and provisions for her. When a man is insisting on 'lordship' over his wife and demands total subservience he is looking to be her 'god.' This is a tendency that was picked up in the garden where man was tempted to raise himself up in pride over others, as did the tempter, Satan.

And then be like God, which means everyone serves you and your purposes because you have now become the central being. In order to do this, you will have to treat your wife as an inferior being that God created, which she certainly is not!

> Genesis 3:5 *"For God knows that in the day you eat of it your eyes will be opened, and **you will be like God**, knowing good and evil." NKJV (emphasis mine)*

Although the Bible describes the woman as the weaker member [10], it also describes her as a helpmate comparable. If she is comparable, she is not inferior in the least. Clearly, she is weaker physically, and emotionally her hormonal state is up and down throughout her monthly cycles, whereas a mans is constant. She is the other half of God's perfect picture for us, together complementing each other with altogether different attributes and abilities. If we go into a church, for example, my wife can remember everything in the room, whereas I have usually only noted where the door is so that we can get out again when it is time.

> Galatians 3:28 *There is neither Jew nor Greek, there is neither slave nor free, there is neither male nor female; for you are all one in Christ Jesus. NKJV*

Women in general are more spiritually and emotionally open than men and will often pick something up intuitively in God more quickly than the gentlemen. However, along with this increased openness comes the potential for deception by other spiritual entities, which is well evidenced with the story of Eve. God has created man as more cognitively based needing to apply logic and reasoning, weighing things up before he is prepared to receive them. Because of this I always value my wife's input and insight in all matters.

> 1 Corinthians 11:10-11 [10] *"For this reason the woman ought to have a symbol of authority on her head, **because of the angels**. [11] Nevertheless, neither is man independent of woman, nor woman independent of man, in the Lord." NKJV (emphasis mine)*

When God first called us to a deeper walk with Him my wife did not respect me and was quite rebellious. (I might point out that much of this was related to unresolved issues from her past!). Let me say though, at that time I was not particularly respectable and I needed to get into God's order myself! I had to learn how to appropriately deal with her and my family according to the Word of God. As I did that, over the years we naturally fell into our Biblical roles. But it began with me, as the covering, conforming to the Word of God before this could happen.

Still today I do not make my wife do anything. I respect her and her freewill and she can choose to follow me as I follow Christ or not, but I certainly would not expect her to submit to controlling attitudes towards her. I understand that just as Christ is the initiator of the ways of God to His bride, the Church, I am to be the initiator in setting the spiritual environment in the home. In fact, the Apostle Paul pointed out that the whole marriage picture was given to us so that we would understand the relationship of Christ and His bride.

> Ephesians 5:31-32 [31] *"For this reason a man shall leave his father and mother and be joined to his wife, and the two shall become one flesh."* [32] *This is a great mystery, but I speak concerning Christ and the church. NKJV*

God's plan is that we are one, working together, and this is His plan for a man and his wife and also a picture of Christ working together in harmony with His Church.

---

10 1 Peter 3:7 *Husbands, likewise, dwell with them with understanding, giving honor to the wife, as to the weaker vessel, and as being heirs together of the grace of life, that your prayers may not be hindered (NKJV).*

In our modern western society, we have seen a dramatic role reversal over the years since the Bible was removed as the standard for living in the early 1960s. Men became pleasure seekers who no longer wanted any responsibilities. As they increasingly abdicated their responsibility to being in long term relationship, and be committed to their wives, the spouses in turn became less and less secure about being looked after, provided for and protected. Whenever this is the case something rises in an individual with some kind of inner decision such as this; *If he is not looking after me/us, I better take over and look after myself and the family!* This understandable response has led increasingly to a role reversal in the home where the woman is the head of the house. It has been going on for so long now that it is almost a cultural norm.

We cannot blame the women at all; it is the failure of the men to fulfill their role, as with Adam, that has led to the problem. This is not to say that the man is to be domineering. Adams role was to hold up the standards and words of God, not to force Eve to do anything. She had free will as well, but if Adam properly set the climate of care, love, provision and protection for his wife, she most likely would have been more than content to work with him in his pursuit of God's will.

Some cultures now have a high percentage of households where the wife is leading. In fact, in a recent national election in Australia, as I travelled around I noted that on the bill boards for the various electorates almost all of the candidates were women. Whether that was the case in every area of the nation or not I could not say, but I was amazed to see perhaps one male out of every 8 or 10 voting options.

In 1 Kings chapter 21 we see King Ahab being too weak to appropriately execute his authority. The result was that his wife Jezebel presumed authority and control, and manipulated the outcome of the situation.

AREAS OF GODLY CONTROL

Before we move on, let us briefly detail some areas that God wants us to be responsible for and have control over.

1. Man over his family.

This is not controlling your wife, as she is already at the age of choice, but is more in exercising fair and godly authority over children in a decreasing manner as they grow up and learn how to control themselves.

2. Pastors and leaders in Churches.

God wants His churches run decently and in order. This does not mean that a Pastor or leader can control his congregation; it means that he instigates God's order and sets the environment as loving, accepting, gracious and acknowledging free will and choice. Authority into people's lives is given by them and not taken from them. People either choose to submit to you as they learn to trust your love and motives or not. Many soulish people who have not read a Bible or have chosen to not obey it will remain carnal, and as in the garden will want the limits thrown off. They will be resistant to anyone suggesting to them what they could do.

This is their free will choice and they can deal with God over it. But it does not mean that they can run amok or that in any way we compromise the standards of God for them. The old saying is that people *vote with their feet*, meaning that if they are self-willed, they will take themselves in and out of church. We just need to respect them in that, but not let them get out of order in services. If they have come into a church they have come under the rules and standards of that church as with any other institution.

There are rare occasions where it is appropriate and godly to control adult people and override their free will and choice. Some instances that I can suggest are; drug addicts, violent people or criminals and people with mental illness. These people have no resistance to spiritual forces manipulating their lives and need help to control themselves.

> Proverbs 25:28 *"Like a city whose walls are broken down is a man who lacks self-control." NIV*

Under normal circumstances God does not control anyone, and respects free will and choice, and so as His children, should we.

LESSON

Evidently God gave all of His creation free will and choice, including the angels. We do not have the right to consider ourselves greater than Him, and seek to take away that which He has given.

Study 2: Ungodly control from insecurity

It was God's intention for mankind to grow up secure in identity, feeling protected, and provided for. When Adam and Eve took themselves out from under these attributes that were provided for them by God, they became insecure and fearful. To a large extent they now felt that they had to be *as God* for themselves, fulfilling these needs. It is now inherent in mankind to try to control his environment in order to feel secure. The problem is that this involves imposing your will on others which is never God's plan for how harmony and peace should operate. You will most likely find insecurity tangled up in every war that promises safety or a better future as an outcome.

The root of ungodly control in general terms is *insecurity*. This insecurity causes us to make things happen for our own provisions. It is demonic in the sense that it is a perversion of the will area of your being, imposing your will on others, beyond intended parameters. This is driven by Satan and is not from God.

> 1 John 5:19 *"We know that we are children of God and that the world around us is under* **the power and control** *of the evil one." NLT (emphasis mine)*

This insecurity leads to controlling others in ways that were not intended by God. For example, children who are grown up and are still subject to the will of the parents. They are not allowed to make their own decisions for themselves without the influence of the family. This is quite common in many European cultures where mum continues the mothering long after the children have grown up and become adults. Sometimes if a wife is not loved properly by her husband, she becomes insecure that there will not be anyone who will care about her, so she simply cannot let her children go even after they are mature people.

Insecure children growing up without firm guidelines and boundaries will even as early as 3 or 4 years old or younger, attempt to take control of their perceived needs. They are trying to make sure that they get what they think they need in terms of attention and provision, by using tantrums and other controlling behavior. The truth is that the parent has been given authority to control the child in a godly manner, but in practice the child is now in authority because the adult is submitting to them. Submission giving authority to the one who is submitted to is a principle. Allowing a spirit to be given access to work through these children by their unwitting cooperation, becomes a serious issue.

> Romans 6:16 *"Do you not know that to whom you present yourselves slaves to obey, you are that one's slaves whom you obey."* NKJV

> 2 Peter 2:19b *" ... for a man is a slave to whatever has mastered him."* NIV

MISUSE OF THE CAPACITY FOR CONTROL

Authority to have some measure of control is linked to responsibility. I could not, for example, walk into a church down the road and begin to tell people what to do. I am not responsible for them and consequently have no authority over them. The same goes for my family and so on. When you see people trying to get others to do things for them, they are exhibiting controlling behavior.

I remember once visiting an event hosted by another church. The hosting Pastor was quite a controlling man who at one point in the service proclaimed; *All the Pastors will now come out and will pray for the people!* It was not what he was doing that was the problem, it was the spirit in which he was doing it. He was imposing his will to make something that he wanted to happen onto everyone, removing their free will and choice.

This was insecurity on his part, that if he requested support, his desires may have been rejected. In the event that you submitted to such a statement you have now just placed yourself under his control and given him authority over you. Let me reiterate the words of the old Jazz song that is a good measure for discerning the spirit behind an action. *It ain't what you do; it's the way how you do it, that's what gets results!* If he had requested; *If there are any Pastors here that would like to come out and pray with people, would you like to do so now?* Then it would have been an entirely different situation, respectful and acknowledging personal sovereignty. I have known churches where people were too afraid to cut their sandwiches without asking the Pastor how it should be done. This is not a healthy, godly situation.

As a Pastor I never tell anyone to do anything. I do not own anyone. I respectfully request if they would be prepared to do this or that and am quite prepared to accept whatever response I receive. People submit to you because they want to, not because they have to. We respond to God as a response to the wonderful way that He treats us, and so it should be with us in relationships. Often people who are *controllers* seem to have used all of their capacity for control on others and consequently lack self-control and their immediate environment is in disarray.

Often controlling people will use the *God told me* or *thus saith the Lord* card to manipulate a situation and have their will carried out. After all who can challenge what God Himself has said! I tend to think that often when people are making these kinds of statements that you are dealing with the *'controlly' spirit* and not the *Holy Spirit*. They are hearing what they want to hear or feel they need to hear, to get what they want or remove their insecurity and thus open themselves up to deception. This will be obvious if the outcome of the use of the Lord's name relates to something that they think should happen.

As I understand it, blasphemy is when you take the Lord's name in vain. This does not necessarily mean swearing, it can mean saying that God said, when He didn't. People need to be more careful than they realize about how they use the Lord's name. Well-meaning mistakes about what we hear will attract grace, but manipulation and imposing your will or what you think should happen on others, attracts nothing but trouble.

In the church environment you may hear prophecies such as; "*Oh my people you are not doing enough, saith the Lord!*" This is most likely proceeding from the spirit of the person who is trying to make something happen that they think should happen. Usually upon examination they are people who have hard and often religious standards towards themselves.

SELF-CONTROL

Listed as a fruit of the Spirit, or evidence that we are cooperating with and giving precedence to the leading of the Holy Spirit, is *self-control*. This is when we are able to discipline ourselves, not to be conformed to the World in some way through some kind of inappropriate *self-indulgence*. As usual, there is a demonic version of this where we make some kind of inner vow and control ourselves in a way that is not in a godly order.

Many years ago, I was at a seminar where we had to list our emotional intensity from 1–10. As I went along, I realized that I was scoring zeros. Initially I thought that I must be very spiritual because I never got, for example, angry. But I began to realize that I never wept, never laughed out loud or never exhibited any emotion at all. I had made an inner vow to suppress or control my emotions, because, I believed as a child that if you laughed too loud or cried, it was not acceptable. *Little children should be seen and not heard* is something that many of us grew up under.

I do not blame my parents for this as it was the cultural norm at the time, however it did have its effect on me. I learnt that Jesus wept, got angry, had joy beyond all of His companions and indeed exhibited a full range of healthy, God given emotions. We can misuse self-control in a way that is the fruit of another spirit.

Note: You never just don't have emotions. If you are holding them back underneath as I was, they will tend to come out in your body or behavior as was the case with myself at that time, and as a result I had a disease. We can safely say, that not having emotions, can be just as big an indicator of *wrong hearts* beliefs and problems as excessive emotions.

IS GOD CONTROLLING?

We are to be 'led' by the Spirit which denotes choice. Jesus began His ministry *led* by the Spirit into the desert and finished it in the garden of Gethsemane, deciding by His own free will and choice, to lay down the easy way in preference to the Father's will. It is perhaps notable that Adam and Eve chose to follow Satan in a garden where everything was going fine, and Jesus to reverse the effects of this chose to suffer to fulfill the Father's desires.

We could state that God is not controlling at all. He instructs us in the way and encourages us and empowers us to fulfill godly choices but does not make us do anything at all. Sometimes it would probably be easier if He did, but He is looking for us to respond to the Love that He initiates and choose Him. Jesus often included words such as; *if, then,* and *but,* which denotes choice. Put another way, He is saying that *if* you choose to walk this way then you can expect this to happen.

John 15:7-8 ⁷**"If** *you abide in Me, and My words abide in you, you will ask what you desire, and **it shall** be done for you.* ⁸ *By this My Father is glorified, that you bear much fruit; so you will be My disciples." NKJV (emphasis mine)*

Matthew 6:15 **"But if** *you do not forgive men their sins, your Father will not forgive your sins. NIV (emphasis mine)*

John 8:31-32 ³¹ *To the Jews who had believed him, Jesus said, "If you hold to my teaching, you are really my disciples.* ³² **Then** *you will know the truth, and the truth will set you free." NIV (emphasis mine)*

We know that Jesus was the perfect representation of the nature of the Father, so was He controlling? Not at all! The following passage helped me a lot in relationships, and also as a young Pastor, in realizing that it was not my job to make anybody do anything. It was simply to teach the way if people were open to hearing, and then offer them whatever help they needed to get there. It would be completely understandable in these following verses, if Jesus had complained to the disciples that He had just invested years in training them and that therefore it is only reasonable that they remain with Him. But instead, He was completely releasing, not in the least bit controlling, and left the decision entirely up to them.

John 6:67-68 ⁶⁷ *Then Jesus said to the twelve, "Do you also want to go away?"* ⁶⁸ *But Simon Peter answered Him, "Lord, to whom shall we go? You have the words of eternal life." NKJV*

LESSON

It is not our job to make anyone do anything. Our mission is to help them understand the ways of God so that they can make the right choices and decisions for themselves. If the ability to do this has been compromised then we have instruction from the Bible to heal them and set them free.

CONTROL EXTREMES AND THE BIG PICTURE

In modern western culture, we see greatly diminished self-control with people being slaves to all kinds of addictions. There is almost an abuse of freedom, with virtually no discipline and few guidelines for general living. It is all about you, what you want, and your rights. As someone has well said, the devil will always give you too little or too much. So as far as how you live, in today's society you can get drunk, have illicit sex, watch pornography, swear publicly, disrespect whoever you like, and in many cases do drugs and nobody pays much attention at all. While personally many people are out of control, at the same time the dark shadow of humanism is coming across our world.

This publication is not meant to touch on controversial subjects but we note that via media, technology and humanism, we are increasingly being controlled in what we may and may not do, and monitored in what we watch and where we go. Rules relating to religious expression are increasingly being imposed with yearly changes. Whilst it is true that *religion* is at the heart of many of the conflicts in our world today, true Christianity is not fundamentally a religion. It is not a set of practices or things that you do to be right with God, it is a relationship with God because you are right with Him through Jesus Christ.

Other more obvious *big picture* controlling ideologies include dictatorships, communism, and controlling religions. We see all of these actively working over cultures across our world today. It is not God's order.

BRANCHES THAT COME FROM UNGODLY CONTROL

1. Manipulation
This could be in the form of kids threatening tantrums, men being physically threatening, wives withholding sex, or people saying that *God said.*

2. Domination
Violence or some kind of abuse is the typical outworking of someone misusing their authority or power.

3. Standards
"You must be how I want you to be and think you should be. You need to do what I want, how I want it or I cannot receive you! You must fit into my plans!"

4. Bitterness and unforgiveness
I will not release you or forgive you for being how you are, or who you are, and not being and doing what I want! This projects rejection because if what you want or do is not good enough then by implication you are unacceptable. That's not fair and so you can expect rebellion as a response to your control.

5. Self-willed; leading to intimidation
If I don't get what I want, get my own way you will pay in some way or I will explode in anger....so look out! (Intimidation)

6. Things have to be a certain way
This could come in the form of perfectionism or obsessive-compulsive behavior which is an extreme form of insecurity and fear compelling you to control details of your life. Things have to be a certain way or there is a fear that something bad will happen. It can be learnt behavior growing up in a household full of fears, or from a controlling environment where there would be some kind of pay out if things were not done according to the will of, for example, a parent with control issues.

Others have grown up not believing that they are cared about and will be looked after. They control those around them to make sure everything is done the right way to meet their needs. The demonic realm certainly can be working in areas of control. In order to identify heart beliefs relating *to insecurity or fear,* the best question that you can ask is; *what will happen if...?* If, for example, you don't check the door over and over, or you don't do things this way or that? It can be a tormenting bondage for many insecure people. If you don't do things how they think things should be done there can be some kind of violent, angry or extreme reaction. Sometimes these people will not trust others to do things for them because they believe that these things MUST be done a certain way.

7. Lack of self-control
We have already mentioned this; it is as if their capacity for self-control is directed outwards in getting others to do things for them, and as a consequence they have little or no self-control or authority over themselves.

8. Tendency to get others to do things for them

Controllers will always be getting others to do things for them. Remember they are insecure, so they are making sure that you care about them because underneath they believe that nobody does. For leaders, often many people are more than willing to help us; it is a good thing if we don't abuse that by getting them to do things that we could easily do ourselves.

9. Blame, fault finding and criticism

They should have done it this way or that way…my way!
They are not good enough! (Usually you make these criticisms because you believe in your heart that in fact you 'are not good enough.' You feel that if you bring them down that you will feel closer to being enough yourself.)

EFFECTS OF UNGODLY CONTROL ON RELATIONSHIPS

We have already discussed the role reversal that is out of God's order for the home that comes as a result of insecurity. We see many couples, Christian couples, in conflict, wrestling backwards and forwards with each other trying to impose their will on each other. This creates instability and an insecure environment in the household which will generationally generate more insecurity down the family line.

Healthy relationships can only exist in the context of free will and choice, where you lay down your right to expect or demand anything from the other. Once you begin to live this way and treat each other this way you will soon find yourselves volunteering and preferring what the other partner wants. In my opinion the best place for sanctification of the will is in the marriage union. I always think that if you won't lay down your wants for your partner then you probably won't for God either. This is an important part of the dying to *self*-process, where life is no longer all about you! When we release people into their own choices about methods, results, and how they want to do things, we are giving them respect and valuing them.

> *Galatians 5:13-15* [13] *You, my brothers, were called to be free. But do not use your freedom to indulge the sinful nature; rather, serve one another in love.* [14] *The entire law is summed up in a single command: "Love your neighbor as yourself."* [15] *If you keep on biting and devouring each other, watch out or you will be destroyed by each other. NIV (emphasis mine)*

While my wife and I were engaged we sold one of our cars to a delightful old lady who took us outside her home and gave us some excellent advice. She pointed up to her roof and made the following comments; *If I threw a rope over my roof and you were one each side of the house trying to pull it off you would have a big struggle and not make much progress. But if you both come around the same side of the house and work together it is as easy as anything!* So, rather than oppose each other contesting for our own will and way, if we lay down our side of the house and give our will to the other without expecting anything in return, then I can tell you from experience and 40+ years of marriage that your life goes from being your worst nightmare to your greatest joy.

> *Luke 6:38 "Give, and it will be given to you: good measure, pressed down, shaken together, and running over will be put into your bosom. For with the same measure that you use, it will be measured back to you." NKJV*

PRACTICAL OUTWORKING OF UNGODLY CONTROL

1. It pushes away the ones that you are **trying to control**. If you are trying to conform somebody else to you, then you are not accepting them for who they are … an individual.

2. It reads as an **unfair projection**. It proposes that they are not good enough as they are and should be something else. It suggests that what they want is worthless, implying that they are nothing.

3. **Love must come by choice**. If you make people do things to show that they care about you it is meaningless, because even if they do your will, in this regard you *know* that you made it happen. It was not something that they did for you just because they wanted to. In this sense a saying that is used in the musical world could be applied; *less is more*. Meaning, sometimes the right thing at the right time is more important than the volume of things done. It is more meaningful if people do less for you of their own accord, than doing a lot that you have compelled them to do.

4. **Controlling God**. Some movements even try to control God. There are extremes of faith where it is taught that if you believe hard enough and long enough that you can get God to give you what you want. Essentially this can be like witchcraft, where you turn God into some kind of vending machine who does your will and becomes your Holy Spirit. Faith principles are for us to receive the promises of God which He initiated and already stated in His word, as that which He has promised to give us. God will not be controlled; you may have to save up for that red sports car yourself.

> *1 John 5:14-15* [14] *"This is the confidence we have in approaching God: that if we ask anything according to his will, he hears us.* [15] *And if we know that he hears us--whatever we ask--we know that we have what we asked of him. NIV (emphasis mine)*

Other people who may have been given everything that they wanted growing up sometimes get angry with God when He does not do the same. You may see resentment and so on towards Him. This is usually rooted in resentment and anger that projects from parents who didn't seem to care about them, and now they believe that God doesn't either if He doesn't supply their *wants*.

5. **Legalistic religions**. There are religions and denominations that demand that you conform to their religious standards for acceptance. They can be very controlling in regards to who you marry, your finances, your spiritual disciplines and so on.

PROBABLE SOURCES OF UNGODLY CONTROL
1. **Insecurity** - as we have detailed in this chapter, the most common reason producing ungodly control are areas in which we don't feel secure.

2. **Modeling** – at times growing up seeing a controlling mother or father can cause us to replicate the behavior, believing that this is simply how you behave and act towards others. As we have previously stated, it is often attached to cultural expectations, and so we see that controlling attitudes can be learnt by osmosis soaking up the environment around us.

3. **Generational issues** - there can be a spiritual element where a weakness or tendency to gravitate towards operating in this manner is present.

WHAT ARE WE LOOKING FOR IN MINISTRY?
Whilst aware of other possibilities, we are primarily looking for *historical insecurity events* matching the current need to control your surroundings. Having noted the fruit of control, you will probably have a much better response if you ask the person if they ever feel a little insecure, as opposed to *telling* them that they are controlling.

ASSOCIATED INNER BELIEFS THAT OVERFLOW FROM THE HEART

1. **Lack of attention** - *nobody cares about me*

2. **Lack of protection** - *I must look after myself*

3. **Abuse** - *I can't trust others to look after my needs, because when I do, I get hurt*

4. **Lack of provision** - *I must get things for myself, nobody really loves me or cares about what I need, so I must get people to provide for me. I must meet my own needs*

5. **Fears** - *I cannot let go of my insecurities and control, what will happen?*

MINISTRY PROTOCOL

1. **Find where the insecurity began**
The womb; (not wanted and therefore not feeling protected or safe?). A life event or theme in the home from early life experiences, osmosis growing up, or the family line.

2. **Deliverance** where applicable, concurrently with healing of the associated beliefs.

3. **Sometimes teaching** as you go with how to be releasing and **hold things loosely**. Some people are not aware of what they are doing, or that it is not God's order. Once you expose the discrepancy and give perspective it leaves them free to decide on their path.

Note: You do not need to remember all of this to minister. It is to help you understand that controlling behavior often flags insecurity beliefs. It is not necessary that you study every detail, just the basic principles.

Sample: Ministry to ungodly control that is presenting from insecurity.

Freda: "My husband says that I am very controlling."
Me: "Give me an example of why he would call you that."
Freda: "Sometimes he gets home later than he should from work. He complains that I am always at him to be on time. He says he feels controlled and can't even stop of at the supermarket on the way home."
Me: "What do you feel will happen if he isn't home on time?"
Freda: Ponders. "Mmmmmm I guess I feel that there will be nobody there for what I need and it's not fair."
Me: "I want you to concentrate on those thoughts that it is not fair that nobody is there for what you need, and see if you can remember another time as early as possible in your life where you felt just like that."
Freda: "As soon as you asked me that, the memory of my first day of school came into my mind. All of the other kids were picked up but my mum didn't arrive for ages."
Me: "As you look at that situation what is the strongest way to describe what you believed as a result of that event?"

Freda: "I guess I believe that I am not important and so nobody is bothering to be there for me. I feel unprotected."

Me: "As you concentrate on that feeling let us see what truth the Lord has for you?"

Prayer: "Lord what would you like Freda to know. She believes that she is not important enough to be there for, she feels unprotected."

Freda: Pause. "It seems like my own thoughts but it seems as if He is saying that I am important to Him, and that He has set His affection on me, and the scripture that He will never leave me nor forsake me has come to my mind."

Me: "Do you still believe that you are not important enough to be there for?"

Freda: "No, I am very important. I also just remembered that my mum had a flat tire and that is why she was late. But I knew that and it didn't seem to fix the problem before."

Me: "That is probably because you took in the belief when you were very upset and emotionally vulnerable. It is what you perceived to be true at the moment of weakness that counts. That conclusion was deeply stored in your heart and as a result it is the inner thought that remained."

"How do you feel about your husband getting home late now?"

Freda: "Fine. I can't believe that it mattered so much to me. It seems a bit ridiculous. He should be able to do some errands if he wants to."

UNIT NINE

Low self-image, Inferiority and Pride

In this Unit we are going to examine the normal fruit associated with the pride tree.

Matthew 12:33b "... for a tree is recognized by its fruit." NIV

Study 1: What is pride?

We could say that pride is fallen confidence. God intended for us to have good self-worth and identity within the context of being satisfied with our own *individual* self. Pride is a condition where we now see ourselves as *above* other people and not equal. It is the imprint that Satan put on mankind tempting them with; *you will be as God. This being your own god* and making your own rules is clearly seen across humanity today. It began with Satan, and we see the five I wills of pride represented in scripture.

Isaiah 14:13 **¹³** *You said* **in your heart,** *"I will* **ascend** *to heaven; I will raise my throne* **above** *the stars of God; I will sit enthroned on the mount of assembly, on* **the utmost heights** *of the sacred mountain.* **¹⁴** *I will ascend* **above** *the tops of the clouds; I will* **make myself** *like the Most High." NIV (emphasis mine)*

This propensity for self-promotion is abundantly evident in the pride profile. We could say that pride is the enemy of success in anything we undertake. God is opposing our being conformed to the likeness of Satan and his nature, and his consequent expression in the Earth through our deception and subsequent co-operation.

James 4:6-7 **⁶** *But he gives us more grace. That is why Scripture says: "God opposes the proud but gives grace to the humble."* **⁷** *Submit yourselves, then, to God. Resist the devil, and he will flee from you. NIV*

Pride would have us have too higher opinion of ourselves, gathering credit or glory for ourselves. It encourages us to believe that we are over or **above** others and to consider ourselves as being superior. This gives us some insight into how Satan engineers it into our lives. It is a deception, and when we believe that we are *inferior* then the solution that he offers is to build an image that we convince ourselves is *superior*. The deception comes as it did with the tree in the Garden of Eden as; *this is what you need, this will make you happy.*

Once we have misinterpreted the situation and received this as being the solution to our inferiority, it leads us to sinful attitudes and practices towards our fellow man. It is the *fallen self-life, old nature* or *'flesh'* exalting itself, as it was with Lucifer placing *self* on a self-made throne. Evidently most people are unaware that they are being influenced by, and hosting, a spiritual nature. It fits well with a performance based, climb the ladder of success society, which promotes achievement as a basis for acceptance and identity.

We would describe it as a *sin of the heart* which appears to be less tolerable to God than *sins and weaknesses in the flesh*. In the following passage, we see a man accepting his human frailty, fleshly weaknesses and sinfulness. Confession means, *say the same as*, and this man is accepting and confessing his shortcomings as measured against the ways of God. This is the basis of forgiveness.

> *Luke 18:10-14* ¹⁰ *"Two men went up to the temple to pray, one a Pharisee and the other a tax collector.* ¹¹ *"The Pharisee stood and prayed thus with himself, 'God, I thank You that I am not like other men; extortioners, unjust, adulterers, or even as this tax collector.* ¹² *'I fast twice a week; I give tithes of all that I possess.'* ¹³ *"And the tax collector, standing afar off, would not so much as raise his eyes to heaven, but beat his breast, saying, 'God, be merciful to me a sinner!'* ¹⁴ *"I tell you, this man went down to his house justified rather than the other; for everyone who exalts himself will be humbled, and he who humbles himself will be exalted." NKJV*

People suffering from beliefs that hold inferiority and low self-image will either give up in self-rejection, and roll over, or gravitate to performance and achievement-based self-worth.

The Bible says that the pride of life is from the world, not from the Father. Remember the fruit of the tree in the garden of Eden was good for making you wise; knowledge puffs up, but love builds up; knowledge can make you look superior, but love will be building up others rather than self.

We have mentioned Peter failing when he denied Jesus, and as a result becoming humble, before God released power through him. It was necessary for Peter to understand his frailty and humanity for him to become humble, with a correct perspective of himself in order for him to be useable. He was then a non-stick Christian who would not let the glory and accolades be attributed to himself. He now knew who he was and made sure that everyone else was aware of his humanity as well, knowing fully that pride was the enemy of revival and harvest. The Bible says that the pride of life is from the world, not from the Father. As illustrated in the following passage, Peter refused to be lifted above anyone else, and made sure that the accolades and glory went to the right place.

> *Acts 3:11-12,16* ¹¹ *"Now as the lame man who was healed held on to Peter and John, all the people ran together to them in the porch which is called Solomon's, greatly amazed.* ¹² *So when Peter saw it, he responded to the people: "Men of Israel, why do you marvel at this? Or why look so intently at us, **as though by our own power or godliness we had made this man walk?** ...* ¹⁶*"And His name, **through faith in His name, has made this man strong**, whom you see and know. Yes, the faith which comes through Him has given him this perfect soundness in the presence of you all." NKJV (emphasis mine)*

Later we see the Apostle Paul making similar statements in Acts chapter 14. These early Christians knew their humanity and weakness, and that God would not let His glory go to another. They knew that they should not be seeking the praises and acknowledgement of man in lifting them *above* others. These men certainly refused to let the glory stick. It was a secret as to why God was able to place His power upon and through them.

> *Acts 14:9-12, 14-15* ⁹ *"This man heard Paul speaking. Paul, observing him intently and seeing that he had faith to be healed,* ¹⁰ *said with a loud voice, "Stand up straight on your feet!" And he leaped and walked.*

*[11] Now when the people saw what Paul had done, they raised their voices, saying in the Lycaonian language, "The gods have come down to us in the likeness of men!" [12] And Barnabas they called Zeus, and Paul, Hermes, because he was the chief speaker. ... [14] But when the apostles Barnabas and Paul heard this, they tore their clothes and ran in among the multitude, crying out. [15] and saying, "Men, why are you doing these things? We also are men with **the same nature as you**." NKJV (emphasis mine)*

Study 2: The fruit, or what will pride look like in behavior and attitudes

Importance

You have to be somebody, you cannot simply be. You have to be important, regarded and valued. Many people and tasks will be beneath you, so as a result of your inferiority and rejection, you are now rejective. In a Christian environment this will probably be manifested as a person who cannot serve nor do small things. It is a breeding ground for *super spirituality* where people are too great in their own eyes to receive from other people and so propose that God talks to them directly. In turn it can be an opening for *false prophecy* where they feel that they always know best about that which God is saying. It will at times be in the form of correcting all of the *lesser* people who aren't doing things right, (according to your standards).

Religiosity also comes into the picture. This happens as people learn all of the spiritual talk and jargon, know more scriptures, listen to more preachers than others etc. to make themselves be greater or above others. We call religion the *try hard* spirit, trying hard to be somebody. Religion declares, *this is what you do to be good enough, this is how you look and what you say!* Religion tries to be good enough by what you do, according to what you think will make you acceptable to man, and possibly be enough to please God.

Very often, as with the Pharisees, it is a man version of what God is supposedly looking for. He wants people who will worship in spirit and truth. This means that they will be very real, as Jesus was on Earth. We don't see Him exhibiting *the religious or hyper spiritual activities* that we see in many churches today. If it doesn't look how Jesus was, I think we can safely discard it. He flew in the face of religious rules and practices, and we don't see Him having special manifestations to be more spiritual than others.

This can also be represented as *masks*, where the person presents as the *mighty anointed* or similar, but at home, off the stage or away from people they are entirely something else. The underlying problem is that they believe that who they *really are* is not good enough and inferior.

Presumption

Have you ever had those people come to visit, who sit down, put their feet up on your furniture, and proceed to change your television channel to what they want to watch? They will probably be overbearing, right about everything, full of their own opinions, arrogant and superior. The *language of the spirit* emanating from their actions and attitudes is something along the lines of; *I am and there is no other!* Have mercy on them. Although they can be annoying remember that usually underneath is a person who has been crushed or neglected, and full of *low self-image*.

In 1 Samuel chapter 15 we see King Saul not fulfilling the instructions of God that he received from Samuel the prophet. He was anointed as King, but not as prophet. He wanted to please the soldiers and be popular. People with these issues will possibly presume to promote themselves to release or anoint people in a church environment, hence promoting themselves over existing authority. In the case of King Saul, Samuel noted that he was once *small in his own eyes*. In other words, his self-promotion and subsequent presumption and rebellion were proceeding from his *low self-image*.

> *1 Samuel 15:17-19* *¹⁷ Samuel said, "Although you were **once small in your own eyes**, did you not become the head of the tribes of Israel? The LORD anointed you king over Israel. ¹⁸ And he sent you on a mission, saying, 'Go and completely destroy those wicked people, the Amalekites; make war on them until you have wiped them out.' ¹⁹ Why did you not obey the LORD? Why did you pounce on the plunder and do evil in the eyes of the LORD?"*
> *NIV (emphasis mine)*

Rebellion against authority often runs closely with pride. This is because authority figures have not provided the identity needed for them to feel that they are sufficient. This is perceived as unjust or unfair and the response is to bypass authority as those in authority are not to be trusted. For Saul, who already suffered with low self-image, there would almost certainly have been *heart beliefs* leading him to this tendency. If he lived now in the dispensation of the Holy Spirit outpouring, he could have easily been set free. In the following verse we see that 'arrogance is like the evil of idolatry.' Let me suggest that this is because arrogance proceeds from the idol that you have made of *self* as a result of low self-image and inferiority.

> *1 Samuel 15:23 "For rebellion is like the sin of divination, and arrogance like the evil of idolatry. Because you have rejected the word of the LORD, he has rejected you as king." NIV (emphasis mine)*

Judgment

These people will often be graceless, harsh, critical and unforgiving towards your shortcomings, imperfections or failures. The hardness and harshness are probably because, at heart level, they have not forgiven themselves for not being up to the mark.

Comparison

We have already mentioned this under the self-rejection heading, but it is a fruit of this tree. I would like to add that when comparison is coupled with low self-image it can lead to self-pity. *Poor me, everyone else is good enough, but I will never be as good as them. I will never be important, worthy or loved. I will never be good enough for love, compliments and attention.* This can be a down side, or depressive side that works in a manic depressive, or as it is now known a bipolar cycle. Swinging from feeling superior as a solution to your perceived inferiority, and then swinging the pendulum back the other way past centre into a depressive state where you feel that you can never be as good as others or be good enough.

Competition

Somehow, we think that if we can climb higher, run faster, gather more money or in some other way prove ourselves then we will feel better about ourselves. I was driving to school to pick my children up years ago, and a lady, who very much carried this whole profile, whizzed past in her car. I found myself accelerating, and then realized that I was being caught up in a *competitive spirit* and so I backed off. These people are often high achievers who will project onto you that you are not enough, don't do enough or have enough. They have arrived and you have not.

Once you are aware that it is *a belief based emotional/spiritual dynamic* that is around them, then you have the option. You can either be a tea bag and soak it all up and respond out of the feelings that it elicits in you; or be a golf ball, which doesn't soak up anything, and can be smacked around and abused quite a bit and remain impervious to its environment without losing its shape at all.

This principle is the same with anything that others are projecting onto you. If it is, however, causing a strong response in you it may be a good opportunity to go *up on the hoist*, so to speak, and get checked over for wrong beliefs or anything out of alignment in yourself.

We have a friend who is a single mother who was constantly wearing out and having to replace the front tires on her car. I suggested that she had someone look a little deeper, and it was found that there was a mechanical problem on her vehicle causing the scrubbed-out tires. Sometimes we do this in the church and just pray well-meaning prayers for each other expecting that we will go better now, when we need to look a little deeper.

The reason that Jesus was so impervious to anything that the devil threw at Him directly or through people, was that He had no wrong beliefs in His heart about Himself or His relationship with the Father. He also understood the ground that gave place to the devil in people that He dealt with that made them agents for the devil to use.

> *John 14:30 "I will no longer talk much with you, for the ruler of this world is coming, and he has nothing in Me." NKJV*

Striving

Trying hard to have the upper hand, being contentious, struggling to be right or regarded, does not promote peace or unity. This possibly shows up in the marriage relationship more than anywhere else. Again, to not have your opinion valued strikes right at the roots of where this most likely all began. Striving may well struggle against the system and rules as well individuals. It is a part of the imprint on fallen man from the garden to want to throw off the rules and limits. This striving is so that our humanity can have a free expression and realization of *self*. This is perhaps nowhere better illustrated in recent times than in the 1960s when the Bible was removed from the schools in the United States.

Without the guidelines regarding enjoying a prosperous life, morality and dealing well with your fellow man, it was not long before people became their *own god*. This meant *'self'* deciding what was right and wrong, and as a result, we saw the emergence of sayings such as; *If it feels good, do it! If it's right for you, it's right. Look out for number one.* Etc.

Many statistics indicate little change for decades up until that time. After the change, for example, violent crime now multiplied more than 6 times by 1990. Divorce rates more than doubled by 1975, while unmarried couples increased by more than 3 times by 1983. Single parent households doubled and premarital sex for teenage girls increased by 3 times by 1990. Pregnancies for unwed girls went up 7 times over the same period with a commensurate increase in abortions. All of this adds up to a lot of unnecessary misery. It really does work better if God is God and we live humbly as the created beings before Him. Again, the attitude can be sourced back to Genesis chapter 3 where Adam and Eve threw off the limits and boundaries. Man is continuing to strive to do this to this day.

Jealousy

Again, King Saul is our example. As we have previously stated, he was once small in his own eyes, or as we would frame it, he suffered from inferiority and low self-image. When David came along, he was exalted by the people. Jealousy occurs when someone else receives what you want. Because of his low self-image, King Saul needed to be praised by men. It ministered to his inner hurt and beliefs to some degree, although clearly it did not bring healing. So, when David received more adulation than him, he burned with jealousy.

> *1 Samuel 18:7-9* [7] *"As they danced, they sang: "Saul has slain his thousands, and David his tens of thousands."* [8] *Saul was very angry; this refrain galled him. "They have credited David with tens of thousands," he thought, "but me with only thousands. What more can he get but the kingdom?"* [9] *And from that time on Saul kept a jealous eye on David." NIV*

This ungodly jealousy gave ground to an evil spirit which promoted a solution to the problem of David's popularity, namely his removal by murder. In today's world, and particularly the church environment this murder will usually come from the tongue by destroying a person's reputation.

> *1 Samuel 18:10-11* [10] *The next day an evil spirit from God came forcefully upon Saul. He was prophesying in his house, while David was playing the harp, as he usually did. Saul had a spear in his hand* [11] *and he hurled it, saying to himself, "I'll pin David to the wall." NIV*

As time went by, we see King Saul relentlessly pursuing David, trying to eradicate him as being the threat to how he is perceived by the people. We can separate out his sinful attitudes and behavior caused by his perceived emotion beliefs and needs, and his true self, which really loved David. I am reminded of the Apostle Paul in Romans chapter 7 where he laments over the fact that his belief-based actions do not match that which he really wants.

> *Romans 7:15 "For what I am doing, I do not understand. For what I will to do, that I do not practice; but what I hate, that I do." NKJV*

Certainly, this double mindedness was evident in King Saul at times; self-conflict evident, having just tried to kill David seemingly now lamenting his own state. Really actually liking or loving David, but jealous and revengeful at the same time because of the shadow that David cast over the perception of his self-image.

> *1 Samuel 24:15-17* [15] *May the LORD be our judge and decide between us. May he consider my cause and uphold it; may he vindicate me by delivering me from your hand."* [16] *When David finished saying this, Saul asked, "Is that your voice, David my son?"* **And he wept aloud**. [17] *"You are more righteous than I," he said. "You have treated me well, but I have treated you badly. NIV (emphasis Mine)*

Note: Many of the presenting symptoms relating to pride issues discussed here were first noted in an excellent study called *Possess the Land* put together by Carroll Thompson from Dallas, Texas, and Published by Carroll Thompson Ministries in 1977.

_{UNIT} # TEN

Rebellion, anger and bitterness

> *2 Thessalonians 2:7 "For the secret power of lawlessness is already at work; but the one who now holds it back will continue to do so till he is taken out of the way." NIV*

Rebellion or lawlessness runs very closely with pride. As we have already seen, Satan as Lucifer' no longer wanted rules. In his proud, self-elevated state he wanted to be above the laws of God and no longer wanted to submit to the authority of God and His commands. God of course would not tolerate this rebellion and Lucifer and those who cooperated with him were cast down to the Earth. He then tempted man to throw off the rules as he had and conform to, or be imprinted with, the likeness of his own behavior.

So, lawlessness or rebellion as we know it is when we won't come under authority and laws, or we set ourselves against authority. Our own will becomes our *god*, subject only to self, and we are no longer prepared to have rules and limits. I will re quote the passage from 1 Samuel 15:23 to make some observations before we move on to examine how the devil engineer's lawlessness into our lives.

> *1 Samuel 15:23 "For rebellion is as the sin of witchcraft, and stubbornness is as iniquity and idolatry." NKJV*

Strong's concordance cites the Hebrew word; 'meriy' as meaning bitterness, i.e. (fig.) rebellion. The reason for this may be that when someone is embittered by injustice or unfairness it will produce rebellion as a predictable response. This will normally be directed towards those who are in authority, who are perceived as not being just and fair.   In the case of the Garden of Eden, Satan was saying did God *really* say do not eat from that tree? He was craftily implying that God was keeping good things from them and did not really care about them. In a sense he was saying; *did God really give you limits, surely that's not fair!*

God was painted as being unjust in keeping that tree from them and mankind doubted His love and character. It is not surprising that the way back to God for humanity is to accept His love, and the grace offered through His merciful character. God has given us the opportunity through Christ to reverse the effect of the fall and consequent separation from him. He has largely limited Himself on Earth to trusting in His nature and love and accessing all that He has for us by faith.

Study 1: Sources of rebellion

We see rebellion and lawlessness enter into mankind at the fall as mankind doubted God's justness and fairness. We decided that we could be *like god* setting our own rules, providing for ourselves, and being accountable only to our own will and wants. Rebellion then is a predictable reaction to perceived or actual unfairness and injustice. We probably consider it to always be sin, but this is not always so; it is a reaction to a situation and what I term a *universal emotion* or response.

For example, the authority figures that Jesus dealt with were the religious leaders of His nation of birth. Jesus clearly rebelled against the heavy religious demands that these teachers were putting on the people. He showed what God actually wanted in relationship, not conformity to man-made rules. His desire was that we would respond to God and obey Him because we love Him and trust in His integrity. Jesus demonstrated the love, mercy and nature of God by meeting the needs of those who came to Him. This included those who had needs on the Sabbath, which infuriated the religious people of the time.

> *Matthew 23:4-5* *⁴ They crush you with impossible religious demands and never lift a finger to help ease the burden. ⁵ "Everything they do is for show." NLT*

Jesus considered these religious burdens and demands on the people to be unfair, unjust and not representative of the Father. His response was rebellion against the existing system. He was not rebellious by nature, but would not come under or submit to their unjust practices. We see that rebellion is a predictable response, or as I term it, a *universal emotion* that any of us can experience when we are either exposed to stressors that produce that reaction, or if we are triggered by a perception of injustice if we hold unfairness issues. There are certainly oppressions and abuses in the world that we should be indignant about and push back against.

REBELLION 'AS WITCHCRAFT'

As we explore this in the context of our falleness, why is rebellion as bad as, or like witchcraft? Those who practice actual witchcraft are taking control, that is not theirs, over the will and outcomes of other people. It is a perversion of the will, imposing your will on another. People in rebellion prefer their will and desires over those of another. They will struggle to submit to the position and will of instituted authority. Christian people with rebellion issues will want to bypass authority and usually consider that they have a *hotline* to heaven hearing directly and correctly from God.

There is a well-illustrated warning for us on two occasions in the book of Numbers. Firstly, with Aaron and his sister Miriam, who considered themselves greater than Moses because of his Ethiopian wife. We see yet again pride, and considering yourself above another, being linked to rebellion. As we have previously stated, Moses was usable because he was humble. After 40 years in the desert, he did not even want the significant leadership position that God had called him to. Being a leader does not necessarily mean that you are greater than others.

> *Numbers 12:2-3* *² So they said, "Has the LORD indeed spoken only through Moses? Has He not spoken through us also?" And the LORD heard it. ³ Now the man Moses was very humble, more than all men who were on the face of the earth. NKJV*

Rebellion inevitably will bring a curse and not a blessing, as is evidenced by the consequences of their heart attitudes.

> *Numbers 12:9-11* *⁹ So the anger of the LORD was aroused against them, and He departed. ¹⁰ And when the cloud departed from above the tabernacle, suddenly Miriam became leprous, as white as snow. Then Aaron turned toward Miriam, and there she was, a leper. ¹¹ So Aaron said to Moses, "Oh, my lord! Please do not lay this sin on us, in which we have done foolishly and in which we have sinned. NKJV*

I am amazed that Christians are not more careful in their attitudes towards their leaders, with examples such as these in the scriptures. Remarkably a few chapters later we see almost the same situation played out again. Someone has said that, *the one thing that we learn from history is that we don't learn from history!* We see the outcome of rebellion played out on Korah and his accomplices as they self-promote their own position.

> *Numbers 16:3 They gathered together against Moses and Aaron, and said to them, "You take too much upon yourselves, for all the congregation is holy, every one of them, and the LORD is among them." NKJV*

If we have rebellion issues it is advisable that we get them dealt with as quickly as possible for the sake of our future prosperity.

> *Numbers 16:32-33* *³² "... and the earth opened its mouth and swallowed them up, with their households and all the men with Korah, with all their goods. ³³ So they and all those with them went down alive into the pit; the earth closed over them, and they perished from among the assembly."*
> *NKJV*

I had a friend a number of years ago who became a Pastor. He visited me a little bit confused, inquiring as to why he was now so unpopular, when previously everyone had loved him. I pointed out to him that when you take on a Senior Pastors role and represent authority, the people with rebellion issues automatically now unconsciously, see you as their *bad, absentee* or *uncaring dad*, or *disapproving school master.*

SOURCES OF REBELLION

Here are some potential beginnings for *beliefs* coming from authority figures. They emanate from real or perceived unfairness and injustice when it seems to a child that they are;

- not valued	- not protected	- not noticed	- not wanted
- not loved	- not cared for	- not affirmed	- not important

These we would consider to be omissions or deficits in terms of emotional nurture that would be justly and fairly expected. They are areas of identity that should have been put into the child that have not. When they are not present the child interprets the situation through their fallen tendencies, with no doubt some inspiration from unholy spirit, as being not fair. The next list covers things that have been done to a person, and should not have been, such as abuses which were *actually* committed and are unjust;

- Physical domination or violence
- Sexual abuse
- Emotional control or manipulation
- Attitudinal: nasty, angry or disapproving looks, shrugged off, indifference
- Verbal abuse: mockery, put down, condemned
- Inappropriate discipline, expectations, or workload

Both of these lists project onto the recipient attitudes, which result in *beliefs* such as; *you are not worth the time, you are a nothing, you are not of any value, I don't care about you* etc. Being made to feel this way really is not fair and is a part of broken heartedness that needs God's healing.

Study 2: Possible struggles for those with rebellion issues

Lusts

People with rebellion issues often have trouble subjecting their flesh. They refuse godly limits and often lack self-control. Very commonly if they have grown up with injustice from authority figures they will take control of their lives as early as possible. Their inner thinking is probably something along the lines of; *If they won't look after me and care about what I need, then I will look after myself!*

This is probably the hardest time in history to be a teenager. Once you have decided to care and provide for yourself you will look to the World for what is available. You are now confronted with masses of addictive material including items such as drugs, cigarettes, alcohol, porn, illicit sex, unhealthy foods, media and much more. The deception behind bondage to addictions is still the same as it was with the temptation in the garden, with a spiritual entity suggesting; *This is what you need; this will make you happy and put you in a better place!* The tree of the knowledge of good and evil in that sense is alive and well. We know for Adam and Eve that it did not make them happy, and the same is very much true for us today.

Protecting our children

> *Ephesians 6:4 "And you, fathers, do not provoke your children to wrath, but bring them up in the training and admonition of the Lord." NKJV*

We can protect our children from rebellion by treating them fairly, being caring and attentive to their needs, and not expecting them to be perfect in a hostile environment. It is not beneficial to try to isolate them from the world but rather teach them how to make good decisions and choices in the world.

When my children were in their early teens, they wanted to go to the pictures with friends from school who were going. I was informed by them that there were no sex scenes but a little bit of swearing. The age that they were, I had to weigh up the situation carefully. If I said no, then it would not be seen as fair because their friends were going. If I said yes, they may have heard some bad language, which doubtless they were already hearing in the school yard. The fact that they were being honest about the movie also demanded that they be respected and trusted to make their own decision at that age. I let them make their own decision and trusted their maturity in weighing the pros and cons.

Our children, now fully grown up, remain great friends that we often travel with. Understanding the roots of responses can help you to bring up your children in the counsel of the Lord. Is God unjust or unfair? Never, in fact His throne is established by being right in all His dealings and on justice. So, if we are to represent Him then we will be just also.

> *Psalm 89:14 "Righteousness and justice are the foundation of Your throne; Mercy and truth go before Your face." NKJV*

Anger, bitterness, and resentment may also be additional responses and reactive emotions to injustice and unfairness. Self-pity could also be present. It is the *nobody cares about me* thinking that can proceed from not being dealt with properly. Lack of trust and insecurity about people's motives may also be evident, which can make it difficult for people with rebellion issues to come and submit to another for help. If you are dealing with somebody presenting with rebellion, my strong recommendation is that you reframe it around the root of the problem as injustice or unfairness issues. This is, not proposing that there is something wrong with them or their behavior, but rather that there is something wrong with how they have been treated or dealt with by others, and consequently they will be far more likely to be willing to receive help.

LESSON
We are God's representatives; He deals with us fairly and graciously in love. If we wisely replicate that nature towards others, we will avoid promoting rebellious responses in them.

Although all of this sounds daunting, and as if there is a lot to deal with, don't forget that all of these may be varying responses that come from one *heart belief* in one memory event. In some cases, it may be just a matter of minutes to resolve lifelong inner conflict and rebellious attitudes. Others have had a life of injustice and may hold a number of unfairness beliefs proceeding from different sources and may require more time.

Rebellion from rejection
Rejection is a source of rebellion as we see in the story of Cain and Abel. Cain felt that it was unfair that Abel's offering was accepted but his was rejected. In truth, Abel showed his heart towards God in bringing the best of what he had. People often feel that if we reject what they do or have then we reject them as a person. In reality, being a great musician or singer for example, is not who we are, it is a gift that we have. It was not Cain himself that the Lord did not accept; it was his attitude to the giving. We have to learn to have sufficient grace as God did to separate what we do from who we are. In any case, Cain rebelled against the warning of God and participated with sin in murdering his brother.

> *Genesis 4:3-7 ³ At harvest time Cain brought to the LORD a gift of his farm produce, ⁴ while Abel brought several choice lambs from the best of his flock. The LORD accepted Abel's offering, ⁵ but he did not accept Cain's. This made Cain very angry and dejected. ⁶ "Why are you so angry?" the LORD asked him. "Why do you look so dejected? ⁷ You will be accepted if you respond in the right way. But if you refuse to respond correctly, then watch out! **Sin is waiting to attack and destroy you, and you must subdue it.**" NLT (emphasis mine)*

Although Cain had to suffer a consequence for his actions it was evident that the Lord still accepted who he was and cared about his safety.

> *Genesis 4:15 The LORD replied, "They will not kill you, for I will give seven times your punishment to anyone who does." Then the LORD put a mark on Cain to warn anyone who might try to kill him. NLT*

Rebellion as a 'Spirit'
Using the *Truth Encounters* principles, we are not looking for evil spirits, but at times along the way we become aware that a problem, such as rebellion, is inordinate in its proportions,

amplified or there is a *stronghold* indicating demonic involvement. We are still primarily interested in the beliefs that are held that produce the rebellion or other issues. Often when we expose the beliefs that are held is the time when the spirit is most likely to manifest and be easily cast out. I have dealt with this in detail in Unit 5. We are primarily focused on the person and along the way we may tell a spirit to go as a part of the process. If we have discovered and resolved the belief and exposed the spirit, the person normally now does no longer want to engage their will in hosting the spirit.

Most, if not all of us, have had some type of rebellious thinking somewhere in our lives because it was a part of our old nature stemming from the fall. In the event of somebody having a *spirit of rebellion* I have observed some fairly easily discernible behavior. People who are captive simply cannot submit to another. In a church setting they may go from church to church airing their opinions, and whilst enjoying the spiritual climate cannot submit to any leadership. There can of course be other reasons for this as well. In relationships they cannot lay down their will in submission to another.

I recall one man who loved to serve in his local church in a variety of ways. But this service always had to be on his terms and his own decision and desire, or in other terms what *he* decided to do. If he was asked if he could help out with this or that the best that he could offer was; *I might.* Good man that he was, he simply could not submit. For him; *I might,* actually meant, *I will,* but he just could not bring himself to come under another will in compliance.

In that instance you will know that it is normally a spirit. People with this problem will often breeze into churches with lots of ideas and projects that they have that will bring people under their agenda and then disappear again. At times the source of a *spirit of rebellion* is the family line where it has passed through generations. Where this is the case, there is very often concurrent evidence of mental illness which we would consider to be a curse and not a blessing.

Autism and rebellion

I have only personally ministered to one autistic person who is now radically changed in terms of the behavior that proceeded from the autism. At times and in certain situations there are some minor signs, if you know what you are looking at, of a residual tendency toward typical autistic behavior. I am certainly not setting myself up as any kind of expert on autism and have not studied it in detail as a condition. I have only ministered to it on one occasion in a Christian context, applying Biblical principles. This involved ministering over time to many of the emotional areas that have been described in this book. This gradually eliminated the autistic behavior. The areas of dramatic change include; rebellion, (as a spirit) self-hatred, violence, withdrawal, anger and insanity. This largely happened through rebuilding the walls of the personality with materials such as; acceptance, encouragement, fairness, godly control, encouragement, security and reframing the person in questions boundaries.

I have had exposure to a number of other people suffering from autism in a general setting. In a number of those cases I have noted an observable *spirit of rebellion* in their fathers. By this I mean that their rebellion was demonic in nature from a spirit inside as opposed to the pressure to be rebellious from the outside of our beings that we all have, or have had elements of. At the same time, I have seen other cases where this is not obvious in either parent but seems to be evident further up the family line. I am certainly not suggesting any kind of standardization based on the few cases that I know of, but simply offer what I have seen in case it helps anyone understand their own loved ones. I have also heard testimonies of autism symptoms improving and reducing through the prayer of faith.

Other Christian commentators have also observed the rebellion and self-rejection issues present with Autism. As we have previously pointed out, a result of rejection can be withdrawal as a countermeasure to extreme fear of rejection, along with self-rejection. At times the withdrawal from relationships is so extreme that the speech or ability to communicate is also not functioning. Some consider this to be an inherited deaf and dumb spirit stemming from Matriarchal control. They consider this ungodly order in the household to be the root cause of the problem. In addition to fathers with rebellion problems I have certainly observed some controlling women and role reversal in the generation lines of children suffering with these problems. Some report changes as these spiritual issues are dealt with.

Autism is one of many disorders that began to emerge after the family unit, from a Biblical perspective, began to disintegrate. Is it a coincidence that we can point to the rapid escalation of autism following the removal of the Bible in the U.S. in the early 1960's, as being the standard of reference? This impacted the world significantly with the proliferation of media from the U.S. and many following this nation as a role model. The problem is that rebellion against God's word and instructions still holds a consequence for subsequent generations, just as it did in the garden at the beginning. I am old enough to have personally witnessed the changes commencing in the 1960's where increasingly women don't work together in leadership, but instead rule the household. One study indicated that in 1975 the incidence of autism was 1 in 5,000. By 1985 it had become 1 in 2,500, 1995 1 in 500, 2001 1 in 250, and by 2012 1 in 88. A very alarming change as the family unit is reframed according to humanistic principles.

> **Note:** The term 'autism' has been in use for around 100 years. It reportedly comes from the Greek word 'autos' which means 'self.' This then describes a state or condition where a person becomes an isolated *self*, withdrawn from social interaction.

REBELLION SUMMARY

Failure to provide love and acceptance, nurture, encouragement and security leaves a void that the child feels that they need to provide for themselves. Nearly all rebellion problems begin in childhood and you can expect them to be networked with other negative emotional reactions stemming from heart beliefs.

MINISTERING TO REBELLION

You will need to go back and look for the origins of rebellion that exists against authority figures and others, usually the parents. In the ministry session we are looking for the feelings of *injustice or unfairness*. We are also being aware of statements emanating from inner beliefs such as, for example, that's *just the way it is for me, nobody ever cares, it's not fair but it's just the way it is!* We have the person focus on the feeling or the statement which connect them to a feeling that is replicated in the past.

Having arrived at the earliest possible memory or impression, have them focus on the feeling and identify the belief, or if they are more cognitive and have the belief first as they look at the situation, have them concentrate on the belief and allow the matching feeling to emerge. Remember, your role is to ask questions to help them identify that which they believe.

Sample Rebellion Session

Me: "What seems to be bothering you Fred?"

Fred: "I've been struggling with angry feelings a bit lately when I come to church."

Me: "If you think about it, what exactly is it that is making you angry?"

Fred: Pause, reflection. "I think it is because the leaders have never shown any interest in the groups that I am starting around the church."

Me: "How does it make you feel as you think that nobody is doing that for you?"

Fred: "It's not fair; they don't care about what I am doing!"

Me: "Why don't you think they care about what you are doing?"

Fred: Reflection, some emotion. "I think it is because I am not very important...."

Me: "Fred, I want you to concentrate on that thought that you are not important. It must be a sad feeling so I want you to let yourself feel that feeling....and now I want you to let your mind connect you with other places where you have felt exactly that way."

Fred: Pause. "As soon as you said that I remembered when I was a little boy, all of the other kids getting a special meal brought home and I wasn't allowed to have any. I was probably about 4 years old."

Me: "So as you look at that situation, why do you think that you were missing out?"

Fred: "I feel a bit angry. They don't care about what I want!"

Me: "So does not caring about what you want mean that they don't care about you....?"

Fred: "Yes, I am not important, I don't matter, and they don't care about me."

Me: "Ok Fred I want you to concentrate on those feelings and see what the Lord has to say to you... His truth, which is the truth." (Then I pray inviting God to communicate truth through the Spirit of truth).

Fred: "It seemed just like my own thoughts, but it seemed like God said that I am important to Him. And I just remembered that passage from 1 Peter 5:7 that says that He cares for me. As I continue to think about it, I have also remembered that I had been sick at the time ... and what I am sensing is that even though they didn't explain it at the time they didn't give me any because I might throw up!"

Me: "So are you important? Cared about?"

Fred: "God thinks so. And apparently my parents cared enough and thought enough about me to not want to make me sick."

Me: "Fred I want you to look in your heart, not your head...is that belief that you are not important still there?"

Fred: "No, which is strange because it has always been there ... but I can't find it any more. I am important, and cared about."

Me: "How do you feel about the leaders not paying attention to your groups now?"

Fred: Ponders. "Well to be honest, I guess that I have never trusted them and let myself connect with them. I wanted them to take up my ideas; I was not interested in working with theirs. I suppose I just expected them to know how I felt which was a bit unreasonable of me I suppose."

Me: "Do you feel alright about approaching them now?"

Fred: "Yes, actually I feel a bit excited about what might be ahead for me!"

Principles of Anger

Many years ago, we lived in a city in inland Australia. It was a very dry area redeemed only by a large river supplying irrigation. At one time we moved into a very old and neglected house. There was nothing alive in the garden and all that remained was one small seemingly dead tree about 5 feet tall. I was going to pull it out but a visitor looked at it and said that it was still alive and that if I watered it that it would recover.

I faithfully began to stand out in the yard in the cool of the evening hosing my 'dead' tree. As I stood watering one night the thought came into my mind; *why don't you play golf anymore?* It was a strange question because I had not played for more than 15 years at the time and was no longer really interested in the game. I considered the question for a while and responded; *I would get too angry.* The next question came into my mind; *And why did you get angry?* After thinking it through for a few moments I replied; *I got angry because I was frustrated.* The next inquiry was; *And why did you get frustrated?* I pondered this for a few moments and came to the conclusion that it was because I could not do what I should be able to do.

The understanding then came into my mind that I became frustrated because something was not how I thought it should be, namely, in this case meeting the standards that I had for my performance on the golf course. When the frustration came to fullness it boiled over in anger. Anger is not a problem in itself; you don't just get angry, or be an angry person, it is coming from something that you believe. From this watering session I established the statement in my mind that *anger comes from unmet expectations or standards,* and more than 20 years on, I have found it always to hold true.

This could relate relationally to a situation such as newlyweds making adjustments with each other. They both come into the marriage with a set of standards and expectations about how the house should run, learnt from their growing up environment. For example, the husband gets frustrated, and then eventually angry because his mother always used to do the dishes straight after their meal. His new bride on the other hand grew up in a household where it was social time after dinner and the dishes were done later in the evening or in the morning. They would both be frustrated and angry with each other trying to enforce their standards and expectations onto each other. The solution is of course to decide to pull down whatever standards and requirements that you are putting onto each other. This holds true for all anger where you are trying to apply your rules to each other. It even extends to people having to meet the unreasonable religious standards of the leaders or denominations in a church environment. Whenever somebody comes to me with an anger problem, I know immediately that I am looking for whatever it is that they believe or perceive, that *isn't how they think that it should be.*

When you apply this to *Truth Encounters* you are looking at *anger beliefs* coming from events where things were considered to not be how they should be. Perhaps this could be a father who never attended school events with their child. The child feels that *this is not how it should be,* based on what other fathers are doing. These unmet expectations or standards are probably out in front of a deeper belief such as; *I am not worth being there for, therefore I am worthless.* Or *I am not as worthy or valued as the other children whose dads make the effort to attend.* Usually when you resolve the hurt belief behind the fruit of anger, the anger is resolved. There can of course be multiple situations and beliefs.

GOD AND EXPECTATIONS
We can be thankful that God dealt with any expectations and standards that could have been applied to us through the cross. Jesus met all of the requirements of the law on our behalf so that God could extend grace to us and we could come as we are, fully accepted and with access to the Father.

In relationships as we learn to be conformed to the likeness of Christ in this, and remove any standards or expectations that we may have learnt from family or society, we find our relationships will flourish. If there are areas where we have difficulty extending this grace, then we are looking for inner beliefs that are being triggered when we are dealing with others.

ANGER AS A 'UNIVERSAL EMOTION'
The principle of anger being a predictable response to things *not being how we think that they should be* is not always sin, and not always inappropriate. At times it is the right thing to do

to show disapproval of activities that *are not how they should be*. This is well illustrated when Jesus became angry at the money changers making His Father's house into something that it was not intended for. It should have been a house of prayer, but it was made into a den of thieves.

> *Matthew 21:12-13* [12] *Then Jesus went into the temple of God and drove out all those who bought and sold in the temple, and overturned the tables of the money changers and the seats of those who sold doves.* [13] *And He said to them, "It is written, 'My house shall be called a house of prayer,' but you have made it a 'den of thieves.'" NKJV*

SELF-ANGER

When there is anger towards others, as with other emotions, it is most often inward as well. If someone comes for ministry and their spouse is for example, reportedly making them angry, for example, because they make them feel as though they are not good enough in some way; as well as being angry at the spouse, they are also most likely angry at themselves for not being what they need to be to be good enough. If they thought they were enough they would not be hurt by the spouse's treatment. So, you are looking for the memory and the pain that related to them 'supposedly,' not being what they are meant to be. Anger is the response and not the problem, so once the hurt relating to the expectations and standards is resolved the anger will disappear.

ANGER AND HEALTH

> *Ephesians 4:26-27* [26] *"In your anger do not sin: Do not let the sun go down while you are still angry,* [27] *and do not give the devil a foothold" (NIV).*

Whether anger is internalized or outward towards others, it is a good idea to take the loving advice of scripture and resolve why we are angry as soon as possible. There are various biological actions that cause us harm if we remain angry. Without taking the time here to go through the mechanisms involved, strong or chronic anger can reportedly lead to problems such as strokes or other physical complaints.

CAN YOU RESOLVE BELIEF-BASED ANGER THROUGH HAVING KNOWLEDGE?

If you have anger that is simply because you have chosen to not forgive others for *not doing things how you think that they should be done*, then understanding this you could well help you make the decision to pull down your standards for them. If you no longer consider that things *should be a particular way*, often your way, then there are no longer grounds for frustration and anger, and the issue is resolved. However, if the reason for the anger is coming from a *heart belief* that is no longer conscious thought then ministry will be required.

Some time ago a man of around 60 years of age came to see me with a problem of unresolved anger that had plagued him all of his life. His counsellor had instructed him to read all of the scriptures regarding anger in the Bible. Now he was an expert on what the Bible said about anger, but this mind knowledge did not change his issue at all. Having identified the *heart belief* that produced the anger responses, the Holy Spirit set him free.

SUMMARY

Whenever somebody comes to me reporting anger issues, I am immediately questioning them in regards to what may be in their lives or in their environment, and then in their history, that is *not how they think that it should be*.

Unforgiveness, resentment and bitterness
'PRESENT TENSE' FORGIVENESS

The bible gives us clear instruction to forgive others. This means that if someone does something that offends you today' then under the guidelines of scripture, we are to forgive them as many times as is necessary. This lifestyle should begin as soon as we know that this is the counsel of scripture. It is the nature of God towards us and we are to go and live likewise. If our next-door neighbour throws his empty beer bottles over the fence every night then we need to choose to forgive him daily for the offense. (There is nothing wrong with dropping by and in love requesting that he stops doing it or some action may need to be taken!).

Forgiveness comes before love. We cannot fully love anyone while we hold onto the things that they have committed towards us, or for that matter, the things that we think that they should have done and haven't. God had to deal with suffering a price for our offences first, before He could extend forgiveness and relationship. In much the same way when people are mistreating us, we have to take up our own crosses, absorb the hurt, and deny ourselves retaliation in order to perpetuate love and grace in the spirit of the gospel.

When my wife and I were first married, for many years, we had a love/hate relationship. That is, we did love the person who was inside behind the behavior, but we did not love the attitudes and hurt that was coming to us from the other person. As we dealt with the issues and learnt to be gracious and forgiving, no longer demanding conformity to each other's standards, our relationship began to blossom.

> Matthew 18:21-22 ²¹ Then Peter came to Him and said, "Lord, how often shall my brother sin against me, and I forgive him? Up to seven times?" ²² Jesus said to him, "I do not say to you, up to seven times, but up to seventy times seven." NKJV

I have been taught that seventy times seven in the Aramaic language in this preceding verse means in an ongoing manner. This means a lifestyle of forgiveness. We once had a couple visit us who had terrible relationship conflicts. Before I began to look into their inner issues, I noted that they could not forgive each other for anything. For example, he could not forgive her for being a woman and not being able to operate machinery as he could. She would not forgive him for not understanding her emotional make up and so on. They simply refused to not hold each other to account for their shortcomings, failings and imperfections.

In our first few years of marriage, I would become frustrated that my wife wasn't as organized as I was, and she could never find her car keys or handbag. Later I began to realize that very creative people are sometimes a bit random in the structure department. After learning forgiveness, I now think it's cute and funny, as long as she doesn't touch my keys!

A 'RECORD OF WRONGS'

> 1 Corinthians 13:4-5 ⁴ "Love is patient, love is kind. It does not envy, it does not boast, it is not proud. ⁵ It is not rude, it is not self-seeking, it is not easily angered, **it keeps no record of wrongs.**" NIV (emphasis mine).

A record of wrongs is when you have a list of grievances against someone. Years ago, I would have considered that I had no unforgiveness towards anyone in the world. That is, I certainly had no deep pain driven hurt or resentment. However, one day I noticed that whenever a particular person came up in conversation that I could not help myself from mentioning various occasions when this person had, in my opinion, acted inappropriately towards us. As I spoke, out would tumble this list of offensive actions that I held. I realized that I had kept a record of wrongs. I made a deep decision to be like our Father in heaven and remember their sins no more. Some people say that God forgets our sins, but I believe that by a deliberate act of His will He chooses to not remember them anymore. I decided to not remember them anymore and began to pray for this person's prosperity, and that God would do for them everything that I would like Him to do in His dealings with me.

Almost immediately my *record of wrongs* list disappeared and was no longer accessed when that person came up in conversation, rather I would find myself saying only positive things. (This was now in effect, *blessing* them, which biblically means *speaking well of them*, rather than cursing them). Could I resurrect the list by trying to remember those grievances? Probably, but now I would have to try to remember, and this is something that I had wilfully decided not to do. For many people, this kind of dealing with resentment and unforgiveness is not possible without healing being done first.

'PAST TENSE' FORGIVENESS

We have talked about the Bible's instruction on forgiveness. So now we know how we should respond to hurts, grievances and offences. Many people come to us having been taught that they must forgive, and as a result, they have spent much of their lives endeavouring to do so but feeling guilty and condemned because they just can't seem to get there.

The problem is that the unforgiveness resides in *hurt received from historical sources*. These situations will make up the majority of times that people will come to you with unforgiveness, resentment and bitterness issues. Under these circumstances we do not initially request that the people forgive those who have offended against them. The reason that they struggle to forgive is because they do not really know what it is that they are forgiving the perpetrator of their unforgivness for.

Let me explain it in this manner. Imagine if someone has suffered, for example, sexual abuse. Clearly, they know that the abuse is the source of their resentment. They most likely are not, however, aware of *the beliefs* that are causing the pain in them. Let us take a common belief that often emanates from this kind of abuse; *I am ruined, I am no longer like other people.* This belief then, is at least a part of the source of the pain, along with other inner thoughts from the event. Once it is discovered, identified and healed by the Spirit of truth, we then ask them how they regard the offender. When the healing is complete and the hurt is resolved, over and over we see that forgiveness comes easily. The abused person may now make some kind of comment such as; *Well I kind of feel sorry for them that they had that problem. Something must have happened to them to make them like that!*

This holds true of people who have been emotionally, physically, verbally or in other ways suffered abuse. It also stands fast in situations where for instance love, acceptance and encouragement have not been given as well. You may hear comments such as; *I know that mum/dad did not get much love themselves, and now that I see it, I feel sorry for them that they had nothing to give!* Usually if a person is all about themselves, they are nursing wounds of some kind. As we get healed of our own issues, we now begin to become aware of the needs of others, making us increasingly available and useable to God.

UNFORGIVENESS OF SELF

As with other emotions, there is an inward version of this unforgiveness towards self. This is where we have a *record of wrongs* regarding our own failings, imperfections and shortcomings. In some instances, we can simply forgive ourselves and move on once we realize that we have held ourselves to account. Most issues that people come for ministry for in this regard may be deeply rooted in an event where a heart belief has come in such as; *I'm not as good as others, I am useless, I am not loveable* for some reason and so on. These need to be healed before you can accept your own self as a normal human being who doesn't always get things right. Again, with healing we hear self-forgiveness statements come such as; *I was only a child; it was ridiculous for me to think that I should know how to do that! Actually, I am ok; it was my parents who had the problem in expecting me to be perfect.*

PROGRESSION OF A LACK OF FORGIVENESS TOWARDS OTHERS OR SELF
For some people, if they refuse to forgive, and they stew on the matters, they will develop eventually into resentment. When resentment becomes deeply seated it can grow into bitterness towards others or self. This is the very toxic form which can end up growing into hatred and can be implicated in various diseases. The old saying; *It is eating them up like a cancer* certainly in my experience is quite accurate. I have witnessed personally as bitterness, self-bitterness and resentment have been strongly present in a number of cancer cases.

A number of years ago, I recommended to a lady that it might be very beneficial for her health in the long run to deal with her unforgiveness which had led to resentment and bitterness. She didn't seem to believe me and was not prepared to let go of her attitudes. Two or three years later she developed cancer and died. I believe that this could have been prevented. Sadly, there are others as well who have not heeded the warning and suffered this or other maladies.

We have also seen cancer healed and know of many others healed by other ministries when the person has come for prayer and help. For some, when the bitterness progresses to hatred it often involves rebellion or retaliation against the perpetrator of the offence. This then can at times involve trying to destroy the other person in some way with the tongue which is not advisable. In the event that the person you are bitter against is yourself, there will be some kind of self-destructive, self-harming, self-punishing behavior as we witness in modern epidemics such as cutting.

God's perfect order is that you are loving and forgiving towards others, and also towards yourself, but often we need His healing before we can live this way. The Lord knows this very well, which is why He promised to heal the broken-hearted and set the captives free if we will come to Him. When you don't love yourself you will probably struggle to love others as well.

> *Matthew 22:39b "You shall love your neighbor as yourself." NKJV*

The 3 LEGS of the 'Jezebelic Spirit'

Rebellion and ungodly control are like witchcraft because they are all about you imposing your will on another and making what you want happen.

> *1 Samuel 15:23 "For rebellion is as the sin of witchcraft, and stubbornness is as iniquity and idolatry." NKJV*

We have already explored this passage in terms of the rebellion aspect. The word normally translated as *stubbornness* here is the Hebrew word; patsar which according to Strong's concordance means; to peck at, i.e. (fig.) stun or dull:--press, urge, stubbornness. Along with rebellion, you have this sense of *pecking at, pressing,* or *urging,* in order to have what you want and impose your will on another, which we would describe as ungodly control. All of this contributes to the *I* syndrome or the *fallen self* on the throne problem that is described in the Bible as the *Flesh* or *sin nature.* We can perhaps summarize it in this way with some easy to remember i words. These may you to help recall the normal roots of the tree problems that we have just discussed;

PRIDE	"I will make myself above"	(Comes mainly from inferiority, or insignificance- aka low self-image)
REBELLION	"I will not submit to another"	(Comes mainly from injustice/ unfairness)
CONTROL	"I will have my way"	(Comes mainly from insecurity)

There have been a number of books written giving a lot of detail in regards to the type of fruit that is associated with what is described as a *Jezebel spirit*. Whilst there is no Jezebel spirit mentioned in the Bible there is the example of behavior that we find in the story of Jezebel that does often have a demonic element. When these spirits are in place, they may respond to any name given when the authority of Christ is exercised.

In my experience the three elements that summarize Jezebelic responses are pride, rebellion and control. From these, all of the other fruit proceeds. Most of us either have or have had one or more of these expressions in some measure and they were not directly held by an evil spirit.

We can of course, point the finger and describe and avoid people with this behavior and run them out of the Church. However, if we look past the fruit as God does, and see the hurt in the heart, we will have grace for them and seek to minister to the beliefs producing the **inferiority, injustice** and **insecurity** that is behind the problems. Many times, they are not open to help because they have difficulty admitting that they may have an issue. They may struggle to trust and submit to someone for ministry. If this is the case then, of course, dealing with their attitudes must be wisely negotiated to protect the Church family.

Many of these people have been hurt and abused more than most, and they are looking for genuine love and understanding. Often, we have to grow in love and grace to reach the person, moving past their offensive attitudes to reach the real person underneath. As the saying goes; *they don't care how much you know until they know how much you care.* We then have to grow in grace and love before these hurting ones that God wants free will open up to us.

> *1 Peter 4:8 "Above all, love each other deeply, because love covers over a multitude of sins." NIV*

> *Proverbs 19:11 "A man's wisdom gives him patience; it is to his glory to overlook an offense." NIV*

JEZEBEL

People with unhealed Jezebelic behavior will present doing the types of things illustrated in the Bible. In 1 Kings chapter 18 Jezebel kills off the Lord's prophets. Today Jezebelic Christians will try to assassinate Pastors, leaders and genuine ministries or authorities. This will usually be with their tongues, through attacks on the spirituality or abilities of the leaders. They often try to gather people to themselves, creating division by starting groups in or out of the church bypassing permission from those in authority. You will often hear that *God told them.* They will usually appear to be very spiritual, as was Jezebel.

In 1 Kings chapter 19 she intimidates Elijah, the man of God. Jezebelic people will often threaten and intimidate people who will not do what they want. Jezebelic people commonly want to bypass the normal processes of being acknowledged in a church and sometimes seek to get in close to senior leadership. From there they can manipulate and influence things in the direction that they desire.

In 1 Kings Chapter 21 we see Jezebel very close to senior leadership in the form of King Ahab her husband. When he was too weak to exercise his kingly authority over Naboth in the purchase of his vineyard, Jezebel stepped in and *made it happen*. These are some of the qualities of her actions that we need to take note of in light of what we can expect from unhealed people with Jezebelic mindsets. She is not submitted to Ahab's leadership. She assumes authority that is not hers. She manipulates and controls people to get what she wants. She instigates lying, false accusation, slander and murder. What began as assassination with the tongue in this case ends up playing out in actual murder as Naboth is removed from the scene. Ultimately Jezebel is cursed for her activities and meets a very sad end.

We certainly do not want to see anyone not finish well, so we need to see these hurting ones as God does, looking inside to the *inferiority, injustice* and *insecurity* that they have been exposed to. Graciously, we need to be extending the hand of help rather than the pointing finger of accusation and judgment.

> *Isaiah 58:9-11 ⁹ Then you will call, and the LORD will answer; you will cry for help, and he will say: Here am I. "If you **do away with the yoke of oppression, with the pointing finger and malicious talk,** ¹⁰ and if you spend yourselves in behalf of the hungry and **satisfy the needs of the oppressed**, then your light will rise in the darkness, and your night will become like the noonday. ¹¹ The LORD will guide you always; he will satisfy your needs in a sun-scorched land and will strengthen your frame. You will be like a well-watered garden, like a spring whose waters never fail. NIV (emphasis mine)*

Other related issues that you may encounter

GUILT AND SHAME

> *Romans 8:1 There is therefore now no condemnation to those who are in Christ Jesus, who do not walk according to the flesh, but according to the Spirit. NKJV*

Guilt is a fruit that will tie into areas such as self-rejection, inferiority and performance anxiety. By that I mean anxiety over our ability to perform to people's expectations. Usually we reject ourselves because we have learnt that we fall short in some way. As a result, we often feel as though we should have done more, been better, been able to please or do what was expected of us and so on. A consequence of these perceived failures is often *low self-image*, and *guilt or shame*.

As we have previously stated, we could summarize that guilt and shame are connected to something that we didn't do that we feel that we should have, or, something that we have done that we shouldn't have. If we have dealt with things that we should not have done from our previous years, we should have received Gods forgiveness' and also our own.

Clearly if we are still doing something that we know that we shouldn't be doing, and could stop in our own strength then guilt is probably an appropriate emotion. In that instance it is not condemnation because we can always repent, but it may well in fact be conviction. Guilt is often tied to other emotional issues and even implicated in depression. It can be one possible trail back to the initial memory for truth and healing.

DEALING WITH GRIEF

Grief is normally associated with loss of some kind. This could include loss of your identity and self-worth if, for example, you have been sexually abused. It could also relate to loss of a relationship or loved one. As with any other belief-based emotion the goal is to identify the thoughts producing the sad feelings.

> *Psalm 31:9-10 ⁹ Have mercy on me, O LORD, for I am in trouble; My eye wastes away with grief, **Yes, my soul and my body!** ¹⁰ For my life is spent with grief, And my years with sighing; My strength fails because of my iniquity, And my bones waste away. NKJV (emphasis mine)*

We take note from the preceding verses, that grief has an impact on both soul and body. At times, we minister to people who look constantly sad, or are continually sighing, resolved to the loss that they have suffered. It is wonderful to see the joy come into them when the Lord sets them free.

UNIT ELEVEN

Sex 'Gods idea!'

PART 1: Gods purpose and order in creating sexuality

Introduction

While we are addressing the problems that are 'common to man' it would be difficult to overlook the area of sexuality. Indeed, most of the World is reeling out of balance in this area, in one direction or another. The Bible describes all that God created as 'good' and this of course includes the sexual act. The devil has worked very hard indeed to distort all of God's creation beyond its intended order and parameters, and in the area of sex this is described as 'sexual immorality' or 'perversion.'

Personally, I feel that it is not my place to make judgments on how anyone has arrived where they are in their sexual life or related problems. As with other areas of life something has happened for us to be in the place that we are in. Perhaps we are simply ignorant of what is right or we have been exposed to things that have caused us to be in our present situation. My purpose is to help people adjust their sexuality to the ways of the Kingdom of God in order for that area of their lives to be free. Then we can be confident that God is pleased with its expression, and we can be sure that the participants will enjoy the blessing that He intended. This is an area very worth attending to. Indeed, Jesus said that we will all be measured and judged by the Word of God, so it is very important to line up with it now in every area of life, including sexuality.

Personally, I feel compassion for the porn addicts, the homosexuals, sexual abusers, the adulterers and all of the sexually immoral. Typically, I find that underneath their immorality they live with guilt and often self-hatred knowing that they are out of order in these areas. Any of us could be drawn into anything given the right environment, exposure, mental programming, emotional conditioning, or things perpetrated against us, but this of course does not make it right.

I often think of it this way. We are all basic generic human beings who have been 'clothed by life' so to speak. Some are clothed by weaknesses inherited from parents or grandparents who have committed sexual sin and have created an opening in our generational line. Others have been exposed to porn in the school yard or at home. Still others have themselves been abused in some way. The list goes on and on, but the point is that God wants to free us of the effects of these things and clothe us in righteousness.

God is always redemptive, always merciful, not wanting any to perish, but wanting all come to repentance in order to be saved.

He is always ready to set us free, and if we are bound, our part in this may be seeking out people of God who are trained to help us deal with our issues.

For those who do not believe in God, or believe in His Word, I make no judgements on you or your decisions. It is not my business how people express their free will and choice. The work we offer here is for those who do believe in God, and His word, and subsequently desire to live in a way that is pleasing to Him.

Study 1: Beginnings

We often find ourselves visiting the events in Genesis that are described as the 'fall of man.' This was where Satan came and tempted Adam and Eve to eat from the tree of the knowledge of good and evil. Eve saw in the fruit on the tree some 'good' aspects for satisfying bodily appetites, and it also appealed to the eyes. This then became a weak area in our fallen human nature. Satan now had a right through our submission to exploit this again and again.

> *Genesis 3:6 When the woman saw that the fruit of the tree <u>was good for food</u> and <u>pleasing to the eye</u>, and also desirable for gaining wisdom, she took some and ate it. She also gave some to her husband, who was with her, and he ate it. NIV (emphasis mine)*

God had commanded in Genesis 2:16-17 that man should not eat from this tree. Basically, what Satan came along proposing was that God was keeping good and beneficial things from mankind. He was suggesting that God doesn't really care about us, that He doesn't want us to have pleasure or fun, and that what He has given us already really isn't enough. Today we have the New Testament writings to guide us, and we understand that this is not true.

> *1 Timothy 6:17b ....But their trust should be in the living God, who richly gives us all we need for our enjoyment. NLT*

The Genesis account sets the scene for the basic attitudinal problem that man, who does not have the revelation of the scriptures, has as a result of the sin of rebellion that was committed at the fall. Really man was unconsciously saying; "I don't want any limits; I will get for myself what is best for me." This generationally inherited perception that God does not have all we need in mind, or care about our pleasure and enjoyment is behind much sin. Consequently, we often choose paths to supposedly meet our own needs, and particularly we do so with choosing to live with the 'limits' off.

For Adam and Eve, it proved that God's boundaries were indeed for their own protection. Sadly, I have often ministered to people who thought that sin like adultery was a good solution to their situation. The reality proved to be heartache, pain, broken families and often emotionally scarred children. What seemed 'good,' was actually bad...throwing off the limits was really not the best way to go.

PUSHING THE LIMITS

A number of years ago I had a man asking me questions about my sex life. I realized that he was trying to work out how far he could go in his own sexual relationship, and what he could get away with before he crossed the line with God. When I went home, I told my wife how this man was exploring the boundaries and wanted to push the limits. Her response was this; "It is almost as if what God has given isn't enough!" Immediately I thought of the Genesis situation where that is exactly what had happened. This was then imprinted on our fallen sinful nature, or flesh as it is sometimes translated. We all, at times, have been tempted to follow our own desires and throw off the boundaries and limits.

1 John 2:16-17 *16 For all that is in the world; the <u>lust of the flesh</u>, the <u>lust of the eyes</u>, and the pride of life; is not of the Father but is of the world. 17 And the world is passing away, and the lust of it; but he who does the will of God abides forever. NKJV (emphasis mine)*

The truth is that God has given us many things in this Earth that are very good indeed. There are many beautiful things that are pleasing to the eye that He has given us. For example, I am sure that the scenery in the Garden of Eden was breathtaking. Regarding the beauty of women, the scripture encourages us to enjoy the appearance of our wives, rather than be attracted to an illicit relationship with another woman. In other words, enjoy what God has provided for you and avoid the 'lust of the eyes' which is the immoral looking at other women.

Proverbs 5:18-20 *18 Let your fountain be blessed, And rejoice with the wife of your youth. 19 As a loving deer and a graceful doe, Let her breasts satisfy you at all times; And always be enraptured with her love. 20 For why should you, my son, be enraptured by an immoral woman, And be embraced in the arms of a seductress? NKJV*

This immoral looking or 'lust' is the wanting to have something or someone that is not for you. So, to enjoy how beautiful things look in the Earth is a gift from God. However, desiring, coveting or looking at a thing that is forbidden for you is sin. In other words, noticing that a member of the opposite sex is attractive is natural and unavoidable. But when you look wanting them for yourselves, or even thinking about them in a sexual way, then the Bible says that it is the same as committing the act. Lust in the Bible means to desire something that is forbidden for you.

Matthew 5:28 "But I say to you that whoever looks at a woman to lust for her has already committed adultery with her in his heart. NKJV

Before we come into the Kingdom of God, we only have our conscience to steer us away from sin. Much of this is put into us by the programming of our moral environment growing up. However, after conversion we have the conviction of the Holy Spirit and the written Word of God to guide our paths. Now we have to choose whether we want to continue to walk after the old nature or flesh and what the fallen self-nature wants, or whether to follow the Spirit.

Romans 8:1 There is therefore now no condemnation to those who are in Christ Jesus, who do not walk according to the flesh, but according to the Spirit.

Romans 8:5-8 *5 For those who live according to the flesh set their minds on the things of the flesh, but those who live according to the Spirit, the things of the Spirit. 6 For to be carnally minded is death, but to be spiritually minded is life and peace. 7 Because the carnal mind is enmity against God; for it is not subject to the law of God, nor indeed can be. 8 So then, those who are in the flesh cannot please God. NKJV*

If we choose to follow the Spirit then we will need to understand Gods order and purposes so that we know how to live.

Study 2: Gods created order and purpose for sexuality

Satan is always trying to distance us from God's perfect, fulfilling and protective ways. He will do anything that he can to take what God has created and pervert and distort it. So, let us have a look in overview at what the Lords purpose is for sexuality.

1. BE FRUITFUL AND MULTIPLY

> Genesis 1:27-28 ²⁷ So God created man in His own image; in the image of God He created him; male and female He created them. ²⁸ Then God blessed them, and God said to them, "Be fruitful and multiply; fill the earth and subdue it. NKJV

God evidently planned for the Earth to be populated with mankind ruling over it and establishing authority and Gods order for it. Everything living on the Earth that I am aware of comes from a seed of some kind. So along with a spiritual inheritance comes wonderful things such as genes and DNA. These are instrumental so that through Gods engineering and purpose, the creation of billions of individually created, one of a kind masterpieces would come about. Us!

2. MAN AND WOMAN JOINING IN CREATION WITH GOD

What a privilege to have a part with God in producing a human being. It is very well documented that there is a bright flash of light that announces the beginning of human life as a sperm meets the egg. As Christians we would deduce that this is the moment where the human spirit and soul as life are placed in us by God, along with the union of the sperm and the egg. Scientists have captured the 'fireworks' on film when an explosion of tiny sparks erupts from the egg at the exact moment of conception. This infusion of power is considered to be the beginning point for individual life and growth in the embryo.

There is typically 250 million to half a billion sperm in a single ejaculation, and even up to 1.2 billion in a healthy male at the peak of his fertility. This means that there are lot of possibilities for the selection of a body for you! If your parents then had between 6 and 20 attempts at getting pregnant, then depending on the sperm numbers the potential for whom you could have been could populate the whole Earth. You are not random; you were selected by God to be exactly who you are!

> Psalm 139:15-16 15 You watched me as I was being formed in utter seclusion, as I was woven together in the dark of the womb. 16 You saw me <u>before I was born</u>. Every day of my life was recorded in your book. Every moment was laid out before a single day had passed. NLT (emphasis mine)

3. KNOWING EACH OTHER INTIMATELY, ONE FLESH

> Genesis 2:24 Therefore a man shall leave his father and mother and be joined to his wife, and they shall become one flesh. NKJV

There is no other relationship that is as close as the bond that comes through sexual intimacy. In the Old Testament we find accounts of Cain and Adam 'knowing' their wives and consequently they became pregnant. This is not the same way as you 'know' other people, it is meant to be unique to marriage. This is a mental, willful, chemical, emotional, and spiritual bonding that is only meant to occur in a marriage relationship between a man and a woman. Some commentators have called the sexual act the superglue of marriage.

I know that often in early marriage when couples are still adjusting to each other, they sometimes 'fall out' with each other through different opinions or emotional hurts. It is many times the strong desire for sexual union that brings them back to reconciliation.

I have heard that behind the Hebrew meaning for 'one flesh' is the concept of being so closely connected that to separate would be like pulling skin off flesh.... where some of the flesh would come away as well as the skin. In Gods economy even chemically, there is a powerful pair bonding hormone called oxytocin that is greatly stimulated when sexual intimacy occurs.

The World tries to tell us that the sexual act is just some pleasure to be had with anyone at will. However, a bond is made on each occasion. Consequently, when we separate there is damage caused to our brain chemistry, as well as mental and emotional states. This is a well-documented result of us trying to trivialize sexual activity.

In modern times the 1960s was a time of rebellion against moral standards. The beginning of this era for many Western nations, as we have previously stated, is marked by the Bible and prayer being removed from the schools in the U.S. in 1962. There was a massive and dramatic negative corresponding increase in statistics in morally related degeneration. Again, man was *'throwing off the limits,'* so to speak. He was disregarding the counsel of safety and spiritual protection outlined in the scriptures that would lead to blessing and happiness.

Sexually transmitted diseases, pregnancies to unwed girls, pre-marital sex, single parent households, unmarried couples living together, divorce rates, rape, abortion, violent crime, alcoholism, drug abuse and so on all skyrocketed.

An increasing number of young people were being admitted to mental hospitals, and many women suffered emotional breakdowns as a result.

Unprotected sex is unmarried sex where there is no spiritual covering by God. Rather as Satan is submitted to, he becomes the covering. We then receive his cursing rather than God's blessing. It is sex that is encouraged, propagated and covered by the spirit of the world. You might like to treat it or consider it as casual and without consequence, but that is far from the truth. In joining with Satan against Gods order we open ourselves to the curses listed in scriptures such as Deuteronomy Chapter 28.

4. PLEASURE AND ENJOYMENT

God created and designed our bodies with various sensual nerve endings that are intended for our pleasure. For example, on the female body is the clitoris which has no other anatomical function other than her pleasure. God is not embarrassed by this; it was His idea, design, and intention all along. Any thoughts that God is against pleasure should be immediately dispelled by the amazing gift of sex. God himself considered it 'very good,' and it was both His idea and of His making and design.

> *Genesis 1:31 Then God saw everything that He had made, and indeed it was very good. NKJV*

God is revealed as relational by nature, and in His provision, He has given us this capacity to give and receive pleasure. This is the ability to enhance and bless our relationships on every level, spiritual, emotional, the will, mind and body. In the past Christianity has proposed some kind of attitude that sex is dirty or impure. What an insult to our loving maker this is! Again, it proposes a God that is trying to keep good things from us...whereas the truth is that all of the parts of our body that give pleasure, whether used immorally or in a Holy way, were originally provided and purposed by Him. The devil takes what is intended for good and seeks to distort and pervert it.

This turns some away from Christianity believing that Disciples of Christ aren't allowed to have fun. I had a young man once tell me that his friends weren't interested in God because Christians can't have sex and don't drink. I suggested that he tell his friends that we are free to drink if we choose to, but we don't get drunk. Tell them also that a healthy Christian marriage potentially has better sex than they do because we have learnt to become 'givers' in our relationships. I might add that we also have the Word of God to teach us how to treat each other and relate in a way that works. We have the offer of God to heal our heart beliefs and emotional issues; this then allows us to be very close to our spouses on all levels. Good, healthy sex then comes as the outworking of the other factors implicated, and is a result of the other parts of our personal and relational lives being in Godly order.

A BIBLICAL PICTURE FOR OUR UNDERSTANDING

Many things in the scriptures that are examples of life in the World are there to help us understand spiritual concepts and realities.

> *Romans 1:20 For since the creation of the world God's invisible qualities--his eternal power and divine nature--have been clearly seen, being understood from what has been made, so that men are without excuse. NIV*

We seem to think that marriage and sexual relations are taken as an example by God from life to help us understand the relationship between Christ and His bride.

But I don't believe that God was just using something that existed so that we could understand this relationship, I believe that He instituted marriage and sexual intimacy so that we could see the spiritual ramifications of our union with Christ Jesus. God of course is always multi-tasking with more than one purpose for everything. In Ephesians chapter five there is an illustration for us explaining how we should fulfil our roles in the marriage covenant.

In verse 32 the Apostle Paul reveals that although he is giving instruction for the proper functioning of marital relations, basing them on how Christ Jesus deals with His bride the church…. He clarifies that he is actually explaining the interaction of we, the Church, responding and relating to Christ.

> *Ephesians 5:21-32 ²¹ Submit to one another out of reverence for Christ. ²² Wives, submit to your husbands as to the Lord. ²³ For the husband is the head of the wife as Christ is the head of the church, his body, of which he is the Savior. ²⁴ Now as the church submits to Christ, so also wives should submit to their husbands in everything. ²⁵ Husbands, love your wives, just as Christ loved the church and gave himself up for her ²⁶ to make her holy, cleansing her by the washing with water through the word, ²⁷ and to present her to himself as a radiant church, without stain or wrinkle or any other blemish, but holy and blameless. ²⁸ In this <u>same way</u>, husbands ought to love their wives as their own bodies. He who loves his wife loves himself. ²⁹ After all, no one ever hated his own body, but he feeds and cares for it, just as Christ does the church—³⁰ for we are members of his body. ³¹ "For this reason a man will leave his father and mother and be united to his wife, and the two will become one flesh." ³² This is a profound mystery--<u>but</u> **I am talking about Christ and the church**. ³³ However, each one of you also must love his wife as he loves himself, and the wife must <u>respect</u> her husband. NIV (emphasis mine)*

Remember that the picture in this passage is Christ as the husband and the Church (Us) as the bride or wife. So, the role that the man has in the relationship is a picture or illustration for us from the natural world to understand the Church and Jesus relationship. This is why the devil works so relentlessly to go against God's order for sexuality in society. He is trying to distort the picture. And he knows that the only way that the marriage relationship can work is in the way that God ordained and intended it. This does not mean that man is in the least bit superior to his wife, it simply means that he has a different role. Consequently, he has been made differently and has dramatically different brain wiring, focus and 'skill set.'

The Bible says that the wife is <u>comparable</u> to the man not inferior. She is equal to him, but different, and with a different God given role and purpose.

> *Genesis 2:18 And the LORD God said, "It is not good that man should be alone; I will make him a helper comparable to him." NKJV (emphasis mine)*

MEN AND WOMEN ARE DIFFERENT IN EVERY WAY

I think my wife and I are a fairly typical sample of what studies report, and what we have observed. Men tend to be more task oriented, providers, protectors, problem solvers, and are looking to the future to make that outboard motor so that you don't have to row your boat everywhere....and can therefore get everywhere more quickly. So, men tend to be more single minded, focused on one thing at a time. The ladies are normally more relationally motivated and live in the day. In the past my wife could be feeling tired, and thinking about the moment, and I have to remind her that we are going on holidays in a couple of days. I am thinking solving the problem, and she is aware of the difficulties of the moment.

Conversely, we can go into a house and she has observed everything that is the building in detail. I have seen nothing except where the door is so that we know how to get back to the car later. So, she is far superior to me in this and many other respects. But in terms of her ability to take my role of responsibility in the home, it is not that she can't do it, but it is more difficult, less natural, and consequently more stressful for her.

Scientists considered that a brain was just a brain until recently. With modern technology they have been able to see that if given the same mathematical problem, that different parts of the female brain are activated than those of the man in working out the same answer. The truth is that there is nothing much the same about men and women mentally, emotionally, physically, hormonally or spiritually. It is not that one is better than the other, just different.

American speaker Mark Gungor has an excellent clip on U-tube titled; 'A Tale of two brains.' He explains that a man isolates his thinking processes into 'boxes.' This means that normally he is just focused on one thing at a time, and subsequently pushes other matters out so that he can finish the task in the 'box' that he is working on. In contrast he describes women's minds as 'a ball of wire.' This means that everything for her is wired into everything else and she is thinking of everything at once. We have observed that this is normally very true, and is an illustration again of the total functional differences of men and women. Not superior or inferior, just different. Equipped specifically for the role that they're going to play.

ROLES IN THE HOUSEHOLD

Biblically God has appointed the man to be responsible for the spiritual climate of the household. It falls to him to be responsible for the emotional wholeness of the relationship and to love his wife sacrificially, or we might say at his own expense. He is to love her first even if it is at personal cost to his own self. The old saying is: "the loved become lovely." It is the principle of sowing and reaping. Love your wife and prefer her and it will come back on your own head, pressed down, shaken together and running over. This may take time but it is a biblical principle and it cannot fail to produce an outcome.

For her part, she is to respect that he has been made responsible to initiate the dynamics in the household, and acknowledge that he will be accountable to God for what their relationship and family looks like. This includes who they serve and follow, a responsibility that Adam did not fulfill. He was given responsibility over everything before Eve was even created. He failed to instruct her that it was not a good idea to listen to the serpent. In our Western culture we often find the women deciding what is best for the family. In much the same way as Adam men just going along with Eves suggestions. Men should not be dominating, but they should be taking responsibility to initiate Godly protocols around the household. This ideally is in consultation with his wife, who holds the other half of the attributes that can make a Godly relationship work.

COVERING

Although we are discussing sexuality, let us digress for a moment onto the relational order that should exist. The following spiritual attitudes, although general, apply to sexuality as well.

Jesus takes full responsibility for setting the spiritual environment that produces a 'Spirit of God' based dynamic for His church. He <u>covers</u> our imperfections and sets the attitudinal standards of the kingdom of God to protect us. These spiritual dynamics are sacrificial giving, unconditional love, (which doesn't demand perfection – as I heard recently; "God's love is not based on us, it is placed on us"), grace, which makes acceptance possible, plus mercy and forgiveness for our shortcomings. He is our 'head' but He does not Lord it over us or demand compliance. He doesn't force His bride to come under the kingdom of God, it is her (our) free will choice. He simply states; "If you love me you will obey me!" It has been well said that Jesus' love language is obedience, and I add, that this obedience is being given by choice not coercion. In all of this we add to the list of spiritual attributes that He institutes over us patience.

FREEWILL AND CHOICE

The choice to submit is hers, she is not dealt with in some kind of dominating, authoritarian kind of manner. Some streams of the church today propose that men should be demanding submission. Actually, the true role of the man is to cover her with these spiritual attributes as Jesus does to us first. He is unbending in them and His stand on Holiness and separation to the ways of the Kingdom, regardless of the activities of His bride. If she (the church) chooses to follow another spiritual kingdom whose precepts are rebellion, control, anger, fear, rejection, resentment or bitterness, this remains her free will choice. A wife is far more likely to gravitate towards these types of responses if she is dealt with in an ungodly, disrespectful kind of way, and by demanding that she submits. This controlling type spirit is not of God. It suits man because in his mind he is 'god' to his wife. Fallen man still wants to be like God, which began in the garden with *you will be like God. (Genesis 3:5)*

If my wife chose to not go to church or not follow God it would not be my place to make her do these things or force her to do anything. God doesn't force her and He is the ultimate authority. My instructions, as a man, are to establish the Jesus modeled spiritual dynamics of the Kingdom which I have previously listed. I am to stand in those and uphold those regardless of her choices. That is covering. If she doesn't want to come under those Kingdom attributes that is her freewill decision. This is what Adam did not do...stand for the instructions of God regardless of any pressures.

So, before we can make judgments on the behaviors of our wives we have to see if we are in the Spirit ourselves. Do we love unconditionally, do we love sacrificially, do we have grace and mercy for things not being exactly how we would like them, and are we patient, are we accepting, are we forgiving? We cannot reasonably expect our wives to submit to Satan's kingdom of fear, control, selfishness, criticism, anger, rejection, resentment, retaliation, and unforgiveness etc. etc. if that is the 'covering' coming from us. These also are spiritual in their nature but not from Gods Kingdom or Spirit.

> *1 Corinthians 11: 3 Now I want you to realize that the head of every man is Christ, and the head of the woman is man, and the head of Christ is God. NIV*

SETTING THE SPIRITUAL CLIMATE
It falls to man to initiate these principles, as God has put him next in line after Christ to establish covering. Many godly women do take up their own biblical role and instructions even though the man is covering her with another spirit, often domination, control and self-serving or self-exaltation in the relationship.

We could summarize this by saying that if my wife is not submitting to me in <u>working with me</u> that it will probably be a reflection on whether or not I am dealing with her in a godly way. Therefore, if she is loved, valued and secure, sharing in her role as joint leaders of the household, then it will be obvious, and she will be my glory in the sense that I have dealt with her as God has instructed me...as next in line in terms of responsibility after Christ.

For her part in the passage from Ephesians 5:21-33 that we have just been examining, the wife is instructed firstly to 'submit' to her husband and in verse 33 she is instructed to respect him.

MAN'S RESPONSIBILITIES
When you realize the responsibility that is on the man to set this Kingdom of God spiritual environment in the household. And when you understand how hard that is to do for him in the face of his own fleshly tendencies, and not only that, but also the spirit of the World pressures and influences that must be overcome to achieve this. And when you consider that he will be accountable to God for this happening, and that he will not be able to blame his wife for submitting to another spirit as Adam did....then you can see why God is encouraging the wife to <u>support him</u> in this and <u>respect him</u> for the burden that he carries.

It is conceivable that she will not have to stand before God in regard to whether or not the Holy Spirit was present, ruling and given place in the household. Perhaps he, largely will have to give account for this. Indeed, the man is to be *the 'initiator'* of Gods order in the household. Man may seek to blame his wife, but as we have related God had already given Him the instructions before she was created.

> *Genesis 3:11-12* [11] *And He said, "Who told you that you were naked? Have you eaten from the tree of which I commanded you that you should not eat?"* [12] *Then the man said, "The woman whom You gave to be with me, she gave me of the tree, and I ate." NKJV*

Additionally, she has been instructed to submit to him. Realizing that God has made the man to be a spiritual covering for her in a practical sense, it stands to reason that it is in her interests to help him to grow into being as good as possible at fulfilling this role. Women in general are more open relationally. When I was a young man, I did some door to door sales work. Both of the companies that I was employed by trained us to convince the housewives through the day that they needed the product. We were then to return in the evening after the wife had talked the man into the purchase and close the sale. Sound familiar? Satan certainly understood this a long time ago.

In general women are more open and feelings based, and men as a rule are a little more analytical and logical. For this reason, it is often the women who are open to the concept of God and are many times converted first. The men are hanging back trying to work it all out… but often eventually follow their wives back to church. Perhaps this is Gods reversal of the garden? The first woman led man astray through her openness and seemingly innocently not expecting anyone to mislead her.

Maybe in Gods economy this willingness to trust is now bringing many back to Him?

'INITIATORS' AND HORMONAL REALITIES
Hormonal differences
It has been often said that hormones make the World go around. Well they make each of our own individual little Worlds and physical function work anyway. Hormones are little chemical messengers that activate physical activities, emotional responses, and processes including appetite and sexual activity. Men and women are dramatically different hormonally. A man's hormones tend to go along much the same from day to day whereas pre menopause, women go through a diversity of changes throughout their monthly cycle. These will impact, amongst other things mood and sexual interest. (Post-menopausal women in general have lower and more stable hormone values)

A man reportedly can have between 10 and 38 times as much testosterone as women, with possibly on average around 20 to 25 times the amount. Testosterone is largely the hormone implicated in sexual thinking and interest. As a result, many women rarely if ever think about sex without the thought or idea being introduced to her. Men on the other hand often think about it quite a lot because of their much higher hormone levels. So, we see from this undeniable level of hormones that man has been created to most often be the initiator of the sexual act.

This is a physical outworking of the spiritual position described in Ephesians Chapter 5 that we have just looked at. Jesus is the initiator of the spiritual relationship with His bride the Church, coming into her to make her fruitful if she will respond. The church is not always willing to respond to her husband Jesus, but when she does it is a great blessing. Women often don't feel very much like sex, but if they respond to the man and accept his overtures, it can be a source of great blessing and intimacy for both.

Perhaps we see a picture of this in Song of Solomon chapter 5 where the lover – a type of Jesus – comes to the door. She has prepared for bed it seems and is not immediately willing to respond and so He leaves. Tired wives who are not feeling like responding to her man's initiating of sex, and possibly can't understand why he is even thinking about it, will often see him leaving emotionally. She also will probably have trouble finding her husband relationally afterwards. A key is for the wife to understand that God has given her husband a relentless sex drive which simply will not go away, it remains even if he is tired. He did not ask for it, it is just there. So, it goes a long way to realize that for the girls it is at times sacrificial in the 1st instance to respond. But it's also good to know that even though it takes a bit longer to get the *'motor running'* it will happen, if she is willing to be willing.

For the man's part he needs to realize that his wife probably doesn't think about sex as he does, and her sexuality is not visually stimulated as his is. Consequently, it is unlikely that if she sees him coming out of the shower that it would be arousing for her as it is for him. This is normal because of how the two different genders are created. So, the male needs to initiate the idea of intimacy by communicating his hopes for connecting on this level. He is far more likely to get a favorable response if he is cherishing and loving his wife, taking care of her needs, and making her feel safe, significant, cared about, and protected. This is how Christ deals with his bride, and this includes covering and having grace for imperfections. We could say that the interaction of sex is the sum of all of these things. Mental agreement, emotional wholeness and spiritual oneness concluding with the physical joining of the two. The sexual encounter improves in quality as all of these other components flourish and come to the fullness of God's order.

All of this is underlined in terms of godly attitudes by the phrase from the passage that we have just quoted;

Ephesians 5:21 Submit to one another out of reverence for Christ. NIV

In practice this means being willing to give of yourself and sometimes lay down that which you want for the sake of unity. If the wife is tired or not in the mood, he can set the tone of the relationship with something like; "that's ok perhaps tomorrow?" This is exhibiting love, patience and self-control. A tip for the men is don't think about sex too much or make too many plans about when it might occur, without putting the idea to your wife, and getting confirmation that it is in fact going to going to happen. This will avoid your body preparing for something that is not going to take place, and then getting all disappointed and upset. For the lady's part, at times she may give of herself and be responsive even though she doesn't feel like it. This giving attitude and being sensitive to each other's needs is incredibly bonding in the relationship as a whole. It says in what I call the 'language of the spirit;' "I value what <u>you</u> want and need, therefore I genuinely care about <u>you</u>."

SUMMARY

We could summarize then by saying that the things that need to be in Gods order for marriage to work, are the same attitudinal things that we must do to be the true bride of Christ. If we can't or won't lay down what <u>we</u> want, and give of, or die to ourselves in our marriages, then we probably won't lay down self, and prefer what Gods wants in relationship with Him either.

How we are in our married state then is often a reflection of our inner attitudes and progress in sanctification. Marriage, although perhaps the hardest relationship to work through, has the greatest potential to put us through the process of becoming Holy, perfected, and sanctified.

I was in Nigeria in the early 2000's and there was a young man there with his fiancé. He was looking for a prophet's confirmation that it was ok to get married to her. Some other Pastors were staying with the young man and I in a dorm situation. I overheard these Pastors 'counseling' the young man to reconsider the marriage idea. In their opinion he was foolish to marry this young lady as in their view she had some 'issues.' A little later I was with him and asked him if he loved her? His answer was yes. I then inquired as to whether they both wanted what God wanted for their lives, and if they were both prepared to let the Lord deal with them? Again, the answer was yes.

So, I explained to him that the easy, 'seemingly' best for yourself path, is actually not many times the best for you in the long run. If we walk away from the hard things in life, we may well be walking away from that which affords God the opportunity to sanctify us. In my experience the 'problems' and 'issues' that people might have are quite simple for God to heal when it is time. The walking through and growing together in finding God for these problems is precious in terms of bonding, and what we ourselves eventually become. The gold comes through the refiners' fire bringing off the dross. We can of course walk away from it, and miss the opportunity to grow in love and grace in the process of becoming Christlike. In any case, in this situation, fortunately for me the 'prophet' confirmed the union as being a good match.

Study 3: Healthy sexuality

Let us put in summary what we are saying here. Healthy sexuality can only fully exist in the context of Gods intended plan for it. Everything that we are endeavoring to do here is aimed at restoring created order for the whole relationship which includes sexuality. Let us examine in brief what these precepts regarding health in sexuality are.

1. Spiritual values. Somebody once described what is called a 'tessellation' to me. These are shapes that can be closely fitted together, and can be stacked up. A triangle is such a shape, and it can be fitted with other triangles to build a massive triangle as big as you want. So, if we imagine a man and woman looking to each other we have a line, and if they are both looking individually to God, we have 2 more lines which make the shape. If we think of many other couples in this configuration, we can imagine how the kingdom of God can be built up, and why the opposer does so much to attack marriage and break down the structure. Consequently, if we are both looking to God to conform our spiritual attitudes to those of Christ Jesus, then we will have common spiritual ground for all aspects of our relationship.

> *Romans 8:29 For those God foreknew he also predestined to be conformed to the likeness of his Son, that he might be the firstborn among many brothers. NIV*

2. Preferring one another in love. Although this is embodied in the last point, I single it out as a vital key to healthy relationships. When most of us were originally married we were probably selfishly thinking that we were engaging with someone whose whole purpose was to meet all of our needs and wants and make us happy. We didn't realize that God's model is the exact opposite of this. For our relationships to work and be functional, we have to know that our part of the team is to unselfishly give of ourselves, and seek to meet the needs of the other.

> *Luke 6:38 Give, and it will be given to you. A good measure, pressed down, shaken together and running over, will be poured into your lap. For with the measure you use, it will be measured to you." NIV*

3. Sowing and reaping. This is a principle that God has instituted. If we sow love, grace, patience and acceptance you can be sure that it will come back on your own head. On the other hand, if you sow criticism, intolerance, rejection and selfishness don't be surprised if these are the attitudes coming back your way! Check your part of the relationship soberly, the condition it is in may well be a reflection on you. My father has always said that life is like a 'sausage machine,' you can only expect to get out of it what you put into it.

4. Willing to be willing. We have already discussed Song of Solomon chapter 5:1-6. This is where the woman was not prepared to respond to her lovers' initiations.

> *1 Corinthians 7:3 The husband should not deprive his wife of sexual intimacy, which is her right as a married woman, nor should the wife deprive her husband. NLT*

The Apostle Paul conceded in 1 Corinthians chapter 7 that because there was so much sexual immorality in the world, that being married and meeting each other's sexual needs in a godly way was the best solution. He acknowledged that because of the sexualized society that they were in, that they were going to be subjected to some level of stimulation through exposure to that environment. He concluded that it was better to deal with sexual appetites appropriately in marriage than to 'burn with lust, or passion.' (Some translations say 'passion' and others 'lust.')

> *1 Corinthians 7:9 But if they cannot control themselves, they should marry,*
> *for it is better to marry than to burn with passion. NIV*

We can deduce then that meeting each other's sexual needs is protecting one another from potential temptations for sexual immorality. The man because of his high levels of sex hormones, and the woman perhaps because of her strong emotional needs…..such as to feel loved and accepted. A good robust sex life is the greatest of defenses against the temptations of a sin sick, excessively sexualized society.

5. Without healthy sexuality every other part of the relationship lacks. Spiritual, mental, emotional, relational and physical intimacies are all activated and showcased in the act of sexual harmony. It is well worth working towards unity in every area of the relationship. The reason that we do the sexuality unit last in the training, is because for it to function as God intended, the areas that I have just mentioned usually need to be restored first.

6. Be fruitful. I have often had ladies complain to me in the ministry room that their husbands are 'animals who just want sex all the time.' *He doesn't love me; he is just an animal.* It is good to realize that behind that much stronger sex drive – that God put on him and he didn't ask for – most likely lays genuine affection and love. For his part he possibly already feels like an 'animal' too because clearly you, the female, do not have the interest for physical intimacy that he does. Indeed, he actually at times may not like himself as a result of his strong urges. If your husband has worked all day and comes in hungry, being loving and affectionate may not be on the top of his list. As with sex, the strong appetite for food is out in front of any romantic thoughts. Once it is satisfied then he is likely to show the affection that he does hold, as well as a bonding appreciation for meeting his needs.

7. Factors that affect the quality of the sexual relationship. Damage from previous experiences may require Gods healing before a healthy physical relationship can occur. Let me just list a few of the potential problems and other considerations that may need to be dealt with.

A] *Beginning your sex life.* Many couples have very poor 1st experiences of sex, even if they are Christians. The church has largely failed to teach about healthy sexuality and adjustment because of some unbiblical prudish religious ideas. As a result, the 'wedding night' or early encounters have not met expectations. These 1st experiences set up a basis for willingness to participate in future engagements. The absence of enjoyment, or the presence of disappointment or anxiety becomes how the sexual act is viewed in the future. It is very important that the church instructs its young people in the area of sexuality. Certainly, the impressions of the Old Testament are earthy robust activities in this area; this could be explained with the older men and women instructing the younger ones.

B] *Past experiences.* Probably for most people today including Christians there are previous sexual relationships in the history. These may have been exciting or romantic times, or bad experiences that left you feeling trashy and cheap. In either case they are to be 'remembered no more.' The connection made to the person or persons are still alive if you think about or replay any of those events in your mind. In that case there is more than one of you in the bed or marriage...and comparisons from memories are extremely counterproductive. They can also be very hurtful if shared with the wrong intention, to hurt or belittle, and can be very damaging to the whole relationship.

C] Unrealistic expectations. Between Hollywood, the movie industry and the proliferation of porn that everyone seems to be exposed to, the devil has confused what the sexual encounter should be. If you use these scripted, acted out models of perfect romance as your guide you may indeed be disappointed. A quick glance at the number of failed marriages that actors and actresses go through should prove that it is indeed all fiction, and that these lifestyles are not working for them. In the porn industry, in reality we hear of physically and emotionally damaged people, and rampant sexually transmitted diseases.

D] Sexual abuse. The statistics that I have viewed for sexual abuse perpetrated towards females in the U.S. are startling, and I feel sure that it would be similar in other 1st world nations. Reportedly there is approximately one out of every three women who have at some time had some form of sexual abuse. This can range from full penetrative sex or rape through to being inappropriately touched by a relative, friend of the family, teacher or even a minister. As I have stated these are the 'reported' cases. In practical experience there are at least as many unreported abuses that have taken place where the victim hasn't for some reason been able to tell anybody.

As we gaze across the church vista, the minority is not those who have been abused, it is more likely those who have not been affected.

We also see an increasing number of males who have also suffered various kinds of sexual abuses and improprieties.

How does this impact the sexual relationship?
Virtually without exception the abuse has had some kind of affect and outworking on the sexuality of the person. For some this means that they come to the position that they believe that they are spoiled, ruined, bad, and now deduce why even try to be good. They then feel that their sexuality means nothing and is a cheap thing and so they can gravitate to becoming promiscuous. Others may come to the conclusion that sex gets them acceptance, and they may confuse this with love.

The majority of those abused that we deal with go the other way. They have taken in various beliefs from the abuse which makes a normal sex life impossible without emotional healing and freedom.

Typically, they associate sex with feelings of guilt, fear, powerlessness, being trapped, dirtiness, or the belief that it is bad and not to be enjoyed, amongst other things.

Many times, they come to us with these negative emotions without being able to report what it is that they believe. To them they are just bad feelings to be avoided, therefore sex should also be avoided.

Often, they do not have memories of the abuse as they have blocked these out in some way. As a result, they come for ministry reporting that these emotions present when approached by their wives or husbands. They may come reporting an inability to express their sexuality or be engaged in the act of sex. They may not even be able to participate at all as a result of their anxieties.

The spouse many times doesn't understand why their partner does not want to engage in the sexual act as they do. Very often the spouse feels rejected, inadequate, undesirable or even not loved. Communication can be very important here so that they do not feel that the problem is with them. Normally the spouse is quite compassionate and relieved when they see that it is not their fault and understands that their partner needs help and healing. It is not uncommon to find that people who have been abused are sexually active and without obvious problems before they are married. *(Clearly, they should not have been, but where they have come from is not for us to judge, only to help them in their situation at the moment.)*

The reason for this is because often before they are married, they don't feel as though they have to have sex.... but when they get married it seems that they don't have a choice, they have to do it. So, they connect to the belief and feeling that they are 'trapped and cannot get away,' which is what they commonly felt in the abusive situation. Along with the overwhelming trapped feeling come all the other feelings which now make the whole act of sex seem repulsive.

It is vitally important to resolve these issues if the gift of sex is to be shared fully in the marriage environment.

 **By all means seek help. You are not stuck; we have seen God free a great many people who have been abused. These people go on to have a normal sexual relationship and produce wonderful children.

*(To reinforce how to be set free of these beliefs and negative feelings see the teaching unit on 'Truth Encounters.'**)*

E] *Relational maladjustment through unresolved emotional issues.* Many Christians do not know how to relate along biblical lines. As a consequence, their marriages and attitudes reflect the values of another worldly kingdom rather than the kingdom of God.

Often it is difficult to live a biblically ideal relational life while we have these unhealed areas or places of bondage.

Partners may take alternate routes to express their sexuality. For example, a man who fears failure or rejection in the bedroom may gravitate towards pornography where there is no perceived pressure, or apparent expectation on him to perform or succeed.
So, for healthy sex to occur many times healing from low self-image, inferiority, selfishness, fear of rejection or failure, guilt, performance anxiety or other emotional problems may need to be resolved. These issues that can relate to belief-based wounds could produce the following attitudes and responses:

Selfishness, (not wanting to give- only wanting to get)
Rejection, etc (misreading the situation if a partner is not wanting to engage)

Beliefs such as;   *'I am nothing, nobody, I don't matter, I am being used.'*
                                   'He/she doesn't really care about me!'
                                   'I am not acceptable, attractive, good enough, etc'
......are some of the types of beliefs that suggest the need for emotional healing.

*(To reinforce how to be set free of these beliefs and negative feelings see the teaching unit on 'Truth Encounters.'**)*

F] The Emotional element of sexuality: Sex appears on face value to be primarily a physical activity. As a result, the modern world has tried to reduce it to being just about pleasure, of no more importance than eating ice-cream.

However, over the years I have come to understand that it is firstly an emotional and relational exercise that involves the use of the body.

Some time ago I was explaining the conclusion that I had come to, to a friend. His response was to ask me if I had seen You Tube clips done by an American man by the name of Pastor Jimmy Evans from Texas in the U.S.A. on the subject. Quoting a study that was done by Dr. Gary and Barb Rosberg in the U.S. he cited the top 5 things that men and women are looking for in marriage.

(Book: The 5 sex needs of men & women, by Dr. Gary & Barbara Rosberg. Tyndale House Publishers.)

You will note that they are all basically how sex affects you emotionally in the process of valuing, accepting and caring enough about each other to serve, rather than selfishly making sex about what you can get for yourself. Here broadly, are the observations, with any additional comments that I make in brackets.

1. Women: To know that before sex that she is appreciated for all that she does, appreciated for being beautiful or attractive.

1. Men: Mutual satisfaction…. that he is pleasing his wife and that she is enjoying it…. having fun. (In part 2 on distorted sexuality we will discuss pornography. You can easily see the emotional lure for men, in that a lot of the excitement is that the women are portrayed as enjoying the sex, and being greatly pleasured by the men involved.) (The following passage from 1 Corinthians 7:33 refers to men who get married spending time working out how to please their wives…in light of this study, might I suggest that they are not worrying about how to please her through doing the dishes, or housework!)

> *1 Corinthians 7:33 But he who is married cares about the things of the world; how he may please his wife. NKJV*

2. This is the same for both men and women…. they want to feel connected with their partner.

3. Women: Non sexual affection.
(This means that she wants to feel loved and valued for who she is regardless of the sexual act.)

APPOINTMENTS
(As was mentioned in this study, we found a number of years ago that one very practical way to do this is make appointments for your physical encounters. How frequent this is may depend on your age and state of health. Let us say to illustrate, that if you are for example 40 years old, and sexual frequency of twice per week was sufficient for you both, then you may agree on Tuesdays, and Saturday nights.

The advantage in this is that for the man, he is no longer thinking about how to make overtures or about sex in general, as he knows his day is coming. For the woman, the advantage is that firstly she is slower to be aroused, so if she knows that it is coming up, she can prepare herself. And secondly, she knows that any affection that she receives on other days is genuine love that doesn't have any other motive involved.

> **Note:** This may not be applicable to early marriage where romance is high and responses are more spontaneous!

3. Men: The responsiveness of the wife saying 'yes,' being interested. (Otherwise he feels rejected, not attractive to you. Eventually, depending on his spiritual walk, this could make him vulnerable to temptations such as pornography where he doesn't need to fear rejection, or possibly to the perceived acceptance of other women. If his rejection is deep, he may even look for it.)

4. Women: Spiritual intimacy with the husband. (Sex is a spiritual act, where you share a deep bonding as spiritual beings. If it is done in the nature of the Spirit of God it will be gracious, accepting, valuing, strengthening and building up)

4. Men: Women to initiate sex at times. (In a practical sense because the man has more testosterone, he is most likely to initiate. But for a wife to be affectionate knowing that it could lead to sex, and that she is open to this possibility is emotionally meaningful to a man. Some women do have stronger sex drives than their husbands, and certainly at the time of the monthly cycle where they are most fertile their sexual interest is often higher.)

5. Women: Romance – that there is more to your love than physical pleasure.
(This could include giving her attention, and taking time to hear what is happening in her life. It may also involve valuing her enough to think to get her a gift that she would like.)

5. Men: Affirmation, that you appreciate him. (Perhaps this could be to do with him being a good provider, or protector, that he is attractive and more than enough for you...that he is pleasing you.)

In all of these points from the study we note that what people are looking for in sex is primarily emotional and relational....and God in His goodness has intended it to be enjoyable. Which leads us into the next element that is required for good sexual function. Being instructed in what to expect in terms of how our bodies work is very important for success in sexual adjustment. Ignorance of the 'mechanics' of sex is a common cause for lack of sexual fulness and enjoyment.

Study 4: Adjusting the physical components of sex

Sex has been described as the glue that sticks a marriage together. It certainly is intended to be an act of unique intimacy, spiritually, mentally, emotionally and chemically bonding. It is an act that in Gods purpose is specific to knowing each other in the commitment of a marriage relationship. It is therefore of prime importance to have it functioning well according to Gods design. As we have already stated, God is not embarrassed or offended by how we are made. It was His design and purpose, not our idea, and I am sure that He is pleased and glorified when we enjoy it...having given us everything that we need for our pleasure and enjoyment. 1 Timothy 6:17

There are physical functional elements of the sexual encounter that need to be considered and learnt. You are much more likely to want to engage with each other in this important relational exercise if it is an enjoyable and satisfying experience, and you are not left frustrated. Both men and women can experience discomfort or pain if they are aroused and do not experience the subsequent release of orgasm. In order for you to be mutually satisfied and pleasured we need to understand and implement the necessary mechanical elements. In many ways the human body is a highly sophisticated and amazing machine, and as with any machine, you need to operate it properly and understand some basic principles to get the best out of it.

You would not consider putting oil in the radiator of your car, and water in the engine and expect it to perform well. When I was younger, I liked to play games such as tennis and golf. I quickly learnt that if I wanted to be any good at them, I had to master principles such as weight transfer, and develop and practice correct techniques. A good lover also needs a good working knowledge of sexual physiology; it normally must be taught and learnt before it can function properly and produce optimum results.

THE NEED FOR HEALTHY INSTRUCTION ON SEXUALITY

I was listening to the radio at a restaurant one day while waiting for my meal to be prepared. There was a talk show on, and the lady being interviewed was talking about her immensely popular media 'blog,' which as I recall, was called something like, *no one is having good sex.* Her 'blog' had thousands of subscribers and comments coming from worldwide, and her audience included well known movie stars. Going by the name of her site it appears that the majority of people outside of Christianity are not well educated in healthy sexual adjustment either. In the church it is our responsibility to teach Gods purposes and give help and instruction.

I would make two comments before I go further on this section. One, to reiterate, God is not disgusted about any bodily function that we have. He designed them and they are perfect. Two; I am not a sex counselor or therapist. There are some excellent Christian authors who are experts on the subject of sexual adjustment, and they can be readily sourced for more detailed studies. Rather than directly quoting word for word in the following passages on sexual adjustment, I am going to indicate where I have referenced the following Christian publications. It will, unless quoted and inserted, be my words, attempting to be faithful to their information on the subject.

I am adding in this fairly graphic study for two reasons. One is that a few years ago while conducting a School in an African nation, when I glossed over the 'how to' part of the need for understanding sexual mechanics, a young Pastor about to get married complained that he wanted to know what to do. Clearly it is necessary to provide some level of instruction for fulness in relationships. Secondly, if we don't instruct our young people, they will go to the world for their information, and get the distorted version promoted through media. The devil loves to work in the dark. We need to bring sexuality out into the light.

** THE GIFT OF SEX   Clifford and Joyce Penner   Word Books
*   SEXUAL HAPPINESS IN MARRIAGE   Herbert J. Miles, Ph.D. Zondervan Books

An additional helpful Christian publication on the subject is:
INTENDED FOR PLEASURE   Ed and Gaye Wheat

UNDERSTANDING OUR BODIES
Female genitals. The predominant female sexual organs are the clitoris and the vagina.

The vagina is the opening or sheath that receives the male organ, the penis, in the sexual act. It is considered that the lower one third where the penis enters, or one and a half to two inches of the vagina is sensitive during sexual arousal. Consequently, as we discuss the male and female parts in sexual intercourse, let us also dispel some of the associated myths.

The assumption that the larger a man's penis, the better he will be able to satisfy a woman just isn't true. First of all, most women don't gain the majority of their sexual satisfaction from the penis being in the vagina, no matter what size the penis. Women tend to be most responsive to generous sensuous body caressing and stimulation of the breasts and external genitalia. **
The clitoris is considered to be the primary organ implicated in the female orgasm. It has no other function than the sexual pleasure of the woman and is exclusively intended for sexual sensation. It is located outside and above the vagina, at the uppermost point where the inner lips meet, on average one and a quarter inches from the vaginal passage. (32mm)

The clitoris is loaded with nerve endings and its stimulation by some means is normally regarded as the primary source of the female orgasm.

Many women report that the most pleasurable place to receive stimulation is around the clitoris, not directly on it. **

Male genitals. The male sexual organ is called the penis, and it is inserted into the vagina in the consummation of the sexual act. Ejaculation with or without orgasm is the primary delivery system for sperm bearing semen that inseminates the woman to become pregnant. Due to the influences of modern media including pornography, many men universally have anxiety about the size and ability of their penis to satisfy their marriage partner.

Women are often concerned that their breast are too big, too small, or too whatever. A man may be concerned with the size of his penis, fearing that a smaller penis is indicative of being less of a man and less able to satisfy a woman.

The truth is that the woman has the organ of accommodation; that is, the vagina changes to accommodate any size penis. Therefore, penis size has little to do with sexual pleasure or satisfaction…. just as the length of a man's penis has little or nothing to do with his effectiveness during sexual intercourse, neither does the circumference or thickness of his penis have any importance for sexual performance.

The woman's PC muscle can tighten so as to completely close the opening to the vagina; therefore, a thin penis can still have firm sensation from the vagina. ** (Note: this is more likely to be the case if the woman is fully aroused before the insertion of the penis. It is well worth doing the necessary preparation before penetration for the enjoyment of both husband and wife.)

The reported size of the penis worldwide in a flaccid state may vary considerably, (flaccid means in a relaxed, unaroused condition) in its state of erection the average is 5 to 6 and a half inches in length.

Masters and Johnson have found that the unaroused (flaccid) penis size does not relate proportionately to erect penis size. A small flaccid penis, upon sexual stimulation, enlarges to a greater extent than does a larger flaccid penis. In their erect state there is not much difference in size between one penis and another, even though they may differ significantly in size when they are not aroused. **

COMMON ANXIETIES

Before we talk about the mechanics of sexual adjustment, let us preface this with the knowledge that achieving good adjustment many times is difficult because of emotional issues that need to be resolved. For example, we have just addressed a common anxiety in men regarding self-image and being equipped to please their wives.

Many women also struggle to relax and enjoy their sexuality for a variety of reasons.

How we feel about ourselves affects how we relate to another person, particularly sexually. It has been found that preorgasmic women (those who have not yet experienced orgasm) who feel unworthy and have difficulty accepting themselves as persons cannot be helped to become orgasmic until they deal with these feelings of low self-worth. **

(To know how to minister to these low self-worth issues, see the unit on 'Truth Encounters.' We have seen that as these seemingly unrelated self-belief problems are resolved, that healthy sexuality is able to occur. This is why this unit is placed last in the training, giving people the opportunity to in part be emotionally whole, maximizing the possibilities, before expecting too much in attempting realistic sexual adjustment.)

It is necessary that we proceed into the sexual act without placing expectations on each other. I recall one young man attending a conference that I was doing in a developing nation, and when I was teaching on this subject, he asked me in the question time; *what if I get a wife and she is no good at sex, do I get rid of her?*

This was fairly obviously a worldly, selfish, sex is about me getting what I want attitude, as opposed to the Godly, what can I give in serving you position. My response to him was;

"Nobody is automatically good at sex, it is like everything else in life, you have to learn how to do it properly if you want to be good at it. In this case it is precious to learn together. (Although I admit that I wanted to say, 'what if you are no good' should she dump you?)"

Sexual anxiety grows out of the demand for performance. This demand may come from within one's self or from one's partner. If we enter the sexual experience with pressure to produce desirable experiences for our loved one or a response in ourselves, that demand will cause anxiety. **

Often people insecure about their self-worth and value will be compulsive in their need for sex, striving to get the bonding, acceptance and connection through the physical act, and meet the emotional fulfillment that they crave.

People with an excessive need to please their partner usually grew up in a situation where they had to work diligently for parental approval. Even with hard work they received little in the way of reward that built their self-worth. These people go through life looking for approval and reinforcement they never received as a child. **

Aside from the need to deal with general emotional issues in order to function well sexually, often anxiety comes in any area of life when we do not know what to do. Therefore, we have a responsibility to each other to study sexuality so that we can be effective in our part of the partnership.

The husband is responsible to meet his wife's sexual needs. He must regularly and lovingly arouse her to a complete sexual experience, climax (or orgasm). Likewise, the wife must meet *her husband's sexual needs. She must regularly and lovingly arouse him to a sexual experience, climax (or orgasm). ***

In a Christian setting, normally it's not that we do not want to do the right thing, it's usually more that we don't know what to do. Which leads us into the next section.

THE 'MECHANISMS' OF THE SEXUAL ACT

*There are two major problems that tend to block good sexual adjustment in marriage. To make it easy to remember these two problems, we will call them "time" and "space" and discuss them in that order.***

The "time" problem

Remember, God created us differently from each other. In His plan for most things to work we have to be prepared to give of ourselves. In the sexual act we find that the first thing that we must deal with is the matter of timing. Men and women have different timing in arousal. A man can become excited very quickly, in part, because he is visually and mentally stimulated. A woman typically takes longer, and being emotionally based is responsive, in part in the first instance, to romance and touch. The man must learn patience if he cares for the pleasure of his partner.

Both man and woman have been given the ability to experience pleasure through orgasm. But another problem emerges. A man can be ready for orgasm in a comparatively short amount of time. His wife may need a considerable amount of stimulation to arouse her before she comes to that place.

*By "time," we refer to the fact that, sexually, male and female bodies are "timed" differently. Sexually, man is timed quickly. He can become aroused through sexual stimulation with his wife and usually reach orgasm in a very short time, two minutes, one minute, or in even less time. This is normal for him. He will gradually learn to control himself, but he will always tend to be "quick on the trigger." The wife should realize that all other women's husbands are "quick on the trigger."***

Remember that success for a man sexually is very important for his self-esteem. The wife then is more likely to get the results that she wants by encouraging him, so that he can grow confident and achieve self-control, rather than deriding him if he lacks endurance, adding to his anxiety.

*On the other hand, sexually, a woman is timed more slowly, sometimes very slowly, as compared with a man. We can safely say that it takes the average woman ten to fifteen minutes or longer from the time that she starts sexual arousal with her husband until she experiences an orgasm. ***

Note: This time would usually include the beginnings of sexual activity, such as kissing and fondling, preparing for, and prior to the stimulation of her more sensitive sexual parts.

*Sometimes she may have an orgasm in ten minutes, five minutes, or even less. A few women on special occasions have an orgasm in one or two minutes. This is the exception. ***

Note: other studies have indicated typically 7 minutes as an average. But there can be many factors involved, such as tiredness, stress, age, and even anxiety from previous experiences.

Many other circumstances such as what is happening in her personal life, or where she is in her monthly cycle may play a role in this, more so than her husband. He should realize that this is the case for all men's wives, and that she is created this way. She takes longer. Perhaps in Gods economy for sexuality to work, the man must be patient and loving, caring more about her needs than his own wants. In fact, in my personal opinion, the man's attitude to sex should be all about her pleasure, and not his own. It truly is better to give than receive. The man who approaches sexuality in this manner will find it far more fulfilling. Indeed, sowing and reaping applies here. The wife, for her part, has to be willing to be willing to be involved in the process, giving herself to him even when initially she may not be aroused, whereas he is excited immediately.

When a young couple understands the difference in their sexual timing and when they accept it and cooperate with it, it is no longer a major problem, but may actually be a blessing. By being a blessing, we mean that this period of sexual stimulation and arousal, whether it be 10 or 20 minutes, may become one of the sweetest, most meaningful and spiritual experiences in husband-wife relationships. *

The "Space" problem

The second major problem that tends to block good sexual adjustment we have called "space." "Space" refers to the distance on the body of the wife between the clitoris and the vaginal passage. The clitoris is the external arousal trigger that sets off orgasm in the woman. It is made up of many nerve endings designed by the creator to arouse a woman to an orgasm. *

As we have already noted, the clitoris is situated about 30mm or one and a quarter inches above the vagina, out in front to some degree at the upper meeting point of the inner lips. It has been described as a 'mini penis' having a shaft and being very sensitive.

When this fact is visualized and understood, it should become clear that in normal intercourse the penis does not touch or contact the clitoris. This fact is of major importance. Since the penis does not move back and forth over the clitoris in intercourse, the wife may not become fully aroused and thus will not have an orgasm. *

It has been suggested that any 'positions' which may allow the penis to contact the clitoris may not be very comfortable for either the wife or the husband. Coupled with this, most husbands cannot control themselves for 10 or 15 minutes so that the wife has sufficient stimulation to have an orgasm.

Since the clitoris is the arousal trigger of the wife, and since the penis does not contact the clitoris in normal intercourse, marriage counselors recommend what is called "direct" stimulation. That is, the husband, in the process of love-play before intercourse starts, will gently stimulate all the erotic zones of his wife's body. This includes kissing her lips and breasts and using his hands and fingers to explore her total body, including the inner thighs, her outer lips, the opening of her vagina, and finally her clitoris.*

If you have not been exposed to these concepts on good sexual mechanics before, you may be struggling in the directness of the quotations.

If you read the book of Song of Songs from the Bible you will find that it is both blatantly descriptive of erotic activity, and poetic and sensual in its illustration of sexual anatomy. It eludes to the activities that are being described in a beautiful and tasteful way.

He will continue the stimulation of the clitoris for ten or fifteen minutes, or whatever time it takes, until he is sure that she is fully aroused sexually and ready for intercourse. *

Note: each woman knows what she prefers in this preparation phase, and this may vary from encounter to encounter. Some women do not want continuous manual stimulation of the clitoris without other touching and caressing taking place. (A sexual meeting can take place beginning with the man giving the wife a back massage, which shows affection, and gives the man's arousal time to settle down before intercourse takes place.)

*The important thing to remember here is that the clitoris is the external arousal trigger; that there must be stimulation of the clitoris and the area near the clitoris for a wife to have an orgasm. The method of stimulation of the clitoris is not so important. ***

On a practical note, there is some kind of lubrication required normally for the stimulation of the wife to not be uncomfortable. This normally would come naturally in the process of touching the moisture around the vaginal area. Many women do not like fingers being inserted deeply into the vagina, if at all. At times some other kind of lubricant may be required, and this may be the case for example, with post-menopausal women who no longer self-lubricate as when they were younger.

To summarize here. After suitable sexual arousal of both man and wife, which will invariably include direct stimulation for her, the penis is inserted and one following the other in movement they move together towards orgasm with the penis inside the vagina.

WHAT IF THIS IS NOT SUFFICIENT FOR BOTH TO ACHIEVE ORGASM AND SATISFACTION?

Let me preface answering this by citing the results of question 54 in the book; SEXUAL HAPPINESS IN MARRIAGE

54. When the wife is aroused near an orgasm, can she reach the orgasm after intromission (inserting the penis in the vagina) during the process of intercourse without further direct stimulation of the clitoris?
*Yes 58.7%   No 41.3% ***

The evidence is that a significant number of women cannot reach orgasm without continued direct stimulation. I have read other more recent statistics stating that this is the case with well over 60% of women.

So, how is this lovingly negotiated, caring for the needs of the wife?

1. One way is as follows. After the arousal period and immediately after intercourse is started, the husband may place the weight of his body on his left arm, put his right hand down on his wife's clitoris, and give her further direct stimulation while intercourse continues. This is somewhat awkward....

2. ......if the wife can have orgasms by direct stimulation but cannot get to an orgasm in intercourse, it is wise for the wife to have further direct stimulation of the clitoris while in the process of intercourse.
*After the arousal period as the husband shifts to start intercourse, the wife may put her finger on her own clitoris and continue giving herself the same direct stimulation that her husband has been giving her. ***

Of the two methods, it is considered that the second one is the most comfortable, and the most efficient. Remember the goal is to work as a team caring about, and meeting each other's needs.

*This pairing of clitoral manipulation with intercourse has been found to be quite effective for many couples. ***

At times as the wife nears orgasm but is taking time to climax the man may be unable to control himself and hold on until she has climaxed. To remove the pressure on each partner and diffuse potential future anxiety, the husband can continue to directly stimulate his wife after his orgasm until she is also fulfilled. The main thing is that emotionally you are accepting of each other's needs, and caring about giving the partner enjoyment and arrival at completion. Indeed, God's gift of sex is to be able to pleasure each other in this way.

Some meaningful time spent together caressing, embracing or resting together is loving way to complete the encounter.

All of this requires good communication about what is liked or disliked to get it to work well. This usually takes time and patience, but if you are dedicated to each other you will get there. Good sex then becomes a strength for your relationship protecting you from the temptations of illicit sexual expression.

PART 2: Distorted sexuality

Sexuality is an area that clearly is very important to God. It is the most intimate of relationships, which includes sharing with Him in creation. As we have pointed out it is a beautiful picture portraying the relationship between Christ and His bride. Faithfulness because of the emotional and relational ramifications of infidelity is vital. And purity because the devil seeks to distort and pervert Gods perfect ways and order for the blessing of mankind, His creation. As a result, we see judgments for sexual immorality listed 19 times in the New Testament from Matthew to Revelation. In the Old Testament it is revealed that the devil's way for sexuality brings a curse for up to 10 generations, highlighting the seriousness of this type of offense. (Deuteronomy 23:2)

BECOMING WHAT WE BEHOLD

In Australia there are programs that show all of the newest video clips that go along with the latest pop songs. In many of these clips are males and particularly females who are dancing erotically and simulating sexual movements. I was told by a young lady that girls who watch one of these shows in particular have usually lost their virginity and become sexually active by the time that they are 13 years old. People who view pornography or other sexually explicit materials including many modern movies often have a distorted perspective of sex. They are programmed by the media to think that what they are viewing is normal, desirable and pleasurable. This underlying subliminal message that doing this will make you happy causes us to want to be what we see. It is a principle that we become like whatever we worship. (Psalm 115:8)

I have heard of non-homosexual men and women wanting to try sex with someone of their own gender because they have viewed it on the screen in a pornographic setting. Or other disturbing things like violent sex, sodomy, (anal sex) incest sex, or bestiality (sex with animals) are all now promoted as something to experiment with in the world of sexual media.

> *Romans 12:2 Do not conform any longer to the pattern of this world, but be transformed by the renewing of your mind. Then you will be able to test and approve what God's will is--his good, pleasing and perfect will. NIV*

SEX AND THE 'MEANING OF LIFE'

Living for sex and being ruled by our primal appetites is clearly wrong. It becomes idolatry of the flesh, of the creation and not the creator. Much modern media seems to make it central, and in a sense, 'the meaning of life.' Personally, I think that it should be regarded as a gift, and even at times an appetite that needs to be dealt with periodically, in order for your relationship with God to not be distracted.

Study 1: Sins of 'Omission'

As with other areas that we have discussed, with sexuality there can be times where the problem is not in things that we have done, but rather, in things that we should have done, but have omitted to do. To deny sexuality as a 'very good' God purposed part of creation is also sin. Sin means 'to offend,' or 'an offense.' To discard God's gift as not good may well be offensive to Him.

I have ministered to a number of well-meaning Christians who thought that it was Holy to abstain from sex. Unfortunately, the spouses often did not share the same values and the relationship was diminished as a result. I have seen otherwise godly couples who look more like any other friends, rather than a bonded, one flesh couple.

This type of ungodly attitude can give grounds for bitterness, or if the need for acceptance through sexuality is high, adultery or some other kind of immorality. At times we see religions that deny marriage and sexuality, who as a result have a high incidence of immoral behavior, often including sexual abuse. You cannot deny being a sexual being because you are going against created order. You can only express it appropriately in a biblical manner. There exists a very small percentage of people who apparently have no sexual interest whatsoever.

The Apostle Paul was very direct in the matter of deliberately trying to deny marital sexual activity.

> 1 Timothy 4:1-3 ¹ The Spirit clearly says that in later times some will abandon the faith and _follow deceiving spirits and things taught by demons_. ² Such teachings come through hypocritical liars, whose consciences have been seared as with a hot iron. ³ _They forbid people to marry_ and order them to abstain from certain foods, _which God created to be received with thanksgiving_ by those who believe and who know the truth. NIV (emphasis mine)

We could summarize all of this by saying that to deny ourselves or our spouses' healthy sexual expression is unhealthy. It leaves us open to temptation, potential immorality, or sinful responses such as bitterness and resentment. Remember rejection can produce rebellion, because in affect it is projecting onto the person that what they need or want means nothing to you. This will read as unfairness or injustice on the recipient as they are feeling that you do not care about them.

> 1 Corinthians 7:2-5 ² But because there is so much sexual immorality, each man should have his own wife, and each woman should have her own husband. ³ The husband should not deprive his wife of sexual intimacy, which is her right as a married woman, nor should the wife deprive her husband. ⁴ The wife gives authority over her body to her husband, and the husband also gives authority over his body to his wife. ⁵ So do not deprive

each other of sexual relations. The only exception to this rule would be the agreement of both husband and wife to refrain from sexual intimacy for a limited time, so they can give themselves more completely to prayer. Afterward they should come together again so that Satan won't be able to tempt them because of their lack of self-control. NLT

SUMMARY

We do not want to be:
- Ignoring or refusing Gods gifts in creation
- Denying your partner blessing and intimacy, acceptance and value
- Trying to deny the God created needs of your own body
- Not be willing to accept and cooperate with Gods order

Denial of your sexuality will not make it go away.

Study 2: Sins of 'Commission'

These are sexual sins that are done, and should not be.

> *1 Corinthians 6:9-10* *⁹ Do you not know that the unrighteous will not inherit the kingdom of God? Do not be deceived. Neither <u>fornicators</u>, nor idolaters, nor <u>adulterers</u>, nor <u>homosexuals</u>, nor <u>sodomites</u>, ¹⁰ nor thieves, nor covetous, nor drunkards, nor revilers, nor extortioners will inherit the kingdom of God. NKJV (emphasis mine)*

The preceding passage outlines some of the immoral practices that we are wanting to cover in this study. Noteworthy the Corinthians passage goes on to say that this is what some of you were. This implies that the early church was equipped to help the genuinely repentant to be set free and move on from these practices.

1. Adultery

Jesus points out that adultery is something that happens at heart level. In the following passage I do not believe that Jesus is talking about a man having a strong reaction to sexually attractive women. For young men at the height of their sexuality this can be difficult as many of them are easily aroused at such a sight. Sadly, this problem is exacerbated by how females dress.... sometimes innocently trying to be in step with fashion....and unaware of how they may appear to men.

I believe that what He is saying is that if you want that woman, or even think about sexual activity with her, then you have crossed the line. I am not saying that it is not an issue to stare at a woman who has a good figure and is provocatively dressed, when clearly it is. I am saying that I don't believe that this is what Jesus is talking about here. Lust is desiring something that is prohibited, and consequently not for you.

> *Matthew 5:28-29* *²⁸ "But I say to you that whoever looks at a woman <u>to lust for her</u> has already committed adultery with her in his heart. ²⁹ "If your right eye causes you to sin, pluck it out and cast it from you; for it is more profitable for you that one of your members perish, than for your whole body to be cast into hell. NKJV (emphasis mine)*

In this context, we can say that there is mental and or emotional adultery. This is where you are desiring emotional interaction with a person other than your spouse. Or thinking affectionately about a person other than your marriage partner. Possibly flirting and seeking acceptance or attention from someone else in an effort to meet your emotional needs. If you are married, the only valid person to receive this from is your marriage partner. Clearly, a healthy relationship at home is the best defense, where your emotional needs are met. But even if they are not being fulfilled, perhaps because healing is needed, there is no biblical basis to justify this behavior. For this reason, it is vital that you embark on a journey of seeking personal healing from God. Then instead of trying to get, to meet your own needs, you can both give, and meet each other's needs that are present.

Having said this, the most common reason that we have found for adultery is the need for acceptance. People who come for ministry who have been involved in adulterous activities invariably suffer from rejection. Often a marriage partner does not build up the person who is drawn into the offense, or even if they do, their efforts simply do not touch the unhealed area that needs acceptance.

Most often the person who falls into adultery receives some kind of attention from a person who is also looking for affirmation. This could be in the form of a particular kind of look, a compliment, inappropriate touching, playful flirting, or perhaps even excessive helpfulness. It is the attitude or projection of intent from the person that can easily be read in the language of the spirit as; "I find you attractive and acceptable, and I desire relational interaction with you." For the person who needs to be valued and treated as significant and important, this ministers to the 'heart beliefs' that they hold about their worth and acceptability. It produces a 'good' feeling because their self-image is being bolstered. This is where the problem comes in. They crave that good feeling and it is desirable to go back for more. Many times, they even mistake that emotion for love. In fact, most of us fell in love with someone who connected with us and accepted, even liked us, which was a good feeling.

We conclude then that most times the best way to avoid this sin is to have emotional healing at heart level. (See the Unit on 'Truth Encounters' for keys to freedom.) Additionally, the spouse may not be completely blameless in driving a susceptible person towards this type of relationship. They may either be ignorant of the needs present, or not understand how to meet those needs from a biblical perspective.

Possibly, they might not care about the person and be busily looking after themselves and their own interests. In some cases, the spouse is the source, as they constantly put down or deride the person of their partner, or are abusive and devaluing. This is probably the result of their own unresolved issues.

2. Fornication

The word fornicator is translated from the Greek word 'pornos,' and along with fornicator it means a whoremonger, or a male prostitute. It carries the sense of someone who gives their body for illicit sexual activity. The dictionary meaning for fornication is consensual intercourse between two people not married to each other.

Satan's intention is to reduce sex to animal urges – just fun for yourself – when in fact it is meant for deep spiritual and emotional bonding. Intended as a vehicle for deep valuing, love, affection, acceptance, security and giving.

When we cooperate with the devils' plan for sexuality, we are joining with him in rebellion against the order of God. In this sense, fornication really is 'unprotected sex,' in that we submit ourselves under Satan's plan for us, and remove God as our covering and protection. The book of revelation reveals that those who participate with a Jezebelic spiritual covering of immorality are inviting a bed of suffering (sickbed) as they serve this spirit. And that they will suffer intensely if they do not repent. The devil has indeed come to destroy those who serve him.

> Revelation 2:20-22 [20] *Nevertheless, I have this against you: You tolerate that woman Jezebel, who calls herself a prophetess. By her teaching she <u>misleads my servants into sexual immorality</u> and the eating of food sacrificed to idols.* [21] *I have given her time to repent of her immorality, but she is unwilling.* [22] *So <u>I will cast her on a bed of suffering</u>, and I will make those who commit adultery with her suffer intensely, unless they repent of her ways. NIV (emphasis mine)*

3. Oral sex

This is a controversial issue. Many, even Christian counsellors consider this to be appropriate and acceptable, as long as both partners don't object. This does sound a bit like the humanistic mindset that we hear; *if it's right for you, it's right!* Basically, this kind of thinking proposes that you are your *own god*, which is a pattern of thinking that began in the garden of Eden. Personally, I am more concerned how God views it, than how I view it! Certainly, our culture has embraced it as normal behavior. Is it perversion? I cannot say with 100% clarity, but let me offer a couple of thoughts for consideration.

Firstly, many Christian and other counsellors that I have read suggest that there is nothing harmful in any of the genital areas that you would expose your mouth to. Remembering that the mouth is intended to be the first stage of digestion.

Statistics report that research has proven that people engaged in oral sex are 58 times more likely to develop throat cancer because of the HPV 16 virus that is reportedly present on the genital area. I am pretty sure that God already knows this! Would you consider that to be a blessing or a curse? It appears that as in the garden of Eden, even with sex, man is wanting to push the boundaries, feeling that what God has given is not enough.

Secondly, does not the very nature of things suggest that oral sex is not a clean activity given the proximity to, and functions of, the genitals in the process of waste disposal. If you were an architect or designer would you build a restaurant in a sewerage outlet?

Thirdly, deliverance sometimes occurs from demons who are attached to people who have been involved in these practices, which at times are producing some kind of throat or mouth problem.

Perhaps the question is, would you do this if you had not heard of it and been encouraged in its normalcy and desirability through peer contact or media?

4. Homosexuality/ Sodomy

Unrepentant sexual activity with someone of the same sex is recorded in the scriptures as behavior that will bring problems now and judgement later. We do not say this to judge people who are caught in it, because sin is sin. But if a bus was about to hit you, I imagine that you would want me to call out a warning. So, in love, without judgement we offer help if you want to be free. We respect your free will and choice, and understand that if you do not believe that there is a God, or for that matter a Satan, then you don't care what anyone says anyway. The responsibility of it being reasonable behavior then falls back on you.

I personally don't deal any differently, or make a greater distinction with homosexuals than with anyone else. They are people that something happened to, just like everyone else. God doesn't want to see them perish, as He does not want anyone else to perish. If you are a drunkard eventually as a result, you might expect liver trouble. A medical friend of mine said that many homosexual men who practice sodomy have problems in the anus (back passage) which was designed for one-way traffic. Women who are sodomized suffer similar problems, and there are very often unclean spirits involved. As with any area of bondage, the attitude of the church should be to help these people receive the Fathers love and grace and be set free.

> *Romans 1:24-27* *24 Therefore God gave them over in the sinful desires of their hearts to sexual impurity for the degrading of their bodies with one another. 25 They exchanged the truth of God for a lie, and worshiped and served created things rather than the Creator--who is forever praised. Amen. 26 Because of this, God gave them over to shameful lusts. Even their women exchanged natural relations for unnatural ones. 27 In the same way the men also abandoned natural relations with women and were inflamed with lust for one another. Men committed indecent acts with other men, and received in themselves the due penalty for their perversion. NIV*

We seem to be experiencing a proliferation of homosexuality in our times. Here are some possible reasons why;

1. The generation line. As sodomy even with women has become a seemingly acceptable and even encouraged practice, these spirits have come in, and gone down the family line.
2. The porn industry and the general decay of societal standards encourage all kinds of immorality, and portrays them as acceptable and to be experimented with.
3. Any kind of promiscuity may open the door to unclean spirits influencing further generations.
4. Confusion about gender is publicly encouraged and applauded.
5. A child may have begun in the womb with expectations of being a particular sex. When they are born, they try to live out that which they believe in their hearts that they should be. They cannot not be a sexual being, as a result they try to conform their sexuality around the role they feel that they should be playing.
6. Possibly one of the best documented and most common reasons is the absence of a significant primary caregiver. For example, if a boy has not received a father's love, when he grows up, he while try to prove that he is worthy of love from a male figure. The same is true for girls who have not received the acceptance of their mother.

SODOMY
Today many young people think that sex in the anus (back passage) is just a normal part of sexual experimentation. Some cultures and even religions promote it as a suitable alternative to 'fornication.' Later they carry the practice into marriage.

5. Sexual abuse
We have already discussed the incredibly damage done to the identity through abuse of this kind. One statistic reports 1 in 4 girls under the age of 10 in the U.S. and almost the same for boys. Sadly, many abusers were themselves abused which gives them a predisposition to this practice. They are infected with sexual and spiritual issues that have to be dealt with. The heart of God is to minister to them and set them free. For those who continue not seeking Gods hand of help in this behavior a fearful judgement awaits.

Matthew 18:6-7 ⁶ *But if anyone causes one of these little ones who trusts in me to lose faith, it would be better for that person to be thrown into the sea with a large millstone tied around the neck.* ⁷ *"How terrible it will be for anyone who causes others to sin. Temptation to do wrong is inevitable, but how terrible it will be for the person who does the tempting. NLT*

6. Incest

In today's world there is what is called 'incest porn' which promotes immorality within the family. Sadly, this is often directed towards children. Regardless, the Bible clearly states that this kind of behavior without repentance and the probable need for deliverance will bring a curse.

Deuteronomy 27: 20, 22-23 ²⁰ *"Cursed is the man who sleeps with his father's wife, for he dishonors his father's bed." Then all the people shall say, "Amen!"*
²² *"Cursed is the man who sleeps with his sister, the daughter of his father or the daughter of his mother." Then all the people shall say, "Amen!"* ²³ *"Cursed is the man who sleeps with his mother-in-law." Then all the people shall say, "Amen!" NIV*

The result of incestuous practices, as with any form of abuse can be tragic. In the story of Tamar in 2 Samuel chapter 13, we see her brother Amnon coercing her into a sexual encounter. The final outcome was that it did not end well with him, and the result was that he was murdered by his brother Absalom. Tamar still carried the pain of the event. The scriptures recorded her as being a 'desolate woman' after the rape. We often minister to people who have a 'tragic' look on their faces as a result of the long-term damage from these types of events.

7. Bestiality

Bestiality is primarily having sexual with an animal. It can also relate to savage and depraved behavior. In the context of animals, it is another area of perversion that is strongly being promoted through pornography as acceptable, and as something to 'try' in our current society; posed as *why not?*

The Bible says clearly that it will bring a curse and open you up to the demonic realm. This sometimes make you wonder about animalistic manifestations that occur even in a church environment…and are certainly evident in some developing countries where this is common practice.

We once ministered to a lovely Christian lady out in the Pacific. She struggled with a tendency towards this which destroyed her sex life with her husband. She was overjoyed at discovering that the problem wasn't that she was a bad person, but because the ancestors on the Island of her birth had practiced this, and this was how the weakness had come upon her. She was delighted at being set free and delivered from this problem that had come through her generation line.

Deuteronomy 27:21 "Cursed is the man who has sexual relations with any animal." Then all the people shall say, "Amen!"

I have even read that in Europe today there are 'bestiality brothels 'where people go and pay to have sex with animals. Lord have mercy on these people!

This is more common than the average person may realize. We have ministered to a number of people who have practiced this, not understanding why they did it, and subsequently living a life filled with tremendous guilt. Most times we have found it to be an inherited weakness coming through the generation line.

8. Pornography

Porn is such a pervasive sin epidemic, that Part 3 is devoted to how to help those bound to be extracted from this destructive bondage.

PART 2: Conclusion and summary

The best way to deal with God given appetites and avoid immorality is to:

1. Eat well – in much the same way as healthy food is good for us, and balance is important, so it is with sexuality. Healthy sexual activity is good for our entire being and relationships. In our times a worldly culture has encouraged living for yourself and remaining single through the highest peak of sexuality, and then later marrying. How young people can survive not sinning within this sexualized society without a robust sex life in marriage is beyond my understanding.

2. Eat enough – the best way to not crave something that is not good for you is to be satisfied. I find with food that if I work too late into the day without a good meal, that when I do eat, I will have anything...junk food...just to satiate the appetite. If your sexuality is fulfilling enough, temptations such as pornography are easily resisted.

3. God is the Creator, and everything that He designed is good – to deny His gift could be disrespectful. We are made in His image. He is creative, and so we can be as well in our sexual expression, within the bounds of propriety and morality.

PART 3: Freedom from Pornography

LIKE A FLOOD

> *ISAIAH 59:19 So shall they fear The name of the LORD from the west, And His glory from the rising of the sun; When the enemy comes in like a flood, The Spirit of the LORD will lift up a standard against him. NKJV*

Over many years of ministry, I have had a significant number of men come to me with the problem of being bound to pornography. Most get free if they are really committed to walking away from it. It <u>IS</u> doable! Some others seem to justify it as 'under grace' and others simply prefer to follow their fleshly desires. Those that take this approach usually lose their families if they are married, and almost all struggle in the area of self-respect. I personally believe that some may also lose their health, perhaps even their lives as a result of the guilt and self-conflict that they carry because of this bondage. Guilt and not liking yourself can have a devastating effect on your health.

Sin and serving the kingdom of this World will always produce some sort of consequence. At some level we all know that it is wrong, and we need to come to God to be set free. It is a problem that is 'common to man' and it is a sin epidemic that is proliferating rapidly in our time across the world. The good news is that God sets the captives free! He will show you a way out and what to do so that you do not need to give in to it again.

> *1 Corinthians 10:13 But remember that the temptations that come into your life are <u>no different from what others experience</u>. And God is faithful. He will keep the temptation from becoming so strong that you can't stand up against it. When you are tempted, <u>he will show you a way out so that you will not give in to it</u>. NLT (emphasis mine)*

Pornography has been described as a mental illness, possibly because it produces a kind of torment of the mind. Many men, and possibly women, cannot stop thinking about sex as a result of their exposure. The Bible describes everything that God created as good, so we can establish right at the beginning that sex and sexuality is a gift from God. However, if it is an obsession, or misused, it has moved from being something that is a natural appetite to be shared with your spouse, to a mental torment status.... DIS-ease. We live in an infected World environment that is sexually distorted with all kinds of perversions.

Media has always had its role in propagating these excesses, with the earliest movies, and even the beginnings of the internet being used almost immediately for explicit pictures. The devil is very much using this in our time to flood the World with sin, and have peoples bound under his power. But we can be free! We know the World will be under this influence, but the church needs to make its stand. As someone has said, "It is ok to have the ship in the sea, but it is not ok to have the sea in the ship. It is ok to have the church in the World, but it is not ok to have the World in the church."

Study 1: The scale of the problem

The West
Let's try to paint a picture of the condition of the World in this regard, and the seriousness of this lust driven malady.

Some of the statistics that are being thrown around are alarming, with some people citing figures such as 96% of 16-year-old boys being addicted to porn in the western world. This is addiction that is quoted, not just occasional viewing. This has many times begun at school, where, I have heard a report that as many as 93% of boys have seen porn on a smart phone by the time that they are 13 years old. The same statistic is reported to be true of girls by 15 years of age. One man that I met who is working in the computer industry suggested to me that there are at least as many teenage girl users if not more. They often initially watch porn to see what they need to do to please the boys. Other viewings may be attributed to peer group pressure and an effort to conform to, and be accepted by the world system.

In the early 2000's I heard a figure of 30 million Americans being <u>addicted</u> to porn, consisting of 72% men and 28% women. This is now many years ago and I shudder to think what the situation would like today.

A Current affairs program in Australia stated that the porn industry there has an estimated turnover of 2 Billion dollars per year...considerably more than the yearly GDP of some nations. The show also said that pornography accounts for 12% of all websites worldwide with 33% of the web being devoted to porn, 25% of all search engine requests, 8% of email requests and 35% of all peer to peer downloads. (2010)

Considering that much of the secular world accepts the viewing of pornography as normal, and even desirable, I would say that we have a problem.

The industry

I recall hearing a speaker about 10 years ago, teaching that Hollywood produces about 400 regular movies in a year. In the same year coming from the same city 10,000 porn movies are produced. Japan in the same era was turning out 12,000 porn movies per annum. Recently I heard that with the advent of smaller more portable cameras the production of these materials is now widespread and coming from many sites and areas.

I saw a documentary some time ago that covered what they described as the 'out of control' sale of pornographic materials in China. This study reported that it had reached a situation where the government didn't know what to do about it.

Other nations

Over the years we have had the privilege of traveling to many nations to train and equip the church. Many years ago, we were out in some Pacific Islands and taught on the porn problem as a part of a teaching on sexuality. Afterwards women thanked me for addressing this problem, as it was a serious issue there. The overseer of the denomination that we were working with was walked in on viewing porn, and even our host for the meetings had porn on his computer. This is truly a far-reaching problem, with people who don't have running water, enough food, or clothing and shelter now having access to the internet.

At times we minister in Africa and so some time ago I asked a friend who is a Pastor there about the situation with them. Previously they mostly have accessed the web through internet cafes. Even then a Pastor may go to the café and buy some time on the computer to do his emails. Very often when he turned on the screen it would still be on a porn site from the last user, and so he would be unintentionally exposed. Many Africans are beginning to have smart phones and so there is a very real danger that they are heading for the same types of problems that the West has been experiencing. We have found the same in many other nations that formerly did not have the technologies, and now have low cost media available.

How is the church doing?

In the church I have found that many if not most young people do not even know that sleeping together before marriage is a sin, let alone that porn is immoral. Porn is rife, and so consequently is the type of distorted sexuality portrayed on the screens visited by young Christians. The church has failed to teach healthy sexuality, so as a result our young people are taking their lessons from a sin sick world.

The percentages of <u>addiction</u> to porn from a study of evangelical churches in the U.S. are quite alarming. Reportedly 65% of Christian men, (another study said 68%), 25% of Christian women and 54% of Pastors are <u>addicted</u> to this problem.
In Australia the claims are 33% of clergy visit sexually explicit websites.

Down spiraling morality

Unfortunately, the old story about the frog hopping in the water in the frying pan when the water is cold, and doesn't notice it heating up until it is too late seems alarmingly like what has happened. We have cited repeatedly that in the 1960's America appears to have led the way in departing from Biblical morality, and moved into what was called the sexual revolution. With the Bible being taken out of the schools early in the 60's 'free love' moved unrestrained to some degree from the hippie culture into mainstream American culture.

Anything goes premarital and extra marital sex was openly flaunted. One outworking was reported by a past president of the American Psychiatric association, who noted an increasing number of young people being admitted to mental hospitals. Since then we have seen an alarming increase in fornication, divorces, abortions, sexual abuse, rape, and the corresponding consequences, premarital pregnancies, single parent homes and sexually transmitted diseases.

Pornography as a next step to licentiousness, has taken the sexual act from not caring with whom you have sex, minimalizing marriage, to distorting what sex actually is meant to be. It has taken sexuality from being without boundaries to exploring and promoting perversion.

I recently saw a documentary where an English lady was going around schools in various nations and working on presenting healthy sex education. What she had found was that the children had learnt how to perform sex from the media that they were viewing. As a result, both boys and girls thought that it was normal to finish intercourse by ejaculating on the girl's face. Anal sex or sodomy as the Bible calls it was also considered to just be a part of normal sexual activity. Consequently, many young girls and boys are suffering from physical problems in that area of their bodies. As I have already made reference to, a friend of mine in the medical profession pointed out that the rectum is designed only for 'one-way traffic' so to speak, so damage is inevitable, and that is sad.

The outworking is that usually without a moral compass to set our direction, that we want to do what we see. Let me repeat that I have even heard that there are bestiality brothels across Europe where people can have sex with animals. I have been told that this has become the new party dare at drunken or drug-soaked parties where people are out of control. 10 years ago, it seemed to be fashionable to dare a girl to kiss a girl or a boy to kiss a boy. We now see this in media everywhere. It just gets worse and worse. Surely sin has nearly reached its fullness again, and judgment is soon coming. I am sure none of us wants to be in the rebellion group when that time arrives.

> **Note:** It is not my purpose here to validate these statistics and reports. They have been gathered from various sources over the years, and they are changing rapidly in an alarming and negative way. Even without substantiating their accuracy, documenting the sources, or evaluating their current ness, it is reasonably clear that we have a problem.

A BIBLICAL PERSPECTIVE

The Greek word used in the New Testament for prostitute is 'porne.' And the word from the Greek used for write or inscribe is 'grapho.' So, when we put the two words together, we get a picture of people selling their bodies in a viewable, repeatable scribing for other people's illicit sexual pleasure.

This means that when a man or woman views pornography they are actually joining with prostitutes for their sexual gratification.

If you are not married fornication is by relating with another person in a sexual act. If you are married, we would consider this to be adultery, because you are meeting your sexual and emotional needs by connecting with someone other than your wives or husbands.

At times I have had wives ask me if they are Biblically able to leave their husbands because of their partners' porn addiction. Sadly, it would be difficult to say with any conviction, that the husband or wife who has gone to porn for their sexual release, is not been unfaithful to their spouses. However, to qualify that, God is always redemptive and always willing to have grace for sin that is confessed and genuinely repented of. If we are to become Christ like then I think that our first position should be forgiveness' and working with the victim if they are willing, before we give up on them.

Having grace, love and compassion for them, and realizing that most often they did not want to find themselves in this trap will go a long way towards a wonderful relationship in the future. Of course, this is dependent on them being genuinely repentant. If they are not then you still need to forgive them even if you choose to separate.

What does scripture say? Let's take a look at 1 Corinthians 6:9-10 to settle the matter. This passage lists behaviors that will NOT inherit the kingdom of God. The word translated fornicator here is from the Greek word 'pornos.'

One commentator that I heard stated that this includes viewing or watching, as well as various other kinds of perversion. This is serious business and not to be treated lightly. The good news in this passage is that the Apostle Paul states that the people formerly bound in these sinful practices were now free. Evidently the fear of God elicited genuine repentance in those times, and the church clearly was well equipped to help set the captives free!

> *1 Corinthians 6:9-11* ⁹ *Do you not know that the unrighteous will not inherit the kingdom of God?* **Do not be deceived**. *Neither <u>fornicators</u>, nor idolaters, nor <u>adulterers</u>, nor homosexuals, nor sodomites,* ¹⁰ *nor thieves, nor covetous, nor drunkards, nor revilers, nor extortioners will inherit the kingdom of God.* ¹¹ *<u>And such</u> **were** <u>some of you</u>. But you were washed, but you were sanctified, but you were justified in the name of the Lord Jesus and by the Spirit of our God. NKJV (emphasis mine)*

Study 2: Steps to Freedom

There are 8 areas that may need to be considered and addressed

I usually use the analogy of cutting off the 8 legs of a spider that has you entrapped in its web. Recently someone who I was helping pointed out that spiders have the ability to grow back their legs. I didn't know that, but after some consideration I concluded that it is still a reasonable example. Once you cripple the beast, as with any addiction you need to be on guard to not reopen pathways. So, I present these 8 areas as places that may need to be dealt with in order to come to freedom, and then maintain the ground that you have repossessed.

You may already be strong in some areas, but need to deal with or build up others. Any area out of God's perfect order can give a <u>place</u> to the devil. As a principle, Ephesians 4:27 speaks of giving the devil a 'place,' which in the Greek language is translated from the word 'topos.' This literally could be translated with words such as: a location, a home, a spot, a position, a place, license to operate, etc. So, we need to be very careful to not cooperate with him and give him a place in our lives to operate from.

Ephesians 4:27 Neither give place to the devil. KJV

Leg 1. The 'Will'

Conforming to the World

Romans 12:2

For non-Christians there are only the standards of the world to base their decisions and actions on. Consequently, many of them watch porn simply <u>because they want</u> to. So, the battle for their choices and the activity of their will is all but nonexistent. The world tells them that it is perfectly acceptable and even desirable to watch explicit material. My wife saw a well-known female movie star appearing on a midday talk show who proudly proclaimed: "Oh, I love Porn." So, people in the world willingly flock to participate with the prince of the power of the air. Satan.

> *Ephesians 2:1-3* [1] *Once you were dead, doomed forever because of your many sins.* [2] *You used to live just like the rest of the world, full of sin, obeying Satan, <u>the mighty prince of the power of the air.</u> He is the spirit at work in the hearts of those who refuse to obey God.* [3] *All of us used to live that way, <u>following the passions and desires</u> of our evil nature. We were born with an evil nature, and we were under God's anger just like everyone else. NLT (emphasis mine)*

Conforming to Christ

Romans 8:29

For Christians however it is not so simple. The scriptures make it clear that we are being tested. Temptation is translated from the Greek word 'peirazo' which literally means testing. The desires of our soul and the lusts of our bodies do not simply disappear at conversion. What has happened now is that we have been indwelt by the Holy Spirit who brings to us a new nature, a nature which desires to follow and please God. Rather than go through all the passages that explain this I will recommend some Bible reading. Firstly, if you read Romans 7:14-25 you will see that the Apostle Paul evidently was struggling with this concept. A part of him wanted to follow God and yet at the same time his 'flesh' wanted to follow a contrary path. It was the pre conversion part of his 'self-life,' already imprinted on and programmed that he was dealing with.

Wooing the will

I find it vital to study passages that instill in me the fear of God and strongly influence my decisions and choices. God is no respecter of persons and we know that we will all be judged by the Word of God. I suggest careful study and meditation on the following passages. We have to 'lean on' our thought life in order to discipline it to move our <u>will</u> in the direction of the 'narrow path of God.'

Further reading: Romans 8:1-14, Galatians 5:16-25 + 6:7-8
Let me just highlight a couple of passages as a sample.

> *Romans 8:1 There is therefore now no condemnation to those who are in Christ Jesus, <u>who do not walk</u> according to the flesh, but according to the Spirit. NKJV (emphasis mine)*

We all want to access the grace of God through a repentant and obedient heart. We want to live without guilt and condemnation and experience the peace and joy of being made right with God through the provision of Jesus our anointed savior. We must therefore examine all of our choices in the light of whether we are following our fleshly lusts and desires, pleasing ourselves, or choosing to please our Father in heaven by following the leading of the Spirit. It is a serious choice that must be considered and weighed carefully.

> *Romans 8:5-8 ⁵ For those who live according to the flesh set their minds on the things of the flesh, but those who live according to the Spirit, the things of the Spirit. ⁶ For to be carnally minded is death, but to be spiritually minded is life and peace. ⁷ Because the carnal mind is enmity against God; for it is not subject to the law of God, nor indeed can be. ⁸ So then, those who are in the flesh cannot please God. NKJV*

There are no shades of grey, the scriptures say what they mean and mean what they say. The following scripture should encourage us to not make choices that suit the 'fallen self or sinful nature.'

> *Romans 8:13-14 ¹³ For if you live according to the sinful nature, you will die; but if by the Spirit you put to death the misdeeds of the body, you will live, ¹⁴ because those who are led by the Spirit of God are sons of God. NKJV*

Romans 12:2 encourages us to renew our minds. When you have settled once and for all whether you are going to follow the flesh or the Spirit, your next port of call is dealing with your mind. Many men struggle with the images already imprinted on their minds from previous exposure. These images push themselves relentlessly into the mind at every opportunity. So, what do you do with them?

Dealing with recorded images and the 'screen' of your conscious mind

To deal with this we must understand that our conscious mind or the viewing place of immediate thought, memory, or imagination is extremely limited. If we liken it to a computer screen, and use it as an example, we might get a glimpse of what we are dealing with. Usually the main page on your computer is called something like the desktop. On the desktop are little 'icons' that represent some other program or file that is not open or seen currently on your screen. For example, it may be an icon that says 'pictures.' If you click on it then onto your screen comes pictures that you can look at. But note that it is limited…you can only look at one full sized picture at a time.

If you are like me you have many icons that are linked to files or programs. For example, on mine I have one that opens my Bible media. Still I can only view my pictures or my Bible program individually. I have to close or at least minimize other programs to one at a time view what I want to see on my screen. Your conscious mind is very much the same. You may be thinking about what you are having for lunch or where you are going for holidays...but not at the same time, even though you may be able to switch very quickly from one subject to another.

The point is that I choose which program that I open and view on my computer screen. Indeed, I could open the internet program, or access stored files and have porn on my screen.

It is MY screen! I choose and decide what I will allow to be viewed on it. In the same way it is YOUR mind, and you totally ALWAYS choose what you are going to allow to be viewed in your consciousness. Somebody could put explicit photos on my computer...and I could be aware that they are there...but you cannot make me bring them onto the screen...I must choose it. Now we may have developed habits of accessing these things that must be broken down. Perhaps we got into the habit through justifying it...or at a weak moment because it was exciting to our 'flesh.' But we always have the final choice as to whether or not we continue the pattern of viewing in our minds.

We know from scripture that God remembers our sins no more. The Bible doesn't say that He has forgotten them. He could access them and view them if He wanted to, but He has chosen not to remember them. We, created in His image, have the same capacity to have images on file but not view them. We too choose to remember them no more. But how do we do it?

Subjecting our thought life

One of the most powerful verses in the Bible pertaining to overcoming this area is found in second Corinthians. It actually tells us that it is necessary to subdue every thought that was initiated from a source outside the Kingdom of God. Now we know many things in our thought lives proceed from things learnt before conversion...and some after.

> 2 Corinthians 10:5 *We demolish arguments and every pretension that sets itself up against the knowledge of God, and we take captive every thought to make it obedient to Christ. NIV*

It begins telling us that we need to demolish and pull down every argument. Let us take time to consider a couple of things before we move on. Firstly, the Greek word most often translated here as 'arguments' is according to Strong's concordance the Greek word '*Logismos.*' The word holds the following meanings, <u>computation</u>, <u>reasoning</u>, <u>imagination</u>, and <u>thought</u>. So, we arrive at arguments and arguing with what we know of God and His ways, by trying to **reason out** or **compute** the Word of God.

We try to process the Word of God and reason it out instead of simply accepting what it says as being so. (This includes if the biblical statements are seemingly ridiculous in terms of what is possible in the natural world.) Many of our western bakeries use flours 'processed' by man to make the bread. The processing has taken all of the goodness out of the grain and there is nothing left that is beneficial or good for us. We must be careful that we don't do this with the Word of God by processing all of the nutrition out of it, and reducing it to what we can understand ourselves.

Secondly, once we entertain a thought or imagining for even a second on the screen of our conscious mind, or begin to reason it out we are in trouble. There is only one way to deal with it! "That doesn't belong in my mind and I absolutely refuse to let it be there for even a millisecond!" This IS the KEY. If you give it any time at all in your mind it will take hold. If you decide that you are going to work this out through reason then you are in trouble because you have let it have a 'place' in your mind. "Perhaps I will give it up tomorrow." No, it has no place in you. "Perhaps I will just think of a few images and stop soon." No, you are giving place to the devil and following your sin nature and flesh. Once you have decided to give it up you cannot afford to give it any 'play' time on the screen of your mind at all. None! You cannot even think of the possibility of letting it into your mind. I have known of people who literally shake their heads as if shaking the thoughts out as they willfully refuse to let their minds be used.

Many are amazed at how quickly they get the victory when they take authority over the screen of their minds!

You can of course choose to remember those images some more. In fact, you can be sure that the devil will return at an 'opportune time' when you are tired, stressed, rejected or weakened in some other way. But having established the victory you will find it fairly easy to resist him...and you have an absolute guarantee that if you do, he will flee!

> *James 4:7-8* ⁷ *Therefore submit to God. <u>Resist the devil and **he will** flee from you</u>.* ⁸ *Draw near to God and He will draw near to you. Cleanse your hands, you sinners; and purify your hearts, you <u>double-minded</u>. NKJV (emphasis mine)*

> **Note:** The double minded statement in this scripture. The mind of the Spirit wants freedom; the mind of the flesh wants to enjoy the pleasures of sin for a while. But the wants of the flesh must be subdued, put off, and brought under the authority of the Spirit. Created order is the human Spirit submitted to God and ruling the soul and the body. (Aka Flesh) See 1 Thessalonians 5:23

Even the decision to not be exposed to outside sources is an argument that must be settled with a one-time decision. I was teaching on avoiding being exposed to something that someone may want to show you on a smartphone in Africa recently. The young man interpreting for me related in the break that a person had tried to entice him to look at an image on his phone. This young interpreter related to me his indignant and forceful response to this person. "I'M A BORN-AGAIN CHRISTIAN! I'M NOT LOOKING AT THAT!" Right answer! Inspiring. If more young people set themselves in such an attitude, cherishing their position in Christ the church would shine in dark times.

Thought Displacement

Another powerful tool in defeating the images that are looking to access the screen of your conscious mind is displacement. This is basically like filling your bath tub right to the top. When you hop in the waters are displaced and go all over the floor. Or if you put compressed air into the ballast tank on a submarine it pushes out all of the water and the vessel rises.

In much the same way we can take control of our minds by pushing out the sinful thought with a Holy one. Many years ago, I heard an old preacher explaining how he overcame sinful thoughts. When the bad thoughts sought access to his mind, and they do, he would fill his mind with praise of Jesus and Father God. The evil thoughts didn't stand a chance! You must eat, but you can replace that chocolate biscuit with a carrot. You must think, but you can replace that demonic thought with a Holy Spirit thought. Not only will the absence of the bad thing be good for you, but also the presence of something good and nutritious will strengthen you and make you healthy. Similarly, you can't stop thinking, so you need to train yourselves to replace the unhealthy thoughts with beneficial thinking.

Conclusion

What a terrible state it is to be in where most of your thought life is consumed with sexual materials. I have heard reports of some men thinking about sex every few minutes all day long. What an empty life this is. The enemy comes to rob you of life. The area of the will needs to be forcefully taken hold of with the mind being brought into subjection.

'Leg' 2. Trigger patterns and associations

Association

Firstly, let us look at some non-pornography examples to help us understand the workings of our minds in regard to association.

Our brain largely operates through memory and association. For example, you may hear a song playing on the radio from when you were a teenager. If it was a good time in your life then you will associate the song with good feelings and feel good. But if it was an unhappy time then you will connect the song to bad times and feel bad. I have observed that many church people's favorite songs are those that were popular around the time of their conversion. Perhaps we associate having unlocked doors in our home with a feeling of danger if we grew up in an area or suburb with social problems.

The connection between association and addiction

Imagine that you are going through a period of time where you are stressed and under load. As a result, you are feeling a bit tired and run down. One day you happen to have a drink of a caffeinated soda drink. The caffeine and sugar give you a bit of a boost and you feel a bit happier and a little more energized. Your brain stores this information in a file titled; 'feeling flat and what to do about it,' in the limbic system area of your chemical mind. The next time you feel flat your brain does a data search on information relating to this problem.

Right on top of the list is a record that drinking caffeinated soda gave you a boost and made you feel a little better in the past. So, your brain has kept a record and created an association between tiredness and the boost received from the drink.

Clearly if you continue to be tired you will continue to access that file titled 'feeling flat and what to do about it.' Before long, you have developed a habit. If you serve the habit long enough over time it becomes an addiction. It is important to create God habits and associations and avoid developing unhealthy habits which end up with mastery over us. We are not 'religiously' suggesting for a moment that drinking caffeinated soda is sin! We are just using it as a possibility for an example of the workings of association and addiction. We do however recognize that it is important to not create habits that potentially can get out of control. It is best we model ourselves on the advice and wisdom of the Apostle Paul.

> *1 Corinthians 6:12-13* [12] *"Everything is permissible for me"--but **not everything is beneficial**. "Everything is permissible for me"--but <u>I will not be mastered by anything</u>.* [13] *"Food for the stomach and the stomach for food"--but God will destroy them both. The body is not meant for sexual immorality, but for the Lord, and the Lord for the body. NIV (emphasis mine)*

Let me also note here, although not related to our subject, that sugar drinks may produce a short-term lift in energy and feeling good. It is however well documented that sugar abuse will actually make you tired. It is reportedly very damaging to organs such as the Thyroid gland. Part of the role of the Thyroid is to help with energy metabolism, so as with many things that are on offer to us that are supposedly 'good,' in fact they damage us and do the opposite in the long run. So, if you don't believe me on this check with Adam and Eve when you get to heaven. They saw that the tree of the knowledge of good and evil was 'good' for certain things, but it actually turned out to be bad for them.

Porn, in the short term may appear exciting, even as with the Garden of Eden, seemingly 'what you need to make you happy.' But in the long run it is a terrible mind destroying bondage.

> Proverbs 6:25-26 ²⁵ Do not lust in your heart after her beauty or let her captivate you with her eyes, ²⁶ for the prostitute reduces you to a loaf of bread, and the adulteress preys upon your very life. NIV

Memory based associations, addictive behavior and trigger patterns

Sometimes your brain establishes a habit that you believe is in your best interests, or perhaps is pleasurable or seemingly beneficial in some way.

Let us take a common addiction, cigarette smoking. In my teenage years it seemed that most young people smoked. It was desirable to fit into the social set and produced some chemical enjoyment at times. The nicotine has very addictive properties and so many people attribute the difficulty giving up to this chemical cycle. The reality is that your amazing body clears this chemical out of your system relatively quickly. The main problem is the trigger patterns and associations that have been established with the habit.

For example, most smokers would consider that they just have a cigarette when they feel like one. What is mostly happening is that they associate having their puff with certain situations. For instance, they believe that they enjoy one after a meal. This goes in the 'when do I smoke?' file. Now when they have a meal their brain makes the association and there is an unconscious prompt that there is something that they should be doing.... namely having a smoke. For some it is when they are driving, morning cup of tea, after working hard, listening to music, having a social drink, or perhaps when they are feeling anxious or rejected. There is a long list of potential 'triggers' that goes on and on. And for the smoker who has anxiety it is an all the time problem, the 'stressor' is virtually continuous!

So how does this relate to porn addiction?

Porn has usually begun with exposure to material that produces intense emotional excitement and response. It also has a chemical element which we will discuss in the next 'Leg.' In order to be free, it is necessary to break down the 'associations' that trigger the behavior. For many men this could be sexual rejection from the wife who is tired, uninterested, or perhaps unable to engage because of her own historical issues relating to previous sexual experiences. This could even include beliefs stemming from a religious background or setting where she (or he) has been taught that sex is dirty or bad.

As with other addictions a part of the power of the bondage to porn is association. For example, imagine a young man goes to his laptop computer to check his emails. Before he gets to his mail box he is confronted with the advertisements on the home page of his internet service supplier. There are ads to click on to see for example; 'Victoria's secrets' which I believe is some kind of skimpy underwear fashion show. Around the year 2000 when I 1st connected to the internet there was an ad on my web suppliers home page suggesting that you click on a link and check out the latest 'grid girls.' Grid girls were, by the picture enticing you to investigate, pretty young ladies in bikini's who started the car races. I never did click on there for a look and later learned how to bypass the home page and go straight to my mailbox.

The point is, that understanding how association works is a defense. If I had let curiosity get the better of me, gone to the site and been visually stimulated by whatever was on those pages, I would have created an association. From that time on if I was thinking of doing work on my laptop, or opened it and turned it on, there would have been an automatic reminder and connection that this was not now merely a laptop computer, but was now an instrument of potential sexual gratification and arousal.

Breaking the media link

Many men have an association between their laptop or now smart phone and their sexuality. My advice to them in regards to this media link is to deal with it harshly and with finality. Jesus said that if your eye is the problem that is causing you to sin, get rid of it! If it is your hand. Get rid of it! If it is your laptop or smart phone, get rid of it! Throw it over the fence. If you have a job that needs a laptop and you can't get control, get yourself a job digging ditches!

> Matthew 5:29-30 ²⁹ *If your right eye causes you to sin, gouge it out and* <u>*throw it away*</u>*. It is* <u>*better for you*</u> *to lose one part of your body than for your whole body to be thrown into hell.* ³⁰ *And if your right hand causes you to sin, cut it off and* <u>*throw it away*</u>*. It is* <u>*better for you*</u> *to lose one part of your body than for your whole body to go into hell.* NKJV (emphasis mine)

You are better off doing this than spending eternity in hell. I am not saying that you are going to hell because you are addicted to porn; I am suggesting that you might be in a bad place if you are not interested in taking the necessary steps that indicate that you are repentant. If you are repentant and wanting to give it up then you are under grace. If you are willfully sinning and have no conviction at all about what you are doing then you may have some problems.

> Hebrews 10:26-27 ²⁶ *If we* <u>*deliberately*</u>* keep on sinning after we have received the knowledge of the truth, no sacrifice for sins is left,* ²⁷ *but only a fearful expectation of judgment and of raging fire that will consume the enemies of God.* NIV (emphasis mine)

NKJV = willfully. From the Greek language this word means - **voluntarily**: --willfully, willingly. From Romans chapter 7 we know that at times the Apostle Paul did, what he did not want to do. His reborn human spirit and renewed mind conflicting with his preprogrammed soul and heart. What I am saying is that there was sin that was in him, that was happening involuntarily, and that his new creation nature was not willfully wanting it to happen. This is not to justify an addiction, but to acknowledge that once captive, although all sin is deliberate and voluntary to some extent, that if the person bound is inwardly groaning and confessing his sin, then God is faithful to forgive. If in their sin they feel they are a wretched person as Paul did, then it is evident that they are repentant, although in need of help to be made free.

I have found that the men who make the necessary decision to break the links and associations by radically dealing with their media get free. This often means saving your marriage and keeping your family. Those who try to justify or rationalize it will most likely remain bound permanently or until they are prepared to bear fruit in keeping with repentance. (Mt 3:8) These men often lose their families and even if single never overcome the guilt and find peace and joy.

I used to have a bag of smart phones in my office from those who were repentant. It was great to observe the blossoming relationships as a result of this commitment to freedom. Phones without internet connecting capabilities are still readily available, and wives are more than willing to share their computers with husbands who are walking away from this illness. After a suitable time of abstinence, it may be possible for some to return to media, having established self-control over their weakness. This would involve fully understanding that even one slip up renews and recreates the association. Equally, each time you use your media equipment, and do not view anything, your mind files it now as something that is not used for sexual gratification.

A key here may be to make up your mind before you turn the item on. You will know in your heart if you are trying to deceive yourself and actually intend to visit the past.

If you have allowed yourself even a very brief thought about what you may view, then you have gone too far. You need to set a deep default decision by thinking it through, that it is not for you, and that is it. Not, I will do it less. I will never do it again!

> Jeremiah 17:9-10 9 *"The heart is deceitful above all things, And desperately wicked; Who can know it?* 10 *I, the LORD, search the heart, I test the mind, Even to give every man according to his ways, According to the fruit of his doings. NKJV*

Other ways that association is relevant to porn

For some men a 'trigger' comes when an association is made between an empty house and watching pornography. So now the wife says that she is going to do the shopping. His mind connects him with the 'what do I do when I have the house to myself' memory file. At the top of the list is an opportunity for going to the internet to watch porn.

For some men (or women) it is the workplace. Reportedly a high percentage of viewing is done where people work. Some companies have found that as a result of putting all of their materials on computers or tablets that they have lost productivity. Instead of using the work programs their employees are found to be watching porn. So simply going to work can 'trigger' use by association.

'Leg' 3. Addictive cycles and chemical programming

Chemical hormonal considerations

Hormones are chemical messengers that help in part to elaborate our thought life into feelings in our bodies. Many of these travel through our bodily systems and attach to receptors, which in turn produce feelings, emotions and various responses. There is a part of our brain that is called the 'Hypothalamus' which is considered to be part brain and part gland. It oversees our central nervous system, (electrical) and our endocrine system, (glandular) as well as being implicated in the operation of other bodily systems. The endocrine system produces and releases hormones in various parts of the body. Basically, when we have a thought it goes to the Hypothalamus, which in turn makes the thought a chemical and electrical reality in our physical selves.

If these realities are emotional events coming from thoughts, we call them feelings. If they are physical body based, we might refer to them as appetites.

An emotional example could be that we are afraid that there is someone out there in the dark. This fearful <u>thought</u> would go to the Hypothalamus which would put the body on the alert, releasing stress hormones and electrical impulses. This would be an emotional response elaborated as a fear feeling.

A physical body example might be if somebody talks about your favorite food. You begin to think about it, and your Hypothalamus makes it a chemical event by releasing the relative hormones and preparing your body to eat. So now you feel hungry and possibly have gastric juices releasing into your stomach getting ready for the incoming food.
In much the same way if we think about sex our body begins to prepare for the act by releasing hormones to stimulate our sexual parts. But remember this arousal was a thought before it became anything else. The problem is once the thinking has happened, even if briefly, the thought has produced a chemical response. This of course includes memories of explicit images. If the devil has your mind, he has you! This is why the section on the 'will' and the 'mind' is so vital in getting free and staying free.

Male sexuality and wiring

I heard some time ago that a male's sexuality, even at its peak is quite manageable without outside stimulus. In other words when a man is exposed to sexual materials it 'hypes' up his system because of the chemical release. We live in a much-sexualized society with media such as television absolutely full of programming based around sexual themes. Even how women dress in the Western World is testing for modern man. I believe that for the most part girls are simply trying to keep up with fashion, not realizing the sexual nature of their appearance. However, if women understood that men do not view them in the same way as women view men, I think many of their habits would change.

A man's sexuality is wired directly into his brain through his eyes. Perhaps this is because God created the man to be the initiator in the multiplication of the population. Man is most likely to think about and suggest a sexual encounter with his wife for this reason. Image, thought, chemical response, overtures and finally activity is pretty much how it goes. So, it is not surprising the roaring lion Satan works so hard to bring down his prey...man...through this area, distorting and supercharging a person's sexual chemistry through pornographic imagery. The Bible does not dispute either the beauty of women or for that matter the physical attractiveness of men to women. However, the counsel of scripture is to fill up visually on the wife that you have been given, and for her to be enough for you. God sets His affection on us by choice. We are blessed if we have chosen to set our affection on our wives.

> *Proverbs 5:18-20* *¹⁸ Let your fountain be blessed, And rejoice with the wife of your youth. ¹⁹ As a loving deer and a graceful doe, Let her breasts satisfy you at all times; And always be enraptured with her love. ²⁰ For why should you, my son, be enraptured by an immoral woman, And be embraced in the arms of a seductress? NKJV*

The Bible does not reveal God as surprised or embarrassed about the erotic and stimulating visual nature of the human body that He designed. If you read the Song of Solomon you will find a strong interaction and appreciation of the physical appearances of the lovers. Notably, this gift does not apply to some kind of devalued general kind of viewing. It is clear from scripture that these visuals are to be enjoyed in the context of a committed marriage relationship.

Media based brain stimulus
Another chemical factor with viewing this type of material is its effect on the pleasure centre in the brain. When this is stimulated there are hormones implicated which produce pleasure feelings. Commentators tell us that masturbation is often involved, or other sexual activities. So, you are also connecting and relating the whole viewing event by associating it to the dopamine release and consequent pleasure in orgasm. Other complex hormones are secreted in the excitement phase which can also be addictive.

The bottom line is that it still all begins with a thought. It could be thinking of memories from past viewing. Or perhaps it could be the thought to look for something of a sexually explicit nature now or in the future. It is your mind, and you are responsible for what goes through it!

'Leg' 4. Dysfunctional sexual relationships

Let me begin this area by saying that sexual issues appear in people's lives because of broken relationships. (*see footnote) The result of the lack of relational wholeness and harmony is going to be unmet emotional and physical needs as well as nurture. One of the problems that we face in our current society, and as we look at this area of meeting sexual needs, is the amount of sexual abuse that we have been exposed to. I reiterate that possibly as many as 2 out of 3 women have endured some kind of sexual abuse in the Western World. In this figure I include inappropriate touching by a friend of the family or a relative. Many men have also suffered abuse of this kind. Some of this is the result of overdriven sexuality from porn that is looking for an expression. Indeed, I have heard reports that even incestuous porn is now in the market place.

For the most part humans want to do what they see others doing. So, when we hear of incest porn, homosexual porn, bestiality porn, and so on, we know that people who see this will inevitably want to try it.

I have heard of 12 and 13-year-old girls who suffer from bowel problems stemming from sodomy. (Anal sex) My wife and I can confirm this as we have ministered to a number of women who have suffered this kind of abuse.

When I am proposing that God's order is to meet each other's sexual needs to the point of not needing stimulus from outside areas, I realize that I am suggesting an ideal, and that other ministry may need to take place before this can become achievable. However, a healthy sex life is Gods perfect order for protecting each other from the temptations of perversion and sexual sin.

As noted, this may well be unrealizable and unrealistic before emotional healing has taken place for the partner who has been abused. They may be unable to be fully engaged before they have received ministry for this problem, and for that matter any related emotional issues, for example fear of failure. Fear of failure could drive a man towards porn because there is no expectation on him to perform or to meet some perceived standard of sexual success. (Refer to the teaching on 'Truth Encounters' to find out how someone who has been abused or has other emotional issues can be set free.)

As previously stated, growing up in a religious or morally rigid environment where it has been taught that sex is undesirable, unholy or unclean could also be a block to being able to engage in a healthy sexual relationship. It is necessary to be able to fulfill each other's needs. It is a form of spiritual covering and protecting each other. The devil works very hard indeed to distort this gift of God and pervert it, so as is evident in society he targets our sexuality in order to take us captive.

> *1 Corinthians 7:3 The husband should not deprive his wife of sexual intimacy, which is her right as a married woman, nor should the wife deprive her husband. NLT*

> *1 Corinthians 7:5 So do not deprive each other of sexual relations. The only exception to this rule would be the agreement of both husband and wife to refrain from sexual intimacy for a limited time, so they can give themselves more completely to prayer. Afterward they should come together again so that Satan won't be able to tempt them <u>because of their lack of self-control</u>.*

> *1 Corinthians 7:9 But if they can't control themselves, they should go ahead and marry. It's better to marry than to <u>burn with lust</u>. NLT (emphasis mine)*

Sex is to some degree an 'appetite' and a part of the natural life. Just like eating it is meant to be expressed and satisfied within proper limits. A healthy 'meal' so to speak, and then no need to think about it again until mealtime comes around again. What the <u>needs</u> are to some degree is dependent on age and health. Gender is another consideration with men having reportedly 20 to 25 times, and even as much as 38 times as much testosterone than women. These levels certainly have men more inclined to think about and therefore desire to initiate sex. This desire to seek sex is the very thing that the devil plays on in his attack on man in particular. Often the men then lead their partners into viewing pornographic materials. So, an understanding wife who is prepared and able to cover a man's sexual needs is an enormous asset in helping him get free and him staying free. It is well worth the effort to work towards a healthy sex life in God's order. It can be a real strength for a man.

---

* Footnote: Some sexual issues come to people through the generational influences of sexual sin in the family line. It can also come through an ungodly sexual bond to someone who has the problem. This increasingly includes a drawing towards porn.

'Leg' 5. Emotional stressors, real or perceived

Rejection

Right at the top of the list I would place rejection. Remember we have discussed associations and memory-based brain 'files.' One of the coping mechanisms for rejection is independence. Basically, somebody rejects you, and a way that you choose to deal with it is by cutting them off. It may not be a conscious thought but in your heart, you are 'saying' "well if you don't want me, then I am going to live a life where I don't need you." Then I don't have to worry about you rejecting me, my needs, or my attempt at having a relationship with you again. So, this is a general response to rejection probably learnt in some environment of hurt in the past. It surfaces when some kind of rejection comes. Then out of the memory bank comes the 'what do I do if people don't receive me or accept my trying to be in relationship.'

A common emotional situation or stressor would be when the person makes overtures for sexual intimacy, and the response is something like; 'in your dreams honey, I am not doing anything tonight, I am tired!' For the rejected person, invariably they will feel not wanted or not good enough, or perhaps not attractive enough. This can be a common stressor for a sense of rejection in men in particular. They already feel that their wives aren't as turned on by their appearance as they are by looking at their wives. And their wives never seem to want sex like they do. Therefore, they reason that they are not attractive! The truth is however that the women do not have their sexuality wired into their eyes as do men, or the strong sex hormones to initiate that a man carries.

In spite of what Hollywood is trying to portray, normally women are not aroused visually as men are. The reason that women typically don't initiate sex is not a lack of interest, it is the comparatively low hormone values that they carry. Men must realize that pretty much everyone's wife is the same. In any case if the man perceives rejection, he may go to his default position of independence. This means that now he will take care of his own sexuality, and choose to not need the response and involvement of his wife. The options for him nowadays are a multiplicity of readily available sexual materials. These are full of women who are portrayed as <u>accepting</u> of men's advances. They are seemingly much more than willing to engage in sexual activities, and apparently want sex as much as the men.

So now we have the association pattern that we talked about, but this time directly relating to emotional feelings and relational reactions. Part of the list of solutions stored in the mind for sexual rejection now is pornography and masturbation. I have seen this over and over. Once explicit materials are used as an emotional bandage, solution or response, then, they are always a 'go to' <u>recorded reaction</u> that will be present. It is mostly no longer a conscious thought process; it has now become an automatized response.

'All men are animals!'

I just want to make a small note here to wives in particular. Because a man can have 20 to 25 times as much testosterone in his body, he will normally be the part of the team who thinks about sex, and consequently makes overtures for it to take place. When a female doesn't understand these chemical differences regarding how they were created, it is easy for her to jump to the conclusion that there is something wrong with her man. She will base this on her own feelings and attitudes towards the sexual act and be mystified as to why he wants it all the time.... even when he's tired. As we have said, some come to the conclusion that 'all men are animals,' and resent them.

The truth is that he did not choose to have a stronger sex drive, it was God's idea. Other women think that their men don't love them; all they want is to use them for sex. Perhaps we can again use the example of missing some meals and being very hungry, then we can grasp the situation. Regardless of gender you are most likely thinking about food rather than being romantic or loving towards your spouse. Does that mean that you don't love them? No! It just means that your appetite for food is your priority until it is dealt with, and behind that strong urge you still love them as much as ever. Once you have had a meal you will probably feel more loving and relational again.

In much the same way behind the man's strong sexual tendencies he loves you just as much as he ever did. In fact, if you grasp the situation of his need and are responsive and accepting, he will probably love how you deal with him more than ever. Not because you gave him sex, but because you cared enough about him to help him satisfy an appetite that he did not choose to have.

We have found an attitude of meeting in the middle very helpful and very bonding. If the husbands need is strong, then a wife who does not feel like it might make a special effort to give of herself for his sake. At other times the man might be trying to initiate the sexual act and sees that his wife is tired or stressed. He lays down what he wants for her sake, and perhaps they make an appointment for another time. This communication and mutual caring is a good tool for working around potential rejective situations from both sides.

I would suggest to men to not go too far in 'thinking' about sex until you have checked with your wife as to whether or not it is a possibility. Remember the thinking will begin to prepare your body for the act. Usually a wife doesn't mind the idea with some advanced warning and consultation. Caring how she feels about it is caring about her. The old saying; 'don't behave like a turkey in the morning if you want to crow like a rooster in the evening' has considerable merit.

Fear of rejection/ fear of failure
Other emotional stressors that may point a man towards the illicit sex arena are fear of rejection and fear of failure. These are sometimes the same thing. A man might be hesitant to seek sexual intimacy in case he cannot meet the perceived standards of society relating to this. Porn itself can create such a picture for men, in that they evidently have to be capable of having their partners groaning or screaming in ecstasy to be a success. Possibly they might have previous failed sexual encounters and, consequently, they fear this happening again with their spouse whose affection and acceptance is more than anyone else vitally important to them. It is surprising how many men do not approach their wives sexually for these kinds of reasons.

Many men and women who have experienced an absence of parental approval seek it from their partners. Perhaps this is most evident in the sexual act because simultaneously you are both most intimate and most vulnerable to rejection. If they feel a failure in their expectations of themselves or their partners in the lovemaking arena, they are likely to gravitate towards alternatives.

Supposedly the point of least resistance and a logical or even unconscious solution for the man is to view pornography where there is no need to fear failure. Perhaps they even identify with the male figures in the pictures that are supposedly having great success in pleasing and satisfying their partners.

Reports and studies actually reveal that for the women acting in pornographic movies that this is not usually the case. The reality is that the girls often suffer considerable emotional and physical duress as they <u>act</u> out the instructions of the movie directors.

Nonetheless porn is a very emotionally stimulating concept for men who have a great desire for this seeming approval, success, and acceptance to be happening to them.

Similarly, the women may see the men being greatly pleased and accepting of the efforts of the girls in these scripted portrayals. Again, this ties into an emotional need to be successful in their attempts to be worthy and acceptable, and often in their needs to please, usually a male figure.

Apparently for some women the attraction and stimulating element of porn is the 'what you need' aspect. Women are looking for a man who will care for them and unselfishly provide for their 'needs.' In the depictions the men are reportedly often portrayed as supplying a service in being great lovers and pleasuring and satisfying the 'needs' of the girls in the pictures.

As we have just illustrated fear of rejection may operate as a result of a rejection profile in a person's life. If they have previously been rejected or dealt with as not good enough even in non-sexual areas, they may fear proving their inadequacy in any or every area of life. A spouse usually represents the most important person to receive acceptance and acknowledgement from. For some the overwhelming pressure to be 'good enough' for them may steer them away from intimacy. Sexual relations with their partner may now seem to be something to be avoided. So, there is on the one hand the desire for closeness and on the other the potential for failure, which means further rejection and emotional anguish. The problem that remains is that your sexuality and need for emotional acceptance will not go away…so if it is not satisfied it will find some other means of expression. The devil has worked hard to provide a lot of avenues for sexual gratification and interest to be catered for, and pornography is high on his list of enticements.

Possible general emotional triggers
> *Proverbs 4:23 Above all else, guard your heart, for it affects everything you do. NLT*

Other 'triggers' could be work pressures, an unhappy home life, even a general dissatisfaction with life. If porn is used as entertainment or escape from these or other emotionally driven situations, then your mind will make the connection. From then on whenever any of these situations present you will gravitate towards the solution that you have encoded in your 'heart.'

This is why the scripture tells us to guard our hearts…be careful what conclusions and solutions that we decide on and establish. This is very important because it affects everything. Relationships with God, others, and even how we consider ourselves.

So emotional stressors and triggers need to be understood and dealt with for freedom and future defenses against temptation.

What do I do about emotional stressors and triggers?
Clearly a wise and understanding wife or husband who is walking with the Lord will want to deal with you in a Biblical way. In other words, how God would like you to be dealt with. Loved, accepted, valued and considerately dealt with. So, a spouse who has discernment and knowledge of the problem can help to alleviate some of the stressors and triggers if they are based around that relationship.

If the 'stressor' is some other life situation such as escape from bad feelings around the workplace or similar, then knowing that porn has become a chosen path to make yourself feel better or distracted, then you must reprogram your responses. Anything that you have decided can be undecided…. you can by a deep 'one-time decision' choose to respond in another way. The <u>power of a made-up mind</u> cannot be underestimated!

It would be advantageous to catalogue some more beneficial options for reacting to those situations, and then be committed to act on them when the pressure comes. For example; Porn is disproportionate worship of something that has been distorted by the World. By implication you are submitting to and worshipping the spirit of lust behind it that is inspiring, encouraging and propagating it. When you are tempted, (Greek =Tested) by it, replace bowing down to it with a serious time of praising God for who He is, thanking Him for the life He has for you, your wife or husband, family and so on. There is no end of things that He can and should be praised for. There can be no darkness where there is light…the light displaces it. You will soon find that if you submit to God and resist the devil he will soon flee.

James 4:7-8 ⁷ Submit yourselves, then, to God. Resist the devil, and he will flee from you. ⁸ Come near to God and he will come near to you. (and the devil will not want to be anywhere near you!) Wash your hands, (deeds/things that you do!) you sinners, and purify your hearts, (motives and what you cherish!) you double-minded. NIV * (double minded = uncommitted, you would like to be free but you also like serving sin at some level!) [Bracketed comments mine. *]

Finally, if you have historical rejection and fear of rejection issues, I would recommend that you seek out emotional healing for this problem. If you don't the anxiety proceeding from the brokenness will continue to cause you problems and leave you potentially vulnerable in the sexual area. These anxieties can also be behind many of the physical problems that relate to sexual dysfunction and the bodily ability to be able to perform. So, it is very much worth the effort to resolve these emotionally driven issues. (see the unit; 'Truth Encounters' to find out how God will set you free and bring healing to these areas.)

'Leg' 6. Sexual 'trauma' (embedded memories from the initial impact)

We have already noted many men struggle with the images already imprinted on their minds from previous exposure. An expert that I was listening to on the subject stated that the images are permanently burned into your mind in 3 tenths of a second. I would liken this to a trauma because of the explicit and impacting nature of the materials. This happens through an electro-chemical process known as protein synthesis. I believe that God could erase these memories and I am sure at times He does. As we have pointed out the vast majorities have these pictures indelibly etched into the brain, and push they themselves relentlessly into the mind at every opportunity.

Our minds <u>do have</u> the capacity to suppress or repress memories and thoughts. The neuroscientists tell us that we have neurological pathways which become stronger the more we use and activate them. But the good news is that the less we use them the less the brain does to maintain them and they breakdown and weaken. We could of course activate them again, and with regular use strengthen them and make them the pathway of choice. We could perhaps liken these pathways to roadways that thoughts pass along in our neural world. When you have the initial trauma, it is like someone has instantly put in a four-lane highway with lighting for all hours. It is a very strong road indeed. It has intersections that bridge the signals called 'axon terminal buttons.' These activate and send signals when stimulated by electrical impulses beginning with thought and release neurotransmitters which light up and connect the brain signal.

The point is that if we refuse to allow these processes to be activated and the roadway to not be used, then your brain doesn't do the maintenance to keep the road open. We go from a four lane super highway to an unused dirt track full of potholes. Eventually it will require deliberate effort to remember the images. They are still there in storage but they are very faded because the roadway to them has become dim and less readily negotiable.

Creating new neurological and thought pathways
In the unit on dealing with fear I shared a story about when I used to drive my children to school. We lived about 6 kilometers from the school so it was necessary to take them and pick them up each day. For many years I traveled the same road. Over time I noticed some people turn off and take a different route, usually arriving at the destination before us. I

didn't really consider changing as I was quite content with the path I was taking. Finally, one day I decided to follow one of these other vehicles and try the alternate way to go. I discovered that it was quicker and just as easy so I decided to travel that way in future. The problem was that if I was day dreaming or listening to a teaching tape or music that I would automatically go the old road. I found that I had to consciously and very deliberately concentrate on following the new way. Eventually the new way became the automatic pathway and I would go that way without thinking. In fact, now if I were driving down that road, I would tend to turn down there by habit, even if I was going somewhere else. I now had to consciously make myself not turn there. The lesson is that, although you may have easily, readily and even automatically followed a thought pathway, simply because that is the way that you always have gone...you can change it. But for a time, it will take conscious effort to think different thoughts.

We used to live on a corner of two fairly large roads. For as long as the stop sign and give way sign system had existed the give way signs had been on one of these roads. This was a period of perhaps 40 years or more. The local council decided to move the give way signs onto the other road, meaning that the road that had right of way and you could drive straight through also changed. People had been driving straight through on the road now bearing the give way signs for so long it was automatic. Even though they put offset traffic islands and warning signs people continued to go straight through.

There were often accidents and we would regularly hear screeching tyres as people slammed on the breaks at the last minute. The point is that in spite of all the warnings, signs and efforts to divert people from danger they continued to follow their previous programming and habit. It takes a very deliberate conscious act to reprogram your mind. We see people successfully doing it all the time in the area of pornography if they are committed to it. You may have to slam the brakes on a few times before you change if you are not purposeful and aware of what you are doing. But you <u>will</u> get there.

We have further discussed how to deal with these images in the section on the will and renewing the mind, so I won't repeat those strategies again here.

'Leg' 7. Natural desires amplified by 'exogenous' [outside] stimulation –

Drag racing cars and indeed some street cars use a product known as 'nitrous oxide.' The effect of adding this to the fuel changes the oxygen mix which in turn allows the fuel to be burned faster. The result of this additive is a massive burst of power supercharging the machines system.

It is considered that a male's sexuality, even at its hormonal peak is quite manageable without outside stimulus. However, when a man is exposed to imagery or literature of a sexual nature, it 'hypes' up and supercharges his hormonal system, increasing the chemical release.

Our society has seemingly made sex 'the meaning of life.' Whilst we continue to thank God for His wonderful gift, if we keep it in perspective it is actually a relatively small part of our existence.

There are times when it is beyond your control to be exposed to women dressed in a sexually provocative manner. There are other times when it is a matter of your personal choice what you see, hear or read. T.V. is full of sexual images, nudity and suggestive or explicit comments. Perhaps it is best to let your wife have the remote control if you must watch T.V. as she does not have the visual weaknesses that you do, and it is important that you acknowledge that you do.

Even better, you may find that if you turn off your media your life might well become much richer and more productive. It is your choice whether you go to the beach in summer where there will be temptation, or what you read and allow to be sent to you via media.

You need to take some control and responsibility for the stimulus that is around your life. Once the exposure has taken place it will likely have some kind of hormonal outworking that perhaps you could have done without.

The alternator in your motor car has something called an 'exciter diode.' A mechanic friend once told me that this diode has to be stimulated before it does its part in letting the electricity go through for charging your battery.
Unlike a generator which can produce power in its own right an alternator first needs power input. So, here is the point; the 'exciter diode' doesn't do anything without first being stimulated by electricity. There has to be some 'power' coming from outside, such as a little bit of current left in your battery before it will work.

Your sexual system is pretty much the same. It needs some kind of stimulus to set it in motion. Once it has begun however, much like an alternator it can generate its own activity and produce by itself. If you are planning to be free from the bondage of pornography it is probably wise to minimize even seemingly harmless sexual exposure.

'Leg' 8. Spiritual powers behind pornography

Dealing with the spiritual factor

> *Ephesians 6:12 For our struggle is not against flesh and blood, but against the rulers, against the authorities, against the powers of this dark world and against the <u>spiritual forces of evil</u> in the heavenly realms.*
> *NIV (emphasis mine)*

We live in a World that is spiritual before it is anything else. Both God's kingdom and the kingdom of darkness are present influencing the natural sense world. We serve, follow and submit to either one of these kingdoms or the other. Whomever we serve becomes lord of that particular area.

If you serve porn then the ruling spirit over your sexuality is not God it is the opposer, Satan. Clearly, he is the instigator and motivator behind this perverted industry. So, when you are serving sin in this area you are submitting to significant 'spiritual forces of evil in the heavenly realms.'

Interestingly the pornography industry has had its greatest and most prolific acceleration and influence through the internet. This along with other misused media comes to us through the 'air.' It is indeed a power of the air in our times.

> *Ephesians 2:1-2 ¹ As for you, you were dead in your transgressions and sins,*
> *² in which you used to live when you followed the ways of this world and of the <u>ruler of the kingdom of the air, the spirit</u> who is now at work in those who are disobedient. NIV (emphasis mine)*

When you offer your sexuality to the devil in this area, he will very happily keep you in bondage and make you miserable. It is vital that we realize that submission, cooperation and participation put you under the authority of the one that you serve and receive from. Jesus' came to free us from the power of sin and forgive us, not to leave us captive to its power. His purpose is always to destroy the works of the devil in our lives. (1 John 3:8) But in order to achieve this, He also requires cooperation and participation. We call this repentance, and it is our most powerful spiritual tool, because it moves us from submitting to an evil spiritual kingdom to serving the kingdom of God. Acts 28:18

> *Romans 6:16 Do you not know that to whom you present yourselves slaves to obey, <u>you are that one's slaves whom you obey</u>, whether of sin leading to death, or of obedience leading to righteousness? NKJV (emphasis mine)*

> *2 Peter 2:19b for a man is a slave to whatever has mastered him. NIV*

> *Romans 6: 12-13 ¹² Therefore do not let sin reign in your mortal body, that you should obey it in its lusts. ¹³ And do not present your members as instruments of unrighteousness to sin, but present yourselves to God as being alive from the dead, and your members as instruments of righteousness to God. NKJV*

Let me repeat, 'repent' is translated from the Greek word, metanoeo: which means according to Strong's concordance, 'to think differently, reconsider.'

When our eyes are opened and we realize that we are submitting to another spirit it puts us in a place of reconsidering the outcome. We think differently about it and come to the understanding that the kingdom that we are serving has an unpleasant reward for our services. I have seen this over and over with the mental torment, physical sickness, emotional self-hatred, broken homes, marriages and ruined children that proceed from following this kingdom of darkness.

The Generational component

 I often ask people who are struggling in this area if anyone in their family line such as a father or grandfather had a problem with this addiction. Very often this is the case and so there is already a spiritual power drawing the victim towards this particular sin. In scripture we understand this power and its limitations if somebody repents and has prayer for freedom. Until we know that it may be a spiritual power that is involved then we probably won't be looking to claim the freedom that is referred to in the New Testament.

> *Galatians 3:13-14 ¹³ Christ redeemed us from the curse of the law by becoming a curse for us, for it is written: "Cursed is everyone who is hung on a tree." ¹⁴ He redeemed us in order that the blessing given to Abraham might come to the Gentiles through Christ Jesus, so that <u>by faith</u> we might receive the <u>promise of the Spirit</u>. NIV (emphasis mine)*

We need to appropriate and receive the finished work of Christ by faith. It is good to find someone who has faith to pray for us for our freedom, and I will describe what that would look like shortly. If you do not understand that there is an inherited spiritual weakness that is drawing you into this, then most likely you will not seek the promise of the Holy Spirit to set you free. This leaves you under the curse of the sin, and you will see your children drawn towards and visited by this weakness as well.

Exodus 20:5-6 ⁵ you shall not bow down to them nor serve them. For I, the LORD your God, am a jealous God, <u>visiting the iniquity</u> of the fathers on the children to the third and fourth generations of those who hate Me, ⁶ but showing mercy to thousands, to those who love Me and keep My commandments. NKJV (emphasis mine)

I have found that many Christians struggle to believe that the curse of sin will visit future generations. Well this visiting didn't start with Exodus; it was a concession and a promise of much blessing to the family line if serving other gods in sin was avoided. Sin actually entered human lineage with Adam, so we were all born under the power of, and tendency towards sin. But this I believe relates to the more specific visiting of particular sins being followed by family lines. We see this with alcoholic or drug addict families. Why are some people drawn to occultist or violent movies, and others are drawn towards fornication or food addictions? King David after his sexual failure with Bathsheba acknowledged that this had been a weakness in him from birth. Later we see the evidence of sexual sin in his family line.

Psalm 51:5 Surely I was sinful at birth, sinful from the time my mother conceived me. NIV

For those who struggle to believe the scriptures on this there is an area of science called 'Epigenetics.' It is an area of brain research that reveals that your habits are passed onto your children and grandchildren. The study states that we not only pass along the DNA sequence to our children, but we also pass epigenetic instructions to them. The epigenetic information sits above the genome that controls the programming of DNA. So, this is the physical outworking of a spiritual reality. As expected, it confirms what scripture has already said, that if we sin in an area it will affect our children in the same area. We have often inherited a weakness that we need to be set free from, and it can be infecting our offspring with the same problems.

Transference

Any sin that is served can lead to the inhabitation of an evil spirit. If you are serving lust then there is every possibility that the spirit promoting lust that is pressuring you from outside of your body will enter into your body where it will have greater influence. This spirit that is holding the sin of lust could gain entry through the trauma of the initial viewing of porn. This would be an emotional opening through the shock of what is being seen...temporarily your normal emotional composure is gone and a door to your personality is open.

It may of course come in through regular deliberate exposure; thereby you are voluntarily participating with an evil spirit. It could enter through an illicit sexual relationship with somebody who already has a spirit that promotes porn. The problem and opportunity for demonization could transfer from a man to a woman, by her being pressured by him to view explicit materials with him. This would also be true of peer pressure where people demonized with lust pressure others to join with them in their sin. For a girl this could come from willfully viewing, even in ignorance of potential consequences, in order to know what to do to please men. An evil spirit doesn't care how; it will take any opportunity to get power.

Demonization

As I have pointed out people often struggle to get free because they do not understand that one part of their problem is demonic power with a stronghold on that area of their personality. Once the evil spirit has gained access it has strong influences on the soul. It will move the will towards more and more sinful activity. Whether you have deliberately or unwittingly joined with it, it now has partial use of the members or parts of your person that you have yielded to it as we have already cited in Romans 6:12-13. In this case it is your eyes, the chemistry in your brain relating to the visuals, your emotions, and your thought life in regard to sexuality.

This is why we see people unable to have normal sexual relationships without perverse acts, and they are subsequently unable to be excited by normal sexuality. It is why people of the opposite sex are compared with the people who have been viewed in media and are considered to fall short. This could possibly be because they are not as sexualized or willing to perform sexual acts as the people appear to be in the movies, or in some instances not as physically attractive.

Separation
Before we pray for a person to be set free from the evil spirit or spirits, they must first have a realization of the demonic activity. They must understand that when they have thoughts urging them to go and view something that in all probability it is not merely their own minds. They readily follow the prompting because they think it is just their own idea, or what they want. You think it is you that wants to look at the material or fantasize about things you have viewed. In fact, it is actually a someone; a spirit being that is in you that wants you to do it.

The reality is that it is something else that is doing the initiating, and wants to be fed and have greater power over you; it does this by drawing you into more and more exposure. Most people desire separation from the evil spirit once they have realized what is really going on. They have been had.... deceived into thinking that they are merely following their own desires. Many have begun with a curious look at something shown at school, or innocently discovering materials at home and found themselves bound and in down spiraling captivity.

What do we do, and how do we pray?
Assuming that the person can discern the spiritual element of their problem, then you can pray a simple prayer commanding the spirit to go in the name of Jesus Christ. The results are more dependent on the person being prayed for wanting to separate from the spirit than your spirituality. Also, they have to be truly repentant and determined to take back control of their minds. You may or may not see something that indicates that the spirit has left. If the person really means it then God will set them free, but God will not be mocked, and if they secretly want to continue at a later date, they may not be delivered. (See Galatians 6:7-8)

If they truly have set their hearts on freedom, then after the spirit is gone it does not mean that there will be no temptation. What they will find is that it will be much easier to resist, as the spirit is now outside of their person. They then need to respect the potential for re-infestation if they return to their sin. The devil will prowl around seeking for an opportune moment to attack, such as when you are tired. He will attack where the wall is lowest, so it is a good idea to work on the strategies that we have detailed. It is vital to walk in the Spirit, be in prayer and read your bible regularly. These should be our basic spiritual daily diet anyway.

With the generational component, we pray the prayer of faith claiming freedom from past influences. Galatians 3:13 is our basis. We break off any spiritual pressures that may be operating against us and command them to go. It is a good practice to forgive our ancestors for bringing this problem on us, and take responsibility in confession for our participation in keeping it active by our continuing and committing the same offense.

Be aware!
If you have a spirit of lust as a result of viewing pornography, the same spirit will probably be finding reasons why you shouldn't get ministry. Or it may justify to you why it is ok. Or

perhaps you may feel very anxious about getting prayer. In reality many of these thoughts and feelings which seem to be your own, are the work of the spirit that you have joined with in sin. It does not want to be evicted and will most probably pressure you away from help. The same is true with many other areas that we might need help with.

---

* Note: for further information on Spiritual freedom see the unit on the subject.

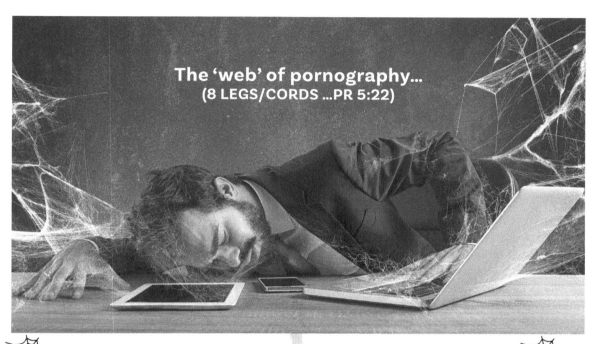

The 'web' of pornography...
(8 LEGS/CORDS ...PR 5:22)

 Natural desires amplified...
(environmental visual stimulation
= 'nitrous oxide' (fuel)
for the sexual machine)

 Emotional stressors
(real or perceived) Rejection, fear of
rejection, loneliness, anxiety:
(Note: fear increases visual arousal)

 Dysfunctional sexual relationship
(in marriage) [appetites not
fulfilled]

 Sexual 'trauma'
(Initial visual shock) (strong
embedded neural memory
pathways from first impact..)
[protein synthesis]

The 'Will' = you just want to!
(given willingly to strong desires,
FLESH, No conviction/the
deception that 'it's o.k.' ECC 1/8

Trigger patterns
(Memory associations with previous
times of opportunity and enactment
situations) i.e. At work, alone, night
contact with girls etc

 Spiritual powers
behind porn: 'demonization'
(perhaps through SIN, the
Generations, or spiritual ties from
ungodly sexual relationships)

 Addiction / Distorted chemical
stimulus 'programming patterns'..

CONCLUSION

I think that we have proven that it is not optional as to whether or not you should be working towards complete freedom in this area. The Good News is that Jesus is the anointed Christ who announced that His purpose and intent is specifically to set the captives free. (Luke 4:18) So you have all of the power of heaven behind you if you decide that you genuinely want to be released.

The only thing that can stop you breaking loose is your own desires and decisions, and perhaps the lack of ministry help that you may need for support. Because Earth is presented to be a testing ground for humanity, God for the most part seems to leave us with free will and choice. God will not override what we choose. It seems that testing and sanctification is for this life, and judgment and punishment for the unrepentant is for the next.

It can be helpful to pray for the gift of repentance and a change of heart.

> *2 Timothy 2:25-26* ²⁵ *In meekness instructing those that <u>oppose themselves</u>; if God peradventure will give them repentance to the acknowledging of the truth;* ²⁶ *And that they may <u>recover themselves</u> out of the snare of the devil, who are taken captive <u>by him at his will</u>.*
> *KJV (emphasis mine)*

Self-deception and self-justification will need to be negotiated, most times with some genuine soul searching done before the Lord. I leave you with a couple of final scriptures to consider. The first is King David's sincere reflection relating to dealing with his sin and being led into eternal life. The second is Jeremiah's acknowledgement that we can deceive ourselves because we have cherished sin in our hearts. This is indeed the deep level that it needs to be dealt with in order to come into freedom.

> *Psalm 139:23-24* ²³ *Search me, O God, and know my heart; test me and know my thoughts.* ²⁴ *Point out anything in me that offends you, and lead me along the path of everlasting life. NLT*

> *Jeremiah 17:9-10* ⁹ *"The human heart is <u>most deceitful</u> and desperately wicked. Who really knows how bad it is?* ¹⁰ *But I know! I, the LORD, search all hearts and examine secret motives. I give all people their due rewards, according to what their actions deserve." NLT (emphasis mine)*

> **Note:** Bible versions which most clearly state what I am proposing have been used and I have added any emphasis where applicable.

FINALLY

I compile this manual in the hope that the body of Christ will be further equipped to not only speak of the good news but to be the good news. There are many who need to be touched by God through believers walking in the Spirit who know how to help. In this, we, as did Jesus, prove God and His word to be true and uphold His integrity.

> *John 15:7-9* ⁷ *'If you remain in me and my words remain in you, ask whatever you wish, and it will be given you.* ⁸ *This is to my Father's glory, that you bear much fruit, showing yourselves to be my disciples."* ⁹ *"As the Father has loved me, so have I loved you. Now remain in my love." NIV*

In all of our efforts we take comfort that our Lord will guide the whole process. I love Psalm 23 which details that we will walk through this hostile environment called Earth, but have the Lords guidance and the promise of restoration for our souls. Verse five encourages us that even in the presence of our enemies He has promised to take us out to lunch!

> *Psalm 23:1-6* ¹ *The LORD is my shepherd; I shall not want.* ² *He makes me to lie down in green pastures; He leads me beside the still waters.* ³ *He restores my soul; He leads me in the paths of righteousness For His name's sake* ⁴ *Yea, though I walk through the valley of the shadow of death, I will fear no evil; For You are with me; Your rod and Your staff, they comfort me.* ⁵ *You prepare a table   before me in the presence of my enemies; You anoint my head with oil; My cup runs over.* ⁶ *Surely goodness and mercy shall follow me All the days of my life; And I will dwell in the house of the LORD Forever. NKJV (emphasis mine)*

APPENDIX ONE

Sample Sessions

SAMPLE MINISTRY TO REJECTION BELIEFS SCENARIO

A person approaches you for help.

Step 1:   Explain the process to the person, and what you are looking for, namely *heart beliefs*. This process could include having them read, view or listen to material such as this explaining the ministry.

Step 2:   The person comes for the actual ministry session.

> **Note:** They already have the problem that they are struggling with so you don't need to come up with anything. It is not your job to fix their whole life, just try to help them with whatever is presenting at the time.

Listen to their story and the issue that they are bringing to you. Make notes of the things that they **say** that may be clues to what they **believe**. Writing things down is good as it means that you don't miss things that may need to later be visited, and you don't need to interrupt their story.

Step 3:   Ministry Example

Fred: I felt very uneasy when I went to try out for the church choir!
Me: Why do you think that you were uncomfortable in that setting?
Fred: I think that I felt that I did not belong there, I was not a part of it.

This could indicate a possible belief such as; *I am not wanted, or I am not accepted.*

Step 4:   We have them concentrate on the feeling produced by the thought that they do not belong, and are not a part of it; rejected by the group. We are looking for the earliest possibly historical place where they learnt beliefs that caused them to feel this way.

Fred: I have just remembered my first day of school. There was a group of kids playing and talking together and they ignored me!
Me: As you concentrate on the memory and feel that rejected feeling, why do you think that they ignored you?
Fred: *Pauses and explores the memory.* I think it is because I am not like them, I am new and so they don't want me. This must be true because they are all accepting each other, but I am on the outside!

Me: Let's ask the Lord what His truth, the real truth is. Lord what do you want Fred to understand about that time where he felt that he was not wanted because he is not like them, because he is new?

Fred: The Lord is reminding me, that these kids went to Kindergarten together and already knew each other. I couldn't get in to Kinder because they were full up.

Me: So, are you not wanted because you are different?

Fred: No, I am the same; I have just not built relationships yet. Later I did make some good friends there.

Me: How do you feel about the church choir now?

Fred: I feel excited about it now; I will be making some new friends it will just take a little time.

Me: Perhaps close in prayer thanking the Lord for His healing, or I may enquire as to whether or not there are other things which require ministry.

Clearly this example is not going to be as deeply painful as rejection often is. Some people may have very painful traumatic rejection situations from some kind of abuse or absence of love in the home. Other people may have a *profile of rejection* composed of multiple less painful beliefs.

SAMPLE MINISTRY: SITUATIONAL OR PHOBIC FEAR

Me: "What can we help you with today?"

Fred: "Well I have a fear of flying."

Me: "So what are you afraid might happen when you get on an aircraft?"

Fred: Ponders "I feel as though I will be out of control"

Me: "I want you to focus on that thought and the feeling that goes with it and see if you remember a time in your life where you felt just like that."

Fred: "I remember being pushed down a steep hill in a little cart we had made. The big kids put me in and sent the cart racing down the hill towards the trees."

Me: "What did you believe might happen while you were afraid?"

Fred: "I guess I felt that I was going to get hurt and nobody could stop it happening. I was terrified!"

Me: "Let's hold that belief up to the Lord that 'nobody can stop what's going to happen, and I will get hurt.'" (Prayer asking the Lord to bring His truth)

Fred: "I just remembered that actually one of the big kids ran after me and eventually did stop the cart before it hit the trees."

Me: "So what does that mean to you?"

Fred: "Well it means that God will always find a way to protect me. He is always in control."

Me: "So think about flying now, are you still afraid of being out of control?"

Fred: Pauses "No. I am still a bit fearful though it is nowhere near as much!"

Me: "Alright focus on the residual fear and see if you can work out what you are afraid of."

Fred: "I have been on a plane before and it felt like there was nothing solid underneath me....it was a scary feeling."

Me: "Okay, I want you to concentrate on the anxious belief that there is nothing solid underneath you." "Lord, would you help Fred to connect with a place where he felt just like that before?"

Fred: "As soon as you said that I remembered being on a cliff edge when we were kids and it caved in underneath me. I slid down the face of it and into the river."

Me: "So you felt as if there was nothing solid under you? And what was the consequence or fear expectation about that situation?"

Fred: "I thought that I was going to die!"

Me:	"Alright, I just want for you to embrace that anxiety and belief in that memory that because there is nothing solid under you, you will die."
Fred:	Pauses "Do you know, that is just not true. What came to mind was the scripture that talks about the circle of the Earth. It's just hung out there in space with nothing under it just because God put it there and supports it, nothing under it, but still suspended."
Me:	"So if you think about there being nothing solid under you on a plane how do you feel about it now?"
Fred:	"You know it's really okay....!"
Me:	"How do you feel about flying now Fred?"
Fred:	"Do you know, it's weird but I think that I am a bit excited!"

Perhaps we might say a prayer thanking the Lord, or certainly make a comment about how amazing our God is in setting us free, and acknowledging Him as being the one who has done the freeing. Either way, God is glorified as He fulfills His promise and the session closes.

SAMPLE MINISTRY: IDENTITY BELIEF-BASED FEAR

Me:	"What seems to be the problem?"
Fred:	"I have been asked to do communion in church next Sunday, but I am petrified and haven't been able to sleep!"
Me:	"I want you to imagine yourself up there in front of all those people. As you feel that anxiety, I would like you to examine it and try to work out exactly what it is that you are afraid might happen."
Fred:	Pause "I am afraid that I might not be able to do it properly."
Me:	"I would like you to feel that anxiety about not doing it properly, and as you do let your mind connect you with a place that held those same feelings. It will be somewhere where you actually couldn't do what was expected."
Fred:	Ponders "I remember in school when I was about 7 years old. The teacher wanted me to write some cursive text on the blackboard, and I wrote it back the front. The teacher made a big fuss over it making fun of me in front of the whole class, and I recall being incredibly embarrassed."
Me:	"As a result of not being able to do it, and the intense embarrassing moment in front of the class, what conclusion about yourself did you come to?"
Fred:	Pause, thoughtful "I'm dumb. I must be dumb because I could not do it right."
Me:	"As you feel that embarrassment and the belief that you are 'dumb' because you could not do it, let us ask the Lord what the real truth is."
Prayer:	"Lord Fred thinks that he is dumb because he could not do the cursive writing on the board. What do you want him to know about that situation?"
Fred:	"Well, I didn't hear any thoughts. But I just sort of understood that none of us had actually been taught cursive yet. And the teacher liked to mock us and make fun of us. She sort of deliberately put me in that position to make sport of me."
Me:	"So are you dumb because you could not do it?"
Fred:	"No, the truth is that none of us could yet. I am feeling that I was alright, there is nothing wrong with me, but I think that the teacher had some issues. I forgive her."
Me:	"Picture yourself doing communion on Sunday, how do you feel about messing it up now?"
Fred:	"I actually feel fine about it; I will work out how to do it as best I can and really everything doesn't have to be perfect. After all, we are all family."

> **Note:** A situation such as public speaking typically may evoke a response from more than one historically learnt fear producing belief. As each one is ministered to the intensity of the anxiety normally goes down. If you just process the beliefs one by one eventually you will achieve peace. It is of course normal to be a little nervous if it is a new situation.

FLOW CHART

The ministry process:

A person comes to you with a problem. This could be a mental, emotional, relational, addictive, spiritual, sexual or physical issue.

↓

They may have been *set off* or *triggered* by a life situation producing for example: anxiety, anger, sadness, bitterness, resentment, guilt, inferiority, rejection and so on.

↓

Your role is to help them focus on these feelings and reactions and to identify the beliefs which they believe at *heart* level, and which they may no longer immediately consciously access.

↓

The key components that you are trying to connect here are: The emotions, the beliefs producing the emotions, and the matching memory pictures. (No pictures could mean it's imbibed prenatal, perhaps connect with a feeling or a sense of something)

↓

You have them focus on the presenting feelings and using questions help them to discover the beliefs producing the emotion, OR

↓

If they have a belief, such as, *I just never think that I am good enough*, have them connect with the feeling that should be associated with such a thought. (The emotion often comes up as the story is related or the memory is accessed and described.)

In the instance of such beliefs as; "I am not good enough, not loveable, not important…" and so on a qualifying phrase can be helpful. For example, ask the question; "why are you not good enough?" You can then offer the belief with the qualifying phrase, such as: "Lord Fred believes that he is not good enough and is dumb **because** he cannot do what others can do."

The conclusion is that he is 'dumb,' but there can be many reasons why he may believe this. So when we offer it to the Lord for truth we make it specific by adding in the phrase that 'he believes that he is dumb, **because** he cannot do what others can do.'

↓

Request that they let memories come to them or wilfully look for the memory picture, if they don't already have it, which contains the beginnings or original source of the thoughts and feelings. (With some pictures that are remembered, it is not always immediately obvious as to why the beliefs have been interpreted here.)

↓

Having refined and identified the belief that was learnt, invite God to bring Truth. (You can be creative in how you request this to avoid being repetitive, but using phrases such as, *Lord, would you like to show Fred how you see this situation? Lord, would you touch Fred by revealing your Truth to replace what he perceives as the truth here? Lord, what would you like Fred to know about the belief that he holds?* and so on.)

APPENDIX TWO

Popular Redemption Scriptures

SCRIPTURES QUALIFYING US FOR HEALING AND FREEDOM

All of the following passages are taken from the New Living Translation of the Bible and the emphasis is mine.

PSALM 103:2-4, 10-12
*² Praise the LORD, I tell myself, and never forget the good things he does for me. ³ He forgives **all** my sins and heals **all** my diseases. ⁴ He ransoms me from death and surrounds me with love and tender mercies.*

.......And.........

*¹⁰ **He has not punished us for all our sins**, nor does he deal with us as we deserve. ¹¹ For his unfailing love toward those who fear him is as great as the height of the heavens above the earth. ¹² **He has removed our rebellious acts as far away from us as the east is from the west.***

ISAIAH 44:22
"I have swept away your sins like the morning mists. I have scattered your offenses like the clouds. Oh, return to me, for I have paid the price to set you free."

ISAIAH 53:5-6, 11
*⁵ But he was wounded and crushed for our sins. He was beaten that we might have peace. He was whipped, and we were healed! ⁶ **All of us** have strayed away like sheep. We have left God's paths to follow our own. Yet the LORD laid on him the guilt and sins **of us all**.*

.......And.........

¹¹ When he sees all that is accomplished by his anguish, he will be satisfied. And because of what he has experienced, my righteous servant will make it possible for many to be counted righteous, for he will bear all their sins.

ROMANS 3:22-25
*²² **We are made right in God's sight when we trust in Jesus Christ to take away our sins**. And we all can be saved in this same way, no matter who we are or what we have done. ²³ For all have sinned; all fall short of God's glorious standard. ²⁴ Yet now God in his gracious kindness declares us not guilty. **He has done this through Christ Jesus, who has freed us by taking away our sins**. ²⁵ For God sent Jesus to take the punishment for our sins and to satisfy God's anger against us. **We are made right with God when we believe that Jesus shed his blood, sacrificing his life for us**.*

1 CORINTHIANS 1:30-31
³⁰ *God alone made it possible for you to be in Christ Jesus. For our benefit God made Christ to be wisdom itself.* **He is the one who made us acceptable to God. He made us pure and holy, and he gave himself to purchase our freedom.** ³¹ *As the Scriptures say,* **"The person who wishes to boast should boast only of what the Lord has done."**

2 CORINTHIANS 5:21
For God made Christ, who never sinned, to be the offering for our sin, **so that we could be made right with God through Christ.**

EPHESIANS 1:4-7
⁴ *Long ago, even before he made the world,* **God loved us and chose us in Christ to be holy and without fault in his eyes.** ⁵ *His unchanging plan has always been to adopt us into his own family by bringing us to himself through Jesus Christ.* **And this gave him great pleasure.** ⁶ *So we praise God for the wonderful kindness he has poured out on us because we belong to his dearly loved Son.* ⁷ *He is so rich in kindness that he purchased our freedom through the blood of his Son,* **and our sins are forgiven.**

EPHESIANS 2:7-9
⁷ *And so God can always point to us as examples of the incredible wealth of his favor and kindness toward us, as shown in all he has done for us through Christ Jesus.* ⁸ *God saved you by his special favor when you believed. And* **you can't take credit for this; it is a gift from God.**
⁹ **Salvation is not a reward for the good things we have done,** *so none of us can boast about it.*

COLOSSIANS 1:22
"yet now he has brought you back as his friends. He has done this through his death on the cross in his own human body. **As a result,** *he has brought you into the very presence of God, and* **you are holy and blameless as you stand before him without a single fault."**

HEBREWS 10:14, 17-18
¹⁴ *For by that one offering* **he perfected forever** *all those whom he is making holy*

......and....

¹⁷ *Then he adds,* **"I will never again remember their sins and lawless deeds."**
¹⁸ *Now when sins have been forgiven, there is no need to offer any more sacrifices.*

APPENDIX THREE

Other Resources from 418Centre

BY STEVE PIDD

SOHAF (SCHOOL OF HEALING AND FREEDOM) BASIC SEMINAR MANUAL
This is the simplified study guide version of the manual. It is provided as a companion to notes for those attending SOHAF Schools or Seminars.

HEALING AND FREEDOM THROUGH TRUTH ENCOUNTERS
This popular book is a complete resource in itself. It contains much of the material found in the SOHAF Comprehensive manual. It is presented in a different order with the focus on explaining the 'Truth Encounters' ministry. It includes explanations on the demonic realm, roots of common issues, and how to work with the Holy Spirit in ministry.

YOU SHALL INDEED BE SET FREE
This publication is an excerpt comprising of the first two Sections from the book 'Healing And Freedom Through Truth Encounters.' It is a much shorter version specifically dealing with the 'Truth Encounters' ministry in isolation.

RECEIVING TRUTH THAT WILL SET YOU FREE
This booklet is designed as a basic introduction to help position those coming for a 'Truth Encounters' ministry session to understand what is involved in receiving their breakthrough.